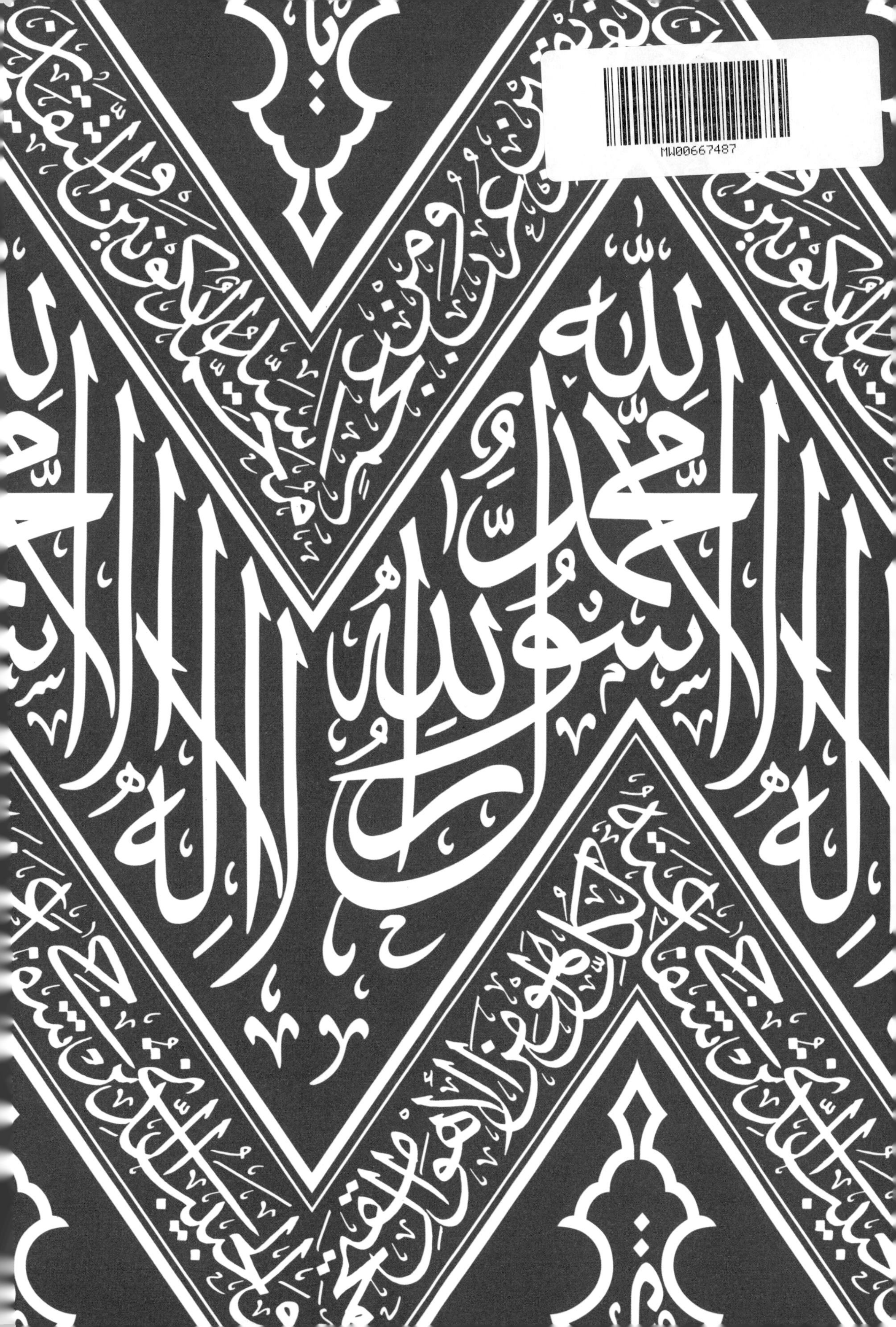
لا إله إلا الله محمد رسول الله
MW00667487

أعوذ بالله من الشيطان الرجيم
بسم الله الرحمن الرحيم

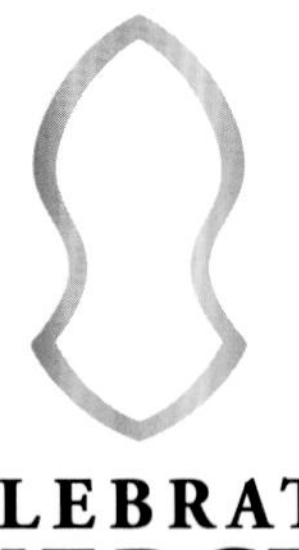

CELEBRATE
MERCY

O LOVE THE PROPHET ﷺ, WE MUST KNOW HIM FIRST.

This book is an excellent first step. Many scholars believe that, for centuries, the Shama'il was – after the Qur'an – one of most popular book in the Muslim world. That's why this beautiful, meticulous translation is so historic. It will help to revive the genre of Shama'il among English-speaking Muslims, bringing Prophetic light into millions of hearts and homes. CelebrateMercy is honoured to be the exclusive distributor for al-Shama'il al-Muhammadiyya in the United States. In 2010, we established CelebrateMercy as a non-profit organisation with one goal: to teach about the Prophet Muhammad's ﷺ life & character. We achieve this through our webinars, conferences, campaigns, and trips. To date, our programs have shared the Prophet ﷺ with over 100,000 people worldwide.

In January 2013, CelebrateMercy hosted its first-ever Portrait of a Prophet® retreat conference. In these quarterly programs, qualified scholars teach the entire 415-hadith Shama'il text in a single weekend. We've seen this book transform the lives of thousands of people as they explore the Prophet's inner and outer beauty.

To bring a one-night lecture on this book or the Portrait of a Prophet® weekend conference to your community, please email info@celebratemercy.com. We would love to read and share your personal reflections. Share your favorite hadiths or sections with the hashtag **#CMShamail**.

~

Al-Shama'il Al-Muhammadiyya

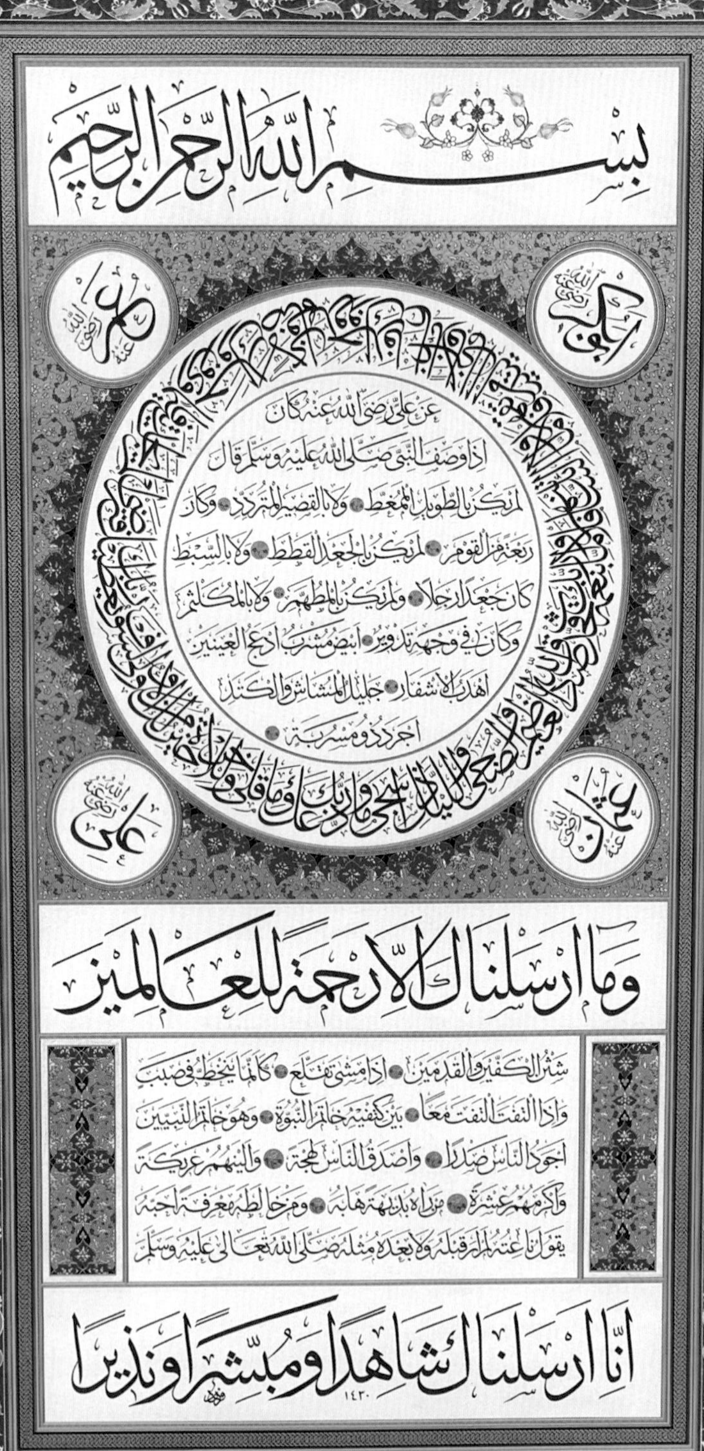

بسم الله الرحمن الرحيم
ابو بكر رضي الله عنه
عمر رضي الله عنه
عن علي رضي الله عنه كان
اذا وصف النبي صلى الله عليه وسلم قال
لم يكن بالطويل الممغط ولا بالقصير المتردد وكان
ربعة من القوم لم يكن بالجعد القطط ولا بالسبط
كان جعدا رجلا ولم يكن بالمطهم ولا بالمكلثم
وكان في وجهه تدوير ابيض مشرب ادعج العينين
اهدب الاشفار جليل المشاش والكتد
اجرد ذو مسربة
عثمان رضي الله عنه
علي رضي الله عنه
وما ارسلناك الا رحمة للعالمين
شثن الكفين والقدمين اذا مشى تقلع كأنما ينحط في صبب
واذا التفت التفت معا بين كتفيه خاتم النبوة وهو خاتم النبيين
اجود الناس صدرا واصدق الناس لهجة والينهم عريكة
واكرمهم عشرة من رآه بديهة هابه ومن خالطه معرفة احبه
يقول ناعته لم ار قبله ولا بعده مثله صلى الله تعالى عليه وسلم
انا ارسلناك شاهدا ومبشرا ونذيرا
١٤٣٠

Al-Shama'il Al-Muhammadiyya

Translation and Commentary by
Abdul Aziz Suraqah & Mohammed Aslam

AL-SHAMA'IL AL-MUHAMMADIYYA
—WWW.THESHAMAIL.com—

IMAM GHAZALI INSTITUTE
106-08 Liberty Avenue
Ozone Park, NY 11417
United States of America
info@imamghazali.org
WWW.IMAMGHAZALI.org

THE CITY OF KNOWLEDGE ACADEMY
113 Golden Hillock Road, Birmingham
West Midlands B10 0DX
United Kingdom
info@cityofknowledge.co.uk
WWW.CITYOFKNOWLEDGE.co.uk

BULK ORDERING INFORMATION: Special discounts are available on quantity purchases by academic institutions, associations, and others. For details, please contact the publishers at the address above.

DESIGN ACKNOWLEDGEMENTS: Our sincere gratitude and heartfelt thanks to (a) *hilya.co.uk* for permission to re-produce the *Hilye-i Şerif* that adorns the frontispiece, (b) Prince Ghazi Trust for Qur'anic Thought for the beautiful calligraphy pieces available at *FreeIslamicCalligraphy.com,* and (c) Sajjad Husain and Rafiah Dada for their support on the final design of the cover.

A list of corrigenda can be found on *TheShamail.com*

Printed and bound in Türkiye Cumhuriyeti (REPUBLIC OF TURKEY)

ISBN: 978-099843805-4 (HARDBACK)
ISBN: 978-099843806-1 (LEATHERBOUND)

First Edition

10 9 8 7 6 5 4 3 2 1

Author
Abu 'Isa Muhammad b. 'Isa
b. Sawra al-Tirmidhi ﷺ

Translators & Researchers
Abdul Aziz Suraqah
Mohammed Aslam

Editor
Kelly El-Yacoubi

Project Managers
Muhammad Tauseef Rehman
Muhammad Adnaan Sattaur

Title Calligraphy
Helmi Sobri

Design & Typesetting
The Noble Ark (SINGAPORE)
Manaqib Productions (UK)

Printer
White Canvas Print

O Allah, remedy the situation of the people
and, O Allah, make the reunification easy.

O Lord, grant Your clear victory to the one
who takes charge and empowers the Deen,

And help him, O You Who are forbearing, and help his party
and fill his heart with what will make him pleasing to You.

O Lord, help our Muhammadan Deen,
and make it end mighty as it began.

Preserve it, O Lord, through the preservation of the scholars,
and raise the minaret of its light to the sky.

Pardon, grant well-being, make up for our deficiency
and forgive our sins and the sins of every Muslim, O our Lord.

O Lord, bless the Chosen one
with Your perfect prayer of blessing.

Your prayer is that which grants success in his affair
as befits his lofty worth.

Then bless his noble family and glorious Companions
and those who have followed them.

Praise belongs to Allah by whose praise
those with an aim completely fulfill that aim.

AL-DU'A AL-NASIRI

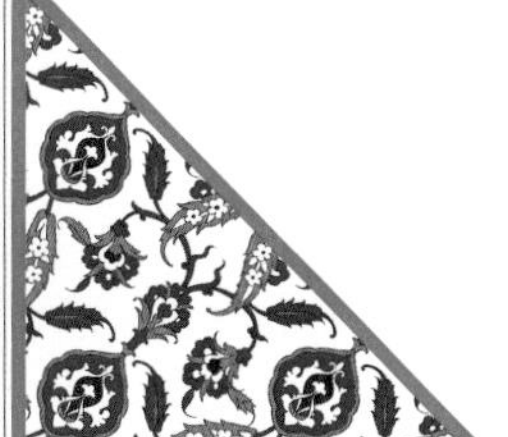

قال ملا علی بن سلطان محمد القاری:

ومن أحسن ما صنف فی شمائله وأخلاقه ﷺ كتاب الترمذی المختصر الجامع فی سيره علی الوجه الأتم بحيث أن مطالع هذا الكتاب ۞ وكأنه يطالع طلعة ذلك الجناب ۞ ويری محاسنه الشريفة فی كل باب ۞

"Among the best books written on his ﷺ description and excellent conduct is the short compendium written by al-Tirmidhi, which completely gathers his hagiography in such a way that it is as if the person who reads this book is looking directly at his noble face and, with each chapter, witnessing his beautiful, noble characteristics."

MULLA ʿALI B. SULTAN MUHAMMAD AL-QARI

CONTENTS

Addenda

FOREWORD

PRAISE BE TO ALLAH, the Fashioner of perfection in human form, and unending salutations and blessings—in a manner that befits his elevated rank—upon the Prophet of Mercy, the locus of divine generosity, Sayyiduna Muhammad ﷺ, his Family and Companions.

In the early lexicon of the Arabic language, the word *Shama'il*, commonly taken to mean character traits, was in some forms used to describe water. Particularly, it referred to a special water source found in arid lands which, when cooled by northerly winds, became pleasant for the drinker who sought to quench his or her thirst.

The primordial nature of man is to seek meaning beyond the ephemeral realm, which is sullied by imperfections. The human being perennially looks for paragons of perfection who embody true comportment with Allah and their fellow men. Just as the body is afflicted by thirst which it seeks to quench, so too does the spirit suffer effects of the lowly world (*dunya*) which gradually scorch its spiritual core. Spiritually thirsty men then seek exemplars of heavenly qualities that nourish their souls. Their qualities are most perfectly embodied in the Prophets. It is these same qualities that are referred to as the *Shama'il*, exemplified in those sent by Allah within whom, as Imam Waliullah al-Dihlawi notes, '...people see the influence of proximity [to Allah] such as miracles and the answering of prayers, so they have no doubt concerning their elevated rank in the heavenly order, that their souls are holy, connected with the angelic, and that they are never disposed to lie about Allah or to carry out any act of disobedience.'

The Islamic tradition has always placed particular focus on collecting these qualities and descriptions of the final Prophet ﷺ in written form. In this regard, *al-Shama'il al-Muhammadiyya wa al-Khasa'il al-Mustafawiyya* of Imam al-Tirmidhi is a foundational tributary that gave rise to an ocean of works on the topic. In composing it, the author laid bare the foundational gems that describe the most perfect of mankind, gems which would then be reworked, set and adorned by those granted divine enabling grace (*tawfiq*) to give life to memory of the Prophet ﷺ.

Imam al-Tirmidlhi intended for the *Shama'il* to be a devotional text rather than simply a compendium in the genre of hadith science. He indicates this by rarely indulging in his usual discussions about the status of the hadith chains or their narrators, though the texts included are certainly of the most pristine caliber.

As in any hadith collection, the opening report grants insight into the aims of the author. In *al-Shama'il al-Muhammadiyya*, the central telos is clear from the first narrations on the blessed physical form and, more precisely, the blessed face of the Prophet ﷺ, a face which conveyed the very message of Islam, from which a thousand poets sought inspiration in devotional verse. 'Abdullah ibn Salam, seeking out the Prophet ﷺ upon his arrival in Medina, gazed upon him to see signs of prophecy and said simply, 'His is not the face of a liar.' [al-Tirmidhi] The poet of the Prophet ﷺ, 'Abdullah ibn Rawaha, placed the same sentiment in verse when he said:

If the noble signs of revelation were yet to descend
it would be his enlightened presence that would grant you the message
—Ibn Hajar al-'Asqalani, *al-Isaba fi Tamyiz al-Sahaba*

❦

It was axiomatic to the first community that the Prophet Muhammad ﷺ was the means by which the divine message, and thereby salvation, is granted. This inherent certainty can be seen in their indisputable outpourings of reverence and attachment to the Prophet ﷺ and his person during his lifetime, which is documented in mass-transmitted (*mutawatir*) reports. That this attachment continued unabated after he passed to the heavenly realm is a testament to how the *Shama'il* left a deep imprint in the heart of every woman and man whose eyes were blessed to have gazed upon such a luminous countenance. Sadly, many modern Muslims may incorrectly deem or even condemn these acts as exaggerated expressions of devotion; in reality they are the most beautiful and natural expressions of hearts that are in an experiential state of *tawhid*.

We see such reverence in the quivering lips of Sayyiduna Bilal al-Habashi ؓ as he struggles to bring himself to utter the Prophet's blessed name ﷺ in the call to prayer after his self-imposed exile from Medina. We encounter it in the frantic search of Sayyiduna Khalid ibn Walid ؓ for his helmet that contained the blessed hair of the Prophet ﷺ even in the midst of battle on the plain of Yarmuk. We bear witness to it while looking upon Sayyiduna 'Amr ibn al-'As ؓ who, while on his death bed in Egypt, requested that a blessed hair of the Prophet ﷺ be placed under his tongue upon death. Far from being isolated instances of attachment, these expressions of love are arguably the unifying trait of the earliest generation. And so it is that every deep ravine and distant valley in Muslim lands stands as a witness to the Companions' absolute conviction that Sayyiduna Muhammad ﷺ is the paragon of human perfection who serves, by Allah's will, as the means by which they are rescued from the claws of wanton barbarism and ignorance and entered into the infinite sanctuary of Allah's merciful-love.

The *Shama'il* works also extol the significance of the personal effects of the Messenger ﷺ, and veneration of this kind was arguably nowhere more pronounced than during the reign of the Ottomans. Their rule was, by definition, predicated on an attachment to his blessed being, an attachment inculcated at every level of Ottoman life, from state structures to personal piety.

It was Sultan Mehmet III who, in the face of successive defeats in their wars with the Austrio-Hungarian forces, led the Ottoman army into battle. He took with him the famed mantle (*burda*) and standard of the Prophet ﷺ. The mantle, granted by the Prophet ﷺ to the poet Sayyiduna Ka'b ibn Zuhayr, had passed through the hands of the Ummayyad and Abbasid caliphs. The standard, named 'Uqba, was fashioned from cloth belonging to Sayyida 'A'isha ؓ and taken to battle by the Prophet ﷺ and the four Rightly Guided Caliphs after him. The battle led by Sultan Mehmet III was fierce, and as it moved ominously to certain defeat, his Shaykh, Sa'd al-Din, implored the Caliph saying, 'As Allah's Caliph striving in His path, it now behooves you to adorn the blessed *burda* and by it beseech Allah's victory!' Initially hesitant, and in the face of inevitable defeat at the Battle of Haçova, Mehmet III did so. Miraculously, the tide turned to victory for the Ottoman Empire. Is it then any wonder that it was honoured by Allah to be the most enduring empire humanity has seen?

❦

It would be a mistake to view *al-Shama'il al-Muhammadiyya* as simply a devotional work. The last Ottoman *Shaykh al-Islam*, Mustafa Sabri (d.1954 CE), identified what lay at the source of the gradual Muslim decline: first, an abandonment of the concept of '*Umma*' in favour of nationalism and second, the 'disenchantment' of the core elements of faith at the behest of crass materialism. With nationalism and materialism came the heartbreaking process of divesting the Prophet ﷺ and his actions of metaphysical significance, a process which unfortunately continues today unabated. In rediscovering this metaphysical significance of the Prophet ﷺ lies the key to Muslim renewal. This is because at the core of the *Shama'il* is the Prophet's ﷺ trait, emanating from a heightened state of *ihsan* (spiritual virtue), of unwavering *i'timad* (reliance) on Allah in the face of unending tribulations.

'There are those', Shaykh Ahmad al-Zarruq comments on the opening *al-Hikam al-Ata'iyya*, 'whose reliance is built upon [an acceptance of] the prior decree and the unfolding command... The sign [of such people] is submission and stillness in the face of events. Such a person's hope does not increase due to any reason, nor does it decrease on account of any cause. If one were to weigh both [fear and hope], they would appear equal in each and every situation. Rather, such a person is "constantly of glad demeanor" [and yet] "always in deep thought", as has been narrated in the descriptive qualities of our Messenger Muhammad ﷺ.'

In the troubled days that the *Umma* is living through, *al-Shama'il al-Muhammadiyya* is as a letter to this now orphaned community. Cut-off from recognising its Prophet ﷺ, his sublime character and values, it has precipitated its own decline., destitute and devoid of meaning, dishonouring his teaching at every turn and in doing so becoming helplessly vulnerable to the the unrelenting vicissitudes of time and the mundane realm. There should therefore be no section of the *Umma* to whom this work does not speak in the most immediate and pressing manner.

To scholars, this work stands as a reminder of their responsibility as the true heirs of the Messenger ﷺ. In the critical times ahead, it behooves the scholars of the *Umma* to embody fully the balanced temperament of the Prophet ﷺ in calling others to Allah. All manifestations of personal rancour and envy should be eschewed.

It is with intense clarity that I remember the gatherings for the study of the *Shama'il* with our honoured teachers. Those were gatherings with an aura distinct to any other sitting of sacred learning. If I were to recall just one of the many unique aspects of such gatherings, it would be the palpable metamorphosis overtaking all in attendance. Even the most illustrious of our esteemed Shaykhs, with their own distinct hues and temperaments (*mizaj*), could be caught weeping. Their own character traits, their personal *shama'il*, were somehow slowly being honed and calibrated as a result of hearing again of the one sent in order to perfect beautiful character (*makaram al-akhlaq*). Whoever attended such gatherings would be humbled and begin to see the shortcomings of his own self, vowing to attend to rectify them. Infallibility is a quality only of the Prophets; blessed are those who recognise the failings of their own souls.

To average believers, *al-Shama'il al-Muhammadiyya* should be a constant companion, frequented and studied until the memory of the generous Prophet ﷺ becomes imprinted on the heart and mind, providing clarity and surety on the path to Allah.

❦

While visiting his teacher, one of the students of the great Damascene reviver of the last century Shaykh Salih al-Farfur (d.1986 CE/1407 AH) cast his eyes at the vast collection of Islamic scholarship contained in his library. With a tinge of dejection, he said, 'The previous scholars came and left no stone unturned in serving this religion, explaining and writing until there was nothing left for us, the later generations, to do.' Shaykh Salih looked at him and said, 'Why don't you say, "Look at how much is left with us, yet to be done"?'

There is indeed so much that has yet to be done, and to deny this would be to deny Allah's continuous generosity to the *Umma* of the Prophet ﷺ. Amongst such pressing needs is a fully annotated translation of *al-Shama'il al-Muhammadiyya* that can provide the English-speaking world with a work that does justice to the reverence in which the original work is rightly held.

The debt owed to this work has been discharged by Shaykh Abdul Aziz Suraqah and my dear friend Shaykh Mohammed Aslam, such that the work has—by the grace of divine providence—been given its due. And yet, we can never show enough reverence and gratitude to Allah and His Messenger ﷺ. By the grace of Allah alone, the translation offered to the reader in these pages is lucid, careful and true to the original meanings. The language is aptly tempered with the reverence and decorum that such an endeavour necessitates. Descriptive prose in Arabic is amongst the most difficult to translate, especially prose that describes nuances of physical qualities in a lexicon that is so deeply rooted in the milieu of Arabia. The care of the translator in executing this task marks it with distinction.

The Arabic print edition that has been relied upon in the translation and notes, that of the contemporary hadith expert Shaykh Muhammad 'Awwama's edition of al-Bajuri's commentary, is to be noted. What sets this edition apart from others is the seniority and the experience of Shaykh Muhammad 'Awwama in the field of hadith which is close to unmatched in this age, as borne out by the unobtrusive yet exact method he utilises in editing the work. More importantly, the core text of *al-Shama'il al-Muhammadiyya* has been verified in light of not only al-Bajuri's commentary, but also a keen engagement with the hadith sources and previous commentators that al-Bajuri drew upon. The result is a printed edition that surpasses other editions which, though focusing on the text of the *Shama'il*, fail to adequately benefit from later commentaries to verify variant wordings of a given hadith.

The copious additional footnotes by both authors are compelling, precise and scholarly, and have managed to encompass the observations of previous scholars. Both authors take great care to draw the reader's attention to the devotional nature of reports within *al-Shama'il al-Muhammadiyya*, identifying and then bringing to life the veneration latent within even the most seemingly simple and 'nondescript' of descriptions. Indeed, how can any description about his blessed being ﷺ be 'nondescript'? It is for this that they are both deserving of our gratitude and supplications.

And so it remains to beseech Allah, who has prescribed proficiency in all things, that this work be granted His acceptance as one that stems from not only a sincere desire to serve this *Umma* for His sake, but from true love of Him and His beloved ﷺ. May Allah grant its original author and its translators proximity to our master, Sayyiduna Muhammad ﷺ, the embodiment of the most perfect of character traits, so that they gaze upon his blessed countenance and quench their thirst on the Day of Rising by drinking the cool draught of al-Kawthar from his blessed hand. *Amin*!

RUZWAN MOHAMMED
Director of iSyllabus
Scotland, April 2018

PUBLISHER'S MESSAGE

IN THE NAME OF ALLAH, THE ALL-MERCIFUL, THE MOST MERCIFUL. All praise is due to Allah, prayers and peace be upon our Master, the Messenger of Allah ﷺ, Muhammad b. Abdullah, and upon his blessed Family and his blessed Companions and those after him. Among the marvels of Allah Most High's creation is the affair of His selecting and electing His creation. Truly the greatest creation that Allah, the Exalted and Sublime, elected and filled with His munificence and generosity is our Master Muhammad (Allah bless him and grant him peace).

More splendid than you my eye hasn't seen.
No woman has mothered one oh so fine!
You are created so free of flaw...
As if made by your own design.
—Based on Hassan ibn Thabit's couplet

Al-Shama'il al-Muhammadiyya ('The Sublime Qualities of the Prophet Muhammad ﷺ') is the most famous collection of narrations detailing the moral, physical, and spiritual perfections of the Prophet Muhammad ﷺ. Commonly referred to as 'The *Shama'il*' and compiled by the prolific, encyclopædic master of Hadith al-Imam Abu 'Isa Muhammad b. 'Isa b. Sawra al-Sulami al-Tirmidhi, this perennial masterpiece connects hearts to the Prophet's blessed being ﷺ. This work that you hold before you is arguably the most indispensable compendium of prophetic sayings relating to his ﷺ blessed biography. You, o noble reader, are no doubt about to embark on a momentous, life-changing journey filled with prophetic love and re-connection to our blessed Prophet ﷺ. And how could this not be the case for the most magnificent work of Imam al-Tirmidhi? Whereas the Sunan of Imam al-Tirmidhi, for want of a better description, is an academic exercise of love, the Shama'il is an outpouring of deep and profound love, as only a lover goes to such lengths to describe his beloved so masterfully. The Shama'il is an undeniable manifestation of the great Imam's love for the Prophet ﷺ.

It has long been our intention to publish an English translation of the *Shama'il.* As Allah would have it, the foundation for this effort was solidified in 2016 by the invitation of Shaykh Mohammed Aslam's City of Knowledge Academy, based in Birmingham, United Kingdom, for collaboration on this project with the Imam Ghazali Institute—a collaboration with Muhammadan love at its core. The task of publishing Imam al-Tirmidhi's *al-Shama'il al-Muhammadiyya* is no small undertaking. This work is a compilation of 415 traditions, and is historically known to have inaugurated this genre of hadith literature. Its acceptance is clear and known for those who are aware. According to the learned *Shaykh al-Islam* and Imam of Masjid al-Azhar, Ibrahim al-Bajuri, *"It is the only book in its genre, unique in its arrangement and content, so much so that it is considered divinely gifted and has been disseminated in the East and the West."*

The *Shama'il* generously invites us to experience the most detailed and exquisite qualities of the message-bearer—the Prophet Muhammad ﷺ. This knowledge fundamentally alters, informs, and orients our understanding of the Message he ﷺ brought. In this project, we have also sought to pay homage to our deep tradition in the realm of art. We were able to manifest our vision into a reality where the notes you see were laid in the style of old historic *Hashiya* texts. The fruit of this labour of love has manifested in the form of not just the intended translation, but a meticulously reviewed vocalised Arabic text inclusive of the sanad, along with nearly one thousand notes to supplement you, o noble reader, on your journey.

The *Shama'il* offers us tastes of delight and joy, and most importantly, engenders sincere love of Allah and His Messenger ﷺ in our hearts. It is our hope and aspiration that this work will serve to introduce, enhance, and solidify the love of the Messenger ﷺ throughout the English-speaking world. It is hoped that by including the vocalized Arabic text along with the sanad that 1) students of Sacred Knowledge will be aided in learning the language of the Qur'an, the Prophet ﷺ, and the 'ulama, and 2) it will serve as a teaching aid for the 'ulama when teaching this text to reference the original work, and 3) to facilitate *majalis* for the *mubarak* recital and transmission of the words of the Messenger ﷺ.

Anything indecorous in this rendering is from our *nafs* and our ignorance, and anything herein which is of benefit is from Allah, the blessing of Imam al-Tirmidhi, and the scholars who transmitted this blessed and noble work. May Allah forgive us for our shortcomings, and may He bless all who teach, read, and study all or part of this work, until the Day of Judgment. May Allah bless the author, the translator, the editors, the proofreaders, the typesetter, and all the members of our team at the City of Knowledge Academy (UK) and the Imam Ghazali Institute (USA). I close by asking that should you, the reader, benefit from this text, kindly remember this poor and needy servant and his family in your duas. *Amin*. And all praise is due to Allah, Lord of the worlds.

MUHAMMAD ADNAAN SATTAUR *(Abu Faris)*
On Behalf of the Imam Ghazali Institute
and the City of Knowledge Academy

Penned from the plains of Arafat on this blessed and most noble of days in the Hajj of 1440 AH

A NOTE OF GRATITUDE

Allah, the Almighty and Wise, says in His Glorious Book, *If you are grateful then I shall surely increase you.* (Quran 14:7) So praise be to Allah the Ennobler of all good acts, and gratitude to His beloved Prophet Muhammad ﷺ for delivering the message, fulfilling the trust, advising the community and striving tirelessly in the way of Allah.

I would humbly like to thank my parents who took me to the gatherings of the righteous scholars from a young age, which shaped my understanding of the religion and allowed me to see living embodiments of our rich tradition. The closest of them to my heart and lineage was my grandfather, Hafiz Muhammad Yusuf, whose striking personality and remarkable achievements of memorising the Quran and studying the sciences of Islam, even though he was born blind, was overwhelming and left a lasting impression on my heart. My thanks also go to my tutor, Mufti Muhammad Akbar Zirak, who became a father figure to me in knowledge and wisdom. His in-depth understanding of this religion, his humble character and his intense love for the Messenger of Allah ﷺ were an inspiration and an encouragement to further my studies in the blessed lands of Sham. My deep gratitude also goes to all of my teachers at Fath al-Islami (Damascus), in particular to 'Allama Shaykh 'Abd al-Razzaq al-Halabi, 'Allama Shaykh Adib al-Kallas, and the Mufti of Damascus, Shaykh 'Abd al-Fattah al-Bizm. May Allah ennoble all my teachers, raise their ranks and increase their benefit until the End of Time. I would like to show my appreciation to all those involved in this great project: the translator, Shaykh Abdul Aziz Suraqah, Hafiz Muhammad Tauseef Rehman for his tireless effort and work, and the publishers, Imam Ghazali Institute and The City of Knowledge Academy. Finally, I pray that this book will be a means of perpetual felicity, continuous blessings, infinite reward, everlasting mercy, and eternal goodness for my sister Ustadha Tahirah Kawthar. Were it not for her aid, support, generosity, and kindness for The City of Knowledge Academy at its inception, we would not have been granted the opportunity to achieve all that which we have achieved thus far.

MOHAMMED ASLAM IBN 'ABDUL QAYUM IBN HAFIZ MUHAMMAD YUSUF

TRANSLATOR'S PREFACE

All praise is due to Allah, the Lord of the Worlds. May Allah send boundless prayers, bountiful blessings and infinite salutations upon the one whose sublime beauty unlocks hearts, whose magnificent countenance removes veils of heedlessness, and whose every statement and action, movement and stillness, gaze and glance, smile and touch move hearts and transform souls. May never-ending prayers and sweet salutations be upon the one whom Allah made His most exquisite creation, the crown jewel of His kingdom and His supreme grace: our master, our beloved, our light, our source and our salvation, Sayyiduna Muhammad, son of 'Abdullah, son of 'Abd al-Muttalib, son of Hashim, son of 'Abd Manaf, son of Qusayy, son of Kilab, son of Murra, son of Ka'b, son of Lu'ayy, son of Ghalib, son of Fihr, son of Malik, son of Nadr, son of Kinana, son of Khuzayma, son of Mudrika, son of Ilyas, son of Mudar, son of Nizar, son of Ma'add, son of 'Adnan!

In Arabic, the word shama'il means qualities of character and nature. As a genre of literature, the *Shama'il* works mention what has been recorded from the Companions ﷺ concerning the descriptions of the Prophet's blessed physical appearance and his clothing, food, belongings, character, worship and lifestyle. The most famous *Shama'il* compilation is the work before you, *al-Shama'il al-Muhammadiyya*, compiled by the preminent hadith master Imam Muhammad ibn 'Isa ibn Sawra al-Tirmidhi (Allah have mercy upon him).

One may ask why the *Shama'il* exists as a distinct genre of Islamic literature when virtually every hadith compilation is already filled with descriptions of the Prophet ﷺ, his recorded statements and his actions. The answer is simple: Learning about the physical and moral qualities of the Prophet Muhammad ﷺ is a *religious necessity* and an essential ingredient of sincere and sound faith. Simply put: **the medium is the message**. The medium of the message of Islam is the one who communicated Islam's contents to us while perfectly reflecting them in his own being—our master the Messenger of Allah, Muhammad ﷺ. Understanding the *Shama'il* is therefore critical to any proper understanding of Islam, for it invites us to experience the most detailed qualities of the message-bearer, thus fundamentally changing how we understand the Message he brought. Knowing the *Shama'il* is a pre-requisite to properly understanding Islam in general and the Prophet's life (*Sira*) in particular, for his beautiful appearance, lifestyle and character provide the ultimate contextualisation needed to correctly understand Islam and, most importantly, apply that understanding. Without a proper understanding of the *Shama'il*, one is left to read Islam and the Prophet's life through the lenses of his or her own socially-conditioned impressions and assumptions.

Knowing the *Shama'il* is a tried and true means of filling one's heart with reverence for the Prophet ﷺ, which, in turn, is how one's heart fills with reverence for his Sacred Law. As Shaykh Muhammad ibn al-Qasim Jasus, a commentator on the *Shama'il*, stated, 'The reverence one gives to speech is proportionate to the reverence one gives the speaker.' That is to say, the more one reveres the speaker the more one reveres his speech. The speech of the Prophet Muhammad ﷺ is the content of Islam, and revering it is a means of acting upon it and preferring it over personal habits and desires.

Knowing the *Shama'il* is knowing the Prophet's sublime beauty. Human beings are naturally disposed to love beauty and those who treat them with kindness and excellence. So what beauty and excellence can rival the beauty and excellence of the Best of Creation, the Prophet Muhammad ﷺ, who said about himself, 'I have not been sent except to perfect the noble qualities of character'? (Ahmad, *Musnad*)

Knowing and learning the *Shama'il* is also a means of rendering service (*khidma*) to the Prophet Muhammad ﷺ. It is a form of praise in its own right and a means of connection, veneration and spiritual transformation. It is an act of worship that draws one near to Allah and His Prophet ﷺ. By reading and reflecting upon the Prophet and his sublimities ﷺ one is 'exposing' himself or herself to gentle breezes of divine mercy and intimate knowledge, as the Prophet ﷺ said, 'Verily in these days of yours are gentle breezes (*nafahat*), so expose yourselves to them.' (al-Tabarani, *al-Mu'jam al-Kabir*)

Knowing the *Shama'il* creates delight and joy within hearts and engenders love of Allah and His Messenger ﷺ. To spend time with the *Shama'il* is to praise Allah and remember Him, for it is He who endows the Prophet Muhammad ﷺ with his beautiful form and unparalleled character.

HOW TO READ
al-Shama'il al-Muhammadiyya

BEFORE VENTURING INTO THE DAZZLING MEADOWS OF THE *Shama'il*, it is essential to prepare our hearts by calling to mind the nature of the Messenger of Allah ﷺ. The first book about the Prophet's sublime qualities is the Quran. It is the first and most excellent *Shama'il*. The beautiful moral, physical and spiritual qualities of the Prophet Muhammad ﷺ are embedded in the Book of Allah. The Quran—the pre-eternal divine speech—is the supreme character reference. Some scholars have said, 'If you want to see the Prophet Muhammad ﷺ, then look into the Quran.' This is undoubtedly true, as Imam al-Tirmidhi recorded in the *Shama'il* (hadith 385) from Anas ibn Malik ؓ, 'I gazed at his blessed face, and it looked like a page from the Quran (*mushaf*)...' The Prophet Muhammad ﷺ, therefore, reflects the Quran just as the Quran reflects him.

The *Shama'il* presents descriptions of the moral, physical and spiritual perfections of the Prophet Muhammad ﷺ. These perfections that Allah bestowed upon him ﷺ encompass every aspect of his blessed being: his outward form, his senses and his internal form. The Prophet Muhammad ﷺ is the most perfect form of created beauty. He possesses the most august, most splendid and most beautiful face, hair, neck, torso, arms, hands, feet, fingers, toes and all other physical aspects of creation. His senses are also perfected: his hearing is absolutely perfect, his sight is absolutely perfect, his smell is absolutely perfect, his taste is absolutely perfect and his touch is absolutely perfect. Likewise, his voice and elocution are absolutely perfect.

The Prophet Muhammad ﷺ is bestowed absolute perfection in his internal form: his blessed heart has been endowed with the most splendid shape, and his blessed liver, heart, spleen, kidneys, lungs and all other organs have the most perfect contours. His blessed blood vessels are in a complete state of balance, and every muscle, tendon, and tissue is flawless. There is no one in creation besides the Prophet Muhammad ﷺ who has complete equilibrium in temperament (*mizaj*).

He has also been given perfection in his inner beauty, such that he carries out divine injunctions sweetly, and perceives Allah's Oneness clearly. His intelligence and sagacity are also absolutely perfect.

The Prophet Muhammad's ﷺ beauties and perfections are unsurpassable. None can rival or outstrip him in any laudable quality or trait. He knows Allah as He should be known. He fears Allah as He should be feared. He loves Allah as He should be loved.

The beautiful character and inward traits of the Prophet Muhammad encompass his whole body and everything about him. His shyness, modesty, kindness, bravery, temperance, fear of Allah, reliance, certainty, contentment, love, devotion, compassion, and many other qualities all pervade his entire body and inward and outward reality.

All of this constitutes the spiritual lens through which the *Shama'il* must be viewed.

To understand many of the hadith in the *Shama'il* that describe the Prophet's human qualities (*bashariyya*) ﷺ, it is essential to know that his sanctified soul has settled within his blessed and pure body in contentment, love and submission. Any veil between soul and body is removed. This means that the 'taste' of the Prophet's noble soul is firmly rooted in his pure, earthen body and penetrates the world as such. His blessed soul is eternally pure, and all his senses diffuse through it. His is the greatest and strongest soul. It was his celestial soul that Allah strengthened to carry the divine speech, concerning which Allah says Had we revealed this Qur'an upon a mountain, you would have seen it humbled and rent asunder by the fear of Allah. (Qur'an 59:21)

All of this should give us pause to reflect: we are not by any means reading about an ordinary man. We must be careful not to understand the descriptions of the Prophet ﷺ through the interpretive lenses of our own flawed human experience. If anything, the descriptions of the Prophet Muhammad ﷺ are always just approximations that attempt to describe utterly sublime beauty through the limited aperture of human language. The Companions of the Prophet Muhammad ﷺ did not have an easy time describing him, because there is nothing within creation to which he may be compared. All creation pales in comparison. The Companions resorted to expressions of transcendence (*tanzih*), saying he was 'neither extremely tall nor short'; when comparing him to objects in creation (*tashbih*), they resorted to approximations, metaphors and signs that point to a higher reality. Imam al-Bajuri said, 'The one who describes him ﷺ only does so through approximations, for none but his Creator know the reality of his qualities!' Simply put, only Allah fully knows the Prophet ﷺ.

When reading the *Shama'il,* in addition to learning about the Prophet's blessed physical features and character, we also learn about his clothing, food, bedding, ring, footwear, weapons, armour and so on ﷺ. It is crucial to remember that every aspect of the Prophet Muhammad ﷺ is bestowed (*wahbi*) by the divine. Nothing about him is happenstance or fortuitous; there are no coincidences. Nothing relating to him is without meaning and significance. Every part of his body witnesses the Divine, and every fibre of his blessed being invites us to Allah. Every movement, every stillness, every statement, every moment of silence, every gesture, every smile, every article of clothing, every belonging—all of them are bestowed and all of them invite humanity to Allah. To look at anything that is from him, on him, or associated with him is to be invited to faith. The part is like the whole (*al-juz' ka al-kull*)!

These are the chief reasons why learning the *Shama'il* and returning to it over and over again are vital to our faith and to the lives of our spiritual hearts. To learn it and meditate upon its descriptions is to not only learn faith but to link our hearts to the strongest support of faith, the one without whom we would have no faith ﷺ. May Allah send endless prayers and salutations upon him and his pure Family!

THIS TRANSLATION

In attempting to translate the *Shama'il,* I readily concede my inability, weakness and incapacity. If the Arabic language—the language of the Prophet Muhammad ﷺ—is unable to fully describe his sublime essence, what about English? No words in any language can *fully* describe the beauties and exquisite qualities of the Messenger of Allah ﷺ. As such, before you is but a meagre attempt to translate the *Shama'il,* during which I have been continually reminded of the poetic lines of Imam Ibn Juzayy al-Kalbi (d. 741 AH):

I attempt to praise the Chosen One but I'm prevented
By my inadequacy in comprehending his merits
How can I possibly encompass the brimming ocean?
How can I possibly count all the grains of sand and the stars?
Had my every muscle turned into a tongue
I would still be unable to attain a portion of his praise
Had all of creation assembled in his honour
They would not fulfil what is truly incumbent
So our tongue has held us back out of awe and courteousness
And out of fear and exaltation to the one of loftiest rank
How often eloquence is found in silence
And how often does speech reprove the speaker!

This translation before you is based on Shaykh Muhammad 'Awwama's edition of *al-Mawahib al-Laduniyya*, Imam Ibrahim ibn Muhammad al-Bajuri's (d. 1277 AH) magisterial commentary on the *Shama'il*. The majority of the footnotes are direct quotations of, or drawn from, Imam al-Bajuri's commentary. In a number of places, I have quoted from other commentaries as well, such as Mulla 'Ali al-Qari's *Jama' al-Wasa'il*, Shaykh Muhammad bin al-Qasim *Jasus' al-Fawa'id al-Bahiyya*, Imam Ibn Hajar al-Haytami's *Ashraf al-Wasa'il*, Imam 'Abd al-Ra'uf al-Munawi's *Sharh al-Shama'il*, and others. The works consulted in this translation and its commentary include, but are not limited to:

1. *Jama' al-Wasa'il fi Sharh al-Shama'il*
   by Mulla 'Ali ibn Sultan al-Qari (d. 1014 AH)
2. *Sharh al-Shama'il li al-Tirmidhi*
   by Shaykh 'Abd al-Ra'uf ibn 'Ali al-Munawi (d. 1031 AH)
3. *Ashraf al-Wasa'il fi Sharh al-Shama'il*
   by Imam Ahmad ibn Hajar al-Haytami (d. 973 AH)
4. *Al-Fawa'id al-Bahiyya 'ala al-Shama'il al-Muhammadiyya*
   by Shaykh Muhammad ibn al-Qasim Jasus (d. 1200 AH)
5. *Sharh al-Mawahib al-Laduniyya*
   by Shaykh Muhammad ibn 'Abd al-Baqi al-Zurqani (d. 1122 AH)
6. *Al-Khasa'is al-Kubra*
   by Imam Jalal al-Din al-Suyuti (d. 911 AH)
7. *Rawd al-Unuf*
   by Shaykh 'Abd al-Rahman al-Suhayli (d. 581 AH)
8. *Al-Sira al-Halabiyya*
   by Shaykh 'Ali ibn Ibrahim al-Halabi (d. 1044 AH)
9. *Al- 'Ujala al-Saniyya 'ala Alfiyya al-Sira al-Nabawiyya*
   by al-Hafiz Zayn al-Din al-'Iraqi (d. 806 AH)
10. *Al-Shifa bi Ta'rif Huquq al-Mustafa*
    by Qadi 'Iyad al-Yahsubi (d. 544 AH)

11. *Subul al-Huda wa al-Rashad*
by Imam Muhammad ibn Yusuf al-Salihi al-Shami (d. 942 AH)
12. *Fath al-Bari*
by al-Hafiz Ibn Hajar al-'Asqalani (d. 852 AH)
13. *Al-Mawahib al-Laduniyya*
by Shaykh Ahmad ibn Muhammad al-Qastalani (d. 923 AH)
14. *Bughyat al-Ra'id*
by Qadi 'Iyad al-Yahsubi (d. 544 AH)
15. *Al-Tibb al-Nabawi*
by Imam Jalal al-Din al-Suyuti (d. 911 AH)
16. *Zahr al-Khama'il 'ala al-Shama'il*
by Imam Jalal al-Din al-Suyuti (d. 911 AH)
17. *Al-Taratib al-Idariyya*
by Shaykh Muhammad ibn Ja'far al-Kittani (d. 1345 AH)
18. *Muntaha al-Sul*
by Shaykh 'Abdullah al-Lahji (d. 1410 AH)
19. *Sayyiduna Muhammad Rasulullah ﷺ Shama'iluhu al-Hamida wa Khasa'ilahu al-Majida,* by Shaykh 'Abdullah Siraj al-Din al-Husayni (d. 1422 AH)

Numerous notes were also written by Shaykh Mohammed Aslam. The initials AA (for Abdul Aziz) and MA (for Mohammed Aslam) are placed after each footnote to distinguish between the commentaries. (Footnotes written by both of us are marked AA, MA.)

Readers will note that throughout this translation, when speaking about the Prophet's limbs ﷺ, the word 'blessed' appears prior—e.g. 'his blessed eyes' and 'his blessed hands'. The word 'blessed' is not mentioned explicitly in the words of Imam al-Tirmidhi or the narrators, but it is a reality that everything of the Prophet ﷺ is blessed, so it has been added out of reverence and to communicate in English something of the awe and love conveyed by the Companions in their original Arabic descriptions.

A comment about some of the word choices used in the translation and notes is in order as well. As Muslims, we believe that the Prophet Muhammad ﷺ is the Perfect Human who is free of every blemish and flaw. His infallibility and perfection (*'isma*) is the centre and vantage point from which we learn about his human qualities. When we come across any description of the Prophet ﷺ that ascribes what may be misconstrued as faults, imperfections, or less-than-sublime qualities, it is imperative that we understand them in light of the clear-cut and unshakable foundation of belief in his perfection. The word choices in this translation and commentary intend to reflect this principle and aim first and foremost to observe the high etiquette (*adab*) required when speaking about the Prophet ﷺ.

TRANSLATOR'S ACKNOWLEDGEMENTS

Our beloved Prophet ﷺ has said, 'Whosoever fails to thank the people has failed to thank Allah.' (Abu Dawud, *Sunan*) In compliance with the prophetic command, and out of love and appreciation, I would like to thank the following individuals for their support.

Firstly, my heartfelt gratitude goes to my teachers who so generously teach me with their words and states. Secondly, I would like to thank Muhammad Adnan Sattaur, Muhammad Tauseef Rehman and Shaykh Mohammed Aslam, who spearheaded this project and whose support and prayers were essential. My thanks also go to Shaykh Muhammad Mendes and Shaykh Abdullah bin Hamid Ali for their fruitful discussions. Thanks also to Kelly El-Yacoubi for her skilful and careful editing eye. My deep appreciation also goes to my teacher, Shaykh Muhammad Sadiq al-'Alawi, for his time, prayers and insights. Thanks also to Abdul-Nur Brooks of Redolent Aromatics for the steady supply of excellent incense that was lit daily while translating this work. And to anyone else I have neglected to mention—may Allah reward you all without measure and bring you under the Banner of the Prophet Muhammad ﷺ on the Last Day. *Amin*!

In conclusion, I seek Allah's forgiveness for falling short, whether through negligence or ignorance, in translating and writing about the descriptions of His beloved ﷺ. The best that can be said when delving into the meanings of the *Shama'il* is the constant refrain: *Allah and His Messenger ﷺ know best!*

ABDUL AZIZ SURAQAH

BIOGRAPHY OF
Imam al-Tirmidhi ﵀

He is Muhammad ibn 'Isa ibn Sawra ibn Musa ibn al-Dahhak al-Sulami al-Tirmidhi, from the city of Tirmidh located in southern Uzbekistan. It is also said that his name was Muhammad ibn 'Isa ibn Yazid ibn Sawra ibn al-Sakan. He was born in the month of Dhu al-Hijja in the year 209 AH. His grandfather Sawra hailed from Merv in present day Turkmenistan and later moved to the village of Bugh. Some historians say Imam al-Tirmidhi was born blind, whereas Imam al-Dhahabi and other scholars mention that he became blind later in life due to many years of rigorous travel in pursuit of sacred knowledge as well as frequent weeping in awe of Allah.

His Pursuit of Sacred Knowledge

Imam al-Tirmidhi began seeking sacred knowledge in his early twenties in his home village of Bugh and eventually studied under scholars in Khorasan, Mecca, Medina, Basra, Kufa, Wasit and Ray (present day Tehran, Iran). In each of these lands he heard hadith from narrators and hadith masters. Although he did not travel to Egypt or the Levant *(Sham)*, he recorded narrations from the hadith scholars of those lands via intermediaries.

His Teachers

Imam al-Tirmidhi had a staggering number of teachers. He studied under the famous hadith masters Imam Muhammad ibn Isma'il al-Bukhari, Imam Muslim ibn Hajjaj al-Naysaburi and Imam Abu Dawud al-Sijistani. He narrated seventy-five reports in his Sunan on the authority of Imam al-Bukhari and quoted him more than one hundred times in his work assessing hadith narrators *(al-Jarh wa al-Ta'dil)*. Imam al-Bukhari is reported to have said to Imam al-Tirmidhi, 'I have benefited from you more than you have benefitted from me!' As for Imam Muslim, although Imam al-Tirmidhi heard narrations from him, he only narrated a single hadith from him in his *Sunan* (hadith 690). As for Imam Abu Dawud, he heard narrations from him and narrated five hadith from him in his *Sunan* (hadith 468, 733, 3148, 3962 and 4158).

Imam al-Dhahabi wrote that Imam al-Tirmidhi narrated on the authority of Qutayba ibn Sa'id, Ishaq ibn Rahawayh, Muhammad ibn 'Amr al-Sawwaq al-Balkhi, Mahmud ibn Ghaylan, Isma'il ibn Musa al-Fizari, Ahmad ibn Mani', Abu Mus'ab al-Zuhri, Bishr ibn Mu'adh al-'Aqadi, Hasan ibn Ahmad ibn Abi Shu'ayb, Abu 'Ammar Husayn b. Hurayth, Ma'mar ibn 'Abdillah ibn Mu'awiya al-Jumahi, 'Abd al-Jabbar ibn al-'Ala', Abu Kurayb, 'Ali ibn Hujr, 'Ali ibn Sa'id ibn Masruq al-Kindi, 'Amr ibn 'Ali al-Fallas, 'Imran ibn Musa al-Qazzaz, Muhammad ibn

Abban al-Mustamli, Muhammad ibn Humayd al-Razi, Muhammad ibn 'Abd al-A'la, Muhammad ibn Rafi', Muhammad ibn 'Abd al-'Aziz ibn Abi Razma, Muhammad ibn 'Abd al-Malik ibn Abi al-Shawarib, Muhammad ibn Yahya al-'Adani, Nasr ibn 'Ali, Harun al-Hammal, Hannad ibn al-Sarri, Abu Hammam al-Walid ibn Shuja', Yahya ibn Aktham, Yahya ibn Habib ibn 'Arabi, Yahya ibn Darsat al-Basri, Yahya ibn Talha al-Yarbu'i, Yusuf ibn Hammad al-Ma'ni, Ishaq ibn Musa al-Khatmi, Ibrahim ibn 'Abdillah al-Harawi and Suwayd ibn Nasr al-Marwazi.

His Students

Imam al-Tirmidhi's most famous students were: Abu Bakr al-Samarqandi, Abu Hamid al-Marwazi, Ahmad ibn 'Ali al-Muqri', Ahmad ibn Yusuf al-Nasafi, Abu al-Harith Asad ibn Hamduwayhi al-Nasafi, Hammad ibn Shakir al-Warraq, Dawud ibn Nasr ibn Suhayl al-Bazdawi, Abu al-Hasan 'Ali ibn 'Umar ibn al-Taqi ibn Kulthum, Abu Ja'far Muhammad ibn Sufyan ibn al-Nadr al-Nasafi, Muhammad ibn al-Mundhir ibn Sa'id al-Harawi, Makhul ibn al-Fadl al-Nasafi, Makki ibn Nuh al-Nasafi al-Muqri' and Haytham ibn Kulayb al-Shashi.

His Virtues & Rank in Scholarship

Imam al-Tirmidhi was held in universal esteem by scholars for both his hadith mastery and personal piety. Hafiz al-Mizzi said of him, 'He is one of the distinguished imams and hadith masters, and one by whom Allah benefitted the Muslims.'

Imam al-Hakim said, 'I heard 'Umar ibn 'Allak say, "Bukhari died and left no one in Khorasan like Abu 'Isa [al-Tirmidhi] in knowledge, memorisation, piety, and worldly renunciation. He wept until he became blind and remained in that condition for years."'

Imam Ibn Kathir said, 'He was one of the imams of hadith in his age and has a number of famous compilations, such as *al-Jami'*, *al-Shama'il*, *Asma' al-Sahaba* and others. The book *al-Jami'* is one of the six [hadith] works that the scholars refer to.'

Abu Ya'la al-Khalili said, 'He is a narrator of probity and precision *(thiqa)*, and there is consensus regarding his status. He was known for his trustworthiness and knowledge.'

Imam al-Dhahabi recorded that Imam al-Tirmidhi said, 'I compiled this work [*al-Jami'*] and presented it to the scholars of the Hejaz, Iraq and Khorasan, and they were pleased with it. Anyone who has this book in his home, it is as if he has the Prophet speaking in his home.'

His Works

Imam al-Tirmidhi wrote:

1. *al-Jami'* (The Compendium). This work is also known as *al-Sunan*, and is a compilation of hadith reports. It is one of the six most prominent hadith collections (commonly referred to as *al-Kutub al-Sitta*, or 'The Six Canonical Books').
2. *al-Shama'il al-Muhammadiyya* (The Muhammadan Qualities). This is a compilation on the physical and moral qualities of the Prophet Muhammad ﷺ.
3. *al-'Ilal* (The Defects). This is a famous work on the subtle defects in chains of transmission.
4. *Asma' al-Sahaba* (The Names of the Companions). This work catalogues the names of the Companions of the Prophet ﷺ.
5. *al-Jarh wa al-Ta'dil* (Creditation and Discreditation). This work details the principles and nomenclature of hadith criticism by which narrators are assessed for their reliability or unreliability.

Imam al-Tirmidhi authored other works not available to us, such as:

1. *Kitab al-Zuhd* (The Book of Worldly Renunciation).
2. *Kitab al-Tarikh* (The Book of History).
3. *al-Asma' wa al-Kuna* (On Names and Agnomens).
4. *al-Athar al-Mawqufa* (The Reports Whose Chains End with Companions).

His Passing

Imam al-Tirmidhi passed away on a Monday, the 13th of Rajab 279 AH, in his home village of Bugh. May Allah Most High have mercy upon him, be pleased with him and admit him to the loftiest Gardens of Paradise in the intimate company of the Prophet Muhammad ﷺ!

Tomb of Imam al-Tirmidhi ﵀.

AUTHORISATION OF *Mohammed Aslam*

أروي بالإجازة عن العلامة الشيخ عبد الرزاق الحلبي ١٤٣٣هـ وعن العلامة الشيخ محمد أديب الكلاس ١٤٣٠هـ وكلاهما يروي عن العلامة الشيخ محمد صالح بن عبد الله الفرفور الحسني ١٤٠٧هـ وهو يروي عن المحدث الأكبر العلامة الشيخ محمد بدر الدين بن يوسف الحسني ١٣٥٤هـ عن الشيخ برهان الدين إبراهيم بن عليّ السقا ١٢٩٨هـ عن الشيخ ثعيلب بن سالم الفشني الضرير ١٢٣٩هـ عن الشيخ شهاب الدين أحمد بن عبد الفتاح الملوي ١١٨٢هـ عن الشيخ عبد الله بن سالم البصري ١١٣٤هـ عن الشيخ محمد بن علاء الدين البابلي ١٠٧٧هـ عن الشيخ أبي النّجا سالم بن محمد السنهوري ١٠١٥هـ عن الشيخ نجم الدين محمد بن أحمد الغيطي ٩٨٢هـ عن شيخ الإسلام القاضي زكريا بن محمد الأنصاري ٩٢٦هـ عن الامام شهاب الدين أحمد بن عليّ بن حجر العسقلاني ٨٥٢هـ عن الشيخ أبي إسحاق إبراهيم بن أحمد التنوخي ٨٠٠هـ عن الشيخ أبي الحسن عليّ بن محمد البندنيجي ٧٣٦هـ عن الشيخ أبي محمد عبد الخالق بن الأنجب النشتبري ٦٤٩هـ عن الشيخ أبي الفتح عبد الملك بن عبد الله الكروخي ٥٤٨هـ عن الشيخ أبي عامر محمود بن قاسم الازدي ٤٨٧هـ عن الشيخ أبي محمد عبد الجبار بن محمد الجراحي المروزي ٤١٢هـ عن الشيخ أبي العباس محمد بن أحمد بن محبوب المروزي ٣٤٦هـ عن إمام المحدثين الحافظ أبي عيسى محمد بن عيسى بن سورة الترمذي ٢٧٩هـ رضي الله عنهم أجمعين.

محمد أسلم بن عبد القيوم بن الحافظ محمد يوسف

I relate al-Shama'il al-Muhammadiyya by way of authorisation from the following scholars, amongst others: ʿAllama Shaykh ʿAbd al-Razzaq al-Halabi (d. 1433 AH) and ʿAllama Shaykh Muhammad Adib al-Kallas (d. 1430 AH), both of whom relate from ʿAllama Shaykh Muhammad Salih ibn ʿAbdullah al-Farfur al-Hasani (d. 1407 AH), who relates from al-Muhadith al-Akbar, ʿAllama Shaykh Muhammad Badr al-Din ibn Yusuf al-Hasani (d. 1354 AH), from Shaykh Burhan al-Din Ibrahim ibn ʿAli al-Saqqa (d. 1298 AH), from Shaykh Thuʿaylib ibn Salim al-Fashani al-Darir (d. 1239 AH), from Shaykh Shihab al-Din Ahmad ibn ʿAbd al-Fattah al-Mulawi (d. 1182 AH), from Shaykh ʿAbdullah ibn Salim al-Basri (d. 1134 AH), from Shaykh Muhammad ibn ʿAla' al-Din al-Babili (d. 1077 AH), from Shaykh Abu al-Naja Salim ibn Muhammad al-Sanhuri (d. 1015 AH), from Shaykh Najm al-Din Muhammad ibn Ahmad al-Ghayti (d. 982 AH), from *Shaykh al-Islam* Qadi Zakariyya ibn Muhammad al-Ansari (d. 926 AH), from Imam Shihab al-Din Ahmad ibn ʿAli ibn Hajar al-ʿAsqalani (d. 852 AH), from Shaykh Abu Ishaq Ibrahim ibn Ahmad al-Tanukhi (d. 800 AH), from Shaykh Abu al-Hasan ʿAli ibn Muhammad al-Bandniji (d. 736 AH), from Shaykh Abu Muhammad ʿAbd al-Khaliq ibn al-Anjab al-Nashtabri (d. 649 AH), from Shaykh Abu al-Fath ʿAbd al-Malik ibn ʿAbdullah al-Karukhi (d. 548 AH), from Shaykh Abu ʿAmir Mahmud ibn Qasim al-Azdi (d. 487 AH), from Shaykh Abu Muhammad ʿAbd al-Jabbar ibn Muhammad al-Jarrahi al-Marwazi (d. 412 AH), from Shaykh Abu al-ʿAbbas Muhammad ibn Ahmad ibn Mahbub al-Marwazi (d. 346 AH), from the author, Imam al-Muhadithin, al-Hafiz Abu ʿIsa Muhammad ibn ʿIsa ibn Sawra al-Tirmidhi (d. 279 AH)—Allah be well pleased with them all.

MOHAMMED ASLAM IBN ʿABDUL QAYUM IBN HAFIZ MUHAMMAD YUSUF

AUTHORISATION OF
Abdul Aziz Suraqah

أروي كتاب الشمائل للإمام الترمذي عن الشيخ السيد يسري جبر الحسيني الشافعي عن الشيخ السيد أبي الفضل عبد الله بن محمد الصديق الغماري الحسني عن مسند العصر سيدي أحمد بن رافع الحسيني القاسمي عن شمس الدين الشيخ محمد الإنيابي عن شيخ الإسلام الشيخ إبراهيم الباجوري عن شيخ الإسلام الشيخ حسن القويسني عن أبي هريرة داود القلعي عن السيد أحمد بن محمد السُحيمي عن الشيخ عبد الله بن عامر الشبراوي عن أحمد بن محمد الخليفي عن الشهاب الدين أحمد البشبيشي عن الشيخ سلطان المزاحي عن أبي النجا سالم السنهوري عن نجم الدين الغيطي عن القاضي زكريا الأنصاري عن أبي الفتح المدني عن الحافظ أبي الفضل عبد الرحيم بن حسين العراقي عن الشيخ عبد الله بن الخبازي عن الشيخ أحمد بن عبد الدايم عن الشيخ أبي شجاع البسطامي عن الشيخ أبي القاسم الخزاعي عن الشيخ أبي سعيد الهيثم بن كليب الشاشي عن الحافظ أبي عيسى محمد بن عيسى بن سورة الترمذي رحمهم الله تعالى ونفعنا بعلومهم في الدارين.

عبد العزيز سراقة

I relate al-Shama'il of Imam al-Tirmidhi by way of authorisation from the following scholars: Shaykh Sayyid Yusri Jabr al-Husayni al-Shafi'i, from Shaykh Abu al-Fadl 'Abdullah ibn Muhammad al-Siddiq al-Ghumari al-Husayni, from al-Musnid Imam Sayyid Ahmad ibn Rafi' al-Husayni al-Qasimi, from Shams al-Din Shaykh Muhammad al-Inyabi, from *Shaykh al-Islam* Imam Ibrahim al-Bajuri, from *Shaykh al-Islam* Imam Hasan al-Quwaysini, from Abu Hurayra Dawud al-Qal'i, from Sayyid Ahmad ibn Muhammad al-Suhaymi, from Shaykh 'Abdullah ibn 'Amir al-Shabrawi, from Shaykh Ahmad ibn Ahmad al-Khalifi, from Shihab al-Din Ahmad al-Bashishi, from Shaykh Sultan al-Mazahi, from Abu al-Naja Salim al-Sanhuri, from Najm al-Din al-Ghayti, from al-Qadi Zakariyya al-Ansari, from Abu al-Fath al-Madani, from al-Hafiz Abu al-Fadl 'Abd al-Rahim ibn Husayn al-'Iraqi, from Shaykh 'Abdullah ibn al-Khabazi, from Shaykh Ahmad ibn 'Abd al-Dayyim, from Shaykh Abu Shuja' al-Bustami, from Shaykh Abu al-Qasim al-Khuza'i, from Shaykh Abu Sa'id al-Haytham ibn Kulayb al-Shashi, from al-Hafiz Abu 'Isa Muhammad ibn 'Isa ibn Sawra al-Tirmidhi—Allah have mercy on them and benefit us by their knowledge in both abodes.

ABDUL AZIZ SURAQAH

"This matter is Religion, so be careful from whom you take your religion."
—Abu Hurayra, Ibn Sirin, Za'ida & others

"Were it not for isnad anyone can say anything."
—Ibn al-Mubarak, as narrated in the introduction to Muslim's *Sahih*

"All the scholars agree that no Muslim is allowed to say: 'The Messenger of Allah ﷺ said this or that' until one has acquired the actual narration of that hadith even in the remotest sense of qualified narration due to what the Prophet ﷺ has said: 'Whoever knowingly attributes a lie to me, let him take his seat in the Hellfire!'"—al-Qari, introduction to *al-Asrar al-Marfu'a*

وَإِنَّكَ لَعَلَىٰ خُلُقٍ عَظِيمٍ

"And verily you are upon an exalted standard of character"

QUR'AN 68:4

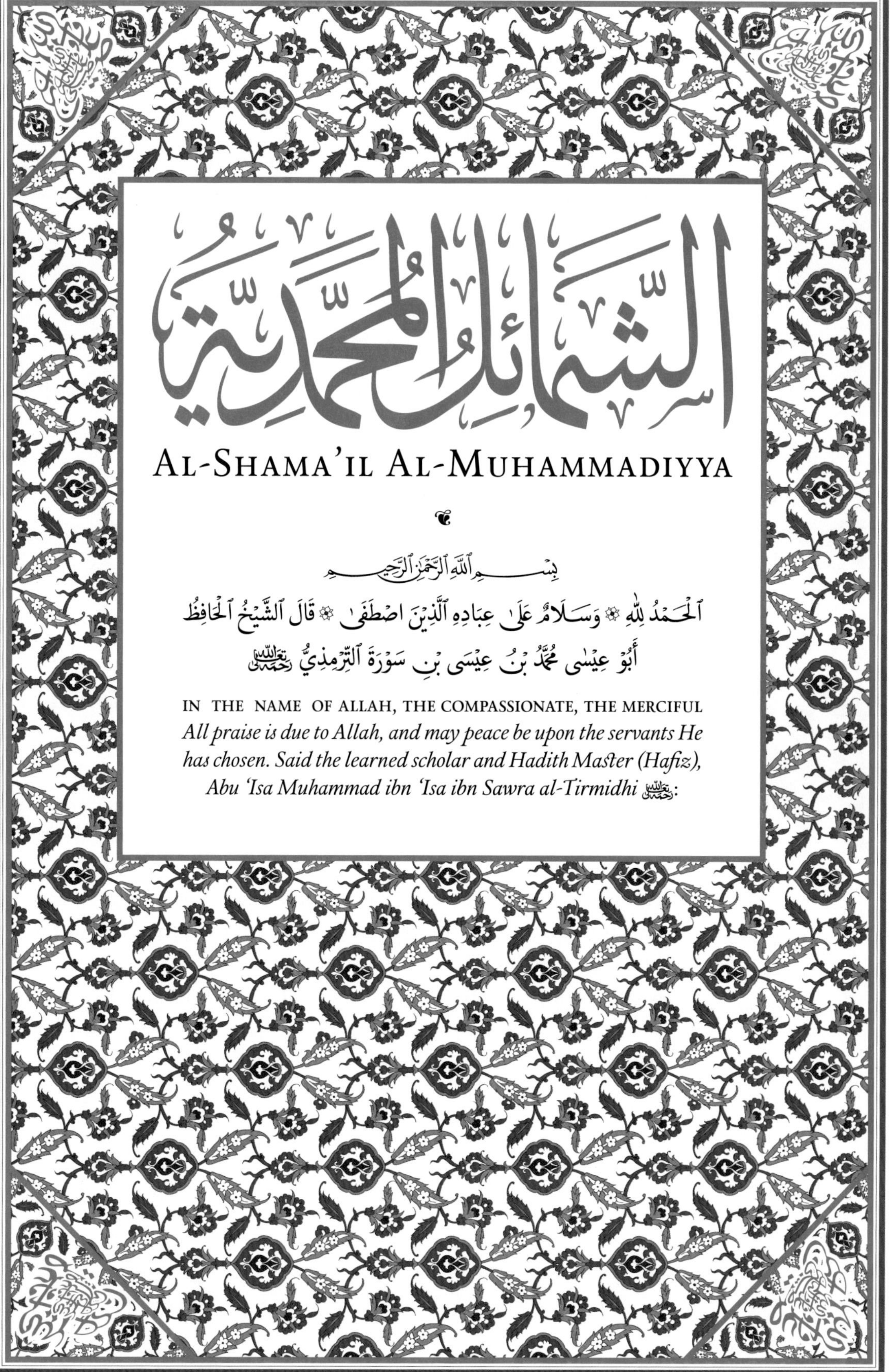

الشمائل المحمدية

Al-Shama'il Al-Muhammadiyya

بِسْمِ اللَّهِ الرَّحْمَٰنِ الرَّحِيمِ

اَلْحَمْدُ لِلَّهِ ۞ وَسَلَامٌ عَلَىٰ عِبَادِهِ ٱلَّذِينَ اصْطَفَىٰ ۞ قَالَ ٱلشَّيْخُ ٱلْحَافِظُ
أَبُو عِيسَىٰ مُحَمَّدُ بْنُ عِيسَى بْنِ سَوْرَةَ ٱلتِّرْمِذِيُّ رَحِمَهُ ٱللَّهُ تَعَالَىٰ

IN THE NAME OF ALLAH, THE COMPASSIONATE, THE MERCIFUL

All praise is due to Allah, and may peace be upon the servants He has chosen. Said the learned scholar and Hadith Master (Hafiz), Abu 'Isa Muhammad ibn 'Isa ibn Sawra al-Tirmidhi رحمه الله تعالى:

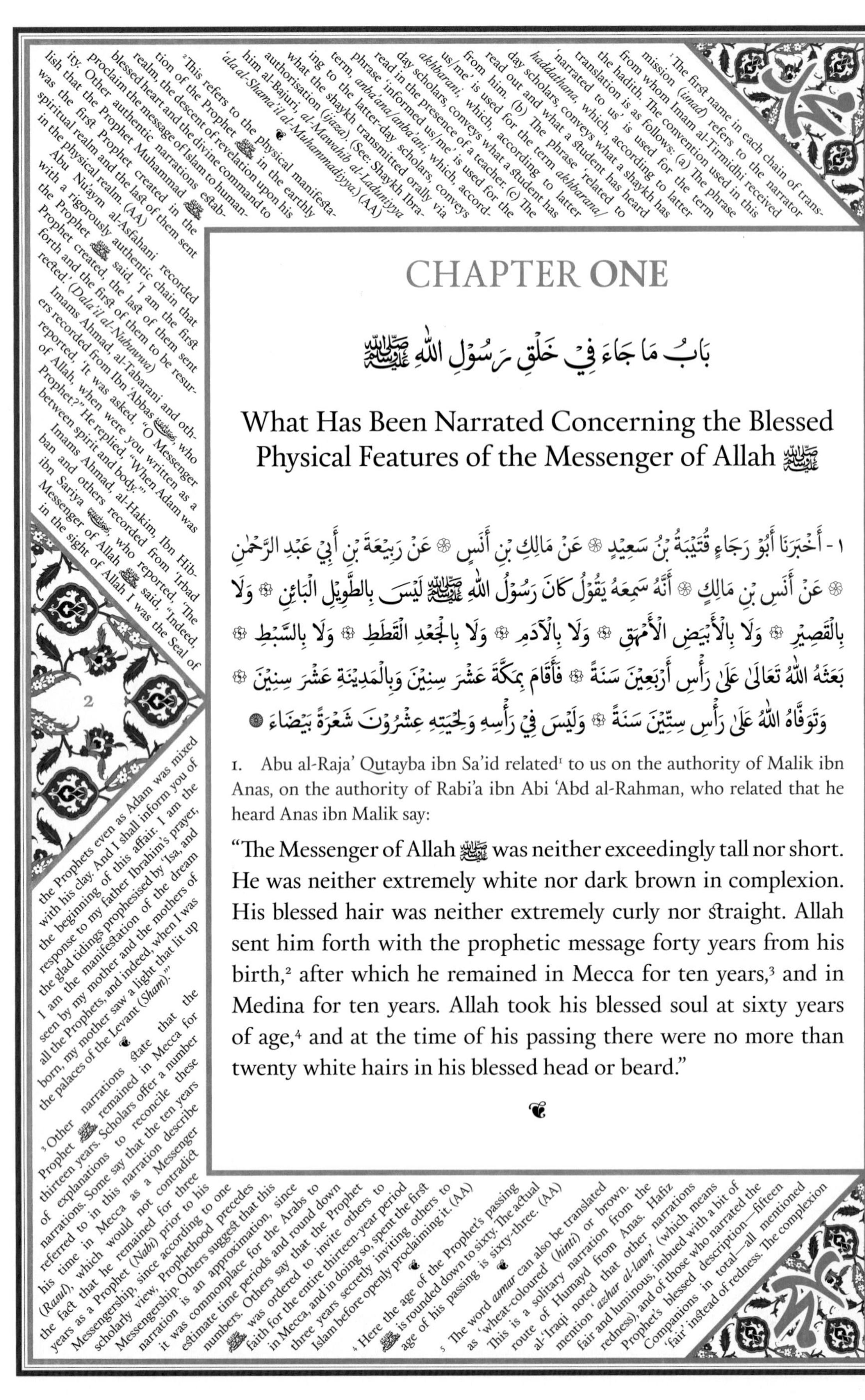

CHAPTER ONE

بَابُ مَا جَاءَ فِي خَلْقِ رَسُولِ اللهِ ﷺ

What Has Been Narrated Concerning the Blessed Physical Features of the Messenger of Allah ﷺ

١ - أَخْبَرَنَا أَبُو رَجَاءٍ قُتَيْبَةُ بْنُ سَعِيدٍ ❁ عَنْ مَالِكِ بْنِ أَنَسٍ ❁ عَنْ رَبِيعَةَ بْنِ أَبِي عَبْدِ الرَّحْمٰنِ ❁ عَنْ أَنَسِ بْنِ مَالِكٍ ❁ أَنَّهُ سَمِعَهُ يَقُولُ كَانَ رَسُولُ اللهِ ﷺ لَيْسَ بِالطَّوِيلِ الْبَائِنِ ❁ وَلَا بِالْقَصِيرِ ❁ وَلَا بِالْأَبْيَضِ الْأَمْهَقِ ❁ وَلَا بِالْآدَمِ ❁ وَلَا بِالْجَعْدِ الْقَطَطِ ❁ وَلَا بِالسَّبْطِ ❁ بَعَثَهُ اللهُ تَعَالَىٰ عَلَىٰ رَأْسِ أَرْبَعِينَ سَنَةً ❁ فَأَقَامَ بِمَكَّةَ عَشْرَ سِنِينَ وَبِالْمَدِينَةِ عَشْرَ سِنِينَ ❁ وَتَوَفَّاهُ اللهُ عَلَىٰ رَأْسِ سِتِّينَ سَنَةً ❁ وَلَيْسَ فِي رَأْسِهِ وَلِحْيَتِهِ عِشْرُونَ شَعْرَةً بَيْضَاءَ ❁

1. Abu al-Raja' Qutayba ibn Sa'id related[1] to us on the authority of Malik ibn Anas, on the authority of Rabi'a ibn Abi 'Abd al-Rahman, who related that he heard Anas ibn Malik say:

"The Messenger of Allah ﷺ was neither exceedingly tall nor short. He was neither extremely white nor dark brown in complexion. His blessed hair was neither extremely curly nor straight. Allah sent him forth with the prophetic message forty years from his birth,[2] after which he remained in Mecca for ten years,[3] and in Medina for ten years. Allah took his blessed soul at sixty years of age,[4] and at the time of his passing there were no more than twenty white hairs in his blessed head or beard."

[1] The first name in each chain of transmission (*isnad*) refers to the narrator from whom Imam al-Tirmidhi received the hadith. The convention used in this translation is as follows: (a) The phrase 'narrated to us' is used for the term *haddathana*, which, according to latter day scholars, conveys what a shaykh has read out and what a student has heard from him. (b) The phrase 'related to us/me' is used for the term *akhbarana/akhbarani*, which, according to latter day scholars, conveys what a student has read in the presence of a teacher. (c) The phrase 'informed us/me' is used for the term *anba'ana/anba'ani*, which, according to the latter-day scholars, conveys what the shaykh transmitted orally via authorisation (*ijaza*). (See: Shaykh Ibrahim al-Bajuri, *al-Mawahib al-Ladumiyya 'ala al-Shama'il al-Muhammadiyya*.) (AA)

[2] This refers to the physical manifestation of the Prophet ﷺ in the earthly realm, the descent of revelation upon his blessed heart and the divine command to proclaim the message of Islam to humanity. Other authentic narrations establish that the Prophet Muhammad ﷺ was the first Prophet created in the spiritual realm and the last of them sent in the physical realm. (AA)

Abu Nu'aym al-Asfahani recorded with a rigorously authentic chain that the Prophet ﷺ said, 'I am the first Prophet created, the last of them sent forth and the first of them to be resurrected.' (*Dala'il al-Nubuwwa*) Imams Ahmad, al-Tabarani and others recorded from Ibn 'Abbas ﷺ, who reported, 'It was asked, "O Messenger of Allah, when were you written as a Prophet?" He replied, "When Adam was between spirit and body."' Imams Ahmad, al-Hakim, Ibn Hibban and others recorded from 'Irbad ibn Sariya ﷺ, who reported, 'The Messenger of Allah ﷺ said, "Indeed, in the sight of Allah I was the Seal of the Prophets even as Adam was mixed with his clay. And I shall inform you of the beginning of this affair. I am the response to my father Ibrahim's prayer, the glad tidings prophesised by 'Isa, and I am the manifestation of the dream seen by my mother and the mothers of all the Prophets, and indeed, when I was born, my mother saw a light that lit up the palaces of the Levant (*Sham*)."'

[3] Other narrations state that the Prophet ﷺ remained in Mecca for thirteen years. Scholars offer a number of explanations to reconcile these narrations. Some say that the ten years referred to in this narration describe his time in Mecca as a Messenger (*Rasul*), which would not contradict the fact that he remained for three years as a Prophet (*Nabi*) prior to his Messengership, since according to one scholarly view, Prophethood precedes Messengership. Others suggest that this narration is an approximation, since it was commonplace for the Arabs to estimate time periods and round down numbers. Others say that the Prophet ﷺ was ordered to invite others to faith for the entire thirteen-year period in Mecca, and in doing so, spent the first three years secretly inviting others to Islam before openly proclaiming it. (AA)

[4] Here the age of the Prophet's passing ﷺ is rounded down to sixty. The actual age of his passing is sixty-three. (AA)

[5] The word *asmar* can also be translated as 'wheat-coloured' (*hinti*) or brown. This is a solitary narration from the route of Humayd from Anas. Hafiz al-'Iraqi noted that other narrations mention '*azhar al-lawn*' (which means fair and luminous, imbued with a bit of redness), and of those who narrated the Prophet's blessed description—fifteen Companions in total—all mentioned 'fair' instead of redness. The complexion

that is negated in the first hadith is dark brown, not the wheat- or brown-complexion mentioned here. Many scholars suggest that what is meant by brown in this narration is redness (*humra*) mixed with the Prophet's ﷺ fair complexion—a balance between extremely white and dark brown. It is critical to note that the word 'fair' in this narration is relative to the complexion of the Arabs of the time, which according to most authorities was wheat-coloured inclining towards dark brown, this being an intermediate complexion between white and dark brown. When reading the Prophet's description as 'fair', it should not be understood that he was pale-skinned (*amhaq*), as in what we would describe as 'white', which is explicitly negated in the first hadith of Anas ﷺ. Allah made His beloved Prophet ﷺ relatable to people of every colour and ethnicity and with a striking complexion that is in the middle of human hues. Allah and His Messenger know best. (AA)

❦

٢ - حَدَّثَنَا حُمَيْدُ بْنُ مَسْعَدَةَ الْبَصْرِيُّ ۞ حَدَّثَنَا عَبْدُ الْوَهَّابِ الثَّقَفِيُّ ۞ عَنْ حُمَيْدٍ ۞ عَنْ أَنَسِ بْنِ مَالِكٍ قَالَ كَانَ رَسُولُ اللهِ ﷺ رَبْعَةً ۞ لَيْسَ بِالطَّوِيلِ وَلَا بِالْقَصِيرِ ۞ حَسَنَ الْجِسْمِ ۞ وَكَانَ شَعْرُهُ لَيْسَ بِجَعْدٍ ۞ وَلَا سَبْطٍ ۞ أَسْمَرَ اللَّوْنِ ۞ إِذَا مَشَى يَتَكَفَّأُ ۞

2. Humayd ibn Mas'ada al-Basri narrated to us, "Abd al-Wahhab al-Thaqafi narrated to us on the authority of Humayd, who related on the authority of Anas ibn Malik, who reported:

"The Messenger of Allah ﷺ was of medium stature, neither exceedingly tall nor short. He had a handsome physique. His blessed hair was neither extremely curly nor straight. His complexion was fair with some redness (*asmar*).[5] When he walked, he would walk swiftly with vigour, and lean forward slightly.""

❦

٣ - حَدَّثَنَا مُحَمَّدُ بْنُ بَشَّارٍ يَعْنِي الْعَبْدِيَّ ۞ حَدَّثَنَا مُحَمَّدُ بْنُ جَعْفَرٍ ۞ حَدَّثَنَا شُعْبَةُ ۞ عَنْ أَبِي إِسْحَاقَ قَالَ سَمِعْتُ الْبَرَاءَ بْنَ عَازِبٍ يَقُولُ كَانَ رَسُولُ اللهِ ﷺ رَجُلًا مَرْبُوعًا ۞ بَعِيدَ مَا بَيْنَ الْمَنْكِبَيْنِ ۞ عَظِيمَ الْجُمَّةِ إِلَى شَحْمَةِ أُذُنَيْهِ ۞ عَلَيْهِ حُلَّةٌ حَمْرَاءُ ۞ مَا رَأَيْتُ شَيْئًا قَطُّ أَحْسَنَ مِنْهُ ۞

3. Muhammad ibn Bashhar—meaning al-'Abdi—narrated to us, 'Muhammad ibn Ja'far narrated to us, "Shu'ba narrated to us on the authority of Abu Ishaq, who said, 'I heard Bara' ibn 'Azib say:

"The Messenger of Allah ﷺ was a man of medium stature. His blessed shoulders were broad.[6] He had a full head of hair (*jumma*) that would reach his blessed earlobes.[7] He was wearing two red garments[8]—I have never seen anything[9] more beautiful than him!""""

❦

[6] Among the Arabs, having the quality of broad shoulders denotes dignity, power, generosity and forbearance. There was not a person Allah ever created who reached the pinnacles of these attributes more than the Messenger of Allah ﷺ. (AA)

❦

[7] In the *Shama'il* works, there are three words used to describe the length of the Prophet's hair ﷺ: (a) *Jumma*: where the hair reaches to the shoulders; (b) *Wafra*: where the hair reaches to the earlobes; (c) *Limma*: where the hair reaches between the earlobes and the shoulders.

In this narration, Bara' ibn 'Azib ﷺ described the Prophet's blessed hair ﷺ with the term *jumma*, and said that it reached his blessed earlobes. But according to the use of these terms, the Prophet's blessed hair ﷺ should have been described here as *wafra*. Imam al-Bajuri and other commentators on the *Shama'il* bring attention to this leniency in terms and suggest that it was stated liberally, with wafra in mind.

The phrase 'would reach' is a translation of the preposition *ila*, often translated as 'to'. There is a difference of opinion amongst grammarians about this preposition and whether or not it includes the end of that to which it extends. For example, if you say in Arabic, *safartu ila al-Madina* ('I travelled to Medina'), does it mean you reached the city limits of Medina or entered Medina proper? The correct position is that it includes the end. This is seen in the verse in the chapter *al-Ma'ida* describing the integrals of ritual purification (*wudu'*), *And wash your faces and arms to the elbows* (Qur'an 5:6). The Prophet ﷺ included his blessed elbows in his washing for prayer, which means one must wash slightly past the elbows and not just the outer edge of the arm before the elbows. In light of this, the narration of Bara ﷺ would mean that the Prophet's blessed hair ﷺ went past his earlobes. (AA)

❦

[8] The word used in this narration and others to come is *hulla*. Traditionally, a *hulla* is a dress consisting of two pieces (an *izar* (loincloth) and tunic). The *izar* and tunic may be matching, or they may be from different materials. Some scholars have said that the *hulla* was solid red and others have said that it had red lines. The word *hulla* can also be interpreted to mean a double layered garment. (AA)

❦

[9] Note that Bara' ﷺ said he had not seen 'anything'—not just anyone—more beautiful than the Prophet ﷺ. The Prophet ﷺ is without doubt the most beautiful of Allah's creation, more beautiful than everything in the cosmos. (AA)

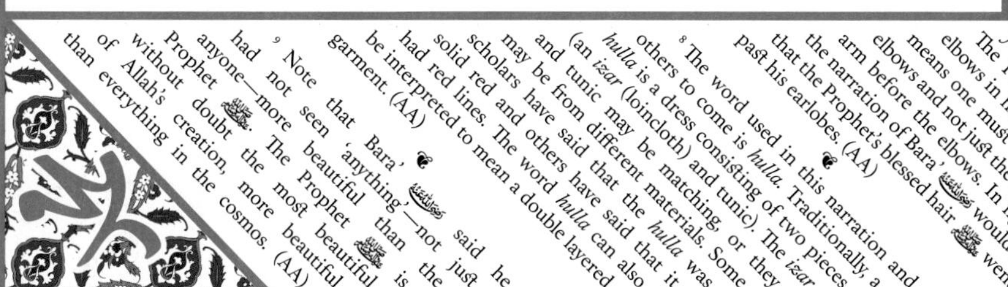

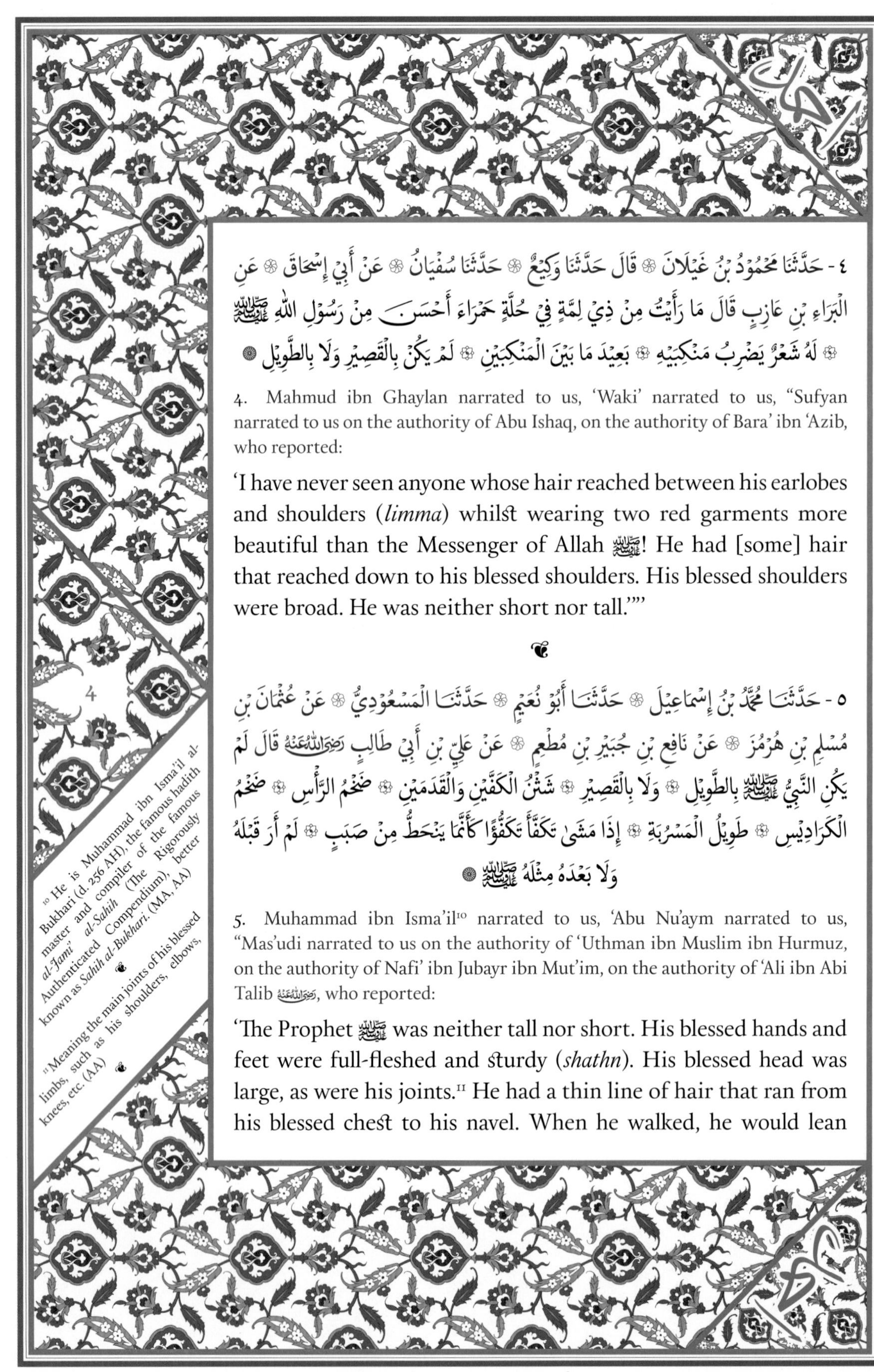

٤ - حَدَّثَنَا مَحْمُودُ بْنُ غَيْلَانَ ❁ قَالَ حَدَّثَنَا وَكِيعٌ ❁ حَدَّثَنَا سُفْيَانُ ❁ عَنْ أَبِي إِسْحَاقَ ❁ عَنِ الْبَرَاءِ بْنِ عَازِبٍ قَالَ مَا رَأَيْتُ مِنْ ذِي لِمَّةٍ فِي حُلَّةٍ حَمْرَاءَ أَحْسَنَ مِنْ رَسُولِ اللهِ ﷺ ❁ لَهُ شَعْرٌ يَضْرِبُ مَنْكِبَيْهِ ❁ بَعِيدَ مَا بَيْنَ الْمَنْكِبَيْنِ ❁ لَمْ يَكُنْ بِالْقَصِيرِ وَلَا بِالطَّوِيلِ ۞

4. Mahmud ibn Ghaylan narrated to us, 'Waki' narrated to us, "Sufyan narrated to us on the authority of Abu Ishaq, on the authority of Bara' ibn 'Azib, who reported:

'I have never seen anyone whose hair reached between his earlobes and shoulders (*limma*) whilst wearing two red garments more beautiful than the Messenger of Allah ﷺ! He had [some] hair that reached down to his blessed shoulders. His blessed shoulders were broad. He was neither short nor tall.'"'

٥ - حَدَّثَنَا مُحَمَّدُ بْنُ إِسْمَاعِيلَ ❁ حَدَّثَنَا أَبُو نُعَيْمٍ ❁ حَدَّثَنَا الْمَسْعُودِيُّ ❁ عَنْ عُثْمَانَ بْنِ مُسْلِمِ بْنِ هُرْمُزَ ❁ عَنْ نَافِعِ بْنِ جُبَيْرِ بْنِ مُطْعِمٍ ❁ عَنْ عَلِيِّ بْنِ أَبِي طَالِبٍ رَضِيَ اللهُ عَنْهُ قَالَ لَمْ يَكُنِ النَّبِيُّ ﷺ بِالطَّوِيلِ ❁ وَلَا بِالْقَصِيرِ ❁ شَثْنُ الْكَفَّيْنِ وَالْقَدَمَيْنِ ❁ ضَخْمُ الرَّأْسِ ❁ ضَخْمُ الْكَرَادِيسِ ❁ طَوِيلُ الْمَسْرُبَةِ ❁ إِذَا مَشَى تَكَفَّأَ تَكَفُّؤًا كَأَنَّمَا يَنْحَطُّ مِنْ صَبَبٍ ❁ لَمْ أَرَ قَبْلَهُ وَلَا بَعْدَهُ مِثْلَهُ ﷺ ۞

5. Muhammad ibn Isma'il[10] narrated to us, 'Abu Nu'aym narrated to us, "Mas'udi narrated to us on the authority of 'Uthman ibn Muslim ibn Hurmuz, on the authority of Nafi' ibn Jubayr ibn Mut'im, on the authority of 'Ali ibn Abi Talib رضي الله عنه, who reported:

'The Prophet ﷺ was neither tall nor short. His blessed hands and feet were full-fleshed and sturdy (*shathn*). His blessed head was large, as were his joints.[11] He had a thin line of hair that ran from his blessed chest to his navel. When he walked, he would lean

[10] He is Muhammad ibn Isma'il al-Bukhari (d. 256 AH), the famous hadith master and compiler of the famous *al-Jami' al-Sahih* (The Rigorously Authenticated Compendium), better known as *Sahih al-Bukhari*. (MA, AA)

[11] Meaning the main joints of his blessed limbs, such as his shoulders, elbows, knees, etc. (AA)

forward slightly, as if descending a height. I saw neither before him nor after him anyone like him!'"'[12]

٦ - حَدَّثَنَا سُفْيَانُ بْنُ وَكِيعٍ ❁ حَدَّثَنَا أَبِي ❁ عَنِ الْمَسْعُودِيِّ ❁ بِهٰذَا الإِسْنَادِ نَحْوَهُ بِمَعْنَاهُ ❁

6. Sufyan ibn Waki' narrated to us, 'My father[13] narrated to us on the authority of al-Mas'udi,[14] who narrated a similar report with this chain of transmission.'

٧ - حَدَّثَنَا أَحْمَدُ بْنُ عَبْدَةَ الضَّبِّيُّ الْبَصْرِيُّ وَعَلِيُّ بْنُ حُجْرٍ وَأَبُو جَعْفَرٍ مُحَمَّدُ بْنُ الْحُسَيْنِ وَهُوَ ابْنُ أَبِي حَلِيمَةَ وَالْمَعْنَىٰ وَاحِدٌ ❁ قَالُوا حَدَّثَنَا عِيسَى بْنُ يُونُسَ ❁ عَنْ عُمَرَ بْنِ عَبْدِ اللهِ مَوْلَىٰ غُفْرَةَ ❁ قَالَ حَدَّثَنِي إِبْرَاهِيمُ بْنُ مُحَمَّدٍ مِنْ وَلَدِ عَلِيِّ بْنِ أَبِي طَالِبٍ رضي الله عنه قَالَ كَانَ عَلِيٌّ إِذَا وَصَفَ رَسُولَ اللهِ ﷺ قَالَ لَمْ يَكُنْ رَسُولُ اللهِ ﷺ بِالطَّوِيلِ الْمُمَغَّطِ ❁ وَلَا بِالْقَصِيرِ الْمُتَرَدِّدِ ❁ وَكَانَ رَبْعَةً مِنَ الْقَوْمِ ❁ وَلَمْ يَكُنْ بِالْجَعْدِ الْقَطَطِ ❁ وَلَا بِالسَّبِطِ ❁ كَانَ جَعْدًا رَجِلًا ❁ وَلَمْ يَكُنْ بِالْمُطَهَّمِ ❁ وَلَا بِالْمُكَلْثَمِ ❁ وَكَانَ فِي وَجْهِهِ تَدْوِيرٌ ❁ أَبْيَضُ مُشْرَبٌ ❁ أَدْعَجُ الْعَيْنَيْنِ ❁ أَهْدَبُ الْأَشْفَارِ ❁ جَلِيلُ الْمُشَاشِ وَالْكَتِدِ ❁ أَجْرَدُ ذُو مَسْرُبَةٍ ❁ شَثْنُ الْكَفَّيْنِ وَالْقَدَمَيْنِ ❁ إِذَا مَشَىٰ تَقَلَّعَ كَأَنَّمَا يَنْحَطُّ مِنْ صَبَبٍ ❁ وَإِذَا الْتَفَتَ الْتَفَتَ مَعًا ❁ بَيْنَ كَتِفَيْهِ خَاتَمُ النُّبُوَّةِ ❁ وَهُوَ خَاتَمُ النَّبِيِّينَ ❁ أَجْوَدُ النَّاسِ صَدْرًا ❁ وَأَصْدَقُ النَّاسِ لَهْجَةً ❁ وَأَلْيَنُهُمْ عَرِيكَةً ❁ وَأَكْرَمُهُمْ عِشْرَةً ❁ مَنْ رَآهُ بَدِيهَةً هَابَهُ ❁ وَمَنْ خَالَطَهُ مَعْرِفَةً أَحَبَّهُ ❁ يَقُولُ نَاعِتُهُ لَمْ أَرَ قَبْلَهُ وَلَا بَعْدَهُ مِثْلَهُ ❁

7. Ahmad ibn 'Abda al-Dabbi al-Basri, 'Ali ibn Hujr and Abu Ja'far Muhammad ibn al-Husayn (who is Ibn Abi Halima all narrated to us (and the meaning was the same), "Isa ibn Yunus narrated to us on the authority of 'Umar ibn 'Abdillah, the freed slave of Ghufra, who said, "Ibrahim ibn Muhammad—from the progeny of 'Ali ibn Abi Talib رضي الله عنه[15]—narrated to me:

[12] This final statement is a summary after elaboration, as though Sayyiduna 'Ali رضي الله عنه was lost for words and in complete awe after describing his beauty and perfection; he sealed his statement, realising he was unable to do full justice to the greatness of the Messenger of Allah ﷺ. Sayyiduna Hassan ibn Thabit رضي الله عنه said in some poetry about the Messenger of Allah ﷺ:

More splendid than you
my eye hasn't seen
No woman has mothered
one oh so fine

You are created
so free of flaw
As if made by
your own design! (MA)

[13] Waki' ibn al-Jarrah. (AA)

[14] He is 'Abd al-Rahman ibn 'Abdillah ibn 'Utba ibn 'Abdillah ibn Mas'ud (d. 160 AH). (AA)

[15] The son of Muhammad ibn al-Hanafiyya, which makes him the grandson of Imam 'Ali ibn Abi Talib رضي الله عنه. (AA)

'When 'Ali described the Messenger of Allah ﷺ, he would say, "The Messenger of Allah ﷺ was neither extremely tall (*mummaghit*) nor extremely short (*mutaraddid*); he was of medium stature among his people.[16] His blessed hair was neither extremely curly (*qatit*) nor straight; rather, it was slightly wavy (*rajil*). He was not corpulent (*mutahham*). His blessed face was not completely circular (*mukaltham*), but was slightly round. His complexion was fair and imbued (*mushrab*) [with a bit of redness].[17] His blessed eyes were very black (*ad'aj*)[18] and his eyelashes were long (*ahdab*). His blessed joints were large (*jalil al-mushash*),[19] and his blessed shoulders (*katad/katid*)[20] were broad. He was not hirsute. A thin line of hair (*masruba*) ran from his blessed chest to his navel. His blessed hands and feet were full-fleshed and sturdy (*shathn*). When he walked, he walked with vigour (*taqalla'*), as if descending a height (*sabab*). When he would turn [to look at someone or something], he would turn with his whole body.[21] Between his blessed shoulders was the Seal of Prophethood[22]—and he is the Seal of the Prophets. His blessed heart was the soundest and most generous of hearts,[23] his speech is the most truthful of speech,[24] and he is the gentlest of all people in nature and the noblest of them in social interactions and companionship (*'ishra*).[25] Whoever saw him unexpectedly (*badiha*) would be awestruck.[26] Whoever interacted with him whilst knowing him would love him.[27] The one who would describe him[28] would say, 'I saw neither before him nor after him anyone like him!'"'"[29]

[16] He ﷺ was of medium stature relative to the average height among his people. When he walked by himself, the Prophet ﷺ would be described as having a medium stature; never did a tall person walk in his company but that the Messenger of Allah ﷺ was taller than him. Imam Abu Bakr ibn Lal recorded in *Makarim al-Akhlaq*, 'At times the Prophet ﷺ would be flanked by two tall men, yet he would appear taller than them; and when they would leave him, they would be described as tall and he would be described as having a medium stature. He ﷺ would say, "All goodness has been placed in moderation."' (AA)

[17] Some commentators say this slight redness would appear when the sun would shine and when the wind would blow; all the while the skin colour under the Prophet's ﷺ garments retained a fair complexion. Those who described the Prophet ﷺ as fair-complexioned meant his skin colour underneath his garments, while those who described him as fair and imbued with a bit of redness meant his appearance in the sun. Allah and His Messenger ﷺ know best.

Point of Benefit

Several narrations mention that during the Prophet's childhood ﷺ, certain miraculous 'prophetic precursors' (*irhasat*) appeared, presaging his emergence as a Prophet and Messenger ﷺ. Among these signs were clouds that would hover over him and shield him from the sun. Ibn Sa'd, Abu Nu'aym and Ibn 'Asakir recorded from Ibn 'Abbas ﷺ, who said, 'It was Halima's [the Prophet's ﷺ wet-nurse] habit to not let him go far from her sight. One hot afternoon, however, she was preoccupied, and a short while later he went with his sister [from suckling] Shayma' to play with the small sheep in their care. Soon afterwards, Halima went out in search of him and finally found him along with Shayma'. She asked Shayma', "How could you venture out with him in this heat?" "Dear mother," replied Shayma', "my brother suffered no heat; I saw that clouds hovered over him, stopping where he stopped, and moving where he moved, until we reached this spot here!"' This was one of the miracles preceding the Prophet's mission. Other narrations show that the Prophet ﷺ stood in the sun at times and was shaded by his Companions, such as Sayyiduna Abu Bakr ﷺ, who shaded his blessed body from the midday sun during the immigration to Medina. (AA)

[18] In Arabic, *adaj al-'aynayn*. This means the irises of his blessed eyes were very black and his sclerae were very white.

[19] Proportionate to his blessed body ﷺ. (AA)

[20] It can be read as either. (AA)

[21] To give importance to the one he was turning towards, for the purpose of speaking with the person or attending to his needs. (MA)

[22] Refer to chapter 2 on the description of the Seal of Prophethood. (MA)

[23] The word used here is *ajwad*, which is either derived from the word *jawda* or the word *jud*. *Jawda* means beauty and purity; *jud* means generosity and largesse. The Prophet's blessed heart ﷺ is the most beautiful, generous, and pure heart, free of every fault and blemish. (MA)

[24] The word used is *lahja*, and literally means tone of voice. The narrator used this word instead of *qawl*, which means statement, because even those who did not accept the truthfulness of the Prophet's statements ﷺ could feel the

NOTES FROM IMAM AL-TIRMIDHI[30]

قَالَ أَبُو عِيسَى سَمِعْتُ أَبَا جَعْفَرٍ مُحَمَّدَ بْنَ الْحُسَيْنِ ❁ يَقُولُ سَمِعْتُ الْأَصْمَعِيَّ يَقُولُ فِي تَفْسِيرِ صِفَةِ النَّبِيِّ ﷺ الْمُمَغَّطُ الذَّاهِبُ طُولًا ❁ وَقَالَ سَمِعْتُ أَعْرَابِيًّا يَقُولُ فِي كَلَامِهِ تَمَغَّطَ فِي نُشَّابَتِهِ ❁ أَيْ مَدَّهَا مَدًّا شَدِيدًا ❁ وَالْمُتَرَدِّدُ الدَّاخِلُ بَعْضُهُ فِي بَعْضٍ قِصَرًا ❁ وَأَمَّا الْقَطَطُ فَالشَّدِيدُ الْجُعُودَةِ ❁ وَالرَّجِلُ الَّذِي فِي شَعْرِهِ حُجُونَةٌ ❁ أَيْ تَثَنٍّ قَلِيلًا ❁ وَأَمَّا الْمُطَهَّمُ فَالْبَادِنُ الْكَثِيرُ اللَّحْمِ ❁ وَالْمُكَلْثَمُ الْمُدَوَّرُ الْوَجْهِ ❁ وَالْمُشْرَبُ الَّذِي فِي بَيَاضِهِ حُمْرَةٌ ❁ وَالْأَدْعَجُ الشَّدِيدُ سَوَادِ الْعَيْنِ ❁ وَالْأَهْدَبُ الطَّوِيلُ الْأَشْفَارِ ❁ وَالْكَتِدُ مُجْتَمَعُ الْكَتِفَيْنِ وَهُوَ الْكَاهِلُ ❁ وَالْمَسْرُبَةُ هُوَ الشَّعْرُ الدَّقِيقُ الَّذِي كَأَنَّهُ قَضِيبٌ مِنَ الصَّدْرِ إِلَى السُّرَّةِ ❁ وَالشَّثْنُ الْغَلِيظُ الْأَصَابِعِ مِنَ الْكَفَّيْنِ وَالْقَدَمَيْنِ ❁ وَالتَّقَلُّعُ أَنْ يَمْشِيَ بِقُوَّةٍ ❁ وَالصَّبَبُ الْحُدُورُ يُقَالُ انْحَدَرْنَا فِي صَبُوبٍ وَصَبَبٍ ❁ وَقَوْلُهُ جَلِيلُ الْمُشَاشِ يُرِيدُ رُؤُوسَ الْمَنَاكِبِ ❁ وَالْعِشْرَةُ الصُّحْبَةُ ❁ وَالْعَشِيرُ الصَّاحِبُ ❁ وَالْبَدِيهَةُ الْمُفَاجَأَةُ ❁ يُقَالُ بَدَهْتُهُ بِأَمْرٍ أَيْ فَجَأْتُهُ بِهِ ۞

I heard Abu Ja'far Muhammad ibn Husayn[31] say, 'I heard al-Asma'i[32] explain the meaning of the word *mummaghit* used to describe the Prophet.[33] He said, "It means excessively tall." He [also said], "I heard a Bedouin Arab once say [figuratively], 'So-and-so *tamaghghata fi nush-shabatihi*'—meaning 'So-and-so lengthened his arrow to an extreme length.' The word *mutaraddid* means one who is so short that he appears compressed.

The word *qatit* means extremely curly. The word *rajil* refers to one whose hair is curvy." That is to say, it is slightly wavy.' As for the word *mutahham,* it means corpulent, having much flesh. *Mukaltham* means one with a circular face. *Mushrab* refers to one whose fairness is imbued with a bit of redness. *Ad'aj* refers to

truthfulness of his tone. Abu Jahl, for example, knew about the truthfulness of the Prophet ﷺ but denied him due to jealousy of Banu Hashim. Allah says about His beloved, *Nor does he speak from caprice; it is but revelation revealed.* (Qur'an 53:3–4) (MA)

25 In other narrations the word used is *'ashira,* which means the noblest of them in lineage and ancestry. (MA)

26 Imam al-Bajuri comments, 'Meaning, whoever saw him before observing his exalted character and splendid states would be struck with awe of him because of his majestic and lordly qualities and his divinely-bestowed, awe-inspiring aura...' (AA) Imam al-Bukhari recorded in al-Adab al-Mufrad that the Prophet ﷺ said, 'The best of my *Umma* are those who, when seen, Allah is remembered.' Scholars say this is due to their hearts being filled with the majesty of Allah and His love, which is mirrored upon their faces and physical forms. If that is the case for those who are the best of his *Umma,* one can only imagine the majesty and greatness of the leader of this *Umma!* (MA)

27 They would love him ﷺ for what he encompassed of perfection, beauty and majesty, and for his high inner and outer qualities of affection, mercy and sincerity for the wellbeing of his *Umma.* (MA)

28 This refers to anyone who would ever describe him. As the Persian poet Hafiz Shirazi said:

O possessor of beauty,
O leader of mankind!
By your illuminated countenance
the moon has found light!
It's impossible to praise you
as you ought to be praised
To cut a long story short: after Allah,
you are the greatest! (MA)

29 Scholars have remarked that this was Sayyiduna 'Ali ؓ, who was described as the 'Door to the City of Knowledge.' Imam al-Tirmidhi, al-Hakim and others recorded that the Prophet ﷺ said, 'I am the City of Knowledge and 'Ali is its Door.' This hadith reveals that Sayyiduna 'Ali ؓ felt completely incapable of describing the Prophet's perfections and greatness—as if to say, 'Who in this world will ever be able to do justice in describing what Allah has granted him?' (MA)

30 A note added by Imam al-Tirmidhi to explain difficult words used in the narration. (MA)

31 He is Abu Ja'far Muhammad ibn Husayn Abu Halima, one of the teachers from whom Imam al-Tirmidhi narrates this hadith. (MA)

32 He is 'Abd al-Malik ibn Qarib, a very famous linguist. He heard hadith from Imam Malik and was regarded as a reliable narrator. (MA)

33 Shaykh Muhammad ibn al-Qasim Jassus notes in his commentary that Abu Ja'far Muhammad ibn Husayn heard the meanings of the words used to describe the Prophet ﷺ from al-Asma'i in general, not in regard to this particular hadith. For this reason, we see that the list of words does not correlate with their appearance in the hadith. (MA)

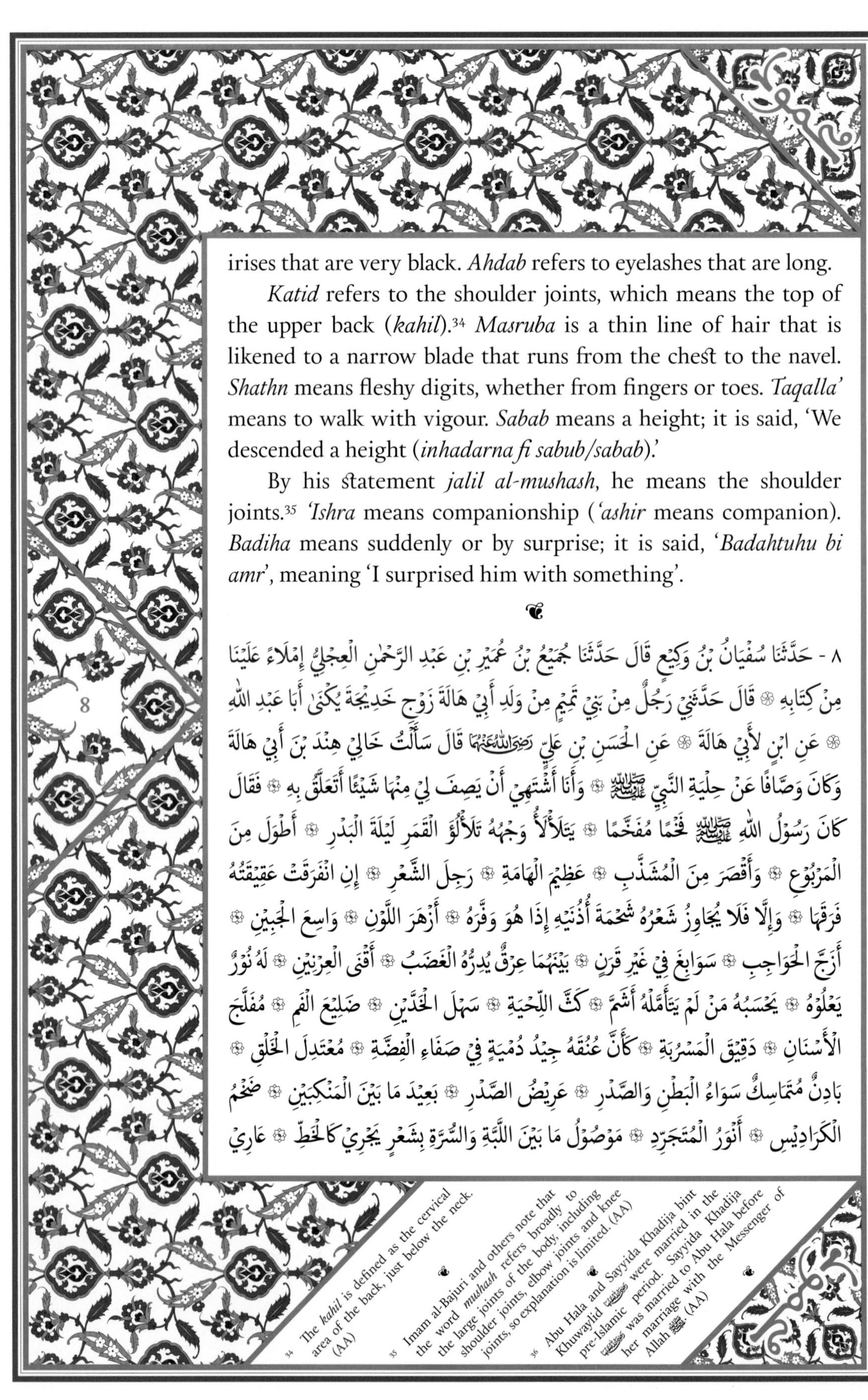

irises that are very black. *Ahdab* refers to eyelashes that are long.

Katid refers to the shoulder joints, which means the top of the upper back (*kahil*).[34] *Masruba* is a thin line of hair that is likened to a narrow blade that runs from the chest to the navel. *Shathn* means fleshy digits, whether from fingers or toes. *Taqalla'* means to walk with vigour. *Sabab* means a height; it is said, 'We descended a height (*inhadarna fi sabub/sabab*).'

By his statement *jalil al-mushash*, he means the shoulder joints.[35] *'Ishra* means companionship (*'ashir* means companion). *Badiha* means suddenly or by surprise; it is said, '*Badahtuhu bi amr*', meaning 'I surprised him with something'.

❦

٨ - حَدَّثَنَا سُفْيَانُ بْنُ وَكِيعٍ قَالَ حَدَّثَنَا جُمَيْعُ بْنُ عُمَيْرِ بْنِ عَبْدِ الرَّحْمٰنِ الْعِجْلِيُّ إِمْلَاءً عَلَيْنَا مِنْ كِتَابِهِ ۞ قَالَ حَدَّثَنِي رَجُلٌ مِنْ بَنِي تَمِيمٍ مِنْ وَلَدِ أَبِي هَالَةَ زَوْجِ خَدِيجَةَ يُكْنَى أَبَا عَبْدِ اللهِ ۞ عَنِ ابْنٍ لِأَبِي هَالَةَ ۞ عَنِ الْحَسَنِ بْنِ عَلِيٍّ رَضِيَ اللهُ عَنْهُمَا قَالَ سَأَلْتُ خَالِي هِنْدَ بْنَ أَبِي هَالَةَ وَكَانَ وَصَّافًا عَنْ حِلْيَةِ النَّبِيِّ صَلَّى اللهُ عَلَيْهِ وَسَلَّمَ ۞ وَأَنَا أَشْتَهِي أَنْ يَصِفَ لِي مِنْهَا شَيْئًا أَتَعَلَّقُ بِهِ ۞ فَقَالَ كَانَ رَسُولُ اللهِ صَلَّى اللهُ عَلَيْهِ وَسَلَّمَ فَخْمًا مُفَخَّمًا ۞ يَتَلَأْلَأُ وَجْهُهُ تَلَأْلُؤَ الْقَمَرِ لَيْلَةَ الْبَدْرِ ۞ أَطْوَلَ مِنَ الْمَرْبُوعِ ۞ وَأَقْصَرَ مِنَ الْمُشَذَّبِ ۞ عَظِيمَ الْهَامَةِ ۞ رَجِلَ الشَّعْرِ ۞ إِنِ انْفَرَقَتْ عَقِيقَتُهُ فَرَقَهَا ۞ وَإِلَّا فَلَا يُجَاوِزُ شَعْرُهُ شَحْمَةَ أُذُنَيْهِ إِذَا هُوَ وَفَّرَهُ ۞ أَزْهَرَ اللَّوْنِ ۞ وَاسِعَ الْجَبِينِ ۞ أَزَجَّ الْحَوَاجِبِ ۞ سَوَابِغَ فِي غَيْرِ قَرَنٍ ۞ بَيْنَهُمَا عِرْقٌ يُدِرُّهُ الْغَضَبُ ۞ أَقْنَى الْعِرْنَيْنِ ۞ لَهُ نُورٌ يَعْلُوهُ ۞ يَحْسَبُهُ مَنْ لَمْ يَتَأَمَّلْهُ أَشَمَّ ۞ كَثَّ اللِّحْيَةِ ۞ سَهْلَ الْخَدَّيْنِ ۞ ضَلِيعَ الْفَمِ ۞ مُفَلَّجَ الْأَسْنَانِ ۞ دَقِيقَ الْمَسْرُبَةِ ۞ كَأَنَّ عُنُقَهُ جِيدُ دُمْيَةٍ فِي صَفَاءِ الْفِضَّةِ ۞ مُعْتَدِلَ الْخَلْقِ ۞ بَادِنٌ مُتَمَاسِكٌ سَوَاءُ الْبَطْنِ وَالصَّدْرِ ۞ عَرِيضُ الصَّدْرِ ۞ بَعِيدَ مَا بَيْنَ الْمَنْكِبَيْنِ ۞ ضَخْمُ الْكَرَادِيسِ ۞ أَنْوَرُ الْمُتَجَرِّدِ ۞ مَوْصُولُ مَا بَيْنَ اللَّبَّةِ وَالسُّرَّةِ بِشَعْرٍ يَجْرِي كَالْخَطِّ ۞ عَارِي

34 The *kahil* is defined as the cervical area of the back, just below the neck. (AA)

35 Imam al-Bajuri and others note that the word *mushash* refers broadly to the large joints of the body, including shoulder joints, elbow joints and knee joints, so explanation is limited. (AA)

36 Abu Hala and Sayyida Khadija bint Khuwaylid رضي الله عنها were married in the pre-Islamic period. Sayyida Khadija رضي الله عنها was married to Abu Hala before her marriage with the Messenger of Allah ﷺ. (AA)

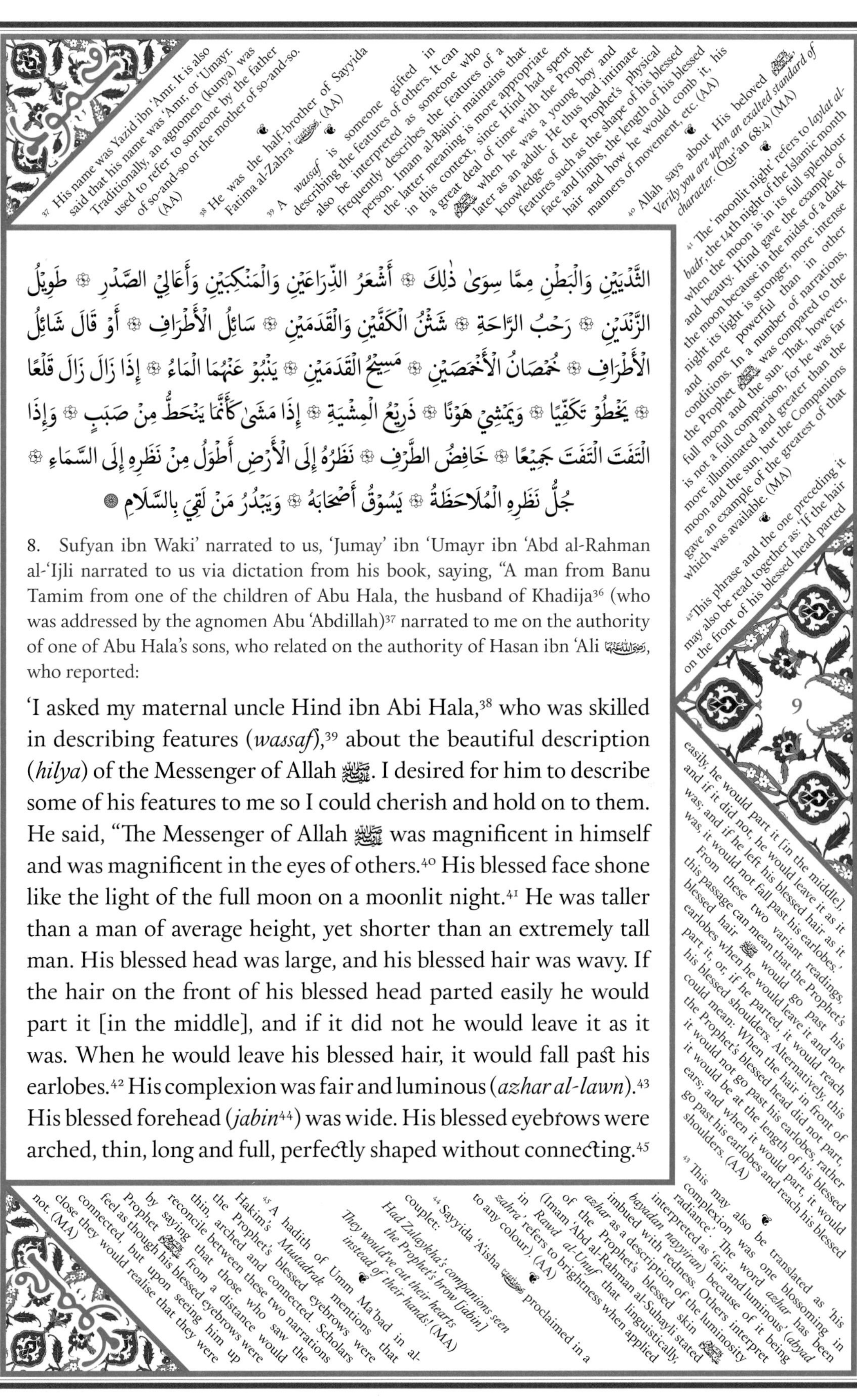

التَّدْيَيْنِ وَالْبَطْنِ مِمَّا سِوَىٰ ذٰلِكَ ۞ أَشْعَرُ الذِّرَاعَيْنِ وَالْمَنْكِبَيْنِ وَأَعَالِي الصَّدْرِ ۞ طَوِيلُ الزَّنْدَيْنِ ۞ رَحْبُ الرَّاحَةِ ۞ شَثْنُ الْكَفَّيْنِ وَالْقَدَمَيْنِ ۞ سَائِلُ الْأَطْرَافِ ۞ أَوْ قَالَ شَائِلُ الْأَطْرَافِ ۞ خُمْصَانُ الْأَخْمَصَيْنِ ۞ مَسِيحُ الْقَدَمَيْنِ ۞ يَنْبُو عَنْهُمَا الْمَاءُ ۞ إِذَا زَالَ زَالَ قَلْعًا ۞ يَخْطُو تَكَفِّيًا ۞ وَيَمْشِي هَوْنًا ۞ ذَرِيعُ الْمِشْيَةِ ۞ إِذَا مَشَىٰ كَأَنَّمَا يَنْحَطُّ مِنْ صَبَبٍ ۞ وَإِذَا الْتَفَتَ الْتَفَتَ جَمِيعًا ۞ خَافِضُ الطَّرْفِ ۞ نَظَرُهُ إِلَى الْأَرْضِ أَطْوَلُ مِنْ نَظَرِهِ إِلَى السَّمَاءِ ۞ جُلُّ نَظَرِهِ الْمُلَاحَظَةُ ۞ يَسُوقُ أَصْحَابَهُ ۞ وَيَبْدُرُ مَنْ لَقِيَ بِالسَّلَامِ ۞

8. Sufyan ibn Waki' narrated to us, 'Jumay' ibn 'Umayr ibn 'Abd al-Rahman al-'Ijli narrated to us via dictation from his book, saying, "A man from Banu Tamim from one of the children of Abu Hala, the husband of Khadija[36] (who was addressed by the agnomen Abu 'Abdillah)[37] narrated to me on the authority of one of Abu Hala's sons, who related on the authority of Hasan ibn 'Ali ﷺ, who reported:

'I asked my maternal uncle Hind ibn Abi Hala,[38] who was skilled in describing features (*wassaf*),[39] about the beautiful description (*hilya*) of the Messenger of Allah ﷺ. I desired for him to describe some of his features to me so I could cherish and hold on to them. He said, "The Messenger of Allah ﷺ was magnificent in himself and was magnificent in the eyes of others.[40] His blessed face shone like the light of the full moon on a moonlit night.[41] He was taller than a man of average height, yet shorter than an extremely tall man. His blessed head was large, and his blessed hair was wavy. If the hair on the front of his blessed head parted easily he would part it [in the middle], and if it did not he would leave it as it was. When he would leave his blessed hair, it would fall past his earlobes.[42] His complexion was fair and luminous (*azhar al-lawn*).[43] His blessed forehead (*jabin*[44]) was wide. His blessed eyebrows were arched, thin, long and full, perfectly shaped without connecting.[45]

[37] His name was Yazid ibn 'Amr. It is also said that his name was 'Amr, or Umayr. Traditionally, an agnomen (*kunya*) was used to refer to someone by the father of so-and-so or the mother of so-and-so. (AA)

[38] He was the half-brother of Sayyida Fatima al-Zahra' ﷺ. (AA)

[39] A *wassaf* is someone gifted in describing the features of others. It can also be interpreted as someone who frequently describes the features of a person. Imam al-Bajuri maintains that the latter meaning is more appropriate in this context, since Hind had spent a great deal of time with the Prophet ﷺ when he was a young boy and later as an adult. He thus had intimate knowledge of the Prophet's physical features such as the shape of his blessed face and limbs, the length of his blessed hair and how he would comb it, his manners of movement, etc. (AA)

[40] Allah says about His beloved ﷺ, *Verily you are upon an exalted standard of character*. (Qur'an 68:4) (MA)

[41] The 'moonlit night' refers to *laylat al-badr*, the 14th night of the Islamic month when the moon is in its full splendour and beauty. Hind gave the example of the moon because in the midst of a dark night its light is stronger, more intense and more powerful than in other conditions. In a number of narrations, the Prophet ﷺ was compared to the full moon and the sun. That, however, is not a full comparison, for he was far more illuminated and greater than the moon and the sun, but the Companions gave an example of the greatest of that which was available. (MA)

[42] This phrase and the one preceding it may also be read together as: 'If the hair on the front of his blessed head parted easily, he would part it [in the middle], and if it did not, he would leave it as it was; and if he left his blessed hair as it was, it would not fall past his earlobes.' From these two variant readings, this passage can mean that the Prophet's blessed hair ﷺ would go past his earlobes when he would leave it and not part it, or, if he parted it, it would reach his blessed shoulders. Alternatively, this could mean: When the hair in front of the Prophet's blessed head did not part, it would not go past his earlobes, rather it would be at the length of his blessed ears; and when it would part, it would go past his earlobes and reach his blessed shoulders. (AA)

[43] This may also be translated as 'his complexion was one blossoming in radiance'. The word *azhar* has been interpreted as fair and luminous (*abyad bayadan nayyiran*) because of it being imbued with redness. Others interpret *azhar* as a description of the luminosity of the Prophet's blessed skin ﷺ. (Imam 'Abd al-Rahman al-Suhayli stated in *Rawd al-Unuf* that linguistically, *zahra'* refers to brightness when applied to any colour). (AA)

[44] Sayyida 'A'isha ﷺ proclaimed in a couplet:
Had Zulaykha's companions seen the Prophet's brow [jabin]
They would've cut their hearts instead of their hands! (MA)

[45] A hadith of Umm Ma'bad in al-Hakim's *Mustadrak* mentions that the Prophet's blessed eyebrows were thin, arched and connected. Scholars reconcile between these two narrations by saying that those who saw the Prophet ﷺ from a distance would feel as though his blessed eyebrows were connected, but upon seeing him up close they would realise that they were not. (MA)

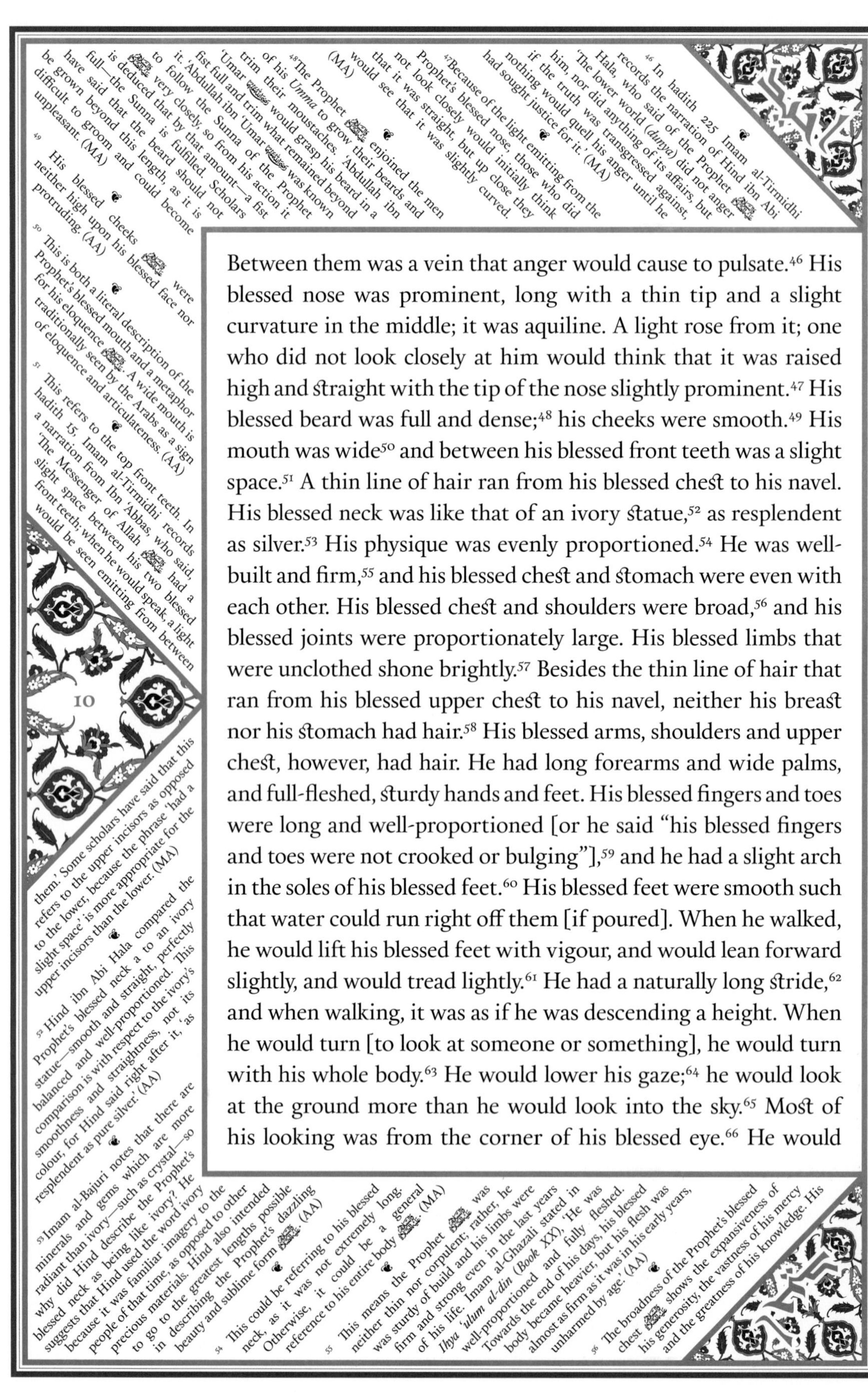

Between them was a vein that anger would cause to pulsate.[46] His blessed nose was prominent, long with a thin tip and a slight curvature in the middle; it was aquiline. A light rose from it; one who did not look closely at him would think that it was raised high and straight with the tip of the nose slightly prominent.[47] His blessed beard was full and dense;[48] his cheeks were smooth.[49] His mouth was wide[50] and between his blessed front teeth was a slight space.[51] A thin line of hair ran from his blessed chest to his navel. His blessed neck was like that of an ivory statue,[52] as resplendent as silver.[53] His physique was evenly proportioned.[54] He was well-built and firm,[55] and his blessed chest and stomach were even with each other. His blessed chest and shoulders were broad,[56] and his blessed joints were proportionately large. His blessed limbs that were unclothed shone brightly.[57] Besides the thin line of hair that ran from his blessed upper chest to his navel, neither his breast nor his stomach had hair.[58] His blessed arms, shoulders and upper chest, however, had hair. He had long forearms and wide palms, and full-fleshed, sturdy hands and feet. His blessed fingers and toes were long and well-proportioned [or he said "his blessed fingers and toes were not crooked or bulging"],[59] and he had a slight arch in the soles of his blessed feet.[60] His blessed feet were smooth such that water could run right off them [if poured]. When he walked, he would lift his blessed feet with vigour, and would lean forward slightly, and would tread lightly.[61] He had a naturally long stride,[62] and when walking, it was as if he was descending a height. When he would turn [to look at someone or something], he would turn with his whole body.[63] He would lower his gaze;[64] he would look at the ground more than he would look into the sky.[65] Most of his looking was from the corner of his blessed eye.[66] He would

[46] In hadith 225 Imam al-Tirmidhi records the narration of Hind ibn Abi Hala, who said of the Prophet ﷺ: 'The lower world (*dunya*) did not anger him, nor did anything of its affairs, but if the truth was transgressed against, nothing would quell his anger until he had sought justice for it.' (MA)

[47] Because of the light emitting from the Prophet's blessed nose, those who did not look closely would initially think that it was straight, but up close they would see that it was slightly curved.

[48] The Prophet ﷺ enjoined the men of his *Umma* to grow their beards and trim their moustaches. 'Abdullah ibn 'Umar ﷺ would grasp his beard in a fist full and trim what remained beyond it. 'Abdullah ibn 'Umar ﷺ was known to follow the Sunna of the Prophet ﷺ very closely, so from his action it is deduced that by that amount—a fist full—the Sunna is fulfilled. Scholars have said that the beard should not be grown beyond this length, as it is difficult to groom and could become unpleasant. (MA)

[49] His blessed cheeks ﷺ were neither high upon his blessed face nor protruding. (AA)

[50] This is both a literal description of the Prophet's blessed mouth and a metaphor for his eloquence ﷺ. A wide mouth is traditionally seen by the Arabs as a sign of eloquence and articulateness. (AA)

[51] This refers to the top front teeth. In hadith 15, Imam al-Tirmidhi records a narration from Ibn 'Abbas, who said, 'The Messenger of Allah ﷺ had a slight space between his two blessed front teeth; when he would speak, a light would be seen emitting from between them.' Some scholars have said that this refers to the upper incisors as opposed to the lower, because the phrase 'had a slight space' is more appropriate for the upper incisors than the lower. (MA)

[52] Hind ibn Abi Hala compared the Prophet's blessed neck to an ivory statue—smooth and straight, perfectly balanced and well-proportioned. This comparison is with respect to the ivory's smoothness and straightness, not its colour, for Hind said right after it, 'as resplendent as pure silver.' (AA)

[53] Imam al-Bajuri notes that there are minerals and gems which are more radiant than ivory—such as crystal—so why did Hind describe the Prophet's blessed neck as being like ivory? He suggests that Hind used the word 'ivory' because it was familiar imagery to the people of that time, as opposed to other precious materials. Hind also intended to go to the greatest lengths possible in describing the Prophet's dazzling beauty and sublime form ﷺ. (AA)

[54] This could be referring to his blessed neck, as it was not extremely long. Otherwise, it could be a general reference to his entire body ﷺ. (MA)

[55] This means the Prophet ﷺ was neither thin nor corpulent; rather, he was sturdy of build and his limbs were firm and strong even in the last years of his life. Imam al-Ghazali stated in *Ihya 'ulum al-din* (*Book XX*), 'He was well-proportioned and fully fleshed. Towards the end of his days, his blessed body became heavier, but his flesh was almost as firm as it was in his early years, unharmed by age.' (AA)

[56] The broadness of the Prophet's blessed chest ﷺ shows the expansiveness of his mercy his generosity, the vastness of his mercy and the greatness of his knowledge. His

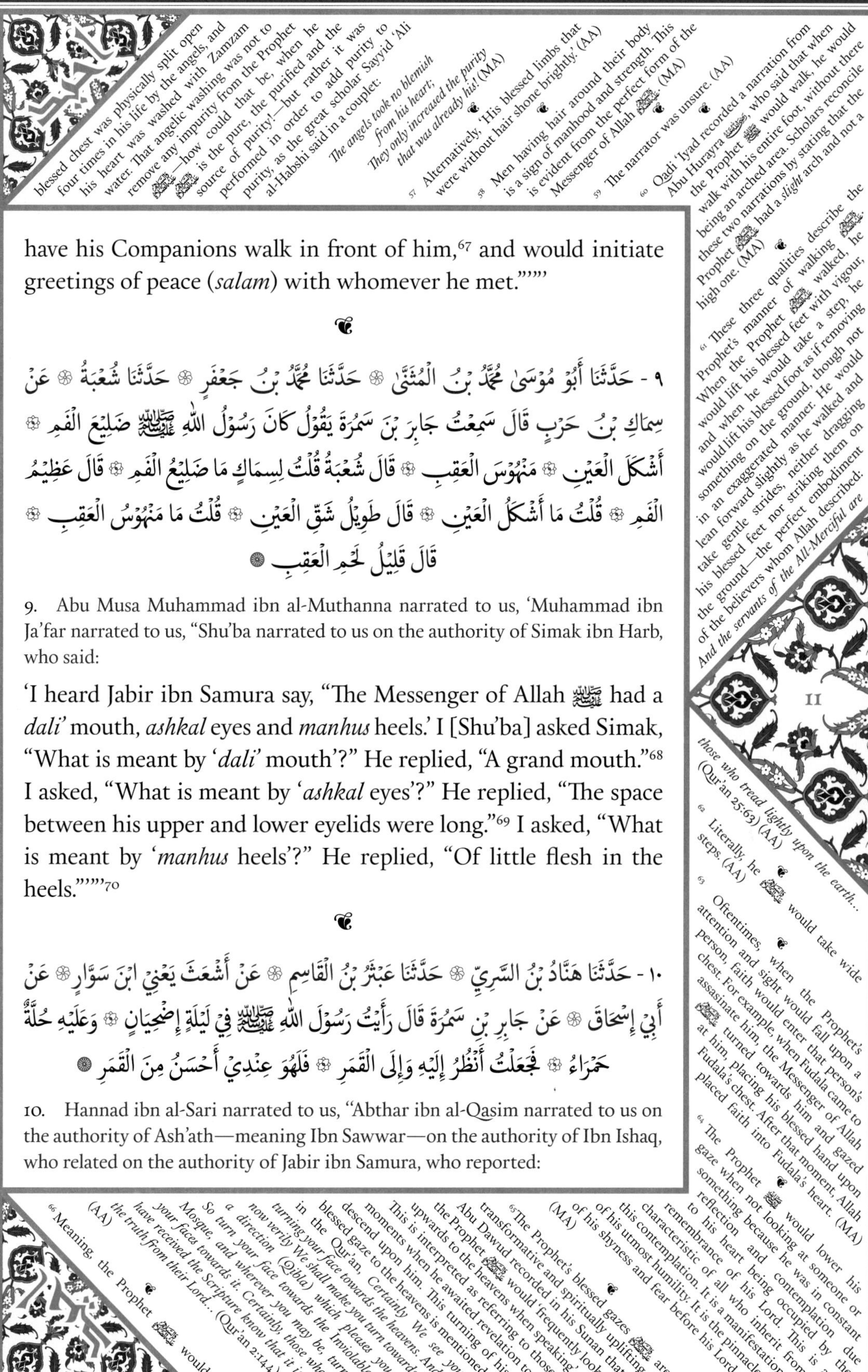

blessed chest was physically split open four times in his life by the angels, and his heart was washed with Zamzam water. That angelic washing was not to remove any impurity from the Prophet ﷺ—how could that be, when he ﷺ is the pure, the purified and the source of purity!—but rather it was performed in order to add purity to purity, as the great scholar Sayyid 'Ali al-Habshi said in a couplet:

The angels took no blemish
from his heart;
They only increased the purity
that was already his! (MA)

57 Alternatively, 'His blessed limbs that were without hair shone brightly.' (AA)

58 Men having hair around their body is a sign of manhood and strength. This is evident from the perfect form of the Messenger of Allah ﷺ. (MA)

59 The narrator was unsure. (AA)

60 Qadi 'Iyad recorded a narration from Abu Hurayra ﷺ, who said that when the Prophet ﷺ would walk, he would walk with his entire foot, without there being an arched area. Scholars reconcile these two narrations by stating that the Prophet ﷺ had a *slight* arch and not a high one. (MA)

have his Companions walk in front of him,[67] and would initiate greetings of peace (*salam*) with whomever he met."'"'

٩ - حَدَّثَنَا أَبُو مُوسَى مُحَمَّدُ بْنُ الْمُثَنَّى ۞ حَدَّثَنَا مُحَمَّدُ بْنُ جَعْفَرٍ ۞ حَدَّثَنَا شُعْبَةُ ۞ عَنْ سِمَاكِ بْنِ حَرْبٍ قَالَ سَمِعْتُ جَابِرَ بْنَ سَمُرَةَ يَقُولُ كَانَ رَسُولُ اللَّهِ ﷺ ضَلِيعَ الْفَمِ ۞ أَشْكَلَ الْعَيْنِ ۞ مَنْهُوسَ الْعَقِبِ ۞ قَالَ شُعْبَةُ قُلْتُ لِسِمَاكٍ مَا ضَلِيعُ الْفَمِ ۞ قَالَ عَظِيمُ الْفَمِ ۞ قُلْتُ مَا أَشْكَلُ الْعَيْنِ ۞ قَالَ طَوِيلُ شَقِّ الْعَيْنِ ۞ قُلْتُ مَا مَنْهُوسُ الْعَقِبِ ۞ قَالَ قَلِيلُ لَحْمِ الْعَقِبِ ۞

9. Abu Musa Muhammad ibn al-Muthanna narrated to us, 'Muhammad ibn Ja'far narrated to us, "Shu'ba narrated to us on the authority of Simak ibn Harb, who said:

'I heard Jabir ibn Samura say, "The Messenger of Allah ﷺ had a *dali'* mouth, *ashkal* eyes and *manhus* heels.' I [Shu'ba] asked Simak, "What is meant by '*dali'* mouth'?" He replied, "A grand mouth."[68] I asked, "What is meant by '*ashkal* eyes'?" He replied, "The space between his upper and lower eyelids were long."[69] I asked, "What is meant by '*manhus* heels'?" He replied, "Of little flesh in the heels."'"'[70]

١٠ - حَدَّثَنَا هَنَّادُ بْنُ السَّرِيِّ ۞ حَدَّثَنَا عَبْثَرُ بْنُ الْقَاسِمِ ۞ عَنْ أَشْعَثَ يَعْنِي ابْنَ سَوَّارٍ ۞ عَنْ أَبِي إِسْحَاقَ ۞ عَنْ جَابِرِ بْنِ سَمُرَةَ قَالَ رَأَيْتُ رَسُولَ اللَّهِ ﷺ فِي لَيْلَةٍ إِضْحِيَانٍ ۞ وَعَلَيْهِ حُلَّةٌ حَمْرَاءُ ۞ فَجَعَلْتُ أَنْظُرُ إِلَيْهِ وَإِلَى الْقَمَرِ ۞ فَلَهُوَ عِنْدِي أَحْسَنُ مِنَ الْقَمَرِ ۞

10. Hannad ibn al-Sari narrated to us, "Abthar ibn al-Qasim narrated to us on the authority of Ash'ath—meaning Ibn Sawwar—on the authority of Ibn Ishaq, who related on the authority of Jabir ibn Samura, who reported:

61 These three qualities describe the Prophet's manner of walking ﷺ. When the Prophet ﷺ walked, he would lift his blessed feet with vigour, and when he would take a step, he would lift his blessed foot as if removing something on the ground, though not in an exaggerated manner. He would lean forward slightly as he walked and take gentle strides, neither dragging his blessed feet nor striking them on the ground—the perfect embodiment of the believers whom Allah described: *And the servants of the All-Merciful are those who tread lightly upon the earth...* (Qur'an 25:63) (AA)

62 Literally, he ﷺ would take wide steps. (AA)

63 Oftentimes, when the Prophet's ﷺ attention and sight would fall upon a person, faith would enter that person's chest. For example, when Fudala came to assassinate him, the Messenger of Allah ﷺ turned towards him and gazed at him, placing his blessed hand upon Fudala's chest. After that moment, Allah placed faith into Fudala's heart. (MA)

64 The Prophet ﷺ would lower his gaze when not looking at someone or something because he was in constant reflection and contemplation due to his heart being occupied by the remembrance of his Lord. This is a characteristic of all who inherit from this contemplation. It is a manifestation of his utmost humility. It is the pinnacle of his shyness and fear before his Lord. (MA)

65 The Prophet's blessed gazes ﷺ are transformative and spiritually uplifting. Abu Dawud recorded in his Sunan that the Prophet ﷺ would 'frequently look upwards to the heavens when speaking'. This is interpreted as referring to those moments when he awaited revelation to descend upon him. This turning of his blessed gaze to the heavens is mentioned in the Qur'an, *Certainly We see you turning your face towards the heavens. And now verily We shall make you turn towards a direction (Qibla) which pleases you. So turn your face towards the Inviolable Mosque, and wherever you may be, turn your faces towards it. Certainly, those who have received the Scripture know that it is the truth from their Lord...* (Qur'an 2:144) (AA)

66 Meaning, the Prophet ﷺ would

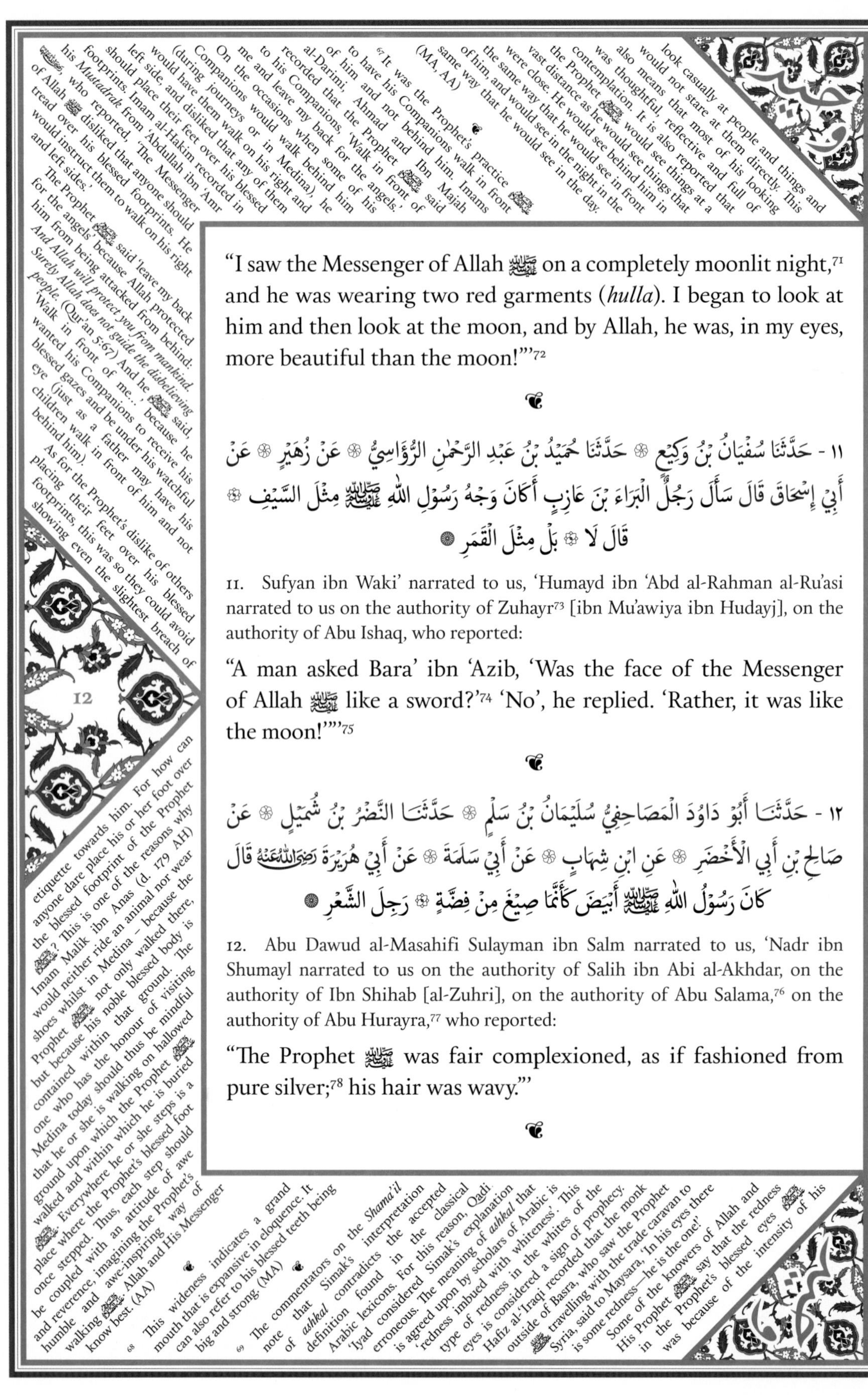

"I saw the Messenger of Allah ﷺ on a completely moonlit night,[71] and he was wearing two red garments (*hulla*). I began to look at him and then look at the moon, and by Allah, he was, in my eyes, more beautiful than the moon!"'[72]

❦

١١ - حَدَّثَنَا سُفْيَانُ بْنُ وَكِيعٍ ۞ حَدَّثَنَا حُمَيْدُ بْنُ عَبْدِ الرَّحْمٰنِ الرُّؤَاسِيُّ ۞ عَنْ زُهَيْرٍ ۞ عَنْ أَبِي إِسْحَاقَ قَالَ سَأَلَ رَجُلٌ الْبَرَاءَ بْنَ عَازِبٍ أَكَانَ وَجْهُ رَسُولِ اللهِ ﷺ مِثْلَ السَّيْفِ ۞ قَالَ لَا ۞ بَلْ مِثْلَ الْقَمَرِ ۞

11. Sufyan ibn Waki' narrated to us, 'Humayd ibn 'Abd al-Rahman al-Ru'asi narrated to us on the authority of Zuhayr[73] [ibn Mu'awiya ibn Hudayj], on the authority of Abu Ishaq, who reported:

"A man asked Bara' ibn 'Azib, 'Was the face of the Messenger of Allah ﷺ like a sword?'[74] 'No', he replied. 'Rather, it was like the moon!'"'[75]

❦

١٢ - حَدَّثَنَا أَبُو دَاوُدَ الْمَصَاحِفِيُّ سُلَيْمَانُ بْنُ سَلْمٍ ۞ حَدَّثَنَا النَّضْرُ بْنُ شُمَيْلٍ ۞ عَنْ صَالِحِ بْنِ أَبِي الْأَخْضَرِ ۞ عَنِ ابْنِ شِهَابٍ ۞ عَنْ أَبِي سَلَمَةَ ۞ عَنْ أَبِي هُرَيْرَةَ رَضِيَ اللهُ عَنْهُ قَالَ كَانَ رَسُولُ اللهِ ﷺ أَبْيَضَ كَأَنَّمَا صِيغَ مِنْ فِضَّةٍ ۞ رَجِلَ الشَّعْرِ ۞

12. Abu Dawud al-Masahifi Sulayman ibn Salm narrated to us, 'Nadr ibn Shumayl narrated to us on the authority of Salih ibn Abi al-Akhdar, on the authority of Ibn Shihab [al-Zuhri], on the authority of Abu Salama,[76] on the authority of Abu Hurayra,[77] who reported:

"The Prophet ﷺ was fair complexioned, as if fashioned from pure silver;[78] his hair was wavy."'

❦

look casually at people and things and would not stare at them directly. This also means that most of his looking was thoughtful, reflective and full of contemplation. It is also reported that the Prophet ﷺ would see things at a vast distance as he would see things that were close. He would see behind him in the same way that he would see in front of him, and would see in the night in the same way that he would see in the day. (MA, AA)

❦

[67] It was the Prophet's ﷺ practice to have his Companions walk in front of him and not behind him. Imams al-Darimi, Ahmad and Ibn Majah recorded that the Prophet ﷺ said to his Companions, 'Walk in front of me and leave my back for the angels.' On the occasions when some of his Companions would walk behind him (during journeys or in Medina), he would have them walk on his right and left side, and disliked that any of them should place their feet over his blessed footprints. Imam al-Hakim recorded in his *Mustadrak* from 'Abdullah ibn 'Amr ﷺ, who reported, 'The Messenger of Allah ﷺ disliked that anyone should tread over his blessed footprints. He would instruct them to walk on his right and left sides.'

The Prophet ﷺ said 'leave my back for the angels' because Allah protected him from being attacked from behind: *And Allah will protect you from mankind. Surely Allah does not guide the disbelieving people.* (Qur'an 5:67) And he ﷺ said, 'Walk in front of me...', because he wanted his Companions to receive his blessed gazes and be under his watchful eye (just as a father may have his children walk in front of him and not behind him).

As for the Prophet's dislike of others placing their feet over his blessed footprints, this was so they could avoid showing even the slightest breach of etiquette towards him. For how can anyone dare place his or her foot over the blessed footprint of the Prophet ﷺ? This is one of the reasons why Imam Malik ibn Anas (d. 179 AH) would neither ride an animal nor wear shoes whilst in Medina – because the Prophet ﷺ not only walked there, but because his noble blessed body is contained within that ground. The one who has the honour of visiting Medina today should thus be mindful that he or she is walking on hallowed ground upon which the Prophet ﷺ walked and within which he is buried. Everywhere he or she steps is a place where the Prophet's blessed foot once stepped. Thus, each step should be coupled with an attitude of awe and reverence, imagining the Prophet's humble and awe-inspiring way of walking ﷺ. Allah and His Messenger ﷺ know best. (AA)

❦

[68] This wideness indicates a grand mouth that is expansive in eloquence. It can also refer to his blessed teeth being big and strong. (MA)

❦

[69] The commentators on the *Shama'il* note that Simak's interpretation of *ashkal* contradicts the accepted definition found in the classical Arabic lexicons. For this reason, Qadi 'Iyad considered Simak's explanation erroneous. The meaning of *ashkal* that is agreed upon by scholars of Arabic is 'redness imbued with whiteness'. This type of redness in the whites of the eyes is considered a sign of prophecy. Hafiz al-'Iraqi recorded that the monk outside of Basra, who saw the Prophet ﷺ travelling with the trade caravan to Syria, said to Maysara, 'In his eyes there is some redness—he is the one!' Some of the knowers of Allah and His Prophet ﷺ say that the redness in the Prophet's blessed eyes was because of the intensity of his

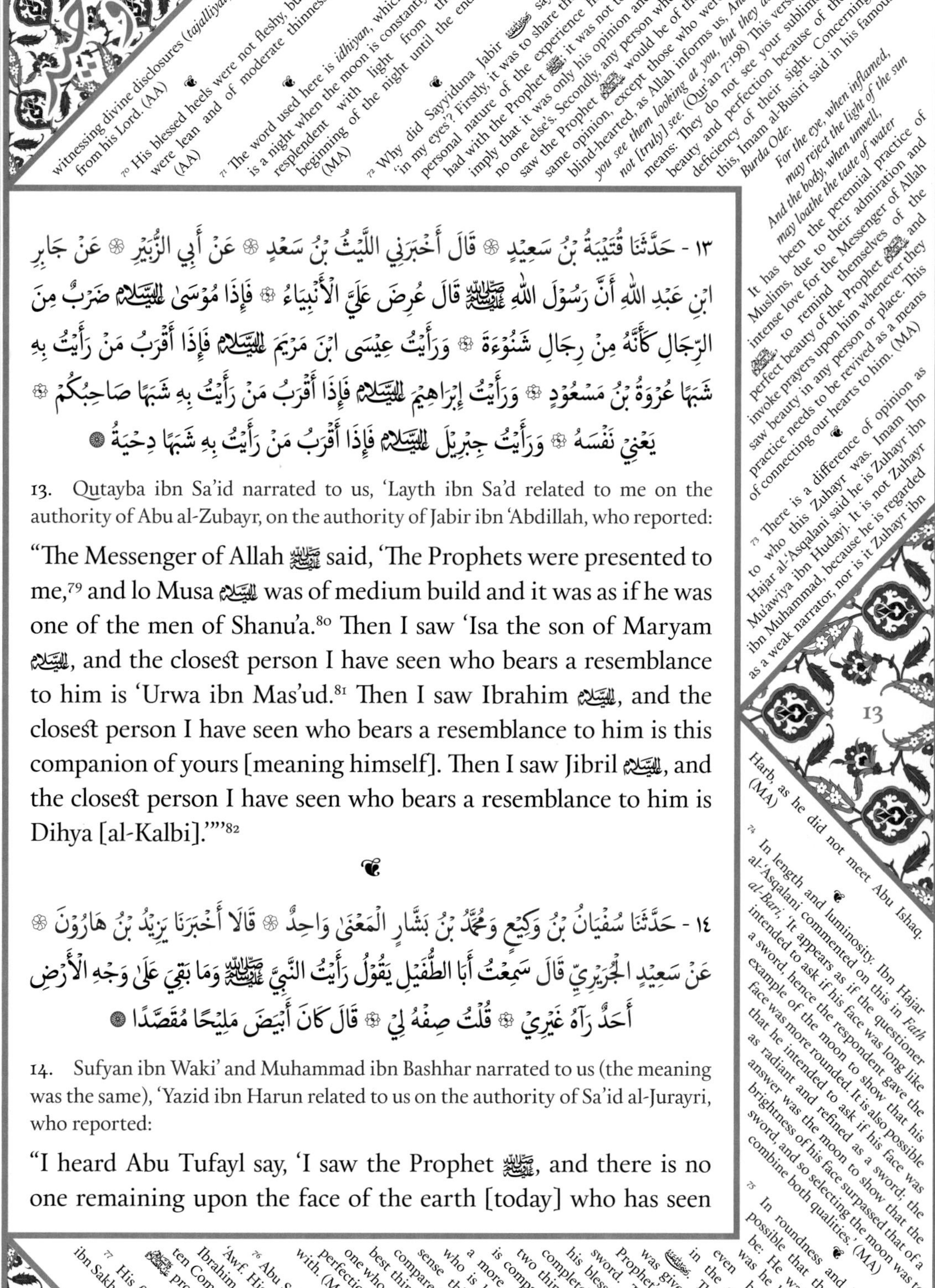

witnessing divine disclosures (*tajalliyat*) from his Lord. (AA)

[70] His blessed heels were not fleshy, but were lean and of moderate thinness. (AA)

[71] The word used here is *idhiyan*, which is a night when the moon is constantly resplendent with light from the beginning of the night until the end. (MA)

[72] Why did Sayyiduna Jabir ﷺ say 'in my eyes'? Firstly, it was to share the personal nature of the experience he had with the Prophet ﷺ; it was not to imply that it was only his opinion and no one else's. Secondly, any person who saw the Prophet ﷺ would be of the same opinion, except those who were blind-hearted, as Allah informs us, *And you see them looking at you, but they do not [truly] see.* (Qur'an 7:198) This verse means: They do not see your sublime beauty and perfection because of the deficiency of their sight. Concerning this, Imam al-Busiri said in his famous Burda Ode:

For the eye, when inflamed, may reject the light of the sun
And the body, when unwell, may loathe the taste of water

It has been the perennial practice of Muslims, due to their admiration and intense love for the Messenger of Allah ﷺ, to remind themselves of the perfect beauty of the Prophet ﷺ and invoke prayers upon him whenever they saw beauty in any person or place. This practice needs to be revived as a means of connecting our hearts to him. (MA)

[73] There is a difference of opinion as to who this Zuhayr was. Imam Ibn Hajar al-'Asqalani said he is Zuhayr ibn Mu'awiya ibn Hudayj. It is not Zuhayr ibn Muhammad, because he is regarded as a weak narrator, nor is it Zuhayr ibn Harb, as he did not meet Abu Ishaq. (MA)

١٣ - حَدَّثَنَا قُتَيْبَةُ بْنُ سَعِيدٍ ۞ قَالَ أَخْبَرَنِي اللَّيْثُ بْنُ سَعْدٍ ۞ عَنْ أَبِي الزُّبَيْرِ ۞ عَنْ جَابِرِ ابْنِ عَبْدِ اللهِ أَنَّ رَسُولَ اللهِ ﷺ قَالَ عُرِضَ عَلَيَّ الْأَنْبِيَاءُ ۞ فَإِذَا مُوسَىٰ عليه السلام ضَرْبٌ مِنَ الرِّجَالِ كَأَنَّهُ مِنْ رِجَالِ شَنُوءَةَ ۞ وَرَأَيْتُ عِيسَى ابْنَ مَرْيَمَ عليه السلام فَإِذَا أَقْرَبُ مَنْ رَأَيْتُ بِهِ شَبَهًا عُرْوَةُ بْنُ مَسْعُودٍ ۞ وَرَأَيْتُ إِبْرَاهِيمَ عليه السلام فَإِذَا أَقْرَبُ مَنْ رَأَيْتُ بِهِ شَبَهًا صَاحِبُكُمْ ۞ يَعْنِي نَفْسَهُ ۞ وَرَأَيْتُ جِبْرِيلَ عليه السلام فَإِذَا أَقْرَبُ مَنْ رَأَيْتُ بِهِ شَبَهًا دِحْيَةُ ۞

13. Qutayba ibn Sa'id narrated to us, 'Layth ibn Sa'd related to me on the authority of Abu al-Zubayr, on the authority of Jabir ibn 'Abdillah, who reported:

"The Messenger of Allah ﷺ said, 'The Prophets were presented to me,[79] and lo Musa عليه السلام was of medium build and it was as if he was one of the men of Shanu'a.[80] Then I saw 'Isa the son of Maryam عليه السلام, and the closest person I have seen who bears a resemblance to him is 'Urwa ibn Mas'ud.[81] Then I saw Ibrahim عليه السلام, and the closest person I have seen who bears a resemblance to him is this companion of yours [meaning himself]. Then I saw Jibril عليه السلام, and the closest person I have seen who bears a resemblance to him is Dihya [al-Kalbi].'"[82]

❦

١٤ - حَدَّثَنَا سُفْيَانُ بْنُ وَكِيعٍ وَمُحَمَّدُ بْنُ بَشَّارٍ الْمَعْنَىٰ وَاحِدٌ ۞ قَالَا أَخْبَرَنَا يَزِيدُ بْنُ هَارُونَ ۞ عَنْ سَعِيدٍ الْجُرَيْرِيِّ قَالَ سَمِعْتُ أَبَا الطُّفَيْلِ يَقُولُ رَأَيْتُ النَّبِيَّ ﷺ وَمَا بَقِيَ عَلَىٰ وَجْهِ الْأَرْضِ أَحَدٌ رَآهُ غَيْرِي ۞ قُلْتُ صِفْهُ لِي ۞ قَالَ كَانَ أَبْيَضَ مَلِيحًا مُقَصَّدًا ۞

14. Sufyan ibn Waki' and Muhammad ibn Bashhar narrated to us (the meaning was the same), 'Yazid ibn Harun related to us on the authority of Sa'id al-Jurayri, who reported:

"I heard Abu Tufayl say, 'I saw the Prophet ﷺ, and there is no one remaining upon the face of the earth [today] who has seen

[74] In length and luminosity. Ibn Hajar al-'Asqalani commented on this in *Fath al-Bari*, 'It appears as if the questioner intended to ask if his face was long like a sword, hence the respondent gave the example of the moon to show that his face was more rounded. It is also possible that he intended to ask if his face was as radiant and refined as a sword; the answer was the moon to show that the brightness of his face surpassed that of a sword, and so selecting the moon was to combine both qualities.' (MA)

[75] In roundness and brightness. It is possible that the meaning could also be: He was not like the sword, nor was he like the moon; rather, he was even better—as previously stated in the statement of Sayyiduna Jabir ﷺ. This comparison to the moon was given to negate the idea that the Prophet's blessed face was long like a sword. This is a partial comparison; his blessed face was rounded but not completely circular. Normally when two things are compared, the one that is compared with has the attribute in a more complete sense than the one who is being compared to it. In this sense this simile is partial, as Bara' compared the Prophet ﷺ with the best thing available, not to say that the one who was being compared was less in perfection than the one being compared with. (MA)

[76] Abu Salama ibn 'Abd al-Rahman ibn 'Awf. His name was either 'Abdullah or Ibrahim. 'Abd al-Rahman was one of ten Companions for whom the Prophet ﷺ promised Paradise. (MA)

[77] His full name was 'Abd al-Rahman ibn Sakhr. (MA)

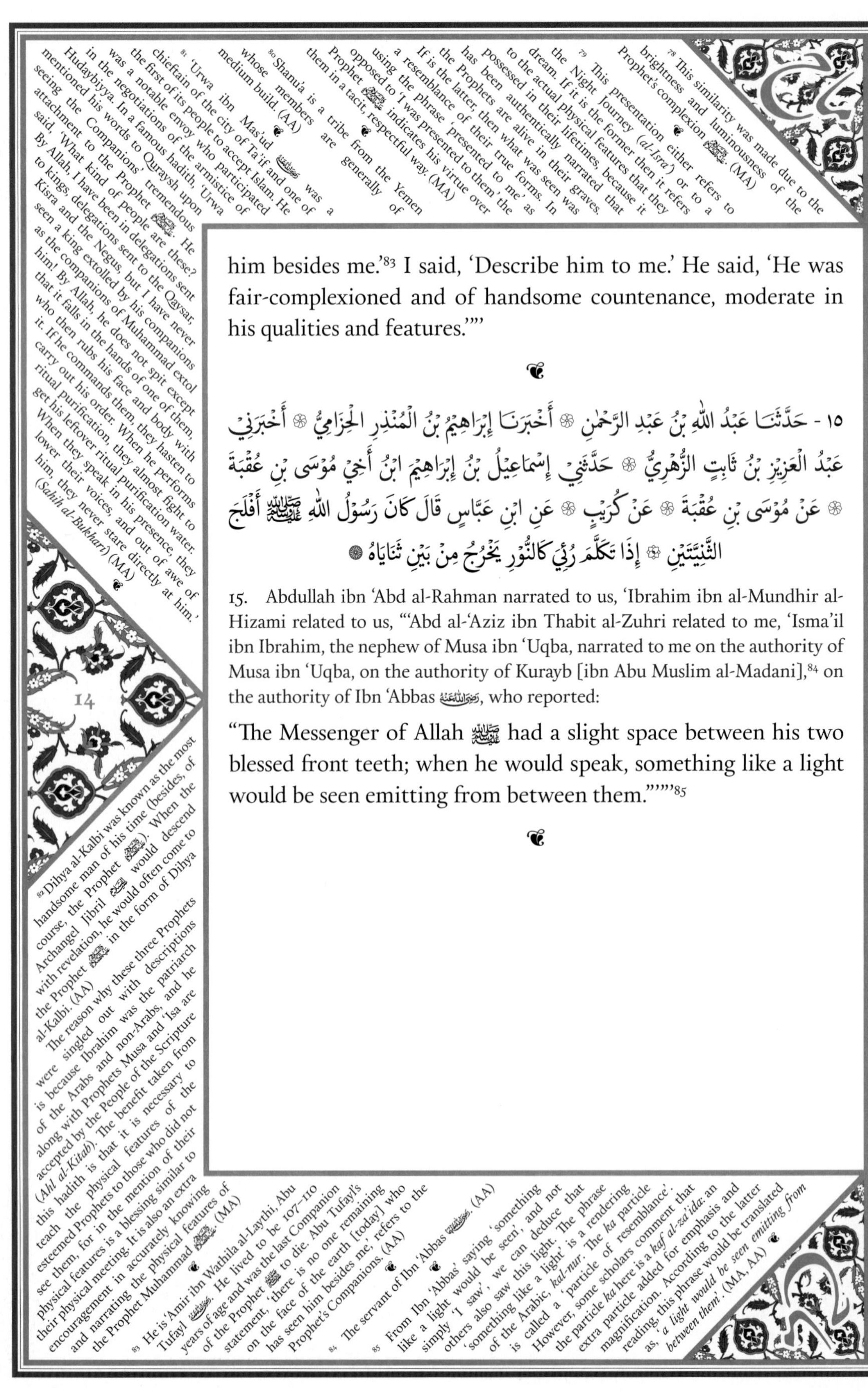

him besides me.'[83] I said, 'Describe him to me.' He said, 'He was fair-complexioned and of handsome countenance, moderate in his qualities and features.'''

١٥ - حَدَّثَنَا عَبْدُ اللهِ بْنُ عَبْدِ الرَّحْمٰنِ ۞ أَخْبَرَنَا إِبْرَاهِيمُ بْنُ الْمُنْذِرِ الْحِزَامِيُّ ۞ أَخْبَرَنِي عَبْدُ الْعَزِيزِ بْنُ ثَابِتٍ الزُّهْرِيُّ ۞ حَدَّثَنِي إِسْمَاعِيلُ بْنُ إِبْرَاهِيمَ ابْنُ أَخِي مُوسَى بْنِ عُقْبَةَ ۞ عَنْ مُوسَى بْنِ عُقْبَةَ ۞ عَنْ كُرَيْبٍ ۞ عَنِ ابْنِ عَبَّاسٍ قَالَ كَانَ رَسُولُ اللهِ ﷺ أَفْلَجَ الثَّنِيَّتَيْنِ ۞ إِذَا تَكَلَّمَ رُئِيَ كَالنُّورِ يَخْرُجُ مِنْ بَيْنِ ثَنَايَاهُ ۞

15. Abdullah ibn 'Abd al-Rahman narrated to us, 'Ibrahim ibn al-Mundhir al-Hizami related to us, "'Abd al-'Aziz ibn Thabit al-Zuhri related to me, 'Isma'il ibn Ibrahim, the nephew of Musa ibn 'Uqba, narrated to me on the authority of Musa ibn 'Uqba, on the authority of Kurayb [ibn Abu Muslim al-Madani],[84] on the authority of Ibn 'Abbas رضي الله عنهما, who reported:

"The Messenger of Allah ﷺ had a slight space between his two blessed front teeth; when he would speak, something like a light would be seen emitting from between them."''''[85]

[78] This similarity was made due to the brightness and luminousness of the Prophet's complexion ﷺ. (MA)

[79] This presentation either refers to the Night Journey (*al-Isra'*) or to a dream. If it is the former then it refers to the actual physical features that they possessed in their lifetimes, because it has been authentically narrated that the Prophets are alive in their graves. If is the latter, then what was seen was a resemblance of their true forms. In using the phrase 'presented to me' as opposed to 'I was presented to them', the Prophet ﷺ indicates his virtue over them in a tacit, respectful way. (MA)

[80] Shanu'a is a tribe from the Yemen whose members are generally of medium build. (AA)

[81] 'Urwa ibn Mas'ud رضي الله عنه was a chieftain of the city of Ta'if and one of the first of its people to accept Islam. He was a notable envoy who participated in the negotiations of the armistice of Hudaybiyya. In a famous hadith, 'Urwa mentioned his words to Quraysh upon seeing the Companions' tremendous attachment to the Prophet ﷺ. He said, 'What kind of people are these? By Allah, I have been in delegations sent to kings, delegations sent to the Qaysar, Kisra and the Negus, but I have never seen a king extolled by his companions as the companions of Muhammad extol him! By Allah, he does not spit except that it falls in the hands of one of them, who then rubs his face and body with it. If he commands them, they hasten to carry out his order. When he performs ritual purification, they almost fight to get his leftover ritual purification water. When they speak in his presence, they lower their voices, and out of awe of him, they never stare directly at him.' (*Sahih al-Bukhari*) (MA)

14

[82] Dihya al-Kalbi was known as the most handsome man of his time (besides, of course, the Prophet ﷺ). When the Archangel Jibril عليه السلام would descend with revelation, he would often come to the Prophet ﷺ in the form of Dihya al-Kalbi. (AA)

The reason why these three Prophets were singled out with descriptions is because Ibrahim was the patriarch of the Arabs and non-Arabs, and he along with Prophets Musa and 'Isa are accepted by the People of the Scripture (*Ahl al-Kitab*). The benefit taken from this hadith is that it is necessary to teach the physical features of the esteemed Prophets to those who did not see them, for in the mention of their physical features is a blessing similar to their physical meeting. It is also an extra encouragement in accurately knowing and narrating the physical features of the Prophet Muhammad ﷺ. (MA)

[83] He is 'Amir ibn Wathila al-Laythi, Abu Tufayl رضي الله عنه. He lived to be 107–110 years of age and was the last Companion of the Prophet ﷺ to die. Abu Tufayl's statement, 'there is no one remaining on the face of the earth [today] who has seen him besides me,' refers to the Prophet's Companions. (AA)

[84] The servant of Ibn 'Abbas رضي الله عنهما. (AA)

[85] From Ibn 'Abbas' saying 'something like a light would be seen', and not simply 'I saw', we can deduce that others also saw this light. The phrase 'something like a light' is a rendering of the Arabic, *kal-nur*. The *ka* particle is called a 'particle of resemblance'. However, some scholars comment that the particle *ka* here is a *kaf al-za'ida*: an extra particle added for emphasis and magnification. According to the latter reading, this phrase would be translated as, '*a light would be seen emitting from between them*'. (MA, AA)

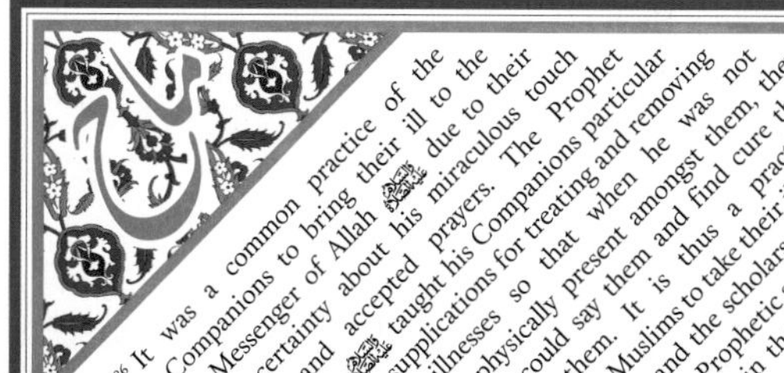

CHAPTER TWO

بَابُ مَا جَاءَ فِي خَاتَمِ النُّبُوَّةِ

What Has Been Narrated Concerning the Seal of Prophethood

١٦ - حَدَّثَنَا أَبُو رَجَاءٍ قُتَيْبَةُ بْنُ سَعِيدٍ ۞ حَدَّثَنَا حَاتِمُ بْنُ إِسْمَاعِيلَ ۞ عَنِ الْجَعْدِ بْنِ عَبْدِ الرَّحْمٰنِ قَالَ سَمِعْتُ السَّائِبَ بْنَ يَزِيدَ يَقُولُ ذَهَبَتْ بِي خَالَتِي إِلَى النَّبِيِّ ﷺ ۞ فَقَالَتْ يَا رَسُولَ اللهِ إِنَّ ابْنَ أُخْتِي وَجِعٌ ۞ فَمَسَحَ ﷺ رَأْسِي ۞ وَدَعَا لِي بِالْبَرَكَةِ ۞ وَتَوَضَّأَ ۞ فَشَرِبْتُ مِنْ وَضُوئِهِ ۞ وَقُمْتُ خَلْفَ ظَهْرِهِ ۞ فَنَظَرْتُ إِلَى الْخَاتَمِ بَيْنَ كَتِفَيْهِ ۞ فَإِذَا هُوَ مِثْلُ زِرِّ الْحَجَلَةِ ۞

16. Abu al-Raja' Qutayba ibn Sa'id narrated to us, 'Hatim ibn Isma'il narrated to us on the authority of Ja'd ibn 'Abd al-Rahman, who said:

"I heard Sa'ib ibn Yazid say, 'My maternal aunt took me to the Prophet ﷺ and said, "O Messenger of Allah, my nephew is suffering from a pain."[86] So he ﷺ wiped his blessed hand on my head and prayed that I be blessed.[87] Then he performed ritual purification (*wudu'*),[88] and I drank from his leftover ritual purification water.[89] I stood behind his blessed back and gazed upon the Seal [of Prophethood] between his blessed shoulders[90] and, lo and behold, it was like a button of a bed canopy [in size].'"[91]

[86] It was a common practice of the Companions to bring their ill to the Messenger of Allah ﷺ due to their certainty about his miraculous touch and accepted prayers. The Prophet ﷺ taught his Companions particular supplications for treating and removing illnesses so that when he was not physically present amongst them, they could say them and find cure through them. It is thus a practice of the Muslims to take their ill to the righteous and the scholars in order to have those Prophetic supplications read upon them in the same way that the Companions practised them with the Prophet ﷺ. A reference book in this area is Imam al-Nawawi's *al-Adhkar*. (MA)

[87] Imam al-Bayhaqi recorded in *Dala'il al-Nubuwwa*, 'Ikrima ibn 'Ammar reported, "'Ata', the freed slave of Sa'ib ibn Yazid, said, 'The hair on Sa'ib's head was black up to here'—and he described it with his hand, showing the location on the front of Sa'ib's head where it was completely black. He ['Ata'] said, 'The back of his head and the front and sides of his beard were all white. I said to him, 'O master! I have never seen anyone with hair as peculiar as yours!' He [Sa'ib] said, 'Do you know why that is, dear son? When I was a young boy, the Messenger of Allah ﷺ passed by and asked me, "Who are you?" "Sa'ib ibn Yazid", I replied. Then he rubbed his blessed hand over my head and said, "May Allah bless you." That area [where he rubbed] will never turn white!'"" In another narration, Ja'd said, "I saw Sa'ib ibn Yazid when he was ninety-four years old. He was healthy and strong, and he said, 'I know that I did not have the luxury of my hearing and sight except through the blessings of the Prophet's supplication ﷺ!'" This points to the utmost gentleness and perfect compassion the Prophet ﷺ had for his Companions, and his transcendence and purity above arrogance and pride. (AA, MA)

[88] Did the Prophet ﷺ perform ritual purification for the sole reason that this child came to him in a state of illness so he could take blessings through his ritual purification water, or was he going to perform ritual purification anyway? If it was the former, we gain new insights into the hadith of Sayyiduna 'Ali and Sayyida Fatima ﷺ and the ritual purification the Prophet ﷺ performed on their wedding night, as well as his ritual purification in order to bless his Companions. If it is the latter, we find that the Prophet ﷺ did not prevent or disapprove his Companions from seeking blessings from his leftover ritual purification water. (MA)

[89] This leftover ritual purification water could have been the water that remained in the vessel used for ritual purification. It could have also been the water that dripped from the Prophet's blessed limbs ﷺ. It was from the practice of the Companions to take the remaining water in the vessel and what dripped from his blessed limbs to seek healing and blessings from it because of its proximity to the Prophet ﷺ. (AA)

[90] In this narration and those that follow, the Prophet's Seal ﷺ is described as being between his blessed shoulders. This, as Imam al-Bajuri and others note, is an approximate description of the Seal's location. Other narrations state that it was adjacent to the left side of the Prophet's blessed shoulder-blade (*naghid*). (AA)

[91] Scholars disagree over the wording and meaning of this final phrase. Imam al-Nawawi and others maintain that it is *zirr al-hajala*, and means a button used on a bed canopy. Others said it is *rizz al-hajala*, and means a pigeon's egg. (AA)

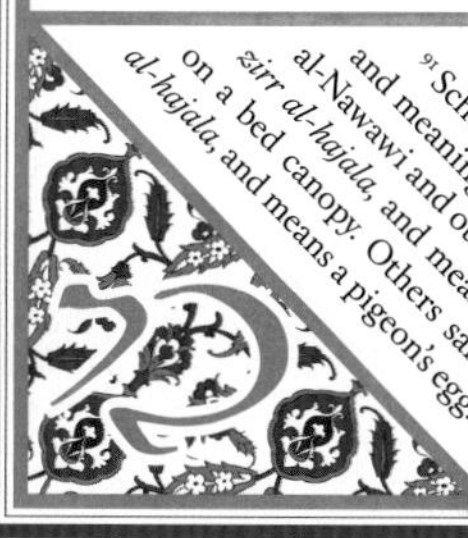

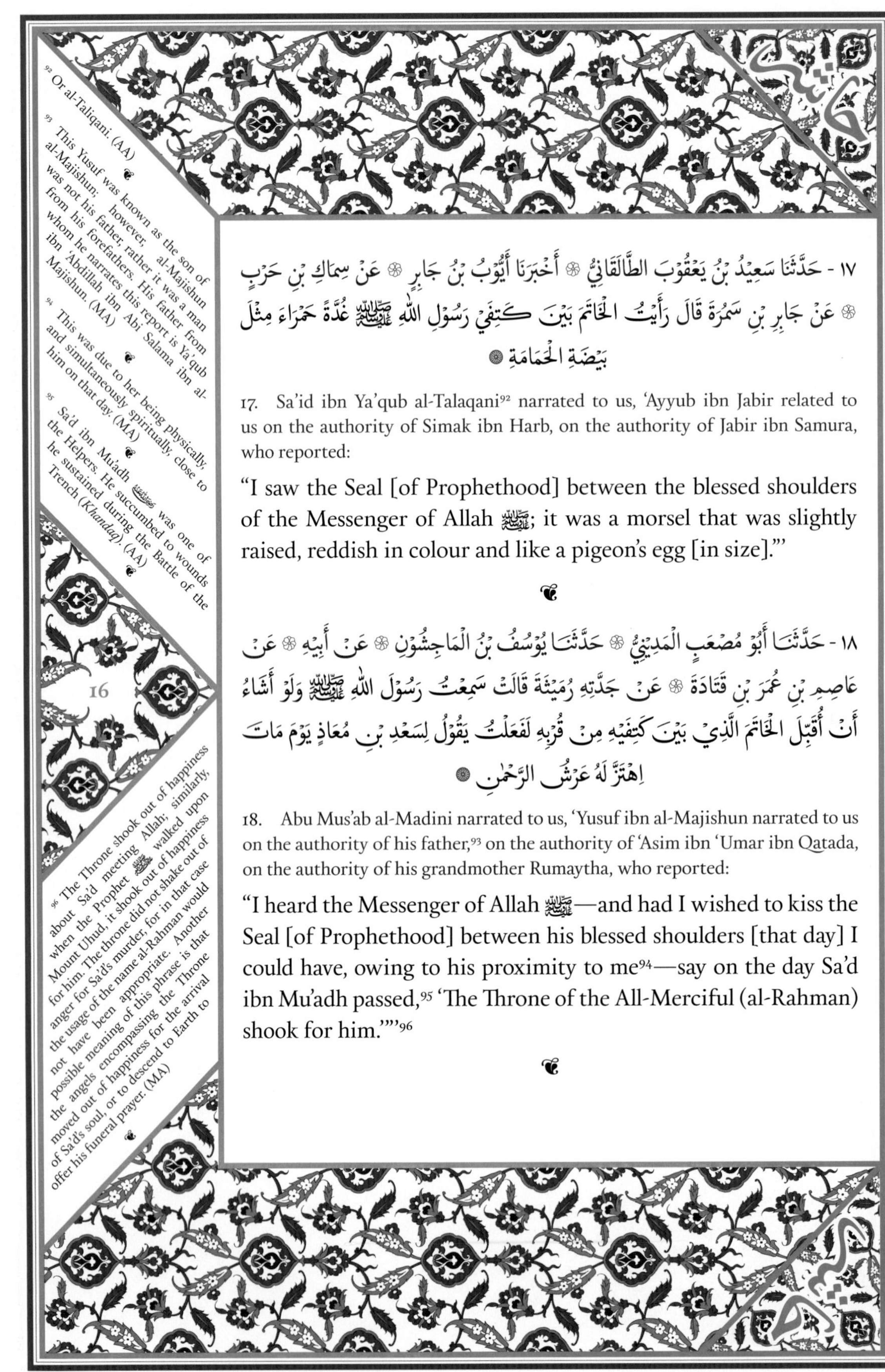

١٧ - حَدَّثَنَا سَعِيْدُ بْنُ يَعْقُوبَ الطَّالَقَانِيُّ ۞ أَخْبَرَنَا أَيُّوبُ بْنُ جَابِرٍ ۞ عَنْ سِمَاكِ بْنِ حَرْبٍ ۞ عَنْ جَابِرِ بْنِ سَمُرَةَ قَالَ رَأَيْتُ الْخَاتَمَ بَيْنَ كَتِفَيْ رَسُوْلِ اللهِ ﷺ غُدَّةً حَمْرَاءَ مِثْلَ بَيْضَةِ الْحَمَامَةِ ۞

17. Sa'id ibn Ya'qub al-Talaqani[92] narrated to us, 'Ayyub ibn Jabir related to us on the authority of Simak ibn Harb, on the authority of Jabir ibn Samura, who reported:

"I saw the Seal [of Prophethood] between the blessed shoulders of the Messenger of Allah ﷺ; it was a morsel that was slightly raised, reddish in colour and like a pigeon's egg [in size]."

١٨ - حَدَّثَنَا أَبُوْ مُصْعَبٍ الْمَدِيْنِيُّ ۞ حَدَّثَنَا يُوْسُفُ بْنُ الْمَاجِشُوْنِ ۞ عَنْ أَبِيْهِ ۞ عَنْ عَاصِمِ بْنِ عُمَرَ بْنِ قَتَادَةَ ۞ عَنْ جَدَّتِهِ رُمَيْثَةَ قَالَتْ سَمِعْتُ رَسُوْلَ اللهِ ﷺ وَلَوْ أَشَاءُ أَنْ أُقَبِّلَ الْخَاتَمَ الَّذِيْ بَيْنَ كَتِفَيْهِ مِنْ قُرْبِهِ لَفَعَلْتُ يَقُوْلُ لِسَعْدِ بْنِ مُعَاذٍ يَوْمَ مَاتَ اهْتَزَّ لَهُ عَرْشُ الرَّحْمٰنِ ۞

18. Abu Mus'ab al-Madini narrated to us, 'Yusuf ibn al-Majishun narrated to us on the authority of his father,[93] on the authority of 'Asim ibn 'Umar ibn Qatada, on the authority of his grandmother Rumaytha, who reported:

"I heard the Messenger of Allah ﷺ—and had I wished to kiss the Seal [of Prophethood] between his blessed shoulders [that day] I could have, owing to his proximity to me[94]—say on the day Sa'd ibn Mu'adh passed,[95] 'The Throne of the All-Merciful (al-Rahman) shook for him.'"[96]

[92] Or al-Taliqani. (AA)

[93] This Yusuf was known as the son of al-Majishun; however, al-Majishun was not his father, rather it was a man from his forefathers. His father from whom he narrates this report is Ya'qub ibn 'Abdillah ibn Abi Salama ibn al-Majishun. (MA)

[94] This was due to her being physically, and simultaneously spiritually, close to him on that day. (MA)

[95] Sa'd ibn Mu'adh رضي الله عنه was one of the Helpers. He succumbed to wounds he sustained during the Battle of the Trench (*Khandaq*). (AA)

[96] The Throne shook out of happiness about Sa'd meeting Allah; similarly, when the Prophet ﷺ walked upon Mount Uhud, it shook out of happiness for him. The throne did not shake out of anger for Sa'd's murder, for in that case the usage of the name al-Rahman would not have been appropriate. Another possible meaning of this phrase is that the angels encompassing the Throne moved out of happiness for the arrival of Sa'd's soul, or to descend to Earth to offer his funeral prayer. (MA)

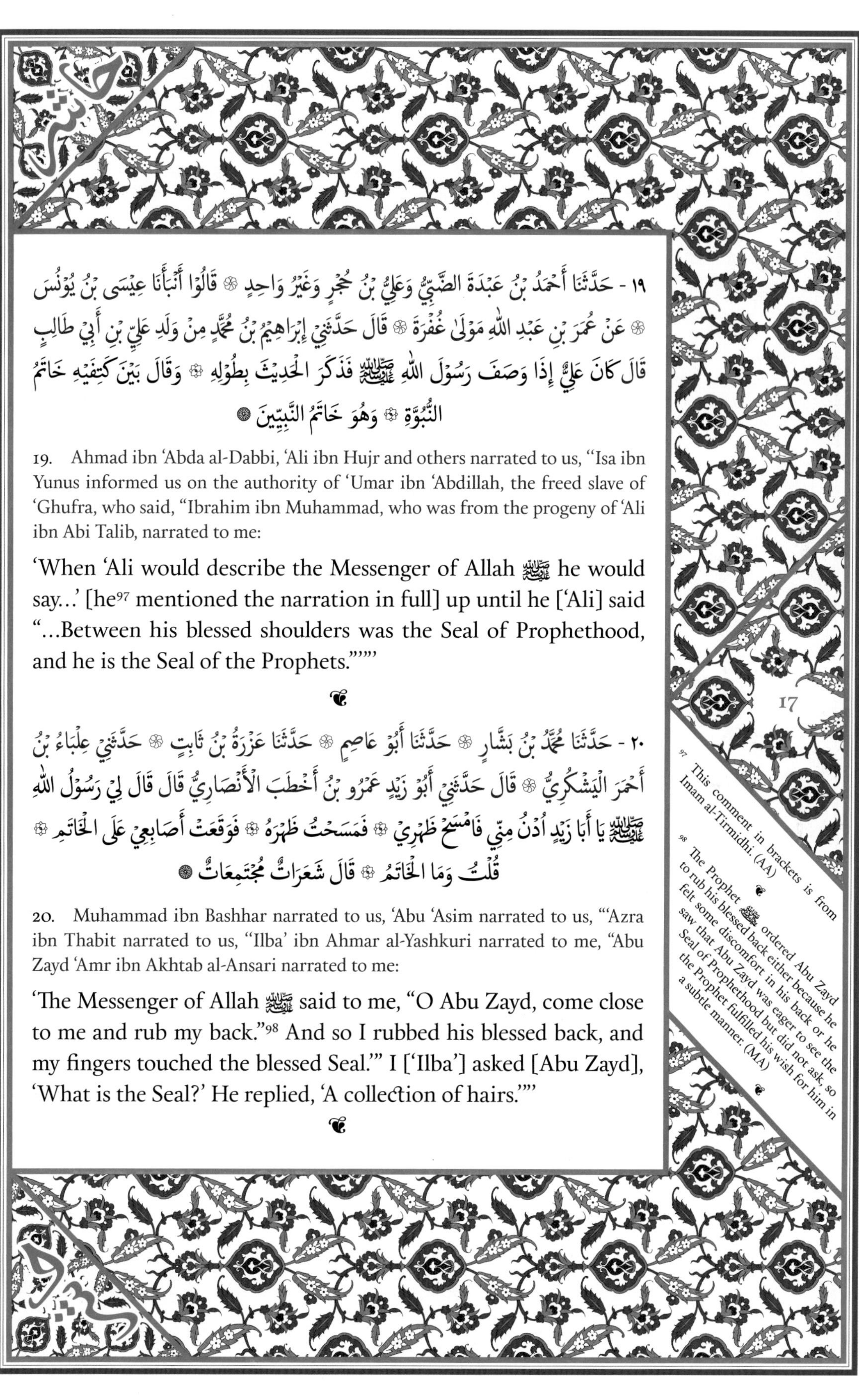

١٩ - حَدَّثَنَا أَحْمَدُ بْنُ عَبْدَةَ الضَّبِّيُّ وَعَلِيُّ بْنُ حُجْرٍ وَغَيْرُ وَاحِدٍ ۞ قَالُوا أَنْبَأَنَا عِيسَى بْنُ يُونُسَ ۞ عَنْ عُمَرَ بْنِ عَبْدِ اللهِ مَوْلَى غُفْرَةَ ۞ قَالَ حَدَّثَنِي إِبْرَاهِيمُ بْنُ مُحَمَّدٍ مِنْ وَلَدِ عَلِيِّ بْنِ أَبِي طَالِبٍ قَالَ كَانَ عَلِيٌّ إِذَا وَصَفَ رَسُولَ اللهِ ﷺ فَذَكَرَ الْحَدِيثَ بِطُولِهِ ۞ وَقَالَ بَيْنَ كَتِفَيْهِ خَاتَمُ النُّبُوَّةِ ۞ وَهُوَ خَاتَمُ النَّبِيِّينَ ۞

19. Ahmad ibn ʿAbda al-Dabbi, ʿAli ibn Hujr and others narrated to us, "ʿIsa ibn Yunus informed us on the authority of ʿUmar ibn ʿAbdillah, the freed slave of ʿGhufra, who said, "Ibrahim ibn Muhammad, who was from the progeny of ʿAli ibn Abi Talib, narrated to me:

'When ʿAli would describe the Messenger of Allah ﷺ he would say...' [he[97] mentioned the narration in full] up until he [ʿAli] said "...Between his blessed shoulders was the Seal of Prophethood, and he is the Seal of the Prophets."""'

٢٠ - حَدَّثَنَا مُحَمَّدُ بْنُ بَشَّارٍ ۞ حَدَّثَنَا أَبُو عَاصِمٍ ۞ حَدَّثَنَا عَزْرَةُ بْنُ ثَابِتٍ ۞ حَدَّثَنِي عِلْبَاءُ بْنُ أَحْمَرَ الْيَشْكُرِيُّ ۞ قَالَ حَدَّثَنِي أَبُو زَيْدٍ عَمْرُو بْنُ أَخْطَبَ الْأَنْصَارِيُّ قَالَ قَالَ لِي رَسُولُ اللهِ ﷺ يَا أَبَا زَيْدٍ اُدْنُ مِنِّي فَامْسَحْ ظَهْرِي ۞ فَمَسَحْتُ ظَهْرَهُ ۞ فَوَقَعَتْ أَصَابِعِي عَلَى الْخَاتَمِ ۞ قُلْتُ وَمَا الْخَاتَمُ ۞ قَالَ شَعَرَاتٌ مُجْتَمِعَاتٌ ۞

20. Muhammad ibn Bashhar narrated to us, ʿAbu ʿAsim narrated to us, "ʿAzra ibn Thabit narrated to us, "Ilba' ibn Ahmar al-Yashkuri narrated to me, "Abu Zayd ʿAmr ibn Akhtab al-Ansari narrated to me:

'The Messenger of Allah ﷺ said to me, "O Abu Zayd, come close to me and rub my back."[98] And so I rubbed his blessed back, and my fingers touched the blessed Seal."' I [ʿIlba'] asked [Abu Zayd], 'What is the Seal?' He replied, 'A collection of hairs.'"'

[97] This comment in brackets is from Imam al-Tirmidhi. (AA)

[98] The Prophet ﷺ ordered Abu Zayd to rub his blessed back either because he felt some discomfort in his back or he saw that Abu Zayd was eager to see the Seal of Prophethood but did not ask, so the Prophet fulfilled his wish for him in a subtle manner. (MA)

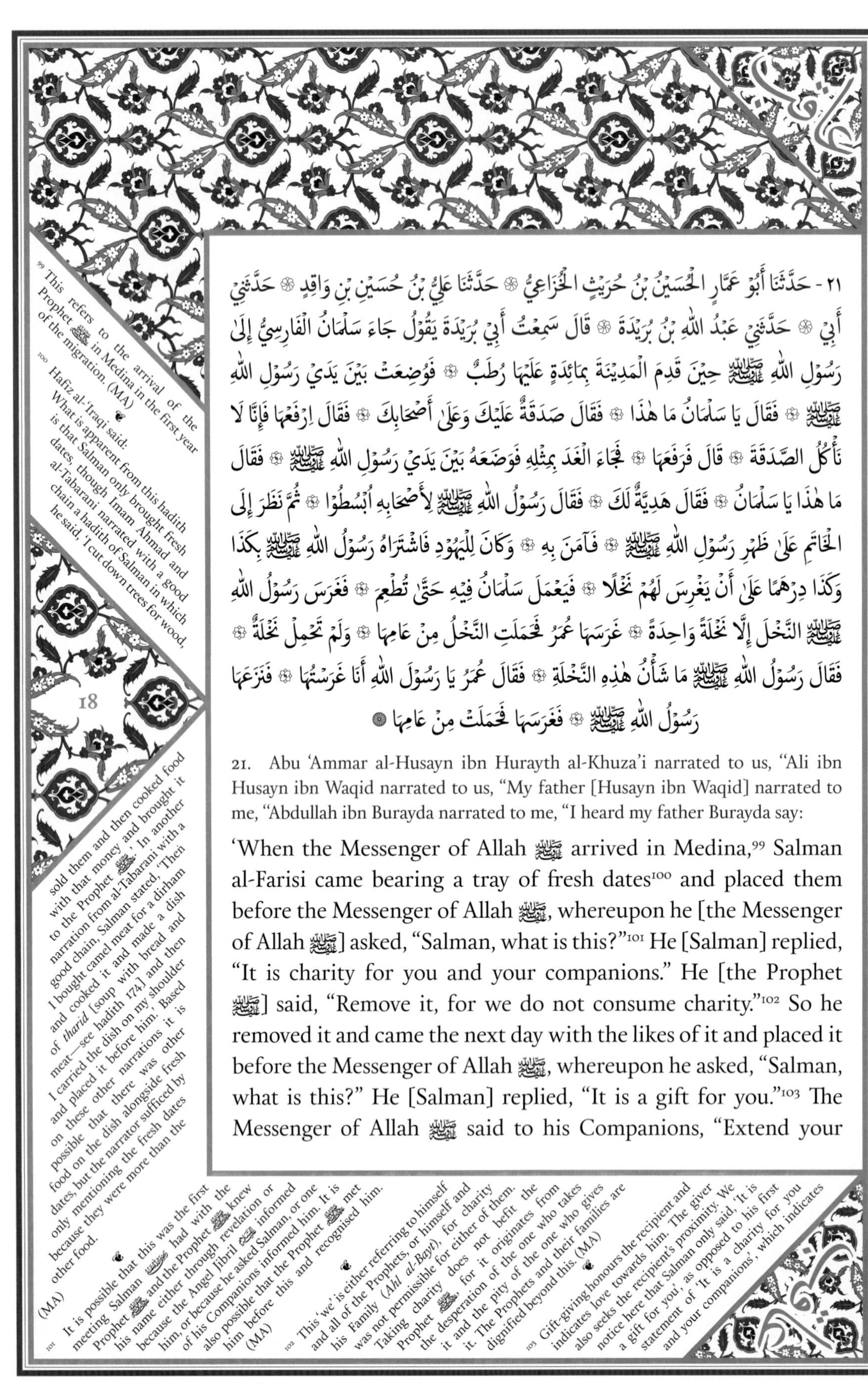

٢١ - حَدَّثَنَا أَبُو عَمَّارٍ الْحُسَيْنُ بْنُ حُرَيْثٍ الْخُزَاعِيُّ ۞ حَدَّثَنَا عَلِيُّ بْنُ حُسَيْنِ بْنِ وَاقِدٍ ۞ حَدَّثَنِي أَبِي ۞ حَدَّثَنِي عَبْدُ اللهِ بْنُ بُرَيْدَةَ ۞ قَالَ سَمِعْتُ أَبِي بُرَيْدَةَ يَقُولُ جَاءَ سَلْمَانُ الْفَارِسِيُّ إِلَىٰ رَسُولِ اللهِ ﷺ حِينَ قَدِمَ الْمَدِينَةَ بِمَائِدَةٍ عَلَيْهَا رُطَبٌ ۞ فَوُضِعَتْ بَيْنَ يَدَيْ رَسُولِ اللهِ ﷺ ۞ فَقَالَ يَا سَلْمَانُ مَا هٰذَا ۞ فَقَالَ صَدَقَةٌ عَلَيْكَ وَعَلَىٰ أَصْحَابِكَ ۞ فَقَالَ ارْفَعْهَا فَإِنَّا لَا نَأْكُلُ الصَّدَقَةَ ۞ قَالَ فَرَفَعَهَا ۞ فَجَاءَ الْغَدَ بِمِثْلِهِ فَوَضَعَهُ بَيْنَ يَدَيْ رَسُولِ اللهِ ﷺ ۞ فَقَالَ مَا هٰذَا يَا سَلْمَانُ ۞ فَقَالَ هَدِيَّةٌ لَكَ ۞ فَقَالَ رَسُولُ اللهِ ﷺ لِأَصْحَابِهِ ابْسُطُوا ۞ ثُمَّ نَظَرَ إِلَى الْخَاتَمِ عَلَىٰ ظَهْرِ رَسُولِ اللهِ ﷺ ۞ فَآمَنَ بِهِ ۞ وَكَانَ لِلْيَهُودِ فَاشْتَرَاهُ رَسُولُ اللهِ ﷺ بِكَذَا وَكَذَا دِرْهَمًا عَلَىٰ أَنْ يَغْرِسَ لَهُمْ نَخْلًا ۞ فَيَعْمَلَ سَلْمَانُ فِيهِ حَتَّىٰ تُطْعِمَ ۞ فَغَرَسَ رَسُولُ اللهِ ﷺ النَّخْلَ إِلَّا نَخْلَةً وَاحِدَةً ۞ غَرَسَهَا عُمَرُ فَحَمَلَتِ النَّخْلُ مِنْ عَامِهَا ۞ وَلَمْ تَحْمِلْ نَخْلَةٌ ۞ فَقَالَ رَسُولُ اللهِ ﷺ مَا شَأْنُ هٰذِهِ النَّخْلَةِ ۞ فَقَالَ عُمَرُ يَا رَسُولَ اللهِ أَنَا غَرَسْتُهَا ۞ فَنَزَعَهَا رَسُولُ اللهِ ﷺ ۞ فَغَرَسَهَا فَحَمَلَتْ مِنْ عَامِهَا ۞

21. Abu 'Ammar al-Husayn ibn Hurayth al-Khuza'i narrated to us, "Ali ibn Husayn ibn Waqid narrated to us, "My father [Husayn ibn Waqid] narrated to me, "Abdullah ibn Burayda narrated to me, "I heard my father Burayda say:

'When the Messenger of Allah ﷺ arrived in Medina,[99] Salman al-Farisi came bearing a tray of fresh dates[100] and placed them before the Messenger of Allah ﷺ, whereupon he [the Messenger of Allah ﷺ] asked, "Salman, what is this?"[101] He [Salman] replied, "It is charity for you and your companions." He [the Prophet ﷺ] said, "Remove it, for we do not consume charity."[102] So he removed it and came the next day with the likes of it and placed it before the Messenger of Allah ﷺ, whereupon he asked, "Salman, what is this?" He [Salman] replied, "It is a gift for you."[103] The Messenger of Allah ﷺ said to his Companions, "Extend your

[99] This refers to the arrival of the Prophet ﷺ in Medina in the first year of the migration. (MA)

[100] Hafiz al-'Iraqi said: What is apparent from this hadith is that Salman only brought fresh dates, though Imam Ahmad and al-Tabarani narrated with a good chain a hadith of Salman in which he said, 'I cut down trees for wood, sold them and then cooked food with that money and brought it to the Prophet ﷺ.' In another narration from al-Tabarani with a good chain, Salman stated, 'Then I bought camel meat for a dirham and cooked it and made a dish of *tharid* [soup with bread and meat—see hadith 174] and then I carried the dish on my shoulder and placed it before him.' Based on these other narrations it is possible that there was other food on the dish alongside fresh dates, but the narrator sufficed by only mentioning the fresh dates because they were more than the other food.

[101] It is possible that this was the first meeting Salman had with the Prophet ﷺ and the Prophet ﷺ knew his name either through revelation or because the Angel Jibril informed him, or because he asked Salman, or one of his Companions informed him. It is also possible that the Prophet ﷺ met him before this and recognised him. (MA)

[102] This 'we' is either referring to himself and all of the Prophets, or himself and his Family (*Ahl al-Bayt*), for charity was not permissible for either of them. Taking charity does not befit the Prophet ﷺ, for it originates from the desperation of the one who takes it and the pity of the one who gives it. The Prophets and their families are dignified beyond this. (MA)

[103] Gift-giving honours the recipient and indicates love towards him. The giver also seeks the recipient's proximity. We notice here that Salman only said, 'It is a gift for you', as opposed to his first statement of 'It is a charity for you and your companions', which indicates

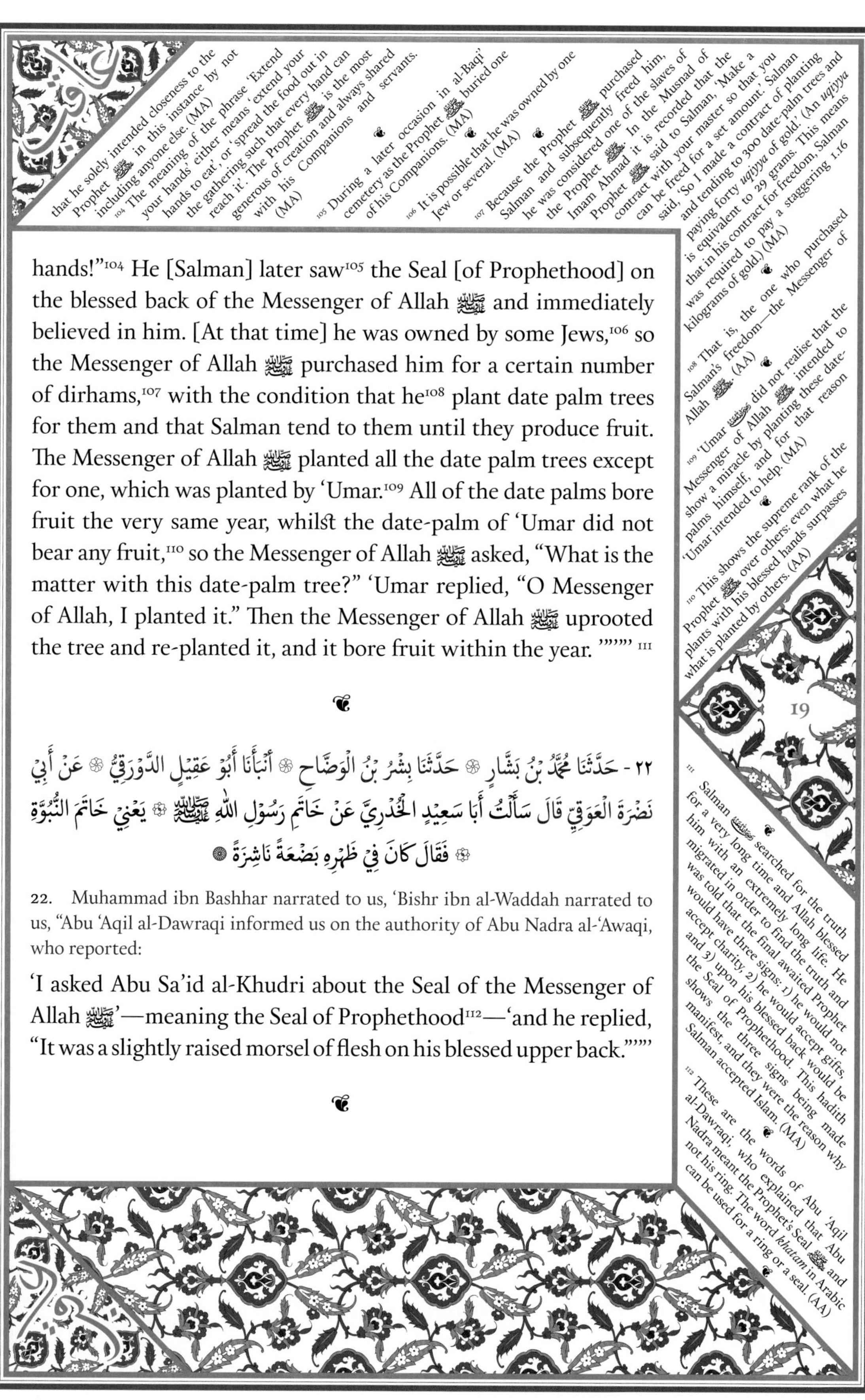

hands!"[104] He [Salman] later saw[105] the Seal [of Prophethood] on the blessed back of the Messenger of Allah ﷺ and immediately believed in him. [At that time] he was owned by some Jews,[106] so the Messenger of Allah ﷺ purchased him for a certain number of dirhams,[107] with the condition that he[108] plant date palm trees for them and that Salman tend to them until they produce fruit. The Messenger of Allah ﷺ planted all the date palm trees except for one, which was planted by 'Umar.[109] All of the date palms bore fruit the very same year, whilst the date-palm of 'Umar did not bear any fruit,[110] so the Messenger of Allah ﷺ asked, "What is the matter with this date-palm tree?" 'Umar replied, "O Messenger of Allah, I planted it." Then the Messenger of Allah ﷺ uprooted the tree and re-planted it, and it bore fruit within the year. '""" [111]

٢٢ - حَدَّثَنَا مُحَمَّدُ بْنُ بَشَّارٍ ۞ حَدَّثَنَا بِشْرُ بْنُ الْوَضَّاحِ ۞ أَنبَأَنَا أَبُو عَقِيلٍ الدَّوْرَقِيُّ ۞ عَنْ أَبِي نَضْرَةَ الْعَوَقِيِّ قَالَ سَأَلْتُ أَبَا سَعِيدٍ الْخُدْرِيَّ عَنْ خَاتَمِ رَسُولِ اللهِ ﷺ ۞ يَعْنِي خَاتَمَ النُّبُوَّةِ ۞ فَقَالَ كَانَ فِي ظَهْرِهِ بَضْعَةً نَاشِزَةً ۞

22. Muhammad ibn Bashhar narrated to us, 'Bishr ibn al-Waddah narrated to us, "Abu 'Aqil al-Dawraqi informed us on the authority of Abu Nadra al-'Awaqi, who reported:

'I asked Abu Sa'id al-Khudri about the Seal of the Messenger of Allah ﷺ'—meaning the Seal of Prophethood[112]—'and he replied, "It was a slightly raised morsel of flesh on his blessed upper back."'"

that he solely intended closeness to the Prophet ﷺ in this instance by not including anyone else. (MA)

104 The meaning of the phrase 'Extend your hands' either means 'extend your hands to eat', or 'spread the food out in the gathering such that every hand can reach it'. The Prophet ﷺ is the most generous of creation and always shared with his Companions and servants. (MA)

105 During a later occasion in al-Baqi' cemetery as the Prophet ﷺ buried one of his Companions. (MA)

106 It is possible that he was owned by one Jew or several. (MA)

107 Because the Prophet ﷺ purchased Salman and subsequently freed him, he was considered one of the slaves of the Prophet ﷺ. In the Musnad of Imam Ahmad it is recorded that the Prophet ﷺ said to Salman, 'Make a contract with your master so that you can be freed for a set amount.' Salman said, 'So I made a contract of planting and tending to 300 date-palm trees and paying forty *uqiyya* of gold.' (An *uqiyya* is equivalent to 29 grams. This means that in his contract for freedom, Salman was required to pay a staggering 1.16 kilograms of gold.) (MA)

108 That is, the one who purchased Salman's freedom—the Messenger of Allah ﷺ. (AA)

109 'Umar ؓ did not realise that the Messenger of Allah ﷺ intended to show a miracle by planting these date-palms himself, and for that reason 'Umar intended to help. (MA)

110 This shows the supreme rank of the Prophet ﷺ over others: even what he plants with his blessed hands surpasses what is planted by others. (AA)

111 Salman ؓ searched for the truth for a very long time and Allah blessed him with an extremely long life. He migrated in order to find the truth and was told that the final awaited Prophet would have three signs: 1) he would not accept charity, 2) he would accept gifts, and 3) upon his blessed back would be the Seal of Prophethood. This hadith shows the three signs being made manifest, and they were the reason why Salman accepted Islam. (MA)

112 These are the words of Abu 'Aqil al-Dawraqi, who explained that Abu Nadra meant the Prophet's Seal ﷺ and not his ring. The word *khatam* in Arabic can be used for a ring or a seal. (AA)

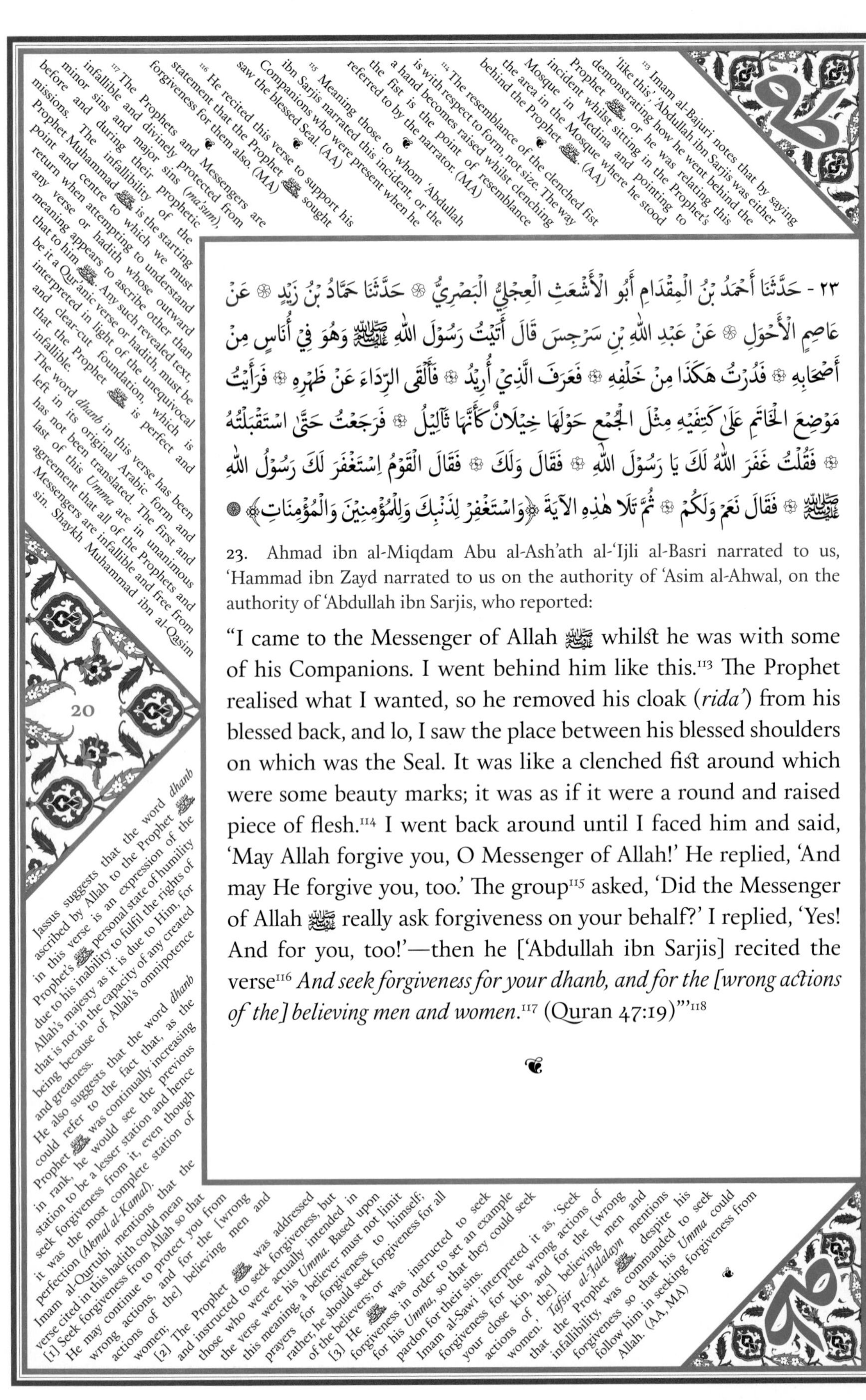

٢٣ - حَدَّثَنَا أَحْمَدُ بْنُ الْمِقْدَامِ أَبُو الْأَشْعَثِ الْعِجْلِيُّ الْبَصْرِيُّ ۞ حَدَّثَنَا حَمَّادُ بْنُ زَيْدٍ ۞ عَنْ عَاصِمٍ الْأَحْوَلِ ۞ عَنْ عَبْدِ اللهِ بْنِ سَرْجِسَ قَالَ أَتَيْتُ رَسُولَ اللهِ ﷺ وَهُوَ فِي أُنَاسٍ مِنْ أَصْحَابِهِ ۞ فَدُرْتُ هٰكَذَا مِنْ خَلْفِهِ ۞ فَعَرَفَ الَّذِي أُرِيدُ ۞ فَأَلْقَى الرِّدَاءَ عَنْ ظَهْرِهِ ۞ فَرَأَيْتُ مَوْضِعَ الْخَاتَمِ عَلَىٰ كَتِفَيْهِ مِثْلَ الْجُمْعِ حَوْلَهَا خِيلَانٌ كَأَنَّهَا ثَآلِيلُ ۞ فَرَجَعْتُ حَتَّىٰ اسْتَقْبَلْتُهُ ۞ فَقُلْتُ غَفَرَ اللهُ لَكَ يَا رَسُولَ اللهِ ۞ فَقَالَ وَلَكَ ۞ فَقَالَ الْقَوْمُ اِسْتَغْفَرَ لَكَ رَسُولُ اللهِ ﷺ ۞ فَقَالَ نَعَمْ وَلَكُمْ ۞ ثُمَّ تَلَا هٰذِهِ الْآيَةَ ﴿وَاسْتَغْفِرْ لِذَنْبِكَ وَلِلْمُؤْمِنِينَ وَالْمُؤْمِنَاتِ﴾ ۞

23. Ahmad ibn al-Miqdam Abu al-Ash'ath al-'Ijli al-Basri narrated to us, 'Hammad ibn Zayd narrated to us on the authority of 'Asim al-Ahwal, on the authority of 'Abdullah ibn Sarjis, who reported:

"I came to the Messenger of Allah ﷺ whilst he was with some of his Companions. I went behind him like this.[113] The Prophet realised what I wanted, so he removed his cloak (*rida'*) from his blessed back, and lo, I saw the place between his blessed shoulders on which was the Seal. It was like a clenched fist around which were some beauty marks; it was as if it were a round and raised piece of flesh.[114] I went back around until I faced him and said, 'May Allah forgive you, O Messenger of Allah!' He replied, 'And may He forgive you, too.' The group[115] asked, 'Did the Messenger of Allah ﷺ really ask forgiveness on your behalf?' I replied, 'Yes! And for you, too!'—then he ['Abdullah ibn Sarjis] recited the verse[116] *And seek forgiveness for your dhanb, and for the [wrong actions of the] believing men and women.*[117] (Quran 47:19)'"[118]

[113] Imam al-Bajuri notes that by saying 'like this', 'Abdullah ibn Sarjis was either demonstrating how he went behind the Prophet ﷺ or he was relating this incident whilst sitting in the Prophet's Mosque in Medina and pointing to the area in the Mosque where he stood behind the Prophet ﷺ. (AA)

[114] The resemblance of the clenched fist is with respect to form, not size. The way a hand becomes raised whilst clenching the fist is the point of resemblance referred to by the narrator. (MA)

[115] Meaning those to whom 'Abdullah ibn Sarjis narrated this incident, or the Companions who were present when he saw the blessed Seal. (AA)

[116] He recited this verse to support his statement that the Prophet ﷺ sought forgiveness for them also. (MA)

[117] The Prophets and Messengers are infallible and divinely protected from minor sins and major sins (*ma'sum*), before and during their prophetic missions. The infallibility of the Prophet Muhammad ﷺ is the starting point and centre to which we must return when attempting to understand any verse or hadith whose outward meaning appears to ascribe other than that to him ﷺ. Any such revealed text, be it a Qur'anic verse or hadith, must be interpreted in light of the unequivocal and clear-cut foundation, which is that the Prophet ﷺ is perfect and infallible. The word *dhanb* in this verse has been left in its original Arabic form and has not been translated. The first and last of this *Umma* are in unanimous agreement that all of the Prophets and Messengers are infallible and free from sin. Shaykh Muhammad ibn al-Qasim Jassus suggests that the word *dhanb* ascribed by Allah to the Prophet ﷺ in this verse is an expression of the Prophet's ﷺ personal state of humility due to his inability to fulfil the rights of Allah's majesty as it is due to Him, for that is not in the capacity of any created being because of Allah's omnipotence and greatness. He also suggests that the word *dhanb* could refer to the fact that, as the Prophet ﷺ was continually increasing in rank, he would see the previous station to be a lesser station and hence seek forgiveness from it, even though it was the most complete station of perfection (*Akmal al-Kamal*). Imam al-Qurtubi mentions that the verse cited in this hadith could mean [1] Seek forgiveness from Allah so that He may continue to protect you from wrong actions, and for the [wrong actions of the] believing men and women; [2] The Prophet ﷺ was addressed and instructed to seek forgiveness, but those who were actually intended in the verse were his *Umma*. Based upon this meaning, a believer must not limit prayers for forgiveness to himself; rather, he should seek forgiveness for all of the believers; or [3] He ﷺ was instructed to seek forgiveness in order to set an example for his *Umma*, so that they could seek pardon for their sins. Imam al-Sawi interpreted it as, 'Seek forgiveness for the wrong actions of your close kin, and for the [wrong actions of the] believing men and women.' *Tafsir al-Jalalayn* mentions that the Prophet ﷺ, despite his infallibility, was commanded to seek forgiveness so that his *Umma* could follow him in seeking forgiveness from Allah. (AA, MA)

CHAPTER THREE

بَابُ مَا جَاءَ فِي شَعْرِ رَسُولِ اللهِ ﷺ

What Has Been Narrated Concerning the Blessed Hair of the Messenger of Allah ﷺ

٢٤ - حَدَّثَنَا عَلِيُّ بْنُ حُجْرٍ ۞ أَنْبَأَنَا إِسْمَاعِيلُ بْنُ إِبْرَاهِيمَ ۞ عَنْ حُمَيْدٍ ۞ عَنْ أَنَسِ بْنِ مَالِكٍ قَالَ كَانَ شَعْرُ رَسُولِ اللهِ ﷺ إِلَى نِصْفِ أُذُنَيْهِ ۞

24. 'Ali ibn Hujr narrated to us, 'Isma'il ibn Ibrahim informed us on the authority of Humayd, on the authority of Anas ibn Malik, who reported:

"The blessed hair of the Messenger of Allah ﷺ reached the middle of his ears."[119]

٢٥ - حَدَّثَنَا هَنَّادُ بْنُ السَّرِيِّ ۞ حَدَّثَنَا عَبْدُ الرَّحْمٰنِ بْنُ أَبِي الزِّنَادِ ۞ عَنْ هِشَامِ بْنِ عُرْوَةَ ۞ عَنْ أَبِيهِ ۞ عَنْ عَائِشَةَ قَالَتْ كُنْتُ أَغْتَسِلُ أَنَا وَرَسُولُ اللهِ ﷺ مِنْ إِنَاءٍ وَاحِدٍ ۞ وَكَانَ لَهُ شَعْرٌ فَوْقَ الْجُمَّةِ وَدُوْنَ الْوَفْرَةِ ۞

25. Hannad ibn al-Sari narrated to us, "Abd al-Rahman ibn Abi al-Zinad narrated to us on the authority of Hisham ibn 'Urwa, on the authority of his father,[120] on the authority of 'A'isha, who reported:

"The Messenger of Allah ﷺ and I would bathe from a single container. His blessed hair was above his shoulders yet reached past his earlobes."'[121]

[118] At the conclusion of this chapter it is fitting to discuss the wisdom behind the Seal of Prophethood being placed between the Prophet's blessed shoulders ﷺ. Most commentaries quote Ibn Dihya and others, who mentioned that the wisdom behind the Seal of Prophethood being placed between his blessed shoulders is that it indicates there will be no other prophet coming after him—meaning 'coming behind him'. Hafiz Ibn Hajar said, 'The scholars say that the secret behind this [placement] is that the heart is in that area.' However, we find a more satisfying answer in a narration from Wahb ibn Munabbih, recorded by Imam al-Hakim in his *Mustadrak*. Wahb reported, 'Allah has not sent forth any Prophet except that he had a mark of prophethood on his right hand—except for our Prophet ﷺ, for his mark of prophethood was between his blessed shoulders.' (See Imam al-Suyuti, *al-Khasa'is al-Kubra* 1:103.) Based on this narration, a number of scholars were of the opinion that the 'Seal', as such, is not exclusive to the Prophet Muhammad ﷺ, but rather what is exclusive to him ﷺ is its location on his blessed body. If each of the previous Prophets had a mark of prophethood on his hand as a sign of his veracity and to distinguish him from others, it begs the question: why is the Seal of the Prophet Muhammad ﷺ on his blessed back, underneath his clothing and not readily visible to others? The answer—and Allah and His Messenger know best—is that his blessed face is so dazzling and his perfect character and form are so sublime, that he does not need a mark or seal as a sign of his prophethood and truthfulness. His beautiful and luminous face suffices as a proof. The Prophets and Messengers are a community unto themselves and a collective, with the Prophet Muhammad ﷺ as their leader—and so in keeping with the divine wont for the Prophets, he was given a seal as one from that collective, though it was on his back and covered by his clothing. Imam al-Tirmidhi recorded in his Sunan from 'Abdullah ibn Salam ﷺ, who reported, 'When the Messenger of Allah entered Medina, the people rushed to see him, and it was said, "The Messenger of Allah has come! The Messenger of Allah has come!" I went along with the people to gaze upon him, and as soon as I saw his blessed face, I knew that it was not the face of a liar!' (AA)

[119] The Prophet Muhammad ﷺ is the most perfect embodiment of servitude and devotion to Allah. Every part of his blessed body, including his hair, worships Allah. His blessed hair was, and is, in a permanent state of prostration before Allah. Imams 'Abd al-Razzaq, Ibn Abi Shayba and al-Tabarani recorded that Sayyiduna 'Abdullah ibn Mas'ud ﷺ once saw a man prostrating in prayer with his hair tied in the back (a ponytail). He went over to the man as he was praying and untied the string around his hair. When the man completed his prayer, Sayyiduna 'Abdullah ibn Mas'ud ﷺ said to him, 'Do not tie your hair [whilst praying], for hair prostrates, and for every hair you will have a reward!' The man replied, 'I only tied it so it would not get dusty!' Sayyiduna 'Abdullah ibn Mas'ud ﷺ replied, 'It is better for you that it gets dusty!' (AA)

[120] 'Urwa ibn al-Zubayr. (AA)

[121] This narration means that the Prophet's blessed hair ﷺ reached between his earlobes and shoulders (also called *limma*). (AA)

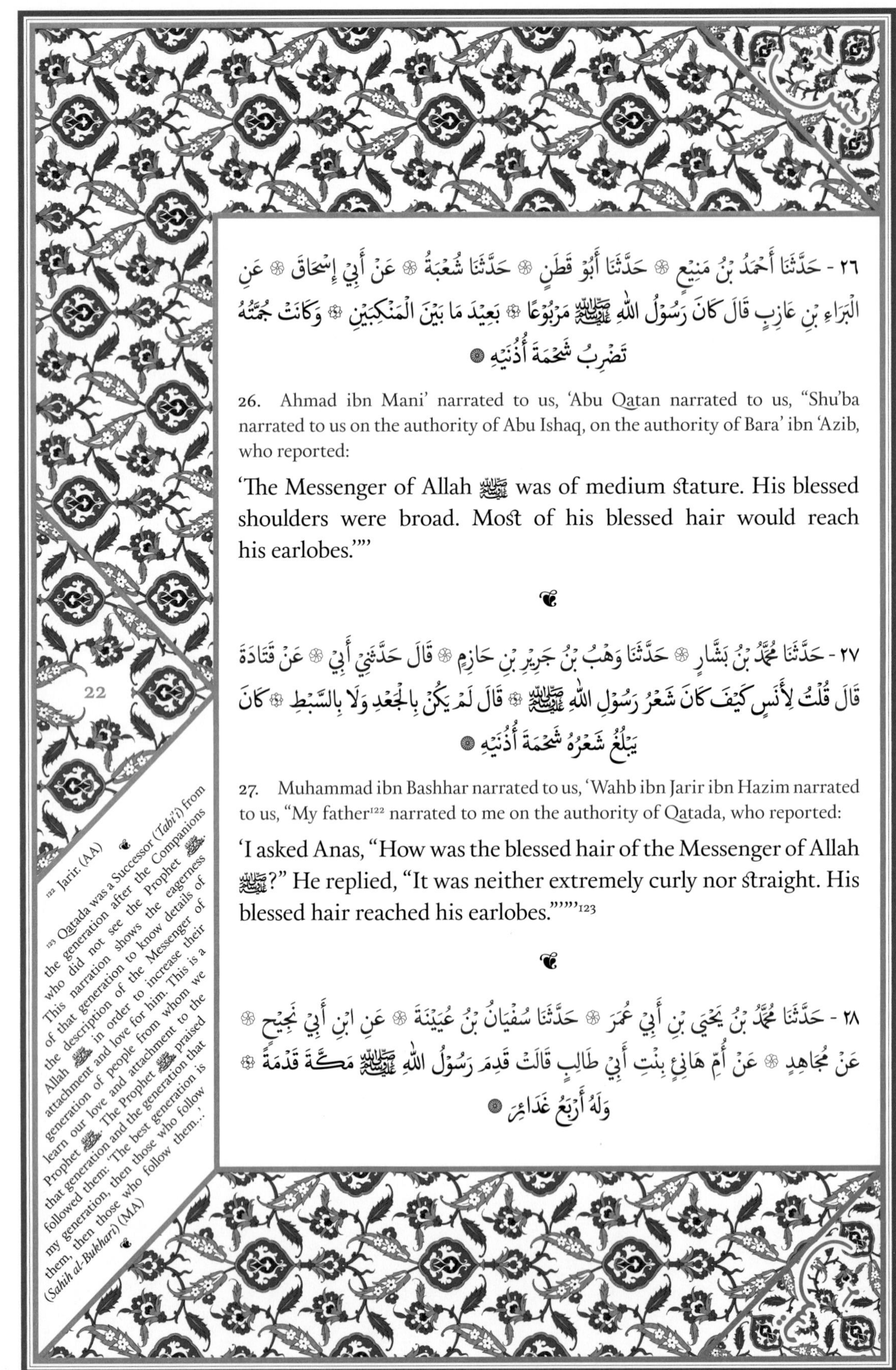

٢٦ - حَدَّثَنَا أَحْمَدُ بْنُ مَنِيعٍ ۞ حَدَّثَنَا أَبُو قَطَنٍ ۞ حَدَّثَنَا شُعْبَةُ ۞ عَنْ أَبِي إِسْحَاقَ ۞ عَنِ الْبَرَاءِ بْنِ عَازِبٍ قَالَ كَانَ رَسُولُ اللهِ ﷺ مَرْبُوعًا ۞ بَعِيدَ مَا بَيْنَ الْمَنْكِبَيْنِ ۞ وَكَانَتْ جُمَّتُهُ تَضْرِبُ شَحْمَةَ أُذُنَيْهِ ۞

26. Ahmad ibn Mani' narrated to us, 'Abu Qatan narrated to us, "Shu'ba narrated to us on the authority of Abu Ishaq, on the authority of Bara' ibn 'Azib, who reported:

'The Messenger of Allah ﷺ was of medium stature. His blessed shoulders were broad. Most of his blessed hair would reach his earlobes.'"'

٢٧ - حَدَّثَنَا مُحَمَّدُ بْنُ بَشَّارٍ ۞ حَدَّثَنَا وَهْبُ بْنُ جَرِيرِ بْنِ حَازِمٍ ۞ قَالَ حَدَّثَنِي أَبِي ۞ عَنْ قَتَادَةَ قَالَ قُلْتُ لِأَنَسٍ كَيْفَ كَانَ شَعْرُ رَسُولِ اللهِ ﷺ ۞ قَالَ لَمْ يَكُنْ بِالْجَعْدِ وَلَا بِالسَّبْطِ ۞ كَانَ يَبْلُغُ شَعْرُهُ شَحْمَةَ أُذُنَيْهِ ۞

27. Muhammad ibn Bashhar narrated to us, 'Wahb ibn Jarir ibn Hazim narrated to us, "My father[122] narrated to me on the authority of Qatada, who reported:

'I asked Anas, "How was the blessed hair of the Messenger of Allah ﷺ?" He replied, "It was neither extremely curly nor straight. His blessed hair reached his earlobes."'"'[123]

٢٨ - حَدَّثَنَا مُحَمَّدُ بْنُ يَحْيَى بْنِ أَبِي عُمَرَ ۞ حَدَّثَنَا سُفْيَانُ بْنُ عُيَيْنَةَ ۞ عَنِ ابْنِ أَبِي نَجِيحٍ ۞ عَنْ مُجَاهِدٍ ۞ عَنْ أُمِّ هَانِئٍ بِنْتِ أَبِي طَالِبٍ قَالَتْ قَدِمَ رَسُولُ اللهِ ﷺ مَكَّةَ قَدْمَةً ۞ وَلَهُ أَرْبَعُ غَدَائِرَ ۞

[122] Jarir. (AA)

[123] Qatada was a Successor (*Tabi'i*) from the generation after the Companions who did not see the Prophet ﷺ. This narration shows the eagerness of that generation to know details of the description of the Messenger of Allah ﷺ in order to increase their attachment and love for him. This is a generation of people from whom we learn our love and attachment to the Prophet ﷺ. The Prophet ﷺ praised that generation and the generation that followed them: 'The best generation is my generation, then those who follow them, then those who follow them...' (*Sahih al-Bukhari*) (MA)

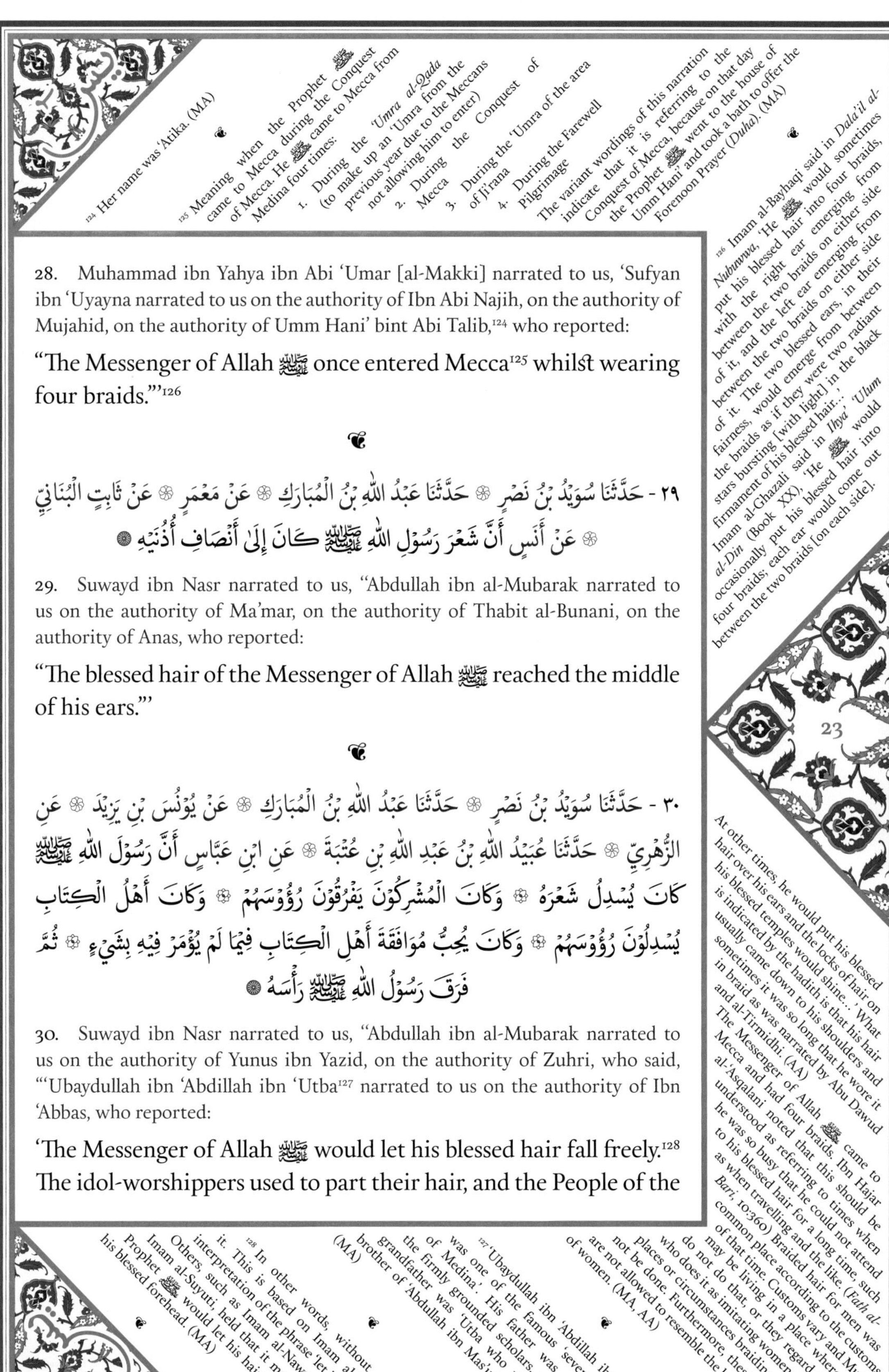

28. Muhammad ibn Yahya ibn Abi 'Umar [al-Makki] narrated to us, 'Sufyan ibn 'Uyayna narrated to us on the authority of Ibn Abi Najih, on the authority of Mujahid, on the authority of Umm Hani' bint Abi Talib,[124] who reported:

"The Messenger of Allah ﷺ once entered Mecca[125] whilst wearing four braids."'[126]

❦

٢٩ - حَدَّثَنَا سُوَيْدُ بْنُ نَصْرٍ ۞ حَدَّثَنَا عَبْدُ اللهِ بْنُ الْمُبَارَكِ ۞ عَنْ مَعْمَرٍ ۞ عَنْ ثَابِتٍ الْبُنَانِيِّ ۞ عَنْ أَنَسٍ أَنَّ شَعْرَ رَسُوْلِ اللهِ ﷺ كَانَ إِلَىٰ أَنْصَافِ أُذُنَيْهِ ۞

29. Suwayd ibn Nasr narrated to us, "Abdullah ibn al-Mubarak narrated to us on the authority of Ma'mar, on the authority of Thabit al-Bunani, on the authority of Anas, who reported:

"The blessed hair of the Messenger of Allah ﷺ reached the middle of his ears."'

❦

٣٠ - حَدَّثَنَا سُوَيْدُ بْنُ نَصْرٍ ۞ حَدَّثَنَا عَبْدُ اللهِ بْنُ الْمُبَارَكِ ۞ عَنْ يُوْنُسَ بْنِ يَزِيْدَ ۞ عَنِ الزُّهْرِيِّ ۞ حَدَّثَنَا عُبَيْدُ اللهِ بْنُ عَبْدِ اللهِ بْنِ عُتْبَةَ ۞ عَنِ ابْنِ عَبَّاسٍ أَنَّ رَسُوْلَ اللهِ ﷺ كَانَ يُسْدِلُ شَعْرَهُ ۞ وَكَانَ الْمُشْرِكُوْنَ يَفْرُقُوْنَ رُؤُوْسَهُمْ ۞ وَكَانَ أَهْلُ الْكِتَابِ يُسْدِلُوْنَ رُؤُوْسَهُمْ ۞ وَكَانَ يُحِبُّ مُوَافَقَةَ أَهْلِ الْكِتَابِ فِيْمَا لَمْ يُؤْمَرْ فِيْهِ بِشَيْءٍ ۞ ثُمَّ فَرَقَ رَسُوْلُ اللهِ ﷺ رَأْسَهُ ۞

30. Suwayd ibn Nasr narrated to us, "Abdullah ibn al-Mubarak narrated to us on the authority of Yunus ibn Yazid, on the authority of Zuhri, who said, "'Ubaydullah ibn 'Abdillah ibn 'Utba[127] narrated to us on the authority of Ibn 'Abbas, who reported:

'The Messenger of Allah ﷺ would let his blessed hair fall freely.[128] The idol-worshippers used to part their hair, and the People of the

[124] Her name was 'Atika. (MA)

[125] Meaning when the Prophet ﷺ came to Mecca during the Conquest of Mecca. He ﷺ came to Mecca from Medina four times:
1. During the *'Umra al-Qada* (to make up an 'Umra from the previous year due to the Meccans not allowing him to enter)
2. During the Conquest of Mecca
3. During the 'Umra of the area of Ji'rana
4. During the Farewell Pilgrimage

The variant wordings of this narration indicate that it is referring to the Conquest of Mecca, because on that day the Prophet ﷺ went to the house of Umm Hani' and took a bath to offer the Forenoon Prayer (*Duha*). (MA)

[126] Imam al-Bayhaqi said in *Dala'il al-Nubuwwa*, 'He ﷺ would sometimes put his blessed hair into four braids, with the right ear emerging from between the two braids on either side of it, and the left ear emerging from between the two braids on either side of it. The two blessed ears, in their fairness, would emerge from between the braids as if they were two radiant stars bursting [with light] in the black firmament of his blessed hair...' Imam al-Ghazali said in *Ihya' 'Ulum al-Din* (Book XX), 'He ﷺ would occasionally put his blessed hair into four braids; each ear would come out between the two braids [on each side]. At other times, he would put his blessed hair over his ears and the locks of hair on his blessed temples would shine...' What is indicated by the hadith is that his hair usually came down to his shoulders and sometimes it was so long that he wore it in braid as was narrated by Abu Dawud and al-Tirmidhi. (AA)

The Messenger of Allah ﷺ came to Mecca and had four braids. Ibn Hajar al-'Asqalani noted that this should be understood as referring to times when he was so busy that he could not attend to his blessed hair for a long time, such as when travelling and the like. (*Fath al-Bari*, 10:360) Braided hair for men was common place according to the customs of that time. Customs vary and Muslims may be living in a place where people do not do that, or they regard the one who does it as imitating women. In such places or circumstances braiding should not be done. Furthermore, these braids are not allowed to resemble the braiding of women. (MA, AA)

[127] 'Ubaydullah ibn 'Abdillah ibn 'Utba was one of the famous 'seven jurists of Medina'. His father was one of the firmly grounded scholars, and his grandfather was 'Utba who was the brother of 'Abdullah ibn Mas'ud. (MA)

[128] In other words, without parting it. This is based on Imam al-Bajuri's interpretation of the phrase 'let it hang'. Others, such as Imam al-Nawawi and Imam al-Suyuti, held that it means the Prophet ﷺ would let his hair fall on his blessed forehead. (MA)

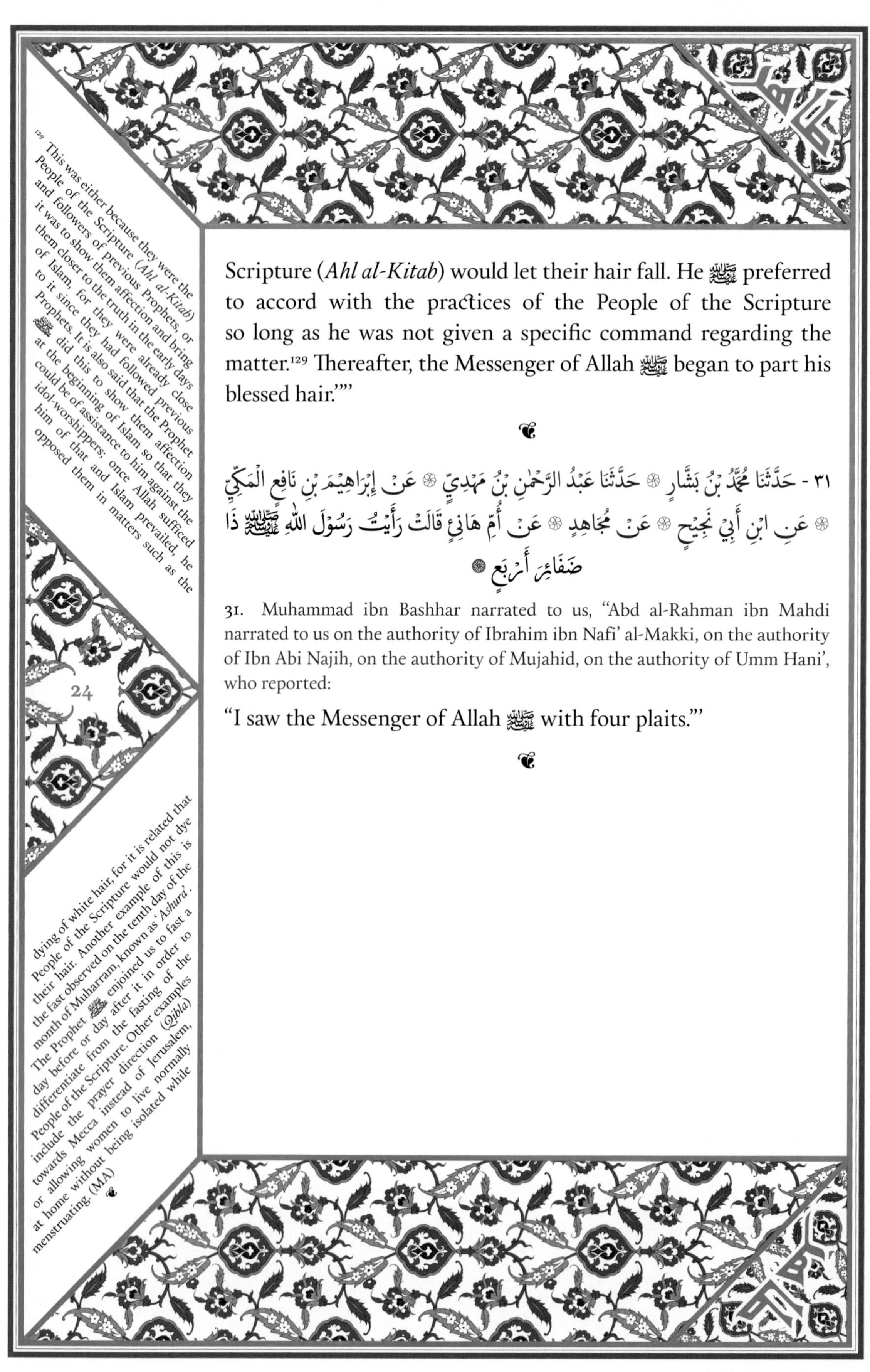

Scripture (*Ahl al-Kitab*) would let their hair fall. He ﷺ preferred to accord with the practices of the People of the Scripture so long as he was not given a specific command regarding the matter.[129] Thereafter, the Messenger of Allah ﷺ began to part his blessed hair.""'

❦

٣١ - حَدَّثَنَا مُحَمَّدُ بْنُ بَشَّارٍ ❁ حَدَّثَنَا عَبْدُ الرَّحْمٰنِ بْنُ مَهْدِيٍّ ❁ عَنْ إِبْرَاهِيمَ بْنِ نَافِعٍ الْمَكِّيِّ ❁ عَنِ ابْنِ أَبِي نَجِيحٍ ❁ عَنْ مُجَاهِدٍ ❁ عَنْ أُمِّ هَانِئٍ قَالَتْ رَأَيْتُ رَسُولَ اللّٰهِ ﷺ ذَا ضَفَائِرَ أَرْبَعٍ ❁

31. Muhammad ibn Bashhar narrated to us, "Abd al-Rahman ibn Mahdi narrated to us on the authority of Ibrahim ibn Nafi' al-Makki, on the authority of Ibn Abi Najih, on the authority of Mujahid, on the authority of Umm Hani', who reported:

"I saw the Messenger of Allah ﷺ with four plaits."'

❦

[129] This was either because they were the People of the Scripture (*Ahl al-Kitab*) and followers of previous Prophets, or it was to show them affection and bring them closer to the truth in the early days of Islam, for they were already close to it since they had followed previous Prophets. It is also said that the Prophet ﷺ did this to show them affection at the beginning of Islam so that they could be of assistance to him against the idol-worshippers; once Allah sufficed him of that and Islam prevailed, he opposed them in matters such as the dying of white hair, for it is related that People of the Scripture would not dye their hair. Another example of this is the fast observed on the tenth day of the month of Muharram, known as *'Ashura'*. The Prophet ﷺ enjoined us to fast a day before or day after it in order to differentiate from the fasting of the People of the Scripture. Other examples include the prayer direction (*Qibla*) towards Mecca instead of Jerusalem, or allowing women to live normally at home without being isolated while menstruating. (MA) ❦

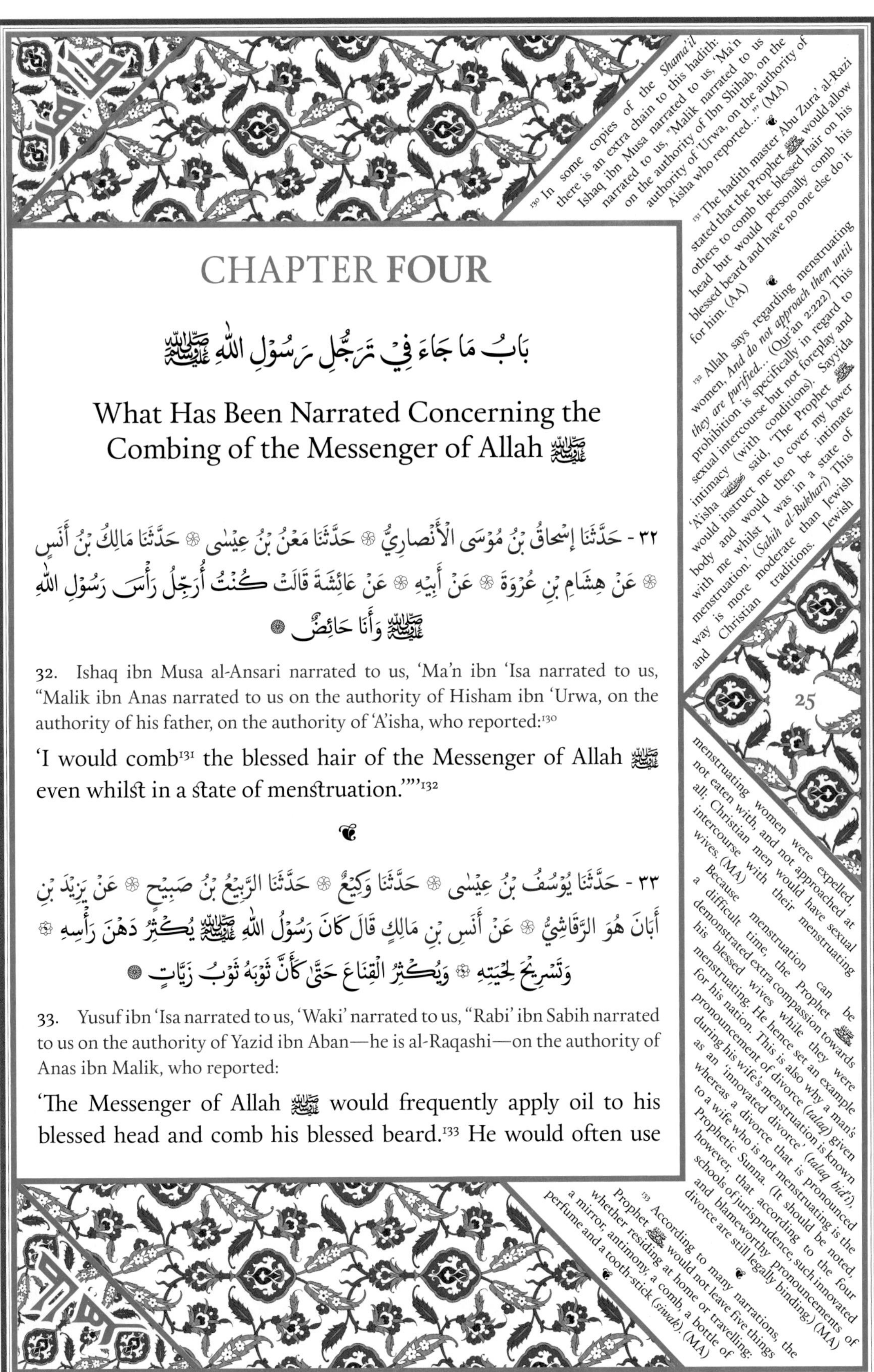

CHAPTER **FOUR**

بَابُ مَا جَاءَ فِي تَرَجُّلِ رَسُولِ اللهِ ﷺ

What Has Been Narrated Concerning the Combing of the Messenger of Allah ﷺ

٣٢ - حَدَّثَنَا إِسْحَاقُ بْنُ مُوسَى الْأَنْصَارِيُّ ۞ حَدَّثَنَا مَعْنُ بْنُ عِيسَى ۞ حَدَّثَنَا مَالِكُ بْنُ أَنَسٍ ۞ عَنْ هِشَامِ بْنِ عُرْوَةَ ۞ عَنْ أَبِيهِ ۞ عَنْ عَائِشَةَ قَالَتْ كُنْتُ أُرَجِّلُ رَأْسَ رَسُولِ اللهِ ﷺ وَأَنَا حَائِضٌ ۞

32. Ishaq ibn Musa al-Ansari narrated to us, 'Ma'n ibn 'Isa narrated to us, "Malik ibn Anas narrated to us on the authority of Hisham ibn 'Urwa, on the authority of his father, on the authority of 'A'isha, who reported:[130]

'I would comb[131] the blessed hair of the Messenger of Allah ﷺ even whilst in a state of menstruation.'"'[132]

❦

٣٣ - حَدَّثَنَا يُوسُفُ بْنُ عِيسَى ۞ حَدَّثَنَا وَكِيعٌ ۞ حَدَّثَنَا الرَّبِيعُ بْنُ صَبِيحٍ ۞ عَنْ يَزِيدَ بْنِ أَبَانَ هُوَ الرَّقَاشِيُّ ۞ عَنْ أَنَسِ بْنِ مَالِكٍ قَالَ كَانَ رَسُولُ اللهِ ﷺ يُكْثِرُ دَهْنَ رَأْسِهِ ۞ وَتَسْرِيحَ لِحْيَتِهِ ۞ وَيُكْثِرُ الْقِنَاعَ حَتَّى كَأَنَّ ثَوْبَهُ ثَوْبُ زَيَّاتٍ ۞

33. Yusuf ibn 'Isa narrated to us, 'Waki' narrated to us, "Rabi' ibn Sabih narrated to us on the authority of Yazid ibn Aban—he is al-Raqashi—on the authority of Anas ibn Malik, who reported:

'The Messenger of Allah ﷺ would frequently apply oil to his blessed head and comb his blessed beard.[133] He would often use

130 In some copies of the *Shama'il* there is an extra chain to this hadith: Ishaq ibn Musa narrated to us, 'Ma'n narrated to us, "Malik narrated to us, on the authority of Ibn Shihab, on the authority of 'Urwa, on the authority of Aisha who reported:..." (MA) ❦

131 The hadith master Abu Zura' al-Razi stated that the Prophet ﷺ would allow others to comb the blessed hair on his head but would personally comb his blessed beard and have no one else do it for him. (AA) ❦

132 Allah says regarding menstruating women, *And do not approach them until they are purified...* (Qur'an 2:222) This prohibition is specifically in regard to sexual intercourse but not foreplay and intimacy (with conditions). Sayyida 'A'isha said, 'The Prophet ﷺ would instruct me to cover my lower body and would then be intimate with me whilst I was in a state of menstruation.' (*Sahih al-Bukhari*) This way is more moderate than Jewish and Christian traditions. Jewish menstruating women were expelled, not eaten with, and not approached at all; Christian men would have sexual intercourse with their menstruating wives. (MA)

Because menstruation can be a difficult time, the Prophet ﷺ demonstrated extra compassion towards his blessed wives while they were menstruating. He hence set an example for his nation. This is also why a man's pronouncement of divorce (*talaq*) given during his wife's menstruation is known as an 'innovated divorce' (*talaq bid'i*), whereas a divorce that is pronounced to a wife who is not menstruating is the Prophetic Sunna. (It should be noted, however, that according to the four schools of jurisprudence, such innovated and blameworthy pronouncements of divorce are still legally binding.) (MA) ❦

133 According to many narrations, the Prophet ﷺ would not leave five things whether residing at home or travelling: a mirror, antimony, a comb, a bottle of perfume and a tooth-stick (*siwak*). (MA) ❦

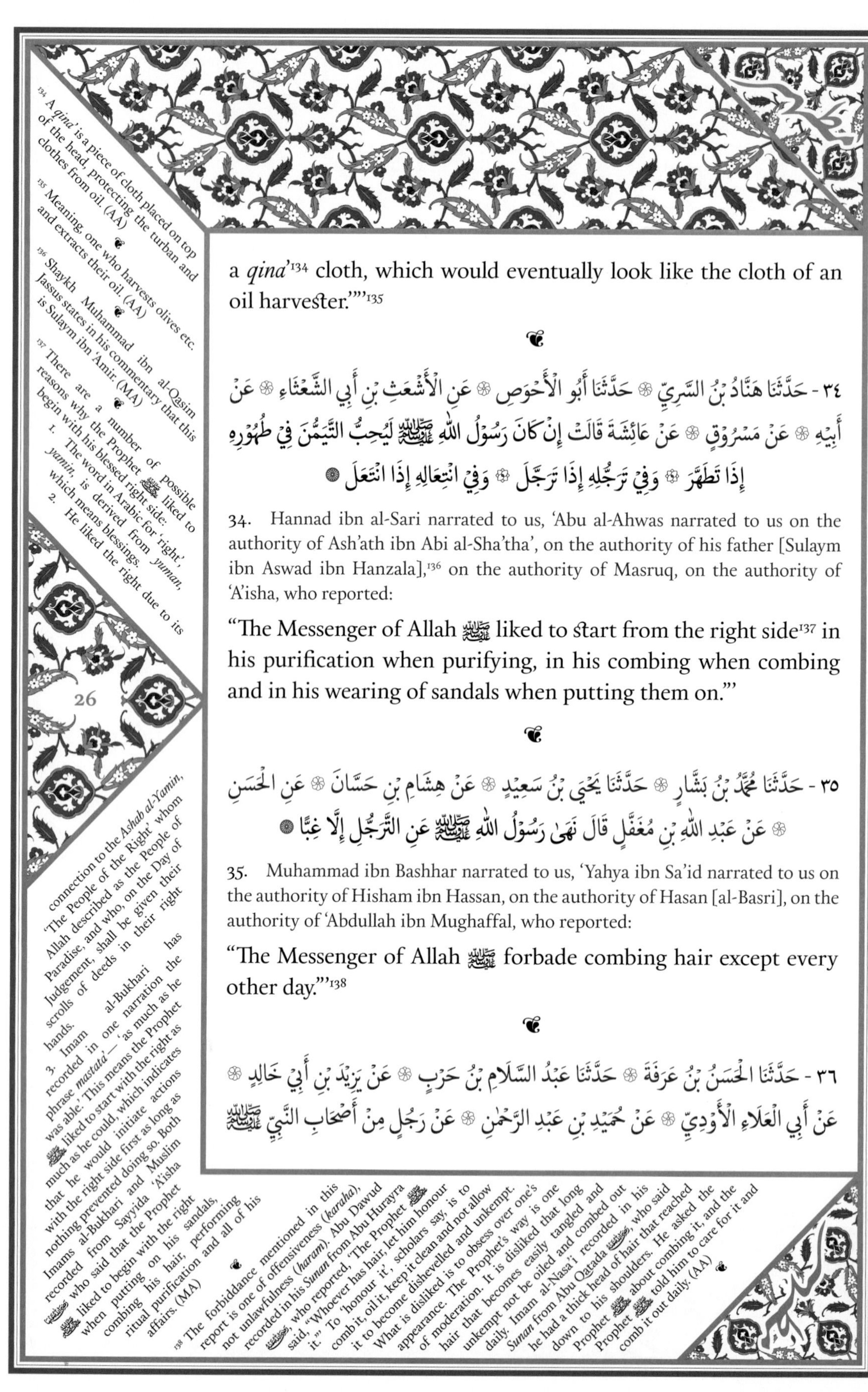

a *qina'*[134] cloth, which would eventually look like the cloth of an oil harvester.'"[135]

٣٤ - حَدَّثَنَا هَنَّادُ بْنُ السَّرِيِّ ۞ حَدَّثَنَا أَبُو الْأَحْوَصِ ۞ عَنِ الْأَشْعَثِ بْنِ أَبِي الشَّعْثَاءِ ۞ عَنْ أَبِيهِ ۞ عَنْ مَسْرُوقٍ ۞ عَنْ عَائِشَةَ قَالَتْ إِنْ كَانَ رَسُولُ اللهِ ﷺ لَيُحِبُّ التَّيَمُّنَ فِي طُهُورِهِ إِذَا تَطَهَّرَ ۞ وَفِي تَرَجُّلِهِ إِذَا تَرَجَّلَ ۞ وَفِي انْتِعَالِهِ إِذَا انْتَعَلَ ۞

34. Hannad ibn al-Sari narrated to us, 'Abu al-Ahwas narrated to us on the authority of Ash'ath ibn Abi al-Sha'tha', on the authority of his father [Sulaym ibn Aswad ibn Hanzala],[136] on the authority of Masruq, on the authority of 'A'isha, who reported:

"The Messenger of Allah ﷺ liked to start from the right side[137] in his purification when purifying, in his combing when combing and in his wearing of sandals when putting them on."'

٣٥ - حَدَّثَنَا مُحَمَّدُ بْنُ بَشَّارٍ ۞ حَدَّثَنَا يَحْيَى بْنُ سَعِيدٍ ۞ عَنْ هِشَامِ بْنِ حَسَّانَ ۞ عَنِ الْحَسَنِ ۞ عَنْ عَبْدِ اللهِ بْنِ مُغَفَّلٍ قَالَ نَهَى رَسُولُ اللهِ ﷺ عَنِ التَّرَجُّلِ إِلَّا غِبًّا ۞

35. Muhammad ibn Bashhar narrated to us, 'Yahya ibn Sa'id narrated to us on the authority of Hisham ibn Hassan, on the authority of Hasan [al-Basri], on the authority of 'Abdullah ibn Mughaffal, who reported:

"The Messenger of Allah ﷺ forbade combing hair except every other day."'[138]

٣٦ - حَدَّثَنَا الْحَسَنُ بْنُ عَرَفَةَ ۞ حَدَّثَنَا عَبْدُ السَّلَامِ بْنُ حَرْبٍ ۞ عَنْ يَزِيدَ بْنِ أَبِي خَالِدٍ ۞ عَنْ أَبِي الْعَلَاءِ الْأَوْدِيِّ ۞ عَنْ حُمَيْدِ بْنِ عَبْدِ الرَّحْمٰنِ ۞ عَنْ رَجُلٍ مِنْ أَصْحَابِ النَّبِيِّ ﷺ

134 A *qina'* is a piece of cloth placed on top of the head, protecting the turban and clothes from oil. (AA)

135 Meaning, one who harvests olives etc. and extracts their oil. (AA)

136 Shaykh Muhammad ibn al-Qasim Jassus states in his commentary that this is Sulaym ibn 'Amir. (MA)

137 There are a number of possible reasons why the Prophet ﷺ liked to begin with his blessed right side:
1. The word in Arabic for 'right', *yamin*, is derived from *yuman*, which means blessings.
2. He liked the right due to its connection to the *Ashab al-Yamin*, 'The People of the Right' whom Allah described as the People of Paradise, and who, on the Day of Judgement, shall be given their scrolls of deeds in their right hands.
3. Imam al-Bukhari has recorded in one narration the phrase *mastata'*—'as much as he was able.' This means the Prophet ﷺ liked to start with the right as much as he could, which indicates that he would initiate actions with the right side first as long as nothing prevented doing so. Both Imams al-Bukhari and Muslim recorded from Sayyida 'A'isha ﷺ who said that the Prophet ﷺ liked to begin with the right when putting on his sandals, combing his hair, performing ritual purification and all of his affairs. (MA)

138 The forbiddance mentioned in this report is one of offensiveness (*karaha*), not unlawfulness (*haram*). Abu Dawud recorded in his *Sunan* from Abu Hurayra ﷺ who reported, 'The Prophet ﷺ said, "Whoever has hair, let him honour it."' To 'honour it', scholars say, is to comb it, oil it, keep it clean and not allow it to become dishevelled and unkempt. What is disliked is to obsess over one's appearance. The Prophet's way is one of moderation. It is disliked that long hair that becomes easily tangled and unkempt not be oiled and combed out daily. Imam al-Nasa'i recorded in his *Sunan* from Abu Qatada ﷺ, who said he had a thick head of hair that reached down to his shoulders. He asked the Prophet ﷺ about combing it, and the Prophet ﷺ told him to care for it and comb it out daily. (AA)

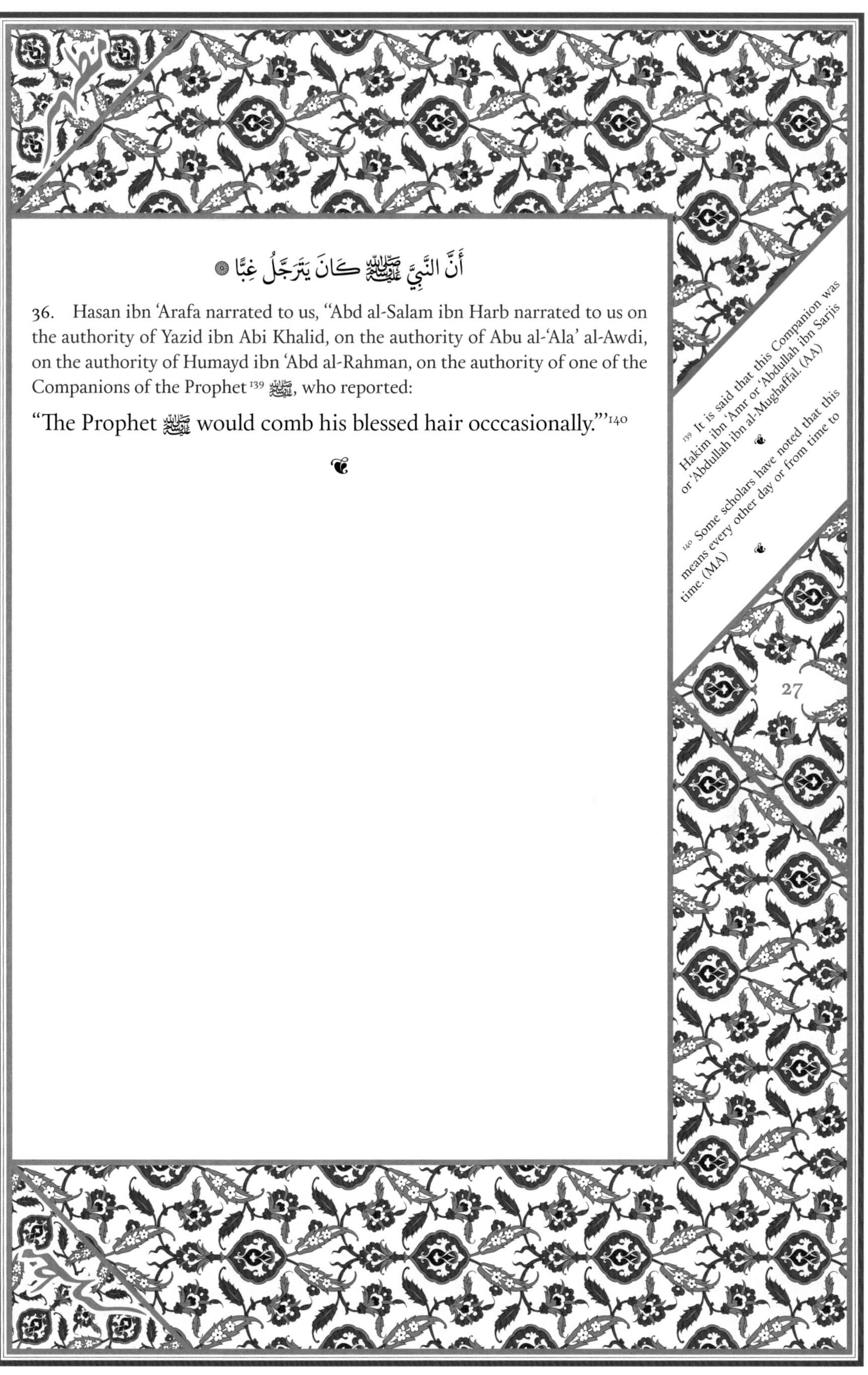

أَنَّ النَّبِيَّ ﷺ كَانَ يَتَرَجَّلُ غِبًّا ۝

36. Hasan ibn 'Arafa narrated to us, "'Abd al-Salam ibn Harb narrated to us on the authority of Yazid ibn Abi Khalid, on the authority of Abu al-'Ala' al-Awdi, on the authority of Humayd ibn 'Abd al-Rahman, on the authority of one of the Companions of the Prophet[139] ﷺ, who reported:

"The Prophet ﷺ would comb his blessed hair occcasionally."'[140]

❦

[139] It is said that this Companion was Hakim ibn 'Amr or 'Abdullah ibn Sarjis or 'Abdullah ibn al-Mughaffal. (AA)

[140] Some scholars have noted that this means every other day or from time to time. (MA)

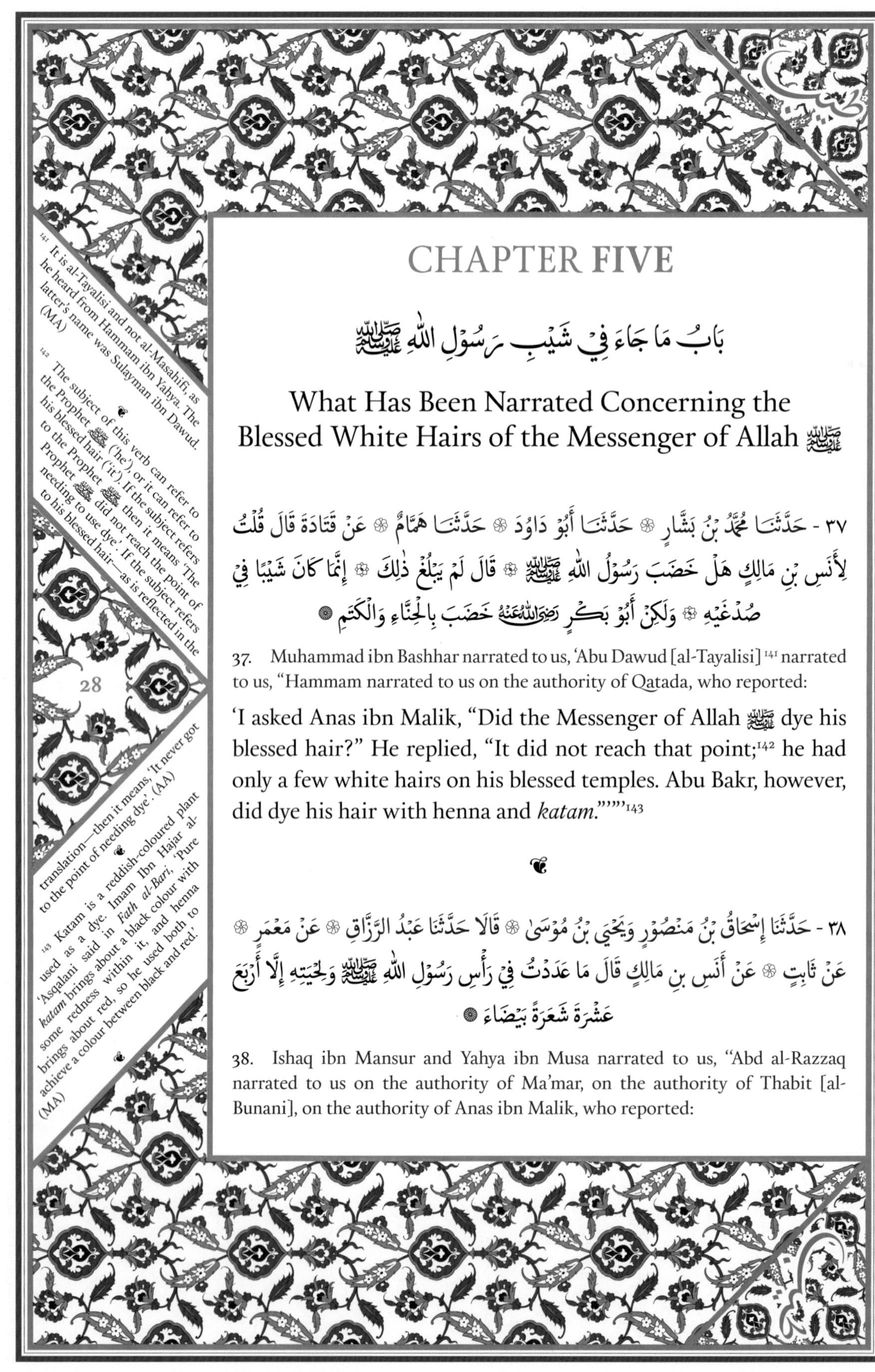

CHAPTER **FIVE**

بَابُ مَا جَاءَ فِي شَيْبِ رَسُولِ اللهِ ﷺ

What Has Been Narrated Concerning the Blessed White Hairs of the Messenger of Allah ﷺ

٣٧ - حَدَّثَنَا مُحَمَّدُ بْنُ بَشَّارٍ ۞ حَدَّثَنَا أَبُو دَاوُدَ ۞ حَدَّثَنَا هَمَّامٌ ۞ عَنْ قَتَادَةَ قَالَ قُلْتُ لِأَنَسِ بْنِ مَالِكٍ هَلْ خَضَبَ رَسُولُ اللهِ ﷺ ۞ قَالَ لَمْ يَبْلُغْ ذٰلِكَ ۞ إِنَّمَا كَانَ شَيْبًا فِي صُدْغَيْهِ ۞ وَلٰكِنْ أَبُو بَكْرٍ رَضِيَ اللهُ عَنْهُ خَضَبَ بِالْحِنَّاءِ وَالْكَتَمِ ۞

37. Muhammad ibn Bashhar narrated to us, 'Abu Dawud [al-Tayalisi] [141] narrated to us, "Hammam narrated to us on the authority of Qatada, who reported:

'I asked Anas ibn Malik, "Did the Messenger of Allah ﷺ dye his blessed hair?" He replied, "It did not reach that point;[142] he had only a few white hairs on his blessed temples. Abu Bakr, however, did dye his hair with henna and *katam*."""'[143]

❦

٣٨ - حَدَّثَنَا إِسْحَاقُ بْنُ مَنْصُورٍ وَيَحْيَى بْنُ مُوسَىٰ ۞ قَالَا حَدَّثَنَا عَبْدُ الرَّزَّاقِ ۞ عَنْ مَعْمَرٍ ۞ عَنْ ثَابِتٍ ۞ عَنْ أَنَسِ بْنِ مَالِكٍ قَالَ مَا عَدَدْتُ فِي رَأْسِ رَسُولِ اللهِ ﷺ وَلِحْيَتِهِ إِلَّا أَرْبَعَ عَشْرَةَ شَعْرَةً بَيْضَاءَ ۞

38. Ishaq ibn Mansur and Yahya ibn Musa narrated to us, "Abd al-Razzaq narrated to us on the authority of Ma'mar, on the authority of Thabit [al-Bunani], on the authority of Anas ibn Malik, who reported:

141 It is al-Tayalisi and not al-Masahifi, as he heard from Hammam ibn Yahya. The latter's name was Sulayman ibn Dawud. (MA)

142 The subject of this verb can refer to the Prophet ﷺ ('he'), or it can refer to his blessed hair ('it'). If the subject refers to the Prophet ﷺ then it means 'The Prophet ﷺ did not reach the point of needing to use dye'. If the subject refers to his blessed hair—as is reflected in the translation—then it means, 'It never got to the point of needing dye'. (AA)

143 Katam is a reddish-coloured plant used as a dye. Imam Ibn Hajar al-'Asqalani said in *Fath al-Bari*, 'Pure *katam* brings about a black colour with some redness within it, and henna brings about red, so he used both to achieve a colour between black and red.' (MA)

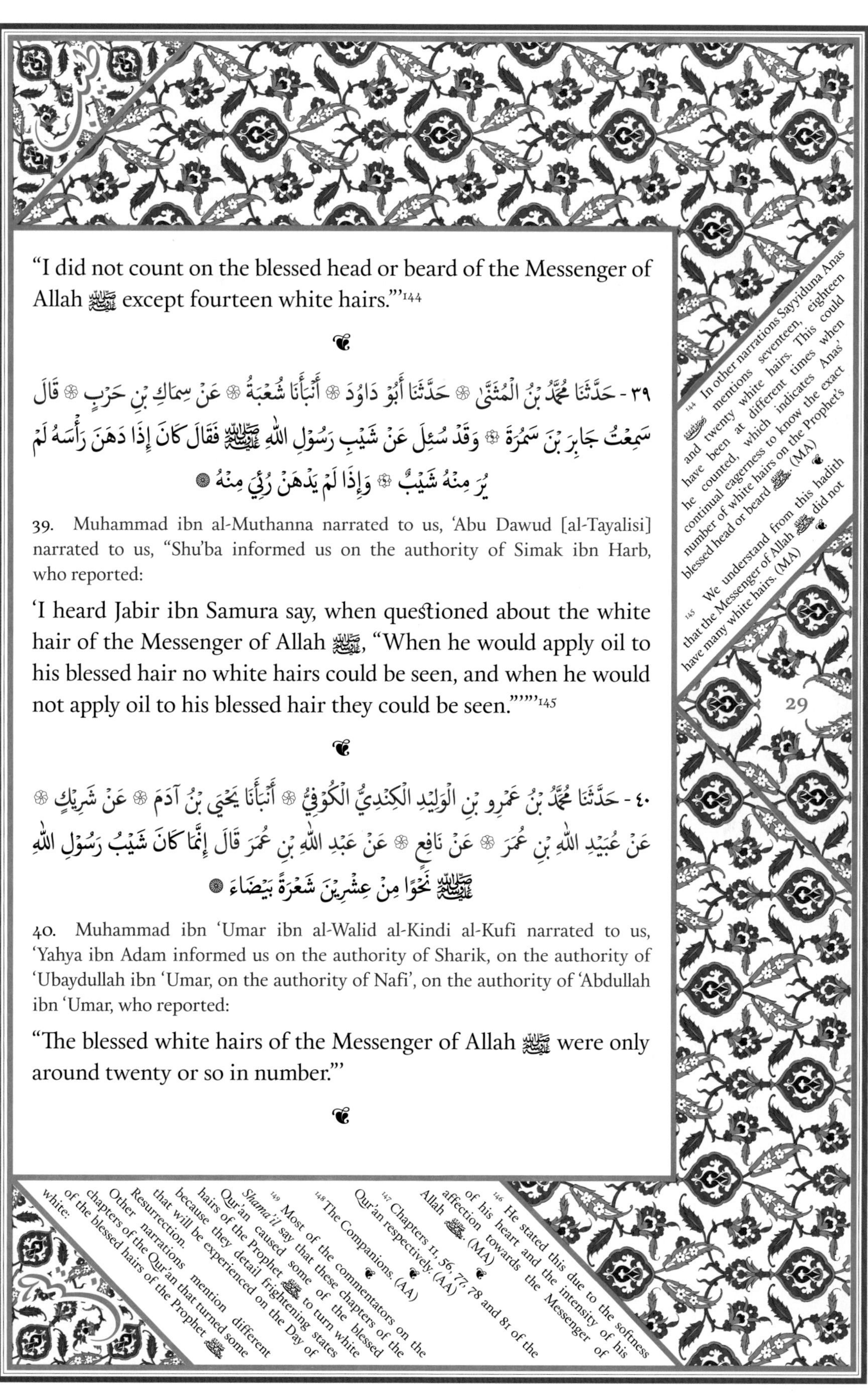

"I did not count on the blessed head or beard of the Messenger of Allah ﷺ except fourteen white hairs."'[144]

❦

٣٩ - حَدَّثَنَا مُحَمَّدُ بْنُ الْمُثَنَّىٰ ۞ حَدَّثَنَا أَبُو دَاوُدَ ۞ أَنبَأَنَا شُعْبَةُ ۞ عَنْ سِمَاكِ بْنِ حَرْبٍ ۞ قَالَ سَمِعْتُ جَابِرَ بْنَ سَمُرَةَ ۞ وَقَدْ سُئِلَ عَنْ شَيْبِ رَسُولِ اللهِ ﷺ فَقَالَ كَانَ إِذَا دَهَنَ رَأْسَهُ لَمْ يُرَ مِنْهُ شَيْبٌ ۞ وَإِذَا لَمْ يَدْهَنْ رُئِيَ مِنْهُ ۞

39. Muhammad ibn al-Muthanna narrated to us, 'Abu Dawud [al-Tayalisi] narrated to us, "Shu'ba informed us on the authority of Simak ibn Harb, who reported:

'I heard Jabir ibn Samura say, when questioned about the white hair of the Messenger of Allah ﷺ, "When he would apply oil to his blessed hair no white hairs could be seen, and when he would not apply oil to his blessed hair they could be seen."'"'[145]

❦

٤٠ - حَدَّثَنَا مُحَمَّدُ بْنُ عَمْرِو بْنِ الْوَلِيدِ الْكِنْدِيُّ الْكُوفِيُّ ۞ أَنبَأَنَا يَحْيَى بْنُ آدَمَ ۞ عَنْ شَرِيكٍ ۞ عَنْ عُبَيْدِ اللهِ بْنِ عُمَرَ ۞ عَنْ نَافِعٍ ۞ عَنْ عَبْدِ اللهِ بْنِ عُمَرَ قَالَ إِنَّمَا كَانَ شَيْبُ رَسُولِ اللهِ ﷺ نَحْوًا مِنْ عِشْرِينَ شَعْرَةً بَيْضَاءَ ۞

40. Muhammad ibn 'Umar ibn al-Walid al-Kindi al-Kufi narrated to us, 'Yahya ibn Adam informed us on the authority of Sharik, on the authority of 'Ubaydullah ibn 'Umar, on the authority of Nafi', on the authority of 'Abdullah ibn 'Umar, who reported:

"The blessed white hairs of the Messenger of Allah ﷺ were only around twenty or so in number."'

❦

144 In other narrations Sayyiduna Anas ﵁ mentions seventeen, eighteen and twenty white hairs. This could have been at different times when he counted, which indicates Anas' continual eagerness to know the exact number of white hairs on the Prophet's blessed head or beard ﷺ. (MA) ❦

145 We understand from this hadith that the Messenger of Allah ﷺ did not have many white hairs. (MA) ❦

146 He stated this due to the softness of his heart and the intensity of his affection towards the Messenger of Allah ﷺ. (MA) ❦

147 Chapters 11, 56, 77, 78 and 81 of the Qur'an respectively. (AA) ❦

148 The Companions. (AA) ❦

149 Most of the commentators on the *Shama'il* say that these chapters of the blessed Qur'an caused some of the blessed hairs of the Prophet ﷺ to turn white because they detail frightening states that will be experienced on the Day of Resurrection. Other narrations mention different chapters of the Qur'an that turned some of the blessed hairs of the Prophet ﷺ white:

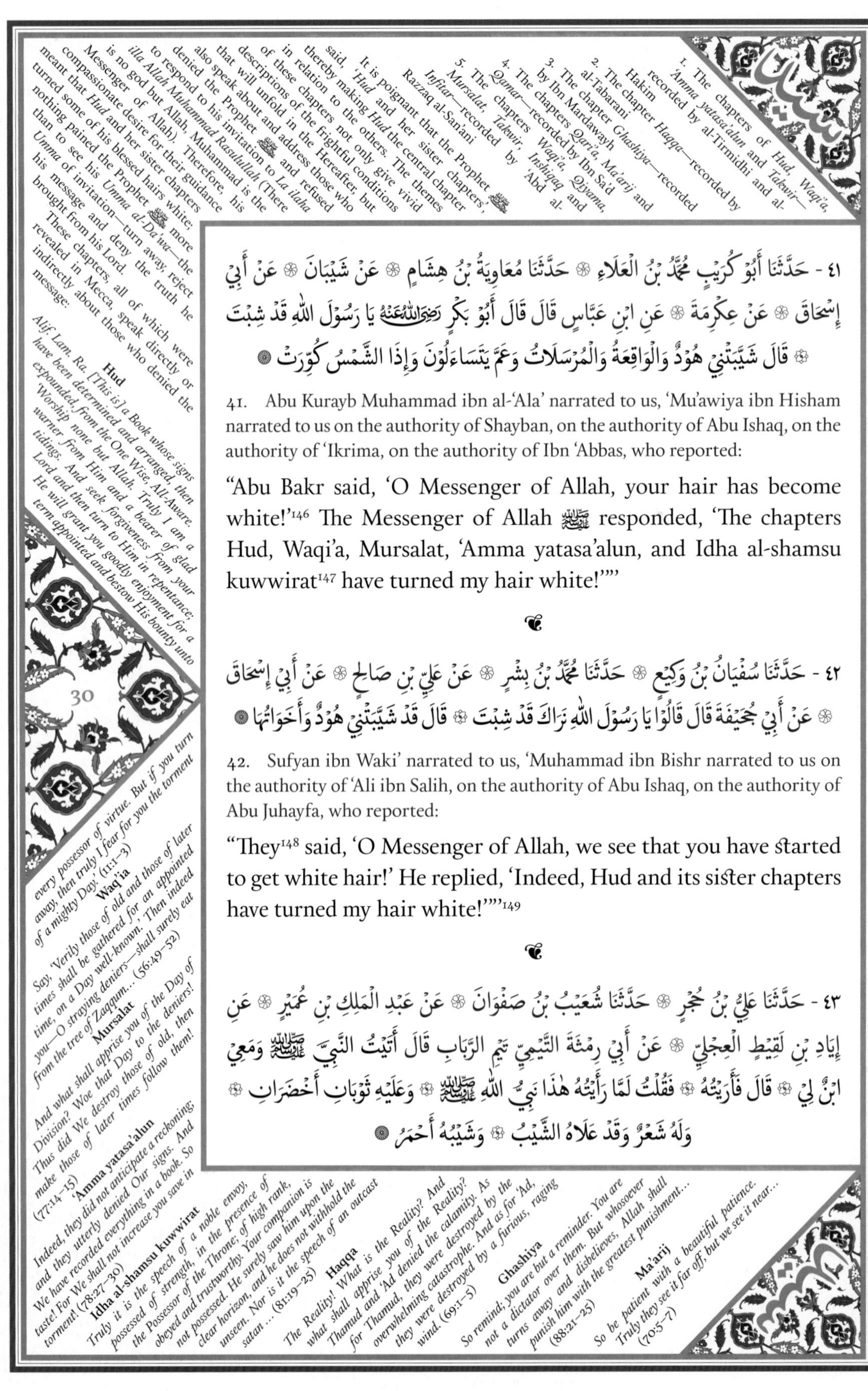

٤١ - حَدَّثَنَا أَبُو كُرَيْبٍ مُحَمَّدُ بْنُ الْعَلَاءِ ۞ حَدَّثَنَا مُعَاوِيَةُ بْنُ هِشَامٍ ۞ عَنْ شَيْبَانَ ۞ عَنْ أَبِي إِسْحَاقَ ۞ عَنْ عِكْرِمَةَ ۞ عَنِ ابْنِ عَبَّاسٍ قَالَ قَالَ أَبُو بَكْرٍ رَضِيَ اللهُ عَنْهُ يَا رَسُولَ اللهِ قَدْ شِبْتَ ۞ قَالَ شَيَّبَتْنِي هُودٌ وَالْوَاقِعَةُ وَالْمُرْسَلَاتُ وَعَمَّ يَتَسَاءَلُونَ وَإِذَا الشَّمْسُ كُوِّرَتْ ۞

41. Abu Kurayb Muhammad ibn al-'Ala' narrated to us, 'Mu'awiya ibn Hisham narrated to us on the authority of Shayban, on the authority of Abu Ishaq, on the authority of 'Ikrima, on the authority of Ibn 'Abbas, who reported:

"Abu Bakr said, 'O Messenger of Allah, your hair has become white!'[146] The Messenger of Allah ﷺ responded, 'The chapters Hud, Waqi'a, Mursalat, 'Amma yatasa'alun, and Idha al-shamsu kuwwirat[147] have turned my hair white!'""

❦

٤٢ - حَدَّثَنَا سُفْيَانُ بْنُ وَكِيعٍ ۞ حَدَّثَنَا مُحَمَّدُ بْنُ بِشْرٍ ۞ عَنْ عَلِيِّ بْنِ صَالِحٍ ۞ عَنْ أَبِي إِسْحَاقَ ۞ عَنْ أَبِي جُحَيْفَةَ قَالَ قَالُوا يَا رَسُولَ اللهِ نَرَاكَ قَدْ شِبْتَ ۞ قَالَ قَدْ شَيَّبَتْنِي هُودٌ وَأَخَوَاتُهَا ۞

42. Sufyan ibn Waki' narrated to us, 'Muhammad ibn Bishr narrated to us on the authority of 'Ali ibn Salih, on the authority of Abu Ishaq, on the authority of Abu Juhayfa, who reported:

"They[148] said, 'O Messenger of Allah, we see that you have started to get white hair!' He replied, 'Indeed, Hud and its sister chapters have turned my hair white!'""[149]

❦

٤٣ - حَدَّثَنَا عَلِيُّ بْنُ حُجْرٍ ۞ حَدَّثَنَا شُعَيْبُ بْنُ صَفْوَانَ ۞ عَنْ عَبْدِ الْمَلِكِ بْنِ عُمَيْرٍ ۞ عَنْ إِيَادِ بْنِ لَقِيطٍ الْعِجْلِيِّ ۞ عَنْ أَبِي رِمْثَةَ التَّيْمِيِّ تَيْمِ الرَّبَابِ قَالَ أَتَيْتُ النَّبِيَّ ﷺ وَمَعِي ابْنٌ لِي ۞ قَالَ فَأُرِيتُهُ ۞ فَقُلْتُ لَمَّا رَأَيْتُهُ هٰذَا نَبِيُّ اللهِ ﷺ ۞ وَعَلَيْهِ ثَوْبَانِ أَخْضَرَانِ ۞ وَلَهُ شَعَرٌ وَقَدْ عَلَاهُ الشَّيْبُ ۞ وَشَيْبُهُ أَحْمَرُ ۞

1. The chapters of Hud, Waqi'a, *'Amma yatasa'alun* and *Takwir*—recorded by al-Tirmidhi and al-Hakim
2. The chapter *Haqqa*—recorded by al-Tabarani
3. The chapter *Ghashiya*—recorded by Ibn Mardawayh
4. The chapters *Qari'a*, *Ma'arij* and *Qamar*—recorded by Ibn Sa'd
5. The chapters *Waqi'a*, *Qiyama*, *Mursalat*, *Takwir*, *Inshiqaq* and *Infitar*—recorded by 'Abd al-Razzaq al-San'ani

It is poignant that the Prophet ﷺ said, '*Hud* and her sister chapters', thereby making *Hud* the central chapter in relation to the others. The themes of these chapters not only give vivid descriptions of the frightful conditions that will unfold in the Hereafter, but also speak about and address those who denied the Prophet ﷺ and refused to respond to his invitation to *La ilaha illa Allah Muhammad Rasulullah* (There is no god but Allah, Muhammad is the Messenger of Allah). Therefore, his compassionate desire for their guidance meant that *Hud* and her sister chapters turned some of his blessed hairs white; nothing pained the Prophet ﷺ more than to see his *Umma al-Da'wa*—the *Umma* of invitation—turn away, reject his message and deny the truth he brought from his Lord.

These chapters, all of which were revealed in Mecca, speak directly or indirectly about those who denied the message:

Hud

Alif, Lam, Ra. [This is] a Book whose signs have been determined and arranged, then expounded, from the One Wise, All-Aware. 'Worship none but Allah. Truly I am a warner from Him and a bearer of glad tidings. And seek forgiveness from your Lord and then turn to Him in repentance; He will grant you goodly enjoyment for a term appointed and bestow His bounty unto every possessor of virtue. But if you turn away, then truly I fear for you the torment of a mighty Day. (11:1–3)

Waq'ia

Say, 'Verily those of old and those of later times shall be gathered for an appointed time, on a Day well-known.' Then indeed you—O straying deniers—shall surely eat from the tree of Zaqqum... (56:49–52)

Mursalat

And what shall apprise you of the Day of Division? Woe that Day to the deniers! Thus did We destroy those of old, then make those of later times follow them! (77:14–15)

'Amma yatasa'alun

Indeed, they did not anticipate a reckoning, and they utterly denied Our signs. And We have recorded everything in a book. So taste! For We shall not increase you save in torment! (78:27–30)

Idha al-shamsu kuwwirat

Truly it is the speech of a noble envoy, possessed of strength, in the presence of the Possessor of the Throne, of high rank, obeyed and trustworthy. Your companion is not possessed. He surely saw him upon the clear horizon, and he does not withhold the unseen. Nor is it the speech of an outcast satan... (81:19–25)

Haqqa

The Reality! What is the Reality? And what shall apprise you of the Reality? Thamud and 'Ad denied the calamity. As for Thamud, they were destroyed by the overwhelming catastrophe. And as for 'Ad, they were destroyed by a furious, raging wind. (69:1–5)

Ghashiya

So remind; you are but a reminder. You are not a dictator over them. But whosoever turns away and disbelieves, Allah shall punish him with the greatest punishment... (88:21–25)

Ma'arij

So be patient with a beautiful patience. Truly they see it far off, but we see it near... (70:5–7)

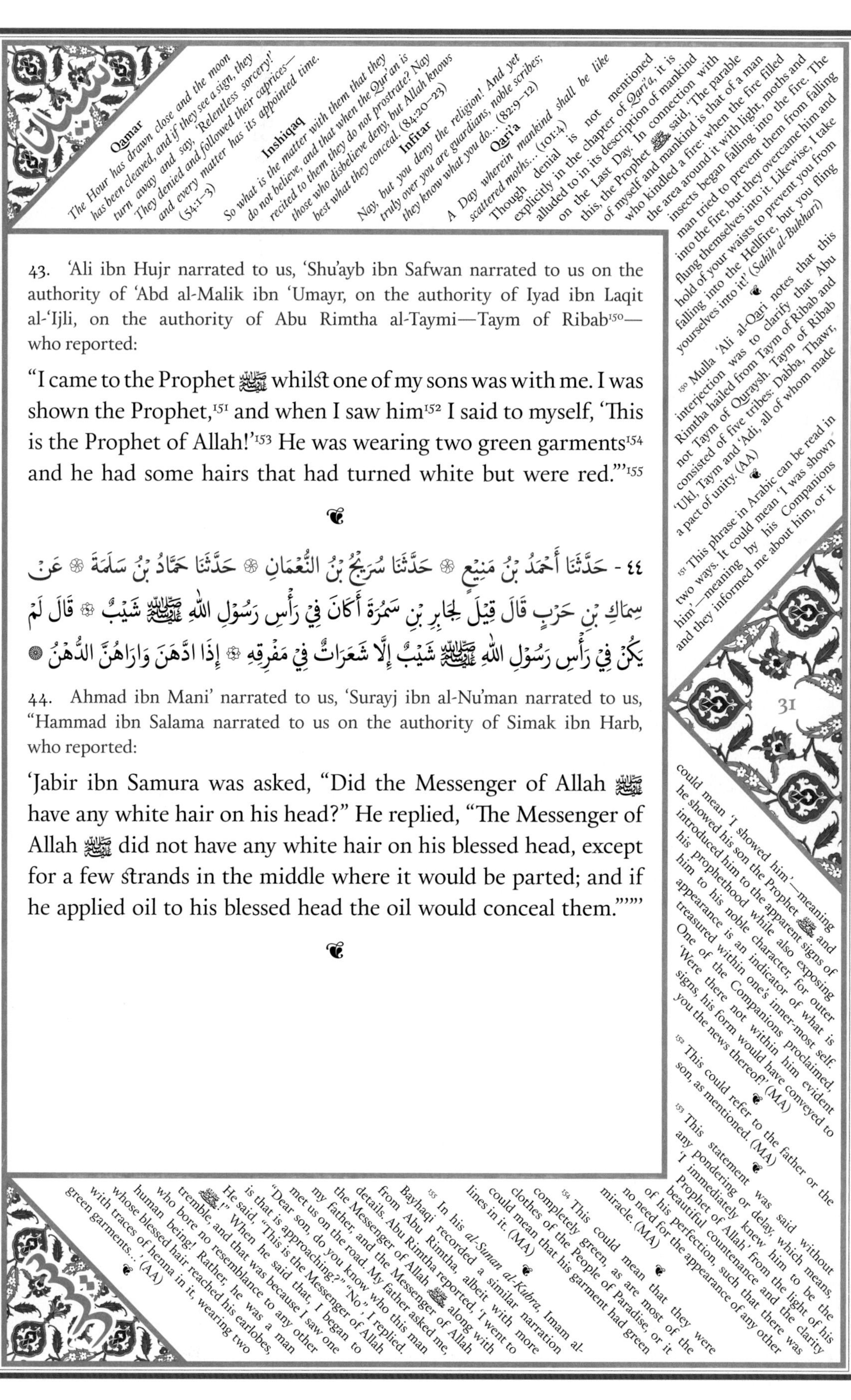

Qamar
The Hour has drawn close and the moon has been cleaved, and if they see a sign, they turn away and say, 'Relentless sorcery!' They denied and followed their caprices—and every matter has its appointed time. (54:1–3)

Inshiqaq
So what is the matter with them that they do not believe, and that when the Qur'an is recited to them they do not prostrate? Nay those who disbelieve deny, but Allah knows best what they conceal. (84:20–23)

Infitar
Nay, but you deny the religion! And yet truly over you are guardians, noble scribes; they know what you do... (82:9–12)

Qari'a
A Day wherein mankind shall be like scattered moths... (101:4)
Though denial is not mentioned explicitly in the chapter of *Qari'a*, it is alluded to in its description of mankind on the Last Day. In connection with this, the Prophet ﷺ said, 'The parable of myself and mankind is that of a man who kindled a fire: when the fire filled the area around it with light, moths and insects began falling into the fire. The man tried to prevent them from falling into the fire, but they overcame him and flung themselves into it. Likewise, I take hold of your waists to prevent you from falling into the Hellfire, but you fling yourselves into it!' (*Sahih al-Bukhari*)

43. 'Ali ibn Hujr narrated to us, 'Shu'ayb ibn Safwan narrated to us on the authority of 'Abd al-Malik ibn 'Umayr, on the authority of Iyad ibn Laqit al-'Ijli, on the authority of Abu Rimtha al-Taymi—Taym of Ribab[150]—who reported:

"I came to the Prophet ﷺ whilst one of my sons was with me. I was shown the Prophet,[151] and when I saw him[152] I said to myself, 'This is the Prophet of Allah!'[153] He was wearing two green garments[154] and he had some hairs that had turned white but were red."'[155]

٤٤ - حَدَّثَنَا أَحْمَدُ بْنُ مَنِيعٍ ۞ حَدَّثَنَا سُرَيْجُ بْنُ النُّعْمَانِ ۞ حَدَّثَنَا حَمَّادُ بْنُ سَلَمَةَ ۞ عَنْ سِمَاكِ بْنِ حَرْبٍ قَالَ قِيلَ لِجَابِرِ بْنِ سَمُرَةَ أَكَانَ فِي رَأْسِ رَسُولِ اللهِ ﷺ شَيْبٌ ۞ قَالَ لَمْ يَكُنْ فِي رَأْسِ رَسُولِ اللهِ ﷺ شَيْبٌ إِلَّا شَعَرَاتٌ فِي مَفْرِقِهِ ۞ إِذَا ادَّهَنَ وَارَاهُنَّ الدُّهْنُ ۞

44. Ahmad ibn Mani' narrated to us, 'Surayj ibn al-Nu'man narrated to us, "Hammad ibn Salama narrated to us on the authority of Simak ibn Harb, who reported:

'Jabir ibn Samura was asked, "Did the Messenger of Allah ﷺ have any white hair on his head?" He replied, "The Messenger of Allah ﷺ did not have any white hair on his blessed head, except for a few strands in the middle where it would be parted; and if he applied oil to his blessed head the oil would conceal them."'"'

[150] Mulla 'Ali al-Qari notes that this interjection was to clarify that Abu Rimtha hailed from Taym of Ribab and not Taym of Quraysh. Taym of Ribab consisted of five tribes: Dabba, Thawr, 'Ukl, Taym and 'Adi, all of whom made a pact of unity. (AA)

[151] This phrase in Arabic can be read in two ways. It could mean 'I was shown him'—meaning by his Companions and they informed me about him, or it could mean 'I showed him'—meaning he showed his son the Prophet ﷺ and introduced him to the apparent signs of his prophethood while also exposing him to his noble character, for outer appearance is an indicator of what is treasured within one's inner-most self. One of the Companions proclaimed, 'Were there not within him evident signs, his form would have conveyed to you the news thereof!' (MA)

[152] This could refer to the father or the son, as mentioned. (MA)

[153] This statement was said without any pondering or delay, which means, 'I immediately knew him to be the Prophet of Allah' from the light of his beautiful countenance and the clarity of his perfection, such that there was no need for the appearance of any other miracle. (MA)

[154] This could mean that they were completely green, as are most of the clothes of the People of Paradise, or it could mean that his garment had green lines in it. (MA)

[155] In his *al-Sunan al-Kubra*, Imam al-Bayhaqi recorded a similar narration from Abu Rimtha, albeit with more details. Abu Rimtha reported, 'I went to the Messenger of Allah ﷺ along with my father, and the Messenger of Allah met us on the road. My father asked me, "Dear son, do you know who this man is that is approaching?" "No," I replied. He said, "This is the Messenger of Allah ﷺ!" When he said that, I began to tremble, and that was because I saw one who bore no resemblance to any other human being! Rather, he was a man whose blessed hair reached his earlobes, with traces of henna in it, wearing two green garments...' (AA)

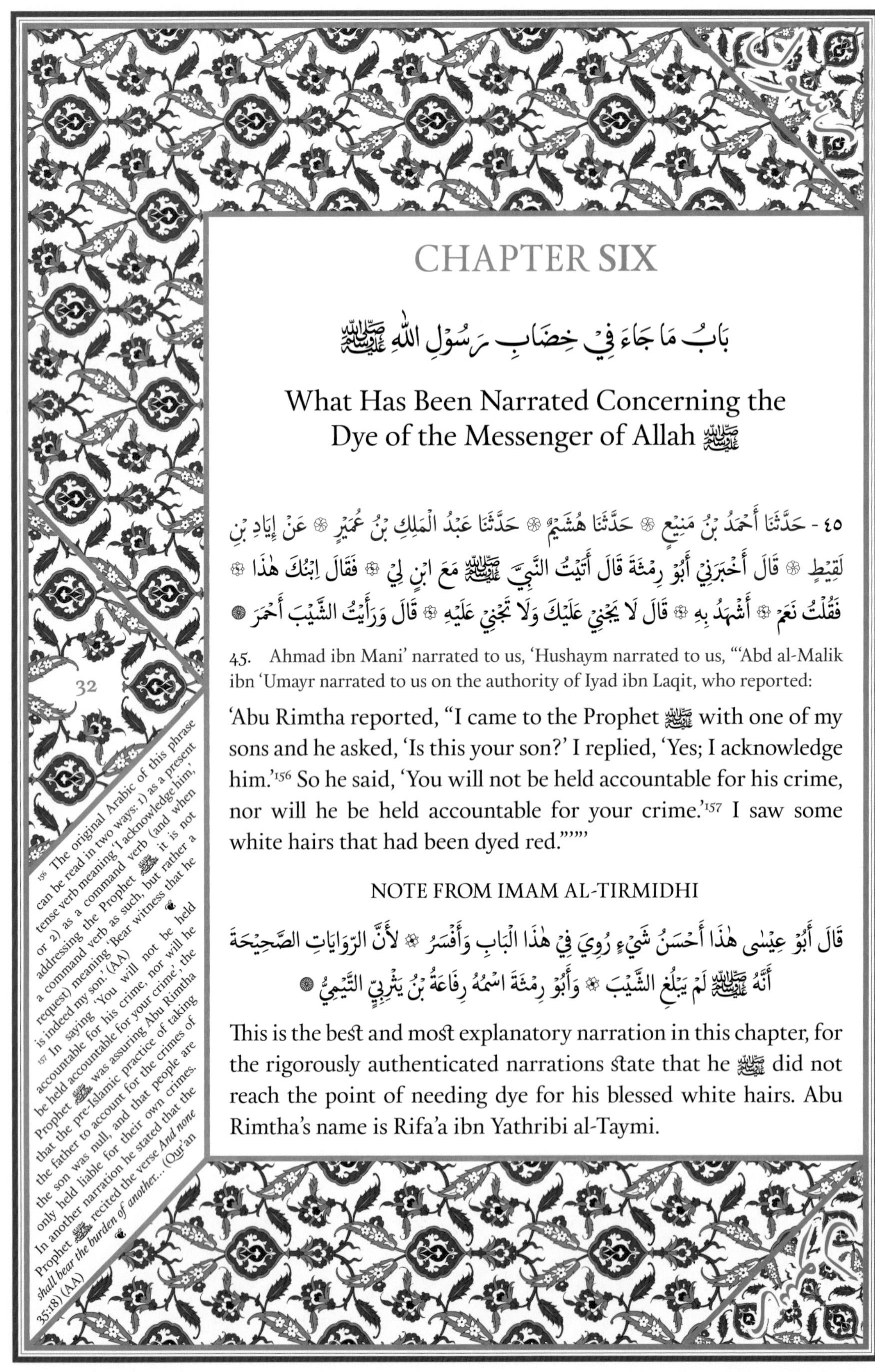

CHAPTER SIX

بَابُ مَا جَاءَ فِي خِضَابِ رَسُولِ اللهِ ﷺ

What Has Been Narrated Concerning the Dye of the Messenger of Allah ﷺ

٤٥ - حَدَّثَنَا أَحْمَدُ بْنُ مَنِيعٍ ❀ حَدَّثَنَا هُشَيْمٌ ❀ حَدَّثَنَا عَبْدُ الْمَلِكِ بْنُ عُمَيْرٍ ❀ عَنْ إِيَادِ بْنِ لَقِيطٍ ❀ قَالَ أَخْبَرَنِي أَبُو رِمْثَةَ قَالَ أَتَيْتُ النَّبِيَّ ﷺ مَعَ ابْنٍ لِي ❀ فَقَالَ ابْنُكَ هٰذَا ❀ فَقُلْتُ نَعَمْ ❀ أَشْهَدُ بِهِ ❀ قَالَ لَا يَجْنِي عَلَيْكَ وَلَا تَجْنِي عَلَيْهِ ❀ قَالَ وَرَأَيْتُ الشَّيْبَ أَحْمَرَ ❀

45. Ahmad ibn Mani' narrated to us, 'Hushaym narrated to us, "'Abd al-Malik ibn 'Umayr narrated to us on the authority of Iyad ibn Laqit, who reported:

'Abu Rimtha reported, "I came to the Prophet ﷺ with one of my sons and he asked, 'Is this your son?' I replied, 'Yes; I acknowledge him.'[156] So he said, 'You will not be held accountable for his crime, nor will he be held accountable for your crime.'[157] I saw some white hairs that had been dyed red."""

NOTE FROM IMAM AL-TIRMIDHI

قَالَ أَبُو عِيسَى هٰذَا أَحْسَنُ شَيْءٍ رُوِيَ فِي هٰذَا الْبَابِ وَأَفْسَرُ ❀ لِأَنَّ الرِّوَايَاتِ الصَّحِيحَةَ أَنَّهُ ﷺ لَمْ يَبْلُغِ الشَّيْبَ ❀ وَأَبُو رِمْثَةَ اسْمُهُ رِفَاعَةُ بْنُ يَثْرِبِيٍّ التَّيْمِيُّ ❀

This is the best and most explanatory narration in this chapter, for the rigorously authenticated narrations state that he ﷺ did not reach the point of needing dye for his blessed white hairs. Abu Rimtha's name is Rifa'a ibn Yathribi al-Taymi.

[156] The original Arabic of this phrase can be read in two ways: 1) as a present tense verb meaning 'I acknowledge him,' or 2) as a command verb (and when addressing the Prophet ﷺ it is not a command verb as such, but rather a request) meaning 'Bear witness that he is indeed my son.' (AA)

[157] In saying 'You will not be held accountable for his crime, nor will he be held accountable for your crime', the Prophet ﷺ was assuring Abu Rimtha that the pre-Islamic practice of taking the father to account for the crimes of the son was null, and that people are only held liable for their own crimes. In another narration he stated that the Prophet ﷺ recited the verse *And none shall bear the burden of another*... (Qur'an 35:18) (AA)

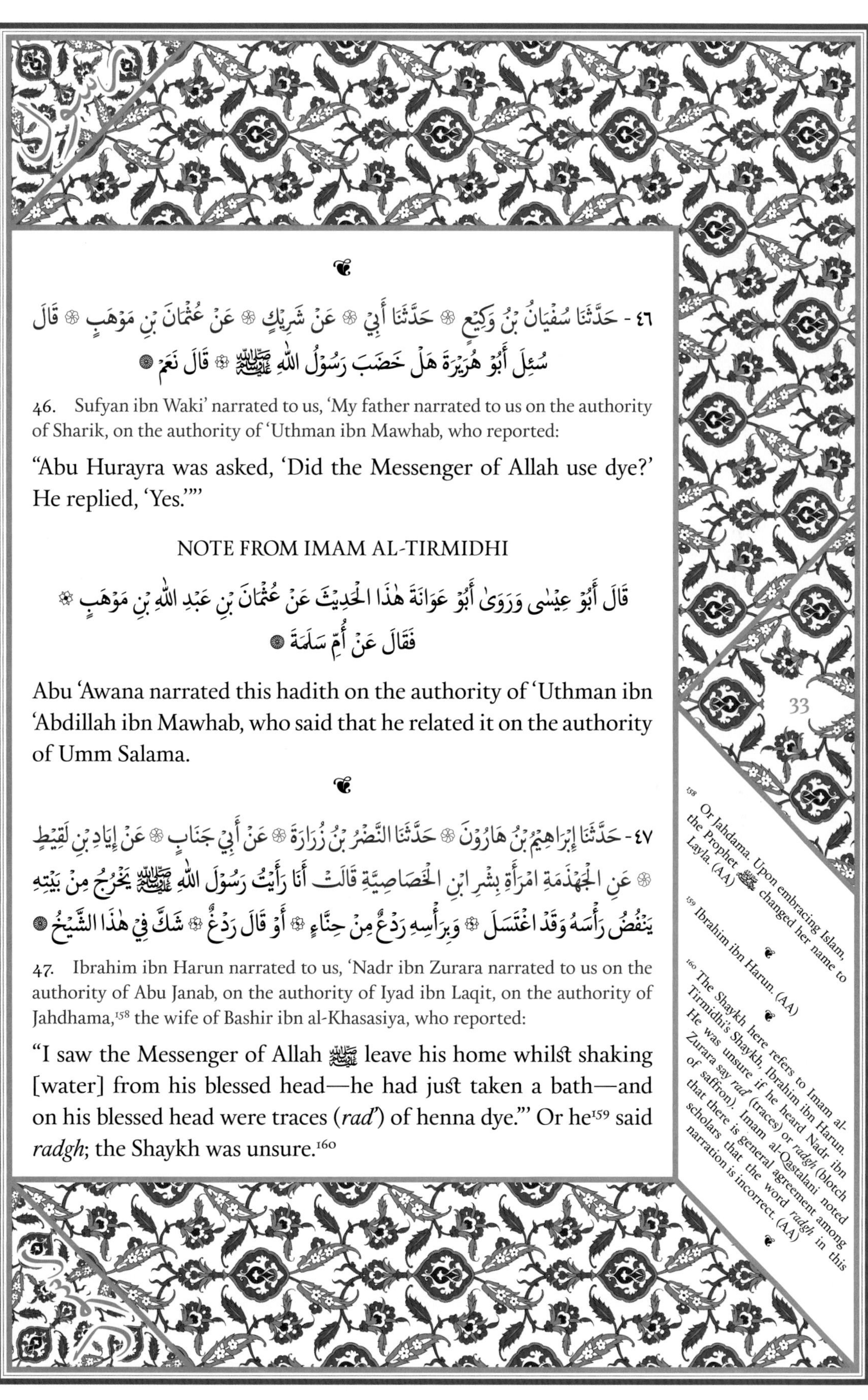

٤٦ - حَدَّثَنَا سُفْيَانُ بْنُ وَكِيعٍ ۞ حَدَّثَنَا أَبِي ۞ عَنْ شَرِيكٍ ۞ عَنْ عُثْمَانَ بْنِ مَوْهَبٍ ۞ قَالَ سُئِلَ أَبُو هُرَيْرَةَ هَلْ خَضَبَ رَسُولُ اللهِ ﷺ ۞ قَالَ نَعَمْ ۞

46. Sufyan ibn Waki' narrated to us, 'My father narrated to us on the authority of Sharik, on the authority of 'Uthman ibn Mawhab, who reported:

"Abu Hurayra was asked, 'Did the Messenger of Allah use dye?' He replied, 'Yes.'"'

NOTE FROM IMAM AL-TIRMIDHI

قَالَ أَبُو عِيسَى وَرَوَى أَبُو عَوَانَةَ هَذَا الْحَدِيثَ عَنْ عُثْمَانَ بْنِ عَبْدِ اللهِ بْنِ مَوْهَبٍ ۞ فَقَالَ عَنْ أُمِّ سَلَمَةَ ۞

Abu 'Awana narrated this hadith on the authority of 'Uthman ibn 'Abdillah ibn Mawhab, who said that he related it on the authority of Umm Salama.

٤٧ - حَدَّثَنَا إِبْرَاهِيمُ بْنُ هَارُونَ ۞ حَدَّثَنَا النَّضْرُ بْنُ زُرَارَةَ ۞ عَنْ أَبِي جَنَابٍ ۞ عَنْ إِيَادِ بْنِ لَقِيطٍ ۞ عَنِ الْجَهْذَمَةِ امْرَأَةِ بِشْرِ ابْنِ الْخَصَاصِيَةِ قَالَتْ أَنَا رَأَيْتُ رَسُولَ اللهِ ﷺ يَخْرُجُ مِنْ بَيْتِهِ يَنْفُضُ رَأْسَهُ وَقَدِ اغْتَسَلَ ۞ وَبِرَأْسِهِ رَدْعٌ مِنْ حِنَّاءٍ ۞ أَوْ قَالَ رَدْغٌ ۞ شَكَّ فِي هَذَا الشَّيْخِ ۞

47. Ibrahim ibn Harun narrated to us, 'Nadr ibn Zurara narrated to us on the authority of Abu Janab, on the authority of Iyad ibn Laqit, on the authority of Jahdhama,[158] the wife of Bashir ibn al-Khasasiya, who reported:

"I saw the Messenger of Allah ﷺ leave his home whilst shaking [water] from his blessed head—he had just taken a bath—and on his blessed head were traces (*rad'*) of henna dye."' Or he[159] said *radgh*; the Shaykh was unsure.[160]

158 Or Jahdama. Upon embracing Islam, the Prophet ﷺ changed her name to Layla. (AA)

159 Ibrahim ibn Harun. (AA)

160 The Shaykh here refers to Imam al-Tirmidhi's Shaykh, Ibrahim ibn Harun. He was unsure if he heard Nadr ibn Zurara say *rad'* (traces) or *radgh* (blotch of saffron). Imam al-Qastalani noted that there is general agreement among scholars that the word *radgh* in this narration is incorrect. (AA)

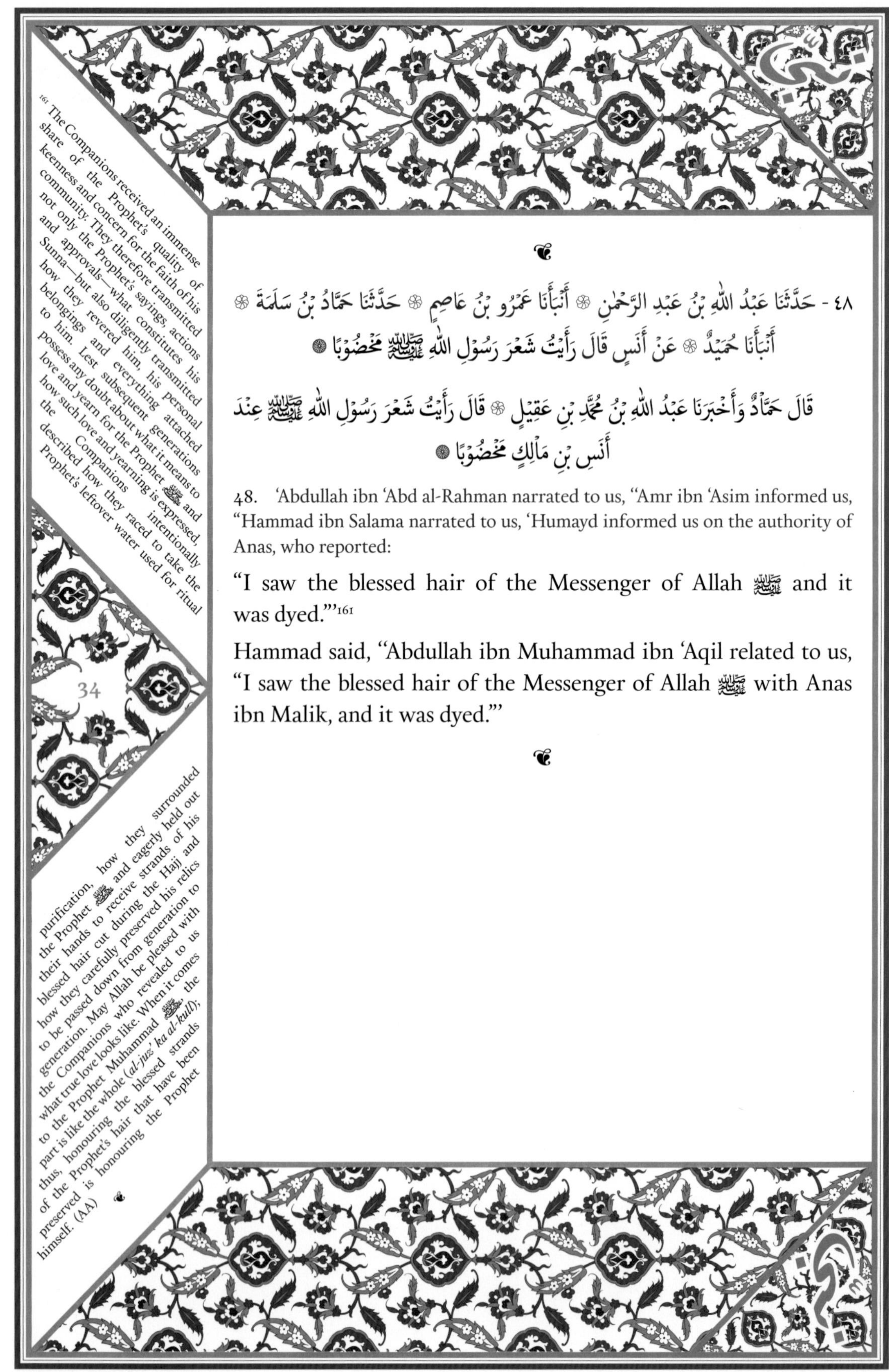

❦

٤٨ - حَدَّثَنَا عَبْدُ اللّٰهِ بْنُ عَبْدِ الرَّحْمٰنِ ❁ أَنْبَأَنَا عَمْرُو بْنُ عَاصِمٍ ❁ حَدَّثَنَا حَمَّادُ بْنُ سَلَمَةَ ❁ أَنْبَأَنَا حُمَيْدٌ ❁ عَنْ أَنَسٍ قَالَ رَأَيْتُ شَعْرَ رَسُولِ اللّٰهِ ﷺ مَخْضُوبًا ❂

قَالَ حَمَّادٌ وَأَخْبَرَنَا عَبْدُ اللّٰهِ بْنُ مُحَمَّدِ بْنِ عَقِيلٍ ❁ قَالَ رَأَيْتُ شَعْرَ رَسُولِ اللّٰهِ ﷺ عِنْدَ أَنَسِ بْنِ مَالِكٍ مَخْضُوبًا ❂

48. ‘Abdullah ibn ‘Abd al-Rahman narrated to us, “Amr ibn ‘Asim informed us, “Hammad ibn Salama narrated to us, ‘Humayd informed us on the authority of Anas, who reported:

“I saw the blessed hair of the Messenger of Allah ﷺ and it was dyed.”’[161]

Hammad said, “Abdullah ibn Muhammad ibn ‘Aqil related to us, “I saw the blessed hair of the Messenger of Allah ﷺ with Anas ibn Malik, and it was dyed.”’

❦

[161] The Companions received an immense share of the Prophet’s quality of keenness and concern for the faith of his community. They therefore transmitted not only the Prophet’s sayings, actions and approvals—what constitutes his Sunna—but also diligently transmitted how they revered him, his personal belongings and everything attached to him. Lest subsequent generations possess any doubt about what it means to love and yearn for the Prophet ﷺ and how such love and yearning is expressed, the Companions intentionally described how they raced to take the Prophet’s leftover water used for ritual purification, how they surrounded the Prophet ﷺ and eagerly held out their hands to receive strands of his blessed hair cut during the Hajj and how they carefully preserved his relics to be passed down from generation to generation. May Allah be pleased with the Companions who revealed to us what true love looks like. When it comes to the Prophet Muhammad ﷺ, the part is like the whole (*al-juz’ ka al-kull*); thus, honouring the blessed strands of the Prophet’s hair that have been preserved is honouring the Prophet himself. (AA) ❦

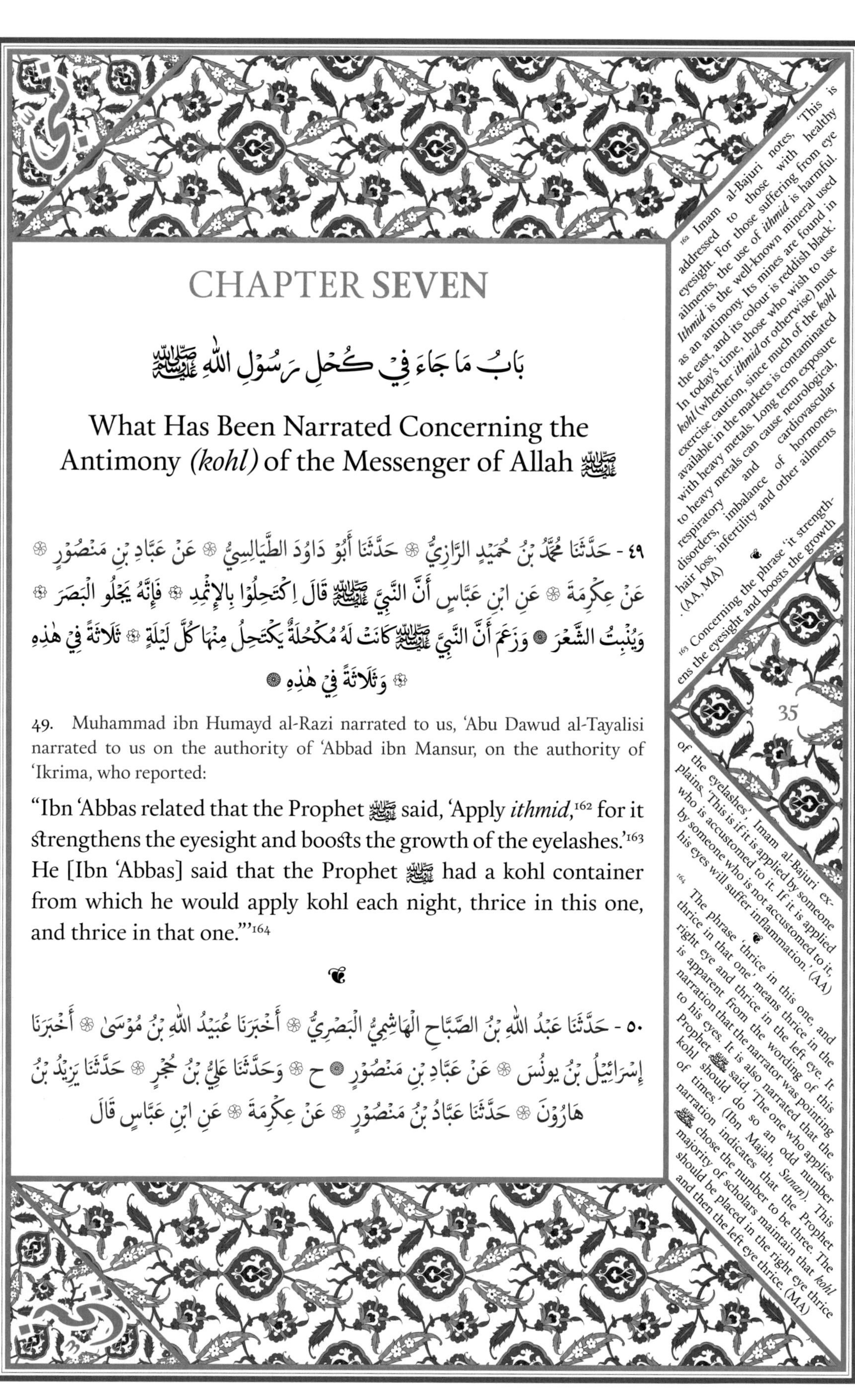

CHAPTER SEVEN

بَابُ مَا جَاءَ فِي كُحْلِ رَسُولِ اللهِ ﷺ

What Has Been Narrated Concerning the Antimony *(kohl)* of the Messenger of Allah ﷺ

٤٩ - حَدَّثَنَا مُحَمَّدُ بْنُ حُمَيْدٍ الرَّازِيُّ ۞ حَدَّثَنَا أَبُو دَاوُدَ الطَّيَالِسِيُّ ۞ عَنْ عَبَّادِ بْنِ مَنْصُورٍ ۞ عَنْ عِكْرِمَةَ ۞ عَنِ ابْنِ عَبَّاسٍ أَنَّ النَّبِيَّ ﷺ قَالَ اِكْتَحِلُوا بِالإِثْمِدِ ۞ فَإِنَّهُ يَجْلُو الْبَصَرَ ۞ وَيُنْبِتُ الشَّعَرَ ۞ وَزَعَمَ أَنَّ النَّبِيَّ ﷺ كَانَتْ لَهُ مُكْحُلَةٌ يَكْتَحِلُ مِنْهَا كُلَّ لَيْلَةٍ ۞ ثَلَاثَةً فِي هٰذِهِ ۞ وَثَلَاثَةً فِي هٰذِهِ ۞

49. Muhammad ibn Humayd al-Razi narrated to us, 'Abu Dawud al-Tayalisi narrated to us on the authority of 'Abbad ibn Mansur, on the authority of 'Ikrima, who reported:

"Ibn 'Abbas related that the Prophet ﷺ said, 'Apply *ithmid*,[162] for it strengthens the eyesight and boosts the growth of the eyelashes.'[163] He [Ibn 'Abbas] said that the Prophet ﷺ had a kohl container from which he would apply kohl each night, thrice in this one, and thrice in that one."'[164]

٥٠ - حَدَّثَنَا عَبْدُ اللهِ بْنُ الصَّبَّاحِ الْهَاشِمِيُّ الْبَصْرِيُّ ۞ أَخْبَرَنَا عُبَيْدُ اللهِ بْنُ مُوسَى ۞ أَخْبَرَنَا إِسْرَائِيلُ بْنُ يونُسَ ۞ عَنْ عَبَّادِ بْنِ مَنْصُورٍ ۞ ح ۞ وَحَدَّثَنَا عَلِيُّ بْنُ حُجْرٍ ۞ حَدَّثَنَا يَزِيدُ بْنُ هَارُونَ ۞ حَدَّثَنَا عَبَّادُ بْنُ مَنْصُورٍ ۞ عَنْ عِكْرِمَةَ ۞ عَنِ ابْنِ عَبَّاسٍ قَالَ

[162] Imam al-Bajuri notes, 'This is addressed to those with healthy eyesight. For those suffering from eye ailments, the use of *ithmid* is harmful. *Ithmid* is the well-known mineral used as an antimony. Its mines are found in the east, and its colour is reddish black.' In today's time, those who wish to use *kohl* (whether *ithmid* or otherwise) must exercise caution, since much of the *kohl* available in the markets is contaminated with heavy metals. Long term exposure to heavy metals can cause neurological, respiratory and cardiovascular disorders, imbalance of hormones, hair loss, infertility and other ailments. (AA, MA)

[163] Concerning the phrase 'it strengthens the eyesight and boosts the growth of the eyelashes', Imam al-Bajuri explains, 'This is if it is applied by someone who is accustomed to it. If it is applied by someone who is not accustomed to it, his eyes will suffer inflammation.' (AA)

[164] The phrase 'thrice in this one, and thrice in that one' means thrice in the right eye and thrice in the left eye. It is apparent from the wording of this narration that the narrator was pointing to his eyes. It is also narrated that the Prophet ﷺ said, 'The one who applies kohl should do so an odd number of times.' (Ibn Majah, *Sunan*). This narration indicates that the Prophet ﷺ chose the number to be three. The majority of scholars maintain that *kohl* should be placed in the right eye thrice and then the left eye thrice. (MA)

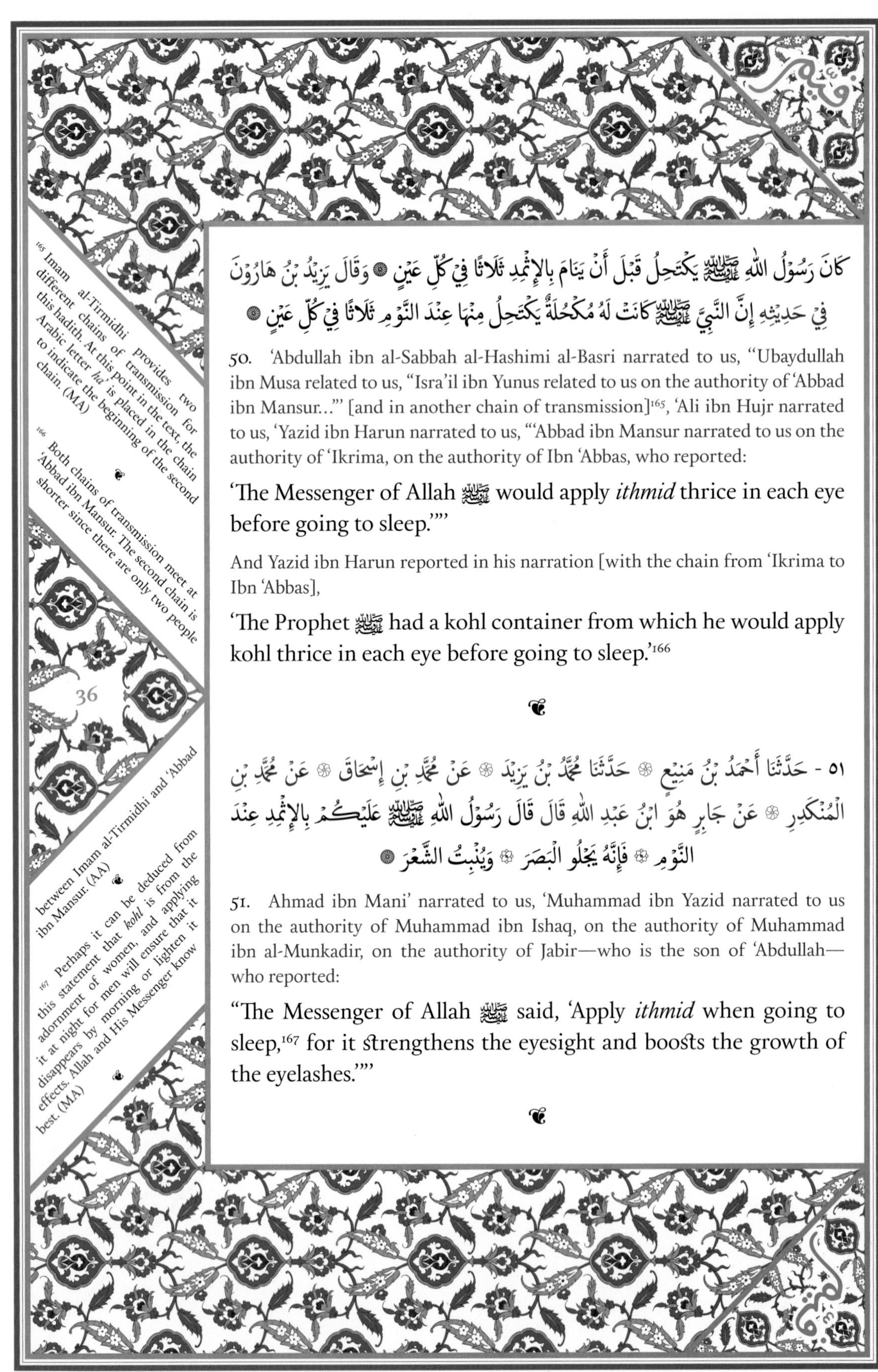

كَانَ رَسُولُ اللهِ ﷺ يَكْتَحِلُ قَبْلَ أَنْ يَنَامَ بِالإِثْمِدِ ثَلَاثًا فِي كُلِّ عَيْنٍ ۞ وَقَالَ يَزِيدُ بْنُ هَارُونَ فِي حَدِيثِهِ إِنَّ النَّبِيَّ ﷺ كَانَتْ لَهُ مُكْحُلَةٌ يَكْتَحِلُ مِنْهَا عِنْدَ النَّوْمِ ثَلَاثًا فِي كُلِّ عَيْنٍ ۞

50. 'Abdullah ibn al-Sabbah al-Hashimi al-Basri narrated to us, "Ubaydullah ibn Musa related to us, "Isra'il ibn Yunus related to us on the authority of 'Abbad ibn Mansur..."' [and in another chain of transmission][165], 'Ali ibn Hujr narrated to us, 'Yazid ibn Harun narrated to us, "'Abbad ibn Mansur narrated to us on the authority of 'Ikrima, on the authority of Ibn 'Abbas, who reported:

'The Messenger of Allah ﷺ would apply *ithmid* thrice in each eye before going to sleep.'"'

And Yazid ibn Harun reported in his narration [with the chain from 'Ikrima to Ibn 'Abbas],

'The Prophet ﷺ had a kohl container from which he would apply kohl thrice in each eye before going to sleep.'[166]

٥١ - حَدَّثَنَا أَحْمَدُ بْنُ مَنِيعٍ ۞ حَدَّثَنَا مُحَمَّدُ بْنُ يَزِيدَ ۞ عَنْ مُحَمَّدِ بْنِ إِسْحَاقَ ۞ عَنْ مُحَمَّدِ بْنِ الْمُنْكَدِرِ ۞ عَنْ جَابِرٍ هُوَ ابْنُ عَبْدِ اللهِ قَالَ قَالَ رَسُولُ اللهِ ﷺ عَلَيْكُمْ بِالإِثْمِدِ عِنْدَ النَّوْمِ ۞ فَإِنَّهُ يَجْلُو الْبَصَرَ ۞ وَيُنْبِتُ الشَّعْرَ ۞

51. Ahmad ibn Mani' narrated to us, 'Muhammad ibn Yazid narrated to us on the authority of Muhammad ibn Ishaq, on the authority of Muhammad ibn al-Munkadir, on the authority of Jabir—who is the son of 'Abdullah—who reported:

"The Messenger of Allah ﷺ said, 'Apply *ithmid* when going to sleep,[167] for it strengthens the eyesight and boosts the growth of the eyelashes.'"'

[165] Imam al-Tirmidhi provides two different chains of transmission for this hadith. At this point in the text, the Arabic letter *ha'* is placed in the chain to indicate the beginning of the second chain. (MA)

[166] Both chains of transmission meet at 'Abbad ibn Mansur. The second chain is shorter since there are only two people between Imam al-Tirmidhi and 'Abbad ibn Mansur. (AA)

[167] Perhaps it can be deduced from this statement that *kohl* is from the adornment of women, and applying it at night for men will ensure that it disappears by morning or lighten its effects. Allah and His Messenger know best. (MA)

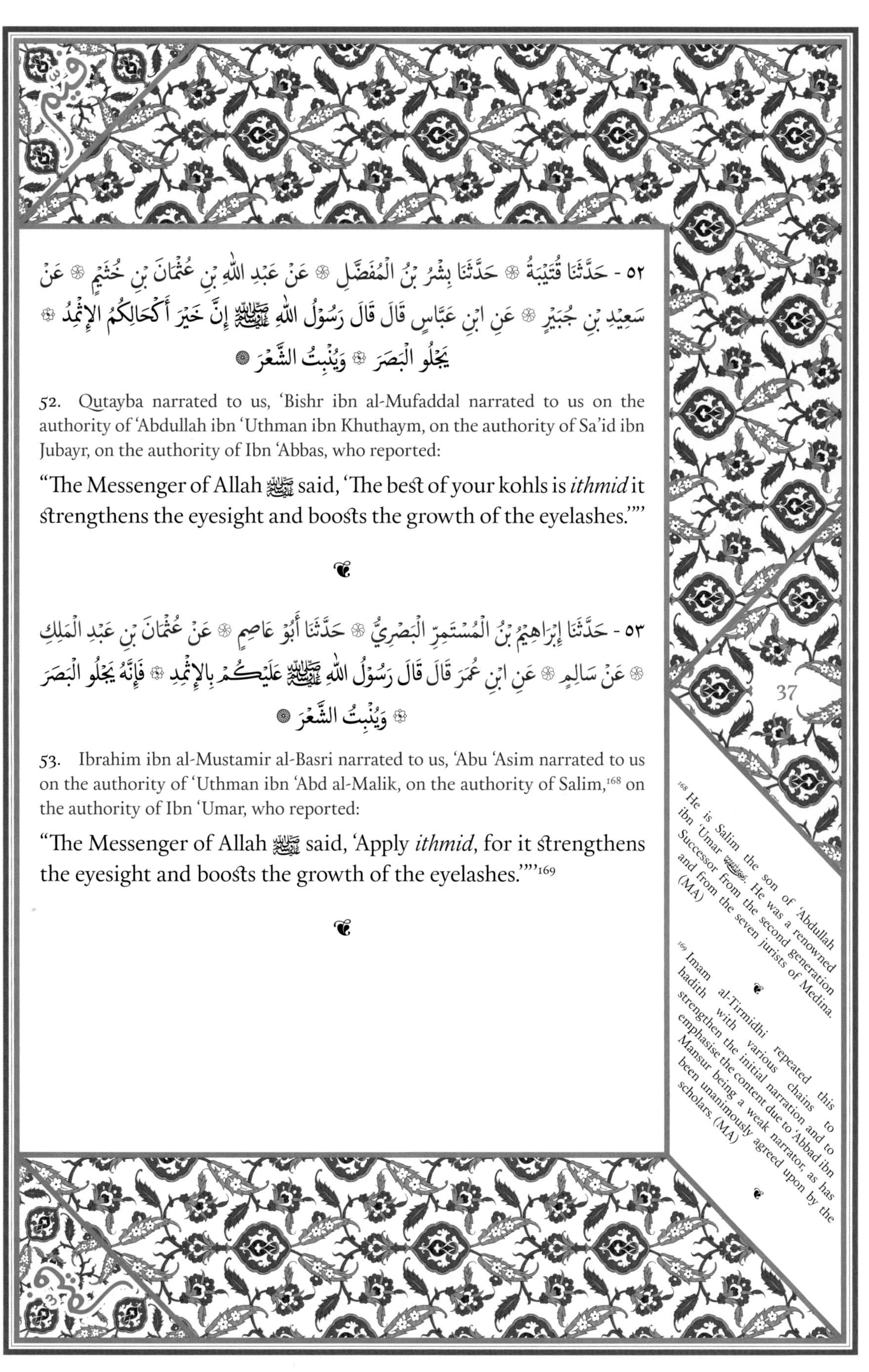

٥٢ - حَدَّثَنَا قُتَيْبَةُ ۞ حَدَّثَنَا بِشْرُ بْنُ الْمُفَضَّلِ ۞ عَنْ عَبْدِ اللهِ بْنِ عُثْمَانَ بْنِ خُثَيْمٍ ۞ عَنْ سَعِيدِ بْنِ جُبَيْرٍ ۞ عَنِ ابْنِ عَبَّاسٍ قَالَ قَالَ رَسُولُ اللهِ ﷺ إِنَّ خَيْرَ أَكْحَالِكُمُ الإِثْمِدُ ۞ يَجْلُو الْبَصَرَ ۞ وَيُنْبِتُ الشَّعْرَ ۞

52. Qutayba narrated to us, 'Bishr ibn al-Mufaddal narrated to us on the authority of 'Abdullah ibn 'Uthman ibn Khuthaym, on the authority of Sa'id ibn Jubayr, on the authority of Ibn 'Abbas, who reported:

"The Messenger of Allah ﷺ said, 'The best of your kohls is *ithmid* it strengthens the eyesight and boosts the growth of the eyelashes.'"'

٥٣ - حَدَّثَنَا إِبْرَاهِيمُ بْنُ الْمُسْتَمِرِّ الْبَصْرِيُّ ۞ حَدَّثَنَا أَبُو عَاصِمٍ ۞ عَنْ عُثْمَانَ بْنِ عَبْدِ الْمَلِكِ ۞ عَنْ سَالِمٍ ۞ عَنِ ابْنِ عُمَرَ قَالَ قَالَ رَسُولُ اللهِ ﷺ عَلَيْكُمْ بِالإِثْمِدِ ۞ فَإِنَّهُ يَجْلُو الْبَصَرَ ۞ وَيُنْبِتُ الشَّعْرَ ۞

53. Ibrahim ibn al-Mustamir al-Basri narrated to us, 'Abu 'Asim narrated to us on the authority of 'Uthman ibn 'Abd al-Malik, on the authority of Salim,[168] on the authority of Ibn 'Umar, who reported:

"The Messenger of Allah ﷺ said, 'Apply *ithmid*, for it strengthens the eyesight and boosts the growth of the eyelashes.'"'[169]

[168] He is Salim the son of 'Abdullah ibn 'Umar ﷺ. He was a renowned Successor from the second generation and from the seven jurists of Medina. (MA)

[169] Imam al-Tirmidhi repeated this hadith with various chains to strengthen the initial narration and to emphasise the content due to 'Abbad ibn Mansur being a weak narrator, as has been unanimously agreed upon by the scholars. (MA)

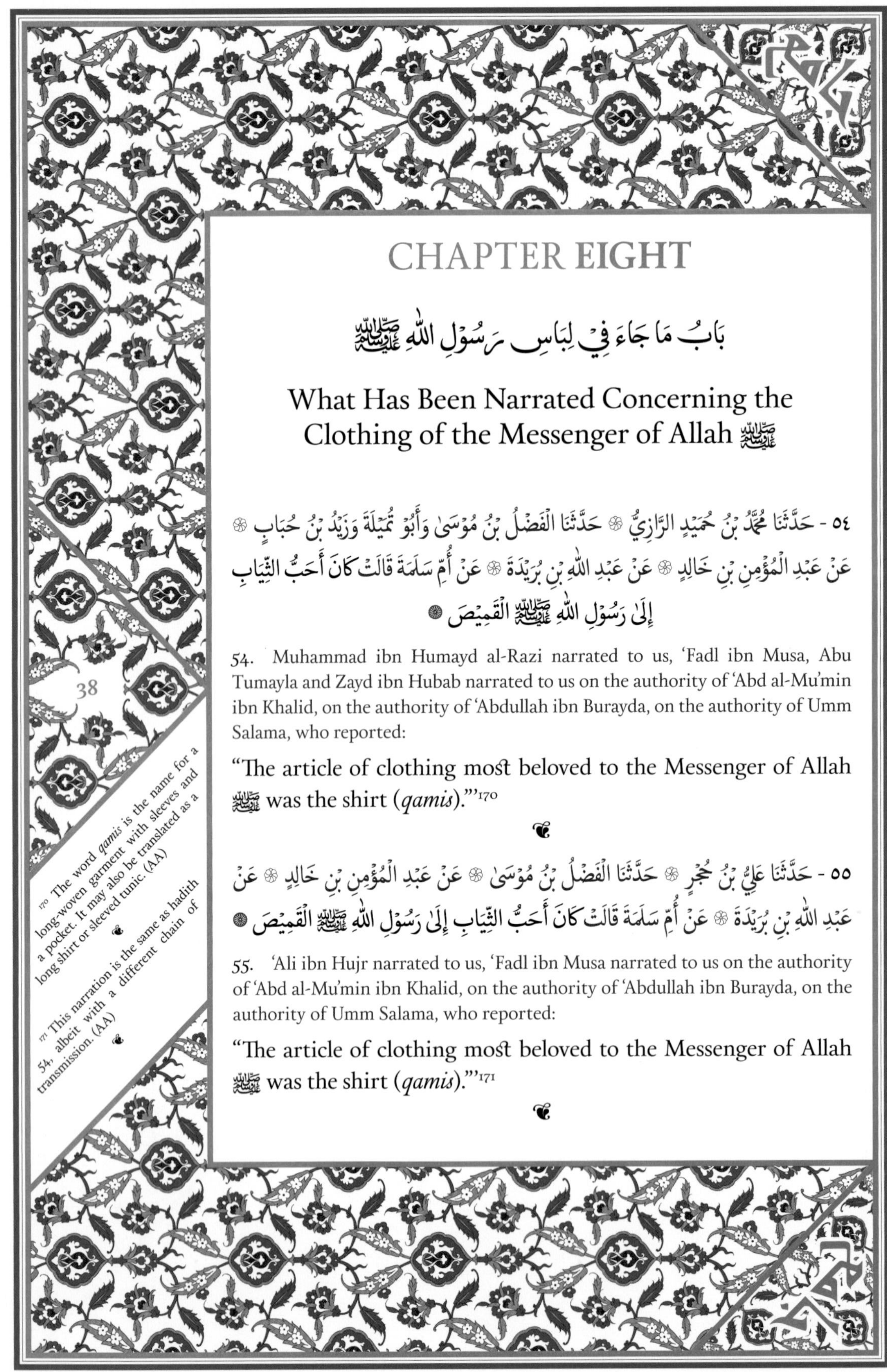

CHAPTER EIGHT

بَابُ مَا جَاءَ فِي لِبَاسِ رَسُولِ اللهِ ﷺ

What Has Been Narrated Concerning the Clothing of the Messenger of Allah ﷺ

٥٤ - حَدَّثَنَا مُحَمَّدُ بْنُ حُمَيْدٍ الرَّازِيُّ ❁ حَدَّثَنَا الْفَضْلُ بْنُ مُوسَىٰ وَأَبُو تُمَيْلَةَ وَزَيْدُ بْنُ حُبَابٍ ❁ عَنْ عَبْدِ الْمُؤْمِنِ بْنِ خَالِدٍ ❁ عَنْ عَبْدِ اللهِ بْنِ بُرَيْدَةَ ❁ عَنْ أُمِّ سَلَمَةَ قَالَتْ كَانَ أَحَبُّ الثِّيَابِ إِلَىٰ رَسُولِ اللهِ ﷺ الْقَمِيصَ ❁

54. Muhammad ibn Humayd al-Razi narrated to us, 'Fadl ibn Musa, Abu Tumayla and Zayd ibn Hubab narrated to us on the authority of 'Abd al-Mu'min ibn Khalid, on the authority of 'Abdullah ibn Burayda, on the authority of Umm Salama, who reported:

"The article of clothing most beloved to the Messenger of Allah ﷺ was the shirt (*qamis*)."[170]

❦

٥٥ - حَدَّثَنَا عَلِيُّ بْنُ حُجْرٍ ❁ حَدَّثَنَا الْفَضْلُ بْنُ مُوسَىٰ ❁ عَنْ عَبْدِ الْمُؤْمِنِ بْنِ خَالِدٍ ❁ عَنْ عَبْدِ اللهِ بْنِ بُرَيْدَةَ ❁ عَنْ أُمِّ سَلَمَةَ قَالَتْ كَانَ أَحَبُّ الثِّيَابِ إِلَىٰ رَسُولِ اللهِ ﷺ الْقَمِيصَ ❁

55. 'Ali ibn Hujr narrated to us, 'Fadl ibn Musa narrated to us on the authority of 'Abd al-Mu'min ibn Khalid, on the authority of 'Abdullah ibn Burayda, on the authority of Umm Salama, who reported:

"The article of clothing most beloved to the Messenger of Allah ﷺ was the shirt (*qamis*)."[171]

❦

170 The word *qamis* is the name for a long-woven garment with sleeves and a pocket. It may also be translated as a long shirt or sleeved tunic. (AA)

171 This narration is the same as hadith 54, albeit with a different chain of transmission. (AA)

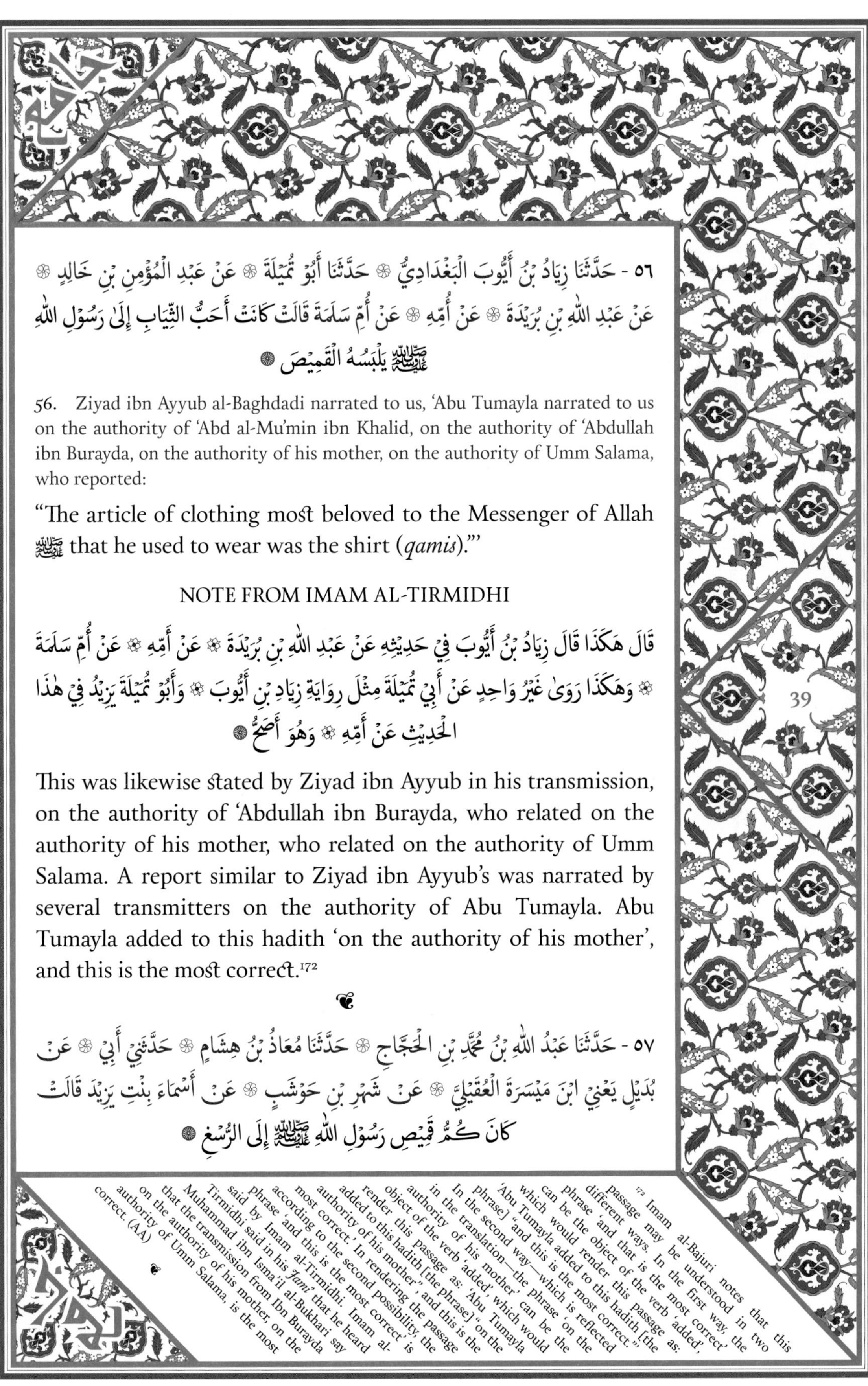

٥٦ - حَدَّثَنَا زِيَادُ بْنُ أَيُّوبَ الْبَغْدَادِيُّ ۞ حَدَّثَنَا أَبُو تُمَيْلَةَ ۞ عَنْ عَبْدِ الْمُؤْمِنِ بْنِ خَالِدٍ ۞ عَنْ عَبْدِ اللهِ بْنِ بُرَيْدَةَ ۞ عَنْ أُمِّهِ ۞ عَنْ أُمِّ سَلَمَةَ قَالَتْ كَانَتْ أَحَبُّ الثِّيَابِ إِلَى رَسُولِ اللهِ ﷺ يَلْبَسُهُ الْقَمِيصَ ۞

56. Ziyad ibn Ayyub al-Baghdadi narrated to us, 'Abu Tumayla narrated to us on the authority of 'Abd al-Mu'min ibn Khalid, on the authority of 'Abdullah ibn Burayda, on the authority of his mother, on the authority of Umm Salama, who reported:

"The article of clothing most beloved to the Messenger of Allah ﷺ that he used to wear was the shirt (*qamis*)."

NOTE FROM IMAM AL-TIRMIDHI

قَالَ هَكَذَا قَالَ زِيَادُ بْنُ أَيُّوبَ فِي حَدِيثِهِ عَنْ عَبْدِ اللهِ بْنِ بُرَيْدَةَ ۞ عَنْ أُمِّهِ ۞ عَنْ أُمِّ سَلَمَةَ ۞ وَهَكَذَا رَوَى غَيْرُ وَاحِدٍ عَنْ أَبِي تُمَيْلَةَ مِثْلَ رِوَايَةِ زِيَادِ بْنِ أَيُّوبَ ۞ وَأَبُو تُمَيْلَةَ يَزِيدُ فِي هَذَا الْحَدِيثِ عَنْ أُمِّهِ ۞ وَهُوَ أَصَحُّ ۞

This was likewise stated by Ziyad ibn Ayyub in his transmission, on the authority of 'Abdullah ibn Burayda, who related on the authority of his mother, who related on the authority of Umm Salama. A report similar to Ziyad ibn Ayyub's was narrated by several transmitters on the authority of Abu Tumayla. Abu Tumayla added to this hadith 'on the authority of his mother', and this is the most correct.[172]

٥٧ - حَدَّثَنَا عَبْدُ اللهِ بْنُ مُحَمَّدِ بْنِ الْحَجَّاجِ ۞ حَدَّثَنَا مُعَاذُ بْنُ هِشَامٍ ۞ حَدَّثَنِي أَبِي ۞ عَنْ بُدَيْلٍ يَعْنِي ابْنَ مَيْسَرَةَ الْعُقَيْلِيَّ ۞ عَنْ شَهْرِ بْنِ حَوْشَبٍ ۞ عَنْ أَسْمَاءَ بِنْتِ يَزِيدَ قَالَتْ كَانَ كُمُّ قَمِيصِ رَسُولِ اللهِ ﷺ إِلَى الرُّسْغِ ۞

172 Imam al-Bajuri notes that this passage may be understood in two different ways. In the first way, the phrase 'and that is the most correct' can be the object of the verb 'added', which would render this passage as: 'Abu Tumayla added to this hadith [the phrase] "and this is the most correct."' In the second way—which is reflected in the translation—the phrase 'on the authority of his mother' can be the object of the verb 'added', which would render this passage as: 'Abu Tumayla added to this hadith [the phrase] "on the authority of his mother", and this is the most correct'. In rendering the passage according to the second possibility, the phrase 'and this is the most correct' is said by Imam al-Tirmidhi. Imam al-Tirmidhi said in his *Jami'* that he heard Muhammad ibn Isma'il al-Bukhari say that the transmission from Ibn Burayda on the authority of his mother, on the authority of Umm Salama, is the most correct. (AA)

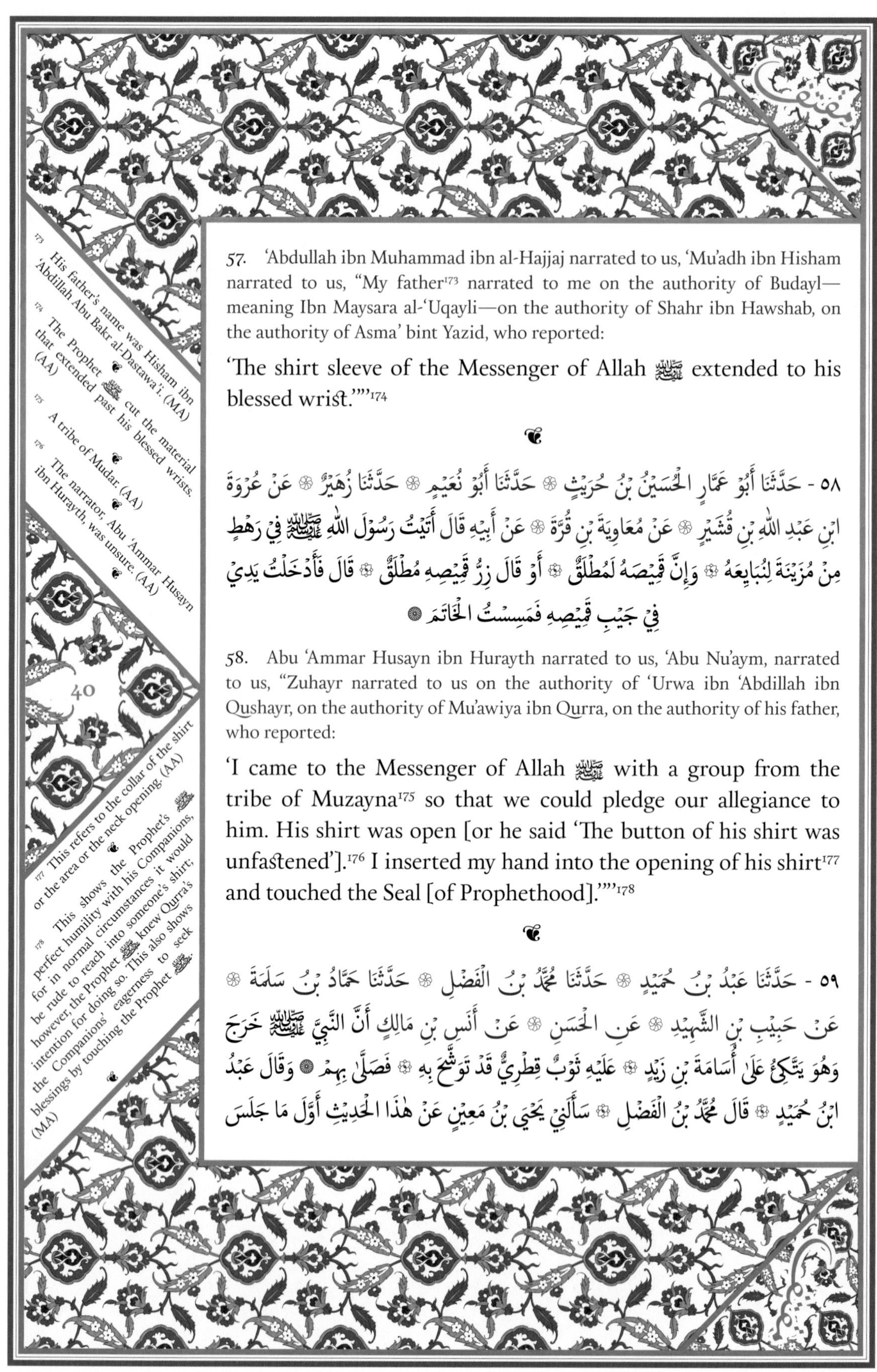

57. 'Abdullah ibn Muhammad ibn al-Hajjaj narrated to us, 'Mu'adh ibn Hisham narrated to us, "My father[173] narrated to me on the authority of Budayl—meaning Ibn Maysara al-'Uqayli—on the authority of Shahr ibn Hawshab, on the authority of Asma' bint Yazid, who reported:

'The shirt sleeve of the Messenger of Allah ﷺ extended to his blessed wrist.'"'[174]

٥٨ - حَدَّثَنَا أَبُو عَمَّارٍ الْحُسَيْنُ بْنُ حُرَيْثٍ ۞ حَدَّثَنَا أَبُو نُعَيْمٍ ۞ حَدَّثَنَا زُهَيْرٌ ۞ عَنْ عُرْوَةَ ابْنِ عَبْدِ اللهِ بْنِ قُشَيْرٍ ۞ عَنْ مُعَاوِيَةَ بْنِ قُرَّةَ ۞ عَنْ أَبِيهِ قَالَ أَتَيْتُ رَسُولَ اللهِ ﷺ فِي رَهْطٍ مِنْ مُزَيْنَةَ لِنُبَايِعَهُ ۞ وَإِنَّ قَمِيصَهُ لَمُطْلَقٌ ۞ أَوْ قَالَ زِرُّ قَمِيصِهِ مُطْلَقٌ ۞ قَالَ فَأَدْخَلْتُ يَدِي فِي جَيْبِ قَمِيصِهِ فَمَسِسْتُ الْخَاتَمَ ۞

58. Abu 'Ammar Husayn ibn Hurayth narrated to us, 'Abu Nu'aym, narrated to us, "Zuhayr narrated to us on the authority of 'Urwa ibn 'Abdillah ibn Qushayr, on the authority of Mu'awiya ibn Qurra, on the authority of his father, who reported:

'I came to the Messenger of Allah ﷺ with a group from the tribe of Muzayna[175] so that we could pledge our allegiance to him. His shirt was open [or he said 'The button of his shirt was unfastened'].[176] I inserted my hand into the opening of his shirt[177] and touched the Seal [of Prophethood].'"'[178]

٥٩ - حَدَّثَنَا عَبْدُ بْنُ حُمَيْدٍ ۞ حَدَّثَنَا مُحَمَّدُ بْنُ الْفَضْلِ ۞ حَدَّثَنَا حَمَّادُ بْنُ سَلَمَةَ ۞ عَنْ حَبِيبِ بْنِ الشَّهِيدِ ۞ عَنِ الْحَسَنِ ۞ عَنْ أَنَسِ بْنِ مَالِكٍ أَنَّ النَّبِيَّ ﷺ خَرَجَ وَهُوَ يَتَّكِئُ عَلَى أُسَامَةَ بْنِ زَيْدٍ ۞ عَلَيْهِ ثَوْبٌ قِطْرِيٌّ قَدْ تَوَشَّحَ بِهِ ۞ فَصَلَّى بِهِمْ ۞ وَقَالَ عَبْدُ ابْنُ حُمَيْدٍ ۞ قَالَ مُحَمَّدُ بْنُ الْفَضْلِ ۞ سَأَلَنِي يَحْيَى بْنُ مَعِينٍ عَنْ هٰذَا الْحَدِيثِ أَوَّلَ مَا جَلَسَ

173 His father's name was Hisham ibn 'Abdillah Abu Bakr al-Dastawa'i. (MA)

174 The Prophet ﷺ cut the material that extended past his blessed wrists. (AA)

175 A tribe of Mudar. (AA)

176 The narrator, Abu 'Ammar Husayn ibn Hurayth, was unsure. (AA)

177 This refers to the collar of the shirt or the area or the neck opening. (AA)

178 This shows the Prophet's ﷺ perfect humility with his Companions, for in normal circumstances it would be rude to reach into someone's shirt; however, the Prophet ﷺ knew Qurra's intention for doing so. This also shows the Companions' eagerness to seek blessings by touching the Prophet ﷺ. (MA)

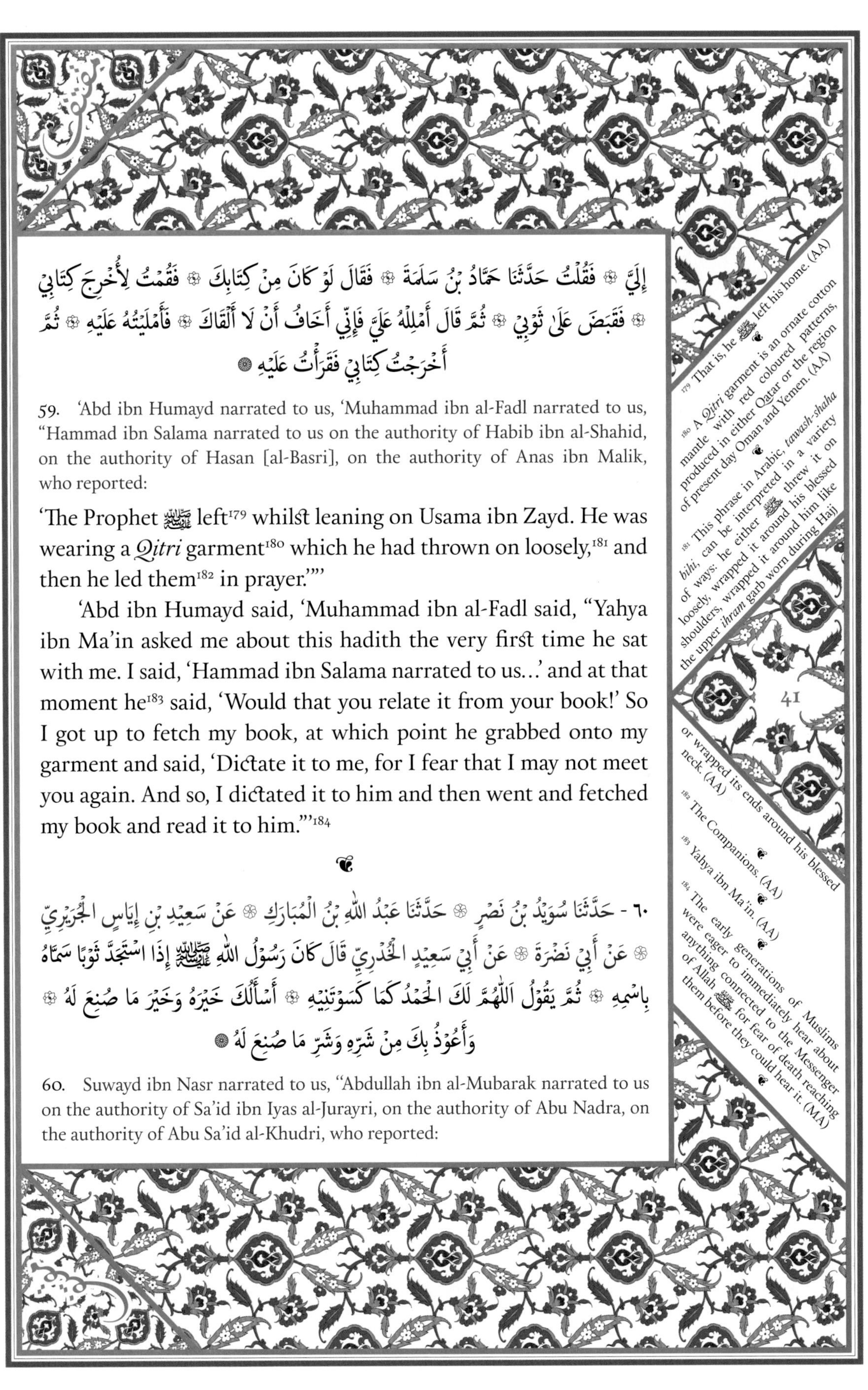

إِلَيَّ ❁ فَقُلْتُ حَدَّثَنَا حَمَّادُ بْنُ سَلَمَةَ ❁ فَقَالَ لَوْ كَانَ مِنْ كِتَابِكَ ❁ فَقُمْتُ لِأُخْرِجَ كِتَابِي ❁ فَقَبَضَ عَلَىٰ ثَوْبِي ❁ ثُمَّ قَالَ أَمْلِلْهُ عَلَيَّ فَإِنِّي أَخَافُ أَنْ لَا أَلْقَاكَ ❁ فَأَمْلَيْتُهُ عَلَيْهِ ❁ ثُمَّ أَخْرَجْتُ كِتَابِي فَقَرَأْتُ عَلَيْهِ ❁

59. 'Abd ibn Humayd narrated to us, 'Muhammad ibn al-Fadl narrated to us, "Hammad ibn Salama narrated to us on the authority of Habib ibn al-Shahid, on the authority of Hasan [al-Basri], on the authority of Anas ibn Malik, who reported:

'The Prophet ﷺ left[179] whilst leaning on Usama ibn Zayd. He was wearing a *Qitri* garment[180] which he had thrown on loosely,[181] and then he led them[182] in prayer.'"'

'Abd ibn Humayd said, 'Muhammad ibn al-Fadl said, "Yahya ibn Ma'in asked me about this hadith the very first time he sat with me. I said, 'Hammad ibn Salama narrated to us...' and at that moment he[183] said, 'Would that you relate it from your book!' So I got up to fetch my book, at which point he grabbed onto my garment and said, 'Dictate it to me, for I fear that I may not meet you again. And so, I dictated it to him and then went and fetched my book and read it to him."'[184]

❦

٦٠ - حَدَّثَنَا سُوَيْدُ بْنُ نَصْرٍ ❁ حَدَّثَنَا عَبْدُ اللهِ بْنُ الْمُبَارَكِ ❁ عَنْ سَعِيدِ بْنِ إِيَاسٍ الْجُرَيْرِيِّ ❁ عَنْ أَبِي نَضْرَةَ ❁ عَنْ أَبِي سَعِيدٍ الْخُدْرِيِّ قَالَ كَانَ رَسُولُ اللهِ ﷺ إِذَا اسْتَجَدَّ ثَوْبًا سَمَّاهُ بِاسْمِهِ ❁ ثُمَّ يَقُولُ اللَّهُمَّ لَكَ الْحَمْدُ كَمَا كَسَوْتَنِيهِ ❁ أَسْأَلُكَ خَيْرَهُ وَخَيْرَ مَا صُنِعَ لَهُ ❁ وَأَعُوذُ بِكَ مِنْ شَرِّهِ وَشَرِّ مَا صُنِعَ لَهُ ❁

60. Suwayd ibn Nasr narrated to us, "Abdullah ibn al-Mubarak narrated to us on the authority of Sa'id ibn Iyas al-Jurayri, on the authority of Abu Nadra, on the authority of Abu Sa'id al-Khudri, who reported:

179 That is, he ﷺ left his home. (AA)

180 A *Qitri* garment is an ornate cotton mantle with red coloured patterns, produced in either Qatar or the region of present day Oman and Yemen. (AA)

181 This phrase in Arabic, *tawash-shaha bihi*, can be interpreted in a variety of ways: he either ﷺ threw it on loosely, wrapped it around his blessed shoulders, wrapped it around him like the upper *ihram* garb worn during Hajj or wrapped its ends around his blessed neck. (AA)

182 The Companions. (AA)

183 Yahya ibn Ma'in. (AA)

184 The early generations of Muslims were eager to immediately hear about anything connected to the Messenger of Allah ﷻ for fear of death reaching them before they could hear it. (MA)

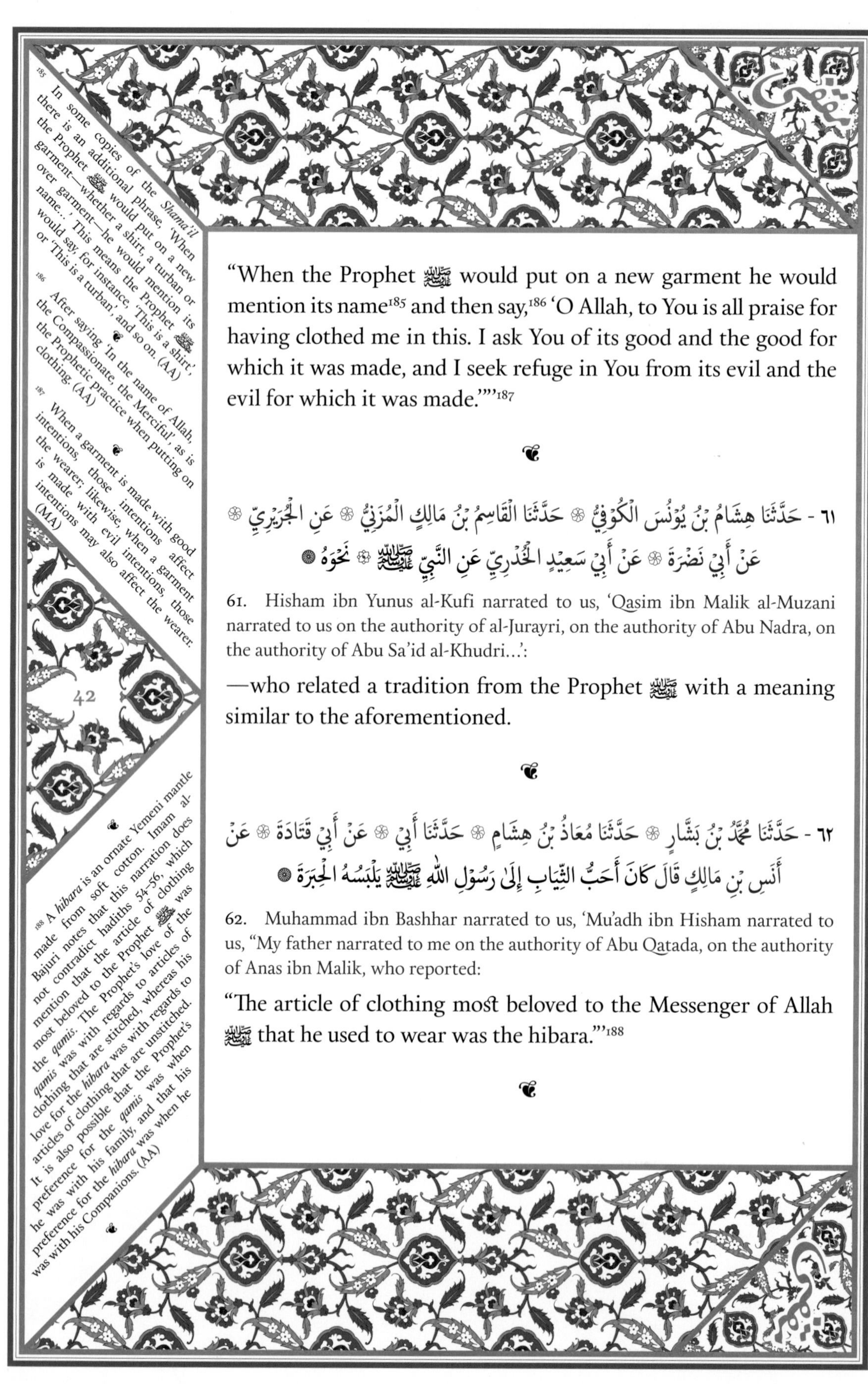

"When the Prophet ﷺ would put on a new garment he would mention its name[185] and then say,[186] 'O Allah, to You is all praise for having clothed me in this. I ask You of its good and the good for which it was made, and I seek refuge in You from its evil and the evil for which it was made.'"'[187]

❦

٦١ - حَدَّثَنَا هِشَامُ بْنُ يُونُسَ الْكُوفِيُّ ۞ حَدَّثَنَا الْقَاسِمُ بْنُ مَالِكٍ الْمُزَنِيُّ ۞ عَنِ الْجُرَيْرِيِّ ۞ عَنْ أَبِي نَضْرَةَ ۞ عَنْ أَبِي سَعِيدٍ الْخُدْرِيِّ عَنِ النَّبِيِّ ﷺ ۞ نَحْوَهُ ۞

61. Hisham ibn Yunus al-Kufi narrated to us, 'Qasim ibn Malik al-Muzani narrated to us on the authority of al-Jurayri, on the authority of Abu Nadra, on the authority of Abu Sa'id al-Khudri...':

—who related a tradition from the Prophet ﷺ with a meaning similar to the aforementioned.

❦

٦٢ - حَدَّثَنَا مُحَمَّدُ بْنُ بَشَّارٍ ۞ حَدَّثَنَا مُعَاذُ بْنُ هِشَامٍ ۞ حَدَّثَنَا أَبِي ۞ عَنْ أَبِي قَتَادَةَ ۞ عَنْ أَنَسِ بْنِ مَالِكٍ قَالَ كَانَ أَحَبُّ الثِّيَابِ إِلَى رَسُولِ اللهِ ﷺ يَلْبَسُهُ الْحِبَرَةَ ۞

62. Muhammad ibn Bashhar narrated to us, 'Mu'adh ibn Hisham narrated to us, "My father narrated to me on the authority of Abu Qatada, on the authority of Anas ibn Malik, who reported:

"The article of clothing most beloved to the Messenger of Allah ﷺ that he used to wear was the hibara."'[188]

❦

185 In some copies of the *Shama'il* there is an additional phrase, 'When the Prophet ﷺ would put on a new garment—whether a shirt, a turban or over garment—he would mention its name...' This means the Prophet ﷺ would say, for instance, 'This is a shirt,' or 'This is a turban,' and so on. (AA)

186 After saying 'In the name of Allah, the Compassionate, the Merciful', as is the Prophetic practice when putting on clothing. (AA)

187 When a garment is made with good intentions, those intentions affect the wearer; likewise, when a garment is made with evil intentions, those intentions may also affect the wearer. (MA)

188 A *hibara* is an ornate Yemeni mantle made from soft cotton. Imam al-Bajuri notes that this narration does not contradict hadiths 54-56, which mention that the article of clothing most beloved to the Prophet ﷺ was the *qamis*. The Prophet's love of the *qamis* was with regards to articles of clothing that are stitched, whereas his love for the *hibara* was with regards to articles of clothing that are unstitched. It is also possible that the Prophet's preference for the *qamis* was when he was with his family, and that his preference for the *hibara* was when he was with his Companions. (AA)

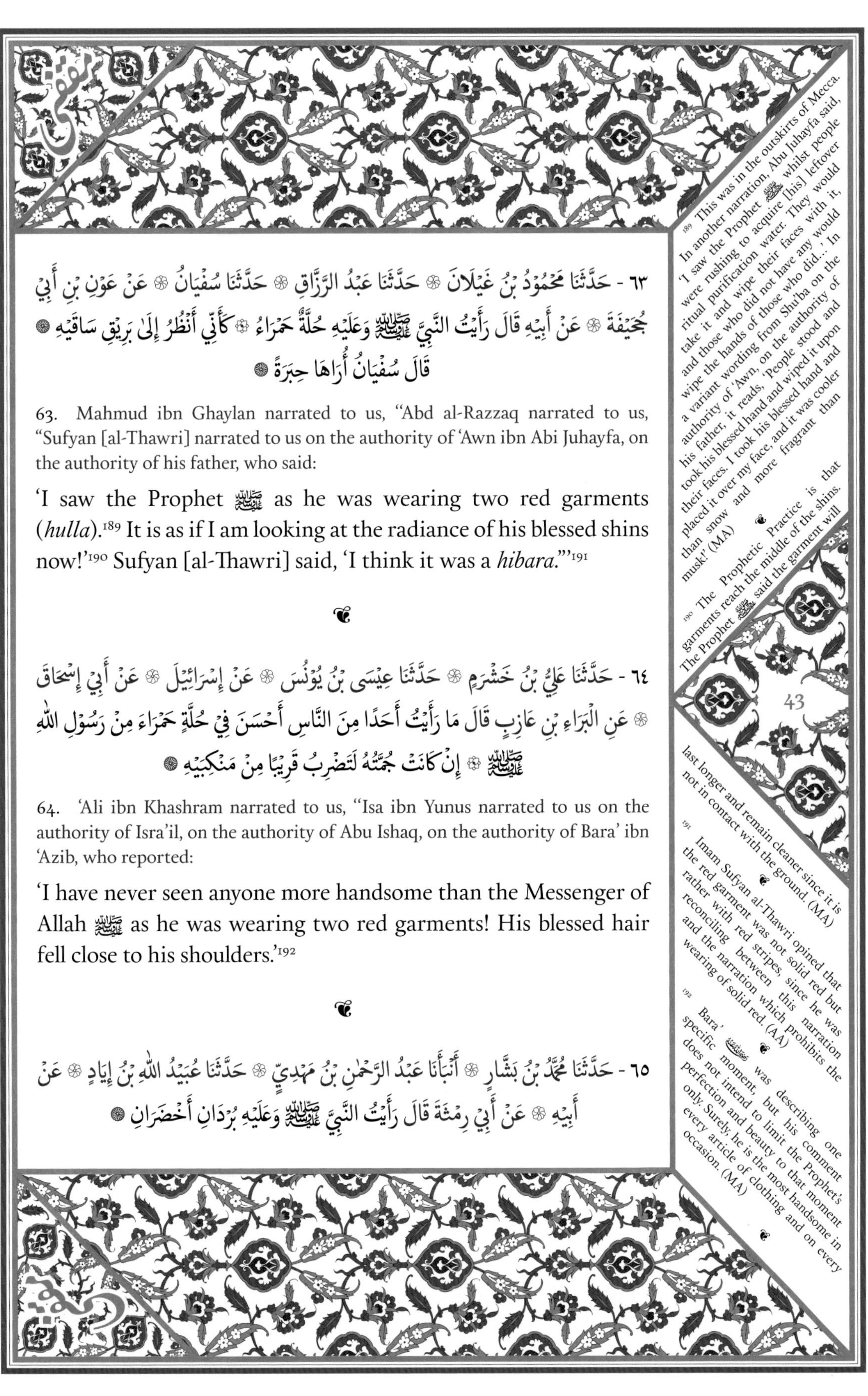

٦٣ - حَدَّثَنَا مَحْمُودُ بْنُ غَيْلَانَ ۞ حَدَّثَنَا عَبْدُ الرَّزَّاقِ ۞ حَدَّثَنَا سُفْيَانُ ۞ عَنْ عَوْنِ بْنِ أَبِي جُحَيْفَةَ ۞ عَنْ أَبِيهِ قَالَ رَأَيْتُ النَّبِيَّ ﷺ وَعَلَيْهِ حُلَّةٌ حَمْرَاءُ ۞ كَأَنِّي أَنْظُرُ إِلَى بَرِيقِ سَاقَيْهِ ۞ قَالَ سُفْيَانُ أُرَاهَا حِبَرَةً ۞

63. Mahmud ibn Ghaylan narrated to us, "Abd al-Razzaq narrated to us, "Sufyan [al-Thawri] narrated to us on the authority of 'Awn ibn Abi Juhayfa, on the authority of his father, who said:

'I saw the Prophet ﷺ as he was wearing two red garments (*hulla*).[189] It is as if I am looking at the radiance of his blessed shins now!'[190] Sufyan [al-Thawri] said, 'I think it was a *hibara*.""[191]

٦٤ - حَدَّثَنَا عَلِيُّ بْنُ خَشْرَمٍ ۞ حَدَّثَنَا عِيسَى بْنُ يُونُسَ ۞ عَنْ إِسْرَائِيلَ ۞ عَنْ أَبِي إِسْحَاقَ ۞ عَنِ الْبَرَاءِ بْنِ عَازِبٍ قَالَ مَا رَأَيْتُ أَحَدًا مِنَ النَّاسِ أَحْسَنَ فِي حُلَّةٍ حَمْرَاءَ مِنْ رَسُولِ اللهِ ﷺ ۞ إِنْ كَانَتْ جُمَّتُهُ لَتَضْرِبُ قَرِيبًا مِنْ مَنْكِبَيْهِ ۞

64. 'Ali ibn Khashram narrated to us, "Isa ibn Yunus narrated to us on the authority of Isra'il, on the authority of Abu Ishaq, on the authority of Bara' ibn 'Azib, who reported:

'I have never seen anyone more handsome than the Messenger of Allah ﷺ as he was wearing two red garments! His blessed hair fell close to his shoulders.'[192]

٦٥ - حَدَّثَنَا مُحَمَّدُ بْنُ بَشَّارٍ ۞ أَنْبَأَنَا عَبْدُ الرَّحْمٰنِ بْنُ مَهْدِيٍّ ۞ حَدَّثَنَا عُبَيْدُ اللهِ بْنُ إِيَادٍ ۞ عَنْ أَبِيهِ ۞ عَنْ أَبِي رِمْثَةَ قَالَ رَأَيْتُ النَّبِيَّ ﷺ وَعَلَيْهِ بُرْدَانِ أَخْضَرَانِ ۞

189 This was in the outskirts of Mecca. In another narration, Abu Juhayfa said, 'I saw the Prophet ﷺ whilst people were rushing to acquire [his] leftover ritual purification water. They would take it and wipe their faces with it, and those who did not have any would wipe the hands of those who did...' In a variant wording from Shu'ba on the authority of 'Awn, on the authority of his father, it reads, 'People stood and took his blessed hand and wiped it upon their faces. I took his blessed hand and placed it over my face, and it was cooler than snow and more fragrant than musk!' (MA)

190 The Prophetic Practice is that garments reach the middle of the shins. The Prophet ﷺ said the garment will last longer and remain cleaner since it is not in contact with the ground. (MA)

191 Imam Sufyan al-Thawri opined that the red garment was not solid red but rather with red stripes, since he was reconciling between this narration and the narration which prohibits the wearing of solid red. (AA)

192 Bara' ﵁ was describing one specific moment, but his comment does not intend to limit the Prophet's perfection and beauty to that moment only. Surely, he is the most handsome in every article of clothing and on every occasion. (MA)

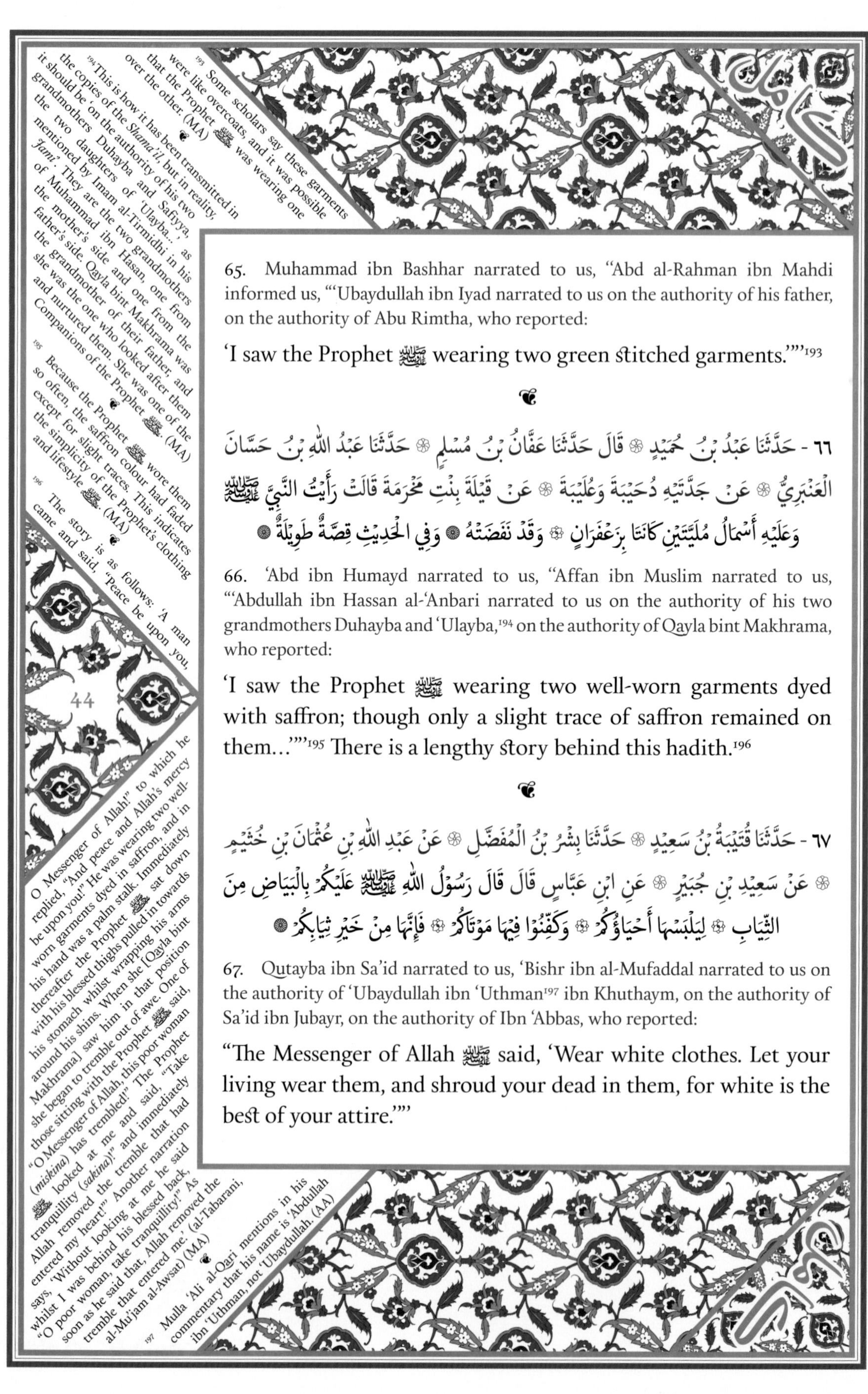

65. Muhammad ibn Bashhar narrated to us, "Abd al-Rahman ibn Mahdi informed us, "'Ubaydullah ibn Iyad narrated to us on the authority of his father, on the authority of Abu Rimtha, who reported:

'I saw the Prophet ﷺ wearing two green stitched garments.'"'[193]

٦٦ - حَدَّثَنَا عَبْدُ بْنُ حُمَيْدٍ ۞ قَالَ حَدَّثَنَا عَفَّانُ بْنُ مُسْلِمٍ ۞ حَدَّثَنَا عَبْدُ اللهِ بْنُ حَسَّانَ الْعَنْبَرِيُّ ۞ عَنْ جَدَّتَيْهِ دُحَيْبَةَ وَعُلَيْبَةَ ۞ عَنْ قَيْلَةَ بِنْتِ مَخْرَمَةَ قَالَتْ رَأَيْتُ النَّبِيَّ ﷺ وَعَلَيْهِ أَسْمَالُ مُلَيَّتَيْنِ كَانَتَا بِزَعْفَرَانٍ ۞ وَقَدْ نَفَضَتْهُ ۞ وَفِي الْحَدِيثِ قِصَّةٌ طَوِيلَةٌ ۞

66. 'Abd ibn Humayd narrated to us, "Affan ibn Muslim narrated to us, "'Abdullah ibn Hassan al-'Anbari narrated to us on the authority of his two grandmothers Duhayba and 'Ulayba,[194] on the authority of Qayla bint Makhrama, who reported:

'I saw the Prophet ﷺ wearing two well-worn garments dyed with saffron; though only a slight trace of saffron remained on them...'"'[195] There is a lengthy story behind this hadith.[196]

٦٧ - حَدَّثَنَا قُتَيْبَةُ بْنُ سَعِيدٍ ۞ حَدَّثَنَا بِشْرُ بْنُ الْمُفَضَّلِ ۞ عَنْ عَبْدِ اللهِ بْنِ عُثْمَانَ بْنِ خُثَيْمٍ ۞ عَنْ سَعِيدِ بْنِ جُبَيْرٍ ۞ عَنِ ابْنِ عَبَّاسٍ قَالَ قَالَ رَسُولُ اللهِ ﷺ عَلَيْكُمْ بِالْبَيَاضِ مِنَ الثِّيَابِ ۞ لِيَلْبَسْهَا أَحْيَاؤُكُمْ ۞ وَكَفِّنُوا فِيهَا مَوْتَاكُمْ ۞ فَإِنَّهَا مِنْ خَيْرِ ثِيَابِكُمْ ۞

67. Qutayba ibn Sa'id narrated to us, 'Bishr ibn al-Mufaddal narrated to us on the authority of 'Ubaydullah ibn 'Uthman[197] ibn Khuthaym, on the authority of Sa'id ibn Jubayr, on the authority of Ibn 'Abbas, who reported:

"The Messenger of Allah ﷺ said, 'Wear white clothes. Let your living wear them, and shroud your dead in them, for white is the best of your attire.'"

193 Some scholars say these garments were like overcoats, and it was possible that the Prophet ﷺ was wearing one over the other. (MA)

194 This is how it has been transmitted in the copies of the *Shama'il*, but in reality, it should be 'on the authority of his two grandmothers Duhayba and Safiyya, the two daughters of 'Ulayba...' as mentioned by Imam al-Tirmidhi in his *Jami'*. They are the two grandmothers of Muhammad ibn Hasan, one from the mother's side and one from the father's side. Qayla bint Makhrama was the grandmother of their father, and she was the one who looked after them and nurtured them. She was one of the Companions of the Prophet ﷺ. (MA)

195 Because the Prophet ﷺ wore them so often, the saffron colour had faded except for slight traces. This indicates the simplicity of the Prophet's clothing and lifestyle ﷺ. (MA)

196 The story is as follows: 'A man came and said, "Peace be upon you, O Messenger of Allah!" to which he replied, "And peace and Allah's mercy be upon you!" He was wearing two well-worn garments dyed in saffron, and in his hand was a palm stalk. Immediately thereafter the Prophet ﷺ sat down with his blessed thighs pulled in towards his stomach whilst wrapping his arms around his shins. When she [Qayla bint Makhrama] saw him in that position she began to tremble out of awe. One of those sitting with the Prophet ﷺ said, "O Messenger of Allah, this poor woman (*miskina*) has trembled!" The Prophet ﷺ looked at me and said, "Take tranquillity (*sakina*)," and immediately Allah removed the tremble that had entered my heart!' Another narration says, 'Without looking at me he said whilst I was behind his blessed back, "O poor woman, take tranquillity!" As soon as he said that, Allah removed the tremble that entered me,' (al-Tabarani, al-Mu'jam al-Awsat) (MA)

197 Mulla 'Ali al-Qari mentions in his commentary that his name is 'Abdullah ibn 'Uthman, not 'Ubaydullah. (AA)

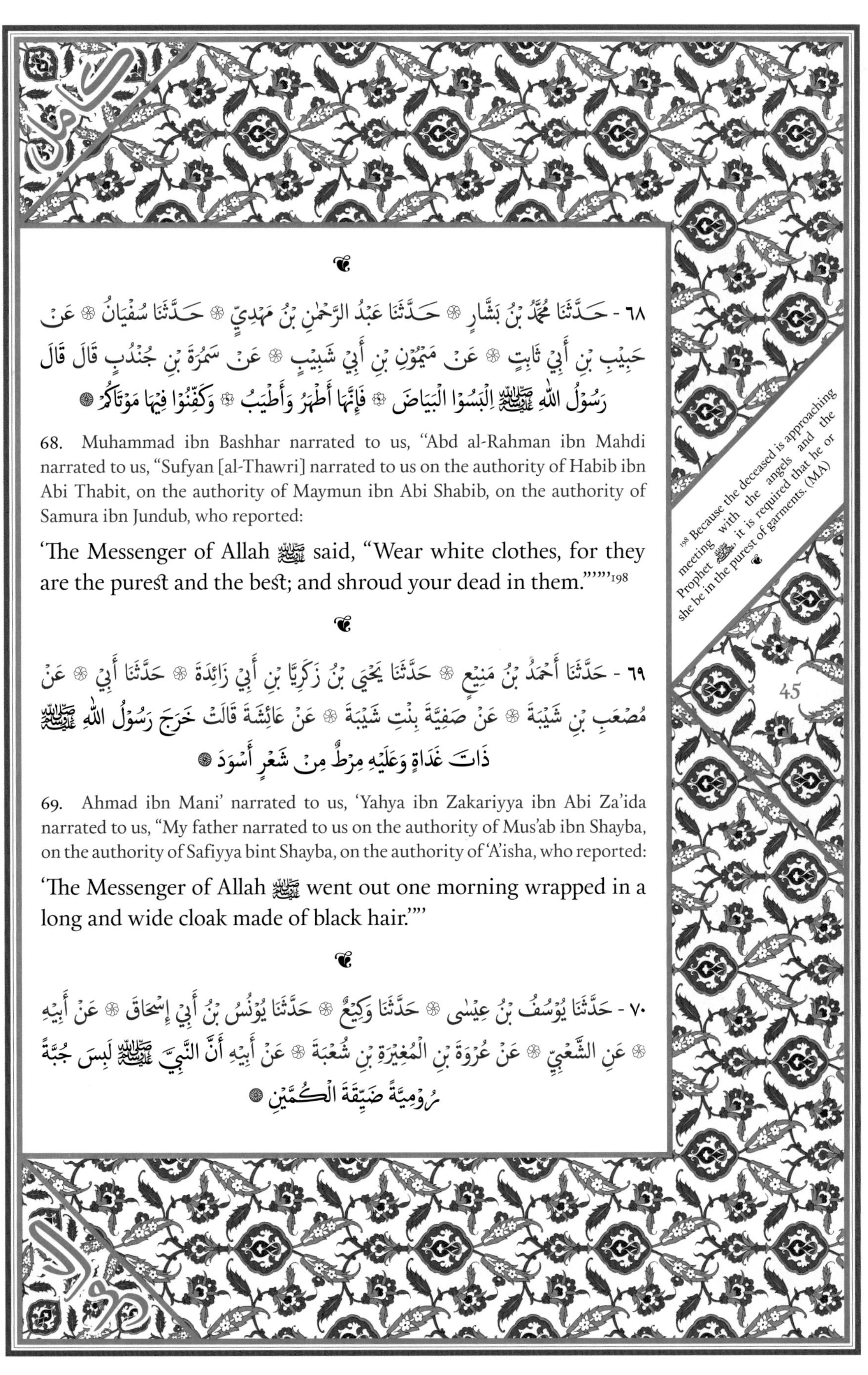

٦٨ - حَدَّثَنَا مُحَمَّدُ بْنُ بَشَّارٍ ۞ حَدَّثَنَا عَبْدُ الرَّحْمٰنِ بْنُ مَهْدِيٍّ ۞ حَدَّثَنَا سُفْيَانُ ۞ عَنْ حَبِيبِ بْنِ أَبِي ثَابِتٍ ۞ عَنْ مَيْمُونِ بْنِ أَبِي شَبِيبٍ ۞ عَنْ سَمُرَةَ بْنِ جُنْدُبٍ قَالَ قَالَ رَسُولُ اللهِ ﷺ اِلْبَسُوا الْبَيَاضَ ۞ فَإِنَّهَا أَطْهَرُ وَأَطْيَبُ ۞ وَكَفِّنُوا فِيهَا مَوْتَاكُمْ ۞

68. Muhammad ibn Bashhar narrated to us, "Abd al-Rahman ibn Mahdi narrated to us, "Sufyan [al-Thawri] narrated to us on the authority of Habib ibn Abi Thabit, on the authority of Maymun ibn Abi Shabib, on the authority of Samura ibn Jundub, who reported:

'The Messenger of Allah ﷺ said, "Wear white clothes, for they are the purest and the best; and shroud your dead in them."''''[198]

٦٩ - حَدَّثَنَا أَحْمَدُ بْنُ مَنِيعٍ ۞ حَدَّثَنَا يَحْيَى بْنُ زَكَرِيَّا بْنِ أَبِي زَائِدَةَ ۞ حَدَّثَنَا أَبِي ۞ عَنْ مُصْعَبِ بْنِ شَيْبَةَ ۞ عَنْ صَفِيَّةَ بِنْتِ شَيْبَةَ ۞ عَنْ عَائِشَةَ قَالَتْ خَرَجَ رَسُولُ اللهِ ﷺ ذَاتَ غَدَاةٍ وَعَلَيْهِ مِرْطٌ مِنْ شَعْرٍ أَسْوَدَ ۞

69. Ahmad ibn Mani' narrated to us, 'Yahya ibn Zakariyya ibn Abi Za'ida narrated to us, "My father narrated to us on the authority of Mus'ab ibn Shayba, on the authority of Safiyya bint Shayba, on the authority of 'A'isha, who reported:

'The Messenger of Allah ﷺ went out one morning wrapped in a long and wide cloak made of black hair.'"'

٧٠ - حَدَّثَنَا يُوسُفُ بْنُ عِيسَى ۞ حَدَّثَنَا وَكِيعٌ ۞ حَدَّثَنَا يُونُسُ بْنُ أَبِي إِسْحَاقَ ۞ عَنْ أَبِيهِ ۞ عَنِ الشَّعْبِيِّ ۞ عَنْ عُرْوَةَ بْنِ الْمُغِيرَةِ بْنِ شُعْبَةَ ۞ عَنْ أَبِيهِ أَنَّ النَّبِيَّ ﷺ لَبِسَ جُبَّةً رُومِيَّةً ضَيِّقَةَ الْكُمَّيْنِ ۞

[198] Because the deceased is approaching meeting with the angels and the Prophet ﷺ, it is required that he or she be in the purest of garments. (MA)

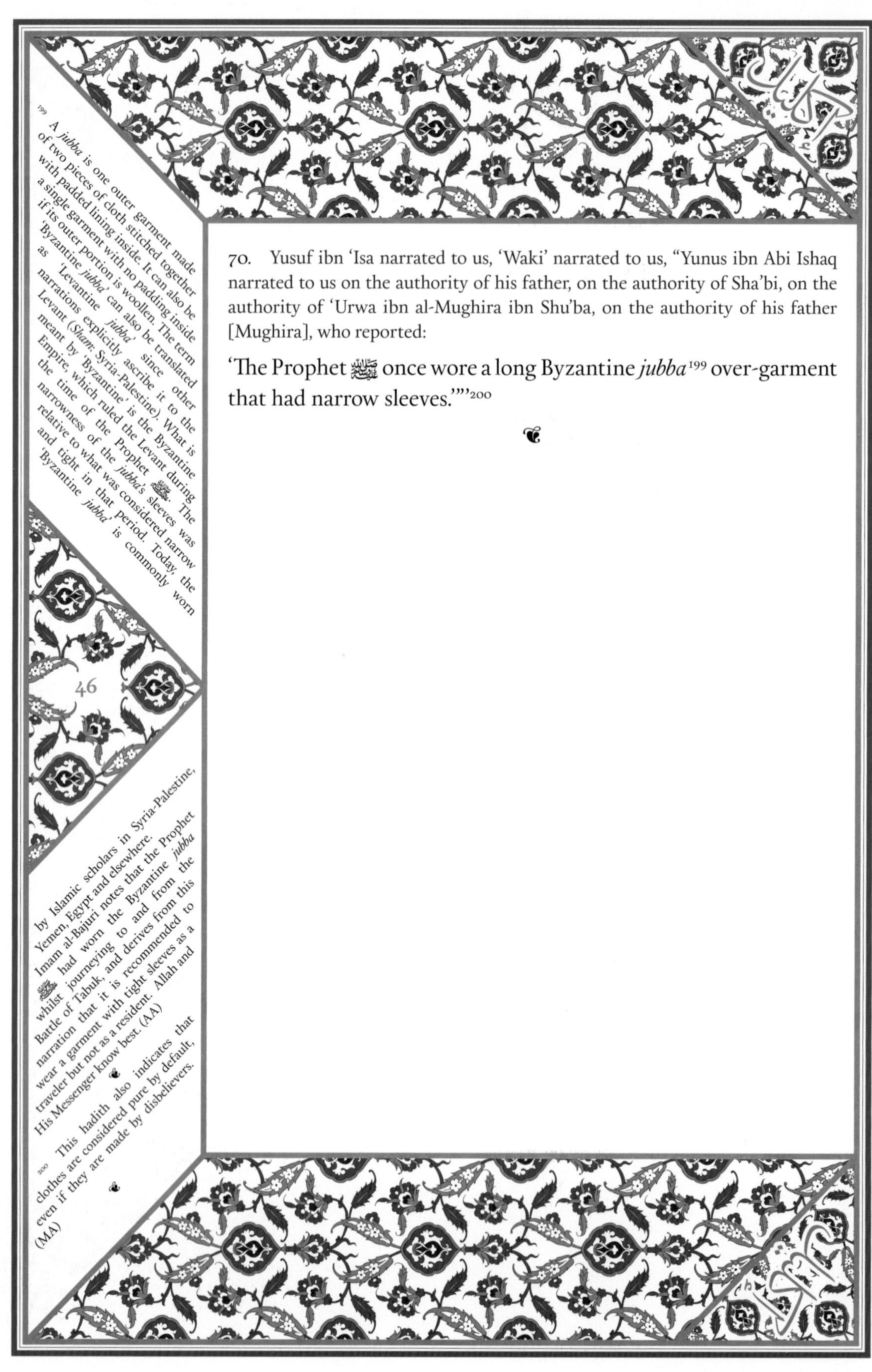

70. Yusuf ibn 'Isa narrated to us, 'Waki' narrated to us, "Yunus ibn Abi Ishaq narrated to us on the authority of his father, on the authority of Sha'bi, on the authority of 'Urwa ibn al-Mughira ibn Shu'ba, on the authority of his father [Mughira], who reported:

'The Prophet ﷺ once wore a long Byzantine *jubba*[199] over-garment that had narrow sleeves.'"[200]

[199] A *jubba* is one outer garment made of two pieces of cloth stitched together with padded lining inside. It can also be a single garment with no padding inside if its outer portion is woollen. The term 'Byzantine *jubba*' can also be translated as 'Levantine *jubba*' since other narrations explicitly ascribe it to the Levant (*Sham*: Syria-Palestine). What is meant by 'Byzantine' is the Byzantine Empire, which ruled the Levant during the time of the Prophet ﷺ. The narrowness of the *jubba's* sleeves was relative to what was considered narrow and tight in that period. Today, the 'Byzantine *jubba*' is commonly worn by Islamic scholars in Syria-Palestine, Yemen, Egypt and elsewhere. Imam al-Bajuri notes that the Prophet ﷺ had worn the Byzantine *jubba* whilst journeying to and from the Battle of Tabuk, and derives from this narration that it is recommended to wear a garment with tight sleeves as a traveler but not as a resident. Allah and His Messenger know best. (AA)

[200] This hadith also indicates that clothes are considered pure by default, even if they are made by disbelievers. (MA)

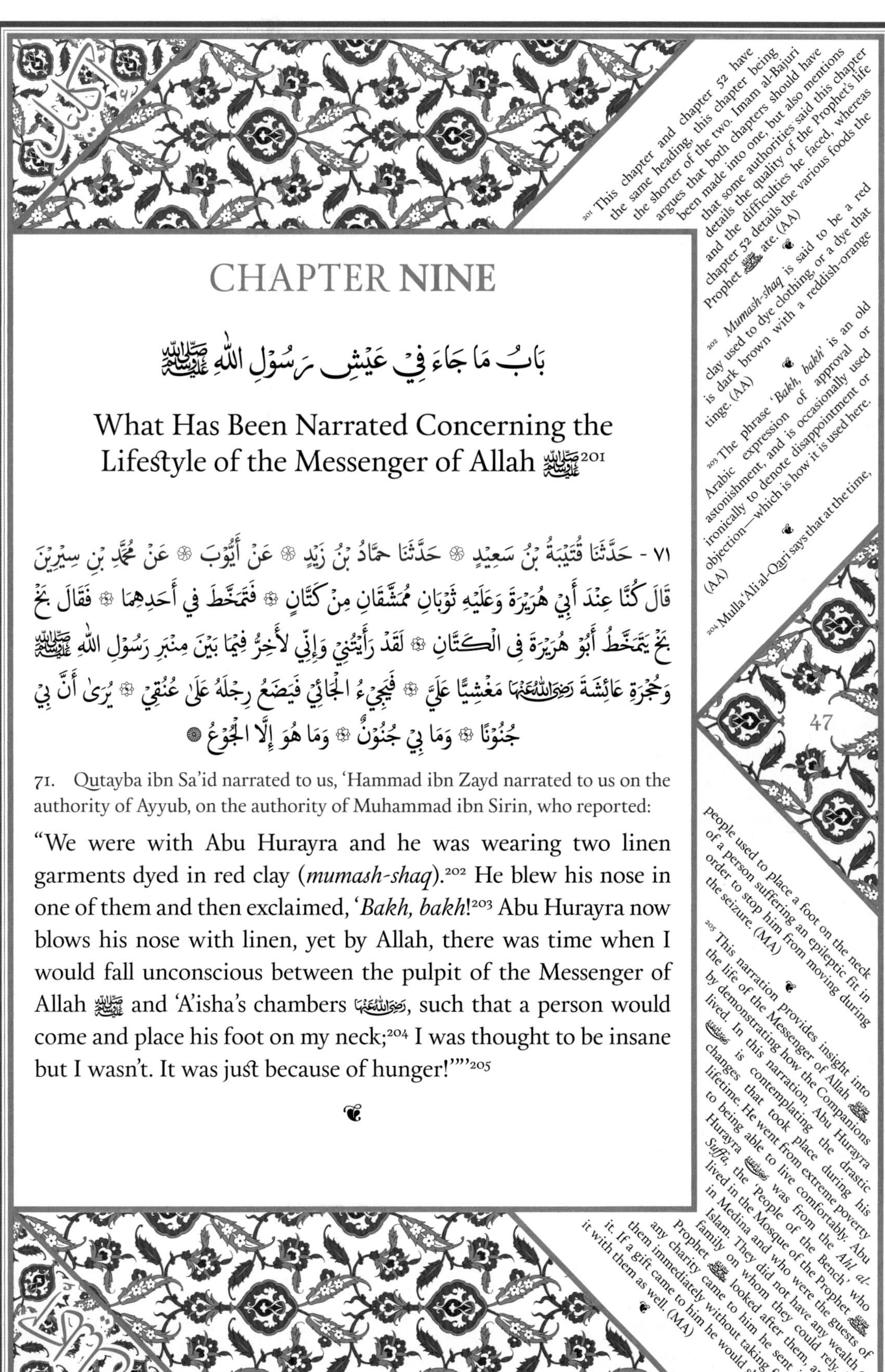

CHAPTER NINE

بَابُ مَا جَاءَ فِي عَيْشِ رَسُولِ اللهِ ﷺ

What Has Been Narrated Concerning the Lifestyle of the Messenger of Allah ﷺ[201]

٧١ - حَدَّثَنَا قُتَيْبَةُ بْنُ سَعِيدٍ ۞ حَدَّثَنَا حَمَّادُ بْنُ زَيْدٍ ۞ عَنْ أَيُّوبَ ۞ عَنْ مُحَمَّدِ بْنِ سِيرِينَ قَالَ كُنَّا عِنْدَ أَبِي هُرَيْرَةَ وَعَلَيْهِ ثَوْبَانِ مُمَشَّقَانِ مِنْ كَتَّانٍ ۞ فَتَمَخَّطَ فِي أَحَدِهِمَا ۞ فَقَالَ بَخْ بَخْ يَتَمَخَّطُ أَبُو هُرَيْرَةَ فِي الْكَتَّانِ ۞ لَقَدْ رَأَيْتُنِي وَإِنِّي لَأَخِرُّ فِيمَا بَيْنَ مِنْبَرِ رَسُولِ اللهِ ﷺ وَحُجْرَةِ عَائِشَةَ رَضِيَ اللهُ عَنْهَا مَغْشِيًّا عَلَيَّ ۞ فَيَجِيءُ الْجَائِي فَيَضَعُ رِجْلَهُ عَلَى عُنُقِي ۞ يُرَى أَنَّ بِي جُنُونًا ۞ وَمَا بِي جُنُونٌ ۞ وَمَا هُوَ إِلَّا الْجُوعُ ۞

71. Qutayba ibn Sa'id narrated to us, 'Hammad ibn Zayd narrated to us on the authority of Ayyub, on the authority of Muhammad ibn Sirin, who reported:

"We were with Abu Hurayra and he was wearing two linen garments dyed in red clay (*mumash-shaq*).[202] He blew his nose in one of them and then exclaimed, '*Bakh, bakh*![203] Abu Hurayra now blows his nose with linen, yet by Allah, there was time when I would fall unconscious between the pulpit of the Messenger of Allah ﷺ and 'A'isha's chambers رضي الله عنها, such that a person would come and place his foot on my neck;[204] I was thought to be insane but I wasn't. It was just because of hunger!'"[205]

201 This chapter and chapter 52 have the same heading, this chapter being the shorter of the two. Imam al-Bajuri argues that both chapters should have been made into one, but also mentions that some authorities said this chapter details the quality of the Prophet's life and the difficulties he faced, whereas chapter 52 details the various foods the Prophet ﷺ ate. (AA)

202 *Mumash-shaq* is said to be a red clay used to dye clothing, or a dye that is dark brown with a reddish-orange tinge. (AA)

203 The phrase '*Bakh, bakh*' is an old Arabic expression of approval or astonishment, and is occasionally used ironically to denote disappointment or objection—which is how it is used here. (AA)

204 Mulla 'Ali al-Qari says that at the time, people used to place a foot on the neck of a person suffering an epileptic fit in order to stop him from moving during the seizure. (MA)

205 This narration provides insight into the life of the Messenger of Allah ﷺ by demonstrating how the Companions lived. In this narration, Abu Hurayra رضي الله عنه is contemplating the drastic changes that took place during his lifetime. He went from extreme poverty to being able to live comfortably. Abu Hurayra رضي الله عنه was from the *Ahl al-Suffa*, the 'People of the Bench,' who lived in the Mosque of the Prophet ﷺ in Medina and who were the guests of Islam. They did not have any wealth or family on whom they could rely. The Prophet ﷺ looked after them, and if any charity came to him he sent it to them immediately without taking from it. If a gift came to him he would share it with them as well. (MA)

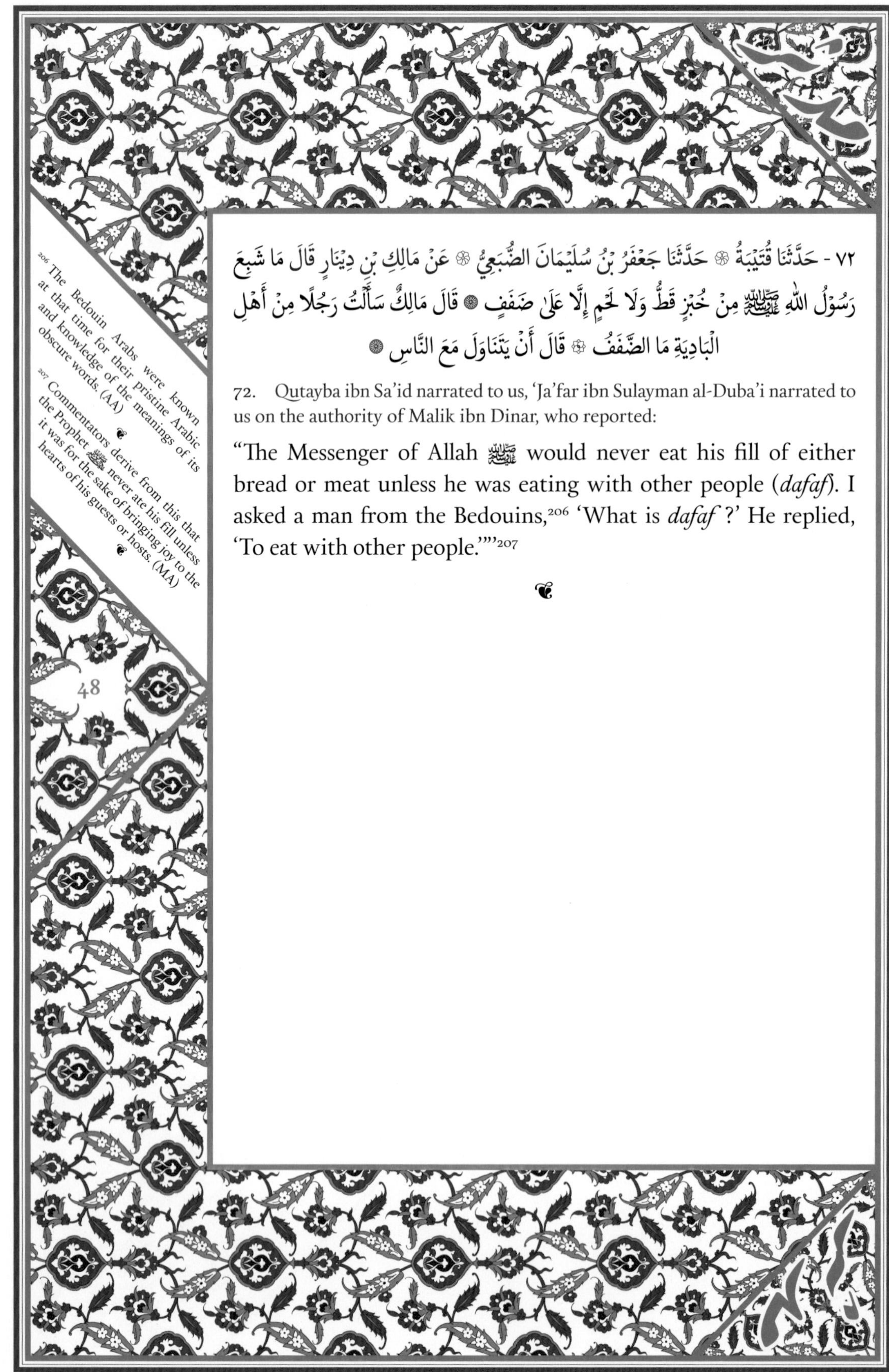

٧٢ - حَدَّثَنَا قُتَيْبَةُ ۞ حَدَّثَنَا جَعْفَرُ بْنُ سُلَيْمَانَ الضُّبَعِيُّ ۞ عَنْ مَالِكِ بْنِ دِينَارٍ قَالَ مَا شَبِعَ رَسُولُ اللهِ ﷺ مِنْ خُبْزٍ قَطُّ وَلَا لَحْمٍ إِلَّا عَلَىٰ ضَفَفٍ ۞ قَالَ مَالِكٌ سَأَلْتُ رَجُلًا مِنْ أَهْلِ الْبَادِيَةِ مَا الضَّفَفُ ۞ قَالَ أَنْ يَتَنَاوَلَ مَعَ النَّاسِ ۞

72. Qutayba ibn Sa'id narrated to us, 'Ja'far ibn Sulayman al-Duba'i narrated to us on the authority of Malik ibn Dinar, who reported:

"The Messenger of Allah ﷺ would never eat his fill of either bread or meat unless he was eating with other people (*dafaf*). I asked a man from the Bedouins,[206] 'What is *dafaf* ?' He replied, 'To eat with other people.'"[207]

[206] The Bedouin Arabs were known at that time for their pristine Arabic and knowledge of the meanings of its obscure words. (AA)

[207] Commentators derive from this that the Prophet ﷺ never ate his fill unless it was for the sake of bringing joy to the hearts of his guests or hosts. (MA)

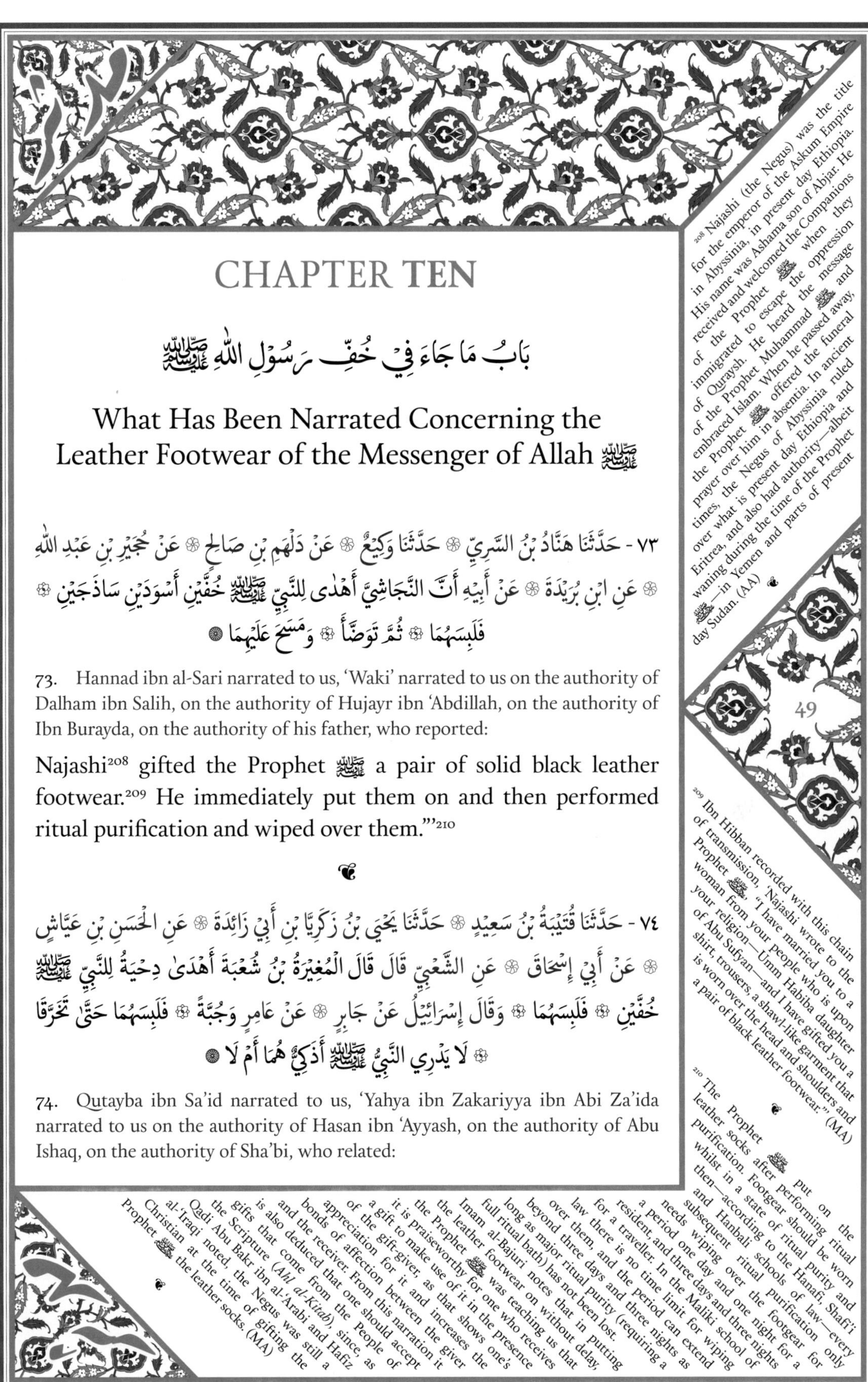

CHAPTER TEN

بَابُ مَا جَاءَ فِي خُفِّ رَسُولِ اللهِ ﷺ

What Has Been Narrated Concerning the Leather Footwear of the Messenger of Allah ﷺ

٧٣ - حَدَّثَنَا هَنَّادُ بْنُ السَّرِيِّ ۞ حَدَّثَنَا وَكِيعٌ ۞ عَنْ دَلْهَمِ بْنِ صَالِحٍ ۞ عَنْ حُجَيْرِ بْنِ عَبْدِ اللهِ ۞ عَنِ ابْنِ بُرَيْدَةَ ۞ عَنْ أَبِيهِ أَنَّ النَّجَاشِيَّ أَهْدَى لِلنَّبِيِّ ﷺ خُفَّيْنِ أَسْوَدَيْنِ سَاذَجَيْنِ ۞ فَلَبِسَهُمَا ۞ ثُمَّ تَوَضَّأَ ۞ وَمَسَحَ عَلَيْهِمَا ۞

73. Hannad ibn al-Sari narrated to us, 'Waki' narrated to us on the authority of Dalham ibn Salih, on the authority of Hujayr ibn 'Abdillah, on the authority of Ibn Burayda, on the authority of his father, who reported:

Najashi[208] gifted the Prophet ﷺ a pair of solid black leather footwear.[209] He immediately put them on and then performed ritual purification and wiped over them.'"[210]

٧٤ - حَدَّثَنَا قُتَيْبَةُ بْنُ سَعِيدٍ ۞ حَدَّثَنَا يَحْيَى بْنُ زَكَرِيَّا بْنِ أَبِي زَائِدَةَ ۞ عَنِ الْحَسَنِ بْنِ عَيَّاشٍ ۞ عَنْ أَبِي إِسْحَاقَ ۞ عَنِ الشَّعْبِيِّ قَالَ قَالَ الْمُغِيرَةُ بْنُ شُعْبَةَ أَهْدَى دِحْيَةُ لِلنَّبِيِّ ﷺ خُفَّيْنِ ۞ فَلَبِسَهُمَا ۞ وَقَالَ إِسْرَائِيلُ عَنْ جَابِرٍ ۞ عَنْ عَامِرٍ وَجُبَّةً ۞ فَلَبِسَهُمَا حَتَّى تَخَرَّقَا ۞ لَا يَدْرِي النَّبِيُّ ﷺ أَذَكِيٌّ هُمَا أَمْ لَا ۞

74. Qutayba ibn Sa'id narrated to us, 'Yahya ibn Zakariyya ibn Abi Za'ida narrated to us on the authority of Hasan ibn 'Ayyash, on the authority of Abu Ishaq, on the authority of Sha'bi, who related:

[208] Najashi (the Negus) was the title for the emperor of the Askum Empire in Abyssinia, in present day Ethiopia. His name was Ashama son of Abjar. He received and welcomed the Companions of the Prophet ﷺ when they immigrated to escape the oppression of Quraysh. He heard the message of the Prophet Muhammad ﷺ and embraced Islam. When he passed away, the Prophet ﷺ offered the funeral prayer over him in absentia. In ancient times, the Negus of Abyssinia ruled over what is present day Ethiopia and Eritrea, and also had authority—albeit waning during the time of the Prophet ﷺ—in Yemen and parts of present day Sudan. (AA)

[209] Ibn Hibban recorded with this chain of transmission, 'Najashi wrote to the Prophet ﷺ, "I have married you to a woman from your people who is upon your religion—Umm Habiba daughter of Abu Sufyan—and I have gifted you a shirt, trousers, a shawl-like garment that is worn over the head and shoulders and a pair of black leather footwear."' (MA)

[210] The Prophet ﷺ put on the leather socks after performing ritual purification. Footgear should be worn whilst in a state of ritual purity and then—according to the Hanafi, Shafi'i and Hanbali schools of law—every subsequent ritual purification only needs wiping over the footgear for a period one day and one night for a resident, and three days and three nights for a traveller. In the Maliki school of law there is no time limit for wiping over them, and the period can extend beyond three days and three nights as long as major ritual purity (requiring a full ritual bath) has not been lost. Imam al-Bajuri notes that in putting the leather footwear on without delay, the Prophet ﷺ was teaching us that it is praiseworthy for one who receives a gift to make use of it in the presence of the gift-giver, as that shows one's appreciation for it and increases the bonds of affection between the giver and the receiver. From this narration it is also deduced that one should accept gifts that come from the People of the Scripture (*Ahl al-Kitab*), since, as Qadi Abu Bakr ibn al-'Arabi and Hafiz al-'Iraqi noted, the Negus was still a Christian at the time of gifting the Prophet ﷺ the leather socks. (MA)

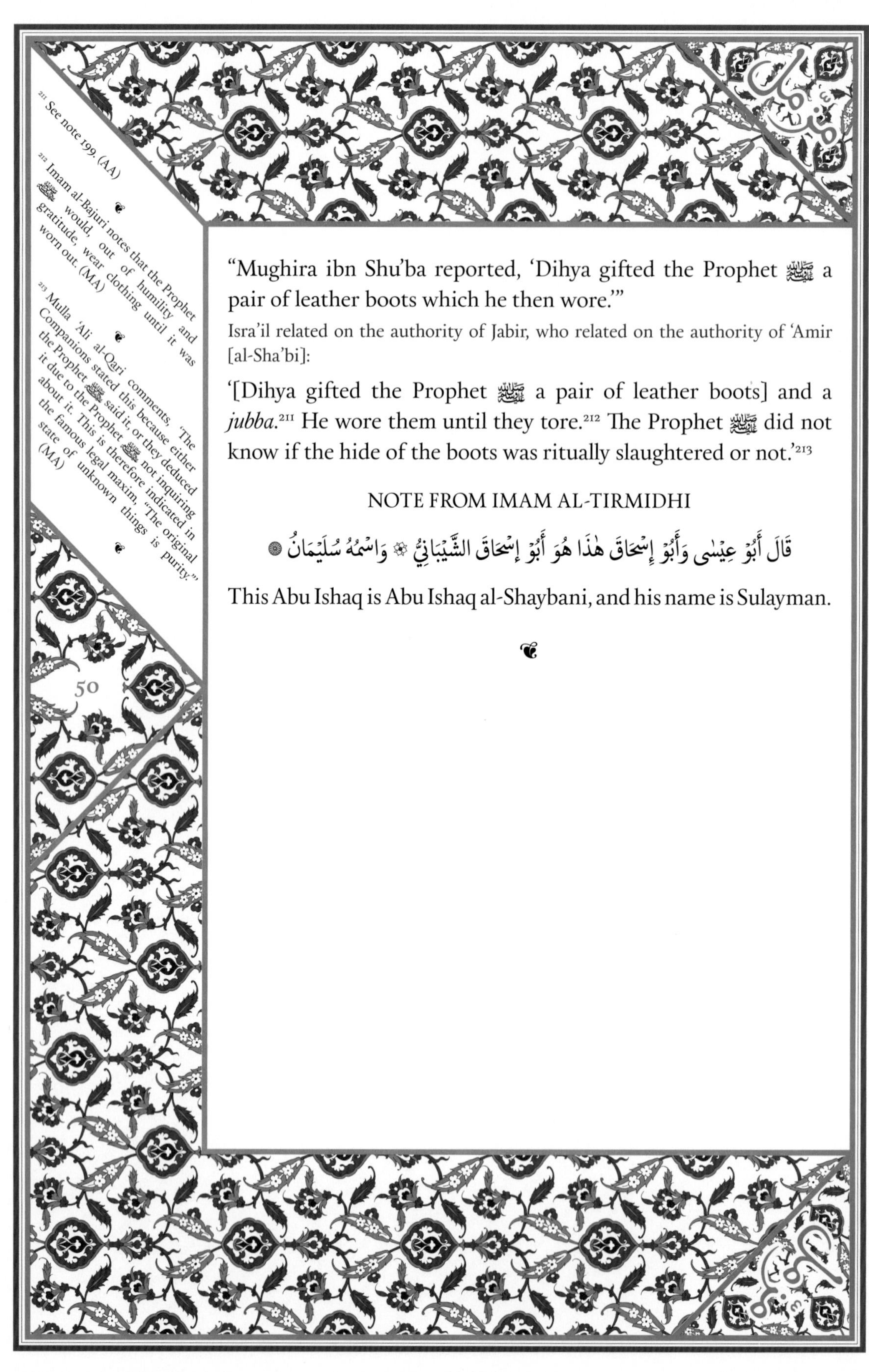

"Mughira ibn Shu'ba reported, 'Dihya gifted the Prophet ﷺ a pair of leather boots which he then wore.'"

Isra'il related on the authority of Jabir, who related on the authority of 'Amir [al-Sha'bi]:

'[Dihya gifted the Prophet ﷺ a pair of leather boots] and a *jubba*.[211] He wore them until they tore.[212] The Prophet ﷺ did not know if the hide of the boots was ritually slaughtered or not.'[213]

NOTE FROM IMAM AL-TIRMIDHI

قَالَ أَبُو عِيسَى وَأَبُو إِسْحَاق هٰذَا هُوَ أَبُو إِسْحَاق الشَّيْبَانِيُّ ۞ وَاسْمُهُ سُلَيْمَانُ ۞

This Abu Ishaq is Abu Ishaq al-Shaybani, and his name is Sulayman.

[211] See note 199. (AA)

[212] Imam al-Bajuri notes that the Prophet ﷺ would, out of humility and gratitude, wear clothing until it was worn out. (MA)

[213] Mulla 'Ali al-Qari comments, 'The Companions stated this because either the Prophet ﷺ said it, or they deduced it due to the Prophet ﷺ not inquiring about it. This is therefore indicated in the famous legal maxim, "The original state of unknown things is purity."' (MA)

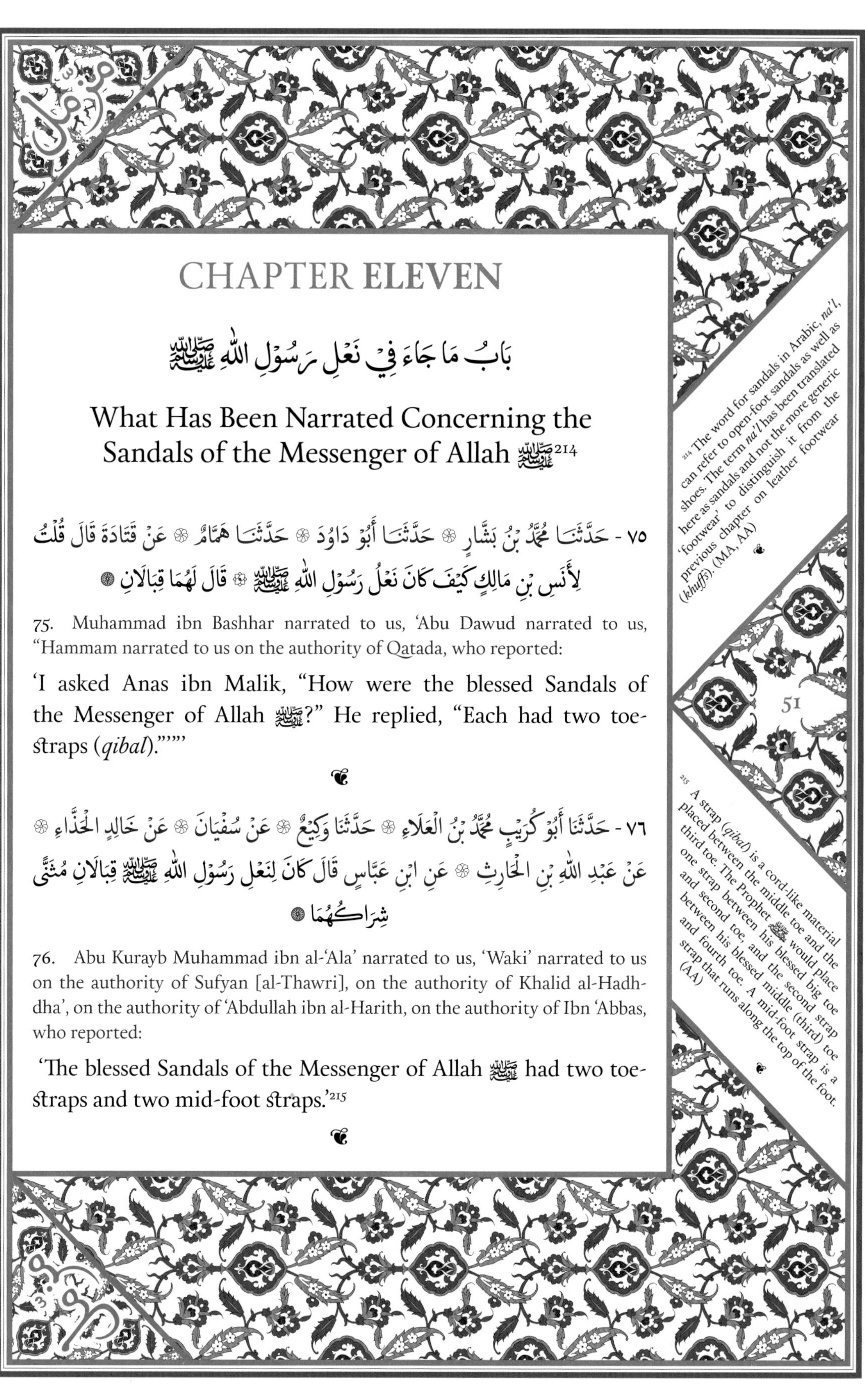

CHAPTER ELEVEN

بَابُ مَا جَاءَ فِي نَعْلِ رَسُولِ اللهِ ﷺ

What Has Been Narrated Concerning the Sandals of the Messenger of Allah ﷺ[214]

٧٥ - حَدَّثَنَا مُحَمَّدُ بْنُ بَشَّارٍ ❁ حَدَّثَنَا أَبُو دَاوُدَ ❁ حَدَّثَنَا هَمَّامٌ ❁ عَنْ قَتَادَةَ قَالَ قُلْتُ لِأَنَسِ بْنِ مَالِكٍ كَيْفَ كَانَ نَعْلُ رَسُولِ اللهِ ﷺ ❁ قَالَ لَهُمَا قِبَالَانِ ❁

75. Muhammad ibn Bashhar narrated to us, 'Abu Dawud narrated to us, "Hammam narrated to us on the authority of Qatada, who reported:

'I asked Anas ibn Malik, "How were the blessed Sandals of the Messenger of Allah ﷺ?" He replied, "Each had two toe-straps (*qibal*).""'

❦

٧٦ - حَدَّثَنَا أَبُو كُرَيْبٍ مُحَمَّدُ بْنُ الْعَلَاءِ ❁ حَدَّثَنَا وَكِيعٌ ❁ عَنْ سُفْيَانَ ❁ عَنْ خَالِدٍ الْحَذَّاءِ ❁ عَنْ عَبْدِ اللهِ بْنِ الْحَارِثِ ❁ عَنِ ابْنِ عَبَّاسٍ قَالَ كَانَ لِنَعْلِ رَسُولِ اللهِ ﷺ قِبَالَانِ مُثَنًّى شِرَاكُهُمَا ❁

76. Abu Kurayb Muhammad ibn al-'Ala' narrated to us, 'Waki' narrated to us on the authority of Sufyan [al-Thawri], on the authority of Khalid al-Hadhdha', on the authority of 'Abdullah ibn al-Harith, on the authority of Ibn 'Abbas, who reported:

'The blessed Sandals of the Messenger of Allah ﷺ had two toe-straps and two mid-foot straps.'[215]

❦

[214] The word for sandals in Arabic, *na'l*, can refer to open-foot sandals as well as shoes. The term *na'l* has been translated here as sandals and not the more generic 'footwear' to distinguish it from the previous chapter on leather footwear (*khuffs*). (MA, AA)

❦

[215] A strap (*qibal*) is a cord-like material placed between the middle toe and the third toe. The Prophet ﷺ would place one strap between his blessed big toe and second toe, and the second strap between his blessed middle (third) toe and fourth toe. A mid-foot strap is a strap that runs along the top of the foot. (AA)

❦

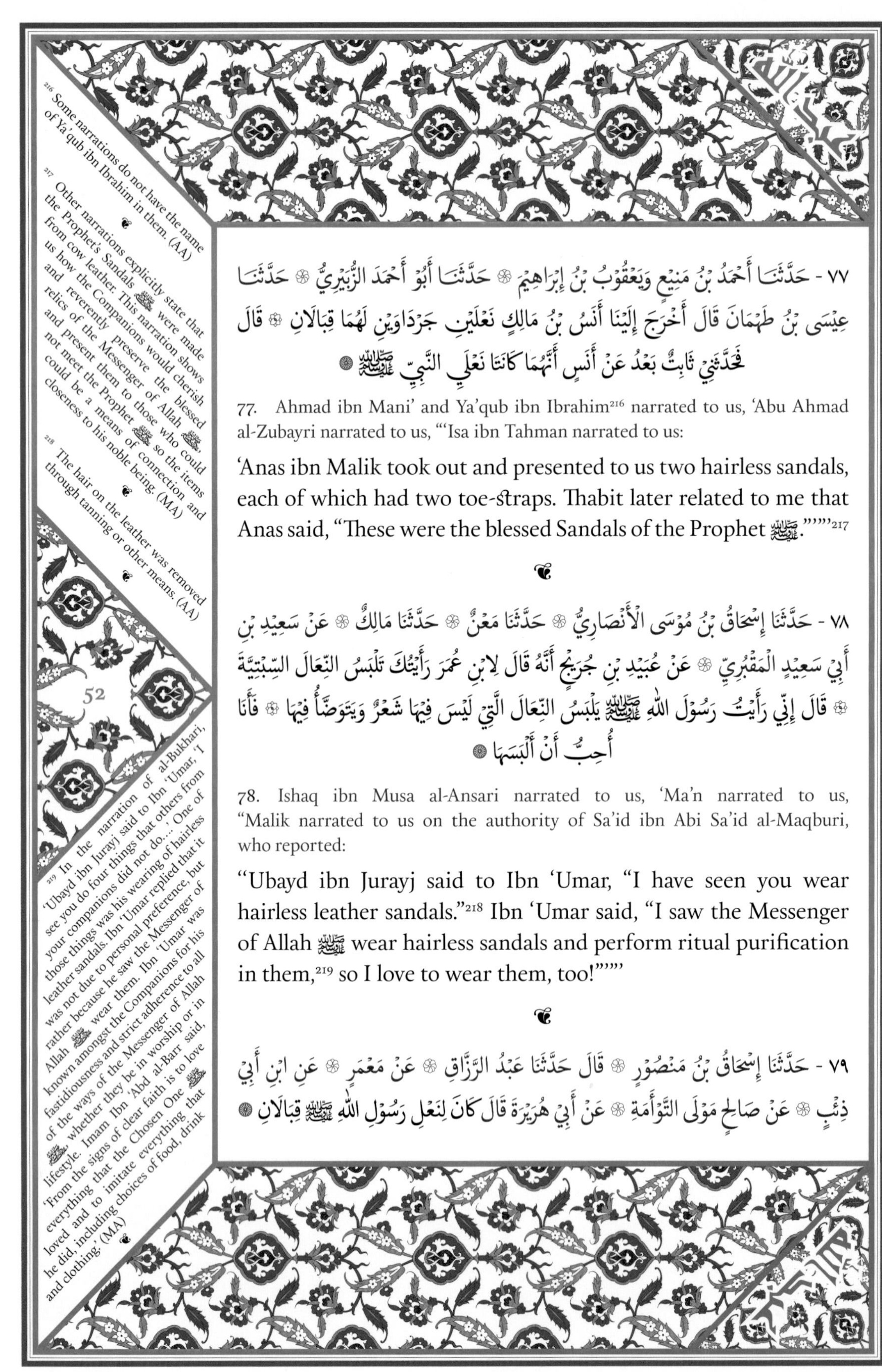

٧٧ - حَدَّثَنَا أَحْمَدُ بْنُ مَنِيعٍ وَيَعْقُوبُ بْنُ إِبْرَاهِيمَ ۞ حَدَّثَنَا أَبُو أَحْمَدَ الزُّبَيْرِيُّ ۞ حَدَّثَنَا عِيسَى بْنُ طَهْمَانَ قَالَ أَخْرَجَ إِلَيْنَا أَنَسُ بْنُ مَالِكٍ نَعْلَيْنِ جَرْدَاوَيْنِ لَهُمَا قِبَالَانِ ۞ قَالَ فَحَدَّثَنِي ثَابِتٌ بَعْدُ عَنْ أَنَسٍ أَنَّهُمَا كَانَتَا نَعْلَيِ النَّبِيِّ ﷺ ۞

77. Ahmad ibn Mani' and Ya'qub ibn Ibrahim[216] narrated to us, 'Abu Ahmad al-Zubayri narrated to us, "'Isa ibn Tahman narrated to us:

'Anas ibn Malik took out and presented to us two hairless sandals, each of which had two toe-straps. Thabit later related to me that Anas said, "These were the blessed Sandals of the Prophet ﷺ."'"'[217]

❦

٧٨ - حَدَّثَنَا إِسْحَاقُ بْنُ مُوسَى الْأَنْصَارِيُّ ۞ حَدَّثَنَا مَعْنٌ ۞ حَدَّثَنَا مَالِكٌ ۞ عَنْ سَعِيدِ بْنِ أَبِي سَعِيدٍ الْمَقْبُرِيِّ ۞ عَنْ عُبَيْدِ بْنِ جُرَيْجٍ أَنَّهُ قَالَ لِابْنِ عُمَرَ رَأَيْتُكَ تَلْبَسُ النِّعَالَ السِّبْتِيَّةَ ۞ قَالَ إِنِّي رَأَيْتُ رَسُولَ اللهِ ﷺ يَلْبَسُ النِّعَالَ الَّتِي لَيْسَ فِيهَا شَعَرٌ وَيَتَوَضَّأُ فِيهَا ۞ فَأَنَا أُحِبُّ أَنْ أَلْبَسَهَا ۞

78. Ishaq ibn Musa al-Ansari narrated to us, 'Ma'n narrated to us, "Malik narrated to us on the authority of Sa'id ibn Abi Sa'id al-Maqburi, who reported:

"Ubayd ibn Jurayj said to Ibn 'Umar, "I have seen you wear hairless leather sandals."[218] Ibn 'Umar said, "I saw the Messenger of Allah ﷺ wear hairless sandals and perform ritual purification in them,[219] so I love to wear them, too!"""'

❦

٧٩ - حَدَّثَنَا إِسْحَاقُ بْنُ مَنْصُورٍ ۞ قَالَ حَدَّثَنَا عَبْدُ الرَّزَّاقِ ۞ عَنْ مَعْمَرٍ ۞ عَنِ ابْنِ أَبِي ذِئْبٍ ۞ عَنْ صَالِحٍ مَوْلَى التَّوْأَمَةِ ۞ عَنْ أَبِي هُرَيْرَةَ قَالَ كَانَ لِنَعْلِ رَسُولِ اللهِ ﷺ قِبَالَانِ ۞

[216] Some narrations do not have the name of Ya'qub ibn Ibrahim in them. (AA)

[217] Other narrations explicitly state that the Prophet's Sandals ﷺ were made from cow leather. This narration shows us how the Companions would cherish and reverently preserve the blessed relics of the Messenger of Allah ﷺ, and present them to those who could not meet the Prophet ﷺ so the items could be a means of connection and closeness to his noble being. (MA)

[218] The hair on the leather was removed through tanning or other means. (AA)

[219] In the narration of al-Bukhari, 'Ubayd ibn Jurayj said to Ibn 'Umar, 'I see you do four things that others from your companions did not do....' One of those things was his wearing of hairless leather sandals. Ibn 'Umar replied that it was not due to personal preference, but rather because he saw the Messenger of Allah ﷺ wear them. Ibn 'Umar was known amongst the Companions for his fastidiousness and strict adherence to all of the ways of the Messenger of Allah ﷺ, whether they be in worship or in lifestyle. Imam Ibn 'Abd al-Barr said, 'From the signs of clear faith is to love everything that the Chosen One ﷺ loved and to imitate everything that he did, including choices of food, drink and clothing.' (MA)

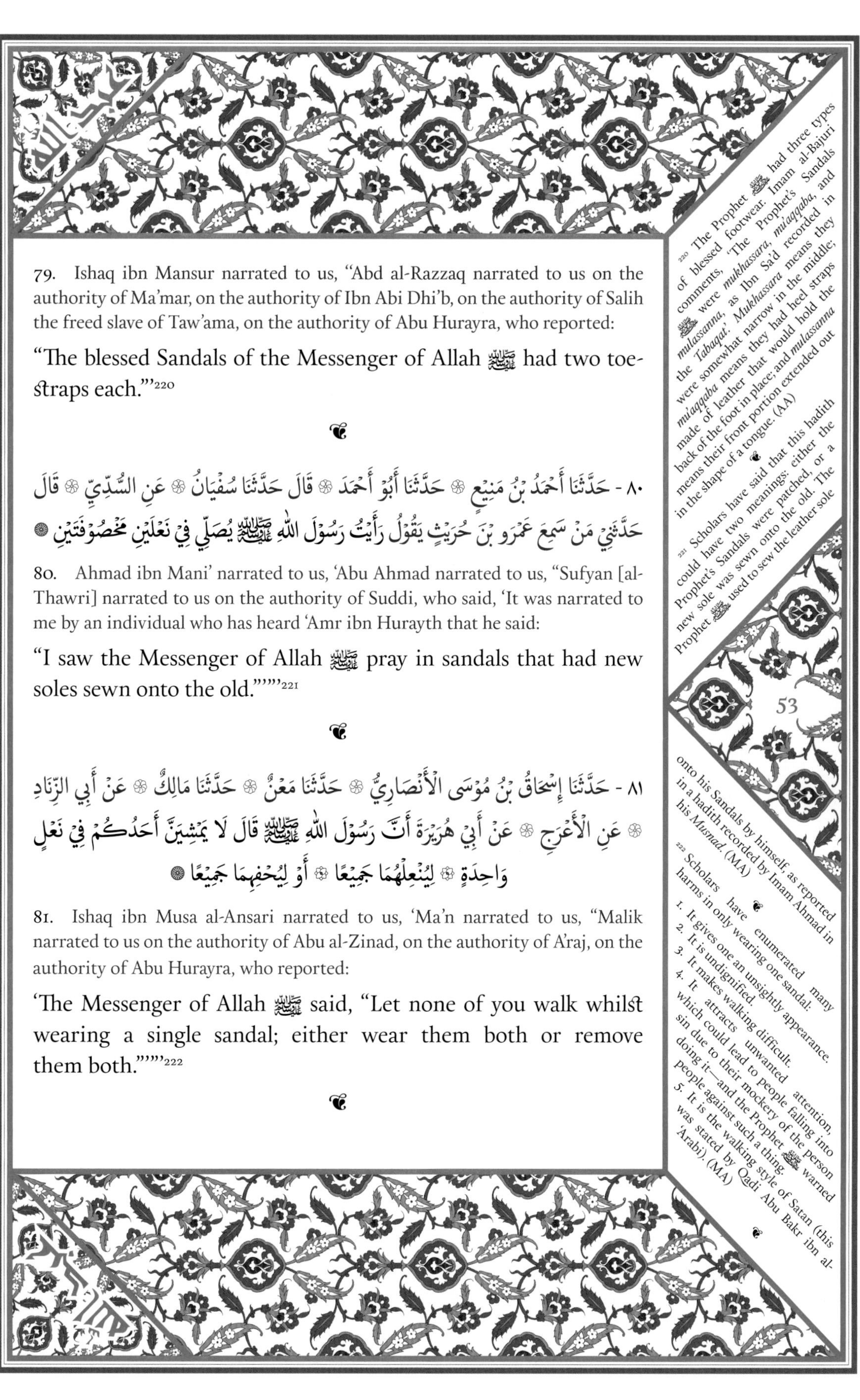

79. Ishaq ibn Mansur narrated to us, "Abd al-Razzaq narrated to us on the authority of Ma'mar, on the authority of Ibn Abi Dhi'b, on the authority of Salih the freed slave of Taw'ama, on the authority of Abu Hurayra, who reported:

"The blessed Sandals of the Messenger of Allah ﷺ had two toe-straps each."'[220]

❦

٨٠ - حَدَّثَنَا أَحْمَدُ بْنُ مَنِيعٍ ۞ حَدَّثَنَا أَبُو أَحْمَدَ ۞ قَالَ حَدَّثَنَا سُفْيَانُ ۞ عَنِ السُّدِّيِّ ۞ قَالَ حَدَّثَنِي مَنْ سَمِعَ عَمْرَو بْنَ حُرَيْثٍ يَقُولُ رَأَيْتُ رَسُولَ اللهِ ﷺ يُصَلِّي فِي نَعْلَيْنِ مَخْصُوفَتَيْنِ ۞

80. Ahmad ibn Mani' narrated to us, 'Abu Ahmad narrated to us, "Sufyan [al-Thawri] narrated to us on the authority of Suddi, who said, 'It was narrated to me by an individual who has heard 'Amr ibn Hurayth that he said:

"I saw the Messenger of Allah ﷺ pray in sandals that had new soles sewn onto the old."'"'[221]

❦

٨١ - حَدَّثَنَا إِسْحَاقُ بْنُ مُوسَى الْأَنْصَارِيُّ ۞ حَدَّثَنَا مَعْنٌ ۞ حَدَّثَنَا مَالِكٌ ۞ عَنْ أَبِي الزِّنَادِ ۞ عَنِ الْأَعْرَجِ ۞ عَنْ أَبِي هُرَيْرَةَ أَنَّ رَسُولَ اللهِ ﷺ قَالَ لَا يَمْشِيَنَّ أَحَدُكُمْ فِي نَعْلٍ وَاحِدَةٍ ۞ لِيُنْعِلْهُمَا جَمِيعًا ۞ أَوْ لِيُحْفِهِمَا جَمِيعًا ۞

81. Ishaq ibn Musa al-Ansari narrated to us, 'Ma'n narrated to us, "Malik narrated to us on the authority of Abu al-Zinad, on the authority of A'raj, on the authority of Abu Hurayra, who reported:

'The Messenger of Allah ﷺ said, "Let none of you walk whilst wearing a single sandal; either wear them both or remove them both."'"'[222]

❦

[220] The Prophet ﷺ had three types of blessed footwear. Imam al-Bajuri comments, 'The Prophet's ﷺ Sandals were *mukhassara*, *mu'aqqaba*, and *mulassanna*, as Ibn Sa'd recorded in the *Tabaqat*.' *Mukhassara* means they were somewhat narrow in the middle; *mu'aqqaba* means they had heel straps made of leather that would hold the back of the foot in place; and *mulassanna* means their front portion extended out in the shape of a tongue. (AA)

❦

[221] Scholars have said that this hadith could have two meanings: either the Prophet's Sandals were patched, or a new sole was sewn onto the old. The Prophet ﷺ used to sew the leather sole onto his Sandals by himself, as reported in a hadith recorded by Imam Ahmad in his *Musnad*. (MA)

❦

[222] Scholars have enumerated many harms in only wearing one sandal:
1. It gives one an unsightly appearance.
2. It is undignified.
3. It makes walking difficult.
4. It attracts unwanted attention, which could lead to people falling into sin due to their mockery of the person doing it—and the Prophet ﷺ warned people against such a thing.
5. It is the walking style of Satan (this was stated by Qadi Abu Bakr ibn al-'Arabi). (MA)

❦

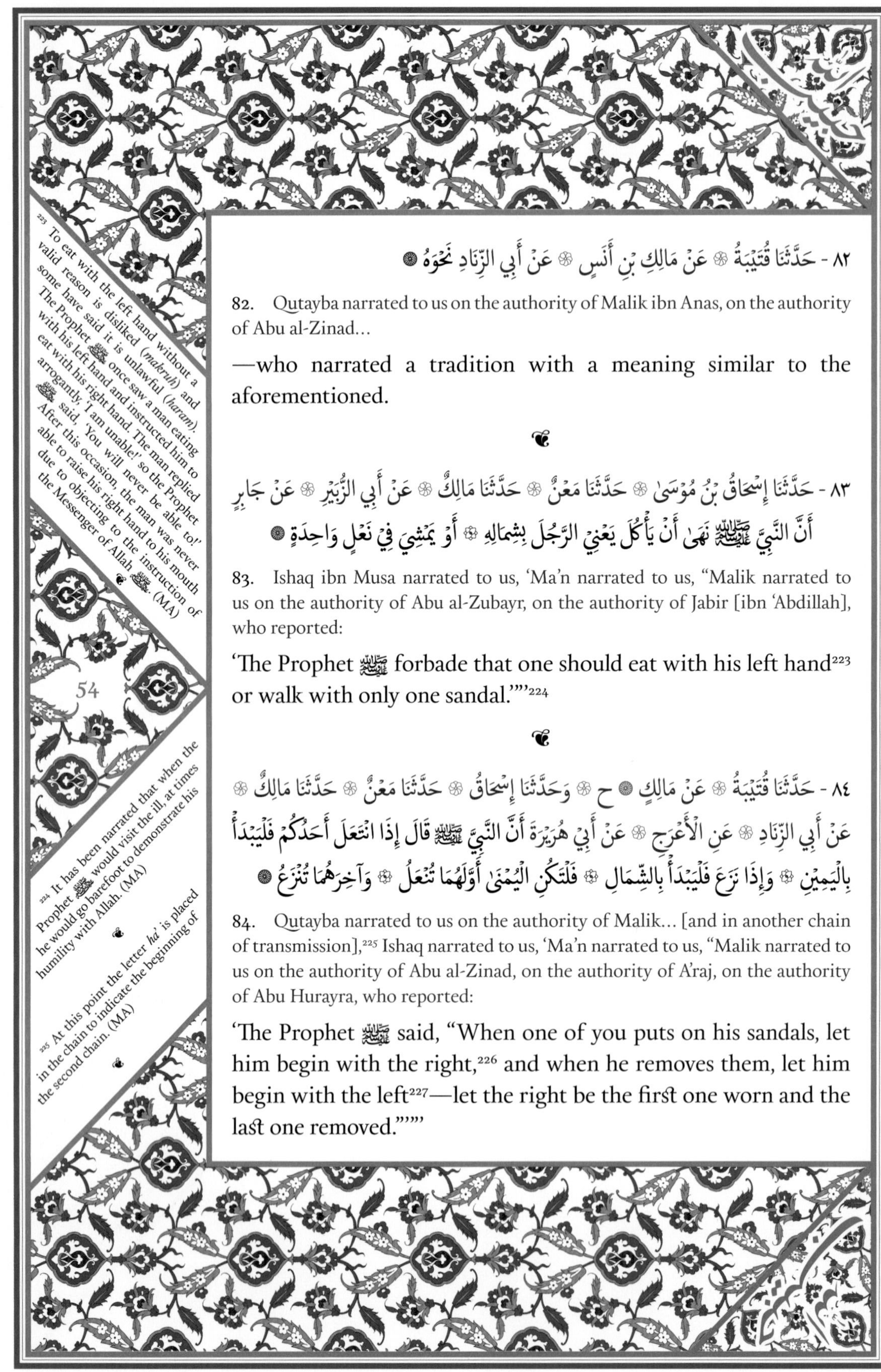

٨٢ - حَدَّثَنَا قُتَيْبَةُ ۞ عَنْ مَالِكِ بْنِ أَنَسٍ ۞ عَنْ أَبِي الزِّنَادِ نَحْوَهُ ۞

82. Qutayba narrated to us on the authority of Malik ibn Anas, on the authority of Abu al-Zinad...

—who narrated a tradition with a meaning similar to the aforementioned.

٨٣ - حَدَّثَنَا إِسْحَاقُ بْنُ مُوسَىٰ ۞ حَدَّثَنَا مَعْنٌ ۞ حَدَّثَنَا مَالِكٌ ۞ عَنْ أَبِي الزُّبَيْرِ ۞ عَنْ جَابِرٍ
أَنَّ النَّبِيَّ ﷺ نَهَى أَنْ يَأْكُلَ يَعْنِي الرَّجُلَ بِشِمَالِهِ ۞ أَوْ يَمْشِيَ فِي نَعْلٍ وَاحِدَةٍ ۞

83. Ishaq ibn Musa narrated to us, 'Ma'n narrated to us, "Malik narrated to us on the authority of Abu al-Zubayr, on the authority of Jabir [ibn 'Abdillah], who reported:

'The Prophet ﷺ forbade that one should eat with his left hand[223] or walk with only one sandal.'"'[224]

٨٤ - حَدَّثَنَا قُتَيْبَةُ ۞ عَنْ مَالِكٍ ۞ ح ۞ وَحَدَّثَنَا إِسْحَاقُ ۞ حَدَّثَنَا مَعْنٌ ۞ حَدَّثَنَا مَالِكٌ ۞
عَنْ أَبِي الزِّنَادِ ۞ عَنِ الْأَعْرَجِ ۞ عَنْ أَبِي هُرَيْرَةَ أَنَّ النَّبِيَّ ﷺ قَالَ إِذَا انْتَعَلَ أَحَدُكُمْ فَلْيَبْدَأْ
بِالْيَمِينِ ۞ وَإِذَا نَزَعَ فَلْيَبْدَأْ بِالشِّمَالِ ۞ فَلْتَكُنِ الْيُمْنَى أَوَّلَهُمَا تُنْعَلُ ۞ وَآخِرَهُمَا تُنْزَعُ ۞

84. Qutayba narrated to us on the authority of Malik... [and in another chain of transmission],[225] Ishaq narrated to us, 'Ma'n narrated to us, "Malik narrated to us on the authority of Abu al-Zinad, on the authority of A'raj, on the authority of Abu Hurayra, who reported:

'The Prophet ﷺ said, "When one of you puts on his sandals, let him begin with the right,[226] and when he removes them, let him begin with the left[227]—let the right be the first one worn and the last one removed."'"'

[223] To eat with the left hand without a valid reason is disliked (*makruh*) and some have said it is unlawful (*haram*). The Prophet ﷺ once saw a man eating with his left hand and instructed him to eat with his right hand. The man replied arrogantly, 'I am unable!' so the Prophet ﷺ said, 'You will never be able to!' After this occasion, the man was never able to raise his right hand to his mouth due to objecting to the instruction of the Messenger of Allah ﷺ. (MA)

[224] It has been narrated that when the Prophet ﷺ would visit the ill, at times he would go barefoot to demonstrate his humility with Allah. (MA)

[225] At this point the letter *ha* is placed in the chain to indicate the beginning of the second chain. (MA)

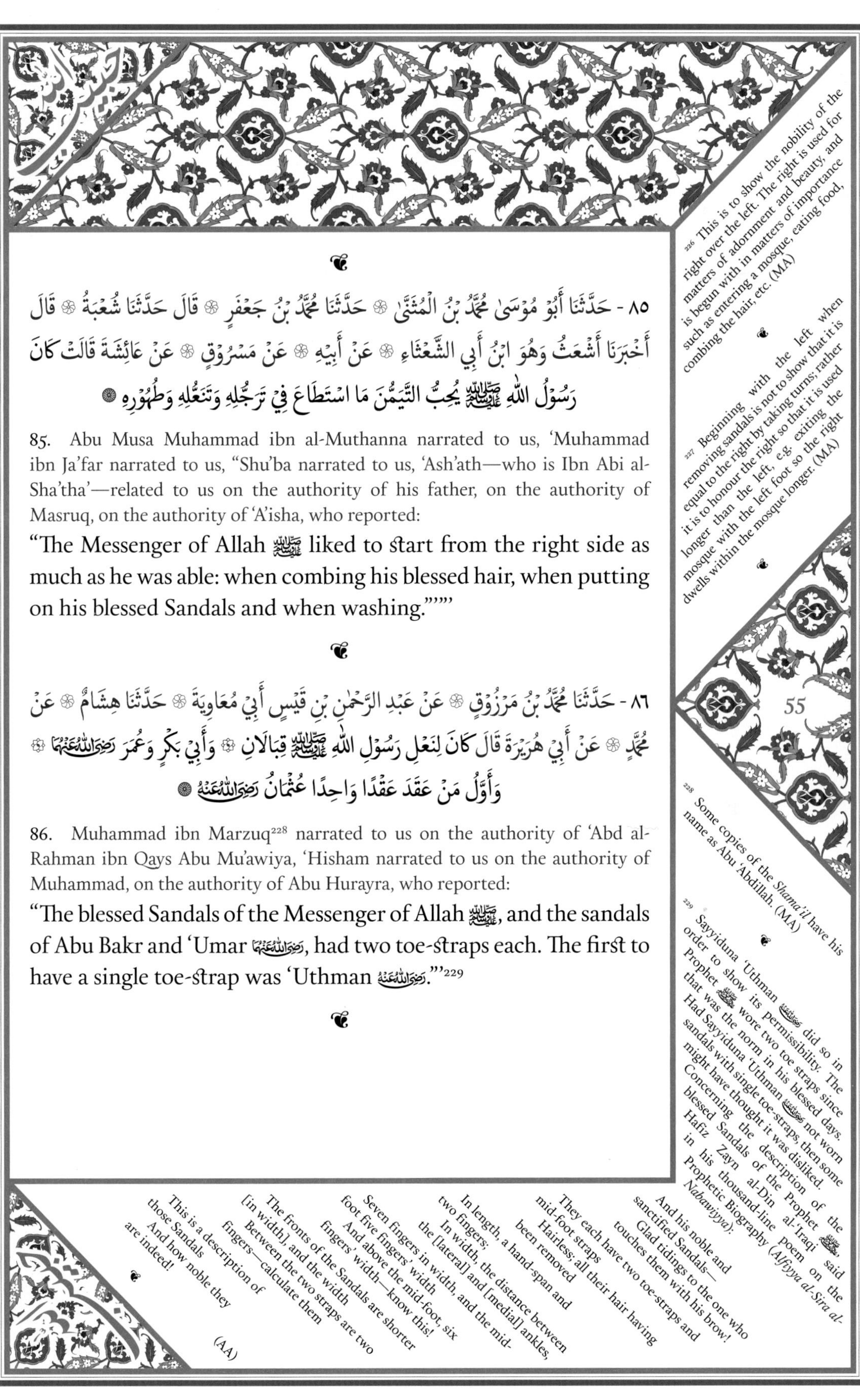

٨٥ - حَدَّثَنَا أَبُو مُوسَىٰ مُحَمَّدُ بْنُ الْمُثَنَّىٰ ۞ حَدَّثَنَا مُحَمَّدُ بْنُ جَعْفَرٍ ۞ قَالَ حَدَّثَنَا شُعْبَةُ ۞ قَالَ أَخْبَرَنَا أَشْعَثُ وَهُوَ ابْنُ أَبِي الشَّعْثَاءِ ۞ عَنْ أَبِيهِ ۞ عَنْ مَسْرُوقٍ ۞ عَنْ عَائِشَةَ قَالَتْ كَانَ رَسُولُ اللهِ ﷺ يُحِبُّ التَّيَمُّنَ مَا اسْتَطَاعَ فِي تَرَجُّلِهِ وَتَنَعُّلِهِ وَطُهُورِهِ ۞

85. Abu Musa Muhammad ibn al-Muthanna narrated to us, 'Muhammad ibn Ja'far narrated to us, "Shu'ba narrated to us, 'Ash'ath—who is Ibn Abi al-Sha'tha'—related to us on the authority of his father, on the authority of Masruq, on the authority of 'A'isha, who reported:

"The Messenger of Allah ﷺ liked to start from the right side as much as he was able: when combing his blessed hair, when putting on his blessed Sandals and when washing."'"'

٨٦ - حَدَّثَنَا مُحَمَّدُ بْنُ مَرْزُوقٍ ۞ عَنْ عَبْدِ الرَّحْمَٰنِ بْنِ قَيْسٍ أَبِي مُعَاوِيَةَ ۞ حَدَّثَنَا هِشَامٌ ۞ عَنْ مُحَمَّدٍ ۞ عَنْ أَبِي هُرَيْرَةَ قَالَ كَانَ لِنَعْلِ رَسُولِ اللهِ ﷺ قِبَالَانِ ۞ وَأَبِي بَكْرٍ وَعُمَرَ رَضِيَ اللهُ عَنْهُمَا ۞ وَأَوَّلُ مَنْ عَقَدَ عَقْدًا وَاحِدًا عُثْمَانُ رَضِيَ اللهُ عَنْهُ ۞

86. Muhammad ibn Marzuq[228] narrated to us on the authority of 'Abd al-Rahman ibn Qays Abu Mu'awiya, 'Hisham narrated to us on the authority of Muhammad, on the authority of Abu Hurayra, who reported:

"The blessed Sandals of the Messenger of Allah ﷺ, and the sandals of Abu Bakr and 'Umar رضي الله عنهما, had two toe-straps each. The first to have a single toe-strap was 'Uthman رضي الله عنه."'[229]

[226] This is to show the nobility of the right over the left. The right is used for matters of adornment and beauty, and is begun with in matters of importance such as entering a mosque, eating food, combing the hair, etc. (MA)

[227] Beginning with the left when removing sandals is not to show that it is equal to the right by taking turns; rather it is to honour the right so that it is used longer than the left, e.g. exiting the mosque with the left foot so the right dwells within the mosque longer. (MA)

[228] Some copies of the *Shama'il* have his name as Abu 'Abdillah. (MA)

[229] Sayyiduna 'Uthman رضي الله عنه did so in order to show its permissibility. The Prophet ﷺ wore two toe straps since that was the norm in his blessed days. Had Sayyiduna 'Uthman رضي الله عنه not worn sandals with single toe-straps, then some might have thought it was disliked. Concerning the description of the blessed Sandals of the Prophet ﷺ, Hafiz Zayn al-Din al-'Iraqi said in his thousand-line poem on the Prophetic Biography (*Alfiyya al-Sira al-Nabawiyya*):

And his noble and sanctified Sandals—
Glad tidings to the one who touches them with his brow!
They each have two toe-straps and mid-foot straps
Hairless; all their hair having been removed
In length, a hand-span and two fingers;
In width, the distance between the [lateral] and [medial] ankles,
Seven fingers in width, and the mid-foot five fingers' width
And above the mid-foot, six fingers' width—know this!
The fronts of the Sandals are shorter [in width], and the width
Between the two straps are two fingers—calculate them
This is a description of those Sandals
And how noble they are indeed!

(AA)

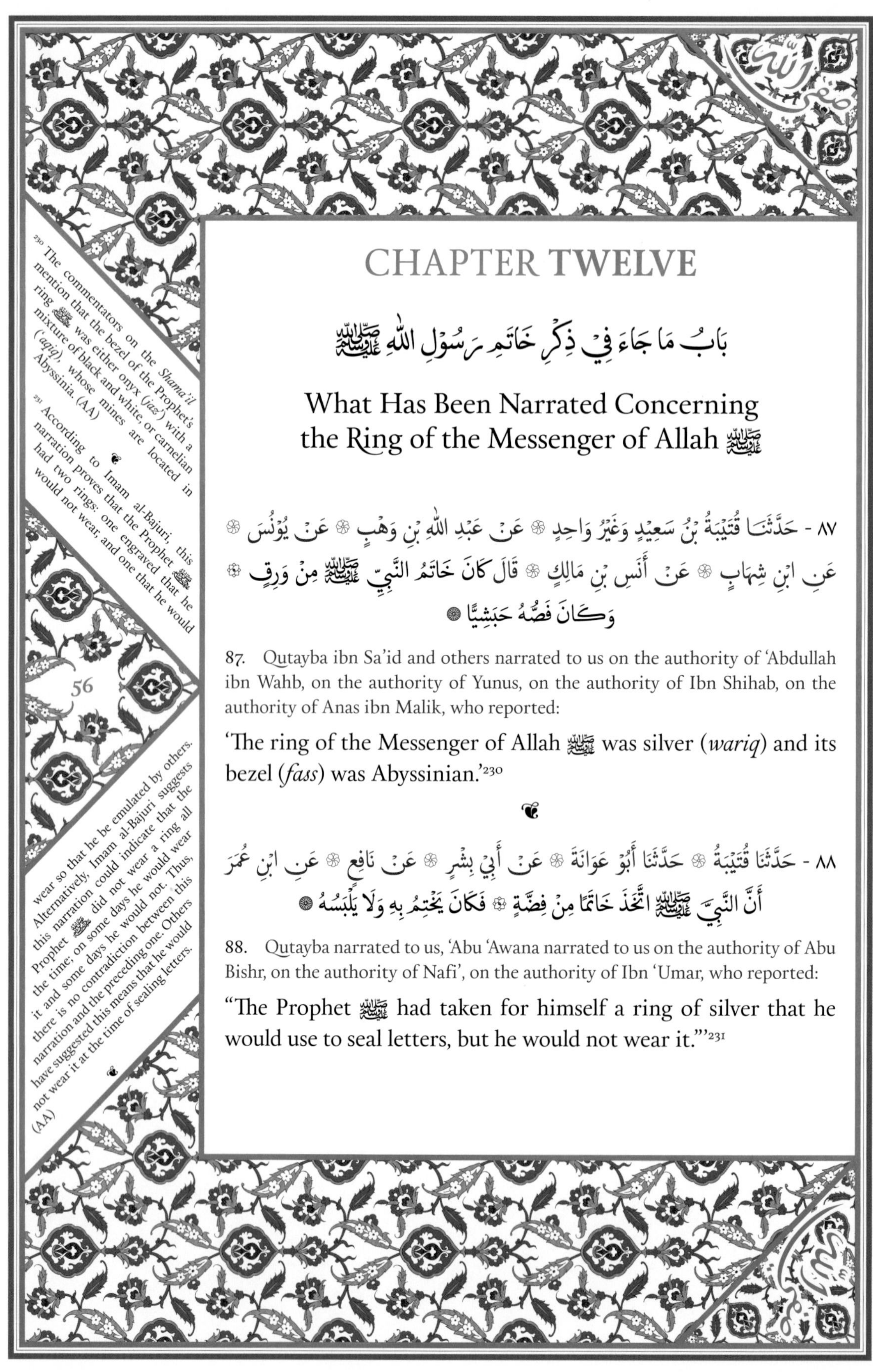

CHAPTER TWELVE

بَابُ مَا جَاءَ فِي ذِكْرِ خَاتَمِ رَسُولِ اللهِ ﷺ

What Has Been Narrated Concerning the Ring of the Messenger of Allah ﷺ

٨٧ - حَدَّثَنَا قُتَيْبَةُ بْنُ سَعِيدٍ وَغَيْرُ وَاحِدٍ ۞ عَنْ عَبْدِ اللهِ بْنِ وَهْبٍ ۞ عَنْ يُونُسَ ۞ عَنِ ابْنِ شِهَابٍ ۞ عَنْ أَنَسِ بْنِ مَالِكٍ ۞ قَالَ كَانَ خَاتَمُ النَّبِيِّ ﷺ مِنْ وَرِقٍ ۞ وَكَانَ فَصُّهُ حَبَشِيًّا ۞

87. Qutayba ibn Sa'id and others narrated to us on the authority of 'Abdullah ibn Wahb, on the authority of Yunus, on the authority of Ibn Shihab, on the authority of Anas ibn Malik, who reported:

'The ring of the Messenger of Allah ﷺ was silver (*wariq*) and its bezel (*fass*) was Abyssinian.'[230]

٨٨ - حَدَّثَنَا قُتَيْبَةُ ۞ حَدَّثَنَا أَبُو عَوَانَةَ ۞ عَنْ أَبِي بِشْرٍ ۞ عَنْ نَافِعٍ ۞ عَنِ ابْنِ عُمَرَ أَنَّ النَّبِيَّ ﷺ اتَّخَذَ خَاتَمًا مِنْ فِضَّةٍ ۞ فَكَانَ يَخْتِمُ بِهِ وَلَا يَلْبَسُهُ ۞

88. Qutayba narrated to us, 'Abu 'Awana narrated to us on the authority of Abu Bishr, on the authority of Nafi', on the authority of Ibn 'Umar, who reported:

"The Prophet ﷺ had taken for himself a ring of silver that he would use to seal letters, but he would not wear it."'[231]

[230] The commentators on the *Shama'il* mention that the bezel of the Prophet's ring ﷺ was either onyx (*jaz'*) with a mixture of black and white, or carnelian (*'aqiq*), whose mines are located in Abyssinia. (AA)

[231] According to Imam al-Bajuri, this narration proves that the Prophet ﷺ had two rings: one engraved that he would not wear, and one that he would wear so that he be emulated by others. Alternatively, Imam al-Bajuri suggests this narration could indicate that the Prophet ﷺ did not wear a ring all the time; on some days he would wear it and some days he would not. Thus, there is no contradiction between this narration and the preceding one. Others have suggested this means that he would not wear it at the time of sealing letters. (AA)

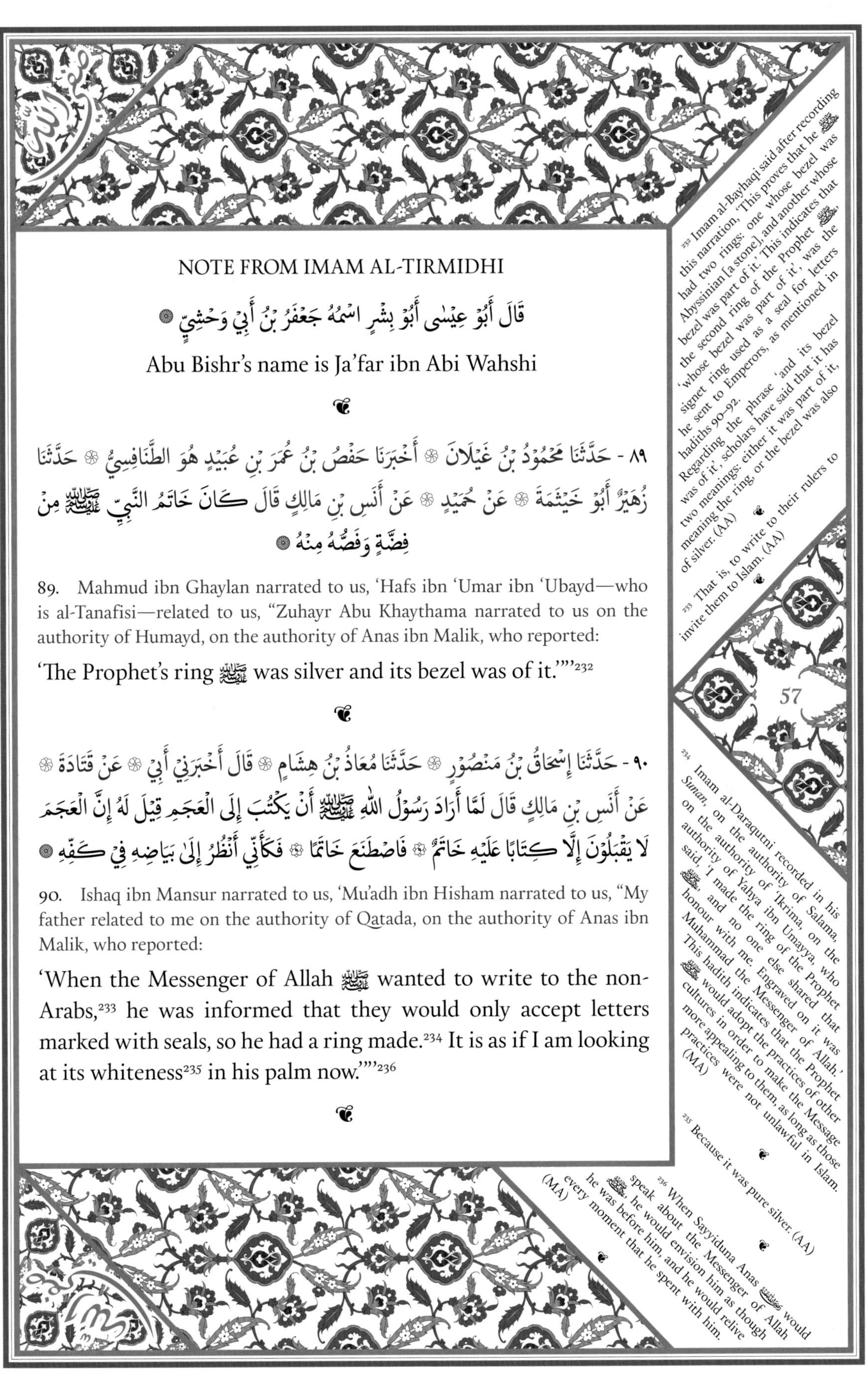

NOTE FROM IMAM AL-TIRMIDHI

قَالَ أَبُو عِيسَى أَبُو بِشْرٍ اسْمُهُ جَعْفَرُ بْنُ أَبِي وَحْشِيٍّ

Abu Bishr's name is Ja'far ibn Abi Wahshi

٨٩ - حَدَّثَنَا مَحْمُودُ بْنُ غَيْلَانَ ۞ أَخْبَرَنَا حَفْصُ بْنُ عُمَرَ بْنِ عُبَيْدٍ هُوَ الطَّنَافِسِيُّ ۞ حَدَّثَنَا زُهَيْرٌ أَبُو خَيْثَمَةَ ۞ عَنْ حُمَيْدٍ ۞ عَنْ أَنَسِ بْنِ مَالِكٍ قَالَ كَانَ خَاتَمُ النَّبِيِّ ﷺ مِنْ فِضَّةٍ وَفَصُّهُ مِنْهُ

89. Mahmud ibn Ghaylan narrated to us, 'Hafs ibn 'Umar ibn 'Ubayd—who is al-Tanafisi—related to us, "Zuhayr Abu Khaythama narrated to us on the authority of Humayd, on the authority of Anas ibn Malik, who reported:

'The Prophet's ring ﷺ was silver and its bezel was of it.'"'[232]

٩٠ - حَدَّثَنَا إِسْحَاقُ بْنُ مَنْصُورٍ ۞ حَدَّثَنَا مُعَاذُ بْنُ هِشَامٍ ۞ قَالَ أَخْبَرَنِي أَبِي ۞ عَنْ قَتَادَةَ ۞ عَنْ أَنَسِ بْنِ مَالِكٍ قَالَ لَمَّا أَرَادَ رَسُولُ اللهِ ﷺ أَنْ يَكْتُبَ إِلَى الْعَجَمِ قِيلَ لَهُ إِنَّ الْعَجَمَ لَا يَقْبَلُونَ إِلَّا كِتَابًا عَلَيْهِ خَاتَمٌ ۞ فَاصْطَنَعَ خَاتَمًا ۞ فَكَأَنِّي أَنْظُرُ إِلَى بَيَاضِهِ فِي كَفِّهِ

90. Ishaq ibn Mansur narrated to us, 'Mu'adh ibn Hisham narrated to us, "My father related to me on the authority of Qatada, on the authority of Anas ibn Malik, who reported:

'When the Messenger of Allah ﷺ wanted to write to the non-Arabs,[233] he was informed that they would only accept letters marked with seals, so he had a ring made.[234] It is as if I am looking at its whiteness[235] in his palm now.'"'[236]

[232] Imam al-Bayhaqi said after recording this narration, 'This proves that he ﷺ had two rings: one whose bezel was Abyssinian [a stone], and another whose bezel was part of it.' This indicates that the second ring of the Prophet ﷺ 'whose bezel was part of it', was the signet ring used as a seal for letters he sent to Emperors, as mentioned in hadiths 90–92. Regarding the phrase 'and its bezel was of it', scholars have said that it has two meanings: either it was part of it, meaning the ring, or the bezel was also of silver. (AA)

[233] That is, to write to their rulers to invite them to Islam. (AA)

[234] Imam al-Daraqutni recorded in his *Sunan*, on the authority of Salama, on the authority of 'Ikrima, on the authority of Yahya ibn Umayya, who said, 'I made the ring of the Prophet ﷺ and no one else shared that honour with me. Engraved on it was Muhammad the Messenger of Allah.' This hadith indicates that the Prophet ﷺ would adopt the practices of other cultures in order to make the Message more appealing to them, as long as those practices were not unlawful in Islam. (MA)

[235] Because it was pure silver. (AA)

[236] When Sayyiduna Anas ؓ would speak about the Messenger of Allah ﷺ, he would envision him as though he was before him, and he would relive every moment that he spent with him. (MA)

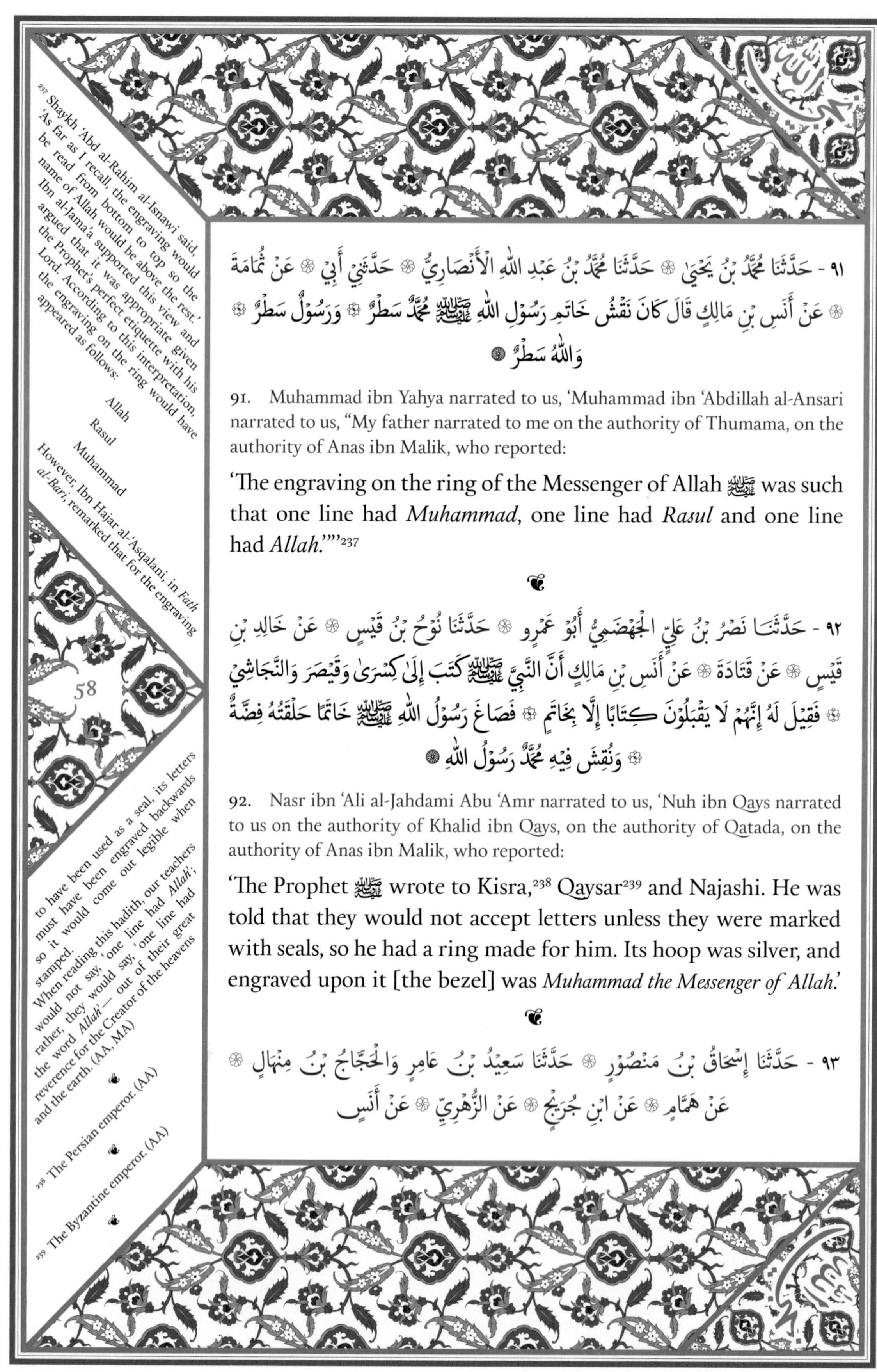

٩١ - حَدَّثَنَا مُحَمَّدُ بْنُ يَحْيَىٰ ۞ حَدَّثَنَا مُحَمَّدُ بْنُ عَبْدِ اللهِ الْأَنْصَارِيُّ ۞ حَدَّثَنِي أَبِي ۞ عَنْ ثُمَامَةَ ۞ عَنْ أَنَسِ بْنِ مَالِكٍ قَالَ كَانَ نَقْشُ خَاتَمِ رَسُولِ اللهِ ﷺ مُحَمَّدٌ سَطْرٌ ۞ وَرَسُولٌ سَطْرٌ ۞ وَاللهُ سَطْرٌ ۞

91. Muhammad ibn Yahya narrated to us, 'Muhammad ibn 'Abdillah al-Ansari narrated to us, "My father narrated to me on the authority of Thumama, on the authority of Anas ibn Malik, who reported:

'The engraving on the ring of the Messenger of Allah ﷺ was such that one line had *Muhammad,* one line had *Rasul* and one line had *Allah*.'"'[237]

٩٢ - حَدَّثَنَا نَصْرُ بْنُ عَلِيٍّ الْجَهْضَمِيُّ أَبُو عَمْرٍو ۞ حَدَّثَنَا نُوحُ بْنُ قَيْسٍ ۞ عَنْ خَالِدِ بْنِ قَيْسٍ ۞ عَنْ قَتَادَةَ ۞ عَنْ أَنَسِ بْنِ مَالِكٍ أَنَّ النَّبِيَّ ﷺ كَتَبَ إِلَىٰ كِسْرَىٰ وَقَيْصَرَ وَالنَّجَاشِيِّ ۞ فَقِيلَ لَهُ إِنَّهُمْ لَا يَقْبَلُونَ كِتَابًا إِلَّا بِخَاتَمٍ ۞ فَصَاغَ رَسُولُ اللهِ ﷺ خَاتَمًا حَلْقَتُهُ فِضَّةٌ ۞ وَنُقِشَ فِيهِ مُحَمَّدٌ رَسُولُ اللهِ ۞

92. Nasr ibn 'Ali al-Jahdami Abu 'Amr narrated to us, 'Nuh ibn Qays narrated to us on the authority of Khalid ibn Qays, on the authority of Qatada, on the authority of Anas ibn Malik, who reported:

'The Prophet ﷺ wrote to Kisra,[238] Qaysar[239] and Najashi. He was told that they would not accept letters unless they were marked with seals, so he had a ring made for him. Its hoop was silver, and engraved upon it [the bezel] was *Muhammad the Messenger of Allah*.'

٩٣ - حَدَّثَنَا إِسْحَاقُ بْنُ مَنْصُورٍ ۞ حَدَّثَنَا سَعِيدُ بْنُ عَامِرٍ وَالْحَجَّاجُ بْنُ مِنْهَالٍ ۞ عَنْ هَمَّامٍ ۞ عَنِ ابْنِ جُرَيْجٍ ۞ عَنِ الزُّهْرِيِّ ۞ عَنْ أَنَسٍ

[237] Shaykh 'Abd al-Rahim al-Isnawi said, 'As far as I recall, the engraving would be read from bottom to top so the name of Allah would be above the rest.' Ibn al-Jama'a supported this view and argued that it was appropriate given the Prophet's perfect etiquette with his Lord. According to this interpretation, the engraving on the ring would have appeared as follows:

Allah
Rasul
Muhammad

However, Ibn Hajar al-'Asqalani, in *Fath al-Bari*, remarked that for the engraving to have been used as a seal, its letters must have been engraved backwards so it would come out legible when stamped.
When reading this hadith, our teachers would not say, 'one line had *Allah*'; rather, they would say, 'one line had the word *Allah*'— out of their great reverence for the Creator of the heavens and the earth. (AA, MA)

[238] The Persian emperor. (AA)

[239] The Byzantine emperor. (AA)

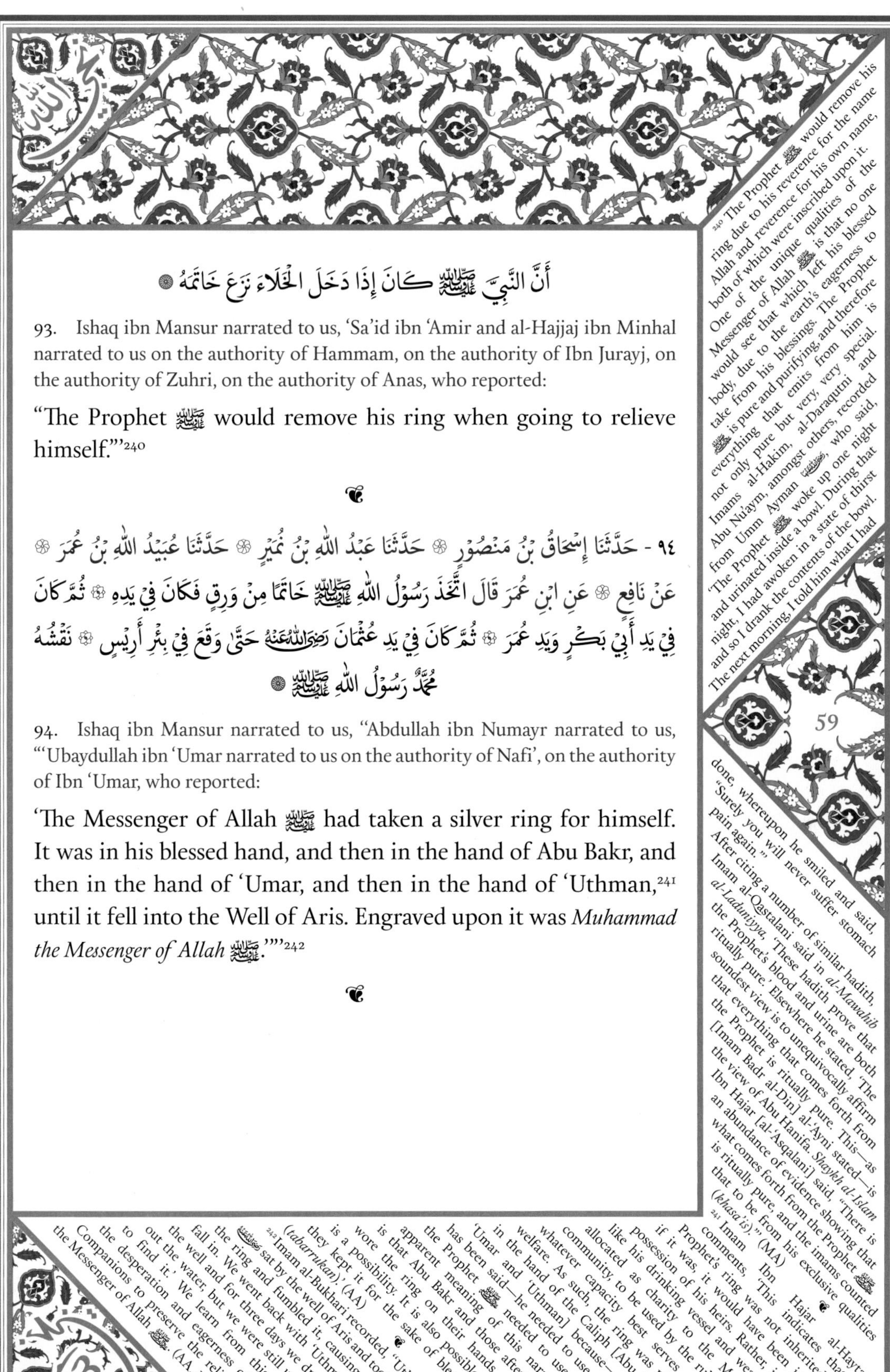

أَنَّ النَّبِيَّ ﷺ كَانَ إِذَا دَخَلَ الْخَلَاءَ نَزَعَ خَاتَمَهُ ۞

93. Ishaq ibn Mansur narrated to us, 'Sa'id ibn 'Amir and al-Hajjaj ibn Minhal narrated to us on the authority of Hammam, on the authority of Ibn Jurayj, on the authority of Zuhri, on the authority of Anas, who reported:

"The Prophet ﷺ would remove his ring when going to relieve himself."'[240]

❦

٩٤ - حَدَّثَنَا إِسْحَاقُ بْنُ مَنْصُورٍ ۞ حَدَّثَنَا عَبْدُ اللهِ بْنُ نُمَيْرٍ ۞ حَدَّثَنَا عُبَيْدُ اللهِ بْنُ عُمَرَ ۞ عَنْ نَافِعٍ ۞ عَنِ ابْنِ عُمَرَ قَالَ اتَّخَذَ رَسُولُ اللهِ ﷺ خَاتَمًا مِنْ وَرِقٍ فَكَانَ فِي يَدِهِ ۞ ثُمَّ كَانَ فِي يَدِ أَبِي بَكْرٍ وَيَدِ عُمَرَ ۞ ثُمَّ كَانَ فِي يَدِ عُثْمَانَ رَضِيَ اللهُ عَنْهُ حَتَّىٰ وَقَعَ فِي بِئْرِ أَرِيسٍ ۞ نَقْشُهُ مُحَمَّدٌ رَسُولُ اللهِ ﷺ ۞

94. Ishaq ibn Mansur narrated to us, "'Abdullah ibn Numayr narrated to us, "'Ubaydullah ibn 'Umar narrated to us on the authority of Nafi', on the authority of Ibn 'Umar, who reported:

'The Messenger of Allah ﷺ had taken a silver ring for himself. It was in his blessed hand, and then in the hand of Abu Bakr, and then in the hand of 'Umar, and then in the hand of 'Uthman,[241] until it fell into the Well of Aris. Engraved upon it was *Muhammad the Messenger of Allah* ﷺ.'''"[242]

❦

240 The Prophet ﷺ would remove his ring due to his reverence for the name of Allah and reverence for his own name, both of which were inscribed upon it. One of the unique qualities of the Messenger of Allah ﷺ is that no one would see that which left his blessed body, due to the earth's eagerness to take from his blessings. The Prophet ﷺ is pure and purifying, and therefore everything that emits from him is not only pure but very, very special. Imams al-Hakim, al-Daraqutni and Abu Nu'aym, amongst others, recorded from Umm Ayman ﷺ, who said, 'The Prophet ﷺ woke up one night and urinated inside a bowl. During that night, I had awoken in a state of thirst and so I drank the contents of the bowl. The next morning, I told him what I had done, whereupon he smiled and said, "Surely you will never suffer stomach pain again."' After citing a number of similar hadith, Imam al-Qastalani said in *al-Mawahib al-Laduniyya*, 'These hadith prove that the Prophet's blood and urine are both ritually pure.' Elsewhere he stated, 'The soundest view is to unequivocally affirm that everything that comes forth from the Prophet is ritually pure. This—as [Imam Badr al-Din] al-'Ayni stated—is the view of Abu Hanifa. *Shaykh al-Islam* Ibn Hajar [al-'Asqalani] said, "There is an abundance of evidence showing that what comes forth from the Prophet ﷺ is ritually pure, and the imams counted that to be from his exclusive qualities (*khasa'is*)."' (MA)

241 Imam Ibn Hajar al-Haytami comments, 'This indicates that the Prophet's ring was not inherited, for if it was, it would have been in the possession of his heirs. Rather, it was like his drinking vessel and weapons: allocated as charity to the Muslim community, to be used by the ruler in whatever capacity best serves their welfare. As such, the ring was placed in the hand of the Caliph [Abu Bakr, 'Umar and 'Uthman] because—as it has been said—he needed to use what the Prophet ﷺ needed to use. The apparent meaning of this narration is that Abu Bakr and those after him wore the ring on their hands. This is a possibility. It is also possible that they kept it for the sake of blessings (*tabarrukan*).' (AA)

❦

242 Imam al-Bukhari recorded, "Uthman ﷺ sat by the well of Aris and took out the ring and fumbled it, causing it to fall in. We went back with 'Uthman to the well and for three days we drained out the water, but we were still unable to find it.' We learn from this also the desperation and eagerness of the Companions to preserve the relics of the Messenger of Allah ﷺ. (AA, MA)

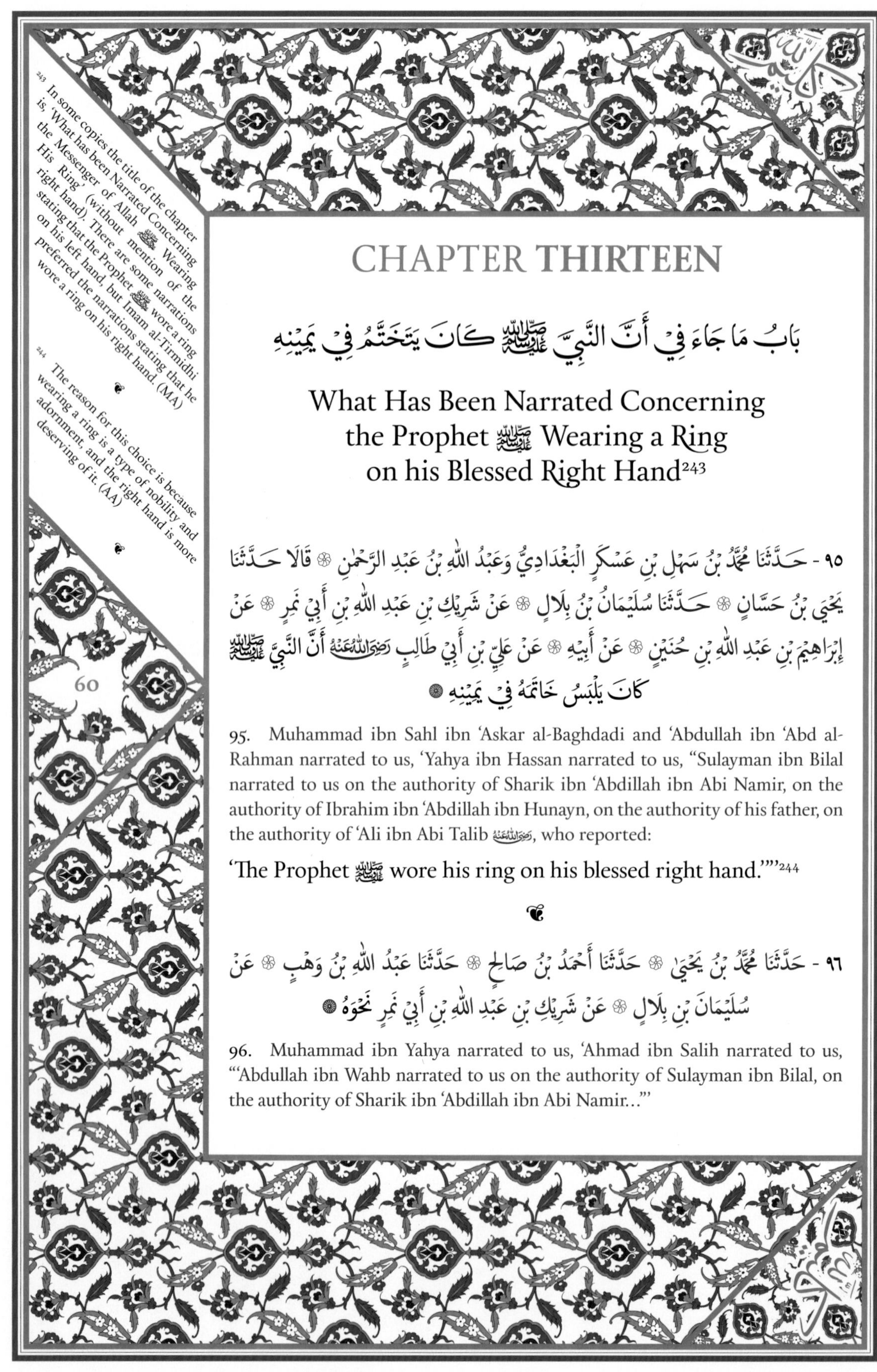

CHAPTER THIRTEEN

بَابُ مَا جَاءَ فِي أَنَّ النَّبِيَّ ﷺ كَانَ يَتَخَتَّمُ فِي يَمِينِهِ

What Has Been Narrated Concerning the Prophet ﷺ Wearing a Ring on his Blessed Right Hand[243]

٩٥ - حَدَّثَنَا مُحَمَّدُ بْنُ سَهْلِ بْنِ عَسْكَرٍ الْبَغْدَادِيُّ وَعَبْدُ اللَّهِ بْنُ عَبْدِ الرَّحْمَٰنِ ۞ قَالَا حَدَّثَنَا يَحْيَى بْنُ حَسَّانٍ ۞ حَدَّثَنَا سُلَيْمَانُ بْنُ بِلَالٍ ۞ عَنْ شَرِيكِ بْنِ عَبْدِ اللَّهِ بْنِ أَبِي نَمِرٍ ۞ عَنْ إِبْرَاهِيمَ بْنِ عَبْدِ اللَّهِ بْنِ حُنَيْنٍ ۞ عَنْ أَبِيهِ ۞ عَنْ عَلِيِّ بْنِ أَبِي طَالِبٍ رَضِيَ اللَّهُ عَنْهُ أَنَّ النَّبِيَّ ﷺ كَانَ يَلْبَسُ خَاتَمَهُ فِي يَمِينِهِ ۝

95. Muhammad ibn Sahl ibn 'Askar al-Baghdadi and 'Abdullah ibn 'Abd al-Rahman narrated to us, 'Yahya ibn Hassan narrated to us, "Sulayman ibn Bilal narrated to us on the authority of Sharik ibn 'Abdillah ibn Abi Namir, on the authority of Ibrahim ibn 'Abdillah ibn Hunayn, on the authority of his father, on the authority of 'Ali ibn Abi Talib رضي الله عنه, who reported:

'The Prophet ﷺ wore his ring on his blessed right hand.'"'[244]

٩٦ - حَدَّثَنَا مُحَمَّدُ بْنُ يَحْيَى ۞ حَدَّثَنَا أَحْمَدُ بْنُ صَالِحٍ ۞ حَدَّثَنَا عَبْدُ اللَّهِ بْنُ وَهْبٍ ۞ عَنْ سُلَيْمَانَ بْنِ بِلَالٍ ۞ عَنْ شَرِيكِ بْنِ عَبْدِ اللَّهِ بْنِ أَبِي نَمِرٍ نَحْوَهُ ۝

96. Muhammad ibn Yahya narrated to us, 'Ahmad ibn Salih narrated to us, "'Abdullah ibn Wahb narrated to us on the authority of Sulayman ibn Bilal, on the authority of Sharik ibn 'Abdillah ibn Abi Namir..."'

243 In some copies the title of the chapter is, 'What has been Narrated Concerning the Messenger of Allah ﷺ Wearing His Ring' (without mention of the right hand). There are some narrations stating that the Prophet ﷺ wore a ring on his left hand, but Imam al-Tirmidhi preferred the narrations stating that he wore a ring on his right hand. (MA)

244 The reason for this choice is because wearing a ring is a type of nobility and adornment, and the right hand is more deserving of it. (AA)

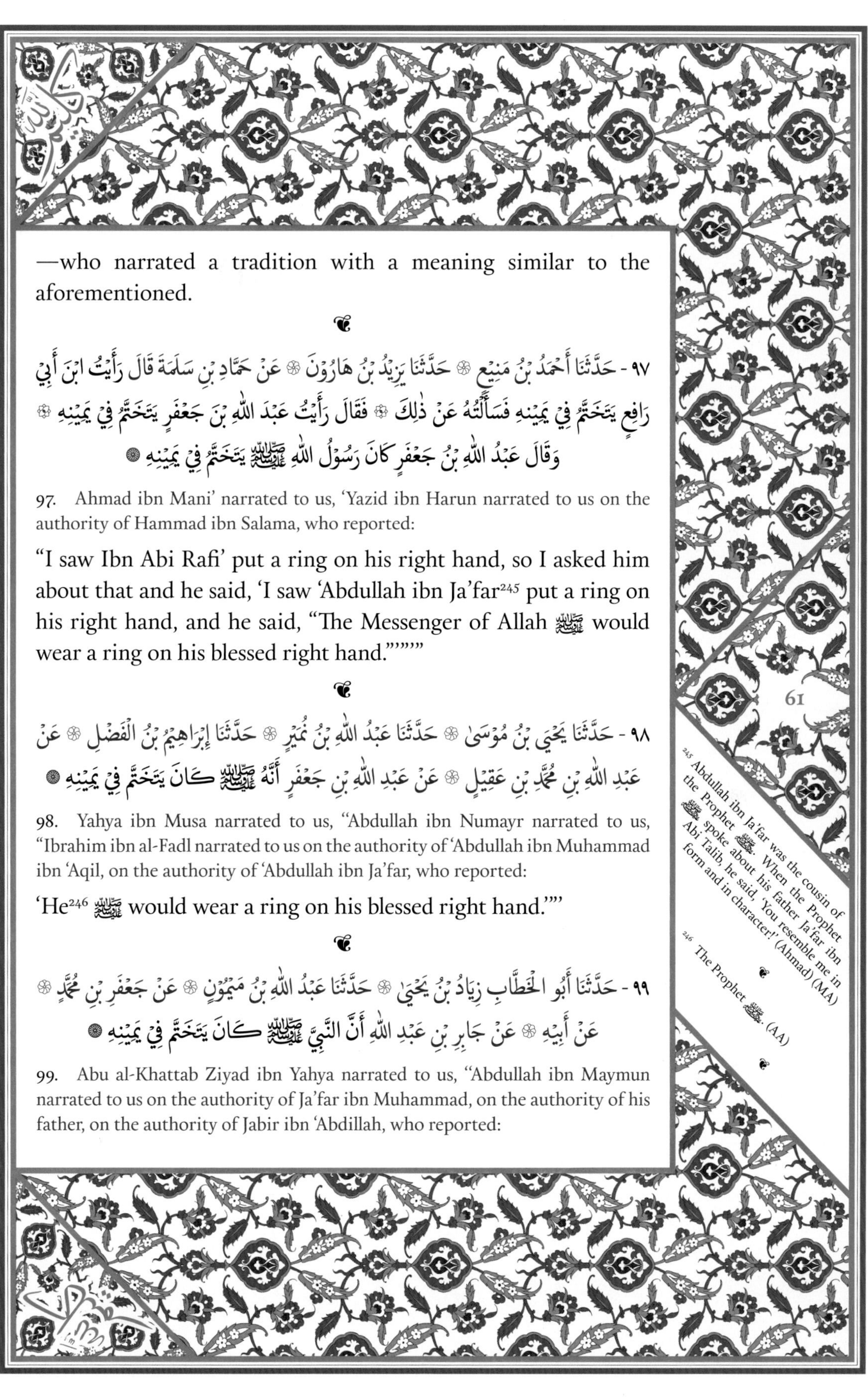

—who narrated a tradition with a meaning similar to the aforementioned.

❦

٩٧ - حَدَّثَنَا أَحْمَدُ بْنُ مَنِيعٍ ۞ حَدَّثَنَا يَزِيدُ بْنُ هَارُونَ ۞ عَنْ حَمَّادِ بْنِ سَلَمَةَ قَالَ رَأَيْتُ ابْنَ أَبِي رَافِعٍ يَتَخَتَّمُ فِي يَمِينِهِ فَسَأَلْتُهُ عَنْ ذٰلِكَ ۞ فَقَالَ رَأَيْتُ عَبْدَ اللهِ بْنَ جَعْفَرٍ يَتَخَتَّمُ فِي يَمِينِهِ ۞ وَقَالَ عَبْدُ اللهِ بْنُ جَعْفَرٍ كَانَ رَسُولُ اللهِ ﷺ يَتَخَتَّمُ فِي يَمِينِهِ ۞

97. Ahmad ibn Mani' narrated to us, 'Yazid ibn Harun narrated to us on the authority of Hammad ibn Salama, who reported:

"I saw Ibn Abi Rafi' put a ring on his right hand, so I asked him about that and he said, 'I saw 'Abdullah ibn Ja'far[245] put a ring on his right hand, and he said, "The Messenger of Allah ﷺ would wear a ring on his blessed right hand."'"'

❦

٩٨ - حَدَّثَنَا يَحْيَى بْنُ مُوسَىٰ ۞ حَدَّثَنَا عَبْدُ اللهِ بْنُ نُمَيْرٍ ۞ حَدَّثَنَا إِبْرَاهِيمُ بْنُ الْفَضْلِ ۞ عَنْ عَبْدِ اللهِ بْنِ مُحَمَّدِ بْنِ عَقِيلٍ ۞ عَنْ عَبْدِ اللهِ بْنِ جَعْفَرٍ أَنَّهُ ﷺ كَانَ يَتَخَتَّمُ فِي يَمِينِهِ ۞

98. Yahya ibn Musa narrated to us, "Abdullah ibn Numayr narrated to us, "Ibrahim ibn al-Fadl narrated to us on the authority of 'Abdullah ibn Muhammad ibn 'Aqil, on the authority of 'Abdullah ibn Ja'far, who reported:

'He[246] ﷺ would wear a ring on his blessed right hand.'"

❦

٩٩ - حَدَّثَنَا أَبُو الْخَطَّابِ زِيَادُ بْنُ يَحْيَىٰ ۞ حَدَّثَنَا عَبْدُ اللهِ بْنُ مَيْمُونٍ ۞ عَنْ جَعْفَرِ بْنِ مُحَمَّدٍ ۞ عَنْ أَبِيهِ ۞ عَنْ جَابِرِ بْنِ عَبْدِ اللهِ أَنَّ النَّبِيَّ ﷺ كَانَ يَتَخَتَّمُ فِي يَمِينِهِ ۞

99. Abu al-Khattab Ziyad ibn Yahya narrated to us, "Abdullah ibn Maymun narrated to us on the authority of Ja'far ibn Muhammad, on the authority of his father, on the authority of Jabir ibn 'Abdillah, who reported:

[245] Abdullah ibn Ja'far was the cousin of the Prophet ﷺ. When the Prophet ﷺ spoke about his father Ja'far ibn Abi Talib, he said, 'You resemble me in form and in character!' (Ahmad) (MA)

[246] The Prophet ﷺ. (AA)

❦

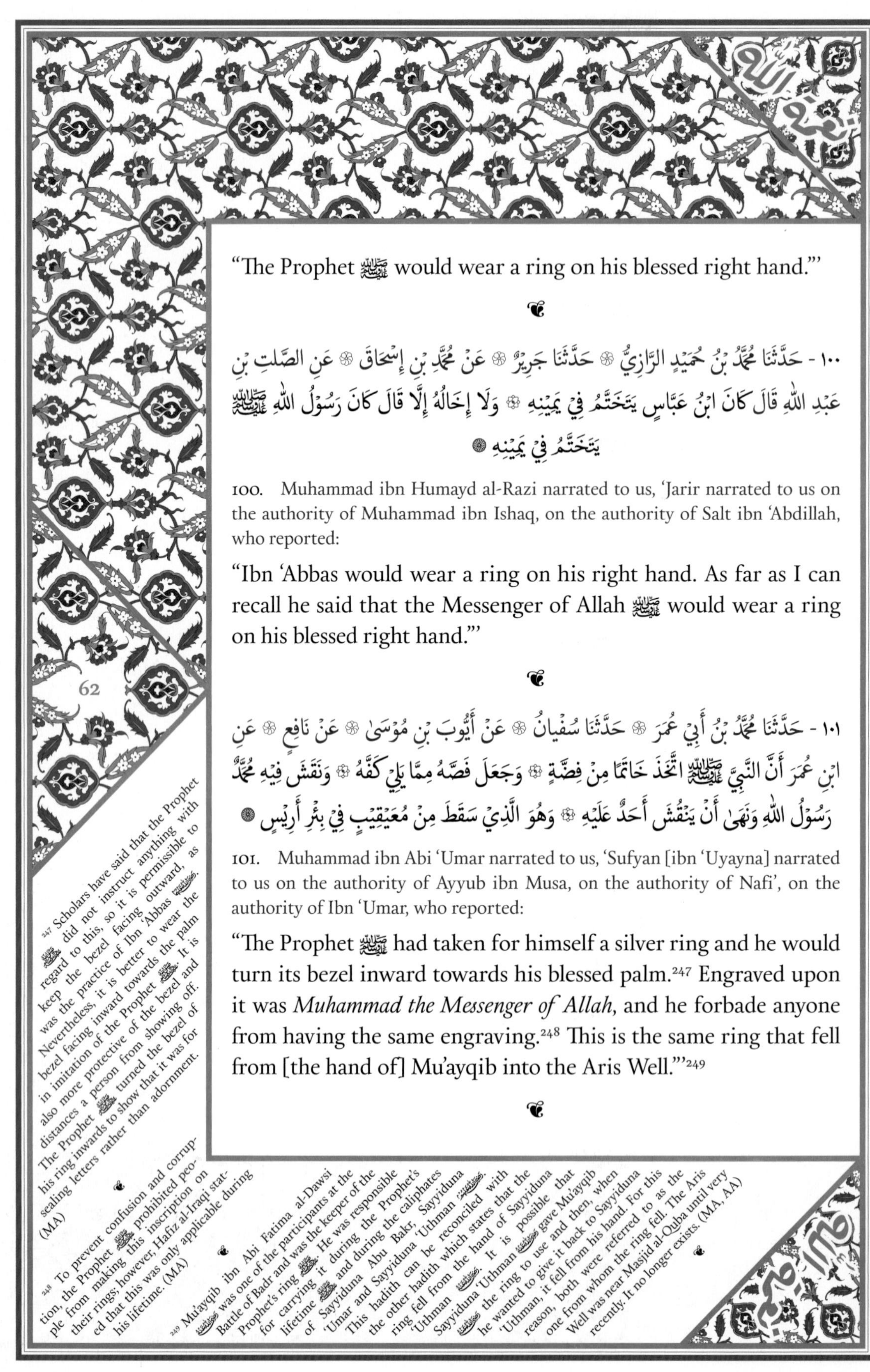

"The Prophet ﷺ would wear a ring on his blessed right hand."'

١٠٠ - حَدَّثَنَا مُحَمَّدُ بْنُ حُمَيْدٍ الرَّازِيُّ ۞ حَدَّثَنَا جَرِيرٌ ۞ عَنْ مُحَمَّدِ بْنِ إِسْحَاقَ ۞ عَنِ الصَّلْتِ بْنِ عَبْدِ اللهِ قَالَ كَانَ ابْنُ عَبَّاسٍ يَتَخَتَّمُ فِي يَمِينِهِ ۞ وَلَا إِخَالُهُ إِلَّا قَالَ كَانَ رَسُولُ اللهِ ﷺ يَتَخَتَّمُ فِي يَمِينِهِ ۞

100. Muhammad ibn Humayd al-Razi narrated to us, 'Jarir narrated to us on the authority of Muhammad ibn Ishaq, on the authority of Salt ibn 'Abdillah, who reported:

"Ibn 'Abbas would wear a ring on his right hand. As far as I can recall he said that the Messenger of Allah ﷺ would wear a ring on his blessed right hand."'

١٠١ - حَدَّثَنَا مُحَمَّدُ بْنُ أَبِي عُمَرَ ۞ حَدَّثَنَا سُفْيَانُ ۞ عَنْ أَيُّوبَ بْنِ مُوسَىٰ ۞ عَنْ نَافِعٍ ۞ عَنِ ابْنِ عُمَرَ أَنَّ النَّبِيَّ ﷺ اتَّخَذَ خَاتَمًا مِنْ فِضَّةٍ ۞ وَجَعَلَ فَصَّهُ مِمَّا يَلِي كَفَّهُ ۞ وَنَقَشَ فِيهِ مُحَمَّدٌ رَسُولُ اللهِ وَنَهَىٰ أَنْ يَنْقُشَ أَحَدٌ عَلَيْهِ ۞ وَهُوَ الَّذِي سَقَطَ مِنْ مُعَيْقِيبٍ فِي بِئْرِ أَرِيسٍ ۞

101. Muhammad ibn Abi 'Umar narrated to us, 'Sufyan [ibn 'Uyayna] narrated to us on the authority of Ayyub ibn Musa, on the authority of Nafi', on the authority of Ibn 'Umar, who reported:

"The Prophet ﷺ had taken for himself a silver ring and he would turn its bezel inward towards his blessed palm.[247] Engraved upon it was *Muhammad the Messenger of Allah,* and he forbade anyone from having the same engraving.[248] This is the same ring that fell from [the hand of] Mu'ayqib into the Aris Well."'[249]

[247] Scholars have said that the Prophet ﷺ did not instruct anything with regard to this, so it is permissible to keep the bezel facing outward, as was the practice of Ibn 'Abbas ﷺ. Nevertheless, it is better to wear the bezel facing inward towards the palm in imitation of the Prophet ﷺ. It is also more protective of the bezel and distances a person from showing off. The Prophet ﷺ turned the bezel of his ring inwards to show that it was for sealing letters rather than adornment. (MA)

[248] To prevent confusion and corruption, the Prophet ﷺ prohibited people from making this inscription on their rings; however, Hafiz al-'Iraqi stated that this was only applicable during his lifetime. (MA)

[249] Mu'ayqib ibn Abi Fatima al-Dawsi ﷺ was one of the participants at the Battle of Badr and was the keeper of the Prophet's ring ﷺ. He was responsible for carrying it during the Prophet's lifetime ﷺ and during the caliphates of Sayyiduna Abu Bakr, Sayyiduna 'Umar and Sayyiduna 'Uthman ﷺ. This hadith can be reconciled with the other hadith which states that the ring fell from the hand of Sayyiduna 'Uthman ﷺ. It is possible that Sayyiduna 'Uthman ﷺ gave Mu'ayqib ﷺ the ring to use and then, when he wanted to give it back to Sayyiduna 'Uthman, it fell from his hand. For this reason, both were referred to as the one from whom the ring fell. The Aris Well was near Masjid al-Quba until very recently. It no longer exists. (MA, AA)

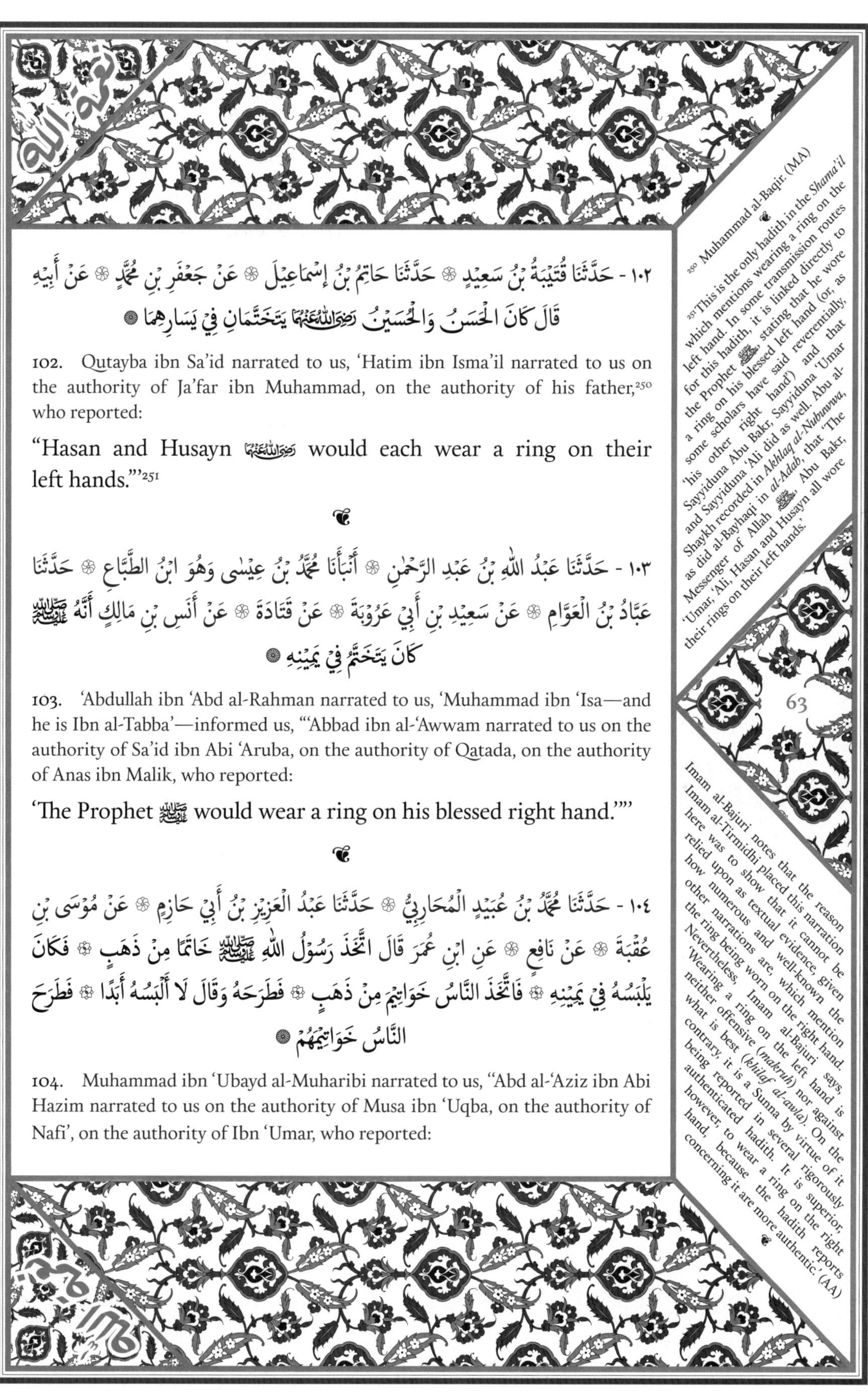

١٠٢ - حَدَّثَنَا قُتَيْبَةُ بْنُ سَعِيدٍ ۞ حَدَّثَنَا حَاتِمُ بْنُ إِسْمَاعِيلَ ۞ عَنْ جَعْفَرِ بْنِ مُحَمَّدٍ ۞ عَنْ أَبِيهِ قَالَ كَانَ الْحَسَنُ وَالْحُسَيْنُ رَضِيَ اللهُ عَنْهُمَا يَتَخَتَّمَانِ فِي يَسَارِهِمَا ۞

102. Qutayba ibn Sa'id narrated to us, 'Hatim ibn Isma'il narrated to us on the authority of Ja'far ibn Muhammad, on the authority of his father,[250] who reported:

"Hasan and Husayn ﷺ would each wear a ring on their left hands."'[251]

١٠٣ - حَدَّثَنَا عَبْدُ اللهِ بْنُ عَبْدِ الرَّحْمٰنِ ۞ أَنْبَأَنَا مُحَمَّدُ بْنُ عِيسَى وَهُوَ ابْنُ الطَّبَّاعِ ۞ حَدَّثَنَا عَبَّادُ بْنُ الْعَوَّامِ ۞ عَنْ سَعِيدِ بْنِ أَبِي عَرُوبَةَ ۞ عَنْ قَتَادَةَ ۞ عَنْ أَنَسِ بْنِ مَالِكٍ أَنَّهُ ﷺ كَانَ يَتَخَتَّمُ فِي يَمِينِهِ ۞

103. 'Abdullah ibn 'Abd al-Rahman narrated to us, 'Muhammad ibn 'Isa—and he is Ibn al-Tabba'—informed us, "'Abbad ibn al-'Awwam narrated to us on the authority of Sa'id ibn Abi 'Aruba, on the authority of Qatada, on the authority of Anas ibn Malik, who reported:

'The Prophet ﷺ would wear a ring on his blessed right hand.'"'

١٠٤ - حَدَّثَنَا مُحَمَّدُ بْنُ عُبَيْدٍ الْمُحَارِبِيُّ ۞ حَدَّثَنَا عَبْدُ الْعَزِيزِ بْنُ أَبِي حَازِمٍ ۞ عَنْ مُوسَى بْنِ عُقْبَةَ ۞ عَنْ نَافِعٍ ۞ عَنِ ابْنِ عُمَرَ قَالَ اتَّخَذَ رَسُولُ اللهِ ﷺ خَاتَمًا مِنْ ذَهَبٍ ۞ فَكَانَ يَلْبَسُهُ فِي يَمِينِهِ ۞ فَاتَّخَذَ النَّاسُ خَوَاتِيمَ مِنْ ذَهَبٍ ۞ فَطَرَحَهُ وَقَالَ لَا أَلْبَسُهُ أَبَدًا ۞ فَطَرَحَ النَّاسُ خَوَاتِيمَهُمْ ۞

104. Muhammad ibn 'Ubayd al-Muharibi narrated to us, "Abd al-'Aziz ibn Abi Hazim narrated to us on the authority of Musa ibn 'Uqba, on the authority of Nafi', on the authority of Ibn 'Umar, who reported:

250 Muhammad al-Baqir. (MA)

251 This is the only hadith in the *Shama'il* which mentions wearing a ring on the left hand. In some transmission routes for this hadith, it is linked directly to the Prophet ﷺ stating that he wore a ring on his blessed left hand (or, as some scholars have said reverentially, 'his other right hand') and that Sayyiduna Abu Bakr, Sayyiduna 'Umar and Sayyiduna 'Ali did as well. Abu al-Shaykh recorded in *Akhlaq al-Nubuwwa*, as did al-Bayhaqi in *al-Adab*, that 'The Messenger of Allah ﷺ, Abu Bakr, 'Umar, 'Ali, Hasan and Husayn all wore their rings on their left hands.'

Imam al-Bajuri notes that the reason Imam al-Tirmidhi placed this narration here was to show that it cannot be relied upon as textual evidence, given how numerous and well-known the other narrations are, which mention the ring being worn on the right hand. Nevertheless, Imam al-Bajuri says, 'Wearing a ring on the left hand is neither offensive (*makruh*) nor against what is best (*khilaf al-awla*). On the contrary, it is a Sunna by virtue of it being reported in several rigorously authenticated hadith. It is superior, however, to wear a ring on the right hand, because the hadith reports concerning it are more authentic.' (AA)

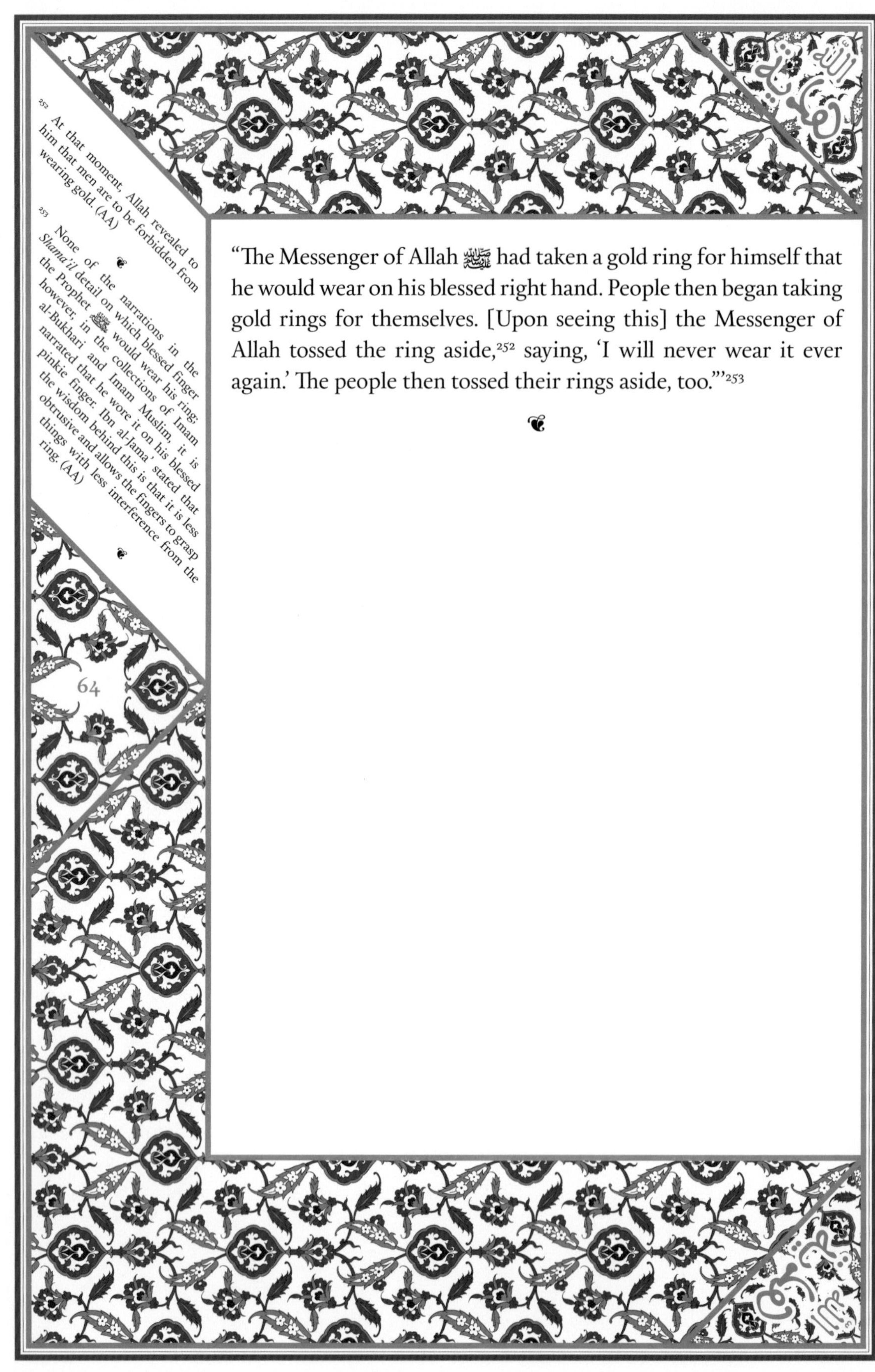

"The Messenger of Allah ﷺ had taken a gold ring for himself that he would wear on his blessed right hand. People then began taking gold rings for themselves. [Upon seeing this] the Messenger of Allah tossed the ring aside,[252] saying, 'I will never wear it ever again.' The people then tossed their rings aside, too."'[253]

❦

[252] At that moment, Allah revealed to him that men are to be forbidden from wearing gold. (AA)

[253] None of the narrations in the *Shama'il* detail on which blessed finger the Prophet ﷺ would wear his ring; however, in the collections of Imam al-Bukhari and Imam Muslim, it is narrated that he wore it on his blessed pinkie finger. Ibn al-Jama' stated that the wisdom behind this is that it is less obtrusive and allows the fingers to grasp things with less interference from the ring. (AA)

CHAPTER FOURTEEN

بَابُ مَا جَاءَ فِي صِفَةِ سَيْفِ رَسُولِ اللهِ ﷺ

What Has Been Narrated Concerning the Description of the Sword of the Messenger of Allah ﷺ

١٠٥ - حَدَّثَنَا مُحَمَّدُ بْنُ بَشَّارٍ ۞ حَدَّثَنَا وَهْبُ بْنُ جَرِيرٍ ۞ حَدَّثَنَا أَبِي ۞ عَنْ قَتَادَةَ ۞ عَنْ أَنَسٍ قَالَ كَانَ قَبِيعَةُ سَيْفِ رَسُولِ اللهِ ﷺ مِنْ فِضَّةٍ ۞

105. Muhammad ibn Bashhar narrated to us, 'Wahb ibn Jarir narrated to us, "My father narrated to us on the authority of Qatada, on the authority of Anas, who reported:

'The pommel of the sword of Allah's Messenger ﷺ was of silver.'"'[254]

١٠٦ - حَدَّثَنَا مُحَمَّدُ بْنُ بَشَّارٍ ۞ حَدَّثَنَا مُعَاذُ بْنُ هِشَامٍ ۞ حَدَّثَنَا أَبِي ۞ عَنْ قَتَادَةَ ۞ عَنْ سَعِيدِ بْنِ أَبِي الْحَسَنِ الْبَصْرِيِّ قَالَ كَانَتْ قَبِيعَةُ سَيْفِ رَسُولِ اللهِ ﷺ مِنْ فِضَّةٍ ۞

106. Muhammad ibn Bashhar narrated to us, 'Mu'adh ibn Hisham narrated to us, "My father narrated to us on the authority of Qatada, on the authority of Sa'id ibn Abi Hasan al-Basri,[255] who reported:

'The pommel of the sword of Allah's Messenger ﷺ was of silver.'"'

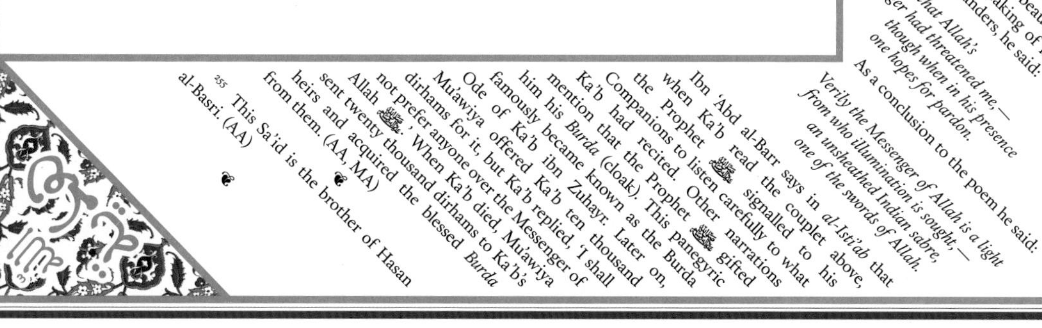

[254] Imam al-Bajuri says, 'The sword referred to in this hadith is the sword named *Dhu al-Faqar*.' Ka'b ibn Zuhayr was from the most skilled and renowned Arab poets of his time. After his brother Bujayr accepted Islam, Ka'b began to lampoon the Prophet ﷺ and used his poetry to instigate people to rise against him. Bujayr accompanied the Prophet during the conquest of Mecca and the subsequent siege of Ta'if, and observed that he did not give a guarantee of safety to other poets who had lampooned him, slandered his noble wives and used their poetry to incite war against the nascent Muslim community. Bujayr wrote a letter to Ka'b informing him of the situation and advised him to come to the Prophet ﷺ and express remorse for his invective poetry. With the seed of faith in his heart, Ka'b arrived to Medina shortly before dawn, as the Prophet was about the lead the Dawn Prayer (*Fajr*), and so he offered his very first prayer behind him. After the Prayer, Ka'b approached the Prophet ﷺ, sat down in front of him, placed his hand in the Prophet's hands and spoke about himself in the third person, 'Ka'b ibn Zuhayr has come as a Muslim and to repent and seek a guarantee of protection. Will you accept that from him if he comes to you?' The Prophet ever ready to forgive those who transgressed against him, said, 'Yes.' Elated, Ka'b said, 'I am Ka'b ibn Zuhayr!' On the way to Medina, Ka'b composed an eloquent panegyric to read before the Prophet ﷺ as an expression of remorse and regret over his past calumnies and transgressions. He stood and recited his poem, in the presence of the Prophet. Here is a translation of its opening lines:

Su'ad has departed, and as a result—my heart has grown sickly and weak today:
enslaved to her in her wake, and shackled—[as though in chains], with no [means of] escape.

Following traditional Arab poetic tradition, Ka'b began his poem by soliloquising amid the traces of his beloved's camp and recalling her beauty. Later in his panegyric, Speaking of his repentance for past slanders, he said:

I was told that Allah's Messenger had threatened me,— though when in his presence one hopes for pardon.

As a conclusion to the poem he said:

Verily the Messenger of Allah is a light from who illumination is sought,— an unsheathed Indian sabre, one of the swords of Allah.

Ibn 'Abd al-Barr says in *al-Isti'ab* that when Ka'b read the couplet above, the Prophet ﷺ signalled to his Companions to listen carefully to what Ka'b had recited. Other narrations mention that the Prophet ﷺ gifted him his *Burda* (cloak). This panegyric famously became known as the Burda Ode of Ka'b ibn Zuhayr. Later on, Mu'awiya offered Ka'b ten thousand dirhams for it, but Ka'b replied, 'I shall not prefer anyone over the Messenger of Allah ﷺ.' When Ka'b died, Mu'awiya sent twenty thousand dirhams to Ka'b's heirs and acquired the blessed *Burda* from them. (AA, MA)

[255] This Sa'id is the brother of Hasan al-Basri. (AA)

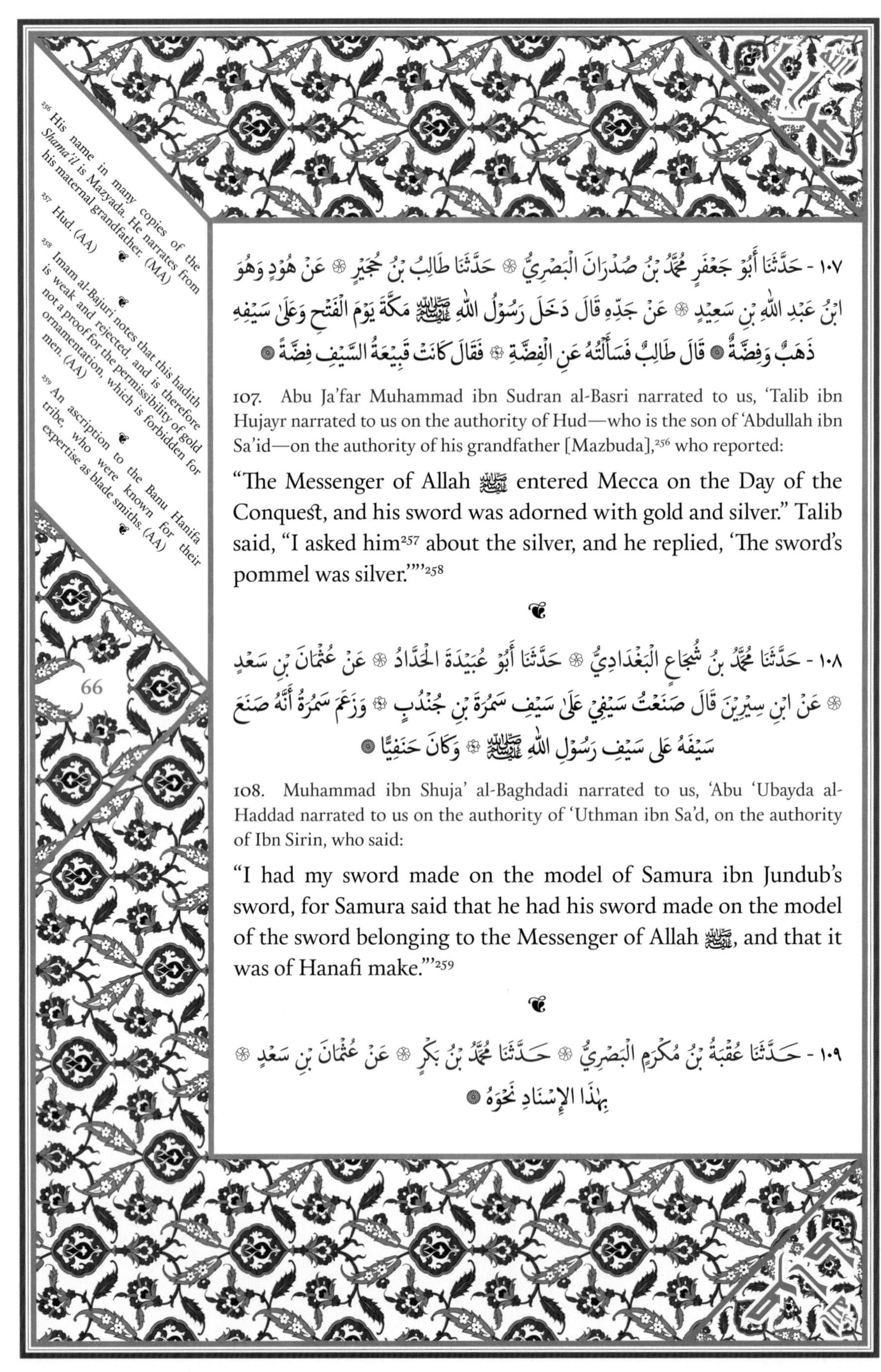

١٠٧ - حَدَّثَنَا أَبُو جَعْفَرٍ مُحَمَّدُ بْنُ صُدْرَانَ الْبَصْرِيُّ ۞ حَدَّثَنَا طَالِبُ بْنُ حُجَيْرٍ ۞ عَنْ هُودٍ وَهُوَ ابْنُ عَبْدِ اللهِ بْنِ سَعِيدٍ ۞ عَنْ جَدِّهِ قَالَ دَخَلَ رَسُولُ اللهِ ﷺ مَكَّةَ يَوْمَ الْفَتْحِ وَعَلَىٰ سَيْفِهِ ذَهَبٌ وَفِضَّةٌ ۞ قَالَ طَالِبٌ فَسَأَلْتُهُ عَنِ الْفِضَّةِ ۞ فَقَالَ كَانَتْ قَبِيعَةُ السَّيْفِ فِضَّةً ۞

107. Abu Ja'far Muhammad ibn Sudran al-Basri narrated to us, 'Talib ibn Hujayr narrated to us on the authority of Hud—who is the son of 'Abdullah ibn Sa'id—on the authority of his grandfather [Mazbuda],[256] who reported:

"The Messenger of Allah ﷺ entered Mecca on the Day of the Conquest, and his sword was adorned with gold and silver." Talib said, "I asked him[257] about the silver, and he replied, 'The sword's pommel was silver.'"'[258]

١٠٨ - حَدَّثَنَا مُحَمَّدُ بْنُ شُجَاعٍ الْبَغْدَادِيُّ ۞ حَدَّثَنَا أَبُو عُبَيْدَةَ الْحَدَّادُ ۞ عَنْ عُثْمَانَ بْنِ سَعْدٍ ۞ عَنِ ابْنِ سِيرِينَ قَالَ صَنَعْتُ سَيْفِي عَلَىٰ سَيْفِ سَمُرَةَ بْنِ جُنْدُبٍ ۞ وَزَعَمَ سَمُرَةُ أَنَّهُ صَنَعَ سَيْفَهُ عَلَى سَيْفِ رَسُولِ اللهِ ﷺ ۞ وَكَانَ حَنَفِيًّا ۞

108. Muhammad ibn Shuja' al-Baghdadi narrated to us, 'Abu 'Ubayda al-Haddad narrated to us on the authority of 'Uthman ibn Sa'd, on the authority of Ibn Sirin, who said:

"I had my sword made on the model of Samura ibn Jundub's sword, for Samura said that he had his sword made on the model of the sword belonging to the Messenger of Allah ﷺ, and that it was of Hanafi make."'[259]

١٠٩ - حَدَّثَنَا عُقْبَةُ بْنُ مُكْرَمٍ الْبَصْرِيُّ ۞ حَدَّثَنَا مُحَمَّدُ بْنُ بَكْرٍ ۞ عَنْ عُثْمَانَ بْنِ سَعْدٍ ۞ بِهَٰذَا الإِسْنَادِ نَحْوَهُ ۞

[256] His name in many copies of the *Shama'il* is Mazyada. He narrates from his maternal grandfather. (MA)

[257] Hud. (AA)

[258] Imam al-Bajuri notes that this hadith is weak and rejected, and is therefore not a proof for the permissibility of gold ornamentation, which is forbidden for men. (AA)

[259] An ascription to the Banu Hanifa tribe, who were known for their expertise as blade smiths. (AA)

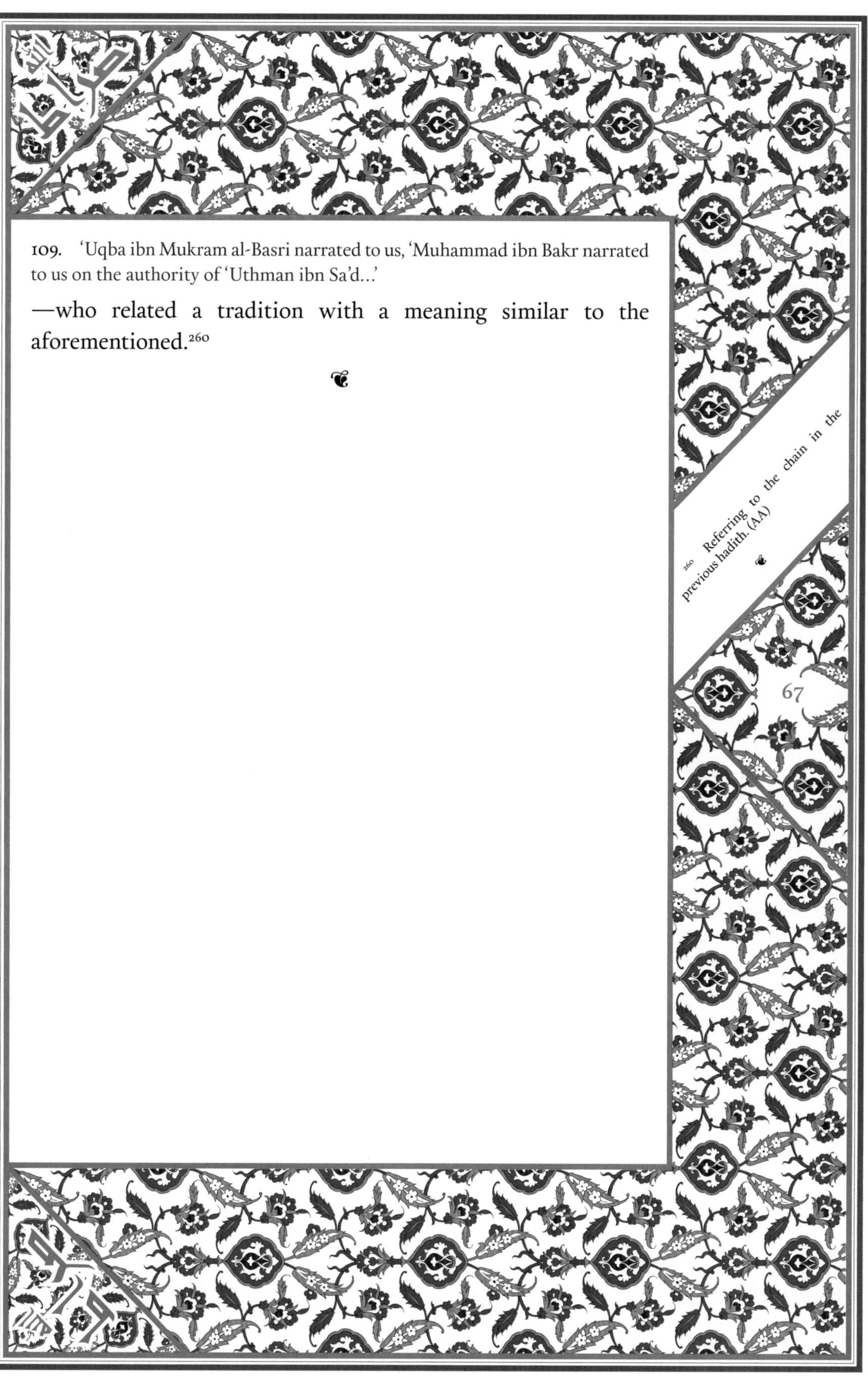

109. ‘Uqba ibn Mukram al-Basri narrated to us, ‘Muhammad ibn Bakr narrated to us on the authority of ‘Uthman ibn Sa’d...’

—who related a tradition with a meaning similar to the aforementioned.[260]

260 Referring to the chain in the previous hadith. (AA)

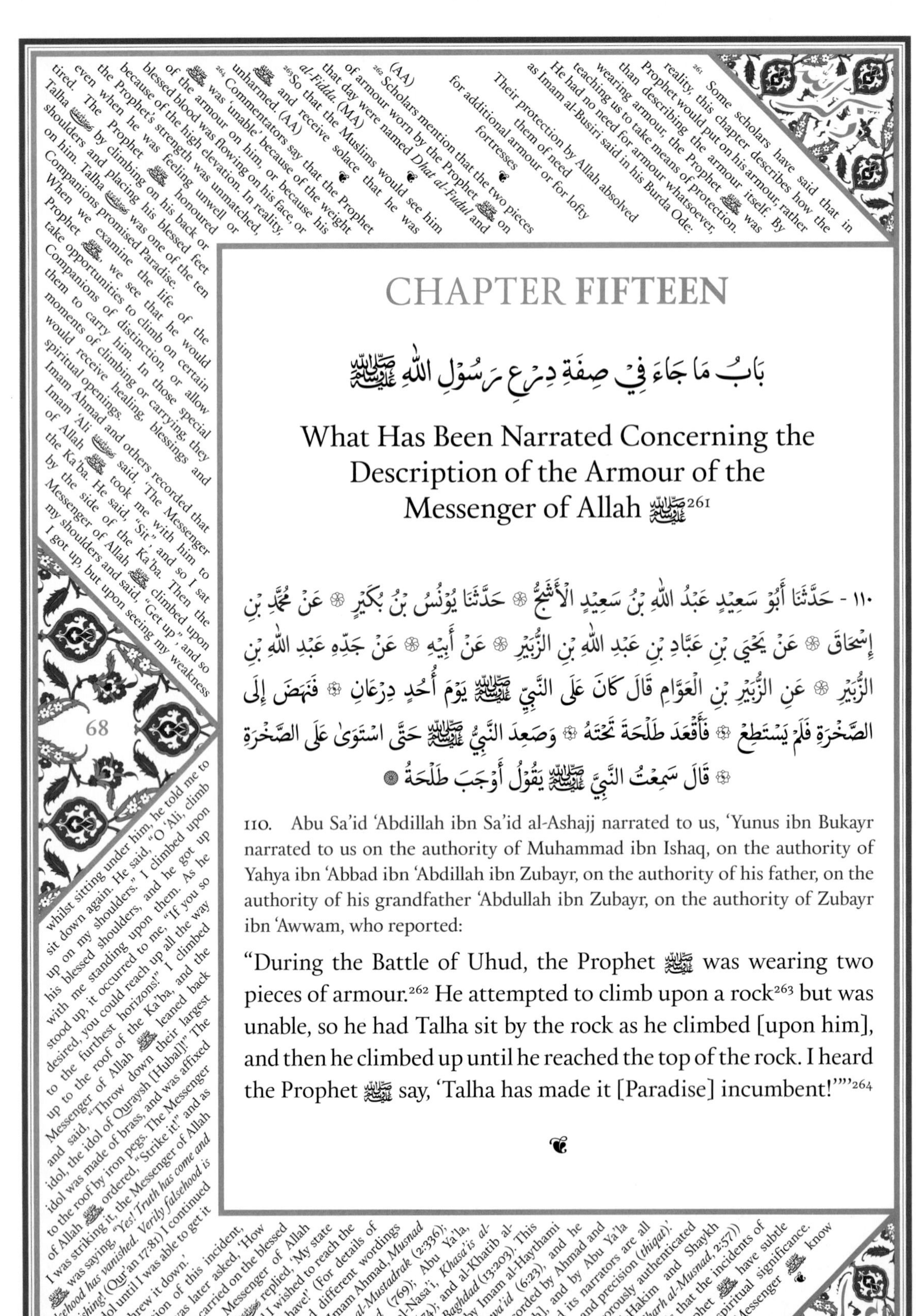

CHAPTER **FIFTEEN**

بَابُ مَا جَاءَ فِي صِفَةِ دِرْعِ رَسُولِ اللهِ ﷺ

What Has Been Narrated Concerning the Description of the Armour of the Messenger of Allah ﷺ[261]

١١٠ - حَدَّثَنَا أَبُو سَعِيدٍ عَبْدُ اللهِ بْنُ سَعِيدٍ الْأَشَجُّ ۞ حَدَّثَنَا يُونُسُ بْنُ بُكَيْرٍ ۞ عَنْ مُحَمَّدِ بْنِ إِسْحَاقَ ۞ عَنْ يَحْيَى بْنِ عَبَّادِ بْنِ عَبْدِ اللهِ بْنِ الزُّبَيْرِ ۞ عَنْ أَبِيهِ ۞ عَنْ جَدِّهِ عَبْدِ اللهِ بْنِ الزُّبَيْرِ ۞ عَنِ الزُّبَيْرِ بْنِ الْعَوَّامِ قَالَ كَانَ عَلَى النَّبِيِّ ﷺ يَوْمَ أُحُدٍ دِرْعَانِ ۞ فَنَهَضَ إِلَى الصَّخْرَةِ فَلَمْ يَسْتَطِعْ ۞ فَأَقْعَدَ طَلْحَةَ تَحْتَهُ ۞ وَصَعِدَ النَّبِيُّ ﷺ حَتَّى اسْتَوَى عَلَى الصَّخْرَةِ ۞ قَالَ سَمِعْتُ النَّبِيَّ ﷺ يَقُولُ أَوْجَبَ طَلْحَةُ ۞

110. Abu Sa'id 'Abdillah ibn Sa'id al-Ashajj narrated to us, 'Yunus ibn Bukayr narrated to us on the authority of Muhammad ibn Ishaq, on the authority of Yahya ibn 'Abbad ibn 'Abdillah ibn Zubayr, on the authority of his father, on the authority of his grandfather 'Abdullah ibn Zubayr, on the authority of Zubayr ibn 'Awwam, who reported:

"During the Battle of Uhud, the Prophet ﷺ was wearing two pieces of armour.[262] He attempted to climb upon a rock[263] but was unable, so he had Talha sit by the rock as he climbed [upon him], and then he climbed up until he reached the top of the rock. I heard the Prophet ﷺ say, 'Talha has made it [Paradise] incumbent!'"'[264]

❦

[261] Some scholars have said that in reality, this chapter describes how the Prophet would put on his armour, rather than describing the armour itself. By wearing armour, the Prophet ﷺ was teaching us to take means of protection. He had no need for armour whatsoever, as Imam al-Busiri said in his Burda Ode:

Their protection by Allah absolved
them of need
for additional armour or for lofty
fortresses ❦

(AA)

[262] Scholars mention that the two pieces of armour worn by the Prophet ﷺ on that day were named *Dhat al-Fudul* and *al-Fidda*. (MA) ❦

[263] So that the Muslims would see him and receive solace that he was unharmed. (AA) ❦

[264] Commentators say that the Prophet ﷺ was 'unable' because of the weight of the armour on him, or because his blessed blood was flowing on his face, or because of the high elevation. In reality, the Prophet's strength was unmatched, even when he was feeling unwell or tired. The Prophet ﷺ honoured Talha by climbing on his back or shoulders and placing his blessed feet on him. Talha was one of the ten Companions promised Paradise. When we examine the life of the Prophet ﷺ we see that he would take opportunities to climb on certain Companions of distinction, or allow them to carry him. In those special moments of climbing or carrying, they would receive healing, blessings and spiritual openings. Imam Ahmad and others recorded that Imam 'Ali said, 'The Messenger of Allah ﷺ took me with him to the Ka'ba. He said, "Sit", and so I sat by the side of the Ka'ba. Then the Messenger of Allah ﷺ climbed upon my shoulders and said, "Get up", and so I got up, but upon seeing my weakness whilst sitting under him, he told me to sit down again. He said, "O 'Ali, climb up on my shoulders," I climbed upon his blessed shoulders, and he got up with me standing upon them. As he stood up, it occurred to me, "If you so desired, you could reach up all the way to the furthest horizons!" I climbed up to the roof of the Ka'ba, and the Messenger of Allah ﷺ leaned back and said, "Throw down their largest idol, the idol of Quraysh [Hubal]!" The idol was made of brass, and was affixed to the roof by iron pegs. The Messenger of Allah ﷺ ordered, "Strike it!" and as I was striking it, the Messenger of Allah ﷺ was saying, "*Yes! Truth has come and falsehood has vanished. Verily falsehood is ever vanishing!* (Qur'an 17:81) I continued to strike the idol until I was able to get it loose, and then I threw it down.' In another narration of this incident, Imam 'Ali was later asked, 'How did you feel being carried on the blessed shoulders of the Messenger of Allah ﷺ?' Imam 'Ali replied, 'My state was such that, had I wished to reach the Pleiades, I could have!' (For details of this narration and different wordings of this event, see: Imam Ahmad, *Musnad* (1:84); al-Hakim, *al-Mustadrak* (2:336); al-Bazzar, *Musnad* (769); Abu Ya'la, *al-Sahih* (1:251); al-Nasa'i, *Khasa'is al-Imam 'Ali* (74); and al-Khatib al-Baghdadi, *Tarikh Baghdad* (13:203). This hadith was cited by Imam al-Haythami in *Majma' al-Zawa'id* (6:23), and he said, 'This was recorded by Ahmad and his son ['Abdullah], and by Abu Ya'la and al-Bazzar, and its narrators are all people of probity and precision (*thiqat*).' This hadith is rigorously authenticated according to al-Hakim and Shaykh Ahmad Shakir. (*Sharh al-Musnad*, 2:57)) The lesson here is that the incidents of carrying the Prophet ﷺ have subtle yet tremendous spiritual significance. Allah and His Messenger ﷺ know best. (AA) ❦

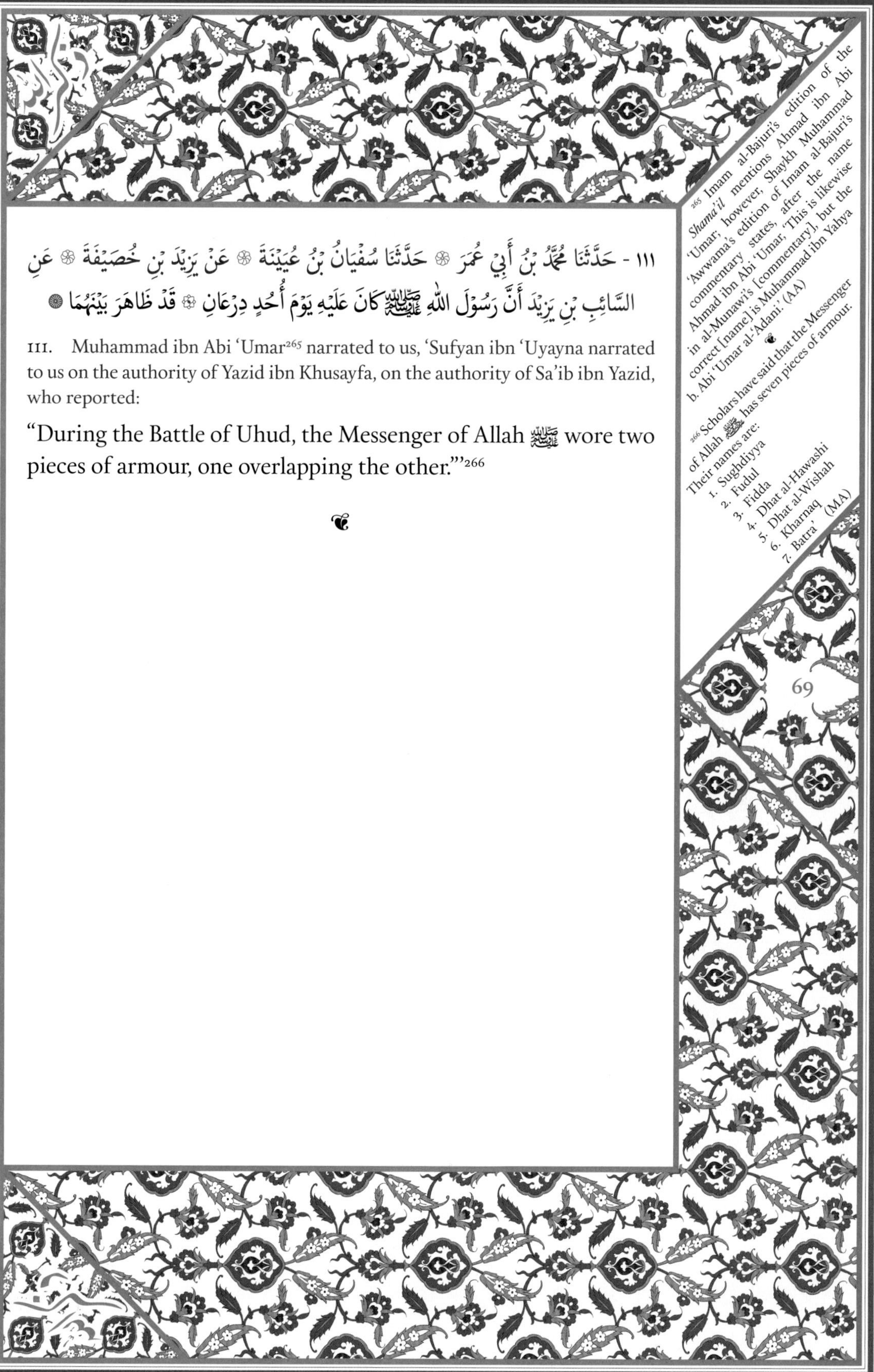

١١١ - حَدَّثَنَا مُحَمَّدُ بْنُ أَبِي عُمَرَ ❁ حَدَّثَنَا سُفْيَانُ بْنُ عُيَيْنَةَ ❁ عَنْ يَزِيْدَ بْنِ خُصَيْفَةَ ❁ عَنِ السَّائِبِ بْنِ يَزِيْدَ أَنَّ رَسُوْلَ اللهِ ﷺ كَانَ عَلَيْهِ يَوْمَ أُحُدٍ دِرْعَانِ ❁ قَدْ ظَاهَرَ بَيْنَهُمَا ❁

111. Muhammad ibn Abi 'Umar[265] narrated to us, 'Sufyan ibn 'Uyayna narrated to us on the authority of Yazid ibn Khusayfa, on the authority of Sa'ib ibn Yazid, who reported:

"During the Battle of Uhud, the Messenger of Allah ﷺ wore two pieces of armour, one overlapping the other."'[266]

❦

[265] Imam al-Bajuri's edition of the *Shama'il* mentions Ahmad ibn Abi 'Umar; however, Shaykh Muhammad 'Awwama's edition of Imam al-Bajuri's commentary states, after the name Ahmad ibn Abi 'Umar, 'This is likewise in al-Munawi's [commentary], but the correct [name] is Muhammad ibn Yahya b. Abi 'Umar al-'Adani.' (AA)

❦

[266] Scholars have said that the Messenger of Allah ﷺ has seven pieces of armour. Their names are:

1. Sughdiyya
2. Fudul
3. Fidda
4. Dhat al-Hawashi
5. Dhat al-Wishah
6. Kharnaq
7. Batra' (MA)

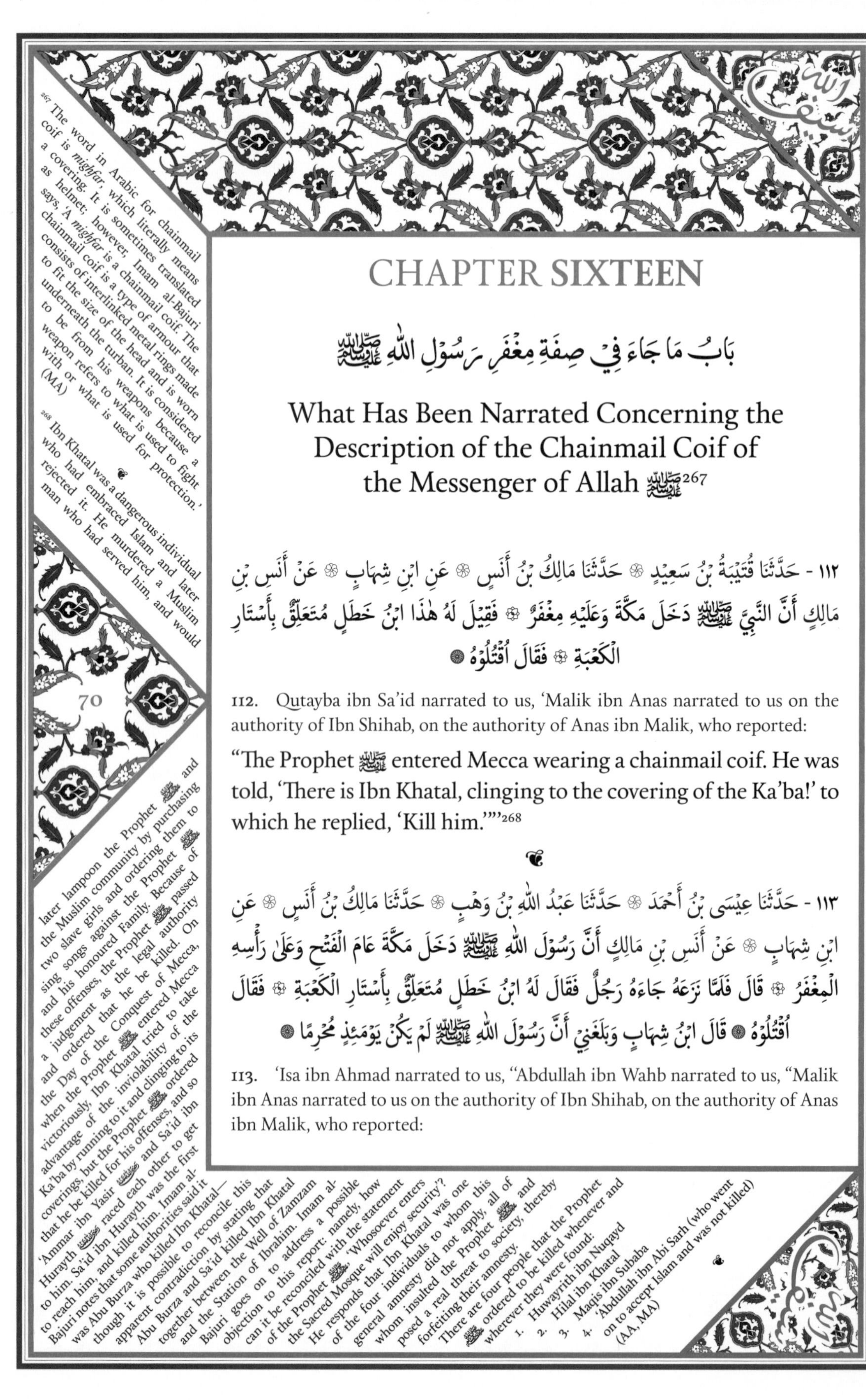

CHAPTER SIXTEEN

بَابُ مَا جَاءَ فِي صِفَةِ مِغْفَرِ رَسُولِ اللهِ ﷺ

What Has Been Narrated Concerning the Description of the Chainmail Coif of the Messenger of Allah ﷺ[267]

١١٢ - حَدَّثَنَا قُتَيْبَةُ بْنُ سَعِيدٍ ۞ حَدَّثَنَا مَالِكُ بْنُ أَنَسٍ ۞ عَنِ ابْنِ شِهَابٍ ۞ عَنْ أَنَسِ بْنِ مَالِكٍ أَنَّ النَّبِيَّ ﷺ دَخَلَ مَكَّةَ وَعَلَيْهِ مِغْفَرٌ ۞ فَقِيلَ لَهُ هٰذَا ابْنُ خَطَلٍ مُتَعَلِّقٌ بِأَسْتَارِ الْكَعْبَةِ ۞ فَقَالَ اُقْتُلُوهُ ۞

112. Qutayba ibn Sa'id narrated to us, 'Malik ibn Anas narrated to us on the authority of Ibn Shihab, on the authority of Anas ibn Malik, who reported:

"The Prophet ﷺ entered Mecca wearing a chainmail coif. He was told, 'There is Ibn Khatal, clinging to the covering of the Ka'ba!' to which he replied, 'Kill him.'"'[268]

١١٣ - حَدَّثَنَا عِيسَى بْنُ أَحْمَدَ ۞ حَدَّثَنَا عَبْدُ اللهِ بْنُ وَهْبٍ ۞ حَدَّثَنَا مَالِكُ بْنُ أَنَسٍ ۞ عَنِ ابْنِ شِهَابٍ ۞ عَنْ أَنَسِ بْنِ مَالِكٍ أَنَّ رَسُولَ اللهِ ﷺ دَخَلَ مَكَّةَ عَامَ الْفَتْحِ وَعَلَىٰ رَأْسِهِ الْمِغْفَرُ ۞ قَالَ فَلَمَّا نَزَعَهُ جَاءَهُ رَجُلٌ فَقَالَ لَهُ ابْنُ خَطَلٍ مُتَعَلِّقٌ بِأَسْتَارِ الْكَعْبَةِ ۞ فَقَالَ اُقْتُلُوهُ ۞ قَالَ ابْنُ شِهَابٍ وَبَلَغَنِي أَنَّ رَسُولَ اللهِ ﷺ لَمْ يَكُنْ يَوْمَئِذٍ مُحْرِمًا ۞

113. 'Isa ibn Ahmad narrated to us, "Abdullah ibn Wahb narrated to us, "Malik ibn Anas narrated to us on the authority of Ibn Shihab, on the authority of Anas ibn Malik, who reported:

[267] The word in Arabic for chainmail coif is *mighfar*, which literally means a covering. It is sometimes translated as helmet; however, Imam al-Bajuri says, 'A *mighfar* is a chainmail coif. The chainmail coif is a type of armour that consists of interlinked metal rings made to fit the size of the head and is worn underneath the turban. It is considered to be from his weapons because a weapon refers to what is used to fight with or what is used for protection.' (MA)

[268] Ibn Khatal was a dangerous individual who had embraced Islam and later rejected it. He murdered a Muslim man who had served him, and would later lampoon the Prophet ﷺ and the Muslim community by purchasing two slave girls and ordering them to sing songs against the Prophet ﷺ and his honoured Family. Because of these offenses, the Prophet ﷺ passed a judgement as the legal authority and ordered that he be killed. On the Day of the Conquest of Mecca, when the Prophet ﷺ entered Mecca victoriously, Ibn Khatal tried to take advantage of the inviolability of the Ka'ba by running to it and clinging to its coverings, but the Prophet ﷺ ordered that he be killed for his offenses, and so 'Ammar ibn Yasir ﷺ and Sa'id ibn Hurayth ﷺ raced each other to get to him. Sa'id ibn Hurayth was the first to reach him, and killed him. Imam al-Bajuri notes that some authorities said it was Abu Burza who killed Ibn Khatal—though it is possible to reconcile this apparent contradiction by stating that Abu Burza and Sa'id killed Ibn Khatal together between the Well of Zamzam and the Station of Ibrahim. Imam al-Bajuri goes on to address a possible objection to this report: namely, how can it be reconciled with the statement of the Prophet ﷺ, 'Whosoever enters the Sacred Mosque will enjoy security'? He responds that Ibn Khatal was one of the four individuals to whom this general amnesty did not apply, all of whom insulted the Prophet ﷺ and posed a real threat to society, thereby forfeiting their amnesty. There are four people that the Prophet ﷺ ordered to be killed whenever and wherever they were found:

1. Huwayrith ibn Nuqayd
2. Hilal ibn Khatal
3. Maqis ibn Subaba
4. 'Abdullah ibn Abi Sarh (who went on to accept Islam and was not killed)

(AA, MA)

'The Messenger of Allah ﷺ entered Mecca on the Day of the Conquest wearing a chainmail coif. After he removed it, a man came to him and said, "Ibn Khatal is clinging to the covering of the Ka'ba!" to which he replied, "Kill him."' Ibn Shihab said, 'It has reached me that the Messenger of Allah ﷺ was not in a state of *ihram*[269] that day.''

[269] To be in a state of *ihram* is to consecrate oneself for the performance of Hajj or 'Umra, by taking a purificatory bath and, for men, putting on an *ihram* garment of a white non-stitched covering and *izar* (loincloth). When in a state of *ihram*, some normally permissible acts are not permissible, i.e. hunting, applying perfume, clipping nails, etc. (MA)

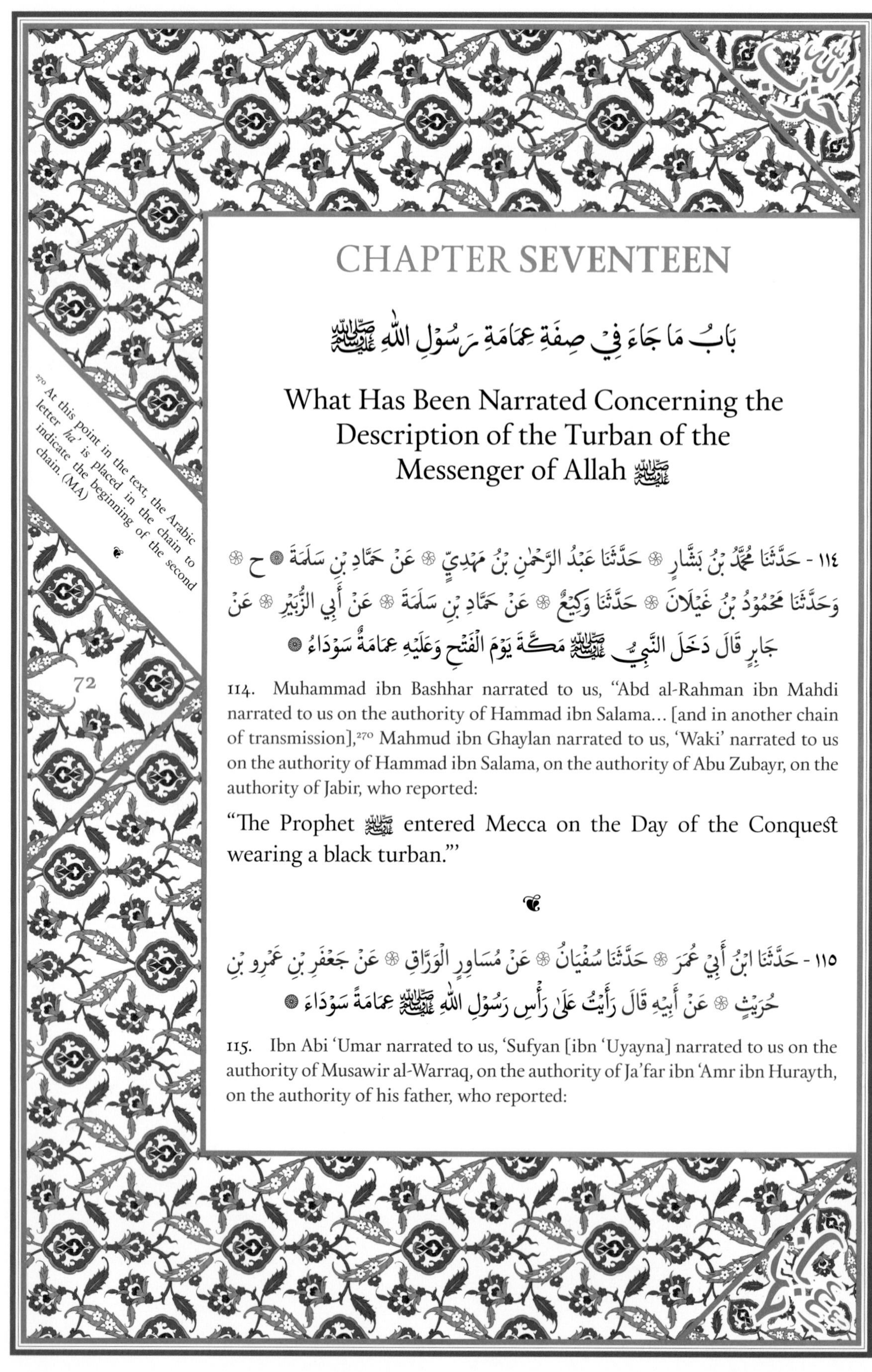

CHAPTER SEVENTEEN

بَابُ مَا جَاءَ فِي صِفَةِ عِمَامَةِ رَسُولِ اللهِ ﷺ

What Has Been Narrated Concerning the Description of the Turban of the Messenger of Allah ﷺ

١١٤ - حَدَّثَنَا مُحَمَّدُ بْنُ بَشَّارٍ ۞ حَدَّثَنَا عَبْدُ الرَّحْمَٰنِ بْنُ مَهْدِيٍّ ۞ عَنْ حَمَّادِ بْنِ سَلَمَةَ ۞ ح ۞ وَحَدَّثَنَا مَحْمُودُ بْنُ غَيْلَانَ ۞ حَدَّثَنَا وَكِيعٌ ۞ عَنْ حَمَّادِ بْنِ سَلَمَةَ ۞ عَنْ أَبِي الزُّبَيْرِ ۞ عَنْ جَابِرٍ قَالَ دَخَلَ النَّبِيُّ ﷺ مَكَّةَ يَوْمَ الْفَتْحِ وَعَلَيْهِ عِمَامَةٌ سَوْدَاءُ ۞

114. Muhammad ibn Bashhar narrated to us, "Abd al-Rahman ibn Mahdi narrated to us on the authority of Hammad ibn Salama... [and in another chain of transmission],[270] Mahmud ibn Ghaylan narrated to us, 'Waki' narrated to us on the authority of Hammad ibn Salama, on the authority of Abu Zubayr, on the authority of Jabir, who reported:

"The Prophet ﷺ entered Mecca on the Day of the Conquest wearing a black turban."'

١١٥ - حَدَّثَنَا ابْنُ أَبِي عُمَرَ ۞ حَدَّثَنَا سُفْيَانُ ۞ عَنْ مُسَاوِرٍ الْوَرَّاقِ ۞ عَنْ جَعْفَرِ بْنِ عَمْرِو بْنِ حُرَيْثٍ ۞ عَنْ أَبِيهِ قَالَ رَأَيْتُ عَلَى رَأْسِ رَسُولِ اللهِ ﷺ عِمَامَةً سَوْدَاءَ ۞

115. Ibn Abi 'Umar narrated to us, 'Sufyan [ibn 'Uyayna] narrated to us on the authority of Musawir al-Warraq, on the authority of Ja'far ibn 'Amr ibn Hurayth, on the authority of his father, who reported:

[270] At this point in the text, the Arabic letter *ha'* is placed in the chain to indicate the beginning of the second chain. (MA)

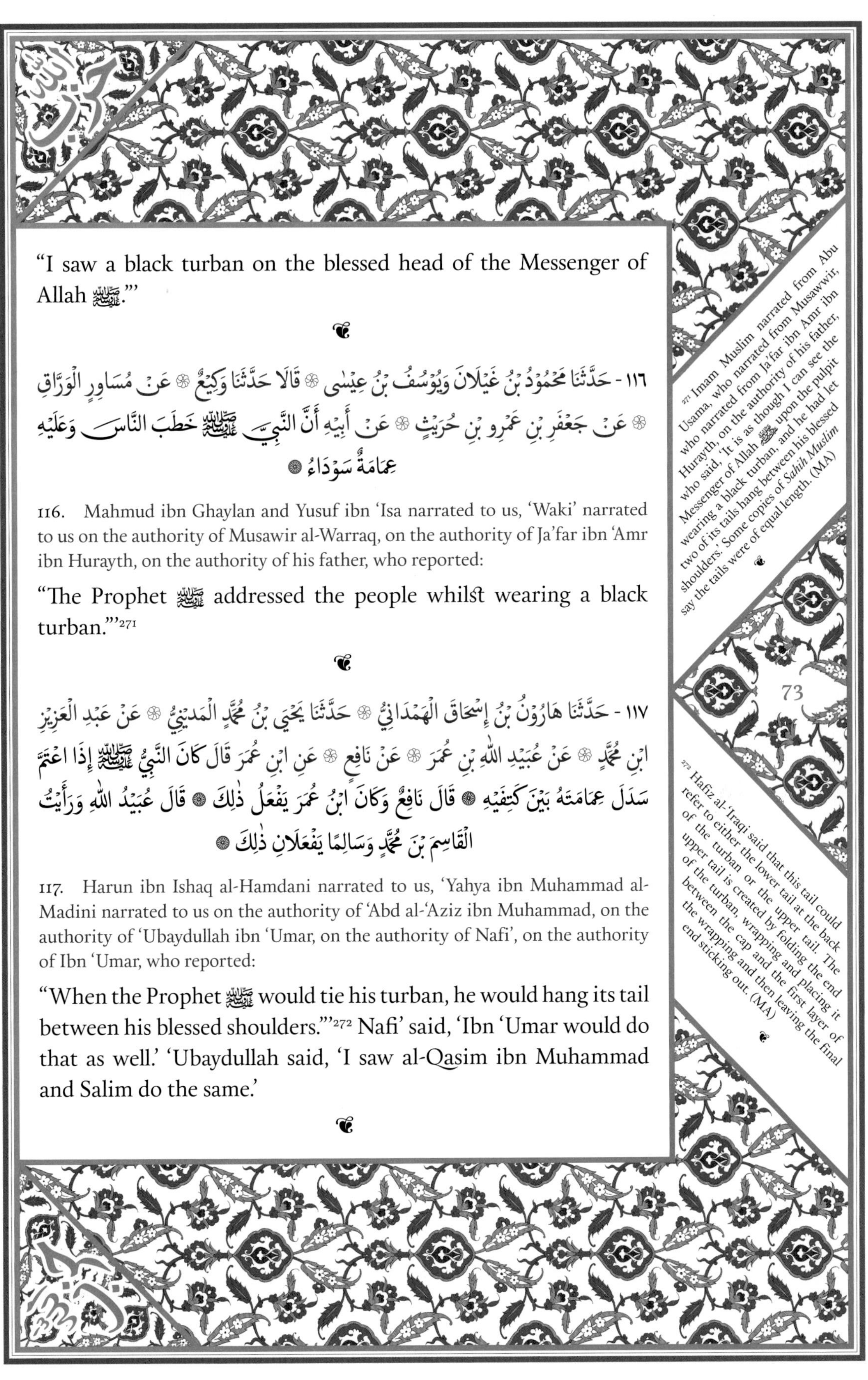

"I saw a black turban on the blessed head of the Messenger of Allah ﷺ.""

١١٦ - حَدَّثَنَا مَحْمُودُ بْنُ غَيْلَانَ وَيُوسُفُ بْنُ عِيسَى ❀ قَالَا حَدَّثَنَا وَكِيعٌ ❀ عَنْ مُسَاوِرٍ الْوَرَّاقِ ❀ عَنْ جَعْفَرِ بْنِ عَمْرِو بْنِ حُرَيْثٍ ❀ عَنْ أَبِيهِ أَنَّ النَّبِيَّ ﷺ خَطَبَ النَّاسَ وَعَلَيْهِ عِمَامَةٌ سَوْدَاءُ ❀

116. Mahmud ibn Ghaylan and Yusuf ibn 'Isa narrated to us, 'Waki' narrated to us on the authority of Musawir al-Warraq, on the authority of Ja'far ibn 'Amr ibn Hurayth, on the authority of his father, who reported:

"The Prophet ﷺ addressed the people whilst wearing a black turban.""[271]

١١٧ - حَدَّثَنَا هَارُونُ بْنُ إِسْحَاقَ الْهَمْدَانِيُّ ❀ حَدَّثَنَا يَحْيَى بْنُ مُحَمَّدٍ الْمَدِينِيُّ ❀ عَنْ عَبْدِ الْعَزِيزِ ابْنِ مُحَمَّدٍ ❀ عَنْ عُبَيْدِ اللهِ بْنِ عُمَرَ ❀ عَنْ نَافِعٍ ❀ عَنِ ابْنِ عُمَرَ قَالَ كَانَ النَّبِيُّ ﷺ إِذَا اعْتَمَّ سَدَلَ عِمَامَتَهُ بَيْنَ كَتِفَيْهِ ❀ قَالَ نَافِعٌ وَكَانَ ابْنُ عُمَرَ يَفْعَلُ ذٰلِكَ ❀ قَالَ عُبَيْدُ اللهِ وَرَأَيْتُ الْقَاسِمَ بْنَ مُحَمَّدٍ وَسَالِمًا يَفْعَلَانِ ذٰلِكَ ❀

117. Harun ibn Ishaq al-Hamdani narrated to us, 'Yahya ibn Muhammad al-Madini narrated to us on the authority of 'Abd al-'Aziz ibn Muhammad, on the authority of 'Ubaydullah ibn 'Umar, on the authority of Nafi', on the authority of Ibn 'Umar, who reported:

"When the Prophet ﷺ would tie his turban, he would hang its tail between his blessed shoulders.""[272] Nafi' said, 'Ibn 'Umar would do that as well.' 'Ubaydullah said, 'I saw al-Qasim ibn Muhammad and Salim do the same.'

[271] Imam Muslim narrated from Abu Usama, who narrated from Musawwir, who narrated from Ja'far ibn Amr ibn Hurayth, on the authority of his father, who said, 'It is as though I can see the Messenger of Allah ﷺ upon the pulpit wearing a black turban, and he had let two of its tails hang between his blessed shoulders.' Some copies of *Sahih Muslim* say the tails were of equal length. (MA)

[272] Hafiz al-'Iraqi said that this tail could refer to either the lower tail at the back of the turban or the upper tail. The upper tail is created by folding the end of the turban, wrapping and placing it between the cap and the first layer of the wrapping and then leaving the final end sticking out. (MA)

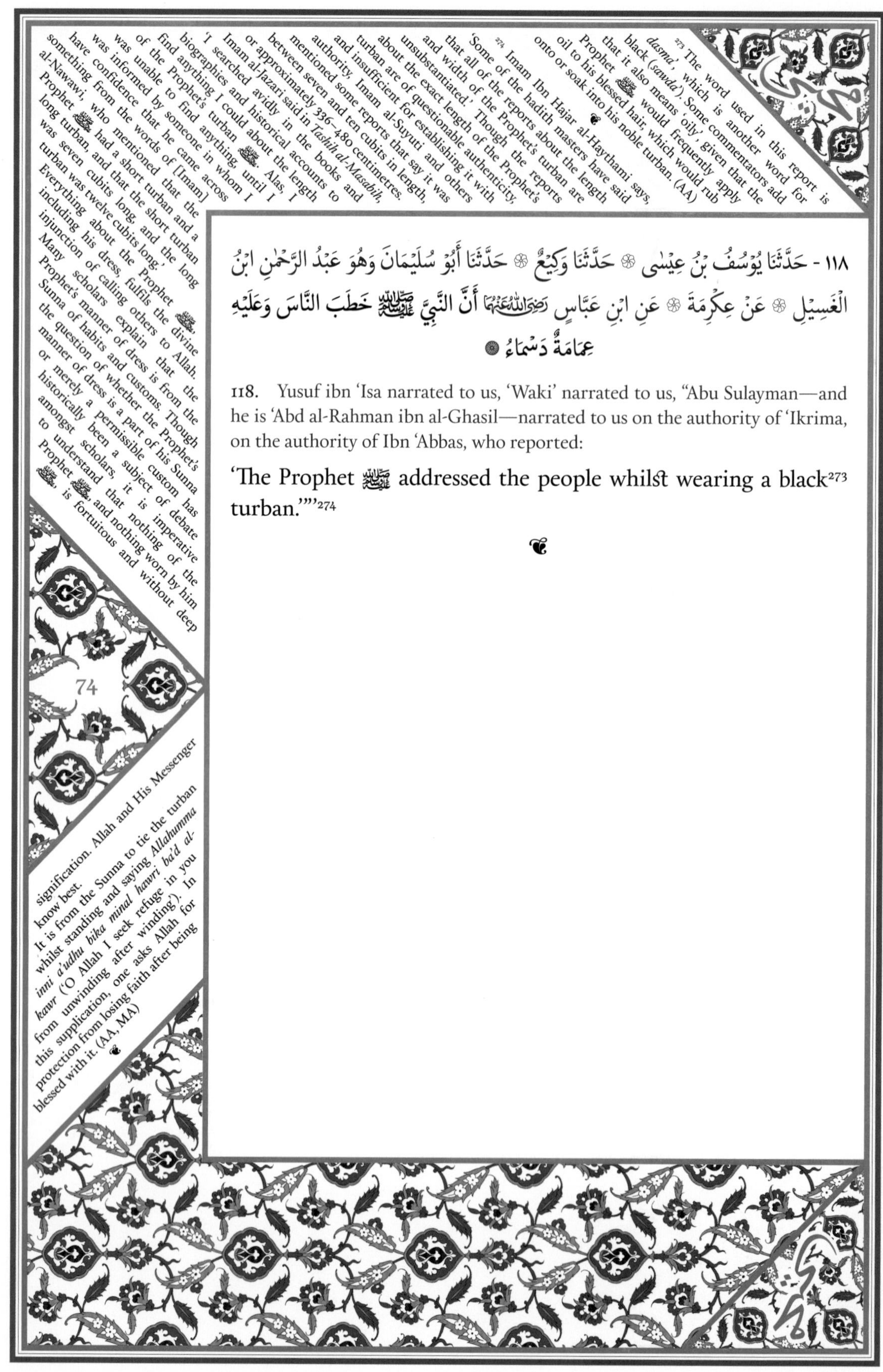

١١٨ - حَدَّثَنَا يُوسُفُ بْنُ عِيسَى ۞ حَدَّثَنَا وَكِيعٌ ۞ حَدَّثَنَا أَبُو سُلَيْمَانَ وَهُوَ عَبْدُ الرَّحْمٰنِ ابْنُ الْغَسِيلِ ۞ عَنْ عِكْرِمَةَ ۞ عَنِ ابْنِ عَبَّاسٍ رَضِيَ اللهُ عَنْهُمَا أَنَّ النَّبِيَّ ﷺ خَطَبَ النَّاسَ وَعَلَيْهِ عِمَامَةٌ دَسْمَاءُ ۞

118. Yusuf ibn 'Isa narrated to us, 'Waki' narrated to us, "Abu Sulayman—and he is 'Abd al-Rahman ibn al-Ghasil—narrated to us on the authority of 'Ikrima, on the authority of Ibn 'Abbas, who reported:

'The Prophet ﷺ addressed the people whilst wearing a black[273] turban.'"[274]

[273] The word used in this report is *dasma'*, which is another word for black (*sawda'*). Some commentators add that it also means 'oily', given that the Prophet ﷺ would frequently apply oil to his blessed hair, which would rub onto or soak into his noble turban. (AA)

[274] Imam Ibn Hajar al-Haythami says, 'Some of the hadith masters have said that all of the reports about the length and width of the Prophet's turban are unsubstantiated'. Though the reports about the exact length of the Prophet's turban are of questionable authenticity, and insufficient for establishing it with authority, Imam al-Suyuti and others mentioned some reports that say it was between seven and ten cubits in length, or approximately 336–480 centimetres. Imam al-Jazari said in *Tashih al-Masabih*, 'I searched avidly in the books and biographies and historical accounts to find anything I could about the length of the Prophet's turban ﷺ. Alas, I was unable to find anything, until I was informed by someone in whom I have confidence that he came across something from the words of [Imam] al-Nawawi, who mentioned that the Prophet ﷺ had a short turban and a long turban, and that the short turban was seven cubits long, and the long turban was twelve cubits long.' Everything about the Prophet ﷺ, including his dress, fulfils the divine injunction of calling others to Allah. Many scholars explain that the Prophet's manner of dress is from the Sunna of habits and customs. Though the question of whether the Prophet's manner of dress is a part of his Sunna or merely a permissible custom has historically been a subject of debate amongst scholars, it is imperative to understand that nothing of the Prophet ﷺ, and nothing worn by him ﷺ, is fortuitous and without deep signification. Allah and His Messenger know best.

It is from the Sunna to tie the turban whilst standing and saying, *Allahumma inni a'udhu bika minal hawri ba'd al-kawr* ('O Allah I seek refuge in you from unwinding after winding'). In this supplication, one asks Allah for protection from losing faith after being blessed with it. (AA, MA)

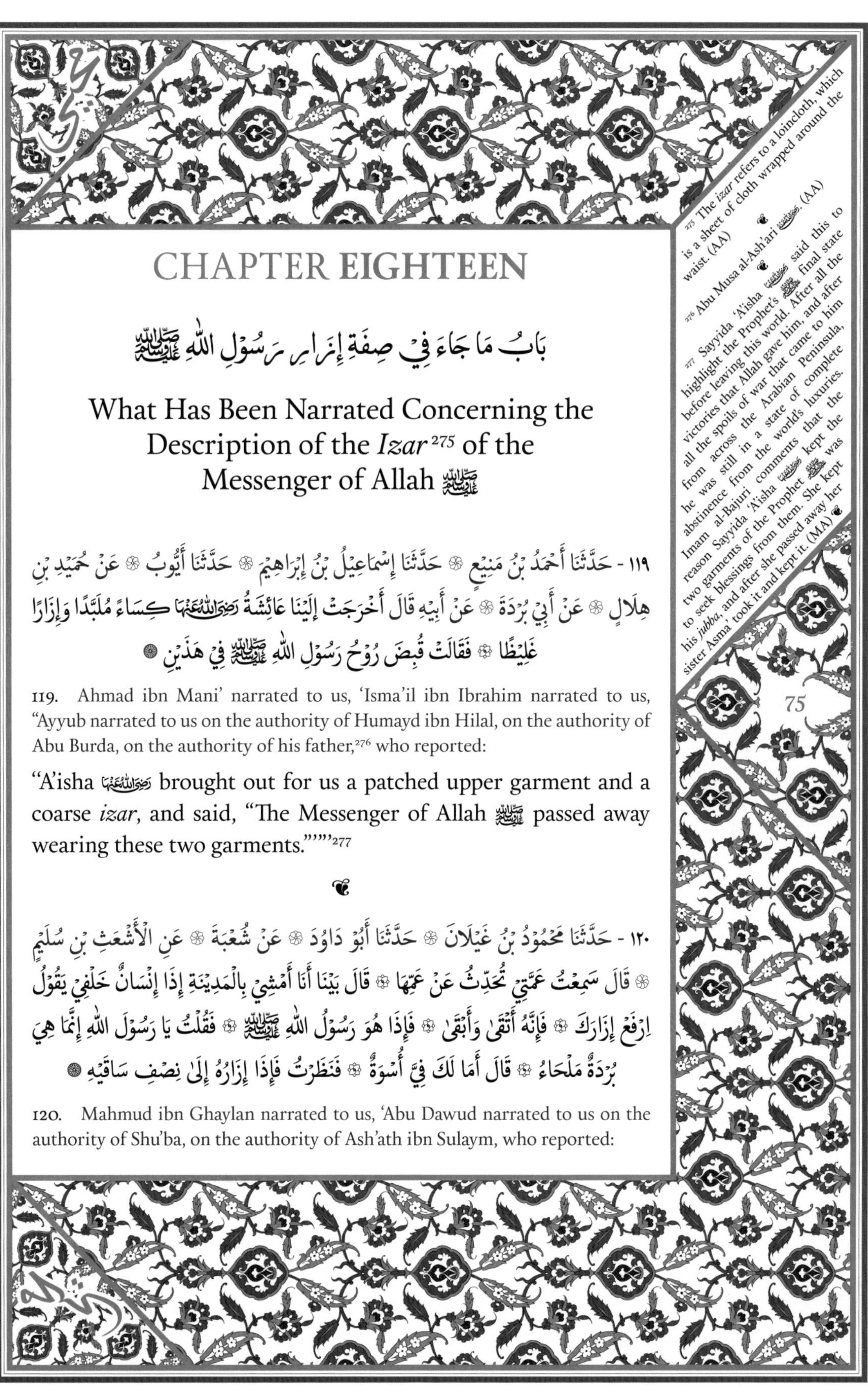

CHAPTER **EIGHTEEN**

بَابُ مَا جَاءَ فِي صِفَةِ إِزَارِ رَسُولِ اللهِ ﷺ

What Has Been Narrated Concerning the Description of the *Izar*[275] of the Messenger of Allah ﷺ

١١٩ - حَدَّثَنَا أَحْمَدُ بْنُ مَنِيعٍ ۞ حَدَّثَنَا إِسْمَاعِيلُ بْنُ إِبْرَاهِيمَ ۞ حَدَّثَنَا أَيُّوبُ ۞ عَنْ حُمَيْدِ بْنِ هِلَالٍ ۞ عَنْ أَبِي بُرْدَةَ ۞ عَنْ أَبِيهِ قَالَ أَخْرَجَتْ إِلَيْنَا عَائِشَةُ رَضِيَ اللهُ عَنْهَا كِسَاءً مُلَبَّدًا وَإِزَارًا غَلِيظًا ۞ فَقَالَتْ قُبِضَ رُوحُ رَسُولِ اللهِ ﷺ فِي هَذَيْنِ ۞

119. Ahmad ibn Mani' narrated to us, 'Isma'il ibn Ibrahim narrated to us, "Ayyub narrated to us on the authority of Humayd ibn Hilal, on the authority of Abu Burda, on the authority of his father,[276] who reported:

"A'isha رضي الله عنها brought out for us a patched upper garment and a coarse *izar*, and said, "The Messenger of Allah ﷺ passed away wearing these two garments.""""[277]

١٢٠ - حَدَّثَنَا مَحْمُودُ بْنُ غَيْلَانَ ۞ حَدَّثَنَا أَبُو دَاوُدَ ۞ عَنْ شُعْبَةَ ۞ عَنِ الْأَشْعَثِ بْنِ سُلَيْمٍ ۞ قَالَ سَمِعْتُ عَمَّتِي تُحَدِّثُ عَنْ عَمِّهَا ۞ قَالَ بَيْنَا أَنَا أَمْشِي بِالْمَدِينَةِ إِذَا إِنْسَانٌ خَلْفِي يَقُولُ ارْفَعْ إِزَارَكَ ۞ فَإِنَّهُ أَتْقَى وَأَبْقَى ۞ فَإِذَا هُوَ رَسُولُ اللهِ ﷺ ۞ فَقُلْتُ يَا رَسُولَ اللهِ إِنَّمَا هِيَ بُرْدَةٌ مَلْحَاءُ ۞ قَالَ أَمَا لَكَ فِيَّ أُسْوَةٌ ۞ فَنَظَرْتُ فَإِذَا إِزَارُهُ إِلَى نِصْفِ سَاقَيْهِ ۞

120. Mahmud ibn Ghaylan narrated to us, 'Abu Dawud narrated to us on the authority of Shu'ba, on the authority of Ash'ath ibn Sulaym, who reported:

275 The *izar* refers to a loincloth, which is a sheet of cloth wrapped around the waist. (AA)

276 Abu Musa al-Ash'ari رضي الله عنه. (AA)

277 Sayyida 'A'isha رضي الله عنها said this to highlight the Prophet's ﷺ final state before leaving this world. After all the victories that Allah gave him, and after all the spoils of war that came to him from across the Arabian Peninsula, he was still in a state of complete abstinence from the world's luxuries. Imam al-Bajuri comments that the reason Sayyida 'A'isha رضي الله عنها kept the two garments of the Prophet ﷺ was to seek blessings from them. She kept his *jubba*, and after she passed away her sister Asma' took it and kept it. (MA)

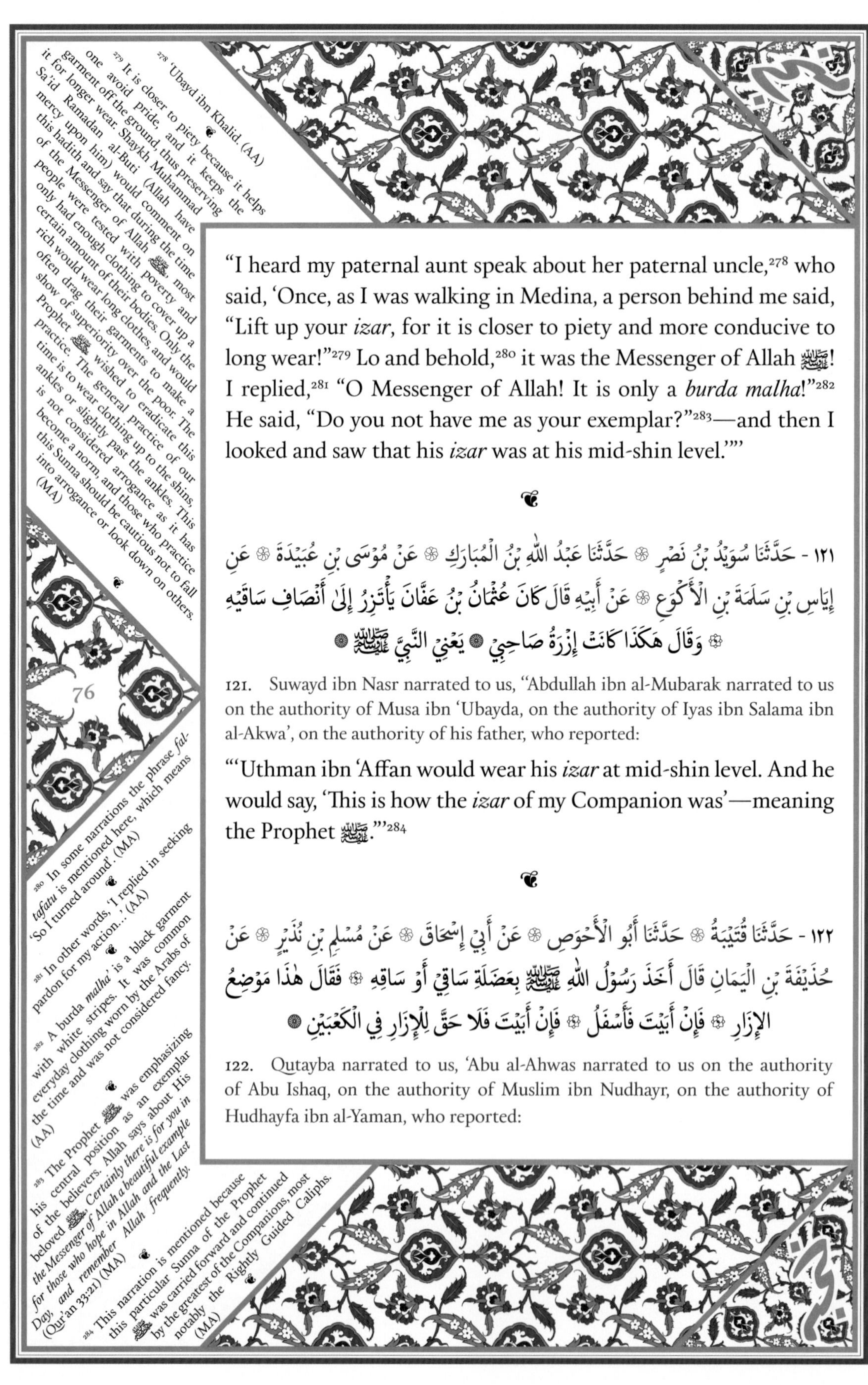

"I heard my paternal aunt speak about her paternal uncle,[278] who said, 'Once, as I was walking in Medina, a person behind me said, "Lift up your *izar*, for it is closer to piety and more conducive to long wear!"[279] Lo and behold,[280] it was the Messenger of Allah ﷺ! I replied,[281] "O Messenger of Allah! It is only a *burda malha*!"[282] He said, "Do you not have me as your exemplar?"[283]—and then I looked and saw that his *izar* was at his mid-shin level.'"

❦

١٢١ - حَدَّثَنَا سُوَيْدُ بْنُ نَصْرٍ ۞ حَدَّثَنَا عَبْدُ اللهِ بْنُ الْمُبَارَكِ ۞ عَنْ مُوسَى بْنِ عُبَيْدَةَ ۞ عَنْ إِيَاسِ بْنِ سَلَمَةَ بْنِ الْأَكْوَعِ ۞ عَنْ أَبِيهِ قَالَ كَانَ عُثْمَانُ بْنُ عَفَّانَ يَأْتَزِرُ إِلَىٰ أَنْصَافِ سَاقَيْهِ ۞ وَقَالَ هٰكَذَا كَانَتْ إِزْرَةُ صَاحِبِي ۞ يَعْنِي النَّبِيَّ ﷺ ۞

121. Suwayd ibn Nasr narrated to us, "Abdullah ibn al-Mubarak narrated to us on the authority of Musa ibn 'Ubayda, on the authority of Iyas ibn Salama ibn al-Akwa', on the authority of his father, who reported:

"'Uthman ibn 'Affan would wear his *izar* at mid-shin level. And he would say, 'This is how the *izar* of my Companion was'—meaning the Prophet ﷺ."[284]

❦

١٢٢ - حَدَّثَنَا قُتَيْبَةُ ۞ حَدَّثَنَا أَبُو الْأَحْوَصِ ۞ عَنْ أَبِي إِسْحَاقَ ۞ عَنْ مُسْلِمِ بْنِ نُذَيْرٍ ۞ عَنْ حُذَيْفَةَ بْنِ الْيَمَانِ قَالَ أَخَذَ رَسُولُ اللهِ ﷺ بِعَضَلَةِ سَاقِي أَوْ سَاقِهِ ۞ فَقَالَ هٰذَا مَوْضِعُ الْإِزَارِ ۞ فَإِنْ أَبَيْتَ فَأَسْفَلُ ۞ فَإِنْ أَبَيْتَ فَلَا حَقَّ لِلْإِزَارِ فِي الْكَعْبَيْنِ ۞

122. Qutayba narrated to us, 'Abu al-Ahwas narrated to us on the authority of Abu Ishaq, on the authority of Muslim ibn Nudhayr, on the authority of Hudhayfa ibn al-Yaman, who reported:

[278] 'Ubayd ibn Khalid. (AA)

[279] It is closer to piety because it helps one avoid pride, and it keeps the garment off the ground, thus preserving it for longer wear. Shaykh Muhammad Sa'id Ramadan al-Buti (Allah have mercy upon him) would comment on this hadith and say that during the time of the Messenger of Allah ﷺ most people were tested with poverty and only had enough clothing to cover up a certain amount of their bodies. Only the rich would wear long clothes, and would often drag their garments to make a show of superiority over the poor. The Prophet ﷺ wished to eradicate this practice. The general practice of our time is to wear clothing up to the shins, ankles or slightly past the ankles. This is not considered arrogance as it has become a norm, and those who practice this Sunna should be cautious not to fall into arrogance or look down on others. (MA)

[280] In some narrations the phrase *fal-tafatu* is mentioned here, which means 'So I turned around'. (MA)

[281] In other words, 'I replied in seeking pardon for my action...' (AA)

[282] A burda *malha'* is a black garment with white stripes. It was common everyday clothing worn by the Arabs of the time and was not considered fancy. (AA)

[283] The Prophet ﷺ was emphasizing his central position as an exemplar of the believers. Allah says about His beloved ﷺ: *Certainly there is for you in the Messenger of Allah a beautiful example for those who hope in Allah and the Last Day, and remember Allah frequently.* (Qur'an 33:21) (MA)

[284] This narration is mentioned because this particular Sunna of the Prophet ﷺ was carried forward and continued by the greatest of the Companions, most notably the Rightly Guided Caliphs. (MA)

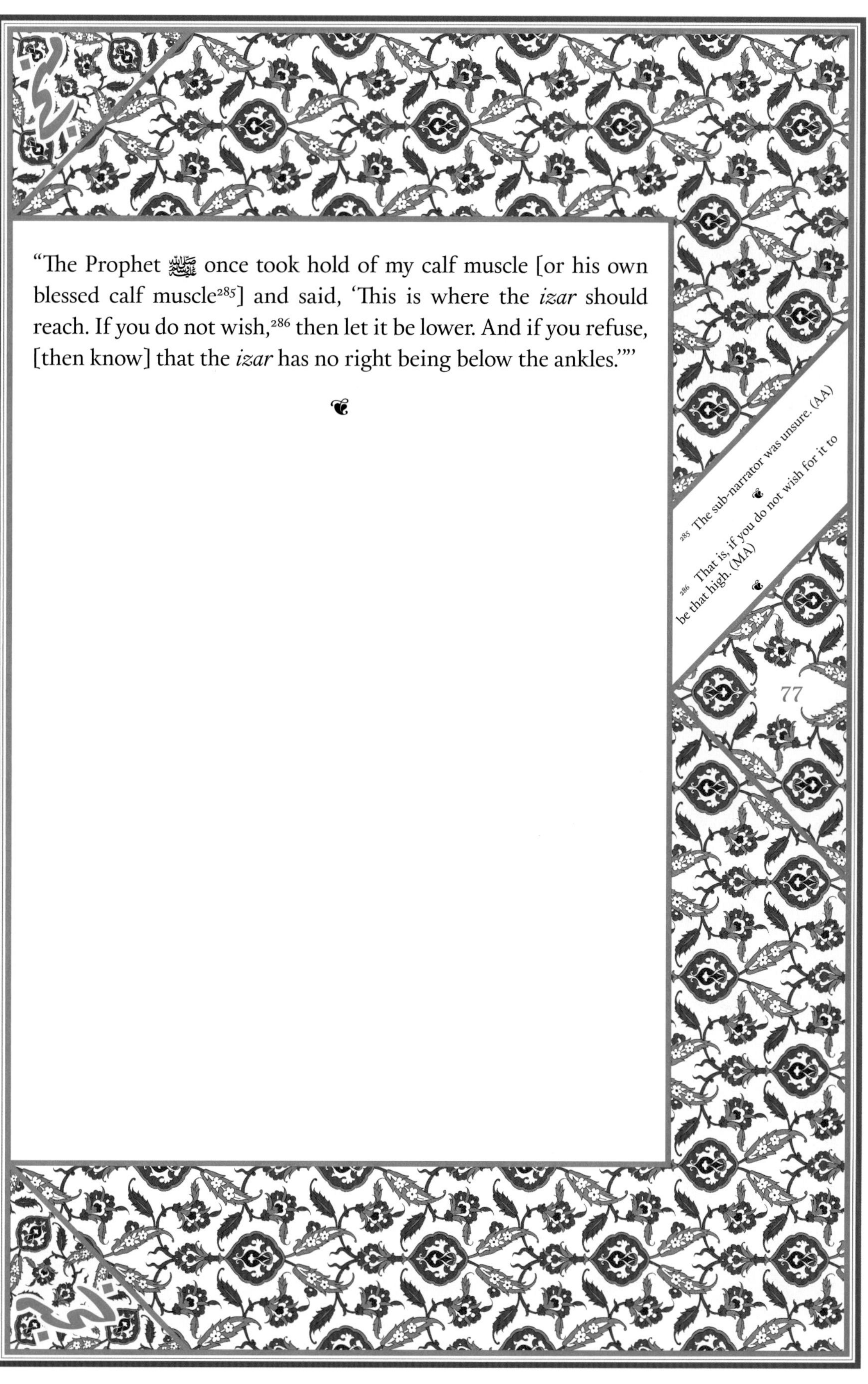

"The Prophet ﷺ once took hold of my calf muscle [or his own blessed calf muscle[285]] and said, 'This is where the *izar* should reach. If you do not wish,[286] then let it be lower. And if you refuse, [then know] that the *izar* has no right being below the ankles.'"

[285] The sub-narrator was unsure. (AA)

[286] That is, if you do not wish for it to be that high. (MA)

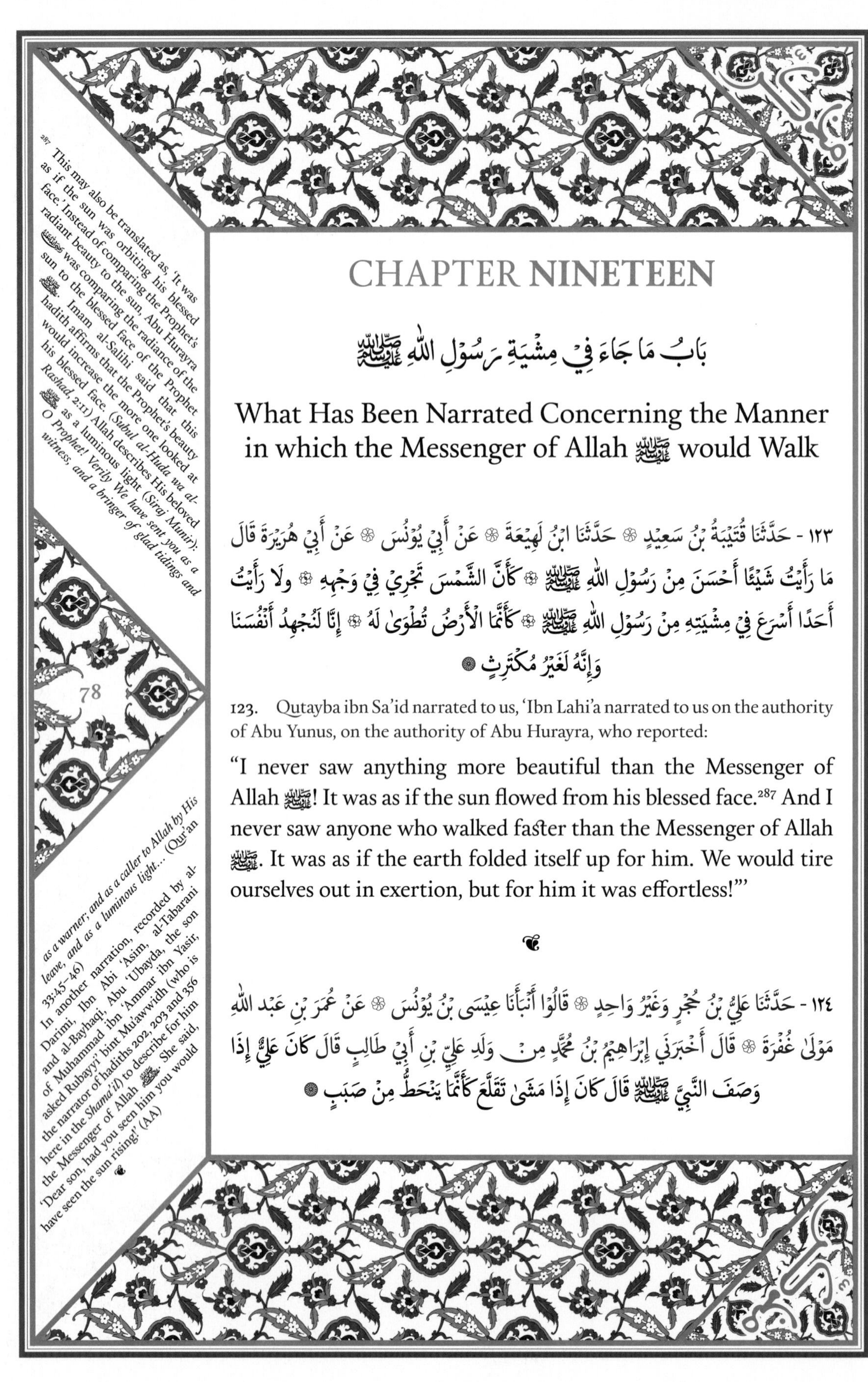

CHAPTER NINETEEN

بَابُ مَا جَاءَ فِي مِشْيَةِ رَسُولِ اللهِ ﷺ

What Has Been Narrated Concerning the Manner in which the Messenger of Allah ﷺ would Walk

١٢٣ - حَدَّثَنَا قُتَيْبَةُ بْنُ سَعِيدٍ ۞ حَدَّثَنَا ابْنُ لَهِيعَةَ ۞ عَنْ أَبِي يُونُسَ ۞ عَنْ أَبِي هُرَيْرَةَ قَالَ مَا رَأَيْتُ شَيْئًا أَحْسَنَ مِنْ رَسُولِ اللهِ ﷺ ۞ كَأَنَّ الشَّمْسَ تَجْرِي فِي وَجْهِهِ ۞ وَلَا رَأَيْتُ أَحَدًا أَسْرَعَ فِي مِشْيَتِهِ مِنْ رَسُولِ اللهِ ﷺ ۞ كَأَنَّمَا الْأَرْضُ تُطْوَى لَهُ ۞ إِنَّا لَنُجْهِدُ أَنْفُسَنَا وَإِنَّهُ لَغَيْرُ مُكْتَرِثٍ ۞

123. Qutayba ibn Sa'id narrated to us, 'Ibn Lahi'a narrated to us on the authority of Abu Yunus, on the authority of Abu Hurayra, who reported:

"I never saw anything more beautiful than the Messenger of Allah ﷺ! It was as if the sun flowed from his blessed face.[287] And I never saw anyone who walked faster than the Messenger of Allah ﷺ. It was as if the earth folded itself up for him. We would tire ourselves out in exertion, but for him it was effortless!'"

١٢٤ - حَدَّثَنَا عَلِيُّ بْنُ حُجْرٍ وَغَيْرُ وَاحِدٍ ۞ قَالُوا أَنْبَأَنَا عِيسَى بْنُ يُونُسَ ۞ عَنْ عُمَرَ بْنِ عَبْدِ اللهِ مَوْلَى غُفْرَةَ ۞ قَالَ أَخْبَرَنِي إِبْرَاهِيمُ بْنُ مُحَمَّدٍ مِنْ وَلَدِ عَلِيِّ بْنِ أَبِي طَالِبٍ قَالَ كَانَ عَلِيٌّ إِذَا وَصَفَ النَّبِيَّ ﷺ قَالَ كَانَ إِذَا مَشَى تَقَلَّعَ كَأَنَّمَا يَنْحَطُّ مِنْ صَبَبٍ ۞

[287] This may also be translated as, 'It was as if the sun was orbiting his blessed face.' Instead of comparing the Prophet's radiant beauty to the sun, Abu Hurayra was comparing the radiance of the sun to the blessed face of the Prophet ﷺ. Imam al-Salihi said that this hadith affirms that the Prophet's beauty would increase the more one looked at his blessed face. (*Subul al-Huda wa al-Rashad*, 2:11) Allah describes His beloved ﷺ as a luminous light (*Siraj Munir*): *O Prophet! Verily We have sent you as a witness, and a bringer of glad tidings and as a warner; and as a caller to Allah by His leave, and as a luminous light...* (Qur'an 33:45-46) In another narration, recorded by al-Darimi, Ibn Abi 'Asim, al-Tabarani and al-Bayhaqi, Abu 'Ubayda, the son of Muhammad ibn 'Ammar ibn Yasir, asked Rubayyi' bint Mu'awwidh (who is the narrator of hadiths 202, 203 and 356 here in the *Shama'il*) to describe for him the Messenger of Allah ﷺ. She said, 'Dear son, had you seen him you would have seen the sun rising!' (AA)

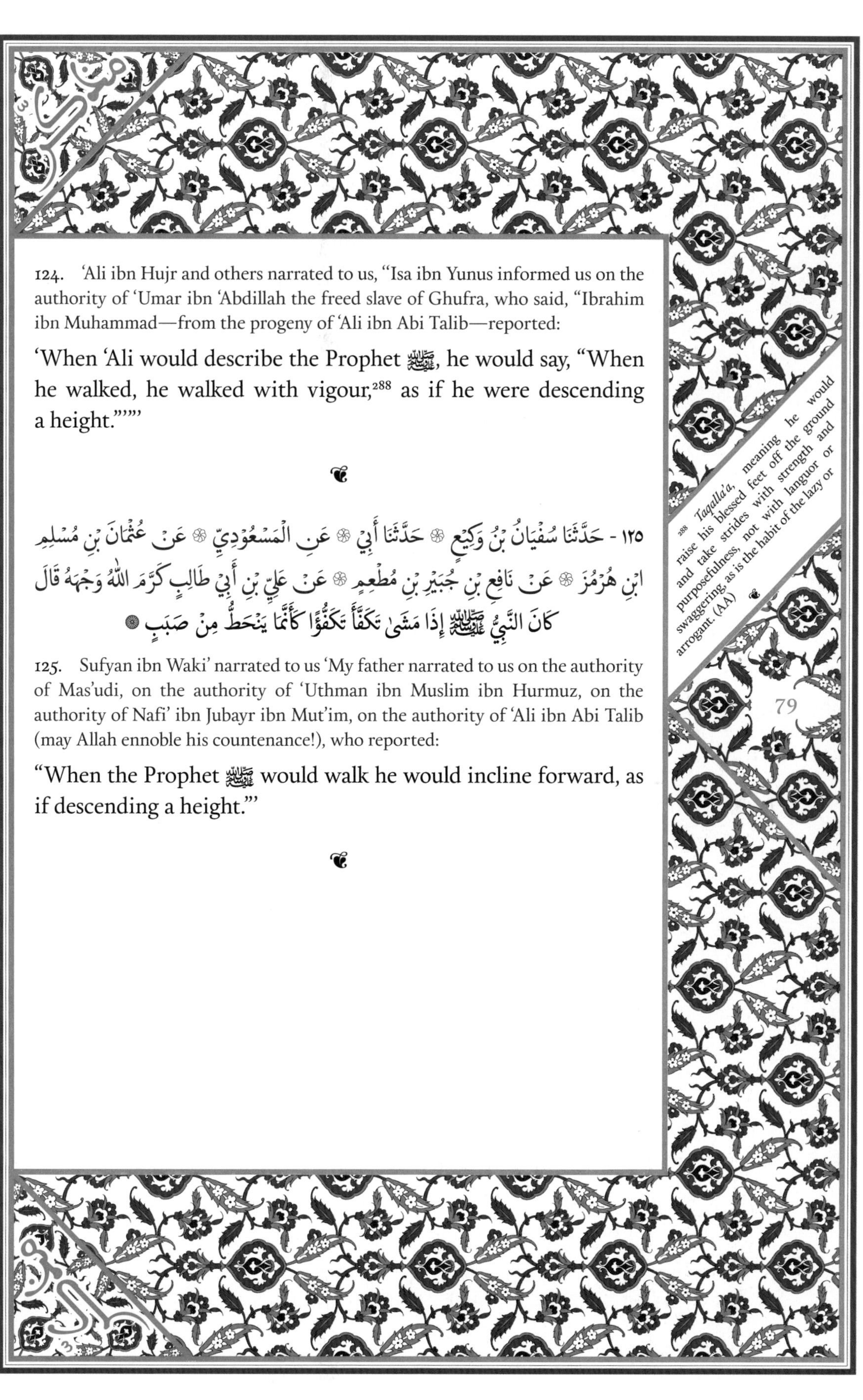

124. 'Ali ibn Hujr and others narrated to us, "Isa ibn Yunus informed us on the authority of 'Umar ibn 'Abdillah the freed slave of Ghufra, who said, "Ibrahim ibn Muhammad—from the progeny of 'Ali ibn Abi Talib—reported:

'When 'Ali would describe the Prophet ﷺ, he would say, "When he walked, he walked with vigour,[288] as if he were descending a height."'""

❦

١٢٥ - حَدَّثَنَا سُفْيَانُ بْنُ وَكِيعٍ ۞ حَدَّثَنَا أَبِي ۞ عَنِ الْمَسْعُودِيِّ ۞ عَنْ عُثْمَانَ بْنِ مُسْلِمِ ابْنِ هُرْمُزَ ۞ عَنْ نَافِعِ بْنِ جُبَيْرِ بْنِ مُطْعِمٍ ۞ عَنْ عَلِيِّ بْنِ أَبِي طَالِبٍ كَرَّمَ اللَّهُ وَجْهَهُ قَالَ كَانَ النَّبِيُّ ﷺ إِذَا مَشَى تَكَفَّأَ تَكَفُّؤًا كَأَنَّمَا يَنْحَطُّ مِنْ صَبَبٍ ۞

125. Sufyan ibn Waki' narrated to us 'My father narrated to us on the authority of Mas'udi, on the authority of 'Uthman ibn Muslim ibn Hurmuz, on the authority of Nafi' ibn Jubayr ibn Mut'im, on the authority of 'Ali ibn Abi Talib (may Allah ennoble his countenance!), who reported:

"When the Prophet ﷺ would walk he would incline forward, as if descending a height."'

❦

288 *Taqalla'a*, meaning he would raise his blessed feet off the ground and take strides with strength and purposefulness, not with languor or swaggering, as is the habit of the lazy or arrogant. (AA) ❦

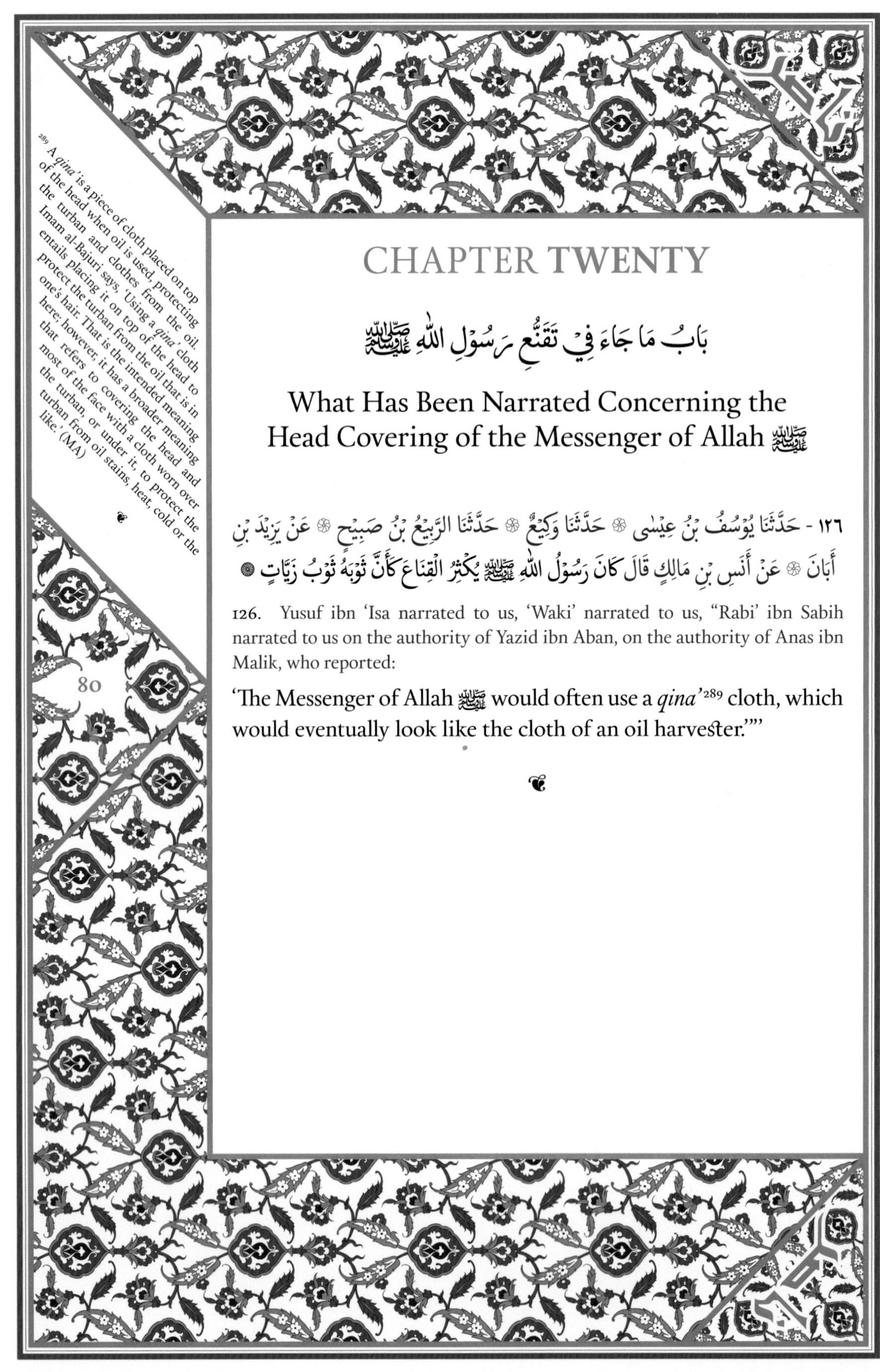

CHAPTER TWENTY

بَابُ مَا جَاءَ فِي تَقَنُّعِ رَسُولِ اللهِ ﷺ

What Has Been Narrated Concerning the Head Covering of the Messenger of Allah ﷺ

١٢٦ - حَدَّثَنَا يُوسُفُ بْنُ عِيسٰى ۞ حَدَّثَنَا وَكِيعٌ ۞ حَدَّثَنَا الرَّبِيعُ بْنُ صَبِيحٍ ۞ عَنْ يَزِيدَ بْنِ أَبَانَ ۞ عَنْ أَنَسِ بْنِ مَالِكٍ قَالَ كَانَ رَسُولُ اللهِ ﷺ يُكْثِرُ الْقِنَاعَ كَأَنَّ ثَوْبَهُ ثَوْبُ زَيَّاتٍ ۞

126. Yusuf ibn 'Isa narrated to us, 'Waki' narrated to us, "Rabi' ibn Sabih narrated to us on the authority of Yazid ibn Aban, on the authority of Anas ibn Malik, who reported:

'The Messenger of Allah ﷺ would often use a *qina'*[289] cloth, which would eventually look like the cloth of an oil harvester.'"

[289] A *qina'* is a piece of cloth placed on top of the head when oil is used, protecting the turban and clothes from the oil. Imam al-Bajuri says, 'Using a *qina'* cloth entails placing it on top of the head to protect the turban from the oil that is in one's hair. That is the intended meaning here; however, it has a broader meaning that refers to covering the head and most of the face with a cloth worn over the turban, or under it, to protect the turban from oil stains, heat, cold or the like.' (MA)

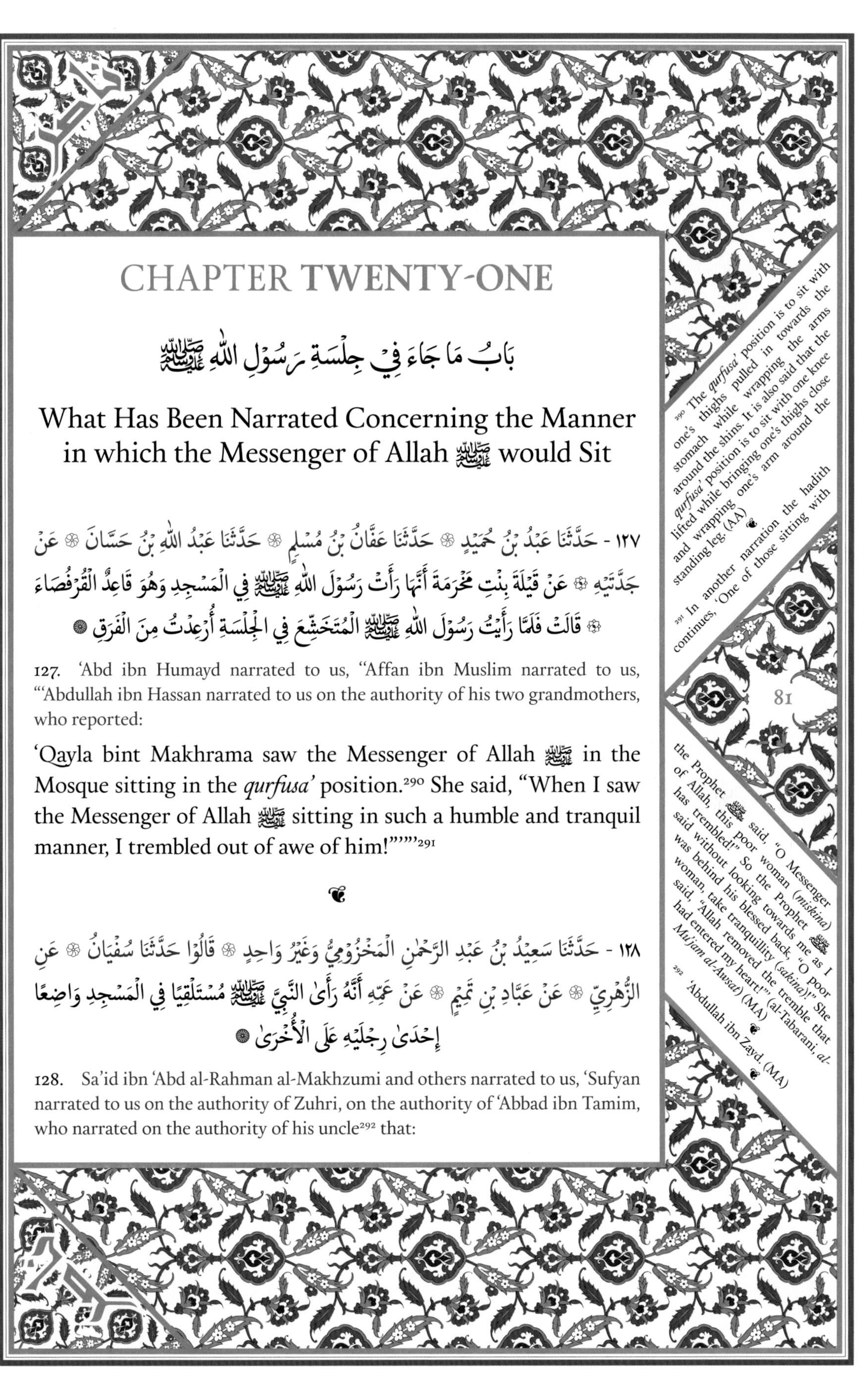

CHAPTER TWENTY-ONE

بَابُ مَا جَاءَ فِي جِلْسَةِ رَسُوْلِ اللهِ ﷺ

What Has Been Narrated Concerning the Manner in which the Messenger of Allah ﷺ would Sit

١٢٧ - حَدَّثَنَا عَبْدُ بْنُ حُمَيْدٍ ❁ حَدَّثَنَا عَفَّانُ بْنُ مُسْلِمٍ ❁ حَدَّثَنَا عَبْدُ اللهِ بْنُ حَسَّانَ ❁ عَنْ جَدَّتَيْهِ ❁ عَنْ قَيْلَةَ بِنْتِ مَخْرَمَةَ أَنَّهَا رَأَتْ رَسُوْلَ اللهِ ﷺ فِي الْمَسْجِدِ وَهُوَ قَاعِدٌ الْقُرْفُصَاءَ ❁ قَالَتْ فَلَمَّا رَأَيْتُ رَسُوْلَ اللهِ ﷺ الْمُتَخَشِّعَ فِي الْجِلْسَةِ أُرْعِدْتُ مِنَ الْفَرَقِ ❁

127. 'Abd ibn Humayd narrated to us, "Affan ibn Muslim narrated to us, "'Abdullah ibn Hassan narrated to us on the authority of his two grandmothers, who reported:

'Qayla bint Makhrama saw the Messenger of Allah ﷺ in the Mosque sitting in the *qurfusa'* position.[290] She said, "When I saw the Messenger of Allah ﷺ sitting in such a humble and tranquil manner, I trembled out of awe of him!"""'[291]

١٢٨ - حَدَّثَنَا سَعِيْدُ بْنُ عَبْدِ الرَّحْمٰنِ الْمَخْزُوْمِيُّ وَغَيْرُ وَاحِدٍ ❁ قَالُوْا حَدَّثَنَا سُفْيَانُ ❁ عَنِ الزُّهْرِيِّ ❁ عَنْ عَبَّادِ بْنِ تَمِيْمٍ ❁ عَنْ عَمِّهِ أَنَّهُ رَأَى النَّبِيَّ ﷺ مُسْتَلْقِيًا فِي الْمَسْجِدِ وَاضِعًا إِحْدَىٰ رِجْلَيْهِ عَلَى الْأُخْرَىٰ ❁

128. Sa'id ibn 'Abd al-Rahman al-Makhzumi and others narrated to us, 'Sufyan narrated to us on the authority of Zuhri, on the authority of 'Abbad ibn Tamim, who narrated on the authority of his uncle[292] that:

[290] The *qurfusa'* position is to sit with one's thighs pulled in towards the stomach while wrapping the arms around the shins. It is also said that the *qurfusa'* position is to sit with one knee lifted while bringing one's thighs close and wrapping one's arm around the standing leg. (AA)

[291] In another narration the hadith continues, 'One of those sitting with the Prophet ﷺ said, "O Messenger of Allah, this poor woman (*miskina*) has trembled!" So the Prophet ﷺ said without looking towards me as I was behind his blessed back, "O poor woman, take tranquillity (*sakina*)!" She said, "Allah removed the tremble that had entered my heart!"' (al-Tabarani, *al-Mu'jam al-Awsat*) (MA)

[292] 'Abdullah ibn Zayd. (MA)

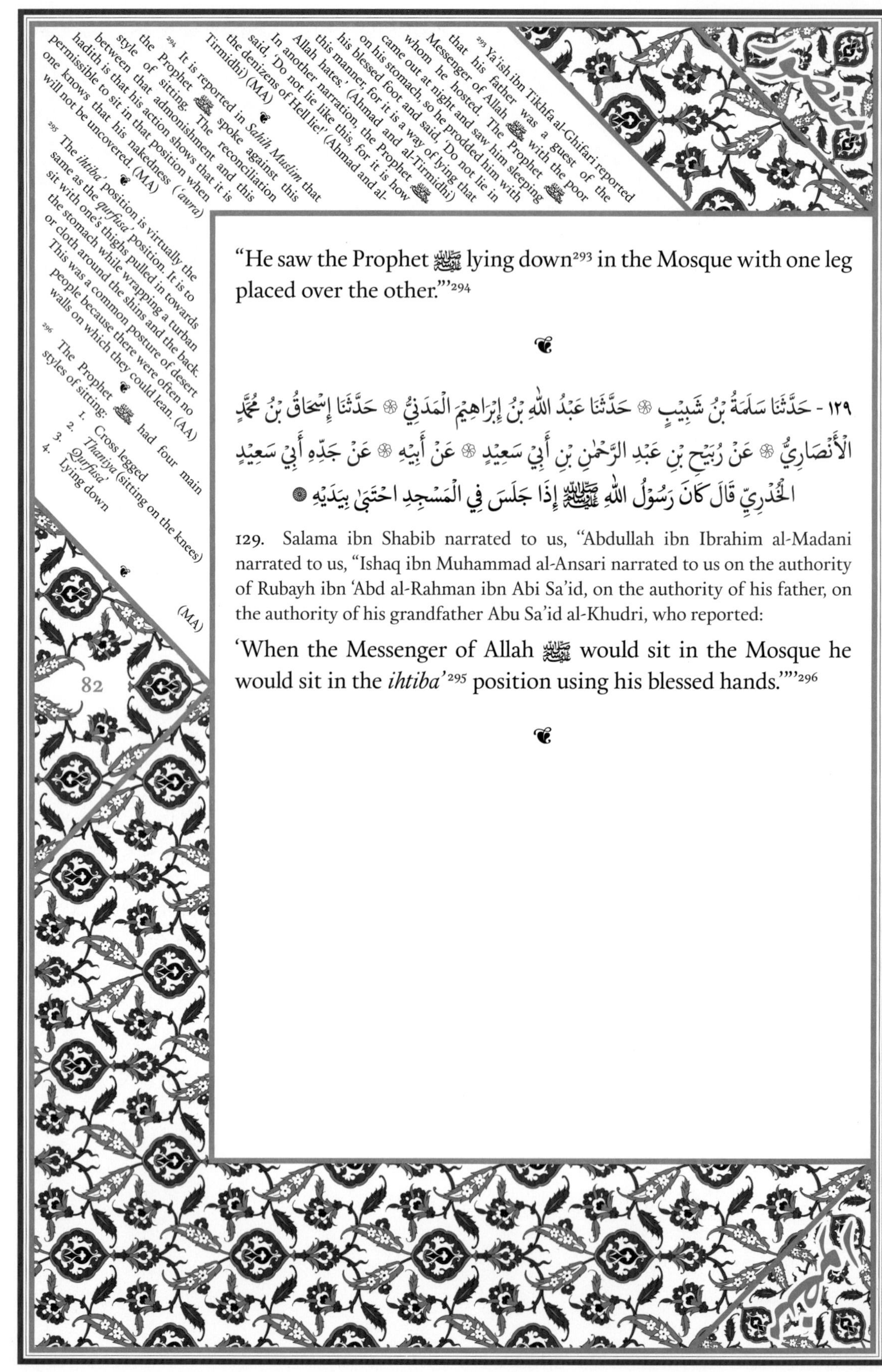

"He saw the Prophet ﷺ lying down[293] in the Mosque with one leg placed over the other."'[294]

❦

١٢٩ - حَدَّثَنَا سَلَمَةُ بْنُ شَبِيبٍ ❀ حَدَّثَنَا عَبْدُ اللهِ بْنُ إِبْرَاهِيمَ الْمَدَنِيُّ ❀ حَدَّثَنَا إِسْحَاقُ بْنُ مُحَمَّدٍ الْأَنْصَارِيُّ ❀ عَنْ رُبَيْحِ بْنِ عَبْدِ الرَّحْمٰنِ بْنِ أَبِي سَعِيدٍ ❀ عَنْ أَبِيهِ ❀ عَنْ جَدِّهِ أَبِي سَعِيدٍ الْخُدْرِيِّ قَالَ كَانَ رَسُولُ اللهِ ﷺ إِذَا جَلَسَ فِي الْمَسْجِدِ احْتَبَىٰ بِيَدَيْهِ ۞

129. Salama ibn Shabib narrated to us, "Abdullah ibn Ibrahim al-Madani narrated to us, "Ishaq ibn Muhammad al-Ansari narrated to us on the authority of Rubayh ibn 'Abd al-Rahman ibn Abi Sa'id, on the authority of his father, on the authority of his grandfather Abu Sa'id al-Khudri, who reported:

'When the Messenger of Allah ﷺ would sit in the Mosque he would sit in the *ihtiba'*[295] position using his blessed hands.'"'[296]

❦

[293] Ya'ish ibn Tikhfa al-Ghifari reported that his father was a guest of the Messenger of Allah ﷺ with the poor whom he hosted. The Prophet ﷺ came out at night and saw him sleeping on his stomach, so he prodded him with his blessed foot and said, 'Do not lie in this manner, for it is a way of lying that Allah hates.' (Ahmad and al-Tirmidhi) In another narration, the Prophet ﷺ said, 'Do not lie like this, for it is how the denizens of Hell lie!' (Ahmad and al-Tirmidhi) (MA)

❦

[294] It is reported in *Sahih Muslim* that the Prophet ﷺ spoke against this style of sitting. The reconciliation between that admonishment and this hadith is that his action shows that it is permissible to sit in that position when one knows that his nakedness (*'awra*) will not be uncovered. (MA)

❦

[295] The *ihtiba'* position is virtually the same as the *qurfusa'* position. It is to sit with one's thighs pulled in towards the stomach while wrapping a turban or cloth around the shins and the back. This was a common posture of desert people because there were often no walls on which they could lean. (AA)

❦

[296] The Prophet ﷺ had four main styles of sitting:

1. Cross legged
2. *Thaniya* (sitting on the knees)
3. *Qurfusa'*
4. Lying down

(MA)

❦

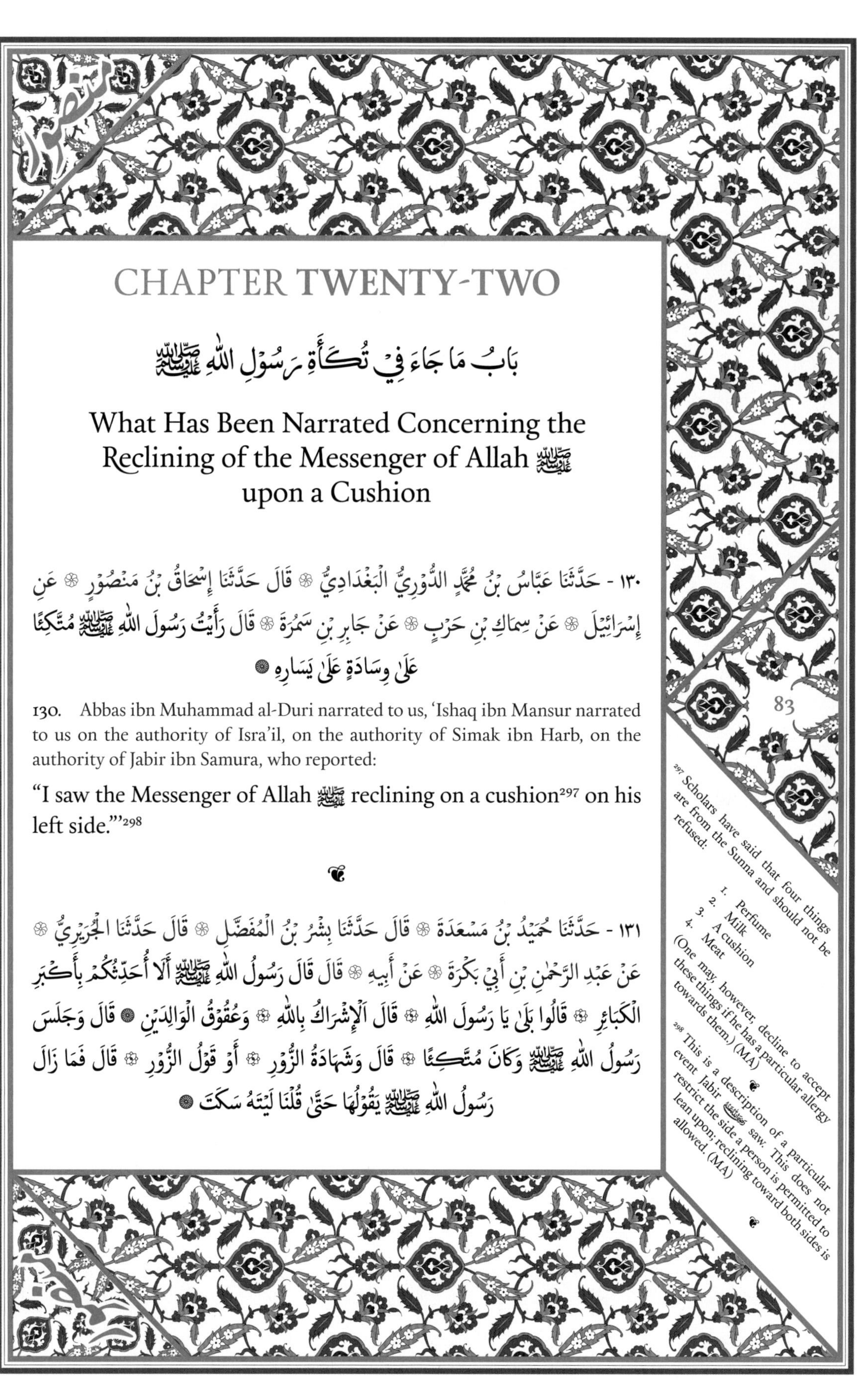

CHAPTER TWENTY-TWO

بَابُ مَا جَاءَ فِي تُكَأَةِ رَسُولِ اللهِ ﷺ

What Has Been Narrated Concerning the Reclining of the Messenger of Allah ﷺ upon a Cushion

١٣٠ - حَدَّثَنَا عَبَّاسُ بْنُ مُحَمَّدٍ الدُّورِيُّ الْبَغْدَادِيُّ ۞ قَالَ حَدَّثَنَا إِسْحَاقُ بْنُ مَنْصُورٍ ۞ عَنِ إِسْرَائِيلَ ۞ عَنْ سِمَاكِ بْنِ حَرْبٍ ۞ عَنْ جَابِرِ بْنِ سَمُرَةَ ۞ قَالَ رَأَيْتُ رَسُولَ اللهِ ﷺ مُتَّكِئًا عَلَىٰ وِسَادَةٍ عَلَىٰ يَسَارِهِ ۞

130. Abbas ibn Muhammad al-Duri narrated to us, 'Ishaq ibn Mansur narrated to us on the authority of Isra'il, on the authority of Simak ibn Harb, on the authority of Jabir ibn Samura, who reported:

"I saw the Messenger of Allah ﷺ reclining on a cushion[297] on his left side."'[298]

١٣١ - حَدَّثَنَا حُمَيْدُ بْنُ مَسْعَدَةَ ۞ قَالَ حَدَّثَنَا بِشْرُ بْنُ الْمُفَضَّلِ ۞ قَالَ حَدَّثَنَا الْجُرَيْرِيُّ ۞ عَنْ عَبْدِ الرَّحْمَٰنِ بْنِ أَبِي بَكْرَةَ ۞ عَنْ أَبِيهِ ۞ قَالَ قَالَ رَسُولُ اللهِ ﷺ أَلَا أُحَدِّثُكُمْ بِأَكْبَرِ الْكَبَائِرِ ۞ قَالُوا بَلَىٰ يَا رَسُولَ اللهِ ۞ قَالَ الْإِشْرَاكُ بِاللهِ ۞ وَعُقُوقُ الْوَالِدَيْنِ ۞ قَالَ وَجَلَسَ رَسُولُ اللهِ ﷺ وَكَانَ مُتَّكِئًا ۞ قَالَ وَشَهَادَةُ الزُّورِ ۞ أَوْ قَوْلُ الزُّورِ ۞ قَالَ فَمَا زَالَ رَسُولُ اللهِ ﷺ يَقُولُهَا حَتَّىٰ قُلْنَا لَيْتَهُ سَكَتَ ۞

[297] Scholars have said that four things are from the Sunna and should not be refused:

1. Perfume
2. Milk
3. A cushion
4. Meat

(One may, however, decline to accept these things if he has a particular allergy towards them.) (MA)

[298] This is a description of a particular event Jabir ؓ saw. This does not restrict the side a person is permitted to lean upon; reclining toward both sides is allowed. (MA)

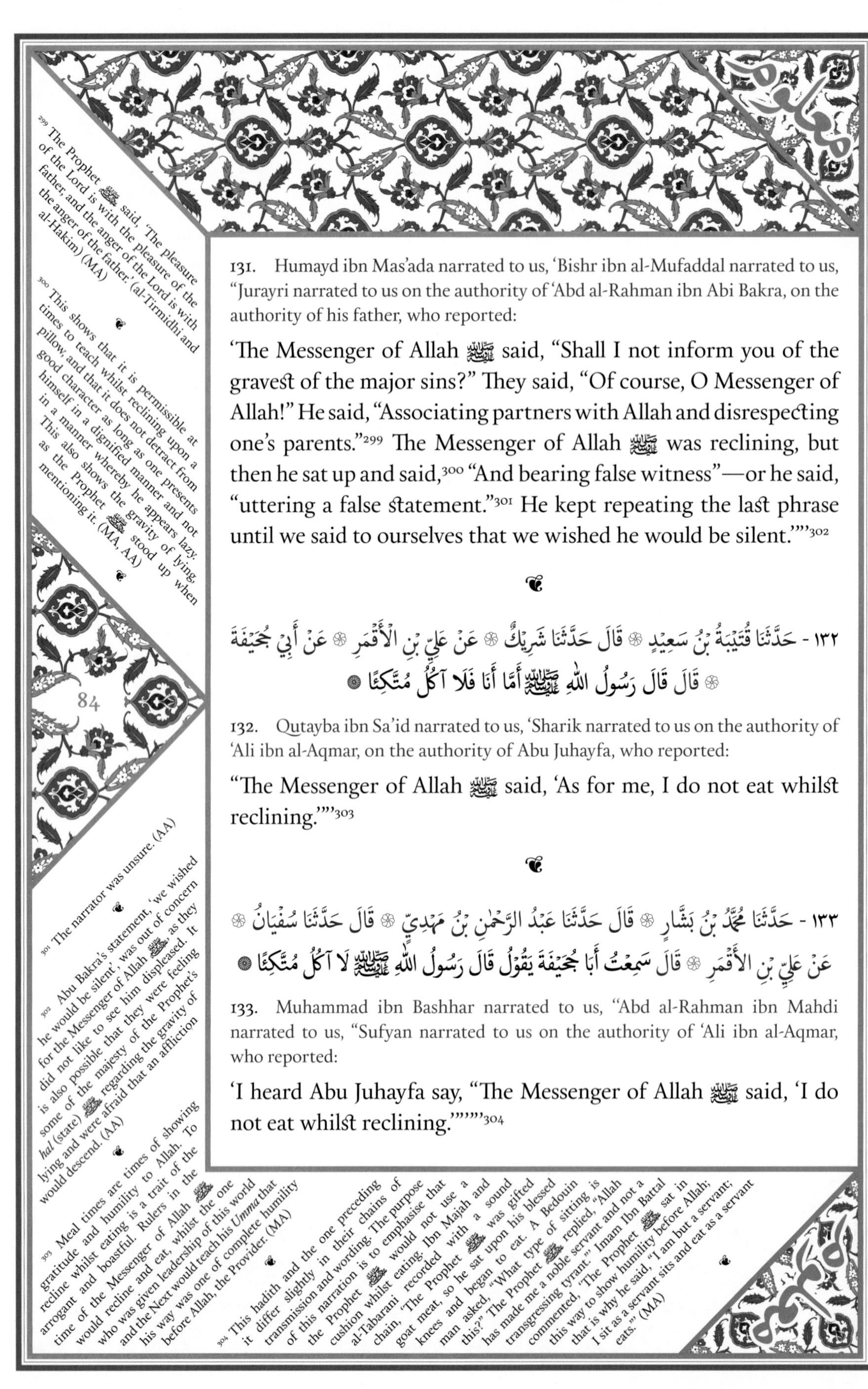

131. Humayd ibn Mas'ada narrated to us, 'Bishr ibn al-Mufaddal narrated to us, "Jurayri narrated to us on the authority of 'Abd al-Rahman ibn Abi Bakra, on the authority of his father, who reported:

'The Messenger of Allah ﷺ said, "Shall I not inform you of the gravest of the major sins?" They said, "Of course, O Messenger of Allah!" He said, "Associating partners with Allah and disrespecting one's parents."[299] The Messenger of Allah ﷺ was reclining, but then he sat up and said,[300] "And bearing false witness"—or he said, "uttering a false statement."[301] He kept repeating the last phrase until we said to ourselves that we wished he would be silent.'"'[302]

❦

١٣٢ - حَدَّثَنَا قُتَيْبَةُ بْنُ سَعِيدٍ ۞ قَالَ حَدَّثَنَا شَرِيكٌ ۞ عَنْ عَلِيِّ بْنِ الأَقْمَرِ ۞ عَنْ أَبِي جُحَيْفَةَ ۞ قَالَ قَالَ رَسُولُ اللهِ ﷺ أَمَّا أَنَا فَلَا آكُلُ مُتَّكِئًا ۞

132. Qutayba ibn Sa'id narrated to us, 'Sharik narrated to us on the authority of 'Ali ibn al-Aqmar, on the authority of Abu Juhayfa, who reported:

"The Messenger of Allah ﷺ said, 'As for me, I do not eat whilst reclining.'"'[303]

❦

١٣٣ - حَدَّثَنَا مُحَمَّدُ بْنُ بَشَّارٍ ۞ قَالَ حَدَّثَنَا عَبْدُ الرَّحْمٰنِ بْنُ مَهْدِيٍّ ۞ قَالَ حَدَّثَنَا سُفْيَانُ ۞ عَنْ عَلِيِّ بْنِ الأَقْمَرِ ۞ قَالَ سَمِعْتُ أَبَا جُحَيْفَةَ يَقُولُ قَالَ رَسُولُ اللهِ ﷺ لَا آكُلُ مُتَّكِئًا ۞

133. Muhammad ibn Bashhar narrated to us, "Abd al-Rahman ibn Mahdi narrated to us, "Sufyan narrated to us on the authority of 'Ali ibn al-Aqmar, who reported:

'I heard Abu Juhayfa say, "The Messenger of Allah ﷺ said, 'I do not eat whilst reclining.'"'"'[304]

299 The Prophet ﷺ said, 'The pleasure of the Lord is with the pleasure of the father, and the anger of the Lord is with the anger of the father.' (al-Tirmidhi and al-Hakim) (MA)

300 This shows that it is permissible at times to teach whilst reclining upon a pillow, and that it does not detract from good character as long as one presents himself in a dignified manner and not in a manner whereby he appears lazy. This also shows the gravity of lying, as the Prophet ﷺ stood up when mentioning it. (MA, AA)

301 The narrator was unsure. (AA)

302 Abu Bakra's statement, 'we wished he would be silent', was out of concern for the Messenger of Allah ﷺ, as they did not like to see him displeased. It is also possible that they were feeling some of the majesty of the Prophet's *hal* (state) ﷺ regarding the gravity of lying and were afraid that an affliction would descend. (AA)

303 Meal times are times of showing gratitude and humility to Allah. To recline whilst eating is a trait of the arrogant and boastful. Rulers in the time of the Messenger of Allah ﷺ would recline and eat, whilst the one who was given leadership of this world and the Next would teach his *Umma* that his way was one of complete humility before Allah, the Provider. (MA)

304 This hadith and the one preceding it differ slightly in their chains of transmission and wording. The purpose of this narration is to emphasise that the Prophet ﷺ would not use a cushion whilst eating. Ibn Majah and al-Tabarani recorded with a sound chain, 'The Prophet ﷺ was gifted goat meat, so he sat upon his blessed knees and began to eat. A Bedouin man asked, "What type of sitting is this?" The Prophet ﷺ replied, "Allah has made me a noble servant and not a transgressing tyrant."' Imam Ibn Battal commented, 'The Prophet ﷺ sat in this way to show humility before Allah; that is why he said, "I am but a servant; I sit as a servant sits and eat as a servant eats."' (MA)

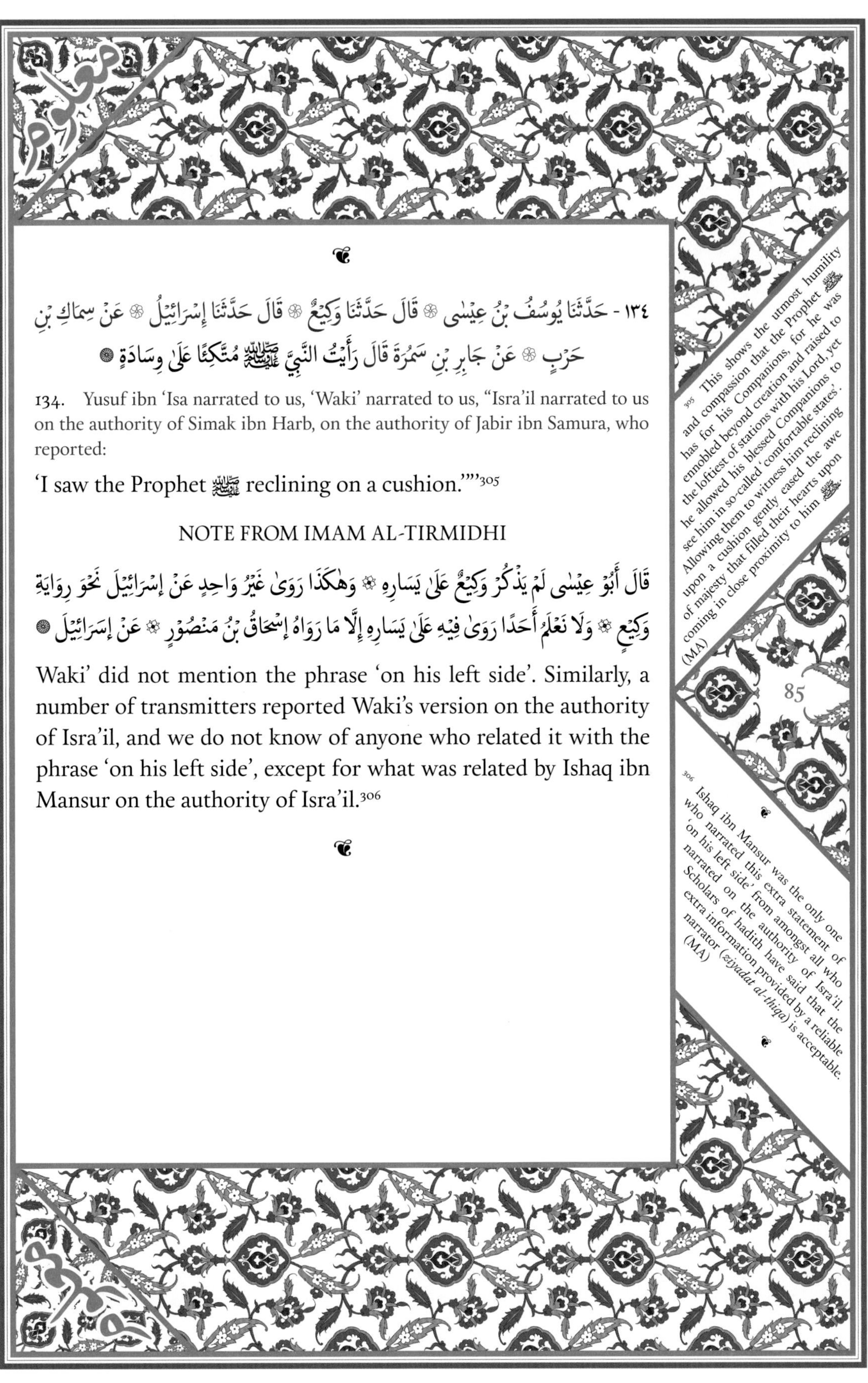

١٣٤ - حَدَّثَنَا يُوسُفُ بْنُ عِيسَى ۞ قَالَ حَدَّثَنَا وَكِيعٌ ۞ قَالَ حَدَّثَنَا إِسْرَائِيلُ ۞ عَنْ سِمَاكِ بْنِ حَرْبٍ ۞ عَنْ جَابِرِ بْنِ سَمُرَةَ قَالَ رَأَيْتُ النَّبِيَّ ﷺ مُتَّكِئًا عَلَىٰ وِسَادَةٍ ۞

134. Yusuf ibn 'Isa narrated to us, 'Waki' narrated to us, "Isra'il narrated to us on the authority of Simak ibn Harb, on the authority of Jabir ibn Samura, who reported:

'I saw the Prophet ﷺ reclining on a cushion.'"[305]

NOTE FROM IMAM AL-TIRMIDHI

قَالَ أَبُو عِيسَى لَمْ يَذْكُرْ وَكِيعٌ عَلَىٰ يَسَارِهِ ۞ وَهٰكَذَا رَوَىٰ غَيْرُ وَاحِدٍ عَنْ إِسْرَائِيلَ نَحْوَ رِوَايَةِ وَكِيعٍ ۞ وَلَا نَعْلَمُ أَحَدًا رَوَىٰ فِيهِ عَلَىٰ يَسَارِهِ إِلَّا مَا رَوَاهُ إِسْحَاقُ بْنُ مَنْصُورٍ ۞ عَنْ إِسْرَائِيلَ ۞

Waki' did not mention the phrase 'on his left side'. Similarly, a number of transmitters reported Waki's version on the authority of Isra'il, and we do not know of anyone who related it with the phrase 'on his left side', except for what was related by Ishaq ibn Mansur on the authority of Isra'il.[306]

[305] This shows the utmost humility and compassion that the Prophet ﷺ has for his Companions, for he was ennobled beyond creation and raised to the loftiest of stations with his Lord, yet he allowed his blessed Companions to see him in so-called 'comfortable states'. Allowing them to witness him reclining upon a cushion gently eased the awe of majesty that filled their hearts upon coming in close proximity to him ﷺ. (MA)

[306] Ishaq ibn Mansur was the only one who narrated this extra statement of 'on his left side' from amongst all who narrated on the authority of Isra'il. Scholars of hadith have said that the extra information provided by a reliable narrator (*ziyadat al-thiqa*) is acceptable. (MA)

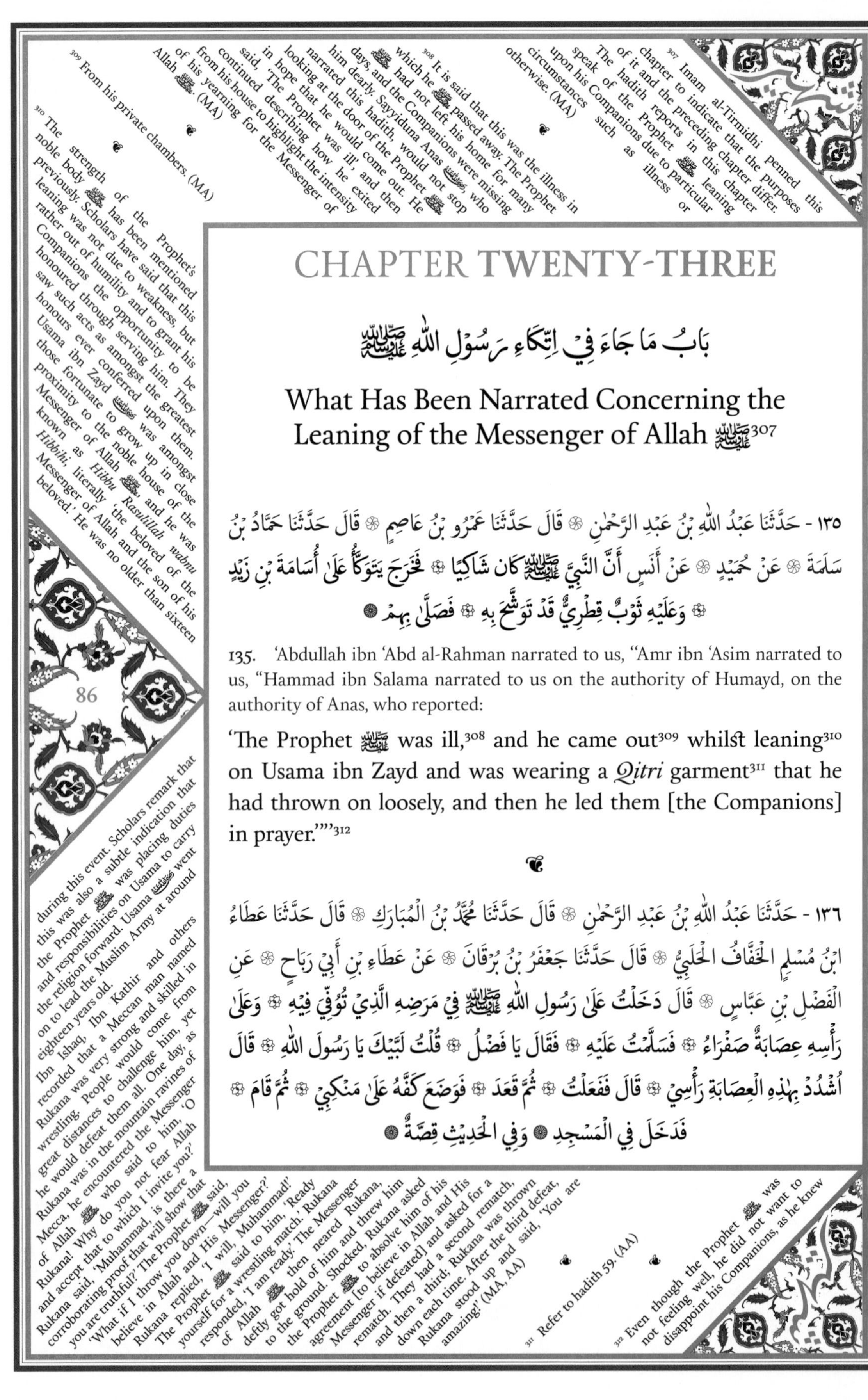

CHAPTER TWENTY-THREE

بَابُ مَا جَاءَ فِي اِتِّكَاءِ رَسُولِ اللهِ ﷺ

What Has Been Narrated Concerning the Leaning of the Messenger of Allah ﷺ[307]

١٣٥ - حَدَّثَنَا عَبْدُ اللهِ بْنُ عَبْدِ الرَّحْمٰنِ ۞ قَالَ حَدَّثَنَا عَمْرُو بْنُ عَاصِمٍ ۞ قَالَ حَدَّثَنَا حَمَّادُ بْنُ سَلَمَةَ ۞ عَنْ حُمَيْدٍ ۞ عَنْ أَنَسٍ أَنَّ النَّبِيَّ ﷺ كَانَ شَاكِيًا ۞ فَخَرَجَ يَتَوَكَّأُ عَلَىٰ أُسَامَةَ بْنِ زَيْدٍ ۞ وَعَلَيْهِ ثَوْبٌ قِطْرِيٌّ قَدْ تَوَشَّحَ بِهِ ۞ فَصَلَّىٰ بِهِمْ ۞

135. ʿAbdullah ibn ʿAbd al-Rahman narrated to us, "ʿAmr ibn ʿAsim narrated to us, "Hammad ibn Salama narrated to us on the authority of Humayd, on the authority of Anas, who reported:

'The Prophet ﷺ was ill,[308] and he came out[309] whilst leaning[310] on Usama ibn Zayd and was wearing a *Qitri* garment[311] that he had thrown on loosely, and then he led them [the Companions] in prayer.'"'[312]

١٣٦ - حَدَّثَنَا عَبْدُ اللهِ بْنُ عَبْدِ الرَّحْمٰنِ ۞ قَالَ حَدَّثَنَا مُحَمَّدُ بْنُ الْمُبَارَكِ ۞ قَالَ حَدَّثَنَا عَطَاءُ ابْنُ مُسْلِمٍ الْخَفَّافُ الْحَلَبِيُّ ۞ قَالَ حَدَّثَنَا جَعْفَرُ بْنُ بُرْقَانَ ۞ عَنْ عَطَاءِ بْنِ أَبِي رَبَاحٍ ۞ عَنِ الْفَضْلِ بْنِ عَبَّاسٍ ۞ قَالَ دَخَلْتُ عَلَىٰ رَسُولِ اللهِ ﷺ فِي مَرَضِهِ الَّذِي تُوُفِّيَ فِيهِ ۞ وَعَلَىٰ رَأْسِهِ عِصَابَةٌ صَفْرَاءُ ۞ فَسَلَّمْتُ عَلَيْهِ ۞ فَقَالَ يَا فَضْلُ ۞ قُلْتُ لَبَّيْكَ يَا رَسُولَ اللهِ ۞ قَالَ اُشْدُدْ بِهٰذِهِ الْعِصَابَةِ رَأْسِي ۞ قَالَ فَفَعَلْتُ ۞ ثُمَّ قَعَدَ ۞ فَوَضَعَ كَفَّهُ عَلَىٰ مَنْكِبِي ۞ ثُمَّ قَامَ فَدَخَلَ فِي الْمَسْجِدِ ۞ وَفِي الْحَدِيثِ قِصَّةٌ ۞

---

307 Imam al-Tirmidhi penned this chapter to indicate that the purposes of it and the preceding chapter differ. The hadith reports in this chapter speak of the Prophet ﷺ leaning upon his Companions due to particular circumstances such as illness or otherwise. (MA)

308 It is said that this was the illness in which he ﷺ passed away. The Prophet ﷺ had not left his home for many days, and the Companions were missing him dearly. Sayyiduna Anas ﷺ, who narrated this hadith, would not stop looking at the door of the Prophet ﷺ in hope that he would come out. He said, 'The Prophet was ill,' and then continued describing how he exited from his house to highlight the intensity of his yearning for the Messenger of Allah ﷺ. (MA)

309 From his private chambers. (MA)

310 The strength of the Prophet's noble body ﷺ has been mentioned previously. Scholars have said that this leaning was not due to weakness, but rather out of humility and to grant his Companions the opportunity to be honoured through serving him. They saw such acts as amongst the greatest honours ever conferred upon them. Usama ibn Zayd ﷺ was amongst those fortunate to grow up in close proximity to the noble house of the Messenger of Allah ﷺ, and he was known as *Hibbu Rasulillah wabnu Hibbihi*, literally 'the beloved of the Messenger of Allah and the son of his beloved.' He was no older than sixteen during this event. Scholars remark that this was also a subtle indication that the Prophet ﷺ was placing duties and responsibilities on Usama to carry the religion forward. Usama ﷺ went on to lead the Muslim Army at around eighteen years old. Ibn Ishaq, Ibn Kathir and others recorded that a Meccan man named Rukana was very strong and skilled in wrestling. People would come from great distances to challenge him, yet he would defeat them all. One day, as Rukana was in the mountain ravines of Mecca, he encountered the Messenger of Allah ﷺ who said to him, 'O Rukana! Why do you not fear Allah and accept that to which I invite you?' Rukana said, 'Muhammad, is there a corroborating proof that will show that you are truthful?' The Prophet ﷺ said, 'What if I throw you down—will you believe in Allah and His Messenger?' Rukana replied, 'I will, Muhammad!' The Prophet ﷺ said to him, 'Ready yourself for a wrestling match.' Rukana responded, 'I am ready.' The Messenger of Allah ﷺ then neared Rukana, deftly got hold of him and threw him to the ground. Shocked, Rukana asked the Prophet ﷺ to absolve him of his agreement [to believe in Allah and His Messenger if defeated] and asked for a rematch. They had a second rematch, and then a third; Rukana was thrown down each time. After the third defeat, Rukana stood up and said, 'You are amazing!' (MA, AA)

311 Refer to hadith 59. (AA)

312 Even though the Prophet ﷺ was not feeling well, he did not want to disappoint his Companions, as he knew

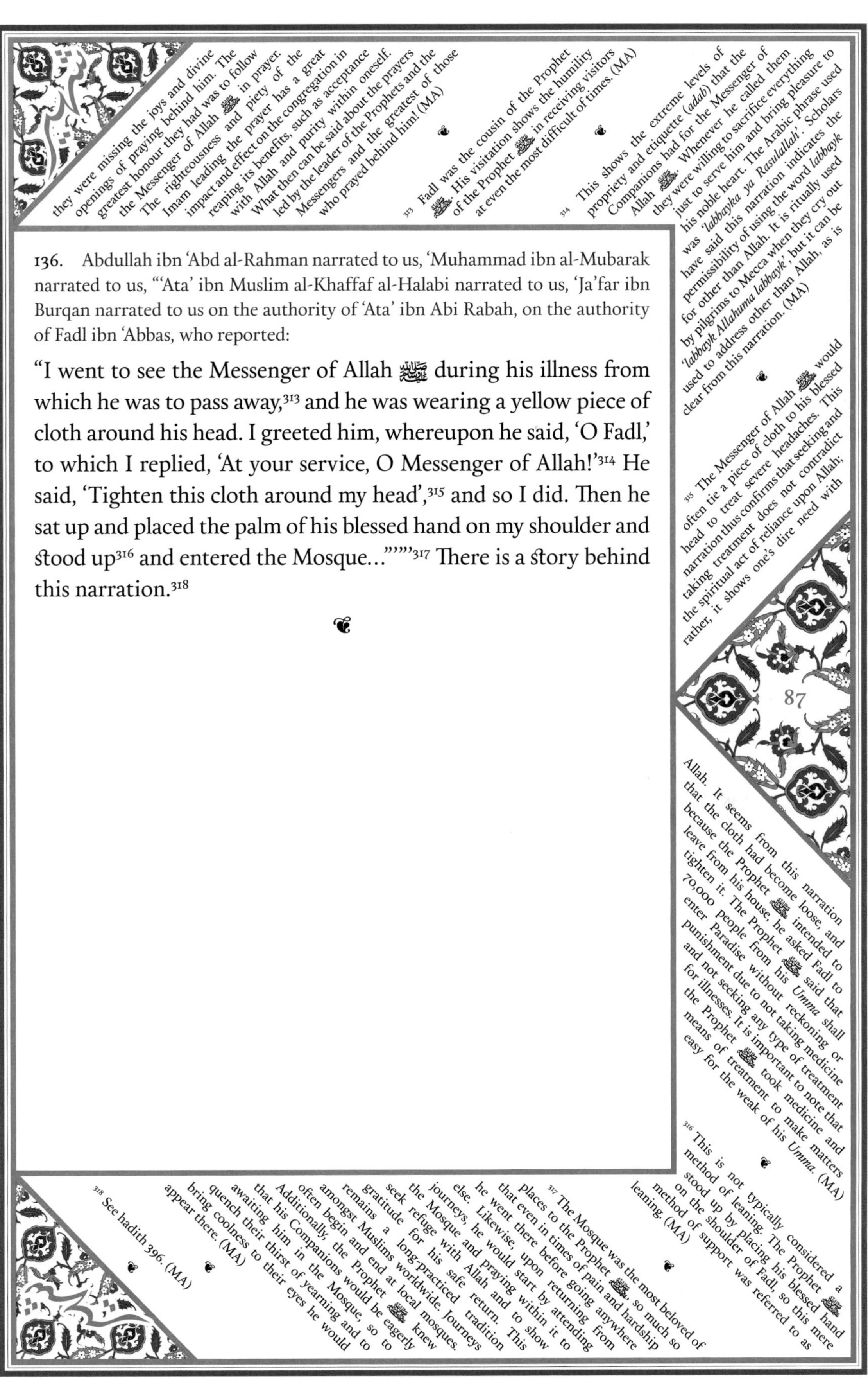

they were missing the joys and divine openings of praying behind him. The greatest honour they had was to follow the Messenger of Allah ﷺ in prayer. The righteousness and piety of the Imam leading the prayer has a great impact and effect on the congregation in reaping its benefits, such as acceptance with Allah and purity within oneself. What then can be said about the prayers led by the leader of the Prophets and the Messengers and the greatest of those who prayed behind him! (MA)

136. Abdullah ibn 'Abd al-Rahman narrated to us, 'Muhammad ibn al-Mubarak narrated to us, "'Ata' ibn Muslim al-Khaffaf al-Halabi narrated to us, 'Ja'far ibn Burqan narrated to us on the authority of 'Ata' ibn Abi Rabah, on the authority of Fadl ibn 'Abbas, who reported:

"I went to see the Messenger of Allah ﷺ during his illness from which he was to pass away,[313] and he was wearing a yellow piece of cloth around his head. I greeted him, whereupon he said, 'O Fadl,' to which I replied, 'At your service, O Messenger of Allah!'[314] He said, 'Tighten this cloth around my head',[315] and so I did. Then he sat up and placed the palm of his blessed hand on my shoulder and stood up[316] and entered the Mosque..."'"'[317] There is a story behind this narration.[318]

[313] Fadl was the cousin of the Prophet ﷺ. His visitation shows the humility of the Prophet ﷺ in receiving visitors at even the most difficult of times. (MA)

[314] This shows the extreme levels of propriety and etiquette (*adab*) that the Companions had for the Messenger of Allah ﷺ. Whenever he called them they were willing to sacrifice everything just to serve him and bring pleasure to his noble heart. The Arabic phrase used was *'labbayka ya Rasulallah'*. Scholars have said this narration indicates the permissibility of using the word *labbayk* for other than Allah. It is ritually used by pilgrims to Mecca when they cry out *'labbayk Allahuma labbayk'*, but it can be used to address other than Allah, as is clear from this narration. (MA)

[315] The Messenger of Allah ﷺ would often tie a piece of cloth to his blessed head to treat severe headaches. This narration thus confirms that seeking and taking treatment does not contradict the spiritual act of reliance upon Allah; rather, it shows one's dire need with Allah. It seems from this narration that the cloth had become loose, and because the Prophet ﷺ intended to leave from his house, he asked Fadl to tighten it. The Prophet ﷺ said that 70,000 people from his *Umma* shall enter Paradise without reckoning or punishment due to not taking medicine and not seeking any type of treatment for illnesses. It is important to note that the Prophet ﷺ took medicine and means of treatment to make matters easy for the weak of his *Umma*. (MA)

[316] This is not typically considered a method of leaning. The Prophet ﷺ stood up by placing his blessed hand on the shoulder of Fadl, so this mere method of support was referred to as leaning. (MA)

[317] The Mosque was the most beloved of places to the Prophet ﷺ, so much so that even in times of pain and hardship he went there before going anywhere else. Likewise, upon returning from journeys, he would start by attending the Mosque and praying within it to seek refuge with Allah and to show gratitude for his safe return. This remains a long-practiced tradition amongst Muslims worldwide. Journeys often begin and end at local mosques. Additionally, the Prophet ﷺ knew that his Companions would be eagerly awaiting him in the Mosque, so to quench their thirst of yearning and to bring coolness to their eyes he would appear there. (MA)

[318] See hadith 396. (MA)

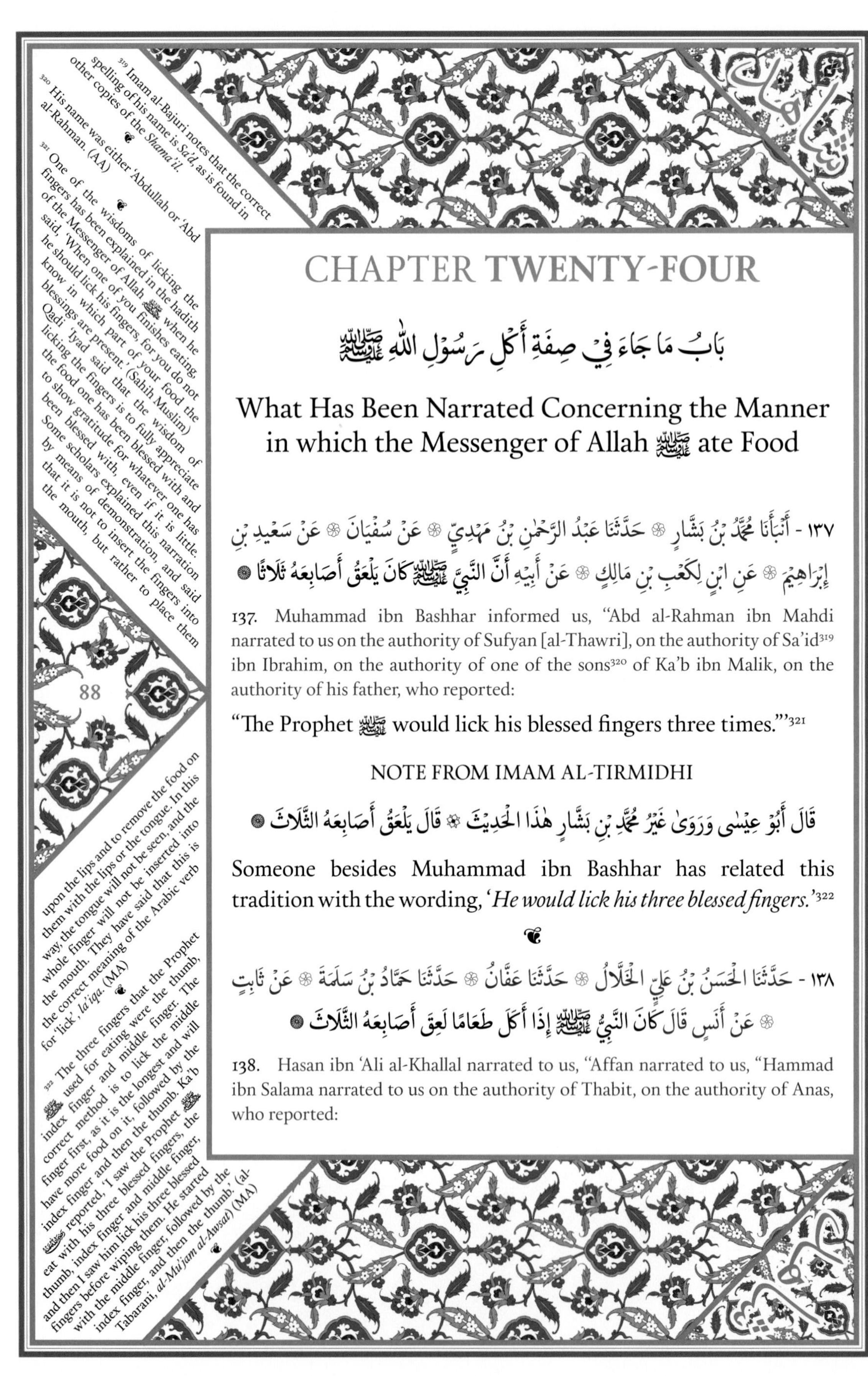

CHAPTER TWENTY-FOUR

بَابُ مَا جَاءَ فِي صِفَةِ أَكْلِ رَسُولِ اللهِ ﷺ

What Has Been Narrated Concerning the Manner in which the Messenger of Allah ﷺ ate Food

١٣٧ - أَنْبَأَنَا مُحَمَّدُ بْنُ بَشَّارٍ ❁ حَدَّثَنَا عَبْدُ الرَّحْمٰنِ بْنُ مَهْدِيٍّ ❁ عَنْ سُفْيَانَ ❁ عَنْ سَعِيدِ بْنِ إِبْرَاهِيمَ ❁ عَنِ ابْنٍ لِكَعْبِ بْنِ مَالِكٍ ❁ عَنْ أَبِيهِ أَنَّ النَّبِيَّ ﷺ كَانَ يَلْعَقُ أَصَابِعَهُ ثَلَاثًا ❁

137. Muhammad ibn Bashhar informed us, "Abd al-Rahman ibn Mahdi narrated to us on the authority of Sufyan [al-Thawri], on the authority of Sa'id[319] ibn Ibrahim, on the authority of one of the sons[320] of Ka'b ibn Malik, on the authority of his father, who reported:

"The Prophet ﷺ would lick his blessed fingers three times."'[321]

NOTE FROM IMAM AL-TIRMIDHI

قَالَ أَبُو عِيسٰى وَرَوٰى غَيْرُ مُحَمَّدِ بْنِ بَشَّارٍ هٰذَا الْحَدِيثَ ❁ قَالَ يَلْعَقُ أَصَابِعَهُ الثَّلَاثَ ❁

Someone besides Muhammad ibn Bashhar has related this tradition with the wording, '*He would lick his three blessed fingers.*'[322]

١٣٨ - حَدَّثَنَا الْحَسَنُ بْنُ عَلِيٍّ الْخَلَّالُ ❁ حَدَّثَنَا عَفَّانُ ❁ حَدَّثَنَا حَمَّادُ بْنُ سَلَمَةَ ❁ عَنْ ثَابِتٍ ❁ عَنْ أَنَسٍ قَالَ كَانَ النَّبِيُّ ﷺ إِذَا أَكَلَ طَعَامًا لَعِقَ أَصَابِعَهُ الثَّلَاثَ ❁

138. Hasan ibn 'Ali al-Khallal narrated to us, "Affan narrated to us, "Hammad ibn Salama narrated to us on the authority of Thabit, on the authority of Anas, who reported:

[319] Imam al-Bajuri notes that the correct spelling of his name is *Sa'd*, as is found in other copies of the *Shama'il*.

[320] His name was either 'Abdullah or 'Abd al-Rahman. (AA)

[321] One of the wisdoms of licking the fingers has been explained in the hadith of the Messenger of Allah ﷺ when he said, 'When one of you finishes eating, he should lick his fingers, for you do not know in which part of your food the blessings are present.' (Sahih Muslim) Qadi 'Iyad said that the wisdom of licking the fingers is to fully appreciate the food one has been blessed with and to show gratitude for whatever one has been blessed with, even if it is little. Some scholars explained this narration by means of demonstration, and said that it is not to insert the fingers into the mouth, but rather to place them upon the lips and to remove the food on them with the lips or the tongue. In this way, the tongue will not be seen, and the whole finger will not be inserted into the mouth. They have said that this is the correct meaning of the Arabic verb for 'lick', *la'iqa*. (MA)

[322] The three fingers that the Prophet ﷺ used for eating were the thumb, index finger and middle finger. The correct method is to lick the middle finger first, as it is the longest and will have more food on it, followed by the index finger and then the thumb. Ka'b ﵁ reported, 'I saw the Prophet ﷺ eat with his three blessed fingers, the thumb, index finger and middle finger, and then I saw him lick his three blessed fingers before wiping them. He started with the middle finger, followed by the index finger, and then the thumb.' (al-Tabarani, *al-Mu'jam al-Awsat*) (MA)

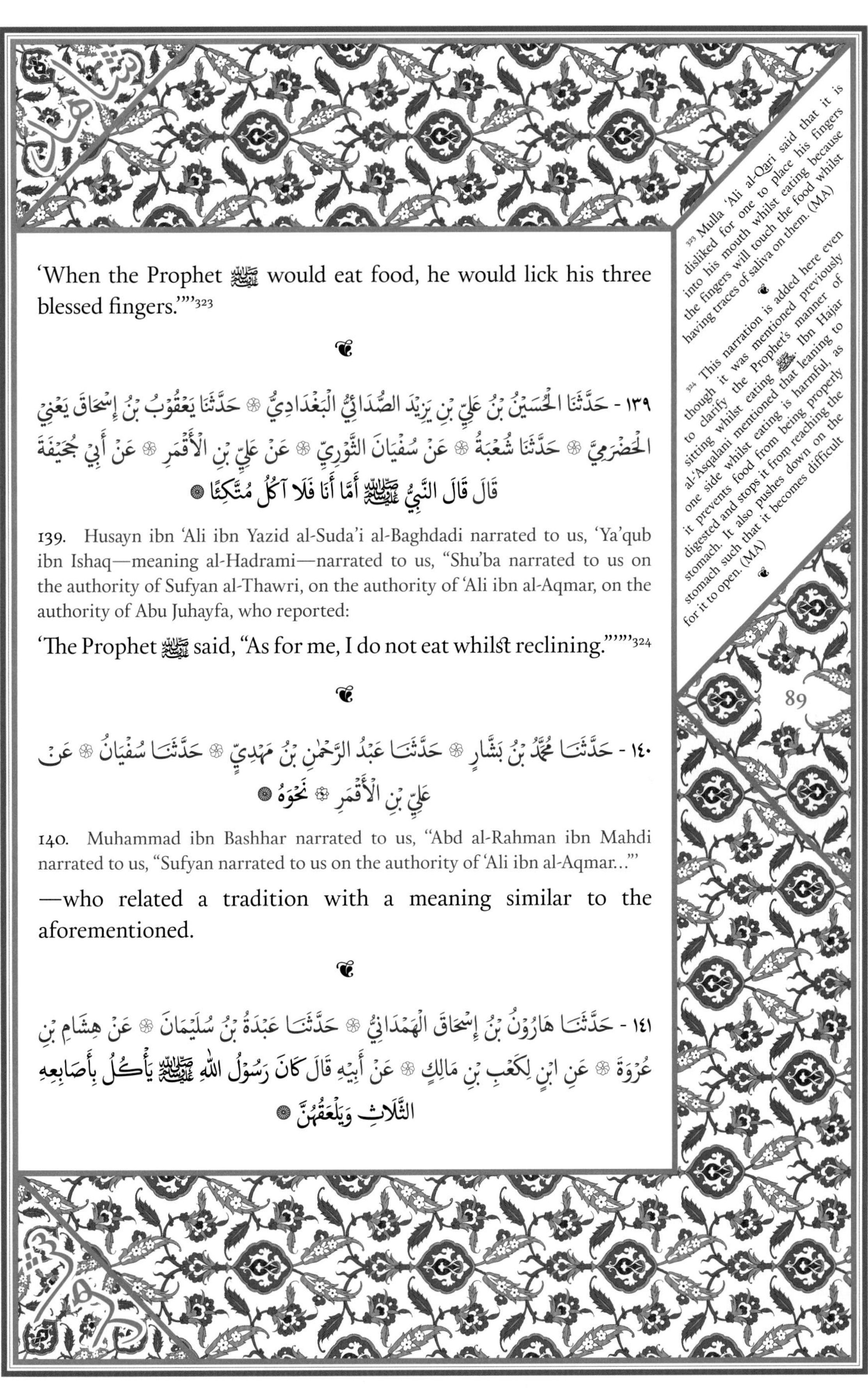

‘When the Prophet ﷺ would eat food, he would lick his three blessed fingers.’”[323]

١٣٩ - حَدَّثَنَا الْحُسَيْنُ بْنُ عَلِيِّ بْنِ يَزِيْدَ الصُّدَائِيُّ الْبَغْدَادِيُّ ۞ حَدَّثَنَا يَعْقُوْبُ بْنُ إِسْحَاقَ يَعْنِي الْحَضْرَمِيَّ ۞ حَدَّثَنَا شُعْبَةُ ۞ عَنْ سُفْيَانَ الثَّوْرِيِّ ۞ عَنْ عَلِيِّ بْنِ الْأَقْمَرِ ۞ عَنْ أَبِي جُحَيْفَةَ قَالَ قَالَ النَّبِيُّ ﷺ أَمَّا أَنَا فَلَا آكُلُ مُتَّكِئًا ۞

139. Husayn ibn ‘Ali ibn Yazid al-Suda’i al-Baghdadi narrated to us, ‘Ya’qub ibn Ishaq—meaning al-Hadrami—narrated to us, “Shu’ba narrated to us on the authority of Sufyan al-Thawri, on the authority of ‘Ali ibn al-Aqmar, on the authority of Abu Juhayfa, who reported:

‘The Prophet ﷺ said, “As for me, I do not eat whilst reclining.”’”’[324]

١٤٠ - حَدَّثَنَا مُحَمَّدُ بْنُ بَشَّارٍ ۞ حَدَّثَنَا عَبْدُ الرَّحْمٰنِ بْنُ مَهْدِيٍّ ۞ حَدَّثَنَا سُفْيَانُ ۞ عَنْ عَلِيِّ بْنِ الْأَقْمَرِ ۞ نَحْوَهُ ۞

140. Muhammad ibn Bashhar narrated to us, “Abd al-Rahman ibn Mahdi narrated to us, “Sufyan narrated to us on the authority of ‘Ali ibn al-Aqmar...”’

—who related a tradition with a meaning similar to the aforementioned.

١٤١ - حَدَّثَنَا هَارُوْنُ بْنُ إِسْحَاقَ الْهَمْدَانِيُّ ۞ حَدَّثَنَا عَبْدَةُ بْنُ سُلَيْمَانَ ۞ عَنْ هِشَامِ بْنِ عُرْوَةَ ۞ عَنِ ابْنٍ لِكَعْبِ بْنِ مَالِكٍ ۞ عَنْ أَبِيْهِ قَالَ كَانَ رَسُوْلُ اللهِ ﷺ يَأْكُلُ بِأَصَابِعِهِ الثَّلَاثِ وَيَلْعَقُهُنَّ ۞

[323] Mulla ‘Ali al-Qari said that it is disliked for one to place his fingers into his mouth whilst eating because the fingers will touch the food whilst having traces of saliva on them. (MA)

[324] This narration is added here even though it was mentioned previously to clarify the Prophet’s manner of sitting whilst eating ﷺ. Ibn Hajar al-‘Asqalani mentioned that leaning to one side whilst eating is harmful, as it prevents food from being properly digested and stops it from reaching the stomach. It also pushes down on the stomach such that it becomes difficult for it to open. (MA)

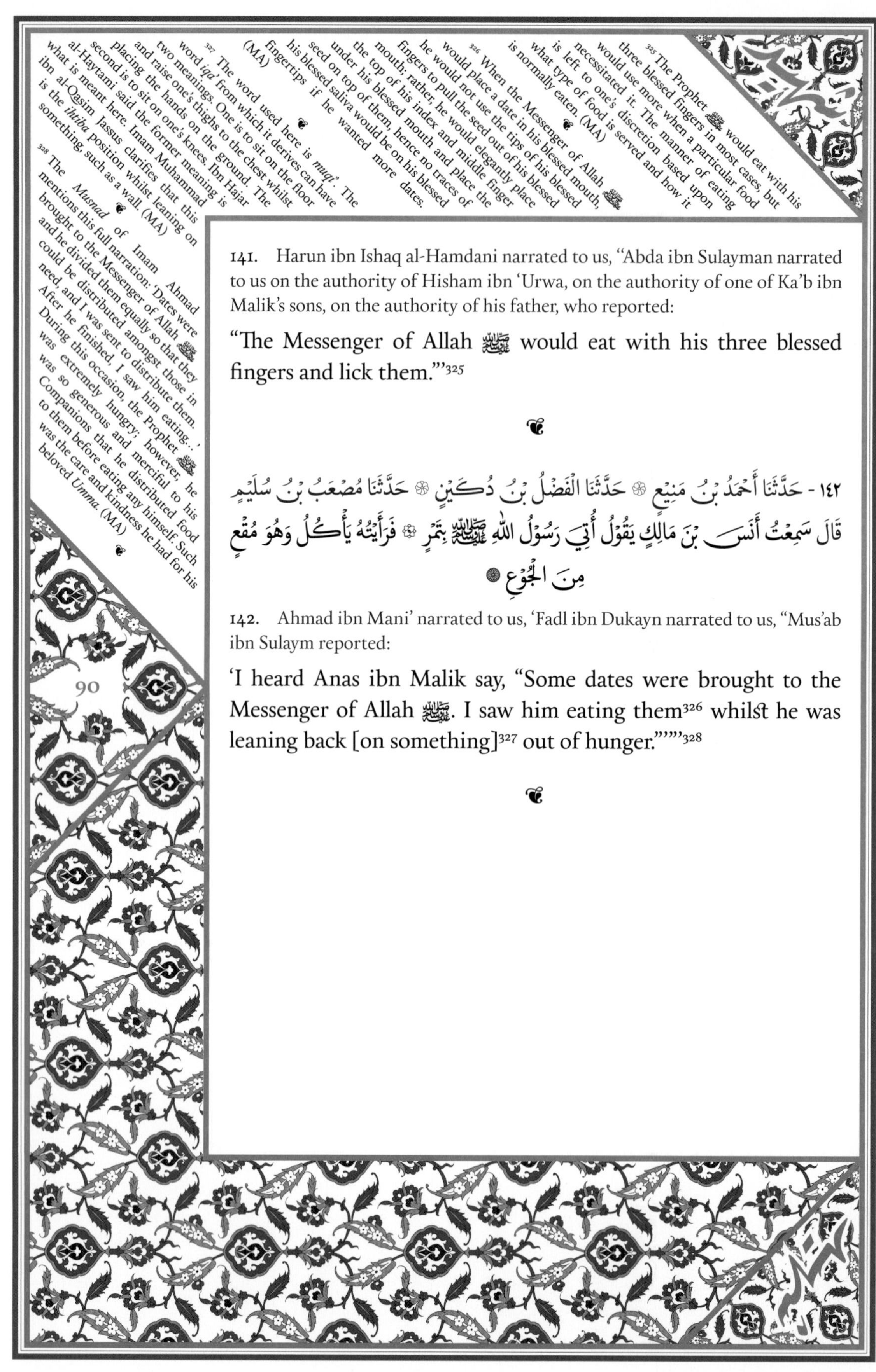

141. Harun ibn Ishaq al-Hamdani narrated to us, "Abda ibn Sulayman narrated to us on the authority of Hisham ibn 'Urwa, on the authority of one of Ka'b ibn Malik's sons, on the authority of his father, who reported:

"The Messenger of Allah ﷺ would eat with his three blessed fingers and lick them."'[325]

١٤٢ - حَدَّثَنَا أَحْمَدُ بْنُ مَنِيعٍ ۞ حَدَّثَنَا الْفَضْلُ بْنُ دُكَيْنٍ ۞ حَدَّثَنَا مُصْعَبُ بْنُ سُلَيْمٍ قَالَ سَمِعْتُ أَنَسَ بْنَ مَالِكٍ يَقُولُ أُتِيَ رَسُولُ اللهِ ﷺ بِتَمْرٍ ۞ فَرَأَيْتُهُ يَأْكُلُ وَهُوَ مُقْعٍ مِنَ الْجُوعِ ۞

142. Ahmad ibn Mani' narrated to us, 'Fadl ibn Dukayn narrated to us, "Mus'ab ibn Sulaym reported:

'I heard Anas ibn Malik say, "Some dates were brought to the Messenger of Allah ﷺ. I saw him eating them[326] whilst he was leaning back [on something][327] out of hunger."'"'[328]

[325] The Prophet ﷺ would eat with his three blessed fingers in most cases, but would use more when a particular food necessitated it. The manner of eating is left to one's discretion based upon what type of food is served and how it is normally eaten. (MA)

[326] When the Messenger of Allah ﷺ would place a date in his blessed mouth, he would not use the tips of his blessed fingers to pull the seed out of his blessed mouth; rather, he would elegantly place the top of his index and middle finger under his blessed mouth and place the seed on top of them, hence no traces of his blessed saliva would be on his blessed fingertips if he wanted more dates. (MA)

[327] The word used here is *muqi'*. The word *iqa'* from which it derives can have two meanings. One is to sit on the floor and raise one's thighs to the chest whilst placing the hands on the ground. The second is to sit on one's knees. Ibn Hajar al-Haytami said the former meaning is what is meant here. Imam Muhammad ibn al-Qasim Jassus clarifies that this is the *ihtiba* position whilst leaning on something, such as a wall. (MA)

[328] The *Musnad* of Imam Ahmad mentions this full narration: 'Dates were brought to the Messenger of Allah ﷺ and he divided them equally so that they could be distributed amongst those in need, and I was sent to distribute them. After he finished, I saw him eating...' During this occasion, the Prophet ﷺ was extremely hungry; however, he was so generous and merciful to his Companions that he distributed food to them before eating any himself. Such was the care and kindness he had for his beloved *Umma*. (MA)

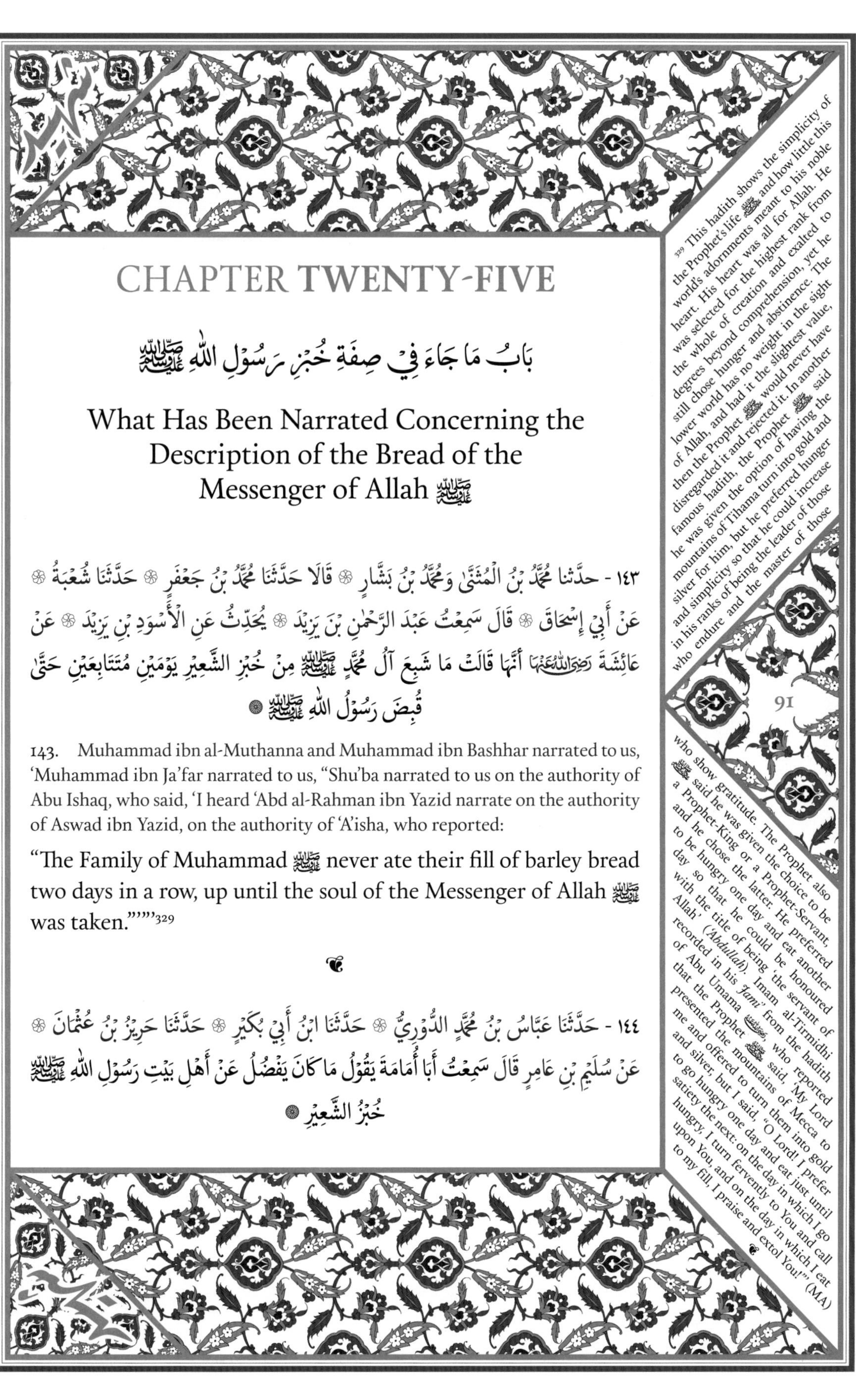

CHAPTER TWENTY-FIVE

بَابُ مَا جَاءَ فِي صِفَةِ خُبْزِ رَسُولِ اللهِ ﷺ

What Has Been Narrated Concerning the Description of the Bread of the Messenger of Allah ﷺ

١٤٣ - حَدَّثَنَا مُحَمَّدُ بْنُ الْمُثَنَّى وَمُحَمَّدُ بْنُ بَشَّارٍ ۞ قَالَا حَدَّثَنَا مُحَمَّدُ بْنُ جَعْفَرٍ ۞ حَدَّثَنَا شُعْبَةُ ۞ عَنْ أَبِي إِسْحَاقَ ۞ قَالَ سَمِعْتُ عَبْدَ الرَّحْمٰنِ بْنَ يَزِيدَ ۞ يُحَدِّثُ عَنِ الْأَسْوَدِ بْنِ يَزِيدَ ۞ عَنْ عَائِشَةَ رَضِيَ اللهُ عَنْهَا أَنَّهَا قَالَتْ مَا شَبِعَ آلُ مُحَمَّدٍ ﷺ مِنْ خُبْزِ الشَّعِيرِ يَوْمَيْنِ مُتَتَابِعَيْنِ حَتَّىٰ قُبِضَ رَسُولُ اللهِ ﷺ ۞

143. Muhammad ibn al-Muthanna and Muhammad ibn Bashhar narrated to us, 'Muhammad ibn Ja'far narrated to us, "Shu'ba narrated to us on the authority of Abu Ishaq, who said, 'I heard 'Abd al-Rahman ibn Yazid narrate on the authority of Aswad ibn Yazid, on the authority of 'A'isha, who reported:

"The Family of Muhammad ﷺ never ate their fill of barley bread two days in a row, up until the soul of the Messenger of Allah ﷺ was taken."'"'[329]

١٤٤ - حَدَّثَنَا عَبَّاسُ بْنُ مُحَمَّدٍ الدُّورِيُّ ۞ حَدَّثَنَا ابْنُ أَبِي بُكَيْرٍ ۞ حَدَّثَنَا حَرِيزُ بْنُ عُثْمَانَ ۞ عَنْ سُلَيْمِ بْنِ عَامِرٍ قَالَ سَمِعْتُ أَبَا أُمَامَةَ يَقُولُ مَا كَانَ يَفْضُلُ عَنْ أَهْلِ بَيْتِ رَسُولِ اللهِ ﷺ خُبْزُ الشَّعِيرِ ۞

[329] This hadith shows the simplicity of the Prophet's life ﷺ and how little this world's adornments meant to his noble heart. His heart was all for Allah. He was selected for the highest rank from the whole of creation and exalted to degrees beyond comprehension, yet he still chose hunger and abstinence. The lower world has no weight in the sight of Allah, and had it the slightest value, then the Prophet ﷺ would never have disregarded it and rejected it. In another famous hadith, the Prophet ﷺ said he was given the option of having the mountains of Tihama turn into gold and silver for him, but he preferred hunger and simplicity so that he could increase in his ranks of being the leader of those who endure and the master of those who show gratitude. The Prophet ﷺ also said he was given the choice to be a Prophet-King or a Prophet-Servant, and he chose the latter. He preferred to be hungry one day and eat another day so that he could be honoured with the title of being 'the servant of Allah' (*'Abdullah*). Imam al-Tirmidhi recorded in his *Jami'* from the hadith of Abu Umama ﷺ, who reported that the Prophet ﷺ said, 'My Lord presented the mountains of Mecca to me and offered to turn them into gold and silver, but I said, "O Lord! I prefer to go hungry one day and eat just until satiety the next: on the day in which I go hungry, I turn fervently to You and call upon You, and on the day in which I eat to my fill, I praise and extol You!"' (MA)

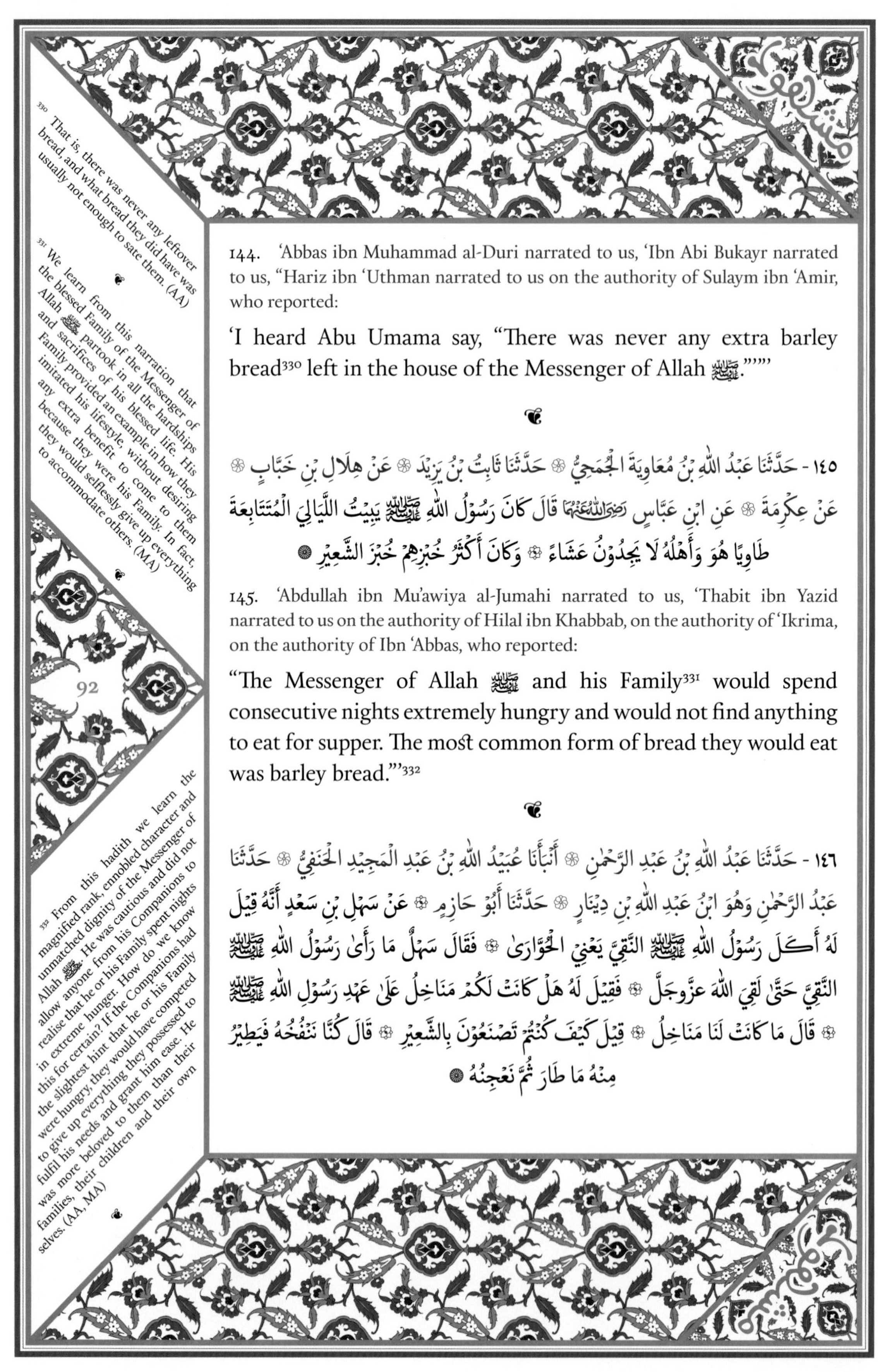

144. 'Abbas ibn Muhammad al-Duri narrated to us, 'Ibn Abi Bukayr narrated to us, "Hariz ibn 'Uthman narrated to us on the authority of Sulaym ibn 'Amir, who reported:

'I heard Abu Umama say, "There was never any extra barley bread[330] left in the house of the Messenger of Allah ﷺ."""'

١٤٥ - حَدَّثَنَا عَبْدُ اللهِ بْنُ مُعَاوِيَةَ الْجُمَحِيُّ ۞ حَدَّثَنَا ثَابِتُ بْنُ يَزِيدَ ۞ عَنْ هِلَالِ بْنِ خَبَّابٍ ۞ عَنْ عِكْرِمَةَ ۞ عَنِ ابْنِ عَبَّاسٍ رَضِيَ اللهُ عَنْهُمَا قَالَ كَانَ رَسُولُ اللهِ ﷺ يَبِيتُ اللَّيَالِيَ الْمُتَتَابِعَةَ طَاوِيًا هُوَ وَأَهْلُهُ لَا يَجِدُونَ عَشَاءً ۞ وَكَانَ أَكْثَرُ خُبْزِهِمْ خُبْزَ الشَّعِيرِ ۞

145. 'Abdullah ibn Mu'awiya al-Jumahi narrated to us, 'Thabit ibn Yazid narrated to us on the authority of Hilal ibn Khabbab, on the authority of 'Ikrima, on the authority of Ibn 'Abbas, who reported:

"The Messenger of Allah ﷺ and his Family[331] would spend consecutive nights extremely hungry and would not find anything to eat for supper. The most common form of bread they would eat was barley bread."'[332]

١٤٦ - حَدَّثَنَا عَبْدُ اللهِ بْنُ عَبْدِ الرَّحْمٰنِ ۞ أَنْبَأَنَا عُبَيْدُ اللهِ بْنُ عَبْدِ الْمَجِيدِ الْحَنَفِيُّ ۞ حَدَّثَنَا عَبْدُ الرَّحْمٰنِ وَهُوَ ابْنُ عَبْدِ اللهِ بْنِ دِينَارٍ ۞ حَدَّثَنَا أَبُو حَازِمٍ ۞ عَنْ سَهْلِ بْنِ سَعْدٍ أَنَّهُ قِيلَ لَهُ أَكَلَ رَسُولُ اللهِ ﷺ النَّقِيَّ يَعْنِي الْحُوَّارَىٰ ۞ فَقَالَ سَهْلٌ مَا رَأَىٰ رَسُولُ اللهِ ﷺ النَّقِيَّ حَتَّىٰ لَقِيَ اللهَ عَزَّوَجَلَّ ۞ فَقِيلَ لَهُ هَلْ كَانَتْ لَكُمْ مَنَاخِلُ عَلَىٰ عَهْدِ رَسُولِ اللهِ ﷺ ۞ قَالَ مَا كَانَتْ لَنَا مَنَاخِلُ ۞ قِيلَ كَيْفَ كُنْتُمْ تَصْنَعُونَ بِالشَّعِيرِ ۞ قَالَ كُنَّا نَنْفُخُهُ فَيَطِيرُ مِنْهُ مَا طَارَ ثُمَّ نَعْجِنُهُ ۞

[330] That is, there was never any leftover bread, and what bread they did have was usually not enough to sate them. (AA)

[331] We learn from this narration that the blessed Family of the Messenger of Allah ﷺ partook in all the hardships and sacrifices of his blessed life. His Family provided an example in how they imitated his lifestyle, without desiring any extra benefit to come to them because they were his Family. In fact, they would selflessly give up everything to accommodate others. (MA)

[332] From this hadith we learn the magnified rank, ennobled character and unmatched dignity of the Messenger of Allah ﷺ. He was cautious and did not allow anyone from his Companions to realise that he or his Family spent nights in extreme hunger. How do we know this for certain? If the Companions had the slightest hint that he or his Family were hungry, they would have competed to give up everything they possessed to fulfil his needs and grant him ease. He was more beloved to them than their families, their children and their own selves. (AA, MA)

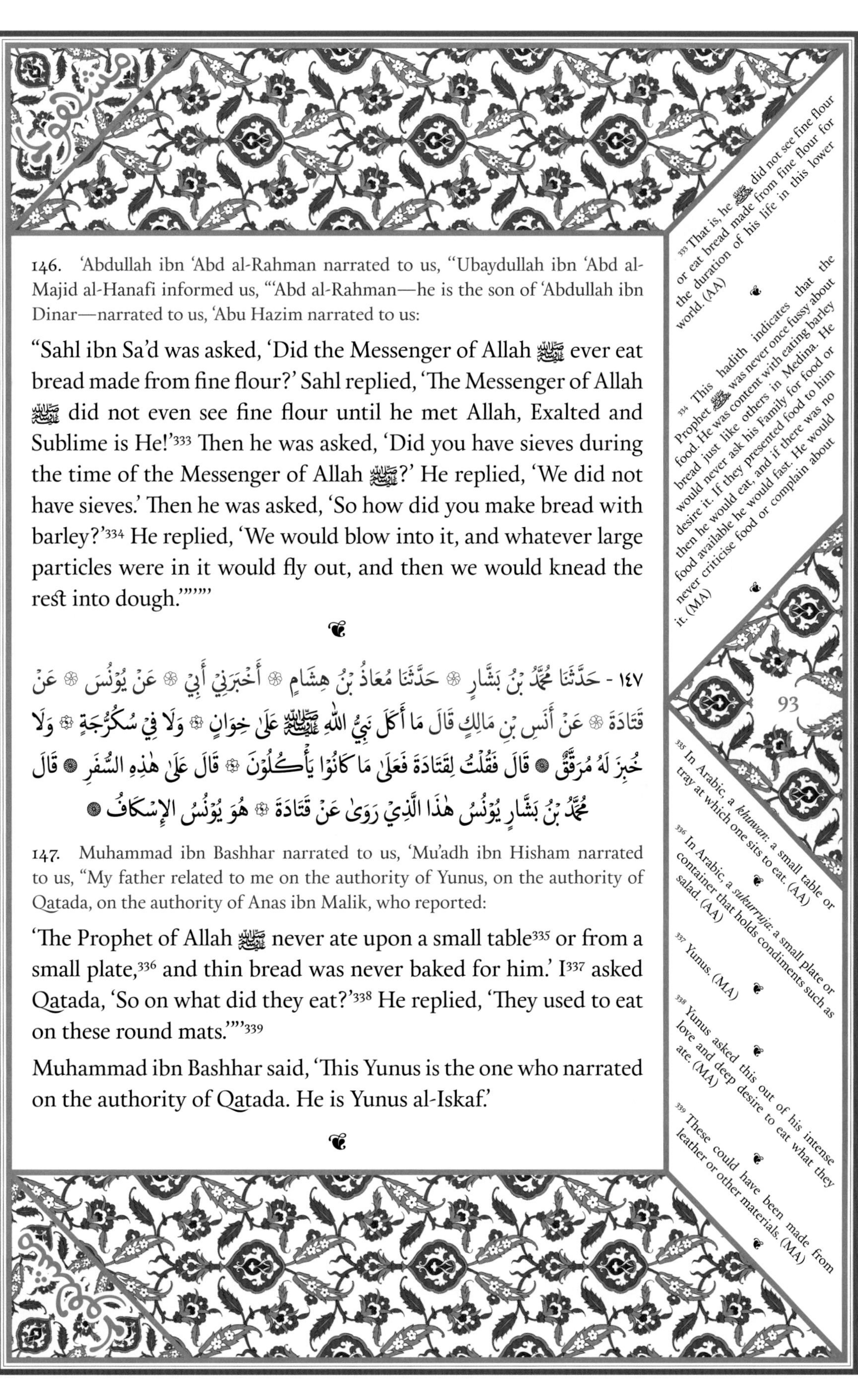

146. ʿAbdullah ibn ʿAbd al-Rahman narrated to us, "ʿUbaydullah ibn ʿAbd al-Majid al-Hanafi informed us, "ʿAbd al-Rahman—he is the son of ʿAbdullah ibn Dinar—narrated to us, ʿAbu Hazim narrated to us:

"Sahl ibn Saʿd was asked, 'Did the Messenger of Allah ﷺ ever eat bread made from fine flour?' Sahl replied, 'The Messenger of Allah ﷺ did not even see fine flour until he met Allah, Exalted and Sublime is He!'[333] Then he was asked, 'Did you have sieves during the time of the Messenger of Allah ﷺ?' He replied, 'We did not have sieves.' Then he was asked, 'So how did you make bread with barley?'[334] He replied, 'We would blow into it, and whatever large particles were in it would fly out, and then we would knead the rest into dough.'""""

١٤٧ - حَدَّثَنَا مُحَمَّدُ بْنُ بَشَّارٍ ۞ حَدَّثَنَا مُعَاذُ بْنُ هِشَامٍ ۞ أَخْبَرَنِي أَبِي ۞ عَنْ يُونُسَ ۞ عَنْ قَتَادَةَ ۞ عَنْ أَنَسِ بْنِ مَالِكٍ قَالَ مَا أَكَلَ نَبِيُّ اللهِ ﷺ عَلَىٰ خِوَانٍ ۞ وَلَا فِي سُكُرُّجَةٍ ۞ وَلَا خُبِزَ لَهُ مُرَقَّقٌ ۞ قَالَ فَقُلْتُ لِقَتَادَةَ فَعَلَىٰ مَا كَانُوا يَأْكُلُونَ ۞ قَالَ عَلَىٰ هٰذِهِ السُّفَرِ ۞ قَالَ مُحَمَّدُ بْنُ بَشَّارٍ يُونُسُ هٰذَا الَّذِي رَوَىٰ عَنْ قَتَادَةَ ۞ هُوَ يُونُسُ الإِسْكَافُ ۞

147. Muhammad ibn Bashhar narrated to us, 'Muʿadh ibn Hisham narrated to us, "My father related to me on the authority of Yunus, on the authority of Qatada, on the authority of Anas ibn Malik, who reported:

'The Prophet of Allah ﷺ never ate upon a small table[335] or from a small plate,[336] and thin bread was never baked for him.' I[337] asked Qatada, 'So on what did they eat?'[338] He replied, 'They used to eat on these round mats.'"'[339]

Muhammad ibn Bashhar said, 'This Yunus is the one who narrated on the authority of Qatada. He is Yunus al-Iskaf.'

[333] That is, he ﷺ did not see fine flour or eat bread made from fine flour for the duration of his life in this lower world. (AA)

[334] This hadith indicates that the Prophet ﷺ was never once fussy about food. He was content with eating barley bread just like others in Medina. He would never ask his Family for food or desire it. If they presented food to him then he would eat, and if there was no food available he would fast. He would never criticise food or complain about it. (MA)

[335] In Arabic, a *khuwan*: a small table or tray at which one sits to eat. (AA)

[336] In Arabic, a *sukurruja*: a small plate or container that holds condiments such as salad. (AA)

[337] Yunus. (MA)

[338] Yunus asked this out of his intense love and deep desire to eat what they ate. (MA)

[339] These could have been made from leather or other materials. (MA)

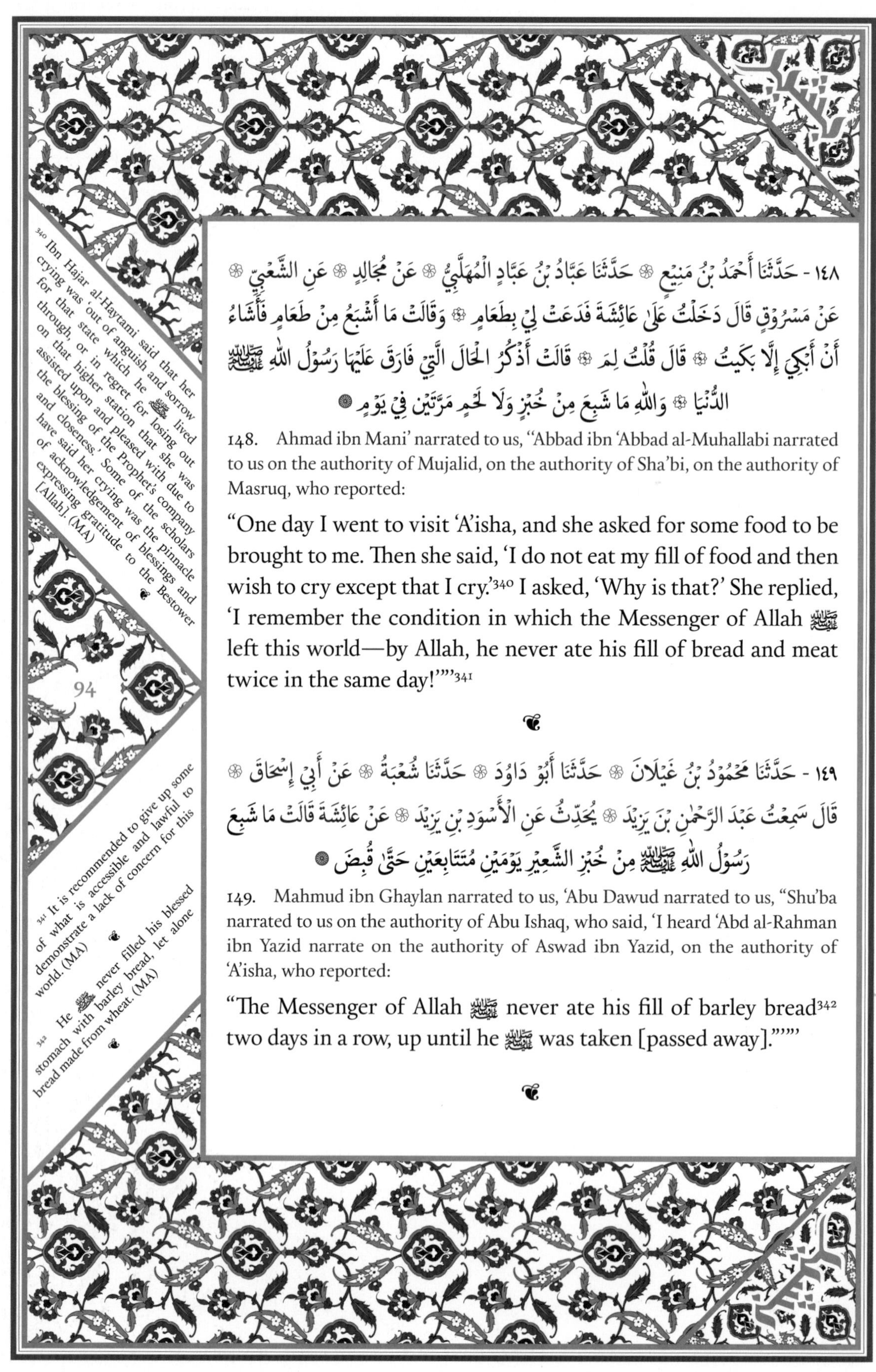

١٤٨ - حَدَّثَنَا أَحْمَدُ بْنُ مَنِيعٍ ۞ حَدَّثَنَا عَبَّادُ بْنُ عَبَّادٍ الْمُهَلَّبِيُّ ۞ عَنْ مُجَالِدٍ ۞ عَنِ الشَّعْبِيِّ ۞ عَنْ مَسْرُوقٍ قَالَ دَخَلْتُ عَلَىٰ عَائِشَةَ فَدَعَتْ لِي بِطَعَامٍ ۞ وَقَالَتْ مَا أَشْبَعُ مِنْ طَعَامٍ فَأَشَاءُ أَنْ أَبْكِيَ إِلَّا بَكَيْتُ ۞ قَالَ قُلْتُ لِمَ ۞ قَالَتْ أَذْكُرُ الْحَالَ الَّتِي فَارَقَ عَلَيْهَا رَسُولُ اللهِ ﷺ الدُّنْيَا ۞ وَاللهِ مَا شَبِعَ مِنْ خُبْزٍ وَلَا لَحْمٍ مَرَّتَيْنِ فِي يَوْمٍ ۞

148. Ahmad ibn Mani' narrated to us, "'Abbad ibn 'Abbad al-Muhallabi narrated to us on the authority of Mujalid, on the authority of Sha'bi, on the authority of Masruq, who reported:

"One day I went to visit 'A'isha, and she asked for some food to be brought to me. Then she said, 'I do not eat my fill of food and then wish to cry except that I cry.'[340] I asked, 'Why is that?' She replied, 'I remember the condition in which the Messenger of Allah ﷺ left this world—by Allah, he never ate his fill of bread and meat twice in the same day!'""[341]

❦

١٤٩ - حَدَّثَنَا مَحْمُودُ بْنُ غَيْلَانَ ۞ حَدَّثَنَا أَبُو دَاوُدَ ۞ حَدَّثَنَا شُعْبَةُ ۞ عَنْ أَبِي إِسْحَاقَ ۞ قَالَ سَمِعْتُ عَبْدَ الرَّحْمَٰنِ بْنَ يَزِيدَ ۞ يُحَدِّثُ عَنِ الْأَسْوَدِ بْنِ يَزِيدَ ۞ عَنْ عَائِشَةَ قَالَتْ مَا شَبِعَ رَسُولُ اللهِ ﷺ مِنْ خُبْزِ الشَّعِيرِ يَوْمَيْنِ مُتَتَابِعَيْنِ حَتَّىٰ قُبِضَ ۞

149. Mahmud ibn Ghaylan narrated to us, 'Abu Dawud narrated to us, "Shu'ba narrated to us on the authority of Abu Ishaq, who said, 'I heard 'Abd al-Rahman ibn Yazid narrate on the authority of Aswad ibn Yazid, on the authority of 'A'isha, who reported:

"The Messenger of Allah ﷺ never ate his fill of barley bread[342] two days in a row, up until he ﷺ was taken [passed away].""""

❦

[340] Ibn Hajar al-Haytami said that her crying was 'out of anguish and sorrow for that state which he ﷺ lived through, or in regret for losing out on that higher station that she was assisted upon and pleased with due to the blessing of the Prophet's company and closeness.' Some of the scholars have said her crying was the pinnacle of acknowledgement of blessings and expressing gratitude to the Bestower [Allah]. (MA) ❦

[341] It is recommended to give up some of what is accessible and lawful to demonstrate a lack of concern for this world. (MA) ❦

[342] He ﷺ never filled his blessed stomach with barley bread, let alone bread made from wheat. (MA) ❦

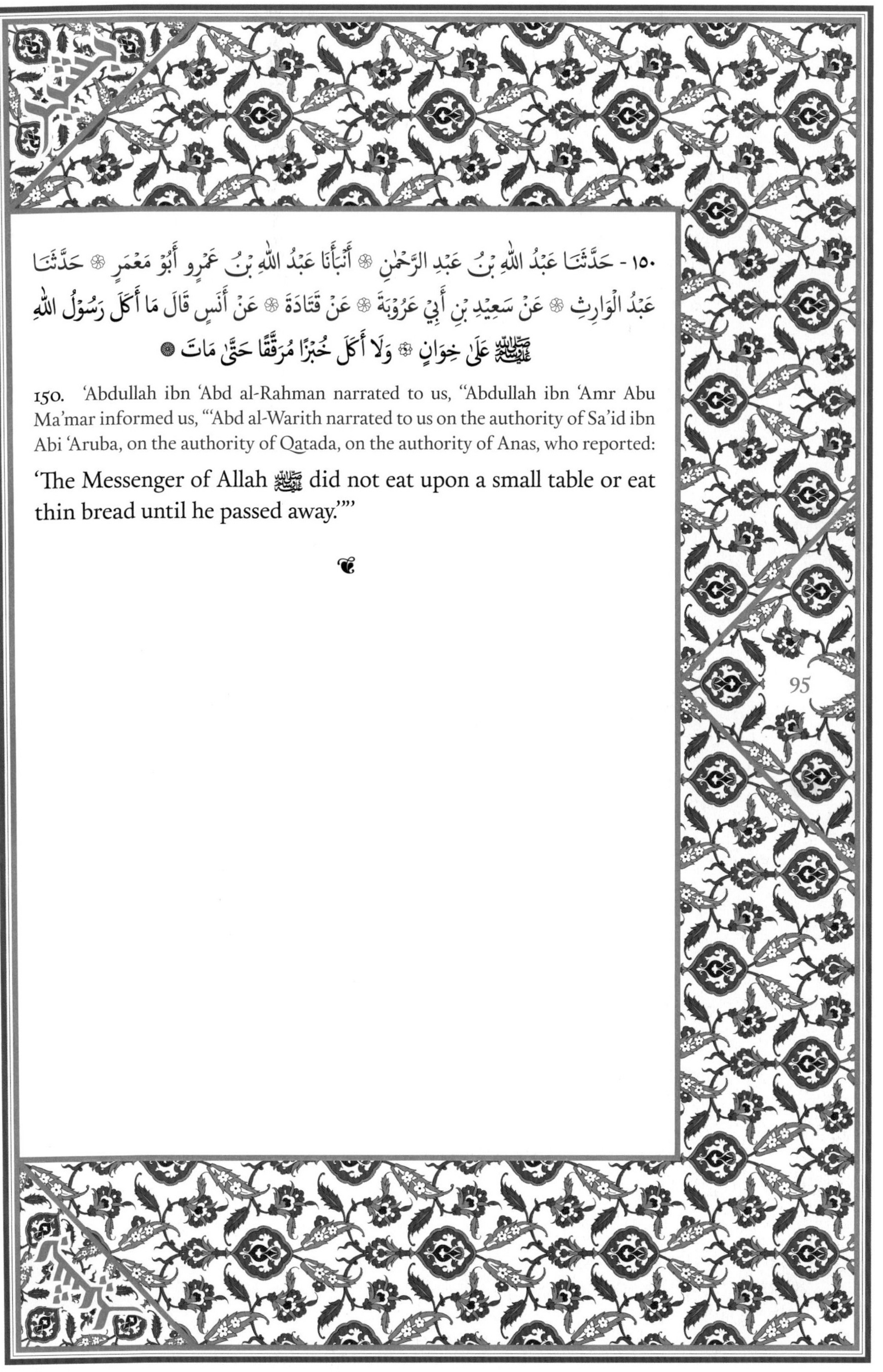

١٥٠ - حَدَّثَنَا عَبْدُ اللهِ بْنُ عَبْدِ الرَّحْمٰنِ ❁ أَنبَأَنَا عَبْدُ اللهِ بْنُ عَمْرٍو أَبُو مَعْمَرٍ ❁ حَدَّثَنَا عَبْدُ الْوَارِثِ ❁ عَنْ سَعِيدِ بْنِ أَبِي عَرُوبَةَ ❁ عَنْ قَتَادَةَ ❁ عَنْ أَنَسٍ قَالَ مَا أَكَلَ رَسُوْلُ اللهِ ﷺ عَلَىٰ خِوَانٍ ❁ وَلَا أَكَلَ خُبْزًا مُرَقَّقًا حَتَّىٰ مَاتَ ❁

150. 'Abdullah ibn 'Abd al-Rahman narrated to us, "Abdullah ibn 'Amr Abu Ma'mar informed us, "'Abd al-Warith narrated to us on the authority of Sa'id ibn Abi 'Aruba, on the authority of Qatada, on the authority of Anas, who reported:

'The Messenger of Allah ﷺ did not eat upon a small table or eat thin bread until he passed away.'""

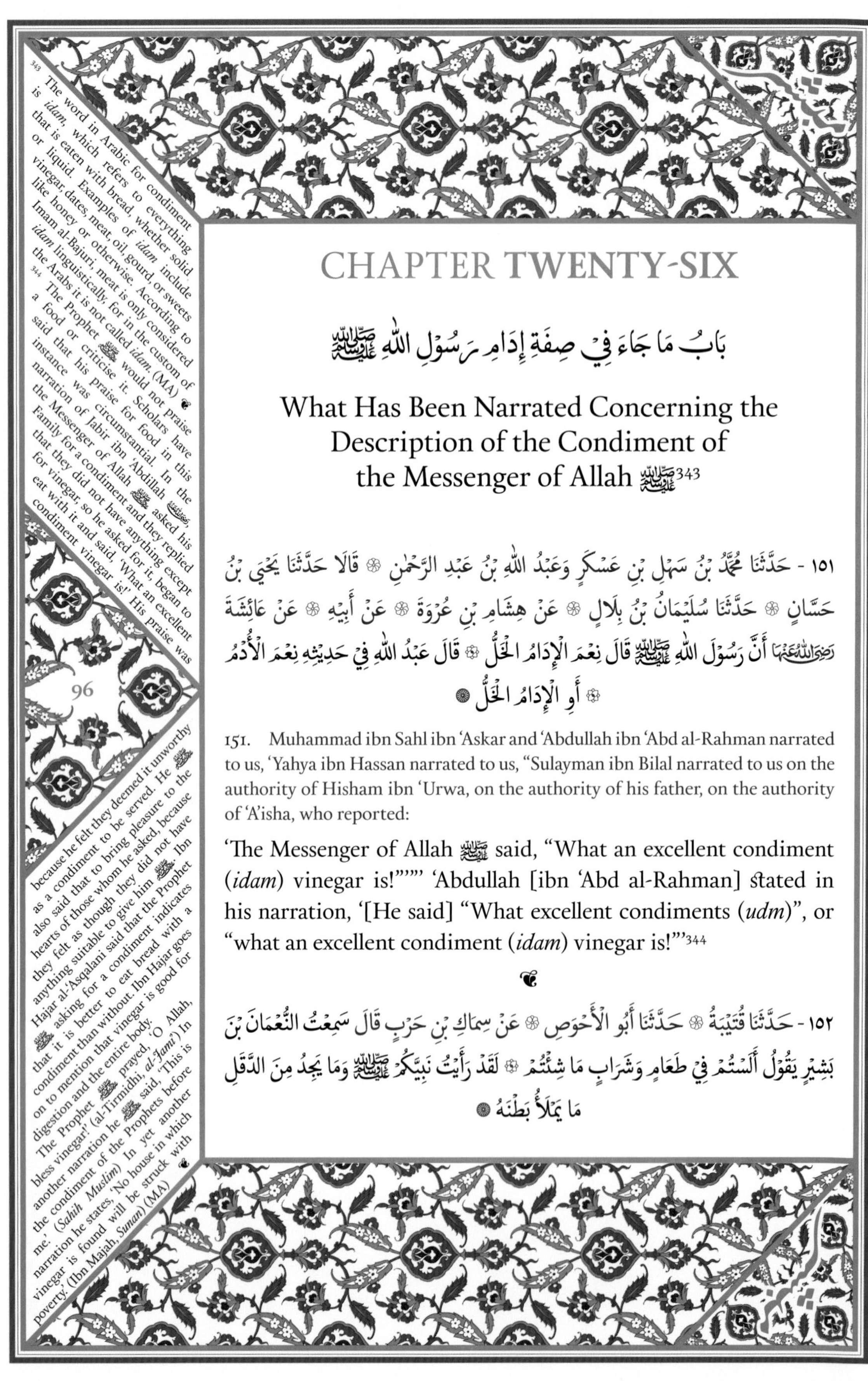

CHAPTER TWENTY-SIX

بَابُ مَا جَاءَ فِي صِفَةِ إِدَامِ رَسُولِ اللهِ ﷺ

What Has Been Narrated Concerning the Description of the Condiment of the Messenger of Allah ﷺ[343]

١٥١ - حَدَّثَنَا مُحَمَّدُ بْنُ سَهْلِ بْنِ عَسْكَرٍ وَعَبْدُ اللهِ بْنُ عَبْدِ الرَّحْمٰنِ ۞ قَالَا حَدَّثَنَا يَحْيَى بْنُ حَسَّانٍ ۞ حَدَّثَنَا سُلَيْمَانُ بْنُ بِلَالٍ ۞ عَنْ هِشَامِ بْنِ عُرْوَةَ ۞ عَنْ أَبِيهِ ۞ عَنْ عَائِشَةَ رَضِيَ اللهُ عَنْهَا أَنَّ رَسُولَ اللهِ ﷺ قَالَ نِعْمَ الْإِدَامُ الْخَلُّ ۞ قَالَ عَبْدُ اللهِ فِي حَدِيثِهِ نِعْمَ الْأُدُمُ ۞ أَوِ الْإِدَامُ الْخَلُّ ۞

151. Muhammad ibn Sahl ibn 'Askar and 'Abdullah ibn 'Abd al-Rahman narrated to us, 'Yahya ibn Hassan narrated to us, "Sulayman ibn Bilal narrated to us on the authority of Hisham ibn 'Urwa, on the authority of his father, on the authority of 'A'isha, who reported:

'The Messenger of Allah ﷺ said, "What an excellent condiment (*idam*) vinegar is!"""' 'Abdullah [ibn 'Abd al-Rahman] stated in his narration, '[He said] "What excellent condiments (*udm*)", or "what an excellent condiment (*idam*) vinegar is!"'[344]

❦

١٥٢ - حَدَّثَنَا قُتَيْبَةُ ۞ حَدَّثَنَا أَبُو الْأَحْوَصِ ۞ عَنْ سِمَاكِ بْنِ حَرْبٍ قَالَ سَمِعْتُ النُّعْمَانَ بْنَ بَشِيرٍ يَقُولُ أَلَسْتُمْ فِي طَعَامٍ وَشَرَابٍ مَا شِئْتُمْ ۞ لَقَدْ رَأَيْتُ نَبِيَّكُمْ ﷺ وَمَا يَجِدُ مِنَ الدَّقَلِ مَا يَمْلَأُ بَطْنَهُ ۞

343 The word in Arabic for condiment is *idam*, which refers to everything that is eaten with bread, whether solid or liquid. Examples of *idam* include vinegar, dates, meat, oil, gourd, or sweets like honey or otherwise. According to Imam al-Bajuri, meat is only considered *idam* linguistically, for in the custom of the Arabs it is not called *idam*. (MA) ❦

344 The Prophet ﷺ would not praise a food or criticise it. Scholars have said that his praise for food in this instance was circumstantial. In the narration of Jabir ibn 'Abdillah رضي الله عنه, the Messenger of Allah ﷺ asked his Family for a condiment and they replied that they did not have anything except for vinegar, so he asked for it, began to eat with it and said, 'What an excellent condiment vinegar is!' His praise was because he felt they deemed it unworthy as a condiment to be served. He ﷺ also said that to bring pleasure to the hearts of those whom he asked, because they felt as though they did not have anything suitable to give him ﷺ. Ibn Hajar al-'Asqalani said that the Prophet ﷺ asking for a condiment indicates that it is better to eat bread with a condiment than without. Ibn Hajar goes on to mention that vinegar is good for digestion and the entire body. The Prophet ﷺ prayed, 'O Allah, bless vinegar!' (al-Tirmidhi, *al-Jami'*) In another narration he ﷺ said, 'This is the condiment of the Prophets before me.' (*Sahih Muslim*) In yet another narration he states, 'No house in which vinegar is found will be struck with poverty.' (Ibn Majah, *Sunan*) (MA) ❦

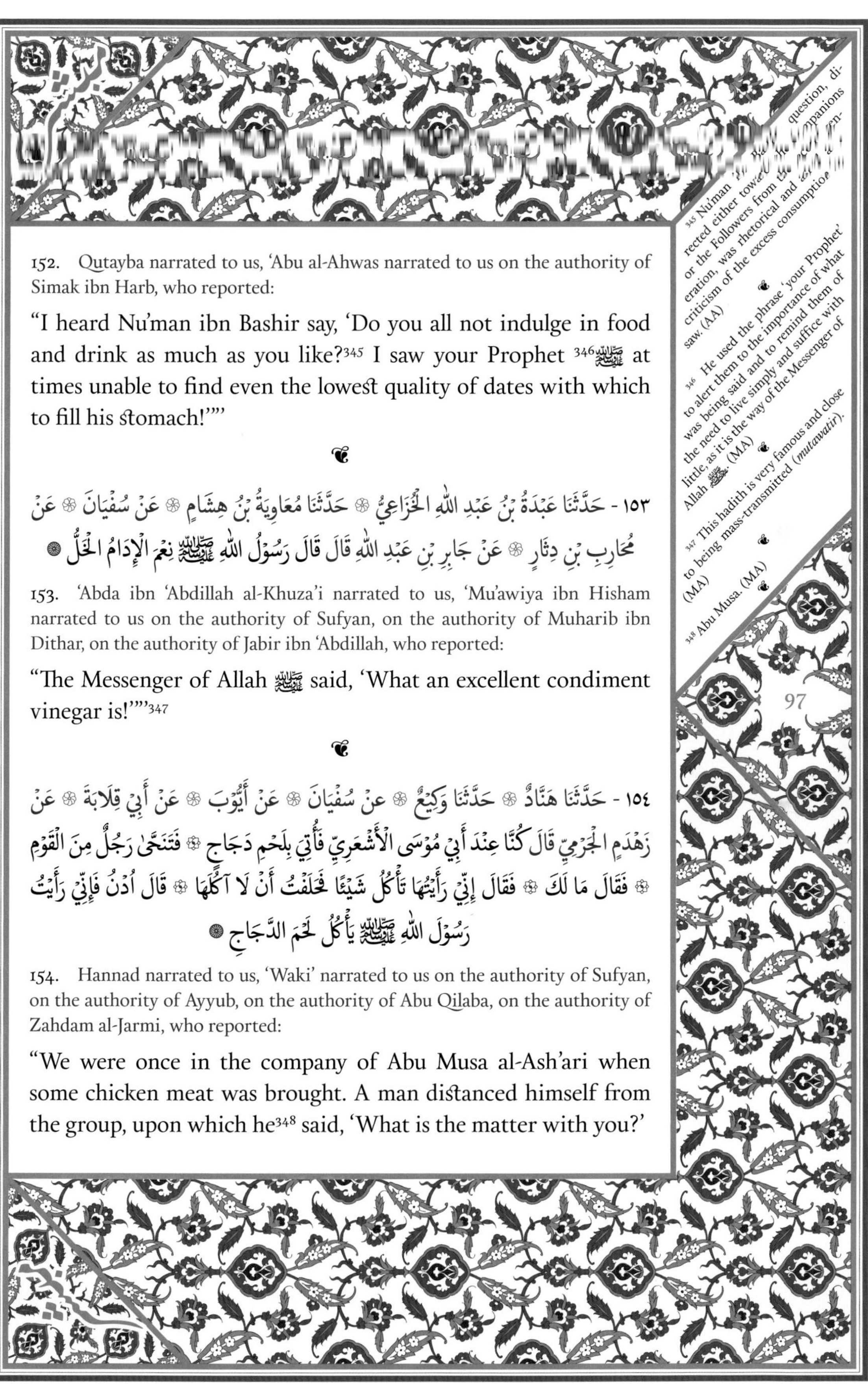

152. Qutayba narrated to us, 'Abu al-Ahwas narrated to us on the authority of Simak ibn Harb, who reported:

"I heard Nu'man ibn Bashir say, 'Do you all not indulge in food and drink as much as you like?[345] I saw your Prophet[346] ﷺ at times unable to find even the lowest quality of dates with which to fill his stomach!'"

١٥٣ - حَدَّثَنَا عَبْدَةُ بْنُ عَبْدِ اللهِ الْخُزَاعِيُّ ۞ حَدَّثَنَا مُعَاوِيَةُ بْنُ هِشَامٍ ۞ عَنْ سُفْيَانَ ۞ عَنْ مُحَارِبِ بْنِ دِثَارٍ ۞ عَنْ جَابِرِ بْنِ عَبْدِ اللهِ قَالَ قَالَ رَسُولُ اللهِ ﷺ نِعْمَ الْإِدَامُ الْخَلُّ ۞

153. 'Abda ibn 'Abdillah al-Khuza'i narrated to us, 'Mu'awiya ibn Hisham narrated to us on the authority of Sufyan, on the authority of Muharib ibn Dithar, on the authority of Jabir ibn 'Abdillah, who reported:

"The Messenger of Allah ﷺ said, 'What an excellent condiment vinegar is!'"[347]

١٥٤ - حَدَّثَنَا هَنَّادٌ ۞ حَدَّثَنَا وَكِيعٌ ۞ عنْ سُفْيَانَ ۞ عَنْ أَيُّوبَ ۞ عَنْ أَبِي قِلَابَةَ ۞ عَنْ زَهْدَمٍ الْجَرْمِيِّ قَالَ كُنَّا عِنْدَ أَبِي مُوسَى الْأَشْعَرِيِّ فَأُتِيَ بِلَحْمِ دَجَاجٍ ۞ فَتَنَحَّى رَجُلٌ مِنَ الْقَوْمِ ۞ فَقَالَ مَا لَكَ ۞ فَقَالَ إِنِّي رَأَيْتُهَا تَأْكُلُ شَيْئًا فَحَلَفْتُ أَنْ لَا آكُلَهَا ۞ قَالَ ادْنُ فَإِنِّي رَأَيْتُ رَسُولَ اللهِ ﷺ يَأْكُلُ لَحْمَ الدَّجَاجِ ۞

154. Hannad narrated to us, 'Waki' narrated to us on the authority of Sufyan, on the authority of Ayyub, on the authority of Abu Qilaba, on the authority of Zahdam al-Jarmi, who reported:

"We were once in the company of Abu Musa al-Ash'ari when some chicken meat was brought. A man distanced himself from the group, upon which he[348] said, 'What is the matter with you?'

[345] Nu'man [illegible] question, directed either tow[illegible] Companions or the Followers from t[illegible] generation, was rhetorical and [illegible] criticism of the excess consumptio[illegible] saw. (AA)

[346] He used the phrase 'your Prophet' to alert them to the importance of what was being said and to remind them of the need to live simply and suffice with little, as it is the way of the Messenger of Allah ﷺ. (MA)

[347] This hadith is very famous and close to being mass-transmitted (*mutawatir*). (MA)

[348] Abu Musa. (MA)

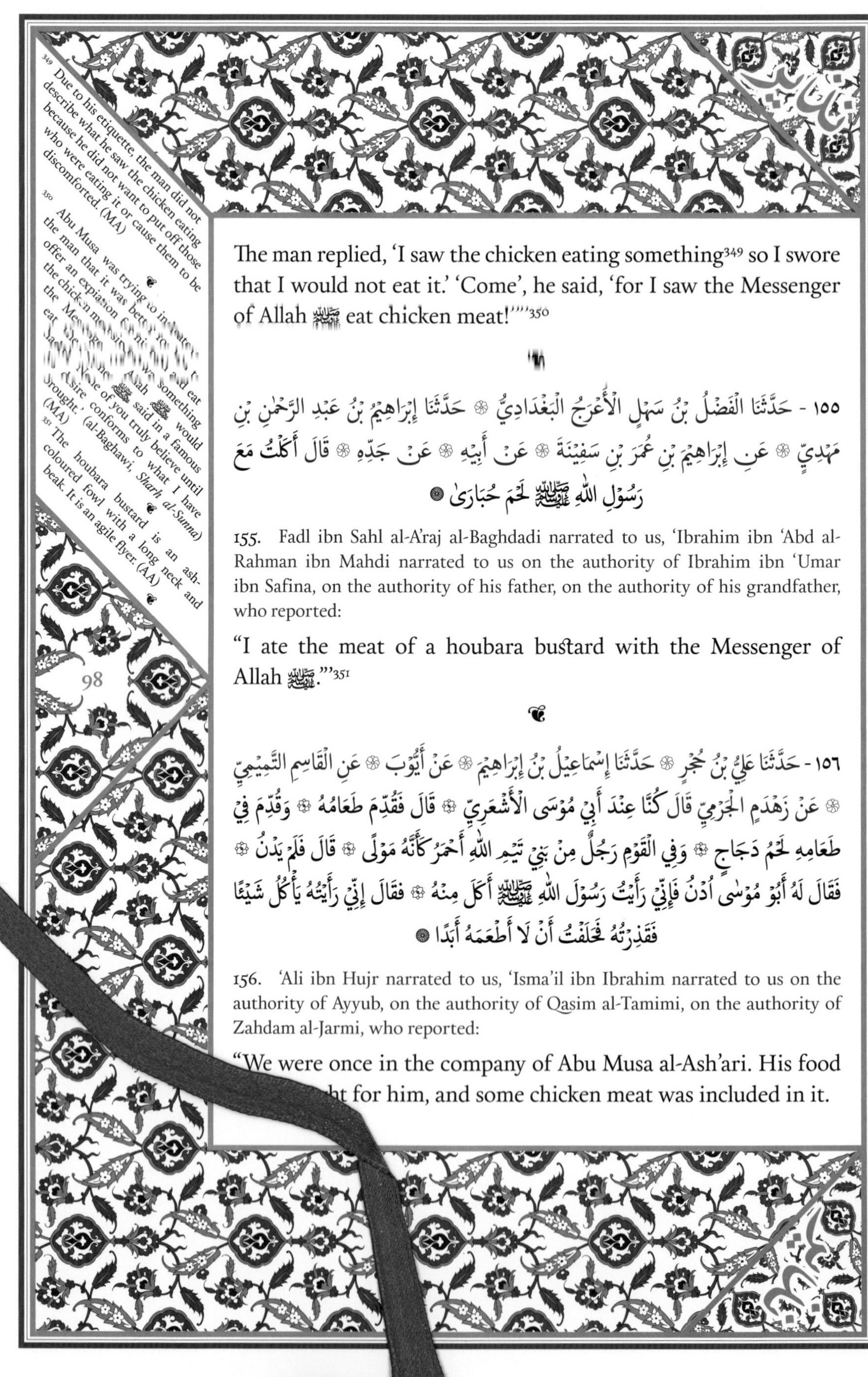

The man replied, 'I saw the chicken eating something[349] so I swore that I would not eat it.' 'Come', he said, 'for I saw the Messenger of Allah ﷺ eat chicken meat!'"'[350]

١٥٥ - حَدَّثَنَا الْفَضْلُ بْنُ سَهْلٍ الْأَعْرَجُ الْبَغْدَادِيُّ ۞ حَدَّثَنَا إِبْرَاهِيمُ بْنُ عَبْدِ الرَّحْمٰنِ بْنِ مَهْدِيٍّ ۞ عَنْ إِبْرَاهِيمَ بْنِ عُمَرَ بْنِ سَفِينَةَ ۞ عَنْ أَبِيهِ ۞ عَنْ جَدِّهِ ۞ قَالَ أَكَلْتُ مَعَ رَسُولِ اللهِ ﷺ لَحْمَ حُبَارَى ۝

155. Fadl ibn Sahl al-A'raj al-Baghdadi narrated to us, 'Ibrahim ibn 'Abd al-Rahman ibn Mahdi narrated to us on the authority of Ibrahim ibn 'Umar ibn Safina, on the authority of his father, on the authority of his grandfather, who reported:

"I ate the meat of a houbara bustard with the Messenger of Allah ﷺ."'[351]

١٥٦ - حَدَّثَنَا عَلِيُّ بْنُ حُجْرٍ ۞ حَدَّثَنَا إِسْمَاعِيلُ بْنُ إِبْرَاهِيمَ ۞ عَنْ أَيُّوبَ ۞ عَنِ الْقَاسِمِ التَّمِيمِيِّ ۞ عَنْ زَهْدَمٍ الْجَرْمِيِّ قَالَ كُنَّا عِنْدَ أَبِي مُوسَى الْأَشْعَرِيِّ ۞ قَالَ فَقُدِّمَ طَعَامُهُ ۞ وَقُدِّمَ فِي طَعَامِهِ لَحْمُ دَجَاجٍ ۞ وَفِي الْقَوْمِ رَجُلٌ مِنْ بَنِي تَيْمِ اللهِ أَحْمَرُ كَأَنَّهُ مَوْلًى ۞ قَالَ فَلَمْ يَدْنُ ۞ فَقَالَ لَهُ أَبُو مُوسَى اُدْنُ فَإِنِّي رَأَيْتُ رَسُولَ اللهِ ﷺ أَكَلَ مِنْهُ ۞ فَقَالَ إِنِّي رَأَيْتُهُ يَأْكُلُ شَيْئًا فَقَذِرْتُهُ فَحَلَفْتُ أَنْ لَا أَطْعَمَهُ أَبَدًا ۝

156. 'Ali ibn Hujr narrated to us, 'Isma'il ibn Ibrahim narrated to us on the authority of Ayyub, on the authority of Qasim al-Tamimi, on the authority of Zahdam al-Jarmi, who reported:

"We were once in the company of Abu Musa al-Ash'ari. His food [illegible]ht for him, and some chicken meat was included in it.

[349] Due to his etiquette, the man did not describe what he saw the chicken eating because he did not want to put off those who were eating it or cause them to be discomforted. (MA)

[350] Abu Musa was trying to in[illegible] the man that it was bett[illegible] offer an expiation f[illegible] the chicken m[illegible] the Mes[illegible] eat [illegible] [illegible]ne[illegible] Allah ﷺ [illegible] something [illegible] would [illegible] None of you ﷺ said in a famous [illegible] desire conforms to what I have brought.' (al-Baghawi, *Sharh al-Sunna*) (MA)

[351] The houbara bustard is an ash-coloured fowl with a long neck and beak. It is an agile flyer. (AA)

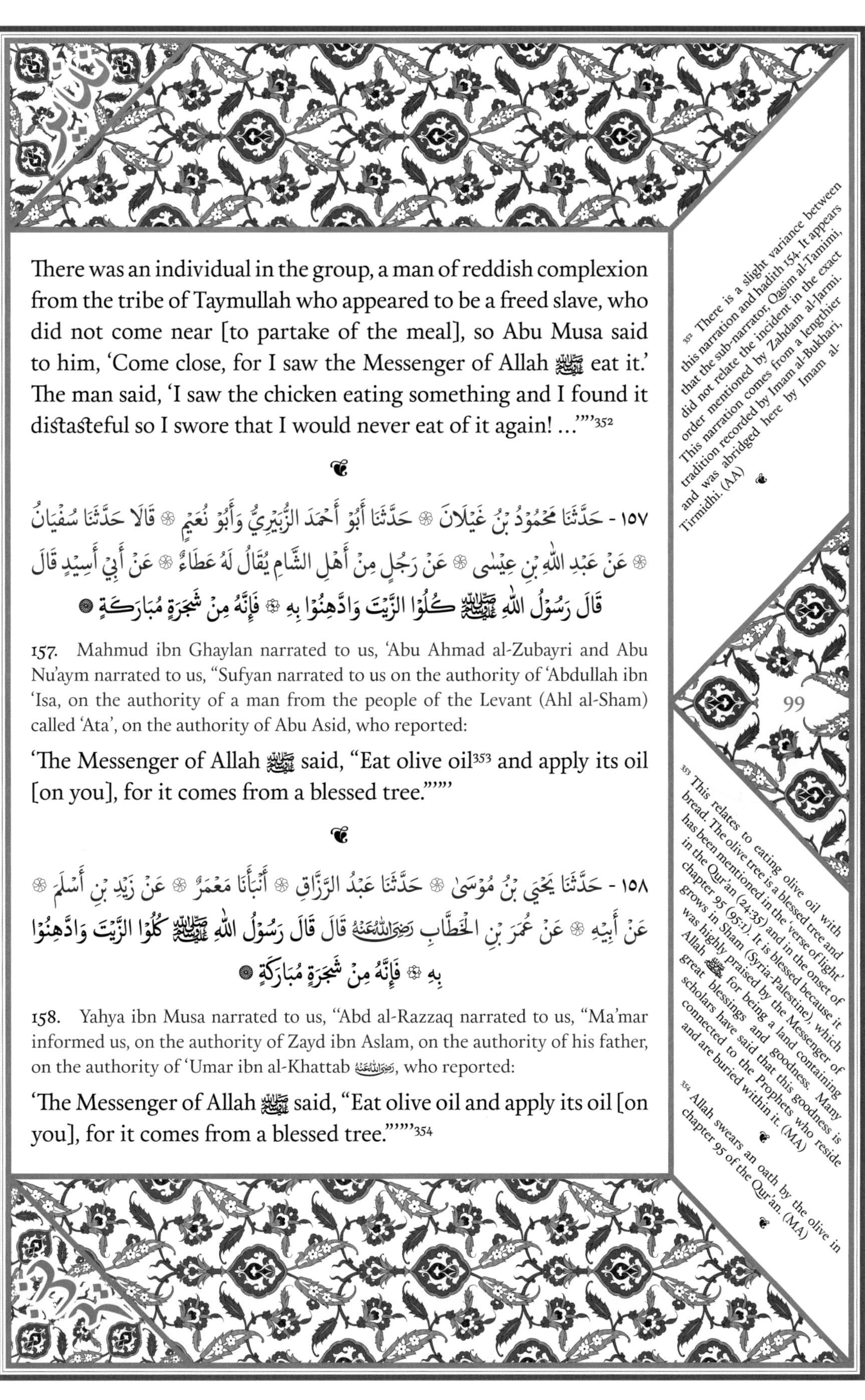

There was an individual in the group, a man of reddish complexion from the tribe of Taymullah who appeared to be a freed slave, who did not come near [to partake of the meal], so Abu Musa said to him, 'Come close, for I saw the Messenger of Allah ﷺ eat it.' The man said, 'I saw the chicken eating something and I found it distasteful so I swore that I would never eat of it again! ...''''[352]

❦

١٥٧ - حَدَّثَنَا مَحْمُودُ بْنُ غَيْلَانَ ۞ حَدَّثَنَا أَبُو أَحْمَدَ الزُّبَيْرِيُّ وَأَبُو نُعَيْمٍ ۞ قَالَا حَدَّثَنَا سُفْيَانُ ۞ عَنْ عَبْدِ اللهِ بْنِ عِيسَى ۞ عَنْ رَجُلٍ مِنْ أَهْلِ الشَّامِ يُقَالُ لَهُ عَطَاءٌ ۞ عَنْ أَبِي أَسِيدٍ قَالَ قَالَ رَسُولُ اللهِ ﷺ كُلُوا الزَّيْتَ وَادَّهِنُوا بِهِ ۞ فَإِنَّهُ مِنْ شَجَرَةٍ مُبَارَكَةٍ ۝

157. Mahmud ibn Ghaylan narrated to us, 'Abu Ahmad al-Zubayri and Abu Nu'aym narrated to us, "Sufyan narrated to us on the authority of 'Abdullah ibn 'Isa, on the authority of a man from the people of the Levant (Ahl al-Sham) called 'Ata', on the authority of Abu Asid, who reported:

'The Messenger of Allah ﷺ said, "Eat olive oil[353] and apply its oil [on you], for it comes from a blessed tree."'''''

❦

١٥٨ - حَدَّثَنَا يَحْيَى بْنُ مُوسَى ۞ حَدَّثَنَا عَبْدُ الرَّزَّاقِ ۞ أَنْبَأَنَا مَعْمَرٌ ۞ عَنْ زَيْدِ بْنِ أَسْلَمَ ۞ عَنْ أَبِيهِ ۞ عَنْ عُمَرَ بْنِ الْخَطَّابِ رَضِيَ اللهُ عَنْهُ قَالَ قَالَ رَسُولُ اللهِ ﷺ كُلُوا الزَّيْتَ وَادَّهِنُوا بِهِ ۞ فَإِنَّهُ مِنْ شَجَرَةٍ مُبَارَكَةٍ ۝

158. Yahya ibn Musa narrated to us, "Abd al-Razzaq narrated to us, "Ma'mar informed us, on the authority of Zayd ibn Aslam, on the authority of his father, on the authority of 'Umar ibn al-Khattab رضي الله عنه, who reported:

'The Messenger of Allah ﷺ said, "Eat olive oil and apply its oil [on you], for it comes from a blessed tree."''''''[354]

[352] There is a slight variance between this narration and hadith 154. It appears that the sub-narrator, Qasim al-Tamimi, did not relate the incident in the exact order mentioned by Zahdam al-Jarmi. This narration comes from a lengthier tradition recorded by Imam al-Bukhari, and was abridged here by Imam al-Tirmidhi. (AA)

❦

[353] This relates to eating olive oil with bread. The olive tree is a blessed tree and has been mentioned in the 'verse of light' in the Qur'an (24:35) and in the onset of chapter 95 (95:1). It is blessed because it grows in Sham (Syria-Palestine), which was highly praised by the Messenger of Allah ﷺ for being a land containing great blessings and goodness. Many scholars have said that this goodness is connected to the Prophets who reside and are buried within it. (MA)

❦

[354] Allah swears an oath by the olive in chapter 95 of the Qur'an. (MA)

❦

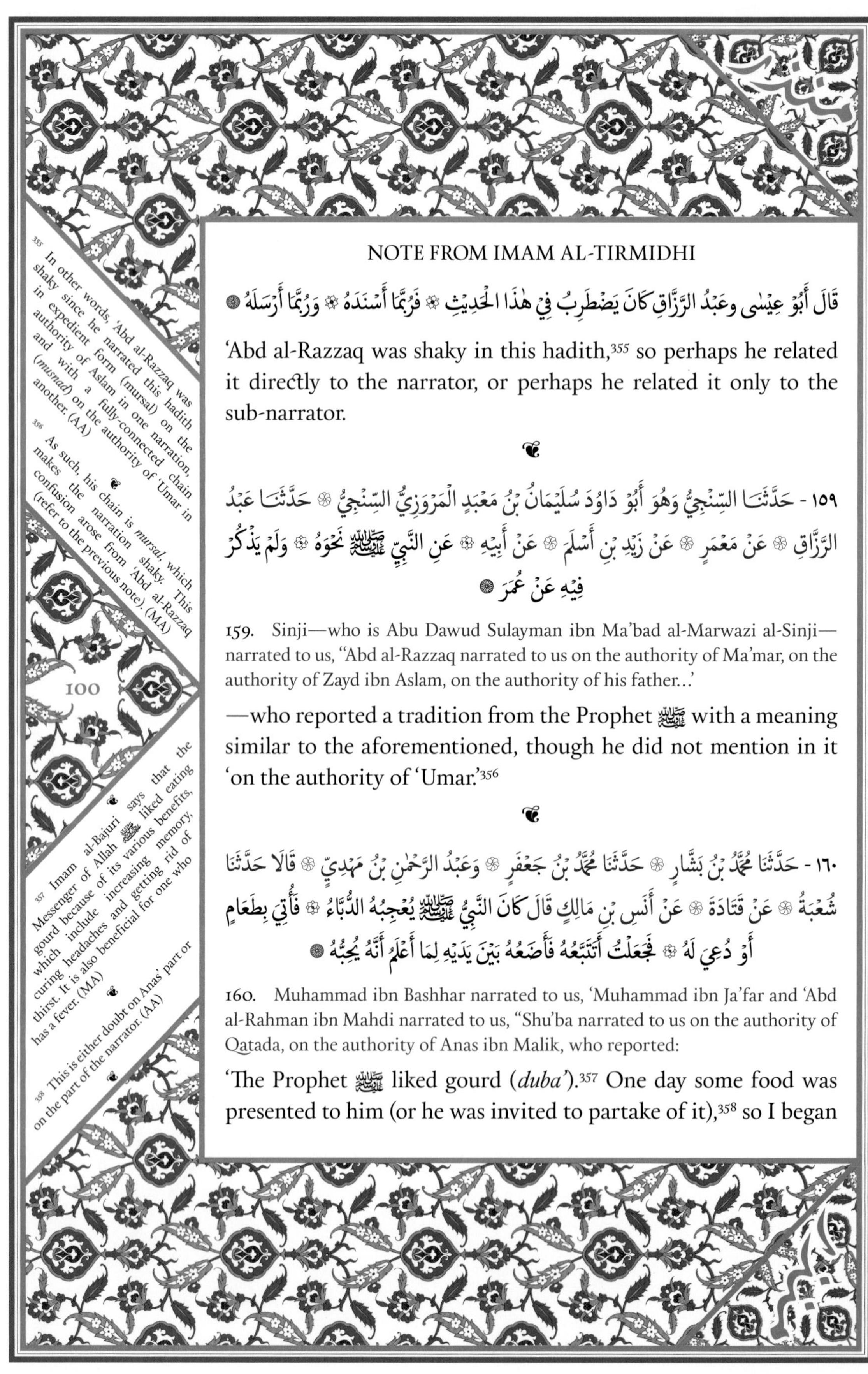

NOTE FROM IMAM AL-TIRMIDHI

قَالَ أَبُو عِيسَى وعَبْدُ الرَّزَّاقِ كَانَ يَضْطَرِبُ فِي هٰذَا الْحَدِيْثِ ۞ فَرُبَّمَا أَسْنَدَهُ ۞ وَرُبَّمَا أَرْسَلَهُ ۞

'Abd al-Razzaq was shaky in this hadith,[355] so perhaps he related it directly to the narrator, or perhaps he related it only to the sub-narrator.

❦

١٥٩ - حَدَّثَنَا السِّنْجِيُّ وَهُوَ أَبُو دَاوُدَ سُلَيْمَانُ بْنُ مَعْبَدٍ الْمَرْوَزِيُّ السِّنْجِيُّ ۞ حَدَّثَنَا عَبْدُ الرَّزَّاقِ ۞ عَنْ مَعْمَرٍ ۞ عَنْ زَيْدِ بْنِ أَسْلَمَ ۞ عَنْ أَبِيهِ ۞ عَنِ النَّبِيِّ ﷺ نَحْوَهُ ۞ وَلَمْ يَذْكُرْ فِيهِ عَنْ عُمَرَ ۞

159. Sinji—who is Abu Dawud Sulayman ibn Ma'bad al-Marwazi al-Sinji—narrated to us, "Abd al-Razzaq narrated to us on the authority of Ma'mar, on the authority of Zayd ibn Aslam, on the authority of his father...'

—who reported a tradition from the Prophet ﷺ with a meaning similar to the aforementioned, though he did not mention in it 'on the authority of 'Umar.'[356]

❦

١٦٠ - حَدَّثَنَا مُحَمَّدُ بْنُ بَشَّارٍ ۞ حَدَّثَنَا مُحَمَّدُ بْنُ جَعْفَرٍ ۞ وَعَبْدُ الرَّحْمٰنِ بْنُ مَهْدِيٍّ ۞ قَالَا حَدَّثَنَا شُعْبَةُ ۞ عَنْ قَتَادَةَ ۞ عَنْ أَنَسِ بْنِ مَالِكٍ قَالَ كَانَ النَّبِيُّ ﷺ يُعْجِبُهُ الدُّبَّاءُ ۞ فَأُتِيَ بِطَعَامٍ أَوْ دُعِيَ لَهُ ۞ فَجَعَلْتُ أَتَتَبَّعُهُ فَأَضَعُهُ بَيْنَ يَدَيْهِ لِمَا أَعْلَمُ أَنَّهُ يُحِبُّهُ ۞

160. Muhammad ibn Bashhar narrated to us, 'Muhammad ibn Ja'far and 'Abd al-Rahman ibn Mahdi narrated to us, "Shu'ba narrated to us on the authority of Qatada, on the authority of Anas ibn Malik, who reported:

'The Prophet ﷺ liked gourd (*duba'*).[357] One day some food was presented to him (or he was invited to partake of it),[358] so I began

[355] In other words, 'Abd al-Razzaq was shaky since he narrated this hadith in expedient form (mursal) on the authority of Aslam in one narration, and with a fully-connected chain (*musnad*) on the authority of 'Umar in another. (AA)

[356] As such, his chain is *mursal*, which makes the narration shaky. This confusion arose from 'Abd al-Razzaq (refer to the previous note). (MA)

[357] Imam al-Bajuri says that the Messenger of Allah ﷺ liked eating gourd because of its various benefits, which include increasing memory, curing headaches and getting rid of thirst. It is also beneficial for one who has a fever. (MA)

[358] This is either doubt on Anas' part or on the part of the narrator. (AA)

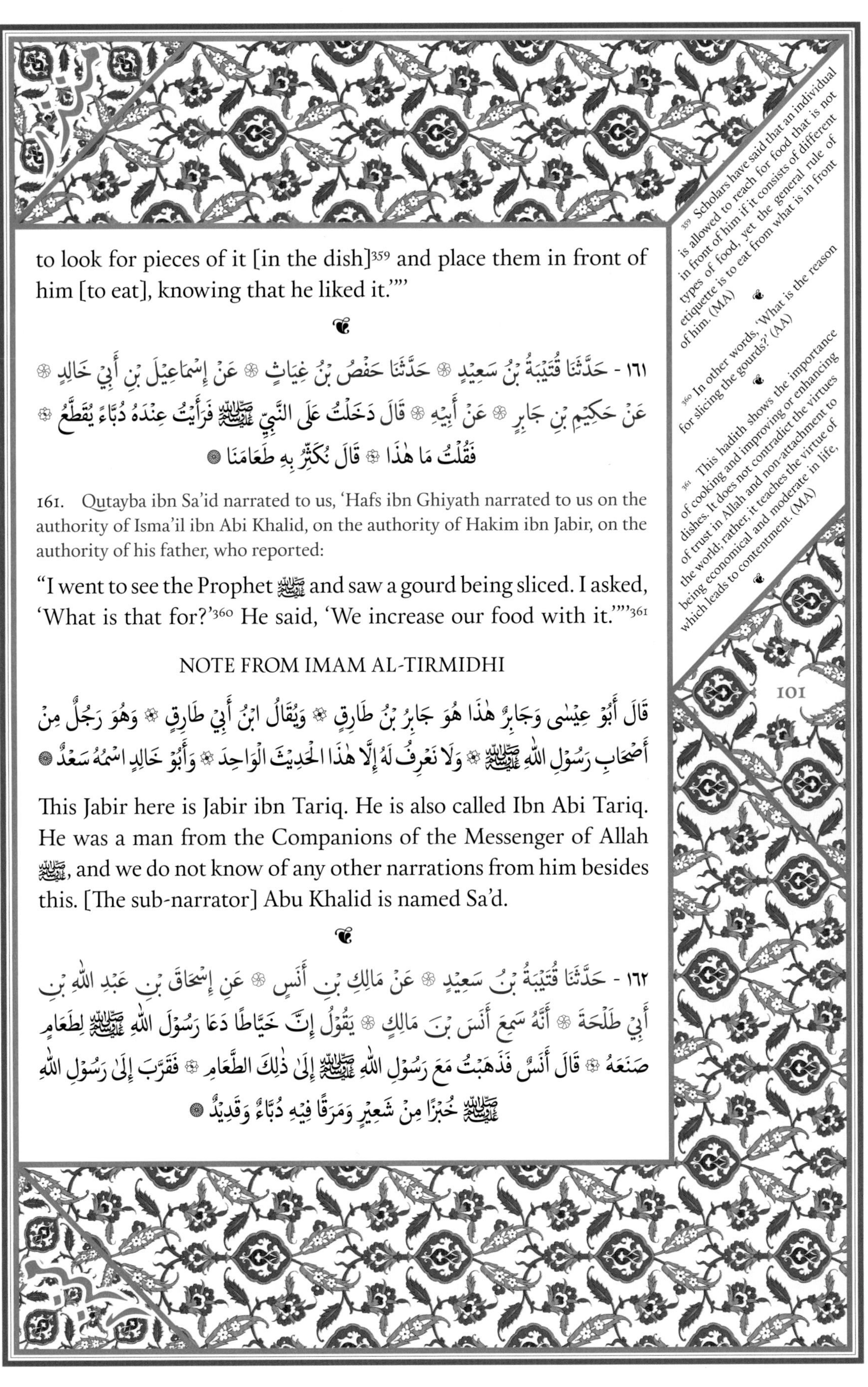

to look for pieces of it [in the dish][359] and place them in front of him [to eat], knowing that he liked it.'"'

❦

١٦١ - حَدَّثَنَا قُتَيْبَةُ بْنُ سَعِيدٍ ۞ حَدَّثَنَا حَفْصُ بْنُ غِيَاثٍ ۞ عَنْ إِسْمَاعِيلَ بْنِ أَبِي خَالِدٍ ۞ عَنْ حَكِيمِ بْنِ جَابِرٍ ۞ عَنْ أَبِيهِ ۞ قَالَ دَخَلْتُ عَلَى النَّبِيِّ ﷺ فَرَأَيْتُ عِنْدَهُ دُبَّاءَ يُقَطَّعُ ۞ فَقُلْتُ مَا هٰذَا ۞ قَالَ نُكَثِّرُ بِهِ طَعَامَنَا ۞

161. Qutayba ibn Sa'id narrated to us, 'Hafs ibn Ghiyath narrated to us on the authority of Isma'il ibn Abi Khalid, on the authority of Hakim ibn Jabir, on the authority of his father, who reported:

"I went to see the Prophet ﷺ and saw a gourd being sliced. I asked, 'What is that for?'[360] He said, 'We increase our food with it.'"'[361]

NOTE FROM IMAM AL-TIRMIDHI

قَالَ أَبُو عِيسَىٰ وَجَابِرٌ هٰذَا هُوَ جَابِرُ بْنُ طَارِقٍ ۞ وَيُقَالُ ابْنُ أَبِي طَارِقٍ ۞ وَهُوَ رَجُلٌ مِنْ أَصْحَابِ رَسُولِ اللهِ ﷺ ۞ وَلَا نَعْرِفُ لَهُ إِلَّا هٰذَا الْحَدِيثَ الْوَاحِدَ ۞ وَأَبُو خَالِدٍ اسْمُهُ سَعْدٌ ۞

This Jabir here is Jabir ibn Tariq. He is also called Ibn Abi Tariq. He was a man from the Companions of the Messenger of Allah ﷺ, and we do not know of any other narrations from him besides this. [The sub-narrator] Abu Khalid is named Sa'd.

❦

١٦٢ - حَدَّثَنَا قُتَيْبَةُ بْنُ سَعِيدٍ ۞ عَنْ مَالِكِ بْنِ أَنَسٍ ۞ عَنْ إِسْحَاقَ بْنِ عَبْدِ اللهِ بْنِ أَبِي طَلْحَةَ ۞ أَنَّهُ سَمِعَ أَنَسَ بْنَ مَالِكٍ ۞ يَقُولُ إِنَّ خَيَّاطًا دَعَا رَسُولَ اللهِ ﷺ لِطَعَامٍ صَنَعَهُ ۞ قَالَ أَنَسٌ فَذَهَبْتُ مَعَ رَسُولِ اللهِ ﷺ إِلَى ذٰلِكَ الطَّعَامِ ۞ فَقَرَّبَ إِلَى رَسُولِ اللهِ ﷺ خُبْزًا مِنْ شَعِيرٍ وَمَرَقًا فِيهِ دُبَّاءٌ وَقَدِيدٌ ۞

[359] Scholars have said that an individual is allowed to reach for food that is not in front of him if it consists of different types of food, yet the general rule of etiquette is to eat from what is in front of him. (MA)

[360] In other words, 'What is the reason for slicing the gourds?' (AA)

[361] This hadith shows the importance of cooking and improving or enhancing dishes. It does not contradict the virtues of trust in Allah and non-attachment to the world; rather, it teaches the virtue of being economical and moderate in life, which leads to contentment. (MA)

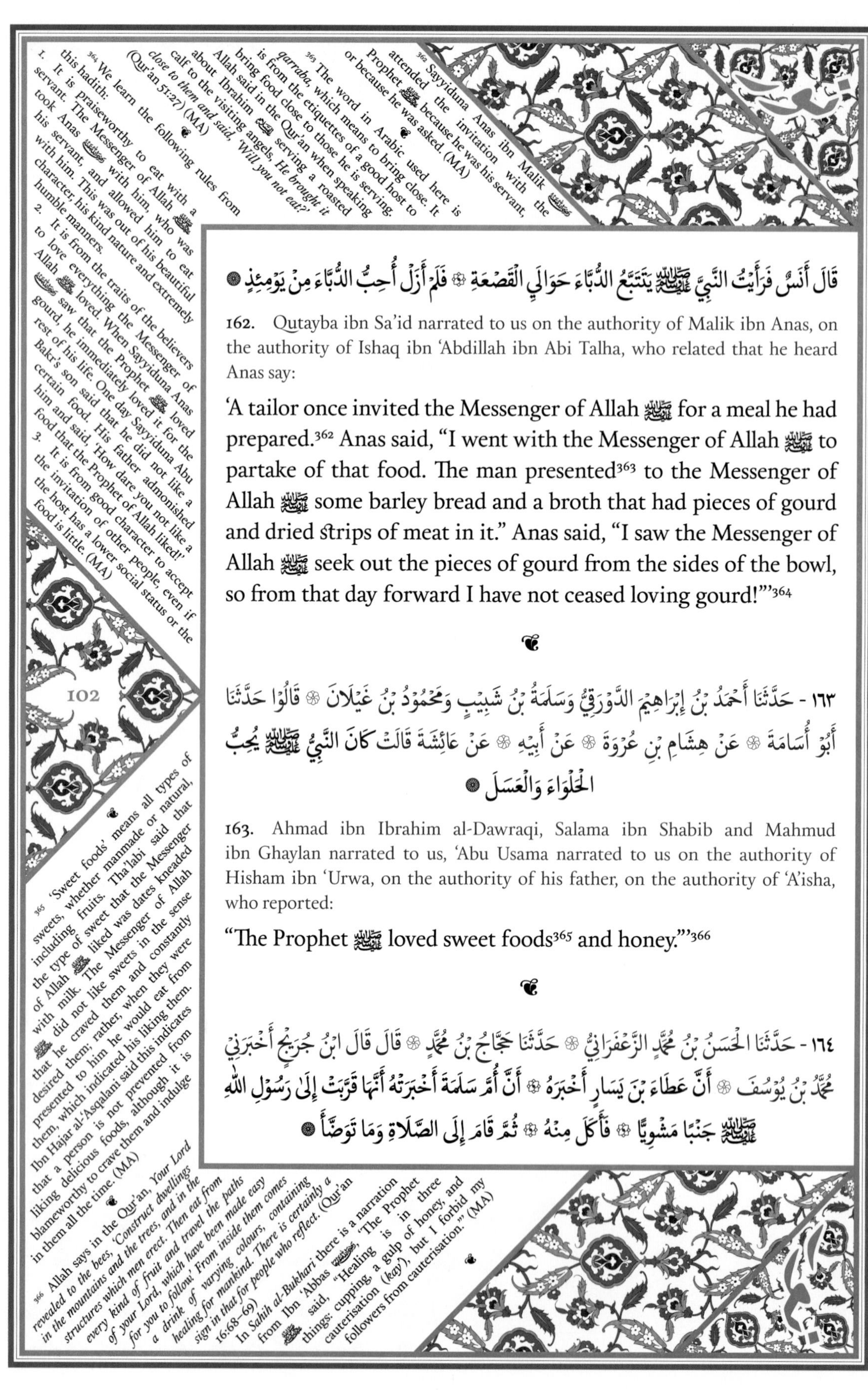

قَالَ أَنَسٌ فَرَأَيْتُ النَّبِيَّ ﷺ يَتَتَبَّعُ الدُّبَّاءَ حَوَالَيِ الْقَصْعَةِ ۞ فَلَمْ أَزَلْ أُحِبُّ الدُّبَّاءَ مِنْ يَوْمِئِذٍ ۞

162. Qutayba ibn Sa'id narrated to us on the authority of Malik ibn Anas, on the authority of Ishaq ibn 'Abdillah ibn Abi Talha, who related that he heard Anas say:

'A tailor once invited the Messenger of Allah ﷺ for a meal he had prepared.[362] Anas said, "I went with the Messenger of Allah ﷺ to partake of that food. The man presented[363] to the Messenger of Allah ﷺ some barley bread and a broth that had pieces of gourd and dried strips of meat in it." Anas said, "I saw the Messenger of Allah ﷺ seek out the pieces of gourd from the sides of the bowl, so from that day forward I have not ceased loving gourd!"'[364]

١٦٣ - حَدَّثَنَا أَحْمَدُ بْنُ إِبْرَاهِيمَ الدَّوْرَقِيُّ وَسَلَمَةُ بْنُ شَبِيبٍ وَمَحْمُودُ بْنُ غَيْلَانَ ۞ قَالُوا حَدَّثَنَا أَبُو أُسَامَةَ ۞ عَنْ هِشَامِ بْنِ عُرْوَةَ ۞ عَنْ أَبِيهِ ۞ عَنْ عَائِشَةَ قَالَتْ كَانَ النَّبِيُّ ﷺ يُحِبُّ الْحَلْوَاءَ وَالْعَسَلَ ۞

163. Ahmad ibn Ibrahim al-Dawraqi, Salama ibn Shabib and Mahmud ibn Ghaylan narrated to us, 'Abu Usama narrated to us on the authority of Hisham ibn 'Urwa, on the authority of his father, on the authority of 'A'isha, who reported:

"The Prophet ﷺ loved sweet foods[365] and honey."'[366]

١٦٤ - حَدَّثَنَا الْحَسَنُ بْنُ مُحَمَّدٍ الزَّعْفَرَانِيُّ ۞ حَدَّثَنَا حَجَّاجُ بْنُ مُحَمَّدٍ ۞ قَالَ قَالَ ابْنُ جُرَيْجٍ أَخْبَرَنِي مُحَمَّدُ بْنُ يُوسُفَ ۞ أَنَّ عَطَاءَ بْنَ يَسَارٍ أَخْبَرَهُ ۞ أَنَّ أُمَّ سَلَمَةَ أَخْبَرَتْهُ أَنَّهَا قَرَّبَتْ إِلَى رَسُولِ اللَّهِ ﷺ جَنْبًا مَشْوِيًّا ۞ فَأَكَلَ مِنْهُ ۞ ثُمَّ قَامَ إِلَى الصَّلَاةِ وَمَا تَوَضَّأَ ۞

[362] Sayyiduna Anas ibn Malik رضي الله عنه attended the invitation with the Prophet ﷺ because he was his servant, or because he was asked. (MA)

[363] The word in Arabic used here is *qarraba*, which means to bring close. It is from the etiquettes of a good host to bring food close to those he is serving. Allah said in the Qur'an when speaking about Ibrahim عليه السلام serving a roasted calf to the visiting angels, *He brought it close to them and said, 'Will you not eat?'* (Qur'an 51:27) (MA)

[364] We learn the following rules from this hadith:
1. It is praiseworthy to eat with a servant. The Messenger of Allah ﷺ took Anas رضي الله عنه with him, who was his servant, and allowed him to eat with him. This was out of his beautiful character, his kind nature and extremely humble manners.
2. It is from the traits of the believers to love everything the Messenger of Allah ﷺ loved. When Sayyiduna Anas رضي الله عنه saw that the Prophet ﷺ loved gourd, he immediately loved it for the rest of his life. One day Sayyiduna Abu Bakr's son said that he did not like a certain food. His father admonished him and said, 'How dare you not like a food that the Prophet of Allah liked!'
3. It is from good character to accept the invitation of other people, even if the host has a lower social status or the food is little. (MA)

[365] 'Sweet foods' means all types of sweets, whether manmade or natural, including fruits. Tha'labi said that the type of sweet that the Messenger of Allah ﷺ liked was dates kneaded with milk. The Messenger of Allah ﷺ did not like sweets in the sense that he craved them and constantly desired them; rather, when they were presented to him he would eat from them, which indicated his liking them. Ibn Hajar al-'Asqalani said this indicates that a person is not prevented from liking delicious foods, although it is blameworthy to crave them and indulge in them all the time. (MA)

[366] Allah says in the Qur'an, *Your Lord revealed to the bees, 'Construct dwellings in the mountains and the trees, and in the structures which men erect. Then eat from every kind of fruit and travel the paths of your Lord, which have been made easy for you to follow.' From inside them comes a drink of varying colours, containing healing for mankind. There is certainly a sign in that for people who reflect.* (Qur'an 16:68–69) In Sahih al-Bukhari there is a narration from Ibn 'Abbas رضي الله عنه, 'The Prophet ﷺ said, "Healing is in three things: cupping, a gulp of honey, and cauterisation (*kay*), but I forbid my followers from cauterisation."' (MA)

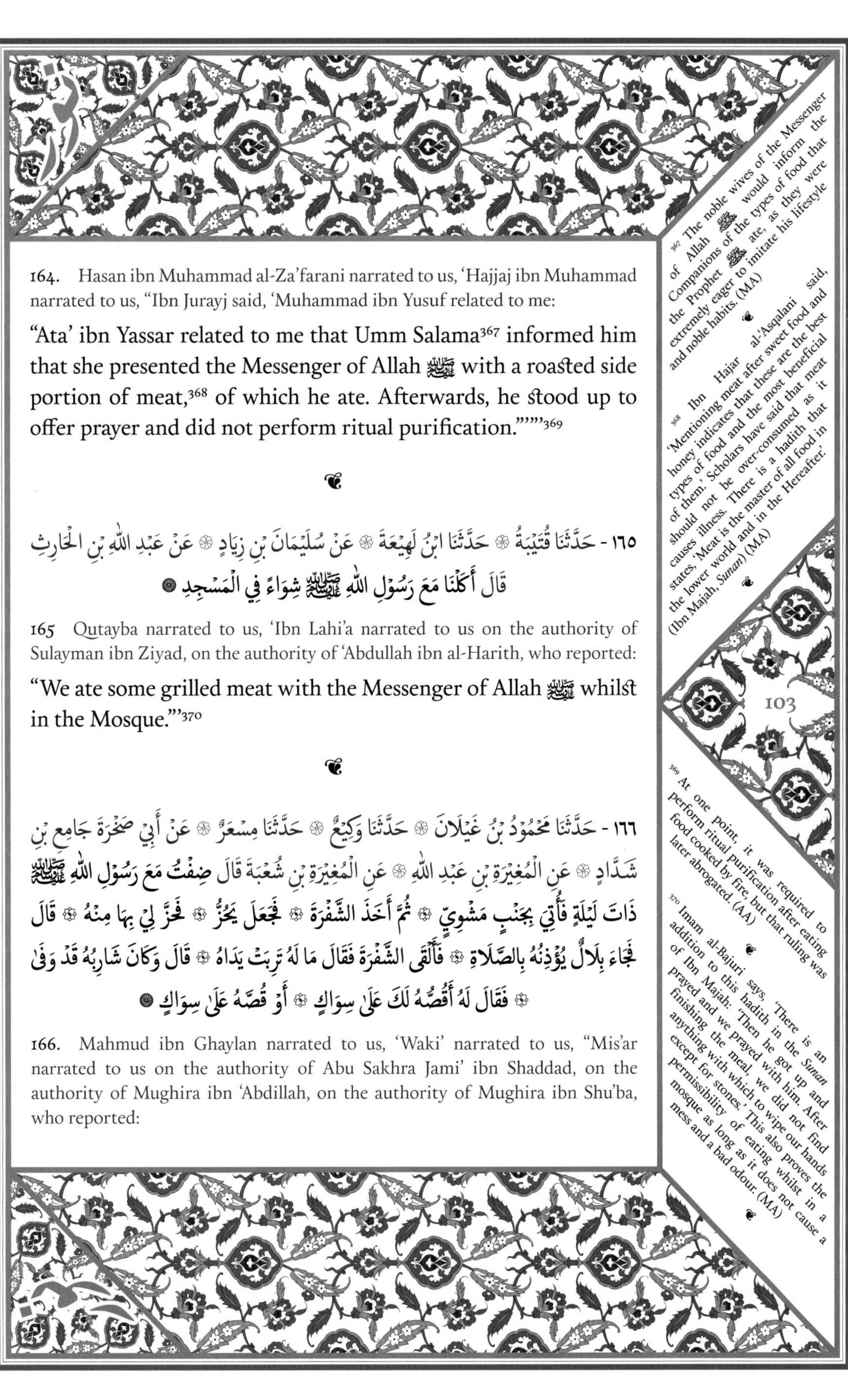

164. Hasan ibn Muhammad al-Za'farani narrated to us, 'Hajjaj ibn Muhammad narrated to us, "Ibn Jurayj said, 'Muhammad ibn Yusuf related to me:

"Ata' ibn Yassar related to me that Umm Salama[367] informed him that she presented the Messenger of Allah ﷺ with a roasted side portion of meat,[368] of which he ate. Afterwards, he stood up to offer prayer and did not perform ritual purification.""'"[369]

❦

١٦٥ - حَدَّثَنَا قُتَيْبَةُ ۞ حَدَّثَنَا ابْنُ لَهِيعَةَ ۞ عَنْ سُلَيْمَانَ بْنِ زِيَادٍ ۞ عَنْ عَبْدِ اللهِ بْنِ الْحَارِثِ قَالَ أَكَلْنَا مَعَ رَسُولِ اللهِ ﷺ شِوَاءً فِي الْمَسْجِدِ ۞

165 Qutayba narrated to us, 'Ibn Lahi'a narrated to us on the authority of Sulayman ibn Ziyad, on the authority of 'Abdullah ibn al-Harith, who reported:

"We ate some grilled meat with the Messenger of Allah ﷺ whilst in the Mosque."'[370]

❦

١٦٦ - حَدَّثَنَا مَحْمُودُ بْنُ غَيْلَانَ ۞ حَدَّثَنَا وَكِيعٌ ۞ حَدَّثَنَا مِسْعَرٌ ۞ عَنْ أَبِي صَخْرَةَ جَامِعِ بْنِ شَدَّادٍ ۞ عَنِ الْمُغِيرَةِ بْنِ عَبْدِ اللهِ ۞ عَنِ الْمُغِيرَةِ بْنِ شُعْبَةَ قَالَ ضِفْتُ مَعَ رَسُولِ اللهِ ﷺ ذَاتَ لَيْلَةٍ فَأُتِيَ بِجَنْبٍ مَشْوِيٍّ ۞ ثُمَّ أَخَذَ الشَّفْرَةَ ۞ فَجَعَلَ يَحُزُّ ۞ فَحَزَّ لِي بِهَا مِنْهُ ۞ قَالَ فَجَاءَ بِلَالٌ يُؤْذِنُهُ بِالصَّلَاةِ ۞ فَأَلْقَى الشَّفْرَةَ فَقَالَ مَا لَهُ تَرِبَتْ يَدَاهُ ۞ قَالَ وَكَانَ شَارِبُهُ قَدْ وَفَى ۞ فَقَالَ لَهُ أَقُصُّهُ لَكَ عَلَى سِوَاكٍ ۞ أَوْ قُصَّهُ عَلَى سِوَاكٍ ۞

166. Mahmud ibn Ghaylan narrated to us, 'Waki' narrated to us, "Mis'ar narrated to us on the authority of Abu Sakhra Jami' ibn Shaddad, on the authority of Mughira ibn 'Abdillah, on the authority of Mughira ibn Shu'ba, who reported:

[367] The noble wives of the Messenger of Allah ﷺ would inform the Companions of the types of food that the Prophet ﷺ ate, as they were extremely eager to imitate his lifestyle and noble habits. (MA)

❦

[368] Ibn Hajar al-'Asqalani said, 'Mentioning meat after sweet food and honey indicates that these are the best types of food and the most beneficial of them. Scholars have said that meat should not be over-consumed as it causes illness. There is a hadith that states, 'Meat is the master of all food in the lower world and in the Hereafter.' (Ibn Majah, *Sunan*) (MA)

❦

[369] At one point, it was required to perform ritual purification after eating food cooked by fire, but that ruling was later abrogated. (AA)

❦

[370] Imam al-Bajuri says, 'There is an addition to this hadith in the *Sunan* of Ibn Majah: 'Then he got up and prayed and we prayed with him. After finishing the meal, we did not find anything with which to wipe our hands except for stones.' This also proves the permissibility of eating whilst in a mosque as long as it does not cause a mess and a bad odour. (MA)

❦

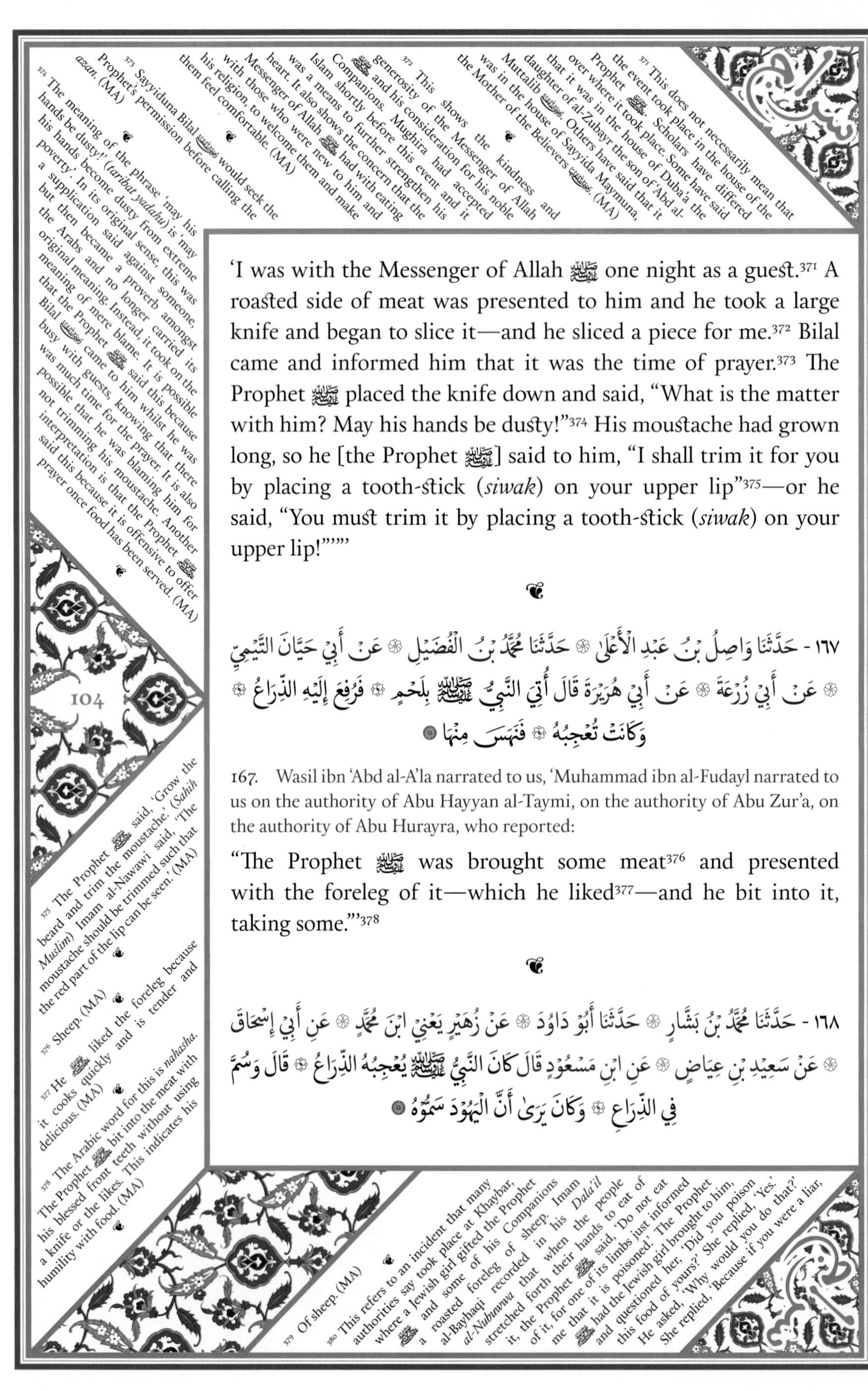

'I was with the Messenger of Allah ﷺ one night as a guest.[371] A roasted side of meat was presented to him and he took a large knife and began to slice it—and he sliced a piece for me.[372] Bilal came and informed him that it was the time of prayer.[373] The Prophet ﷺ placed the knife down and said, "What is the matter with him? May his hands be dusty!"[374] His moustache had grown long, so he [the Prophet ﷺ] said to him, "I shall trim it for you by placing a tooth-stick (*siwak*) on your upper lip"[375]—or he said, "You must trim it by placing a tooth-stick (*siwak*) on your upper lip!""'

١٦٧ - حَدَّثَنَا وَاصِلُ بْنُ عَبْدِ الْأَعْلَى ۞ حَدَّثَنَا مُحَمَّدُ بْنُ الْفُضَيْلِ ۞ عَنْ أَبِي حَيَّانَ التَّيْمِيِّ ۞ عَنْ أَبِي زُرْعَةَ ۞ عَنْ أَبِي هُرَيْرَةَ قَالَ أُتِيَ النَّبِيُّ ﷺ بِلَحْمٍ ۞ فَرُفِعَ إِلَيْهِ الذِّرَاعُ ۞ وَكَانَتْ تُعْجِبُهُ ۞ فَنَهَسَ مِنْهَا ۞

167. Wasil ibn 'Abd al-A'la narrated to us, 'Muhammad ibn al-Fudayl narrated to us on the authority of Abu Hayyan al-Taymi, on the authority of Abu Zur'a, on the authority of Abu Hurayra, who reported:

"The Prophet ﷺ was brought some meat[376] and presented with the foreleg of it—which he liked[377]—and he bit into it, taking some."'[378]

١٦٨ - حَدَّثَنَا مُحَمَّدُ بْنُ بَشَّارٍ ۞ حَدَّثَنَا أَبُو دَاوُدَ ۞ عَنْ زُهَيْرٍ يَعْنِي ابْنَ مُحَمَّدٍ ۞ عَنْ أَبِي إِسْحَاقَ ۞ عَنْ سَعِيدِ بْنِ عِيَاضٍ ۞ عَنِ ابْنِ مَسْعُودٍ قَالَ كَانَ النَّبِيُّ ﷺ يُعْجِبُهُ الذِّرَاعُ ۞ قَالَ وَسُمَّ فِي الذِّرَاعِ ۞ وَكَانَ يَرَى أَنَّ الْيَهُودَ سَمُّوهُ ۞

[371] This does not necessarily mean that the event took place in the house of the Prophet ﷺ. Scholars have differed over where it took place. Some have said that it was in the house of Duba'a the daughter of al-Zubayr the son of 'Abd al-Muttalib ﷺ. Others have said that it was in the house of Sayyida Maymuna, the Mother of the Believers ﷺ. (MA)

[372] This shows the kindness and generosity of the Messenger of Allah ﷺ and his consideration for his noble Companions. Mughira had accepted Islam shortly before this event and it was a means to further strengthen his heart. It also shows the concern that the Messenger of Allah ﷺ had with eating with those who were new to him and his religion, to welcome them and make them feel comfortable. (MA)

[373] Sayyiduna Bilal ﷺ would seek the Prophet's permission before calling the *azan*. (MA)

[374] The meaning of the phrase 'may his hands be dusty!' (*taribat yadahu*) is 'may his hands become dusty from extreme poverty'. In its original sense, this was a supplication said against someone, but then became a proverb amongst the Arabs and no longer carried its original meaning. Instead, it took on the meaning of mere blame. It is possible that the Prophet ﷺ said this because Bilal ﷺ came to him whilst he was busy with guests, knowing that there was much time for the prayer. It is also possible that he was blaming him for not trimming his moustache. Another interpretation is that the Prophet ﷺ said this because it is offensive to offer prayer once food has been served. (MA)

[375] The Prophet ﷺ said, 'Grow the beard and trim the moustache.' (*Sahih Muslim*) Imam al-Nawawi said, 'The moustache should be trimmed such that the red part of the lip can be seen.' (MA)

[376] Sheep. (MA)

[377] He ﷺ liked the foreleg because it cooks quickly and is tender and delicious. (MA)

[378] The Arabic word for this is *nahasha*. The Prophet ﷺ bit into the meat with his blessed front teeth without using a knife or the likes. This indicates his humility with food. (MA)

[379] Of sheep. (MA)

[380] This refers to an incident that many authorities say took place at Khaybar, where a Jewish girl gifted the Prophet ﷺ and some of his Companions a roasted foreleg of sheep. Imam al-Bayhaqi recorded in his *Dala'il al-Nubuwwa* that when the people stretched forth their hands to eat of it, the Prophet ﷺ said, 'Do not eat of it, for one of its limbs just informed me that it is poisoned.' The Prophet ﷺ had the Jewish girl brought to him, and questioned her, 'Did you poison this food of yours?' She replied, 'Yes.' He asked, 'Why would you do that?' She replied, 'Because if you were a liar,

I wanted to rid the people of you, and if you were truthful, I knew that Allah would disclose it to you.' After that, the Prophet ﷺ said to his Companions, 'Eat in the name of Allah.' They began to eat of it and no harm came to any of them.

Other narrations indicate that the Prophet ﷺ put a morsel of the poisoned lamb in his blessed mouth, whereupon the cooked lamb spoke to him and informed him that it was poisoned. In *Sahih al-Bukhari* there is a narration from Sayyida 'A'isha ﷺ who reported, 'The Prophet ﷺ would say during his final illness from which he would pass away, "O 'A'isha, I still feel the pain of the food I ate at Khaybar, and I feel as if my aorta is being cut from that poison."' Imam al-Zurqani mentioned in his commentary on *al-Mawahib al-Laduniyya* that 'Abdullah ibn Mas'ud ﷺ felt that the Prophet ﷺ was taken as a martyr as a result of the poison in the lamb, and that the delay in the poison's effect (which was three or four years) was a prophetic miracle. Allah and His Messenger know best. (AA, MA)

168. Muhammad ibn Bashhar narrated to us, 'Abu Dawud narrated to us on the authority of Zuhayr—meaning Ibn Muhammad—on the authority of Abu Ishaq, on the authority of Sa'd ibn 'Iyad, on the authority of Ibn Mas'ud, who reported:

"The Prophet ﷺ liked the foreleg.[379] He said (Ibn Mas'ud), "It was a foreleg that was poisoned, and it was suspected that the Jews had poisoned him."'[380]

١٦٩ - حَدَّثَنَا مُحَمَّدُ بْنُ بَشَّارٍ ۞ حَدَّثَنَا مُسْلِمُ بْنُ إِبْرَاهِيمَ ۞ عَنْ أَبَانَ بْنِ يَزِيدَ ۞ عَنْ قَتَادَةَ ۞ عَنْ شَهْرِ بْنِ حَوْشَبٍ ۞ عَنْ أَبِي عُبَيْدٍ قَالَ طَبَخْتُ لِلنَّبِيِّ ﷺ قِدْرًا ۞ وَكَانَ يُعْجِبُهُ الذِّرَاعُ ۞ فَنَاوَلْتُهُ الذِّرَاعَ ۞ ثُمَّ قَالَ نَاوِلْنِي الذِّرَاعَ فَنَاوَلْتُهُ ۞ ثُمَّ قَالَ نَاوِلْنِي الذِّرَاعَ ۞ فَقُلْتُ يَا رَسُولَ اللهِ وَكَمْ لِلشَّاةِ مِنْ ذِرَاعٍ ۞ فَقَالَ وَالَّذِي نَفْسِي بِيَدِهِ لَوْ سَكَتَّ لَنَاوَلْتَنِي الذِّرَاعَ مَا دَعَوْتُ ۞

169. Muhammad ibn Bashhar narrated to us, 'Muslim ibn Ibrahim narrated to us on the authority of Aban ibn Yazid, on the authority of Qatada, on the authority of Shahr ibn Hawshab, on the authority of Abu 'Ubayda,[381] who reported:

"I cooked a pot of food[382] for the Prophet ﷺ. He liked the foreleg, so I gave him a foreleg from it. Then he said, 'Pass me another foreleg', so I passed it to him. Then he said, 'Pass me another foreleg.' I asked him, 'O Messenger of Allah! How many forelegs does a sheep have?'[383] He replied, 'By Him in Whose Hand is my soul,[384] if only you had been silent, you would have given me as many forelegs as I asked for!'"'[385]

381 Some commentators note that his name was Abu 'Ubayd, one of the servants of the Messenger of Allah ﷺ. His agnomen (*kunya*) was his name. (MA)

382 With sheep. (AA)

383 His question was not out of doubt or denial, but rather out of amazement and surprise. The Companions would not doubt the Prophet ﷺ, and were aware that he knew beyond what they did. The Prophet ﷺ replied without mentioning the number of forelegs a sheep possesses, but with additional wise advice. (MA)

384 The Prophet ﷺ would use this expression when he wanted to emphasise an important matter, so its usage here indicates something greater than the number of forelegs that the sheep had. It was to alert this *Umma* to the great gifts that Allah had blessed him with, of miracles and blessings. (MA)

385 Imam al-Zurqani stated in *Sharh al-Mawahib al-Laduniyya*, commenting on another narration in which the same thing occurred with another Companion (Abu Rafi' ﷺ): The meaning of the Prophet's words ﷺ 'if only you had been silent, you would have passed me foreleg after foreleg,' is that Allah would have created foreleg after foreleg as a miracle for him ﷺ if he [Abu Rafi'] had remained silent. However, his [Abu Rafi's] human instinct for haste made him say, 'But a sheep only has two forelegs,' and so the divine succour was cut off. Such bestowal could only come from the succour of the Magnanimous (*al-Karim*), Exalted is He, as an honour to the Finest of His Creation ﷺ. Had he [Abu Rafi'] only responded with proper manners and remained silently alert to this wonder, it would have been an expression of gratitude from him sufficient to merit the blessing of this divine succour being channelled through his own hands. However, since he responded with dubiety, the blessing went back whence it came, since it did not find a suitable place to manifest. It is not fitting that one should witness such a tremendous miracle—the witnessing of which is a type of honour conferred upon the one who sees it—unless his submission is perfect and there remains not within him even the slightest trace of personal motive or independent will. (AA)

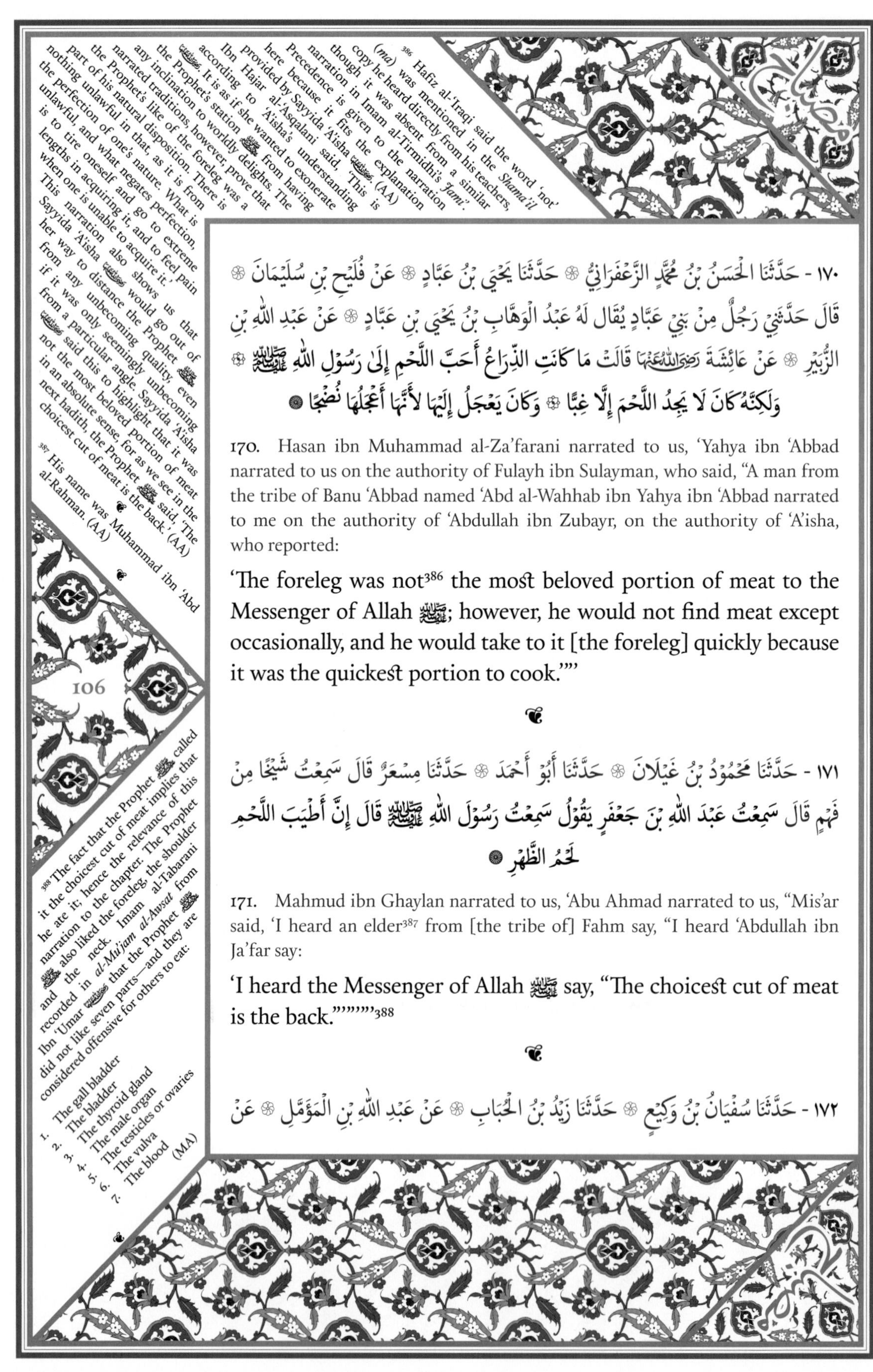

١٧٠ - حَدَّثَنَا الْحَسَنُ بْنُ مُحَمَّدٍ الزَّعْفَرَانِيُّ ۞ حَدَّثَنَا يَحْيَى بْنُ عَبَّادٍ ۞ عَنْ فُلَيْحِ بْنِ سُلَيْمَانَ ۞ قَالَ حَدَّثَنِي رَجُلٌ مِنْ بَنِي عَبَّادٍ يُقَالُ لَهُ عَبْدُ الْوَهَّابِ بْنُ يَحْيَى بْنِ عَبَّادٍ ۞ عَنْ عَبْدِ اللهِ بْنِ الزُّبَيْرِ ۞ عَنْ عَائِشَةَ رَضِيَ اللهُ عَنْهَا قَالَتْ مَا كَانَتِ الذِّرَاعُ أَحَبَّ اللَّحْمِ إِلَى رَسُولِ اللهِ ﷺ ۞ وَلَكِنَّهُ كَانَ لَا يَجِدُ اللَّحْمَ إِلَّا غِبًّا ۞ وَكَانَ يَعْجَلُ إِلَيْهَا لِأَنَّهَا أَعْجَلُهَا نُضْجًا ۞

170. Hasan ibn Muhammad al-Za'farani narrated to us, 'Yahya ibn 'Abbad narrated to us on the authority of Fulayh ibn Sulayman, who said, "A man from the tribe of Banu 'Abbad named 'Abd al-Wahhab ibn Yahya ibn 'Abbad narrated to me on the authority of 'Abdullah ibn Zubayr, on the authority of 'A'isha, who reported:

'The foreleg was not[386] the most beloved portion of meat to the Messenger of Allah ﷺ; however, he would not find meat except occasionally, and he would take to it [the foreleg] quickly because it was the quickest portion to cook.'"'

❦

١٧١ - حَدَّثَنَا مَحْمُودُ بْنُ غَيْلَانَ ۞ حَدَّثَنَا أَبُو أَحْمَدَ ۞ حَدَّثَنَا مِسْعَرٌ قَالَ سَمِعْتُ شَيْخًا مِنْ فَهْمٍ قَالَ سَمِعْتُ عَبْدَ اللهِ بْنَ جَعْفَرٍ يَقُولُ سَمِعْتُ رَسُولَ اللهِ ﷺ قَالَ إِنَّ أَطْيَبَ اللَّحْمِ لَحْمُ الظَّهْرِ ۞

171. Mahmud ibn Ghaylan narrated to us, 'Abu Ahmad narrated to us, "Mis'ar said, 'I heard an elder[387] from [the tribe of] Fahm say, "I heard 'Abdullah ibn Ja'far say:

'I heard the Messenger of Allah ﷺ say, "The choicest cut of meat is the back."'"'"'[388]

❦

١٧٢ - حَدَّثَنَا سُفْيَانُ بْنُ وَكِيعٍ ۞ حَدَّثَنَا زَيْدُ بْنُ الْحُبَابِ ۞ عَنْ عَبْدِ اللهِ بْنِ الْمُؤَمَّلِ ۞ عَنْ

[386] Hafiz al-'Iraqi said the word 'not' (*ma*) was mentioned in the *Shama'il* copy he heard directly from his teachers, though it was absent from a similar narration in Imam al-Tirmidhi's *Jami'*. Precedence is given to the narration here because it fits the explanation provided by Sayyida 'A'isha. (AA) Ibn Hajar al-'Asqalani said, 'This is according to 'A'isha's understanding. It is as if she wanted to exonerate the Prophet's ﷺ station from having any inclination to worldly delights. The narrated traditions, however, prove that the Prophet's like of the foreleg was a part of his natural disposition. There is nothing unlawful in that, as it is from the perfection of one's nature. What is unlawful, and what negates perfection, is to tire oneself and go to extreme lengths in acquiring it, and to feel pain when one is unable to acquire it.' This narration also shows us that Sayyida 'A'isha would go out of her way to distance the Prophet ﷺ from any unbecoming quality, even if it was only seemingly unbecoming from a particular angle. Sayyida 'A'isha said this to highlight that it was not the most beloved portion of meat in an absolute sense, for as we see in the next hadith, the Prophet ﷺ said, 'The choicest cut of meat is the back.' (AA)

❦

[387] His name was Muhammad ibn 'Abd al-Rahman. (AA)

❦

[388] The fact that the Prophet ﷺ called it the choicest cut of meat implies that he ate it; hence the relevance of this narration to the chapter. The Prophet ﷺ also liked the foreleg, the shoulder and the neck. Imam al-Tabarani recorded in *al-Mu'jam al-Awsat* from Ibn 'Umar that the Prophet ﷺ did not like seven parts—and they are considered offensive for others to eat:

1. The gall bladder
2. The bladder
3. The thyroid gland
4. The male organ
5. The testicles or ovaries
6. The vulva
7. The blood

(MA)

❦

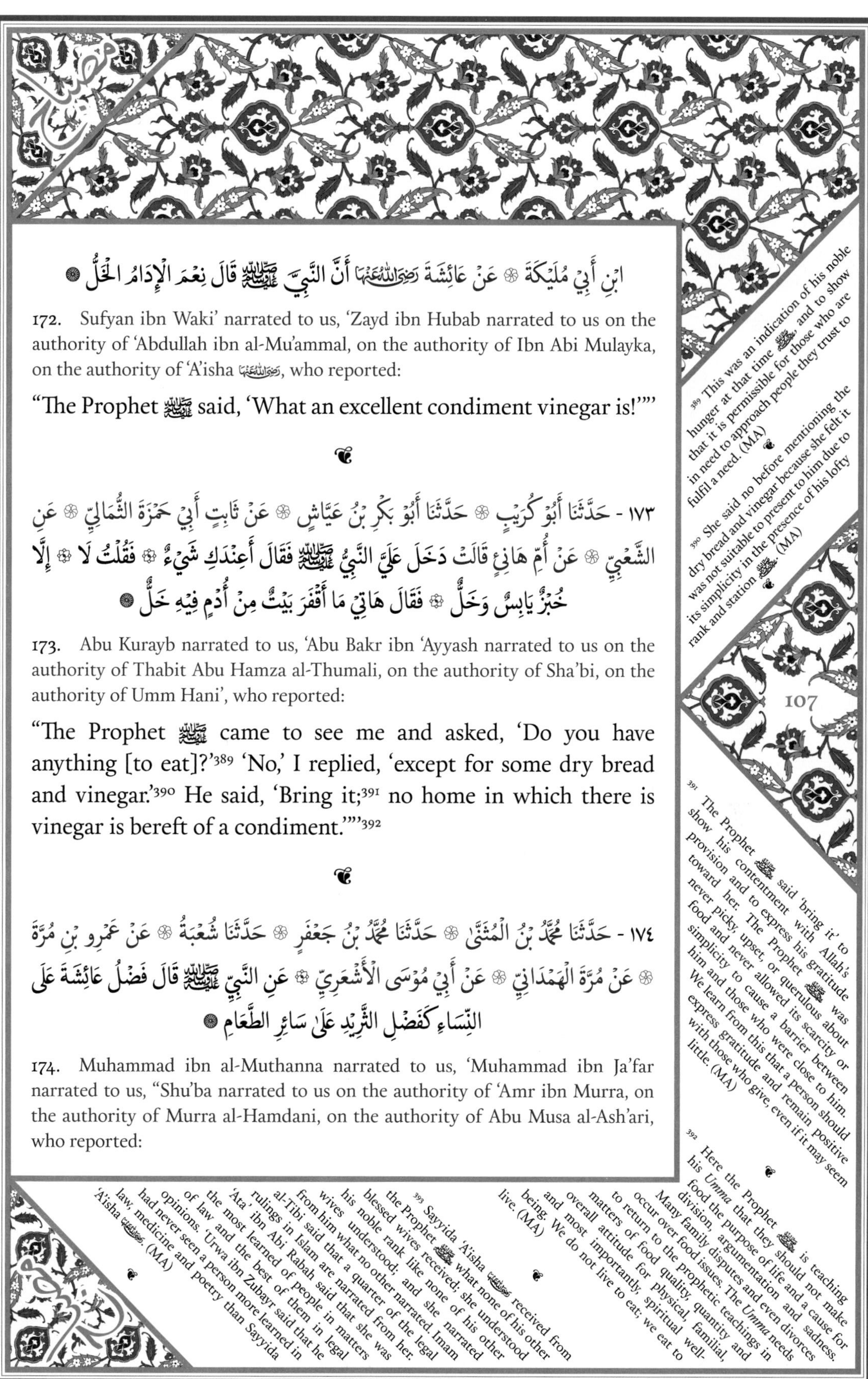

ابنِ أَبِي مُلَيْكَةَ ۞ عَنْ عَائِشَةَ رَضِيَ اللهُ عَنْهَا أَنَّ النَّبِيَّ ﷺ قَالَ نِعْمَ الْإِدَامُ الْخَلُّ ۞

172. Sufyan ibn Waki' narrated to us, 'Zayd ibn Hubab narrated to us on the authority of 'Abdullah ibn al-Mu'ammal, on the authority of Ibn Abi Mulayka, on the authority of 'A'isha رضي الله عنها, who reported:

"The Prophet ﷺ said, 'What an excellent condiment vinegar is!'"'

❦

١٧٣ - حَدَّثَنَا أَبُو كُرَيْبٍ ۞ حَدَّثَنَا أَبُو بَكْرِ بْنُ عَيَّاشٍ ۞ عَنْ ثَابِتٍ أَبِي حَمْزَةَ الثُّمَالِيِّ ۞ عَنِ الشَّعْبِيِّ ۞ عَنْ أُمِّ هَانِئٍ قَالَتْ دَخَلَ عَلَيَّ النَّبِيُّ ﷺ فَقَالَ أَعِنْدَكِ شَيْءٌ ۞ فَقُلْتُ لَا ۞ إِلَّا خُبْزٌ يَابِسٌ وَخَلٌّ ۞ فَقَالَ هَاتِي مَا أَقْفَرَ بَيْتٌ مِنْ أُدْمٍ فِيهِ خَلٌّ ۞

173. Abu Kurayb narrated to us, 'Abu Bakr ibn 'Ayyash narrated to us on the authority of Thabit Abu Hamza al-Thumali, on the authority of Sha'bi, on the authority of Umm Hani', who reported:

"The Prophet ﷺ came to see me and asked, 'Do you have anything [to eat]?'[389] 'No,' I replied, 'except for some dry bread and vinegar.'[390] He said, 'Bring it;[391] no home in which there is vinegar is bereft of a condiment.'"'[392]

❦

١٧٤ - حَدَّثَنَا مُحَمَّدُ بْنُ الْمُثَنَّى ۞ حَدَّثَنَا مُحَمَّدُ بْنُ جَعْفَرٍ ۞ حَدَّثَنَا شُعْبَةُ ۞ عَنْ عَمْرِو بْنِ مُرَّةَ ۞ عَنْ مُرَّةَ الْهَمْدَانِيِّ ۞ عَنْ أَبِي مُوسَى الْأَشْعَرِيِّ ۞ عَنِ النَّبِيِّ ﷺ قَالَ فَضْلُ عَائِشَةَ عَلَى النِّسَاءِ كَفَضْلِ الثَّرِيدِ عَلَى سَائِرِ الطَّعَامِ ۞

174. Muhammad ibn al-Muthanna narrated to us, 'Muhammad ibn Ja'far narrated to us, "Shu'ba narrated to us on the authority of 'Amr ibn Murra, on the authority of Murra al-Hamdani, on the authority of Abu Musa al-Ash'ari, who reported:

[389] This was an indication of his noble hunger at that time ﷺ, and to show that it is permissible for those who are in need to approach people they trust to fulfil a need. (MA)

[390] She said no before mentioning the dry bread and vinegar because she felt it was not suitable to present to him due to its simplicity in the presence of his lofty rank and station ﷺ. (MA)

[391] The Prophet ﷺ said 'bring it' to show his contentment with Allah's provision and to express his gratitude toward her. The Prophet ﷺ was never picky, upset, or querulous about food and never allowed its scarcity or simplicity to cause a barrier between him and those who were close to him. We learn from this that a person should express gratitude and remain positive with those who give, even if it may seem little. (MA)

[392] Here the Prophet ﷺ is teaching his *Umma* that they should not make food the purpose of life and a cause for division, argumentation and sadness. Many family disputes and even divorces occur over food issues. The *Umma* needs to return to the prophetic teachings in matters of food quality, quantity and overall attitude for physical, familial, and most importantly, spiritual well-being. We do not live to eat; we eat to live. (MA)

[393] Sayyida 'A'isha رضي الله عنها received from the Prophet ﷺ what none of his other blessed wives received; she understood his noble rank like none of his other wives understood; and she narrated from him what no other narrated. Imam al-Tibi said that a quarter of the legal rulings in Islam are narrated from her. 'Ata' ibn Abi Rabah said that she was the most learned of people in matters of law and the best of them in legal opinions. Urwa ibn Zubayr said that he had never seen a person more learned in law, medicine and poetry than Sayyida 'A'isha رضي الله عنها. (MA)

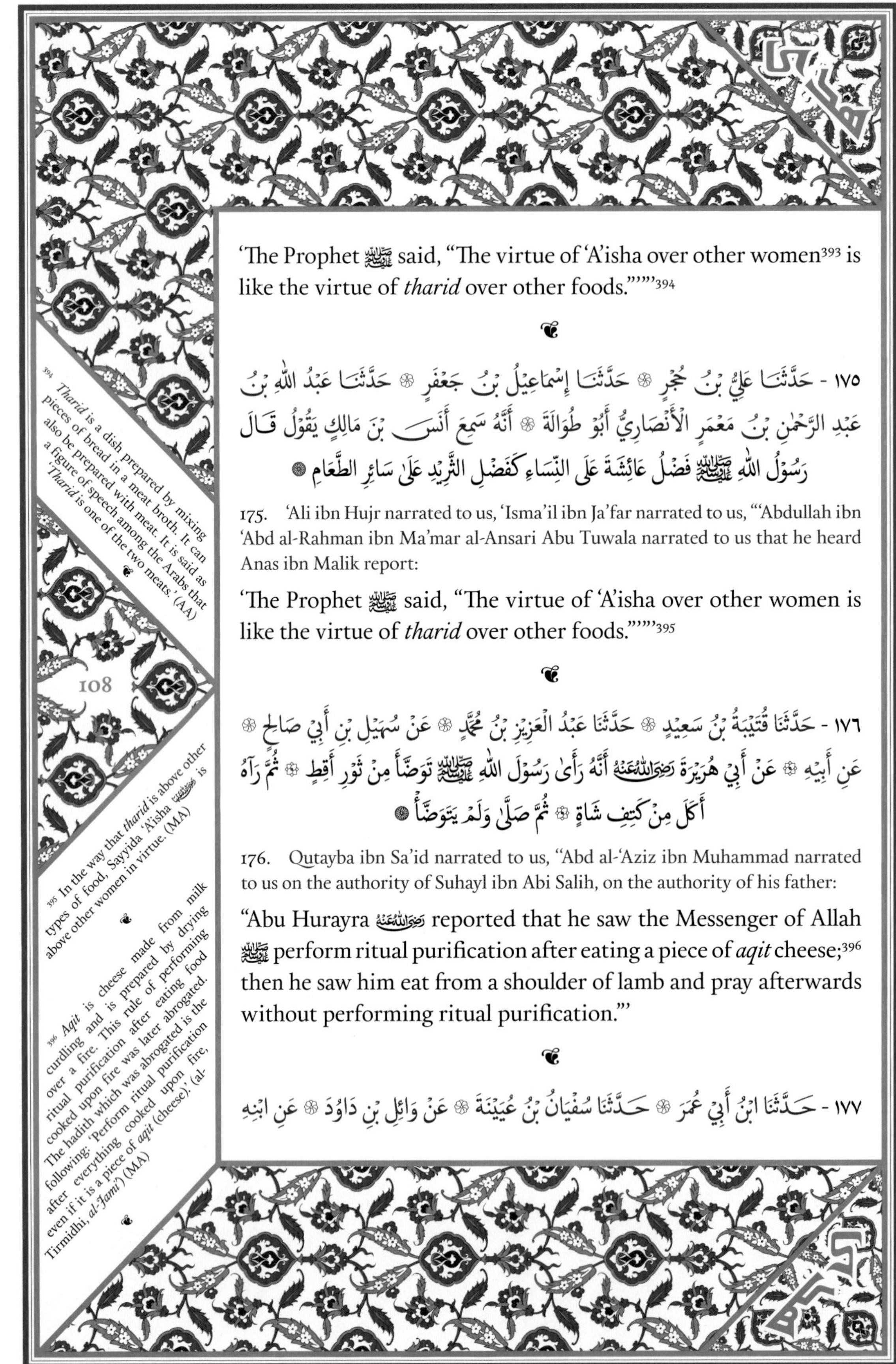

'The Prophet ﷺ said, "The virtue of 'A'isha over other women[393] is like the virtue of *tharid* over other foods."'''[394]

١٧٥ - حَدَّثَنَا عَلِيُّ بْنُ حُجْرٍ ۞ حَدَّثَنَا إِسْمَاعِيلُ بْنُ جَعْفَرٍ ۞ حَدَّثَنَا عَبْدُ اللهِ بْنُ عَبْدِ الرَّحْمٰنِ بْنُ مَعْمَرٍ الْأَنْصَارِيُّ أَبُو طُوَالَةَ ۞ أَنَّهُ سَمِعَ أَنَسَ بْنَ مَالِكٍ يَقُولُ قَالَ رَسُولُ اللهِ ﷺ فَضْلُ عَائِشَةَ عَلَى النِّسَاءِ كَفَضْلِ الثَّرِيدِ عَلَىٰ سَائِرِ الطَّعَامِ ۞

175. 'Ali ibn Hujr narrated to us, 'Isma'il ibn Ja'far narrated to us, "'Abdullah ibn 'Abd al-Rahman ibn Ma'mar al-Ansari Abu Tuwala narrated to us that he heard Anas ibn Malik report:

'The Prophet ﷺ said, "The virtue of 'A'isha over other women is like the virtue of *tharid* over other foods."'''[395]

١٧٦ - حَدَّثَنَا قُتَيْبَةُ بْنُ سَعِيدٍ ۞ حَدَّثَنَا عَبْدُ الْعَزِيزِ بْنُ مُحَمَّدٍ ۞ عَنْ سُهَيْلِ بْنِ أَبِي صَالِحٍ ۞ عَنْ أَبِيهِ ۞ عَنْ أَبِي هُرَيْرَةَ رَضِيَ اللهُ عَنْهُ أَنَّهُ رَأَىٰ رَسُولَ اللهِ ﷺ تَوَضَّأَ مِنْ ثَوْرِ أَقِطٍ ۞ ثُمَّ رَآهُ أَكَلَ مِنْ كَتِفِ شَاةٍ ۞ ثُمَّ صَلَّىٰ وَلَمْ يَتَوَضَّأْ ۞

176. Qutayba ibn Sa'id narrated to us, "Abd al-'Aziz ibn Muhammad narrated to us on the authority of Suhayl ibn Abi Salih, on the authority of his father:

"Abu Hurayra رضي الله عنه reported that he saw the Messenger of Allah ﷺ perform ritual purification after eating a piece of *aqit* cheese;[396] then he saw him eat from a shoulder of lamb and pray afterwards without performing ritual purification."'

١٧٧ - حَدَّثَنَا ابْنُ أَبِي عُمَرَ ۞ حَدَّثَنَا سُفْيَانُ بْنُ عُيَيْنَةَ ۞ عَنْ وَائِلِ بْنِ دَاوُدَ ۞ عَنِ ابْنِهِ

[394] *Tharid* is a dish prepared by mixing pieces of bread in a meat broth. It can also be prepared with meat. It is said as a figure of speech among the Arabs that '*Tharid* is one of the two meats.' (AA)

[395] In the way that *tharid* is above other types of food, Sayyida 'A'isha رضي الله عنها is above other women in virtue. (MA)

[396] *Aqit* is cheese made from milk curdling and is prepared by drying over a fire. This rule of performing ritual purification after eating food cooked upon fire was later abrogated. The hadith which was abrogated is the following: 'Perform ritual purification after everything cooked upon fire, even if it is a piece of *aqit* (cheese).' (al-Tirmidhi, *al-Jami'*) (MA)

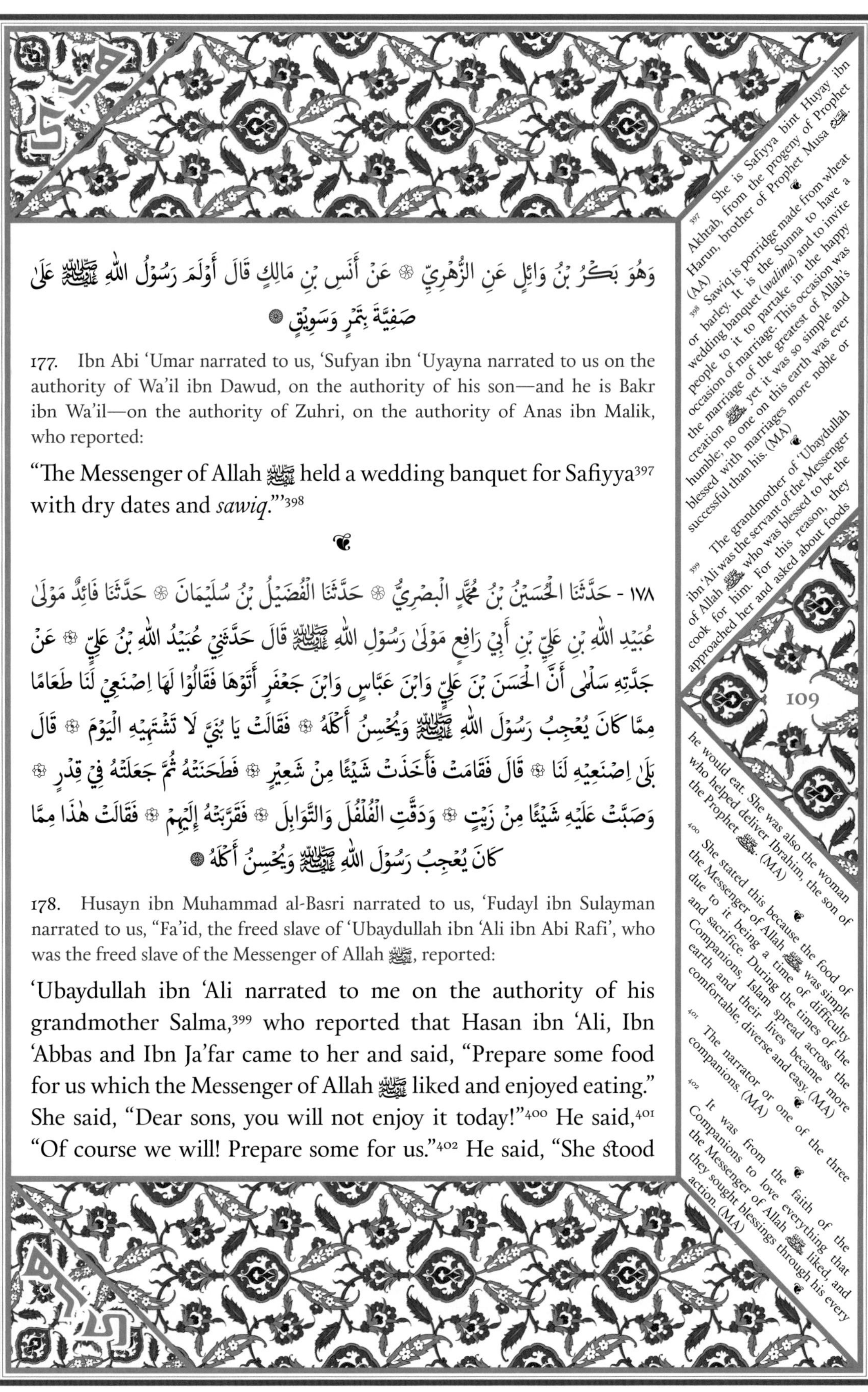

وَهُوَ بَكْرُ بْنُ وَائِلٍ عَنِ الزُّهْرِيِّ ۞ عَنْ أَنَسِ بْنِ مَالِكٍ قَالَ أَوْلَمَ رَسُولُ اللهِ ﷺ عَلَى صَفِيَّةَ بِتَمْرٍ وَسَوِيقٍ ۞

177. Ibn Abi 'Umar narrated to us, 'Sufyan ibn 'Uyayna narrated to us on the authority of Wa'il ibn Dawud, on the authority of his son—and he is Bakr ibn Wa'il—on the authority of Zuhri, on the authority of Anas ibn Malik, who reported:

"The Messenger of Allah ﷺ held a wedding banquet for Safiyya[397] with dry dates and *sawiq*."'[398]

١٧٨ - حَدَّثَنَا الْحُسَيْنُ بْنُ مُحَمَّدٍ الْبَصْرِيُّ ۞ حَدَّثَنَا الْفُضَيْلُ بْنُ سُلَيْمَانَ ۞ حَدَّثَنَا فَائِدٌ مَوْلَى عُبَيْدِ اللهِ بْنِ عَلِيِّ بْنِ أَبِي رَافِعٍ مَوْلَى رَسُولِ اللهِ ﷺ قَالَ حَدَّثَنِي عُبَيْدُ اللهِ بْنُ عَلِيٍّ ۞ عَنْ جَدَّتِهِ سَلْمَى أَنَّ الْحَسَنَ بْنَ عَلِيٍّ وَابْنَ عَبَّاسٍ وَابْنَ جَعْفَرٍ أَتَوْهَا فَقَالُوا لَهَا اِصْنَعِي لَنَا طَعَامًا مِمَّا كَانَ يُعْجِبُ رَسُولَ اللهِ ﷺ وَيُحْسِنُ أَكْلَهُ ۞ فَقَالَتْ يَا بُنَيَّ لَا تَشْتَهِيهِ الْيَوْمَ ۞ قَالَ بَلَى اِصْنَعِيهِ لَنَا ۞ قَالَ فَقَامَتْ فَأَخَذَتْ شَيْئًا مِنْ شَعِيرٍ ۞ فَطَحَنَتْهُ ثُمَّ جَعَلَتْهُ فِي قِدْرٍ ۞ وَصَبَّتْ عَلَيْهِ شَيْئًا مِنْ زَيْتٍ ۞ وَدَقَّتِ الْفُلْفُلَ وَالتَّوَابِلَ ۞ فَقَرَّبَتْهُ إِلَيْهِمْ ۞ فَقَالَتْ هٰذَا مِمَّا كَانَ يُعْجِبُ رَسُولَ اللهِ ﷺ وَيُحْسِنُ أَكْلَهُ ۞

178. Husayn ibn Muhammad al-Basri narrated to us, 'Fudayl ibn Sulayman narrated to us, "Fa'id, the freed slave of 'Ubaydullah ibn 'Ali ibn Abi Rafi', who was the freed slave of the Messenger of Allah ﷺ, reported:

'Ubaydullah ibn 'Ali narrated to me on the authority of his grandmother Salma,[399] who reported that Hasan ibn 'Ali, Ibn 'Abbas and Ibn Ja'far came to her and said, "Prepare some food for us which the Messenger of Allah ﷺ liked and enjoyed eating." She said, "Dear sons, you will not enjoy it today!"[400] He said,[401] "Of course we will! Prepare some for us."[402] He said, "She stood

397 She is Safiyya bint Huyay ibn Akhtab, from the progeny of Prophet Harun, brother of Prophet Musa ﷺ. (AA)

398 Sawiq is porridge made from wheat or barley. It is the Sunna to have a wedding banquet (*walima*) and to invite people to it to partake in the happy occasion of marriage. This occasion was the marriage of the greatest of Allah's creation ﷺ yet it was so simple and humble; no one on this earth was ever blessed with marriages more noble or successful than his. (MA)

399 The grandmother of 'Ubaydullah ibn 'Ali was the servant of the Messenger of Allah ﷺ who was blessed to be the cook for him. For this reason, they approached her and asked about foods he would eat. She was also the woman who helped deliver Ibrahim, the son of the Prophet ﷺ. (MA)

400 She stated this because the food of the Messenger of Allah ﷺ was simple due to it being a time of difficulty and sacrifice. During the times of the Companions, Islam spread across the earth and their lives became more comfortable, diverse and easy. (MA)

401 The narrator or one of the three companions. (MA)

402 It was from the faith of the Companions to love everything that the Messenger of Allah ﷺ liked, and they sought blessings through his every action. (MA)

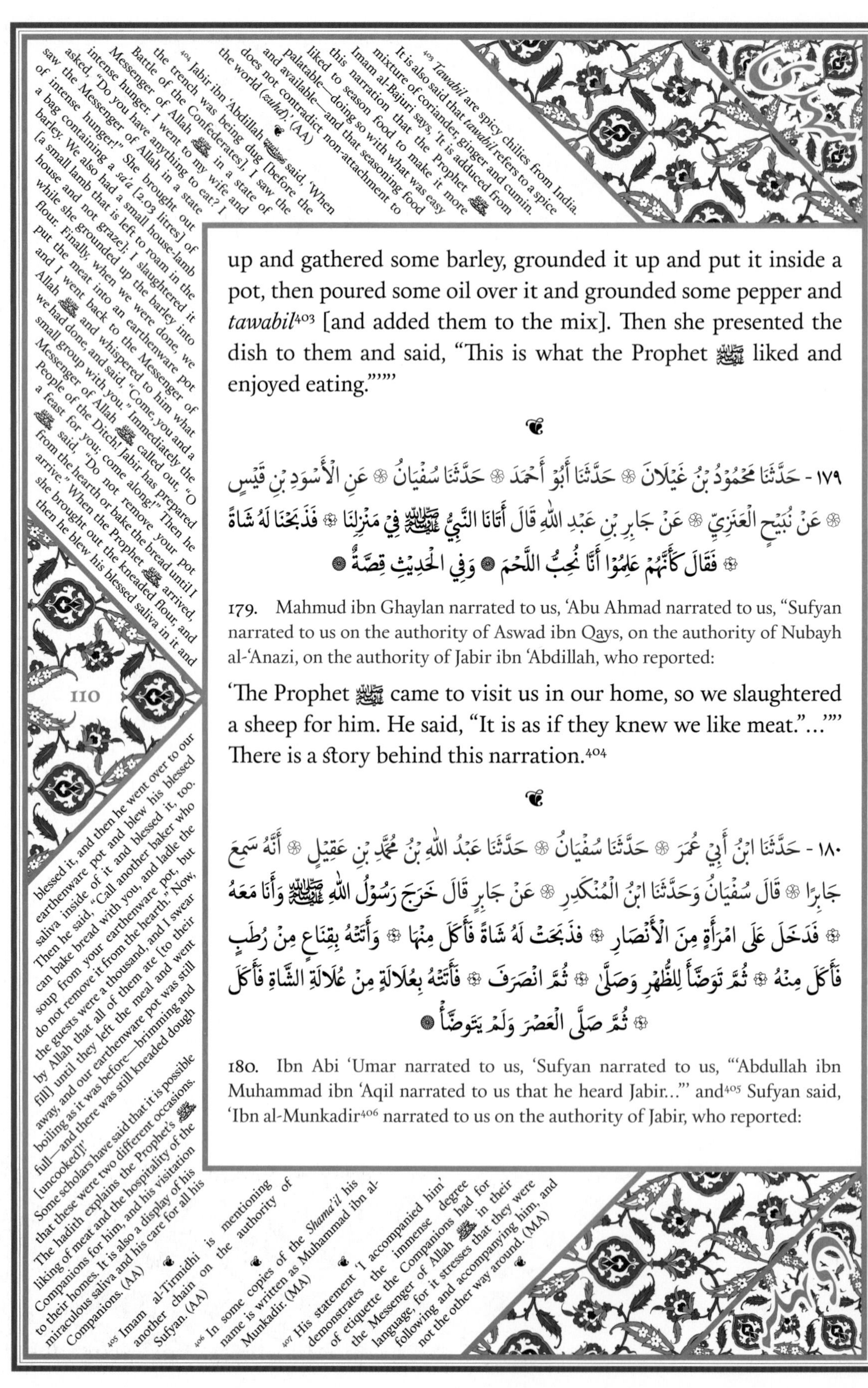

up and gathered some barley, grounded it up and put it inside a pot, then poured some oil over it and grounded some pepper and *tawabil*[403] [and added them to the mix]. Then she presented the dish to them and said, "This is what the Prophet ﷺ liked and enjoyed eating."'"'

❦

١٧٩ - حَدَّثَنَا مَحْمُودُ بْنُ غَيْلَانَ ۞ حَدَّثَنَا أَبُو أَحْمَدَ ۞ حَدَّثَنَا سُفْيَانُ ۞ عَنِ الْأَسْوَدِ بْنِ قَيْسٍ ۞ عَنْ نُبَيْحٍ الْعَنَزِيِّ ۞ عَنْ جَابِرِ بْنِ عَبْدِ اللهِ قَالَ أَتَانَا النَّبِيُّ ﷺ فِي مَنْزِلِنَا ۞ فَذَبَحْنَا لَهُ شَاةً ۞ فَقَالَ كَأَنَّهُمْ عَلِمُوا أَنَّا نُحِبُّ اللَّحْمَ ۞ وَفِي الْحَدِيثِ قِصَّةٌ ۞

179. Mahmud ibn Ghaylan narrated to us, 'Abu Ahmad narrated to us, "Sufyan narrated to us on the authority of Aswad ibn Qays, on the authority of Nubayh al-'Anazi, on the authority of Jabir ibn 'Abdillah, who reported:

'The Prophet ﷺ came to visit us in our home, so we slaughtered a sheep for him. He said, "It is as if they knew we like meat."...'"' There is a story behind this narration.[404]

❦

١٨٠ - حَدَّثَنَا ابْنُ أَبِي عُمَرَ ۞ حَدَّثَنَا سُفْيَانُ ۞ حَدَّثَنَا عَبْدُ اللهِ بْنُ مُحَمَّدِ بْنِ عَقِيلٍ ۞ أَنَّهُ سَمِعَ جَابِرًا ۞ قَالَ سُفْيَانُ وَحَدَّثَنَا ابْنُ الْمُنْكَدِرِ ۞ عَنْ جَابِرٍ قَالَ خَرَجَ رَسُولُ اللهِ ﷺ وَأَنَا مَعَهُ ۞ فَدَخَلَ عَلَى امْرَأَةٍ مِنَ الْأَنْصَارِ ۞ فَذَبَحَتْ لَهُ شَاةً فَأَكَلَ مِنْهَا ۞ وَأَتَتْهُ بِقِنَاعٍ مِنْ رُطَبٍ فَأَكَلَ مِنْهُ ۞ ثُمَّ تَوَضَّأَ لِلظُّهْرِ وَصَلَّى ۞ ثُمَّ انْصَرَفَ ۞ فَأَتَتْهُ بِعُلَالَةٍ مِنْ عُلَالَةِ الشَّاةِ فَأَكَلَ ۞ ثُمَّ صَلَّى الْعَصْرَ وَلَمْ يَتَوَضَّأْ ۞

180. Ibn Abi 'Umar narrated to us, 'Sufyan narrated to us, "'Abdullah ibn Muhammad ibn 'Aqil narrated to us that he heard Jabir..."' and[405] Sufyan said, 'Ibn al-Munkadir[406] narrated to us on the authority of Jabir, who reported:

[403] *Tawabil* are spicy chilies from India. It is also said that *tawabil* refers to a spice mixture of coriander, ginger and cumin. Imam al-Bajuri says, 'It is adduced from this narration that the Prophet ﷺ liked to season food to make it more palatable—doing so with what was easy and available—and that seasoning food does not contradict non-attachment to the world (*zuhd*).' (AA)

❦

[404] Jabir ibn 'Abdillah ﷺ said, 'When the trench was being dug [before the Battle of the Confederates], I saw the Messenger of Allah ﷺ in a state of intense hunger. I went to my wife and asked, "Do you have anything to eat? I saw the Messenger of Allah in a state of intense hunger!" She brought out a bag containing a *sa'a* [2.03 litres] of barley. We also had a small house-lamb [a small lamb that is left to roam in the house and not graze]; I slaughtered it while she grounded up the barley into flour. Finally, when we were done, we put the meat into an earthenware pot and I went back to the Messenger of Allah ﷺ and whispered to him what we had done, and said, "Come, you and a small group with you." Immediately the Messenger of Allah ﷺ called out, "O People of the Ditch! Jabir has prepared a feast for you; come along!" Then he ﷺ said, "Do not remove your pot from the hearth or bake the bread until I arrive." When the Prophet ﷺ arrived, she brought out the kneaded flour, and then he blew his blessed saliva in it and blessed it, and then he went over to our earthenware pot and blew his blessed saliva inside of it and blessed it, too. Then he said, "Call another baker who can bake bread with you, and ladle the soup from your earthenware pot, but do not remove it from the hearth." Now, the guests were a thousand, and I swear by Allah that all of them ate [to their fill] until they left the meal and went away, and our earthenware pot was still boiling as it was before—brimming and full—and there was still kneaded dough [uncooked]!' Some scholars have said that it is possible that these were two different occasions. The hadith explains the Prophet's ﷺ liking of meat and the hospitality of the Companions for him, and his visitation to their homes. It is also a display of his miraculous saliva and his care for all his Companions. (AA)

❦

[405] Imam al-Tirmidhi is mentioning another chain on the authority of Sufyan. (AA)

❦

[406] In some copies of the *Shama'il* his name is written as Muhammad ibn al-Munkadir. (MA)

❦

[407] His statement 'I accompanied him' demonstrates the immense degree of etiquette the Companions had for the Messenger of Allah ﷺ in their language, for it stresses that they were following and accompanying him, and not the other way around. (MA)

❦

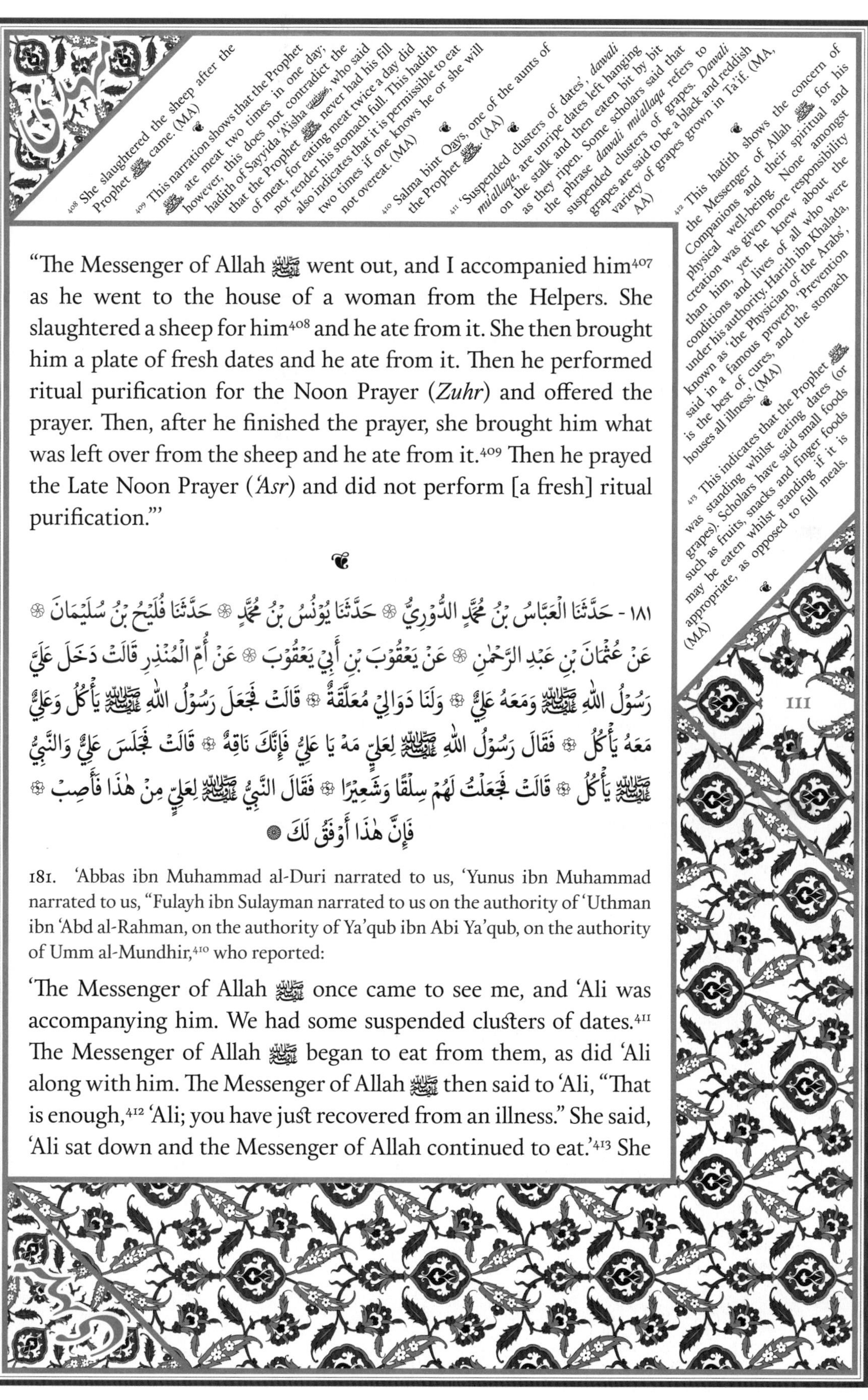

"The Messenger of Allah ﷺ went out, and I accompanied him[407] as he went to the house of a woman from the Helpers. She slaughtered a sheep for him[408] and he ate from it. She then brought him a plate of fresh dates and he ate from it. Then he performed ritual purification for the Noon Prayer (*Zuhr*) and offered the prayer. Then, after he finished the prayer, she brought him what was left over from the sheep and he ate from it.[409] Then he prayed the Late Noon Prayer (*'Asr*) and did not perform [a fresh] ritual purification."'

١٨١ - حَدَّثَنَا الْعَبَّاسُ بْنُ مُحَمَّدٍ الدُّورِيُّ ۞ حَدَّثَنَا يُونُسُ بْنُ مُحَمَّدٍ ۞ حَدَّثَنَا فُلَيْحُ بْنُ سُلَيْمَانَ ۞ عَنْ عُثْمَانَ بْنِ عَبْدِ الرَّحْمٰنِ ۞ عَنْ يَعْقُوبَ بْنِ أَبِي يَعْقُوبَ ۞ عَنْ أُمِّ الْمُنْذِرِ قَالَتْ دَخَلَ عَلَيَّ رَسُولُ اللهِ ﷺ وَمَعَهُ عَلِيٌّ ۞ وَلَنَا دَوَالِي مُعَلَّقَةٌ ۞ قَالَتْ فَجَعَلَ رَسُولُ اللهِ ﷺ يَأْكُلُ وَعَلِيٌّ مَعَهُ يَأْكُلُ ۞ فَقَالَ رَسُولُ اللهِ ﷺ لِعَلِيٍّ مَهْ يَا عَلِيُّ فَإِنَّكَ نَاقِهٌ ۞ قَالَتْ فَجَلَسَ عَلِيٌّ وَالنَّبِيُّ ﷺ يَأْكُلُ ۞ قَالَتْ فَجَعَلْتُ لَهُمْ سِلْقًا وَشَعِيرًا ۞ فَقَالَ النَّبِيُّ ﷺ لِعَلِيٍّ مِنْ هٰذَا فَأَصِبْ ۞ فَإِنَّ هٰذَا أَوْفَقُ لَكَ ۞

181. 'Abbas ibn Muhammad al-Duri narrated to us, 'Yunus ibn Muhammad narrated to us, "Fulayh ibn Sulayman narrated to us on the authority of 'Uthman ibn 'Abd al-Rahman, on the authority of Ya'qub ibn Abi Ya'qub, on the authority of Umm al-Mundhir,[410] who reported:

'The Messenger of Allah ﷺ once came to see me, and 'Ali was accompanying him. We had some suspended clusters of dates.[411] The Messenger of Allah ﷺ began to eat from them, as did 'Ali along with him. The Messenger of Allah ﷺ then said to 'Ali, "That is enough,[412] 'Ali; you have just recovered from an illness." She said, 'Ali sat down and the Messenger of Allah continued to eat.'[413] She

[408] She slaughtered the sheep after the Prophet ﷺ came. (MA)

[409] This narration shows that the Prophet ﷺ ate meat two times in one day; however, this does not contradict the hadith of Sayyida 'A'isha رضي الله عنها, who said that the Prophet ﷺ never had his fill of meat, for eating meat twice a day did not render his stomach full. This hadith also indicates that it is permissible to eat two times if one knows he or she will not overeat. (MA)

[410] Salma bint Qays, one of the aunts of the Prophet ﷺ. (AA)

[411] 'Suspended clusters of dates', *dawali mu'allaqa*, are unripe dates left hanging on the stalk and then eaten bit by bit as they ripen. Some scholars said that the phrase *dawali mu'allaqa* refers to suspended clusters of grapes. *Dawali* grapes are said to be a black and reddish variety of grapes grown in Ta'if. (MA, AA)

[412] This hadith shows the concern of the Messenger of Allah ﷺ for his Companions and their spiritual and physical well-being. None amongst creation was given more responsibility than him, yet he knew about the conditions and lives of all who were under his authority. Harith ibn Khalada, known as 'the Physician of the Arabs', said in a famous proverb, 'Prevention is the best of cures, and the stomach houses all illness.' (MA)

[413] This indicates that the Prophet ﷺ was standing whilst eating dates (or grapes). Scholars have said small foods such as fruits, snacks and finger foods may be eaten whilst standing if it is appropriate, as opposed to full meals. (MA)

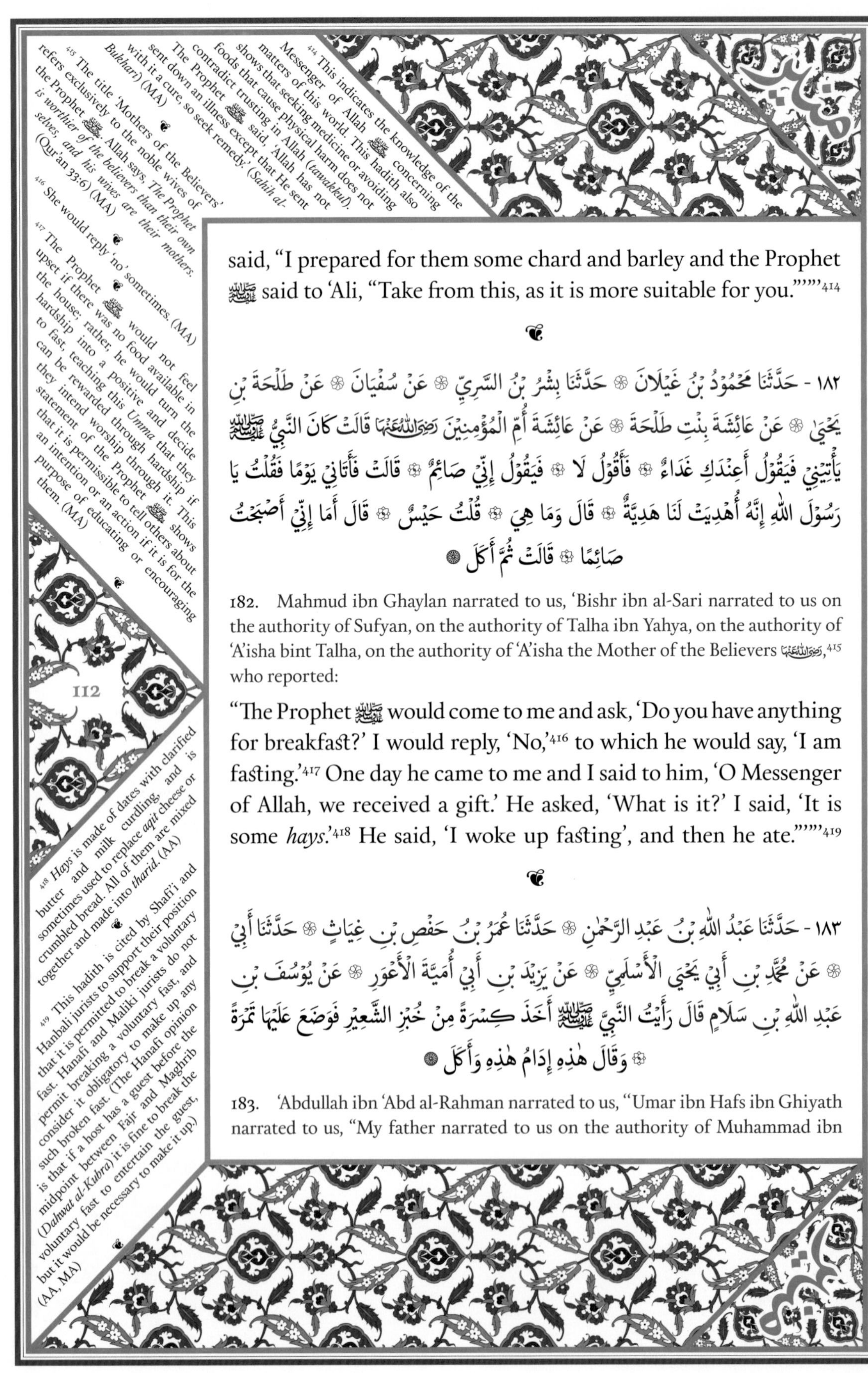

said, "I prepared for them some chard and barley and the Prophet ﷺ said to 'Ali, "Take from this, as it is more suitable for you."""[414]

١٨٢ - حَدَّثَنَا مَحْمُودُ بْنُ غَيْلَانَ ۞ حَدَّثَنَا بِشْرُ بْنُ السَّرِيِّ ۞ عَنْ سُفْيَانَ ۞ عَنْ طَلْحَةَ بْنِ يَحْيَىٰ ۞ عَنْ عَائِشَةَ بِنْتِ طَلْحَةَ ۞ عَنْ عَائِشَةَ أُمِّ الْمُؤْمِنِينَ رَضِيَ اللهُ عَنْهَا قَالَتْ كَانَ النَّبِيُّ ﷺ يَأْتِينِي فَيَقُولُ أَعِنْدَكِ غَدَاءٌ ۞ فَأَقُولُ لَا ۞ فَيَقُولُ إِنِّي صَائِمٌ ۞ قَالَتْ فَأَتَانِي يَوْمًا فَقُلْتُ يَا رَسُولَ اللهِ إِنَّهُ أُهْدِيَتْ لَنَا هَدِيَّةٌ ۞ قَالَ وَمَا هِيَ ۞ قُلْتُ حَيْسٌ ۞ قَالَ أَمَا إِنِّي أَصْبَحْتُ صَائِمًا ۞ قَالَتْ ثُمَّ أَكَلَ ۞

182. Mahmud ibn Ghaylan narrated to us, 'Bishr ibn al-Sari narrated to us on the authority of Sufyan, on the authority of Talha ibn Yahya, on the authority of 'A'isha bint Talha, on the authority of 'A'isha the Mother of the Believers رضي الله عنها,[415] who reported:

"The Prophet ﷺ would come to me and ask, 'Do you have anything for breakfast?' I would reply, 'No,'[416] to which he would say, 'I am fasting.'[417] One day he came to me and I said to him, 'O Messenger of Allah, we received a gift.' He asked, 'What is it?' I said, 'It is some *hays*.'[418] He said, 'I woke up fasting', and then he ate."""[419]

١٨٣ - حَدَّثَنَا عَبْدُ اللهِ بْنُ عَبْدِ الرَّحْمٰنِ ۞ حَدَّثَنَا عُمَرُ بْنُ حَفْصِ بْنِ غِيَاثٍ ۞ حَدَّثَنَا أَبِي ۞ عَنْ مُحَمَّدِ بْنِ أَبِي يَحْيَى الْأَسْلَمِيِّ ۞ عَنْ يَزِيدَ بْنِ أَبِي أُمَيَّةَ الْأَعْوَرِ ۞ عَنْ يُوسُفَ بْنِ عَبْدِ اللهِ بْنِ سَلَامٍ قَالَ رَأَيْتُ النَّبِيَّ ﷺ أَخَذَ كِسْرَةً مِنْ خُبْزِ الشَّعِيرِ فَوَضَعَ عَلَيْهَا تَمْرَةً ۞ وَقَالَ هٰذِهِ إِدَامُ هٰذِهِ وَأَكَلَ ۞

183. 'Abdullah ibn 'Abd al-Rahman narrated to us, "'Umar ibn Hafs ibn Ghiyath narrated to us, "My father narrated to us on the authority of Muhammad ibn

414 This indicates the knowledge of the Messenger of Allah ﷺ concerning matters of this world. This hadith also shows that seeking medicine or avoiding foods that cause physical harm does not contradict trusting in Allah (*tawakkul*). The Prophet ﷺ said, 'Allah has not sent down an illness except that He sent with it a cure, so seek remedy.' (*Sahih al-Bukhari*) (MA)

415 The title 'Mothers of the Believers' refers exclusively to the noble wives of the Prophet ﷺ. Allah says, *The Prophet is worthier of the believers than their own selves, and his wives are their mothers.* (Qur'an 33:6) (MA)

416 She would reply 'no' sometimes. (MA)

417 The Prophet ﷺ would not feel upset if there was no food available in the house; rather, he would turn the hardship into a positive and decide to fast, teaching this *Umma* that they can be rewarded through hardship if they intend worship through it. This statement of the Prophet ﷺ shows that it is permissible to tell others about an intention or an action if it is for the purpose of educating or encouraging them. (MA)

418 *Hays* is made of dates with clarified butter and milk curdling, and is sometimes used to replace *aqit* cheese or crumbled bread. All of them are mixed together and made into *tharid*. (AA)

419 This hadith is cited by Shafi'i and Hanbali jurists to support their position that it is permitted to break a voluntary fast. Hanafi and Maliki jurists do not permit breaking a voluntary fast, and consider it obligatory to make up any such broken fast. (The Hanafi opinion is that if a host has a guest before the midpoint between Fajr and Maghrib (*Dahwat al-Kubra*) it is fine to break the voluntary fast to entertain the guest, but it would be necessary to make it up.) (AA, MA)

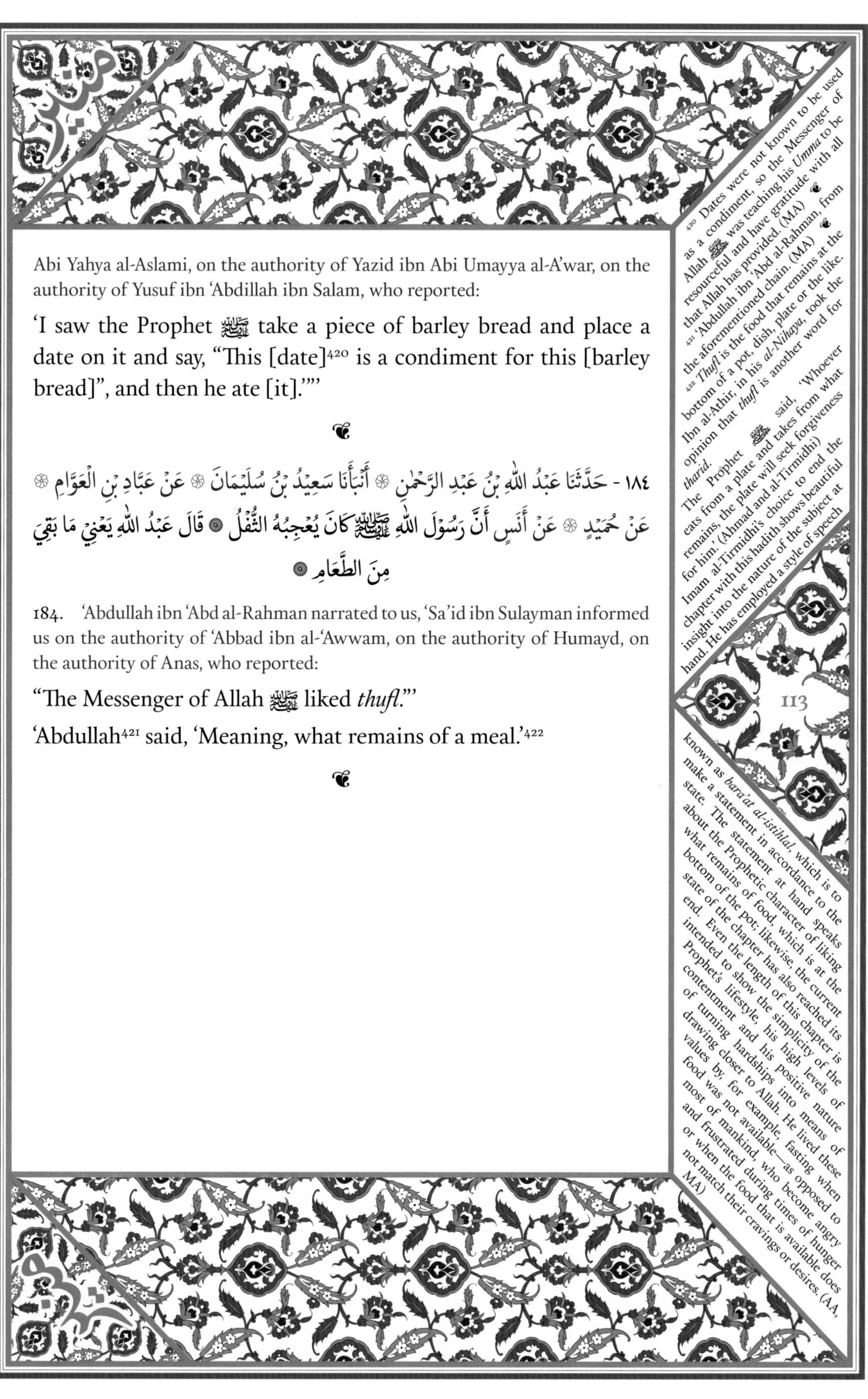

Abi Yahya al-Aslami, on the authority of Yazid ibn Abi Umayya al-A'war, on the authority of Yusuf ibn 'Abdillah ibn Salam, who reported:

'I saw the Prophet ﷺ take a piece of barley bread and place a date on it and say, "This [date][420] is a condiment for this [barley bread]", and then he ate [it].'"

❦

١٨٤ - حَدَّثَنَا عَبْدُ اللهِ بْنُ عَبْدِ الرَّحْمٰنِ ۞ أَنْبَأَنَا سَعِيدُ بْنُ سُلَيْمَانَ ۞ عَنْ عَبَّادِ بْنِ الْعَوَّامِ ۞ عَنْ حُمَيْدٍ ۞ عَنْ أَنَسٍ أَنَّ رَسُولَ اللهِ ﷺ كَانَ يُعْجِبُهُ الثُّفْلُ ۞ قَالَ عَبْدُ اللهِ يَعْنِي مَا بَقِيَ مِنَ الطَّعَامِ ۞

184. 'Abdullah ibn 'Abd al-Rahman narrated to us, 'Sa'id ibn Sulayman informed us on the authority of 'Abbad ibn al-'Awwam, on the authority of Humayd, on the authority of Anas, who reported:

"The Messenger of Allah ﷺ liked *thufl*."

'Abdullah[421] said, 'Meaning, what remains of a meal.'[422]

❦

[420] Dates were not known to be used as a condiment, so the Messenger of Allah ﷺ was teaching his *Umma* to be resourceful and have gratitude with all that Allah has provided. (MA) ❦

[421] 'Abdullah ibn 'Abd al-Rahman, from the aforementioned chain. (MA) ❦

[422] *Thufl* is the food that remains at the bottom of a pot, dish, plate or the like. Ibn al-Athir, in his *al-Nihaya*, took the opinion that *thufl* is another word for *tharid*. The Prophet ﷺ said, 'Whoever eats from a plate and takes from what remains, the plate will seek forgiveness for him.' (Ahmad and al-Tirmidhi) Imam al-Tirmidhi's choice to end the chapter with this hadith shows beautiful insight into the nature of the subject at hand. He has employed a style of speech known as *bara'at al-istihlal*, which is to make a statement in accordance to the state. The statement at hand speaks about the Prophetic character of liking what remains of food, which is at the bottom of the pot; likewise, the current state of the chapter has also reached its end. Even the length of this chapter is intended to show the simplicity of the Prophet's lifestyle, his high levels of contentment and his positive nature of turning hardships into means of drawing closer to Allah. He lived these values by, for example, fasting when food was not available—as opposed to most of mankind, who become angry and frustrated during times of hunger or when the food that is available does not match their cravings or desires. (AA, MA)

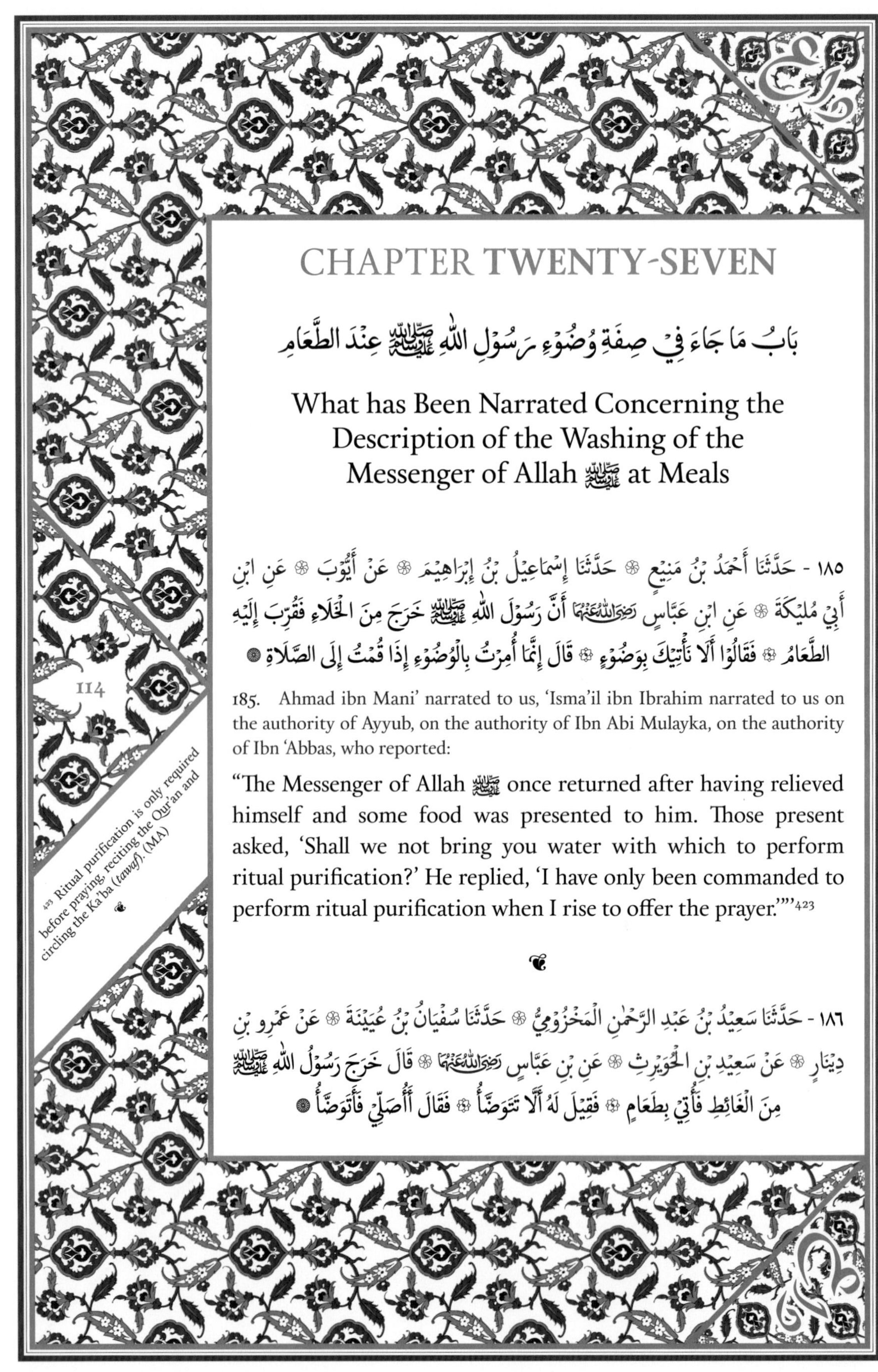

CHAPTER TWENTY-SEVEN

بَابُ مَا جَاءَ فِي صِفَةِ وُضُوءِ رَسُولِ اللهِ ﷺ عِنْدَ الطَّعَامِ

What has Been Narrated Concerning the Description of the Washing of the Messenger of Allah ﷺ at Meals

١٨٥ - حَدَّثَنَا أَحْمَدُ بْنُ مَنِيعٍ ۞ حَدَّثَنَا إِسْمَاعِيلُ بْنُ إِبْرَاهِيمَ ۞ عَنْ أَيُّوبَ ۞ عَنِ ابْنِ أَبِي مُلَيْكَةَ ۞ عَنِ ابْنِ عَبَّاسٍ رَضِيَ اللهُ عَنْهُمَا أَنَّ رَسُولَ اللهِ ﷺ خَرَجَ مِنَ الْخَلَاءِ فَقُرِّبَ إِلَيْهِ الطَّعَامُ ۞ فَقَالُوا أَلَا نَأْتِيكَ بِوَضُوءٍ ۞ قَالَ إِنَّمَا أُمِرْتُ بِالْوُضُوءِ إِذَا قُمْتُ إِلَى الصَّلَاةِ ۞

185. Ahmad ibn Mani' narrated to us, 'Isma'il ibn Ibrahim narrated to us on the authority of Ayyub, on the authority of Ibn Abi Mulayka, on the authority of Ibn 'Abbas, who reported:

"The Messenger of Allah ﷺ once returned after having relieved himself and some food was presented to him. Those present asked, 'Shall we not bring you water with which to perform ritual purification?' He replied, 'I have only been commanded to perform ritual purification when I rise to offer the prayer.'"[423]

١٨٦ - حَدَّثَنَا سَعِيدُ بْنُ عَبْدِ الرَّحْمٰنِ الْمَخْزُومِيُّ ۞ حَدَّثَنَا سُفْيَانُ بْنُ عُيَيْنَةَ ۞ عَنْ عَمْرِو بْنِ دِينَارٍ ۞ عَنْ سَعِيدِ بْنِ الْحُوَيْرِثِ ۞ عَنِ بْنِ عَبَّاسٍ رَضِيَ اللهُ عَنْهُمَا ۞ قَالَ خَرَجَ رَسُولُ اللهِ ﷺ مِنَ الْغَائِطِ فَأُتِيَ بِطَعَامٍ ۞ فَقِيلَ لَهُ أَلَّا تَتَوَضَّأُ ۞ فَقَالَ أَأُصَلِّي فَأَتَوَضَّأُ ۞

423 Ritual purification is only required before praying, reciting the Qur'an and circling the Ka'ba (*tawaf*). (MA)

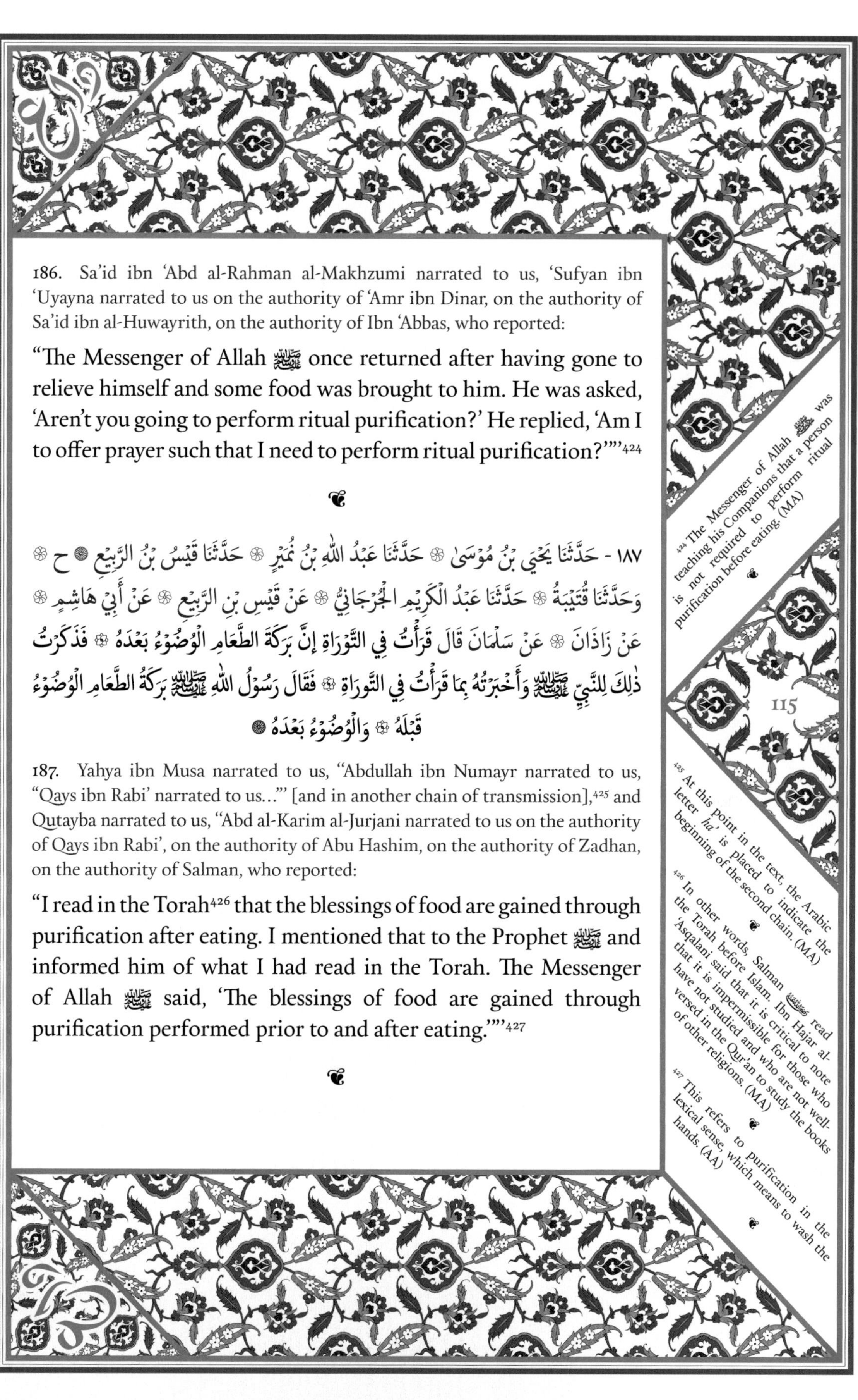

186. Sa'id ibn 'Abd al-Rahman al-Makhzumi narrated to us, 'Sufyan ibn 'Uyayna narrated to us on the authority of 'Amr ibn Dinar, on the authority of Sa'id ibn al-Huwayrith, on the authority of Ibn 'Abbas, who reported:

"The Messenger of Allah ﷺ once returned after having gone to relieve himself and some food was brought to him. He was asked, 'Aren't you going to perform ritual purification?' He replied, 'Am I to offer prayer such that I need to perform ritual purification?'"'[424]

❦

١٨٧ - حَدَّثَنَا يَحْيَى بْنُ مُوسَىٰ ۞ حَدَّثَنَا عَبْدُ اللهِ بْنُ نُمَيْرٍ ۞ حَدَّثَنَا قَيْسُ بْنُ الرَّبِيعِ ● ح ۞ وَحَدَّثَنَا قُتَيْبَةُ ۞ حَدَّثَنَا عَبْدُ الْكَرِيمِ الْجُرْجَانِيُّ ۞ عَنْ قَيْسِ بْنِ الرَّبِيعِ ۞ عَنْ أَبِي هَاشِمٍ ۞ عَنْ زَاذَانَ ۞ عَنْ سَلْمَانَ قَالَ قَرَأْتُ فِي التَّوْرَاةِ إِنَّ بَرَكَةَ الطَّعَامِ الْوُضُوءُ بَعْدَهُ ۞ فَذَكَرْتُ ذٰلِكَ لِلنَّبِيِّ ﷺ وَأَخْبَرْتُهُ بِمَا قَرَأْتُ فِي التَّوْرَاةِ ۞ فَقَالَ رَسُولُ اللهِ ﷺ بَرَكَةُ الطَّعَامِ الْوُضُوءُ قَبْلَهُ ۞ وَالْوُضُوءُ بَعْدَهُ ●

187. Yahya ibn Musa narrated to us, "Abdullah ibn Numayr narrated to us, "Qays ibn Rabi' narrated to us..."' [and in another chain of transmission],[425] and Qutayba narrated to us, "Abd al-Karim al-Jurjani narrated to us on the authority of Qays ibn Rabi', on the authority of Abu Hashim, on the authority of Zadhan, on the authority of Salman, who reported:

"I read in the Torah[426] that the blessings of food are gained through purification after eating. I mentioned that to the Prophet ﷺ and informed him of what I had read in the Torah. The Messenger of Allah ﷺ said, 'The blessings of food are gained through purification performed prior to and after eating.'"'[427]

❦

[424] The Messenger of Allah ﷺ was teaching his Companions that a person is not required to perform ritual purification before eating. (MA)

[425] At this point in the text, the Arabic letter *ha'* is placed to indicate the beginning of the second chain. (MA)

[426] In other words, Salman رضي الله عنه read the Torah before Islam. Ibn Hajar al-'Asqalani said that it is critical to note that it is impermissible for those who have not studied and who are not well-versed in the Qur'an to study the books of other religions. (MA)

[427] This refers to purification in the lexical sense, which means to wash the hands. (AA)

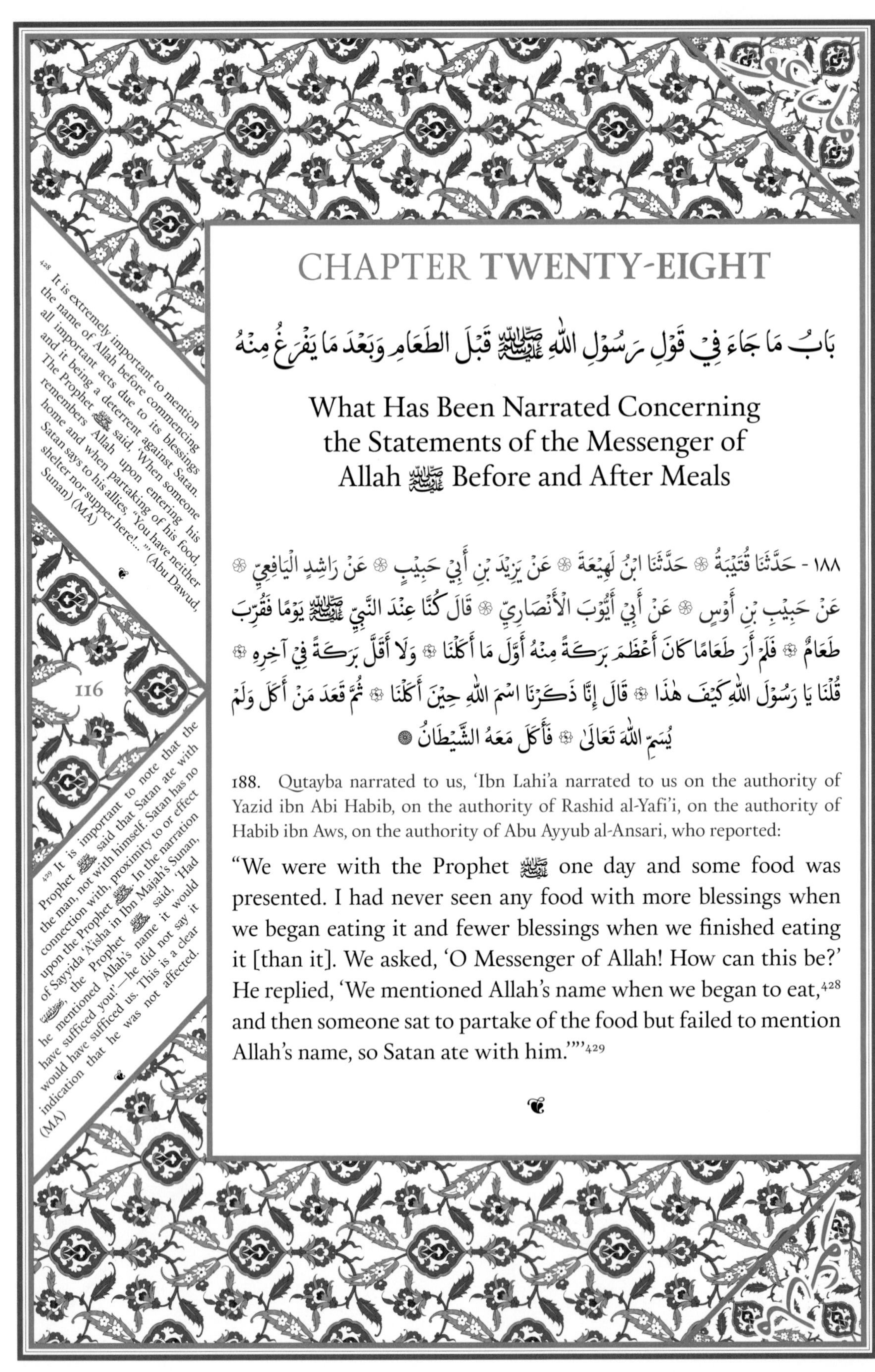

CHAPTER TWENTY-EIGHT

بَابُ مَا جَاءَ فِي قَوْلِ رَسُوْلِ اللهِ ﷺ قَبْلَ الطَّعَامِ وَبَعْدَ مَا يَفْرَغُ مِنْهُ

What Has Been Narrated Concerning the Statements of the Messenger of Allah ﷺ Before and After Meals

١٨٨ - حَدَّثَنَا قُتَيْبَةُ ❁ حَدَّثَنَا ابْنُ لَهِيعَةَ ❁ عَنْ يَزِيْدَ بْنِ أَبِي حَبِيْبٍ ❁ عَنْ رَاشِدٍ الْيَافِعِيِّ ❁ عَنْ حَبِيْبِ بْنِ أَوْسٍ ❁ عَنْ أَبِي أَيُّوبَ الْأَنْصَارِيِّ ❁ قَالَ كُنَّا عِنْدَ النَّبِيِّ ﷺ يَوْمًا فَقُرِّبَ طَعَامٌ ❁ فَلَمْ أَرَ طَعَامًا كَانَ أَعْظَمَ بَرَكَةً مِنْهُ أَوَّلَ مَا أَكَلْنَا ❁ وَلَا أَقَلَّ بَرَكَةً فِي آخِرِهِ ❁ قُلْنَا يَا رَسُوْلَ اللهِ كَيْفَ هٰذَا ❁ قَالَ إِنَّا ذَكَرْنَا اسْمَ اللهِ حِيْنَ أَكَلْنَا ❁ ثُمَّ قَعَدَ مَنْ أَكَلَ وَلَمْ يُسَمِّ اللهَ تَعَالَىٰ ❁ فَأَكَلَ مَعَهُ الشَّيْطَانُ ◉

188. Qutayba narrated to us, 'Ibn Lahi'a narrated to us on the authority of Yazid ibn Abi Habib, on the authority of Rashid al-Yafi'i, on the authority of Habib ibn Aws, on the authority of Abu Ayyub al-Ansari, who reported:

"We were with the Prophet ﷺ one day and some food was presented. I had never seen any food with more blessings when we began eating it and fewer blessings when we finished eating it [than it]. We asked, 'O Messenger of Allah! How can this be?' He replied, 'We mentioned Allah's name when we began to eat,[428] and then someone sat to partake of the food but failed to mention Allah's name, so Satan ate with him.'"[429]

[428] It is extremely important to mention the name of Allah before commencing all important acts due to its blessings and it being a deterrent against Satan. The Prophet ﷺ said, 'When someone remembers Allah upon entering his home and when partaking of his food, Satan says to his allies, "You have neither shelter nor supper here!..."' (Abu Dawud, Sunan) (MA)

[429] It is important to note that the Prophet ﷺ said that Satan ate with the man, not with himself. Satan has no connection with, proximity to or effect upon the Prophet ﷺ. In the narration of Sayyida 'A'isha ﷺ in Ibn Majah's Sunan, the Prophet ﷺ said, 'Had he mentioned Allah's name it would have sufficed you!'—he did not say it would have sufficed us. This is a clear indication that he was not affected. (MA)

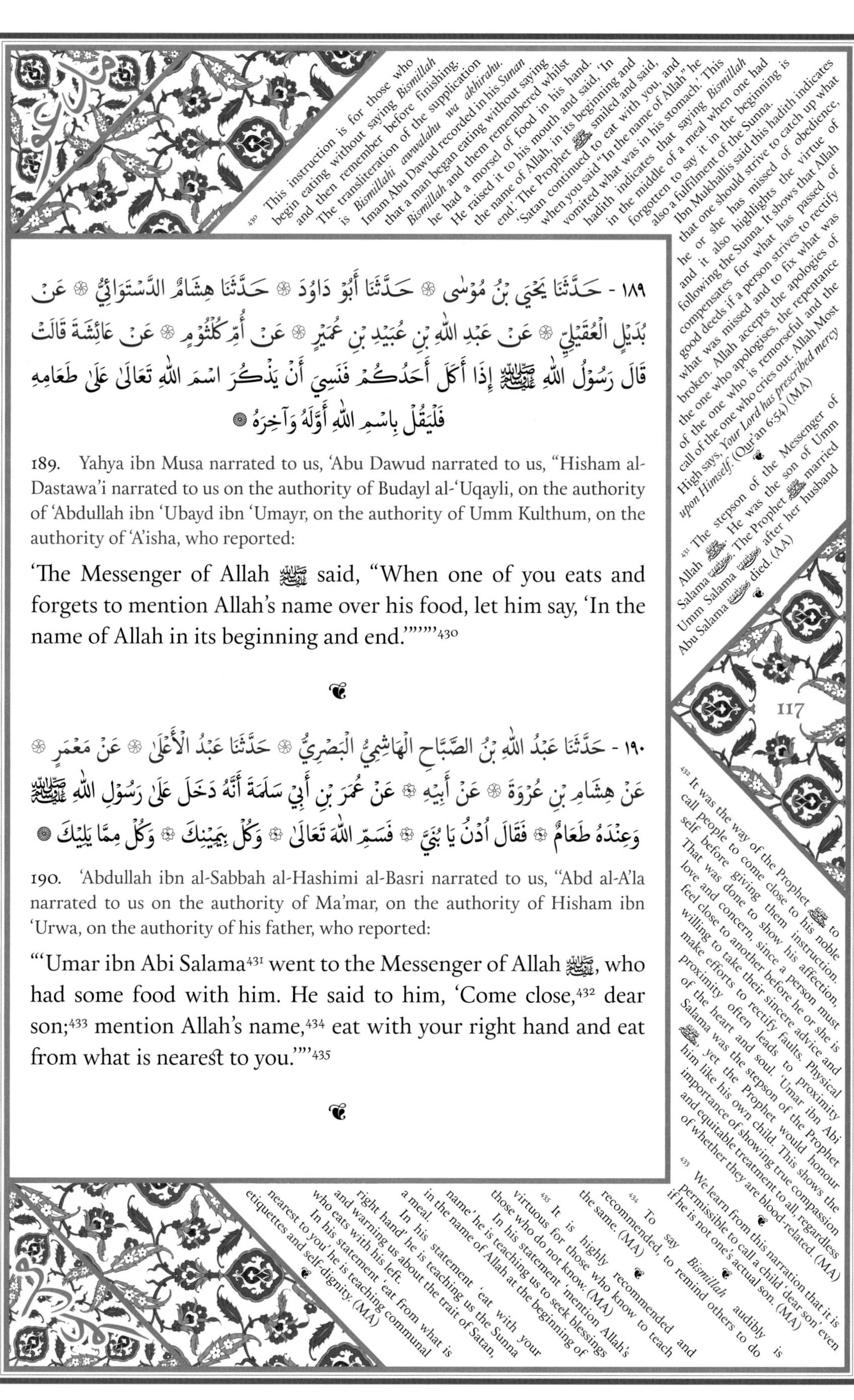

١٨٩ - حَدَّثَنَا يَحْيَى بْنُ مُوسَى ۞ حَدَّثَنَا أَبُو دَاوُدَ ۞ حَدَّثَنَا هِشَامٌ الدَّسْتَوَائِيُّ ۞ عَنْ بُدَيْلٍ الْعُقَيْلِيِّ ۞ عَنْ عَبْدِ اللهِ بْنِ عُبَيْدِ بْنِ عُمَيْرٍ ۞ عَنْ أُمِّ كُلْثُومٍ ۞ عَنْ عَائِشَةَ قَالَتْ قَالَ رَسُولُ اللهِ ﷺ إِذَا أَكَلَ أَحَدُكُمْ فَنَسِيَ أَنْ يَذْكُرَ اسْمَ اللهِ تَعَالَى عَلَى طَعَامِهِ فَلْيَقُلْ بِاسْمِ اللهِ أَوَّلَهُ وَآخِرَهُ ۞

189. Yahya ibn Musa narrated to us, 'Abu Dawud narrated to us, "Hisham al-Dastawa'i narrated to us on the authority of Budayl al-'Uqayli, on the authority of 'Abdullah ibn 'Ubayd ibn 'Umayr, on the authority of Umm Kulthum, on the authority of 'A'isha, who reported:

'The Messenger of Allah ﷺ said, "When one of you eats and forgets to mention Allah's name over his food, let him say, 'In the name of Allah in its beginning and end.'"'"'[430]

❦

١٩٠ - حَدَّثَنَا عَبْدُ اللهِ بْنُ الصَّبَّاحِ الْهَاشِمِيُّ الْبَصْرِيُّ ۞ حَدَّثَنَا عَبْدُ الْأَعْلَى ۞ عَنْ مَعْمَرٍ ۞ عَنْ هِشَامِ بْنِ عُرْوَةَ ۞ عَنْ أَبِيهِ ۞ عَنْ عُمَرَ بْنِ أَبِي سَلَمَةَ أَنَّهُ دَخَلَ عَلَى رَسُولِ اللهِ ﷺ وَعِنْدَهُ طَعَامٌ ۞ فَقَالَ ادْنُ يَا بُنَيَّ ۞ فَسَمِّ اللهَ تَعَالَى ۞ وَكُلْ بِيَمِينِكَ ۞ وَكُلْ مِمَّا يَلِيكَ ۞

190. 'Abdullah ibn al-Sabbah al-Hashimi al-Basri narrated to us, "Abd al-A'la narrated to us on the authority of Ma'mar, on the authority of Hisham ibn 'Urwa, on the authority of his father, who reported:

"'Umar ibn Abi Salama[431] went to the Messenger of Allah ﷺ, who had some food with him. He said to him, 'Come close,[432] dear son;[433] mention Allah's name,[434] eat with your right hand and eat from what is nearest to you.'"'[435]

❦

[430] This instruction is for those who begin eating without saying *Bismillah* and then remember before finishing. The transliteration of the supplication is *Bismillahi awwalahu wa akhirahu*. Imam Abu Dawud recorded in his *Sunan* that a man began eating without saying *Bismillah* and them remembered whilst he had a morsel of food in his hand. He raised it to his mouth and said, 'In the name of Allah, in its beginning and end.' The Prophet ﷺ smiled and said, 'Satan continued to eat with you, and when you said "In the name of Allah" he vomited what was in his stomach.' This hadith indicates that saying *Bismillah* in the middle of a meal when one had forgotten to say it in the beginning is also a fulfilment of the Sunna. Ibn Mukhallis said this hadith indicates that one should strive to catch up what he or she has missed of obedience, and it also highlights the virtue of following the Sunna. It shows that Allah compensates for what has passed of good deeds if a person strives to rectify what was missed and to fix what was broken. Allah accepts the apologies of the one who apologises, the repentance of the one who is remorseful and the call of the one who cries out. Allah Most High says, *Your Lord has prescribed mercy upon Himself.* (Qur'an 6:54) (MA) ❦

[431] The stepson of the Messenger of Allah ﷺ. He was the son of Umm Salama. The Prophet ﷺ married Umm Salama after her husband Abu Salama died. (AA)

[432] It was the way of the Prophet ﷺ to call people to come close to his noble self before giving them instruction. That was done to show his affection, love and concern, since a person must feel close to another before he or she is willing to take their sincere advice and make efforts to rectify faults. Physical proximity often leads to proximity of the heart and soul. 'Umar ibn Abi Salama was the stepson of the Prophet ﷺ, yet the Prophet would honour him like his own child. This shows the importance of showing true compassion and equitable treatment to all, regardless of whether they are blood-related. (MA) ❦

[433] We learn from this narration that it is permissible to call a child 'dear son' even if he is not one's actual son. (MA) ❦

[434] To say *Bismillah* audibly is recommended, to remind others to do the same. (MA) ❦

[435] It is highly recommended and virtuous for those who know to teach those who do not know. (MA) In his statement 'mention Allah's name' he is teaching us to seek blessings in the name of Allah at the beginning of a meal. In his statement 'eat with your right hand' he is teaching us the Sunna and warning us about the trait of Satan, who eats with his left. In his statement 'eat from what is nearest to you' he is teaching communal etiquettes and self-dignity. (MA) ❦

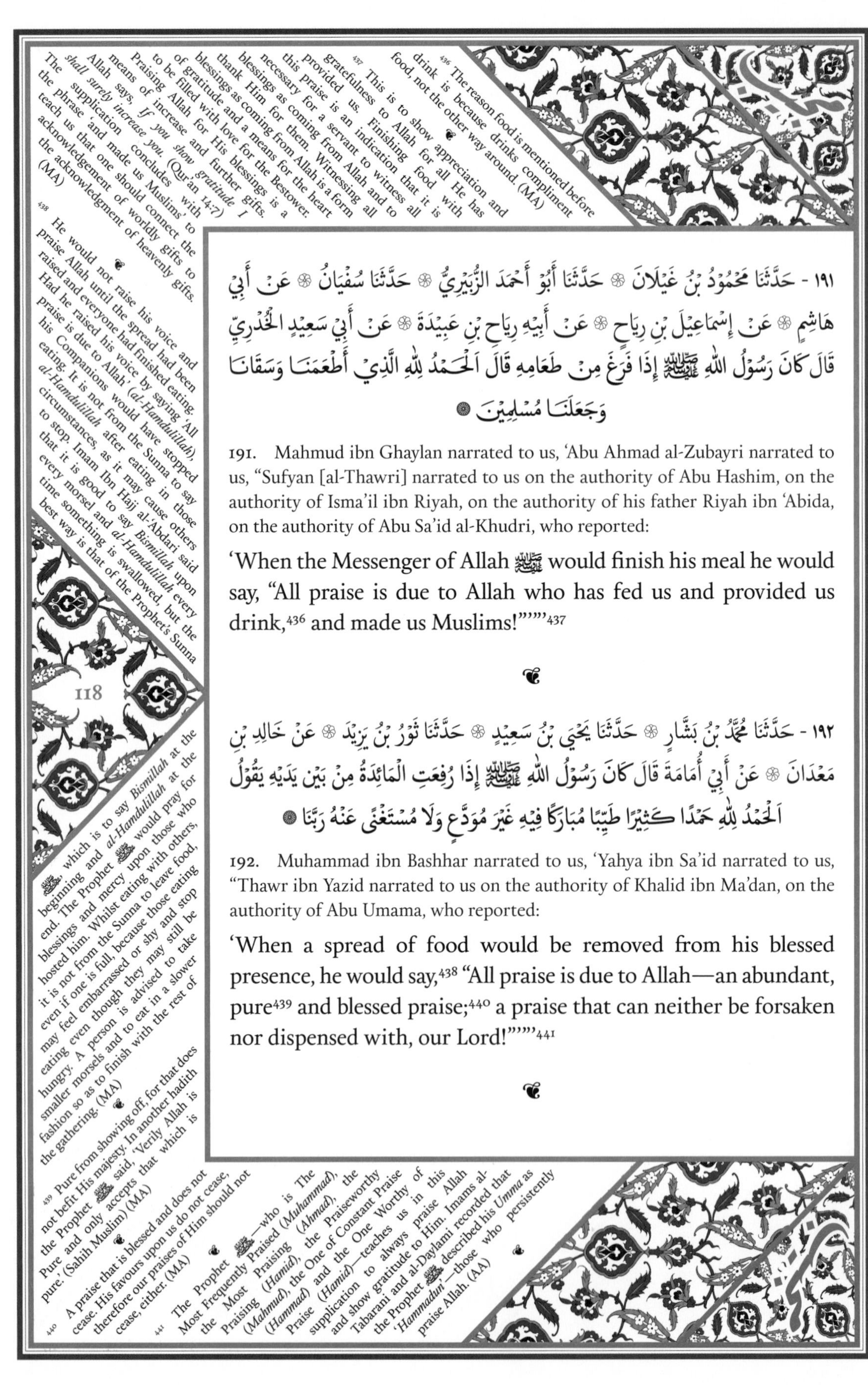

١٩١ - حَدَّثَنَا مَحْمُودُ بْنُ غَيْلَانَ ۞ حَدَّثَنَا أَبُو أَحْمَدَ الزُّبَيْرِيُّ ۞ حَدَّثَنَا سُفْيَانُ ۞ عَنْ أَبِي هَاشِمٍ ۞ عَنْ إِسْمَاعِيلَ بْنِ رِيَاحٍ ۞ عَنْ أَبِيهِ رِيَاحِ بْنِ عَبِيدَةَ ۞ عَنْ أَبِي سَعِيدٍ الْخُدْرِيِّ قَالَ كَانَ رَسُولُ اللهِ ﷺ إِذَا فَرَغَ مِنْ طَعَامِهِ قَالَ اَلْحَمْدُ لِلّٰهِ الَّذِي أَطْعَمَنَا وَسَقَانَا وَجَعَلَنَا مُسْلِمِينَ ۞

191. Mahmud ibn Ghaylan narrated to us, 'Abu Ahmad al-Zubayri narrated to us, "Sufyan [al-Thawri] narrated to us on the authority of Abu Hashim, on the authority of Isma'il ibn Riyah, on the authority of his father Riyah ibn 'Abida, on the authority of Abu Sa'id al-Khudri, who reported:

'When the Messenger of Allah ﷺ would finish his meal he would say, "All praise is due to Allah who has fed us and provided us drink,[436] and made us Muslims!"""'[437]

❦

١٩٢ - حَدَّثَنَا مُحَمَّدُ بْنُ بَشَّارٍ ۞ حَدَّثَنَا يَحْيَى بْنُ سَعِيدٍ ۞ حَدَّثَنَا ثَوْرُ بْنُ يَزِيدَ ۞ عَنْ خَالِدِ بْنِ مَعْدَانَ ۞ عَنْ أَبِي أُمَامَةَ قَالَ كَانَ رَسُولُ اللهِ ﷺ إِذَا رُفِعَتِ الْمَائِدَةُ مِنْ بَيْنِ يَدَيْهِ يَقُولُ اَلْحَمْدُ لِلّٰهِ حَمْدًا كَثِيرًا طَيِّبًا مُبَارَكًا فِيهِ غَيْرَ مُوَدَّعٍ وَلَا مُسْتَغْنًى عَنْهُ رَبَّنَا ۞

192. Muhammad ibn Bashhar narrated to us, 'Yahya ibn Sa'id narrated to us, "Thawr ibn Yazid narrated to us on the authority of Khalid ibn Ma'dan, on the authority of Abu Umama, who reported:

'When a spread of food would be removed from his blessed presence, he would say,[438] "All praise is due to Allah—an abundant, pure[439] and blessed praise;[440] a praise that can neither be forsaken nor dispensed with, our Lord!"""'[441]

❦

436 The reason food is mentioned before drink is because drinks compliment food, not the other way around. (MA)

437 This is to show appreciation and gratefulness to Allah for all He has provided us. Finishing food with this praise is an indication that it is necessary for a servant to witness all blessings as coming from Allah and to thank Him for them. Witnessing all blessings as coming from Allah is a form of gratitude and a means for the heart to be filled with love for the Bestower. Praising Allah for His blessings is a means of increase and further gifts. Allah says, *If you show gratitude I shall surely increase you.* (Qur'an 14:7) The supplication concludes with the phrase 'and made us Muslims' to teach us that one should connect the acknowledgement of worldly gifts to the acknowledgment of heavenly gifts. (MA)

438 He would not raise his voice and praise Allah until the spread had been raised and everyone had finished eating. Had he raised his voice by saying 'All praise is due to Allah' (*al-Hamdulillah*), his Companions would have stopped eating. It is not from the Sunna to say *al-Hamdulillah* after eating in those circumstances, as it may cause others to stop. Imam Ibn Hajj al-'Abdari said that it is good to say *Bismillah* and *al-Hamdulillah* upon every morsel and every time something is swallowed, but the best way is that of the Prophet's Sunna ﷺ which is to say *Bismillah* at the beginning and *al-Hamdulillah* at the end. The Prophet ﷺ would pray for blessings and mercy upon those who hosted him. Whilst eating with others, it is not from the Sunna to leave food, even if one is full, because those eating may feel embarrassed or shy and stop eating even though they may still be hungry. A person is advised to take smaller morsels and to eat in a slower fashion so as to finish with the rest of the gathering. (MA)

439 Pure from showing off, for that does not befit His majesty. In another hadith the Prophet ﷺ said, 'Verily Allah is Pure and only accepts that which is pure.' (Sahih Muslim) (MA)

440 A praise that is blessed and does not cease. His favours upon us do not cease, therefore our praises of Him should not cease, either. (MA)

441 The Prophet ﷺ—who is The Most Frequently Praised (*Muhammad*), the Most Praising (*Ahmad*), the Praiseworthy (*Mahmud*), the One of Constant Praise (*Hammad*) and the One Worthy of Praise (*Hamid*)—teaches us in this supplication to always praise Allah and show gratitude to Him. Imams al-Tabarani and al-Daylami recorded that the Prophet ﷺ described his *Umma* as '*Hammadun*'—those who persistently praise Allah. (AA)

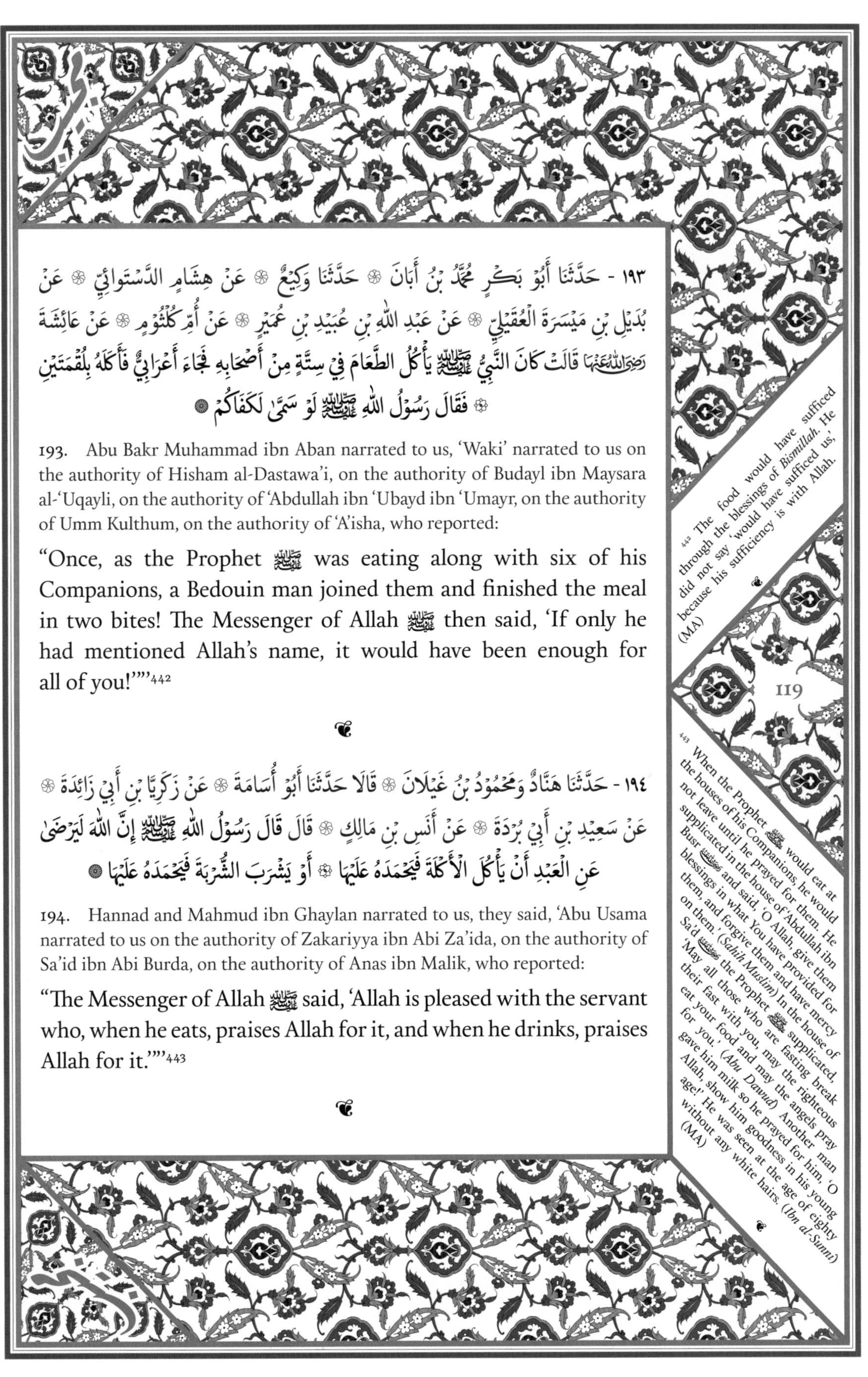

١٩٣ - حَدَّثَنَا أَبُو بَكْرٍ مُحَمَّدُ بْنُ أَبَانَ ۞ حَدَّثَنَا وَكِيعٌ ۞ عَنْ هِشَامٍ الدَّسْتَوائِيِّ ۞ عَنْ بُدَيْلِ بْنِ مَيْسَرَةَ الْعُقَيْلِيِّ ۞ عَنْ عَبْدِ اللهِ بْنِ عُبَيْدِ بْنِ عُمَيْرٍ ۞ عَنْ أُمِّ كُلْثُومٍ ۞ عَنْ عَائِشَةَ رَضِيَ اللهُ عَنْهَا قَالَتْ كَانَ النَّبِيُّ ﷺ يَأْكُلُ الطَّعَامَ فِي سِتَّةٍ مِنْ أَصْحَابِهِ فَجَاءَ أَعْرَابِيٌّ فَأَكَلَهُ بِلُقْمَتَيْنِ ۞ فَقَالَ رَسُولُ اللهِ ﷺ لَوْ سَمَّى لَكَفَاكُمْ ۞

193. Abu Bakr Muhammad ibn Aban narrated to us, 'Waki' narrated to us on the authority of Hisham al-Dastawa'i, on the authority of Budayl ibn Maysara al-'Uqayli, on the authority of 'Abdullah ibn 'Ubayd ibn 'Umayr, on the authority of Umm Kulthum, on the authority of 'A'isha, who reported:

"Once, as the Prophet ﷺ was eating along with six of his Companions, a Bedouin man joined them and finished the meal in two bites! The Messenger of Allah ﷺ then said, 'If only he had mentioned Allah's name, it would have been enough for all of you!'"'[442]

١٩٤ - حَدَّثَنَا هَنَّادٌ وَمَحْمُودُ بْنُ غَيْلَانَ ۞ قَالَا حَدَّثَنَا أَبُو أُسَامَةَ ۞ عَنْ زَكَرِيَّا بْنِ أَبِي زَائِدَةَ ۞ عَنْ سَعِيدِ بْنِ أَبِي بُرْدَةَ ۞ عَنْ أَنَسِ بْنِ مَالِكٍ ۞ قَالَ قَالَ رَسُولُ اللهِ ﷺ إِنَّ اللهَ لَيَرْضَى عَنِ الْعَبْدِ أَنْ يَأْكُلَ الْأَكْلَةَ فَيَحْمَدَهُ عَلَيْهَا ۞ أَوْ يَشْرَبَ الشَّرْبَةَ فَيَحْمَدَهُ عَلَيْهَا ۞

194. Hannad and Mahmud ibn Ghaylan narrated to us, they said, 'Abu Usama narrated to us on the authority of Zakariyya ibn Abi Za'ida, on the authority of Sa'id ibn Abi Burda, on the authority of Anas ibn Malik, who reported:

"The Messenger of Allah ﷺ said, 'Allah is pleased with the servant who, when he eats, praises Allah for it, and when he drinks, praises Allah for it.'"'[443]

[442] The food would have sufficed through the blessings of *Bismillah*. He did not say 'would have sufficed us,' because his sufficiency is with Allah. (MA)

[443] When the Prophet ﷺ would eat at the houses of his Companions, he would not leave until he prayed for them. He supplicated in the house of 'Abdullah ibn Busr ﷺ and said, 'O Allah, give them blessings in what You have provided for them, and forgive them and have mercy on them.' (*Sahih Muslim*) In the house of Sa'd ﷺ the Prophet ﷺ supplicated, 'May all those who are fasting break their fast with you, may the righteous eat your food and may the angels pray for you.' (*Abu Dawud*) Another man gave him milk so he prayed for him, 'O Allah, show him goodness in his young age!' He was seen at the age of eighty without any white hairs. (*Ibn al-Sunni*) (MA)

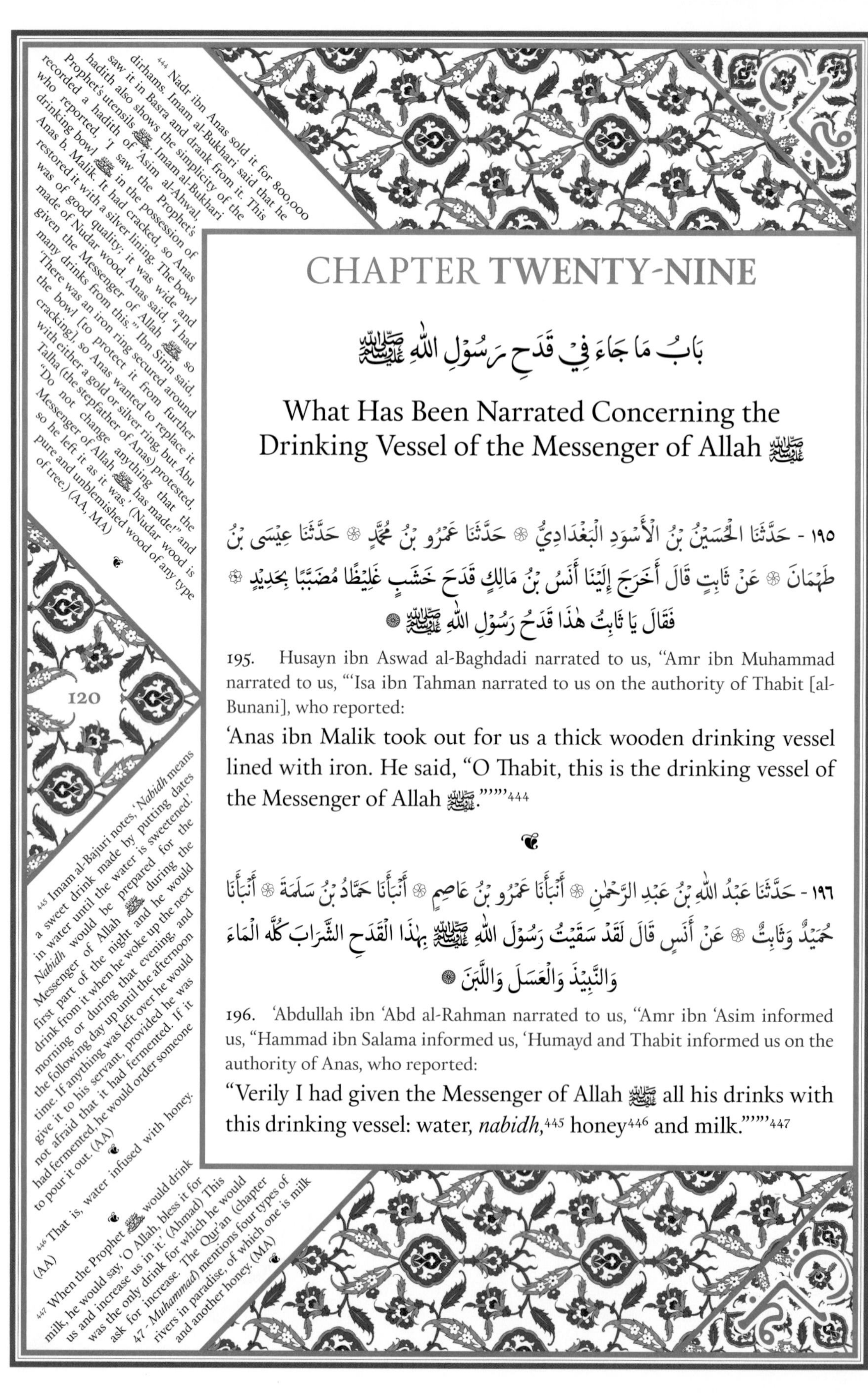

CHAPTER TWENTY-NINE

بَابُ مَا جَاءَ فِي قَدَحِ رَسُولِ اللهِ ﷺ

What Has Been Narrated Concerning the Drinking Vessel of the Messenger of Allah ﷺ

١٩٥ - حَدَّثَنَا الْحُسَيْنُ بْنُ الْأَسْوَدِ الْبَغْدَادِيُّ ۞ حَدَّثَنَا عَمْرُو بْنُ مُحَمَّدٍ ۞ حَدَّثَنَا عِيسَى بْنُ طَهْمَانَ ۞ عَنْ ثَابِتٍ قَالَ أَخْرَجَ إِلَيْنَا أَنَسُ بْنُ مَالِكٍ قَدَحَ خَشَبٍ غَلِيظًا مُضَبَّبًا بِحَدِيدٍ ۞ فَقَالَ يَا ثَابِتُ هٰذَا قَدَحُ رَسُولِ اللهِ ﷺ ۞

195. Husayn ibn Aswad al-Baghdadi narrated to us, "Amr ibn Muhammad narrated to us, "'Isa ibn Tahman narrated to us on the authority of Thabit [al-Bunani], who reported:

'Anas ibn Malik took out for us a thick wooden drinking vessel lined with iron. He said, "O Thabit, this is the drinking vessel of the Messenger of Allah ﷺ."'""[444]

١٩٦ - حَدَّثَنَا عَبْدُ اللهِ بْنُ عَبْدِ الرَّحْمٰنِ ۞ أَنْبَأَنَا عَمْرُو بْنُ عَاصِمٍ ۞ أَنْبَأَنَا حَمَّادُ بْنُ سَلَمَةَ ۞ أَنْبَأَنَا حُمَيْدٌ وَثَابِتٌ ۞ عَنْ أَنَسٍ قَالَ لَقَدْ سَقَيْتُ رَسُولَ اللهِ ﷺ بِهٰذَا الْقَدَحِ الشَّرَابَ كُلَّهُ الْمَاءَ وَالنَّبِيذَ وَالْعَسَلَ وَاللَّبَنَ ۞

196. 'Abdullah ibn 'Abd al-Rahman narrated to us, "Amr ibn 'Asim informed us, "Hammad ibn Salama informed us, 'Humayd and Thabit informed us on the authority of Anas, who reported:

"Verily I had given the Messenger of Allah ﷺ all his drinks with this drinking vessel: water, *nabidh*,[445] honey[446] and milk."'""[447]

[444] Nadr ibn Anas sold it for 800,000 dirhams. Imam al-Bukhari said that he saw it in Basra and drank from it. This hadith also shows the simplicity of the Prophet's utensils ﷺ. Imam al-Bukhari recorded a hadith of 'Asim al-Ahwal, who reported, 'I saw the Prophet's drinking bowl ﷺ in the possession of Anas b. Malik. It had cracked, so Anas restored it with a silver lining. The bowl was of good quality; it was wide and made of Nudar wood. Anas said, 'I had given the Messenger of Allah ﷺ so many drinks from this.'' Ibn Sirin said, 'There was an iron ring secured around the bowl [to protect it from further cracking], so Anas wanted to replace it with either a gold or silver ring, but Abu Talha (the stepfather of Anas) protested, 'Do not change anything that the Messenger of Allah ﷺ has made!' and so he left it as it was.' (Nudar wood is pure and unblemished wood of any type of tree.) (AA, MA)

[445] Imam al-Bajuri notes, '*Nabidh* means a sweet drink made by putting dates in water until the water is sweetened'. *Nabidh* would be prepared for the Messenger of Allah ﷺ during the first part of the night and he would drink from it when he woke up the next morning or during that evening, and the following day up until the afternoon time. If anything was left over he would give it to his servant, provided he was not afraid that it had fermented. If it had fermented, he would order someone to pour it out. (AA)

[446] That is, water infused with honey. (AA)

[447] When the Prophet ﷺ would drink milk, he would say, 'O Allah, bless it for us and increase us in it.' (Ahmad) This was the only drink for which he would ask for increase. The Qur'an (chapter 47 - *Muhammad*) mentions four types of rivers in paradise, of which one is milk and another honey. (MA)

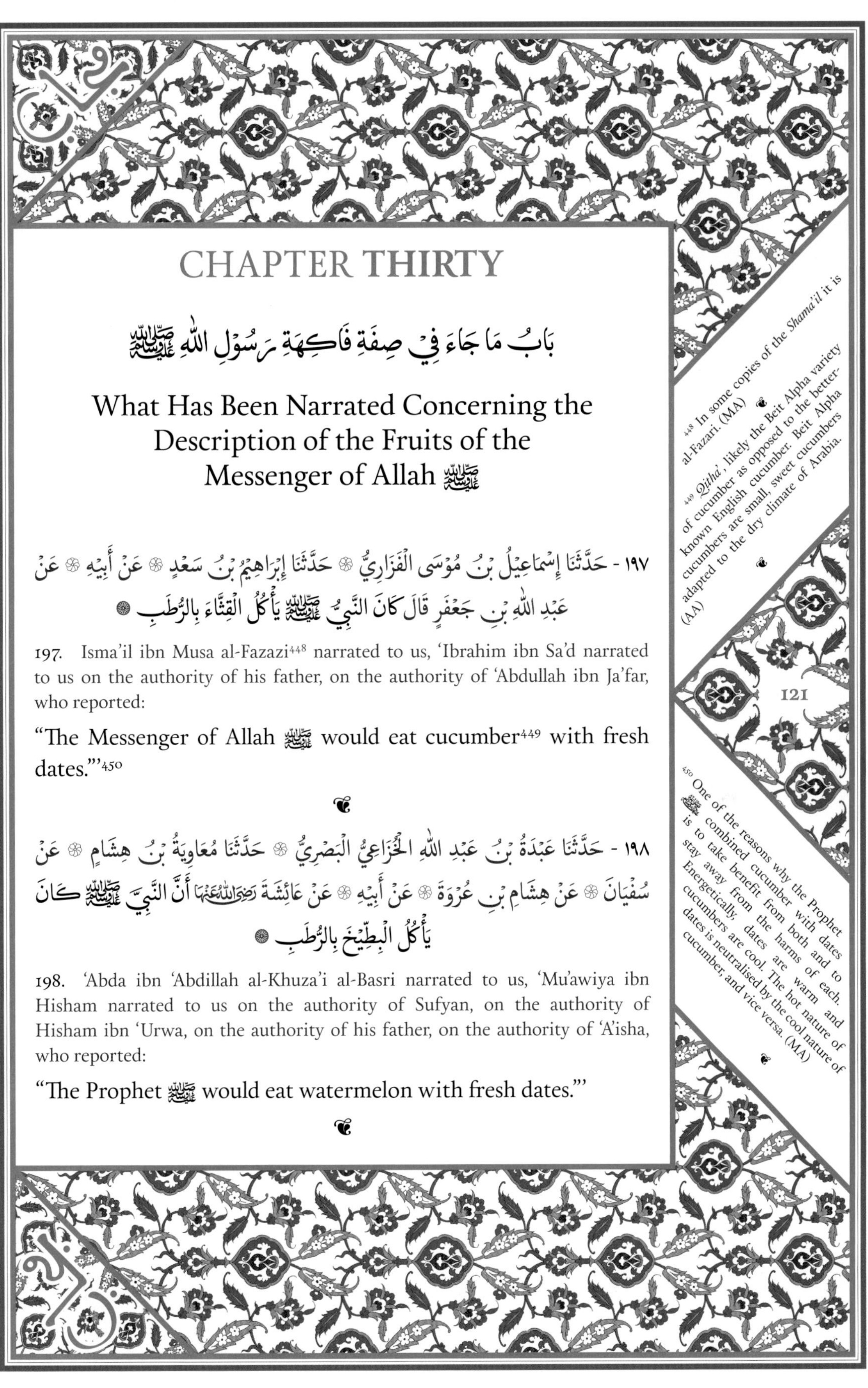

CHAPTER THIRTY

بَابُ مَا جَاءَ فِي صِفَةِ فَاكِهَةِ رَسُولِ اللهِ ﷺ

What Has Been Narrated Concerning the Description of the Fruits of the Messenger of Allah ﷺ

١٩٧ - حَدَّثَنَا إِسْمَاعِيلُ بْنُ مُوسَى الْفَزَارِيُّ ۞ حَدَّثَنَا إِبْرَاهِيمُ بْنُ سَعْدٍ ۞ عَنْ أَبِيهِ ۞ عَنْ عَبْدِ اللهِ بْنِ جَعْفَرٍ قَالَ كَانَ النَّبِيُّ ﷺ يَأْكُلُ الْقِثَّاءَ بِالرُّطَبِ ۞

197. Isma'il ibn Musa al-Fazazi[448] narrated to us, 'Ibrahim ibn Sa'd narrated to us on the authority of his father, on the authority of 'Abdullah ibn Ja'far, who reported:

"The Messenger of Allah ﷺ would eat cucumber[449] with fresh dates."'[450]

١٩٨ - حَدَّثَنَا عَبْدَةُ بْنُ عَبْدِ اللهِ الْخُزَاعِيُّ الْبَصْرِيُّ ۞ حَدَّثَنَا مُعَاوِيَةُ بْنُ هِشَامٍ ۞ عَنْ سُفْيَانَ ۞ عَنْ هِشَامِ بْنِ عُرْوَةَ ۞ عَنْ أَبِيهِ ۞ عَنْ عَائِشَةَ رَضِيَ اللهُ عَنْهَا أَنَّ النَّبِيَّ ﷺ كَانَ يَأْكُلُ الْبِطِّيخَ بِالرُّطَبِ ۞

198. 'Abda ibn 'Abdillah al-Khuza'i al-Basri narrated to us, 'Mu'awiya ibn Hisham narrated to us on the authority of Sufyan, on the authority of Hisham ibn 'Urwa, on the authority of his father, on the authority of 'A'isha, who reported:

"The Prophet ﷺ would eat watermelon with fresh dates."'

[448] In some copies of the *Shama'il* it is al-Fazari. (MA)

[449] *Qitha'*, likely the Beit Alpha variety of cucumber as opposed to the better-known English cucumber. Beit Alpha cucumbers are small, sweet cucumbers adapted to the dry climate of Arabia. (AA)

[450] One of the reasons why the Prophet ﷺ combined cucumber with dates is to take benefit from both and to stay away from the harms of each. Energetically, dates are warm and cucumbers are cool. The hot nature of dates is neutralised by the cool nature of cucumber, and vice versa. (MA)

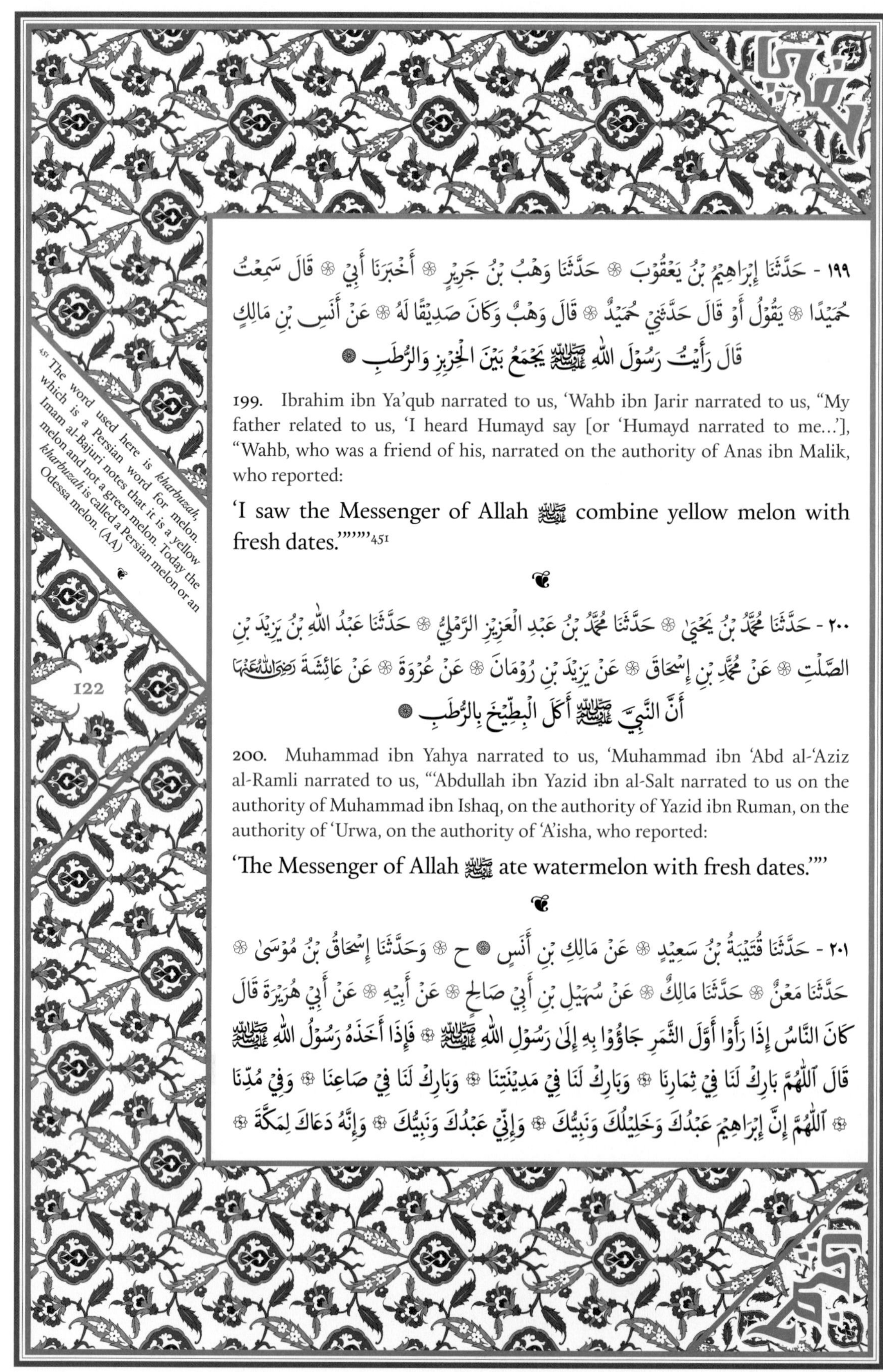

١٩٩ - حَدَّثَنَا إِبْرَاهِيمُ بْنُ يَعْقُوبَ ۞ حَدَّثَنَا وَهْبُ بْنُ جَرِيرٍ ۞ أَخْبَرَنَا أَبِي ۞ قَالَ سَمِعْتُ حُمَيْدًا ۞ يَقُولُ أَوْ قَالَ حَدَّثَنِي حُمَيْدٌ ۞ قَالَ وَهْبٌ وَكَانَ صَدِيقًا لَهُ ۞ عَنْ أَنَسِ بْنِ مَالِكٍ قَالَ رَأَيْتُ رَسُولَ اللهِ ﷺ يَجْمَعُ بَيْنَ الْخِرْبِزِ وَالرُّطَبِ ۞

199. Ibrahim ibn Ya'qub narrated to us, 'Wahb ibn Jarir narrated to us, "My father related to us, 'I heard Humayd say [or 'Humayd narrated to me...'], "Wahb, who was a friend of his, narrated on the authority of Anas ibn Malik, who reported:

'I saw the Messenger of Allah ﷺ combine yellow melon with fresh dates.''''''[451]

١٩٩ - حَدَّثَنَا مُحَمَّدُ بْنُ يَحْيَىٰ ۞ حَدَّثَنَا مُحَمَّدُ بْنُ عَبْدِ الْعَزِيزِ الرَّمْلِيُّ ۞ حَدَّثَنَا عَبْدُ اللهِ بْنُ يَزِيدَ بْنِ الصَّلْتِ ۞ عَنْ مُحَمَّدِ بْنِ إِسْحَاقَ ۞ عَنْ يَزِيدَ بْنِ رُومَانَ ۞ عَنْ عُرْوَةَ ۞ عَنْ عَائِشَةَ رَضِيَ اللهُ عَنْهَا أَنَّ النَّبِيَّ ﷺ أَكَلَ الْبِطِّيخَ بِالرُّطَبِ ۞

200. Muhammad ibn Yahya narrated to us, 'Muhammad ibn 'Abd al-'Aziz al-Ramli narrated to us, "'Abdullah ibn Yazid ibn al-Salt narrated to us on the authority of Muhammad ibn Ishaq, on the authority of Yazid ibn Ruman, on the authority of 'Urwa, on the authority of 'A'isha, who reported:

'The Messenger of Allah ﷺ ate watermelon with fresh dates.'''

٢٠١ - حَدَّثَنَا قُتَيْبَةُ بْنُ سَعِيدٍ ۞ عَنْ مَالِكِ بْنِ أَنَسٍ ۞ ح ۞ وَحَدَّثَنَا إِسْحَاقُ بْنُ مُوسَىٰ ۞ حَدَّثَنَا مَعْنٌ ۞ حَدَّثَنَا مَالِكٌ ۞ عَنْ سُهَيْلِ بْنِ أَبِي صَالِحٍ ۞ عَنْ أَبِيهِ ۞ عَنْ أَبِي هُرَيْرَةَ قَالَ كَانَ النَّاسُ إِذَا رَأَوْا أَوَّلَ الثَّمَرِ جَاؤُوا بِهِ إِلَىٰ رَسُولِ اللهِ ﷺ ۞ فَإِذَا أَخَذَهُ رَسُولُ اللهِ ﷺ قَالَ اللَّهُمَّ بَارِكْ لَنَا فِي ثِمَارِنَا ۞ وَبَارِكْ لَنَا فِي مَدِينَتِنَا ۞ وَبَارِكْ لَنَا فِي صَاعِنَا ۞ وَفِي مُدِّنَا ۞ اللَّهُمَّ إِنَّ إِبْرَاهِيمَ عَبْدُكَ وَخَلِيلُكَ وَنَبِيُّكَ ۞ وَإِنِّي عَبْدُكَ وَنَبِيُّكَ ۞ وَإِنَّهُ دَعَاكَ لِمَكَّةَ ۞

[451] The word used here is *kharbuzah*, which is a Persian word for melon. Imam al-Bajuri notes that it is a yellow melon and not a green melon. Today the *kharbuzah* is called a Persian melon or an Odessa melon. (AA)

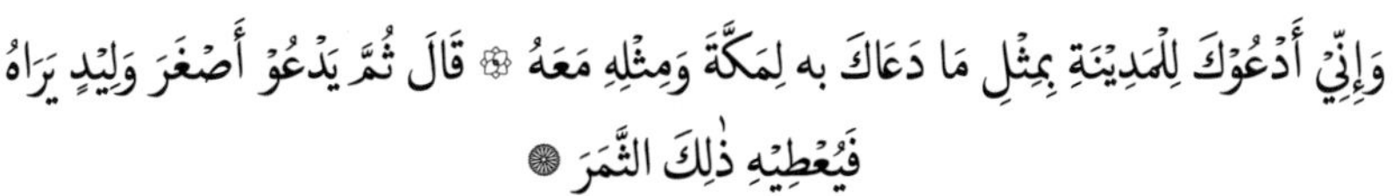

وَإِنِّي أَدْعُوكَ لِلْمَدِينَةِ بِمِثْلِ مَا دَعَاكَ بِهِ لِمَكَّةَ وَمِثْلِهِ مَعَهُ ۞ قَالَ ثُمَّ يَدْعُو أَصْغَرَ وَلِيدٍ يَرَاهُ فَيُعْطِيهِ ذَٰلِكَ الثَّمَرَ ۞

201. Qutayba ibn Sa'id narrated to us on the authority of Anas ibn Malik... [and in another chain of transmission][452] Ishaq ibn Musa narrated to us, 'Ma'n narrated to us, "Malik narrated to us on the authority of Suhayl ibn Abi Salih, on the authority of his father, on the authority of Abu Hurayra, who reported:

'When people would see the new fruits [of the harvest],[453] they would bring them to the Messenger of Allah ﷺ.[454] When the Messenger of Allah ﷺ would take the fruit, he would supplicate, "O Allah! Bless our fruit, bless our Medina and bless our *sa'a* and our *mudd*.[455] O Allah! Verily Ibrahim is Your servant and Your intimate friend (*khalil*)[456] and Your Prophet—and I am Your servant and Your Prophet. He supplicated to You for Mecca, and I supplicate to You for Medina with the likes of which he supplicated to You regarding Mecca, and the likes thereof along with it."[457] Then he would call for the youngest child he saw and give him[458] some of that fruit."''[459]

❦

٢٠٢ - حَدَّثَنَا مُحَمَّدُ بْنُ حُمَيْدٍ الرَّازِيُّ ۞ أَنْبَأَنَا إِبْرَاهِيمُ بْنُ الْمُخْتَارِ ۞ عَنْ مُحَمَّدِ بْنِ إِسْحَاقَ ۞ عَنْ أَبِي عُبَيْدَةَ بْنِ مُحَمَّدِ بْنِ عَمَّارِ بْنِ يَاسِرٍ ۞ عَنِ الرُّبَيِّعِ بِنْتِ مُعَوِّذٍ ابْنِ عَفْرَاءَ قَالَتْ بَعَثَنِي مُعَاذٌ بِقِنَاعٍ مِنْ رُطَبٍ وَعَلَيْهِ أَجْرٍ[٤٦٠] مِنْ قِثَّاءٍ زُغْبٍ ۞ وَكَانَ النَّبِيُّ ﷺ يُحِبُّ الْقِثَّاءَ فَأَتَيْتُهُ بِهِ ۞ وَعِنْدَهُ حِلْيَةٌ قَدْ قَدِمَتْ عَلَيْهِ مِنَ الْبَحْرَيْنِ ۞ فَمَلَأَ يَدَهُ مِنْهَا فَأَعْطَانِيهِ ۞

202. Muhammad ibn Humayd al-Razi narrated to us, 'Ibrahim ibn al-Mukhtar informed us on the authority of Muhammad ibn Ishaq, on the authority of Abu 'Ubayda ibn Muhammad ibn 'Ammar ibn Yasir, on the authority of Rubayyi' bint al-Mu'awwidh ibn 'Afra', who reported:

452 At this point in the text, the Arabic letter *ha'* is placed to indicate the beginning of the second chain. (MA)

453 Imam al-Suyuti recorded in *al-Jami al-Saghir*, 'When newly picked fruits were brought to the Prophet ﷺ, he would place them on his blessed eyes and lips and supplicate, "O Allah, as You have shown us the first of it, show us the last of it!" and then he would give them to the children around him.' (MA)

454 Because he was the most beloved person in the world to them, they desired to bring their most precious and beloved things to him in order to attain the pleasure of his heart and the blessings of his supplications. (MA)

455 A *sa'a* is 2.03 litres and a *mudd* is 0.51 litres. (AA)

456 The Prophet Muhammad ﷺ is also the 'intimate friend of Allah' (*Khalilullah*), but in this particular prayer he did not mention this title for himself. That was either because of his love, honour and reverence for his grandfather, Prophet Ibrahim ﷺ, or because of his humility before his Lord; Allah had granted him a station far beyond the rank of a *Khalil* and his nobility surpassed all of the Prophets and Messengers. The final station of every Prophet is just the beginning station of Sayyiduna Muhammad ﷺ. (MA)

457 That is, 'I supplicate to You for more than what Ibrahim ﷺ supplicated for Mecca.' The two greatest cities on earth are Mecca and Medina. According to the opinions of Imam Abu Hanifa, Imam al-Shafi'i and Imam Ahmad, Mecca is superior to Medina, but according to Imam Malik, Medina has greater virtue. Despite this difference of opinion, scholars are in unanimous agreement that the greatest piece of the created universe is the earth which touches the noble body of the Messenger of Allah ﷺ in his blessed grave, for it is better than the heavens and the earth. (AA, MA)

458 Here we see the extreme generosity, kindness and beauty of the Messenger of Allah ﷺ, for he chose not to take from the fruits himself even though he was the leader of mankind; rather, he chose to bless the youngest of the city with that honour. From the characteristics of the people of nobility and pure souls is that they do not desire to enjoy anything until they see all those around them being given priority and preference. (MA)

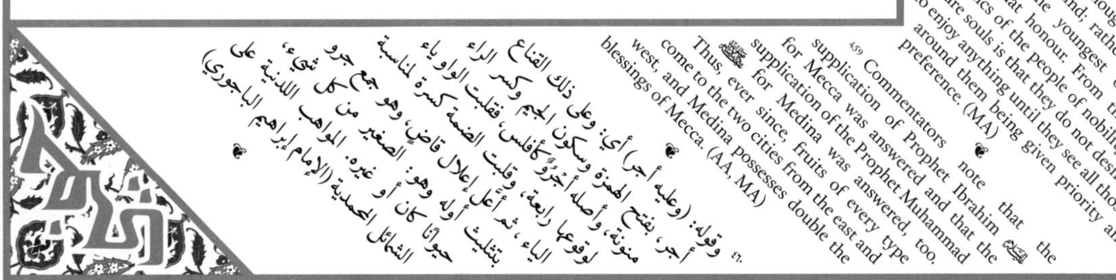

459 Commentators note that the supplication of Prophet Ibrahim ﷺ for Mecca was answered and that the supplication of the Prophet Muhammad ﷺ for Medina was answered, too. Thus, ever since, fruits of every type come to the two cities from the east and west, and Medina possesses double the blessings of Mecca. (AA, MA)

٤٦٠ قوله: (وعليه أجر) أي: وعلى ذلك القناع أجر، بفتح الهمزة وسكون الجيم وكسر الراء منونة، وأصله أجرُوٌ كأفلس، فقلبت الواو ياء لوقوعها رابعة، وقلبت الضمة كسرة لمناسبة الياء، ثم أُعل إعلال قاض، وهو جمع جرو بتثليث أوله وهو: الصغير من كل شيء، حيوانا كان أو غيره. المواهب اللدنية على الشمائل المحمدية (الإمام إبراهيم الباجوري)

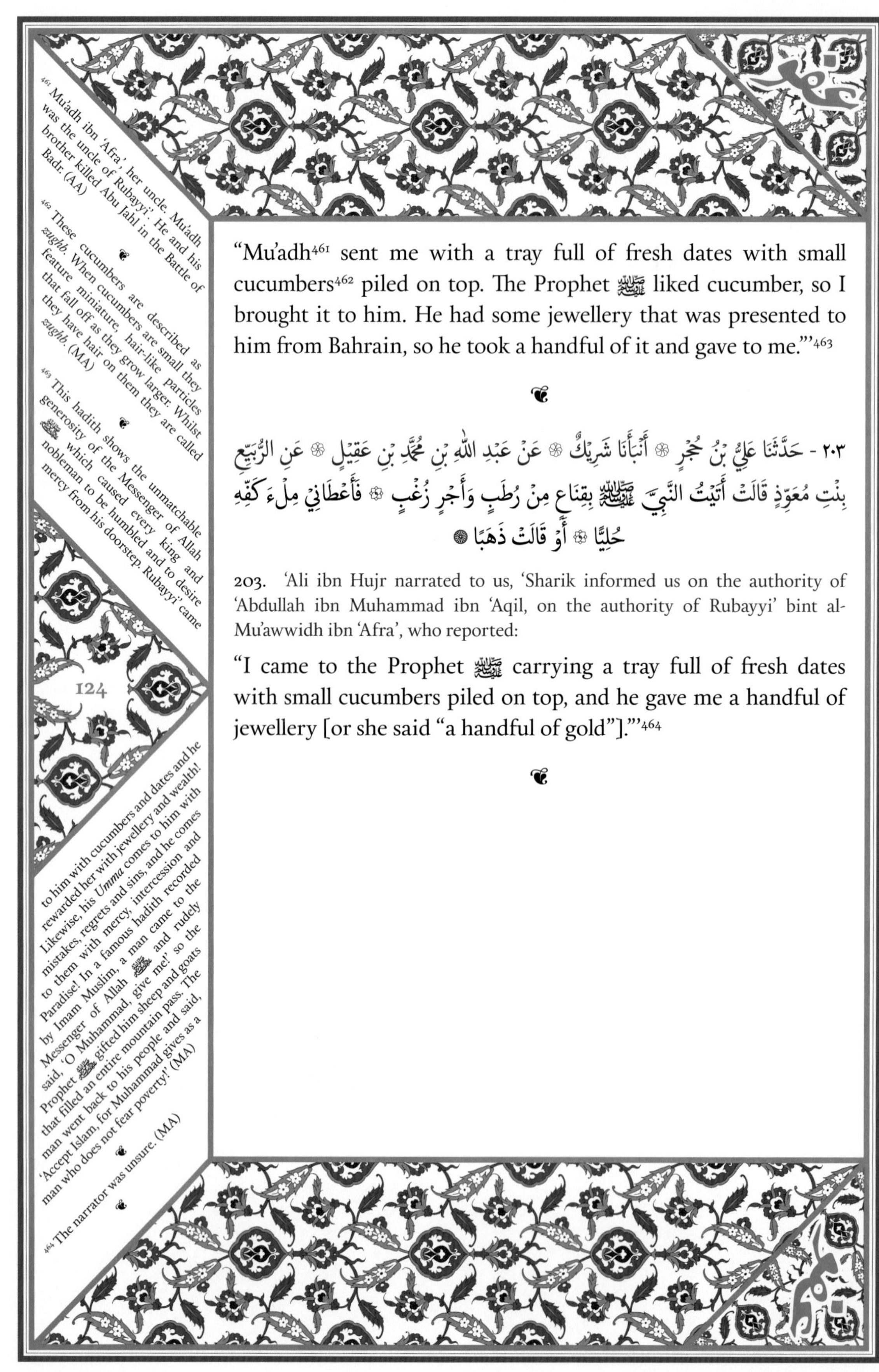

"Mu'adh[461] sent me with a tray full of fresh dates with small cucumbers[462] piled on top. The Prophet ﷺ liked cucumber, so I brought it to him. He had some jewellery that was presented to him from Bahrain, so he took a handful of it and gave to me."'[463]

٢٠٣ - حَدَّثَنَا عَلِيُّ بْنُ حُجْرٍ ۞ أَنبَأَنَا شَرِيكٌ ۞ عَنْ عَبْدِ اللهِ بْنِ مُحَمَّدِ بْنِ عَقِيلٍ ۞ عَنِ الرُّبَيِّعِ بِنْتِ مُعَوِّذٍ قَالَتْ أَتَيْتُ النَّبِيَّ ﷺ بِقِنَاعٍ مِنْ رُطَبٍ وَأَجْرٍ زُغْبٍ ۞ فَأَعْطَانِي مِلْءَ كَفِّهِ حُلِيًّا ۞ أَوْ قَالَتْ ذَهَبًا ۞

203. 'Ali ibn Hujr narrated to us, 'Sharik informed us on the authority of 'Abdullah ibn Muhammad ibn 'Aqil, on the authority of Rubayyi' bint al-Mu'awwidh ibn 'Afra', who reported:

"I came to the Prophet ﷺ carrying a tray full of fresh dates with small cucumbers piled on top, and he gave me a handful of jewellery [or she said "a handful of gold"]."'[464]

[461] Mu'adh ibn 'Afra', her uncle. Mu'adh was the uncle of Rubayyi'. He and his brother killed Abu Jahl in the Battle of Badr. (AA)

[462] These cucumbers are described as *zughb*. When cucumbers are small they feature miniature, hair-like particles that fall off as they grow larger. Whilst they have hair on them they are called *zughb*. (MA)

[463] This hadith shows the unmatchable generosity of the Messenger of Allah ﷺ which caused every king and nobleman to be humbled and to desire mercy from his doorstep. Rubayyi' came to him with cucumbers and dates and he rewarded her with jewellery and wealth! Likewise, his *Umma* comes to him with mistakes, regrets and sins, and he comes to them with mercy, intercession and Paradise! In a famous hadith recorded by Imam Muslim, a man came to the Messenger of Allah ﷺ and rudely said, 'O Muhammad, give me!' so the Prophet ﷺ gifted him sheep and goats that filled an entire mountain pass. The man went back to his people and said, 'Accept Islam, for Muhammad gives as a man who does not fear poverty!' (MA)

[464] The narrator was unsure. (MA)

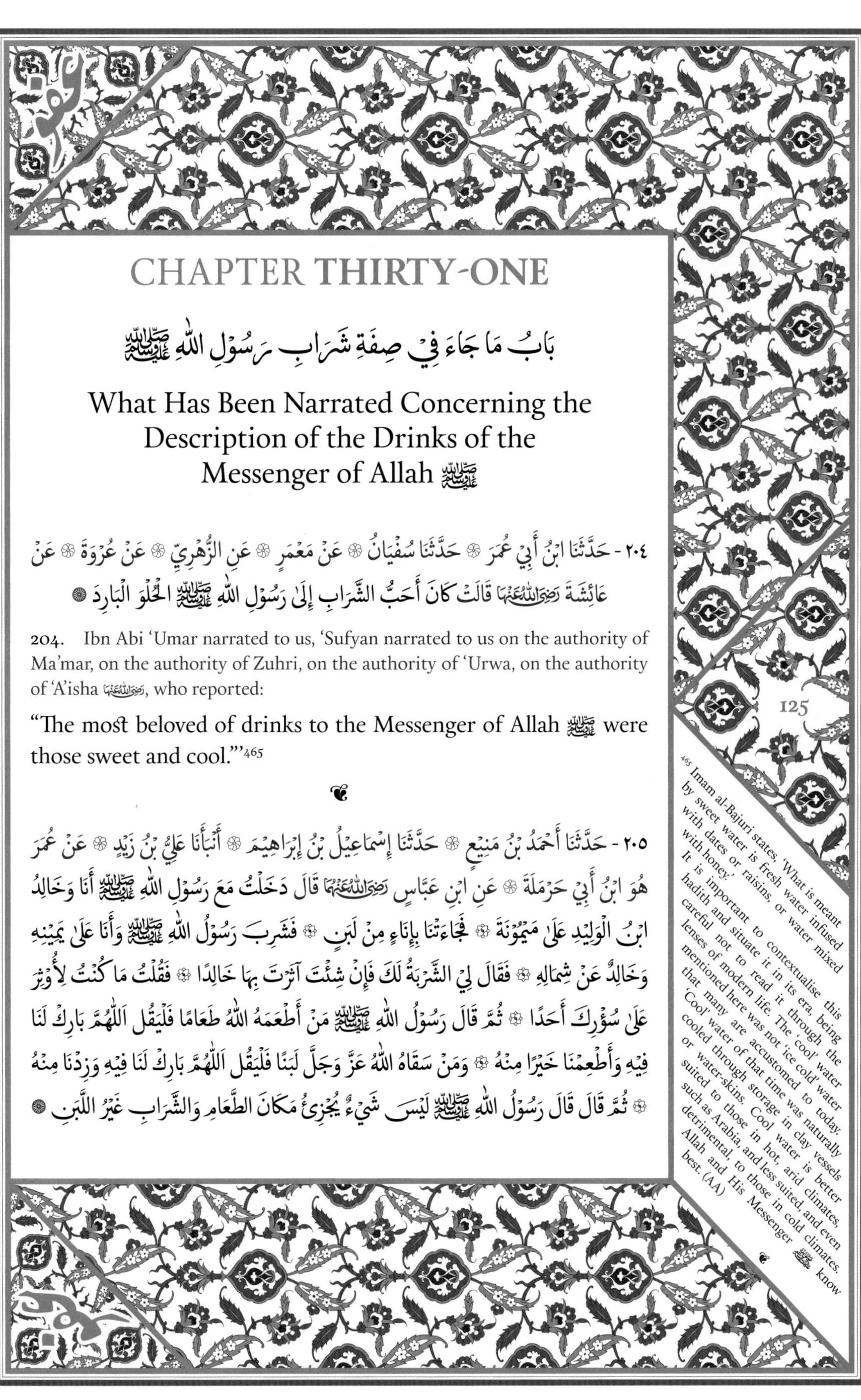

CHAPTER THIRTY-ONE

بَابُ مَا جَاءَ فِي صِفَةِ شَرَابِ رَسُولِ اللَّهِ ﷺ

What Has Been Narrated Concerning the Description of the Drinks of the Messenger of Allah ﷺ

٢٠٤ - حَدَّثَنَا ابْنُ أَبِي عُمَرَ ❀ حَدَّثَنَا سُفْيَانُ ❀ عَنْ مَعْمَرٍ ❀ عَنِ الزُّهْرِيِّ ❀ عَنْ عُرْوَةَ ❀ عَنْ عَائِشَةَ رَضِيَ اللَّهُ عَنْهَا قَالَتْ كَانَ أَحَبُّ الشَّرَابِ إِلَى رَسُولِ اللَّهِ ﷺ الْحُلْوَ الْبَارِدَ ❀

204. Ibn Abi 'Umar narrated to us, 'Sufyan narrated to us on the authority of Ma'mar, on the authority of Zuhri, on the authority of 'Urwa, on the authority of 'A'isha رضي الله عنها, who reported:

"The most beloved of drinks to the Messenger of Allah ﷺ were those sweet and cool."'[465]

٢٠٥ - حَدَّثَنَا أَحْمَدُ بْنُ مَنِيعٍ ❀ حَدَّثَنَا إِسْمَاعِيلُ بْنُ إِبْرَاهِيمَ ❀ أَنْبَأَنَا عَلِيُّ بْنُ زَيْدٍ ❀ عَنْ عُمَرَ هُوَ ابْنُ أَبِي حَرْمَلَةَ ❀ عَنِ ابْنِ عَبَّاسٍ رَضِيَ اللَّهُ عَنْهُمَا قَالَ دَخَلْتُ مَعَ رَسُولِ اللَّهِ ﷺ أَنَا وَخَالِدُ ابْنُ الْوَلِيدِ عَلَى مَيْمُونَةَ ❀ فَجَاءَتْنَا بِإِنَاءٍ مِنْ لَبَنٍ ❀ فَشَرِبَ رَسُولُ اللَّهِ ﷺ وَأَنَا عَلَى يَمِينِهِ وَخَالِدٌ عَنْ شِمَالِهِ ❀ فَقَالَ لِي الشَّرْبَةُ لَكَ فَإِنْ شِئْتَ آثَرْتَ بِهَا خَالِدًا ❀ فَقُلْتُ مَا كُنْتُ لِأُوثِرَ عَلَى سُؤْرِكَ أَحَدًا ❀ ثُمَّ قَالَ رَسُولُ اللَّهِ ﷺ مَنْ أَطْعَمَهُ اللَّهُ طَعَامًا فَلْيَقُلِ اللَّهُمَّ بَارِكْ لَنَا فِيهِ وَأَطْعِمْنَا خَيْرًا مِنْهُ ❀ وَمَنْ سَقَاهُ اللَّهُ عَزَّ وَجَلَّ لَبَنًا فَلْيَقُلِ اللَّهُمَّ بَارِكْ لَنَا فِيهِ وَزِدْنَا مِنْهُ ❀ ثُمَّ قَالَ قَالَ رَسُولُ اللَّهِ ﷺ لَيْسَ شَيْءٌ يُجْزِئُ مَكَانَ الطَّعَامِ وَالشَّرَابِ غَيْرُ اللَّبَنِ ❀

[465] Imam al-Bajuri states, 'What is meant by sweet water is fresh water infused with dates or raisins, or water mixed with honey.' It is important to contextualise this hadith and situate it in its era, being careful not to read it through the lenses of modern life. The 'cool' water mentioned here was not 'ice cold' water that many are accustomed to today. 'Cool' water of that time was naturally cooled through storage in clay vessels or water-skins. Cool water is better suited to those in hot, arid climates, such as Arabia, and less suited, and even detrimental, to those in cold climates. Allah and His Messenger ﷺ know best. (AA)

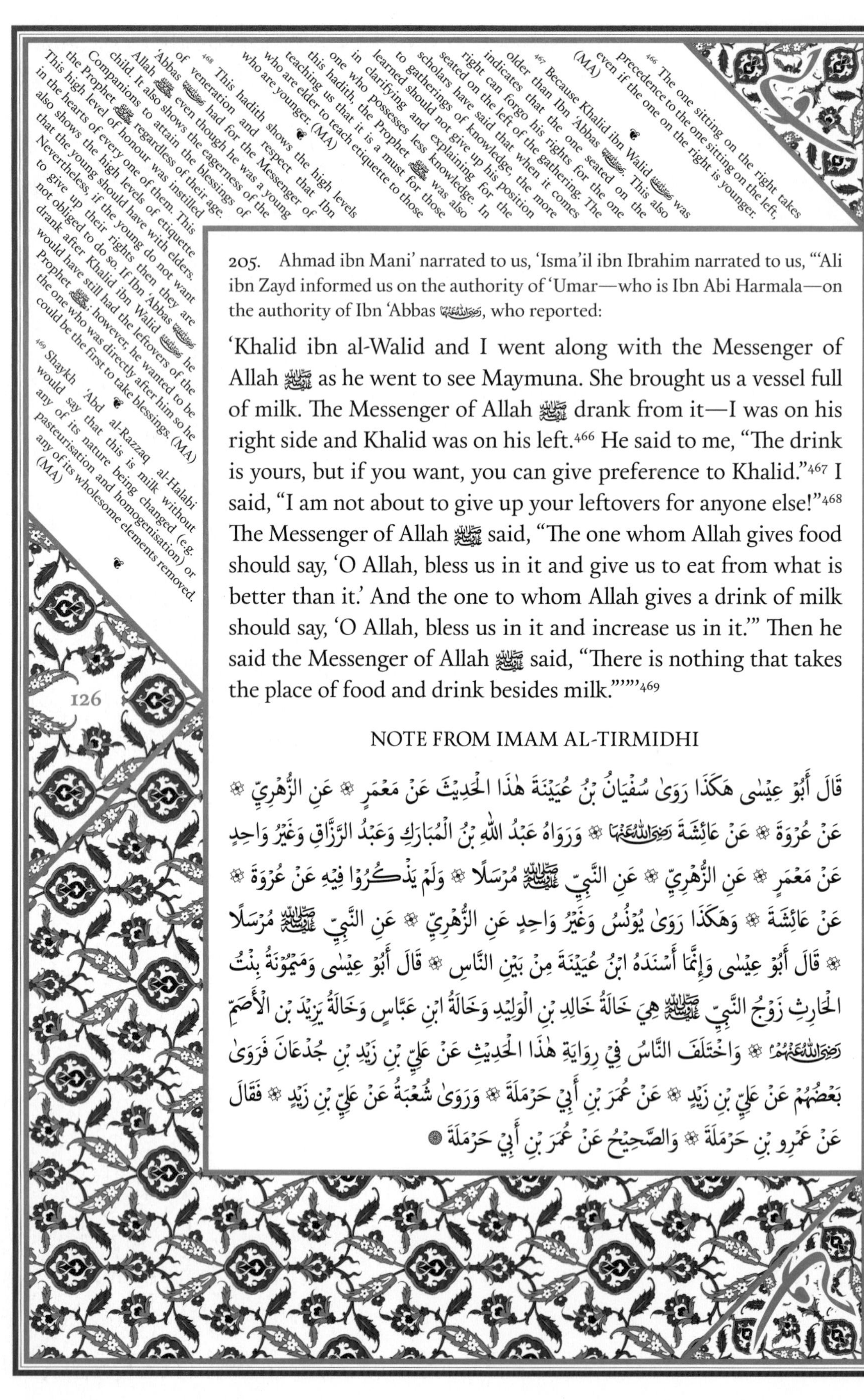

205. Ahmad ibn Mani' narrated to us, 'Isma'il ibn Ibrahim narrated to us, "'Ali ibn Zayd informed us on the authority of 'Umar—who is Ibn Abi Harmala—on the authority of Ibn 'Abbas رضي الله عنهما, who reported:

'Khalid ibn al-Walid and I went along with the Messenger of Allah ﷺ as he went to see Maymuna. She brought us a vessel full of milk. The Messenger of Allah ﷺ drank from it—I was on his right side and Khalid was on his left.[466] He said to me, "The drink is yours, but if you want, you can give preference to Khalid."[467] I said, "I am not about to give up your leftovers for anyone else!"[468] The Messenger of Allah ﷺ said, "The one whom Allah gives food should say, 'O Allah, bless us in it and give us to eat from what is better than it.' And the one to whom Allah gives a drink of milk should say, 'O Allah, bless us in it and increase us in it.'" Then he said the Messenger of Allah ﷺ said, "There is nothing that takes the place of food and drink besides milk."'"[469]

NOTE FROM IMAM AL-TIRMIDHI

قَالَ أَبُو عِيسَىٰ هَكَذَا رَوَىٰ سُفْيَانُ بْنُ عُيَيْنَةَ هٰذَا الْحَدِيثَ عَنْ مَعْمَرٍ ❁ عَنِ الزُّهْرِيِّ ❁ عَنْ عُرْوَةَ ❁ عَنْ عَائِشَةَ رَضِيَ اللهُ عَنْهَا ❁ وَرَوَاهُ عَبْدُ اللهِ بْنُ الْمُبَارَكِ وَعَبْدُ الرَّزَّاقِ وَغَيْرُ وَاحِدٍ عَنْ مَعْمَرٍ ❁ عَنِ الزُّهْرِيِّ ❁ عَنِ النَّبِيِّ ﷺ مُرْسَلًا ❁ وَلَمْ يَذْكُرُوا فِيهِ عَنْ عُرْوَةَ ❁ عَنْ عَائِشَةَ ❁ وَهَكَذَا رَوَىٰ يُونُسُ وَغَيْرُ وَاحِدٍ عَنِ الزُّهْرِيِّ ❁ عَنِ النَّبِيِّ ﷺ مُرْسَلًا ❁ قَالَ أَبُو عِيسَىٰ وَإِنَّمَا أَسْنَدَهُ ابْنُ عُيَيْنَةَ مِنْ بَيْنِ النَّاسِ ❁ قَالَ أَبُو عِيسَىٰ وَمَيْمُونَةُ بِنْتُ الْحَارِثِ زَوْجُ النَّبِيِّ ﷺ هِيَ خَالَةُ خَالِدِ بْنِ الْوَلِيدِ وَخَالَةُ ابْنِ عَبَّاسٍ وَخَالَةُ يَزِيدَ بْنِ الْأَصَمِّ رَضِيَ اللهُ عَنْهُمْ ❁ وَاخْتَلَفَ النَّاسُ فِي رِوَايَةِ هٰذَا الْحَدِيثِ عَنْ عَلِيِّ بْنِ زَيْدِ بْنِ جُدْعَانَ فَرَوَىٰ بَعْضُهُمْ عَنْ عَلِيِّ بْنِ زَيْدٍ ❁ عَنْ عُمَرَ بْنِ أَبِي حَرْمَلَةَ ❁ وَرَوَىٰ شُعْبَةُ عَنْ عَلِيِّ بْنِ زَيْدٍ ❁ فَقَالَ عَنْ عَمْرِو بْنِ حَرْمَلَةَ ❁ وَالصَّحِيحُ عَنْ عُمَرَ بْنِ أَبِي حَرْمَلَةَ ۞

466 The one sitting on the right takes precedence to the one sitting on the left, even if the one on the right is younger. (MA)

467 Because Khalid ibn Walid رضي الله عنه was older than Ibn 'Abbas رضي الله عنهما. This also indicates that the one seated on the right can forgo his rights for the one seated on the left of the gathering. The scholars have said that when it comes to gatherings of knowledge, the more learned should not give up his position in clarifying and explaining for the one who possesses less knowledge. In this hadith, the Prophet ﷺ was also teaching us that it is a must for those who are elder to teach etiquette to those who are younger. (MA)

468 This hadith shows the high levels of veneration and respect that Ibn 'Abbas رضي الله عنهما had for the Messenger of Allah ﷺ even though he was a young child. It also shows the eagerness of the Companions to attain the blessings of the Prophet ﷺ regardless of their age. This high level of honour was instilled in the hearts of every one of them. This also shows the high levels of etiquette that the young should have with elders. Nevertheless, if the young do not want to give up their rights then they are not obliged to do so. If Ibn 'Abbas رضي الله عنهما had drank after Khalid ibn Walid رضي الله عنه he would have still had the leftovers of the Prophet ﷺ; however, he wanted to be the one who was directly after him so he could be the first to take blessings. (MA)

469 Shaykh 'Abd al-Razzaq al-Halabi would say that this is milk without any of its nature being changed (e.g. pasteurisation and homogenisation) or any of its wholesome elements removed. (MA)

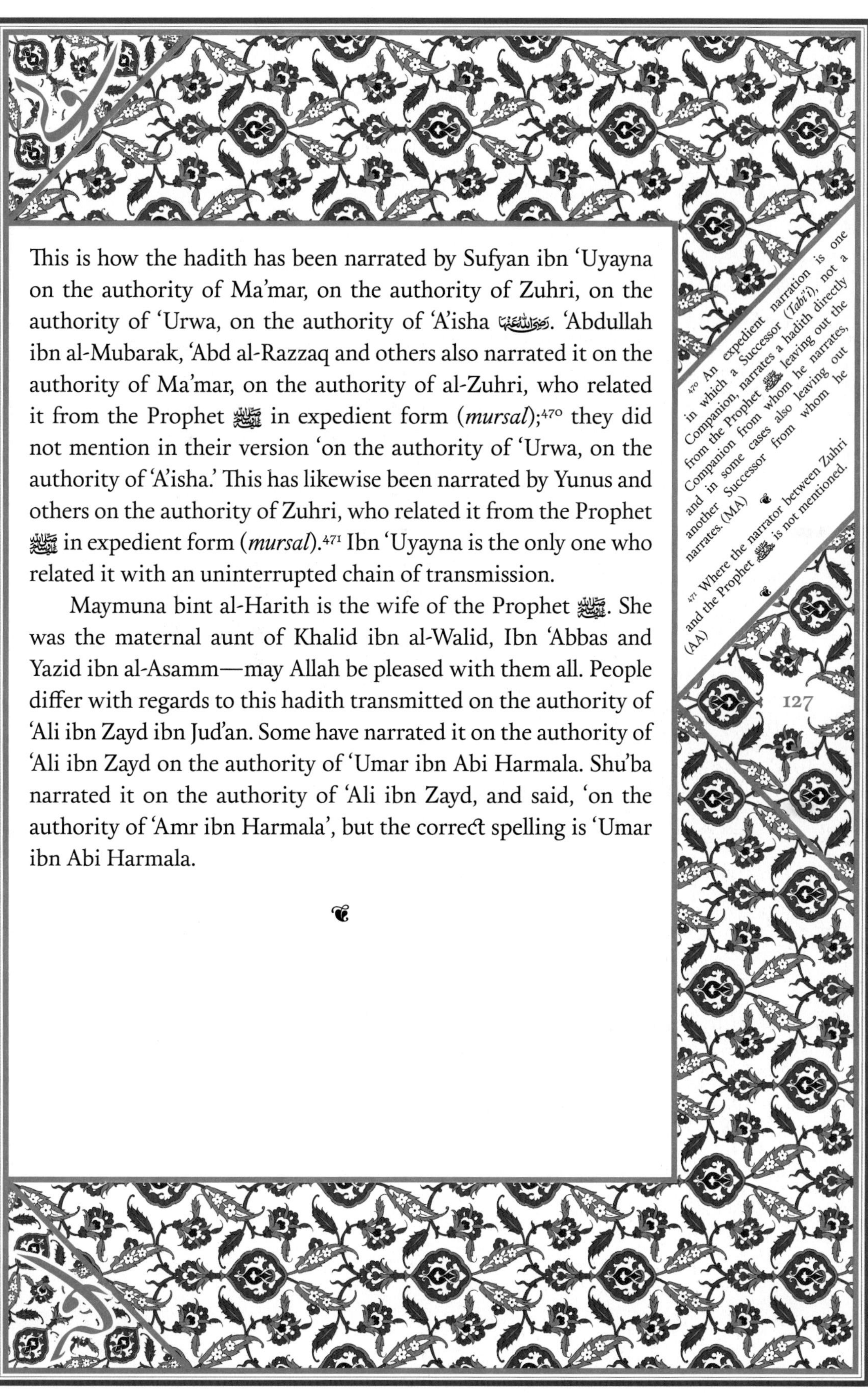

This is how the hadith has been narrated by Sufyan ibn 'Uyayna on the authority of Ma'mar, on the authority of Zuhri, on the authority of 'Urwa, on the authority of 'A'isha رضي الله عنها. 'Abdullah ibn al-Mubarak, 'Abd al-Razzaq and others also narrated it on the authority of Ma'mar, on the authority of al-Zuhri, who related it from the Prophet ﷺ in expedient form (*mursal*);[470] they did not mention in their version 'on the authority of 'Urwa, on the authority of 'A'isha.' This has likewise been narrated by Yunus and others on the authority of Zuhri, who related it from the Prophet ﷺ in expedient form (*mursal*).[471] Ibn 'Uyayna is the only one who related it with an uninterrupted chain of transmission.

Maymuna bint al-Harith is the wife of the Prophet ﷺ. She was the maternal aunt of Khalid ibn al-Walid, Ibn 'Abbas and Yazid ibn al-Asamm—may Allah be pleased with them all. People differ with regards to this hadith transmitted on the authority of 'Ali ibn Zayd ibn Jud'an. Some have narrated it on the authority of 'Ali ibn Zayd on the authority of 'Umar ibn Abi Harmala. Shu'ba narrated it on the authority of 'Ali ibn Zayd, and said, 'on the authority of 'Amr ibn Harmala', but the correct spelling is 'Umar ibn Abi Harmala.

❦

[470] An expedient narration is one in which a Successor (*Tabi'i*), not a Companion, narrates a hadith directly from the Prophet ﷺ leaving out the Companion from whom he narrates, and in some cases also leaving out another Successor from whom he narrates. (MA)

[471] Where the narrator between Zuhri and the Prophet ﷺ is not mentioned. (AA)

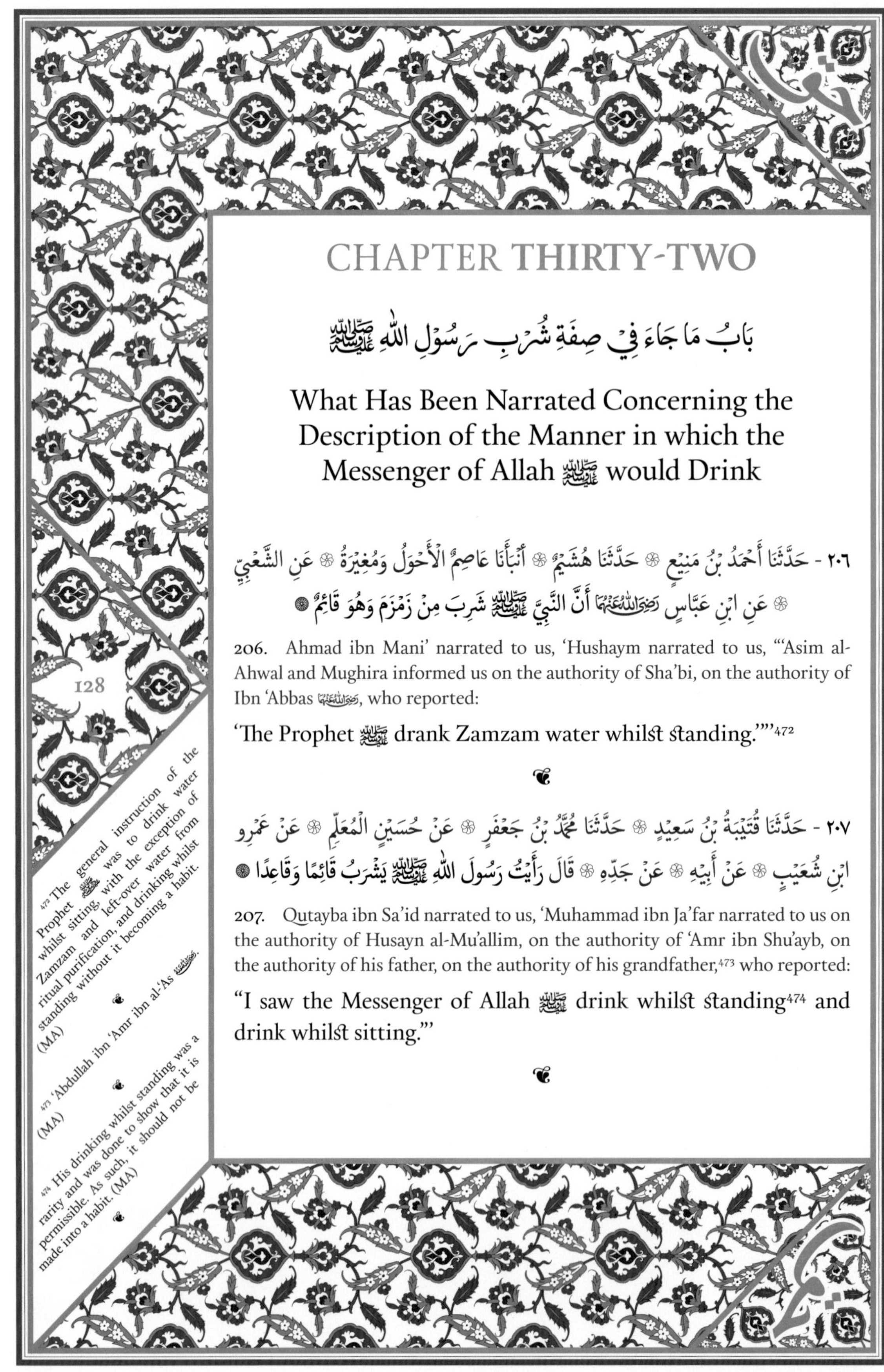

CHAPTER THIRTY-TWO

بَابُ مَا جَاءَ فِي صِفَةِ شُرْبِ رَسُولِ اللهِ ﷺ

What Has Been Narrated Concerning the Description of the Manner in which the Messenger of Allah ﷺ would Drink

٢٠٦ - حَدَّثَنَا أَحْمَدُ بْنُ مَنِيعٍ ۞ حَدَّثَنَا هُشَيْمٌ ۞ أَنْبَأَنَا عَاصِمٌ الْأَحْوَلُ وَمُغِيرَةُ ۞ عَنِ الشَّعْبِيِّ
۞ عَنِ ابْنِ عَبَّاسٍ رَضِيَ اللهُ عَنْهُمَا أَنَّ النَّبِيَّ ﷺ شَرِبَ مِنْ زَمْزَمَ وَهُوَ قَائِمٌ ۞

206. Ahmad ibn Mani' narrated to us, 'Hushaym narrated to us, "'Asim al-Ahwal and Mughira informed us on the authority of Sha'bi, on the authority of Ibn 'Abbas رضي الله عنهما, who reported:

'The Prophet ﷺ drank Zamzam water whilst standing.'"'[472]

❦

٢٠٧ - حَدَّثَنَا قُتَيْبَةُ بْنُ سَعِيدٍ ۞ حَدَّثَنَا مُحَمَّدُ بْنُ جَعْفَرٍ ۞ عَنْ حُسَيْنٍ الْمُعَلِّمِ ۞ عَنْ عَمْرِو
ابْنِ شُعَيْبٍ ۞ عَنْ أَبِيهِ ۞ عَنْ جَدِّهِ ۞ قَالَ رَأَيْتُ رَسُولَ اللهِ ﷺ يَشْرَبُ قَائِمًا وَقَاعِدًا ۞

207. Qutayba ibn Sa'id narrated to us, 'Muhammad ibn Ja'far narrated to us on the authority of Husayn al-Mu'allim, on the authority of 'Amr ibn Shu'ayb, on the authority of his father, on the authority of his grandfather,[473] who reported:

"I saw the Messenger of Allah ﷺ drink whilst standing[474] and drink whilst sitting."'

❦

[472] The general instruction of the Prophet ﷺ was to drink water whilst sitting, with the exception of Zamzam and left-over water from ritual purification, and drinking whilst standing without it becoming a habit. (MA)

[473] 'Abdullah ibn 'Amr ibn al-'As رضي الله عنهما. (MA)

[474] His drinking whilst standing was a rarity and was done to show that it is permissible. As such, it should not be made into a habit. (MA)

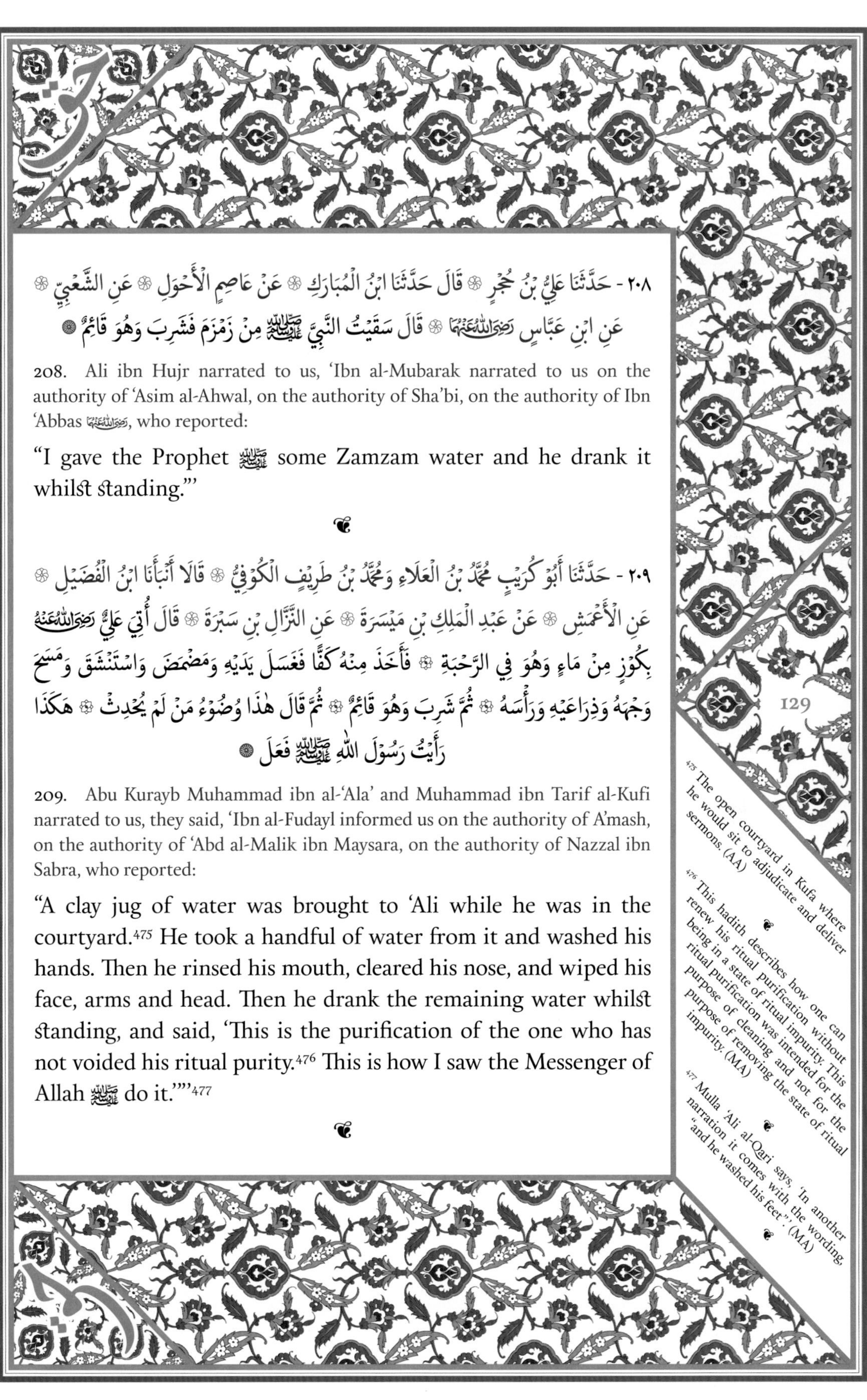

٢٠٨ - حَدَّثَنَا عَلِيُّ بْنُ حُجْرٍ ۞ قَالَ حَدَّثَنَا ابْنُ الْمُبَارَكِ ۞ عَنْ عَاصِمٍ الْأَحْوَلِ ۞ عَنِ الشَّعْبِيِّ ۞ عَنِ ابْنِ عَبَّاسٍ رَضِيَ اللَّهُ عَنْهُمَا ۞ قَالَ سَقَيْتُ النَّبِيَّ ﷺ مِنْ زَمْزَمَ فَشَرِبَ وَهُوَ قَائِمٌ ۞

208. Ali ibn Hujr narrated to us, 'Ibn al-Mubarak narrated to us on the authority of 'Asim al-Ahwal, on the authority of Sha'bi, on the authority of Ibn 'Abbas رضي الله عنهما, who reported:

"I gave the Prophet ﷺ some Zamzam water and he drank it whilst standing."'

٢٠٩ - حَدَّثَنَا أَبُو كُرَيْبٍ مُحَمَّدُ بْنُ الْعَلَاءِ وَمُحَمَّدُ بْنُ طَرِيفٍ الْكُوفِيُّ ۞ قَالَا أَنْبَأَنَا ابْنُ الْفُضَيْلِ ۞ عَنِ الْأَعْمَشِ ۞ عَنْ عَبْدِ الْمَلِكِ بْنِ مَيْسَرَةَ ۞ عَنِ النَّزَّالِ بْنِ سَبْرَةَ ۞ قَالَ أُتِيَ عَلِيٌّ رَضِيَ اللَّهُ عَنْهُ بِكُوزٍ مِنْ مَاءٍ وَهُوَ فِي الرَّحْبَةِ ۞ فَأَخَذَ مِنْهُ كَفًّا فَغَسَلَ يَدَيْهِ وَمَضْمَضَ وَاسْتَنْشَقَ وَمَسَحَ وَجْهَهُ وَذِرَاعَيْهِ وَرَأْسَهُ ۞ ثُمَّ شَرِبَ وَهُوَ قَائِمٌ ۞ ثُمَّ قَالَ هَٰذَا وُضُوءُ مَنْ لَمْ يُحْدِثْ ۞ هَكَذَا رَأَيْتُ رَسُولَ اللَّهِ ﷺ فَعَلَ ۞

209. Abu Kurayb Muhammad ibn al-'Ala' and Muhammad ibn Tarif al-Kufi narrated to us, they said, 'Ibn al-Fudayl informed us on the authority of A'mash, on the authority of 'Abd al-Malik ibn Maysara, on the authority of Nazzal ibn Sabra, who reported:

"A clay jug of water was brought to 'Ali while he was in the courtyard.[475] He took a handful of water from it and washed his hands. Then he rinsed his mouth, cleared his nose, and wiped his face, arms and head. Then he drank the remaining water whilst standing, and said, 'This is the purification of the one who has not voided his ritual purity.[476] This is how I saw the Messenger of Allah ﷺ do it.'"'[477]

[475] The open courtyard in Kufa where he would sit to adjudicate and deliver sermons. (AA)

[476] This hadith describes how one can renew his ritual purification without being in a state of ritual impurity. This ritual purification was intended for the purpose of cleaning and not for the purpose of removing the state of ritual impurity. (MA)

[477] Mulla 'Ali al-Qari says, 'In another narration it comes with the wording, "and he washed his feet".' (MA)

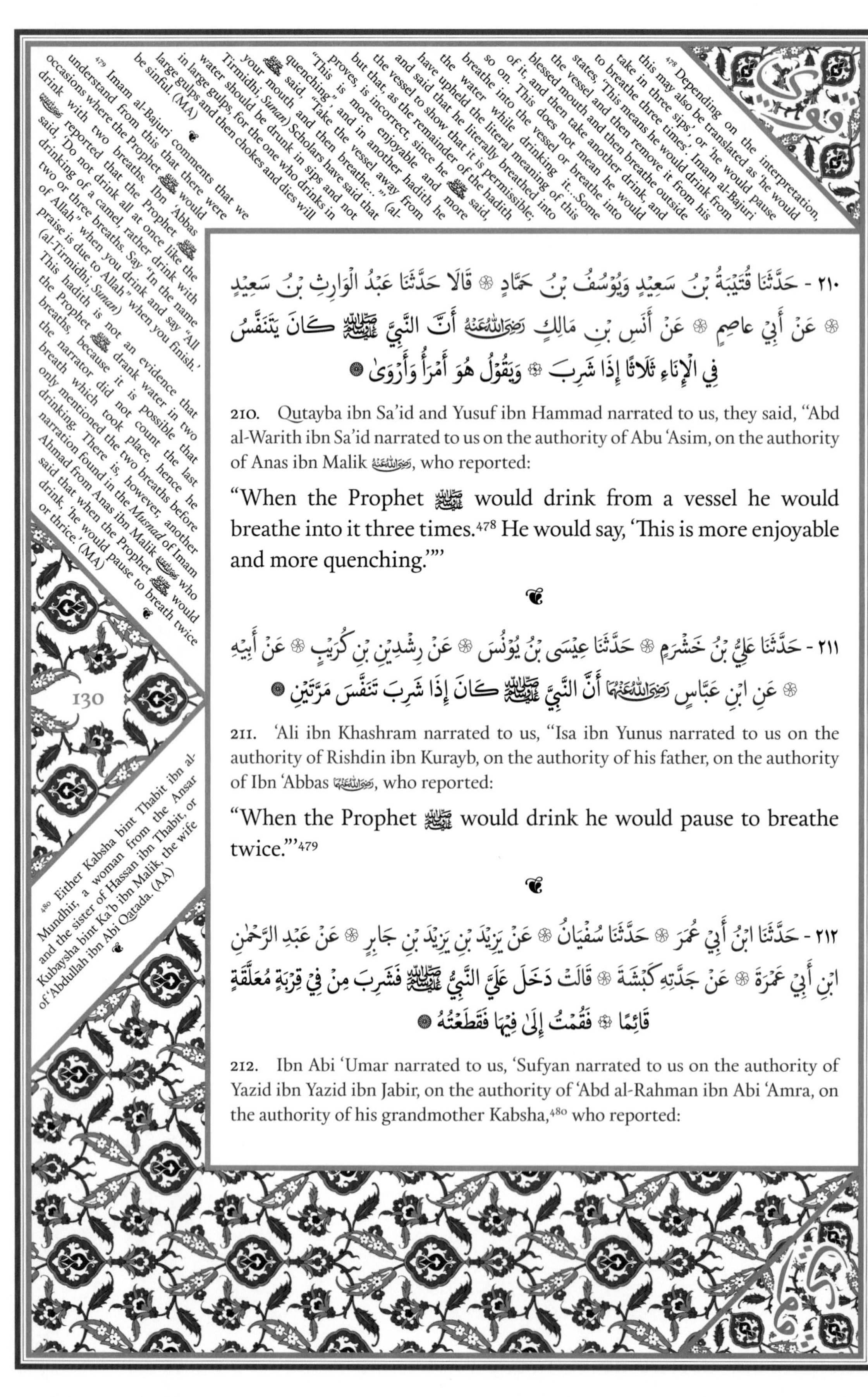

٢١٠ - حَدَّثَنَا قُتَيْبَةُ بْنُ سَعِيدٍ وَيُوسُفُ بْنُ حَمَّادٍ ❀ قَالَا حَدَّثَنَا عَبْدُ الْوَارِثِ بْنُ سَعِيدٍ ❀ عَنْ أَبِي عَاصِمٍ ❀ عَنْ أَنَسِ بْنِ مَالِكٍ رَضِيَ اللَّهُ عَنْهُ أَنَّ النَّبِيَّ ﷺ كَانَ يَتَنَفَّسُ فِي الْإِنَاءِ ثَلَاثًا إِذَا شَرِبَ ❀ وَيَقُولُ هُوَ أَمْرَأُ وَأَرْوَىٰ ●

210. Qutayba ibn Sa'id and Yusuf ibn Hammad narrated to us, they said, "Abd al-Warith ibn Sa'id narrated to us on the authority of Abu 'Asim, on the authority of Anas ibn Malik رضي الله عنه, who reported:

"When the Prophet ﷺ would drink from a vessel he would breathe into it three times.[478] He would say, 'This is more enjoyable and more quenching.'"

❦

٢١١ - حَدَّثَنَا عَلِيُّ بْنُ خَشْرَمٍ ❀ حَدَّثَنَا عِيسَى بْنُ يُونُسَ ❀ عَنْ رِشْدِينَ بْنِ كُرَيْبٍ ❀ عَنْ أَبِيهِ ❀ عَنِ ابْنِ عَبَّاسٍ رَضِيَ اللَّهُ عَنْهُمَا أَنَّ النَّبِيَّ ﷺ كَانَ إِذَا شَرِبَ تَنَفَّسَ مَرَّتَيْنِ ●

211. 'Ali ibn Khashram narrated to us, "Isa ibn Yunus narrated to us on the authority of Rishdin ibn Kurayb, on the authority of his father, on the authority of Ibn 'Abbas رضي الله عنهما, who reported:

"When the Prophet ﷺ would drink he would pause to breathe twice."'[479]

❦

٢١٢ - حَدَّثَنَا ابْنُ أَبِي عُمَرَ ❀ حَدَّثَنَا سُفْيَانُ ❀ عَنْ يَزِيدَ بْنِ يَزِيدَ بْنِ جَابِرٍ ❀ عَنْ عَبْدِ الرَّحْمَٰنِ ابْنِ أَبِي عَمْرَةَ ❀ عَنْ جَدَّتِهِ كَبْشَةَ ❀ قَالَتْ دَخَلَ عَلَيَّ النَّبِيُّ ﷺ فَشَرِبَ مِنْ فِي قِرْبَةٍ مُعَلَّقَةٍ قَائِمًا ❀ فَقُمْتُ إِلَىٰ فِيهَا فَقَطَعْتُهُ ●

212. Ibn Abi 'Umar narrated to us, 'Sufyan narrated to us on the authority of Yazid ibn Yazid ibn Jabir, on the authority of 'Abd al-Rahman ibn Abi 'Amra, on the authority of his grandmother Kabsha,[480] who reported:

[478] Depending on the interpretation, this may also be translated as 'he would take in three sips', or 'he would pause to breathe three times'. Imam al-Bajuri states, 'This means he would drink from the vessel and then remove it from his blessed mouth and then breathe outside of it, and then take another drink, and so on. This does not mean he would breathe into the vessel or breathe into the water while drinking it... Some have upheld the literal meaning of this and said that he literally breathed into the vessel to show that it is permissible; but that, as the remainder of the hadith proves, is incorrect, since he ﷺ said, "This is more enjoyable and more quenching", and in another hadith he ﷺ said, "Take the vessel away from your mouth and then breathe..." (al-Tirmidhi, *Sunan*) Scholars have said that water should be drunk in sips and not in large gulps, for the one who drinks in large gulps and then chokes and dies will be sinful. (MA) ❦

[479] Imam al-Bajuri comments that we understand from this that there were occasions where the Prophet ﷺ would drink with two breaths. Ibn 'Abbas ﷺ reported that the Prophet ﷺ said, 'Do not drink all at once like the drinking of a camel, rather drink with two or three breaths. Say "In the name of Allah" when you drink and say "All praise is due to Allah" when you finish.' (al-Tirmidhi, *Sunan*) This hadith is not an evidence that the Prophet ﷺ drank water in two breaths, because it is possible that the narrator did not count the last breath which took place, hence he only mentioned the two breaths before drinking. There is, however, another narration found in the *Musnad* of Imam Ahmad from Anas ibn Malik ﷺ who said that when the Prophet ﷺ would drink, 'he would pause to breath twice or thrice.' (MA) ❦

[480] Either Kabsha bint Thabit ibn al-Mundhir, a woman from the Ansar and the sister of Hassan ibn Thabit, or Kubaysha bint Ka'b ibn Malik, the wife of 'Abdullah ibn Abi Qatada. (AA) ❦

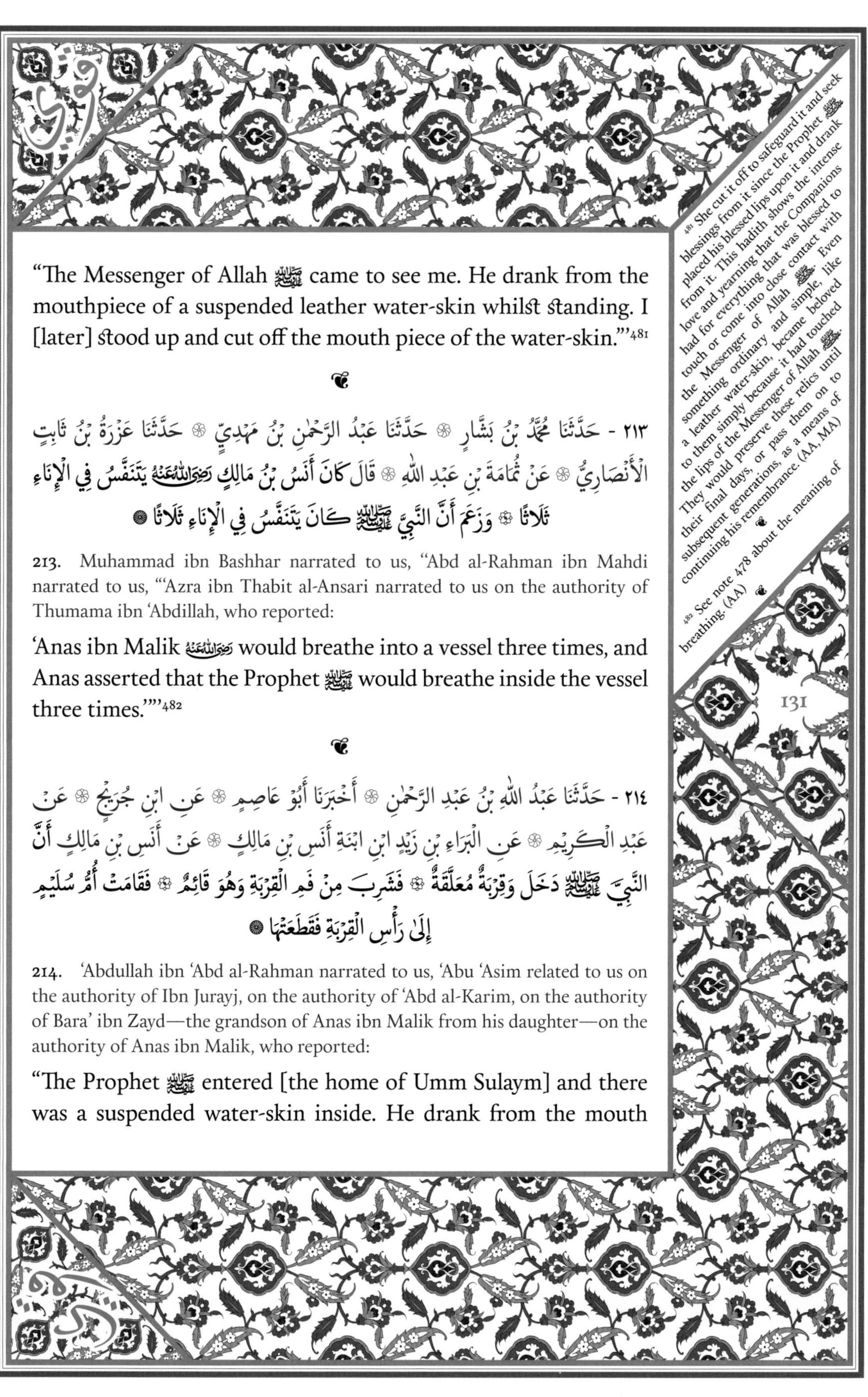

"The Messenger of Allah ﷺ came to see me. He drank from the mouthpiece of a suspended leather water-skin whilst standing. I [later] stood up and cut off the mouth piece of the water-skin."'[481]

٢١٣ - حَدَّثَنَا مُحَمَّدُ بْنُ بَشَّارٍ ۞ حَدَّثَنَا عَبْدُ الرَّحْمَٰنِ بْنُ مَهْدِيٍّ ۞ حَدَّثَنَا عَزْرَةُ بْنُ ثَابِتٍ الْأَنْصَارِيُّ ۞ عَنْ ثُمَامَةَ بْنِ عَبْدِ اللهِ ۞ قَالَ كَانَ أَنَسُ بْنُ مَالِكٍ رَضِيَ اللهُ عَنْهُ يَتَنَفَّسُ فِي الْإِنَاءِ ثَلَاثًا ۞ وَزَعَمَ أَنَّ النَّبِيَّ ﷺ كَانَ يَتَنَفَّسُ فِي الْإِنَاءِ ثَلَاثًا ۞

213. Muhammad ibn Bashhar narrated to us, "Abd al-Rahman ibn Mahdi narrated to us, "'Azra ibn Thabit al-Ansari narrated to us on the authority of Thumama ibn 'Abdillah, who reported:

'Anas ibn Malik رضي الله عنه would breathe into a vessel three times, and Anas asserted that the Prophet ﷺ would breathe inside the vessel three times.'"'[482]

٢١٤ - حَدَّثَنَا عَبْدُ اللهِ بْنُ عَبْدِ الرَّحْمَٰنِ ۞ أَخْبَرَنَا أَبُو عَاصِمٍ ۞ عَنِ ابْنِ جُرَيْجٍ ۞ عَنْ عَبْدِ الْكَرِيمِ ۞ عَنِ الْبَرَاءِ بْنِ زَيْدٍ ابْنِ ابْنَةِ أَنَسِ بْنِ مَالِكٍ ۞ عَنْ أَنَسِ بْنِ مَالِكٍ أَنَّ النَّبِيَّ ﷺ دَخَلَ وَقِرْبَةٌ مُعَلَّقَةٌ ۞ فَشَرِبَ مِنْ فَمِ الْقِرْبَةِ وَهُوَ قَائِمٌ ۞ فَقَامَتْ أُمُّ سُلَيْمٍ إِلَى رَأْسِ الْقِرْبَةِ فَقَطَعَتْهَا ۞

214. 'Abdullah ibn 'Abd al-Rahman narrated to us, 'Abu 'Asim related to us on the authority of Ibn Jurayj, on the authority of 'Abd al-Karim, on the authority of Bara' ibn Zayd—the grandson of Anas ibn Malik from his daughter—on the authority of Anas ibn Malik, who reported:

"The Prophet ﷺ entered [the home of Umm Sulaym] and there was a suspended water-skin inside. He drank from the mouth

[481] She cut it off to safeguard it and seek blessings from it since the Prophet ﷺ placed his blessed lips upon it and drank from it. This hadith shows the intense love and yearning that the Companions had for everything that was blessed to touch or come into close contact with the Messenger of Allah ﷺ. Even something ordinary and simple, like a leather water-skin, became beloved to them simply because it had touched the lips of the Messenger of Allah ﷺ. They would preserve these relics until their final days, or pass them on to subsequent generations, as a means of continuing his remembrance. (AA, MA)

[482] See note 478 about the meaning of breathing. (AA)

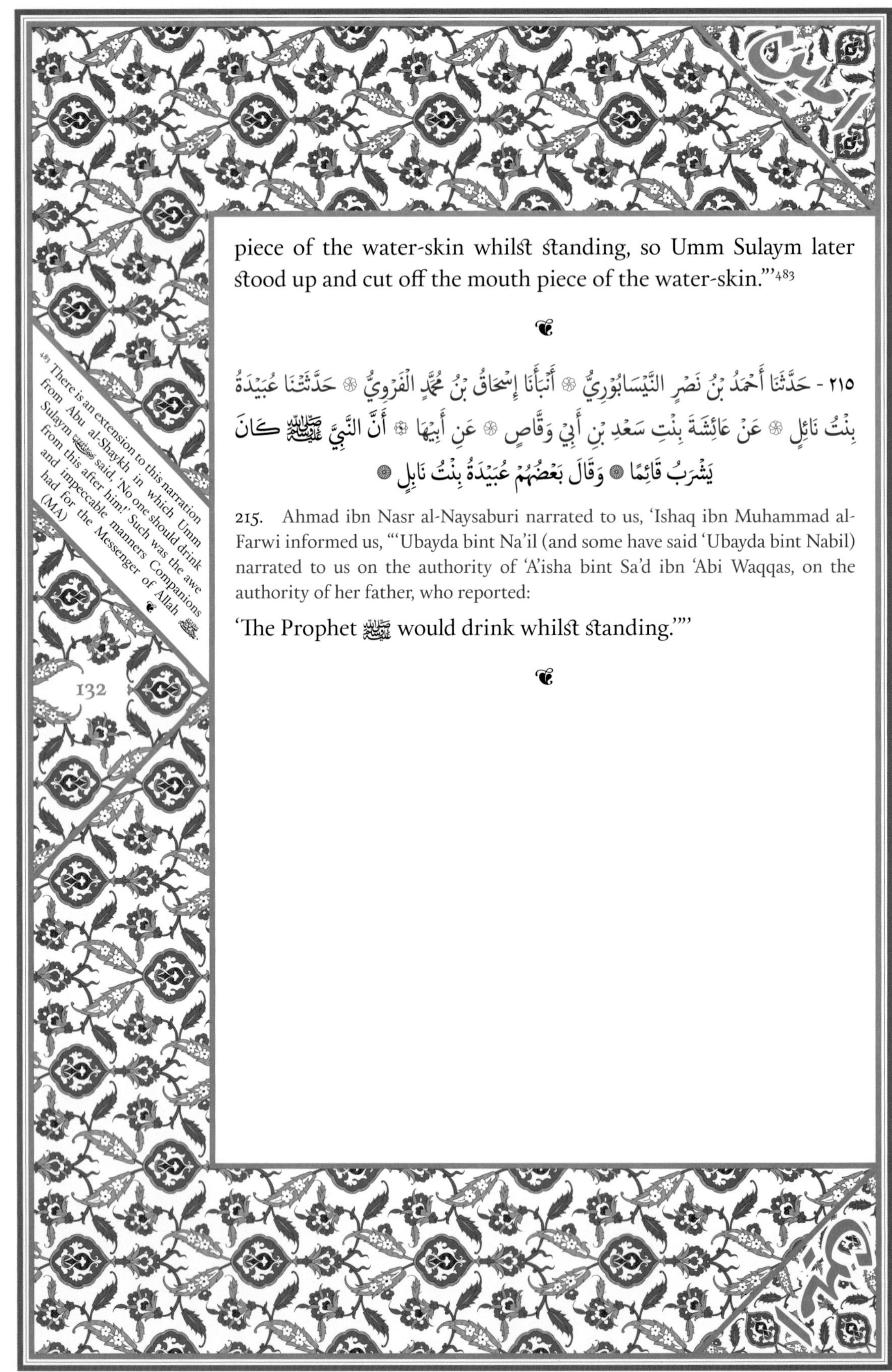

piece of the water-skin whilst standing, so Umm Sulaym later stood up and cut off the mouth piece of the water-skin.'"[483]

۞

٢١٥ - حَدَّثَنَا أَحْمَدُ بْنُ نَصْرٍ النَّيْسَابُورِيُّ ۞ أَنبَأَنَا إِسْحَاقُ بْنُ مُحَمَّدٍ الْفَرْوِيُّ ۞ حَدَّثَتْنَا عُبَيْدَةُ بِنْتُ نَائِلٍ ۞ عَنْ عَائِشَةَ بِنْتِ سَعْدِ بْنِ أَبِي وَقَّاصٍ ۞ عَنْ أَبِيهَا ۞ أَنَّ النَّبِيَّ ﷺ كَانَ يَشْرَبُ قَائِمًا ۞ وَقَالَ بَعْضُهُمْ عُبَيْدَةُ بِنْتُ نَابِلٍ ۞

215. Ahmad ibn Nasr al-Naysaburi narrated to us, 'Ishaq ibn Muhammad al-Farwi informed us, "'Ubayda bint Na'il (and some have said 'Ubayda bint Nabil) narrated to us on the authority of 'A'isha bint Sa'd ibn 'Abi Waqqas, on the authority of her father, who reported:

'The Prophet ﷺ would drink whilst standing.'"

۞

[483] There is an extension to this narration from Abu al-Shaykh in which Umm Sulaym said, 'No one should drink from this after him!' Such was the awe and impeccable manners Companions had for the Messenger of Allah ﷺ. (MA) ۞

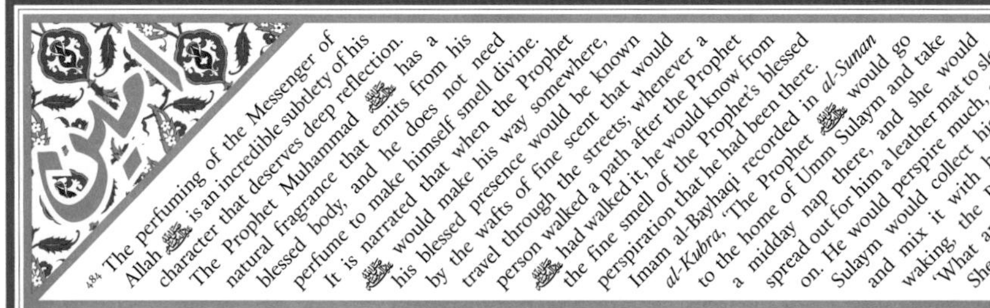

CHAPTER THIRTY-THREE

بَابُ مَا جَاءَ فِي تَعَطُّرِ رَسُولِ اللهِ ﷺ

What Has Been Narrated Concerning the Perfuming of the Messenger of Allah ﷺ[484]

٢١٦ - حَدَّثَنَا مُحَمَّدُ بْنُ رَافِعٍ وَغَيْرُ وَاحِدٍ ۞ قَالُوا أَنْبَأَنَا أَبُو أَحْمَدَ الزُّبَيْرِيُّ ۞ حَدَّثَنَا شَيْبَانُ ۞ عَنْ عَبْدِ اللهِ بْنِ الْمُخْتَارِ ۞ عَنْ مُوسَى بْنِ أَنَسِ بْنِ مَالِكٍ ۞ عَنْ أَبِيهِ ۞ قَالَ كَانَ لِرَسُولِ اللهِ ﷺ سُكَّةٌ يَتَطَيَّبُ مِنْهَا ۞

216. Muhammad ibn Rafi' and others narrated to us, 'Abu Ahmad al-Zubayri informed us, "Shayban narrated to us on the authority of 'Abdullah ibn al-Mukhtar, on the authority of Musa ibn Anas ibn Malik, on the authority of his father [Anas ibn Malik], who reported:

'The Messenger of Allah ﷺ had sukka perfume he would apply on himself.'"'[485]

❦

٢١٧ - حَدَّثَنَا مُحَمَّدُ بْنُ بَشَّارٍ ۞ حَدَّثَنَا عَبْدُ الرَّحْمٰنِ بْنُ مَهْدِيٍّ ۞ حَدَّثَنَا عَزْرَةُ بْنُ ثَابِتٍ ۞ عَنْ ثُمَامَةَ بْنِ عَبْدِ اللهِ ۞ قَالَ كَانَ أَنَسُ بْنُ مَالِكٍ لَا يَرُدُّ الطِّيبَ ۞ وَقَالَ أَنَسٌ إِنَّ النَّبِيَّ ﷺ كَانَ لَا يَرُدُّ الطِّيبَ ۞

217. Muhammad ibn Bashhar narrated to us, "Abd al-Rahman ibn Mahdi narrated to us, "'Azra ibn Thabit narrated to us on the authority of Thumama ibn 'Abdillah, who reported:

'Anas ibn Malik would never refuse perfume. Anas said, "The Prophet ﷺ would never refuse perfume."'"'[486]

484 The perfuming of the Messenger of Allah ﷺ is an incredible subtlety of his character that deserves deep reflection. The Prophet Muhammad ﷺ has a natural fragrance that emits from his blessed body, and he does not need perfume to make himself smell divine. It is narrated that when the Prophet ﷺ would make his way somewhere, his blessed presence would be known by the wafts of fine scent that would travel through the streets; whenever a person walked a path after the Prophet ﷺ had walked it, he would know from the fine smell of the Prophet's blessed perspiration that he had been there. Imam al-Bayhaqi recorded in *al-Sunan al-Kubra*, 'The Prophet ﷺ would go to the home of Umm Sulaym and take a midday nap there, and she would spread out for him a leather mat to sleep on. He would perspire much, so Umm Sulaym would collect his perspiration and mix it with her perfume. Upon waking, the Prophet ﷺ asked her, 'What are you doing, Umm Sulaym?' She said, "We use your perspiration as perfume, and it is the finest of scents!' And in another narration, Umm Sulaym said, 'O Messenger of Allah! We seek its blessings for our young children.' The Prophet ﷺ said to her, 'You are correct.' Why did the Prophet Muhammad ﷺ apply perfume to his blessed body when his perspiration smells finer than the finest of scents? What is the nature of the Ahmadan-Muhammadan Redolence? Is it biological? Several dimensions of this phenomenon should be considered. Firstly, it is evident that by applying perfume, the Prophet ﷺ was establishing it as a Sunna for his community to follow after him. Thus, it is recommended for men specifically to wear perfume on Friday (*Jumu'a*), the two Eids, when putting on the *ihram* garb before Hajj and 'Umra, when attending gatherings of remembrance or sacred knowledge, when reciting the Qur'an, when sitting to invoke Allah and when spending intimate time with one's wife. It is recommended for women to wear perfume in their homes. Secondly, smell is the most powerful sense in human beings. The sense of smell is closely linked with memory, and smells often trigger memories of experiences. The sense of smell is also highly emotive. Much of our emotional responses to things are governed by association and temperament (*mizaj*), which is why different people can have completely different perceptions of the same smell. In perfume, for example, what one person finds 'aromatic' and 'nice', another person may find 'overpowering' or 'nauseating'. Thirdly, the bestowed (*wahbi*) scent of the Messenger of Allah ﷺ is celestial in nature and not of this lower world. It is not biological as such. In fact, every biological component of the Prophet ﷺ in its essential essence (*haqiqa*) is mysteriously celestial. Just as he ﷺ is the best and most beautiful of Allah's creation, his blessed scent is likewise the finest scent in Allah's creation—Paradise or otherwise. In hadith 221, the Prophet ﷺ tells us that the scent of *rayhan* (which is the fragrant plant sweet-basil, but can also be interpreted as any fragrant plant) comes from Paradise. Scholars typically interpret this hadith by saying it reminds of us Paradise, so what can possibly be said about the blessed scent of the Prophet's blessed perspiration ﷺ? What does it remind us of? Fourthly, the beauties of the Prophet ﷺ (which include his blessed scent) do not manifest in this world to their fullest extent, for if they did, no one would be able to withstand the intensity of their sublimity, purity and effulgent lights. If humanity were able to behold the full extent of the Prophet's beauties, or smell

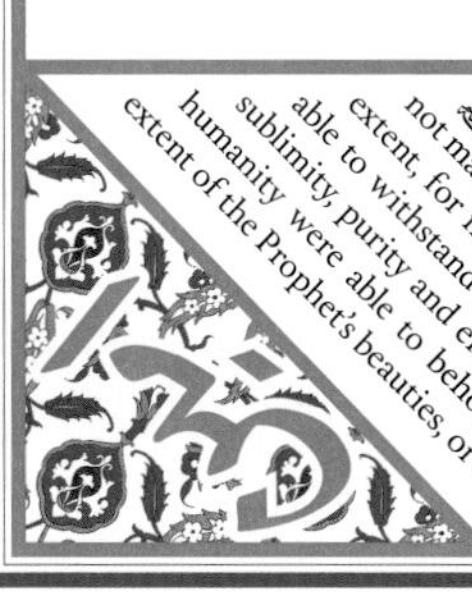

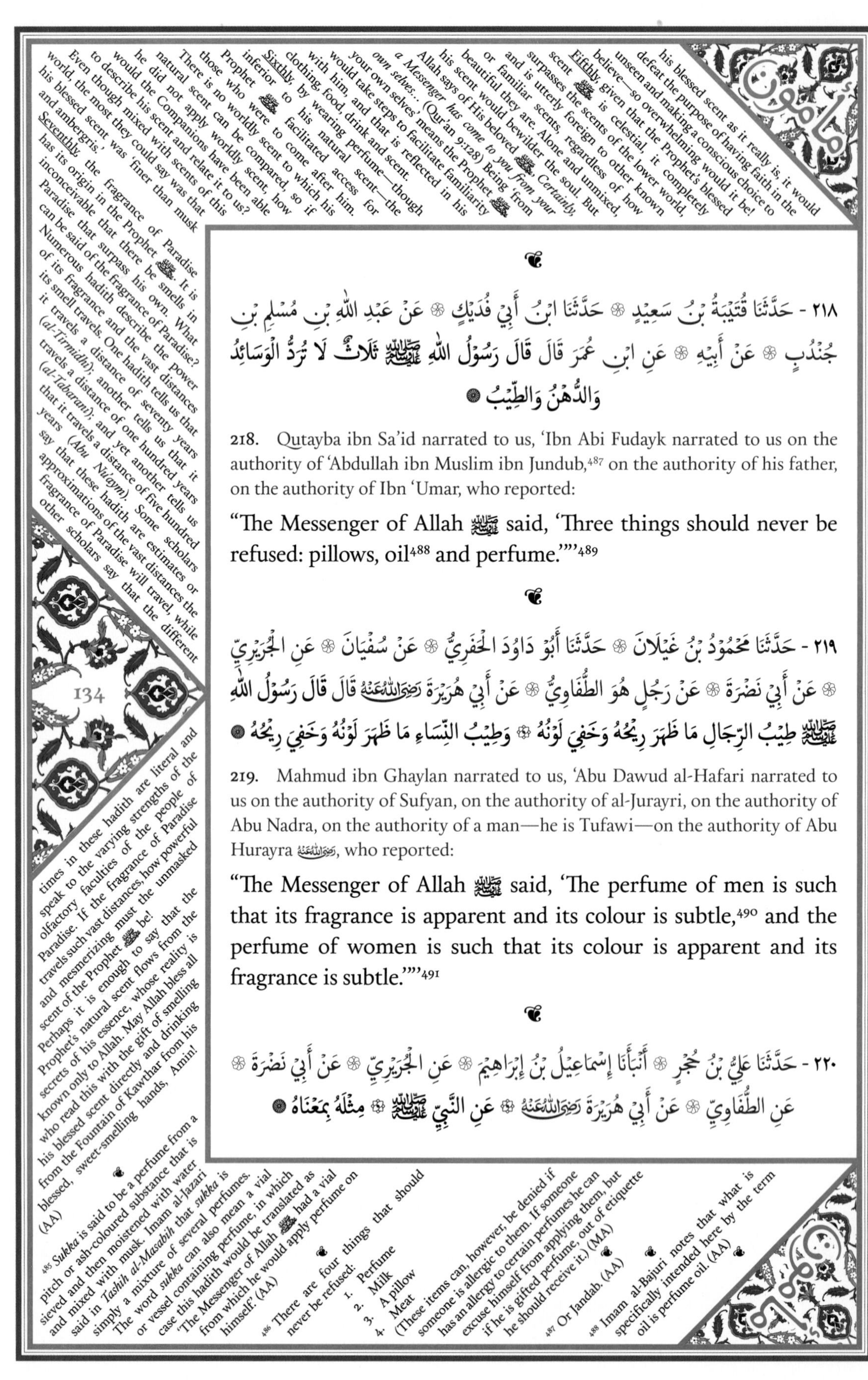

٢١٨ - حَدَّثَنَا قُتَيْبَةُ بْنُ سَعِيدٍ ۞ حَدَّثَنَا ابْنُ أَبِي فُدَيْكٍ ۞ عَنْ عَبْدِ اللهِ بْنِ مُسْلِمِ بْنِ جُنْدُبٍ ۞ عَنْ أَبِيهِ ۞ عَنِ ابْنِ عُمَرَ قَالَ قَالَ رَسُولُ اللهِ ﷺ ثَلَاثٌ لَا تُرَدُّ الْوَسَائِدُ وَالدُّهْنُ وَالطِّيبُ ۞

218. Qutayba ibn Sa'id narrated to us, 'Ibn Abi Fudayk narrated to us on the authority of 'Abdullah ibn Muslim ibn Jundub,[487] on the authority of his father, on the authority of Ibn 'Umar, who reported:

"The Messenger of Allah ﷺ said, 'Three things should never be refused: pillows, oil[488] and perfume.'"[489]

٢١٩ - حَدَّثَنَا مَحْمُودُ بْنُ غَيْلَانَ ۞ حَدَّثَنَا أَبُو دَاوُدَ الْحَفَرِيُّ ۞ عَنْ سُفْيَانَ ۞ عَنِ الْجُرَيْرِيِّ ۞ عَنْ أَبِي نَضْرَةَ ۞ عَنْ رَجُلٍ هُوَ الطُّفَاوِيُّ ۞ عَنْ أَبِي هُرَيْرَةَ رَضِيَ اللهُ عَنْهُ قَالَ قَالَ رَسُولُ اللهِ ﷺ طِيبُ الرِّجَالِ مَا ظَهَرَ رِيحُهُ وَخَفِيَ لَوْنُهُ ۞ وَطِيبُ النِّسَاءِ مَا ظَهَرَ لَوْنُهُ وَخَفِيَ رِيحُهُ ۞

219. Mahmud ibn Ghaylan narrated to us, 'Abu Dawud al-Hafari narrated to us on the authority of Sufyan, on the authority of al-Jurayri, on the authority of Abu Nadra, on the authority of a man—he is Tufawi—on the authority of Abu Hurayra رضي الله عنه, who reported:

"The Messenger of Allah ﷺ said, 'The perfume of men is such that its fragrance is apparent and its colour is subtle,[490] and the perfume of women is such that its colour is apparent and its fragrance is subtle.'"[491]

٢٢٠ - حَدَّثَنَا عَلِيُّ بْنُ حُجْرٍ ۞ أَنْبَأَنَا إِسْمَاعِيلُ بْنُ إِبْرَاهِيمَ ۞ عَنِ الْجُرَيْرِيِّ ۞ عَنْ أَبِي نَضْرَةَ ۞ عَنِ الطُّفَاوِيِّ ۞ عَنْ أَبِي هُرَيْرَةَ رَضِيَ اللهُ عَنْهُ ۞ عَنِ النَّبِيِّ ﷺ ۞ مِثْلَهُ بِمَعْنَاهُ ۞

his blessed scent as it really is, it would defeat the purpose of having faith in the unseen and making a conscious choice to believe—so overwhelming would it be! Fifthly, given that the Prophet's blessed scent ﷺ is celestial, it completely surpasses the scents of the lower world, and is utterly foreign to other known or familiar scents, regardless of how beautiful they are. Alone and unmixed, his scent would bewilder the soul. But Allah says of His beloved ﷺ, *Certainly, a Messenger has come to you from your own selves...* (Qur'an 9:128) Being 'from your own selves' means the Prophet ﷺ would take steps to facilitate familiarity with him, and that is reflected in his clothing, food, drink and scent. Sixthly, by wearing perfume—though inferior to his natural scent—the Prophet ﷺ facilitated access for those who were to come after him. There is no worldly scent to which his natural scent can be compared, so if he did not apply worldly scent, how would the Companions have been able to describe his scent and relate it to us? Even though mixed with scents of this world, the most they could say was that his blessed scent was 'finer than musk and ambergris.' Seventhly, the fragrance of Paradise has its origin in the Prophet ﷺ. It is inconceivable that there be smells in Paradise that surpass his own. What can be said of the fragrance of Paradise? Numerous hadith describe the power of its fragrance and the vast distances its smell travels. One hadith tells us that it travels a distance of seventy years (*al-Tirmidhi*); another tells us that it travels a distance of one hundred years (*al-Tabarani*); and yet another tells us that it travels a distance of five hundred years (*Abu Nu'aym*). Some scholars say that these hadith are estimates or approximations of the vast distances the fragrance of Paradise will travel, while other scholars say that the different times in these hadith are literal and speak to the varying strengths of the olfactory faculties of the people of Paradise. If the fragrance of Paradise travels such vast distances, how powerful and mesmerizing must the unmasked scent of the Prophet ﷺ be! Perhaps it is enough to say that the Prophet's natural scent flows from the secrets of his essence, whose reality is known only to Allah. May Allah bless all who read this with the gift of smelling his blessed scent directly and drinking from the Fountain of Kawthar from his blessed, sweet-smelling hands, Amin! (AA)

[485] *Sukka* is said to be a perfume from a pitch or ash-coloured substance that is sieved and then moistened with water and mixed with musk. Imam al-Jazari said in *Tashih al-Masabih* that *sukka* is simply a mixture of several perfumes. The word *sukka* can also mean a vial or vessel containing perfume, in which case this hadith would be translated as 'The Messenger of Allah ﷺ had a vial from which he would apply perfume on himself.' (AA)

[486] There are four things that should never be refused:
1. Perfume
2. Milk
3. A pillow
4. Meat

(These items can, however, be denied if someone is allergic to them. If someone has an allergy to certain perfumes he can excuse himself from applying them, but if he is gifted perfume, out of etiquette he should receive it.) (MA)

[487] Or Jandab. (AA)

[488] Imam al-Bajuri notes that what is specifically intended here by the term oil is perfume oil. (AA)

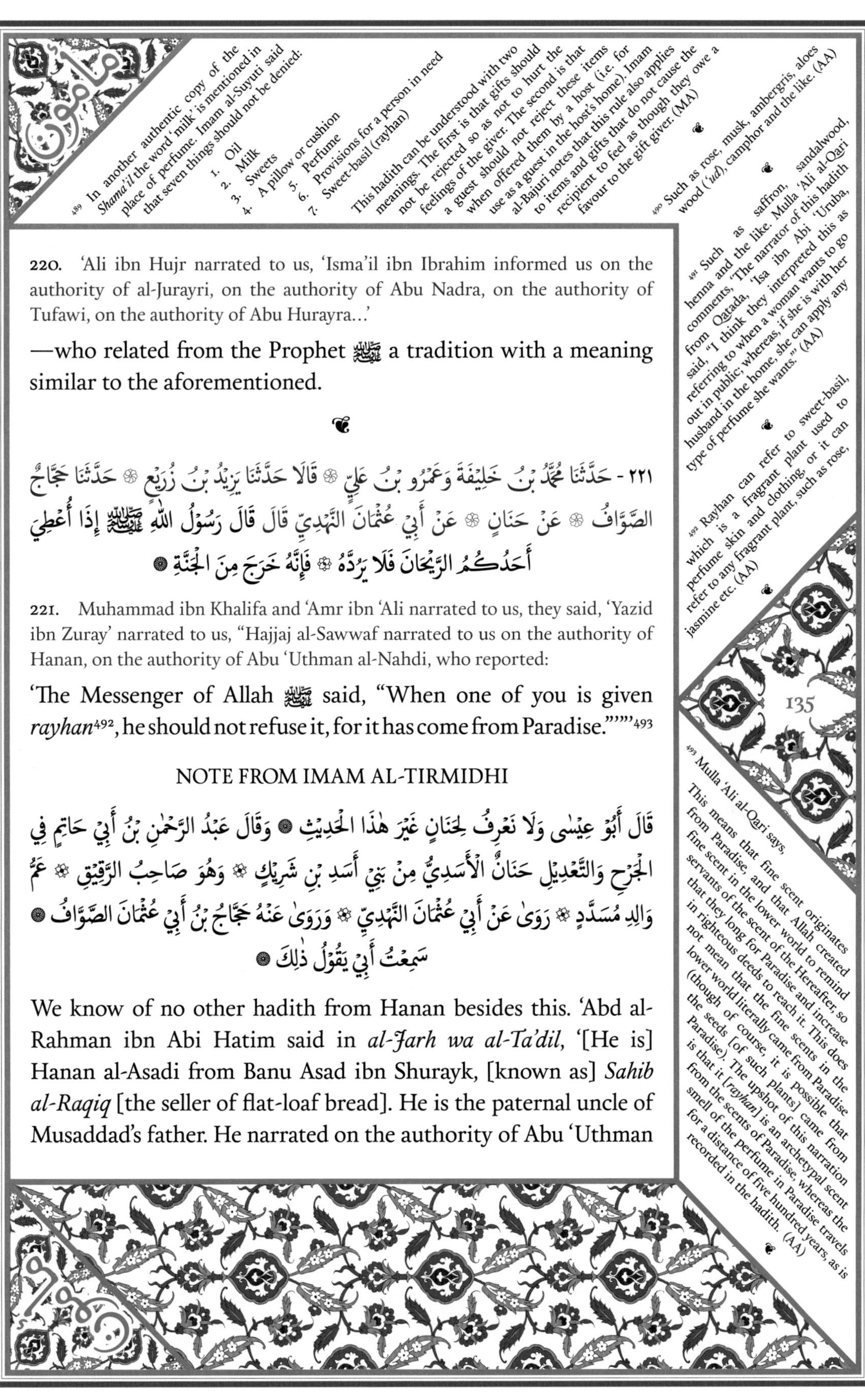

220. 'Ali ibn Hujr narrated to us, 'Isma'il ibn Ibrahim informed us on the authority of al-Jurayri, on the authority of Abu Nadra, on the authority of Tufawi, on the authority of Abu Hurayra...'

—who related from the Prophet ﷺ a tradition with a meaning similar to the aforementioned.

٢٢١ - حَدَّثَنَا مُحَمَّدُ بْنُ خَلِيفَةَ وَعَمْرُو بْنُ عَلِيٍّ ۞ قَالَا حَدَّثَنَا يَزِيدُ بْنُ زُرَيْعٍ ۞ حَدَّثَنَا حَجَّاجٌ الصَّوَّافُ ۞ عَنْ حَنَانٍ ۞ عَنْ أَبِي عُثْمَانَ النَّهْدِيِّ قَالَ قَالَ رَسُولُ اللهِ ﷺ إِذَا أُعْطِيَ أَحَدُكُمُ الرَّيْحَانَ فَلَا يَرُدَّهُ ۞ فَإِنَّهُ خَرَجَ مِنَ الْجَنَّةِ ۞

221. Muhammad ibn Khalifa and 'Amr ibn 'Ali narrated to us, they said, 'Yazid ibn Zuray' narrated to us, "Hajjaj al-Sawwaf narrated to us on the authority of Hanan, on the authority of Abu 'Uthman al-Nahdi, who reported:

'The Messenger of Allah ﷺ said, "When one of you is given *rayhan*[492], he should not refuse it, for it has come from Paradise."""'[493]

NOTE FROM IMAM AL-TIRMIDHI

قَالَ أَبُو عِيسٰى وَلَا نَعْرِفُ لِحَنَانٍ غَيْرَ هٰذَا الْحَدِيثِ ۞ وَقَالَ عَبْدُ الرَّحْمٰنِ بْنُ أَبِي حَاتِمٍ فِي الْجَرْحِ وَالتَّعْدِيلِ حَنَانٌ الْأَسَدِيُّ مِنْ بَنِي أَسَدِ بْنِ شَرِيكٍ ۞ وَهُوَ صَاحِبُ الرَّقِيقِ ۞ عَمُّ وَالِدِ مُسَدَّدٍ ۞ رَوَى عَنْ أَبِي عُثْمَانَ النَّهْدِيِّ ۞ وَرَوَى عَنْهُ حَجَّاجُ بْنُ أَبِي عُثْمَانَ الصَّوَّافُ ۞ سَمِعْتُ أَبِي يَقُولُ ذٰلِكَ ۞

We know of no other hadith from Hanan besides this. 'Abd al-Rahman ibn Abi Hatim said in *al-Jarh wa al-Ta'dil*, '[He is] Hanan al-Asadi from Banu Asad ibn Shurayk, [known as] *Sahib al-Raqiq* [the seller of flat-loaf bread]. He is the paternal uncle of Musaddad's father. He narrated on the authority of Abu 'Uthman

489 In another authentic copy of the *Shama'il* the word 'milk' is mentioned in place of perfume. Imam al-Suyuti said that seven things should not be denied:

1. Oil
2. Milk
3. Sweets
4. A pillow or cushion
5. Perfume
6. Provisions for a person in need
7. Sweet-basil (rayhan)

This hadith can be understood with two meanings. The first is that gifts should not be rejected so as not to hurt the feelings of the giver. The second is that a guest should not reject these items when offered them by a host (i.e. for use as a guest in the host's home). Imam al-Bajuri notes that this rule also applies to items and gifts that do not cause the recipient to feel as though they owe a favour to the gift giver. (MA)

490 Such as rose, musk, ambergris, aloes wood (*'ud*), camphor and the like. (AA)

491 Such as saffron, sandalwood, henna and the like. Mulla 'Ali al-Qari comments, 'The narrator of this hadith from Qatada, 'Isa ibn Abi 'Uruba, said, "I think they interpreted this as referring to when a woman wants to go out in public; whereas, if she is with her husband in the home, she can apply any type of perfume she wants." (AA)

492 Rayhan can refer to sweet-basil, which is a fragrant plant used to perfume skin and clothing, or it can refer to any fragrant plant, such as rose, jasmine etc. (AA)

493 Mulla 'Ali al-Qari says,

This means that fine scent originates from Paradise, and that Allah created fine scent in the lower world to remind servants of the scent of the Hereafter, so that they long for Paradise and increase in righteous deeds to reach it. This does not mean that the fine scents in the lower world literally came from Paradise (though of course, it is possible that the seeds [of such plants] came from Paradise). The upshot of this narration is that it [*rayhan*] is an archetypal scent from the scents of Paradise, whereas the smell of the perfume in Paradise travels for a distance of five hundred years, as is recorded in the hadith. (AA)

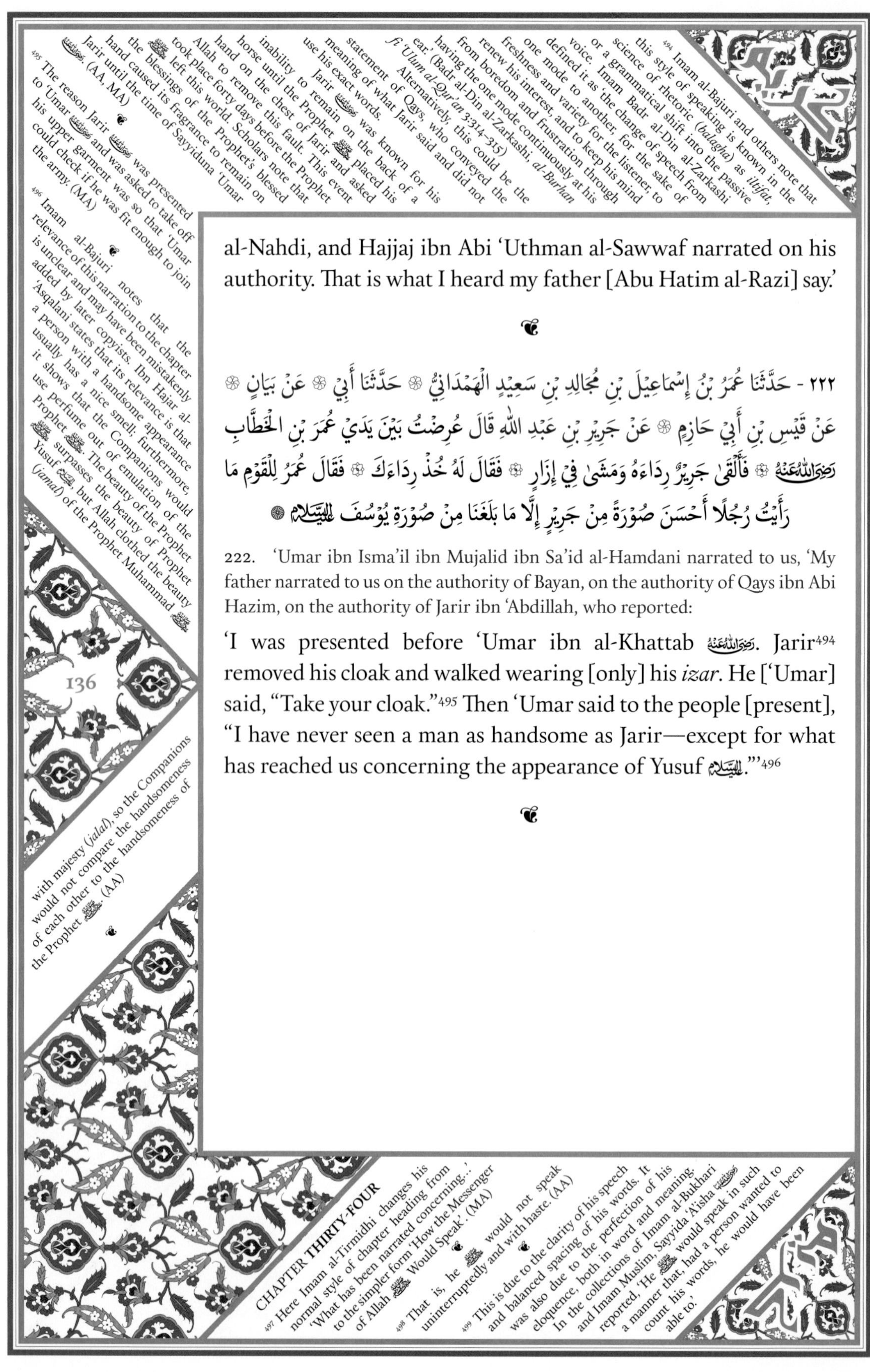

al-Nahdi, and Hajjaj ibn Abi 'Uthman al-Sawwaf narrated on his authority. That is what I heard my father [Abu Hatim al-Razi] say.'

٢٢٢ - حَدَّثَنَا عُمَرُ بْنُ إِسْمَاعِيلَ بْنِ مُجَالِدِ بْنِ سَعِيدٍ الْهَمْدَانِيُّ ۞ حَدَّثَنَا أَبِي ۞ عَنْ بَيَانٍ ۞ عَنْ قَيْسِ بْنِ أَبِي حَازِمٍ ۞ عَنْ جَرِيرِ بْنِ عَبْدِ اللهِ قَالَ عُرِضْتُ بَيْنَ يَدَيْ عُمَرَ بْنِ الْخَطَّابِ رَضِيَ اللهُ عَنْهُ ۞ فَأَلْقَى جَرِيرٌ رِدَاءَهُ وَمَشَى فِي إِزَارٍ ۞ فَقَالَ لَهُ خُذْ رِدَاءَكَ ۞ فَقَالَ عُمَرُ لِلْقَوْمِ مَا رَأَيْتُ رَجُلًا أَحْسَنَ صُورَةً مِنْ جَرِيرٍ إِلَّا مَا بَلَغَنَا مِنْ صُورَةِ يُوسُفَ عَلَيْهِ السَّلَامُ ۞

222. 'Umar ibn Isma'il ibn Mujalid ibn Sa'id al-Hamdani narrated to us, 'My father narrated to us on the authority of Bayan, on the authority of Qays ibn Abi Hazim, on the authority of Jarir ibn 'Abdillah, who reported:

'I was presented before 'Umar ibn al-Khattab رضي الله عنه. Jarir[494] removed his cloak and walked wearing [only] his *izar*. He ['Umar] said, "Take your cloak."[495] Then 'Umar said to the people [present], "I have never seen a man as handsome as Jarir—except for what has reached us concerning the appearance of Yusuf عليه السلام."'[496]

[494] Imam al-Bajuri and others note that this style of speaking is known in the science of rhetoric (*balagha*) as *iltifat*, or a grammatical shift into the passive voice. Imam Badr al-Din al-Zarkashi defined it as 'the change of speech from one mode to another, for the sake of freshness and variety for the listener, to renew his interest, and to keep his mind from boredom and frustration through having the one mode continuously at his ear.' (Badr al-Din al-Zarkashi, *al-Burhan fi 'Ulum al-Qur'an* 3:314–315) Alternatively, this could be the statement of Qays, who conveyed the meaning of what Jarir said and did not use his exact words. Jarir رضي الله عنه was known for his inability to remain on the back of a horse until the Prophet ﷺ placed his hand on the chest of Jarir and asked Allah to remove this fault. This event took place forty days before the Prophet ﷺ left this world. Scholars note that the blessings of the Prophet's blessed hand caused its fragrance to remain on Jarir until the time of Sayyiduna 'Umar رضي الله عنه. (AA, MA)

[495] The reason Jarir رضي الله عنه was presented to 'Umar رضي الله عنه and was asked to take off his upper garment was so that 'Umar could check if he was fit enough to join the army. (MA)

[496] Imam al-Bajuri notes that the relevance of this narration to the chapter is unclear and may have been mistakenly added by later copyists. Ibn Hajar al-'Asqalani states that its relevance is that a person with a handsome appearance usually has a nice smell; furthermore, it shows that the Companions would use perfume out of emulation of the Prophet ﷺ. The beauty of the Prophet ﷺ surpasses the beauty of Prophet Yusuf عليه السلام, but Allah clothed the beauty (*jamal*) of the Prophet Muhammad ﷺ with majesty (*jalal*), so the Companions would not compare the handsomeness of each other to the handsomeness of the Prophet ﷺ. (AA)

CHAPTER THIRTY-FOUR

[497] Here Imam al-Tirmidhi changes his normal style of chapter heading from 'What has been narrated concerning...' to the simpler form 'How the Messenger of Allah ﷺ Would Speak'. (MA)

[498] That is, he ﷺ would not speak uninterruptedly and with haste. (AA)

[499] This is due to the clarity of his speech and balanced spacing of his words. It was also due to the perfection of his eloquence, both in word and meaning. In the collections of Imam al-Bukhari and Imam Muslim, Sayyida 'A'isha رضي الله عنها reported, 'He ﷺ would speak in such a manner that, had a person wanted to count his words, he would have been able to.'

CHAPTER THIRTY-FOUR

How the Messenger of Allah ﷺ would Speak[497]

٢٢٣ - حَدَّثَنَا حُمَيْدُ بْنُ مَسْعَدَةَ الْبَصْرِيُّ ❁ حَدَّثَنَا حُمَيْدُ بْنُ الْأَسْوَدِ ❁ عَنْ أُسَامَةَ بْنِ زَيْدٍ ❁ عَنِ الزُّهْرِيِّ ❁ عَنْ عُرْوَةَ ❁ عَنْ عَائِشَةَ رَضِيَ اللهُ عَنْهَا قَالَتْ مَا كَانَ رَسُولُ اللهِ ﷺ يَسْرُدُ كَسَرْدِكُمْ هٰذَا ❁ وَلَكِنَّهُ كَانَ يَتَكَلَّمُ بِكَلَامٍ بَيِّنٍ فَصْلٍ ❁ يَحْفَظُهُ مَنْ جَلَسَ إِلَيْهِ ❁

223. Humayd ibn Mas'ada al-Basri narrated to us, 'Humayd ibn Aswad narrated to us on the authority of Usama ibn Zayd, on the authority of Zuhri, on the authority of 'Urwa, on the authority of 'A'isha رضي الله عنها, who reported:

"The Messenger of Allah ﷺ would not draw out his speech[498] as you all do. He would speak clearly and lucidly and would space out his words. Anyone who sat with him would remember what he had said."'[499]

❦

٢٢٤ - حَدَّثَنَا مُحَمَّدُ بْنُ يَحْيَىٰ ❁ حَدَّثَنَا أَبُو قُتَيْبَةَ سَلْمُ بْنُ قُتَيْبَةَ ❁ عَنْ عَبْدِ اللهِ بْنِ الْمُثَنَّىٰ ❁ عَنْ ثُمَامَةَ ❁ عَنْ أَنَسِ بْنِ مَالِكٍ قَالَ كَانَ رَسُولُ اللهِ ﷺ يُعِيدُ الْكَلِمَةَ ثَلَاثًا لِتُعْقَلَ عَنْهُ ❁

224. Muhammad ibn Yahya narrated to us, 'Abu Qutayba Salm ibn Qutayba narrated to us on the authority of 'Abdullah ibn al-Muthanna, on the authority of Thumama, on the authority of Anas ibn Malik, who reported:

"The Messenger of Allah ﷺ would repeat a word three times so he could be understood."'[500]

Another reason the Companions remembered exactly what he said is because each person's speech is covered with the garment of the heart from which it came. The garment of the sound heart is light, and there is no light comparable to the light of the Messenger of Allah ﷺ, therefore no speech matches his in adornment, beauty, majesty and perfection. For this reason, it captures hearts and captivates intellects, causing them both to submit. Through the Prophet's speech ﷺ Allah united scattered nations and gathered the Arabs and non-Arabs. Its sweetness made parents forget children and children forget parents. Due to stillness and absorption in his speech, it appeared as though birds were perched atop the heads of those listening to him ﷺ. When he would instruct the Companions, they would immediately respond without hesitation. (MA)

[500] He would repeat a word three times. It is important to note, however, that this was not always done. He repeated words:

1. To make sure that listeners understood what he said.
2. To emphasise a particular word which was extremely important in the sentence.
3. To ensure everyone heard what he said.

This was due to the great care the Prophet ﷺ had for everyone in his gathering, and his eagerness for them to increase in guidance and knowledge. Teachers who follow his path should also speak in a way that allows everyone attending to understand and take benefit. Students who follow his path should listen in a way that models focus and reverence. (MA)

[501] In Arabic, *mutawasil al-ahzan*. Imam al-Bajuri comments, 'The Prophet ﷺ was "in a continual state of worry" because of his constant contemplation and immersion in witnessing the majesty of his Lord.' First and foremost, this refers to the state of the Prophet's noble speech ﷺ. He was always in a continual state of worry when addressing his Companions regarding the matters of the Hereafter and whilst instructing them to compete in goodness and refrain from what Allah forbade. His is the speech of one who perceives the realities of this world and the Next, including the realities of death, the questioning of the grave, the reckoning on the Day of Judgement, the lofty stations of people of Paradise, the terrible punishment of the inhabitants of Hellfire, the value of his Lord's pleasure and the weight of His wrath. He ﷺ saw the Divine Judgement, the Traverse (*Sirat*) and all the afterworldly trials that are to come. By this knowledge, his every word was filled with compassion, care, and concern for his *Umma*, with the desire that they be granted ease and relief from all pains and tribulations at every level of existence. Secondly, scholars have said that this state of worry refers to when the Prophet ﷺ would sit privately in contemplation, during which he would fill with awe and reverence for his Lord. When seen in public, however, he ﷺ would be seen with a smile on his blessed face in order to welcome others and bring their hearts closer to Islam. One Companion said that from the day he accepted Islam he never saw the Prophet ﷺ except that he had a smile upon his blessed and beautiful face. The Prophet's worry should not be understood to mean depression or anxiety, for Allah protected him from such things and answered his prayer, 'O Allah, I seek refuge in You from worry and sorrow...' (*Sahih al-Bukhari*). Another interpretation states that the Prophet's worry was a manifestation of

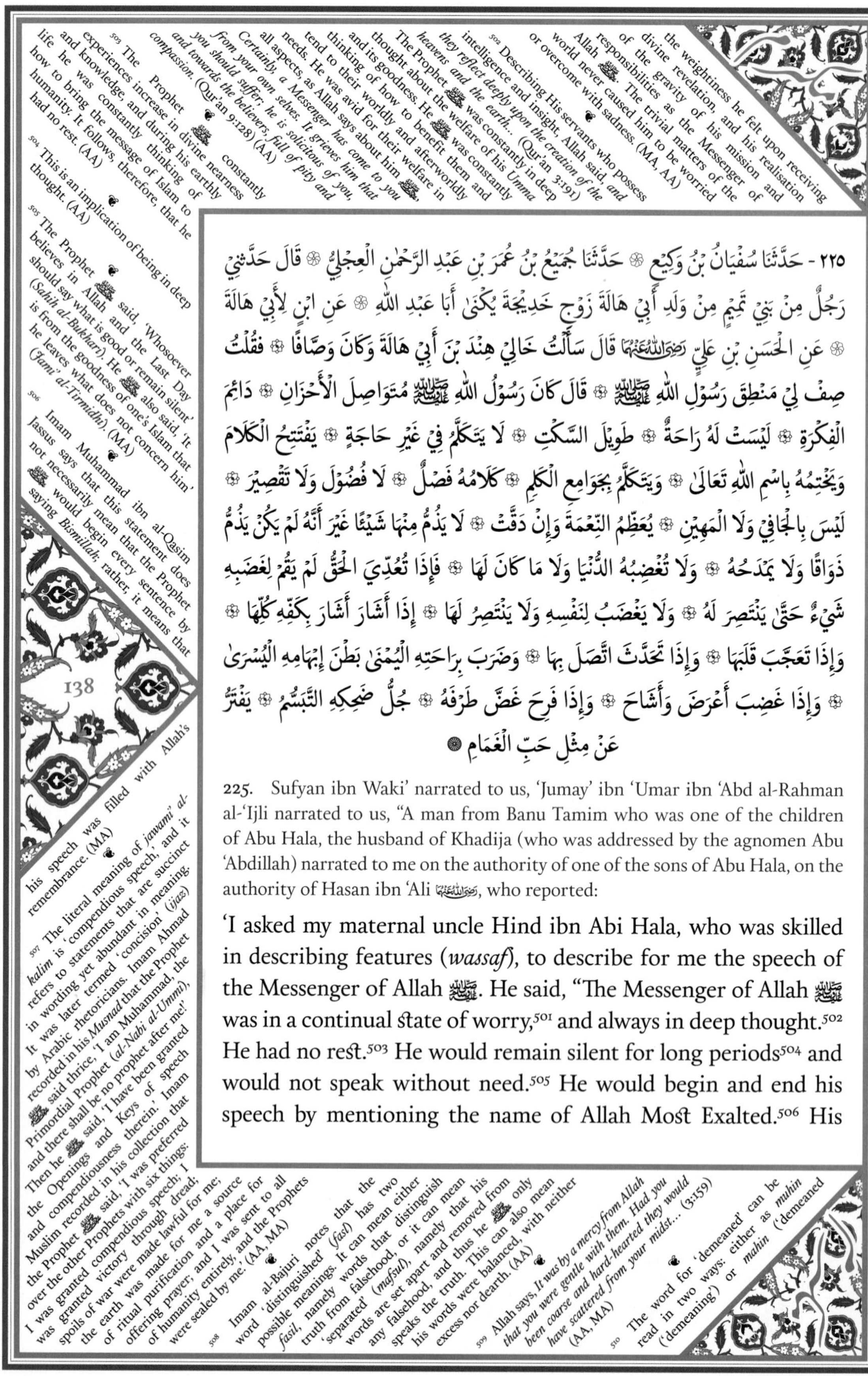

٢٢٥ - حَدَّثَنَا سُفْيَانُ بْنُ وَكِيعٍ ۞ حَدَّثَنَا جُمَيْعُ بْنُ عُمَرَ بْنِ عَبْدِ الرَّحْمٰنِ الْعِجْلِيُّ ۞ قَالَ حَدَّثَنِي رَجُلٌ مِنْ بَنِي تَمِيمٍ مِنْ وَلَدِ أَبِي هَالَةَ زَوْجِ خَدِيجَةَ يُكْنَىٰ أَبَا عَبْدِ اللهِ ۞ عَنِ ابْنٍ لِأَبِي هَالَةَ ۞ عَنِ الْحَسَنِ بْنِ عَلِيٍّ رَضِيَ اللهُ عَنْهُمَا قَالَ سَأَلْتُ خَالِي هِنْدَ بْنَ أَبِي هَالَةَ وَكَانَ وَصَّافًا ۞ فَقُلْتُ صِفْ لِي مَنْطِقَ رَسُولِ اللهِ ﷺ ۞ قَالَ كَانَ رَسُولُ اللهِ ﷺ مُتَوَاصِلَ الْأَحْزَانِ ۞ دَائِمَ الْفِكْرَةِ ۞ لَيْسَتْ لَهُ رَاحَةٌ ۞ طَوِيلَ السَّكْتِ ۞ لَا يَتَكَلَّمُ فِي غَيْرِ حَاجَةٍ ۞ يَفْتَتِحُ الْكَلَامَ وَيَخْتِمُهُ بِاسْمِ اللهِ تَعَالَىٰ ۞ وَيَتَكَلَّمُ بِجَوَامِعِ الْكَلِمِ ۞ كَلَامُهُ فَصْلٌ ۞ لَا فُضُولَ وَلَا تَقْصِيرَ ۞ لَيْسَ بِالْجَافِي وَلَا الْمَهِينِ ۞ يُعَظِّمُ النِّعْمَةَ وَإِنْ دَقَّتْ ۞ لَا يَذُمُّ مِنْهَا شَيْئًا غَيْرَ أَنَّهُ لَمْ يَكُنْ يَذُمُّ ذَوَاقًا وَلَا يَمْدَحُهُ ۞ وَلَا تُغْضِبُهُ الدُّنْيَا وَلَا مَا كَانَ لَهَا ۞ فَإِذَا تُعُدِّيَ الْحَقُّ لَمْ يَقُمْ لِغَضَبِهِ شَيْءٌ حَتَّىٰ يَنْتَصِرَ لَهُ ۞ وَلَا يَغْضَبُ لِنَفْسِهِ وَلَا يَنْتَصِرُ لَهَا ۞ إِذَا أَشَارَ أَشَارَ بِكَفِّهِ كُلِّهَا ۞ وَإِذَا تَعَجَّبَ قَلَبَهَا ۞ وَإِذَا تَحَدَّثَ اتَّصَلَ بِهَا ۞ وَضَرَبَ بِرَاحَتِهِ الْيُمْنَىٰ بَطْنَ إِبْهَامِهِ الْيُسْرَىٰ ۞ وَإِذَا غَضِبَ أَعْرَضَ وَأَشَاحَ ۞ وَإِذَا فَرِحَ غَضَّ طَرْفَهُ ۞ جُلُّ ضَحِكِهِ التَّبَسُّمُ ۞ يَفْتَرُّ عَنْ مِثْلِ حَبِّ الْغَمَامِ ۞

225. Sufyan ibn Waki' narrated to us, 'Jumay' ibn 'Umar ibn 'Abd al-Rahman al-'Ijli narrated to us, "A man from Banu Tamim who was one of the children of Abu Hala, the husband of Khadija (who was addressed by the agnomen Abu 'Abdillah) narrated to me on the authority of one of the sons of Abu Hala, on the authority of Hasan ibn 'Ali رضي الله عنهما, who reported:

'I asked my maternal uncle Hind ibn Abi Hala, who was skilled in describing features (*wassaf*), to describe for me the speech of the Messenger of Allah ﷺ. He said, "The Messenger of Allah ﷺ was in a continual state of worry,[501] and always in deep thought.[502] He had no rest.[503] He would remain silent for long periods[504] and would not speak without need.[505] He would begin and end his speech by mentioning the name of Allah Most Exalted.[506] His

the weightiness he felt upon receiving divine revelation, and his realisation of the gravity of his mission and responsibilities as the Messenger of Allah ﷺ. The trivial matters of the world never caused him to be worried or overcome with sadness. (MA, AA)

502 Describing His servants who possess intelligence and insight, Allah said, *and they reflect deeply upon the creation of the heavens and the earth...* (Qur'an 3:191) The Prophet ﷺ was constantly in deep thought about the welfare of his Umma and its goodness. He ﷺ was constantly thinking of how to benefit them and tend to their worldly and afterworldly needs. He was avid for their welfare in all aspects, as Allah says about him ﷺ, *Certainly, a Messenger has come to you from your own selves. It grieves him that you should suffer; he is solicitous of you, and towards the believers, full of pity and compassion.* (Qur'an 9:128) (AA)

503 The Prophet ﷺ constantly experiences increase in divine nearness and knowledge, and during his earthly life he was constantly thinking of how to bring the message of Islam to humanity. It follows, therefore, that he had no rest. (AA)

504 This is an implication of being in deep thought. (AA)

505 The Prophet ﷺ said, 'Whosoever believes in Allah and the Last Day should say what is good or remain silent' (*Sahih al-Bukhari*). He ﷺ also said, 'It is from the goodness of one's Islam that he leaves what does not concern him' (*Jami' al-Tirmidhi*). (MA)

506 Imam Muhammad ibn al-Qasim Jassus says that this statement does not necessarily mean that the Prophet ﷺ would begin every sentence by saying *Bismillah*; rather, it means that his speech was filled with Allah's remembrance. (MA)

507 The literal meaning of *jawami' al-kalim* is 'compendious speech,' and it refers to statements that are succinct in wording yet abundant in meaning. It was later termed 'concision' (*ijaz*) by Arabic rhetoricians. Imam Ahmad recorded in his *Musnad* that the Prophet ﷺ said thrice, 'I am Muhammad, the Primordial Prophet (*al-Nabi al-Ummi*), and there shall be no prophet after me!' Then he ﷺ said, 'I have been granted the Openings and Keys of speech and the compendiousness therein.' Imam Muslim recorded in his collection that the Prophet ﷺ said, 'I was preferred over the other Prophets with six things: I was granted compendious speech; I was granted victory through dread; spoils of war were made lawful for me; the earth was made for me a source of ritual purification and a place for offering prayer; and I was sent to all of humanity entirely, and the Prophets were sealed by me.' (AA, MA)

508 Imam al-Bajuri notes that the word 'distinguished' (*fasl*) has two possible meanings. It can mean either *fasil*, namely words that distinguish truth from falsehood, or it can mean 'separated' (*mafsul*), namely that his words are set apart and removed from any falsehood, and thus he ﷺ only speaks the truth. This can also mean his words were balanced, with neither excess nor dearth. (AA)

509 Allah says, *It was by a mercy from Allah that you were gentle with them. Had you been coarse and hard-hearted they would have scattered from your midst...* (3:159) (AA, MA)

510 The word for 'demeaned' can be read in two ways: either as *muhin* ('demeaning') or *mahin* ('demeaned

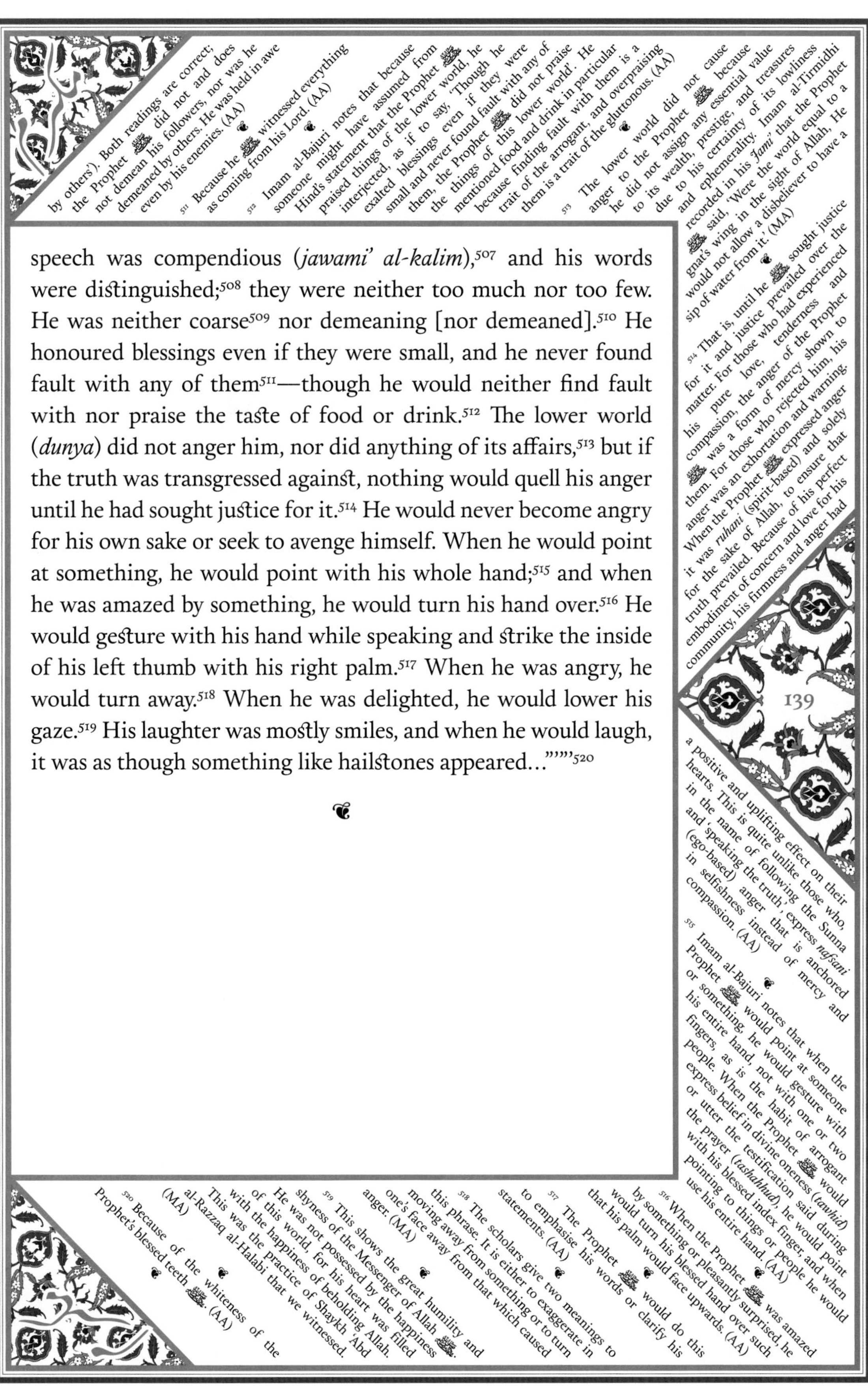

speech was compendious (*jawami' al-kalim*),[507] and his words were distinguished;[508] they were neither too much nor too few. He was neither coarse[509] nor demeaning [nor demeaned].[510] He honoured blessings even if they were small, and he never found fault with any of them[511]—though he would neither find fault with nor praise the taste of food or drink.[512] The lower world (*dunya*) did not anger him, nor did anything of its affairs,[513] but if the truth was transgressed against, nothing would quell his anger until he had sought justice for it.[514] He would never become angry for his own sake or seek to avenge himself. When he would point at something, he would point with his whole hand;[515] and when he was amazed by something, he would turn his hand over.[516] He would gesture with his hand while speaking and strike the inside of his left thumb with his right palm.[517] When he was angry, he would turn away.[518] When he was delighted, he would lower his gaze.[519] His laughter was mostly smiles, and when he would laugh, it was as though something like hailstones appeared…""""[520]

❦

by others'). Both readings are correct; the Prophet ﷺ did not and does not demean his followers, nor was he demeaned by others. He was held in awe even by his enemies. (AA)

511 Because he ﷺ witnessed everything as coming from his Lord. (AA)

512 Imam al-Bajuri notes that because someone might have assumed from Hind's statement that the Prophet ﷺ praised things of the lower world, he interjected, as if to say, 'Though he exalted blessings even if they were small and never found fault with any of them, the Prophet ﷺ did not praise the things of this lower world'. He mentioned food and drink in particular because finding fault with them is a trait of the arrogant, and overpraising them is a trait of the gluttonous. (AA)

513 The lower world did not cause anger to the Prophet ﷺ because he did not assign any essential value to its wealth, prestige, and treasures due to his certainty of its lowliness and ephemerality. Imam al-Tirmidhi recorded in his *Jami'* that the Prophet ﷺ said, 'Were the world equal to a gnat's wing in the sight of Allah, He would not allow a disbeliever to have a sip of water from it.' (MA)

514 That is, until he ﷺ sought justice for it and justice prevailed over the matter. For those who had experienced his pure love, tenderness and compassion, the anger of the Prophet ﷺ was a form of mercy shown to them. For those who rejected him, his anger was an exhortation and warning. When the Prophet ﷺ expressed anger it was *ruhani* (spirit-based) and solely for the sake of Allah, to ensure that truth prevailed. Because of his perfect embodiment of concern and love for his community, his firmness and anger had a positive and uplifting effect on their hearts. This is quite unlike those who, in the name of following the Sunna and 'speaking the truth', express *nafsani* (ego-based) anger that is anchored in selfishness instead of mercy and compassion. (AA)

515 Imam al-Bajuri notes that when the Prophet ﷺ would point at someone or something, he would gesture with his entire hand, not with one or two fingers, as is the habit of arrogant people. When the Prophet ﷺ would express belief in divine oneness (*tawhid*) or utter the testification said during the prayer (*tashahhud*), he would point with his blessed index finger, and when pointing to things or people he would use his entire hand. (AA)

516 When the Prophet ﷺ was amazed by something or pleasantly surprised, he would turn his blessed hand over such that his palm would face upwards. (AA)

517 The Prophet ﷺ would do this to emphasise his words or clarify his statements. (AA)

518 The scholars give two meanings to this phrase. It is either to exaggerate in moving away from something or to turn one's face away from that which caused anger. (MA)

519 This shows the great humility and shyness of the Messenger of Allah ﷺ. He was not possessed by the happiness of this world, for his heart was filled with the happiness of beholding Allah. This was the practice of Shaykh 'Abd al-Razzaq al-Halabi that we witnessed. (MA)

520 Because of the whiteness of the Prophet's blessed teeth ﷺ. (AA)

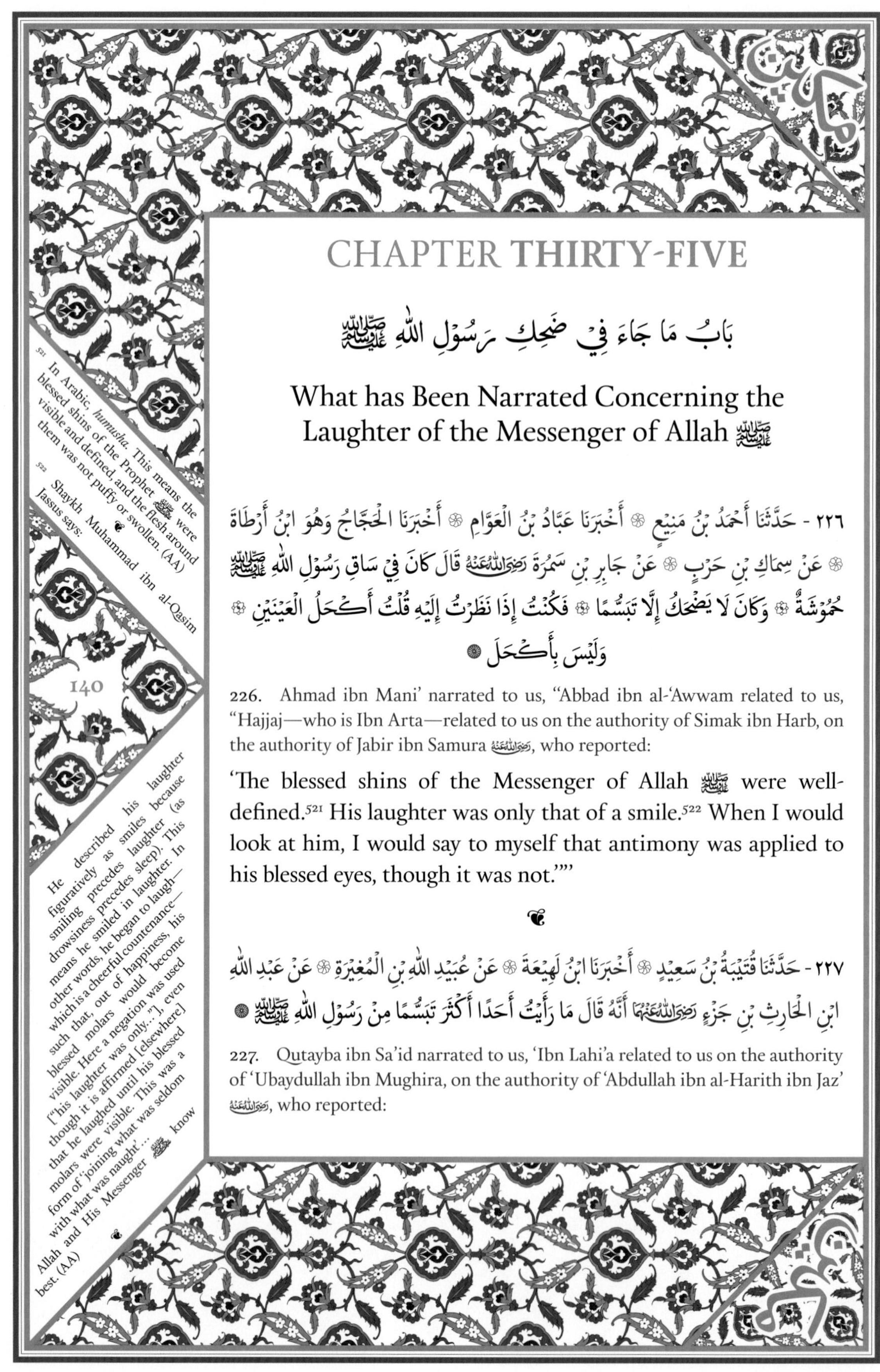

CHAPTER THIRTY-FIVE

بَابُ مَا جَاءَ فِي ضَحِكِ رَسُولِ اللهِ ﷺ

What has Been Narrated Concerning the Laughter of the Messenger of Allah ﷺ

٢٢٦ - حَدَّثَنَا أَحْمَدُ بْنُ مَنِيعٍ ۞ أَخْبَرَنَا عَبَّادُ بْنُ الْعَوَّامِ ۞ أَخْبَرَنَا الْحَجَّاجُ وَهُوَ ابْنُ أَرْطَاةَ ۞ عَنْ سِمَاكِ بْنِ حَرْبٍ ۞ عَنْ جَابِرِ بْنِ سَمُرَةَ رَضِيَ اللهُ عَنْهُ قَالَ كَانَ فِي سَاقِ رَسُولِ اللهِ ﷺ حُمُوشَةٌ ۞ وَكَانَ لَا يَضْحَكُ إِلَّا تَبَسُّمًا ۞ فَكُنْتُ إِذَا نَظَرْتُ إِلَيْهِ قُلْتُ أَكْحَلُ الْعَيْنَيْنِ ۞ وَلَيْسَ بِأَكْحَلَ ۞

226. Ahmad ibn Mani' narrated to us, "Abbad ibn al-'Awwam related to us, "Hajjaj—who is Ibn Arta—related to us on the authority of Simak ibn Harb, on the authority of Jabir ibn Samura رضي الله عنه, who reported:

'The blessed shins of the Messenger of Allah ﷺ were well-defined.[521] His laughter was only that of a smile.[522] When I would look at him, I would say to myself that antimony was applied to his blessed eyes, though it was not.'"

٢٢٧ - حَدَّثَنَا قُتَيْبَةُ بْنُ سَعِيدٍ ۞ أَخْبَرَنَا ابْنُ لَهِيعَةَ ۞ عَنْ عُبَيْدِ اللهِ بْنِ الْمُغِيرَةِ ۞ عَنْ عَبْدِ اللهِ ابْنِ الْحَارِثِ بْنِ جَزْءٍ رَضِيَ اللهُ عَنْهُمَا أَنَّهُ قَالَ مَا رَأَيْتُ أَحَدًا أَكْثَرَ تَبَسُّمًا مِنْ رَسُولِ اللهِ ﷺ ۞

227. Qutayba ibn Sa'id narrated to us, 'Ibn Lahi'a related to us on the authority of 'Ubaydullah ibn Mughira, on the authority of 'Abdullah ibn al-Harith ibn Jaz' رضي الله عنه, who reported:

[521] In Arabic, *humusha*. This means the blessed shins of the Prophet ﷺ were visible and defined, and the flesh around them was not puffy or swollen. (AA)

[522] Shaykh Muhammad ibn al-Qasim Jassus says: He described his laughter figuratively as smiles because smiling precedes laughter (as drowsiness precedes sleep). This means he smiled in laughter. In other words, he began to laugh—which is a cheerful countenance—such that, out of happiness, his blessed molars would become visible. Here a negation was used ["his laughter was only…"], even though it is affirmed [elsewhere] that he laughed until his blessed molars were visible. This was a form of 'joining what was seldom with what was naught'… Allah and His Messenger ﷺ know best. (AA)

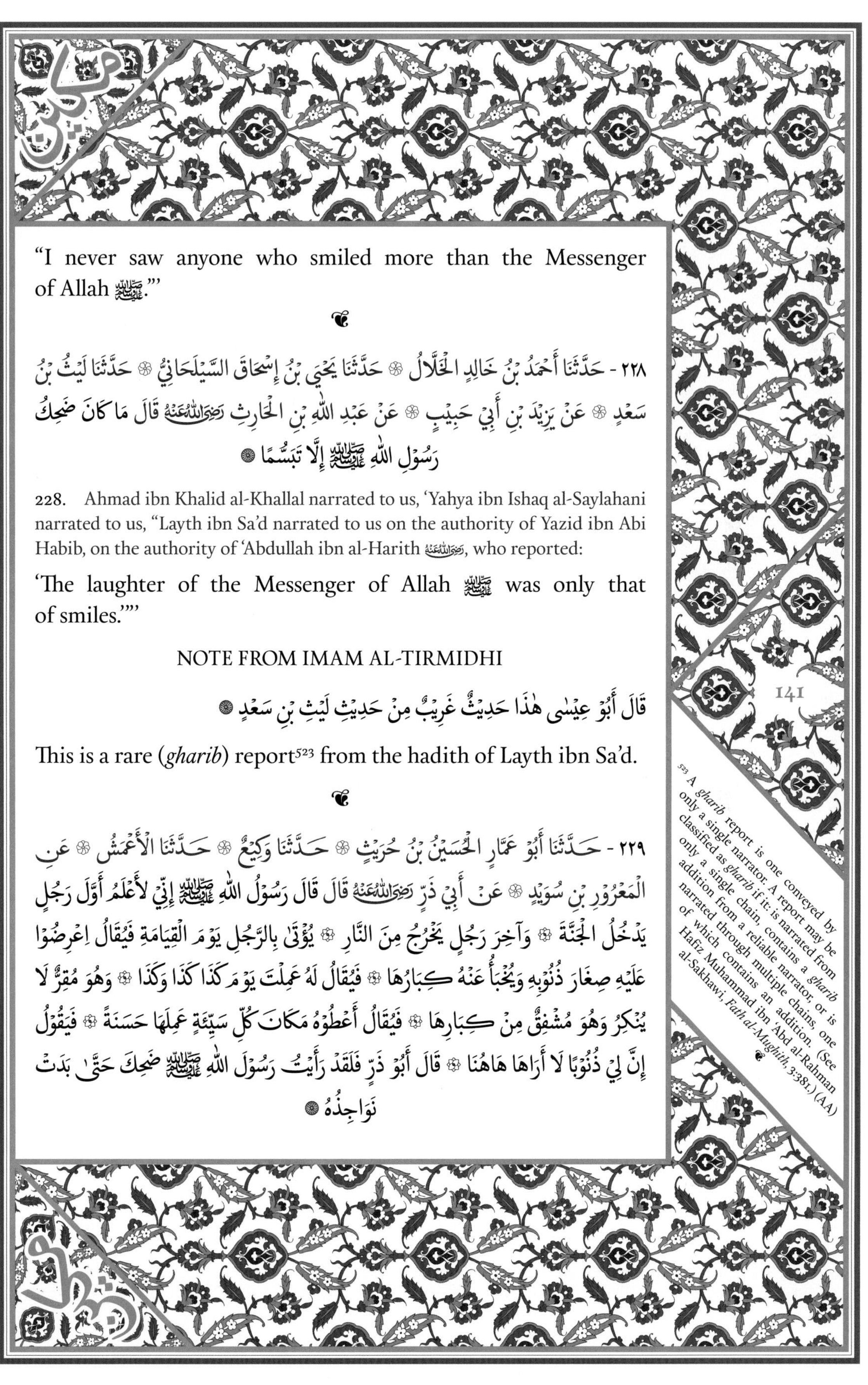

"I never saw anyone who smiled more than the Messenger of Allah ﷺ.'"

❦

٢٢٨ - حَدَّثَنَا أَحْمَدُ بْنُ خَالِدٍ الْخَلَّالُ ۞ حَدَّثَنَا يَحْيَى بْنُ إِسْحَاقَ السَّيْلَحَانِيُّ ۞ حَدَّثَنَا لَيْثُ بْنُ سَعْدٍ ۞ عَنْ يَزِيدَ بْنِ أَبِي حَبِيبٍ ۞ عَنْ عَبْدِ اللَّهِ بْنِ الْحَارِثِ رَضِيَ اللَّهُ عَنْهُ قَالَ مَا كَانَ ضَحِكُ رَسُولِ اللَّهِ ﷺ إِلَّا تَبَسُّمًا ۞

228. Ahmad ibn Khalid al-Khallal narrated to us, 'Yahya ibn Ishaq al-Saylahani narrated to us, "Layth ibn Sa'd narrated to us on the authority of Yazid ibn Abi Habib, on the authority of 'Abdullah ibn al-Harith رضي الله عنه, who reported:

'The laughter of the Messenger of Allah ﷺ was only that of smiles.'"'

NOTE FROM IMAM AL-TIRMIDHI

قَالَ أَبُو عِيسَى هَٰذَا حَدِيثٌ غَرِيبٌ مِنْ حَدِيثِ لَيْثِ بْنِ سَعْدٍ ۞

This is a rare (*gharib*) report[523] from the hadith of Layth ibn Sa'd.

❦

٢٢٩ - حَدَّثَنَا أَبُو عَمَّارٍ الْحُسَيْنُ بْنُ حُرَيْثٍ ۞ حَدَّثَنَا وَكِيعٌ ۞ حَدَّثَنَا الْأَعْمَشُ ۞ عَنِ الْمَعْرُورِ بْنِ سُوَيْدٍ ۞ عَنْ أَبِي ذَرٍّ رَضِيَ اللَّهُ عَنْهُ قَالَ قَالَ رَسُولُ اللَّهِ ﷺ إِنِّي لَأَعْلَمُ أَوَّلَ رَجُلٍ يَدْخُلُ الْجَنَّةَ ۞ وَآخِرَ رَجُلٍ يَخْرُجُ مِنَ النَّارِ ۞ يُؤْتَى بِالرَّجُلِ يَوْمَ الْقِيَامَةِ فَيُقَالُ اعْرِضُوا عَلَيْهِ صِغَارَ ذُنُوبِهِ وَيُخَبَّأُ عَنْهُ كِبَارُهَا ۞ فَيُقَالُ لَهُ عَمِلْتَ يَوْمَ كَذَا كَذَا وَكَذَا ۞ وَهُوَ مُقِرٌّ لَا يُنْكِرُ وَهُوَ مُشْفِقٌ مِنْ كِبَارِهَا ۞ فَيُقَالُ أَعْطُوهُ مَكَانَ كُلِّ سَيِّئَةٍ عَمِلَهَا حَسَنَةً ۞ فَيَقُولُ إِنَّ لِي ذُنُوبًا لَا أَرَاهَا هَاهُنَا ۞ قَالَ أَبُو ذَرٍّ فَلَقَدْ رَأَيْتُ رَسُولَ اللَّهِ ﷺ ضَحِكَ حَتَّىٰ بَدَتْ نَوَاجِذُهُ ۞

[523] A *gharib* report is one conveyed by only a single narrator. A report may be classified as *gharib* if it: is narrated from only a single chain, contains a *gharib* addition from a reliable narrator, or is narrated through multiple chains, one of which contains an addition. (See Hafiz Muhammad ibn 'Abd al-Rahman al-Sakhawi, *Fath al-Mughith*, 3:381.) (AA)

❦

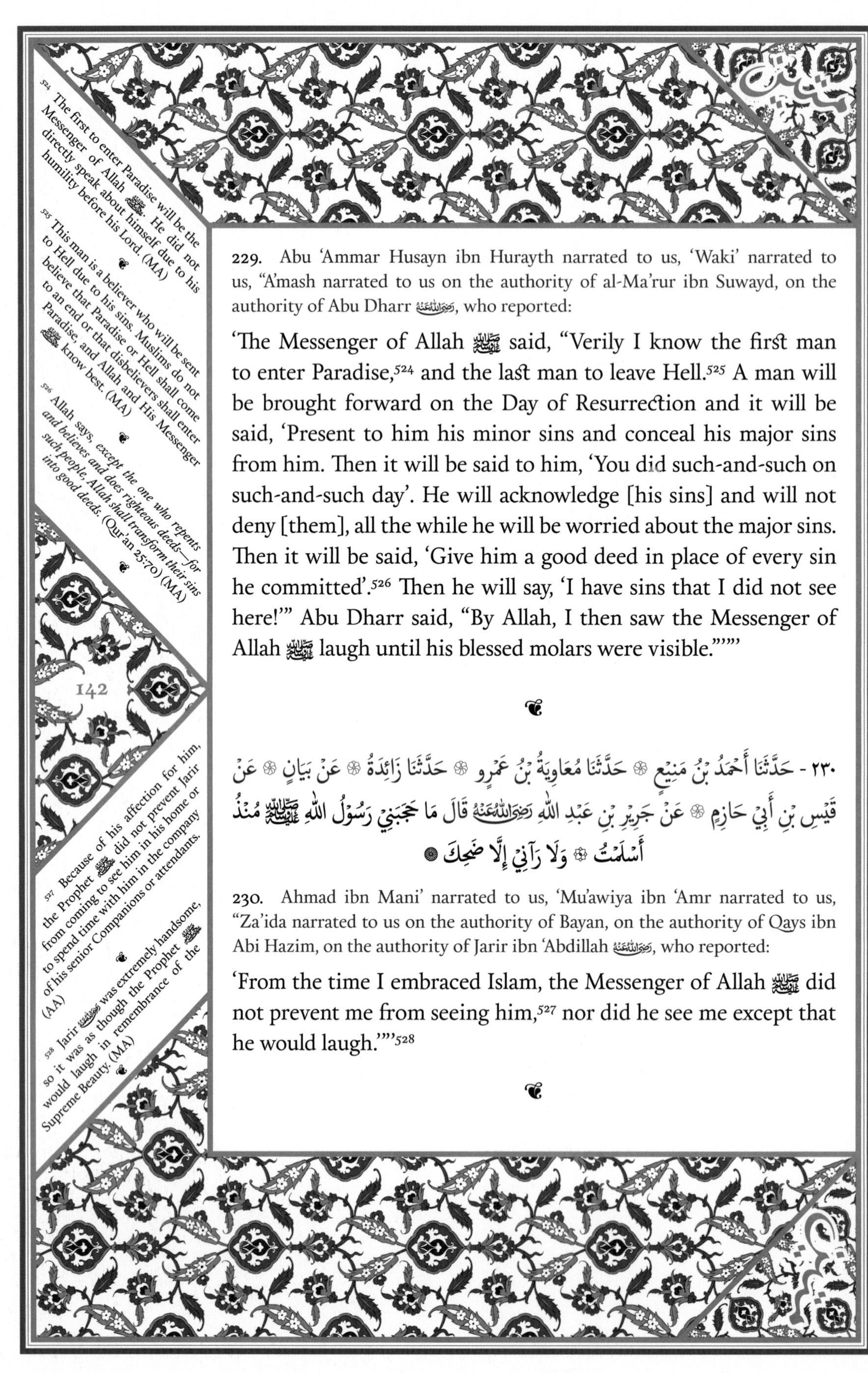

229. Abu 'Ammar Husayn ibn Hurayth narrated to us, 'Waki' narrated to us, "A'mash narrated to us on the authority of al-Ma'rur ibn Suwayd, on the authority of Abu Dharr رضي الله عنه, who reported:

'The Messenger of Allah ﷺ said, "Verily I know the first man to enter Paradise,[524] and the last man to leave Hell.[525] A man will be brought forward on the Day of Resurrection and it will be said, 'Present to him his minor sins and conceal his major sins from him. Then it will be said to him, 'You did such-and-such on such-and-such day'. He will acknowledge [his sins] and will not deny [them], all the while he will be worried about the major sins. Then it will be said, 'Give him a good deed in place of every sin he committed'.[526] Then he will say, 'I have sins that I did not see here!'" Abu Dharr said, "By Allah, I then saw the Messenger of Allah ﷺ laugh until his blessed molars were visible."'"

٢٣٠ - حَدَّثَنَا أَحْمَدُ بْنُ مَنِيعٍ ۞ حَدَّثَنَا مُعَاوِيَةُ بْنُ عَمْرٍو ۞ حَدَّثَنَا زَائِدَةُ ۞ عَنْ بَيَانٍ ۞ عَنْ قَيْسِ بْنِ أَبِي حَازِمٍ ۞ عَنْ جَرِيرِ بْنِ عَبْدِ اللهِ رَضِيَ اللهُ عَنْهُ قَالَ مَا حَجَبَنِي رَسُولُ اللهِ ﷺ مُنْذُ أَسْلَمْتُ ۞ وَلَا رَآنِي إِلَّا ضَحِكَ ۞

230. Ahmad ibn Mani' narrated to us, 'Mu'awiya ibn 'Amr narrated to us, "Za'ida narrated to us on the authority of Bayan, on the authority of Qays ibn Abi Hazim, on the authority of Jarir ibn 'Abdillah رضي الله عنه, who reported:

'From the time I embraced Islam, the Messenger of Allah ﷺ did not prevent me from seeing him,[527] nor did he see me except that he would laugh.'"[528]

[524] The first to enter Paradise will be the Messenger of Allah ﷺ. He did not directly speak about himself due to his humility before his Lord. (MA)

[525] This man is a believer who will be sent to Hell due to his sins. Muslims do not believe that Paradise or Hell shall come to an end or that disbelievers shall enter Paradise, and Allah and His Messenger ﷺ know best. (MA)

[526] Allah says, *except the one who repents and believes and does righteous deeds—for such people, Allah shall transform their sins into good deeds.* (Qur'an 25:70) (MA)

[527] Because of his affection for him, the Prophet ﷺ did not prevent Jarir from coming to see him in his home or to spend time with him in the company of his senior Companions or attendants. (AA)

[528] Jarir رضي الله عنه was extremely handsome, so it was as though the Prophet ﷺ would laugh in remembrance of the Supreme Beauty. (MA)

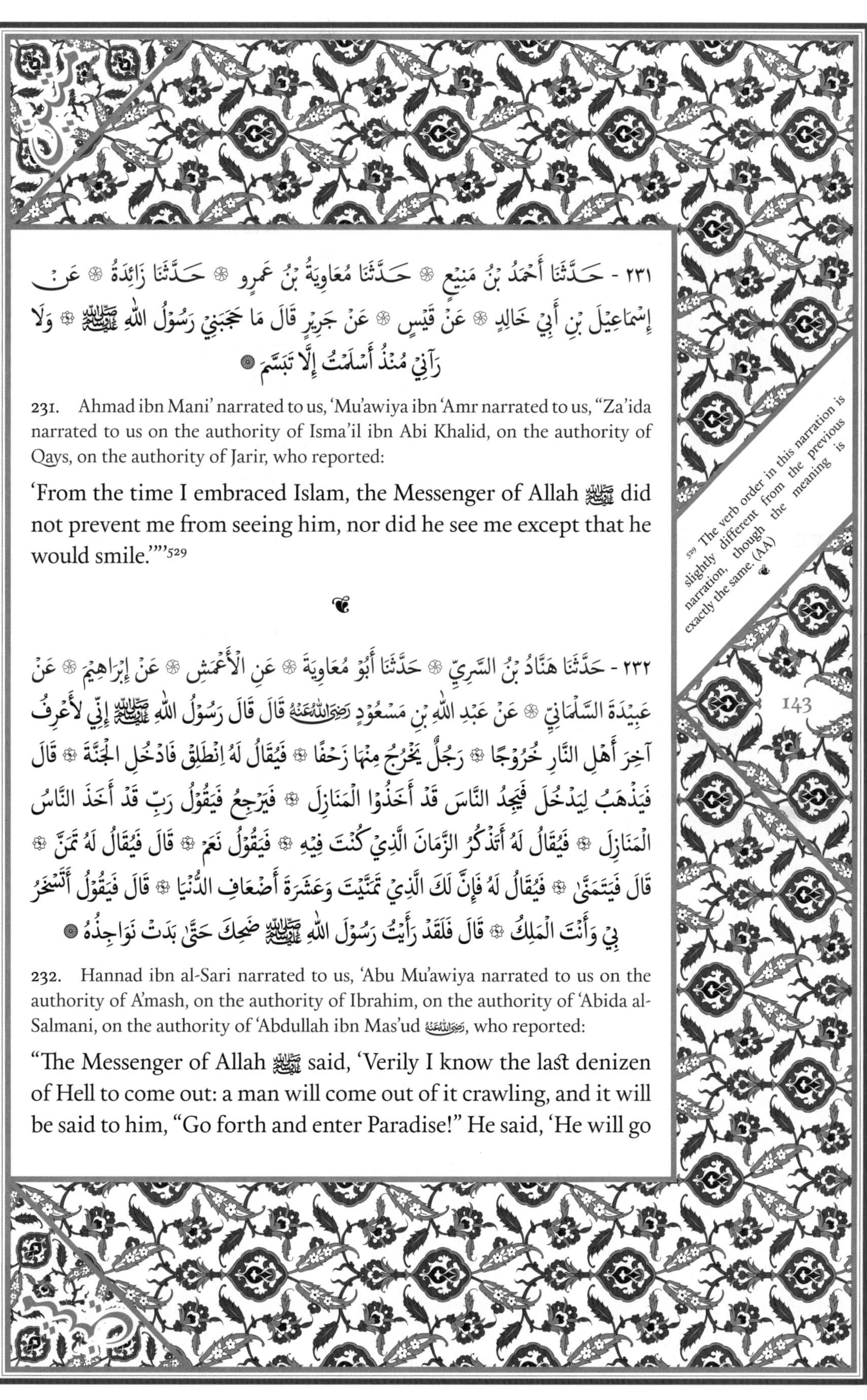

٢٣١ - حَدَّثَنَا أَحْمَدُ بْنُ مَنِيعٍ ❀ حَدَّثَنَا مُعَاوِيَةُ بْنُ عَمْرٍو ❀ حَدَّثَنَا زَائِدَةُ ❀ عَنْ إِسْمَاعِيلَ بْنِ أَبِي خَالِدٍ ❀ عَنْ قَيْسٍ ❀ عَنْ جَرِيرٍ قَالَ مَا حَجَبَنِي رَسُولُ اللهِ ﷺ ❀ وَلَا رَآنِي مُنْذُ أَسْلَمْتُ إِلَّا تَبَسَّمَ ❀

231. Ahmad ibn Mani' narrated to us, 'Mu'awiya ibn 'Amr narrated to us, "Za'ida narrated to us on the authority of Isma'il ibn Abi Khalid, on the authority of Qays, on the authority of Jarir, who reported:

'From the time I embraced Islam, the Messenger of Allah ﷺ did not prevent me from seeing him, nor did he see me except that he would smile.'"'[529]

٢٣٢ - حَدَّثَنَا هَنَّادُ بْنُ السَّرِيِّ ❀ حَدَّثَنَا أَبُو مُعَاوِيَةَ ❀ عَنِ الْأَعْمَشِ ❀ عَنْ إِبْرَاهِيمَ ❀ عَنْ عَبِيدَةَ السَّلْمَانِيِّ ❀ عَنْ عَبْدِ اللهِ بْنِ مَسْعُودٍ رَضِيَ اللهُ عَنْهُ قَالَ قَالَ رَسُولُ اللهِ ﷺ إِنِّي لَأَعْرِفُ آخِرَ أَهْلِ النَّارِ خُرُوجًا ❀ رَجُلٌ يَخْرُجُ مِنْهَا زَحْفًا ❀ فَيُقَالُ لَهُ انْطَلِقْ فَادْخُلِ الْجَنَّةَ ❀ قَالَ فَيَذْهَبُ لِيَدْخُلَ فَيَجِدُ النَّاسَ قَدْ أَخَذُوا الْمَنَازِلَ ❀ فَيَرْجِعُ فَيَقُولُ رَبِّ قَدْ أَخَذَ النَّاسُ الْمَنَازِلَ ❀ فَيُقَالُ لَهُ أَتَذْكُرُ الزَّمَانَ الَّذِي كُنْتَ فِيهِ ❀ فَيَقُولُ نَعَمْ ❀ قَالَ فَيُقَالُ لَهُ تَمَنَّ ❀ قَالَ فَيَتَمَنَّى ❀ فَيُقَالُ لَهُ فَإِنَّ لَكَ الَّذِي تَمَنَّيْتَ وَعَشَرَةَ أَضْعَافِ الدُّنْيَا ❀ قَالَ فَيَقُولُ أَتَسْخَرُ بِي وَأَنْتَ الْمَلِكُ ❀ قَالَ فَلَقَدْ رَأَيْتُ رَسُولَ اللهِ ﷺ ضَحِكَ حَتَّى بَدَتْ نَوَاجِذُهُ ❀

232. Hannad ibn al-Sari narrated to us, 'Abu Mu'awiya narrated to us on the authority of A'mash, on the authority of Ibrahim, on the authority of 'Abida al-Salmani, on the authority of 'Abdullah ibn Mas'ud رضي الله عنه, who reported:

"The Messenger of Allah ﷺ said, 'Verily I know the last denizen of Hell to come out: a man will come out of it crawling, and it will be said to him, "Go forth and enter Paradise!" He said, 'He will go

[529] The verb order in this narration is slightly different from the previous narration, though the meaning is exactly the same. (AA)

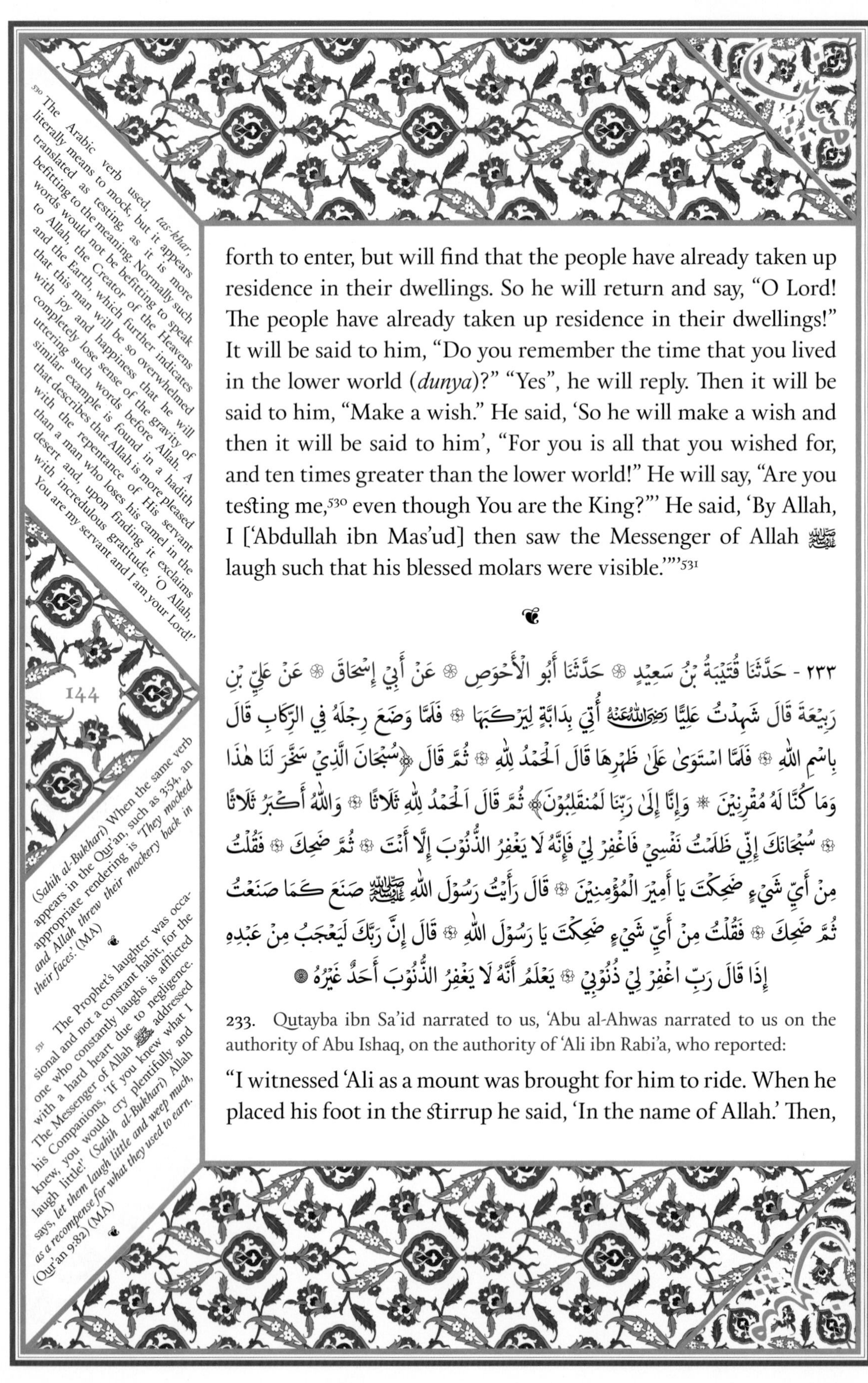

forth to enter, but will find that the people have already taken up residence in their dwellings. So he will return and say, "O Lord! The people have already taken up residence in their dwellings!" It will be said to him, "Do you remember the time that you lived in the lower world (*dunya*)?" "Yes", he will reply. Then it will be said to him, "Make a wish." He said, 'So he will make a wish and then it will be said to him', "For you is all that you wished for, and ten times greater than the lower world!" He will say, "Are you testing me,[530] even though You are the King?"' He said, 'By Allah, I ['Abdullah ibn Mas'ud] then saw the Messenger of Allah ﷺ laugh such that his blessed molars were visible.'"'[531]

❦

٢٣٣ - حَدَّثَنَا قُتَيْبَةُ بْنُ سَعِيدٍ ۞ حَدَّثَنَا أَبُو الْأَحْوَصِ ۞ عَنْ أَبِي إِسْحَاقَ ۞ عَنْ عَلِيِّ بْنِ رَبِيعَةَ قَالَ شَهِدْتُ عَلِيًّا رَضِيَ اللَّهُ عَنْهُ أُتِيَ بِدَابَّةٍ لِيَرْكَبَهَا ۞ فَلَمَّا وَضَعَ رِجْلَهُ فِي الرِّكَابِ قَالَ بِاسْمِ اللهِ ۞ فَلَمَّا اسْتَوَىٰ عَلَىٰ ظَهْرِهَا قَالَ الْحَمْدُ لِلَّهِ ۞ ثُمَّ قَالَ ﴿سُبْحَانَ الَّذِي سَخَّرَ لَنَا هَٰذَا وَمَا كُنَّا لَهُ مُقْرِنِينَ ۞ وَإِنَّا إِلَىٰ رَبِّنَا لَمُنقَلِبُونَ﴾ ثُمَّ قَالَ الْحَمْدُ لِلَّهِ ثَلَاثًا ۞ وَاللهُ أَكْبَرُ ثَلَاثًا ۞ سُبْحَانَكَ إِنِّي ظَلَمْتُ نَفْسِي فَاغْفِرْ لِي فَإِنَّهُ لَا يَغْفِرُ الذُّنُوبَ إِلَّا أَنْتَ ۞ ثُمَّ ضَحِكَ ۞ فَقُلْتُ مِنْ أَيِّ شَيْءٍ ضَحِكْتَ يَا أَمِيرَ الْمُؤْمِنِينَ ۞ قَالَ رَأَيْتُ رَسُولَ اللهِ ﷺ صَنَعَ كَمَا صَنَعْتُ ثُمَّ ضَحِكَ ۞ فَقُلْتُ مِنْ أَيِّ شَيْءٍ ضَحِكْتَ يَا رَسُولَ اللهِ ۞ قَالَ إِنَّ رَبَّكَ لَيَعْجَبُ مِنْ عَبْدِهِ إِذَا قَالَ رَبِّ اغْفِرْ لِي ذُنُوبِي ۞ يَعْلَمُ أَنَّهُ لَا يَغْفِرُ الذُّنُوبَ أَحَدٌ غَيْرُهُ ۞

233. Qutayba ibn Sa'id narrated to us, 'Abu al-Ahwas narrated to us on the authority of Abu Ishaq, on the authority of 'Ali ibn Rabi'a, who reported:

"I witnessed 'Ali as a mount was brought for him to ride. When he placed his foot in the stirrup he said, 'In the name of Allah.' Then,

[530] The Arabic verb used, *tas-khar*, literally means to mock, but it appears translated as testing, as it is more befitting to the meaning. Normally such words would not be befitting to speak to Allah, the Creator of the Heavens and the Earth, which further indicates that this man will be so overwhelmed with joy and happiness that he will completely lose sense of the gravity of uttering such words before Allah. A similar example is found in a hadith that describes that Allah is more pleased with the repentance of His servant than a man who loses his camel in the desert and, upon finding it exclaims with incredulous gratitude, 'O Allah, You are my servant and I am your Lord!' (*Sahih al-Bukhari*) When the same verb appears in the Qur'an, such as 3:54, an appropriate rendering is '*They mocked and Allah threw their mockery back in their faces.*' (MA)

[531] The Prophet's laughter was occasional and not a constant habit, for the one who constantly laughs is afflicted with a hard heart due to negligence. The Messenger of Allah ﷺ addressed his Companions, 'If you knew what I knew, you would cry plentifully and laugh little!' (*Sahih al-Bukhari*) Allah says, *let them laugh little and weep much, as a recompense for what they used to earn.* (Qur'an 9:82) (MA)

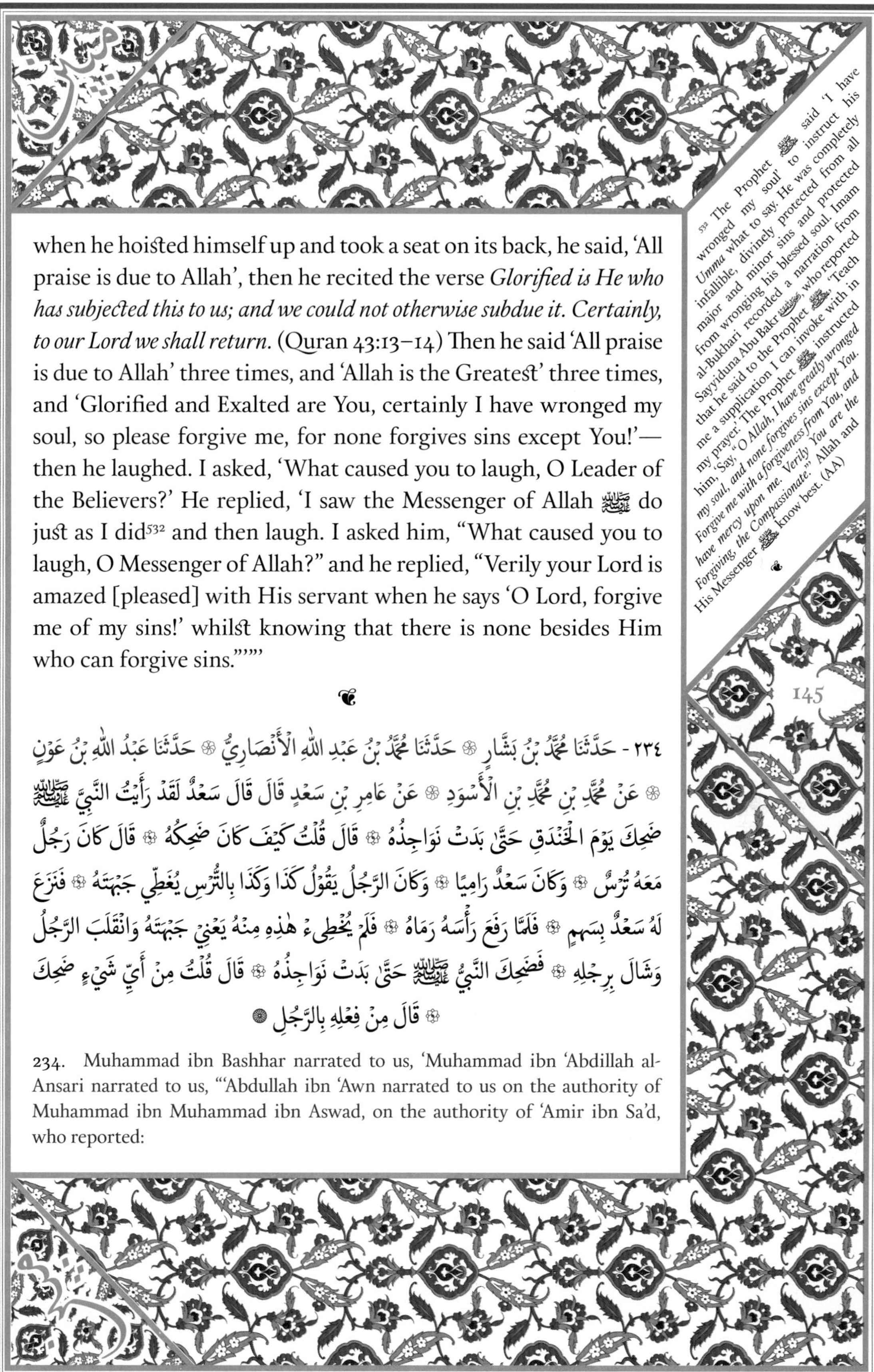

when he hoisted himself up and took a seat on its back, he said, 'All praise is due to Allah', then he recited the verse *Glorified is He who has subjected this to us; and we could not otherwise subdue it. Certainly, to our Lord we shall return.* (Quran 43:13–14) Then he said 'All praise is due to Allah' three times, and 'Allah is the Greatest' three times, and 'Glorified and Exalted are You, certainly I have wronged my soul, so please forgive me, for none forgives sins except You!'—then he laughed. I asked, 'What caused you to laugh, O Leader of the Believers?' He replied, 'I saw the Messenger of Allah ﷺ do just as I did[532] and then laugh. I asked him, "What caused you to laugh, O Messenger of Allah?" and he replied, "Verily your Lord is amazed [pleased] with His servant when he says 'O Lord, forgive me of my sins!' whilst knowing that there is none besides Him who can forgive sins."'"'

❦

٢٣٤ - حَدَّثَنَا مُحَمَّدُ بْنُ بَشَّارٍ ۞ حَدَّثَنَا مُحَمَّدُ بْنُ عَبْدِ اللهِ الْأَنْصَارِيُّ ۞ حَدَّثَنَا عَبْدُ اللهِ بْنُ عَوْنٍ ۞ عَنْ مُحَمَّدِ بْنِ مُحَمَّدِ بْنِ الْأَسْوَدِ ۞ عَنْ عَامِرِ بْنِ سَعْدٍ قَالَ قَالَ سَعْدٌ لَقَدْ رَأَيْتُ النَّبِيَّ ﷺ ضَحِكَ يَوْمَ الْخَنْدَقِ حَتَّىٰ بَدَتْ نَوَاجِذُهُ ۞ قَالَ قُلْتُ كَيْفَ كَانَ ضَحِكُهُ ۞ قَالَ كَانَ رَجُلٌ مَعَهُ تُرْسٌ ۞ وَكَانَ سَعْدٌ رَامِيًا ۞ وَكَانَ الرَّجُلُ يَقُولُ كَذَا وَكَذَا بِالتُّرْسِ يُغَطِّي جَبْهَتَهُ ۞ فَنَزَعَ لَهُ سَعْدٌ بِسَهْمٍ ۞ فَلَمَّا رَفَعَ رَأْسَهُ رَمَاهُ ۞ فَلَمْ يُخْطِئْ هٰذِهِ مِنْهُ يَعْنِي جَبْهَتَهُ وَانْقَلَبَ الرَّجُلُ وَشَالَ بِرِجْلِهِ ۞ فَضَحِكَ النَّبِيُّ ﷺ حَتَّىٰ بَدَتْ نَوَاجِذُهُ ۞ قَالَ قُلْتُ مِنْ أَيِّ شَيْءٍ ضَحِكَ ۞ قَالَ مِنْ فِعْلِهِ بِالرَّجُلِ ۞

234. Muhammad ibn Bashhar narrated to us, 'Muhammad ibn 'Abdillah al-Ansari narrated to us, "'Abdullah ibn 'Awn narrated to us on the authority of Muhammad ibn Muhammad ibn Aswad, on the authority of 'Amir ibn Sa'd, who reported:

532 The Prophet ﷺ said 'I have wronged my soul' to instruct his *Umma* what to say. He was completely infallible, divinely protected from all major and minor sins and protected from wronging his blessed soul. Imam al-Bukhari recorded a narration from Sayyiduna Abu Bakr, who reported that he said to the Prophet ﷺ, 'Teach me a supplication I can invoke with in my prayer.' The Prophet ﷺ instructed him, 'Say, "*O Allah, I have greatly wronged my soul, and none forgives sins except You. Forgive me with a forgiveness from You, and have mercy upon me. Verily You are the Forgiving, the Compassionate.*"' Allah and His Messenger ﷺ know best. (AA)

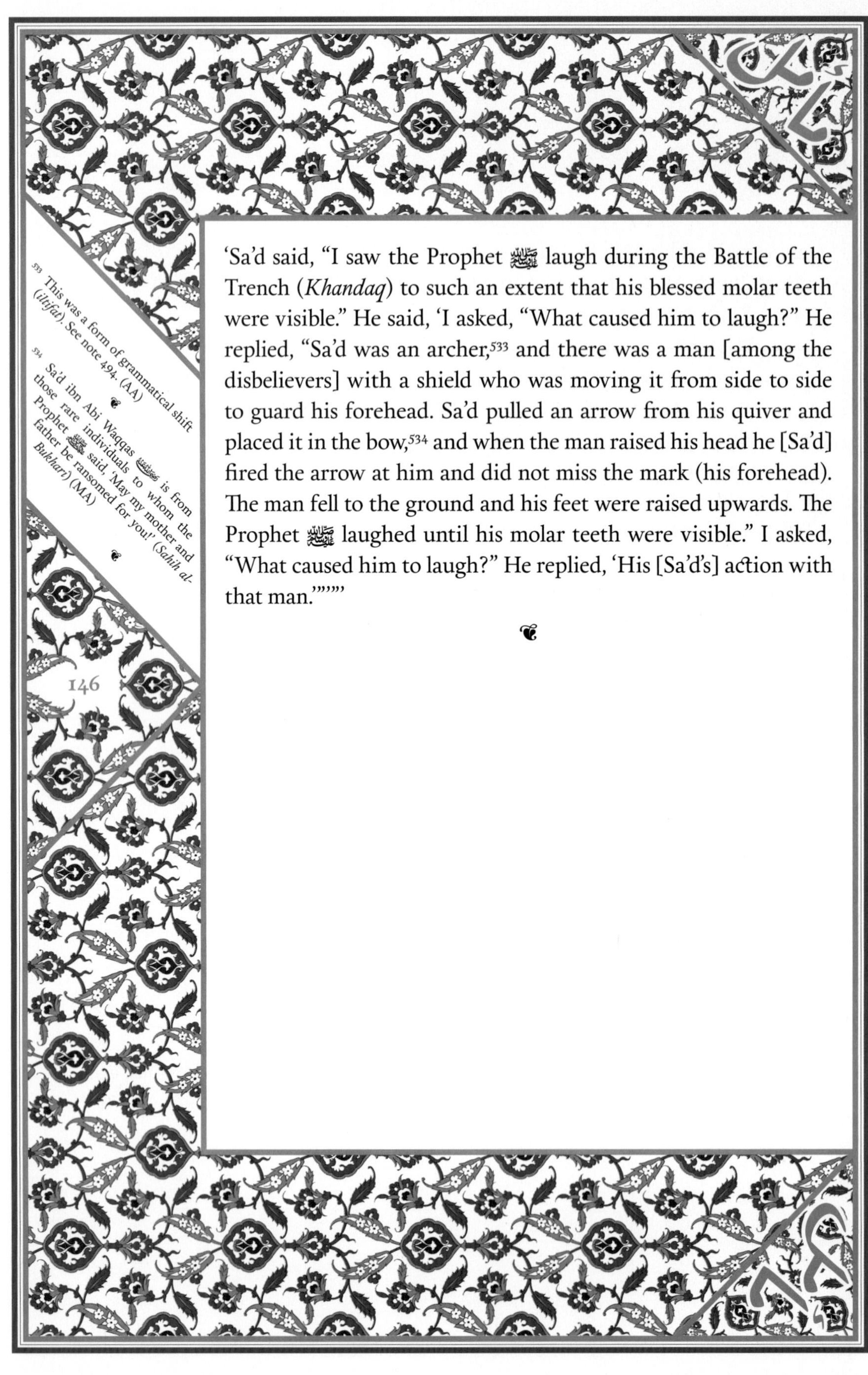

'Sa'd said, "I saw the Prophet ﷺ laugh during the Battle of the Trench (*Khandaq*) to such an extent that his blessed molar teeth were visible." He said, 'I asked, "What caused him to laugh?" He replied, "Sa'd was an archer,[533] and there was a man [among the disbelievers] with a shield who was moving it from side to side to guard his forehead. Sa'd pulled an arrow from his quiver and placed it in the bow,[534] and when the man raised his head he [Sa'd] fired the arrow at him and did not miss the mark (his forehead). The man fell to the ground and his feet were raised upwards. The Prophet ﷺ laughed until his molar teeth were visible." I asked, "What caused him to laugh?" He replied, 'His [Sa'd's] action with that man.'"'"'

❦

[533] This was a form of grammatical shift (*iltifat*). See note 494. (AA)

[534] Sa'd ibn Abi Waqqas رضي الله عنه is from those rare individuals to whom the Prophet ﷺ said, 'May my mother and father be ransomed for you!' (*Sahih al-Bukhari*) (MA)

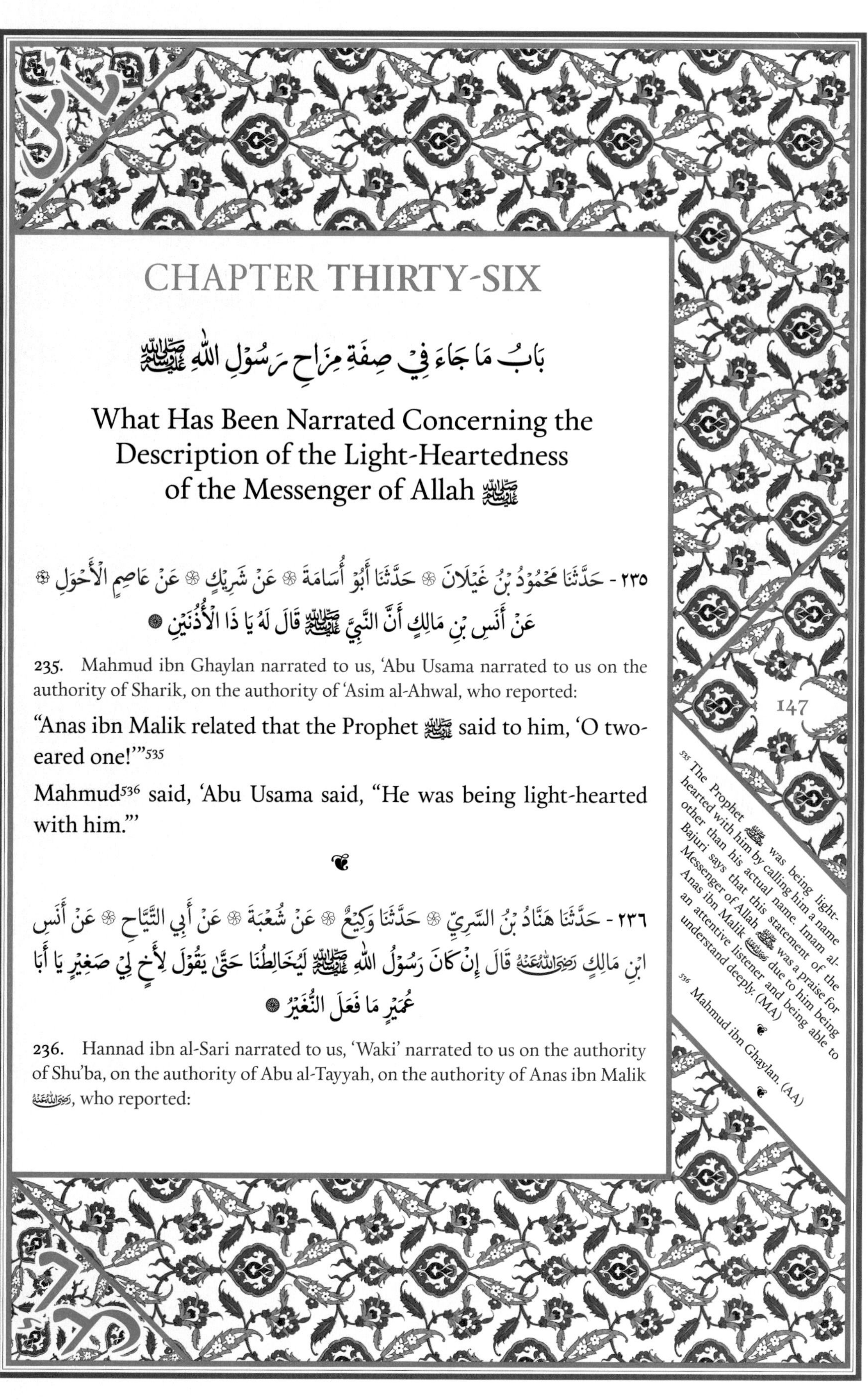

CHAPTER THIRTY-SIX

بَابُ مَا جَاءَ فِي صِفَةِ مِزَاحِ رَسُولِ اللَّهِ ﷺ

What Has Been Narrated Concerning the Description of the Light-Heartedness of the Messenger of Allah ﷺ

٢٣٥ - حَدَّثَنَا مَحْمُودُ بْنُ غَيْلَانَ ۞ حَدَّثَنَا أَبُو أُسَامَةَ ۞ عَنْ شَرِيكٍ ۞ عَنْ عَاصِمٍ الْأَحْوَلِ ۞ عَنْ أَنَسِ بْنِ مَالِكٍ أَنَّ النَّبِيَّ ﷺ قَالَ لَهُ يَا ذَا الْأُذُنَيْنِ ۞

235. Mahmud ibn Ghaylan narrated to us, 'Abu Usama narrated to us on the authority of Sharik, on the authority of 'Asim al-Ahwal, who reported:

"Anas ibn Malik related that the Prophet ﷺ said to him, 'O two-eared one!'"[535]

Mahmud[536] said, 'Abu Usama said, "He was being light-hearted with him."'

❦

٢٣٦ - حَدَّثَنَا هَنَّادُ بْنُ السَّرِيِّ ۞ حَدَّثَنَا وَكِيعٌ ۞ عَنْ شُعْبَةَ ۞ عَنْ أَبِي التَّيَّاحِ ۞ عَنْ أَنَسِ بْنِ مَالِكٍ رَضِيَ اللَّهُ عَنْهُ قَالَ إِنْ كَانَ رَسُولُ اللَّهِ ﷺ لَيُخَالِطُنَا حَتَّى يَقُولَ لِأَخٍ لِي صَغِيرٍ يَا أَبَا عُمَيْرٍ مَا فَعَلَ النُّغَيْرُ ۞

236. Hannad ibn al-Sari narrated to us, 'Waki' narrated to us on the authority of Shu'ba, on the authority of Abu al-Tayyah, on the authority of Anas ibn Malik رضي الله عنه, who reported:

[535] The Prophet ﷺ was being light-hearted with him by calling him a name other than his actual name. Imam al-Bajuri says that this statement of the Messenger of Allah ﷺ was a praise for Anas ibn Malik رضي الله عنه due to him being an attentive listener and being able to understand deeply. (MA)

[536] Mahmud ibn Ghaylan. (AA)

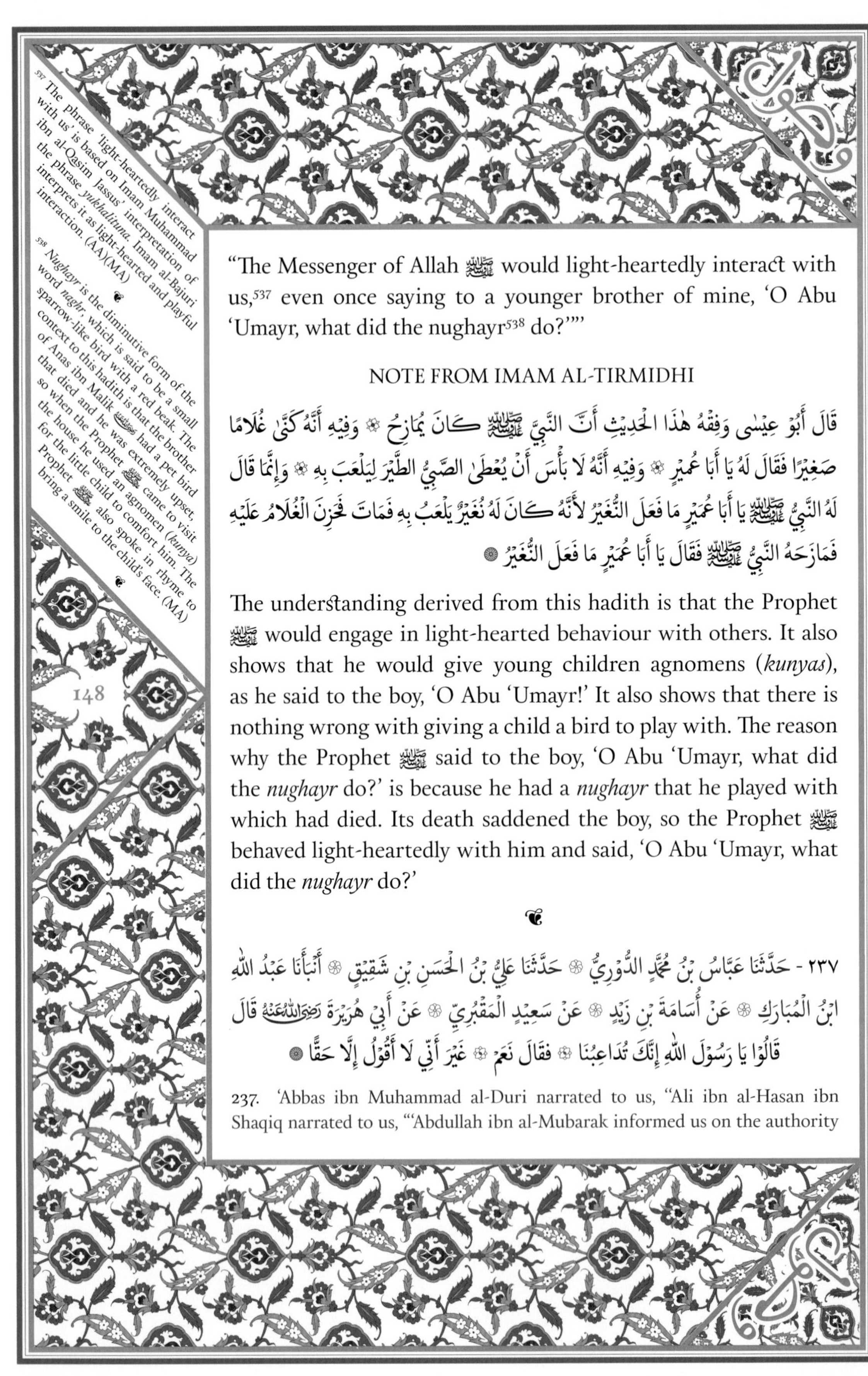

"The Messenger of Allah ﷺ would light-heartedly interact with us,[537] even once saying to a younger brother of mine, 'O Abu 'Umayr, what did the nughayr[538] do?'"'

NOTE FROM IMAM AL-TIRMIDHI

قَالَ أَبُو عِيسَى وَفِقْهُ هٰذَا الْحَدِيثِ أَنَّ النَّبِيَّ ﷺ كَانَ يُمَازِحُ ۞ وَفِيهِ أَنَّهُ كَنَّى غُلَامًا صَغِيرًا فَقَالَ لَهُ يَا أَبَا عُمَيْرٍ ۞ وَفِيهِ أَنَّهُ لَا بَأْسَ أَنْ يُعْطَى الصَّبِيُّ الطَّيْرَ لِيَلْعَبَ بِهِ ۞ وَإِنَّمَا قَالَ لَهُ النَّبِيُّ ﷺ يَا أَبَا عُمَيْرٍ مَا فَعَلَ النُّغَيْرُ لِأَنَّهُ كَانَ لَهُ نُغَيْرٌ يَلْعَبُ بِهِ فَمَاتَ فَحَزِنَ الْغُلَامُ عَلَيْهِ فَمَازَحَهُ النَّبِيُّ ﷺ فَقَالَ يَا أَبَا عُمَيْرٍ مَا فَعَلَ النُّغَيْرُ ۞

The understanding derived from this hadith is that the Prophet ﷺ would engage in light-hearted behaviour with others. It also shows that he would give young children agnomens (*kunyas*), as he said to the boy, 'O Abu 'Umayr!' It also shows that there is nothing wrong with giving a child a bird to play with. The reason why the Prophet ﷺ said to the boy, 'O Abu 'Umayr, what did the *nughayr* do?' is because he had a *nughayr* that he played with which had died. Its death saddened the boy, so the Prophet ﷺ behaved light-heartedly with him and said, 'O Abu 'Umayr, what did the *nughayr* do?'

❦

٢٣٧ - حَدَّثَنَا عَبَّاسُ بْنُ مُحَمَّدٍ الدُّورِيُّ ۞ حَدَّثَنَا عَلِيُّ بْنُ الْحَسَنِ بْنِ شَقِيقٍ ۞ أَنْبَأَنَا عَبْدُ اللهِ ابْنُ الْمُبَارَكِ ۞ عَنْ أُسَامَةَ بْنِ زَيْدٍ ۞ عَنْ سَعِيدٍ الْمَقْبُرِيِّ ۞ عَنْ أَبِي هُرَيْرَةَ رَضِيَ اللهُ عَنْهُ قَالَ قَالُوا يَا رَسُولَ اللهِ إِنَّكَ تُدَاعِبُنَا ۞ فَقَالَ نَعَمْ ۞ غَيْرَ أَنِّي لَا أَقُولُ إِلَّا حَقًّا ۞

237. 'Abbas ibn Muhammad al-Duri narrated to us, "Ali ibn al-Hasan ibn Shaqiq narrated to us, "'Abdullah ibn al-Mubarak informed us on the authority

[537] The phrase 'light-heartedly interact with us' is based on Imam Muhammad ibn al-Qasim Jassus' interpretation of the phrase *yukhalituna*. Imam al-Bajuri interprets it as light-hearted and playful interaction. (AA)(MA)

❦

[538] *Nughayr* is the diminutive form of the word *naghr*, which is said to be a small sparrow-like bird with a red beak. The context to this hadith is that the brother of Anas ibn Malik رضي الله عنه had a pet bird that died and he was extremely upset, so when the Prophet ﷺ came to visit the house he used an agnomen (*kunya*) for the little child to comfort him. The Prophet ﷺ also spoke in rhyme to bring a smile to the child's face. (MA)

❦

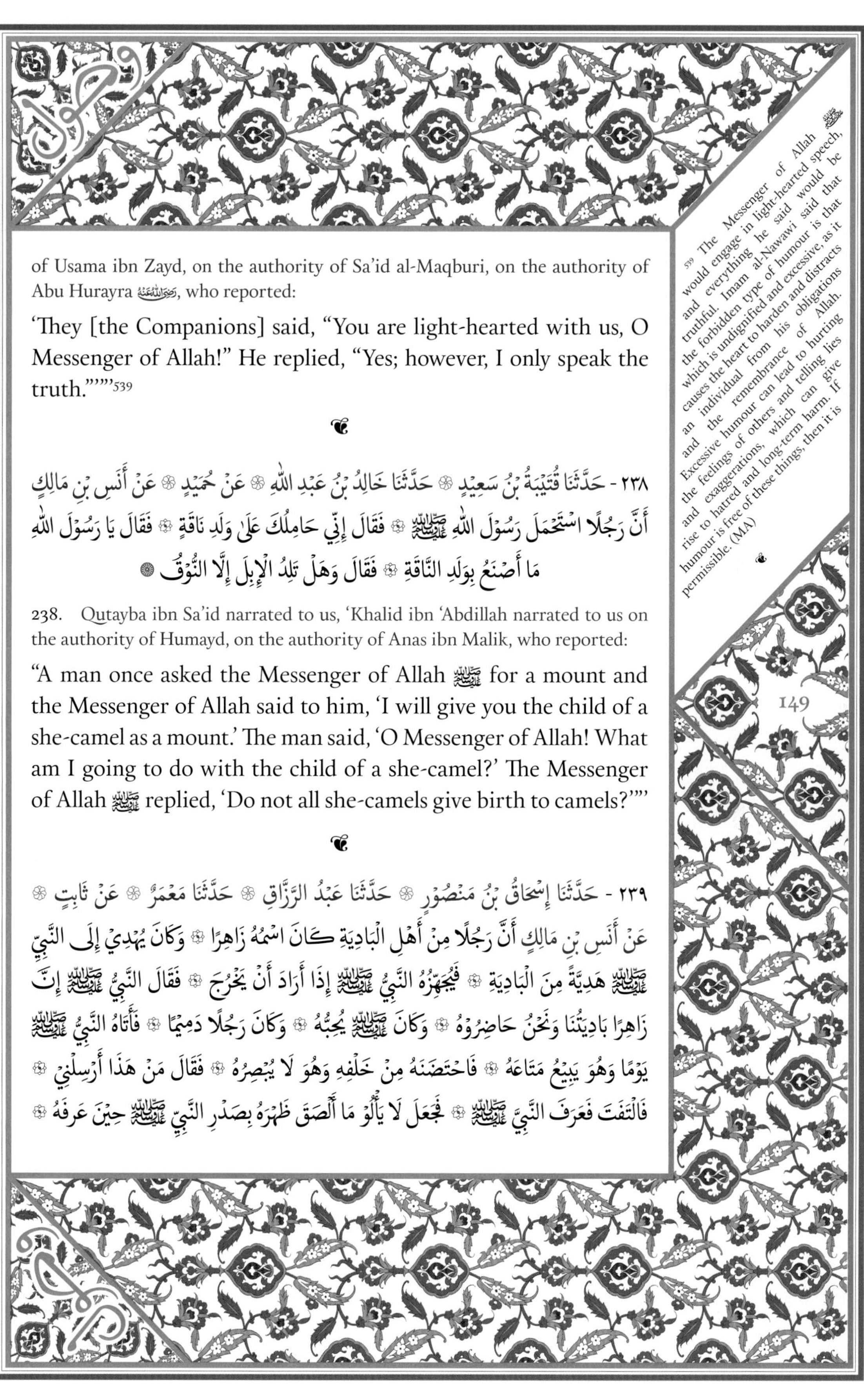

of Usama ibn Zayd, on the authority of Sa'id al-Maqburi, on the authority of Abu Hurayra رضي الله عنه, who reported:

'They [the Companions] said, "You are light-hearted with us, O Messenger of Allah!" He replied, "Yes; however, I only speak the truth."''[539]

٢٣٨ - حَدَّثَنَا قُتَيْبَةُ بْنُ سَعِيدٍ ۞ حَدَّثَنَا خَالِدُ بْنُ عَبْدِ اللهِ ۞ عَنْ حُمَيْدٍ ۞ عَنْ أَنَسِ بْنِ مَالِكٍ أَنَّ رَجُلًا اسْتَحْمَلَ رَسُولَ اللهِ ﷺ ۞ فَقَالَ إِنِّي حَامِلُكَ عَلَى وَلَدِ نَاقَةٍ ۞ فَقَالَ يَا رَسُولَ اللهِ مَا أَصْنَعُ بِوَلَدِ النَّاقَةِ ۞ فَقَالَ وَهَلْ تَلِدُ الْإِبِلَ إِلَّا النُّوقُ ۞

238. Qutayba ibn Sa'id narrated to us, 'Khalid ibn 'Abdillah narrated to us on the authority of Humayd, on the authority of Anas ibn Malik, who reported:

"A man once asked the Messenger of Allah ﷺ for a mount and the Messenger of Allah said to him, 'I will give you the child of a she-camel as a mount.' The man said, 'O Messenger of Allah! What am I going to do with the child of a she-camel?' The Messenger of Allah ﷺ replied, 'Do not all she-camels give birth to camels?''"

٢٣٩ - حَدَّثَنَا إِسْحَاقُ بْنُ مَنْصُورٍ ۞ حَدَّثَنَا عَبْدُ الرَّزَّاقِ ۞ حَدَّثَنَا مَعْمَرٌ ۞ عَنْ ثَابِتٍ ۞ عَنْ أَنَسِ بْنِ مَالِكٍ أَنَّ رَجُلًا مِنْ أَهْلِ الْبَادِيَةِ كَانَ اسْمُهُ زَاهِرًا ۞ وَكَانَ يُهْدِي إِلَى النَّبِيِّ ﷺ هَدِيَّةً مِنَ الْبَادِيَةِ ۞ فَيُجَهِّزُهُ النَّبِيُّ ﷺ إِذَا أَرَادَ أَنْ يَخْرُجَ ۞ فَقَالَ النَّبِيُّ ﷺ إِنَّ زَاهِرًا بَادِيَتُنَا وَنَحْنُ حَاضِرُوهُ ۞ وَكَانَ ﷺ يُحِبُّهُ ۞ وَكَانَ رَجُلًا دَمِيمًا ۞ فَأَتَاهُ النَّبِيُّ ﷺ يَوْمًا وَهُوَ يَبِيعُ مَتَاعَهُ ۞ فَاحْتَضَنَهُ مِنْ خَلْفِهِ وَهُوَ لَا يُبْصِرُهُ ۞ فَقَالَ مَنْ هَذَا أَرْسِلْنِي ۞ فَالْتَفَتَ فَعَرَفَ النَّبِيَّ ﷺ ۞ فَجَعَلَ لَا يَأْلُو مَا أَلْصَقَ ظَهْرَهُ بِصَدْرِ النَّبِيِّ ﷺ حِينَ عَرَفَهُ ۞

[539] The Messenger of Allah ﷺ would engage in light-hearted speech, and everything he said would be truthful. Imam al-Nawawi said that the forbidden type of humour is that which is undignified and excessive, as it causes the heart to harden and distracts an individual from his obligations and the remembrance of Allah. Excessive humour can lead to hurting the feelings of others and telling lies and exaggerations, which can give rise to hatred and long-term harm. If humour is free of these things, then it is permissible. (MA)

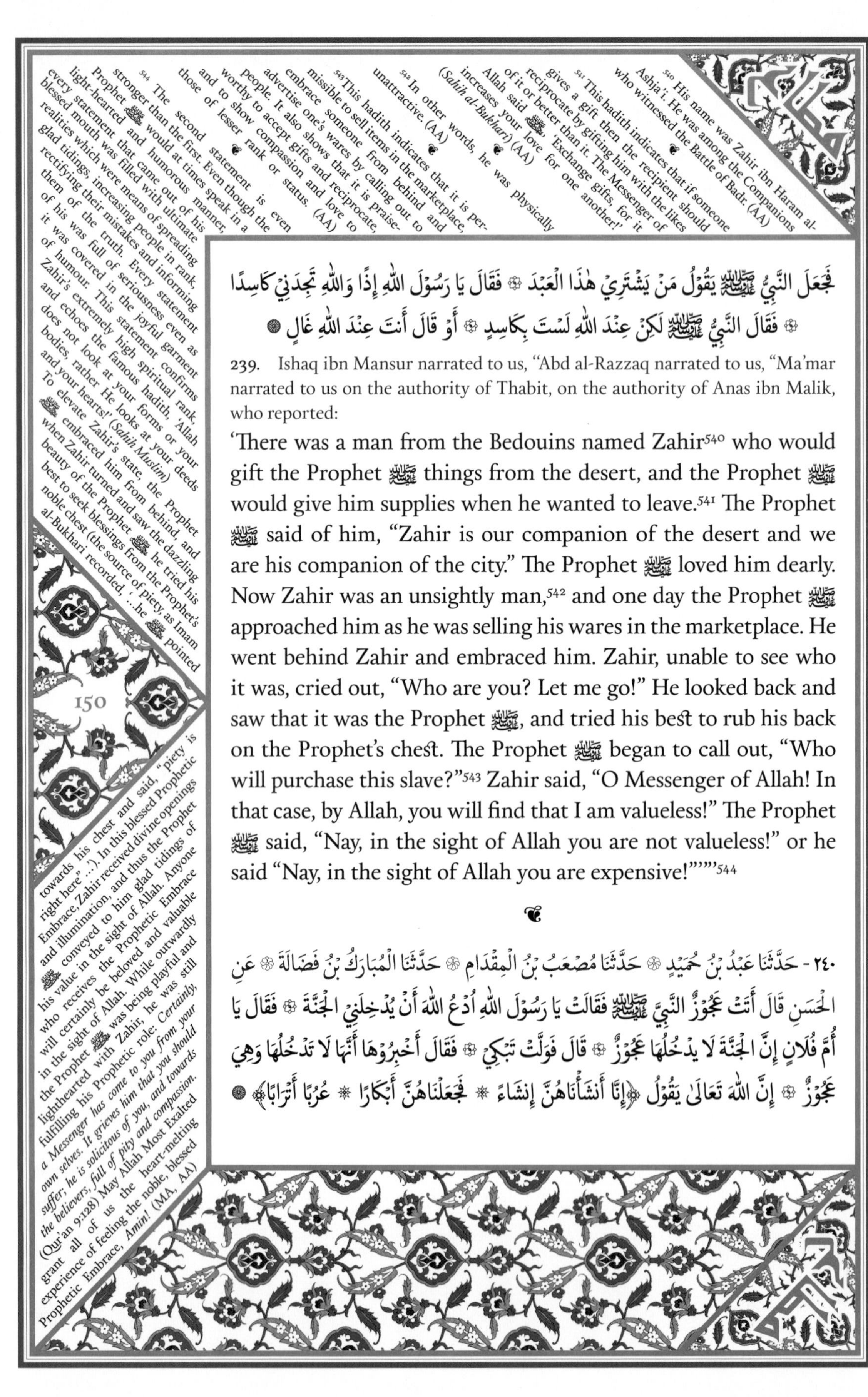

فَجَعَلَ النَّبِيُّ ﷺ يَقُوْلُ مَنْ يَشْتَرِي هٰذَا الْعَبْدَ ۞ فَقَالَ يَا رَسُوْلَ اللهِ إِذًا وَاللهِ تَجِدُنِي كَاسِدًا ۞ فَقَالَ النَّبِيُّ ﷺ لٰكِنْ عِنْدَ اللهِ لَسْتَ بِكَاسِدٍ ۞ أَوْ قَالَ أَنْتَ عِنْدَ اللهِ غَالٍ ۞

239. Ishaq ibn Mansur narrated to us, "Abd al-Razzaq narrated to us, "Ma'mar narrated to us on the authority of Thabit, on the authority of Anas ibn Malik, who reported:

'There was a man from the Bedouins named Zahir[540] who would gift the Prophet ﷺ things from the desert, and the Prophet ﷺ would give him supplies when he wanted to leave.[541] The Prophet ﷺ said of him, "Zahir is our companion of the desert and we are his companion of the city." The Prophet ﷺ loved him dearly. Now Zahir was an unsightly man,[542] and one day the Prophet ﷺ approached him as he was selling his wares in the marketplace. He went behind Zahir and embraced him. Zahir, unable to see who it was, cried out, "Who are you? Let me go!" He looked back and saw that it was the Prophet ﷺ, and tried his best to rub his back on the Prophet's chest. The Prophet ﷺ began to call out, "Who will purchase this slave?"[543] Zahir said, "O Messenger of Allah! In that case, by Allah, you will find that I am valueless!" The Prophet ﷺ said, "Nay, in the sight of Allah you are not valueless!" or he said "Nay, in the sight of Allah you are expensive!"""'[544]

٢٤٠ - حَدَّثَنَا عَبْدُ بْنُ حُمَيْدٍ ۞ حَدَّثَنَا مُصْعَبُ بْنُ الْمِقْدَامِ ۞ حَدَّثَنَا الْمُبَارَكُ بْنُ فَضَالَةَ ۞ عَنِ الْحَسَنِ قَالَ أَتَتْ عَجُوْزٌ النَّبِيَّ ﷺ فَقَالَتْ يَا رَسُوْلَ اللهِ ادْعُ اللهَ أَنْ يُدْخِلَنِي الْجَنَّةَ ۞ فَقَالَ يَا أُمَّ فُلَانٍ إِنَّ الْجَنَّةَ لَا يَدْخُلُهَا عَجُوْزٌ ۞ قَالَ فَوَلَّتْ تَبْكِي ۞ فَقَالَ أَخْبِرُوْهَا أَنَّهَا لَا تَدْخُلُهَا وَهِيَ عَجُوْزٌ ۞ إِنَّ اللهَ تَعَالَىٰ يَقُوْلُ ﴿إِنَّا أَنشَأْنَاهُنَّ إِنشَاءً ۞ فَجَعَلْنَاهُنَّ أَبْكَارًا ۞ عُرُبًا أَتْرَابًا﴾ ۞

[540] His name was Zahir ibn Haram al-Ashja'i. He was among the Companions who witnessed the Battle of Badr. (AA)

[541] This hadith indicates that if someone gives a gift then the recipient should reciprocate by gifting him with the likes of it or better than it. The Messenger of Allah ﷺ said 'Exchange gifts, for it increases your love for one another!' (*Sahih al-Bukhari*) (AA)

[542] In other words, he was physically unattractive. (AA)

[543] This hadith indicates that it is permissible to sell items in the marketplace, embrace someone from behind and advertise one's wares by calling out to people. It also shows that it is praiseworthy to accept gifts and reciprocate, and to show compassion and love to those of lesser rank or status. (AA)

[544] The second statement is even stronger than the first. Even though the Prophet ﷺ would at times speak in a light-hearted and humorous manner, every statement that came out of his blessed mouth was filled with ultimate realities which were means of spreading glad tidings, increasing people in rank, rectifying their mistakes and informing them of the truth. Every statement of his was full of seriousness even as it was covered in the joyful garment of humour. This statement confirms Zahir's extremely high spiritual rank, and echoes the famous hadith, 'Allah does not look at your forms or your bodies, rather He looks at your deeds and your hearts!' (*Sahih Muslim*) To elevate Zahir's state, the Prophet ﷺ embraced him from behind, and when Zahir turned and saw the dazzling beauty of the Prophet ﷺ he tried his best to seek blessings from the Prophet's noble chest (the source of piety, as Imam al-Bukhari recorded, '...he ﷺ pointed towards his chest and said, "piety is right here" ...'). In this blessed Prophetic Embrace, Zahir received divine openings and illumination, and thus the Prophet ﷺ conveyed to him glad tidings of his value in the sight of Allah. Anyone who receives the Prophetic Embrace will certainly be beloved and valuable in the sight of Allah. While outwardly the Prophet ﷺ was being playful and lighthearted with Zahir, he was still fulfilling his Prophetic role: *Certainly, a Messenger has come to you from your own selves. It grieves him that you should suffer; he is solicitous of you, and towards the believers, full of pity and compassion.* (Qur'an 9:128) May Allah Most Exalted grant all of us the heart-melting experience of feeling the noble, blessed Prophetic Embrace, *Amin!* (MA, AA)

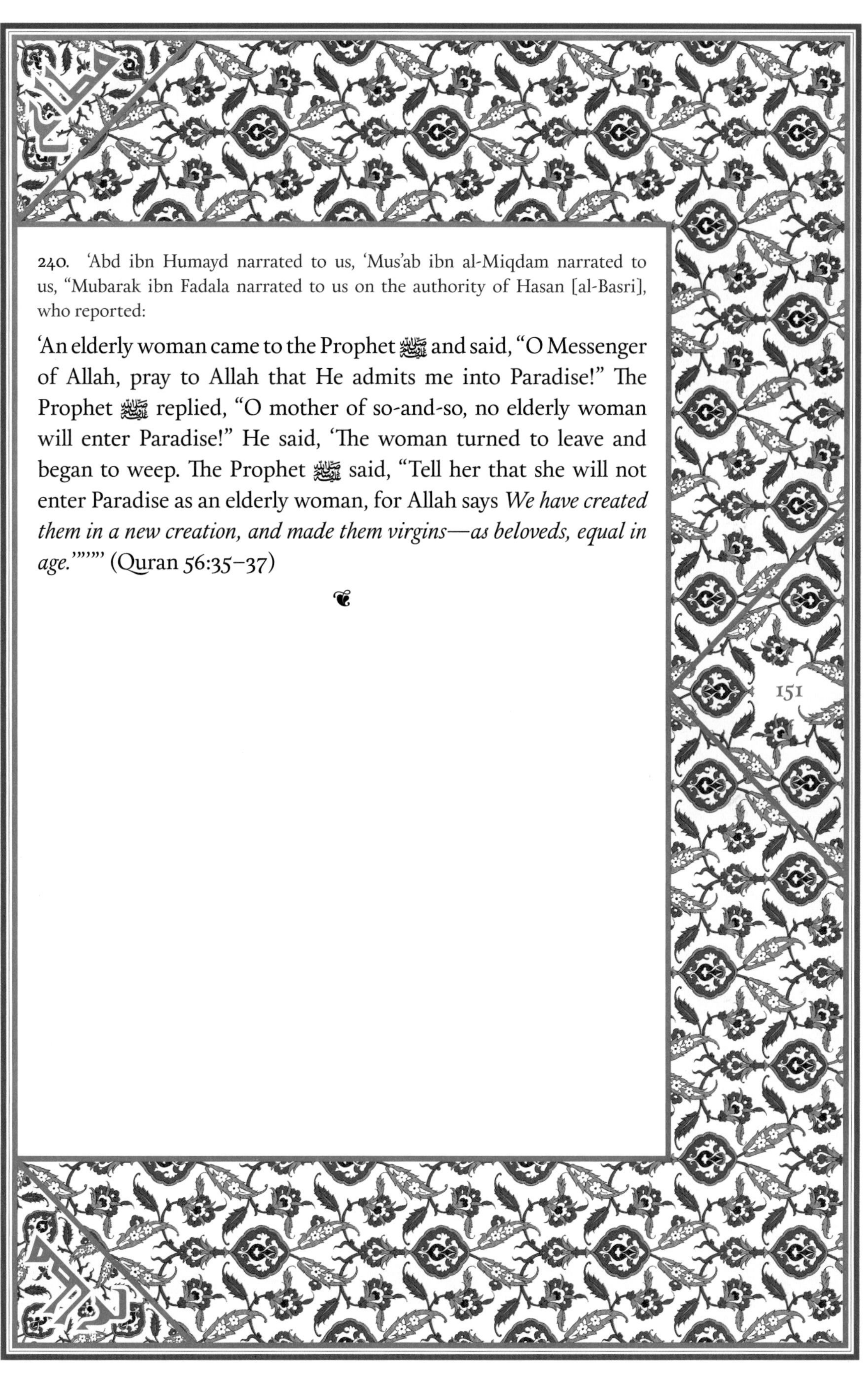

240. 'Abd ibn Humayd narrated to us, 'Mus'ab ibn al-Miqdam narrated to us, "Mubarak ibn Fadala narrated to us on the authority of Hasan [al-Basri], who reported:

'An elderly woman came to the Prophet ﷺ and said, "O Messenger of Allah, pray to Allah that He admits me into Paradise!" The Prophet ﷺ replied, "O mother of so-and-so, no elderly woman will enter Paradise!" He said, 'The woman turned to leave and began to weep. The Prophet ﷺ said, "Tell her that she will not enter Paradise as an elderly woman, for Allah says *We have created them in a new creation, and made them virgins—as beloveds, equal in age.*"'"'" (Quran 56:35–37)

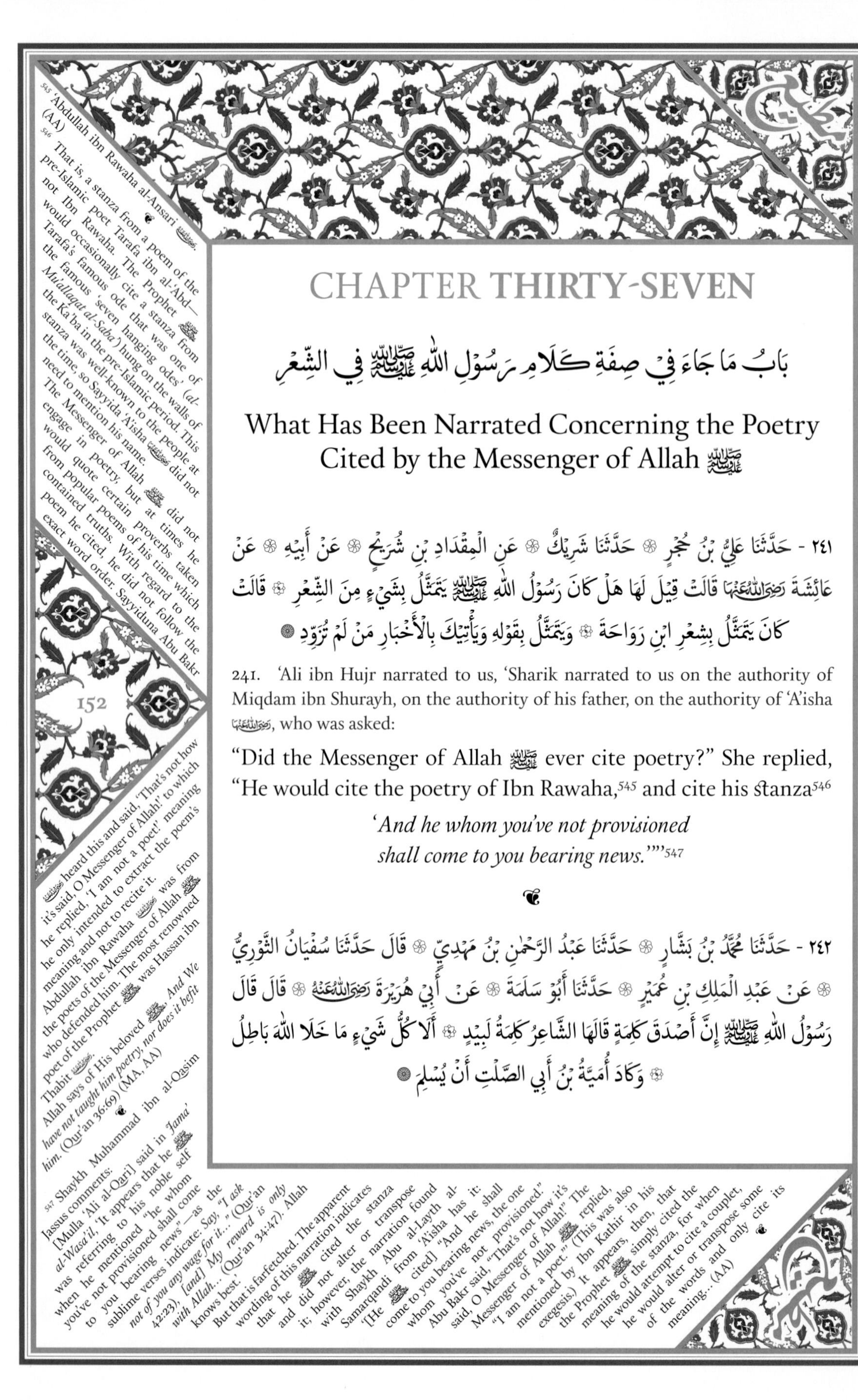

CHAPTER THIRTY-SEVEN

بَابُ مَا جَاءَ فِي صِفَةِ كَلَامِ رَسُولِ اللهِ ﷺ فِي الشِّعْرِ

What Has Been Narrated Concerning the Poetry Cited by the Messenger of Allah ﷺ

٢٤١ - حَدَّثَنَا عَلِيُّ بْنُ حُجْرٍ ۞ حَدَّثَنَا شَرِيكٌ ۞ عَنِ الْمِقْدَادِ بْنِ شُرَيْحٍ ۞ عَنْ أَبِيهِ ۞ عَنْ عَائِشَةَ رَضِيَ اللهُ عَنْهَا قَالَتْ قِيلَ لَهَا هَلْ كَانَ رَسُولُ اللهِ ﷺ يَتَمَثَّلُ بِشَيْءٍ مِنَ الشِّعْرِ ۞ قَالَتْ كَانَ يَتَمَثَّلُ بِشِعْرِ ابْنِ رَوَاحَةَ ۞ وَيَتَمَثَّلُ بِقَوْلِهِ وَيَأْتِيكَ بِالْأَخْبَارِ مَنْ لَمْ تُزَوِّدِ ۞

241. 'Ali ibn Hujr narrated to us, 'Sharik narrated to us on the authority of Miqdam ibn Shurayh, on the authority of his father, on the authority of 'A'isha رضي الله عنها, who was asked:

"Did the Messenger of Allah ﷺ ever cite poetry?" She replied, "He would cite the poetry of Ibn Rawaha,[545] and cite his stanza[546]

'And he whom you've not provisioned
shall come to you bearing news.'"'[547]

٢٤٢ - حَدَّثَنَا مُحَمَّدُ بْنُ بَشَّارٍ ۞ حَدَّثَنَا عَبْدُ الرَّحْمٰنِ بْنُ مَهْدِيٍّ ۞ قَالَ حَدَّثَنَا سُفْيَانُ الثَّوْرِيُّ ۞ عَنْ عَبْدِ الْمَلِكِ بْنِ عُمَيْرٍ ۞ حَدَّثَنَا أَبُو سَلَمَةَ ۞ عَنْ أَبِي هُرَيْرَةَ رَضِيَ اللهُ عَنْهُ ۞ قَالَ قَالَ رَسُولُ اللهِ ﷺ إِنَّ أَصْدَقَ كَلِمَةٍ قَالَهَا الشَّاعِرُ كَلِمَةُ لَبِيدٍ ۞ أَلَا كُلُّ شَيْءٍ مَا خَلَا اللهَ بَاطِلُ ۞ وَكَادَ أُمَيَّةُ بْنُ أَبِي الصَّلْتِ أَنْ يُسْلِمَ ۞

[545] 'Abdullah ibn Rawaha al-Ansari رضي الله عنه. (AA)

[546] That is, a stanza from a poem of the pre-Islamic poet Tarafa ibn al-'Abd—not Ibn Rawaha. The Prophet ﷺ would occasionally cite a stanza from Tarafa's famous ode that was one of the famous 'seven hanging odes' (*al-Mu'allaqat al-Saba'*) hung on the walls of the Ka'ba in the pre-Islamic period. This stanza was well-known to the people at the time, so Sayyida 'A'isha رضي الله عنها did not need to mention his name. The Messenger of Allah ﷺ did not engage in poetry, but at times he would quote certain proverbs taken from popular poems of his time which contained truths. With regard to the poem he cited, he did not follow the exact word order. Sayyiduna Abu Bakr رضي الله عنه heard this and said, 'That's not how it's said, O Messenger of Allah!' to which he replied, 'I am not a poet!' meaning he only intended to extract the poem's meaning and not to recite it. 'Abdullah ibn Rawaha رضي الله عنه was from the poets of the Messenger of Allah ﷺ who defended him. The most renowned poet of the Prophet ﷺ was Hassan ibn Thabit رضي الله عنه. Allah says of His beloved ﷺ, *And We have not taught him poetry, nor does it befit him.* (Qur'an 36:69) (MA, AA)

[547] Shaykh Muhammad ibn al-Qasim Jassus comments: [Mulla 'Ali al-Qari] said in *Jama' al-Wasa'il*, 'It appears that he ﷺ was referring to his noble self when he mentioned "he whom you've not provisioned shall come to you bearing news"—as the sublime verses indicate: *Say, "I ask not of you any wage for it..."* (Qur'an 42:23), *[and] My reward is only with Allah...* (Qur'an 34:47). Allah knows best.' But that is farfetched. The apparent wording of this narration indicates that he ﷺ cited the stanza and did not alter or transpose it, however, the narration found with Shaykh Abu al-Layth al-Samarqandi from 'A'isha has it: [He ﷺ cited] "And he shall come to you bearing news, the one whom you've not provisioned." Abu Bakr said, "That's not how it's said, O Messenger of Allah!" The Messenger of Allah ﷺ replied, "I am not a poet." (This was also mentioned by Ibn Kathir in his exegesis.) It appears, then, that the Prophet ﷺ simply cited the meaning of the stanza, for when he would attempt to cite a couplet, he would alter or transpose some of the words and only cite its meaning... (AA)

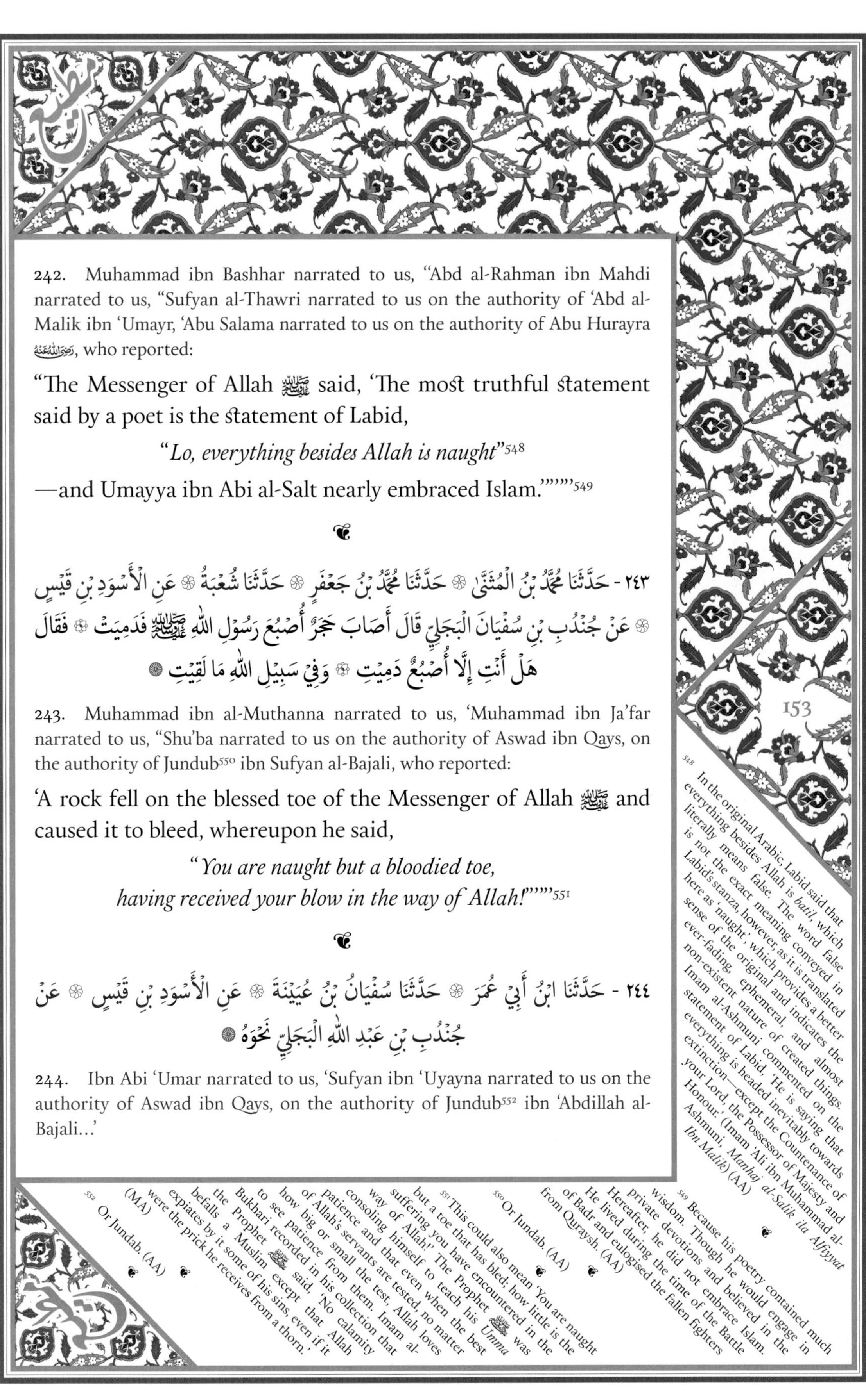

242. Muhammad ibn Bashhar narrated to us, "'Abd al-Rahman ibn Mahdi narrated to us, "Sufyan al-Thawri narrated to us on the authority of 'Abd al-Malik ibn 'Umayr, 'Abu Salama narrated to us on the authority of Abu Hurayra رضي الله عنه, who reported:

"The Messenger of Allah ﷺ said, 'The most truthful statement said by a poet is the statement of Labid,

"Lo, everything besides Allah is naught"[548]

—and Umayya ibn Abi al-Salt nearly embraced Islam.'"""'[549]

❦

٢٤٣ - حَدَّثَنَا مُحَمَّدُ بْنُ الْمُثَنَّى ۞ حَدَّثَنَا مُحَمَّدُ بْنُ جَعْفَرٍ ۞ حَدَّثَنَا شُعْبَةُ ۞ عَنِ الْأَسْوَدِ بْنِ قَيْسٍ ۞ عَنْ جُنْدُبِ بْنِ سُفْيَانَ الْبَجَلِيِّ قَالَ أَصَابَ حَجَرٌ أُصْبُعَ رَسُولِ اللهِ ﷺ فَدَمِيَتْ ۞ فَقَالَ هَلْ أَنْتِ إِلَّا أُصْبُعٌ دَمِيتِ ۞ وَفِي سَبِيلِ اللهِ مَا لَقِيتِ ۞

243. Muhammad ibn al-Muthanna narrated to us, 'Muhammad ibn Ja'far narrated to us, "Shu'ba narrated to us on the authority of Aswad ibn Qays, on the authority of Jundub[550] ibn Sufyan al-Bajali, who reported:

'A rock fell on the blessed toe of the Messenger of Allah ﷺ and caused it to bleed, whereupon he said,

"You are naught but a bloodied toe,
having received your blow in the way of Allah!"'"'[551]

❦

٢٤٤ - حَدَّثَنَا ابْنُ أَبِي عُمَرَ ۞ حَدَّثَنَا سُفْيَانُ بْنُ عُيَيْنَةَ ۞ عَنِ الْأَسْوَدِ بْنِ قَيْسٍ ۞ عَنْ جُنْدُبِ بْنِ عَبْدِ اللهِ الْبَجَلِيِّ نَحْوَهُ ۞

244. Ibn Abi 'Umar narrated to us, 'Sufyan ibn 'Uyayna narrated to us on the authority of Aswad ibn Qays, on the authority of Jundub[552] ibn 'Abdillah al-Bajali...'

[548] In the original Arabic, Labid said that everything besides Allah is *batil*, which literally means false. The word false is not the exact meaning conveyed in Labid's stanza, however, as it is translated here as 'naught', which provides a better sense of the original and indicates the ever-fading, ephemeral, and almost non-existent nature of created things. Imam al-Ashmuni commented on the statement of Labid, 'He is saying that everything is headed inevitably towards extinction—except the Countenance of your Lord, the Possessor of Majesty and Honour.' (Imam 'Ali ibn Muhammad al-Ashmuni, *Manhaj al-Salik ila Alfiyyat Ibn Malik*) (AA) ❦

[549] Because his poetry contained much wisdom. Though he would engage in private devotions and believed in the Hereafter, he did not embrace Islam. He lived during the time of the Battle of Badr and eulogised the fallen fighters from Quraysh. (AA) ❦

[550] Or Jundab. (AA) ❦

[551] This could also mean 'You are naught but a toe that has bled; how little is the suffering you have encountered in the way of Allah!' The Prophet ﷺ was consoling himself to teach his *Umma* patience and that even when the best of Allah's servants are tested, no matter how big or small the test, Allah loves to see patience from them. Imam al-Bukhari recorded in his collection that the Prophet ﷺ said, 'No calamity befalls a Muslim except that Allah expiates by it some of his sins, even if it were the prick he receives from a thorn.' (MA) ❦

[552] Or Jundab. (AA) ❦

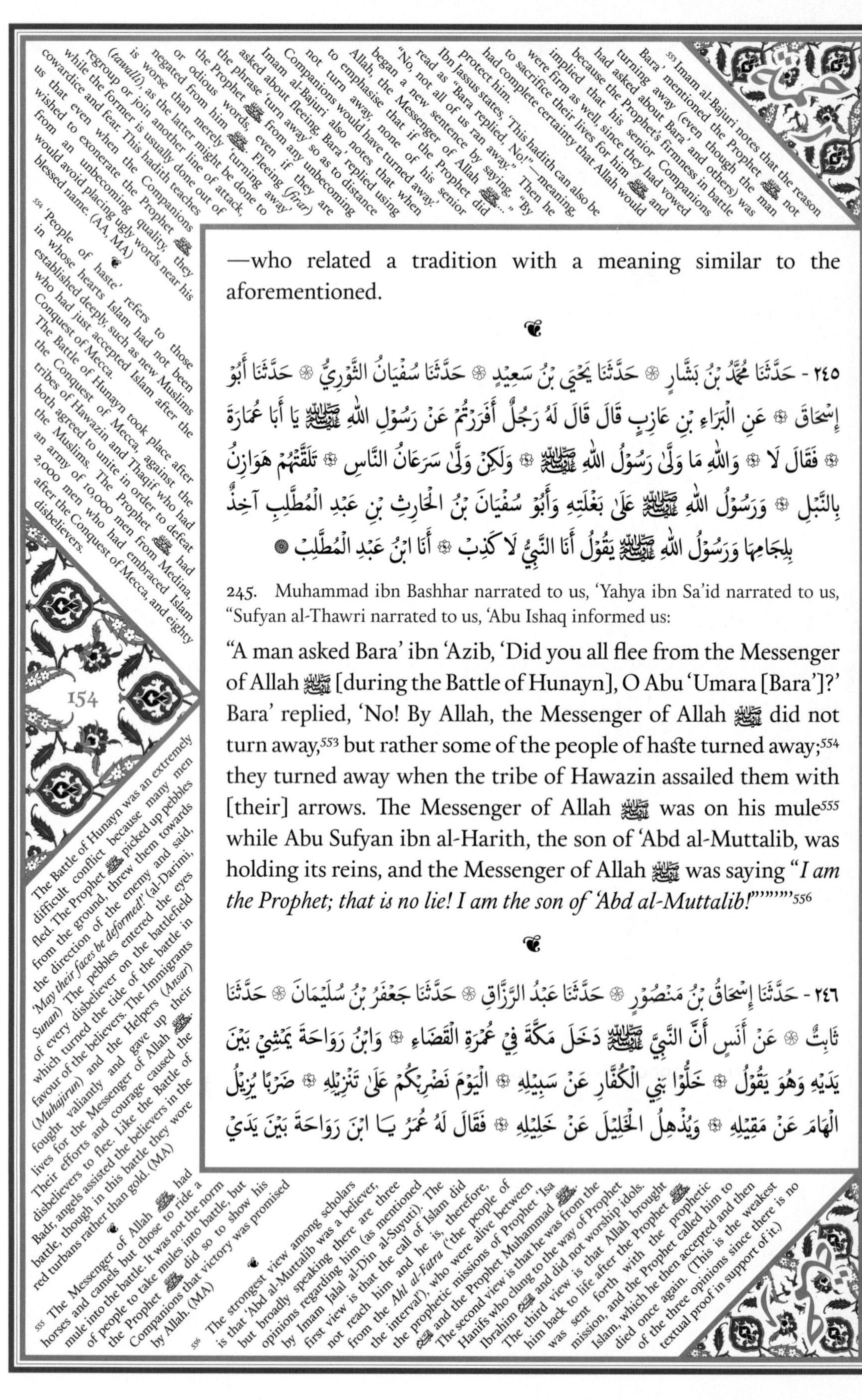

—who related a tradition with a meaning similar to the aforementioned.

٢٤٥ - حَدَّثَنَا مُحَمَّدُ بْنُ بَشَّارٍ ۞ حَدَّثَنَا يَحْيَى بْنُ سَعِيدٍ ۞ حَدَّثَنَا سُفْيَانُ الثَّوْرِيُّ ۞ حَدَّثَنَا أَبُو إِسْحَاقَ ۞ عَنِ الْبَرَاءِ بْنِ عَازِبٍ قَالَ قَالَ لَهُ رَجُلٌ أَفَرَرْتُمْ عَنْ رَسُولِ اللهِ ﷺ يَا أَبَا عُمَارَةَ ۞ فَقَالَ لَا ۞ وَاللهِ مَا وَلَّى رَسُولُ اللهِ ﷺ ۞ وَلَكِنْ وَلَّى سَرَعَانُ النَّاسِ ۞ تَلَقَّتْهُمْ هَوَازِنُ بِالنَّبْلِ ۞ وَرَسُولُ اللهِ ﷺ عَلَى بَغْلَتِهِ وَأَبُو سُفْيَانَ بْنُ الْحَارِثِ بْنِ عَبْدِ الْمُطَّلِبِ آخِذٌ بِلِجَامِهَا وَرَسُولُ اللهِ ﷺ يَقُولُ أَنَا النَّبِيُّ لَا كَذِبْ ۞ أَنَا ابْنُ عَبْدِ الْمُطَّلِبْ ۞

245. Muhammad ibn Bashhar narrated to us, 'Yahya ibn Sa'id narrated to us, "Sufyan al-Thawri narrated to us, 'Abu Ishaq informed us:

"A man asked Bara' ibn 'Azib, 'Did you all flee from the Messenger of Allah ﷺ [during the Battle of Hunayn], O Abu 'Umara [Bara']?' Bara' replied, 'No! By Allah, the Messenger of Allah ﷺ did not turn away,[553] but rather some of the people of haste turned away;[554] they turned away when the tribe of Hawazin assailed them with [their] arrows. The Messenger of Allah ﷺ was on his mule[555] while Abu Sufyan ibn al-Harith, the son of 'Abd al-Muttalib, was holding its reins, and the Messenger of Allah ﷺ was saying "*I am the Prophet; that is no lie! I am the son of 'Abd al-Muttalib!*"'"'"[556]

٢٤٦ - حَدَّثَنَا إِسْحَاقُ بْنُ مَنْصُورٍ ۞ حَدَّثَنَا عَبْدُ الرَّزَّاقِ ۞ حَدَّثَنَا جَعْفَرُ بْنُ سُلَيْمَانَ ۞ حَدَّثَنَا ثَابِتٌ ۞ عَنْ أَنَسٍ أَنَّ النَّبِيَّ ﷺ دَخَلَ مَكَّةَ فِي عُمْرَةِ الْقَضَاءِ ۞ وَابْنُ رَوَاحَةَ يَمْشِي بَيْنَ يَدَيْهِ وَهُوَ يَقُولُ ۞ خَلُّوا بَنِي الْكُفَّارِ عَنْ سَبِيلِهِ ۞ الْيَوْمَ نَضْرِبْكُمْ عَلَى تَنْزِيلِهِ ۞ ضَرْبًا يُزِيلُ الْهَامَ عَنْ مَقِيلِهِ ۞ وَيُذْهِلُ الْخَلِيلَ عَنْ خَلِيلِهِ ۞ فَقَالَ لَهُ عُمَرُ يَا ابْنَ رَوَاحَةَ بَيْنَ يَدَيْ

553 Imam al-Bajuri notes that the reason Bara' mentioned the Prophet ﷺ not turning away (even though the man had asked about Bara' and others) was because the Prophet's firmness in battle implied that his senior Companions were firm as well, since they had vowed to sacrifice their lives for him ﷺ and had complete certainty that Allah would protect him. Ibn Jassus states, 'This hadith can also be read as "Bara replied, No!"—meaning, "No, not all of us ran away." Then he began a new sentence by saying, "By Allah, the Messenger of Allah ﷺ..." to emphasise that if the Prophet did not turn away, none of his senior Companions would have turned away.' Imam al-Bajuri also notes that when asked about fleeing, Bara' replied using the phrase 'turn away' so as to distance the Prophet ﷺ from any unbecoming or odious words, even if they are negated from him ﷺ. Fleeing (*firar*) is worse than merely 'turning away' (*tawalli*), as the latter might be done to regroup or join another line of attack, while the former is usually done out of cowardice and fear. This hadith teaches us that even when the Companions wished to exonerate the Prophet ﷺ from an unbecoming quality, they would avoid placing ugly words near his blessed name. (AA, MA)

554 'People of haste' refers to those in whose hearts Islam had not been established deeply, such as new Muslims who had just accepted Islam after the Conquest of Mecca. The Battle of Hunayn took place after the Conquest of Mecca, against the tribes of Hawazin and Thaqif who had both agreed to unite in order to defeat the Muslims. The Prophet ﷺ had an army of 10,000 men from Medina, 2,000 men who had embraced Islam after the Conquest of Mecca, and eighty disbelievers.

The Battle of Hunayn was an extremely difficult conflict because many men fled. The Prophet ﷺ picked up pebbles from the ground, threw them towards the direction of the enemy and said, '*May their faces be deformed!*' (al-Darimi, *Sunan*) The pebbles entered the eyes of every disbeliever on the battlefield which turned the tide of the battle in favour of the believers. The Immigrants (*Muhajirun*) and the Helpers (*Ansar*) fought valiantly and gave up their lives for the Messenger of Allah ﷺ. Their efforts and courage caused the disbelievers to flee. Like the Battle of Badr, angels assisted the believers in the battle, though in this battle they wore red turbans rather than gold. (MA)

555 The Messenger of Allah ﷺ had horses and camels but chose to ride a mule into the battle. It was not the norm of people to take mules into battle, but the Prophet ﷺ did so to show his Companions that victory was promised by Allah. (MA)

556 The strongest view among scholars is that 'Abd al-Muttalib was a believer, but broadly speaking there are three opinions regarding him (as mentioned by Imam Jalal al-Din al-Suyuti). The first view is that the call of Islam did not reach him and he is, therefore, from the *Ahl al-Fatra* ('the people of the interval'), who were alive between the prophetic missions of Prophet 'Isa ﷺ and the Prophet Muhammad ﷺ. The second view is that he was from the Hanifs who clung to the way of Prophet Ibrahim ﷺ and did not worship idols. The third view is that Allah brought him back to life after the Prophet ﷺ was sent forth with the prophetic mission, and the Prophet called him to Islam, which he then accepted and then died once again. (This is the weakest of the three opinions since there is no textual proof in support of it.)

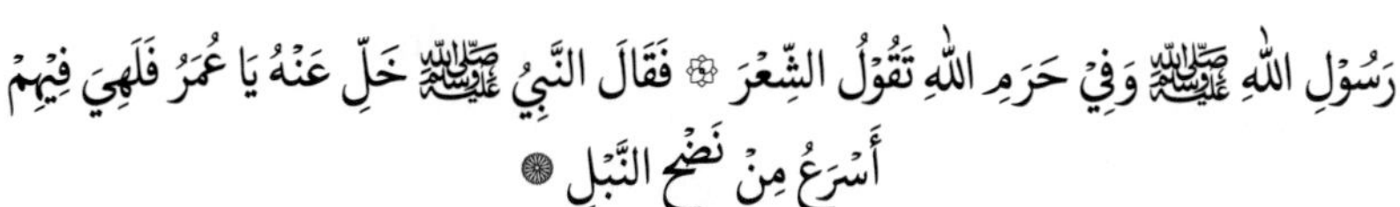
رَسُولِ اللهِ ﷺ وَفِي حَرَمِ اللهِ تَقُولُ الشِّعْرَ ۞ فَقَالَ النَّبِيُّ ﷺ خَلِّ عَنْهُ يَا عُمَرُ فَلَهِيَ فِيهِمْ أَسْرَعُ مِنْ نَضْحِ النَّبْلِ ۞

246. Ishaq ibn Mansur narrated to us, "Abd al-Razzaq narrated to us, "Ja'far ibn Sulayman narrated to us, 'Thabit narrated to us on the authority of Anas, who reported:

"The Prophet ﷺ entered Mecca to perform 'Umra[557] and Ibn Rawaha was walking in front of him and saying [in poetic metre]

'Clear his path, O sons of an unbelieving folk!
Today we will strike you upon his arrival
with such a blow that will sever their heads from their necks
and cause intimate friends to forget one another!'

Upon hearing this, 'Umar said to him, 'O Ibn Rawaha, how dare you recite poetry before the Messenger of Allah ﷺ, and while in the Sacred Precinct [*al-Haram*] at that!'[558] The Messenger of Allah ﷺ said to him, 'Leave him be, 'Umar, for those words are swifter against them than a shower of arrows!'""""[559]

۞

٢٤٧ - حَدَّثَنَا عَلِيُّ بْنُ حُجْرٍ ۞ حَدَّثَنَا شَرِيكٌ ۞ عَنْ سِمَاكِ بْنِ حَرْبٍ ۞ عَنْ جَابِرِ بْنِ سَمُرَةَ قَالَ جَالَسْتُ النَّبِيَّ ﷺ أَكْثَرَ مِنْ مِئَةِ مَرَّةٍ ۞ وَكَانَ أَصْحَابُهُ يَتَنَاشَدُونَ الشِّعْرَ ۞ وَيَتَذَاكَرُونَ أَشْيَاءَ مِنْ أَمْرِ الْجَاهِلِيَّةِ وَهُوَ سَاكِتٌ ۞ وَرُبَّمَا تَبَسَّمَ مَعَهُمْ ۞

247. 'Ali ibn Hujr narrated to us, 'Sharik narrated to us on the authority of Simak ibn Harb, on the authority of Jabir ibn Samura, who reported:

"I sat with the Prophet ﷺ over a hundred times; his Companions would rehearse poetry in his presence recall events that took

Proofs that 'Abd al-Muttalib was a believer and not an idol-worshipper include narrations that mention the pure lineage of the Prophet ﷺ and how he hailed from pure loins, unsoiled by either fornication or idol-worship. Imam al-Bayhaqi reported in his *Sunan* that Ibn 'Abbas (رضي الله عنه) said, 'The Messenger of Allah ﷺ said, "Nothing of me hailed from the fornication of the period of ignorance (*jahiliyya*). I was only born through the union of Islam."' Abu Nuaym, al-Tabarani and Ibn 'Asakir recorded from 'Ali b. Abi Talib (رضي الله عنه), who reported that the Prophet ﷺ said, 'I was born in wedlock, and I was not transmitted through the loins of a fornicator from the time of Adam until I was born to my mother and father; I was not touched by any of the fornication of the period of ignorance (*jahiliyya*).' Abu Nu'aym also reported from Ibn 'Abbas (رضي الله عنه), 'None of my forefathers ever committed fornication, and Allah continued to transmit me from the pure loins of fathers to the pure wombs of mothers. Never would a family line branch out in two except that I was in the best of the two.'

We see from these narrations that the Prophet Muhammad ﷺ hailed from pure loins: from forefathers who never worshipped idols or fornicated. We also find that 'Abd al-Muttalib refused the pagan practice of divination through arrows and chose instead to draw lots. Allah also honoured him with a true dream revealing to him the source of the treasure of Zamzam, and gave him a life-saving miracle, both of which have been narrated by Muhammad ibn Ishaq al-Fakihi in *Akhbar Makka* with a fully connected chain of transmission. Fakihi said, 'Abdullah ibn Zubayr al-Ghafiqi reported that he heard 'Ali ibn Abi Talib (رضي الله عنه) narrate the story of the well of Zamzam, when 'Abd al-Muttalib was instructed to dig it up. 'Ali said, "'Abd al-Muttalib said, 'I was sleeping in the

Hijr [inside the Ka'ba] when a figure came to me and said, "Dig purity." "What is purity?" I asked. But the figure vanished so I went back to sleep. The next night the figure appeared to me again and said, "Dig beneficence." "What is beneficence?" I asked. But the figure vanished. The next night the figure appeared yet again and said, "Dig Zamzam." "What is Zamzam?" I asked. The figure replied, "It shall never dry up or become scarce, and it shall provide drink to the pilgrims on the Greatest Pilgrimage (*al-Hajj al-Akbar*). It lies in a place where there is dung, blood, pecking ravens and an ant nest." When the status of the well and its location became clear to 'Abd al-Muttalib, and he realised that the figure spoke the truth, he took his pickaxe and brought with him Harith ibn 'Abd al-Muttalib, who was his only son. When he eventually struck the well-stone and shouted Allah's praises, Quraysh realised that he found what he was looking for, so they stood up and covering and proclaimed, 'O 'Abd al-Muttalib! This is our inheritance from our father Isma'il and we have a right to share in it, so give us our share!' But 'Abd al-Muttalib refused, 'No! I have been chosen with this to the exclusion of all of you; I have been granted it alone!' Quraysh replied, 'Deal with us fairly, for we won't leave you until we seek a judgment regarding it!' 'Abd al-Muttalib retorted, 'Place anyone you wish between you and me; I will plead my case against you before the diviners of Banu Sa'd ibn Hudhaym!' Pleased with this arrangement, Quraysh agreed and said, 'Fine.' Banu Sa'd ibn Hudhaym were with noblemen in the Levant (*Sham*), so 'Abd al-Muttalib and a group of his cousins from Banu 'Abd Manaf and a small group from every tribe set out on a journey to the Levant. During that time the route was through a desert wasteland, and when they reached an area situated between the

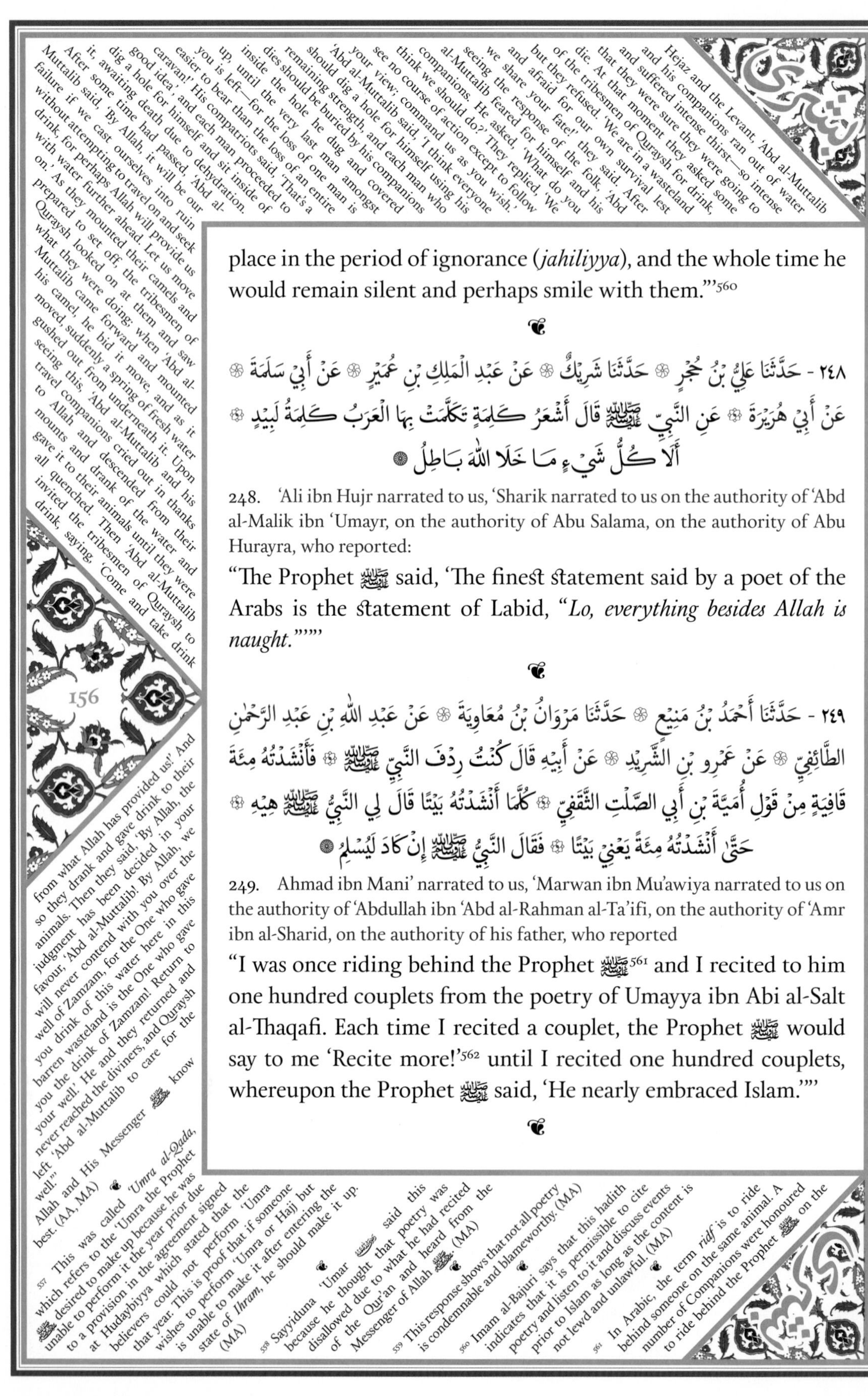

place in the period of ignorance (*jahiliyya*), and the whole time he would remain silent and perhaps smile with them."'[560]

٢٤٨ - حَدَّثَنَا عَلِيُّ بْنُ حُجْرٍ ۞ حَدَّثَنَا شَرِيكٌ ۞ عَنْ عَبْدِ الْمَلِكِ بْنِ عُمَيْرٍ ۞ عَنْ أَبِي سَلَمَةَ ۞ عَنْ أَبِي هُرَيْرَةَ ۞ عَنِ النَّبِيِّ ﷺ قَالَ أَشْعَرُ كَلِمَةٍ تَكَلَّمَتْ بِهَا الْعَرَبُ كَلِمَةُ لَبِيدٍ ۞ أَلَا كُلُّ شَيْءٍ مَا خَلَا اللهَ بَاطِلُ ۞

248. 'Ali ibn Hujr narrated to us, 'Sharik narrated to us on the authority of 'Abd al-Malik ibn 'Umayr, on the authority of Abu Salama, on the authority of Abu Hurayra, who reported:

"The Prophet ﷺ said, 'The finest statement said by a poet of the Arabs is the statement of Labid, "*Lo, everything besides Allah is naught.*"'""

٢٤٩ - حَدَّثَنَا أَحْمَدُ بْنُ مَنِيعٍ ۞ حَدَّثَنَا مَرْوَانُ بْنُ مُعَاوِيَةَ ۞ عَنْ عَبْدِ اللهِ بْنِ عَبْدِ الرَّحْمٰنِ الطَّائِفِيِّ ۞ عَنْ عَمْرِو بْنِ الشَّرِيدِ ۞ عَنْ أَبِيهِ قَالَ كُنْتُ رِدْفَ النَّبِيِّ ﷺ ۞ فَأَنْشَدْتُهُ مِئَةَ قَافِيَةٍ مِنْ قَوْلِ أُمَيَّةَ بْنِ أَبِي الصَّلْتِ الثَّقَفِيِّ ۞ كُلَّمَا أَنْشَدْتُهُ بَيْتًا قَالَ لِي النَّبِيُّ ﷺ هِيهْ ۞ حَتَّىٰ أَنْشَدْتُهُ مِئَةً يَعْنِي بَيْتًا ۞ فَقَالَ النَّبِيُّ ﷺ إِنْ كَادَ لَيُسْلِمُ ۞

249. Ahmad ibn Mani' narrated to us, 'Marwan ibn Mu'awiya narrated to us on the authority of 'Abdullah ibn 'Abd al-Rahman al-Ta'ifi, on the authority of 'Amr ibn al-Sharid, on the authority of his father, who reported

"I was once riding behind the Prophet ﷺ[561] and I recited to him one hundred couplets from the poetry of Umayya ibn Abi al-Salt al-Thaqafi. Each time I recited a couplet, the Prophet ﷺ would say to me 'Recite more!'[562] until I recited one hundred couplets, whereupon the Prophet ﷺ said, 'He nearly embraced Islam.'"

Hejaz and the Levant, 'Abd al-Muttalib and his companions ran out of water and suffered intense thirst—so intense that they were sure they were going to die. At that moment they asked some of the tribesmen of Quraysh for drink, but they refused. 'We are in a wasteland and afraid for our own survival lest we share your fate!' they said. After seeing the response of the folk, 'Abd al-Muttalib feared for himself and his companions. He asked, 'What do you think we should do?' They replied, 'We see no course of action except to follow your view; command us as you wish.' 'Abd al-Muttalib said, 'I think everyone should dig a hole for himself using his remaining strength, and each man who dies should be buried by his companions inside the hole he dug and covered up, until the very last man amongst you is left—for the loss of one man is easier to bear than the loss of an entire caravan!' His compatriots said, 'That's a good idea', and each man proceeded to dig a hole for himself and sit inside of it, awaiting death due to dehydration. After some time had passed, 'Abd al-Muttalib said, 'By Allah, it will be our failure if we cast ourselves into ruin without attempting to travel on and seek drink, for perhaps Allah will provide us with water further ahead. Let us move on.' As they mounted their camels and prepared to set off, the tribesmen of Quraysh looked on at them and saw what they were doing; when 'Abd al-Muttalib came forward and mounted his camel, he bid it move, and as it moved, suddenly a spring of fresh water gushed out from underneath it. Upon seeing this, 'Abd al-Muttalib and his travel companions cried out in thanks to Allah and descended from their mounts and drank of the water and gave it to their animals until they were all quenched. Then 'Abd al-Muttalib invited the tribesmen of Quraysh to drink, saying, 'Come and take drink from what Allah has provided us!' And so they drank and gave drink to their animals. Then they said, 'By Allah, the judgment has been decided in your favour, 'Abd al-Muttalib! By Allah, we will never contend with you over the well of Zamzam, for the One who gave you drink of this water here in this barren wasteland is the One who gave you the drink of Zamzam! Return to your well.' He and they returned and never reached the diviners, and Quraysh left 'Abd al-Muttalib to care for the well." Allah and His Messenger ﷺ know best. (AA, MA)

557 This was called *'Umra al-Qada*, which refers to the 'Umra the Prophet ﷺ desired to make up because he was unable to perform it the year prior due to a provision in the agreement signed at Hudaybiyya which stated that the believers could not perform 'Umra that year. This is proof that if someone wishes to perform 'Umra or Hajj but is unable to make it after entering the state of *Ihram*, he should make it up. (MA)

558 Sayyiduna 'Umar ﷺ said this because he thought that poetry was disallowed due to what he had recited of the Qur'an and heard from the Messenger of Allah ﷺ. (MA)

559 This response shows that not all poetry is condemnable and blameworthy. (MA)

560 Imam al-Bajuri says that this hadith indicates that it is permissible to cite poetry and listen to it and discuss events prior to Islam as long as the content is not lewd and unlawful. (MA)

561 In Arabic, the term *ridf* is to ride behind someone on the same animal. A number of Companions were honoured to ride behind the Prophet ﷺ on the

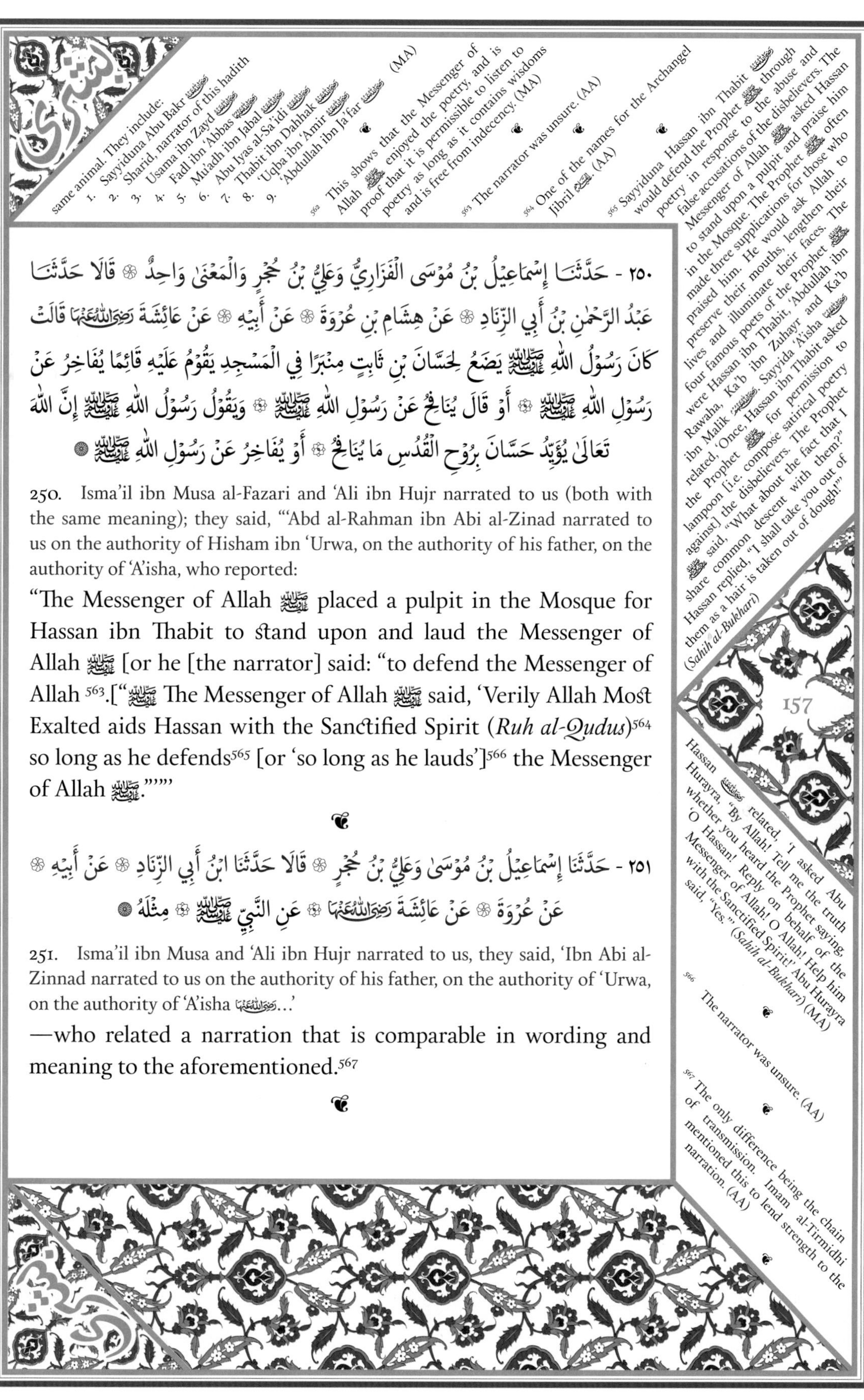

٢٥٠ - حَدَّثَنَا إِسْمَاعِيلُ بْنُ مُوسَى الْفَزَارِيُّ وَعَلِيُّ بْنُ حُجْرٍ وَالْمَعْنَىٰ وَاحِدٌ ۞ قَالَا حَدَّثَنَا عَبْدُ الرَّحْمٰنِ بْنُ أَبِي الزِّنَادِ ۞ عَنْ هِشَامِ بْنِ عُرْوَةَ ۞ عَنْ أَبِيهِ ۞ عَنْ عَائِشَةَ رَضِيَ اللهُ عَنْهَا قَالَتْ كَانَ رَسُولُ اللهِ ﷺ يَضَعُ لِحَسَّانَ بْنِ ثَابِتٍ مِنْبَرًا فِي الْمَسْجِدِ يَقُومُ عَلَيْهِ قَائِمًا يُفَاخِرُ عَنْ رَسُولِ اللهِ ﷺ ۞ أَوْ قَالَ يُنَافِحُ عَنْ رَسُولِ اللهِ ﷺ ۞ وَيَقُولُ رَسُولُ اللهِ ﷺ إِنَّ اللهَ تَعَالَىٰ يُؤَيِّدُ حَسَّانَ بِرُوحِ الْقُدُسِ مَا يُنَافِحُ ۞ أَوْ يُفَاخِرُ عَنْ رَسُولِ اللهِ ﷺ ۞

250. Isma'il ibn Musa al-Fazari and 'Ali ibn Hujr narrated to us (both with the same meaning); they said, "'Abd al-Rahman ibn Abi al-Zinad narrated to us on the authority of Hisham ibn 'Urwa, on the authority of his father, on the authority of 'A'isha, who reported:

"The Messenger of Allah ﷺ placed a pulpit in the Mosque for Hassan ibn Thabit to stand upon and laud the Messenger of Allah ﷺ [or he [the narrator] said: "to defend the Messenger of Allah [563].["ﷺ The Messenger of Allah ﷺ said, 'Verily Allah Most Exalted aids Hassan with the Sanctified Spirit (*Ruh al-Qudus*)[564] so long as he defends[565] [or 'so long as he lauds'][566] the Messenger of Allah ﷺ.''''"

٢٥١ - حَدَّثَنَا إِسْمَاعِيلُ بْنُ مُوسَىٰ وَعَلِيُّ بْنُ حُجْرٍ ۞ قَالَا حَدَّثَنَا ابْنُ أَبِي الزِّنَادِ ۞ عَنْ أَبِيهِ ۞ عَنْ عُرْوَةَ ۞ عَنْ عَائِشَةَ رَضِيَ اللهُ عَنْهَا ۞ عَنِ النَّبِيِّ ﷺ ۞ مِثْلَهُ ۞

251. Isma'il ibn Musa and 'Ali ibn Hujr narrated to us, they said, 'Ibn Abi al-Zinnad narrated to us on the authority of his father, on the authority of 'Urwa, on the authority of 'A'isha ...'

—who related a narration that is comparable in wording and meaning to the aforementioned.[567]

same animal. They include:
1. Sayyiduna Abu Bakr
2. Sharid, narrator of this hadith
3. Usama ibn Zayd
4. Fadl ibn 'Abbas
5. Mu'adh ibn Jabal
6. Abu Iyas al-Sa'idi
7. Thabit ibn Dahhak
8. 'Uqba ibn 'Amir
9. 'Abdullah ibn Ja'far (MA)

562 This shows that the Messenger of Allah ﷺ enjoyed the poetry, and is proof that it is permissible to listen to poetry as long as it contains wisdoms and is free from indecency. (MA)

563 The narrator was unsure. (AA)

564 One of the names for the Archangel Jibril. (AA)

565 Sayyiduna Hassan ibn Thabit would defend the Prophet ﷺ through poetry in response to the abuse and false accusations of the disbelievers. The Messenger of Allah ﷺ asked Hassan to stand upon a pulpit and praise him in the Mosque. The Prophet ﷺ often made three supplications for those who praised him. He would ask Allah to preserve their mouths, lengthen their lives and illuminate their faces. The four famous poets of the Prophet ﷺ were Hassan ibn Thabit, 'Abdullah ibn Rawaha, Ka'b ibn Zuhayr and Ka'b ibn Malik. Sayyida 'A'isha related, 'Once, Hassan ibn Thabit asked the Prophet ﷺ for permission to lampoon [i.e. compose satirical poetry against] the disbelievers. The Prophet ﷺ said, "What about the fact that I share common descent with them?" Hassan replied, "I shall take you out of them as a hair is taken out of dough!"' (*Sahih al-Bukhari*)

Hassan related, 'I asked Abu Hurayra, "By Allah! Tell me the truth whether you heard the Prophet saying, 'O Hassan! Reply on behalf of the Messenger of Allah! O Allah! Help him with the Sanctified Spirit!' Abu Hurayra said, "Yes." ' (*Sahih al-Bukhari*) (MA)

566 The narrator was unsure. (AA)

567 The only difference being the chain of transmission. Imam al-Tirmidhi mentioned this to lend strength to the narration. (AA)

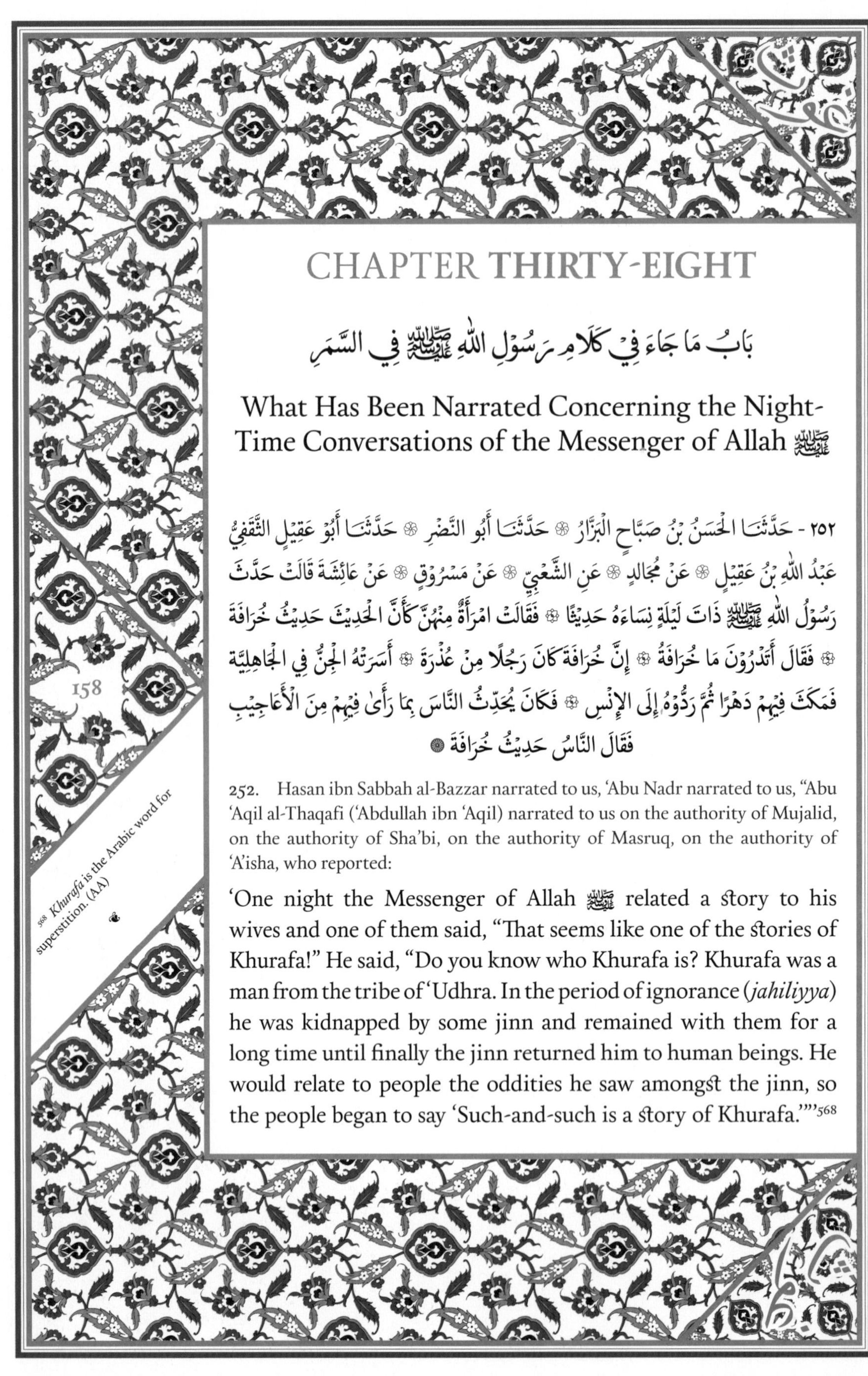

CHAPTER THIRTY-EIGHT

بَابُ مَا جَاءَ فِي كَلَامِ رَسُولِ اللهِ ﷺ فِي السَّمَرِ

What Has Been Narrated Concerning the Night-Time Conversations of the Messenger of Allah ﷺ

٢٥٢ - حَدَّثَنَا الْحَسَنُ بْنُ صَبَّاحٍ الْبَزَّارُ ۞ حَدَّثَنَا أَبُو النَّضْرِ ۞ حَدَّثَنَا أَبُو عَقِيلٍ الثَّقَفِيُّ عَبْدُ اللهِ بْنُ عَقِيلٍ ۞ عَنْ مُجَالِدٍ ۞ عَنِ الشَّعْبِيِّ ۞ عَنْ مَسْرُوقٍ ۞ عَنْ عَائِشَةَ قَالَتْ حَدَّثَ رَسُولُ اللهِ ﷺ ذَاتَ لَيْلَةٍ نِسَاءَهُ حَدِيثًا ۞ فَقَالَتِ امْرَأَةٌ مِنْهُنَّ كَأَنَّ الْحَدِيثَ حَدِيثُ خُرَافَةَ ۞ فَقَالَ أَتَدْرُونَ مَا خُرَافَةُ ۞ إِنَّ خُرَافَةَ كَانَ رَجُلًا مِنْ عُذْرَةَ ۞ أَسَرَتْهُ الْجِنُّ فِي الْجَاهِلِيَّةِ فَمَكَثَ فِيهِمْ دَهْرًا ثُمَّ رَدُّوهُ إِلَى الإِنْسِ ۞ فَكَانَ يُحَدِّثُ النَّاسَ بِمَا رَأَى فِيهِمْ مِنَ الأَعَاجِيبِ فَقَالَ النَّاسُ حَدِيثُ خُرَافَةَ ۞

252. Hasan ibn Sabbah al-Bazzar narrated to us, 'Abu Nadr narrated to us, "Abu 'Aqil al-Thaqafi ('Abdullah ibn 'Aqil) narrated to us on the authority of Mujalid, on the authority of Sha'bi, on the authority of Masruq, on the authority of 'A'isha, who reported:

'One night the Messenger of Allah ﷺ related a story to his wives and one of them said, "That seems like one of the stories of Khurafa!" He said, "Do you know who Khurafa is? Khurafa was a man from the tribe of 'Udhra. In the period of ignorance (*jahiliyya*) he was kidnapped by some jinn and remained with them for a long time until finally the jinn returned him to human beings. He would relate to people the oddities he saw amongst the jinn, so the people began to say 'Such-and-such is a story of Khurafa.'"'[568]

568 *Khurafa* is the Arabic word for superstition. (AA)

حَدِيثُ أُمِّ زَرْعٍ

٢٥٣ - حَدَّثَنَا عَلِيُّ بْنُ حُجْرٍ ۞ أَخْبَرَنَا عِيسَى بْنُ يُونُسَ ۞ عَنْ هِشَامِ بْنِ عُرْوَةَ ۞ عَنْ أَخِيهِ عَبْدِ اللهِ بْنِ عُرْوَةَ ۞ عَنْ عُرْوَةَ ۞ عَنْ عَائِشَةَ قَالَتْ جَلَسَتْ إِحْدَىٰ عَشْرَةَ امْرَأَةً فَتَعَاهَدْنَ وَتَعَاقَدْنَ أَنْ لَا يَكْتُمْنَ مِنْ أَخْبَارِ أَزْوَاجِهِنَّ شَيْئًا ۞ فَقَالَتِ الْأُولَىٰ زَوْجِي لَحْمُ جَمَلٍ غَثٍّ عَلَىٰ رَأْسِ جَبَلٍ وَعْرٍ ۞ لَا سَهْلٍ فَيُرْتَقَىٰ ۞ وَلَا سَمِينٍ فَيُنْتَقَلُ ۞ قَالَتِ الثَّانِيَةُ زَوْجِي لَا أُثِيرُ خَبَرَهُ ۞ إِنِّي أَخَافُ أَنْ لَا أَذَرَهُ ۞ إِنْ أَذْكُرْهُ أَذْكُرْ عُجَرَهُ وَبُجَرَهُ ۞ قَالَتِ الثَّالِثَةُ زَوْجِي الْعَشَنَّقُ ۞ إِنْ أَنْطِقْ أُطَلَّقْ ۞ وَإِنْ أَسْكُتْ أُعَلَّقْ ۞ قَالَتِ الرَّابِعَةُ زَوْجِي كَلَيْلِ تِهَامَةَ ۞ لَا حَرٌّ وَلَا قُرٌّ وَلَا مَخَافَةَ وَلَا سَآمَةَ ۞ قَالَتِ الْخَامِسَةُ زَوْجِي إِنْ دَخَلَ فَهِدَ ۞ وَإِنْ خَرَجَ أَسِدَ ۞ وَلَا يَسْأَلُ عَمَّا عَهِدَ ۞ قَالَتِ السَّادِسَةُ زَوْجِي إِنْ أَكَلَ لَفَّ ۞ وَإِنْ شَرِبَ اشْتَفَّ ۞ وَإِنِ اضْطَجَعَ الْتَفَّ ۞ وَلَا يُولِجُ الْكَفَّ لِيَعْلَمَ الْبَثَّ ۞ قَالَتِ السَّابِعَةُ زَوْجِي عَيَايَاءُ أَوْ غَيَايَاءُ طَبَاقَاءُ ۞ كُلُّ دَاءٍ لَهُ دَاءٌ ۞ شَجَّكِ أَوْ فَلَّكِ ۞ أَوْ جَمَعَ كُلًّا لَكِ ۞ قَالَتِ الثَّامِنَةُ زَوْجِي الْمَسُّ مَسُّ أَرْنَبٍ ۞ وَالرِّيحُ رِيحُ زَرْنَبٍ ۞ قَالَتِ التَّاسِعَةُ زَوْجِي رَفِيعُ الْعِمَادِ ۞ طَوِيلُ النِّجَادِ ۞ عَظِيمُ الرَّمَادِ ۞ قَرِيبُ الْبَيْتِ مِنَ النَّادِ ۞ قَالَتِ الْعَاشِرَةُ زَوْجِي مَالِكٌ ۞ وَمَا مَالِكٌ ۞ مَالِكٌ خَيْرٌ مِنْ ذَٰلِكِ ۞ لَهُ إِبِلٌ كَثِيرَاتُ الْمَبَارِكِ ۞ قَلِيلَاتُ الْمَسَارِحِ ۞ إِذَا سَمِعْنَ صَوْتَ الْمِزْهَرِ أَيْقَنَّ أَنَّهُنَّ هَوَالِكُ ۞ قَالَتِ الْحَادِيَةَ عَشْرَةَ زَوْجِي أَبُو زَرْعٍ ۞ وَمَا أَبُو زَرْعٍ ۞ أَنَاسَ مِنْ حُلِيٍّ أُذُنَيَّ ۞ وَمَلَأَ مِنْ شَحْمٍ عَضُدَيَّ ۞ وَبَجَّحَنِي فَبَجِحَتْ إِلَيَّ نَفْسِي ۞ وَجَدَنِي فِي أَهْلِ غُنَيْمَةٍ بِشَقٍّ ۞ فَجَعَلَنِي فِي أَهْلِ صَهِيلٍ وَأَطِيطٍ وَدَائِسٍ وَمُنَقٍّ ۞ فَعِنْدَهُ أَقُولُ فَلَا أُقَبَّحُ ۞ وَأَرْقُدُ فَأَتَصَبَّحُ ۞ وَأَشْرَبُ فَأَتَقَمَّحُ ۞ أُمُّ أَبِي زَرْعٍ ۞ فَمَا أُمُّ أَبِي زَرْعٍ ۞ عُكُومُهَا رَدَاحٌ ۞ وَبَيْتُهَا فَسَاحٌ ۞ ابْنُ أَبِي زَرْعٍ ۞ فَمَا ابْنُ أَبِي زَرْعٍ ۞ مَضْجَعُهُ كَمَسَلِّ شَطْبَةٍ ۞ وَتُشْبِعُهُ ذِرَاعُ الْجَفْرَةِ

569 In other words, he is emotionally distant and inaccessible; even if he were accessible, his company would bring little benefit. (AA)

570 Commentators on this tradition disagree about the meaning of this phrase. Some say that it means 'I fear that if I start mentioning his faults, I won't be able to stop.' Some say that the word 'not' is extraneous (used for rhetorical effect), while others say it is intended. The first interpretation would mean she fears that if she starts mentioning her husband's faults, she will want to leave him. The second interpretation would mean she does not want to reveal her husband's faults, because she fears she will be unable to leave him. (AA)

571 In this passive description of her husband, the second wife speaks of him negatively and does not conceal anything about him, even though she does not mention any particular bad quality. (AA)

572 Because of his foolishness and ill-temperament, if she speaks about his faults he will divorce her. (AA)

573 Meaning, if she remains silent and does not mention his bad qualities, she will be 'left hanging' (*muʿallaqa*), which refers to a woman who is left in a state of 'suspended animation', neither enjoying the benefits of marriage nor the status of being single. (AA)

574 Tihama refers to Mecca and her surrounding areas. This means he is completely balanced in nature, amiable in character and of pleasant disposition. (AA)

575 He is mild like a spring night in Tihama. He is not a source of fear or malaise, and he never acts like he is bored with his wife. He listens attentively without cutting her off or acting bored and uninterested. In saying he was not fearsome, she is saying she isn't afraid of being terrorised or embarrassed by him. In another narration of this tradition, the wife added, 'nor is he boorish'. (AA)

576 Commentators disagree over whether this tradition is a statement of praise or criticism. Imam al-Bajuri states, 'That is, when he comes to her desiring intercourse, he pounces on her like a leopard. Or it means he strikes her when he comes home. Or it means he resembles a leopard in his overbearingness and deep sleep.... This statement carries the possibility of being a praise or a criticism. If the former is intended, it means he is like a leopard in his playfulness when intimate with her, or he is like a leopard who sleeps heavily, and who, out of nobility and clemency, overlooks her shortcomings in her household duties. If the latter is intended, it means he is like a leopard in that he pounces on her to strike her, and he is overbearing, sleeps heavily and ignores her...' (AA)

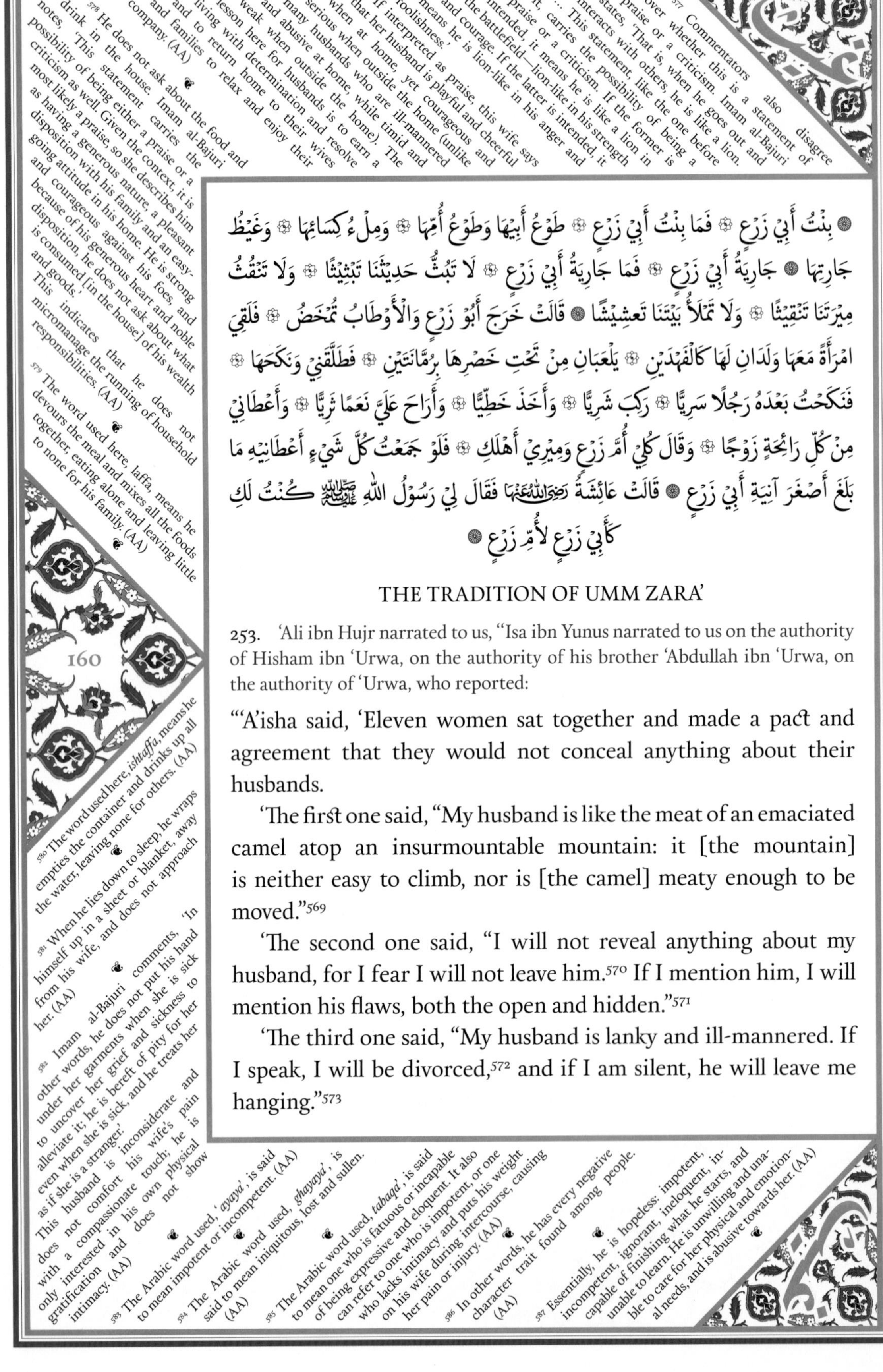

۞ بِنْتُ أَبِي زَرْعٍ ۞ فَمَا بِنْتُ أَبِي زَرْعٍ ۞ طَوْعُ أَبِيهَا وَطَوْعُ أُمِّهَا ۞ وَمِلْءُ كِسَائِهَا ۞ وَغَيْظُ جَارَتِهَا ۞ جَارِيَةُ أَبِي زَرْعٍ ۞ فَمَا جَارِيَةُ أَبِي زَرْعٍ ۞ لَا تَبُثُّ حَدِيثَنَا تَبْثِيثًا ۞ وَلَا تُنَقِّثُ مِيرَتَنَا تَنْقِيثًا ۞ وَلَا تَمْلَأُ بَيْتَنَا تَعْشِيشًا ۞ قَالَتْ خَرَجَ أَبُو زَرْعٍ وَالْأَوْطَابُ تُمْخَضُ ۞ فَلَقِيَ امْرَأَةً مَعَهَا وَلَدَانِ لَهَا كَالْفَهْدَيْنِ ۞ يَلْعَبَانِ مِنْ تَحْتِ خَصْرِهَا بِرُمَّانَتَيْنِ ۞ فَطَلَّقَنِي وَنَكَحَهَا ۞ فَنَكَحْتُ بَعْدَهُ رَجُلًا سَرِيًّا ۞ رَكِبَ شَرِيًّا ۞ وَأَخَذَ خَطِّيًّا ۞ وَأَرَاحَ عَلَيَّ نَعَمًا ثَرِيًّا ۞ وَأَعْطَانِي مِنْ كُلِّ رَائِحَةٍ زَوْجًا ۞ وَقَالَ كُلِي أُمَّ زَرْعٍ وَمِيرِي أَهْلَكِ ۞ فَلَوْ جَمَعْتُ كُلَّ شَيْءٍ أَعْطَانِيهِ مَا بَلَغَ أَصْغَرَ آنِيَةِ أَبِي زَرْعٍ ۞ قَالَتْ عَائِشَةُ رَضِيَ اللَّهُ عَنْهَا فَقَالَ لِي رَسُولُ اللَّهِ ﷺ كُنْتُ لَكِ كَأَبِي زَرْعٍ لِأُمِّ زَرْعٍ ۞

THE TRADITION OF UMM ZARA'

253. 'Ali ibn Hujr narrated to us, "Isa ibn Yunus narrated to us on the authority of Hisham ibn 'Urwa, on the authority of his brother 'Abdullah ibn 'Urwa, on the authority of 'Urwa, who reported:

"'A'isha said, 'Eleven women sat together and made a pact and agreement that they would not conceal anything about their husbands.

'The first one said, "My husband is like the meat of an emaciated camel atop an insurmountable mountain: it [the mountain] is neither easy to climb, nor is [the camel] meaty enough to be moved."[569]

'The second one said, "I will not reveal anything about my husband, for I fear I will not leave him.[570] If I mention him, I will mention his flaws, both the open and hidden."[571]

'The third one said, "My husband is lanky and ill-mannered. If I speak, I will be divorced,[572] and if I am silent, he will leave me hanging."[573]

577 Commentators also disagree over whether this is a statement of praise or a criticism. Imam al-Bajuri states, 'That is, when he goes out and interacts with others, he is like a lion. ... This statement, like the one before it, carries the possibility of being a praise or a criticism. If the former is intended, it means he is like a lion in the battlefield—lion-like in his strength and courage. If the latter is intended, it means he is lion-like in his anger and foolishness.' If interpreted as praise, this wife says that her husband is playful and cheerful when at home, yet courageous and serious when outside the home (unlike many husbands who are ill-mannered and abusive at home, while timid and weak when outside the home). The lesson here for husbands is to earn a living with determination and resolve and to return home to their wives and families to relax and enjoy their company. (AA)

578 He does not ask about the food and drink in the house. Imam al-Bajuri notes, 'This statement carries the possibility of being either a praise or a criticism as well. Given the context, it is most likely a praise, so she describes him as having a generous nature, a pleasant disposition with his family and an easy-going attitude in his home. He is strong and courageous against his foes, and because of his generous heart and noble disposition, he does not ask about what is consumed [in the house] of his wealth and goods.' This indicates that he does not micromanage the running of household responsibilities. (AA)

579 The word used here, laffa, means he devours the meal and mixes all the foods together, eating alone and leaving little to none for his family. (AA)

580 The word used here, *ishtaffa*, means he empties the container and drinks up all the water, leaving none for others. (AA)

581 When he lies down to sleep, he wraps himself up in a sheet or blanket, away from his wife, and does not approach her. (AA)

582 Imam al-Bajuri comments, 'In other words, he does not put his hand under her garments when she is sick to uncover her grief and sickness to alleviate it; he is bereft of pity for her even when she is sick, and he treats her as if she is a stranger.' This husband is inconsiderate and does not comfort his wife's pain with a compassionate touch; he is only interested in his own physical gratification and does not show intimacy. (AA)

583 The Arabic word used, '*ayaya*', is said to mean impotent or incompetent. (AA)

584 The Arabic word used, *ghayaya*', is said to mean iniquitous, lost and sullen. (AA)

585 The Arabic word used, *tabaqa*', is said to mean one who is fatuous or incapable of being expressive and eloquent. It also can refer to one who is impotent, or one who lacks intimacy and puts his weight on his wife during intercourse, causing her pain or injury. (AA)

586 In other words, he has every negative character trait found among people. (AA)

587 Essentially, he is hopeless: impotent, incompetent, ignorant, ineloquent, incapable of finishing what he starts, and unable to learn. He is unwilling and unable to care for her physical and emotional needs, and is abusive towards her. (AA)

'The forth one said, "My husband is like a night in Tihama:[574] neither hot nor cold, nor fearsome nor dull."[575]

'The fifth one said, "When my husband enters [the house], he is like a leopard,[576] and when he goes out, he is like a lion,[577] and he does not ask about what he entrusts me with."[578]

'The sixth one said, "When my husband eats, he gobbles it all up![579] And when he drinks, he gulps it all down![580] When he lies down, he wraps himself up[581] and does not extend his hand to uncover any grief!"[582]

'The seventh one said, "My husband is completely useless[583] [or she said "he is wicked"[584]] and dim-witted.[585] Every illness is his.[586] If he strikes you he will either wound your head or break your bones, or both."[587]

'The eighth one said, "My husband has the touch of a rabbit[588] and the fragrance of perfume."[589]

'The ninth one said, "My husband is of noble stature,[590] his scabbard is long,[591] his ash heap is large[592] and his home is near the gathering-place."[593]

'The tenth one said, "My husband is Malik—and how great is Malik! Malik is better than that![594] He has camels housed in several pens[595] and they are seldom roaming.[596] When they hear the sound of the lute they know they are about to be slaughtered!"

'The eleventh one said, "My husband was Abu Zara'[597]—how great was Abu Zara'! He made my ears dangle with jewellery,[598] and made my arms plump.[599] He delighted me until I delighted myself.[600] He found me in a family of few sheep, living in hardship,[601] and he brought me to a family in which were heard the neighs of horses and the cries of camels, and the sounds of threshing and cleaning grains.[602] When in his presence I could

588 He is soft to touch and gentle-natured. (AA)

589 This perfume, *zarnab*, is said to be from a fragrant plant, or from saffron. (AA)

590 In Arabic, this is *Rafi' al-'imad*, which literally means 'The pillars of his house are lofty.' In the context of Arabic rhetoric, this is known as *kinaya*, or metonymy, which means 'the replacement of one word by another word which has a logical connection with it.' By saying *Rafi' al-'imad*, it is inferred that the wife means he is noble in character and hospitable with guests and kin, and capable of entertaining large crowds. (AA)

591 That is, he is both tall and brave. Because his scabbard is long, it is deduced that he is tall, and because he carries a sword, it is deduced that he is brave. (AA)

592 In other words, he is generous since he has heaps of ashes from fires used to cook food for his many guests. (AA)

593 The congregational 'gathering-place' hall—the *nadi*—was a common feature of ancient Arabian society and was used for the guests of a tribe. In saying that her husband's home is close to the gathering-place, she is telling the other women that he is eager to entertain guests. (AA)

594 Imam al-Bajuri comments, 'In other words, "he is better than the aforementioned husbands", or "he is better than the ninth husband", or "he surpasses what I am going to say about him".' (AA)

595 This can also mean that he has many camels kneeling and close at hand for milking or slaughtering. (AA)

596 In other words, they are kept close in their pens and are seldom left to roam in pastures because he has them readied for milking or slaughter in order to feed his guests. (AA)

597 Literally, 'the Father of Crops'. (AA)

598 He gifted her expensive jewellery. It did not fling around; rather, it was heavy and caused her earlobes to dangle. (AA)

599 He fed her well, causing her to gain weight. The Arabs of that time found heavyset women attractive. (AA)

600 He praised her and loved her so much that she grew in self-esteem. (AA)

601 Or a family owning only a few sheep, living by the side of a mountain. (AA)

602 In other words, she was brought to a large farming family that owned many horses and camels and spent their time harvesting crops, separating grains from plants and cleaning them. (AA)

603 Her mother-in-law. (AA)

604 Her step-son. (AA)

605 He was lean of build and so light that he could sleep on a thin surface easily without complaint. (AA)

606 Her step-daughter. (AA)

607 Literally, 'She was obedience to her father and obedience to her mother.' This means she was so dutiful to her parents that she was described as obedience itself. Imam al-Bajuri notes that the father and mother are mentioned separately as an indication that each are to be obeyed independently. (AA)

speak and would not be rebuked, and I could sleep through the morning and drink till I was quenched. And the mother of Abu Zara'—how great was the mother of Abu Zara'![603] Her food containers were large, heavy and plentiful, and her home was spacious. And the son of Abu Zara'—how great was the son of Abu Zara'![604] His bed was like a slice of a palm leaf,[605] and a single foreleg of a lean lamb was enough to sate him. And the daughter of Abu Zara'—how great was the daughter of Abu Zara'![606] To her father she was extremely obedient, and to her mother she was extremely obedient.[607] She filled out her garment[608] and infuriated her co-wife.[609] And the slave girl of Abu Zara'—how great was the slave girl of Abu Zara'! She did not divulge our conversations to others, nor did she purloin our food, nor did she fill our house with litter. She said, 'One day, Abu Zara' went out as the milkers were churning butter.[610] While out, he met a woman with two boys who were like leopards, and they were playing beneath her waist with pomegranates.[611] He divorced me and married her. After him I married a noble man with a swift and tireless steed, and he was skilful with the spear. He showered me with many valuables and gave me a pair of every kind of cattle. He said to me, 'Eat, O Umm Zara', and take some [food] to your kin.' If I had gathered everything that he gave me, it would not amount to the smallest vessel of Abu Zara'."

['A'isha said] 'The Messenger of Allah ﷺ said to me, "I am unto you as Abu Zara' was unto Umm Zara'."'"'"[612]

❦

[608] She had a plump and shapely figure. (AA)

[609] Because of her beauty and character. (AA)

[610] It was the custom of the Arabs to leave their homes for commerce when milk was abundant. (AA)

[611] The phrase 'they were playing beneath her waist with pomegranates' is a euphemistic way of saying she had a shapely bosom. Imam al-Bajuri notes that this wife mentioned the two sons and their qualities because they were one of the factors that motivated Abu Zara' to marry the woman. This, Imam al-Bajuri says, 'is because the Arabs desired progeny and abundant offspring, so it is possible that when Abu Zara' saw this woman and was pleased with her appearance and the appearance of her two sons and saw signs of intelligence in them, he wanted to marry her.' (AA)

[612] In al-Tabarani's version of this tradition there is the addition, '...except that he divorced her, and I will never divorce you.' Imam al-Nasa'i and al-Tabarani both recorded that Sayyida 'A'isha said, 'O Messenger of Allah, you are better than Abu Zara'!' In the narration of this hadith from Zubayr it reads, 'May my mother and father be ransomed for you, you are far better for me than Abu Zara' is for Umm Zara'!' The entire narration was leading to this final section. Entire books have been written about the eloquent language and lessons contained in the tradition of Umm Zara'. Scholars have mentioned several lessons and points of benefit derived from it, amongst them:

1. The excellence of observing beautiful character with one's wife through intimacy and conversation about permissible matters.
2. The permissibility of joking around occasionally and being playful with one's wife and expressing love for her.
3. The prohibition of boasting about one's wealth.
4. The permissibility of a wife mentioning her husband's good qualities to others.
5. The permissibility of mentioning the stories of previous nations and deriving lessons from them.
6. The encouragement of women to be loyal to their husbands.
7. The permissibility of praising someone to his face provided it is known that such praise will not corrupt him.
8. The beautiful etiquette of the Prophet ﷺ who listened attentively to his wife 'A'isha as she recounted the descriptions of the wives. He did not interrupt her, and only commented after she was finished.
9. The intelligence, eloquence and linguistic prowess of Sayyida 'A'isha.
10. The permissibility, rather encouragement, to have light-hearted night time conversations with one's spouse.
11. The permissibility of a husband reminding his wife of his kindness in order to strengthen the bonds of love between him and her and to prevent disgruntlement. (AA)

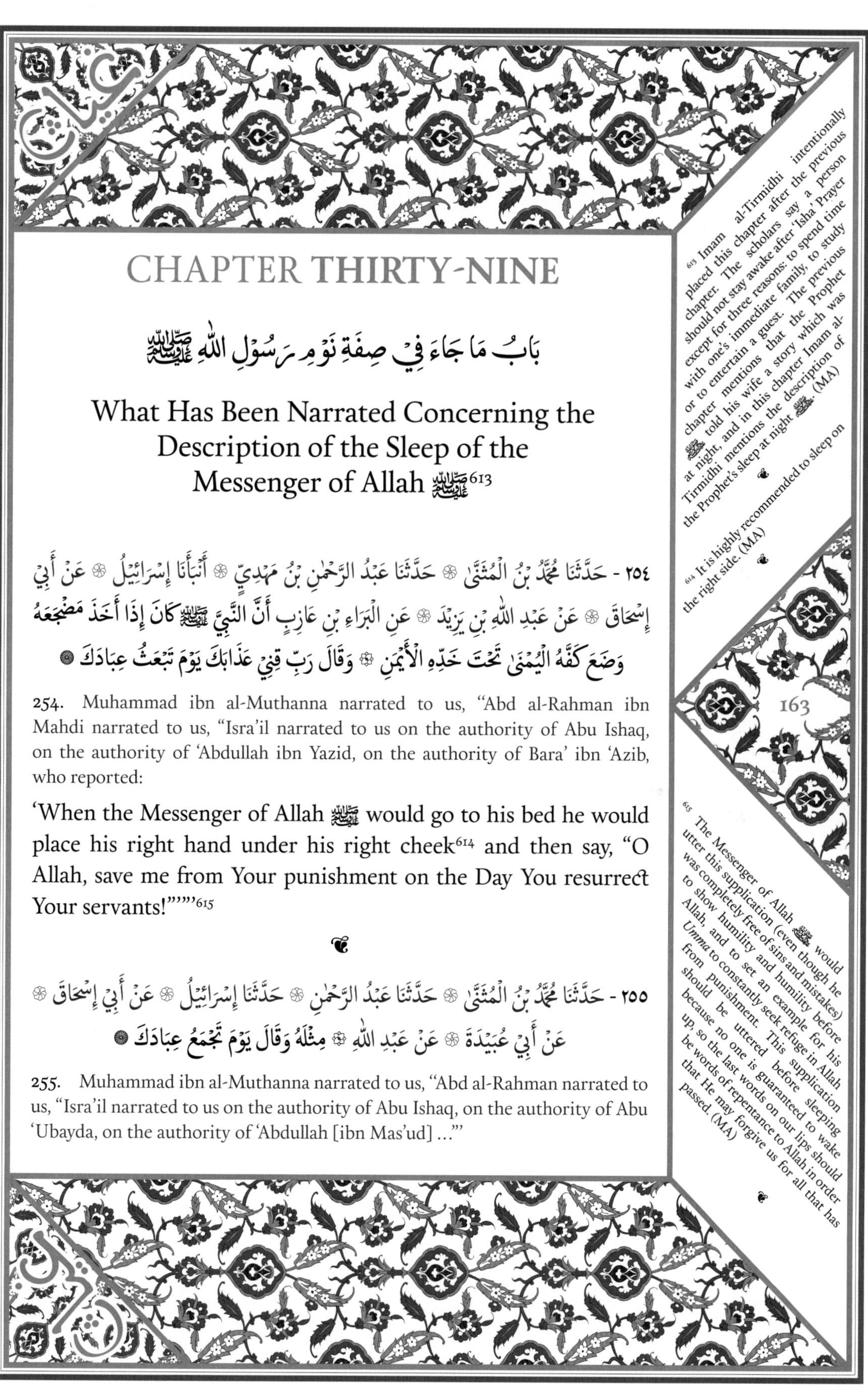

CHAPTER THIRTY-NINE

بَابُ مَا جَاءَ فِي صِفَةِ نَوْمِ رَسُولِ اللهِ ﷺ

What Has Been Narrated Concerning the Description of the Sleep of the Messenger of Allah ﷺ[613]

٢٥٤ - حَدَّثَنَا مُحَمَّدُ بْنُ الْمُثَنَّى ۞ حَدَّثَنَا عَبْدُ الرَّحْمٰنِ بْنُ مَهْدِيٍّ ۞ أَنْبَأَنَا إِسْرَائِيلُ ۞ عَنْ أَبِي إِسْحَاقَ ۞ عَنْ عَبْدِ اللهِ بْنِ يَزِيدَ ۞ عَنِ الْبَرَاءِ بْنِ عَازِبٍ أَنَّ النَّبِيَّ ﷺ كَانَ إِذَا أَخَذَ مَضْجَعَهُ وَضَعَ كَفَّهُ الْيُمْنَى تَحْتَ خَدِّهِ الْأَيْمَنِ ۞ وَقَالَ رَبِّ قِنِي عَذَابَكَ يَوْمَ تَبْعَثُ عِبَادَكَ ۞

254. Muhammad ibn al-Muthanna narrated to us, "Abd al-Rahman ibn Mahdi narrated to us, "Isra'il narrated to us on the authority of Abu Ishaq, on the authority of 'Abdullah ibn Yazid, on the authority of Bara' ibn 'Azib, who reported:

'When the Messenger of Allah ﷺ would go to his bed he would place his right hand under his right cheek[614] and then say, "O Allah, save me from Your punishment on the Day You resurrect Your servants!"'"'[615]

٢٥٥ - حَدَّثَنَا مُحَمَّدُ بْنُ الْمُثَنَّى ۞ حَدَّثَنَا عَبْدُ الرَّحْمٰنِ ۞ حَدَّثَنَا إِسْرَائِيلُ ۞ عَنْ أَبِي إِسْحَاقَ ۞ عَنْ أَبِي عُبَيْدَةَ ۞ عَنْ عَبْدِ اللهِ ۞ مِثْلَهُ وَقَالَ يَوْمَ تَجْمَعُ عِبَادَكَ ۞

255. Muhammad ibn al-Muthanna narrated to us, "Abd al-Rahman narrated to us, "Isra'il narrated to us on the authority of Abu Ishaq, on the authority of Abu 'Ubayda, on the authority of 'Abdullah [ibn Mas'ud] ..."'

[613] Imam al-Tirmidhi intentionally placed this chapter after the previous chapter. The scholars say a person should not stay awake after 'Isha' Prayer except for three reasons: to spend time with one's immediate family, to study or to entertain a guest. The previous chapter mentions that the Prophet ﷺ told his wife a story which was at night, and in this chapter Imam al-Tirmidhi mentions the description of the Prophet's sleep at night ﷺ. (MA)

[614] It is highly recommended to sleep on the right side. (MA)

[615] The Messenger of Allah ﷺ would utter this supplication (even though he was completely free of sins and mistakes) to show humility and humility before Allah, and to set an example for his *Umma* to constantly seek refuge in Allah from punishment. This supplication should be uttered before sleeping because no one is guaranteed to wake up, so the last words on our lips should be words of repentance to Allah in order that He may forgive us for all that has passed. (MA)

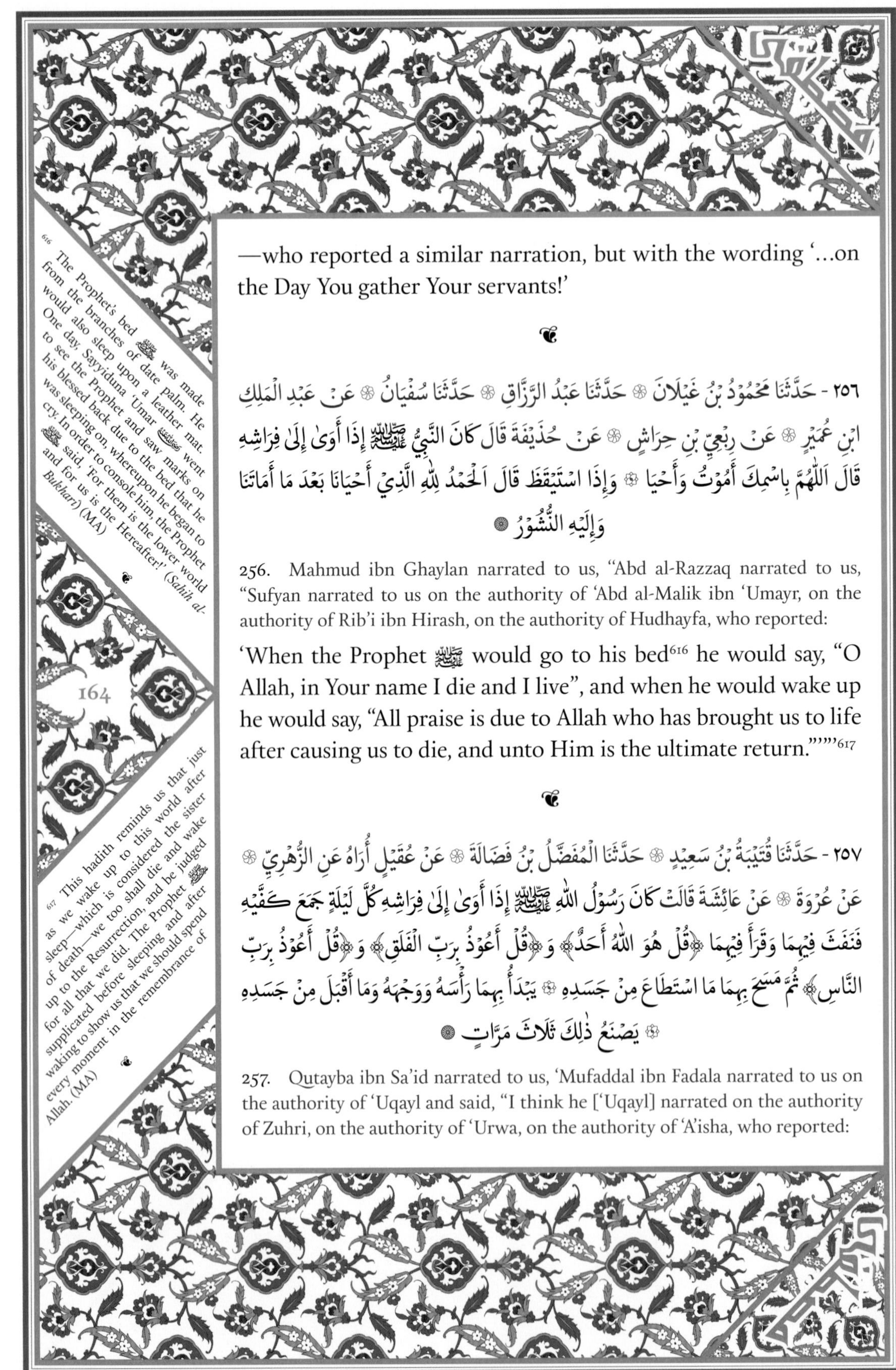

—who reported a similar narration, but with the wording '...on the Day You gather Your servants!'

٢٥٦ - حَدَّثَنَا مَحْمُودُ بْنُ غَيْلَانَ ۞ حَدَّثَنَا عَبْدُ الرَّزَّاقِ ۞ حَدَّثَنَا سُفْيَانُ ۞ عَنْ عَبْدِ الْمَلِكِ ابْنِ عُمَيْرٍ ۞ عَنْ رِبْعِيِّ بْنِ حِرَاشٍ ۞ عَنْ حُذَيْفَةَ قَالَ كَانَ النَّبِيُّ ﷺ إِذَا أَوَىٰ إِلَىٰ فِرَاشِهِ قَالَ اَللّٰهُمَّ بِاسْمِكَ أَمُوتُ وَأَحْيَا ۞ وَإِذَا اسْتَيْقَظَ قَالَ اَلْحَمْدُ لِلّٰهِ الَّذِي أَحْيَانَا بَعْدَ مَا أَمَاتَنَا وَإِلَيْهِ النُّشُورُ ۞

256. Mahmud ibn Ghaylan narrated to us, "Abd al-Razzaq narrated to us, "Sufyan narrated to us on the authority of 'Abd al-Malik ibn 'Umayr, on the authority of Rib'i ibn Hirash, on the authority of Hudhayfa, who reported:

'When the Prophet ﷺ would go to his bed[616] he would say, "O Allah, in Your name I die and I live", and when he would wake up he would say, "All praise is due to Allah who has brought us to life after causing us to die, and unto Him is the ultimate return."""'[617]

٢٥٧ - حَدَّثَنَا قُتَيْبَةُ بْنُ سَعِيدٍ ۞ حَدَّثَنَا الْمُفَضَّلُ بْنُ فَضَالَةَ ۞ عَنْ عُقَيْلٍ أُرَاهُ عَنِ الزُّهْرِيِّ ۞ عَنْ عُرْوَةَ ۞ عَنْ عَائِشَةَ قَالَتْ كَانَ رَسُولُ اللّٰهِ ﷺ إِذَا أَوَىٰ إِلَىٰ فِرَاشِهِ كُلَّ لَيْلَةٍ جَمَعَ كَفَّيْهِ فَنَفَثَ فِيهِمَا وَقَرَأَ فِيهِمَا ﴿قُلْ هُوَ اللّٰهُ أَحَدٌ﴾ وَ ﴿قُلْ أَعُوذُ بِرَبِّ الْفَلَقِ﴾ وَ ﴿قُلْ أَعُوذُ بِرَبِّ النَّاسِ﴾ ثُمَّ مَسَحَ بِهِمَا مَا اسْتَطَاعَ مِنْ جَسَدِهِ ۞ يَبْدَأُ بِهِمَا رَأْسَهُ وَوَجْهَهُ وَمَا أَقْبَلَ مِنْ جَسَدِهِ ۞ يَصْنَعُ ذٰلِكَ ثَلَاثَ مَرَّاتٍ ۞

257. Qutayba ibn Sa'id narrated to us, 'Mufaddal ibn Fadala narrated to us on the authority of 'Uqayl and said, "I think he ['Uqayl] narrated on the authority of Zuhri, on the authority of 'Urwa, on the authority of 'A'isha, who reported:

616 The Prophet's bed ﷺ was made from the branches of date palm. He would also sleep upon a leather mat. One day, Sayyiduna 'Umar ﷺ went to see the Prophet and saw marks on his blessed back due to the bed that he was sleeping on, whereupon he began to cry. In order to console him, the Prophet ﷺ said, 'For them is the lower world and for us is the Hereafter!' (*Sahih al-Bukhari*) (MA)

617 This hadith reminds us that just as we wake up to this world after sleep—which is considered the sister of death—we too shall die and wake up to the Resurrection, and be judged for all that we did. The Prophet ﷺ supplicated before sleeping and after waking to show us that we should spend every moment in the remembrance of Allah. (MA)

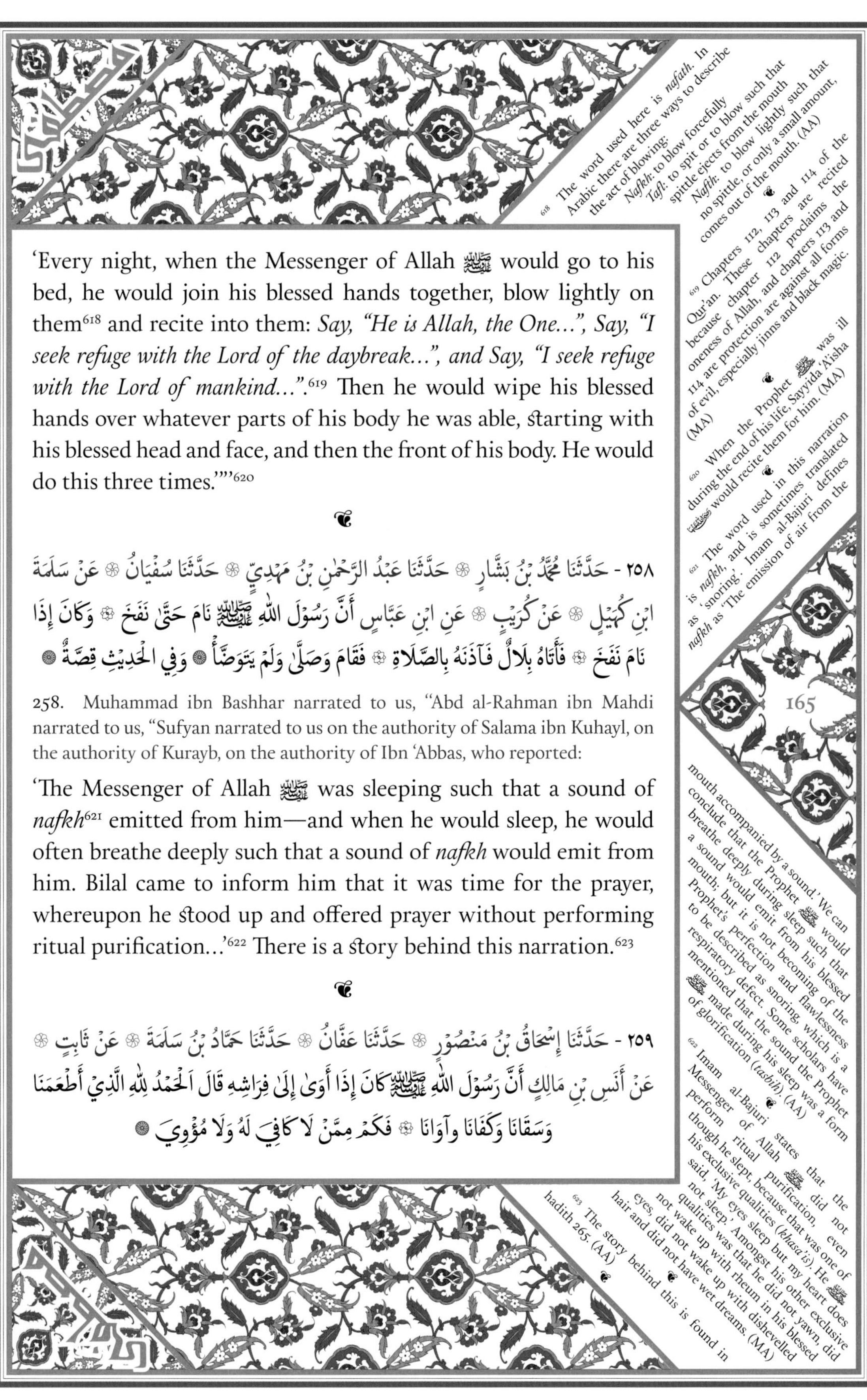

'Every night, when the Messenger of Allah ﷺ would go to his bed, he would join his blessed hands together, blow lightly on them[618] and recite into them: *Say, "He is Allah, the One...", Say, "I seek refuge with the Lord of the daybreak...", and Say, "I seek refuge with the Lord of mankind..."*.[619] Then he would wipe his blessed hands over whatever parts of his body he was able, starting with his blessed head and face, and then the front of his body. He would do this three times.'"[620]

٢٥٨ - حَدَّثَنَا مُحَمَّدُ بْنُ بَشَّارٍ ۞ حَدَّثَنَا عَبْدُ الرَّحْمَٰنِ بْنُ مَهْدِيٍّ ۞ حَدَّثَنَا سُفْيَانُ ۞ عَنْ سَلَمَةَ ابْنِ كُهَيْلٍ ۞ عَنْ كُرَيْبٍ ۞ عَنِ ابْنِ عَبَّاسٍ أَنَّ رَسُولَ اللهِ ﷺ نَامَ حَتَّىٰ نَفَخَ ۞ وَكَانَ إِذَا نَامَ نَفَخَ ۞ فَأَتَاهُ بِلَالٌ فَآذَنَهُ بِالصَّلَاةِ ۞ فَقَامَ وَصَلَّىٰ وَلَمْ يَتَوَضَّأْ ۞ وَفِي الْحَدِيثِ قِصَّةٌ ۞

258. Muhammad ibn Bashhar narrated to us, "'Abd al-Rahman ibn Mahdi narrated to us, "Sufyan narrated to us on the authority of Salama ibn Kuhayl, on the authority of Kurayb, on the authority of Ibn 'Abbas, who reported:

'The Messenger of Allah ﷺ was sleeping such that a sound of *nafkh*[621] emitted from him—and when he would sleep, he would often breathe deeply such that a sound of *nafkh* would emit from him. Bilal came to inform him that it was time for the prayer, whereupon he stood up and offered prayer without performing ritual purification...'[622] There is a story behind this narration.[623]

٢٥٩ - حَدَّثَنَا إِسْحَاقُ بْنُ مَنْصُورٍ ۞ حَدَّثَنَا عَفَّانُ ۞ حَدَّثَنَا حَمَّادُ بْنُ سَلَمَةَ ۞ عَنْ ثَابِتٍ ۞ عَنْ أَنَسِ بْنِ مَالِكٍ أَنَّ رَسُولَ اللهِ ﷺ كَانَ إِذَا أَوَىٰ إِلَىٰ فِرَاشِهِ قَالَ الْحَمْدُ لِلَّهِ الَّذِي أَطْعَمَنَا وَسَقَانَا وَكَفَانَا وَآوَانَا ۞ فَكَمْ مِمَّنْ لَا كَافِيَ لَهُ وَلَا مُؤْوِيَ ۞

618 The word used here is *nafath*. In Arabic there are three ways to describe the act of blowing:
Nafkh: to blow forcefully
Tafl: to spit or to blow such that spittle ejects from the mouth
Nafth: to blow lightly such that no spittle, or only a small amount, comes out of the mouth. (AA)

619 Chapters 112, 113 and 114 of the Qur'an. These chapters are recited because chapter 112 proclaims the oneness of Allah, and chapters 113 and 114 are protection are against all forms of evil, especially jinns and black magic. (MA)

620 When the Prophet ﷺ was ill during the end of his life, Sayyida 'A'isha would recite them for him. (MA)

621 The word used in this narration is *nafkh*, and is sometimes translated as 'snoring'. Imam al-Bajuri defines *nafkh* as 'The emission of air from the mouth accompanied by a sound.' We can conclude that the Prophet ﷺ would breathe deeply during sleep such that a sound would emit from his blessed mouth; but it is not becoming of the Prophet's perfection and flawlessness to be described as snoring, which is a respiratory defect. Some scholars have mentioned that the sound the Prophet ﷺ made during his sleep was a form of glorification (*tasbih*). (AA)

622 Imam al-Bajuri states that the Messenger of Allah ﷺ did not perform ritual purification, even though he slept, because that was one of his exclusive qualities (*khasa'is*). He ﷺ said, 'My eyes sleep but my heart does not sleep.' Amongst his other exclusive qualities was that he did not yawn, did not wake up with rheum in his blessed eyes, did not wake up with dishevelled hair and did not have wet dreams. (MA)

623 The story behind this is found in hadith 265. (AA)

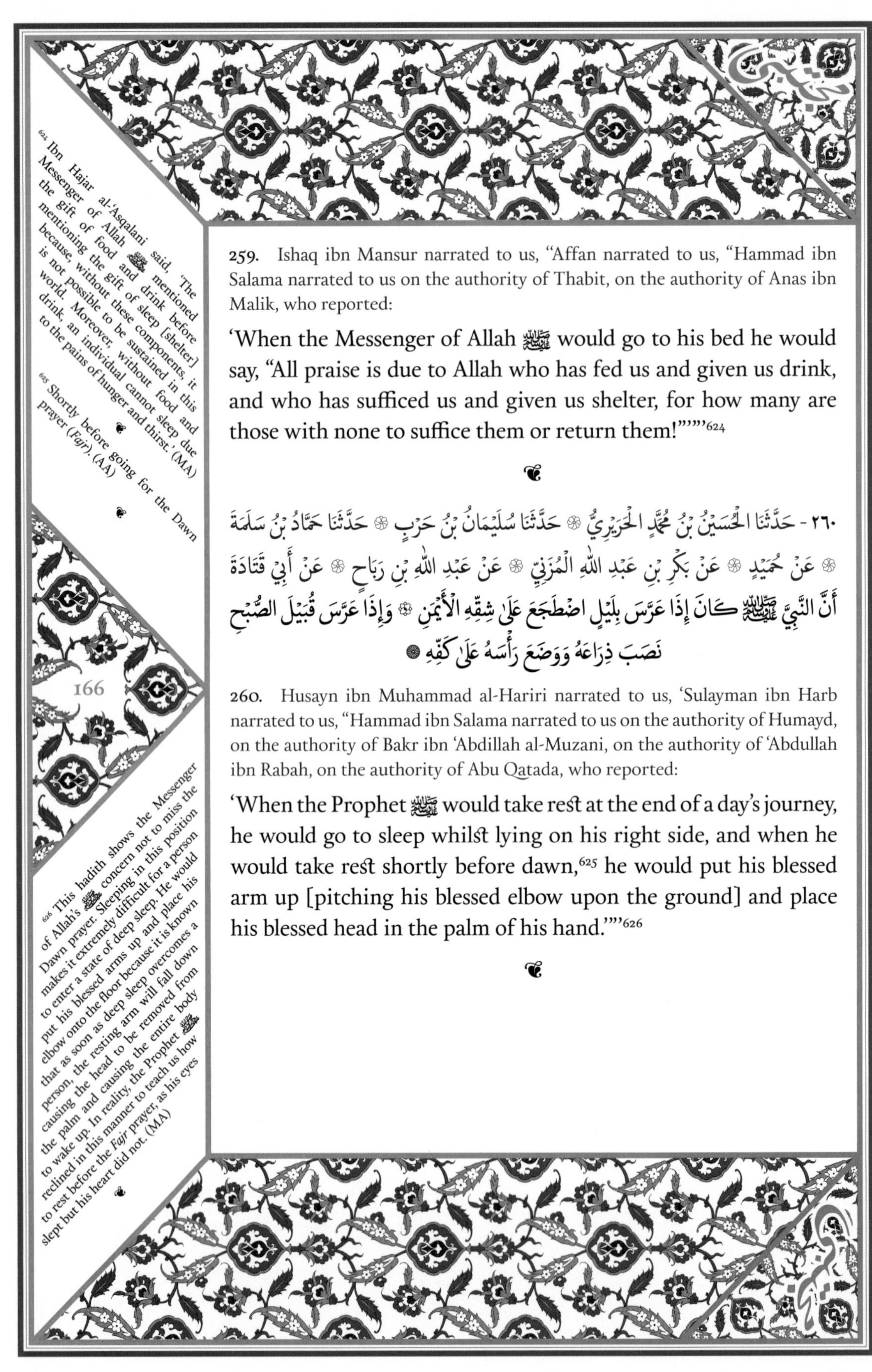

259. Ishaq ibn Mansur narrated to us, "Affan narrated to us, "Hammad ibn Salama narrated to us on the authority of Thabit, on the authority of Anas ibn Malik, who reported:

'When the Messenger of Allah ﷺ would go to his bed he would say, "All praise is due to Allah who has fed us and given us drink, and who has sufficed us and given us shelter, for how many are those with none to suffice them or return them!"""'[624]

٢٦٠ - حَدَّثَنَا الْحُسَيْنُ بْنُ مُحَمَّدٍ الْحَرِيرِيُّ ۞ حَدَّثَنَا سُلَيْمَانُ بْنُ حَرْبٍ ۞ حَدَّثَنَا حَمَّادُ بْنُ سَلَمَةَ ۞ عَنْ حُمَيْدٍ ۞ عَنْ بَكْرِ بْنِ عَبْدِ اللهِ الْمُزَنِيِّ ۞ عَنْ عَبْدِ اللهِ بْنِ رَبَاحٍ ۞ عَنْ أَبِي قَتَادَةَ أَنَّ النَّبِيَّ ﷺ كَانَ إِذَا عَرَّسَ بِلَيْلٍ اضْطَجَعَ عَلَىٰ شِقِّهِ الْأَيْمَنِ ۞ وَإِذَا عَرَّسَ قُبَيْلَ الصُّبْحِ نَصَبَ ذِرَاعَهُ وَوَضَعَ رَأْسَهُ عَلَىٰ كَفِّهِ ۞

260. Husayn ibn Muhammad al-Hariri narrated to us, 'Sulayman ibn Harb narrated to us, "Hammad ibn Salama narrated to us on the authority of Humayd, on the authority of Bakr ibn 'Abdillah al-Muzani, on the authority of 'Abdullah ibn Rabah, on the authority of Abu Qatada, who reported:

'When the Prophet ﷺ would take rest at the end of a day's journey, he would go to sleep whilst lying on his right side, and when he would take rest shortly before dawn,[625] he would put his blessed arm up [pitching his blessed elbow upon the ground] and place his blessed head in the palm of his hand.'"'[626]

[624] Ibn Hajar al-'Asqalani said, 'The Messenger of Allah ﷺ mentioned the gift of food and drink before mentioning the gift of sleep [shelter] because, without these components, it is not possible to be sustained in this world. Moreover, without food and drink, an individual cannot sleep due to the pains of hunger and thirst.' (MA)

[625] Shortly before going for the Dawn prayer (*Fajr*). (AA)

[626] This hadith shows the Messenger of Allah's ﷺ concern not to miss the Dawn prayer. Sleeping in this position makes it extremely difficult for a person to enter a state of deep sleep. He would put his blessed arms up and place his elbow onto the floor because it is known that as soon as deep sleep overcomes a person, the resting arm will fall down causing the head to be removed from the palm and causing the entire body to wake up. In reality, the Prophet ﷺ reclined in this manner to teach us how to rest before the *Fajr* prayer, as his eyes slept but his heart did not. (MA)

CHAPTER FORTY

بَابُ مَا جَاءَ فِي عِبَادَةِ رَسُولِ اللهِ ﷺ

What Has Been Narrated Concerning the Worship of the Messenger of Allah ﷺ[627]

٢٦١ - حَدَّثَنَا قُتَيْبَةُ بْنُ سَعِيدٍ وَبِشْرُ بْنُ مُعَاذٍ ❁ قَالَا حَدَّثَنَا أَبُو عَوَانَةَ ❁ عَنْ زِيَادِ بْنِ عِلَاقَةَ ❁ عَنِ الْمُغِيرَةِ بْنِ شُعْبَةَ رَضِيَ اللهُ عَنْهُ قَالَ صَلَّى رَسُولُ اللهِ ﷺ حَتَّى انْتَفَخَتْ قَدَمَاهُ ❁ فَقِيلَ لَهُ أَتَتَكَلَّفُ هٰذَا وَقَدْ غَفَرَ اللهُ لَكَ مَا تَقَدَّمَ مِنْ ذَنْبِكَ وَمَا تَأَخَّرَ ❁ قَالَ أَفَلَا أَكُونُ عَبْدًا شَكُورًا ●

261. Qutayba ibn Sa'id and Bishr ibn Mu'adh narrated to us, 'Abu 'Awana narrated to us on the authority of Ziyad ibn 'Ilaqa, on the authority of Mughira ibn Shu'ba رضي الله عنه, who reported:

"The Messenger of Allah ﷺ prayed so long that his blessed feet swelled. He was asked, 'You take it upon yourself to do this even though Allah has forgiven, by means of you, the sins of those who came before and the sins of those who are to come!'[629] He replied, 'Shall I not, then, be a grateful servant?'"[630]

❦

٢٦٢ - حَدَّثَنَا أَبُو عَمَّارٍ الْحُسَيْنُ بْنُ حُرَيْثٍ ❁ أَخْبَرَنَا الْفَضْلُ بْنُ مُوسَىٰ ❁ عَنْ مُحَمَّدِ بْنِ عَمْرٍو ❁ عَنْ أَبِي سَلَمَةَ ❁ عَنْ أَبِي هُرَيْرَةَ رَضِيَ اللهُ عَنْهُ قَالَ كَانَ رَسُولُ اللهِ ﷺ يُصَلِّي حَتَّىٰ تَرِمَ قَدَمَاهُ ❁ قَالَ فَقِيلَ لَهُ أَتَفْعَلُ هٰذَا وَقَدْ جَاءَكَ أَنَّ اللهَ تَعَالَىٰ قَدْ غَفَرَ لَكَ مَا تَقَدَّمَ مِنْ ذَنْبِكَ وَمَا تَأَخَّرَ ❁ قَالَ أَفَلَا أَكُونُ عَبْدًا شَكُورًا ●

[627] Imam al-Bajuri says, 'He [Imam al-Tirmidhi] placed the chapter on worship after the chapter on sleep because the Prophet's sleep ﷺ was one of the noblest forms of worship and most perfect acts of obedience…' This also teaches us that we should rise from sleep, which is one of the most comfortable of states, for the sake of the remembrance of Allah. Imam al-Tirmidhi also intentionally made this the fortieth chapter. It was at the age of forty that the Messenger of Allah ﷺ received revelation and invited people to the worship of Allah. This chapter indicates the efforts that Messenger of Allah ﷺ exerted in the worship of Allah, through night vigil (*tahajjud*) and extra voluntary actions during the day. It also notes the seriousness of his devotions. There is no doubt that he was the greatest of creation in worship, obedience, and gratitude. The objective of all worship is to praise Allah through one's speech and actions, and to venerate and magnify Him through brokenness and humbleness. The praise and humility of every individual is based upon his knowledge of Allah; no creation knew Allah better than the Prophet ﷺ. He therefore fulfilled all of Allah's rights upon him, which no other can do. Though this chapter speaks about the Prophet's ﷺ extra voluntary prayers during day and night, all of his states, actions, movements and stillness were also of the highest forms of worship, as he did not do anything except seek the pleasure of his Lord. (MA)

❦

[628] The verb in Arabic that translates as 'You take it upon yourself' is *tatakallafu*, and comes from the word *takalluf*, which denotes 'burden', 'responsibility', 'being charged with duty' etc. In reality, the Prophet ﷺ never had to 'force himself' to worship Allah. Every state of his ﷺ—when awake, when

asleep, when moving, when still, when speaking, or when silent—was an act of worship in one way or another, and none of his devotions had to be 'forced'. The Prophet's exertion in worship was an expression of his perfect servitude (*'ubudiyya*) and love of Allah. Allah Most Exalted says, *Allah does not task a soul more than it can bear.* (Qur'an 2:286) And He says, *Allah does not task a soul more than He has given it.* (Qur'an 65:7) So one must ask: what is the capacity of the Prophet's ﷺ blessed soul? What does his blessed soul bear? What has Allah given it? Allah tasked him with the divine message, caused him to bear the divine speech (Qur'an) in his blessed heart and gave him intimate knowledge of Him. It follows, therefore, that his supreme capacity would manifest in various exertions that bewildered his Companions ﷺ. The questioner was amazed by the worship of the Messenger of Allah ﷺ and was absolutely taken back by his struggle and striving despite the fact that he was infallible and free of sin. The Prophet ﷺ replied by informing him that his worship has nothing to do with sins and forgiveness, but rather with fulfilling the rights of Allah upon him by remembering, honouring, worshipping, venerating, and thanking Him. This hadith demonstrates the perfection of the Prophet's motivation ﷺ, and is an encouragement to others to strive in worship, for he did so whilst knowing his station with his Lord. If this is the devotion of the best of creation who is sinless, it follows that we who are sinful should exert more efforts—even though it is not possible to even approach the level of the Prophet's ﷺ devotions in any way, shape or form. Imam al-Bukhari recorded a hadith from Anas ibn Malik ﷺ, who reported that a group of three companions came to one of the houses of the Prophet's wives and inquired about his worship.

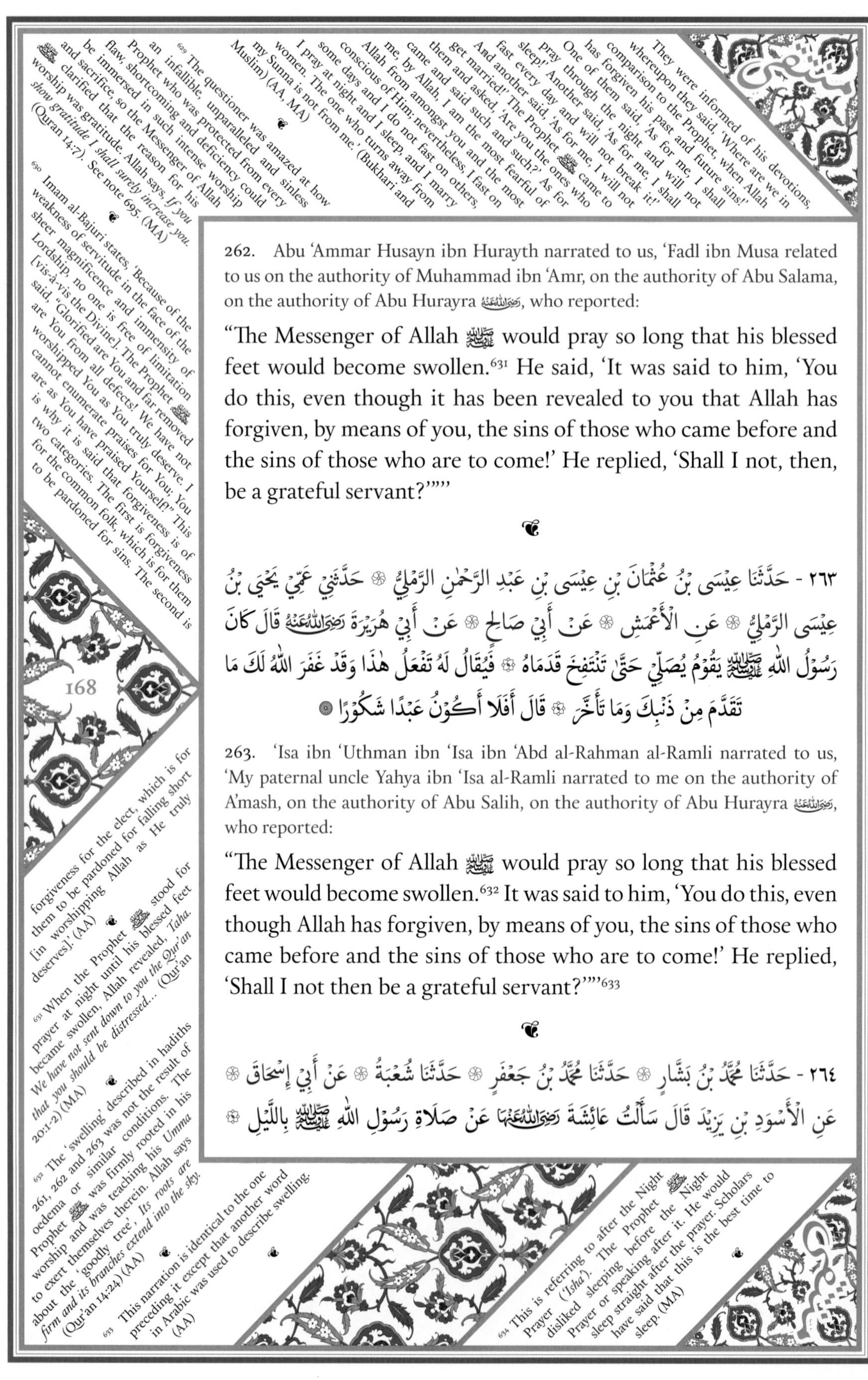

262. Abu 'Ammar Husayn ibn Hurayth narrated to us, 'Fadl ibn Musa related to us on the authority of Muhammad ibn 'Amr, on the authority of Abu Salama, on the authority of Abu Hurayra ﵁, who reported:

"The Messenger of Allah ﷺ would pray so long that his blessed feet would become swollen.[631] He said, 'It was said to him, 'You do this, even though it has been revealed to you that Allah has forgiven, by means of you, the sins of those who came before and the sins of those who are to come!' He replied, 'Shall I not, then, be a grateful servant?''''

٢٦٣ - حَدَّثَنَا عِيسَى بْنُ عُثْمَانَ بْنِ عِيسَى بْنِ عَبْدِ الرَّحْمٰنِ الرَّمْلِيُّ ❁ حَدَّثَنِي عَمِّي يَحْيَى بْنُ عِيسَى الرَّمْلِيُّ ❁ عَنِ الْأَعْمَشِ ❁ عَنْ أَبِي صَالِحٍ ❁ عَنْ أَبِي هُرَيْرَةَ ﵁ قَالَ كَانَ رَسُولُ اللهِ ﷺ يَقُومُ يُصَلِّي حَتَّىٰ تَنْتَفِخَ قَدَمَاهُ ❁ فَيُقَالُ لَهُ تَفْعَلُ هٰذَا وَقَدْ غَفَرَ اللهُ لَكَ مَا تَقَدَّمَ مِنْ ذَنْبِكَ وَمَا تَأَخَّرَ ❁ قَالَ أَفَلَا أَكُونُ عَبْدًا شَكُورًا ❁

263. 'Isa ibn 'Uthman ibn 'Isa ibn 'Abd al-Rahman al-Ramli narrated to us, 'My paternal uncle Yahya ibn 'Isa al-Ramli narrated to me on the authority of A'mash, on the authority of Abu Salih, on the authority of Abu Hurayra ﵁, who reported:

"The Messenger of Allah ﷺ would pray so long that his blessed feet would become swollen.[632] It was said to him, 'You do this, even though Allah has forgiven, by means of you, the sins of those who came before and the sins of those who are to come!' He replied, 'Shall I not then be a grateful servant?''''[633]

٢٦٤ - حَدَّثَنَا مُحَمَّدُ بْنُ بَشَّارٍ ❁ حَدَّثَنَا مُحَمَّدُ بْنُ جَعْفَرٍ ❁ حَدَّثَنَا شُعْبَةُ ❁ عَنْ أَبِي إِسْحَاقَ ❁ عَنِ الْأَسْوَدِ بْنِ يَزِيدَ قَالَ سَأَلْتُ عَائِشَةَ ﵂ عَنْ صَلَاةِ رَسُولِ اللهِ ﷺ بِاللَّيْلِ ❁

They were informed of his devotions, whereupon they said, 'Where are we in comparison to the Prophet, when Allah has forgiven his past and future sins!' One of them said, 'As for me, I shall pray through the night and will not sleep!' Another said, 'As for me, I shall fast every day and will not break it!' And another said, 'As for me, I will not get married!' The Prophet ﷺ came to them and asked, 'Are you the ones who came and said such and such?' As for me, by Allah, I am the most fearful of Allah from amongst you and the most conscious of Him; nevertheless, I fast on some days and I do not fast on others, I pray at night and I sleep, and I marry women. The one who turns away from my Sunna is not from me.' (Bukhari and Muslim) (AA, MA)

629 The questioner was amazed at how an infallible, unparalleled and sinless Prophet who was protected from every flaw, shortcoming and deficiency could be immersed in such intense worship and sacrifice, so the Messenger of Allah ﷺ clarified that the reason for his worship was gratitude. Allah says, *If you show gratitude I shall surely increase you.* (Quran 14:7). See note 695. (MA)

630 Imam al-Bajuri states, 'Because of the weakness of servitude in the face of the sheer magnificence and immensity of Lordship, no one is free of limitation [vis-à-vis the Divine]. The Prophet ﷺ said, "Glorified are You and far removed are You from all defects! We have not worshipped You as You truly deserve. I cannot enumerate praises for You; You are as You have praised Yourself!" This is why it is said that forgiveness is of two categories. The first is forgiveness for the common folk, which is for them to be pardoned for sins. The second is forgiveness for the elect, which is for them to be pardoned for falling short [in worshipping Allah as He truly deserves].' (AA)

631 When the Prophet ﷺ stood for prayer at night until his blessed feet became swollen, Allah revealed, *Taha. We have not sent down to you the Qur'an that you should be distressed...* (Qur'an 20:1-2) (MA)

632 The 'swelling' described in hadiths 261, 262 and 263 was not the result of oedema or similar conditions. The Prophet ﷺ was firmly rooted in his worship and was teaching his Umma to exert themselves therein. Allah says about the 'goodly tree', *Its roots are firm and its branches extend into the sky.* (Qur'an 14:24) (AA)

633 This narration is identical to the one preceding it except that another word in Arabic was used to describe swelling. (AA)

634 This is referring to after the Night Prayer ('*Isha*'). The Prophet ﷺ disliked sleeping before the Night Prayer or speaking after it. He would sleep straight after the prayer. Scholars have said that this is the best time to sleep. (MA)

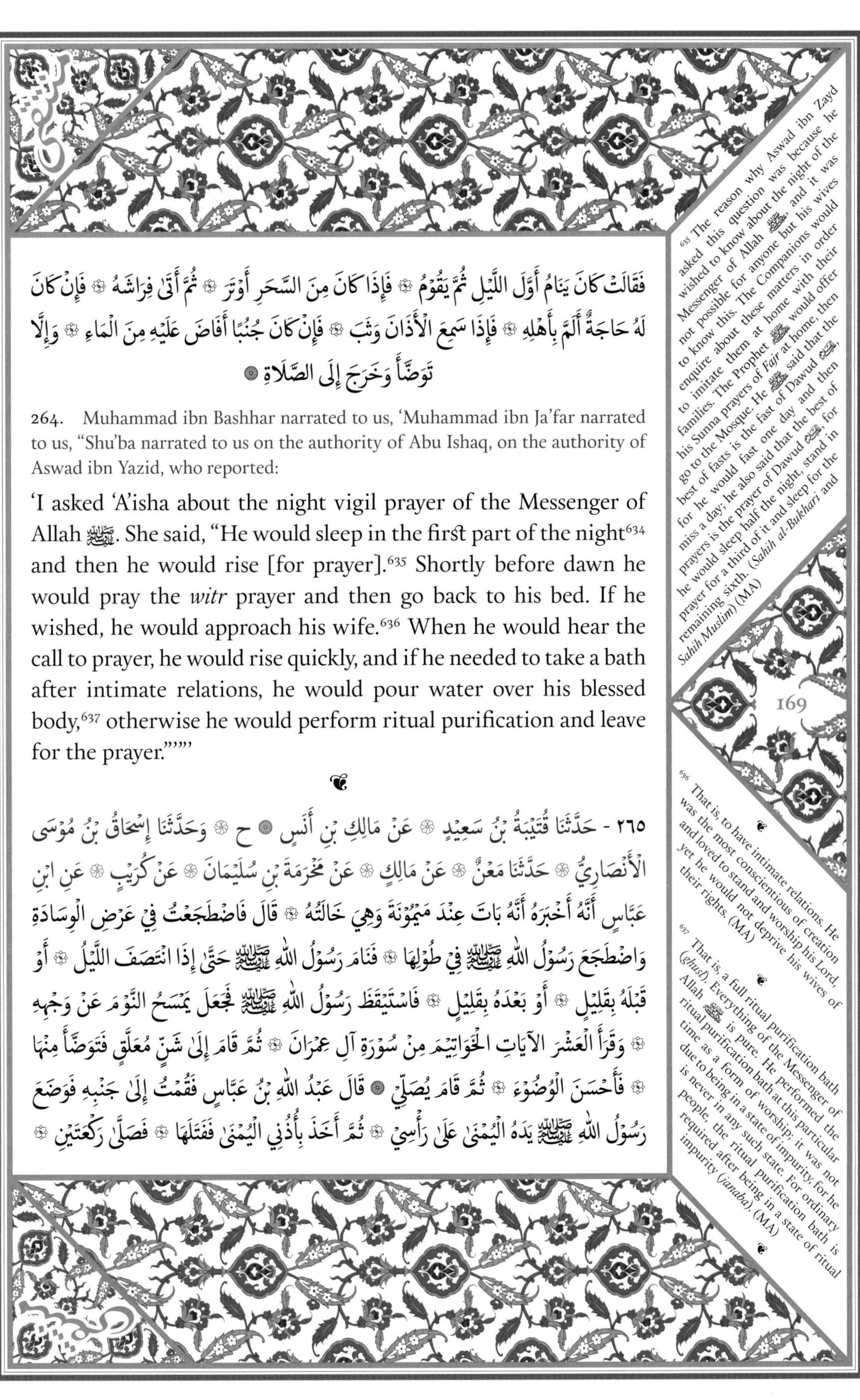

فَقَالَتْ كَانَ يَنَامُ أَوَّلَ اللَّيْلِ ثُمَّ يَقُومُ ۞ فَإِذَا كَانَ مِنَ السَّحَرِ أَوْتَرَ ۞ ثُمَّ أَتَى فِرَاشَهُ ۞ فَإِنْ كَانَ لَهُ حَاجَةٌ أَلَمَّ بِأَهْلِهِ ۞ فَإِذَا سَمِعَ الْأَذَانَ وَثَبَ ۞ فَإِنْ كَانَ جُنُبًا أَفَاضَ عَلَيْهِ مِنَ الْمَاءِ ۞ وَإِلَّا تَوَضَّأَ وَخَرَجَ إِلَى الصَّلَاةِ ۞

264. Muhammad ibn Bashhar narrated to us, 'Muhammad ibn Ja'far narrated to us, "Shu'ba narrated to us on the authority of Abu Ishaq, on the authority of Aswad ibn Yazid, who reported:

'I asked 'A'isha about the night vigil prayer of the Messenger of Allah ﷺ. She said, "He would sleep in the first part of the night[634] and then he would rise [for prayer].[635] Shortly before dawn he would pray the *witr* prayer and then go back to his bed. If he wished, he would approach his wife.[636] When he would hear the call to prayer, he would rise quickly, and if he needed to take a bath after intimate relations, he would pour water over his blessed body,[637] otherwise he would perform ritual purification and leave for the prayer."""'

٢٦٥ - حَدَّثَنَا قُتَيْبَةُ بْنُ سَعِيدٍ ۞ عَنْ مَالِكِ بْنِ أَنَسٍ ۞ ح ۞ وَحَدَّثَنَا إِسْحَاقُ بْنُ مُوسَى الْأَنْصَارِيُّ ۞ حَدَّثَنَا مَعْنٌ ۞ عَنْ مَالِكٍ ۞ عَنْ مَخْرَمَةَ بْنِ سُلَيْمَانَ ۞ عَنْ كُرَيْبٍ ۞ عَنِ ابْنِ عَبَّاسٍ أَنَّهُ أَخْبَرَهُ أَنَّهُ بَاتَ عِنْدَ مَيْمُونَةَ وَهِيَ خَالَتُهُ ۞ قَالَ فَاضْطَجَعْتُ فِي عَرْضِ الْوِسَادَةِ وَاضْطَجَعَ رَسُولُ اللهِ ﷺ فِي طُولِهَا ۞ فَنَامَ رَسُولُ اللهِ ﷺ حَتَّى إِذَا انْتَصَفَ اللَّيْلُ ۞ أَوْ قَبْلَهُ بِقَلِيلٍ ۞ أَوْ بَعْدَهُ بِقَلِيلٍ ۞ فَاسْتَيْقَظَ رَسُولُ اللهِ ﷺ فَجَعَلَ يَمْسَحُ النَّوْمَ عَنْ وَجْهِهِ ۞ وَقَرَأَ الْعَشْرَ الْآيَاتِ الْخَوَاتِيمَ مِنْ سُورَةِ آلِ عِمْرَانَ ۞ ثُمَّ قَامَ إِلَى شَنٍّ مُعَلَّقٍ فَتَوَضَّأَ مِنْهَا ۞ فَأَحْسَنَ الْوُضُوءَ ۞ ثُمَّ قَامَ يُصَلِّي ۞ قَالَ عَبْدُ اللهِ بْنُ عَبَّاسٍ فَقُمْتُ إِلَى جَنْبِهِ فَوَضَعَ رَسُولُ اللهِ ﷺ يَدَهُ الْيُمْنَى عَلَى رَأْسِي ۞ ثُمَّ أَخَذَ بِأُذُنِي الْيُمْنَى فَفَتَلَهَا ۞ فَصَلَّى رَكْعَتَيْنِ ۞

[635] The reason why Aswad ibn Zayd asked this question was because he wished to know about the night of the Messenger of Allah ﷺ, and it was not possible for anyone but his wives to know this. The Companions would enquire about these matters in order to imitate them at home with their families. The Prophet ﷺ would offer his Sunna prayers of *Fajr* at home, then go to the Mosque. He ﷺ said that the best of fasts is the fast of Dawud ﷺ, for he would fast one day and then miss a day; he also said that the best of prayers is the prayer of Dawud ﷺ, for he would sleep half the night, stand in prayer for a third of it and sleep for the remaining sixth. (*Sahih al-Bukhari* and *Sahih Muslim*) (MA)

[636] That is, to have intimate relations. He was the most conscientious of creation and loved to stand and worship his Lord, yet he would not deprive his wives of their rights. (MA)

[637] That is, a full ritual purification bath (*ghusl*). Everything of the Messenger of Allah ﷺ is pure. He performed the ritual purification bath at this particular time as a form of worship; it was not due to being in a state of impurity, for he is never in any such state. For ordinary people, the ritual purification bath is required after being in a state of ritual impurity (*janaba*). (MA)

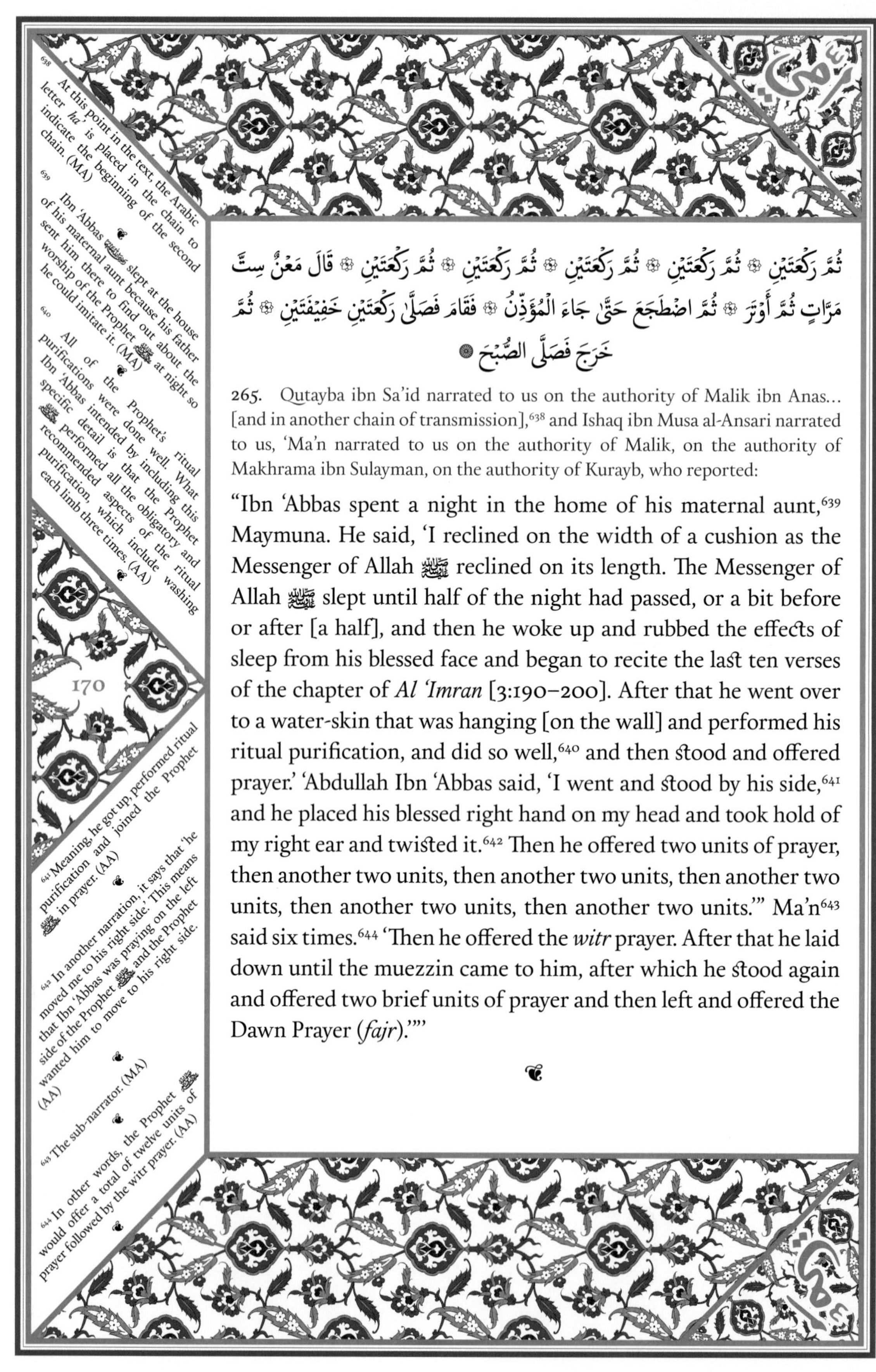

ثُمَّ رَكْعَتَيْنِ ۞ ثُمَّ رَكْعَتَيْنِ ۞ ثُمَّ رَكْعَتَيْنِ ۞ ثُمَّ رَكْعَتَيْنِ ۞ ثُمَّ رَكْعَتَيْنِ ۞ قَالَ مَعْنٌ سِتَّ
مَرَّاتٍ ثُمَّ أَوْتَرَ ۞ ثُمَّ اضْطَجَعَ حَتَّىٰ جَاءَ الْمُؤَذِّنُ ۞ فَقَامَ فَصَلَّىٰ رَكْعَتَيْنِ خَفِيفَتَيْنِ ۞ ثُمَّ
خَرَجَ فَصَلَّى الصُّبْحَ ۞

265. Qutayba ibn Sa'id narrated to us on the authority of Malik ibn Anas... [and in another chain of transmission],[638] and Ishaq ibn Musa al-Ansari narrated to us, 'Ma'n narrated to us on the authority of Malik, on the authority of Makhrama ibn Sulayman, on the authority of Kurayb, who reported:

"Ibn 'Abbas spent a night in the home of his maternal aunt,[639] Maymuna. He said, 'I reclined on the width of a cushion as the Messenger of Allah ﷺ reclined on its length. The Messenger of Allah ﷺ slept until half of the night had passed, or a bit before or after [a half], and then he woke up and rubbed the effects of sleep from his blessed face and began to recite the last ten verses of the chapter of *Al 'Imran* [3:190–200]. After that he went over to a water-skin that was hanging [on the wall] and performed his ritual purification, and did so well,[640] and then stood and offered prayer.' 'Abdullah Ibn 'Abbas said, 'I went and stood by his side,[641] and he placed his blessed right hand on my head and took hold of my right ear and twisted it.[642] Then he offered two units of prayer, then another two units, then another two units, then another two units, then another two units, then another two units.'" Ma'n[643] said six times.[644] 'Then he offered the *witr* prayer. After that he laid down until the muezzin came to him, after which he stood again and offered two brief units of prayer and then left and offered the Dawn Prayer (*fajr*).'"

638 At this point in the text, the Arabic letter *ha'* is placed in the chain to indicate the beginning of the second chain. (MA)

639 Ibn 'Abbas ﷺ slept at the house of his maternal aunt because his father sent him there to find out about the worship of the Prophet ﷺ at night so he could imitate it. (MA)

640 All of the Prophet's ritual purifications were done well. What Ibn 'Abbas intended by including this specific detail is that the Prophet ﷺ performed all the obligatory and recommended aspects of the ritual purification, which include washing each limb three times. (AA)

641 Meaning, he got up, performed ritual purification and joined the Prophet ﷺ in prayer. (AA)

642 In another narration, it says that 'he moved me to his right side.' This means that Ibn 'Abbas was praying on the left side of the Prophet ﷺ and the Prophet wanted him to move to his right side. (AA)

643 The sub-narrator. (MA)

644 In other words, the Prophet ﷺ would offer a total of twelve units of prayer followed by the witr prayer. (AA)

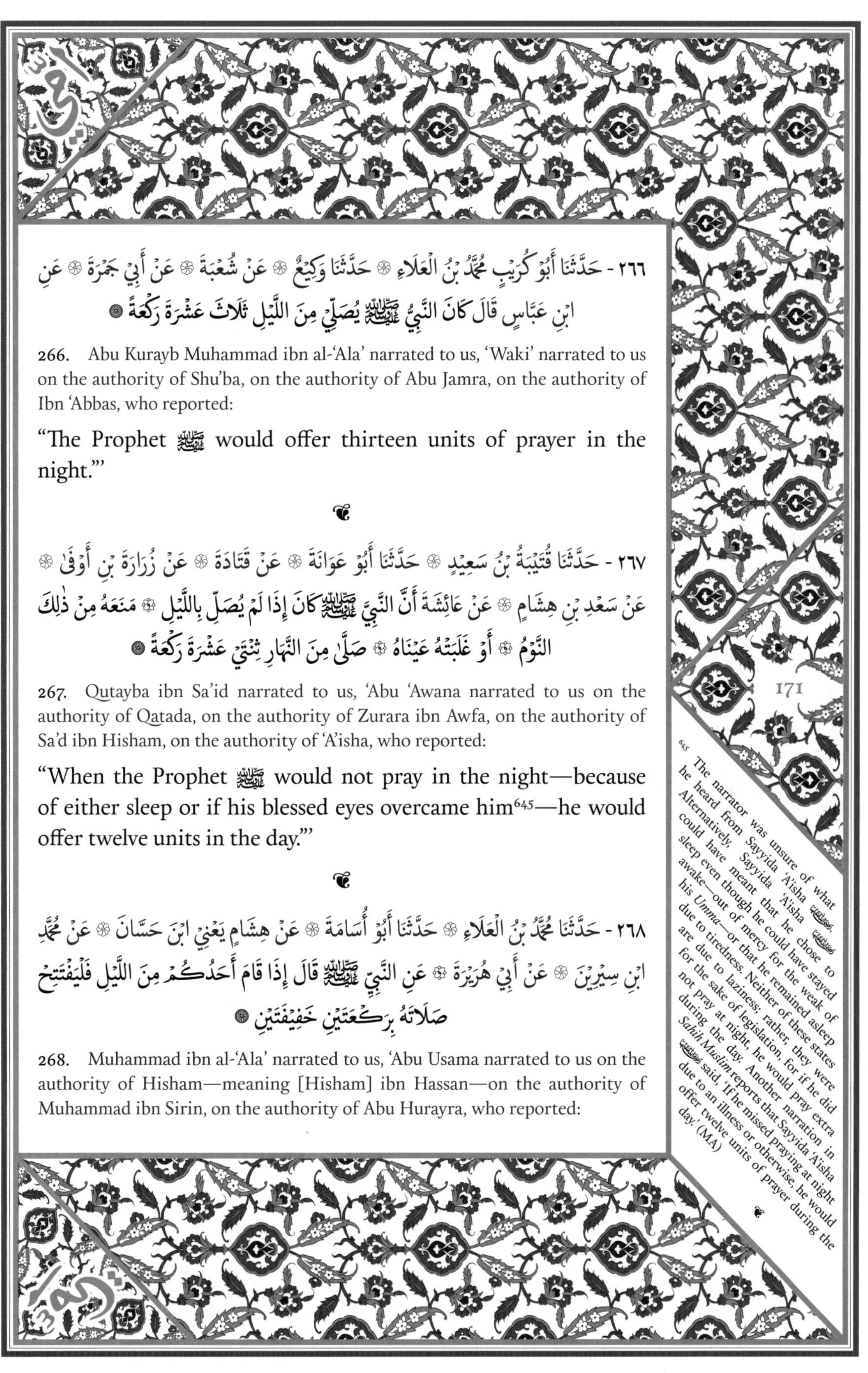

٢٦٦ - حَدَّثَنَا أَبُو كُرَيْبٍ مُحَمَّدُ بْنُ الْعَلَاءِ ❁ حَدَّثَنَا وَكِيعٌ ❁ عَنْ شُعْبَةَ ❁ عَنْ أَبِي جَمْرَةَ ❁ عَنِ ابْنِ عَبَّاسٍ قَالَ كَانَ النَّبِيُّ ﷺ يُصَلِّي مِنَ اللَّيْلِ ثَلَاثَ عَشْرَةَ رَكْعَةً ❁

266. Abu Kurayb Muhammad ibn al-'Ala' narrated to us, 'Waki' narrated to us on the authority of Shu'ba, on the authority of Abu Jamra, on the authority of Ibn 'Abbas, who reported:

"The Prophet ﷺ would offer thirteen units of prayer in the night."'

❦

٢٦٧ - حَدَّثَنَا قُتَيْبَةُ بْنُ سَعِيدٍ ❁ حَدَّثَنَا أَبُو عَوَانَةَ ❁ عَنْ قَتَادَةَ ❁ عَنْ زُرَارَةَ بْنِ أَوْفَى ❁ عَنْ سَعْدِ بْنِ هِشَامٍ ❁ عَنْ عَائِشَةَ أَنَّ النَّبِيَّ ﷺ كَانَ إِذَا لَمْ يُصَلِّ بِاللَّيْلِ ❁ مَنَعَهُ مِنْ ذَٰلِكَ النَّوْمُ ❁ أَوْ غَلَبَتْهُ عَيْنَاهُ ❁ صَلَّى مِنَ النَّهَارِ ثِنْتَيْ عَشْرَةَ رَكْعَةً ❁

267. Qutayba ibn Sa'id narrated to us, 'Abu 'Awana narrated to us on the authority of Qatada, on the authority of Zurara ibn Awfa, on the authority of Sa'd ibn Hisham, on the authority of 'A'isha, who reported:

"When the Prophet ﷺ would not pray in the night—because of either sleep or if his blessed eyes overcame him[645]—he would offer twelve units in the day."'

❦

٢٦٨ - حَدَّثَنَا مُحَمَّدُ بْنُ الْعَلَاءِ ❁ حَدَّثَنَا أَبُو أُسَامَةَ ❁ عَنْ هِشَامٍ يَعْنِي ابْنَ حَسَّانَ ❁ عَنْ مُحَمَّدِ ابْنِ سِيرِينَ ❁ عَنْ أَبِي هُرَيْرَةَ ❁ عَنِ النَّبِيِّ ﷺ قَالَ إِذَا قَامَ أَحَدُكُمْ مِنَ اللَّيْلِ فَلْيَفْتَتِحْ صَلَاتَهُ بِرَكْعَتَيْنِ خَفِيفَتَيْنِ ❁

268. Muhammad ibn al-'Ala' narrated to us, 'Abu Usama narrated to us on the authority of Hisham—meaning [Hisham] ibn Hassan—on the authority of Muhammad ibn Sirin, on the authority of Abu Hurayra, who reported:

645 The narrator was unsure of what he heard from Sayyida 'A'isha ﷺ. Alternatively, Sayyida 'A'isha ﷺ could have meant that he chose to sleep even though he could have stayed awake—out of mercy for the weak of his *Umma*—or that he remained asleep due to tiredness. Neither of these states are due to laziness; rather, they were for the sake of legislation, for if he did not pray at night, he would pray extra during the day. Another narration in *Sahih Muslim* reports that Sayyida 'A'isha ﷺ said, 'If he missed praying at night due to an illness or otherwise, he would offer twelve units of prayer during the day.' (MA)

❦

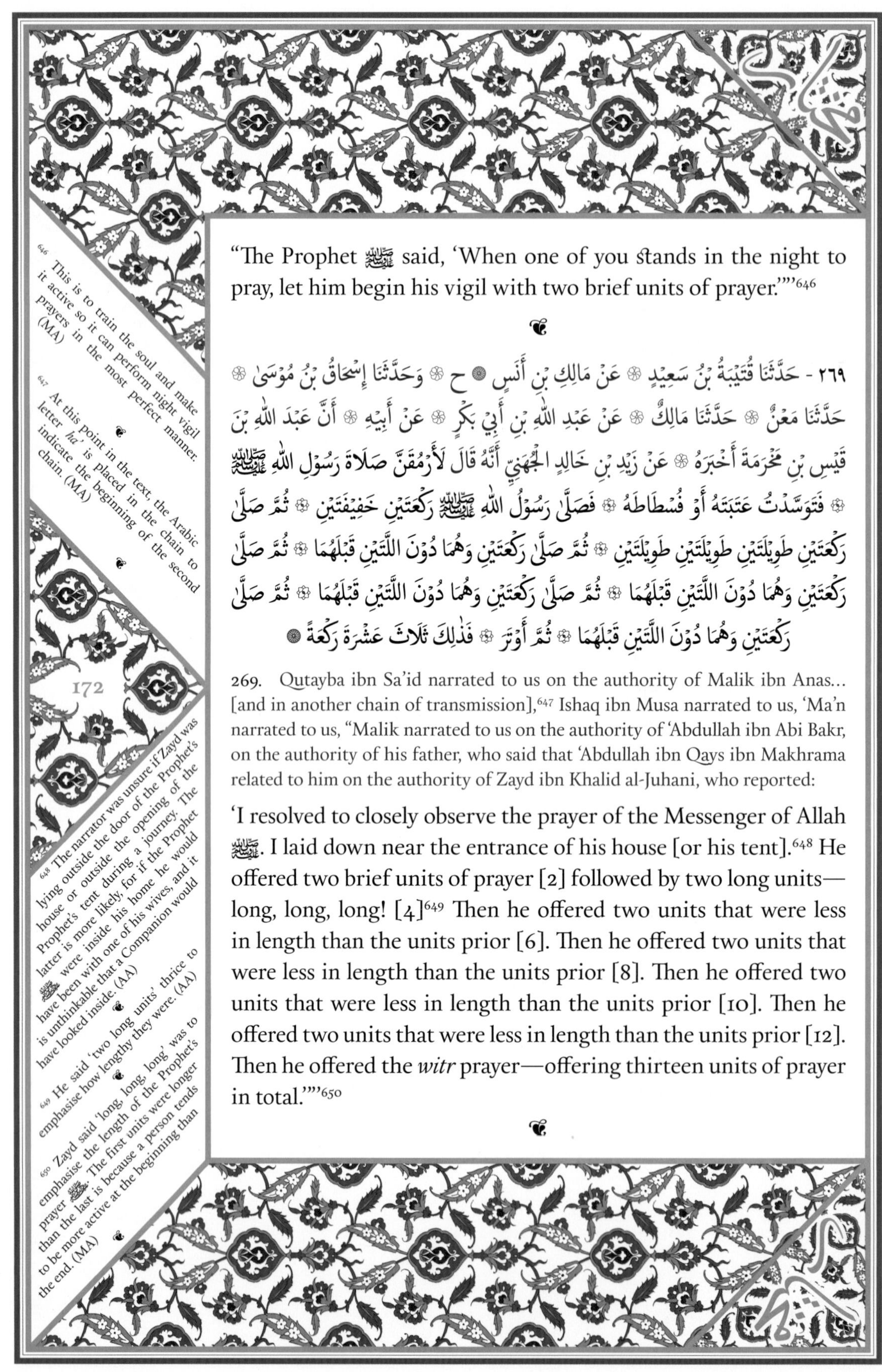

"The Prophet ﷺ said, 'When one of you stands in the night to pray, let him begin his vigil with two brief units of prayer.'"'[646]

٢٦٩ - حَدَّثَنَا قُتَيْبَةُ بْنُ سَعِيدٍ ۞ عَنْ مَالِكِ بْنِ أَنَسٍ ۞ ح ۞ وَحَدَّثَنَا إِسْحَاقُ بْنُ مُوسَىٰ ۞ حَدَّثَنَا مَعْنٌ ۞ حَدَّثَنَا مَالِكٌ ۞ عَنْ عَبْدِ اللهِ بْنِ أَبِي بَكْرٍ ۞ عَنْ أَبِيهِ ۞ أَنَّ عَبْدَ اللهِ بْنَ قَيْسِ بْنِ مَخْرَمَةَ أَخْبَرَهُ ۞ عَنْ زَيْدِ بْنِ خَالِدٍ الْجُهَنِيِّ أَنَّهُ قَالَ لَأَرْمُقَنَّ صَلَاةَ رَسُولِ اللهِ ﷺ ۞ فَتَوَسَّدْتُ عَتَبَتَهُ أَوْ فُسْطَاطَهُ ۞ فَصَلَّىٰ رَسُولُ اللهِ ﷺ رَكْعَتَيْنِ خَفِيفَتَيْنِ ۞ ثُمَّ صَلَّىٰ رَكْعَتَيْنِ طَوِيلَتَيْنِ طَوِيلَتَيْنِ طَوِيلَتَيْنِ ۞ ثُمَّ صَلَّىٰ رَكْعَتَيْنِ وَهُمَا دُونَ اللَّتَيْنِ قَبْلَهُمَا ۞ ثُمَّ صَلَّىٰ رَكْعَتَيْنِ وَهُمَا دُونَ اللَّتَيْنِ قَبْلَهُمَا ۞ ثُمَّ صَلَّىٰ رَكْعَتَيْنِ وَهُمَا دُونَ اللَّتَيْنِ قَبْلَهُمَا ۞ ثُمَّ صَلَّىٰ رَكْعَتَيْنِ وَهُمَا دُونَ اللَّتَيْنِ قَبْلَهُمَا ۞ ثُمَّ أَوْتَرَ ۞ فَذَٰلِكَ ثَلَاثَ عَشْرَةَ رَكْعَةً ۞

269. Qutayba ibn Sa'id narrated to us on the authority of Malik ibn Anas... [and in another chain of transmission],[647] Ishaq ibn Musa narrated to us, 'Ma'n narrated to us, "Malik narrated to us on the authority of 'Abdullah ibn Abi Bakr, on the authority of his father, who said that 'Abdullah ibn Qays ibn Makhrama related to him on the authority of Zayd ibn Khalid al-Juhani, who reported:

'I resolved to closely observe the prayer of the Messenger of Allah ﷺ. I laid down near the entrance of his house [or his tent].[648] He offered two brief units of prayer [2] followed by two long units—long, long, long! [4][649] Then he offered two units that were less in length than the units prior [6]. Then he offered two units that were less in length than the units prior [8]. Then he offered two units that were less in length than the units prior [10]. Then he offered two units that were less in length than the units prior [12]. Then he offered the *witr* prayer—offering thirteen units of prayer in total.'"'[650]

646 This is to train the soul and make it active so it can perform night vigil prayers in the most perfect manner. (MA)

647 At this point in the text, the Arabic letter *ha'* is placed in the chain to indicate the beginning of the second chain. (MA)

648 The narrator was unsure if Zayd was lying outside the door of the Prophet's house or outside the opening of the Prophet's tent during a journey. The latter is more likely, for if the Prophet ﷺ were inside his home he would have been with one of his wives, and it is unthinkable that a Companion would have looked inside. (AA)

649 He said 'two long units' thrice to emphasise how lengthy they were. (AA)

650 Zayd said 'long, long, long' was to emphasise the length of the Prophet's prayer ﷺ. The first units were longer than the last is because a person tends to be more active at the beginning than the end. (MA)

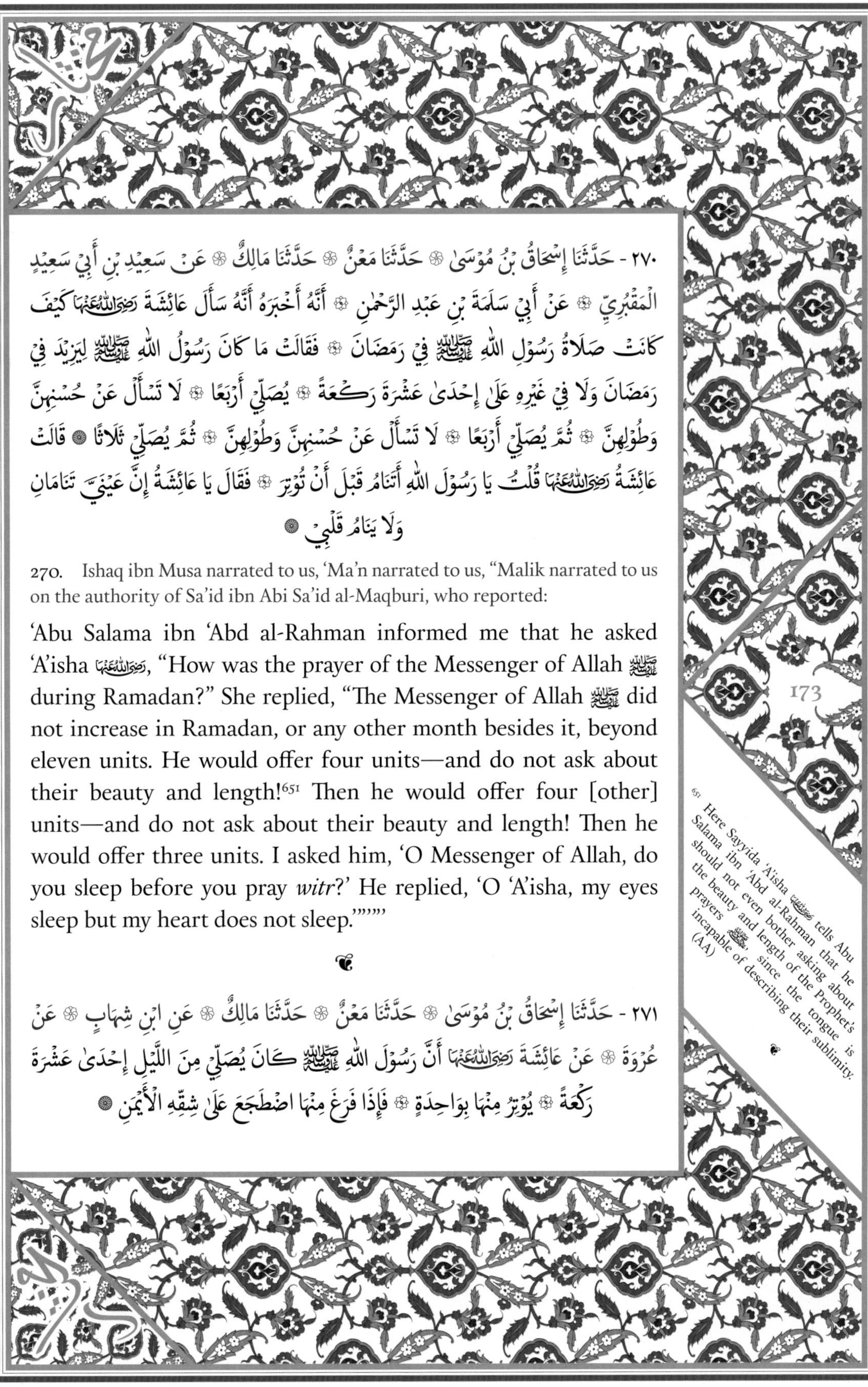

٢٧٠ - حَدَّثَنَا إِسْحَاقُ بْنُ مُوسَىٰ ۞ حَدَّثَنَا مَعْنٌ ۞ حَدَّثَنَا مَالِكٌ ۞ عَنْ سَعِيدِ بْنِ أَبِي سَعِيدٍ الْمَقْبُرِيِّ ۞ عَنْ أَبِي سَلَمَةَ بْنِ عَبْدِ الرَّحْمَٰنِ ۞ أَنَّهُ أَخْبَرَهُ أَنَّهُ سَأَلَ عَائِشَةَ رَضِيَ اللَّهُ عَنْهَا كَيْفَ كَانَتْ صَلَاةُ رَسُولِ اللَّهِ ﷺ فِي رَمَضَانَ ۞ فَقَالَتْ مَا كَانَ رَسُولُ اللَّهِ ﷺ لِيَزِيدَ فِي رَمَضَانَ وَلَا فِي غَيْرِهِ عَلَىٰ إِحْدَىٰ عَشْرَةَ رَكْعَةً ۞ يُصَلِّي أَرْبَعًا ۞ لَا تَسْأَلْ عَنْ حُسْنِهِنَّ وَطُولِهِنَّ ۞ ثُمَّ يُصَلِّي أَرْبَعًا ۞ لَا تَسْأَلْ عَنْ حُسْنِهِنَّ وَطُولِهِنَّ ۞ ثُمَّ يُصَلِّي ثَلَاثًا ۞ قَالَتْ عَائِشَةُ رَضِيَ اللَّهُ عَنْهَا قُلْتُ يَا رَسُولَ اللَّهِ أَتَنَامُ قَبْلَ أَنْ تُوتِرَ ۞ فَقَالَ يَا عَائِشَةُ إِنَّ عَيْنَيَّ تَنَامَانِ وَلَا يَنَامُ قَلْبِي ۞

270. Ishaq ibn Musa narrated to us, 'Ma'n narrated to us, "Malik narrated to us on the authority of Sa'id ibn Abi Sa'id al-Maqburi, who reported:

'Abu Salama ibn 'Abd al-Rahman informed me that he asked 'A'isha رضي الله عنها, "How was the prayer of the Messenger of Allah ﷺ during Ramadan?" She replied, "The Messenger of Allah ﷺ did not increase in Ramadan, or any other month besides it, beyond eleven units. He would offer four units—and do not ask about their beauty and length![651] Then he would offer four [other] units—and do not ask about their beauty and length! Then he would offer three units. I asked him, 'O Messenger of Allah, do you sleep before you pray *witr*?' He replied, 'O 'A'isha, my eyes sleep but my heart does not sleep.'"'"'

❦

٢٧١ - حَدَّثَنَا إِسْحَاقُ بْنُ مُوسَىٰ ۞ حَدَّثَنَا مَعْنٌ ۞ حَدَّثَنَا مَالِكٌ ۞ عَنِ ابْنِ شِهَابٍ ۞ عَنْ عُرْوَةَ ۞ عَنْ عَائِشَةَ رَضِيَ اللَّهُ عَنْهَا أَنَّ رَسُولَ اللَّهِ ﷺ كَانَ يُصَلِّي مِنَ اللَّيْلِ إِحْدَىٰ عَشْرَةَ رَكْعَةً ۞ يُوتِرُ مِنْهَا بِوَاحِدَةٍ ۞ فَإِذَا فَرَغَ مِنْهَا اضْطَجَعَ عَلَىٰ شِقِّهِ الْأَيْمَنِ ۞

[651] Here Sayyida 'A'isha رضي الله عنها tells Abu Salama ibn 'Abd al-Rahman that he should not even bother asking about the beauty and length of the Prophet's prayers ﷺ, since the tongue is incapable of describing their sublimity. (AA)

❦

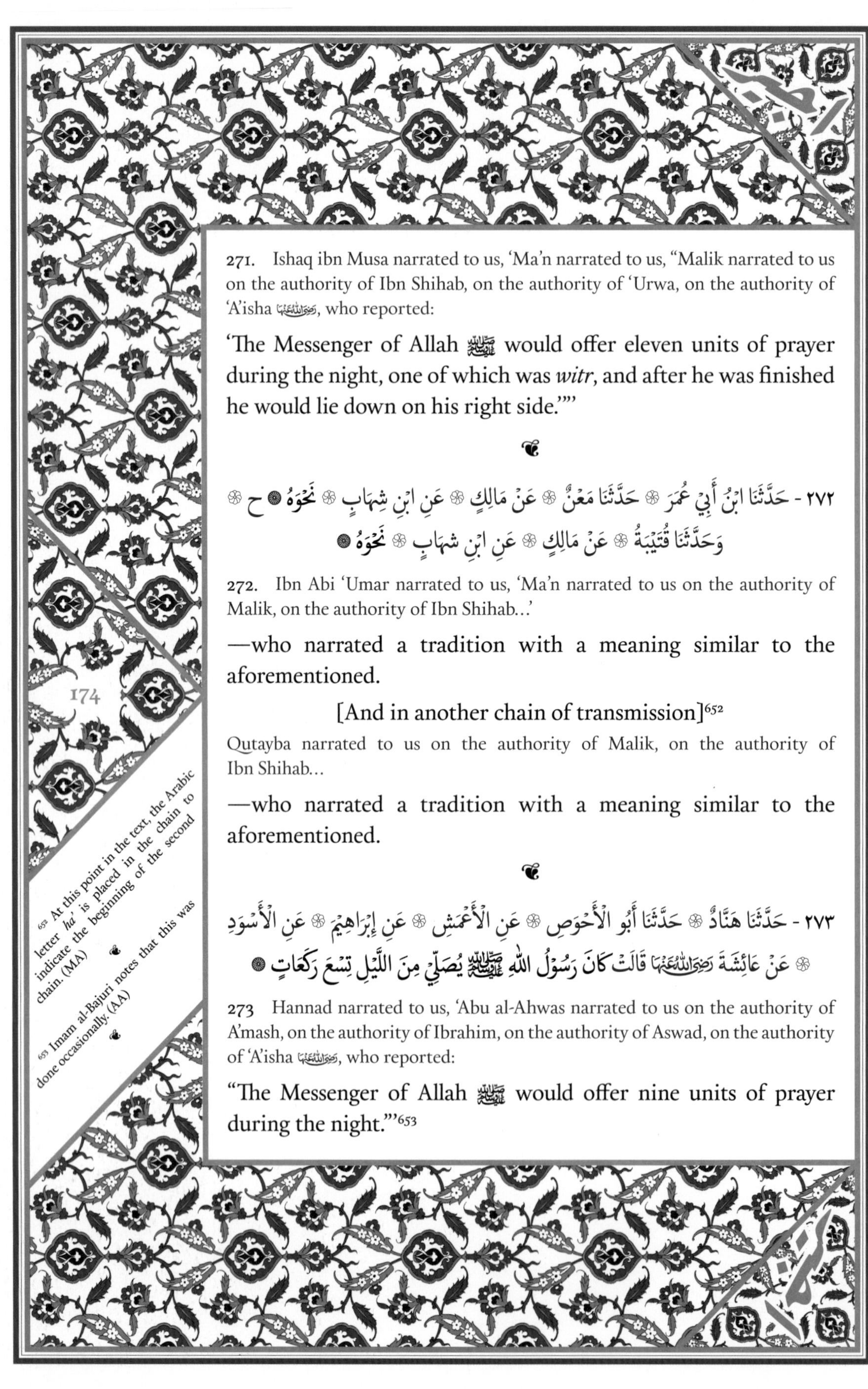

271. Ishaq ibn Musa narrated to us, 'Ma'n narrated to us, "Malik narrated to us on the authority of Ibn Shihab, on the authority of 'Urwa, on the authority of 'A'isha ﵂, who reported:

'The Messenger of Allah ﷺ would offer eleven units of prayer during the night, one of which was *witr*, and after he was finished he would lie down on his right side.'"'

❦

٢٧٢ - حَدَّثَنَا ابْنُ أَبِي عُمَرَ ۞ حَدَّثَنَا مَعْنٌ ۞ عَنْ مَالِكٍ ۞ عَنِ ابْنِ شِهَابٍ ۞ نَحْوَهُ ۞ ح ۞
وَحَدَّثَنَا قُتَيْبَةُ ۞ عَنْ مَالِكٍ ۞ عَنِ ابْنِ شهَابٍ ۞ نَحْوَهُ ۞

272. Ibn Abi 'Umar narrated to us, 'Ma'n narrated to us on the authority of Malik, on the authority of Ibn Shihab…'

—who narrated a tradition with a meaning similar to the aforementioned.

[And in another chain of transmission][652]

Qutayba narrated to us on the authority of Malik, on the authority of Ibn Shihab…

—who narrated a tradition with a meaning similar to the aforementioned.

❦

٢٧٣ - حَدَّثَنَا هَنَّادٌ ۞ حَدَّثَنَا أَبُو الْأَحْوَصِ ۞ عَنِ الْأَعْمَشِ ۞ عَنْ إِبْرَاهِيمَ ۞ عَنِ الْأَسْوَدِ
۞ عَنْ عَائِشَةَ رَضِيَ اللهُ عَنْهَا قَالَتْ كَانَ رَسُولُ اللهِ ﷺ يُصَلِّي مِنَ اللَّيْلِ تِسْعَ رَكَعَاتٍ ۞

273 Hannad narrated to us, 'Abu al-Ahwas narrated to us on the authority of A'mash, on the authority of Ibrahim, on the authority of Aswad, on the authority of 'A'isha ﵂, who reported:

"The Messenger of Allah ﷺ would offer nine units of prayer during the night."'[653]

[652] At this point in the text, the Arabic letter *ha'* is placed in the chain to indicate the beginning of the second chain. (MA)

[653] Imam al-Bajuri notes that this was done occasionally. (AA)

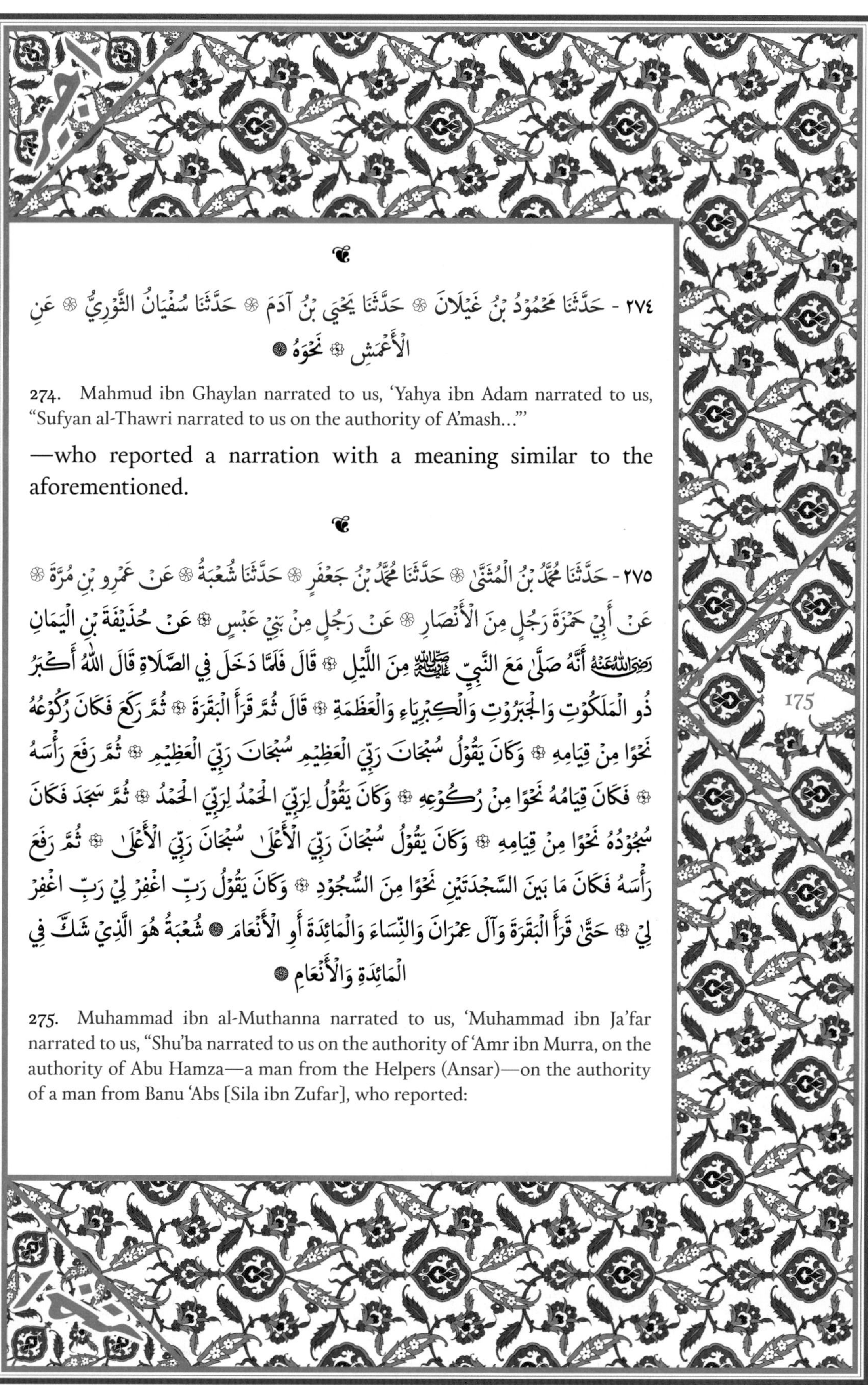

❦

٢٧٤ - حَدَّثَنَا مَحْمُودُ بْنُ غَيْلَانَ ۞ حَدَّثَنَا يَحْيَى بْنُ آدَمَ ۞ حَدَّثَنَا سُفْيَانُ الثَّوْرِيُّ ۞ عَنِ الْأَعْمَشِ ۞ نَحْوَهُ ۞

274. Mahmud ibn Ghaylan narrated to us, 'Yahya ibn Adam narrated to us, "Sufyan al-Thawri narrated to us on the authority of A'mash..."'

—who reported a narration with a meaning similar to the aforementioned.

❦

٢٧٥ - حَدَّثَنَا مُحَمَّدُ بْنُ الْمُثَنَّى ۞ حَدَّثَنَا مُحَمَّدُ بْنُ جَعْفَرٍ ۞ حَدَّثَنَا شُعْبَةُ ۞ عَنْ عَمْرِو بْنِ مُرَّةَ ۞ عَنْ أَبِي حَمْزَةَ رَجُلٍ مِنَ الْأَنْصَارِ ۞ عَنْ رَجُلٍ مِنْ بَنِي عَبْسٍ ۞ عَنْ حُذَيْفَةَ بْنِ الْيَمَانِ رَضِيَ اللَّهُ عَنْهُ أَنَّهُ صَلَّى مَعَ النَّبِيِّ ﷺ مِنَ اللَّيْلِ ۞ قَالَ فَلَمَّا دَخَلَ فِي الصَّلَاةِ قَالَ اللَّهُ أَكْبَرُ ذُو الْمَلَكُوتِ وَالْجَبَرُوتِ وَالْكِبْرِيَاءِ وَالْعَظَمَةِ ۞ قَالَ ثُمَّ قَرَأَ الْبَقَرَةَ ۞ ثُمَّ رَكَعَ فَكَانَ رُكُوعُهُ نَحْوًا مِنْ قِيَامِهِ ۞ وَكَانَ يَقُولُ سُبْحَانَ رَبِّيَ الْعَظِيمِ سُبْحَانَ رَبِّيَ الْعَظِيمِ ۞ ثُمَّ رَفَعَ رَأْسَهُ ۞ فَكَانَ قِيَامُهُ نَحْوًا مِنْ رُكُوعِهِ ۞ وَكَانَ يَقُولُ لِرَبِّيَ الْحَمْدُ لِرَبِّيَ الْحَمْدُ ۞ ثُمَّ سَجَدَ فَكَانَ سُجُودُهُ نَحْوًا مِنْ قِيَامِهِ ۞ وَكَانَ يَقُولُ سُبْحَانَ رَبِّيَ الْأَعْلَى سُبْحَانَ رَبِّيَ الْأَعْلَى ۞ ثُمَّ رَفَعَ رَأْسَهُ فَكَانَ مَا بَيْنَ السَّجْدَتَيْنِ نَحْوًا مِنَ السُّجُودِ ۞ وَكَانَ يَقُولُ رَبِّ اغْفِرْ لِي رَبِّ اغْفِرْ لِي ۞ حَتَّى قَرَأَ الْبَقَرَةَ وَآلَ عِمْرَانَ وَالنِّسَاءَ وَالْمَائِدَةَ أَوِ الْأَنْعَامَ ۞ شُعْبَةُ هُوَ الَّذِي شَكَّ فِي الْمَائِدَةِ وَالْأَنْعَامِ ۞

275. Muhammad ibn al-Muthanna narrated to us, 'Muhammad ibn Ja'far narrated to us, "Shu'ba narrated to us on the authority of 'Amr ibn Murra, on the authority of Abu Hamza—a man from the Helpers (Ansar)—on the authority of a man from Banu 'Abs [Sila ibn Zufar], who reported:

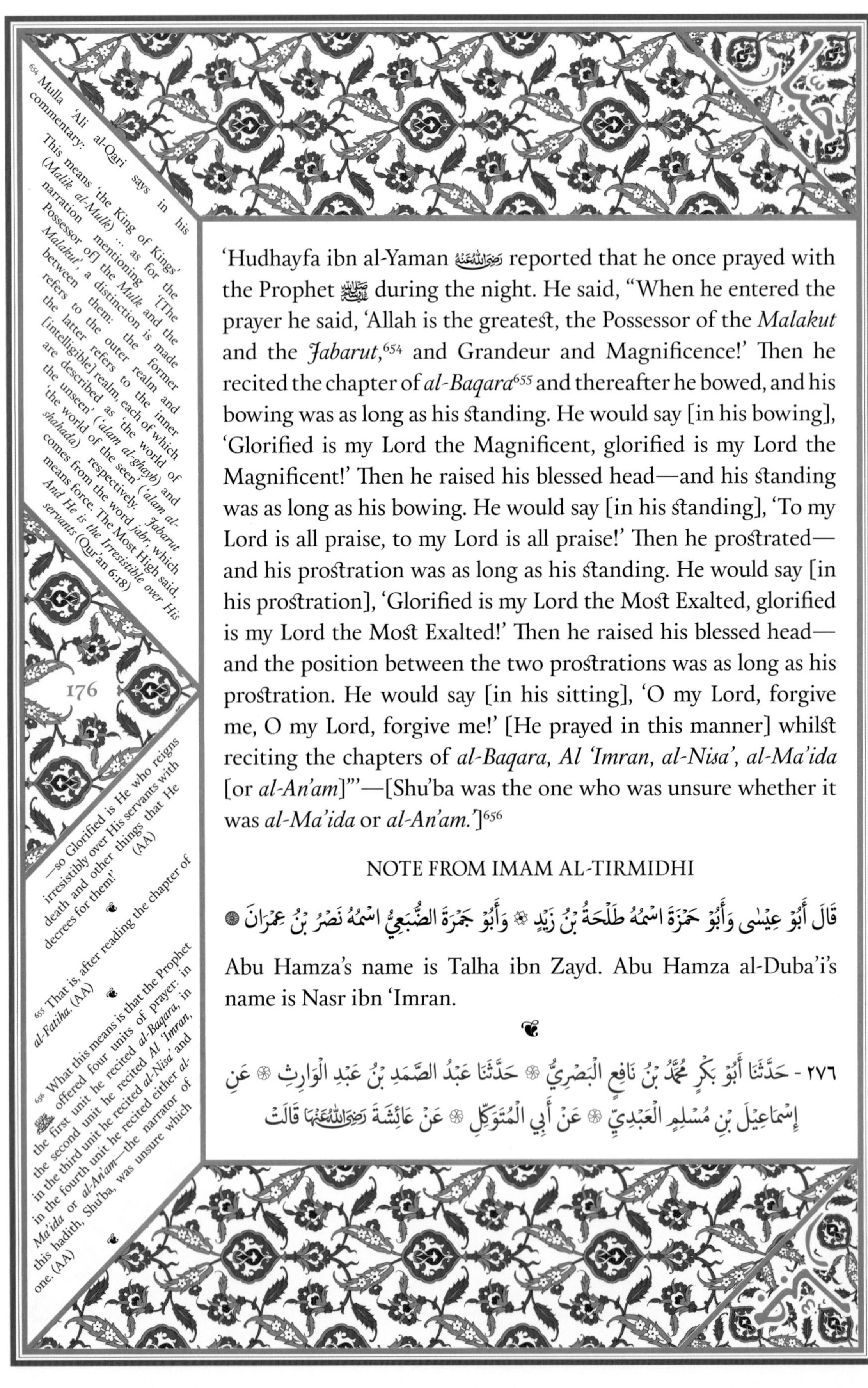

'Hudhayfa ibn al-Yaman ﵁ reported that he once prayed with the Prophet ﷺ during the night. He said, "When he entered the prayer he said, 'Allah is the greatest, the Possessor of the *Malakut* and the *Jabarut*,[654] and Grandeur and Magnificence!' Then he recited the chapter of *al-Baqara*[655] and thereafter he bowed, and his bowing was as long as his standing. He would say [in his bowing], 'Glorified is my Lord the Magnificent, glorified is my Lord the Magnificent!' Then he raised his blessed head—and his standing was as long as his bowing. He would say [in his standing], 'To my Lord is all praise, to my Lord is all praise!' Then he prostrated—and his prostration was as long as his standing. He would say [in his prostration], 'Glorified is my Lord the Most Exalted, glorified is my Lord the Most Exalted!' Then he raised his blessed head—and the position between the two prostrations was as long as his prostration. He would say [in his sitting], 'O my Lord, forgive me, O my Lord, forgive me!' [He prayed in this manner] whilst reciting the chapters of *al-Baqara, Al 'Imran, al-Nisa', al-Ma'ida* [or *al-An'am*]"'—[Shu'ba was the one who was unsure whether it was *al-Ma'ida* or *al-An'am.'*][656]

NOTE FROM IMAM AL-TIRMIDHI

قَالَ أَبُو عِيسَىٰ وَأَبُو حَمْزَةَ اسْمُهُ طَلْحَةُ بْنُ زَيْدٍ ۞ وَأَبُو جَمْرَةَ الضُّبَعِيُّ اسْمُهُ نَصْرُ بْنُ عِمْرَانَ ۞

Abu Hamza's name is Talha ibn Zayd. Abu Hamza al-Duba'i's name is Nasr ibn 'Imran.

٢٧٦ - حَدَّثَنَا أَبُو بَكْرٍ مُحَمَّدُ بْنُ نَافِعٍ الْبَصْرِيُّ ۞ حَدَّثَنَا عَبْدُ الصَّمَدِ بْنُ عَبْدِ الْوَارِثِ ۞ عَنْ إِسْمَاعِيلَ بْنِ مُسْلِمٍ الْعَبْدِيِّ ۞ عَنْ أَبِي الْمُتَوَكِّلِ ۞ عَنْ عَائِشَةَ رَضِيَ اللَّهُ عَنْهَا قَالَتْ

[654] Mulla 'Ali al-Qari says in his commentary: This means 'the King of Kings' (*Malik al-Mulk*) ... as for the narration mentioning '[The Possessor of] the *Mulk* and the *Malakut*', a distinction is made between them: the former refers to the outer realm and the latter refers to the inner [intelligible] realm, each of which are described as 'the world of the unseen' (*'alam al-ghayb*) and 'the world of the seen' (*'alam al-shahada*) respectively. *Jabarut* comes from the word *jabr*, which means force. The Most High said, *And He is the Irresistible over His servants* (Qur'an 6:18)—so Glorified is He who reigns irresistibly over His servants with death and other things that He decrees for them!' (AA)

[655] That is, after reading the chapter of *al-Fatiha*. (AA)

[656] What this means is that the Prophet ﷺ offered four units of prayer: in the first unit he recited *al-Baqara*, in the second unit he recited *Al 'Imran*, in the third unit he recited *al-Nisa'* and in the fourth unit he recited either *al-Ma'ida* or *al-An'am*—the narrator of this hadith, Shu'ba, was unsure which one. (AA)

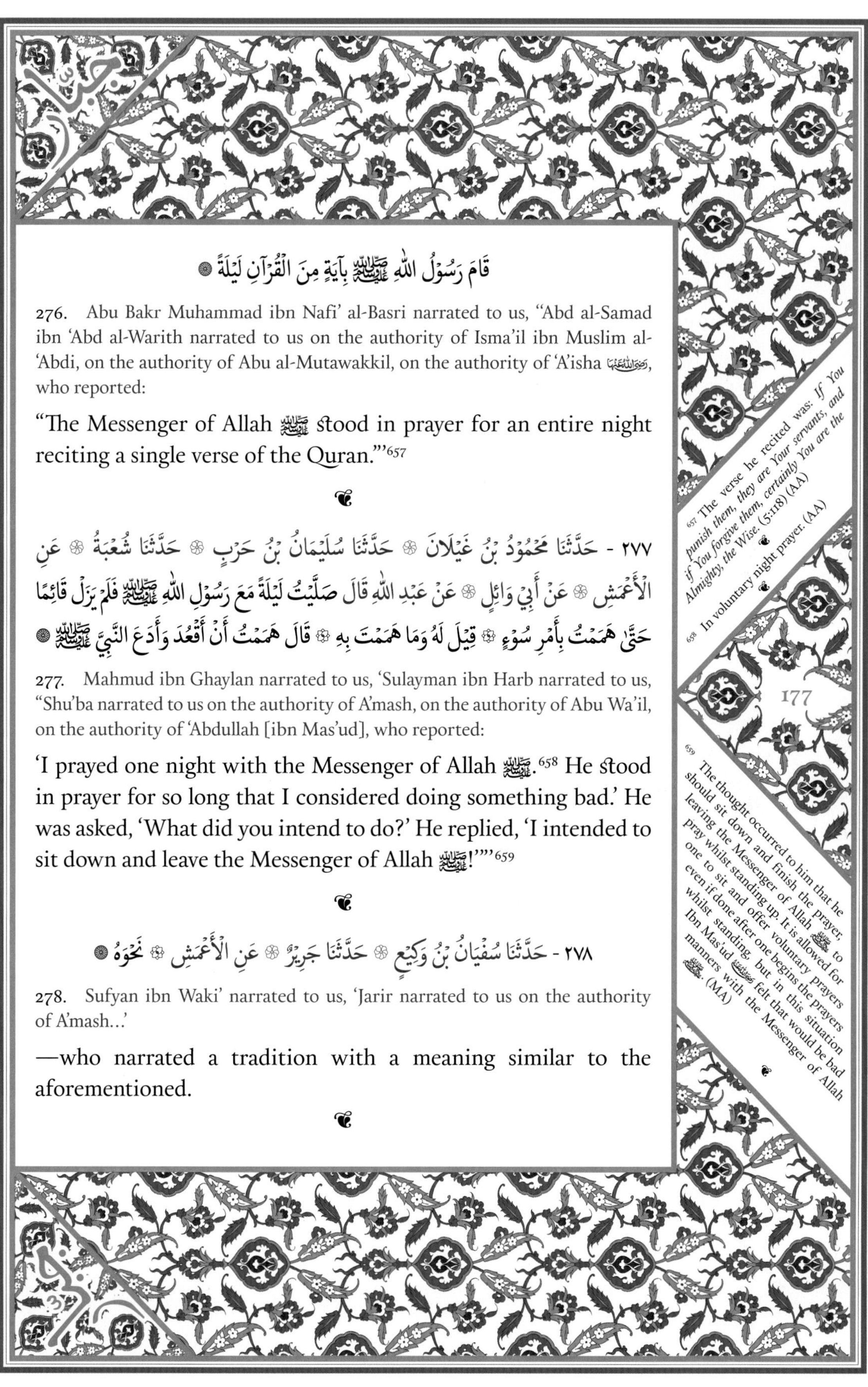

قَامَ رَسُولُ اللهِ ﷺ بِآيَةٍ مِنَ الْقُرْآنِ لَيْلَةً

276. Abu Bakr Muhammad ibn Nafi' al-Basri narrated to us, "Abd al-Samad ibn 'Abd al-Warith narrated to us on the authority of Isma'il ibn Muslim al-'Abdi, on the authority of Abu al-Mutawakkil, on the authority of 'A'isha ﵂, who reported:

"The Messenger of Allah ﷺ stood in prayer for an entire night reciting a single verse of the Quran."'[657]

٢٧٧ - حَدَّثَنَا مَحْمُودُ بْنُ غَيْلَانَ ۞ حَدَّثَنَا سُلَيْمَانُ بْنُ حَرْبٍ ۞ حَدَّثَنَا شُعْبَةُ ۞ عَنِ الْأَعْمَشِ ۞ عَنْ أَبِي وَائِلٍ ۞ عَنْ عَبْدِ اللهِ قَالَ صَلَّيْتُ لَيْلَةً مَعَ رَسُولِ اللهِ ﷺ فَلَمْ يَزَلْ قَائِمًا حَتَّىٰ هَمَمْتُ بِأَمْرِ سُوءٍ ۞ قِيلَ لَهُ وَمَا هَمَمْتَ بِهِ ۞ قَالَ هَمَمْتُ أَنْ أَقْعُدَ وَأَدَعَ النَّبِيَّ ﷺ

277. Mahmud ibn Ghaylan narrated to us, 'Sulayman ibn Harb narrated to us, "Shu'ba narrated to us on the authority of A'mash, on the authority of Abu Wa'il, on the authority of 'Abdullah [ibn Mas'ud], who reported:

'I prayed one night with the Messenger of Allah ﷺ.[658] He stood in prayer for so long that I considered doing something bad.' He was asked, 'What did you intend to do?' He replied, 'I intended to sit down and leave the Messenger of Allah ﷺ!'"'[659]

٢٧٨ - حَدَّثَنَا سُفْيَانُ بْنُ وَكِيعٍ ۞ حَدَّثَنَا جَرِيرٌ ۞ عَنِ الْأَعْمَشِ ۞ نَحْوَهُ

278. Sufyan ibn Waki' narrated to us, 'Jarir narrated to us on the authority of A'mash...'

—who narrated a tradition with a meaning similar to the aforementioned.

[657] The verse he recited was: *If You punish them, they are Your servants, and if You forgive them, certainly You are the Almighty, the Wise.* (5:118) (AA)

[658] In voluntary night prayer. (AA)

[659] The thought occurred to him that he should sit down and finish the prayer, leaving the Messenger of Allah ﷺ to pray whilst standing up. It is allowed for one to sit and offer voluntary prayers even if done after one begins the prayers whilst standing, but in this situation Ibn Mas'ud ﵁ felt that would be bad manners with the Messenger of Allah ﷺ. (MA)

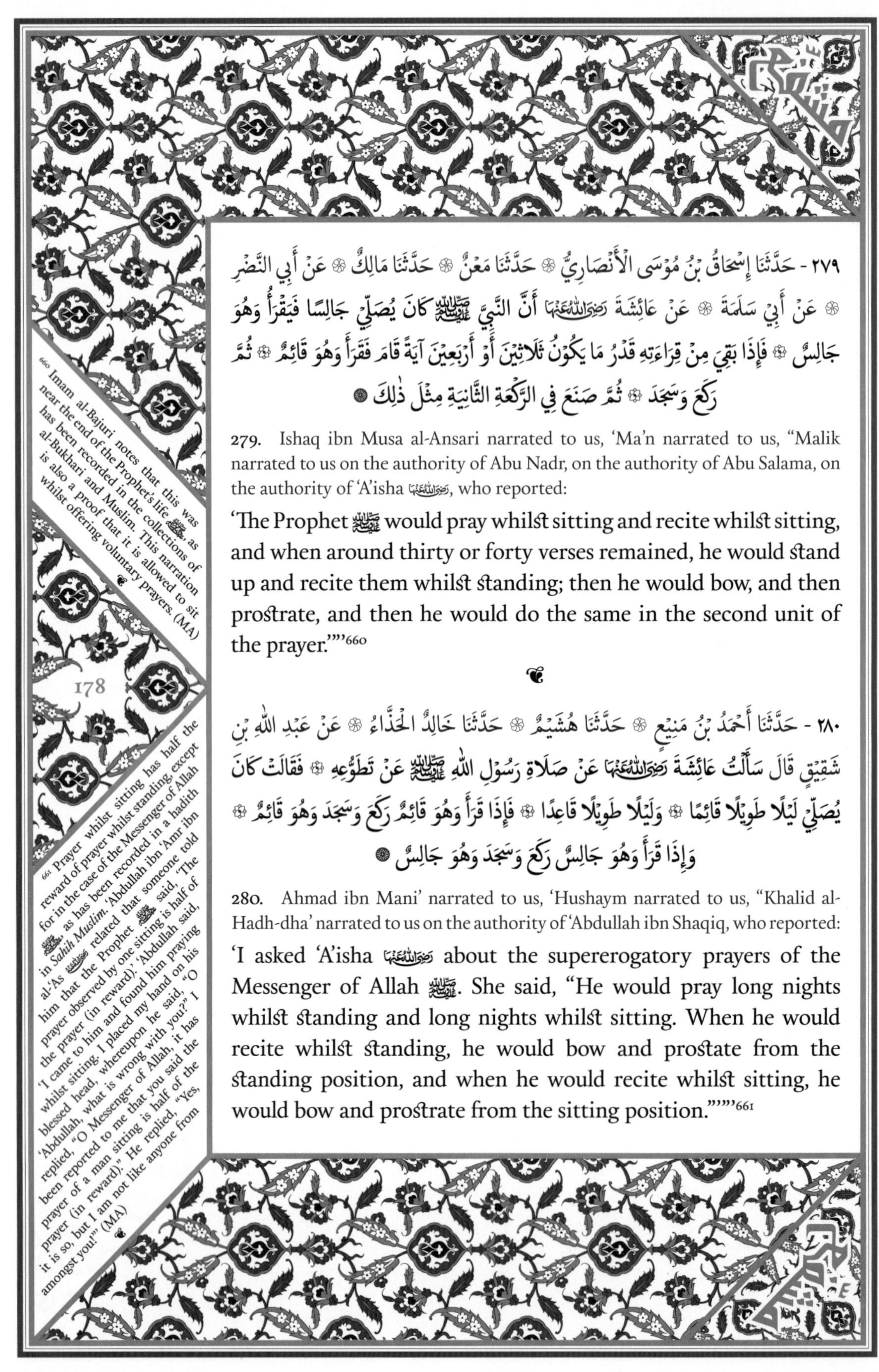

٢٧٩ - حَدَّثَنَا إِسْحَاقُ بْنُ مُوسَى الْأَنْصَارِيُّ ۞ حَدَّثَنَا مَعْنٌ ۞ حَدَّثَنَا مَالِكٌ ۞ عَنْ أَبِي النَّضْرِ ۞ عَنْ أَبِي سَلَمَةَ ۞ عَنْ عَائِشَةَ رَضِيَ اللهُ عَنْهَا أَنَّ النَّبِيَّ ﷺ كَانَ يُصَلِّي جَالِسًا فَيَقْرَأُ وَهُوَ جَالِسٌ ۞ فَإِذَا بَقِيَ مِنْ قِرَاءَتِهِ قَدْرُ مَا يَكُونُ ثَلَاثِينَ أَوْ أَرْبَعِينَ آيَةً قَامَ فَقَرَأَ وَهُوَ قَائِمٌ ۞ ثُمَّ رَكَعَ وَسَجَدَ ۞ ثُمَّ صَنَعَ فِي الرَّكْعَةِ الثَّانِيَةِ مِثْلَ ذٰلِكَ ۞

279. Ishaq ibn Musa al-Ansari narrated to us, 'Ma'n narrated to us, "Malik narrated to us on the authority of Abu Nadr, on the authority of Abu Salama, on the authority of 'A'isha رضي الله عنها, who reported:

'The Prophet ﷺ would pray whilst sitting and recite whilst sitting, and when around thirty or forty verses remained, he would stand up and recite them whilst standing; then he would bow, and then prostrate, and then he would do the same in the second unit of the prayer.'"'[660]

❦

٢٨٠ - حَدَّثَنَا أَحْمَدُ بْنُ مَنِيعٍ ۞ حَدَّثَنَا هُشَيْمٌ ۞ حَدَّثَنَا خَالِدٌ الْحَذَّاءُ ۞ عَنْ عَبْدِ اللهِ بْنِ شَقِيقٍ قَالَ سَأَلْتُ عَائِشَةَ رَضِيَ اللهُ عَنْهَا عَنْ صَلَاةِ رَسُولِ اللهِ ﷺ عَنْ تَطَوُّعِهِ ۞ فَقَالَتْ كَانَ يُصَلِّي لَيْلًا طَوِيلًا قَائِمًا ۞ وَلَيْلًا طَوِيلًا قَاعِدًا ۞ فَإِذَا قَرَأَ وَهُوَ قَائِمٌ رَكَعَ وَسَجَدَ وَهُوَ قَائِمٌ ۞ وَإِذَا قَرَأَ وَهُوَ جَالِسٌ رَكَعَ وَسَجَدَ وَهُوَ جَالِسٌ ۞

280. Ahmad ibn Mani' narrated to us, 'Hushaym narrated to us, "Khalid al-Hadh-dha' narrated to us on the authority of 'Abdullah ibn Shaqiq, who reported:

'I asked 'A'isha رضي الله عنها about the supererogatory prayers of the Messenger of Allah ﷺ. She said, "He would pray long nights whilst standing and long nights whilst sitting. When he would recite whilst standing, he would bow and prostrate from the standing position, and when he would recite whilst sitting, he would bow and prostrate from the sitting position."'"'[661]

[660] Imam al-Bajuri notes that this was near the end of the Prophet's life ﷺ, as has been recorded in the collections of al-Bukhari and Muslim. This narration is also a proof that it is allowed to sit whilst offering voluntary prayers. (MA) ❦

[661] Prayer whilst sitting has half the reward of prayer whilst standing, except for in the case of the Messenger of Allah ﷺ as has been recorded in a hadith in *Sahih Muslim*. 'Abdullah ibn 'Amr ibn al-'As رضي الله عنهما related that someone told him that the Prophet ﷺ said, 'The prayer observed by one sitting is half of the prayer (in reward).' 'Abdullah said, 'I came to him and found him praying whilst sitting. I placed my hand on his blessed head, whereupon he said, "O 'Abdullah, what is wrong with you?" I replied, "O Messenger of Allah, it has been reported to me that you said the prayer of a man sitting is half of the prayer (in reward)." He replied, "Yes, it is so, but I am not like anyone from amongst you!"' (MA) ❦

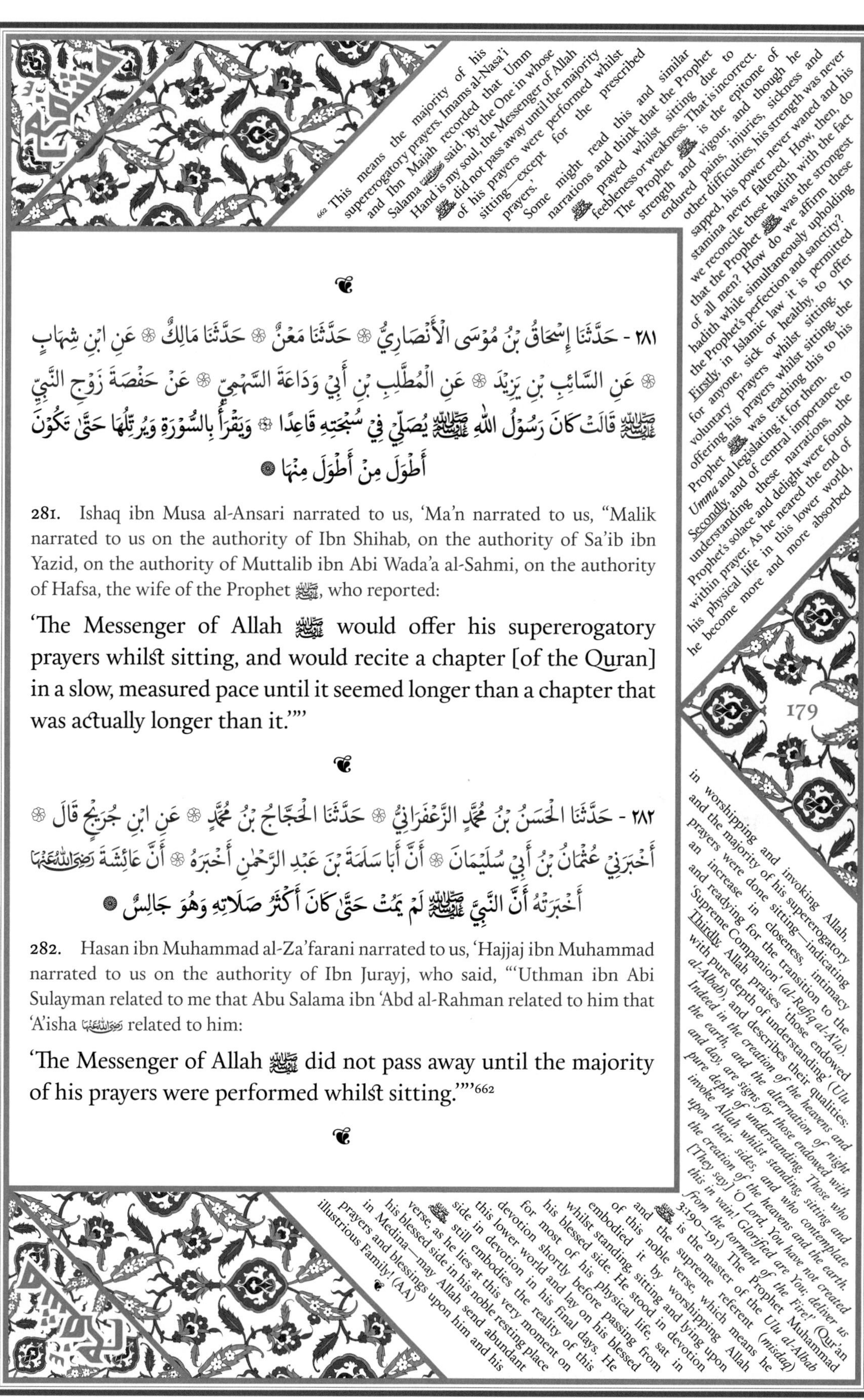

❦

٢٨١ - حَدَّثَنَا إِسْحَاقُ بْنُ مُوسَى الْأَنْصَارِيُّ ❁ حَدَّثَنَا مَعْنٌ ❁ حَدَّثَنَا مَالِكٌ ❁ عَنِ ابْنِ شِهَابٍ ❁ عَنِ السَّائِبِ بْنِ يَزِيدَ ❁ عَنِ الْمُطَّلِبِ بْنِ أَبِي وَدَاعَةَ السَّهْمِيِّ ❁ عَنْ حَفْصَةَ زَوْجِ النَّبِيِّ ﷺ قَالَتْ كَانَ رَسُولُ اللهِ ﷺ يُصَلِّي فِي سُبْحَتِهِ قَاعِدًا ❁ وَيَقْرَأُ بِالسُّورَةِ وَيُرَتِّلُهَا حَتَّىٰ تَكُونَ أَطْوَلَ مِنْ أَطْوَلَ مِنْهَا ۝

281. Ishaq ibn Musa al-Ansari narrated to us, 'Ma'n narrated to us, "Malik narrated to us on the authority of Ibn Shihab, on the authority of Sa'ib ibn Yazid, on the authority of Muttalib ibn Abi Wada'a al-Sahmi, on the authority of Hafsa, the wife of the Prophet ﷺ, who reported:

'The Messenger of Allah ﷺ would offer his supererogatory prayers whilst sitting, and would recite a chapter [of the Quran] in a slow, measured pace until it seemed longer than a chapter that was actually longer than it.'"'

❦

٢٨٢ - حَدَّثَنَا الْحَسَنُ بْنُ مُحَمَّدٍ الزَّعْفَرَانِيُّ ❁ حَدَّثَنَا الْحَجَّاجُ بْنُ مُحَمَّدٍ ❁ عَنِ ابْنِ جُرَيْجٍ قَالَ ❁ أَخْبَرَنِي عُثْمَانُ بْنُ أَبِي سُلَيْمَانَ ❁ أَنَّ أَبَا سَلَمَةَ بْنَ عَبْدِ الرَّحْمٰنِ أَخْبَرَهُ ❁ أَنَّ عَائِشَةَ رَضِيَ اللهُ عَنْهَا أَخْبَرَتْهُ أَنَّ النَّبِيَّ ﷺ لَمْ يَمُتْ حَتَّىٰ كَانَ أَكْثَرُ صَلَاتِهِ وَهُوَ جَالِسٌ ۝

282. Hasan ibn Muhammad al-Za'farani narrated to us, 'Hajjaj ibn Muhammad narrated to us on the authority of Ibn Jurayj, who said, "'Uthman ibn Abi Sulayman related to me that Abu Salama ibn 'Abd al-Rahman related to him that 'A'isha رضي الله عنها related to him:

'The Messenger of Allah ﷺ did not pass away until the majority of his prayers were performed whilst sitting.'"'[662]

❦

[662] This means the majority of his supererogatory prayers. Imams al-Nasa'i and Ibn Majah recorded that Umm Salama رضي الله عنها said, 'By the One in whose Hand is my soul, the Messenger of Allah ﷺ did not pass away until the majority of his prayers were performed whilst sitting—except for the prescribed prayers.' Some might read this and similar narrations and think that the Prophet ﷺ prayed whilst sitting due to feebleness or weakness. That is incorrect. The Prophet ﷺ is the epitome of strength and vigour, and though he endured pains, injuries, sickness and other difficulties, his strength was never sapped, his power never waned and his stamina never faltered. How, then, do we reconcile these hadith with the fact that the Prophet ﷺ was the strongest of all men? How do we affirm these hadith while simultaneously upholding the Prophet's perfection and sanctity? Firstly, in Islamic law it is permitted for anyone, sick or healthy, to offer voluntary prayers whilst sitting. In offering his prayers whilst sitting, the Prophet ﷺ was teaching this to his *Umma* and legislating it for them. Secondly, and of central importance to understanding these narrations, the Prophet's solace and delight were found within prayer. As he neared the end of his physical life in this lower world, he become more and more absorbed in worshipping and invoking Allah, and the majority of his supererogatory prayers were done sitting—indicating an increase in closeness, intimacy and readying for the transition to the 'Supreme Companion' (*al-Rafiq al-A'la*). Thirdly, Allah praises 'those endowed with pure depth of understanding' (*Ulu al-Albab*), and describes their qualities: *Indeed in the creation of the heavens and the earth, and the alternation of night and day, are signs for those endowed with pure depth of understanding. Those who invoke Allah whilst standing, sitting and upon their sides, and who contemplate the creation of the heavens and the earth. [They say] 'O Lord, You have not created this in vain! Glorified are You; deliver us from the torment of the Fire!'* (Qur'an 3:190–191) The Prophet Muhammad ﷺ is the master of the *Ulu al-Albab* and the supreme referent (*misdaq*) of this noble verse, which means he embodied it by worshipping Allah whilst standing, sitting and lying upon his blessed side. He stood in devotion for most of his physical life, sat in devotion shortly before passing from this lower world and lay on his blessed side in devotion in his final days. He still embodies the reality of this verse, as he lies at this very moment on his blessed side in his noble resting place in Medina—may Allah send abundant prayers and blessings upon him and his illustrious Family! (AA) ❦

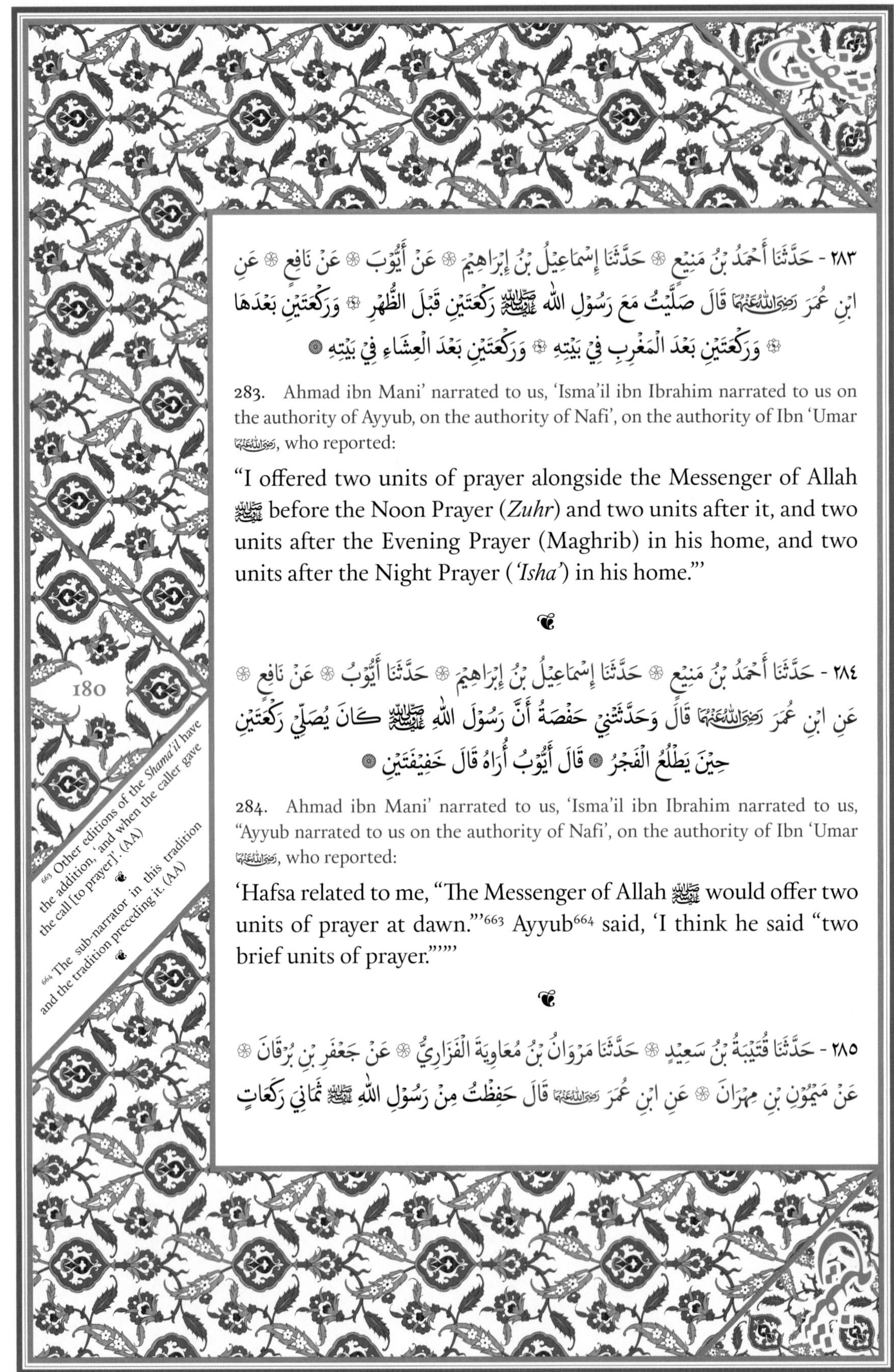

٢٨٣ - حَدَّثَنَا أَحْمَدُ بْنُ مَنِيعٍ ۞ حَدَّثَنَا إِسْمَاعِيلُ بْنُ إِبْرَاهِيمَ ۞ عَنْ أَيُّوبَ ۞ عَنْ نَافِعٍ ۞ عَنِ ابْنِ عُمَرَ رَضِيَ اللَّهُ عَنْهُمَا قَالَ صَلَّيْتُ مَعَ رَسُولِ اللهِ ﷺ رَكْعَتَيْنِ قَبْلَ الظُّهْرِ ۞ وَرَكْعَتَيْنِ بَعْدَهَا ۞ وَرَكْعَتَيْنِ بَعْدَ الْمَغْرِبِ فِي بَيْتِهِ ۞ وَرَكْعَتَيْنِ بَعْدَ الْعِشَاءِ فِي بَيْتِهِ ۞

283. Ahmad ibn Mani' narrated to us, 'Isma'il ibn Ibrahim narrated to us on the authority of Ayyub, on the authority of Nafi', on the authority of Ibn 'Umar رضي الله عنهما, who reported:

"I offered two units of prayer alongside the Messenger of Allah ﷺ before the Noon Prayer (*Zuhr*) and two units after it, and two units after the Evening Prayer (Maghrib) in his home, and two units after the Night Prayer (*'Isha'*) in his home."'

٢٨٤ - حَدَّثَنَا أَحْمَدُ بْنُ مَنِيعٍ ۞ حَدَّثَنَا إِسْمَاعِيلُ بْنُ إِبْرَاهِيمَ ۞ حَدَّثَنَا أَيُّوبُ ۞ عَنْ نَافِعٍ ۞ عَنِ ابْنِ عُمَرَ رَضِيَ اللَّهُ عَنْهُمَا قَالَ وَحَدَّثَتْنِي حَفْصَةُ أَنَّ رَسُولَ اللهِ ﷺ كَانَ يُصَلِّي رَكْعَتَيْنِ حِينَ يَطْلُعُ الْفَجْرُ ۞ قَالَ أَيُّوبُ أُرَاهُ قَالَ خَفِيفَتَيْنِ ۞

284. Ahmad ibn Mani' narrated to us, 'Isma'il ibn Ibrahim narrated to us, "Ayyub narrated to us on the authority of Nafi', on the authority of Ibn 'Umar رضي الله عنهما, who reported:

'Hafsa related to me, "The Messenger of Allah ﷺ would offer two units of prayer at dawn."'[663] Ayyub[664] said, 'I think he said "two brief units of prayer."'"'

٢٨٥ - حَدَّثَنَا قُتَيْبَةُ بْنُ سَعِيدٍ ۞ حَدَّثَنَا مَرْوَانُ بْنُ مُعَاوِيَةَ الْفَزَارِيُّ ۞ عَنْ جَعْفَرِ بْنِ بُرْقَانَ ۞ عَنْ مَيْمُونِ بْنِ مِهْرَانَ ۞ عَنِ ابْنِ عُمَرَ رَضِيَ اللَّهُ عَنْهُمَا قَالَ حَفِظْتُ مِنْ رَسُولِ اللهِ ﷺ ثَمَانِيَ رَكَعَاتٍ

663 Other editions of the *Shama'il* have the addition, 'and when the caller gave the call [to prayer]'. (AA)

664 The sub-narrator in this tradition and the tradition preceding it. (AA)

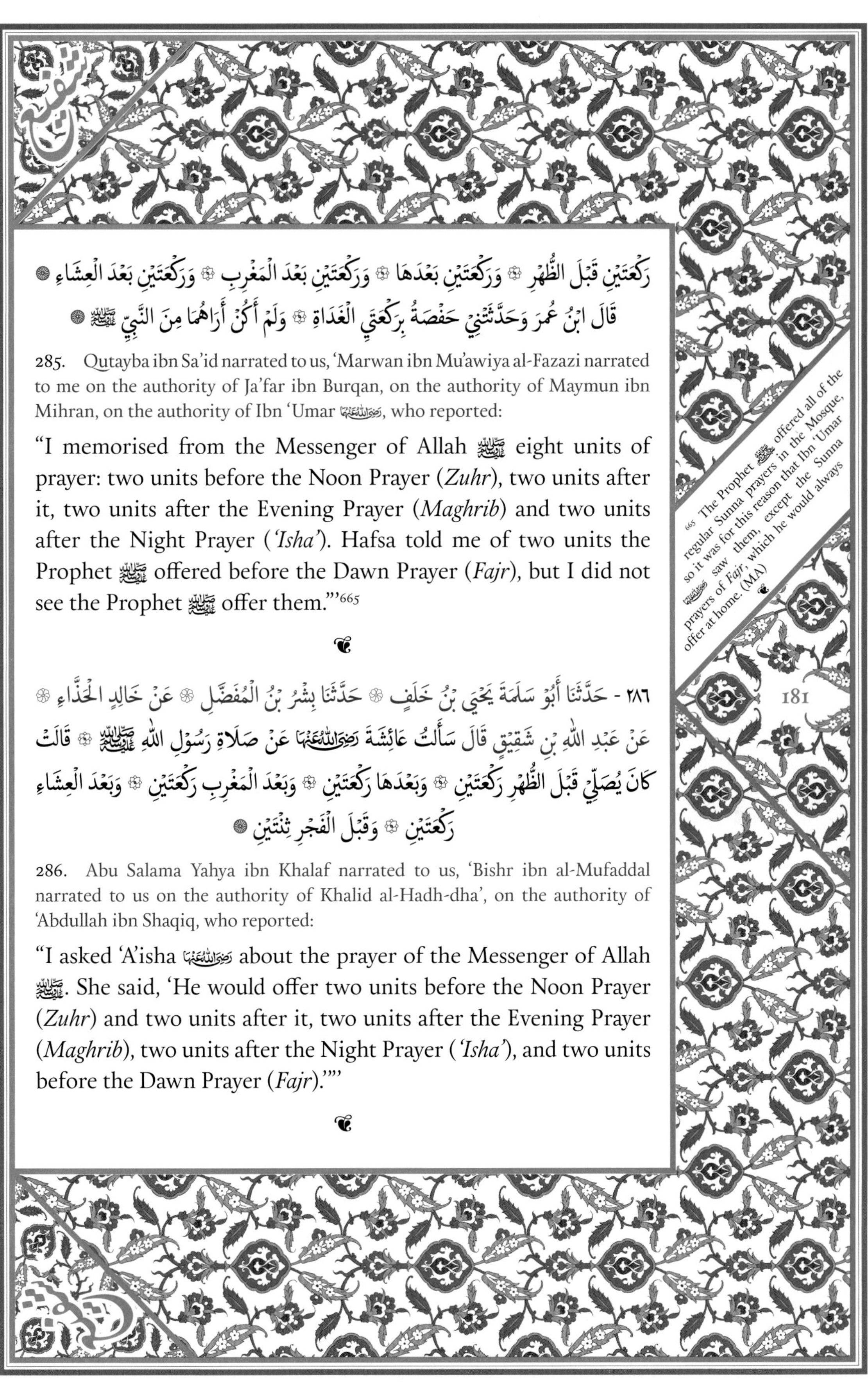

رَكْعَتَيْنِ قَبْلَ الظُّهْرِ ۞ وَرَكْعَتَيْنِ بَعْدَهَا ۞ وَرَكْعَتَيْنِ بَعْدَ الْمَغْرِبِ ۞ وَرَكْعَتَيْنِ بَعْدَ الْعِشَاءِ ۞
قَالَ ابْنُ عُمَرَ وَحَدَّثَتْنِي حَفْصَةُ بِرَكْعَتَي الْغَدَاةِ ۞ وَلَمْ أَكُنْ أَرَاهُمَا مِنَ النَّبِيِّ ﷺ ۞

285. Qutayba ibn Sa'id narrated to us, 'Marwan ibn Mu'awiya al-Fazazi narrated to me on the authority of Ja'far ibn Burqan, on the authority of Maymun ibn Mihran, on the authority of Ibn 'Umar رضي الله عنه, who reported:

"I memorised from the Messenger of Allah ﷺ eight units of prayer: two units before the Noon Prayer (*Zuhr*), two units after it, two units after the Evening Prayer (*Maghrib*) and two units after the Night Prayer (*'Isha'*). Hafsa told me of two units the Prophet ﷺ offered before the Dawn Prayer (*Fajr*), but I did not see the Prophet ﷺ offer them."'[665]

٢٨٦ - حَدَّثَنَا أَبُو سَلَمَةَ يَحْيَى بْنُ خَلَفٍ ۞ حَدَّثَنَا بِشْرُ بْنُ الْمُفَضَّلِ ۞ عَنْ خَالِدٍ الْحَذَّاءِ ۞ عَنْ عَبْدِ اللهِ بْنِ شَقِيقٍ قَالَ سَأَلْتُ عَائِشَةَ رَضِيَ اللهُ عَنْهَا عَنْ صَلَاةِ رَسُولِ اللهِ ﷺ ۞ قَالَتْ كَانَ يُصَلِّي قَبْلَ الظُّهْرِ رَكْعَتَيْنِ ۞ وَبَعْدَهَا رَكْعَتَيْنِ ۞ وَبَعْدَ الْمَغْرِبِ رَكْعَتَيْنِ ۞ وَبَعْدَ الْعِشَاءِ رَكْعَتَيْنِ ۞ وَقَبْلَ الْفَجْرِ ثِنْتَيْنِ ۞

286. Abu Salama Yahya ibn Khalaf narrated to us, 'Bishr ibn al-Mufaddal narrated to us on the authority of Khalid al-Hadh-dha', on the authority of 'Abdullah ibn Shaqiq, who reported:

"I asked 'A'isha رضي الله عنها about the prayer of the Messenger of Allah ﷺ. She said, 'He would offer two units before the Noon Prayer (*Zuhr*) and two units after it, two units after the Evening Prayer (*Maghrib*), two units after the Night Prayer (*'Isha'*), and two units before the Dawn Prayer (*Fajr*).'"'

[665] The Prophet ﷺ offered all of the regular Sunna prayers in the Mosque, so it was for this reason that Ibn 'Umar رضي الله عنه saw them, except the Sunna prayers of *Fajr*, which he would always offer at home. (MA)

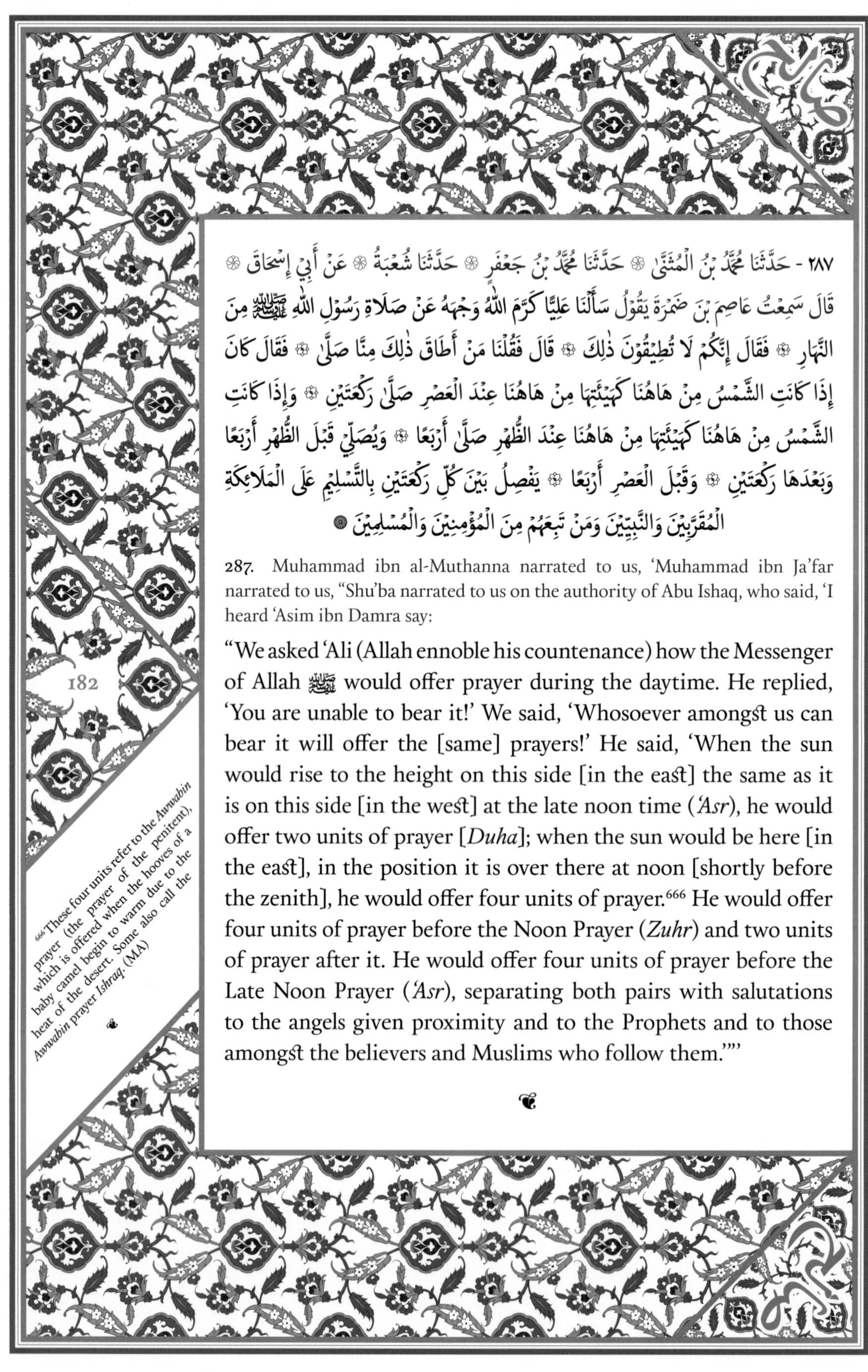

٢٨٧ - حَدَّثَنَا مُحَمَّدُ بْنُ الْمُثَنَّى ۞ حَدَّثَنَا مُحَمَّدُ بْنُ جَعْفَرٍ ۞ حَدَّثَنَا شُعْبَةُ ۞ عَنْ أَبِي إِسْحَاقَ ۞ قَالَ سَمِعْتُ عَاصِمَ بْنَ ضَمْرَةَ يَقُولُ سَأَلْنَا عَلِيًّا كَرَّمَ اللهُ وَجْهَهُ عَنْ صَلَاةِ رَسُولِ اللهِ ﷺ مِنَ النَّهَارِ ۞ فَقَالَ إِنَّكُمْ لَا تُطِيقُونَ ذٰلِكَ ۞ قَالَ فَقُلْنَا مَنْ أَطَاقَ ذٰلِكَ مِنَّا صَلَّى ۞ فَقَالَ كَانَ إِذَا كَانَتِ الشَّمْسُ مِنْ هَاهُنَا كَهَيْئَتِهَا مِنْ هَاهُنَا عِنْدَ الْعَصْرِ صَلَّى رَكْعَتَيْنِ ۞ وَإِذَا كَانَتِ الشَّمْسُ مِنْ هَاهُنَا كَهَيْئَتِهَا مِنْ هَاهُنَا عِنْدَ الظُّهْرِ صَلَّى أَرْبَعًا ۞ وَيُصَلِّي قَبْلَ الظُّهْرِ أَرْبَعًا وَبَعْدَهَا رَكْعَتَيْنِ ۞ وَقَبْلَ الْعَصْرِ أَرْبَعًا ۞ يَفْصِلُ بَيْنَ كُلِّ رَكْعَتَيْنِ بِالتَّسْلِيمِ عَلَى الْمَلَائِكَةِ الْمُقَرَّبِينَ وَالنَّبِيِّينَ وَمَنْ تَبِعَهُمْ مِنَ الْمُؤْمِنِينَ وَالْمُسْلِمِينَ ۞

287. Muhammad ibn al-Muthanna narrated to us, 'Muhammad ibn Ja'far narrated to us, "Shu'ba narrated to us on the authority of Abu Ishaq, who said, 'I heard 'Asim ibn Damra say:

"We asked 'Ali (Allah ennoble his countenance) how the Messenger of Allah ﷺ would offer prayer during the daytime. He replied, 'You are unable to bear it!' We said, 'Whosoever amongst us can bear it will offer the [same] prayers!' He said, 'When the sun would rise to the height on this side [in the east] the same as it is on this side [in the west] at the late noon time (*'Asr*), he would offer two units of prayer [*Duha*]; when the sun would be here [in the east], in the position it is over there at noon [shortly before the zenith], he would offer four units of prayer.[666] He would offer four units of prayer before the Noon Prayer (*Zuhr*) and two units of prayer after it. He would offer four units of prayer before the Late Noon Prayer (*'Asr*), separating both pairs with salutations to the angels given proximity and to the Prophets and to those amongst the believers and Muslims who follow them.'"'

[666] These four units refer to the *Awwabin* prayer (the prayer of the penitent), which is offered when the hooves of a baby camel begin to warm due to the heat of the desert. Some also call the *Awwabin* prayer *Ishraq*. (MA)

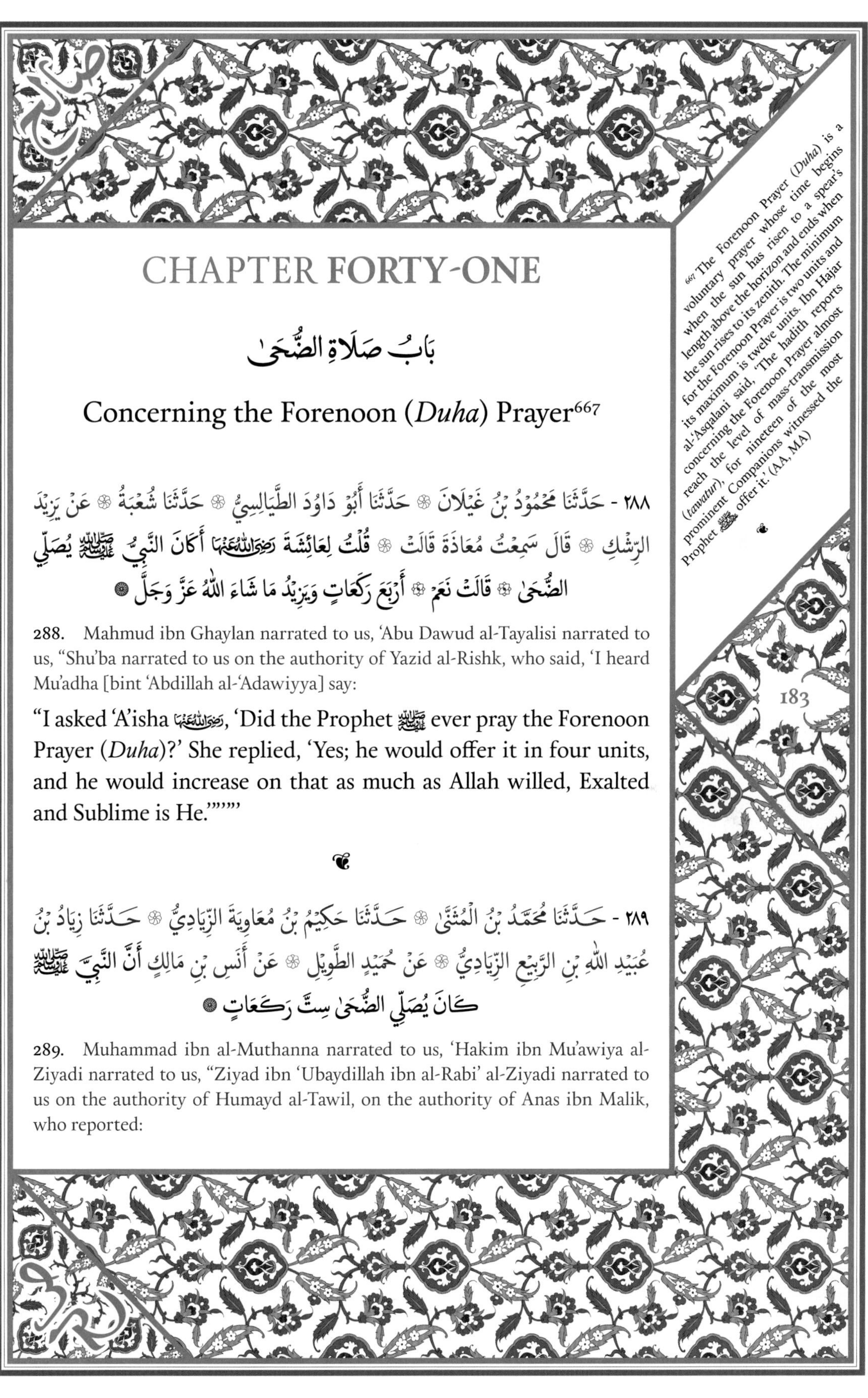

CHAPTER FORTY-ONE

بَابُ صَلَاةِ الضُّحَىٰ

Concerning the Forenoon (*Duha*) Prayer[667]

٢٨٨ - حَدَّثَنَا مَحْمُودُ بْنُ غَيْلَانَ ۞ حَدَّثَنَا أَبُو دَاوُدَ الطَّيَالِسِيُّ ۞ حَدَّثَنَا شُعْبَةُ ۞ عَنْ يَزِيدَ الرِّشْكِ ۞ قَالَ سَمِعْتُ مُعَاذَةَ قَالَتْ ۞ قُلْتُ لِعَائِشَةَ رَضِيَ اللهُ عَنْهَا أَكَانَ النَّبِيُّ ﷺ يُصَلِّي الضُّحَىٰ ۞ قَالَتْ نَعَمْ ۞ أَرْبَعَ رَكَعَاتٍ وَيَزِيدُ مَا شَاءَ اللهُ عَزَّ وَجَلَّ ۞

288. Mahmud ibn Ghaylan narrated to us, 'Abu Dawud al-Tayalisi narrated to us, "Shu'ba narrated to us on the authority of Yazid al-Rishk, who said, 'I heard Mu'adha [bint 'Abdillah al-'Adawiyya] say:

"I asked 'A'isha رضي الله عنها, 'Did the Prophet ﷺ ever pray the Forenoon Prayer (*Duha*)?' She replied, 'Yes; he would offer it in four units, and he would increase on that as much as Allah willed, Exalted and Sublime is He.'"'"'

٢٨٩ - حَدَّثَنَا مُحَمَّدُ بْنُ الْمُثَنَّىٰ ۞ حَدَّثَنَا حَكِيمُ بْنُ مُعَاوِيَةَ الزِّيَادِيُّ ۞ حَدَّثَنَا زِيَادُ بْنُ عُبَيْدِ اللهِ بْنِ الرَّبِيعِ الزِّيَادِيُّ ۞ عَنْ حُمَيْدٍ الطَّوِيلِ ۞ عَنْ أَنَسِ بْنِ مَالِكٍ أَنَّ النَّبِيَّ ﷺ كَانَ يُصَلِّي الضُّحَىٰ سِتَّ رَكَعَاتٍ ۞

289. Muhammad ibn al-Muthanna narrated to us, 'Hakim ibn Mu'awiya al-Ziyadi narrated to us, "Ziyad ibn 'Ubaydillah ibn al-Rabi' al-Ziyadi narrated to us on the authority of Humayd al-Tawil, on the authority of Anas ibn Malik, who reported:

[667] The Forenoon Prayer (*Duha*) is a voluntary prayer whose time begins when the sun has risen to a spear's length above the horizon and ends when the sun rises to its zenith. The minimum for the Forenoon Prayer is two units and its maximum is twelve units. Ibn Hajar al-'Asqalani said, 'The hadith reports concerning the Forenoon Prayer almost reach the level of mass-transmission (*tawatur*), for nineteen of the most prominent Companions witnessed the Prophet ﷺ offer it.' (AA, MA)

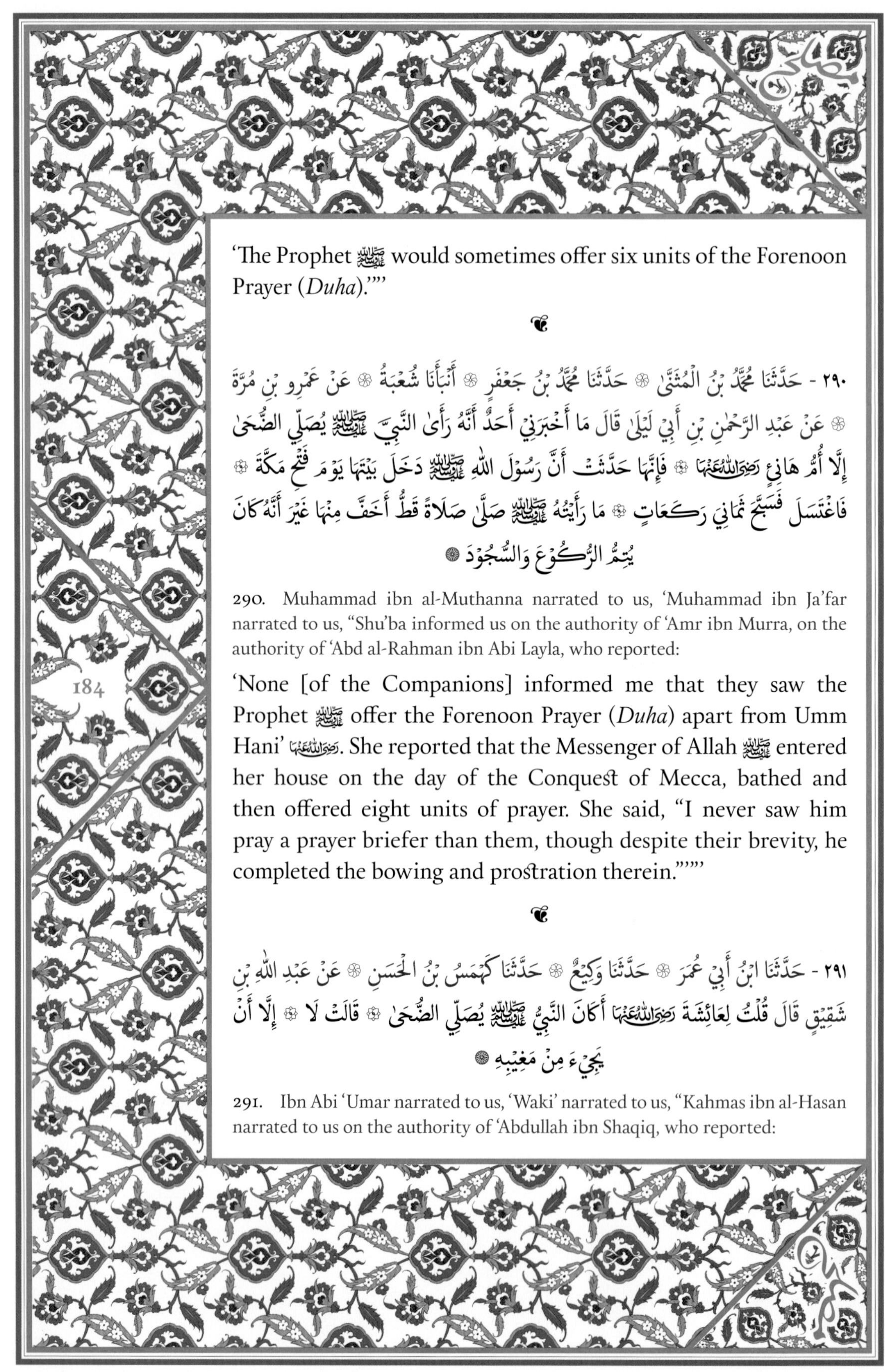

'The Prophet ﷺ would sometimes offer six units of the Forenoon Prayer (*Duha*).''''

❦

٢٩٠ - حَدَّثَنَا مُحَمَّدُ بْنُ الْمُثَنَّىٰ ۞ حَدَّثَنَا مُحَمَّدُ بْنُ جَعْفَرٍ ۞ أَنْبَأَنَا شُعْبَةُ ۞ عَنْ عَمْرِو بْنِ مُرَّةَ ۞ عَنْ عَبْدِ الرَّحْمَٰنِ بْنِ أَبِي لَيْلَىٰ قَالَ مَا أَخْبَرَنِي أَحَدٌ أَنَّهُ رَأَىٰ النَّبِيَّ ﷺ يُصَلِّي الضُّحَىٰ إِلَّا أُمُّ هَانِئٍ رَضِيَ اللَّهُ عَنْهَا ۞ فَإِنَّهَا حَدَّثَتْ أَنَّ رَسُولَ اللَّهِ ﷺ دَخَلَ بَيْتَهَا يَوْمَ فَتْحِ مَكَّةَ ۞ فَاغْتَسَلَ فَسَبَّحَ ثَمَانِيَ رَكَعَاتٍ ۞ مَا رَأَيْتُهُ ﷺ صَلَّىٰ صَلَاةً قَطُّ أَخَفَّ مِنْهَا غَيْرَ أَنَّهُ كَانَ يُتِمُّ الرُّكُوعَ وَالسُّجُودَ ۞

290. Muhammad ibn al-Muthanna narrated to us, 'Muhammad ibn Ja'far narrated to us, "Shu'ba informed us on the authority of 'Amr ibn Murra, on the authority of 'Abd al-Rahman ibn Abi Layla, who reported:

'None [of the Companions] informed me that they saw the Prophet ﷺ offer the Forenoon Prayer (*Duha*) apart from Umm Hani' رضي الله عنها. She reported that the Messenger of Allah ﷺ entered her house on the day of the Conquest of Mecca, bathed and then offered eight units of prayer. She said, "I never saw him pray a prayer briefer than them, though despite their brevity, he completed the bowing and prostration therein.""''

❦

٢٩١ - حَدَّثَنَا ابْنُ أَبِي عُمَرَ ۞ حَدَّثَنَا وَكِيعٌ ۞ حَدَّثَنَا كَهْمَسُ بْنُ الْحَسَنِ ۞ عَنْ عَبْدِ اللَّهِ بْنِ شَقِيقٍ قَالَ قُلْتُ لِعَائِشَةَ رَضِيَ اللَّهُ عَنْهَا أَكَانَ النَّبِيُّ ﷺ يُصَلِّي الضُّحَىٰ ۞ قَالَتْ لَا ۞ إِلَّا أَنْ يَجِيءَ مِنْ مَغِيبِهِ ۞

291. Ibn Abi 'Umar narrated to us, 'Waki' narrated to us, "Kahmas ibn al-Hasan narrated to us on the authority of 'Abdullah ibn Shaqiq, who reported:

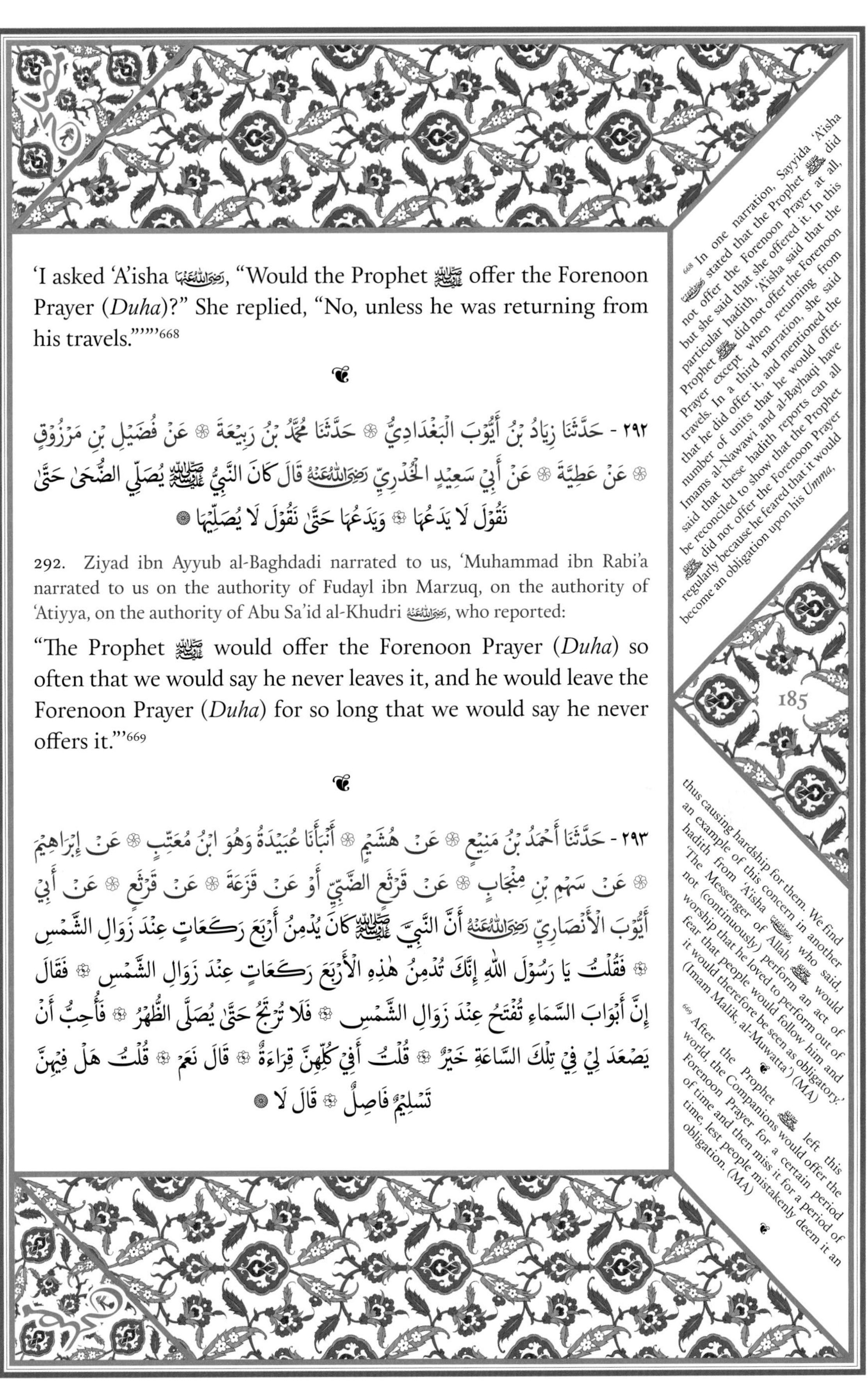

'I asked 'A'isha رضي الله عنها, "Would the Prophet ﷺ offer the Forenoon Prayer (*Duha*)?" She replied, "No, unless he was returning from his travels."""'[668]

٢٩٢ - حَدَّثَنَا زِيَادُ بْنُ أَيُّوبَ الْبَغْدَادِيُّ ۞ حَدَّثَنَا مُحَمَّدُ بْنُ رَبِيعَةَ ۞ عَنْ فُضَيْلِ بْنِ مَرْزُوقٍ ۞ عَنْ عَطِيَّةَ ۞ عَنْ أَبِي سَعِيدٍ الْخُدْرِيِّ رَضِيَ اللهُ عَنْهُ قَالَ كَانَ النَّبِيُّ ﷺ يُصَلِّي الضُّحَىٰ حَتَّىٰ نَقُولَ لَا يَدَعُهَا ۞ وَيَدَعُهَا حَتَّىٰ نَقُولَ لَا يُصَلِّيهَا ۞

292. Ziyad ibn Ayyub al-Baghdadi narrated to us, 'Muhammad ibn Rabi'a narrated to us on the authority of Fudayl ibn Marzuq, on the authority of 'Atiyya, on the authority of Abu Sa'id al-Khudri رضي الله عنه, who reported:

"The Prophet ﷺ would offer the Forenoon Prayer (*Duha*) so often that we would say he never leaves it, and he would leave the Forenoon Prayer (*Duha*) for so long that we would say he never offers it."'[669]

٢٩٣ - حَدَّثَنَا أَحْمَدُ بْنُ مَنِيعٍ ۞ عَنْ هُشَيْمٍ ۞ أَنْبَأَنَا عُبَيْدَةُ وَهُوَ ابْنُ مُعَتِّبٍ ۞ عَنْ إِبْرَاهِيمَ ۞ عَنْ سَهْمِ بْنِ مِنْجَابٍ ۞ عَنْ قَرْثَعٍ الضَّبِّيِّ أَوْ عَنْ قَزَعَةَ ۞ عَنْ قَرْثَعٍ ۞ عَنْ أَبِي أَيُّوبَ الْأَنْصَارِيِّ رَضِيَ اللهُ عَنْهُ أَنَّ النَّبِيَّ ﷺ كَانَ يُدْمِنُ أَرْبَعَ رَكَعَاتٍ عِنْدَ زَوَالِ الشَّمْسِ ۞ فَقُلْتُ يَا رَسُولَ اللهِ إِنَّكَ تُدْمِنُ هٰذِهِ الْأَرْبَعَ رَكَعَاتٍ عِنْدَ زَوَالِ الشَّمْسِ ۞ فَقَالَ إِنَّ أَبْوَابَ السَّمَاءِ تُفْتَحُ عِنْدَ زَوَالِ الشَّمْسِ ۞ فَلَا تُرْتَجُ حَتَّىٰ يُصَلَّى الظُّهْرُ ۞ فَأُحِبُّ أَنْ يَصْعَدَ لِي فِي تِلْكَ السَّاعَةِ خَيْرٌ ۞ قُلْتُ أَفِي كُلِّهِنَّ قِرَاءَةٌ ۞ قَالَ نَعَمْ ۞ قُلْتُ هَلْ فِيهِنَّ تَسْلِيمٌ فَاصِلٌ ۞ قَالَ لَا ۞

[668] In one narration, Sayyida 'A'isha رضي الله عنها stated that the Prophet ﷺ did not offer the Forenoon Prayer at all, but she said that she offered it. In this particular hadith, 'A'isha said that the Prophet ﷺ did not offer the Forenoon Prayer except when returning from travels. In a third narration, she said that he did offer it, and mentioned the number of units that he would offer. Imams al-Nawawi and al-Bayhaqi have said that these hadith reports can all be reconciled to show that the Prophet ﷺ did not offer the Forenoon Prayer regularly because he feared that it would become an obligation upon his *Umma*, thus causing hardship for them. We find an example of this concern in another hadith from 'A'isha رضي الله عنها, who said, 'The Messenger of Allah ﷺ would not (continuously) perform an act of worship that he loved to perform out of fear that people would follow him and it would therefore be seen as obligatory.' (Imam Malik, al-Muwatta') (MA)

[669] After the Prophet ﷺ left this world, the Companions would offer the Forenoon Prayer for a certain period of time and then miss it for a period of time, lest people mistakenly deem it an obligation. (MA)

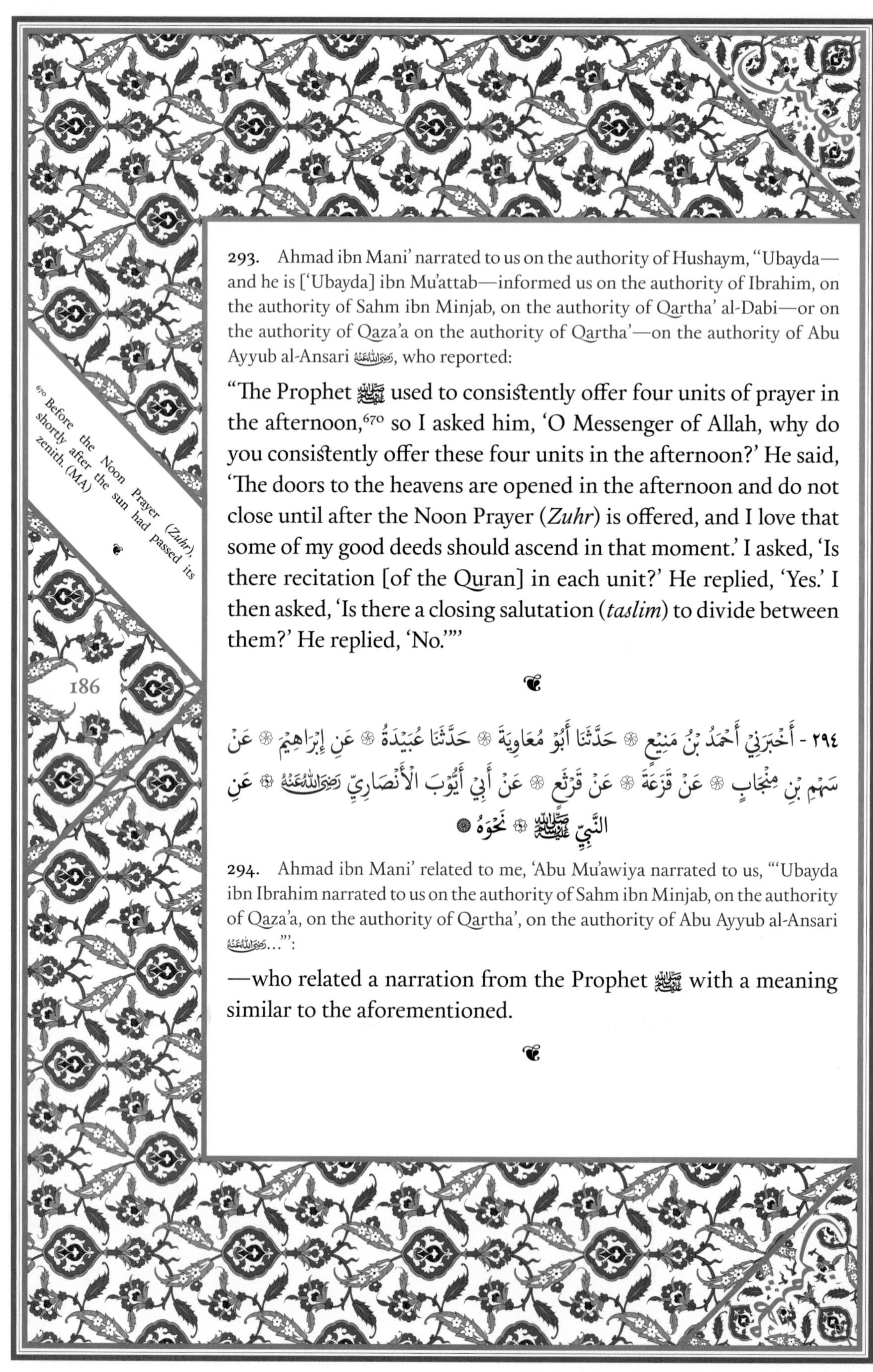

293. Ahmad ibn Mani' narrated to us on the authority of Hushaym, "Ubayda—and he is ['Ubayda] ibn Mu'attab—informed us on the authority of Ibrahim, on the authority of Sahm ibn Minjab, on the authority of Qartha' al-Dabi—or on the authority of Qaza'a on the authority of Qartha'—on the authority of Abu Ayyub al-Ansari رضي الله عنه, who reported:

"The Prophet ﷺ used to consistently offer four units of prayer in the afternoon,[670] so I asked him, 'O Messenger of Allah, why do you consistently offer these four units in the afternoon?' He said, 'The doors to the heavens are opened in the afternoon and do not close until after the Noon Prayer (*Zuhr*) is offered, and I love that some of my good deeds should ascend in that moment.' I asked, 'Is there recitation [of the Quran] in each unit?' He replied, 'Yes.' I then asked, 'Is there a closing salutation (*taslim*) to divide between them?' He replied, 'No.'"

٢٩٤ - أَخْبَرَنِي أَحْمَدُ بْنُ مَنِيعٍ ۞ حَدَّثَنَا أَبُو مُعَاوِيَةَ ۞ حَدَّثَنَا عُبَيْدَةُ ۞ عَنْ إِبْرَاهِيمَ ۞ عَنْ سَهْمِ بْنِ مِنْجَابٍ ۞ عَنْ قَزَعَةَ ۞ عَنْ قَرْثَعٍ ۞ عَنْ أَبِي أَيُّوبَ الأَنْصَارِيِّ رَضِيَ اللهُ عَنْهُ ۞ عَنِ النَّبِيِّ ﷺ ۞ نَحْوَهُ ۞

294. Ahmad ibn Mani' related to me, 'Abu Mu'awiya narrated to us, "'Ubayda ibn Ibrahim narrated to us on the authority of Sahm ibn Minjab, on the authority of Qaza'a, on the authority of Qartha', on the authority of Abu Ayyub al-Ansari رضي الله عنه..."':

—who related a narration from the Prophet ﷺ with a meaning similar to the aforementioned.

[670] Before the Noon Prayer (*Zuhr*), shortly after the sun had passed its zenith. (MA)

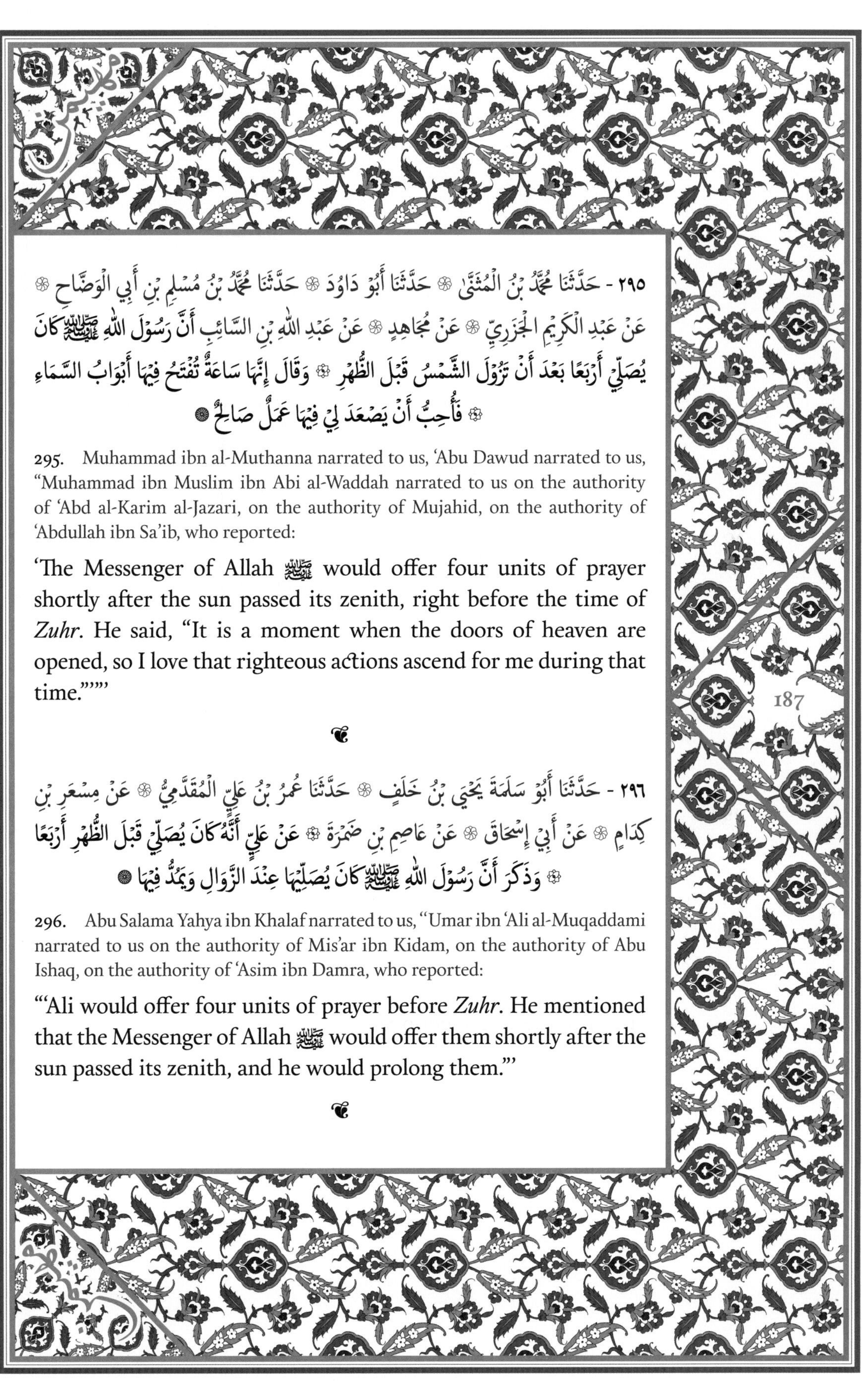

٢٩٥ - حَدَّثَنَا مُحَمَّدُ بْنُ الْمُثَنَّى ۞ حَدَّثَنَا أَبُو دَاوُدَ ۞ حَدَّثَنَا مُحَمَّدُ بْنُ مُسْلِمِ بْنِ أَبِي الْوَضَّاحِ ۞ عَنْ عَبْدِ الْكَرِيمِ الْجَزَرِيِّ ۞ عَنْ مُجَاهِدٍ ۞ عَنْ عَبْدِ اللهِ بْنِ السَّائِبِ أَنَّ رَسُولَ اللهِ ﷺ كَانَ يُصَلِّي أَرْبَعًا بَعْدَ أَنْ تَزُولَ الشَّمْسُ قَبْلَ الظُّهْرِ ۞ وَقَالَ إِنَّهَا سَاعَةٌ تُفْتَحُ فِيهَا أَبْوَابُ السَّمَاءِ ۞ فَأُحِبُّ أَنْ يَصْعَدَ لِي فِيهَا عَمَلٌ صَالِحٌ ۞

295. Muhammad ibn al-Muthanna narrated to us, 'Abu Dawud narrated to us, "Muhammad ibn Muslim ibn Abi al-Waddah narrated to us on the authority of 'Abd al-Karim al-Jazari, on the authority of Mujahid, on the authority of 'Abdullah ibn Sa'ib, who reported:

'The Messenger of Allah ﷺ would offer four units of prayer shortly after the sun passed its zenith, right before the time of *Zuhr*. He said, "It is a moment when the doors of heaven are opened, so I love that righteous actions ascend for me during that time."'"'

٢٩٦ - حَدَّثَنَا أَبُو سَلَمَةَ يَحْيَى بْنُ خَلَفٍ ۞ حَدَّثَنَا عُمَرُ بْنُ عَلِيٍّ الْمُقَدَّمِيُّ ۞ عَنْ مِسْعَرِ بْنِ كِدَامٍ ۞ عَنْ أَبِي إِسْحَاقَ ۞ عَنْ عَاصِمِ بْنِ ضَمْرَةَ ۞ عَنْ عَلِيٍّ أَنَّهُ كَانَ يُصَلِّي قَبْلَ الظُّهْرِ أَرْبَعًا ۞ وَذَكَرَ أَنَّ رَسُولَ اللهِ ﷺ كَانَ يُصَلِّيهَا عِنْدَ الزَّوَالِ وَيَمُدُّ فِيهَا ۞

296. Abu Salama Yahya ibn Khalaf narrated to us, "Umar ibn 'Ali al-Muqaddami narrated to us on the authority of Mis'ar ibn Kidam, on the authority of Abu Ishaq, on the authority of 'Asim ibn Damra, who reported:

"'Ali would offer four units of prayer before *Zuhr*. He mentioned that the Messenger of Allah ﷺ would offer them shortly after the sun passed its zenith, and he would prolong them."'

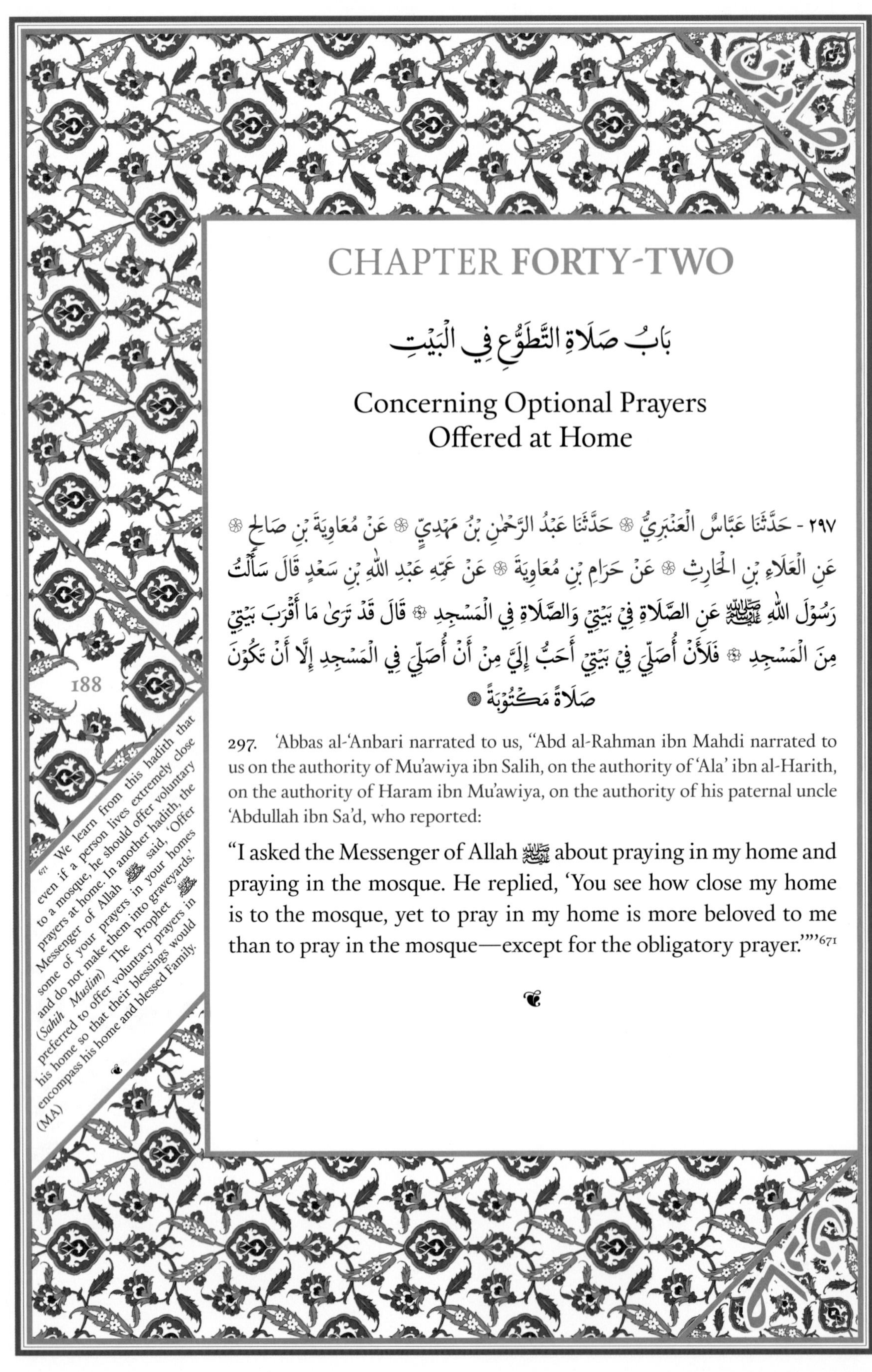

CHAPTER FORTY-TWO

بَابُ صَلَاةِ التَّطَوُّعِ فِي الْبَيْتِ

Concerning Optional Prayers Offered at Home

٢٩٧ - حَدَّثَنَا عَبَّاسٌ الْعَنْبَرِيُّ ۞ حَدَّثَنَا عَبْدُ الرَّحْمٰنِ بْنُ مَهْدِيٍّ ۞ عَنْ مُعَاوِيَةَ بْنِ صَالِحٍ ۞ عَنِ الْعَلَاءِ بْنِ الْحَارِثِ ۞ عَنْ حَرَامِ بْنِ مُعَاوِيَةَ ۞ عَنْ عَمِّهِ عَبْدِ اللهِ بْنِ سَعْدٍ قَالَ سَأَلْتُ رَسُولَ اللهِ ﷺ عَنِ الصَّلَاةِ فِي بَيْتِي وَالصَّلَاةِ فِي الْمَسْجِدِ ۞ قَالَ قَدْ تَرَىٰ مَا أَقْرَبَ بَيْتِي مِنَ الْمَسْجِدِ ۞ فَلَأَنْ أُصَلِّيَ فِي بَيْتِي أَحَبُّ إِلَيَّ مِنْ أَنْ أُصَلِّيَ فِي الْمَسْجِدِ إِلَّا أَنْ تَكُونَ صَلَاةً مَكْتُوبَةً ۞

297. ʿAbbas al-ʿAnbari narrated to us, "ʿAbd al-Rahman ibn Mahdi narrated to us on the authority of Mu'awiya ibn Salih, on the authority of ʿAla' ibn al-Harith, on the authority of Haram ibn Mu'awiya, on the authority of his paternal uncle ʿAbdullah ibn Sa'd, who reported:

"I asked the Messenger of Allah ﷺ about praying in my home and praying in the mosque. He replied, 'You see how close my home is to the mosque, yet to pray in my home is more beloved to me than to pray in the mosque—except for the obligatory prayer.'"[671]

[671] We learn from this hadith that even if a person lives extremely close to a mosque, he should offer voluntary prayers at home. In another hadith, the Messenger of Allah ﷺ said, 'Offer some of your prayers in your homes and do not make them into graveyards.' (*Sahih Muslim*) The Prophet ﷺ preferred to offer voluntary prayers in his home so that their blessings would encompass his home and blessed Family. (MA)

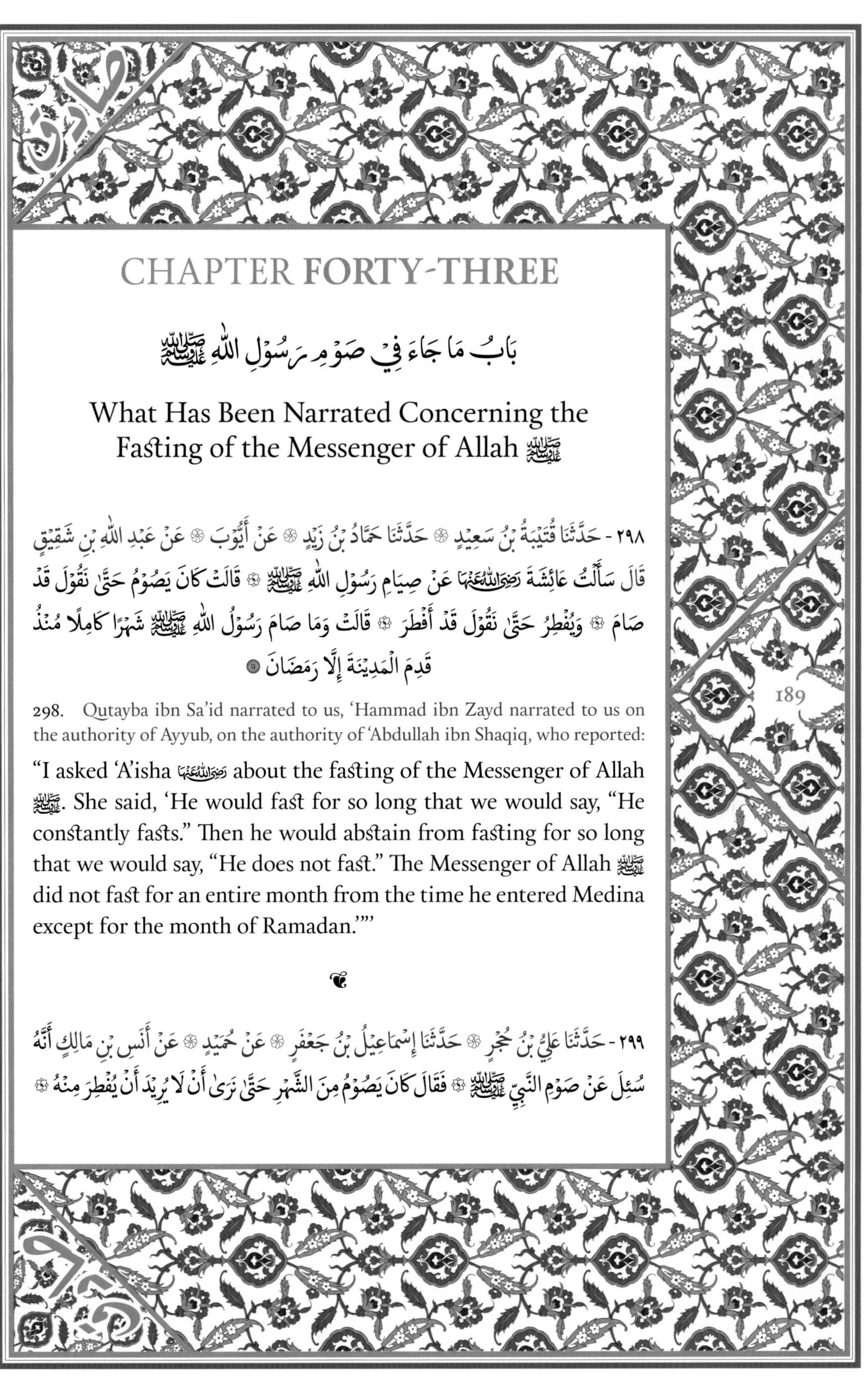

CHAPTER FORTY-THREE

بَابُ مَا جَاءَ فِي صَوْمِ رَسُولِ اللهِ ﷺ

What Has Been Narrated Concerning the Fasting of the Messenger of Allah ﷺ

٢٩٨ - حَدَّثَنَا قُتَيْبَةُ بْنُ سَعِيدٍ ❁ حَدَّثَنَا حَمَّادُ بْنُ زَيْدٍ ❁ عَنْ أَيُّوبَ ❁ عَنْ عَبْدِ اللهِ بْنِ شَقِيقٍ قَالَ سَأَلْتُ عَائِشَةَ رَضِيَ اللهُ عَنْهَا عَنْ صِيَامِ رَسُولِ اللهِ ﷺ ❁ قَالَتْ كَانَ يَصُومُ حَتَّىٰ نَقُولَ قَدْ صَامَ ❁ وَيُفْطِرُ حَتَّىٰ نَقُولَ قَدْ أَفْطَرَ ❁ قَالَتْ وَمَا صَامَ رَسُولُ اللهِ ﷺ شَهْرًا كَامِلًا مُنْذُ قَدِمَ الْمَدِينَةَ إِلَّا رَمَضَانَ ۝

298. Qutayba ibn Sa'id narrated to us, 'Hammad ibn Zayd narrated to us on the authority of Ayyub, on the authority of 'Abdullah ibn Shaqiq, who reported:

"I asked 'A'isha رضي الله عنها about the fasting of the Messenger of Allah ﷺ. She said, 'He would fast for so long that we would say, "He constantly fasts." Then he would abstain from fasting for so long that we would say, "He does not fast." The Messenger of Allah ﷺ did not fast for an entire month from the time he entered Medina except for the month of Ramadan.'"

٢٩٩ - حَدَّثَنَا عَلِيُّ بْنُ حُجْرٍ ❁ حَدَّثَنَا إِسْمَاعِيلُ بْنُ جَعْفَرٍ ❁ عَنْ حُمَيْدٍ ❁ عَنْ أَنَسِ بْنِ مَالِكٍ أَنَّهُ سُئِلَ عَنْ صَوْمِ النَّبِيِّ ﷺ ❁ فَقَالَ كَانَ يَصُومُ مِنَ الشَّهْرِ حَتَّىٰ نَرَىٰ أَنْ لَا يُرِيدَ أَنْ يُفْطِرَ مِنْهُ ❁

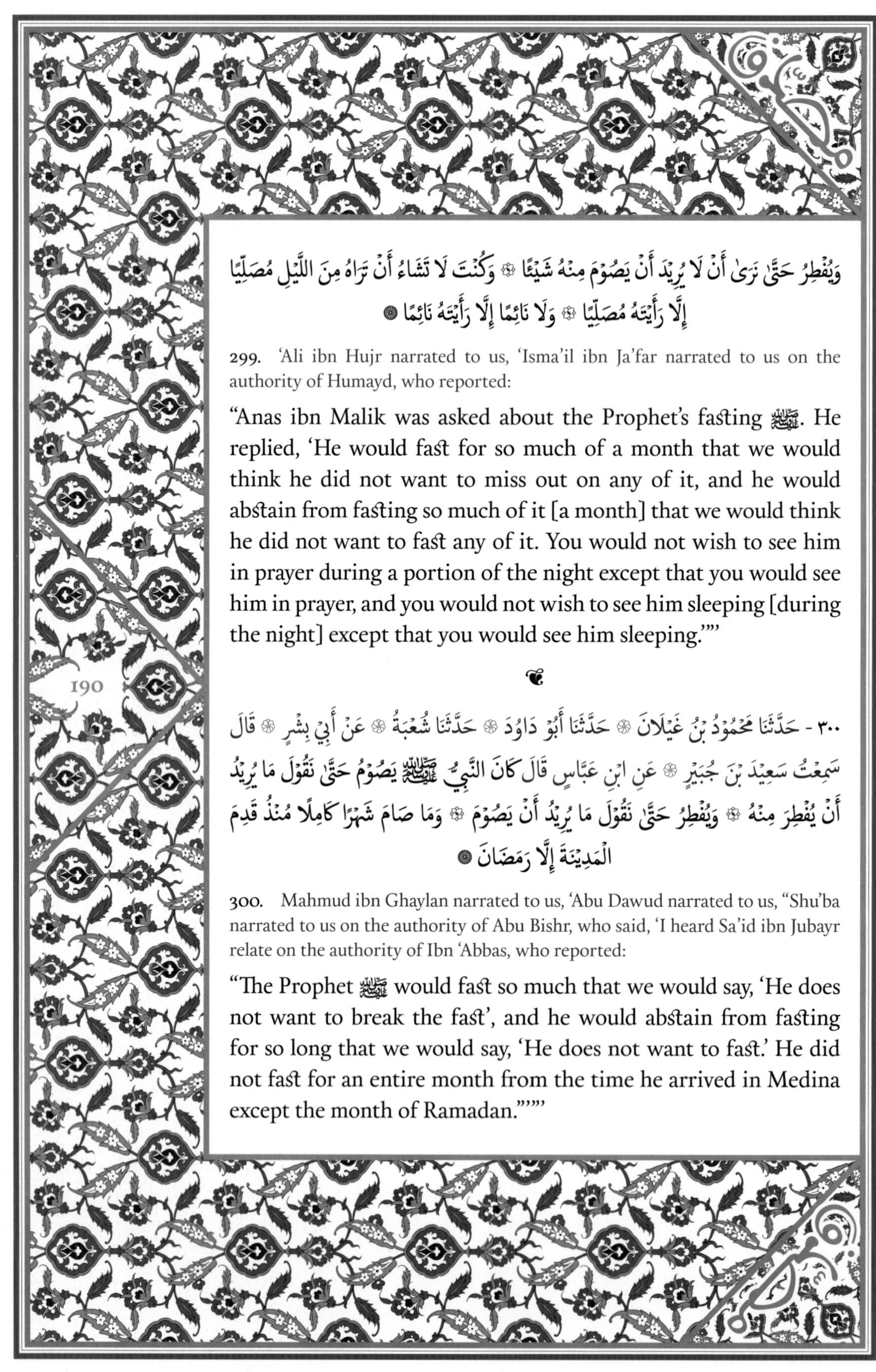

وَيُفْطِرُ حَتَّىٰ نَرَىٰ أَنْ لَا يُرِيدَ أَنْ يَصُومَ مِنْهُ شَيْئًا ۞ وَكُنْتَ لَا تَشَاءُ أَنْ تَرَاهُ مِنَ اللَّيْلِ مُصَلِّيًا إِلَّا رَأَيْتَهُ مُصَلِّيًا ۞ وَلَا نَائِمًا إِلَّا رَأَيْتَهُ نَائِمًا ۞

299. 'Ali ibn Hujr narrated to us, 'Isma'il ibn Ja'far narrated to us on the authority of Humayd, who reported:

"Anas ibn Malik was asked about the Prophet's fasting ﷺ. He replied, 'He would fast for so much of a month that we would think he did not want to miss out on any of it, and he would abstain from fasting so much of it [a month] that we would think he did not want to fast any of it. You would not wish to see him in prayer during a portion of the night except that you would see him in prayer, and you would not wish to see him sleeping [during the night] except that you would see him sleeping.'"

٣٠٠ - حَدَّثَنَا مَحْمُودُ بْنُ غَيْلَانَ ۞ حَدَّثَنَا أَبُو دَاوُدَ ۞ حَدَّثَنَا شُعْبَةُ ۞ عَنْ أَبِي بِشْرٍ ۞ قَالَ سَمِعْتُ سَعِيدَ بْنَ جُبَيْرٍ ۞ عَنِ ابْنِ عَبَّاسٍ قَالَ كَانَ النَّبِيُّ ﷺ يَصُومُ حَتَّىٰ نَقُولَ مَا يُرِيدُ أَنْ يُفْطِرَ مِنْهُ ۞ وَيُفْطِرُ حَتَّىٰ نَقُولَ مَا يُرِيدُ أَنْ يَصُومَ ۞ وَمَا صَامَ شَهْرًا كَامِلًا مُنْذُ قَدِمَ الْمَدِينَةَ إِلَّا رَمَضَانَ ۞

300. Mahmud ibn Ghaylan narrated to us, 'Abu Dawud narrated to us, "Shu'ba narrated to us on the authority of Abu Bishr, who said, 'I heard Sa'id ibn Jubayr relate on the authority of Ibn 'Abbas, who reported:

"The Prophet ﷺ would fast so much that we would say, 'He does not want to break the fast', and he would abstain from fasting for so long that we would say, 'He does not want to fast.' He did not fast for an entire month from the time he arrived in Medina except the month of Ramadan.""""

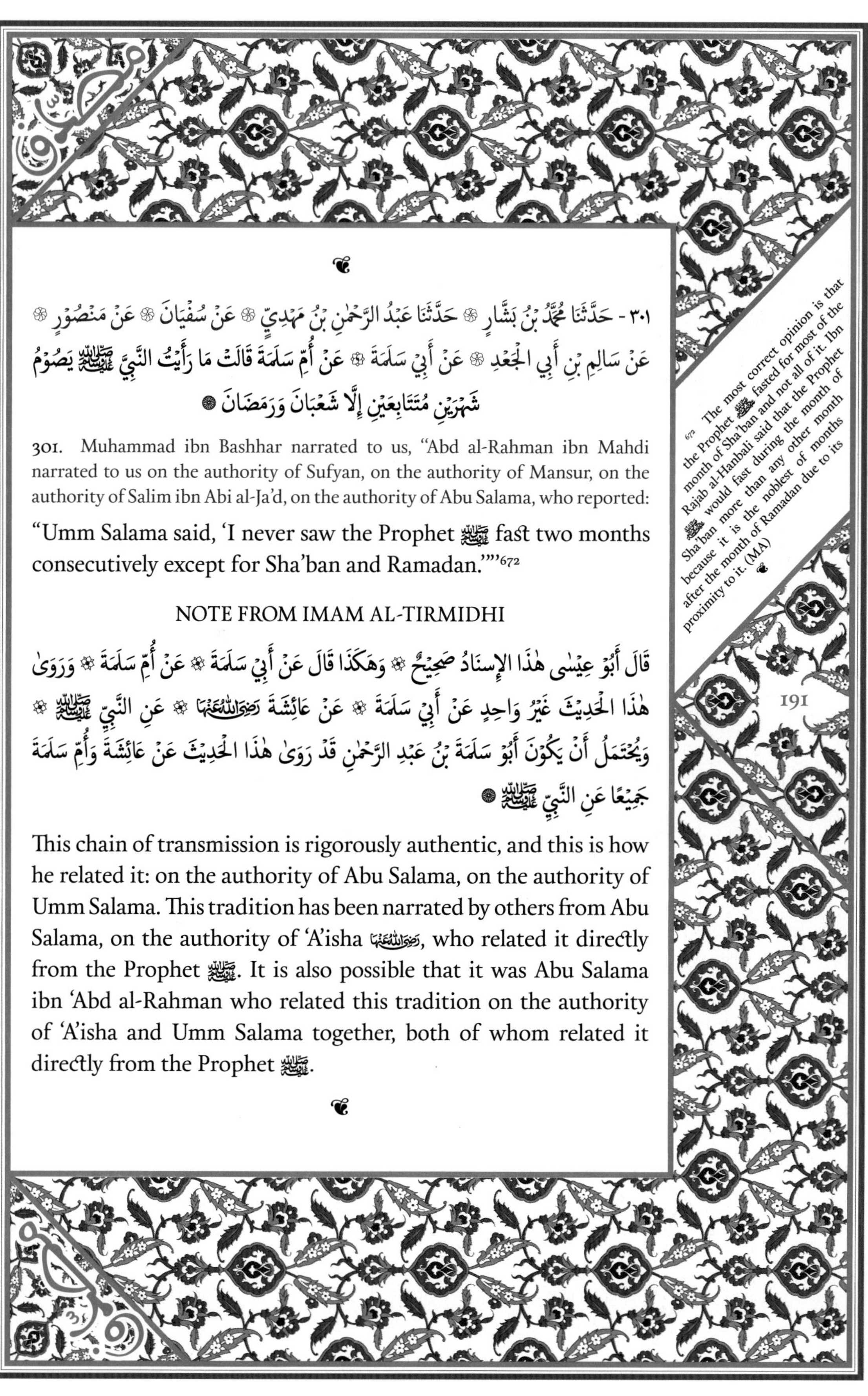

٣٠١ - حَدَّثَنَا مُحَمَّدُ بْنُ بَشَّارٍ ۞ حَدَّثَنَا عَبْدُ الرَّحْمٰنِ بْنُ مَهْدِيٍّ ۞ عَنْ سُفْيَانَ ۞ عَنْ مَنْصُورٍ ۞ عَنْ سَالِمِ بْنِ أَبِي الْجَعْدِ ۞ عَنْ أَبِي سَلَمَةَ ۞ عَنْ أُمِّ سَلَمَةَ قَالَتْ مَا رَأَيْتُ النَّبِيَّ ﷺ يَصُومُ شَهْرَيْنِ مُتَتَابِعَيْنِ إِلَّا شَعْبَانَ وَرَمَضَانَ ۞

301. Muhammad ibn Bashhar narrated to us, "Abd al-Rahman ibn Mahdi narrated to us on the authority of Sufyan, on the authority of Mansur, on the authority of Salim ibn Abi al-Ja'd, on the authority of Abu Salama, who reported:

"Umm Salama said, 'I never saw the Prophet ﷺ fast two months consecutively except for Sha'ban and Ramadan.'"[672]

NOTE FROM IMAM AL-TIRMIDHI

قَالَ أَبُو عِيسٰى هٰذَا الإِسْنَادُ صَحِيحٌ ۞ وَهٰكَذَا قَالَ عَنْ أَبِي سَلَمَةَ ۞ عَنْ أُمِّ سَلَمَةَ ۞ وَرَوٰى هٰذَا الْحَدِيثَ غَيْرُ وَاحِدٍ عَنْ أَبِي سَلَمَةَ ۞ عَنْ عَائِشَةَ رَضِيَ اللهُ عَنْهَا ۞ عَنِ النَّبِيِّ ﷺ ۞ وَيُحْتَمَلُ أَنْ يَكُونَ أَبُو سَلَمَةَ بْنُ عَبْدِ الرَّحْمٰنِ قَدْ رَوٰى هٰذَا الْحَدِيثَ عَنْ عَائِشَةَ وَأُمِّ سَلَمَةَ جَمِيعًا عَنِ النَّبِيِّ ﷺ ۞

This chain of transmission is rigorously authentic, and this is how he related it: on the authority of Abu Salama, on the authority of Umm Salama. This tradition has been narrated by others from Abu Salama, on the authority of 'A'isha رضي الله عنها, who related it directly from the Prophet ﷺ. It is also possible that it was Abu Salama ibn 'Abd al-Rahman who related this tradition on the authority of 'A'isha and Umm Salama together, both of whom related it directly from the Prophet ﷺ.

[672] The most correct opinion is that the Prophet ﷺ fasted for most of the month of Sha'ban and not all of it. Ibn Rajab al-Hanbali said that the Prophet ﷺ would fast during the month of Sha'ban more than any other month because it is the noblest of months after the month of Ramadan due to its proximity to it. (MA)

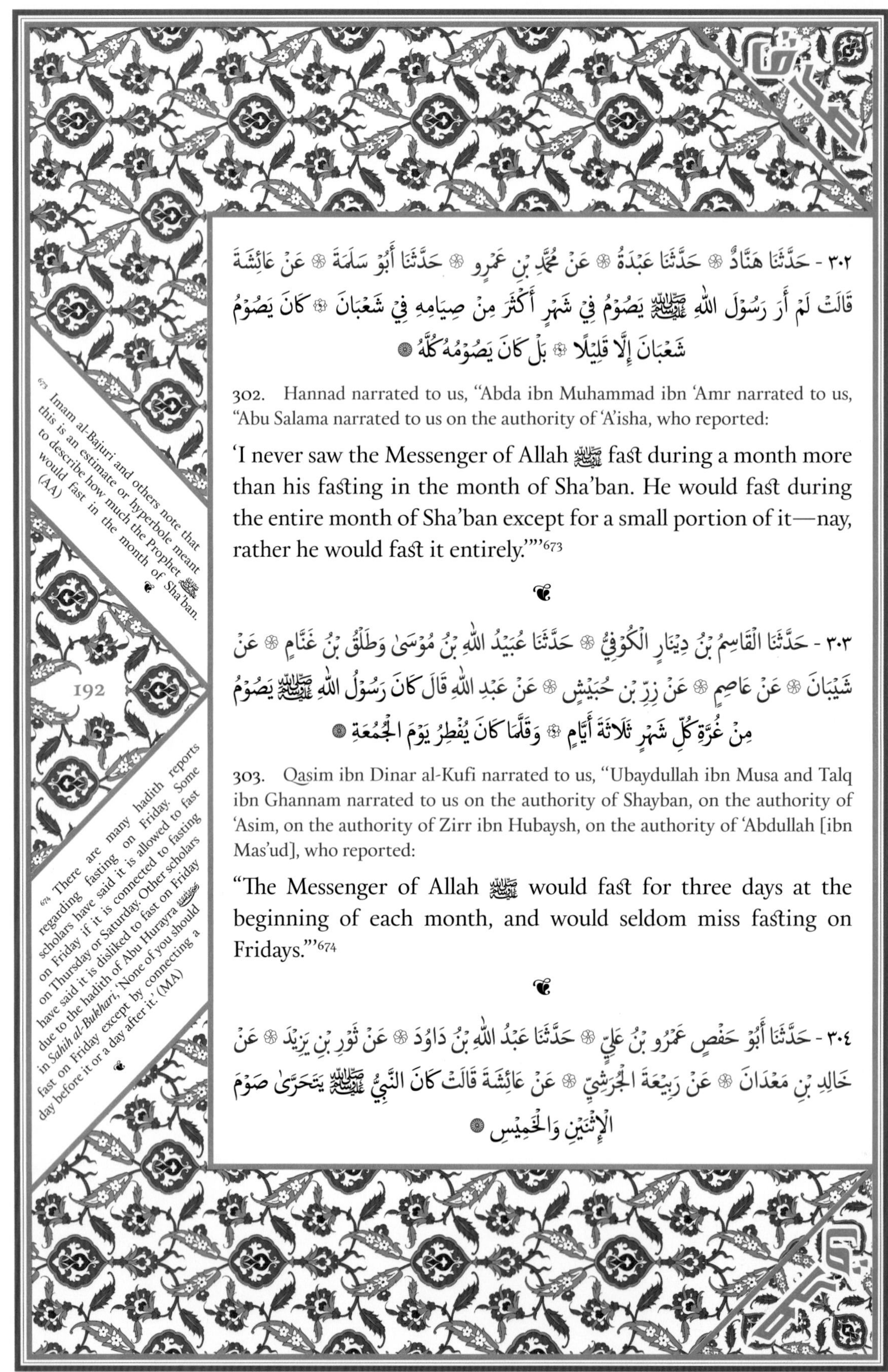

٣٠٢ - حَدَّثَنَا هَنَّادٌ ۞ حَدَّثَنَا عَبْدَةُ ۞ عَنْ مُحَمَّدِ بْنِ عَمْرٍو ۞ حَدَّثَنَا أَبُو سَلَمَةَ ۞ عَنْ عَائِشَةَ قَالَتْ لَمْ أَرَ رَسُولَ اللهِ ﷺ يَصُومُ فِي شَهْرٍ أَكْثَرَ مِنْ صِيَامِهِ فِي شَعْبَانَ ۞ كَانَ يَصُومُ شَعْبَانَ إِلَّا قَلِيلًا ۞ بَلْ كَانَ يَصُومُهُ كُلَّهُ ۞

302. Hannad narrated to us, "Abda ibn Muhammad ibn 'Amr narrated to us, "Abu Salama narrated to us on the authority of 'A'isha, who reported:

'I never saw the Messenger of Allah ﷺ fast during a month more than his fasting in the month of Sha'ban. He would fast during the entire month of Sha'ban except for a small portion of it—nay, rather he would fast it entirely.'''[673]

❦

٣٠٣ - حَدَّثَنَا الْقَاسِمُ بْنُ دِينَارٍ الْكُوفِيُّ ۞ حَدَّثَنَا عُبَيْدُ اللهِ بْنُ مُوسَى وَطَلْقُ بْنُ غَنَّامٍ ۞ عَنْ شَيْبَانَ ۞ عَنْ عَاصِمٍ ۞ عَنْ زِرِّ بْنِ حُبَيْشٍ ۞ عَنْ عَبْدِ اللهِ قَالَ كَانَ رَسُولُ اللهِ ﷺ يَصُومُ مِنْ غُرَّةِ كُلِّ شَهْرٍ ثَلَاثَةَ أَيَّامٍ ۞ وَقَلَّمَا كَانَ يُفْطِرُ يَوْمَ الْجُمُعَةِ ۞

303. Qasim ibn Dinar al-Kufi narrated to us, "Ubaydullah ibn Musa and Talq ibn Ghannam narrated to us on the authority of Shayban, on the authority of 'Asim, on the authority of Zirr ibn Hubaysh, on the authority of 'Abdullah [ibn Mas'ud], who reported:

"The Messenger of Allah ﷺ would fast for three days at the beginning of each month, and would seldom miss fasting on Fridays."'[674]

❦

٣٠٤ - حَدَّثَنَا أَبُو حَفْصٍ عَمْرُو بْنُ عَلِيٍّ ۞ حَدَّثَنَا عَبْدُ اللهِ بْنُ دَاوُدَ ۞ عَنْ ثَوْرِ بْنِ يَزِيدَ ۞ عَنْ خَالِدِ بْنِ مَعْدَانَ ۞ عَنْ رَبِيعَةَ الْجُرَشِيِّ ۞ عَنْ عَائِشَةَ قَالَتْ كَانَ النَّبِيُّ ﷺ يَتَحَرَّى صَوْمَ الْإِثْنَيْنِ وَالْخَمِيسِ ۞

[673] Imam al-Bajuri and others note that this is an estimate or hyperbole meant to describe how much the Prophet ﷺ would fast in the month of Sha'ban. (AA)

[674] There are many hadith reports regarding fasting on Friday. Some scholars have said it is allowed to fast on Friday if it is connected to fasting on Thursday or Saturday. Other scholars have said it is disliked to fast on Friday due to the hadith of Abu Hurayra ؓ in *Sahih al-Bukhari*, 'None of you should fast on Friday except by connecting a day before it or a day after it.' (MA)

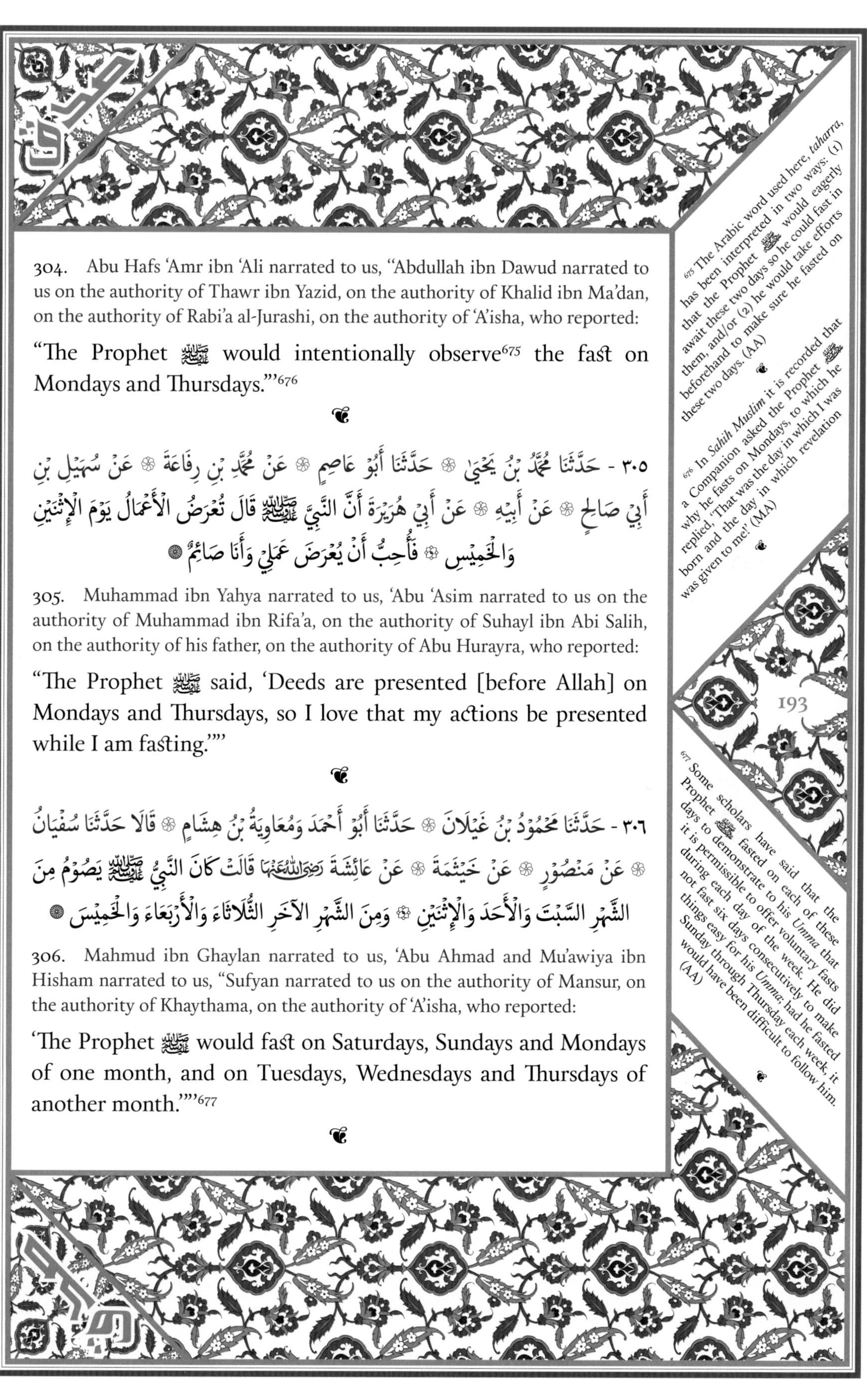

304. Abu Hafs 'Amr ibn 'Ali narrated to us, "Abdullah ibn Dawud narrated to us on the authority of Thawr ibn Yazid, on the authority of Khalid ibn Ma'dan, on the authority of Rabi'a al-Jurashi, on the authority of 'A'isha, who reported:

"The Prophet ﷺ would intentionally observe[675] the fast on Mondays and Thursdays."'[676]

❦

٣٠٥ - حَدَّثَنَا مُحَمَّدُ بْنُ يَحْيَىٰ ۞ حَدَّثَنَا أَبُو عَاصِمٍ ۞ عَنْ مُحَمَّدِ بْنِ رِفَاعَةَ ۞ عَنْ سُهَيْلِ بْنِ أَبِي صَالِحٍ ۞ عَنْ أَبِيهِ ۞ عَنْ أَبِي هُرَيْرَةَ أَنَّ النَّبِيَّ ﷺ قَالَ تُعْرَضُ الْأَعْمَالُ يَوْمَ الْإِثْنَيْنِ وَالْخَمِيسِ ۞ فَأُحِبُّ أَنْ يُعْرَضَ عَمَلِي وَأَنَا صَائِمٌ ۞

305. Muhammad ibn Yahya narrated to us, 'Abu 'Asim narrated to us on the authority of Muhammad ibn Rifa'a, on the authority of Suhayl ibn Abi Salih, on the authority of his father, on the authority of Abu Hurayra, who reported:

"The Prophet ﷺ said, 'Deeds are presented [before Allah] on Mondays and Thursdays, so I love that my actions be presented while I am fasting.'"'

❦

٣٠٦ - حَدَّثَنَا مَحْمُودُ بْنُ غَيْلَانَ ۞ حَدَّثَنَا أَبُو أَحْمَدَ وَمُعَاوِيَةُ بْنُ هِشَامٍ ۞ قَالَا حَدَّثَنَا سُفْيَانُ ۞ عَنْ مَنْصُورٍ ۞ عَنْ خَيْثَمَةَ ۞ عَنْ عَائِشَةَ رَضِيَ اللهُ عَنْهَا قَالَتْ كَانَ النَّبِيُّ ﷺ يَصُومُ مِنَ الشَّهْرِ السَّبْتَ وَالْأَحَدَ وَالْإِثْنَيْنِ ۞ وَمِنَ الشَّهْرِ الْآخَرِ الثُّلَاثَاءَ وَالْأَرْبَعَاءَ وَالْخَمِيسَ ۞

306. Mahmud ibn Ghaylan narrated to us, 'Abu Ahmad and Mu'awiya ibn Hisham narrated to us, "Sufyan narrated to us on the authority of Mansur, on the authority of Khaythama, on the authority of 'A'isha, who reported:

'The Prophet ﷺ would fast on Saturdays, Sundays and Mondays of one month, and on Tuesdays, Wednesdays and Thursdays of another month.'"'[677]

❦

[675] The Arabic word used here, *taharra*, has been interpreted in two ways: (1) that the Prophet ﷺ would eagerly await these two days so he could fast in them, and/or (2) he would take efforts beforehand to make sure he fasted on these two days. (AA)

❦

[676] In *Sahih Muslim* it is recorded that a Companion asked the Prophet ﷺ why he fasts on Mondays, to which he replied, 'That was the day in which I was born and the day in which revelation was given to me!' (MA)

❦

[677] Some scholars have said that the Prophet ﷺ fasted on each of these days to demonstrate to his *Umma* that it is permissible to offer voluntary fasts during each day of the week. He did not fast six days consecutively to make things easy for his *Umma*; had he fasted Sunday through Thursday each week, it would have been difficult to follow him. (AA)

❦

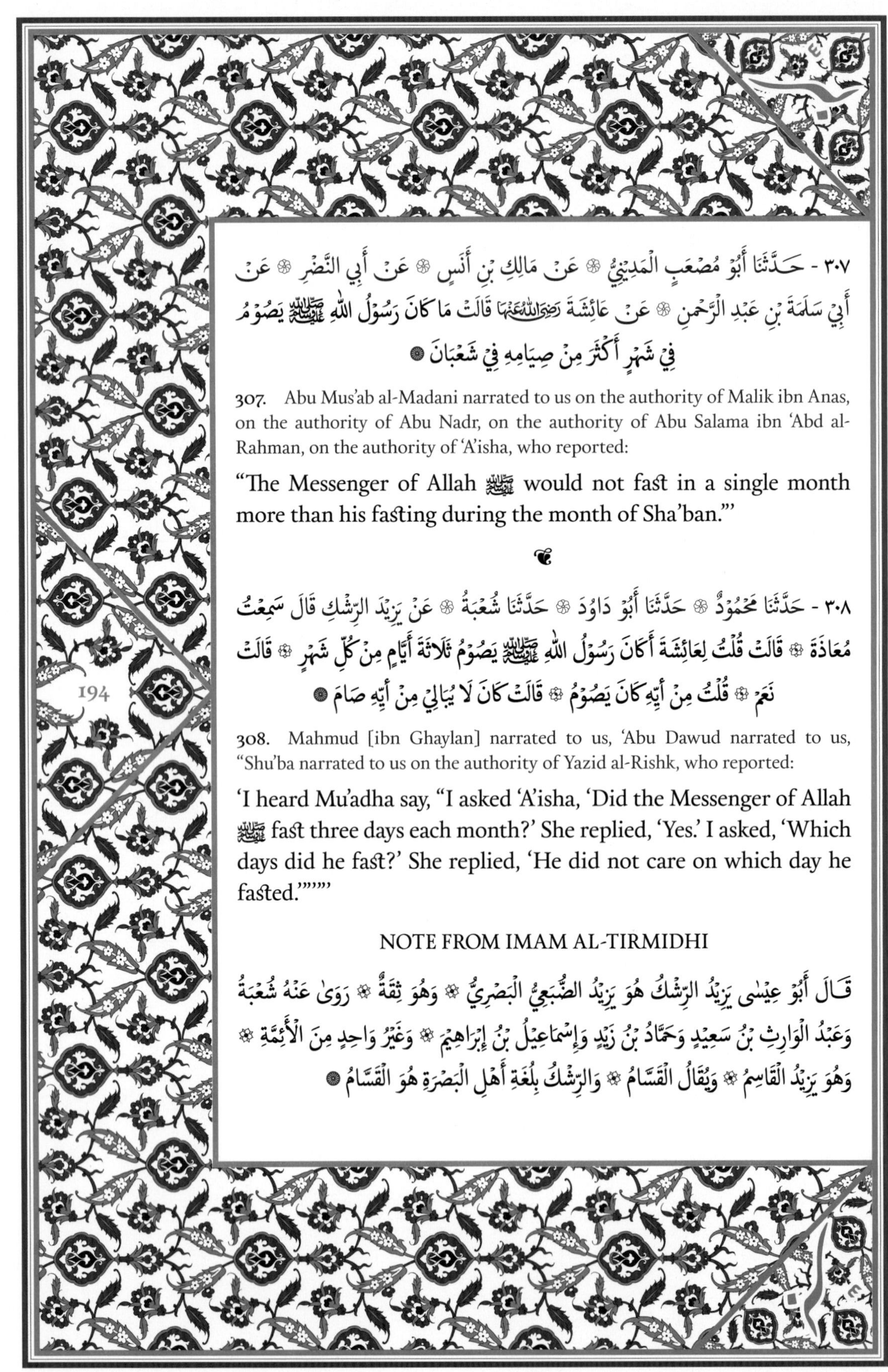

٣٠٧ - حَدَّثَنَا أَبُو مُصْعَبٍ الْمَدِينِيُّ ۞ عَنْ مَالِكِ بْنِ أَنَسٍ ۞ عَنْ أَبِي النَّضْرِ ۞ عَنْ أَبِي سَلَمَةَ بْنِ عَبْدِ الرَّحْمٰنِ ۞ عَنْ عَائِشَةَ رَضِيَ اللهُ عَنْهَا قَالَتْ مَا كَانَ رَسُولُ اللهِ ﷺ يَصُومُ فِي شَهْرٍ أَكْثَرَ مِنْ صِيَامِهِ فِي شَعْبَانَ ۞

307. Abu Mus'ab al-Madani narrated to us on the authority of Malik ibn Anas, on the authority of Abu Nadr, on the authority of Abu Salama ibn 'Abd al-Rahman, on the authority of 'A'isha, who reported:

"The Messenger of Allah ﷺ would not fast in a single month more than his fasting during the month of Sha'ban."'

❦

٣٠٨ - حَدَّثَنَا مَحْمُودٌ ۞ حَدَّثَنَا أَبُو دَاوُدَ ۞ حَدَّثَنَا شُعْبَةُ ۞ عَنْ يَزِيدَ الرِّشْكِ قَالَ سَمِعْتُ مُعَاذَةَ ۞ قَالَتْ قُلْتُ لِعَائِشَةَ أَكَانَ رَسُولُ اللهِ ﷺ يَصُومُ ثَلَاثَةَ أَيَّامٍ مِنْ كُلِّ شَهْرٍ ۞ قَالَتْ نَعَمْ ۞ قُلْتُ مِنْ أَيِّهِ كَانَ يَصُومُ ۞ قَالَتْ كَانَ لَا يُبَالِي مِنْ أَيِّهِ صَامَ ۞

308. Mahmud [ibn Ghaylan] narrated to us, 'Abu Dawud narrated to us, "Shu'ba narrated to us on the authority of Yazid al-Rishk, who reported:

'I heard Mu'adha say, "I asked 'A'isha, 'Did the Messenger of Allah ﷺ fast three days each month?' She replied, 'Yes.' I asked, 'Which days did he fast?' She replied, 'He did not care on which day he fasted.'"'"'

NOTE FROM IMAM AL-TIRMIDHI

قَالَ أَبُو عِيسَى يَزِيدُ الرِّشْكُ هُوَ يَزِيدُ الضُّبَعِيُّ الْبَصْرِيُّ ۞ وَهُوَ ثِقَةٌ ۞ رَوَى عَنْهُ شُعْبَةُ وَعَبْدُ الْوَارِثِ بْنُ سَعِيدٍ وَحَمَّادُ بْنُ زَيْدٍ وَإِسْمَاعِيلُ بْنُ إِبْرَاهِيمَ ۞ وَغَيْرُ وَاحِدٍ مِنَ الْأَئِمَّةِ ۞ وَهُوَ يَزِيدُ الْقَاسِمُ ۞ وَيُقَالُ الْقَسَّامُ ۞ وَالرِّشْكُ بِلُغَةِ أَهْلِ الْبَصْرَةِ هُوَ الْقَسَّامُ ۞

Yazid al-Rishk is Yazid al-Duba'i al-Basri, and he is a narrator of probity and precision (*thiqa*). Shu'ba, 'Abd al-Warith ibn Sa'id, Hammad ibn Zayd, Isma'il ibn Ibrahim and other Imams all narrated on his authority. He is [also called] Yazid al-Qasim, or al-Qassam, and in the dialect of the people of Basra, the word Rishk means Qassam.[678]

❦

٣٠٩ - حَدَّثَنَا هَارُونُ بْنُ إِسْحَاقَ الْهَمْدَانِيُّ ۞ حَدَّثَنَا عَبْدَةُ بْنُ سُلَيْمَانَ ۞ عَنْ هِشَامِ بْنِ عُرْوَةَ ۞ عَنْ أَبِيهِ ۞ عَنْ عَائِشَةَ قَالَتْ كَانَ عَاشُورَاءُ يَوْمًا تَصُومُهُ قُرَيْشٌ فِي الْجَاهِلِيَّةِ ۞ وَكَانَ رَسُولُ اللهِ ﷺ يَصُومُهُ ۞ فَلَمَّا قَدِمَ الْمَدِينَةَ صَامَهُ وَأَمَرَ بِصِيَامِهِ ۞ فَلَمَّا افْتُرِضَ رَمَضَانُ كَانَ رَمَضَانُ هُوَ الْفَرِيضَةَ ۞ وَتُرِكَ عَاشُورَاءُ ۞ فَمَنْ شَاءَ صَامَهُ وَمَنْ شَاءَ تَرَكَهُ ۞

309. Harun ibn Ishaq al-Hamdani narrated to us, "Abda ibn Sulayman narrated to us on the authority of Hisham ibn 'Urwa, on the authority of his father, on the authority of 'A'isha, who reported:

"''Ashura' was a day that the tribe of Quraysh would fast during the period of ignorance (*jahiliyya*), and the Messenger of Allah ﷺ would fast during it, too.[679] When he entered Medina[680] he would fast during it [the day of 'Ashura'][681] and order [others] to fast during it as well. When [fasting in] Ramadan was made compulsory, it became the obligatory fast, and fasting on 'Ashura' was left, so now whosoever wants can fast during it, and whosoever wants can leave it.'"

❦

٣١٠ - حَدَّثَنَا مُحَمَّدُ بْنُ بَشَّارٍ ۞ حَدَّثَنَا عَبْدُ الرَّحْمٰنِ بْنُ مَهْدِيٍّ ۞ حَدَّثَنَا سُفْيَانُ ۞ عَنْ مَنْصُورٍ ۞ عَنْ إِبْرَاهِيمَ ۞ عَنْ عَلْقَمَةَ قَالَ سَأَلْتُ عَائِشَةَ رَضِيَ اللهُ عَنْهَا أَكَانَ رَسُولُ اللهِ ﷺ يَخُصُّ مِنَ الْأَيَّامِ شَيْئًا ۞ قَالَتْ كَانَ عَمَلُهُ دِيمَةً ۞ وَأَيُّكُمْ يُطِيقُ مَا كَانَ رَسُولُ اللهِ ﷺ يُطِيقُ ۞

678 The meaning of Qassam is distributor. The reason he was given this name was because he was skilled in distributing land between business partners and estate heirs. (MA)

679 'Ashura' is the tenth day of the sacred lunar month of Muharram. Allah says in the Qur'an, *Verily the number of months in the sight of Allah is twelve months [ordained] in the Book of Allah, the day He created the heavens and the earth. Of them, four are sacred. That is the upright way, so wrong not yourselves during them...* (Qur'an 9:36) Abu Bakr related that the Prophet ﷺ said, 'The year consists of twelve months, four of which are sacred: the three consecutive months of Dhu al-Qa'da, Dhu al-Hijja and Muharram, and Rajab Mudar, which comes between Jumada and Sha'ban.' (*Sahih al-Bukhari*) The day of 'Ashura' has been a day of significance and sacredness from the earliest of times. Imam Ahmad al-Sawi collated many narrations (of various levels of authenticity) from different sources which describe events that occurred on 'Ashura' throughout history. Amongst them:
1. Allah accepted the repentance of Prophet Adam on 'Ashura'.
2. The Ark of Prophet Nuh landed on Mount Judi on 'Ashura'.
3. Prophet Ibrahim was born on 'Ashura'.
4. Prophet Ibrahim received the title *Khalilullah* (The Intimate Friend of Allah) on 'Ashura'.
5. Prophet Ibrahim was thrown by Nimrud into a fire that Allah made cool on 'Ashura'.
6. Allah granted relief to Prophet Ayyub on 'Ashura'.
7. Allah granted victory to Prophet Musa against Pharaoh on 'Ashura'.
8. Prophet Yunus, after spending forty days in the belly of a whale, was cast onto shore on 'Ashura'.
9. Prophet Sulayman was made a king with rulership over men and jinn on 'Ashura'.
10. Imam Husayn, the blessed grandson of the Prophet ﷺ and the leader of the youth in Paradise, was martyred on 'Ashura'.
11. The Day of Judgement will occur on 'Ashura'.

(Shaykh Ahmad al-Sawi, *Hashiyat al-Sawi 'ala Tafsir al-Jalalayn*.)

'Ashura' is a day of great sanctity (*hurma*) and reward. Imam al-Bukhari recorded that the Prophet ﷺ would fast on 'Ashura' in Mecca before ordering the nascent Muslim community to fast. When he migrated to Medina, he found the Jews fasting on 'Ashura' and then he enjoined the Muslims to fast it as well. Ibn 'Abbas related, 'When the Messenger of Allah ﷺ arrived in Medina, he found the Jews fasting 'Ashura', and so he asked them, "What is this day you are fasting?" They replied, "This is a tremendous day—on this day Allah delivered Musa and his people and drowned Pharaoh and his people. Musa fasted on this day out of gratitude, and so we fast it, too." The Messenger of Allah ﷺ said, "We have more right to Musa than you!" So he fasted that day and enjoined others to fast it.' (*Sahih al-Bukhari*) The Prophet ﷺ also said, 'Fasting the day of 'Arafa—I hope that Allah will expiate by it [the sins] of the year before it and the year after it. And fasting the day of 'Ashura'—I hope that Allah will expiate by it [the sins] of the year before it.' (*Sahih Muslim*) (AA, MA)

680 When he ﷺ emigrated to Medina. (AA)

681 Ibn 'Abbas reported, 'I never saw the Messenger of Allah ﷺ so keen to fast any day and give it priority over any other than this day, the day of 'Ashura', and this month, Ramadan.' (*Sahih al-Bukhari*) Abu Qatada reported that the Prophet ﷺ said, 'Fasting the day of 'Ashura'—

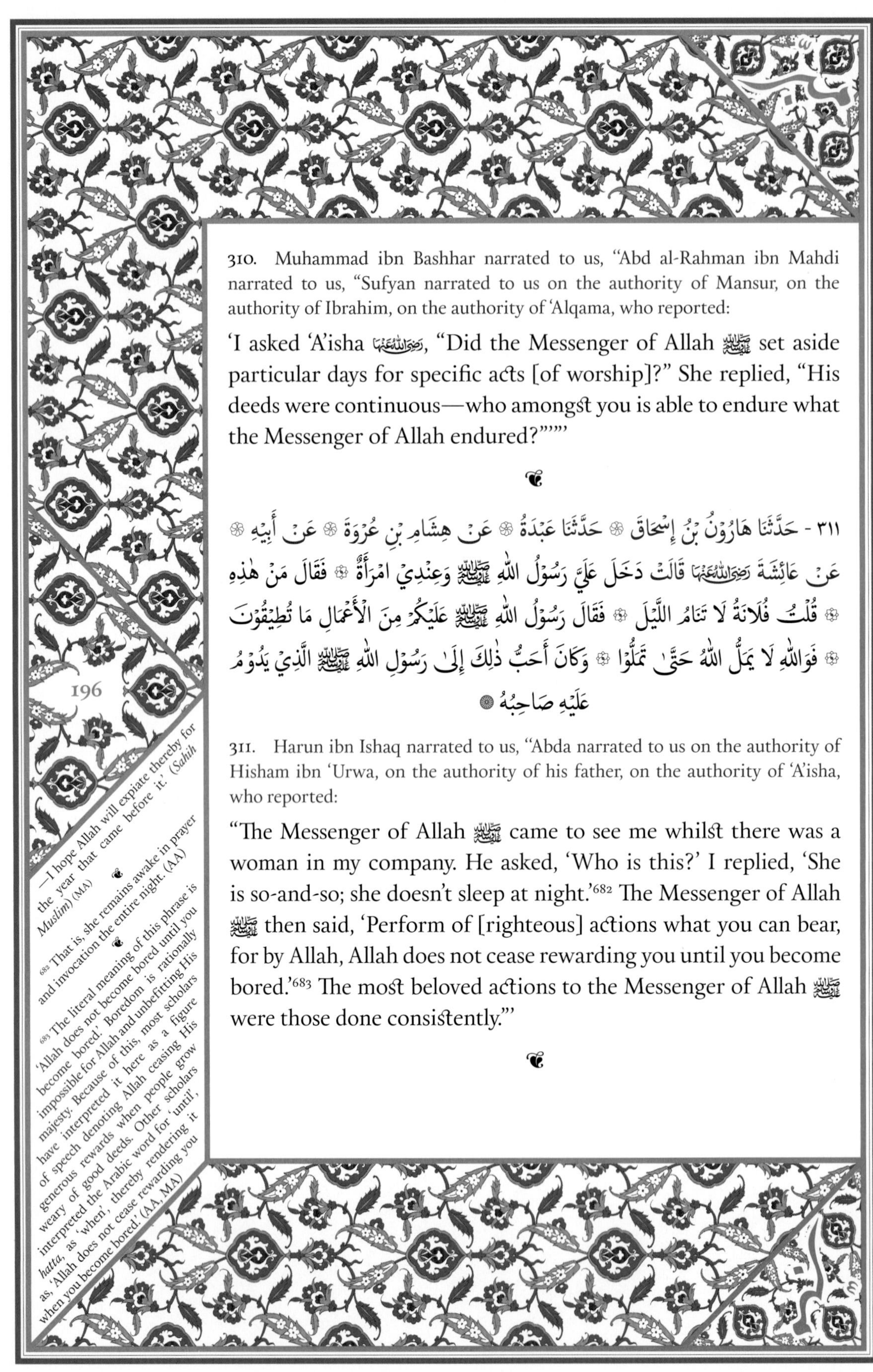

310. Muhammad ibn Bashhar narrated to us, "Abd al-Rahman ibn Mahdi narrated to us, "Sufyan narrated to us on the authority of Mansur, on the authority of Ibrahim, on the authority of 'Alqama, who reported:

'I asked 'A'isha ﵂, "Did the Messenger of Allah ﷺ set aside particular days for specific acts [of worship]?" She replied, "His deeds were continuous—who amongst you is able to endure what the Messenger of Allah endured?"'""

❦

٣١١ - حَدَّثَنَا هَارُونُ بْنُ إِسْحَاقَ ۞ حَدَّثَنَا عَبْدَةُ ۞ عَنْ هِشَامِ بْنِ عُرْوَةَ ۞ عَنْ أَبِيهِ ۞ عَنْ عَائِشَةَ رَضِيَ اللهُ عَنْهَا قَالَتْ دَخَلَ عَلَيَّ رَسُولُ اللهِ ﷺ وَعِنْدِي امْرَأَةٌ ۞ فَقَالَ مَنْ هٰذِهِ ۞ قُلْتُ فُلَانَةُ لَا تَنَامُ اللَّيْلَ ۞ فَقَالَ رَسُولُ اللهِ ﷺ عَلَيْكُمْ مِنَ الْأَعْمَالِ مَا تُطِيقُونَ ۞ فَوَاللهِ لَا يَمَلُّ اللهُ حَتَّىٰ تَمَلُّوا ۞ وَكَانَ أَحَبُّ ذٰلِكَ إِلَىٰ رَسُولِ اللهِ ﷺ الَّذِي يَدُومُ عَلَيْهِ صَاحِبُهُ ۞

311. Harun ibn Ishaq narrated to us, "Abda narrated to us on the authority of Hisham ibn 'Urwa, on the authority of his father, on the authority of 'A'isha, who reported:

"The Messenger of Allah ﷺ came to see me whilst there was a woman in my company. He asked, 'Who is this?' I replied, 'She is so-and-so; she doesn't sleep at night.'[682] The Messenger of Allah ﷺ then said, 'Perform of [righteous] actions what you can bear, for by Allah, Allah does not cease rewarding you until you become bored.'[683] The most beloved actions to the Messenger of Allah ﷺ were those done consistently.""

❦

—I hope Allah will expiate thereby for the year that came before it.' (*Sahih Muslim*) (MA)

682 That is, she remains awake in prayer and invocation the entire night. (AA)

683 The literal meaning of this phrase is 'Allah does not become bored until you become bored.' Boredom is rationally impossible for Allah and unbefitting His majesty. Because of this, most scholars have interpreted it here as a figure of speech denoting Allah ceasing His generous rewards when people grow weary of good deeds. Other scholars interpreted the Arabic word for 'until', *hatta*, as 'when', thereby rendering it as, 'Allah does not cease rewarding you when you become bored.' (AA, MA)

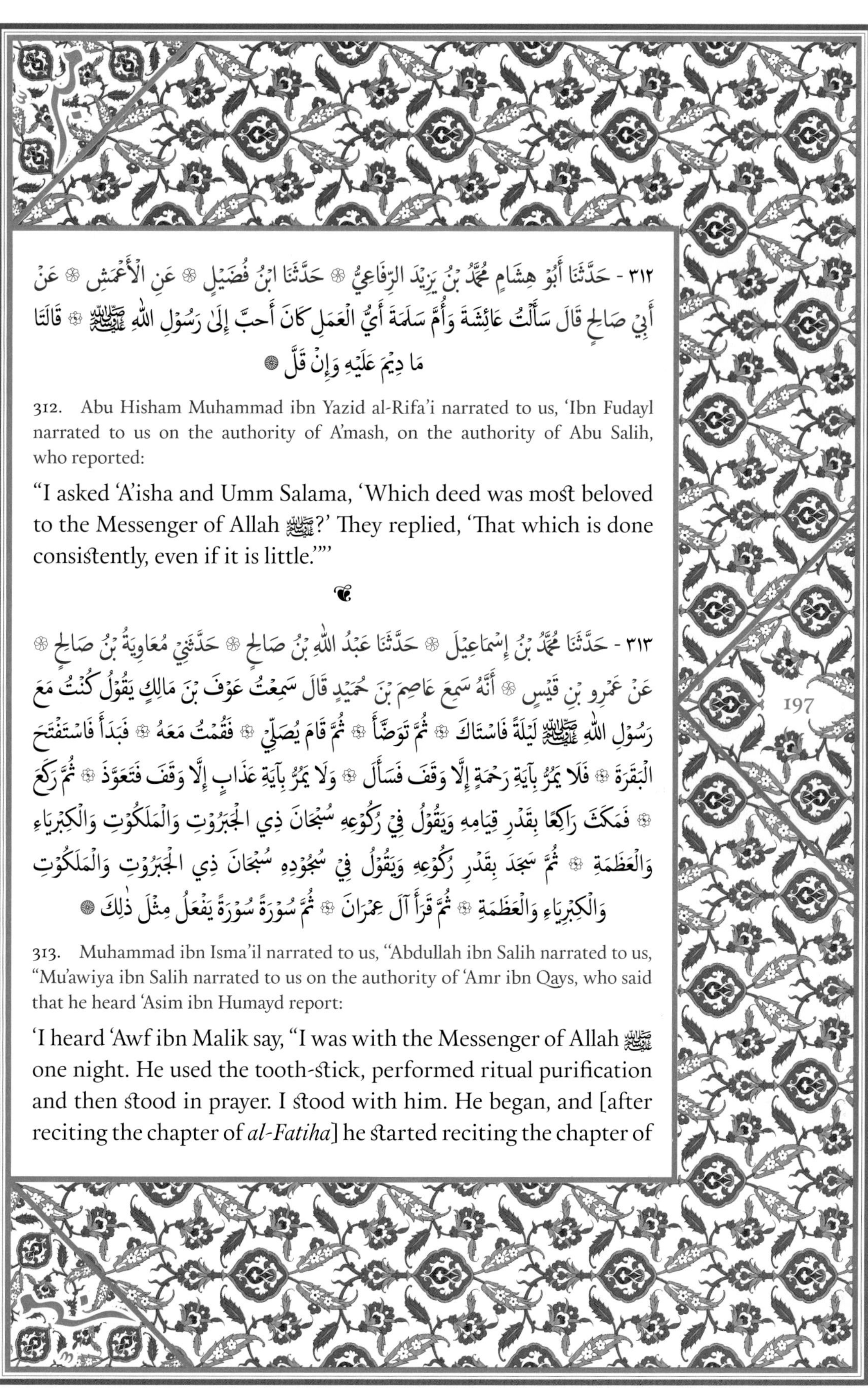

٣١٢ - حَدَّثَنَا أَبُو هِشَامٍ مُحَمَّدُ بْنُ يَزِيدَ الرِّفَاعِيُّ ۞ حَدَّثَنَا ابْنُ فُضَيْلٍ ۞ عَنِ الْأَعْمَشِ ۞ عَنْ أَبِي صَالِحٍ قَالَ سَأَلْتُ عَائِشَةَ وَأُمَّ سَلَمَةَ أَيُّ الْعَمَلِ كَانَ أَحَبَّ إِلَى رَسُولِ اللهِ ﷺ ۞ قَالَتَا مَا دِيمَ عَلَيْهِ وَإِنْ قَلَّ ۞

312. Abu Hisham Muhammad ibn Yazid al-Rifa'i narrated to us, 'Ibn Fudayl narrated to us on the authority of A'mash, on the authority of Abu Salih, who reported:

"I asked 'A'isha and Umm Salama, 'Which deed was most beloved to the Messenger of Allah ﷺ?' They replied, 'That which is done consistently, even if it is little.''"

٣١٣ - حَدَّثَنَا مُحَمَّدُ بْنُ إِسْمَاعِيلَ ۞ حَدَّثَنَا عَبْدُ اللهِ بْنُ صَالِحٍ ۞ حَدَّثَنِي مُعَاوِيَةُ بْنُ صَالِحٍ ۞ عَنْ عَمْرِو بْنِ قَيْسٍ ۞ أَنَّهُ سَمِعَ عَاصِمَ بْنَ حُمَيْدٍ قَالَ سَمِعْتُ عَوْفَ بْنَ مَالِكٍ يَقُولُ كُنْتُ مَعَ رَسُولِ اللهِ ﷺ لَيْلَةً فَاسْتَاكَ ۞ ثُمَّ تَوَضَّأَ ۞ ثُمَّ قَامَ يُصَلِّي ۞ فَقُمْتُ مَعَهُ ۞ فَبَدَأَ فَاسْتَفْتَحَ الْبَقَرَةَ ۞ فَلَا يَمُرُّ بِآيَةِ رَحْمَةٍ إِلَّا وَقَفَ فَسَأَلَ ۞ وَلَا يَمُرُّ بِآيَةِ عَذَابٍ إِلَّا وَقَفَ فَتَعَوَّذَ ۞ ثُمَّ رَكَعَ ۞ فَمَكَثَ رَاكِعًا بِقَدْرِ قِيَامِهِ وَيَقُولُ فِي رُكُوعِهِ سُبْحَانَ ذِي الْجَبَرُوتِ وَالْمَلَكُوتِ وَالْكِبْرِيَاءِ وَالْعَظَمَةِ ۞ ثُمَّ سَجَدَ بِقَدْرِ رُكُوعِهِ وَيَقُولُ فِي سُجُودِهِ سُبْحَانَ ذِي الْجَبَرُوتِ وَالْمَلَكُوتِ وَالْكِبْرِيَاءِ وَالْعَظَمَةِ ۞ ثُمَّ قَرَأَ آلَ عِمْرَانَ ۞ ثُمَّ سُورَةً سُورَةً يَفْعَلُ مِثْلَ ذَٰلِكَ ۞

313. Muhammad ibn Isma'il narrated to us, "Abdullah ibn Salih narrated to us, "Mu'awiya ibn Salih narrated to us on the authority of 'Amr ibn Qays, who said that he heard 'Asim ibn Humayd report:

'I heard 'Awf ibn Malik say, "I was with the Messenger of Allah ﷺ one night. He used the tooth-stick, performed ritual purification and then stood in prayer. I stood with him. He began, and [after reciting the chapter of *al-Fatiha*] he started reciting the chapter of

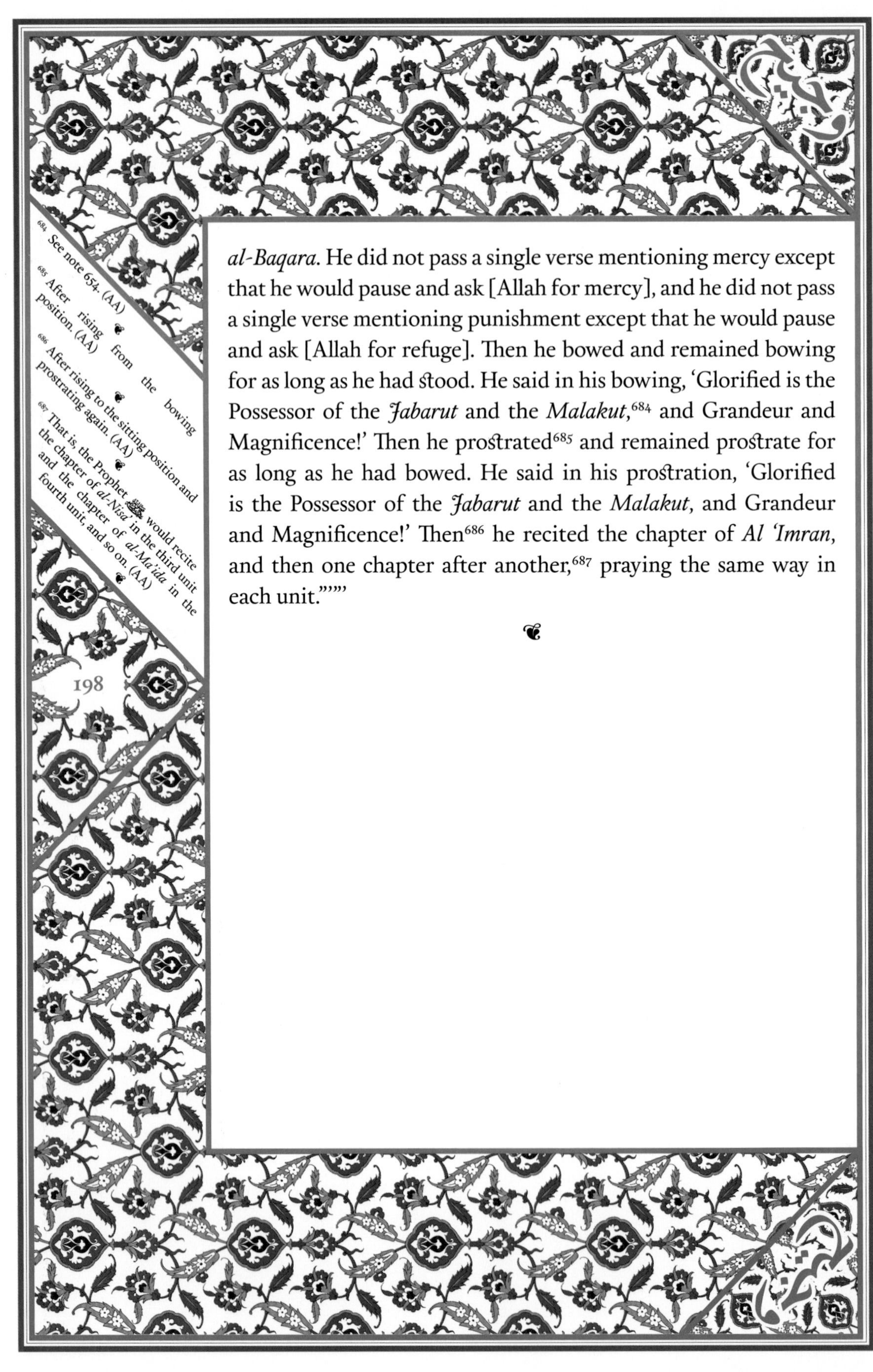

al-Baqara. He did not pass a single verse mentioning mercy except that he would pause and ask [Allah for mercy], and he did not pass a single verse mentioning punishment except that he would pause and ask [Allah for refuge]. Then he bowed and remained bowing for as long as he had stood. He said in his bowing, 'Glorified is the Possessor of the *Jabarut* and the *Malakut*,[684] and Grandeur and Magnificence!' Then he prostrated[685] and remained prostrate for as long as he had bowed. He said in his prostration, 'Glorified is the Possessor of the *Jabarut* and the *Malakut*, and Grandeur and Magnificence!' Then[686] he recited the chapter of *Al 'Imran*, and then one chapter after another,[687] praying the same way in each unit.''''

❦

[684] See note 654. (AA)

[685] After rising from the bowing position. (AA)

[686] After rising to the sitting position and prostrating again. (AA)

[687] That is, the Prophet ﷺ would recite the chapter of *al-Nisa'* in the third unit and the chapter of *al-Ma'ida* in the fourth unit, and so on. (AA)

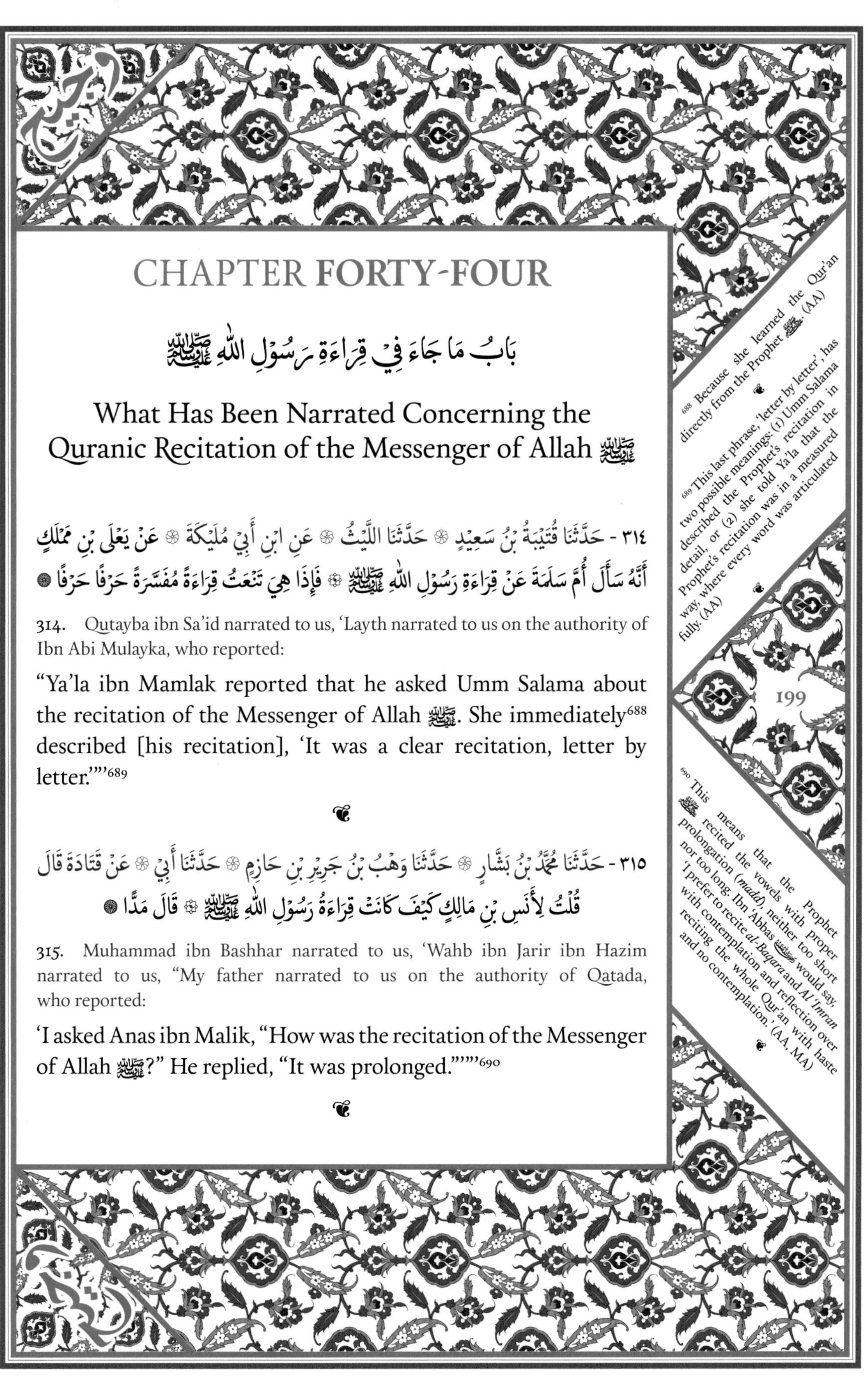

CHAPTER FORTY-FOUR

بَابُ مَا جَاءَ فِي قِرَاءَةِ رَسُولِ اللهِ ﷺ

What Has Been Narrated Concerning the Quranic Recitation of the Messenger of Allah ﷺ

٣١٤ - حَدَّثَنَا قُتَيْبَةُ بْنُ سَعِيدٍ ۞ حَدَّثَنَا اللَّيْثُ ۞ عَنِ ابْنِ أَبِي مُلَيْكَةَ ۞ عَنْ يَعْلَى بْنِ مَمْلَكٍ أَنَّهُ سَأَلَ أُمَّ سَلَمَةَ عَنْ قِرَاءَةِ رَسُولِ اللهِ ﷺ ۞ فَإِذَا هِيَ تَنْعَتُ قِرَاءَةً مُفَسَّرَةً حَرْفًا حَرْفًا ۞

314. Qutayba ibn Sa'id narrated to us, 'Layth narrated to us on the authority of Ibn Abi Mulayka, who reported:

"Ya'la ibn Mamlak reported that he asked Umm Salama about the recitation of the Messenger of Allah ﷺ. She immediately[688] described [his recitation], 'It was a clear recitation, letter by letter.'"'[689]

٣١٥ - حَدَّثَنَا مُحَمَّدُ بْنُ بَشَّارٍ ۞ حَدَّثَنَا وَهْبُ بْنُ جَرِيرِ بْنِ حَازِمٍ ۞ حَدَّثَنَا أَبِي ۞ عَنْ قَتَادَةَ قَالَ قُلْتُ لِأَنَسِ بْنِ مَالِكٍ كَيْفَ كَانَتْ قِرَاءَةُ رَسُولِ اللهِ ﷺ ۞ قَالَ مَدًّا ۞

315. Muhammad ibn Bashhar narrated to us, 'Wahb ibn Jarir ibn Hazim narrated to us, "My father narrated to us on the authority of Qatada, who reported:

'I asked Anas ibn Malik, "How was the recitation of the Messenger of Allah ﷺ?" He replied, "It was prolonged."'"'[690]

[688] Because she learned the Qur'an directly from the Prophet ﷺ. (AA)

[689] This last phrase, 'letter by letter', has two possible meanings: (1) Umm Salama described the Prophet's recitation in detail, or (2) she told Ya'la that the Prophet's recitation was in a measured way, where every word was articulated fully. (AA)

[690] This means that the Prophet ﷺ recited the vowels with proper prolongation (*madd*), neither too short nor too long. Ibn 'Abbas would say, 'I prefer to recite *al-Baqara* and *Al 'Imran* with contemplation and reflection over reciting the whole Qur'an with haste and no contemplation.' (AA, MA)

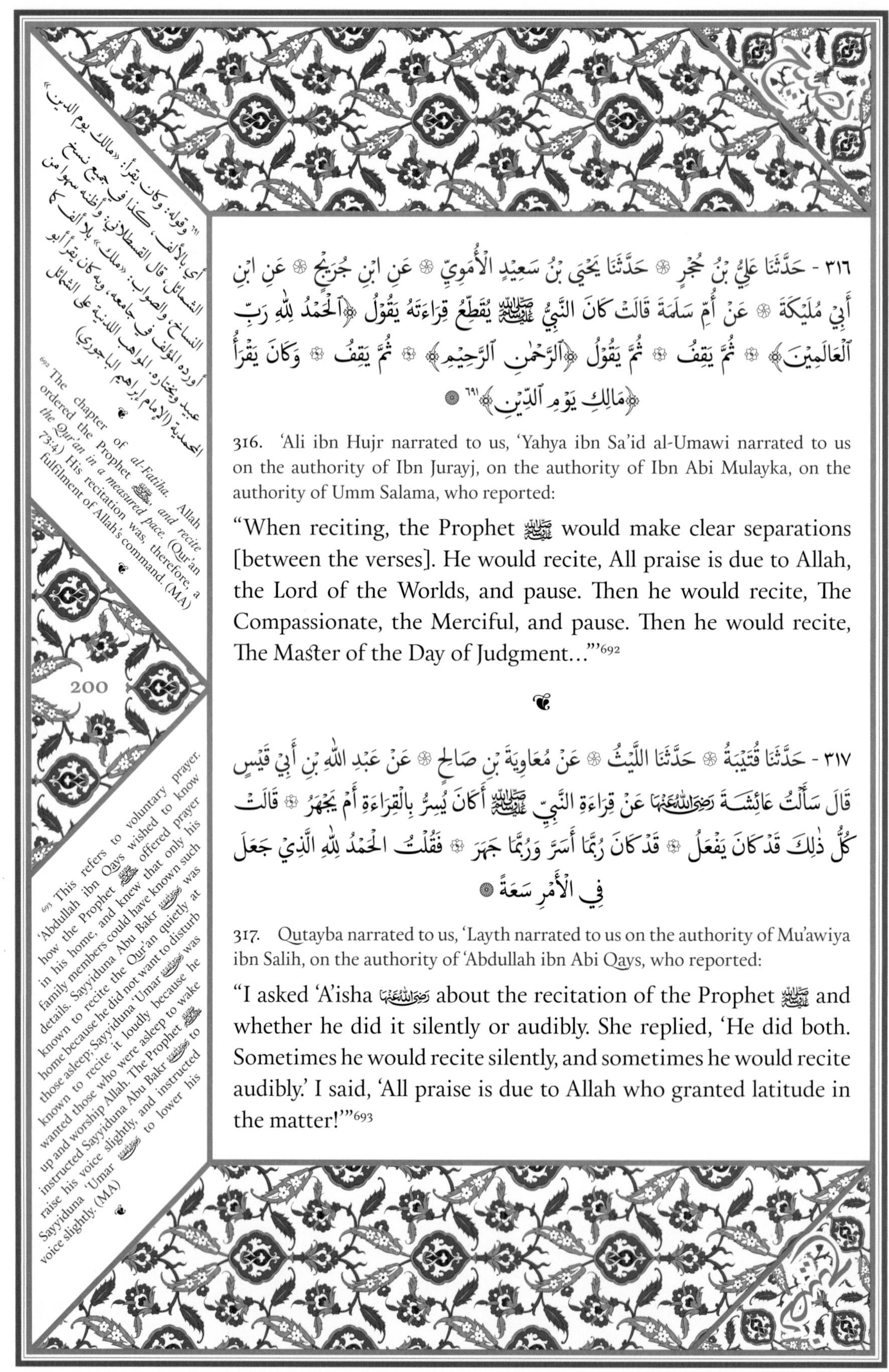

٣١٦ - حَدَّثَنَا عَلِيُّ بْنُ حُجْرٍ ۞ حَدَّثَنَا يَحْيَى بْنُ سَعِيدٍ الْأُمَوِيّ ۞ عَنِ ابْنِ جُرَيْجٍ ۞ عَنِ ابْنِ أَبِي مُلَيْكَةَ ۞ عَنْ أُمِّ سَلَمَةَ قَالَتْ كَانَ النَّبِيُّ ﷺ يُقَطِّعُ قِرَاءَتَهُ يَقُولُ ﴿ٱلْحَمْدُ لِلَّهِ رَبِّ ٱلْعَالَمِينَ﴾ ۞ ثُمَّ يَقِفُ ۞ ثُمَّ يَقُولُ ﴿ٱلرَّحْمَٰنِ ٱلرَّحِيمِ﴾ ۞ ثُمَّ يَقِفُ ۞ وَكَانَ يَقْرَأُ ﴿مَالِكِ يَوْمِ ٱلدِّينِ﴾[٦٩١]

316. 'Ali ibn Hujr narrated to us, 'Yahya ibn Sa'id al-Umawi narrated to us on the authority of Ibn Jurayj, on the authority of Ibn Abi Mulayka, on the authority of Umm Salama, who reported:

"When reciting, the Prophet ﷺ would make clear separations [between the verses]. He would recite, All praise is due to Allah, the Lord of the Worlds, and pause. Then he would recite, The Compassionate, the Merciful, and pause. Then he would recite, The Master of the Day of Judgment…"'[692]

٣١٧ - حَدَّثَنَا قُتَيْبَةُ ۞ حَدَّثَنَا اللَّيْثُ ۞ عَنْ مُعَاوِيَةَ بْنِ صَالِحٍ ۞ عَنْ عَبْدِ اللهِ بْنِ أَبِي قَيْسٍ قَالَ سَأَلْتُ عَائِشَةَ رَضِيَ اللهُ عَنْهَا عَنْ قِرَاءَةِ النَّبِيِّ ﷺ أَكَانَ يُسِرُّ بِالْقِرَاءَةِ أَمْ يَجْهَرُ ۞ قَالَتْ كُلُّ ذٰلِكَ قَدْ كَانَ يَفْعَلُ ۞ قَدْ كَانَ رُبَّمَا أَسَرَّ وَرُبَّمَا جَهَرَ ۞ فَقُلْتُ الْحَمْدُ لِلَّهِ الَّذِي جَعَلَ فِي الْأَمْرِ سَعَةً

317. Qutayba narrated to us, 'Layth narrated to us on the authority of Mu'awiya ibn Salih, on the authority of 'Abdullah ibn Abi Qays, who reported:

"I asked 'A'isha رضي الله عنها about the recitation of the Prophet ﷺ and whether he did it silently or audibly. She replied, 'He did both. Sometimes he would recite silently, and sometimes he would recite audibly.' I said, 'All praise is due to Allah who granted latitude in the matter!'"'[693]

٦٩١ قوله: وكان يقرأ: «مالك يوم الدين» أي بالألف، كذا في جميع نسخ الشمائل، قال القسطلاني: وأظنه سهوا من النساخ، والصواب: «ملك» بلا ألف كما أورده المؤلف في جامعه، وبه كان يقرأ أبو عبيد ويختاره. المواهب اللدنية على الشمائل المحمدية (الإمام إبراهيم الباجوري)

692 The chapter of *al-Fatiha*. Allah ordered the Prophet ﷺ, *and recite the Qur'an in a measured pace.* (Qur'an 73:4) His recitation was, therefore, a fulfilment of Allah's command. (MA)

693 This refers to voluntary prayer. 'Abdullah ibn Qays wished to know how the Prophet ﷺ offered prayer in his home, and knew that only his family members could have known such details. Sayyiduna Abu Bakr رضي الله عنه was known to recite the Qur'an quietly at home because he did not want to disturb those asleep. Sayyiduna 'Umar رضي الله عنه was known to recite it loudly because he wanted those who were asleep to wake up and worship Allah. The Prophet ﷺ instructed Sayyiduna Abu Bakr رضي الله عنه to raise his voice slightly, and instructed Sayyiduna 'Umar رضي الله عنه to lower his voice slightly. (MA)

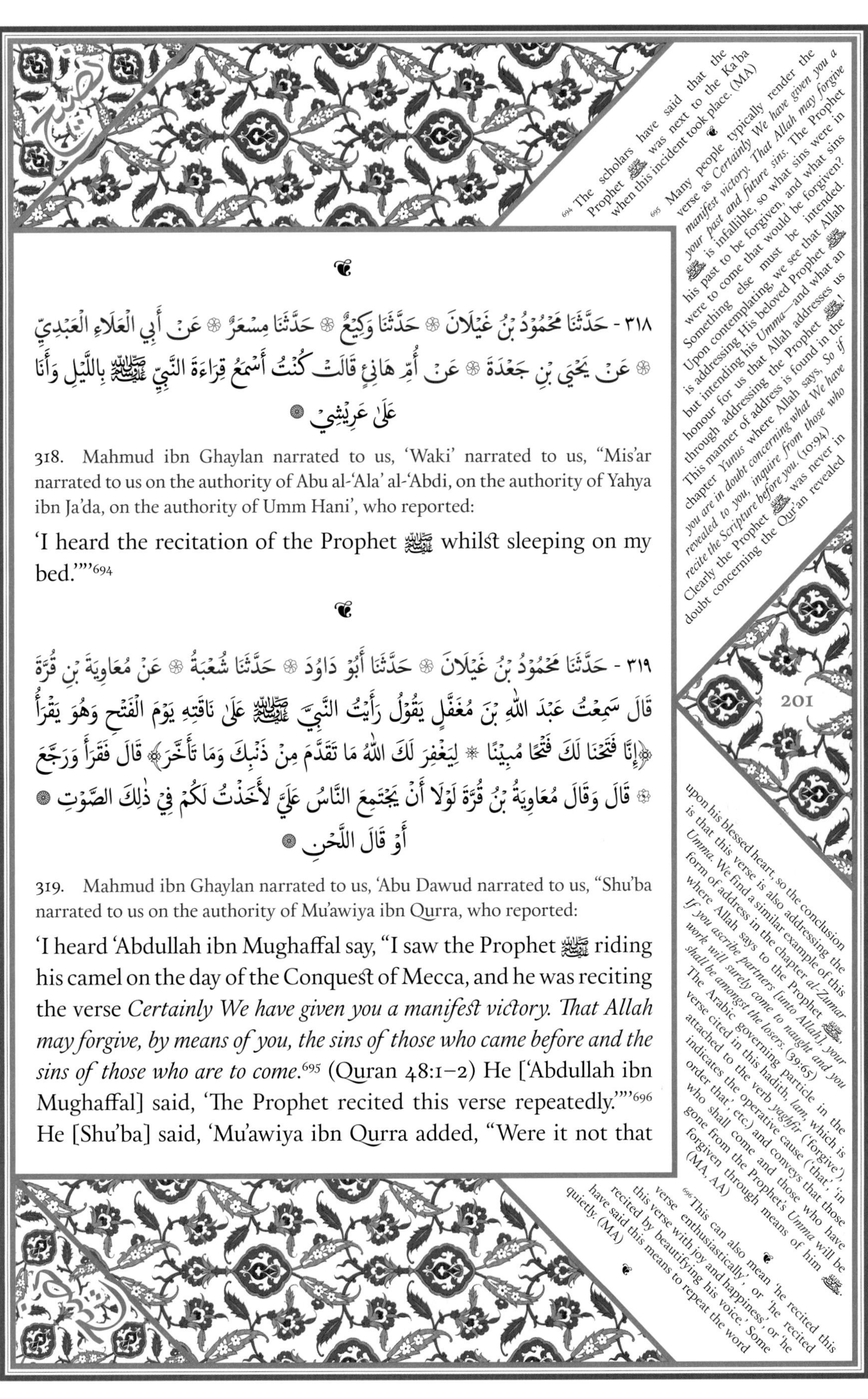

٣١٨ - حَدَّثَنَا مَحْمُودُ بْنُ غَيْلَانَ ۞ حَدَّثَنَا وَكِيعٌ ۞ حَدَّثَنَا مِسْعَرٌ ۞ عَنْ أَبِي الْعَلَاءِ الْعَبْدِيِّ ۞ عَنْ يَحْيَى بْنِ جَعْدَةَ ۞ عَنْ أُمِّ هَانِئٍ قَالَتْ كُنْتُ أَسْمَعُ قِرَاءَةَ النَّبِيِّ ﷺ بِاللَّيْلِ وَأَنَا عَلَى عَرِيشِي ۞

318. Mahmud ibn Ghaylan narrated to us, 'Waki' narrated to us, "Mis'ar narrated to us on the authority of Abu al-'Ala' al-'Abdi, on the authority of Yahya ibn Ja'da, on the authority of Umm Hani', who reported:

'I heard the recitation of the Prophet ﷺ whilst sleeping on my bed.'"'[694]

٣١٩ - حَدَّثَنَا مَحْمُودُ بْنُ غَيْلَانَ ۞ حَدَّثَنَا أَبُو دَاوُدَ ۞ حَدَّثَنَا شُعْبَةُ ۞ عَنْ مُعَاوِيَةَ بْنِ قُرَّةَ قَالَ سَمِعْتُ عَبْدَ اللهِ بْنَ مُغَفَّلٍ يَقُولُ رَأَيْتُ النَّبِيَّ ﷺ عَلَى نَاقَتِهِ يَوْمَ الْفَتْحِ وَهُوَ يَقْرَأُ ﴿إِنَّا فَتَحْنَا لَكَ فَتْحًا مُبِينًا ۞ لِيَغْفِرَ لَكَ اللهُ مَا تَقَدَّمَ مِنْ ذَنْبِكَ وَمَا تَأَخَّرَ﴾ قَالَ فَقَرَأَ وَرَجَّعَ ۞ قَالَ وَقَالَ مُعَاوِيَةُ بْنُ قُرَّةَ لَوْلَا أَنْ يَجْتَمِعَ النَّاسُ عَلَيَّ لَأَخَذْتُ لَكُمْ فِي ذٰلِكَ الصَّوْتِ ۞ أَوْ قَالَ اللَّحْنِ ۞

319. Mahmud ibn Ghaylan narrated to us, 'Abu Dawud narrated to us, "Shu'ba narrated to us on the authority of Mu'awiya ibn Qurra, who reported:

'I heard 'Abdullah ibn Mughaffal say, "I saw the Prophet ﷺ riding his camel on the day of the Conquest of Mecca, and he was reciting the verse *Certainly We have given you a manifest victory. That Allah may forgive, by means of you, the sins of those who came before and the sins of those who are to come.*[695] (Quran 48:1–2) He ['Abdullah ibn Mughaffal] said, 'The Prophet recited this verse repeatedly.'"'[696] He [Shu'ba] said, 'Mu'awiya ibn Qurra added, "Were it not that

[694] The scholars have said that the Prophet ﷺ was next to the Ka'ba when this incident took place. (MA)

[695] Many people typically render the verse as *Certainly We have given you a manifest victory. That Allah may forgive your past and future sins.* The Prophet ﷺ is infallible, so what sins were in his past to be forgiven, and what sins were to come that would be forgiven? Something else must be intended. Upon contemplating, we see that Allah is addressing His beloved Prophet ﷺ but intending his *Umma*—and what an honour for us that Allah addresses us through addressing the Prophet ﷺ! This manner of address is found in the chapter *Yunus* where Allah says, *So if you are in doubt concerning what We have revealed to you, inquire from those who recite the Scripture before you.* (10:94) Clearly the Prophet ﷺ was never in doubt concerning the Qur'an revealed upon his blessed heart, so the conclusion is that this verse is also addressing the *Umma*. We find a similar example of this form of address in the chapter *al-Zumar* where Allah says to the Prophet ﷺ, *If you ascribe partners [unto Allah], your work will surely come to naught and you shall be amongst the losers.* (39:65) The Arabic governing particle in the verse cited in this hadith, *lam*, which is attached to the verb *yaghfir* ('forgive'), indicates the operative cause ('that', 'in order that', etc.) and conveys that those who shall come and those who have gone from the Prophet's *Umma* will be forgiven through means of him ﷺ. (MA, AA)

[696] This can also mean 'he recited this verse enthusiastically', or 'he recited this verse with joy and happiness', or 'he recited by beautifying his voice'. Some have said this means to repeat the word quietly. (MA)

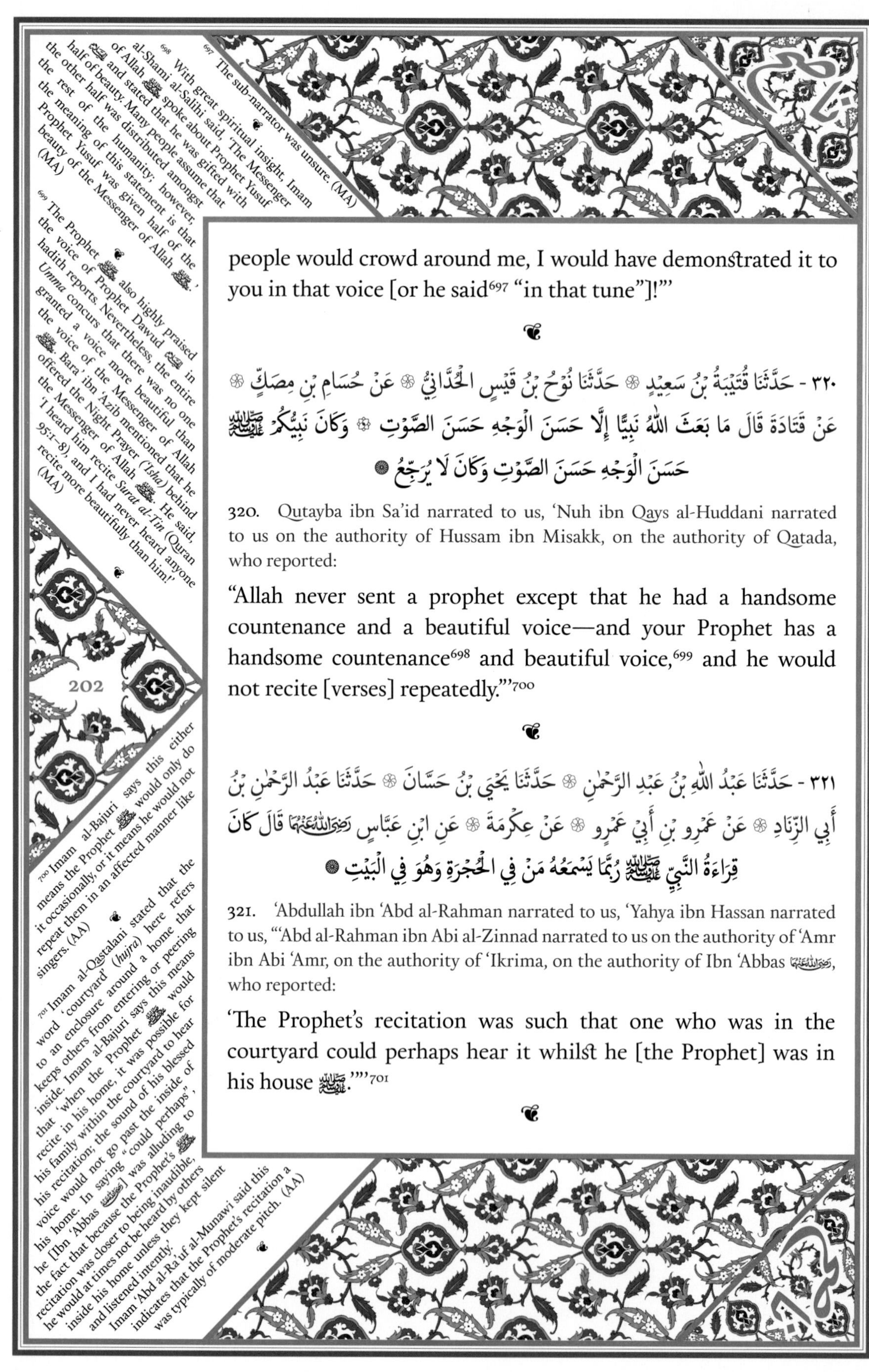

people would crowd around me, I would have demonstrated it to you in that voice [or he said[697] "in that tune"]!'"

٣٢٠ - حَدَّثَنَا قُتَيْبَةُ بْنُ سَعِيدٍ ❁ حَدَّثَنَا نُوحُ بْنُ قَيْسٍ الْحُدَّانِيُّ ❁ عَنْ حُسَامِ بْنِ مِصَكٍّ ❁ عَنْ قَتَادَةَ قَالَ مَا بَعَثَ اللهُ نَبِيًّا إِلَّا حَسَنَ الْوَجْهِ حَسَنَ الصَّوْتِ ❁ وَكَانَ نَبِيُّكُمْ ﷺ حَسَنَ الْوَجْهِ حَسَنَ الصَّوْتِ وَكَانَ لَا يُرَجِّعُ ❁

320. Qutayba ibn Sa'id narrated to us, 'Nuh ibn Qays al-Huddani narrated to us on the authority of Hussam ibn Misakk, on the authority of Qatada, who reported:

"Allah never sent a prophet except that he had a handsome countenance and a beautiful voice—and your Prophet has a handsome countenance[698] and beautiful voice,[699] and he would not recite [verses] repeatedly."'[700]

٣٢١ - حَدَّثَنَا عَبْدُ اللهِ بْنُ عَبْدِ الرَّحْمٰنِ ❁ حَدَّثَنَا يَحْيَى بْنُ حَسَّانَ ❁ حَدَّثَنَا عَبْدُ الرَّحْمٰنِ بْنُ أَبِي الزِّنَادِ ❁ عَنْ عَمْرِو بْنِ أَبِي عَمْرٍو ❁ عَنْ عِكْرِمَةَ ❁ عَنِ ابْنِ عَبَّاسٍ رَضِيَ اللهُ عَنْهُمَا قَالَ كَانَ قِرَاءَةُ النَّبِيِّ ﷺ رُبَّمَا يَسْمَعُهُ مَنْ فِي الْحُجْرَةِ وَهُوَ فِي الْبَيْتِ ❁

321. 'Abdullah ibn 'Abd al-Rahman narrated to us, 'Yahya ibn Hassan narrated to us, "'Abd al-Rahman ibn Abi al-Zinnad narrated to us on the authority of 'Amr ibn Abi 'Amr, on the authority of 'Ikrima, on the authority of Ibn 'Abbas رضي الله عنهما, who reported:

'The Prophet's recitation was such that one who was in the courtyard could perhaps hear it whilst he [the Prophet] was in his house ﷺ.'"'[701]

697 The sub-narrator was unsure. (MA)

698 With great spiritual insight, Imam al-Shami al-Salihi said, 'The Messenger of Allah ﷺ spoke about Prophet Yusuf ﷺ and stated that he was gifted with half of beauty. Many people assume that the other half was distributed amongst the rest of the humanity; however, the meaning of this statement is that Prophet Yusuf was given half of the beauty of the Messenger of Allah ﷺ.' (MA)

699 The Prophet ﷺ also highly praised the voice of Prophet Dawud ﷺ in hadith reports. Nevertheless, the entire *Umma* concurs that there was no one granted a voice more beautiful than the voice of the Messenger of Allah ﷺ. Bara ibn 'Azib mentioned that he offered the Night Prayer (*Isha*) behind the Messenger of Allah ﷺ. He said, 'I heard him recite *Surat al-Tin* (Quran 95:1–8), and I had never heard anyone recite more beautifully than him!' (MA)

700 Imam al-Bajuri says this either means the Prophet ﷺ would only do it occasionally, or it means he would not repeat them in an affected manner like singers. (AA)

701 Imam al-Qastalani stated that the word 'courtyard' (*hujra*) here refers to an enclosure around a home that keeps others from entering or peering inside. Imam al-Bajuri says this means that 'when the Prophet ﷺ would recite in his home, it was possible for his family within the courtyard to hear his recitation; the sound of his blessed voice would not go past the inside of his home. In saying "could perhaps", he [Ibn 'Abbas ﷺ] was alluding to the fact that because the Prophet's ﷺ recitation was closer to being inaudible, he would at times not be heard by others inside his home unless they kept silent and listened intently.' Imam 'Abd al-Ra'uf al-Munawi said this indicates that the Prophet's recitation a was typically of moderate pitch. (AA)

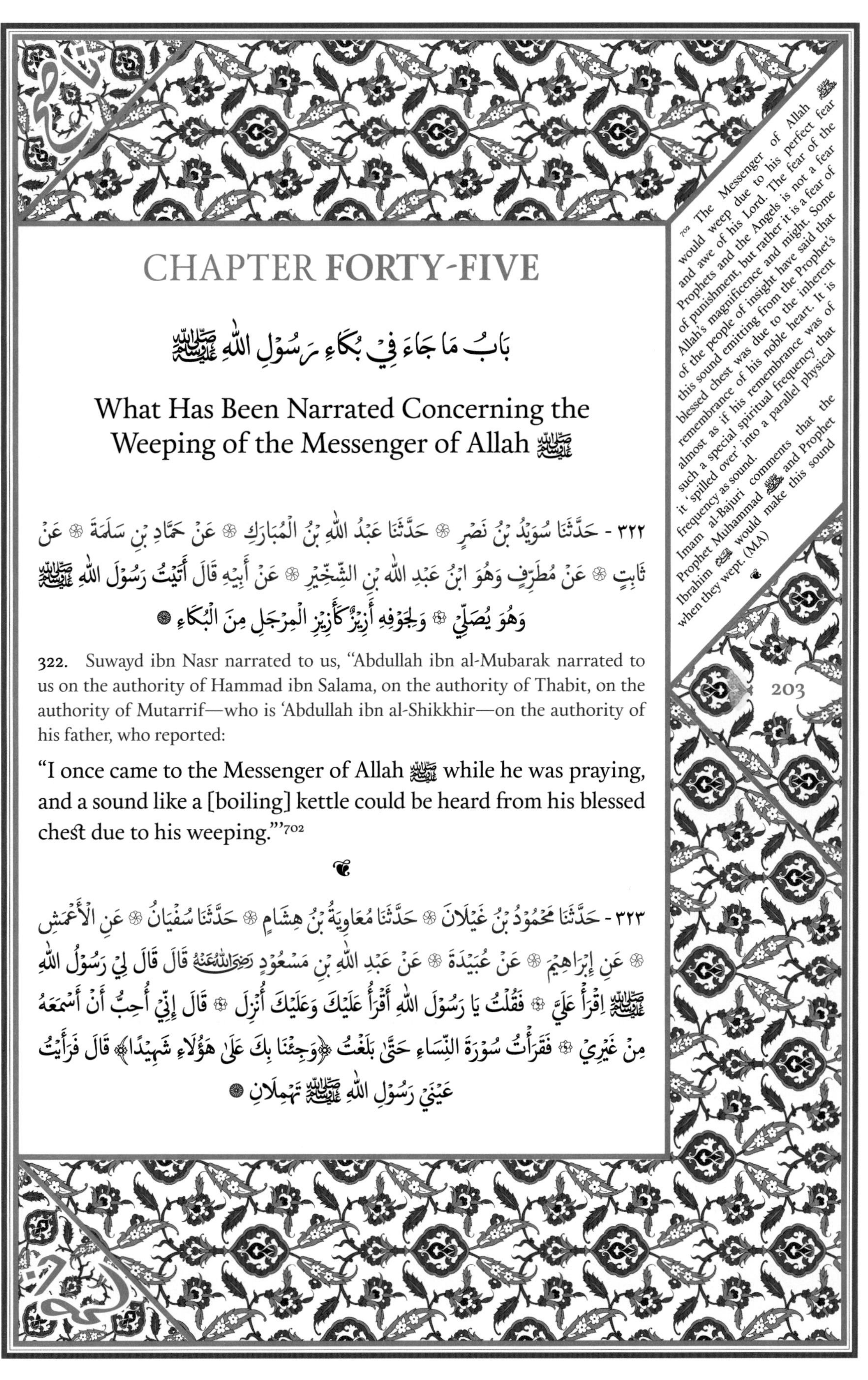

CHAPTER FORTY-FIVE

بَابُ مَا جَاءَ فِي بُكَاءِ رَسُولِ اللهِ ﷺ

What Has Been Narrated Concerning the Weeping of the Messenger of Allah ﷺ

٣٢٢ - حَدَّثَنَا سُوَيْدُ بْنُ نَصْرٍ ۞ حَدَّثَنَا عَبْدُ اللهِ بْنُ الْمُبَارَكِ ۞ عَنْ حَمَّادِ بْنِ سَلَمَةَ ۞ عَنْ ثَابِتٍ ۞ عَنْ مُطَرِّفٍ وَهُوَ ابْنُ عَبْدِ اللهِ بْنِ الشِّخِّيرِ ۞ عَنْ أَبِيهِ قَالَ أَتَيْتُ رَسُولَ اللهِ ﷺ وَهُوَ يُصَلِّي ۞ وَلِجَوْفِهِ أَزِيزٌ كَأَزِيزِ الْمِرْجَلِ مِنَ الْبُكَاءِ ۞

322. Suwayd ibn Nasr narrated to us, "Abdullah ibn al-Mubarak narrated to us on the authority of Hammad ibn Salama, on the authority of Thabit, on the authority of Mutarrif—who is 'Abdullah ibn al-Shikkhir—on the authority of his father, who reported:

"I once came to the Messenger of Allah ﷺ while he was praying, and a sound like a [boiling] kettle could be heard from his blessed chest due to his weeping."'[702]

٣٢٣ - حَدَّثَنَا مَحْمُودُ بْنُ غَيْلَانَ ۞ حَدَّثَنَا مُعَاوِيَةُ بْنُ هِشَامٍ ۞ حَدَّثَنَا سُفْيَانُ ۞ عَنِ الْأَعْمَشِ ۞ عَنْ إِبْرَاهِيمَ ۞ عَنْ عُبَيْدَةَ ۞ عَنْ عَبْدِ اللهِ بْنِ مَسْعُودٍ رَضِيَ اللهُ عَنْهُ قَالَ قَالَ لِي رَسُولُ اللهِ ﷺ اقْرَأْ عَلَيَّ ۞ فَقُلْتُ يَا رَسُولَ اللهِ أَقْرَأُ عَلَيْكَ وَعَلَيْكَ أُنْزِلَ ۞ قَالَ إِنِّي أُحِبُّ أَنْ أَسْمَعَهُ مِنْ غَيْرِي ۞ فَقَرَأْتُ سُورَةَ النِّسَاءِ حَتَّى بَلَغْتُ ﴿وَجِئْنَا بِكَ عَلَى هَؤُلَاءِ شَهِيدًا﴾ قَالَ فَرَأَيْتُ عَيْنَيْ رَسُولِ اللهِ ﷺ تَهْمِلَانِ ۞

702 The Messenger of Allah ﷺ would weep due to his perfect fear and awe of his Lord. The fear of the Prophets and the Angels is not a fear of punishment, but rather it is a fear of Allah's magnificence and might. Some of the people of insight have said that this sound emitting from the Prophet's blessed chest was due to the inherent remembrance of his noble heart. It is almost as if his remembrance was of such a special spiritual frequency that it 'spilled over' into a parallel physical frequency as sound. Imam al-Bajuri comments that the Prophet Muhammad ﷺ and Prophet Ibrahim ﷺ would make this sound when they wept. (MA)

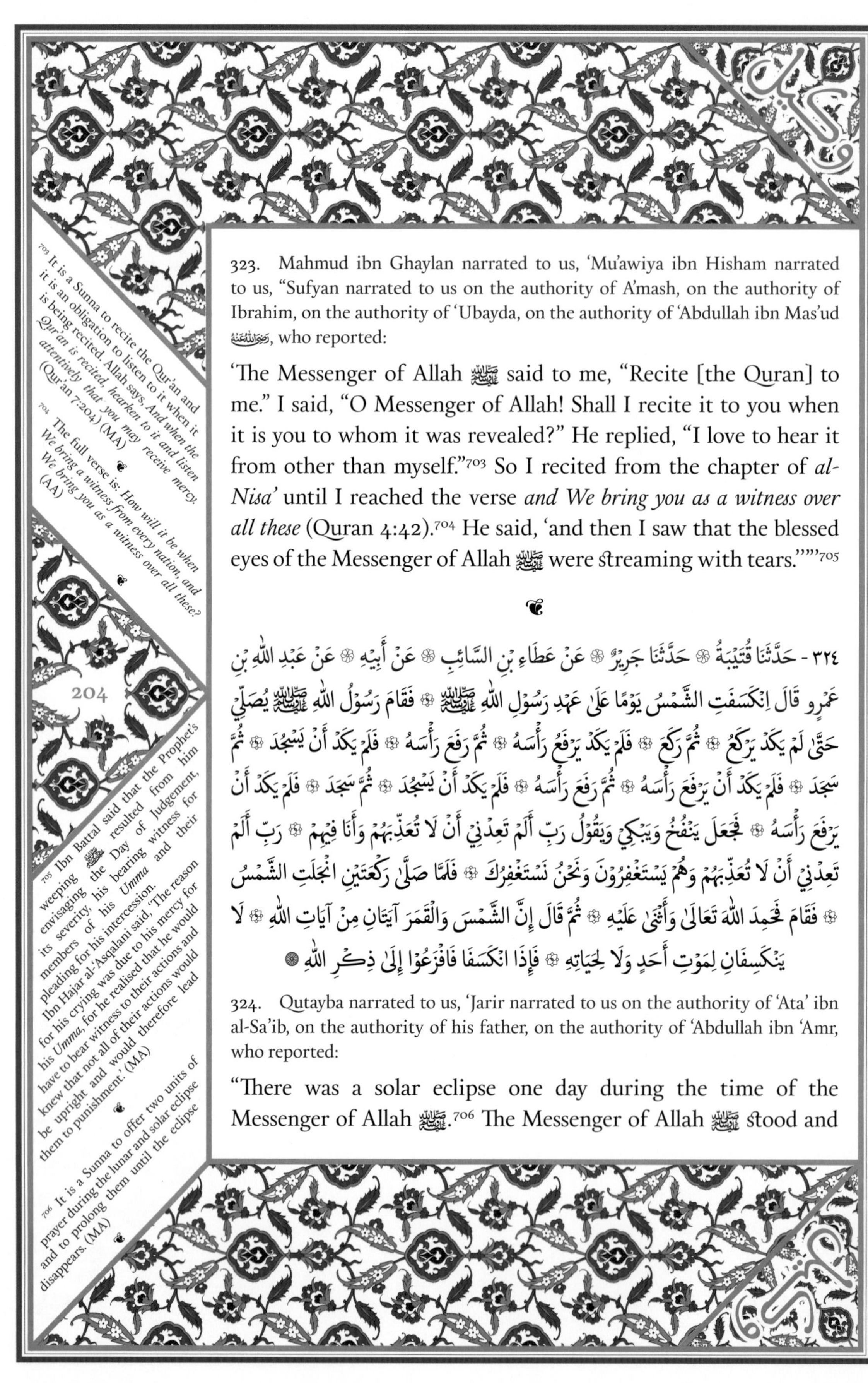

323. Mahmud ibn Ghaylan narrated to us, 'Mu'awiya ibn Hisham narrated to us, "Sufyan narrated to us on the authority of A'mash, on the authority of Ibrahim, on the authority of 'Ubayda, on the authority of 'Abdullah ibn Mas'ud رضي الله عنه, who reported:

'The Messenger of Allah ﷺ said to me, "Recite [the Quran] to me." I said, "O Messenger of Allah! Shall I recite it to you when it is you to whom it was revealed?" He replied, "I love to hear it from other than myself."[703] So I recited from the chapter of *al-Nisa'* until I reached the verse *and We bring you as a witness over all these* (Quran 4:42).[704] He said, 'and then I saw that the blessed eyes of the Messenger of Allah ﷺ were streaming with tears.'"'[705]

❦

٣٢٤ - حَدَّثَنَا قُتَيْبَةُ ۞ حَدَّثَنَا جَرِيرٌ ۞ عَنْ عَطَاءِ بْنِ السَّائِبِ ۞ عَنْ أَبِيهِ ۞ عَنْ عَبْدِ اللَّهِ بْنِ عَمْرٍو قَالَ انْكَسَفَتِ الشَّمْسُ يَوْمًا عَلَىٰ عَهْدِ رَسُولِ اللَّهِ ﷺ ۞ فَقَامَ رَسُولُ اللَّهِ ﷺ يُصَلِّي حَتَّىٰ لَمْ يَكَدْ يَرْكَعُ ۞ ثُمَّ رَكَعَ ۞ فَلَمْ يَكَدْ يَرْفَعُ رَأْسَهُ ۞ ثُمَّ رَفَعَ رَأْسَهُ ۞ فَلَمْ يَكَدْ أَنْ يَسْجُدَ ۞ ثُمَّ سَجَدَ ۞ فَلَمْ يَكَدْ أَنْ يَرْفَعَ رَأْسَهُ ۞ ثُمَّ رَفَعَ رَأْسَهُ ۞ فَلَمْ يَكَدْ أَنْ يَسْجُدَ ۞ ثُمَّ سَجَدَ ۞ فَلَمْ يَكَدْ أَنْ يَرْفَعَ رَأْسَهُ ۞ فَجَعَلَ يَنْفُخُ وَيَبْكِي وَيَقُولُ رَبِّ أَلَمْ تَعِدْنِي أَنْ لَا تُعَذِّبَهُمْ وَأَنَا فِيهِمْ ۞ رَبِّ أَلَمْ تَعِدْنِي أَنْ لَا تُعَذِّبَهُمْ وَهُمْ يَسْتَغْفِرُونَ وَنَحْنُ نَسْتَغْفِرُكَ ۞ فَلَمَّا صَلَّىٰ رَكْعَتَيْنِ انْجَلَتِ الشَّمْسُ ۞ فَقَامَ فَحَمِدَ اللَّهَ تَعَالَىٰ وَأَثْنَىٰ عَلَيْهِ ۞ ثُمَّ قَالَ إِنَّ الشَّمْسَ وَالْقَمَرَ آيَتَانِ مِنْ آيَاتِ اللَّهِ ۞ لَا يَنْكَسِفَانِ لِمَوْتِ أَحَدٍ وَلَا لِحَيَاتِهِ ۞ فَإِذَا انْكَسَفَا فَافْزَعُوا إِلَىٰ ذِكْرِ اللَّهِ ۞

324. Qutayba narrated to us, 'Jarir narrated to us on the authority of 'Ata' ibn al-Sa'ib, on the authority of his father, on the authority of 'Abdullah ibn 'Amr, who reported:

"There was a solar eclipse one day during the time of the Messenger of Allah ﷺ.[706] The Messenger of Allah ﷺ stood and

[703] It is a Sunna to recite the Qur'an and it is an obligation to listen to it when it is being recited. Allah says, *And when the Qur'an is recited, hearken to it and listen attentively that you may receive mercy.* (Qur'an 7:204) (MA)

[704] The full verse is: *How will it be when We bring a witness from every nation, and We bring you as a witness over all these?* (AA)

[705] Ibn Battal said that the Prophet's ﷺ weeping resulted from him envisaging the Day of Judgement, its severity, his bearing witness for members of his *Umma* and their pleading for his intercession. Ibn Hajar al-'Asqalani said, 'The reason for his crying was due to his mercy for his *Umma*, for he realised that he would have to bear witness to their actions and knew that not all of their actions would be upright and would therefore lead them to punishment.' (MA)

[706] It is a Sunna to offer two units of prayer during the lunar and solar eclipse and to prolong them until the eclipse disappears. (MA)

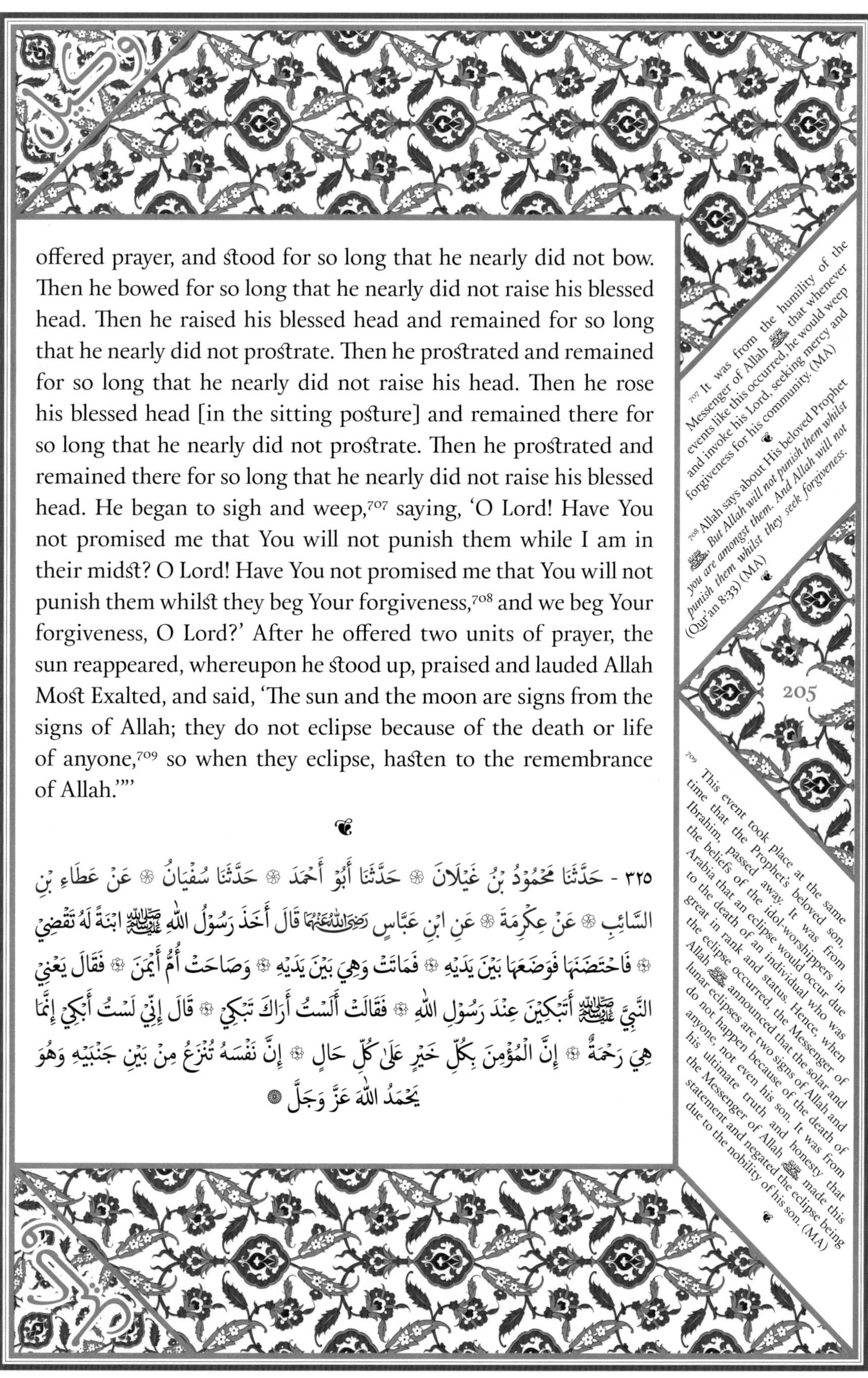

offered prayer, and stood for so long that he nearly did not bow. Then he bowed for so long that he nearly did not raise his blessed head. Then he raised his blessed head and remained for so long that he nearly did not prostrate. Then he prostrated and remained for so long that he nearly did not raise his head. Then he rose his blessed head [in the sitting posture] and remained there for so long that he nearly did not prostrate. Then he prostrated and remained there for so long that he nearly did not raise his blessed head. He began to sigh and weep,[707] saying, 'O Lord! Have You not promised me that You will not punish them while I am in their midst? O Lord! Have You not promised me that You will not punish them whilst they beg Your forgiveness,[708] and we beg Your forgiveness, O Lord?' After he offered two units of prayer, the sun reappeared, whereupon he stood up, praised and lauded Allah Most Exalted, and said, 'The sun and the moon are signs from the signs of Allah; they do not eclipse because of the death or life of anyone,[709] so when they eclipse, hasten to the remembrance of Allah.'"'

٣٢٥ - حَدَّثَنَا مَحْمُودُ بْنُ غَيْلَانَ ۞ حَدَّثَنَا أَبُو أَحْمَدَ ۞ حَدَّثَنَا سُفْيَانُ ۞ عَنْ عَطَاءِ بْنِ السَّائِبِ ۞ عَنْ عِكْرِمَةَ ۞ عَنِ ابْنِ عَبَّاسٍ رَضِيَ اللهُ عَنْهُمَا قَالَ أَخَذَ رَسُولُ اللهِ ﷺ ابْنَةً لَهُ تَقْضِي ۞ فَاحْتَضَنَهَا فَوَضَعَهَا بَيْنَ يَدَيْهِ ۞ فَمَاتَتْ وَهِيَ بَيْنَ يَدَيْهِ ۞ وَصَاحَتْ أُمُّ أَيْمَنَ ۞ فَقَالَ يَعْنِي النَّبِيَّ ﷺ أَتَبْكِينَ عِنْدَ رَسُولِ اللهِ ۞ فَقَالَتْ أَلَسْتُ أَرَاكَ تَبْكِي ۞ قَالَ إِنِّي لَسْتُ أَبْكِي إِنَّمَا هِيَ رَحْمَةٌ ۞ إِنَّ الْمُؤْمِنَ بِكُلِّ خَيْرٍ عَلَى كُلِّ حَالٍ ۞ إِنَّ نَفْسَهُ تُنْزَعُ مِنْ بَيْنِ جَنْبَيْهِ وَهُوَ يَحْمَدُ اللهَ عَزَّ وَجَلَّ ۞

[707] It was from the humility of the Messenger of Allah ﷺ that whenever events like this occurred, he would weep and invoke his Lord, seeking mercy and forgiveness for his community. (MA)

[708] Allah says about His beloved Prophet ﷺ, *But Allah will not punish them whilst you are amongst them. And Allah will not punish them whilst they seek forgiveness.* (Qur'an 8:33) (MA)

[709] This event took place at the same time that the Prophet's beloved son, Ibrahim, passed away. It was from the beliefs of the idol-worshippers in Arabia that an eclipse would occur due to the death of an individual who was great in rank and status. Hence, when the eclipse occurred, the Messenger of Allah ﷺ announced that the solar and lunar eclipses are two signs of Allah and do not happen because of the death of anyone, not even his son. It was from his ultimate truth and honesty that the Messenger of Allah ﷺ made this statement and negated the eclipse being due to the nobility of his son. (MA)

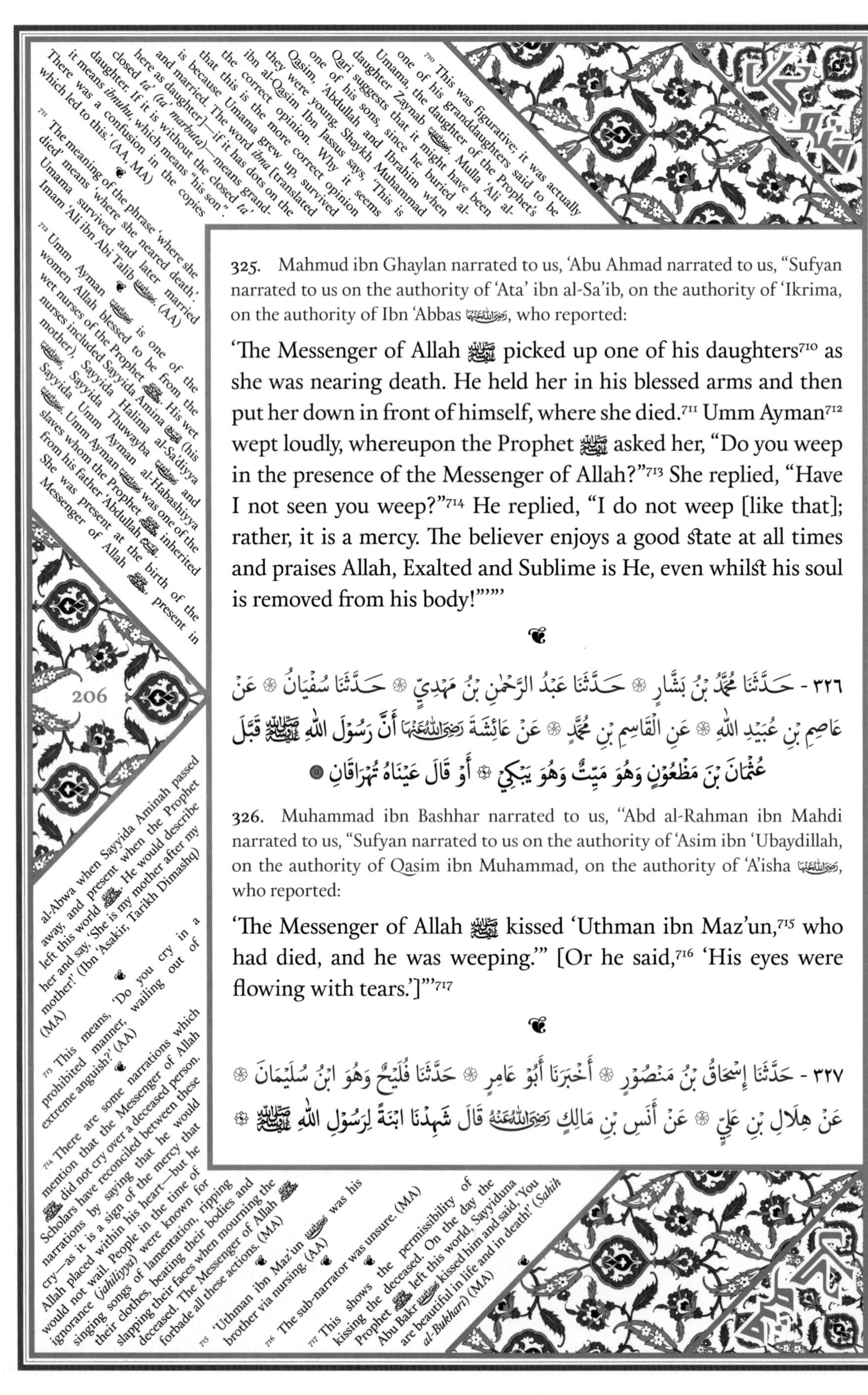

325. Mahmud ibn Ghaylan narrated to us, 'Abu Ahmad narrated to us, "Sufyan narrated to us on the authority of 'Ata' ibn al-Sa'ib, on the authority of 'Ikrima, on the authority of Ibn 'Abbas, who reported:

'The Messenger of Allah picked up one of his daughters[710] as she was nearing death. He held her in his blessed arms and then put her down in front of himself, where she died.[711] Umm Ayman[712] wept loudly, whereupon the Prophet asked her, "Do you weep in the presence of the Messenger of Allah?"[713] She replied, "Have I not seen you weep?"[714] He replied, "I do not weep [like that]; rather, it is a mercy. The believer enjoys a good state at all times and praises Allah, Exalted and Sublime is He, even whilst his soul is removed from his body!"""'

٣٢٦ - حَدَّثَنَا مُحَمَّدُ بْنُ بَشَّارٍ ۞ حَدَّثَنَا عَبْدُ الرَّحْمَٰنِ بْنُ مَهْدِيٍّ ۞ حَدَّثَنَا سُفْيَانُ ۞ عَنْ عَاصِمِ بْنِ عُبَيْدِ اللهِ ۞ عَنِ الْقَاسِمِ بْنِ مُحَمَّدٍ ۞ عَنْ عَائِشَةَ رَضِيَ اللهُ عَنْهَا أَنَّ رَسُولَ اللهِ ﷺ قَبَّلَ عُثْمَانَ بْنَ مَظْعُونٍ وَهُوَ مَيِّتٌ وَهُوَ يَبْكِي ۞ أَوْ قَالَ عَيْنَاهُ تُهَرَاقَانِ ۞

326. Muhammad ibn Bashhar narrated to us, "Abd al-Rahman ibn Mahdi narrated to us, "Sufyan narrated to us on the authority of 'Asim ibn 'Ubaydillah, on the authority of Qasim ibn Muhammad, on the authority of 'A'isha, who reported:

'The Messenger of Allah kissed 'Uthman ibn Maz'un,[715] who had died, and he was weeping.'" [Or he said,[716] 'His eyes were flowing with tears.']"'[717]

٣٢٧ - حَدَّثَنَا إِسْحَاقُ بْنُ مَنْصُورٍ ۞ أَخْبَرَنَا أَبُو عَامِرٍ ۞ حَدَّثَنَا فُلَيْحٌ وَهُوَ ابْنُ سُلَيْمَانَ ۞ عَنْ هِلَالِ بْنِ عَلِيٍّ ۞ عَنْ أَنَسِ بْنِ مَالِكٍ رَضِيَ اللهُ عَنْهُ قَالَ شَهِدْنَا ابْنَةً لِرَسُولِ اللهِ ﷺ ۞

[710] This was figurative; it was actually one of his granddaughters said to be Umama, the daughter of the Prophet's daughter Zaynab. Mulla 'Ali al-Qari suggests that it might have been one of his sons, since he buried al-Qasim, 'Abdullah and Ibrahim when they were young. Shaykh Muhammad ibn al-Qasim Ibn Jassus says, 'This is the correct opinion. Why it seems that this is the more correct opinion is because Umama grew up, survived and married. The word *ibna* [translated here as daughter]—if it has dots on the closed *ta'* (*ta' marbuta*)—means granddaughter. If it is without the closed *ta'* it means *ibnuhu*, which means "his son". There was a confusion in the copies which led to this.' (AA, MA)

[711] The meaning of the phrase 'where she died' means 'where she neared death'. Umama survived and later married Imam 'Ali ibn Abi Talib. (AA)

[712] Umm Ayman is one of the women Allah blessed to be from the wet nurses of the Prophet. His wet nurses included Sayyida Amina (his mother), Sayyida Halima al-Sa'diyya, Sayyida Thuwayba and Sayyida Umm Ayman al-Habashiyya. Umm Ayman was one of the slaves whom the Prophet inherited from his father 'Abdullah. She was present at the birth of the Messenger of Allah, present in al-Abwa when Sayyida Aminah passed away, and present when the Prophet left this world. He would describe her and say, 'She is my mother after my mother!' (Ibn 'Asakir, Tarikh Dimashq) (MA)

[713] This means, 'Do you cry in a prohibited manner, wailing out of extreme anguish?' (AA)

[714] There are some narrations which mention that the Messenger of Allah did not cry over a deceased person. Scholars have reconciled between these narrations by saying that he would cry—as it is a sign of the mercy that Allah placed within his heart—but he would not wail. People in the time of ignorance (*jahiliyya*) were known for singing songs of lamentation, ripping their clothes, beating their bodies and slapping their faces when mourning the deceased. The Messenger of Allah forbade all these actions. (MA)

[715] 'Uthman ibn Maz'un was his brother via nursing. (AA)

[716] The sub-narrator was unsure. (MA)

[717] This shows the permissibility of kissing the deceased. On the day the Prophet left this world, Sayyiduna Abu Bakr kissed him and said, 'You are beautiful in life and in death!' (*Sahih al-Bukhari*) (MA)

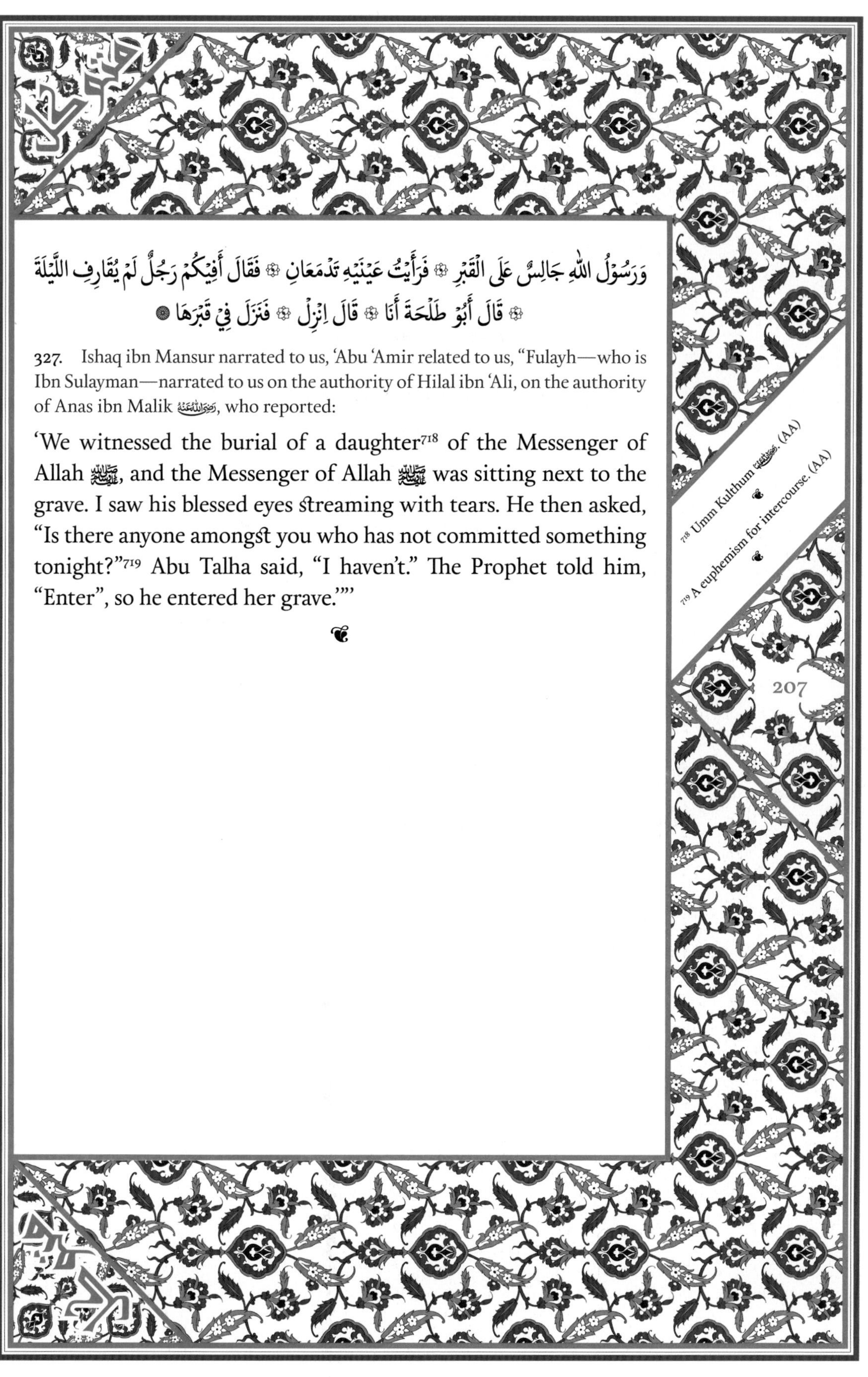

وَرَسُوْلُ اللهِ جَالِسٌ عَلَى الْقَبْرِ ۞ فَرَأَيْتُ عَيْنَيْهِ تَدْمَعَانِ ۞ فَقَالَ أَفِيْكُمْ رَجُلٌ لَمْ يُقَارِفِ اللَّيْلَةَ
۞ قَالَ أَبُوْ طَلْحَةَ أَنَا ۞ قَالَ انْزِلْ ۞ فَنَزَلَ فِيْ قَبْرِهَا ۞

327. Ishaq ibn Mansur narrated to us, 'Abu 'Amir related to us, "Fulayh—who is Ibn Sulayman—narrated to us on the authority of Hilal ibn 'Ali, on the authority of Anas ibn Malik رضي الله عنه, who reported:

'We witnessed the burial of a daughter[718] of the Messenger of Allah ﷺ, and the Messenger of Allah ﷺ was sitting next to the grave. I saw his blessed eyes streaming with tears. He then asked, "Is there anyone amongst you who has not committed something tonight?"[719] Abu Talha said, "I haven't." The Prophet told him, "Enter", so he entered her grave.'"

[718] Umm Kulthum رضي الله عنها. (AA)

[719] A euphemism for intercourse. (AA)

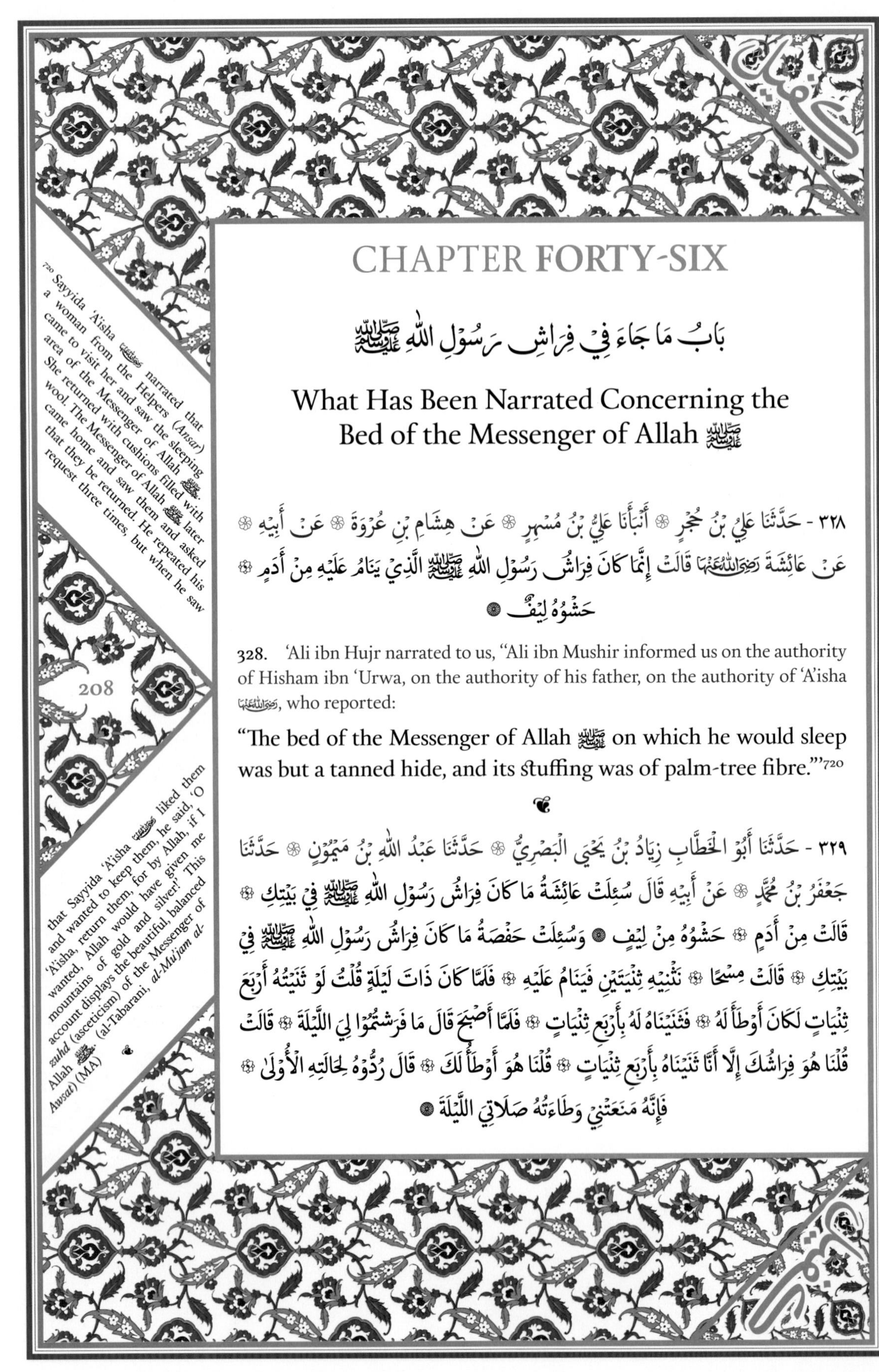

CHAPTER FORTY-SIX

بَابُ مَا جَاءَ فِي فِرَاشِ رَسُولِ اللهِ ﷺ

What Has Been Narrated Concerning the Bed of the Messenger of Allah ﷺ

٣٢٨ - حَدَّثَنَا عَلِيُّ بْنُ حُجْرٍ ۞ أَنْبَأَنَا عَلِيُّ بْنُ مُسْهِرٍ ۞ عَنْ هِشَامِ بْنِ عُرْوَةَ ۞ عَنْ أَبِيهِ ۞ عَنْ عَائِشَةَ رَضِيَ اللهُ عَنْهَا قَالَتْ إِنَّمَا كَانَ فِرَاشُ رَسُولِ اللهِ ﷺ الَّذِي يَنَامُ عَلَيْهِ مِنْ أَدَمٍ ۞ حَشْوُهُ لِيفٌ ۞

328. 'Ali ibn Hujr narrated to us, "Ali ibn Mushir informed us on the authority of Hisham ibn 'Urwa, on the authority of his father, on the authority of 'A'isha رضي الله عنها, who reported:

"The bed of the Messenger of Allah ﷺ on which he would sleep was but a tanned hide, and its stuffing was of palm-tree fibre."'[720]

٣٢٩ - حَدَّثَنَا أَبُو الْخَطَّابِ زِيَادُ بْنُ يَحْيَى الْبَصْرِيُّ ۞ حَدَّثَنَا عَبْدُ اللهِ بْنُ مَيْمُونٍ ۞ حَدَّثَنَا جَعْفَرُ بْنُ مُحَمَّدٍ ۞ عَنْ أَبِيهِ قَالَ سُئِلَتْ عَائِشَةُ مَا كَانَ فِرَاشُ رَسُولِ اللهِ ﷺ فِي بَيْتِكِ ۞ قَالَتْ مِنْ أَدَمٍ ۞ حَشْوُهُ مِنْ لِيفٍ ۞ وَسُئِلَتْ حَفْصَةُ مَا كَانَ فِرَاشُ رَسُولِ اللهِ ﷺ فِي بَيْتِكِ ۞ قَالَتْ مِسْحًا ۞ نَثْنِيهِ ثِنْيَتَيْنِ فَيَنَامُ عَلَيْهِ ۞ فَلَمَّا كَانَ ذَاتَ لَيْلَةٍ قُلْتُ لَوْ ثَنَيْتَهُ أَرْبَعَ ثِنْيَاتٍ لَكَانَ أَوْطَأَ لَهُ ۞ فَثَنَيْنَاهُ لَهُ بِأَرْبَعِ ثِنْيَاتٍ ۞ فَلَمَّا أَصْبَحَ قَالَ مَا فَرَشْتُمُوا لِيَ اللَّيْلَةَ ۞ قَالَتْ قُلْنَا هُوَ فِرَاشُكَ إِلَّا أَنَّا ثَنَيْنَاهُ بِأَرْبَعِ ثِنْيَاتٍ ۞ قُلْنَا هُوَ أَوْطَأُ لَكَ ۞ قَالَ رُدُّوهُ لِحَالَتِهِ الْأُولَى ۞ فَإِنَّهُ مَنَعَتْنِي وَطَاءَتُهُ صَلَاتِيَ اللَّيْلَةَ ۞

[720] Sayyida 'A'isha رضي الله عنها narrated that a woman from the Helpers (*Ansar*) came to visit her and saw the sleeping area of the Messenger of Allah ﷺ. She returned with cushions filled with wool. The Messenger of Allah ﷺ later came home and saw them and asked that they be returned. He repeated his request three times, but when he saw that Sayyida 'A'isha رضي الله عنها liked them and wanted to keep them, he said, 'O 'A'isha, return them, for by Allah, if I wanted, Allah would have given me mountains of gold and silver!' This account displays the beautiful, balanced *zuhd* (asceticism) of the Messenger of Allah ﷺ. (al-Tabarani, *al-Mu'jam al-Awsat*) (MA)

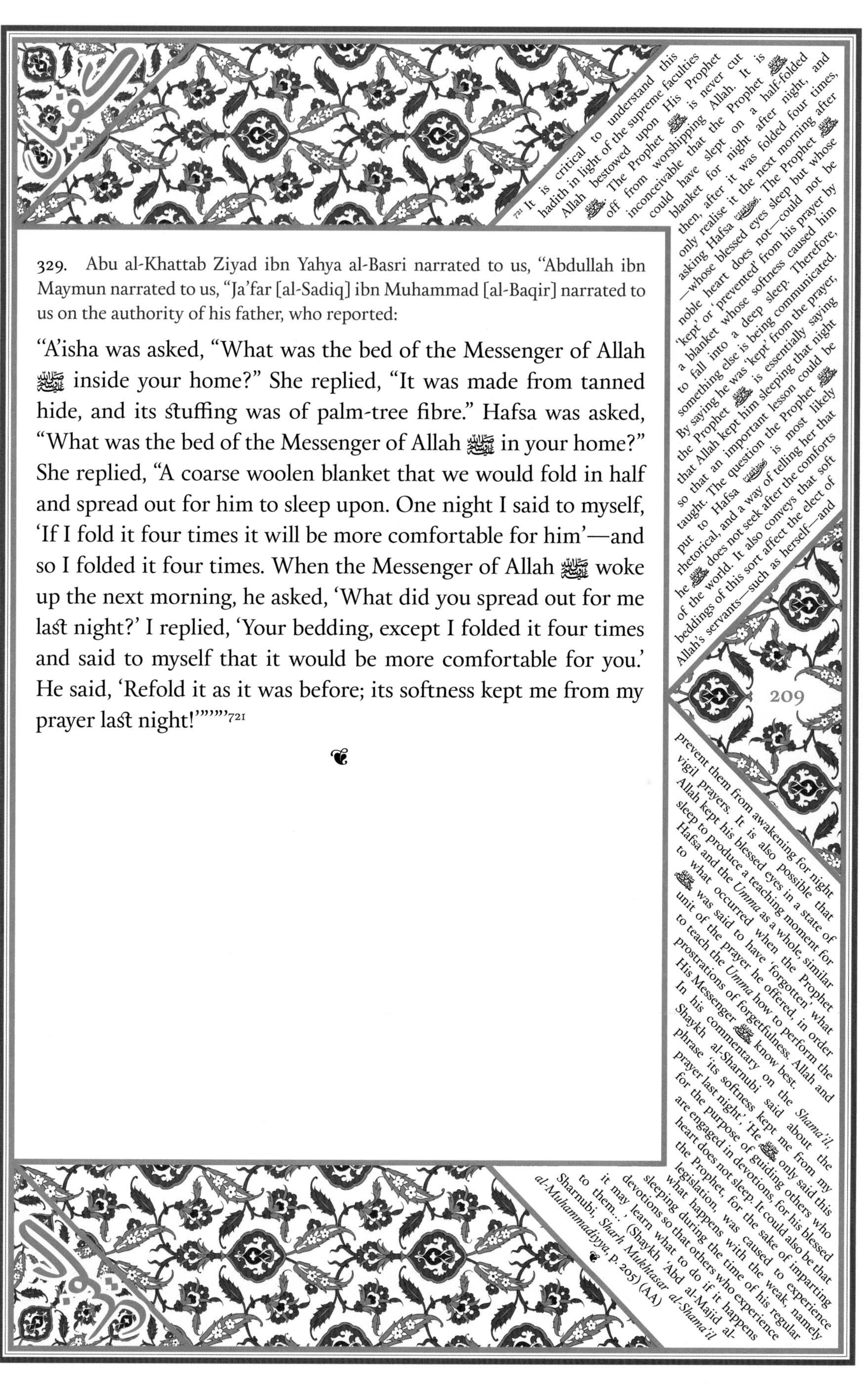

329. Abu al-Khattab Ziyad ibn Yahya al-Basri narrated to us, "Abdullah ibn Maymun narrated to us, "Ja'far [al-Sadiq] ibn Muhammad [al-Baqir] narrated to us on the authority of his father, who reported:

"A'isha was asked, "What was the bed of the Messenger of Allah ﷺ inside your home?" She replied, "It was made from tanned hide, and its stuffing was of palm-tree fibre." Hafsa was asked, "What was the bed of the Messenger of Allah ﷺ in your home?" She replied, "A coarse woolen blanket that we would fold in half and spread out for him to sleep upon. One night I said to myself, 'If I fold it four times it will be more comfortable for him'—and so I folded it four times. When the Messenger of Allah ﷺ woke up the next morning, he asked, 'What did you spread out for me last night?' I replied, 'Your bedding, except I folded it four times and said to myself that it would be more comfortable for you.' He said, 'Refold it as it was before; its softness kept me from my prayer last night!'"""[721]

[721] It is critical to understand this hadith in light of the supreme faculties Allah bestowed upon His Prophet ﷺ. The Prophet ﷺ is never cut off from worshipping Allah. It is inconceivable that the Prophet ﷺ could have slept on a half-folded blanket for night after night, and then, after it was folded four times, only realise it the next morning after asking Hafsa. The Prophet ﷺ—whose blessed eyes sleep but whose noble heart does not—could not be 'kept' or 'prevented' from his prayer by a blanket whose softness caused him to fall into a deep sleep. Therefore, something else is being communicated. By saying he was 'kept' from the prayer, the Prophet ﷺ is essentially saying that Allah kept him sleeping that night so that an important lesson could be taught. The question the Prophet ﷺ put to Hafsa is most likely rhetorical, and a way of telling her that he ﷺ does not seek after the comforts of the world. It also conveys that soft beddings of this sort affect the elect of Allah's servants—such as herself—and prevent them from awakening for night vigil prayers. It is also possible that Allah kept his blessed eyes in a state of sleep to produce a teaching moment for Hafsa and the *Umma* as a whole, similar to what occurred when the Prophet ﷺ was said to have 'forgotten' what unit of the prayer he offered, in order to teach the *Umma* how to perform the prostrations of forgetfulness. Allah and His Messenger ﷺ know best. In his commentary on the *Shama'il*, Shaykh al-Sharnubi said about the phrase 'its softness kept me from my prayer last night', 'He ﷺ only said this for the purpose of guiding others who are engaged in devotions, for his blessed heart does not sleep. It could also be that the Prophet, for the sake of imparting legislation, was caused to experience what happens with the weak, namely sleeping during the time of his regular devotions so that others who experience it may learn what to do if it happens to them...' (Shaykh 'Abd al-Majid al-Sharnubi, *Sharh Mukhtasar al-Shama'il al-Muhammadiyya*, p. 205) (AA)

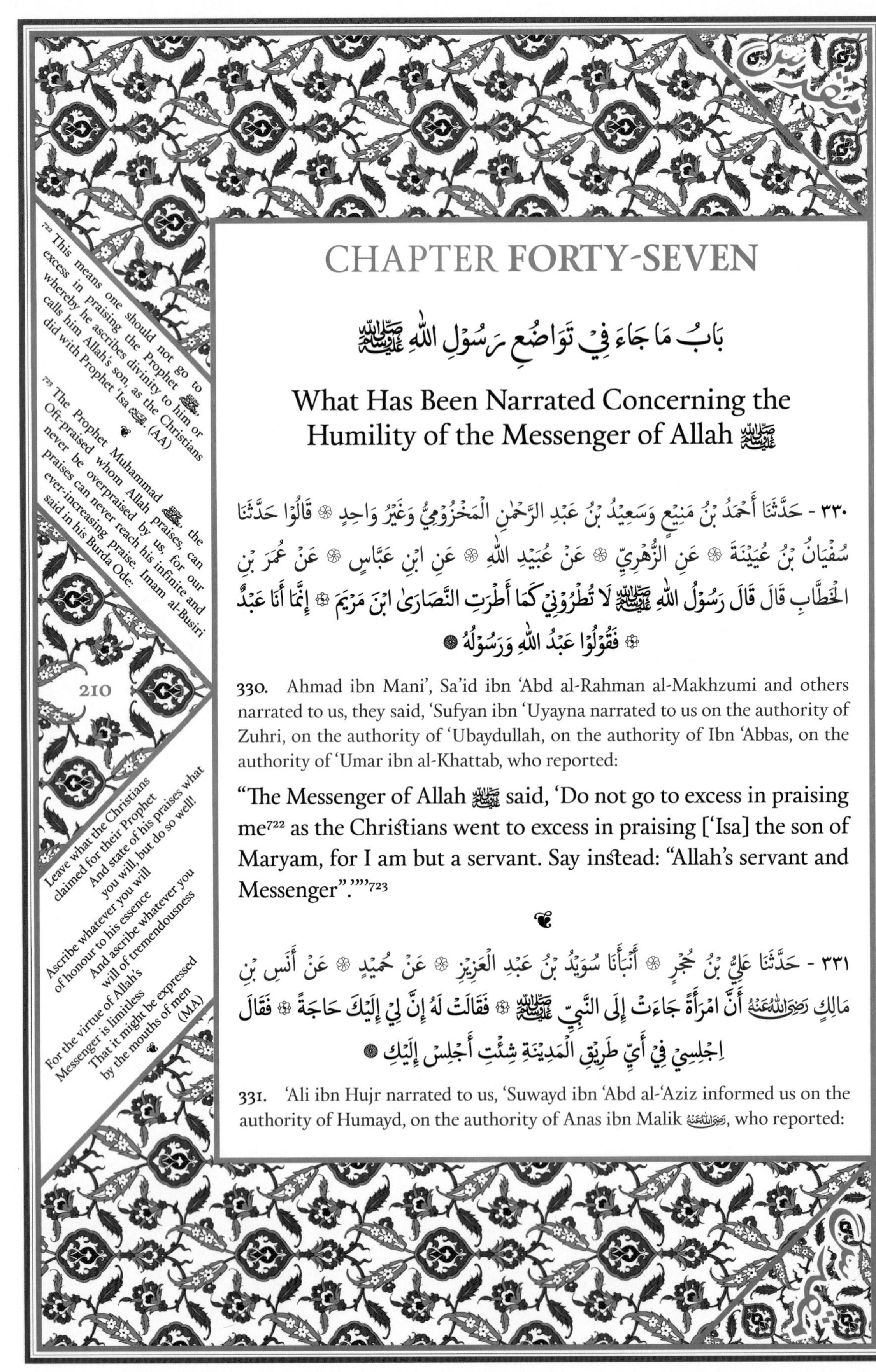

CHAPTER FORTY-SEVEN

بَابُ مَا جَاءَ فِي تَوَاضُعِ رَسُولِ اللهِ ﷺ

What Has Been Narrated Concerning the Humility of the Messenger of Allah ﷺ

٣٣٠ - حَدَّثَنَا أَحْمَدُ بْنُ مَنِيعٍ وَسَعِيدُ بْنُ عَبْدِ الرَّحْمَٰنِ الْمَخْزُومِيُّ وَغَيْرُ وَاحِدٍ ۞ قَالُوا حَدَّثَنَا سُفْيَانُ بْنُ عُيَيْنَةَ ۞ عَنِ الزُّهْرِيِّ ۞ عَنْ عُبَيْدِ اللهِ ۞ عَنِ ابْنِ عَبَّاسٍ ۞ عَنْ عُمَرَ بْنِ الْخَطَّابِ قَالَ قَالَ رَسُولُ اللهِ ﷺ لَا تُطْرُونِي كَمَا أَطْرَتِ النَّصَارَىٰ ابْنَ مَرْيَمَ ۞ إِنَّمَا أَنَا عَبْدٌ ۞ فَقُولُوا عَبْدُ اللهِ وَرَسُولُهُ ۞

330. Ahmad ibn Mani', Sa'id ibn 'Abd al-Rahman al-Makhzumi and others narrated to us, they said, 'Sufyan ibn 'Uyayna narrated to us on the authority of Zuhri, on the authority of 'Ubaydullah, on the authority of Ibn 'Abbas, on the authority of 'Umar ibn al-Khattab, who reported:

"The Messenger of Allah ﷺ said, 'Do not go to excess in praising me[722] as the Christians went to excess in praising ['Isa] the son of Maryam, for I am but a servant. Say instead: "Allah's servant and Messenger".'"[723]

٣٣١ - حَدَّثَنَا عَلِيُّ بْنُ حُجْرٍ ۞ أَنْبَأَنَا سُوَيْدُ بْنُ عَبْدِ الْعَزِيزِ ۞ عَنْ حُمَيْدٍ ۞ عَنْ أَنَسِ بْنِ مَالِكٍ رضي الله عنه أَنَّ امْرَأَةً جَاءَتْ إِلَى النَّبِيِّ ﷺ ۞ فَقَالَتْ لَهُ إِنَّ لِي إِلَيْكَ حَاجَةً ۞ فَقَالَ اجْلِسِي فِي أَيِّ طَرِيقِ الْمَدِينَةِ شِئْتِ أَجْلِسْ إِلَيْكِ ۞

331. 'Ali ibn Hujr narrated to us, 'Suwayd ibn 'Abd al-'Aziz informed us on the authority of Humayd, on the authority of Anas ibn Malik رضي الله عنه, who reported:

[722] This means one should not go to excess in praising the Prophet ﷺ, whereby he ascribes divinity to him or calls him Allah's son, as the Christians did with Prophet 'Isa عليه السلام. (AA)

[723] The Prophet Muhammad ﷺ, the Oft-praised whom Allah praises, can never be overpraised by us, for our praises can never reach his infinite and ever-increasing praise. Imam al-Busiri said in his Burda Ode:

Leave what the Christians claimed for their Prophet
And state of his praises what you will, but do so well!
Ascribe whatever you will of honour to his essence
And ascribe whatever you will of tremendousness
For the virtue of Allah's Messenger is limitless
That it might be expressed by the mouths of men
(MA)

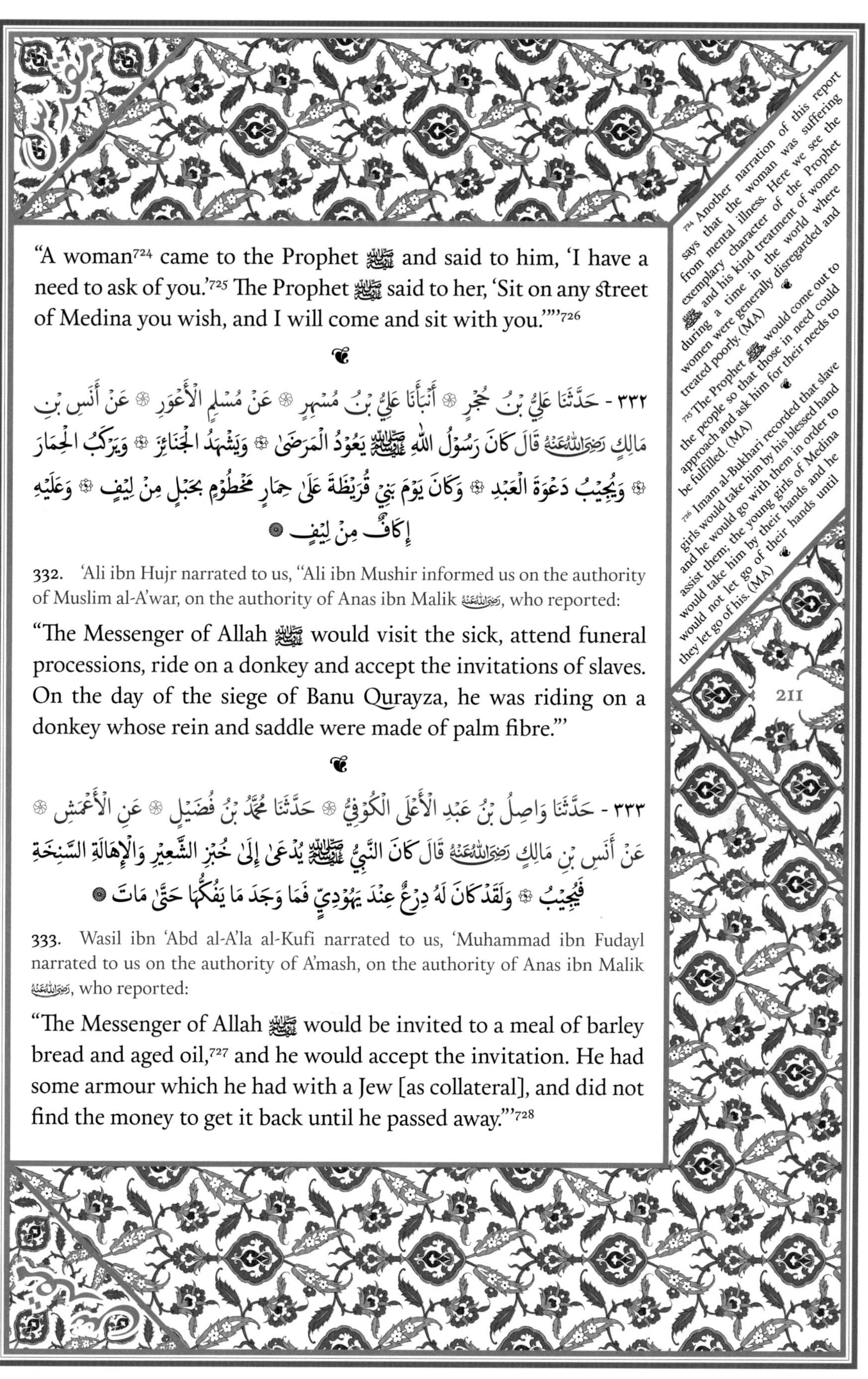

"A woman[724] came to the Prophet ﷺ and said to him, 'I have a need to ask of you.'[725] The Prophet ﷺ said to her, 'Sit on any street of Medina you wish, and I will come and sit with you.'"'[726]

❦

٣٣٢ - حَدَّثَنَا عَلِيُّ بْنُ حُجْرٍ ۞ أَنْبَأَنَا عَلِيُّ بْنُ مُسْهِرٍ ۞ عَنْ مُسْلِمٍ الْأَعْوَرِ ۞ عَنْ أَنَسِ بْنِ مَالِكٍ رَضِيَ اللَّهُ عَنْهُ قَالَ كَانَ رَسُولُ اللَّهِ ﷺ يَعُودُ الْمَرْضَىٰ ۞ وَيَشْهَدُ الْجَنَائِزَ ۞ وَيَرْكَبُ الْحِمَارَ ۞ وَيُجِيبُ دَعْوَةَ الْعَبْدِ ۞ وَكَانَ يَوْمَ بَنِي قُرَيْظَةَ عَلَىٰ حِمَارٍ مَخْطُومٍ بِحَبْلٍ مِنْ لِيفٍ ۞ وَعَلَيْهِ إِكَافٌ مِنْ لِيفٍ ۞

332. 'Ali ibn Hujr narrated to us, "Ali ibn Mushir informed us on the authority of Muslim al-A'war, on the authority of Anas ibn Malik رضي الله عنه, who reported:

"The Messenger of Allah ﷺ would visit the sick, attend funeral processions, ride on a donkey and accept the invitations of slaves. On the day of the siege of Banu Qurayza, he was riding on a donkey whose rein and saddle were made of palm fibre."'

❦

٣٣٣ - حَدَّثَنَا وَاصِلُ بْنُ عَبْدِ الْأَعْلَى الْكُوفِيُّ ۞ حَدَّثَنَا مُحَمَّدُ بْنُ فُضَيْلٍ ۞ عَنِ الْأَعْمَشِ ۞ عَنْ أَنَسِ بْنِ مَالِكٍ رَضِيَ اللَّهُ عَنْهُ قَالَ كَانَ النَّبِيُّ ﷺ يُدْعَىٰ إِلَىٰ خُبْزِ الشَّعِيرِ وَالْإِهَالَةِ السَّنِخَةِ فَيُجِيبُ ۞ وَلَقَدْ كَانَ لَهُ دِرْعٌ عِنْدَ يَهُودِيٍّ فَمَا وَجَدَ مَا يَفُكُّهَا حَتَّىٰ مَاتَ ۞

333. Wasil ibn 'Abd al-A'la al-Kufi narrated to us, 'Muhammad ibn Fudayl narrated to us on the authority of A'mash, on the authority of Anas ibn Malik رضي الله عنه, who reported:

"The Messenger of Allah ﷺ would be invited to a meal of barley bread and aged oil,[727] and he would accept the invitation. He had some armour which he had with a Jew [as collateral], and did not find the money to get it back until he passed away."'[728]

[724] Another narration of this report says that the woman was suffering from mental illness. Here we see the exemplary character of the Prophet ﷺ and his kind treatment of women during a time in the world where women were generally disregarded and treated poorly. (MA)

[725] The Prophet ﷺ would come out to the people so that those in need could approach and ask him for their needs to be fulfilled. (MA)

[726] Imam al-Bukhari recorded that slave girls would take him by his blessed hand and he would go with them in order to assist them; the young girls of Medina would take him by their hands and he would not let go of their hands until they let go of his. (MA)

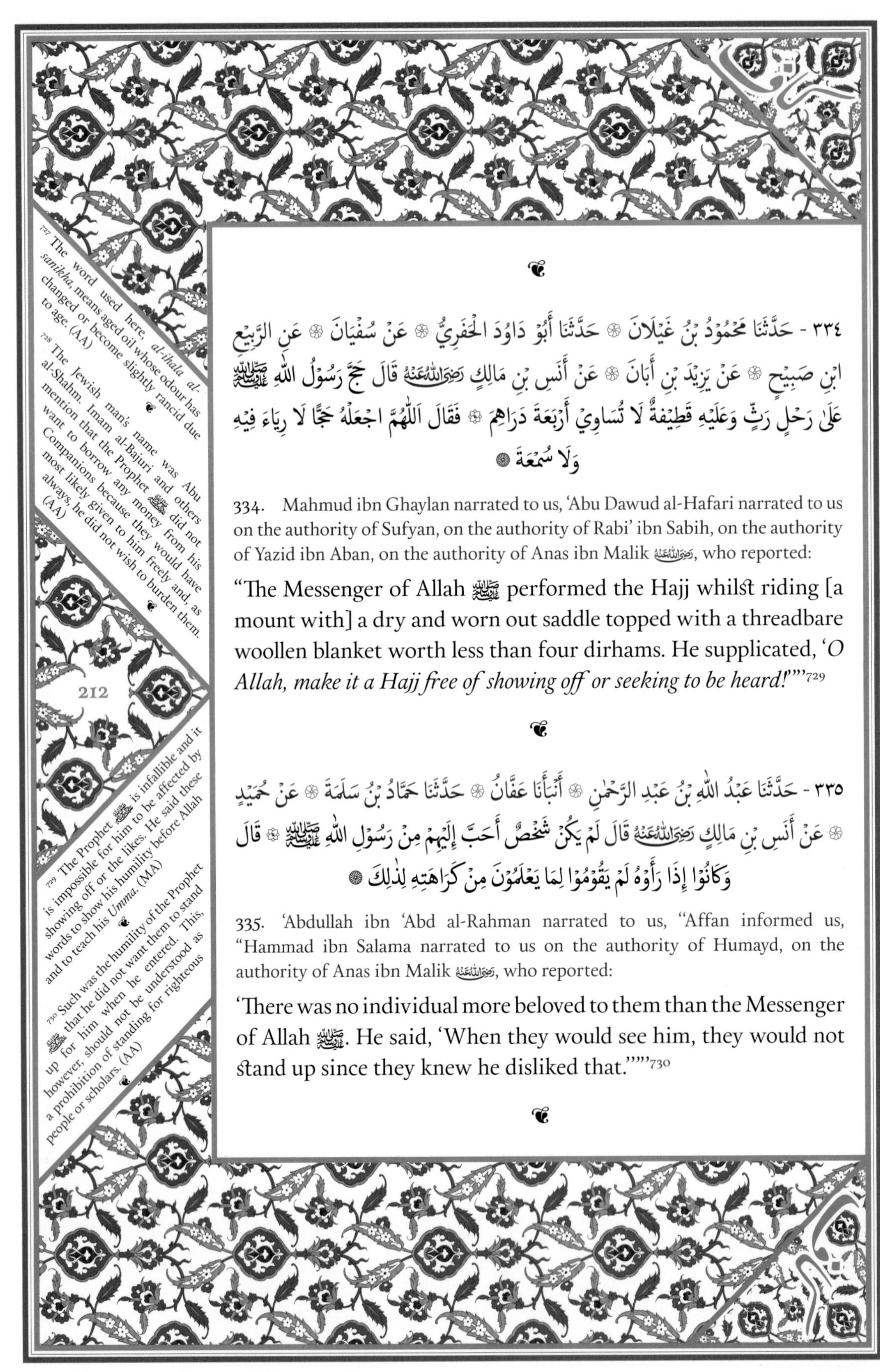

٣٣٤ - حَدَّثَنَا مَحْمُودُ بْنُ غَيْلَانَ ۞ حَدَّثَنَا أَبُو دَاوُدَ الْحَفَرِيُّ ۞ عَنْ سُفْيَانَ ۞ عَنِ الرَّبِيعِ ابْنِ صَبِيحٍ ۞ عَنْ يَزِيدَ بْنِ أَبَانَ ۞ عَنْ أَنَسِ بْنِ مَالِكٍ رَضِيَ اللَّهُ عَنْهُ قَالَ حَجَّ رَسُولُ اللهِ صَلَّى اللهُ عَلَيْهِ وَسَلَّمَ عَلَى رَحْلٍ رَثٍّ وَعَلَيْهِ قَطِيفَةٌ لَا تُسَاوِي أَرْبَعَةَ دَرَاهِمَ ۞ فَقَالَ اللَّهُمَّ اجْعَلْهُ حَجًّا لَا رِيَاءَ فِيهِ وَلَا سُمْعَةَ ۞

334. Mahmud ibn Ghaylan narrated to us, 'Abu Dawud al-Hafari narrated to us on the authority of Sufyan, on the authority of Rabi' ibn Sabih, on the authority of Yazid ibn Aban, on the authority of Anas ibn Malik رضي الله عنه, who reported:

"The Messenger of Allah ﷺ performed the Hajj whilst riding [a mount with] a dry and worn out saddle topped with a threadbare woollen blanket worth less than four dirhams. He supplicated, '*O Allah, make it a Hajj free of showing off or seeking to be heard!*'"'[729]

٣٣٥ - حَدَّثَنَا عَبْدُ اللهِ بْنُ عَبْدِ الرَّحْمٰنِ ۞ أَنْبَأَنَا عَفَّانُ ۞ حَدَّثَنَا حَمَّادُ بْنُ سَلَمَةَ ۞ عَنْ حُمَيْدٍ ۞ عَنْ أَنَسِ بْنِ مَالِكٍ رَضِيَ اللَّهُ عَنْهُ قَالَ لَمْ يَكُنْ شَخْصٌ أَحَبَّ إِلَيْهِمْ مِنْ رَسُولِ اللهِ صَلَّى اللهُ عَلَيْهِ وَسَلَّمَ ۞ قَالَ وَكَانُوا إِذَا رَأَوْهُ لَمْ يَقُومُوا لِمَا يَعْلَمُونَ مِنْ كَرَاهَتِهِ لِذٰلِكَ ۞

335. 'Abdullah ibn 'Abd al-Rahman narrated to us, "Affan informed us, "Hammad ibn Salama narrated to us on the authority of Humayd, on the authority of Anas ibn Malik رضي الله عنه, who reported:

'There was no individual more beloved to them than the Messenger of Allah ﷺ. He said, 'When they would see him, they would not stand up since they knew he disliked that.'"''[730]

[727] The word used here, *al-ihala al-sanikha*, means aged oil whose odour has changed or become slightly rancid due to age. (AA)

[728] The Jewish man's name was Abu al-Shahm. Imam al-Bajuri and others mention that the Prophet ﷺ did not want to borrow any money from his Companions because they would have most likely given to him freely and, as always, he did not wish to burden them. (AA)

[729] The Prophet ﷺ is infallible and it is impossible for him to be affected by showing off or the likes. He said these words to show his humility before Allah and to teach his *Umma*. (MA)

[730] Such was the humility of the Prophet ﷺ that he did not want them to stand up for him when he entered. This, however, should not be understood as a prohibition of standing for righteous people or scholars. (AA)

٣٣٦ - حَدَّثَنَا سُفيَانُ بْنُ وَكِيعٍ ۞ حَدَّثَنَا جُمَيْعُ بْنُ عُمَرَ بْنِ عَبْدِ الرَّحْمَنِ الْعِجْلِيُّ ۞ أَنْبَأَنَا رَجُلٌ مِنْ بَنِي تَمِيمٍ مِنْ وَلَدِ أَبِي هَالَةَ زَوْجِ خَدِيجَةَ رَضِيَ اللهُ عَنْهَا يُكْنَى أَبَا عَبْدِ اللهِ ۞ عَنِ ابْنٍ لِأَبِي هَالَةَ ۞ عَنِ الْحَسَنِ بْنِ عَلِيٍّ قَالَ سَأَلْتُ خَالِي هِنْدَ بْنَ أَبِي هَالَةَ وَكَانَ وَصَّافًا عَنْ حِلْيَةِ رَسُولِ اللهِ ﷺ ۞ وَأَنَا أَشْتَهِي أَنْ يَصِفَ لِي مِنْهَا شَيْئًا ۞ فَقَالَ كَانَ رَسُولُ اللهِ ﷺ فَخْمًا مُفَخَّمًا ۞ يَتَلَأْلَأُ وَجْهُهُ تَلَأْلُؤَ الْقَمَرِ لَيْلَةَ الْبَدْرِ ۞ فَذَكَرَ الْحَدِيثَ بِطُولِهِ ۞ قَالَ الْحَسَنُ فَكَتَمْتُهَا الْحُسَيْنَ زَمَانًا ۞ ثُمَّ حَدَّثْتُهُ ۞ فَوَجَدْتُهُ قَدْ سَبَقَنِي إِلَيْهِ ۞ فَسَأَلَهُ عَمَّا سَأَلْتُهُ عَنْهُ ۞ وَوَجَدْتُهُ قَدْ سَأَلَ أَبَاهُ عَنْ مَدْخَلِهِ وَمَخْرَجِهِ وَشَكْلِهِ فَلَمْ يَدَعْ مِنْهُ شَيْئًا ۞ قَالَ الْحُسَيْنُ فَسَأَلْتُ أَبِي عَنْ دُخُولِ رَسُولِ اللهِ ﷺ ۞ فَقَالَ كَانَ إِذَا أَوَى إِلَى مَنْزِلِهِ جَزَّأَ دُخُولَهُ ثَلَاثَةَ أَجْزَاءٍ ۞ جُزْءًا لِلهِ ۞ وَجُزْءًا لِأَهْلِهِ ۞ وَجُزْءًا لِنَفْسِهِ ۞ ثُمَّ جَزَّأَ جُزْأَهُ بَيْنَهُ وَبَيْنَ النَّاسِ ۞ فَيَرُدُّ ذَٰلِكَ بِالْخَاصَّةِ عَلَى الْعَامَّةِ ۞ وَلَا يَدَّخِرُ عَنْهُمْ شَيْئًا ۞ وَكَانَ مِنْ سِيرَتِهِ فِي جُزْءِ الْأُمَّةِ إِيثَارُ أَهْلِ الْفَضْلِ بِإِذْنِهِ ۞ وَقَسْمُهُ عَلَىٰ قَدْرِ فَضْلِهِمْ فِي الدِّينِ ۞ فَمِنْهُمْ ذُو الْحَاجَةِ ۞ وَمِنْهُمْ ذُو الْحَاجَتَيْنِ ۞ وَمِنْهُمْ ذُو الْحَوَائِجِ ۞ فَيَتَشَاغَلُ بِهِمْ ۞ وَيَشْغَلُهُمْ فِيمَا يُصْلِحُهُمْ وَالْأُمَّةَ مِنْ مَسْأَلَتِهِمْ عَنْهُ ۞ وَإِخْبَارِهِمْ بِالَّذِي يَنْبَغِي لَهُمْ ۞ وَيَقُولُ لِيُبَلِّغِ الشَّاهِدُ مِنْكُمُ الْغَائِبَ ۞ وَأَبْلِغُونِي حَاجَةَ مَنْ لَا يَسْتَطِيعُ إِبْلَاغَهَا ۞ فَإِنَّهُ مَنْ أَبْلَغَ سُلْطَانًا حَاجَةَ مَنْ لَا يَسْتَطِيعُ إِبْلَاغَهَا ثَبَّتَ اللهُ قَدَمَيْهِ يَوْمَ الْقِيَامَةِ ۞ لَا يُذْكَرُ عِنْدَهُ إِلَّا ذَٰلِكَ ۞ وَلَا يَقْبَلُ مِنْ أَحَدٍ غَيْرَهُ ۞ يَدْخُلُونَ رُوَّادًا ۞ وَلَا يَفْتَرِقُونَ إِلَّا عَنْ ذَوَاقٍ ۞ وَيَخْرُجُونَ أَدِلَّةً ۞ يَعْنِي عَلَى الْخَيْرِ ۞ قَالَ فَسَأَلْتُهُ عَنْ مَخْرَجِهِ كَيْفَ كَانَ يَصْنَعُ فِيهِ ۞ قَالَ كَانَ رَسُولُ اللهِ ﷺ يَخْزُنُ لِسَانَهُ إِلَّا فِيمَا يَعْنِيهِ ۞ وَيُؤَلِّفُهُمْ وَلَا يُنَفِّرُهُمْ ۞ وَيُكْرِمُ كَرِيمَ كُلِّ قَوْمٍ وَيُوَلِّيهِ عَلَيْهِمْ ۞ وَيَحْذَرُ النَّاسَ وَيَحْتَرِسُ مِنْهُمْ مِنْ غَيْرِ أَنْ يَطْوِيَ عَنْ أَحَدٍ مِنْهُمْ بِشْرَهُ وَخُلُقَهُ ۞ وَيَتَفَقَّدُ أَصْحَابَهُ ۞ وَيَسْأَلُ النَّاسَ عَمَّا فِي النَّاسِ ۞ وَيُحَسِّنُ الْحَسَنَ وَيُقَوِّيهِ ۞ وَيُقَبِّحُ الْقَبِيحَ وَيُوَهِّيهِ ۞ مُعْتَدِلُ الْأَمْرِ غَيْرُ مُخْتَلِفٍ ۞ لَا يَغْفُلُ

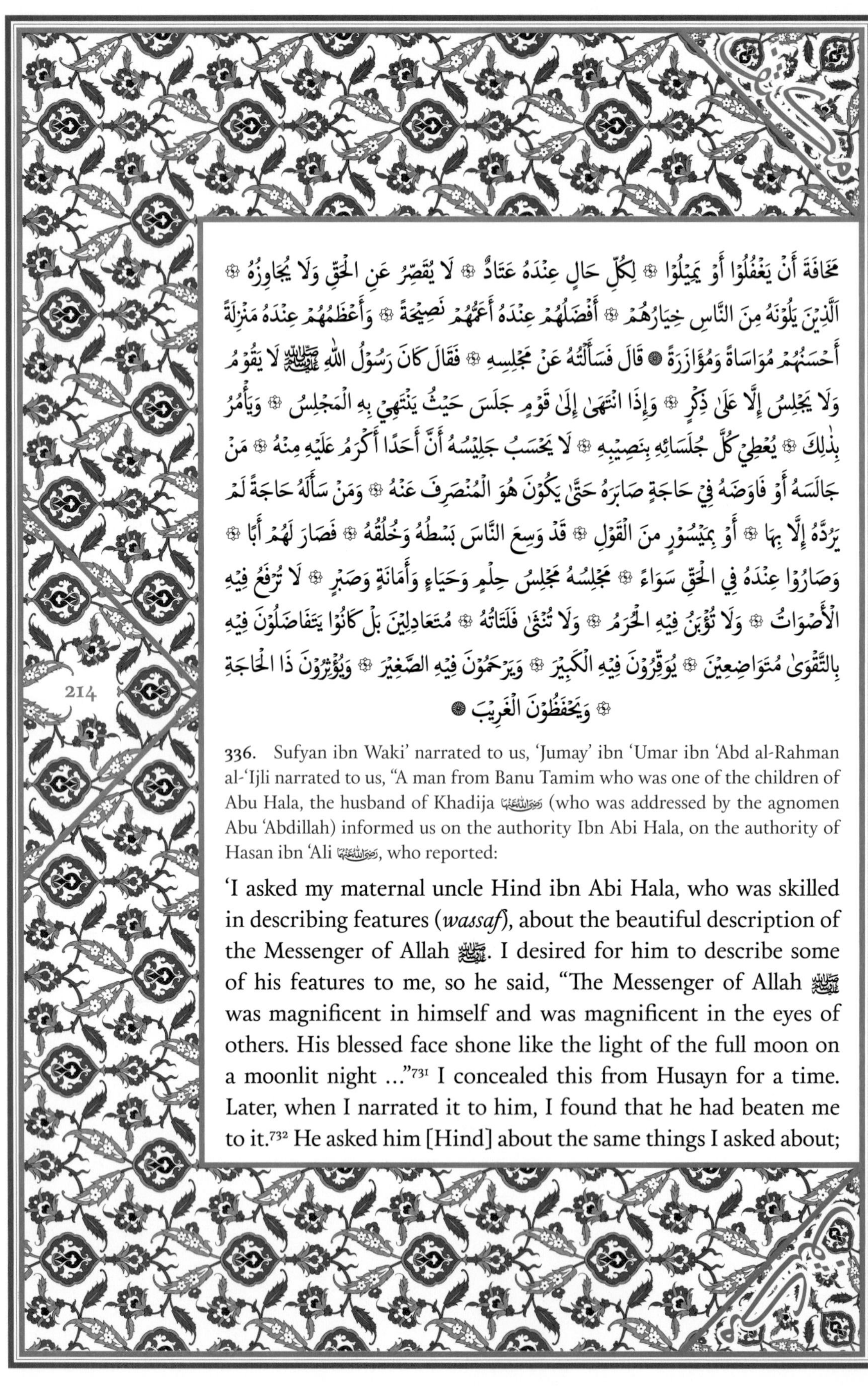

مَخَافَةَ أَنْ يَغْفُلُوا أَوْ يَمِيلُوا ۞ لِكُلِّ حَالٍ عِنْدَهُ عَتَادٌ ۞ لَا يُقَصِّرُ عَنِ الْحَقِّ وَلَا يُجَاوِزُهُ ۞
اَلَّذِينَ يَلُونَهُ مِنَ النَّاسِ خِيَارُهُمْ ۞ أَفْضَلُهُمْ عِنْدَهُ أَعَمُّهُمْ نَصِيحَةً ۞ وَأَعْظَمُهُمْ عِنْدَهُ مَنْزِلَةً
أَحْسَنُهُمْ مُوَاسَاةً وَمُؤَازَرَةً ۝ قَالَ فَسَأَلْتُهُ عَنْ مَجْلِسِهِ ۞ فَقَالَ كَانَ رَسُولُ اللهِ ﷺ لَا يَقُومُ
وَلَا يَجْلِسُ إِلَّا عَلَىٰ ذِكْرٍ ۞ وَإِذَا انْتَهَىٰ إِلَىٰ قَوْمٍ جَلَسَ حَيْثُ يَنْتَهِي بِهِ الْمَجْلِسُ ۞ وَيَأْمُرُ
بِذٰلِكَ ۞ يُعْطِي كُلَّ جُلَسَائِهِ بِنَصِيبِهِ ۞ لَا يَحْسَبُ جَلِيسُهُ أَنَّ أَحَدًا أَكْرَمُ عَلَيْهِ مِنْهُ ۞ مَنْ
جَالَسَهُ أَوْ فَاوَضَهُ فِي حَاجَةٍ صَابَرَهُ حَتَّىٰ يَكُونَ هُوَ الْمُنْصَرِفَ عَنْهُ ۞ وَمَنْ سَأَلَهُ حَاجَةً لَمْ
يَرُدَّهُ إِلَّا بِهَا ۞ أَوْ بِمَيْسُورٍ مِنَ الْقَوْلِ ۞ قَدْ وَسِعَ النَّاسَ بَسْطُهُ وَخُلُقُهُ ۞ فَصَارَ لَهُمْ أَبًا ۞
وَصَارُوا عِنْدَهُ فِي الْحَقِّ سَوَاءً ۞ مَجْلِسُهُ مَجْلِسُ حِلْمٍ وَحَيَاءٍ وَأَمَانَةٍ وَصَبْرٍ ۞ لَا تُرْفَعُ فِيهِ
الْأَصْوَاتُ ۞ وَلَا تُؤْبَنُ فِيهِ الْحُرَمُ ۞ وَلَا تُثْنَىٰ فَلَتَاتُهُ ۞ مُتَعَادِلِينَ بَلْ كَانُوا يَتَفَاضَلُونَ فِيهِ
بِالتَّقْوَىٰ مُتَوَاضِعِينَ ۞ يُوَقِّرُونَ فِيهِ الْكَبِيرَ ۞ وَيَرْحَمُونَ فِيهِ الصَّغِيرَ ۞ وَيُؤْثِرُونَ ذَا الْحَاجَةِ
۞ وَيَحْفَظُونَ الْغَرِيبَ ۝

336. Sufyan ibn Waki' narrated to us, 'Jumay' ibn 'Umar ibn 'Abd al-Rahman al-'Ijli narrated to us, "A man from Banu Tamim who was one of the children of Abu Hala, the husband of Khadija ﵂ (who was addressed by the agnomen Abu 'Abdillah) informed us on the authority Ibn Abi Hala, on the authority of Hasan ibn 'Ali ﵄, who reported:

'I asked my maternal uncle Hind ibn Abi Hala, who was skilled in describing features (*wassaf*), about the beautiful description of the Messenger of Allah ﷺ. I desired for him to describe some of his features to me, so he said, "The Messenger of Allah ﷺ was magnificent in himself and was magnificent in the eyes of others. His blessed face shone like the light of the full moon on a moonlit night ..."[731] I concealed this from Husayn for a time. Later, when I narrated it to him, I found that he had beaten me to it.[732] He asked him [Hind] about the same things I asked about;

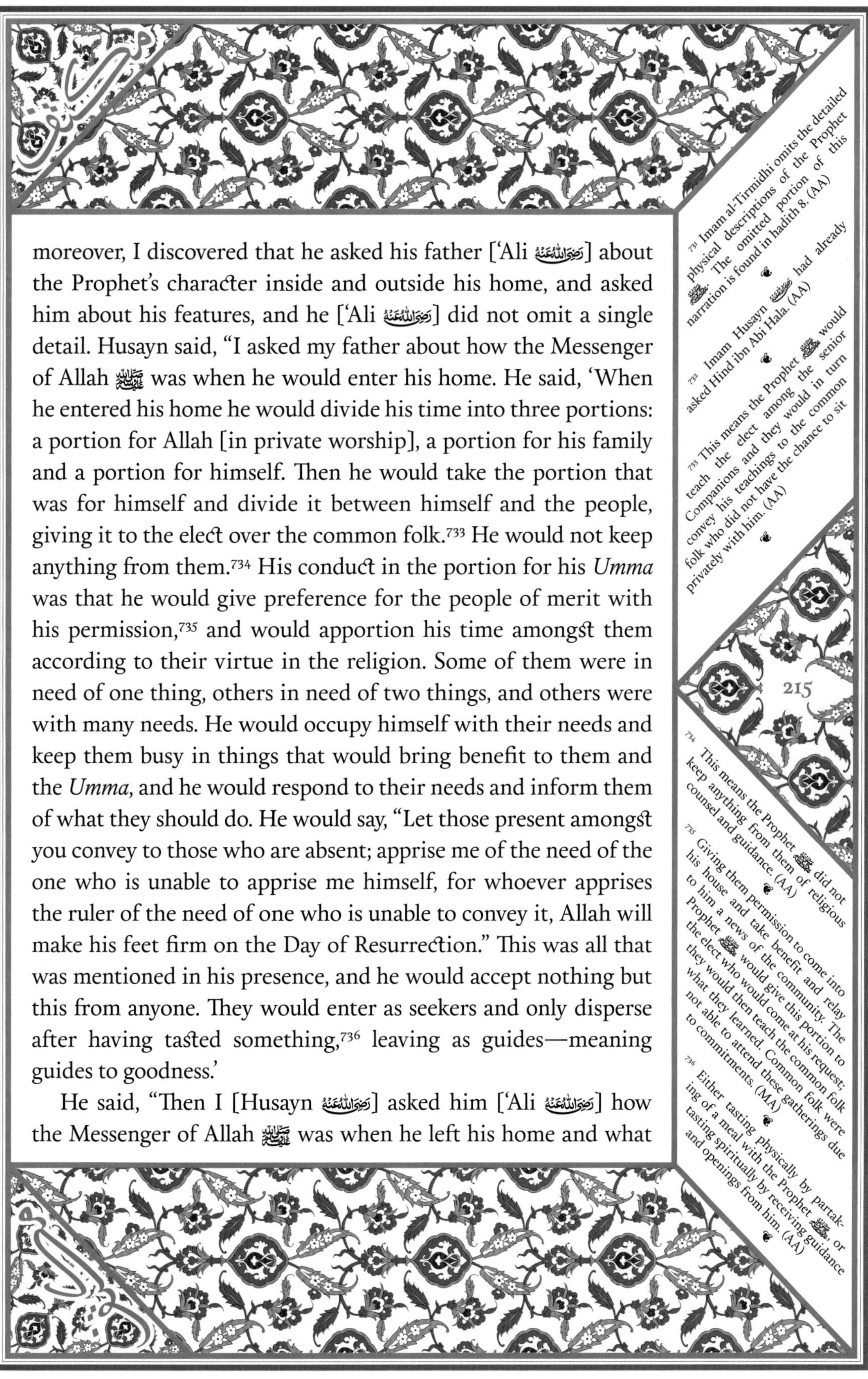

moreover, I discovered that he asked his father ['Ali رضي الله عنه] about the Prophet's character inside and outside his home, and asked him about his features, and he ['Ali رضي الله عنه] did not omit a single detail. Husayn said, "I asked my father about how the Messenger of Allah ﷺ was when he would enter his home. He said, 'When he entered his home he would divide his time into three portions: a portion for Allah [in private worship], a portion for his family and a portion for himself. Then he would take the portion that was for himself and divide it between himself and the people, giving it to the elect over the common folk.[733] He would not keep anything from them.[734] His conduct in the portion for his *Umma* was that he would give preference for the people of merit with his permission,[735] and would apportion his time amongst them according to their virtue in the religion. Some of them were in need of one thing, others in need of two things, and others were with many needs. He would occupy himself with their needs and keep them busy in things that would bring benefit to them and the *Umma*, and he would respond to their needs and inform them of what they should do. He would say, "Let those present amongst you convey to those who are absent; apprise me of the need of the one who is unable to apprise me himself, for whoever apprises the ruler of the need of one who is unable to convey it, Allah will make his feet firm on the Day of Resurrection." This was all that was mentioned in his presence, and he would accept nothing but this from anyone. They would enter as seekers and only disperse after having tasted something,[736] leaving as guides—meaning guides to goodness.'

He said, "Then I [Husayn رضي الله عنه] asked him ['Ali رضي الله عنه] how the Messenger of Allah ﷺ was when he left his home and what

731 Imam al-Tirmidhi omits the detailed physical descriptions of the Prophet ﷺ. The omitted portion of this narration is found in hadith 8. (AA)

732 Imam Husayn رضي الله عنه had already asked Hind ibn Abi Hala. (AA)

733 This means the Prophet ﷺ would teach the elect among the senior Companions and they would in turn convey his teachings to the common folk who did not have the chance to sit privately with him. (AA)

734 This means the Prophet ﷺ did not keep anything from them of religious counsel and guidance. (AA)

735 Giving them permission to come into his house and take benefit and relay to him a news of the community. The Prophet ﷺ would give this portion to the elect who would come at his request; they would then teach the common folk what they learned. Common folk were not able to attend these gatherings due to commitments. (MA)

736 Either tasting physically by partaking of a meal with the Prophet ﷺ, or tasting spiritually by receiving guidance and openings from him. (AA)

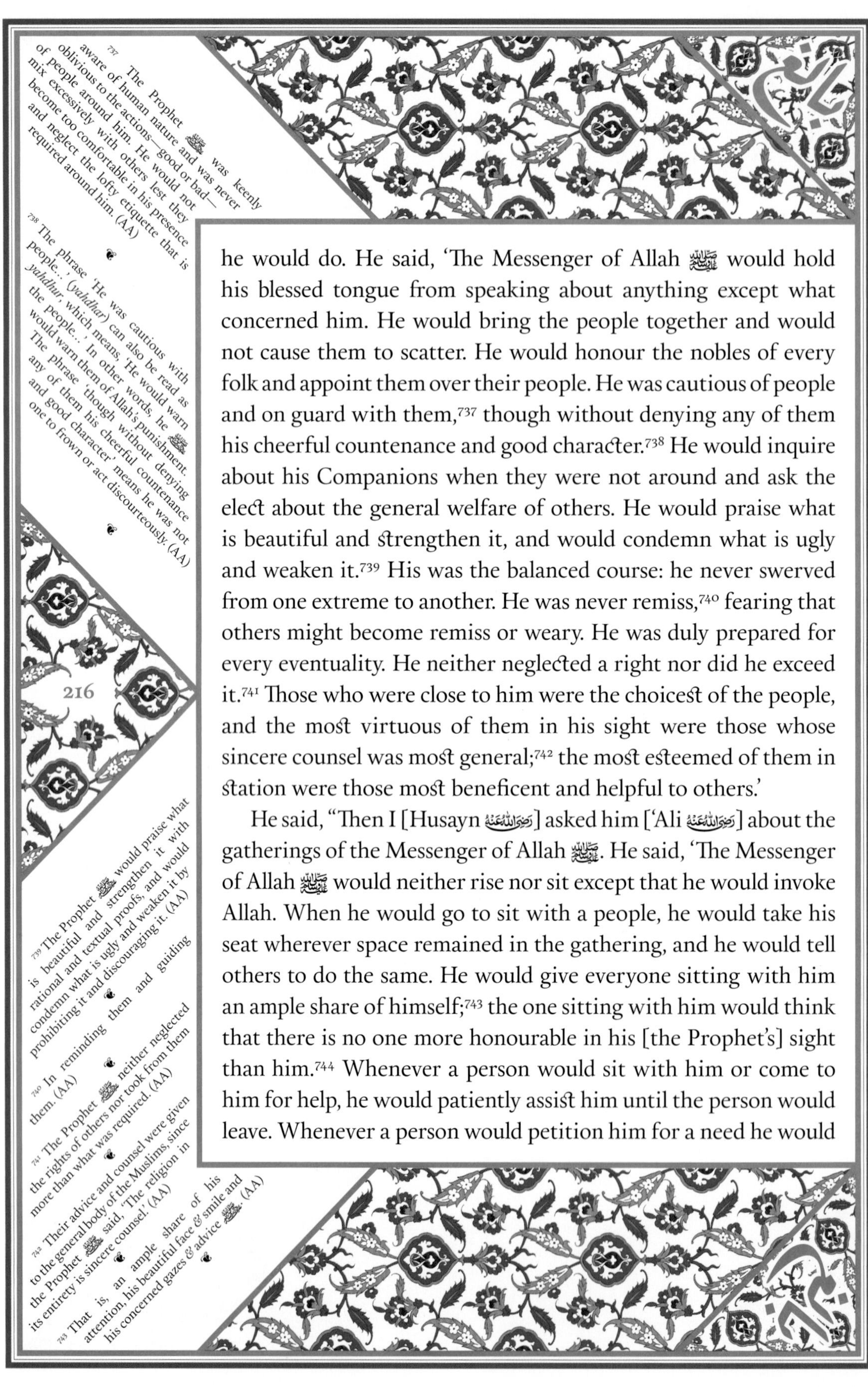

he would do. He said, 'The Messenger of Allah ﷺ would hold his blessed tongue from speaking about anything except what concerned him. He would bring the people together and would not cause them to scatter. He would honour the nobles of every folk and appoint them over their people. He was cautious of people and on guard with them,[737] though without denying any of them his cheerful countenance and good character.[738] He would inquire about his Companions when they were not around and ask the elect about the general welfare of others. He would praise what is beautiful and strengthen it, and would condemn what is ugly and weaken it.[739] His was the balanced course: he never swerved from one extreme to another. He was never remiss,[740] fearing that others might become remiss or weary. He was duly prepared for every eventuality. He neither neglected a right nor did he exceed it.[741] Those who were close to him were the choicest of the people, and the most virtuous of them in his sight were those whose sincere counsel was most general;[742] the most esteemed of them in station were those most beneficent and helpful to others.'

He said, "Then I [Husayn رضي الله عنه] asked him ['Ali رضي الله عنه] about the gatherings of the Messenger of Allah ﷺ. He said, 'The Messenger of Allah ﷺ would neither rise nor sit except that he would invoke Allah. When he would go to sit with a people, he would take his seat wherever space remained in the gathering, and he would tell others to do the same. He would give everyone sitting with him an ample share of himself;[743] the one sitting with him would think that there is no one more honourable in his [the Prophet's] sight than him.[744] Whenever a person would sit with him or come to him for help, he would patiently assist him until the person would leave. Whenever a person would petition him for a need he would

737 The Prophet ﷺ was keenly aware of human nature and was never oblivious to the actions—good or bad—of people around him. He would not mix excessively with others lest they become too comfortable in his presence and neglect the lofty etiquette that is required around him. (AA)

738 The phrase 'He was cautious with people...' (*yahdhar*) can also be read as *yuhdhir*, which means, 'He would warn the people...' In other words, he ﷺ would warn them of Allah's punishment. The phrase 'though without denying any of them his cheerful countenance and good character' means he was not one to frown or act discourteously. (AA)

739 The Prophet ﷺ would praise what is beautiful and strengthen it with rational and textual proofs, and would condemn what is ugly and weaken it by prohibiting it and discouraging it. (AA)

740 In reminding them and guiding them. (AA)

741 The Prophet ﷺ neither neglected the rights of others nor took from them more than what was required. (AA)

742 Their advice and counsel were given to the general body of the Muslims, since the Prophet ﷺ said, 'The religion in its entirety is sincere counsel.' (AA)

743 That is, an ample share of his attention, his beautiful face & smile and his concerned gazes & advice ﷺ. (AA)

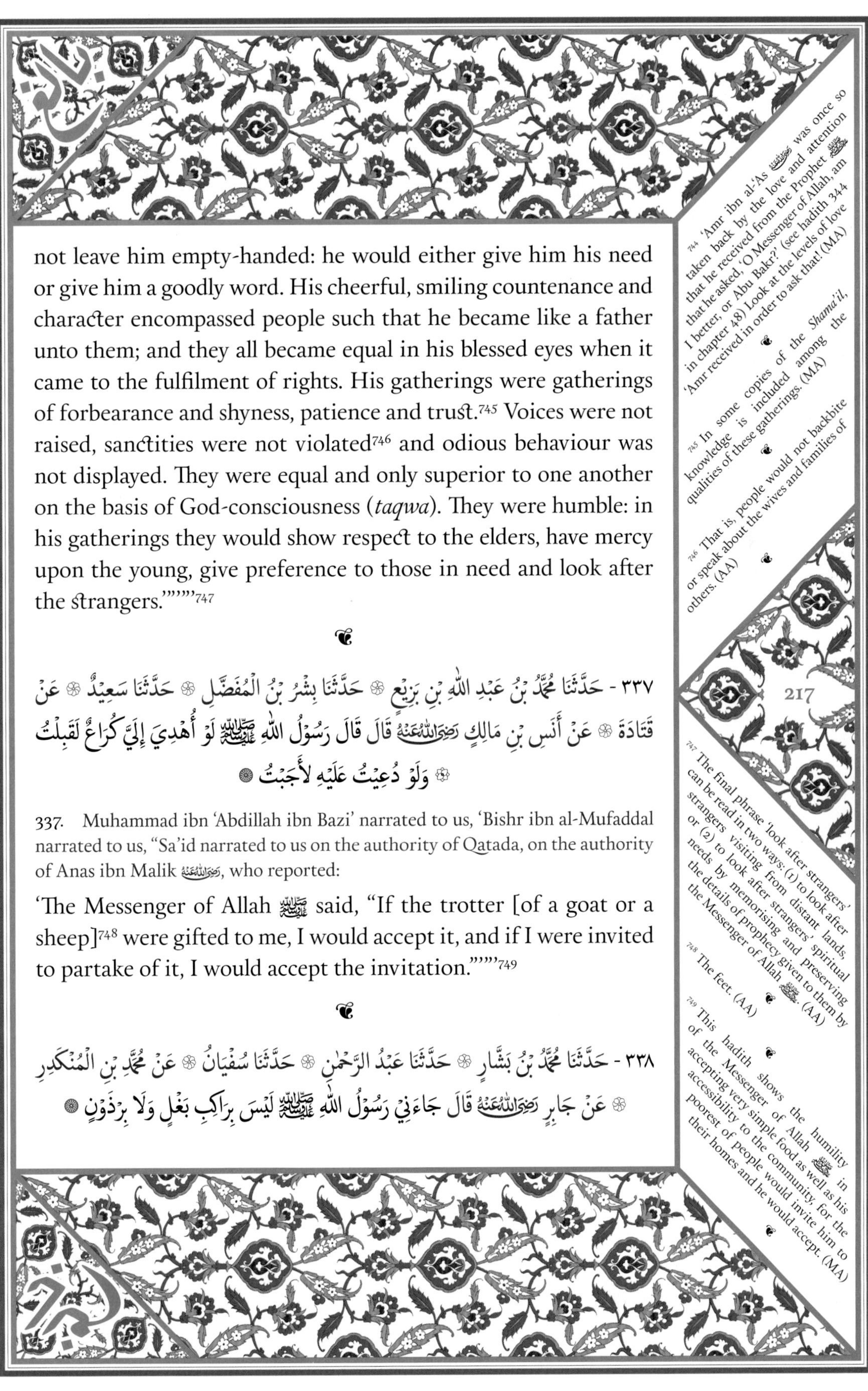

not leave him empty-handed: he would either give him his need or give him a goodly word. His cheerful, smiling countenance and character encompassed people such that he became like a father unto them; and they all became equal in his blessed eyes when it came to the fulfilment of rights. His gatherings were gatherings of forbearance and shyness, patience and trust.[745] Voices were not raised, sanctities were not violated[746] and odious behaviour was not displayed. They were equal and only superior to one another on the basis of God-consciousness (*taqwa*). They were humble: in his gatherings they would show respect to the elders, have mercy upon the young, give preference to those in need and look after the strangers.''''''[747]

٣٣٧ - حَدَّثَنَا مُحَمَّدُ بْنُ عَبْدِ اللهِ بْنِ بَزِيعٍ ۞ حَدَّثَنَا بِشْرُ بْنُ الْمُفَضَّلِ ۞ حَدَّثَنَا سَعِيدٌ ۞ عَنْ قَتَادَةَ ۞ عَنْ أَنَسِ بْنِ مَالِكٍ رَضِيَ اللهُ عَنْهُ قَالَ قَالَ رَسُولُ اللهِ ﷺ لَوْ أُهْدِيَ إِلَيَّ كُرَاعٌ لَقَبِلْتُ ۞ وَلَوْ دُعِيتُ عَلَيْهِ لَأَجَبْتُ ۞

337. Muhammad ibn 'Abdillah ibn Bazi' narrated to us, 'Bishr ibn al-Mufaddal narrated to us, "Sa'id narrated to us on the authority of Qatada, on the authority of Anas ibn Malik رضي الله عنه, who reported:

'The Messenger of Allah ﷺ said, "If the trotter [of a goat or a sheep][748] were gifted to me, I would accept it, and if I were invited to partake of it, I would accept the invitation."'''[749]

٣٣٨ - حَدَّثَنَا مُحَمَّدُ بْنُ بَشَّارٍ ۞ حَدَّثَنَا عَبْدُ الرَّحْمٰنِ ۞ حَدَّثَنَا سُفْيَانُ ۞ عَنْ مُحَمَّدِ بْنِ الْمُنْكَدِرِ ۞ عَنْ جَابِرٍ رَضِيَ اللهُ عَنْهُ قَالَ جَاءَنِي رَسُولُ اللهِ ﷺ لَيْسَ بِرَاكِبِ بَغْلٍ وَلَا بِرْذَوْنٍ ۞

[744] 'Amr ibn al-'As رضي الله عنه was once so taken back by the love and attention that he received from the Prophet ﷺ that he asked, 'O Messenger of Allah, am I better, or Abu Bakr?' (see hadith 344 in chapter 48) Look at the levels of love 'Amr received in order to ask that! (MA)

[745] In some copies of the *Shama'il*, knowledge is included among the qualities of these gatherings. (MA)

[746] That is, people would not backbite or speak about the wives and families of others. (AA)

[747] The final phrase 'look after strangers' can be read in two ways: (1) to look after strangers visiting from distant lands, or (2) to look after strangers' spiritual needs by memorising and preserving the details of prophecy given to them by the Messenger of Allah ﷺ. (AA)

[748] The feet. (AA)

[749] This hadith shows the humility of the Messenger of Allah ﷺ in accepting very simple food as well as his accessibility to the community, for the poorest of people would invite him to their homes and he would accept. (MA)

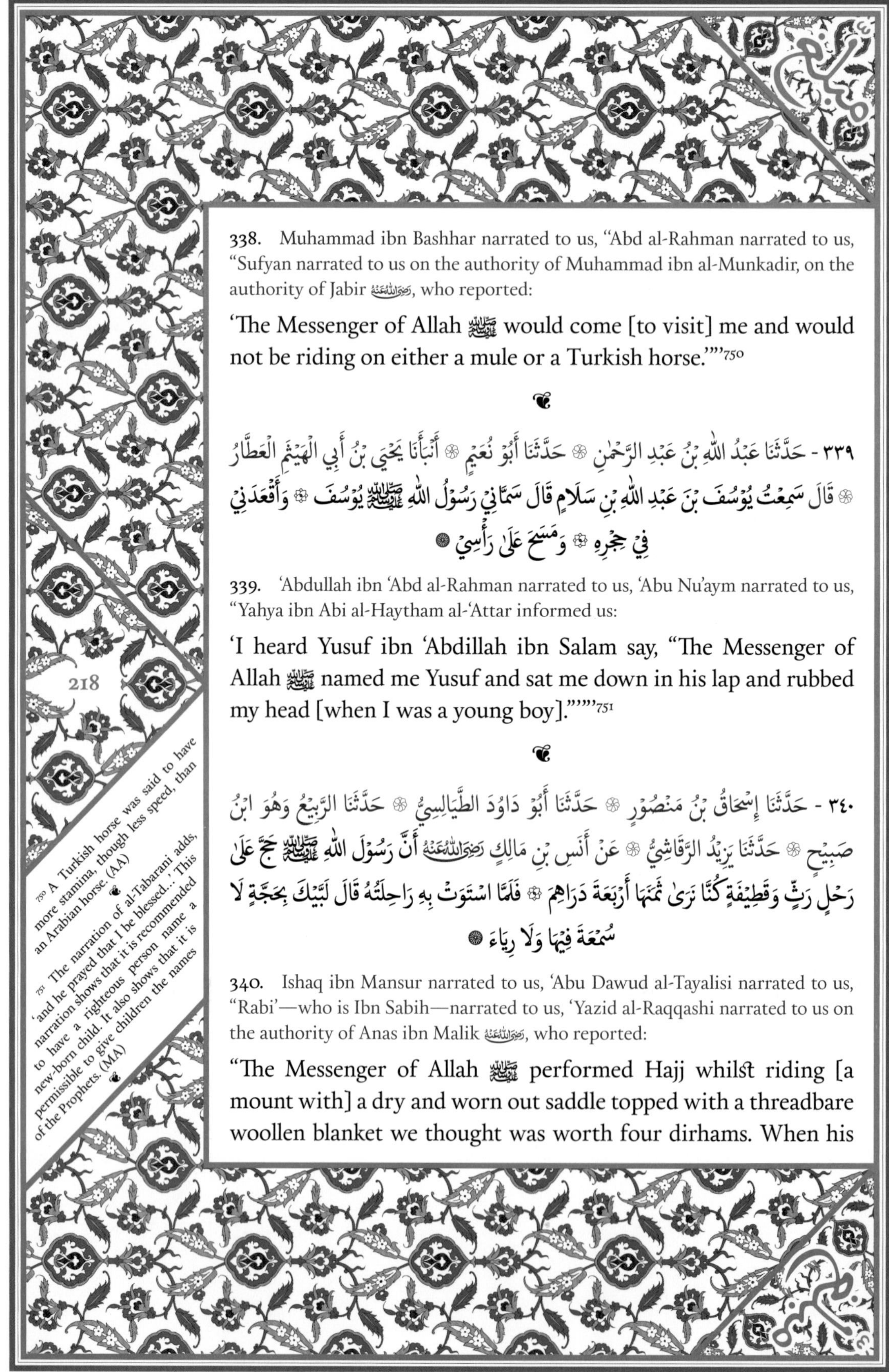

338. Muhammad ibn Bashhar narrated to us, "Abd al-Rahman narrated to us, "Sufyan narrated to us on the authority of Muhammad ibn al-Munkadir, on the authority of Jabir رضي الله عنه, who reported:

'The Messenger of Allah ﷺ would come [to visit] me and would not be riding on either a mule or a Turkish horse.'"'[750]

٣٣٩ - حَدَّثَنَا عَبْدُ اللهِ بْنُ عَبْدِ الرَّحْمٰنِ ۞ حَدَّثَنَا أَبُو نُعَيْمٍ ۞ أَنبَأَنَا يَحْيَى بْنُ أَبِي الْهَيْثَمِ الْعَطَّارُ ۞ قَالَ سَمِعْتُ يُوسُفَ بْنَ عَبْدِ اللهِ بْنِ سَلَامٍ قَالَ سَمَّانِي رَسُولُ اللهِ ﷺ يُوسُفَ ۞ وَأَقْعَدَنِي فِي حِجْرِهِ ۞ وَمَسَحَ عَلَى رَأْسِي ۞

339. 'Abdullah ibn 'Abd al-Rahman narrated to us, 'Abu Nu'aym narrated to us, "Yahya ibn Abi al-Haytham al-'Attar informed us:

'I heard Yusuf ibn 'Abdillah ibn Salam say, "The Messenger of Allah ﷺ named me Yusuf and sat me down in his lap and rubbed my head [when I was a young boy].""'"[751]

٣٤٠ - حَدَّثَنَا إِسْحَاقُ بْنُ مَنْصُورٍ ۞ حَدَّثَنَا أَبُو دَاوُدَ الطَّيَالِسِيُّ ۞ حَدَّثَنَا الرَّبِيعُ وَهُوَ ابْنُ صَبِيحٍ ۞ حَدَّثَنَا يَزِيدُ الرَّقَاشِيُّ ۞ عَنْ أَنَسِ بْنِ مَالِكٍ رضي الله عنه أَنَّ رَسُولَ اللهِ ﷺ حَجَّ عَلَى رَحْلٍ رَثٍّ وَقَطِيفَةٍ كُنَّا نَرَى ثَمَنَهَا أَرْبَعَةَ دَرَاهِمَ ۞ فَلَمَّا اسْتَوَتْ بِهِ رَاحِلَتُهُ قَالَ لَبَّيْكَ بِحَجَّةٍ لَا سُمْعَةَ فِيهَا وَلَا رِيَاءَ ۞

340. Ishaq ibn Mansur narrated to us, 'Abu Dawud al-Tayalisi narrated to us, "Rabi'—who is Ibn Sabih—narrated to us, 'Yazid al-Raqqashi narrated to us on the authority of Anas ibn Malik رضي الله عنه, who reported:

"The Messenger of Allah ﷺ performed Hajj whilst riding [a mount with] a dry and worn out saddle topped with a threadbare woollen blanket we thought was worth four dirhams. When his

[750] A Turkish horse was said to have more stamina, though less speed, than an Arabian horse. (AA)

[751] The narration of al-Tabarani adds, 'and he prayed that I be blessed...' This narration shows that it is recommended to have a righteous person name a new-born child. It also shows that it is permissible to give children the names of the Prophets. (MA)

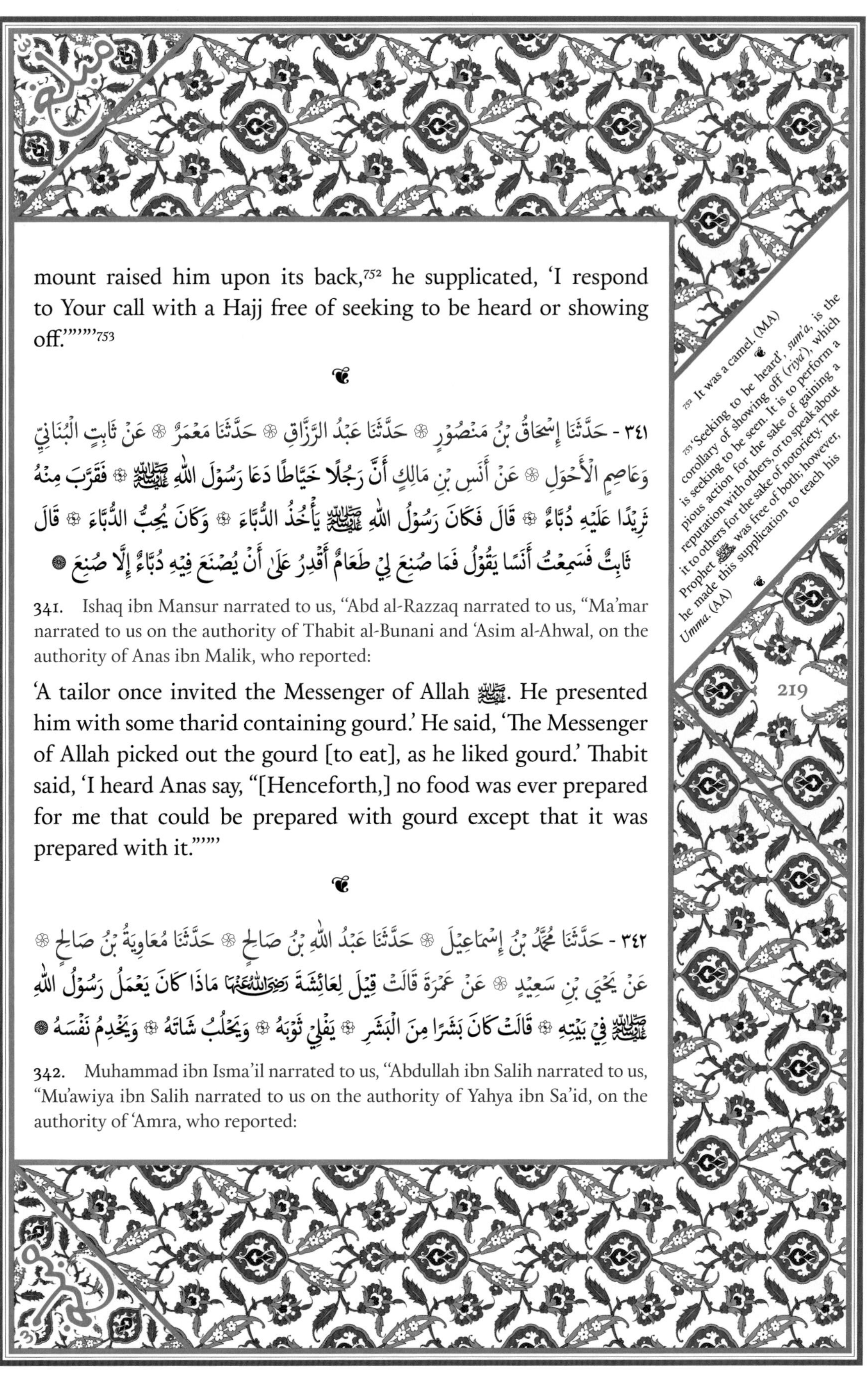

mount raised him upon its back,[752] he supplicated, 'I respond to Your call with a Hajj free of seeking to be heard or showing off.'"""'[753]

❦

٣٤١ - حَدَّثَنَا إِسْحَاقُ بْنُ مَنْصُورٍ ۞ حَدَّثَنَا عَبْدُ الرَّزَّاقِ ۞ حَدَّثَنَا مَعْمَرٌ ۞ عَنْ ثَابِتٍ الْبُنَانِيِّ وَعَاصِمٍ الْأَحْوَلِ ۞ عَنْ أَنَسِ بْنِ مَالِكٍ أَنَّ رَجُلًا خَيَّاطًا دَعَا رَسُولَ اللهِ ﷺ ۞ فَقَرَّبَ مِنْهُ ثَرِيدًا عَلَيْهِ دُبَّاءٌ ۞ قَالَ فَكَانَ رَسُولُ اللهِ ﷺ يَأْخُذُ الدُّبَّاءَ ۞ وَكَانَ يُحِبُّ الدُّبَّاءَ ۞ قَالَ ثَابِتٌ فَسَمِعْتُ أَنَسًا يَقُولُ فَمَا صُنِعَ لِي طَعَامٌ أَقْدِرُ عَلَىٰ أَنْ يُصْنَعَ فِيهِ دُبَّاءٌ إِلَّا صُنِعَ ۞

341. Ishaq ibn Mansur narrated to us, "Abd al-Razzaq narrated to us, "Ma'mar narrated to us on the authority of Thabit al-Bunani and 'Asim al-Ahwal, on the authority of Anas ibn Malik, who reported:

'A tailor once invited the Messenger of Allah ﷺ. He presented him with some tharid containing gourd.' He said, 'The Messenger of Allah picked out the gourd [to eat], as he liked gourd.' Thabit said, 'I heard Anas say, "[Henceforth,] no food was ever prepared for me that could be prepared with gourd except that it was prepared with it."'""

❦

٣٤٢ - حَدَّثَنَا مُحَمَّدُ بْنُ إِسْمَاعِيلَ ۞ حَدَّثَنَا عَبْدُ اللهِ بْنُ صَالِحٍ ۞ حَدَّثَنَا مُعَاوِيَةُ بْنُ صَالِحٍ ۞ عَنْ يَحْيَى بْنِ سَعِيدٍ ۞ عَنْ عَمْرَةَ قَالَتْ قِيلَ لِعَائِشَةَ رَضِيَ اللهُ عَنْهَا مَاذَا كَانَ يَعْمَلُ رَسُولُ اللهِ ﷺ فِي بَيْتِهِ ۞ قَالَتْ كَانَ بَشَرًا مِنَ الْبَشَرِ ۞ يَفْلِي ثَوْبَهُ ۞ وَيَحْلُبُ شَاتَهُ ۞ وَيَخْدُمُ نَفْسَهُ ۞

342. Muhammad ibn Isma'il narrated to us, "Abdullah ibn Salih narrated to us, "Mu'awiya ibn Salih narrated to us on the authority of Yahya ibn Sa'id, on the authority of 'Amra, who reported:

[752] It was a camel. (MA)

[753] 'Seeking to be heard', *sum'a*, is the corollary of showing off (*riya'*), which is seeking to be seen. It is to perform a pious action for the sake of gaining a reputation with others, or to speak about it to others for the sake of notoriety. The Prophet ﷺ was free of both; however, he made this supplication to teach his *Umma*. (AA)

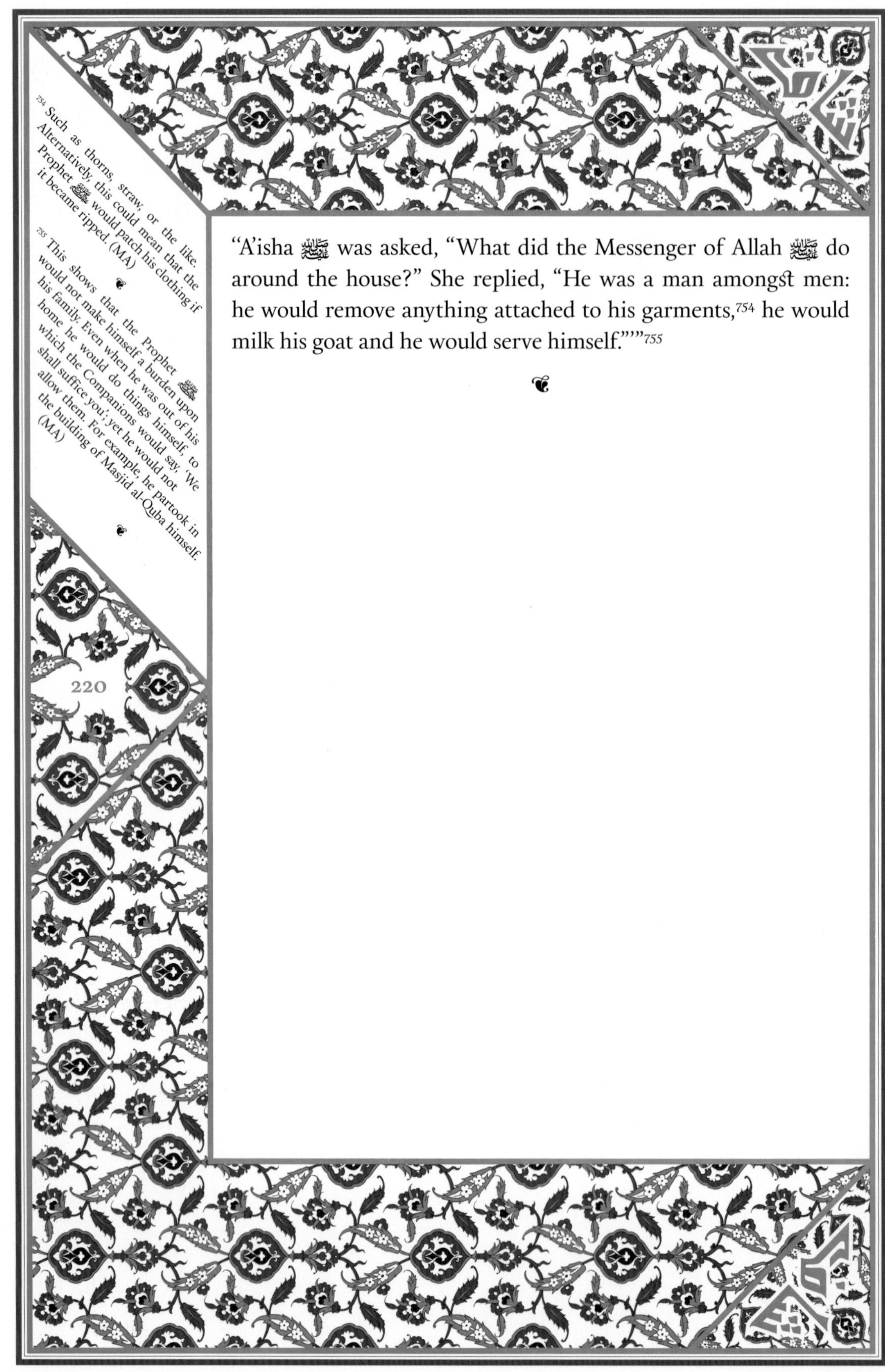

"A'isha رضي الله عنها was asked, "What did the Messenger of Allah ﷺ do around the house?" She replied, "He was a man amongst men: he would remove anything attached to his garments,[754] he would milk his goat and he would serve himself.""[755]

[754] Such as thorns, straw, or the like. Alternatively, this could mean that the Prophet ﷺ would patch his clothing if it became ripped. (MA)

[755] This shows that the Prophet ﷺ would not make himself a burden upon his family. Even when he was out of his home he would do things himself, to which the Companions would say, 'We shall suffice you'; yet he would not allow them. For example, he partook in the building of Masjid al-Quba himself. (MA)

CHAPTER FORTY-EIGHT

بَابُ مَا جَاءَ فِي خُلُقِ رَسُولِ اللهِ ﷺ

What Has Been Narrated Concerning the Character of the Messenger of Allah ﷺ

٣٤٣ - حَدَّثَنَا عَبَّاسُ بْنُ مُحَمَّدٍ الدُّورِيُّ ۞ حَدَّثَنَا عَبْدُ اللهِ بْنُ يَزِيدَ الْمُقْرِئُ ۞ حَدَّثَنَا لَيْثُ بْنُ سَعْدٍ ۞ حَدَّثَنَا أَبُو عُثْمَانَ الْوَلِيدُ بْنُ أَبِي الْوَلِيدِ ۞ عَنْ سُلَيْمَانَ بْنِ خَارِجَةَ ۞ عَنْ خَارِجَةَ ابْنِ زَيْدِ بْنِ ثَابِتٍ قَالَ دَخَلَ نَفَرٌ عَلَىٰ زَيْدِ بْنِ ثَابِتٍ ۞ فَقَالُوا لَهُ حَدِّثْنَا أَحَادِيثَ رَسُولِ اللهِ ﷺ ۞ قَالَ مَاذَا أُحَدِّثُكُمْ ۞ كُنْتُ جَارَهُ فَكَانَ إِذَا نَزَلَ عَلَيْهِ الْوَحْيُ بَعَثَ إِلَيَّ فَكَتَبْتُهُ لَهُ ۞ فَكُنَّا إِذَا ذَكَرْنَا الدُّنْيَا ذَكَرَهَا مَعَنَا ۞ وَإِذَا ذَكَرْنَا الْآخِرَةَ ذَكَرَهَا مَعَنَا ۞ وَإِذَا ذَكَرْنَا الطَّعَامَ ذَكَرَهُ مَعَنَا ۞ فَكُلُّ هٰذَا أُحَدِّثُكُمْ عَنْ رَسُولِ اللهِ ﷺ ۞

343. ʿAbbas ibn Muhammad al-Duri narrated to us, "Abdullah ibn Yazid al-Muqri' narrated to us, "Layth ibn Sa'd narrated to us, 'Abu ʿUthman al-Walid ibn Abi al-Walid narrated to us on the authority of Sulayman ibn Kharija ibn Zayd ibn Thabit, who reported:

"A group of people went to see Zayd ibn Thabit. They said to him, 'Narrate to us some traditions about the Messenger of Allah ﷺ.' He said, 'What shall I narrate to you? I was his neighbour. When revelation would descend upon him, he would send for me to write it down. When we would speak about worldly matters, he would speak about them as well,[756] and when we would speak about the Hereafter, he would participate with us. When we would speak about food he would speak about it likewise[757]—all of this is what I can narrate to you from the Messenger of Allah!'''''

[756] They knew that he was the most knowledgeable of creation and that he was blessed with indescribable levels of insight, so they would come to him to seek advice about the world. (MA)

[757] The Prophet ﷺ would speak about the varieties of foods and drinks and mention their rulings, properties and particular harms and benefits, the details of which are recorded in the collections on Prophetic Medicine (*al-Tibb al-Nabawi*). (AA)

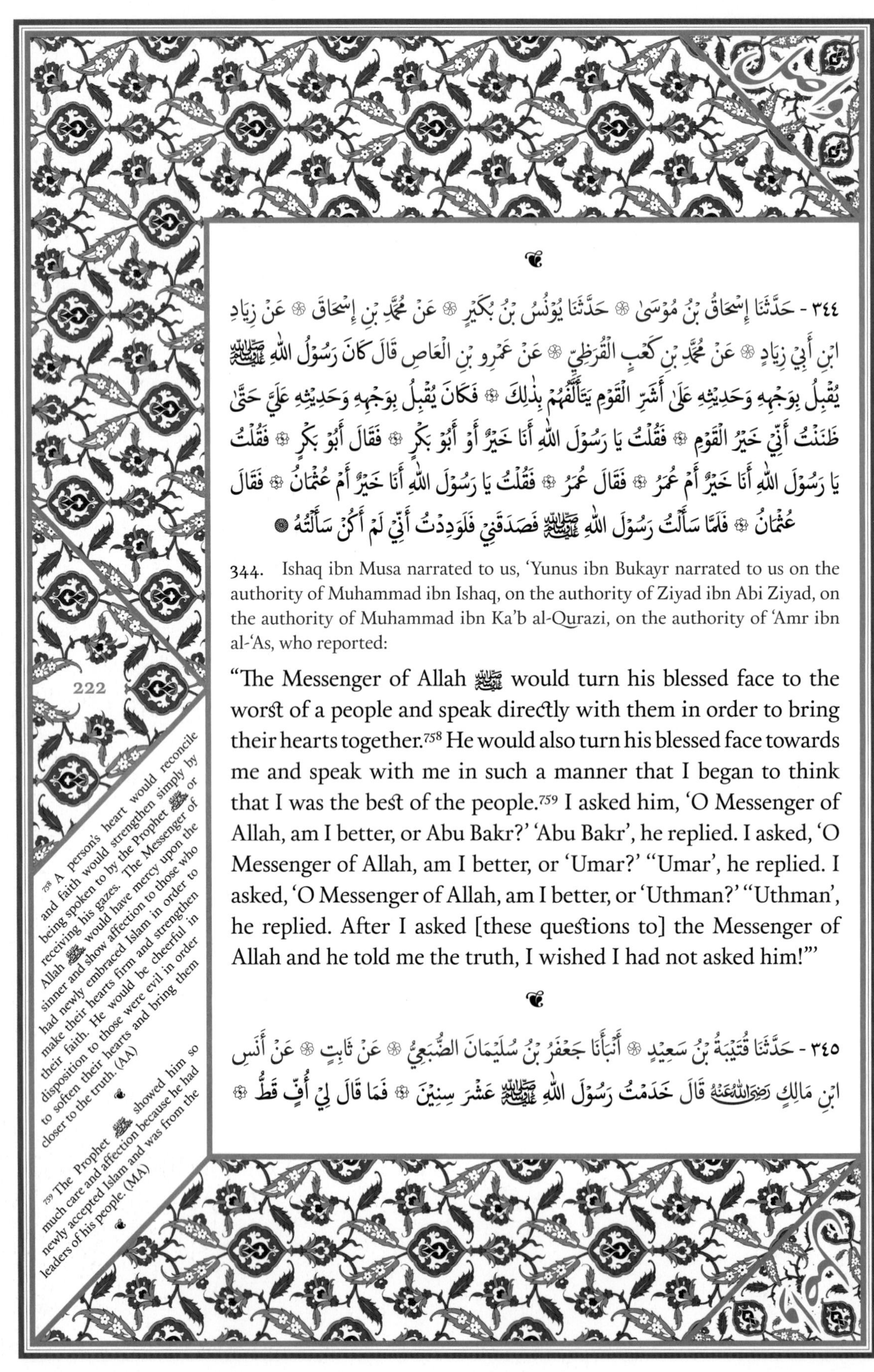

٣٤٤ - حَدَّثَنَا إِسْحَاقُ بْنُ مُوسَىٰ ۞ حَدَّثَنَا يُونُسُ بْنُ بُكَيْرٍ ۞ عَنْ مُحَمَّدِ بْنِ إِسْحَاقَ ۞ عَنْ زِيَادِ ابْنِ أَبِي زِيَادٍ ۞ عَنْ مُحَمَّدِ بْنِ كَعْبٍ الْقُرَظِيِّ ۞ عَنْ عَمْرِو بْنِ الْعَاصِ قَالَ كَانَ رَسُولُ اللهِ ﷺ يُقْبِلُ بِوَجْهِهِ وَحَدِيثِهِ عَلَىٰ أَشَرِّ الْقَوْمِ يَتَأَلَّفُهُمْ بِذَٰلِكَ ۞ فَكَانَ يُقْبِلُ بِوَجْهِهِ وَحَدِيثِهِ عَلَيَّ حَتَّىٰ ظَنَنْتُ أَنِّي خَيْرُ الْقَوْمِ ۞ فَقُلْتُ يَا رَسُولَ اللهِ أَنَا خَيْرٌ أَوْ أَبُو بَكْرٍ ۞ فَقَالَ أَبُو بَكْرٍ ۞ فَقُلْتُ يَا رَسُولَ اللهِ أَنَا خَيْرٌ أَمْ عُمَرُ ۞ فَقَالَ عُمَرُ ۞ فَقُلْتُ يَا رَسُولَ اللهِ أَنَا خَيْرٌ أَمْ عُثْمَانُ ۞ فَقَالَ عُثْمَانُ ۞ فَلَمَّا سَأَلْتُ رَسُولَ اللهِ ﷺ فَصَدَقَنِي فَلَوَدِدْتُ أَنِّي لَمْ أَكُنْ سَأَلْتُهُ ۞

344. Ishaq ibn Musa narrated to us, 'Yunus ibn Bukayr narrated to us on the authority of Muhammad ibn Ishaq, on the authority of Ziyad ibn Abi Ziyad, on the authority of Muhammad ibn Ka'b al-Qurazi, on the authority of 'Amr ibn al-'As, who reported:

"The Messenger of Allah ﷺ would turn his blessed face to the worst of a people and speak directly with them in order to bring their hearts together.[758] He would also turn his blessed face towards me and speak with me in such a manner that I began to think that I was the best of the people.[759] I asked him, 'O Messenger of Allah, am I better, or Abu Bakr?' 'Abu Bakr', he replied. I asked, 'O Messenger of Allah, am I better, or 'Umar?' ''Umar', he replied. I asked, 'O Messenger of Allah, am I better, or 'Uthman?' ''Uthman', he replied. After I asked [these questions to] the Messenger of Allah and he told me the truth, I wished I had not asked him!'"

٣٤٥ - حَدَّثَنَا قُتَيْبَةُ بْنُ سَعِيدٍ ۞ أَنْبَأَنَا جَعْفَرُ بْنُ سُلَيْمَانَ الضُّبَعِيُّ ۞ عَنْ ثَابِتٍ ۞ عَنْ أَنَسِ ابْنِ مَالِكٍ رَضِيَ اللهُ عَنْهُ قَالَ خَدَمْتُ رَسُولَ اللهِ ﷺ عَشْرَ سِنِينَ ۞ فَمَا قَالَ لِي أُفٍّ قَطُّ ۞

[758] A person's heart would reconcile and faith would strengthen simply by being spoken to by the Prophet ﷺ or receiving his gazes. The Messenger of Allah ﷺ would have mercy upon the sinner and show affection to those who had newly embraced Islam in order to make their hearts firm and strengthen their faith. He would be cheerful in disposition to those were evil in order to soften their hearts and bring them closer to the truth. (AA)

[759] The Prophet ﷺ showed him so much care and affection because he had newly accepted Islam and was from the leaders of his people. (MA)

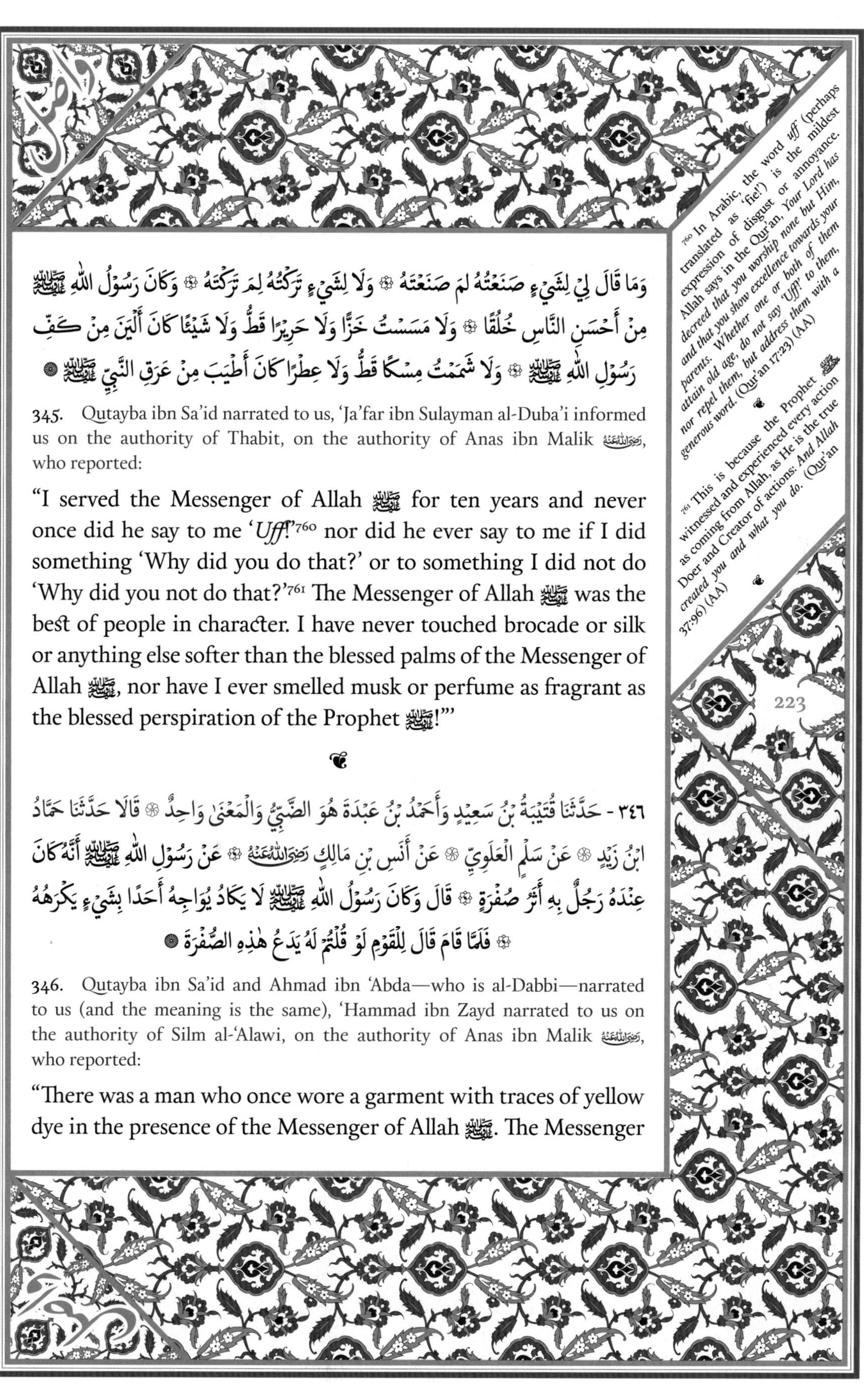

وَمَا قَالَ لِي لِشَيْءٍ صَنَعْتُهُ لِمَ صَنَعْتَهُ ۞ وَلَا لِشَيْءٍ تَرَكْتُهُ لِمَ تَرَكْتَهُ ۞ وَكَانَ رَسُولُ اللهِ ﷺ مِنْ أَحْسَنِ النَّاسِ خُلُقًا ۞ وَلَا مَسَسْتُ خَزًّا وَلَا حَرِيرًا قَطُّ وَلَا شَيْئًا كَانَ أَلْيَنَ مِنْ كَفِّ رَسُولِ اللهِ ﷺ ۞ وَلَا شَمَمْتُ مِسْكًا قَطُّ وَلَا عِطْرًا كَانَ أَطْيَبَ مِنْ عَرَقِ النَّبِيِّ ﷺ ۞

345. Qutayba ibn Sa'id narrated to us, 'Ja'far ibn Sulayman al-Duba'i informed us on the authority of Thabit, on the authority of Anas ibn Malik رضي الله عنه, who reported:

"I served the Messenger of Allah ﷺ for ten years and never once did he say to me '*Uff!*'[760] nor did he ever say to me if I did something 'Why did you do that?' or to something I did not do 'Why did you not do that?'[761] The Messenger of Allah ﷺ was the best of people in character. I have never touched brocade or silk or anything else softer than the blessed palms of the Messenger of Allah ﷺ, nor have I ever smelled musk or perfume as fragrant as the blessed perspiration of the Prophet ﷺ!'"

❦

٣٤٦ - حَدَّثَنَا قُتَيْبَةُ بْنُ سَعِيدٍ وَأَحْمَدُ بْنُ عَبْدَةَ هُوَ الضَّبِّيُّ وَالْمَعْنَىٰ وَاحِدٌ ۞ قَالَا حَدَّثَنَا حَمَّادُ ابْنُ زَيْدٍ ۞ عَنْ سَلْمٍ الْعَلَوِيِّ ۞ عَنْ أَنَسِ بْنِ مَالِكٍ رَضِيَ اللهُ عَنْهُ ۞ عَنْ رَسُولِ اللهِ ﷺ أَنَّهُ كَانَ عِنْدَهُ رَجُلٌ بِهِ أَثَرُ صُفْرَةٍ ۞ قَالَ وَكَانَ رَسُولُ اللهِ ﷺ لَا يَكَادُ يُوَاجِهُ أَحَدًا بِشَيْءٍ يَكْرَهُهُ ۞ فَلَمَّا قَامَ قَالَ لِلْقَوْمِ لَوْ قُلْتُمْ لَهُ يَدَعُ هٰذِهِ الصُّفْرَةَ ۞

346. Qutayba ibn Sa'id and Ahmad ibn 'Abda—who is al-Dabbi—narrated to us (and the meaning is the same), 'Hammad ibn Zayd narrated to us on the authority of Silm al-'Alawi, on the authority of Anas ibn Malik رضي الله عنه, who reported:

"There was a man who once wore a garment with traces of yellow dye in the presence of the Messenger of Allah ﷺ. The Messenger

[760] In Arabic, the word *uff* (perhaps translated as 'fie!') is the mildest expression of disgust or annoyance. Allah says in the Qur'an, *Your Lord has decreed that you worship none but Him, and that you show excellence towards your parents. Whether one or both of them attain old age, do not say 'Uff!' to them, nor repel them, but address them with a generous word.* (Qur'an 17:23) (AA)

❦

[761] This is because the Prophet ﷺ witnessed and experienced every action as coming from Allah, as He is the true Doer and Creator of actions: *And Allah created you and what you do.* (Qur'an 37:96) (AA)

❦

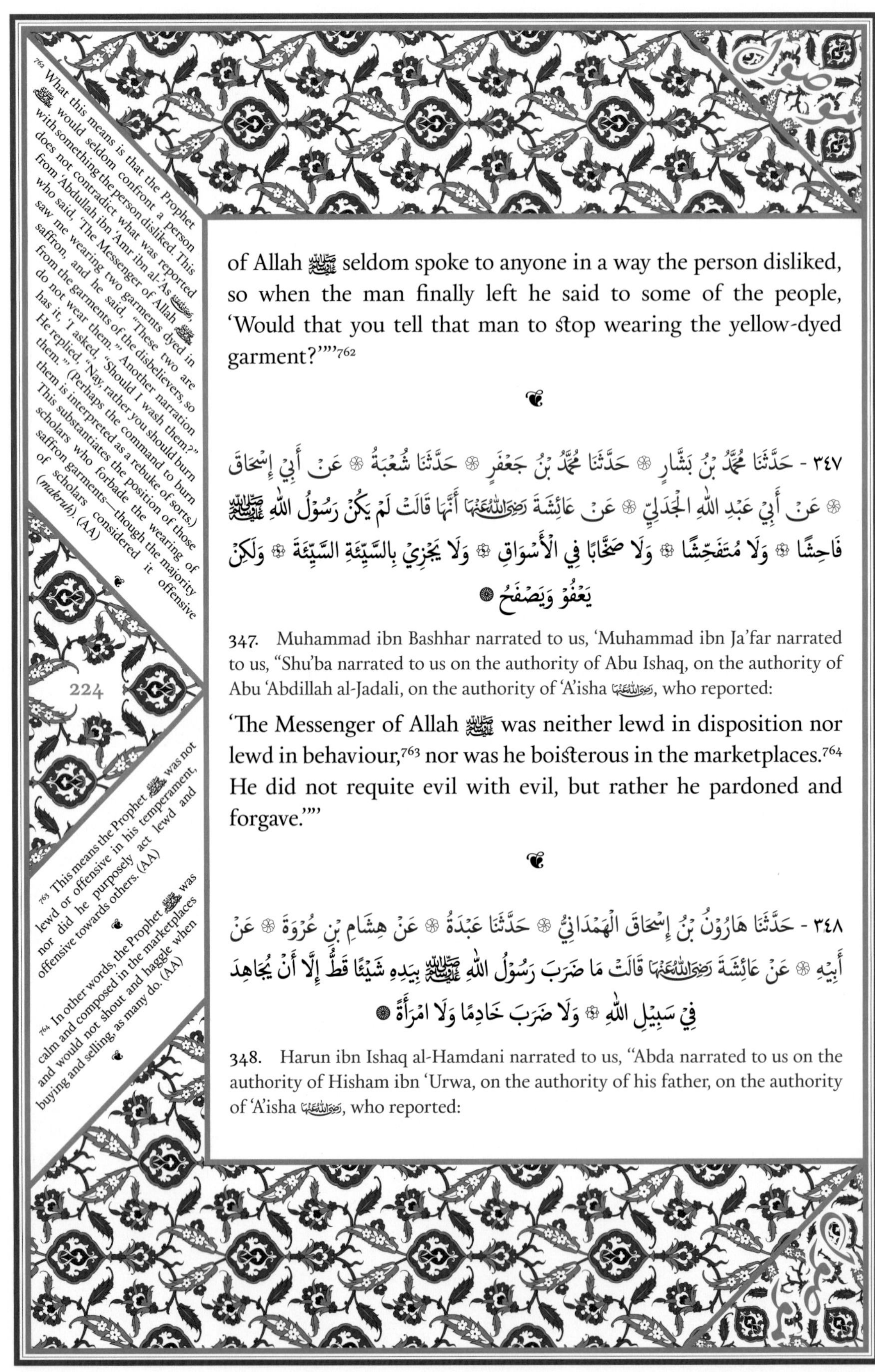

of Allah ﷺ seldom spoke to anyone in a way the person disliked, so when the man finally left he said to some of the people, 'Would that you tell that man to stop wearing the yellow-dyed garment?'"'[762]

❦

٣٤٧ - حَدَّثَنَا مُحَمَّدُ بْنُ بَشَّارٍ ۞ حَدَّثَنَا مُحَمَّدُ بْنُ جَعْفَرٍ ۞ حَدَّثَنَا شُعْبَةُ ۞ عَنْ أَبِي إِسْحَاقَ ۞ عَنْ أَبِي عَبْدِ اللهِ الْجَدَلِيِّ ۞ عَنْ عَائِشَةَ رَضِيَ اللهُ عَنْهَا أَنَّهَا قَالَتْ لَمْ يَكُنْ رَسُولُ اللهِ ﷺ فَاحِشًا ۞ وَلَا مُتَفَحِّشًا ۞ وَلَا صَخَّابًا فِي الْأَسْوَاقِ ۞ وَلَا يَجْزِي بِالسَّيِّئَةِ السَّيِّئَةَ ۞ وَلَكِنْ يَعْفُو وَيَصْفَحُ ۞

347. Muhammad ibn Bashhar narrated to us, 'Muhammad ibn Ja'far narrated to us, "Shu'ba narrated to us on the authority of Abu Ishaq, on the authority of Abu 'Abdillah al-Jadali, on the authority of 'A'isha رضي الله عنها, who reported:

'The Messenger of Allah ﷺ was neither lewd in disposition nor lewd in behaviour,[763] nor was he boisterous in the marketplaces.[764] He did not requite evil with evil, but rather he pardoned and forgave.'"'

❦

٣٤٨ - حَدَّثَنَا هَارُونُ بْنُ إِسْحَاقَ الْهَمْدَانِيُّ ۞ حَدَّثَنَا عَبْدَةُ ۞ عَنْ هِشَامِ بْنِ عُرْوَةَ ۞ عَنْ أَبِيهِ ۞ عَنْ عَائِشَةَ رَضِيَ اللهُ عَنْهَا قَالَتْ مَا ضَرَبَ رَسُولُ اللهِ ﷺ بِيَدِهِ شَيْئًا قَطُّ إِلَّا أَنْ يُجَاهِدَ فِي سَبِيلِ اللهِ ۞ وَلَا ضَرَبَ خَادِمًا وَلَا امْرَأَةً ۞

348. Harun ibn Ishaq al-Hamdani narrated to us, "Abda narrated to us on the authority of Hisham ibn 'Urwa, on the authority of his father, on the authority of 'A'isha رضي الله عنها, who reported:

[762] What this means is that the Prophet ﷺ would seldom confront a person with something the person disliked. This does not contradict what was reported from 'Abdullah ibn 'Amr ibn al-'As رضي الله عنهما, who said, 'The Messenger of Allah ﷺ saw me wearing two garments dyed in saffron, and he said, "These two are from the garments of the disbelievers, so do not wear them." Another narration has it, 'I asked, "Should I wash them?" He replied, "Nay, rather you should burn them."' (Perhaps the command to burn them is interpreted as a rebuke of sorts.) This substantiates the position of those scholars who forbade the wearing of saffron garments—though the majority of scholars considered it offensive (*makruh*). (AA)

❦

[763] This means the Prophet ﷺ was not lewd or offensive in his temperament, nor did he purposely act lewd and offensive towards others. (AA)

❦

[764] In other words, the Prophet ﷺ was calm and composed in the marketplaces and would not shout and haggle when buying and selling, as many do. (AA)

❦

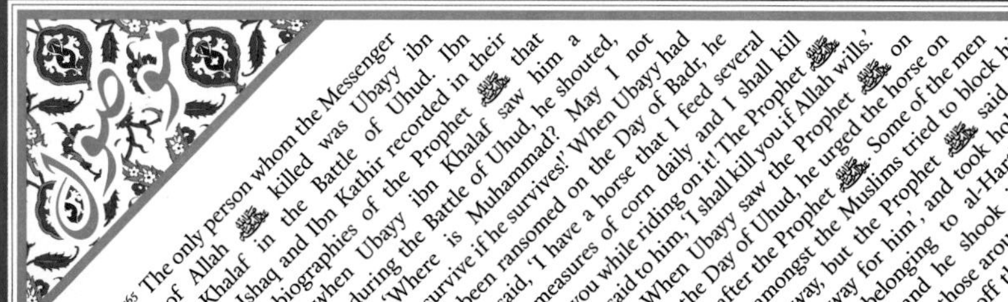

"The Messenger of Allah ﷺ never struck anything with his blessed hand unless he was waging jihad in the way of Allah;[765] he struck neither a servant nor a woman."'[766]

٣٤٩ - حَدَّثَنَا أَحْمَدُ بْنُ عَبْدَةَ الضَّبِّيُّ ۞ حَدَّثَنَا فُضَيْلُ بْنُ عِيَاضٍ ۞ عَنْ مَنْصُورٍ ۞ عَنِ الزُّهْرِيِّ ۞ عَنْ عُرْوَةَ ۞ عَنْ عَائِشَةَ رَضِيَ اللَّهُ عَنْهَا قَالَتْ مَا رَأَيْتُ رَسُولَ اللَّهِ ﷺ مُنْتَصِرًا مِنْ مَظْلَمَةٍ ظُلِمَهَا قَطُّ مَالَمْ يُنْتَهَكْ مِنْ مَحَارِمِ اللَّهِ شَيْءٌ ۞ فَإِذَا انْتُهِكَ مِنْ مَحَارِمِ اللَّهِ شَيْءٌ كَانَ مِنْ أَشَدِّهِمْ فِي ذَٰلِكَ غَضَبًا ۞ وَمَا خُيِّرَ بَيْنَ أَمْرَيْنِ إِلَّا اخْتَارَ أَيْسَرَهُمَا مَا لَمْ يَكُنْ مَأْثَمًا ۞

349. Ahmad ibn 'Abda al-Dabbi narrated to us, 'Fudayl ibn 'Iyad narrated to us on the authority of Mansur, on the authority of Zuhri, on the authority of 'Urwa, on the authority of 'A'isha ؓ, who reported:

"I never saw the Messenger of Allah ﷺ exact revenge for a personal injustice done against him, so long as the sanctities of Allah were not violated. If any of Allah's sanctities were violated, he would be the angriest of people for that. He was never put in the position to choose between two things except that he chose the easiest[767]—unless that choice entailed sin."'

٣٥٠ - حَدَّثَنَا ابْنُ أَبِي عُمَرَ ۞ حَدَّثَنَا سُفْيَانُ ۞ عَنْ مُحَمَّدِ بْنِ الْمُنْكَدِرِ ۞ عَنْ عُرْوَةَ ۞ عَنْ عَائِشَةَ رَضِيَ اللَّهُ عَنْهَا قَالَتْ اِسْتَأْذَنَ رَجُلٌ عَلَى رَسُولِ اللَّهِ ﷺ وَأَنَا عِنْدَهُ ۞ فَقَالَ بِئْسَ ابْنُ الْعَشِيرَةِ أَوْ أَخُو الْعَشِيرَةِ ۞ ثُمَّ أَذِنَ لَهُ ۞ فَلَمَّا دَخَلَ فَأَلَانَ لَهُ الْقَوْلَ ۞ فَلَمَّا خَرَجَ قُلْتُ يَا رَسُولَ اللَّهِ قُلْتَ مَا قُلْتَ ثُمَّ أَلَنْتَ لَهُ الْقَوْلَ ۞ فَقَالَ يَا عَائِشَةُ إِنَّ مِنْ شَرِّ النَّاسِ مَنْ تَرَكَهُ النَّاسُ ۞ أَوْ وَدَعَهُ النَّاسُ اتِّقَاءَ فُحْشِهِ ۞

[765] The only person whom the Messenger of Allah ﷺ killed was Ubayy ibn Khalaf in the Battle of Uhud. Ibn Ishaq and Ibn Kathir recorded in their biographies of the Prophet ﷺ that when Ubayy ibn Khalaf saw him a during the Battle of Uhud, he shouted, 'Where is Muhammad? May I not survive if he survives!' When Ubayy had been ransomed on the Day of Badr, he said, 'I have a horse that I feed several measures of corn daily and I shall kill you while riding on it!' The Prophet ﷺ said to him, 'I shall kill you if Allah wills.' When Ubayy saw the Prophet ﷺ on the Day of Uhud, he urged the horse on after the Prophet ﷺ. Some of the men amongst the Muslims tried to block his way, but the Prophet ﷺ said, 'Make way for him', and took hold of a spear belonging to al-Harith ibn al-Simma, and he shook it in such a way that those around him took flight as flies fly off the back of a camel when it shakes itself. Then the Prophet ﷺ turned to face Ubayy and pierced him in the neck, causing him to fall from his horse. It was said that he had broken one of his ribs. When he returned to Quraysh, Ubayy said, 'Muhammad has killed me!' They said, 'There is nothing wrong with you at all!' He replied, 'Had everyone here received the injury that I have they would all be killed—did he not say "I shall kill you"? By Allah, had he spat upon me it would have killed me!' Ubayy died as the caravan was making its way back to Mecca. This killing was therefore a fulfilment of Prophecy. (MA)

[766] What is negated in this tradition is painful striking or striking out of anger, for there are narrations showing that the Prophet ﷺ lightly struck certain animals or people. As for the Prophet ﷺ lightly striking animals, Imam al-Bukhari recorded in his collection that Jabir ؓ reported, 'I was with the Prophet ﷺ during a military expedition and my camel was slow and exhausted. The Prophet ﷺ came up to me and said, "O Jabir!" I replied, "Yes!" He asked, "What is going on with you?" I replied, "My camel is slow and exhausted, so I've lagged behind." Then he got down and poked the camel with his stick and said, "Ride." I mounted the camel and rode it, and it became so fast that I had to hold it back from going ahead of the Messenger of Allah ﷺ!...' As for the Prophet ﷺ lightly striking people, Imam Muslim recorded in his collection that Ubayy ibn Ka'b ؓ reported, 'I was in the Mosque when a man entered and prayed and recited [the Qur'an] in a style to which I objected. Then another man entered and recited in a style different from the first. When we finished the prayer, we all went to Messenger of Allah ﷺ and said to him "This man recited in a style to which I objected, and the other entered and recited in a style different from him!" The Messenger of Allah ﷺ asked them to recite, and so they recited, and the Messenger of Allah ﷺ expressed approval of both. At that moment, there occurred in my mind a sort of denial which did not occur to me even during the days of ignorance (*jahiliyya*). When the Messenger of Allah ﷺ saw how I was affected, he lightly struck my chest, whereupon I broke into a sweat and felt as though I were looking at Allah in a state of fear!' (AA)

[767] That was to bring ease for his *Umma* ﷺ. (MA)

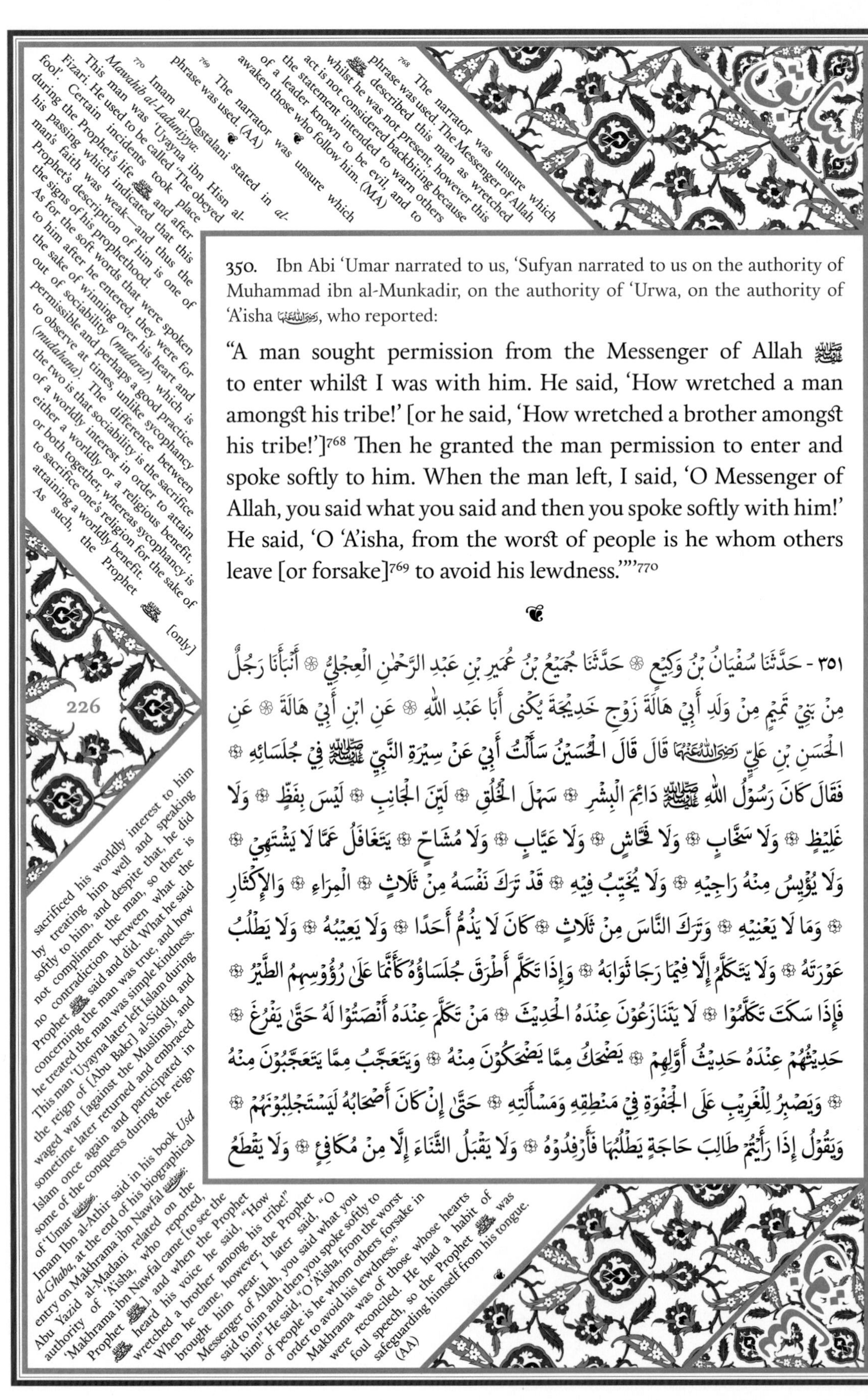

350. Ibn Abi 'Umar narrated to us, 'Sufyan narrated to us on the authority of Muhammad ibn al-Munkadir, on the authority of 'Urwa, on the authority of 'A'isha رضي الله عنها, who reported:

"A man sought permission from the Messenger of Allah ﷺ to enter whilst I was with him. He said, 'How wretched a man amongst his tribe!' [or he said, 'How wretched a brother amongst his tribe!'][768] Then he granted the man permission to enter and spoke softly to him. When the man left, I said, 'O Messenger of Allah, you said what you said and then you spoke softly with him!' He said, 'O 'A'isha, from the worst of people is he whom others leave [or forsake][769] to avoid his lewdness."''[770]

❁

٣٥١ - حَدَّثَنَا سُفْيَانُ بْنُ وَكِيعٍ ❁ حَدَّثَنَا جُمَيْعُ بْنُ عُمَيْرِ بْنِ عَبْدِ الرَّحْمٰنِ الْعِجْلِيُّ ❁ أَنْبَأَنَا رَجُلٌ
مِنْ بَنِي تَمِيمٍ مِنْ وَلَدِ أَبِي هَالَةَ زَوْجِ خَدِيجَةَ يُكْنَى أَبَا عَبْدِ اللهِ ❁ عَنِ ابْنِ أَبِي هَالَةَ ❁ عَنِ
الْحَسَنِ بْنِ عَلِيٍّ رَضِيَ اللهُ عَنْهُمَا قَالَ قَالَ الْحُسَيْنُ سَأَلْتُ أَبِي عَنْ سِيرَةِ النَّبِيِّ ﷺ فِي جُلَسَائِهِ ❁
فَقَالَ كَانَ رَسُولُ اللهِ ﷺ دَائِمَ الْبِشْرِ ❁ سَهْلَ الْخُلُقِ ❁ لَيِّنَ الْجَانِبِ ❁ لَيْسَ بِفَظٍّ ❁ وَلَا
غَلِيظٍ ❁ وَلَا سَخَّابٍ ❁ وَلَا فَحَّاشٍ ❁ وَلَا عَيَّابٍ ❁ وَلَا مُشَاحٍّ ❁ يَتَغَافَلُ عَمَّا لَا يَشْتَهِي ❁
وَلَا يُؤْيِسُ مِنْهُ رَاجِيَهُ ❁ وَلَا يُخَيِّبُ فِيهِ ❁ قَدْ تَرَكَ نَفْسَهُ مِنْ ثَلَاثٍ ❁ الْمِرَاءِ ❁ وَالْإِكْثَارِ
❁ وَمَا لَا يَعْنِيهِ ❁ وَتَرَكَ النَّاسَ مِنْ ثَلَاثٍ ❁ كَانَ لَا يَذُمُّ أَحَدًا ❁ وَلَا يَعِيبُهُ ❁ وَلَا يَطْلُبُ
عَوْرَتَهُ ❁ وَلَا يَتَكَلَّمُ إِلَّا فِيمَا رَجَا ثَوَابَهُ ❁ وَإِذَا تَكَلَّمَ أَطْرَقَ جُلَسَاؤُهُ كَأَنَّمَا عَلَى رُؤُوسِهِمُ الطَّيْرُ ❁
فَإِذَا سَكَتَ تَكَلَّمُوا ❁ لَا يَتَنَازَعُونَ عِنْدَهُ الْحَدِيثَ ❁ مَنْ تَكَلَّمَ عِنْدَهُ أَنْصَتُوا لَهُ حَتَّى يَفْرُغَ ❁
حَدِيثُهُمْ عِنْدَهُ حَدِيثُ أَوَّلِهِمْ ❁ يَضْحَكُ مِمَّا يَضْحَكُونَ مِنْهُ ❁ وَيَتَعَجَّبُ مِمَّا يَتَعَجَّبُونَ مِنْهُ
❁ وَيَصْبِرُ لِلْغَرِيبِ عَلَى الْجَفْوَةِ فِي مَنْطِقِهِ وَمَسْأَلَتِهِ ❁ حَتَّى إِنْ كَانَ أَصْحَابُهُ لَيَسْتَجْلِبُونَهُمْ ❁
وَيَقُولُ إِذَا رَأَيْتُمْ طَالِبَ حَاجَةٍ يَطْلُبُهَا فَأَرْفِدُوهُ ❁ وَلَا يَقْبَلُ الثَّنَاءَ إِلَّا مِنْ مُكَافِئٍ ❁ وَلَا يَقْطَعُ

768 The narrator was unsure which phrase was used. The Messenger of Allah ﷺ described this man as wretched whilst he was not present, however this act is not considered backbiting because the statement intended to warn others of a leader known to be evil, and to awaken those who follow him. (MA)

769 The narrator was unsure which phrase was used. (AA)

770 Imam al-Qastalani stated in *al-Mawahib al-Ladunniyya*: This man was 'Uyayna ibn Hisn al-Fizari. He used to be called 'The obeyed fool'. Certain incidents took place during the Prophet's life ﷺ and after his passing which indicated that this man's faith was weak—and thus the Prophet's description of him is one of the signs of his prophethood. As for the soft words that were spoken to him after he entered, they were for the sake of winning over his heart and out of sociability (*mudarat*), which is permissible and perhaps a good practice to observe at times, unlike sycophancy (*mudahana*). The difference between the two is that sociability is the sacrifice of a worldly interest in order to attain either a worldly or a religious benefit, or both together, whereas sycophancy is to sacrifice one's religion for the sake of attaining a worldly benefit. As such, the Prophet ﷺ [only] sacrificed his worldly interest to him by treating him well and speaking softly to him, and despite that, he did not compliment the man, so there is no contradiction between what the Prophet ﷺ said and did. What he said concerning the man was true, and how he treated the man was simple kindness. This man 'Uyayna later left Islam during the reign of [Abu Bakr] al-Siddiq and waged war [against the Muslims], and sometime later returned and embraced Islam once again and participated in some of the conquests during the reign of 'Umar رضي الله عنه. Imam Ibn al-Athir said in his book *Usd al-Ghaba*, at the end of his biographical entry on Makhrama ibn Nawfal رضي الله عنه: Abu Yazid al-Madani related on the authority of 'A'isha, who reported, 'Makhrama ibn Nawfal came [to see the Prophet ﷺ], and when the Prophet ﷺ heard his voice he said, "How wretched a brother among his tribe!" When he came, however, the Prophet brought him near. I later said, "O Messenger of Allah, you said what you said and then you spoke softly to him!" He said, "O 'A'isha, from the worst of people is he whom others forsake in order to avoid his lewdness."' Makhrama was of those whose hearts were reconciled. He had a habit of foul speech, so the Prophet ﷺ was safeguarding himself from his tongue. (AA)

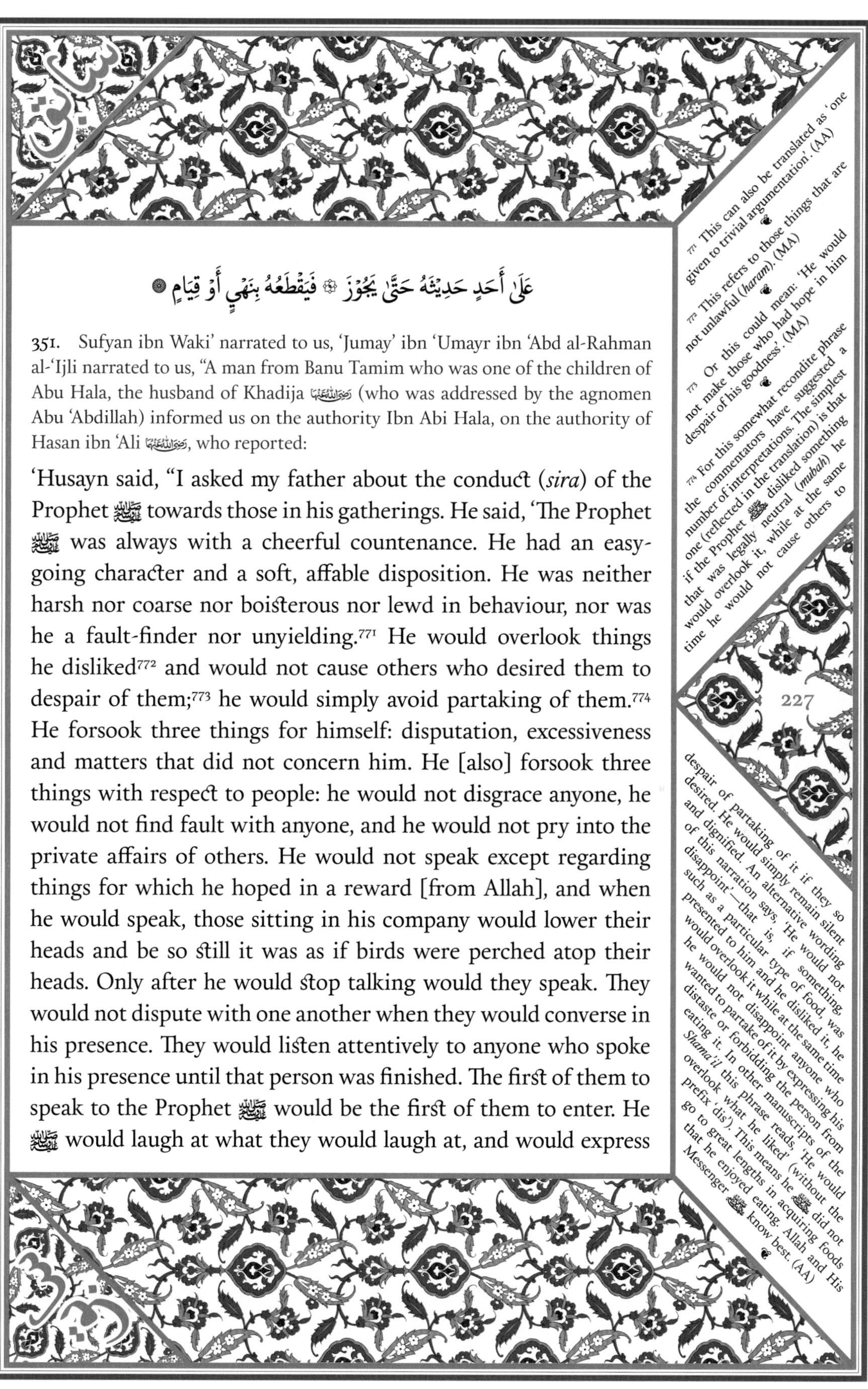

عَلَىٰ أَحَدٍ حَدِيثَهُ حَتَّىٰ يَجُوزَ ۞ فَيَقْطَعُهُ بِنَهْيٍ أَوْ قِيَامٍ ۞

351. Sufyan ibn Waki' narrated to us, 'Jumay' ibn 'Umayr ibn 'Abd al-Rahman al-'Ijli narrated to us, "A man from Banu Tamim who was one of the children of Abu Hala, the husband of Khadija رضي الله عنها (who was addressed by the agnomen Abu 'Abdillah) informed us on the authority Ibn Abi Hala, on the authority of Hasan ibn 'Ali رضي الله عنهما, who reported:

'Husayn said, "I asked my father about the conduct (*sira*) of the Prophet ﷺ towards those in his gatherings. He said, 'The Prophet ﷺ was always with a cheerful countenance. He had an easy-going character and a soft, affable disposition. He was neither harsh nor coarse nor boisterous nor lewd in behaviour, nor was he a fault-finder nor unyielding.[771] He would overlook things he disliked[772] and would not cause others who desired them to despair of them;[773] he would simply avoid partaking of them.[774] He forsook three things for himself: disputation, excessiveness and matters that did not concern him. He [also] forsook three things with respect to people: he would not disgrace anyone, he would not find fault with anyone, and he would not pry into the private affairs of others. He would not speak except regarding things for which he hoped in a reward [from Allah], and when he would speak, those sitting in his company would lower their heads and be so still it was as if birds were perched atop their heads. Only after he would stop talking would they speak. They would not dispute with one another when they would converse in his presence. They would listen attentively to anyone who spoke in his presence until that person was finished. The first of them to speak to the Prophet ﷺ would be the first of them to enter. He ﷺ would laugh at what they would laugh at, and would express

[771] This can also be translated as 'one given to trivial argumentation'. (AA)

[772] This refers to those things that are not unlawful (*haram*). (MA)

[773] Or this could mean: 'He would not make those who had hope in him despair of his goodness'. (MA)

[774] For this somewhat recondite phrase the commentators have suggested a number of interpretations. The simplest one (reflected in the translation) is that if the Prophet ﷺ disliked something that was legally neutral (*mubah*) he would overlook it, while at the same time he would not cause others to despair of partaking of it if they so desired. He would simply remain silent and dignified. An alternative wording of this narration says, 'He would not disappoint'—that is, if something, such as a particular type of food, was presented to him and he disliked it, he would overlook it while at the same time he would not disappoint anyone who wanted to partake of it by expressing his distaste or forbidding the person from eating it. In other manuscripts of the *Shama'il* this phrase reads, 'He would overlook what he liked' (without the prefix 'dis'). This means he ﷺ did not go to great lengths in acquiring foods that he enjoyed eating. Allah and His Messenger ﷺ know best. (AA)

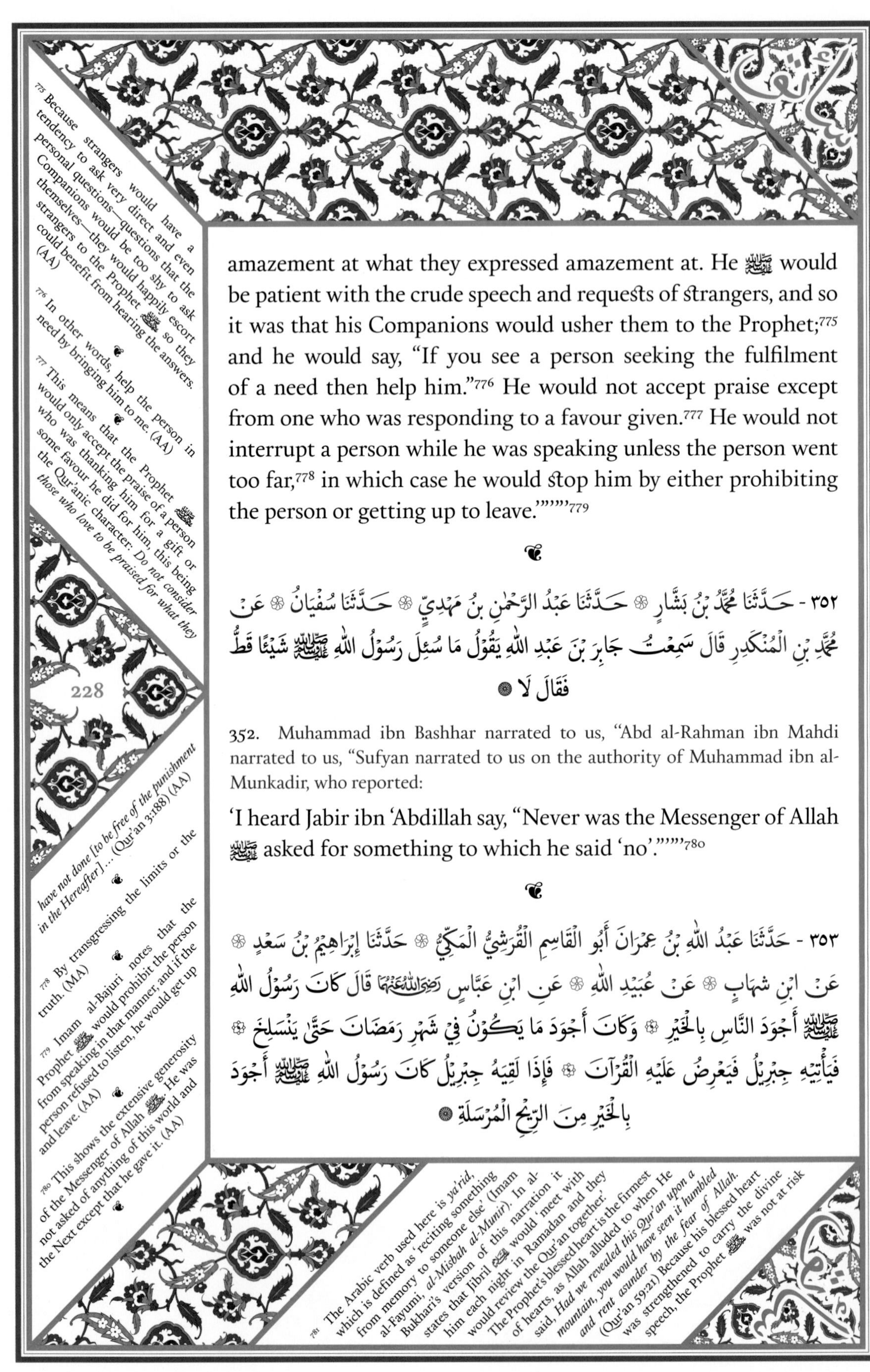

amazement at what they expressed amazement at. He ﷺ would be patient with the crude speech and requests of strangers, and so it was that his Companions would usher them to the Prophet;[775] and he would say, "If you see a person seeking the fulfilment of a need then help him."[776] He would not accept praise except from one who was responding to a favour given.[777] He would not interrupt a person while he was speaking unless the person went too far,[778] in which case he would stop him by either prohibiting the person or getting up to leave.'"""[779]

٣٥٢ - حَدَّثَنَا مُحَمَّدُ بْنُ بَشَّارٍ ۞ حَدَّثَنَا عَبْدُ الرَّحْمٰنِ بْنُ مَهْدِيٍّ ۞ حَدَّثَنَا سُفْيَانُ ۞ عَنْ مُحَمَّدِ بْنِ الْمُنْكَدِرِ قَالَ سَمِعْتُ جَابِرَ بْنَ عَبْدِ اللهِ يَقُولُ مَا سُئِلَ رَسُولُ اللهِ ﷺ شَيْئًا قَطُّ فَقَالَ لَا ۞

352. Muhammad ibn Bashhar narrated to us, "Abd al-Rahman ibn Mahdi narrated to us, "Sufyan narrated to us on the authority of Muhammad ibn al-Munkadir, who reported:

'I heard Jabir ibn 'Abdillah say, "Never was the Messenger of Allah ﷺ asked for something to which he said 'no'."'""[780]

٣٥٣ - حَدَّثَنَا عَبْدُ اللهِ بْنُ عِمْرَانَ أَبُو الْقَاسِمِ الْقُرَشِيُّ الْمَكِّيُّ ۞ حَدَّثَنَا إِبْرَاهِيمُ بْنُ سَعْدٍ ۞ عَنِ ابْنِ شِهَابٍ ۞ عَنْ عُبَيْدِ اللهِ ۞ عَنِ ابْنِ عَبَّاسٍ رَضِيَ اللهُ عَنْهُمَا قَالَ كَانَ رَسُولُ اللهِ ﷺ أَجْوَدَ النَّاسِ بِالْخَيْرِ ۞ وَكَانَ أَجْوَدَ مَا يَكُونُ فِي شَهْرِ رَمَضَانَ حَتَّى يَنْسَلِخَ ۞ فَيَأْتِيهِ جِبْرِيلُ فَيَعْرِضُ عَلَيْهِ الْقُرْآنَ ۞ فَإِذَا لَقِيَهُ جِبْرِيلُ كَانَ رَسُولُ اللهِ ﷺ أَجْوَدَ بِالْخَيْرِ مِنَ الرِّيحِ الْمُرْسَلَةِ ۞

[775] Because strangers would have a tendency to ask very direct and even personal questions—questions that the Companions would be too shy to ask themselves—they would happily escort strangers to the Prophet ﷺ so they could benefit from hearing the answers. (AA)

[776] In other words, help the person in need by bringing him to me. (AA)

[777] This means that the Prophet ﷺ would only accept the praise of a person who was thanking him for a gift or some favour he did for him, this being the Qur'anic character: *Do not consider those who love to be praised for what they have not done [to be free of the punishment in the Hereafter]*... (Qur'an 3:188) (AA)

[778] By transgressing the limits or the truth. (MA)

[779] Imam al-Bajuri notes that the Prophet ﷺ would prohibit the person from speaking in that manner, and if the person refused to listen, he would get up and leave. (AA)

[780] This shows the extensive generosity of the Messenger of Allah ﷺ. He was not asked of anything of this world and the Next except that he gave it. (AA)

[781] The Arabic verb used here is *ya'rid*, which is defined as 'reciting something from memory to someone else' (Imam al-Fayumi, *al-Misbah al-Munir*). In al-Bukhari's version of this narration it states that Jibril ﷺ would 'meet with him each night in Ramadan and they would review the Qur'an together.' The Prophet's blessed heart is the firmest of hearts, as Allah alluded to when He said, *Had we revealed this Qur'an upon a mountain, you would have seen it humbled and rent asunder by the fear of Allah.* (Qur'an 59:21) Because his blessed heart was strengthened to carry the divine speech, the Prophet ﷺ was not at risk

of forgetting the Qur'an; nevertheless, out of love he was keen to review it, and also sought to demonstrate to his *Umma* the importance of continually reviewing it. Allah told the Prophet ﷺ that it is He who would teach him the Qur'an: *We shall teach you to recite and so you will not forget.* (Qur'an 87:6) In another verse, Allah says that it is for Him—Glorified and Exalted is He—to gather the Qur'an in the Prophet's blessed chest and ensure that he recites it properly: *Verily it is for Us to gather it and to recite it.* (Qur'an 75:17) Scholars say the primary role of Jibril ﷺ was as a servant (*khadim*) to the Prophet ﷺ and to be the means by which the Prophet ﷺ—and thereby his community—received the Qur'an. Because Allah has placed human beings in a world of means, Allah revealed His scriptures to various Prophets through the means of the Angel Jibril ﷺ. The Prophet ﷺ enjoyed hearing the Qur'an recited by others (see hadith 323 in chapter 45). So too would the Prophet ﷺ experience joy when listening to Jibril recite. Through these yearly 'reviews' of the Qur'an with the Angel Jibril ﷺ, the Prophet was teaching his *Umma* the importance of continually reciting and preserving it. These narrations demonstrate the Prophet's concern that his *Umma* stays attached to the Qur'an. Allah and His Messenger ﷺ know best. (AA, MA)

353. 'Abdullah ibn 'Imran Abu al-Qasim al-Qurashi al-Makki narrated to us, 'Ibrahim ibn Sa'd narrated to us on the authority of Ibn Shihab, on the authority of 'Ubaydullah, on the authority of Ibn 'Abbas ﷺ, who reported:

"The Messenger of Allah ﷺ was the most generous of people in goodness. He was most generous during the month of Ramadan, until the end of it, when Jibril would come to him and he would recite to him the Quran from memory.[781] When Jibril would meet with him, the Messenger of Allah ﷺ was more generous with good than a strong wind that brings forth rain."'[782]

٣٥٤ - حَدَّثَنَا قُتَيْبَةُ بْنُ سَعِيدٍ ۞ حَدَّثَنَا جَعْفَرُ بْنُ سُلَيْمَانَ ۞ عَنْ ثَابِتٍ ۞ عَنْ أَنَسِ بْنِ مَالِكٍ رَضِيَ اللَّهُ عَنْهُ قَالَ كَانَ النَّبِيُّ ﷺ لَا يَدَّخِرُ شَيْئًا لِغَدٍ ۞

354. Qutayba ibn Sa'id narrated to us, 'Ja'far ibn Sulayman narrated to us on the authority of Thabit, on the authority of Anas ibn Malik ﷺ, who reported:

"The Messenger of Allah ﷺ never stored anything for the next day."'[783]

٣٥٥ - حَدَّثَنَا هَارُونُ بْنُ مُوسَى بْنِ أَبِي عَلْقَمَةَ الْمَدَنِيُّ ۞ حَدَّثَنِي أَبِي ۞ عَنْ هِشَامِ بْنِ سَعْدٍ ۞ عَنْ زَيْدِ بْنِ أَسْلَمَ ۞ عَنْ أَبِيهِ ۞ عَنْ عُمَرَ بْنِ الْخَطَّابِ رَضِيَ اللَّهُ عَنْهُ أَنَّ رَجُلًا جَاءَ إِلَى النَّبِيِّ ﷺ فَسَأَلَهُ أَنْ يُعْطِيَهُ ۞ فَقَالَ النَّبِيُّ ﷺ مَا عِنْدِي شَيْءٌ وَلَكِنِ ابْتَعْ عَلَيَّ فَإِذَا جَاءَنِي شَيْءٌ قَضَيْتُهُ ۞ فَقَالَ عُمَرُ يَا رَسُولَ اللَّهِ قَدْ أَعْطَيْتَهُ ۞ فَمَا كَلَّفَكَ اللَّهُ مَا لَا تَقْدِرُ عَلَيْهِ ۞ فَكَرِهَ النَّبِيُّ ﷺ قَوْلَ عُمَرَ ۞ فَقَالَ رَجُلٌ مِنَ الْأَنْصَارِ يَا رَسُولَ اللَّهِ أَنْفِقْ وَلَا تَخَفْ مِنْ ذِي الْعَرْشِ إِقْلَالًا ۞ فَتَبَسَّمَ رَسُولُ اللَّهِ ﷺ وَعُرِفَ فِي وَجْهِهِ الْبِشْرُ لِقَوْلِ الْأَنْصَارِيِّ ۞ ثُمَّ قَالَ بِهَذَا أُمِرْتُ ۞

[782] Imam al-Bajuri comments, 'The Prophet ﷺ was most generous in the month of Ramadan because it is a time of abundant goodness and a time in which goodness is on the increase. Allah bestows favours upon His servants in this month to a degree that He does not bestow in other months, and thus the Prophet ﷺ adopts his Lord's qualities of character.' The Prophet ﷺ is therefore bountiful like a wind bringing forth fresh rain: his care and concern, his guidance and gazes, his beautiful character and example all bring forth spiritual rain to drench dry hearts. He offers hope and life to all of humanity, whether rich or poor, good or bad, high or low. Just as rain brings life back to land, the Prophet's goodness brings life back to hearts. The generosity of the Prophet ﷺ is in fact beyond the generosity of a strong wind that brings forth rain, for rain comes and goes, while the generosity of the Prophet ﷺ does not. This generosity would occur with Jibril ﷺ because it was the moment that he, the best of the Angels, would come to meet the Prophet ﷺ, the best of Allah's creation. In the same way that rain falls on all types of earth, so too does the flow of the Prophet's generosity extend to all people. The scholars say that the *Umma* should be a nation of generosity and kindness in the month of Ramadan in imitation of their Prophet ﷺ. (AA)

[783] That is, he ﷺ never kept any leftover provisions for the next day. This is with regard to the Prophet ﷺ himself, since there are other narrations showing that he stored a year's worth of provisions for his Family. Imam al-Ghazali said in *Ihya' 'Ulum al-Din*, 'The Prophet ﷺ would not take of the things which Allah gave him except his provision of a year, and of that, only the simplest foodstuffs he found, such as dates and barley, the rest of which he gave in charity for the sake of Allah. He ﷺ was never asked for anything except that he gave it, after which he would return to his provision for the year and prefer [the seeker over himself], often being in need before the end of the year if nothing came to him.' (AA)

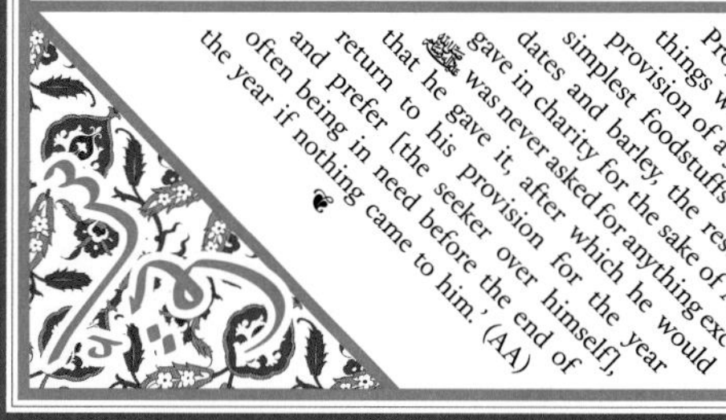

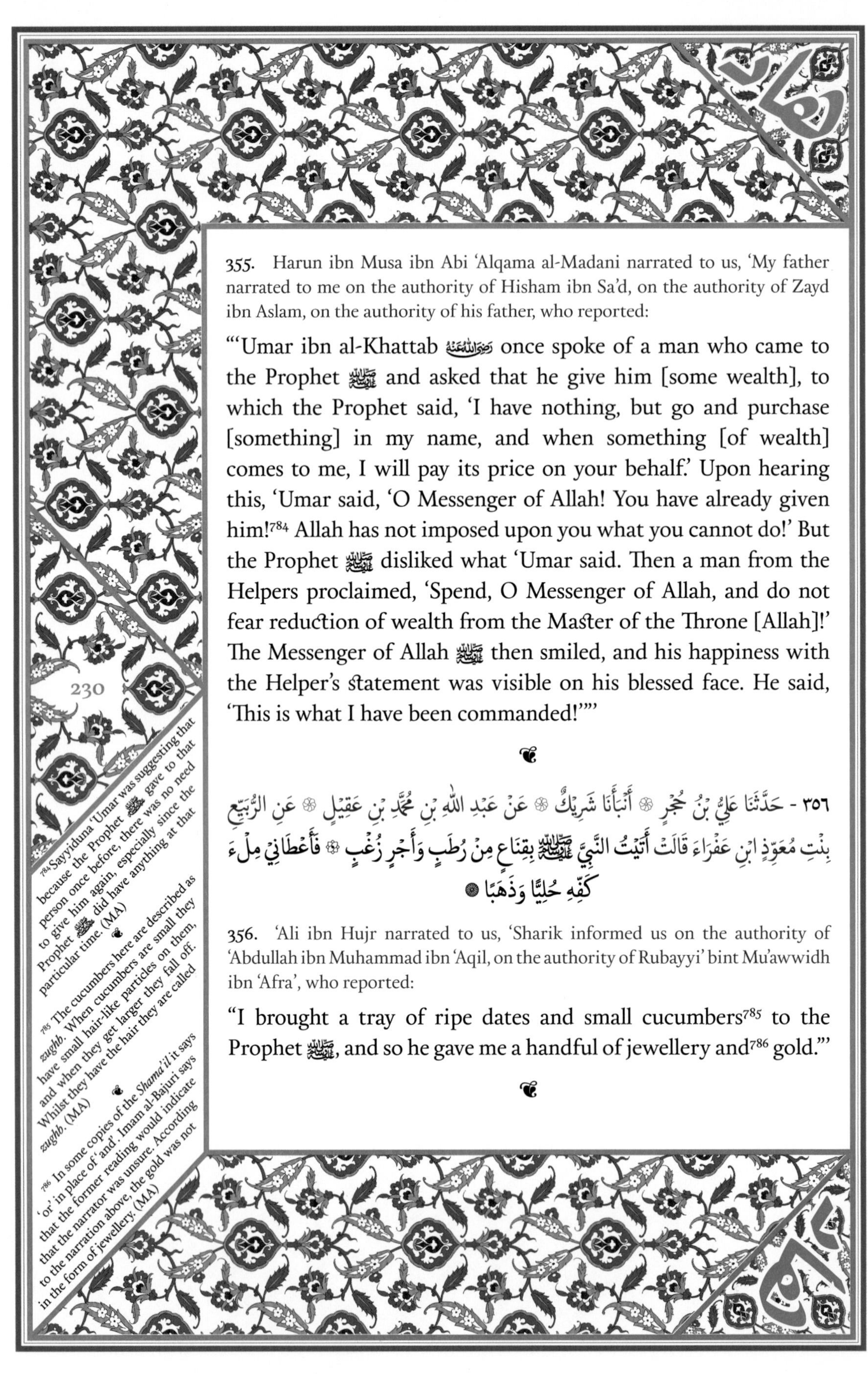

355. Harun ibn Musa ibn Abi 'Alqama al-Madani narrated to us, 'My father narrated to me on the authority of Hisham ibn Sa'd, on the authority of Zayd ibn Aslam, on the authority of his father, who reported:

"'Umar ibn al-Khattab ﵁ once spoke of a man who came to the Prophet ﷺ and asked that he give him [some wealth], to which the Prophet said, 'I have nothing, but go and purchase [something] in my name, and when something [of wealth] comes to me, I will pay its price on your behalf.' Upon hearing this, 'Umar said, 'O Messenger of Allah! You have already given him![784] Allah has not imposed upon you what you cannot do!' But the Prophet ﷺ disliked what 'Umar said. Then a man from the Helpers proclaimed, 'Spend, O Messenger of Allah, and do not fear reduction of wealth from the Master of the Throne [Allah]!' The Messenger of Allah ﷺ then smiled, and his happiness with the Helper's statement was visible on his blessed face. He said, 'This is what I have been commanded!'"'

٣٥٦ - حَدَّثَنَا عَلِيُّ بْنُ حُجْرٍ ۞ أَنْبَأَنَا شَرِيكٌ ۞ عَنْ عَبْدِ اللهِ بْنِ مُحَمَّدِ بْنِ عَقِيلٍ ۞ عَنِ الرُّبَيِّعِ بِنْتِ مُعَوِّذِ ابْنِ عَفْرَاءَ قَالَتْ أَتَيْتُ النَّبِيَّ ﷺ بِقِنَاعٍ مِنْ رُطَبٍ وَأَجْرٍ زُغْبٍ ۞ فَأَعْطَانِي مِلْءَ كَفِّهِ حُلِيًّا وَذَهَبًا ۞

356. 'Ali ibn Hujr narrated to us, 'Sharik informed us on the authority of 'Abdullah ibn Muhammad ibn 'Aqil, on the authority of Rubayyi' bint Mu'awwidh ibn 'Afra', who reported:

"I brought a tray of ripe dates and small cucumbers[785] to the Prophet ﷺ, and so he gave me a handful of jewellery and[786] gold."'

[784] Sayyiduna 'Umar was suggesting that because the Prophet ﷺ gave to that person once before, there was no need to give him again, especially since the Prophet ﷺ did have anything at that particular time. (MA)

[785] The cucumbers here are described as *zughb*. When cucumbers are small they have small hair-like particles on them, and when they get larger they fall off. Whilst they have the hair they are called *zughb*. (MA)

[786] In some copies of the *Shama'il* it says 'or' in place of 'and'. Imam al-Bajuri says that the former reading would indicate that the narrator was unsure. According to the narration above, the gold was not in the form of jewellery. (MA)

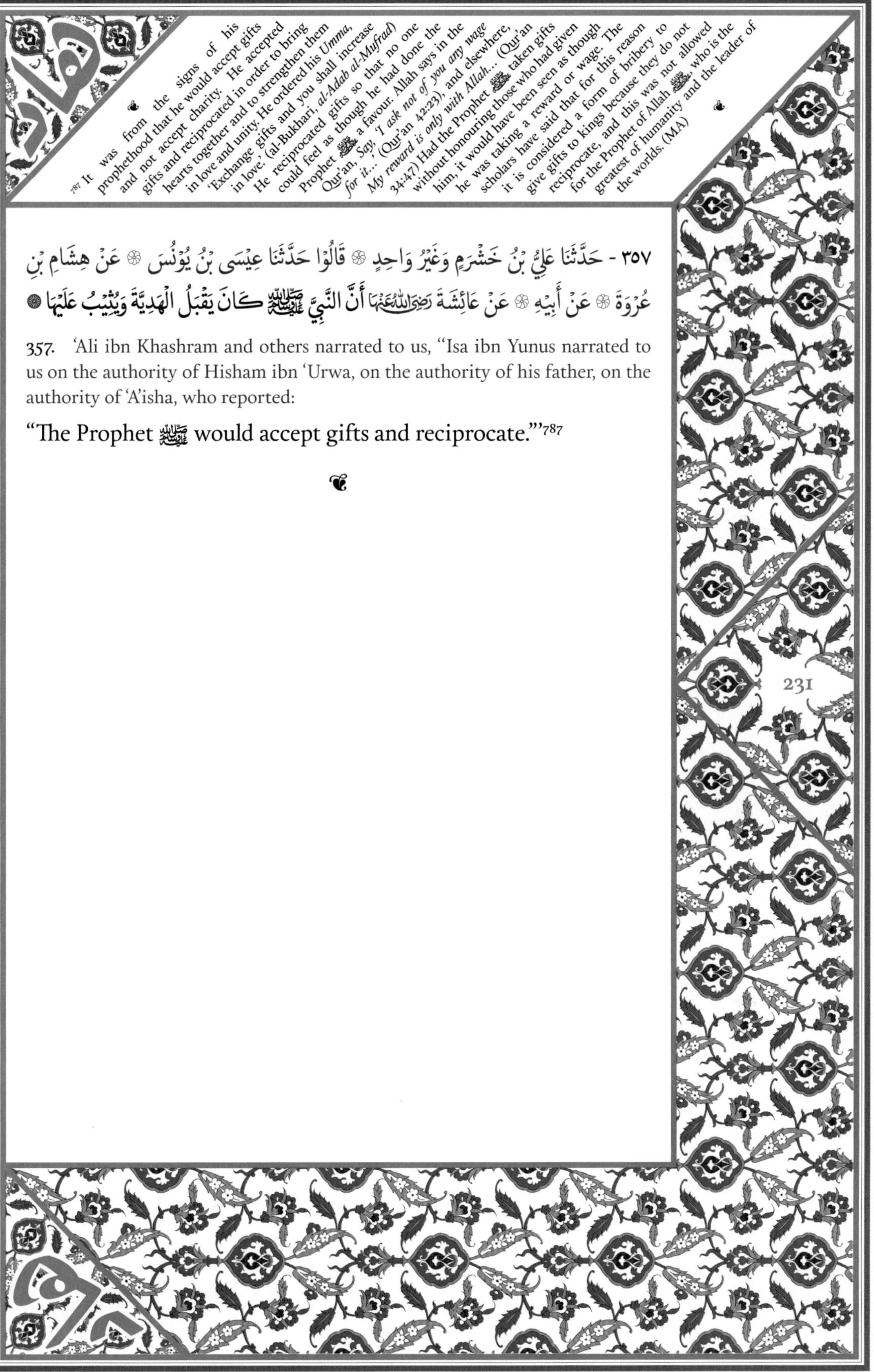

٣٥٧ - حَدَّثَنَا عَلِيُّ بْنُ خَشْرَمٍ وَغَيْرُ وَاحِدٍ ۞ قَالُوا حَدَّثَنَا عِيسَى بْنُ يُونُسَ ۞ عَنْ هِشَامِ بْنِ عُرْوَةَ ۞ عَنْ أَبِيهِ ۞ عَنْ عَائِشَةَ رَضِيَ اللهُ عَنْهَا أَنَّ النَّبِيَّ ﷺ كَانَ يَقْبَلُ الْهَدِيَّةَ وَيُثِيبُ عَلَيْهَا ۞

357. 'Ali ibn Khashram and others narrated to us, "Isa ibn Yunus narrated to us on the authority of Hisham ibn 'Urwa, on the authority of his father, on the authority of 'A'isha, who reported:

"The Prophet ﷺ would accept gifts and reciprocate."'[787]

[787] It was from the signs of his prophethood that he would accept gifts and not accept charity. He accepted gifts and reciprocated in order to bring hearts together and to strengthen them in love and unity. He ordered his *Umma*, 'Exchange gifts and you shall increase in love.' (al-Bukhari, *al-Adab al-Mufrad*) He reciprocated gifts so that no one could feel as though he had done the Prophet ﷺ a favour. Allah says in the Qur'an, *Say, 'I ask not of you any wage for it...'* (Qur'an 42:23), and elsewhere, *My reward is only with Allah...* (Qur'an 34:47) Had the Prophet ﷺ taken gifts without honouring those who had given him, it would have been seen as though he was taking a reward or wage. The scholars have said that for this reason it is considered a form of bribery to give gifts to kings because they do not reciprocate, and this was not allowed for the Prophet of Allah ﷺ, who is the greatest of humanity and the leader of the worlds. (MA)

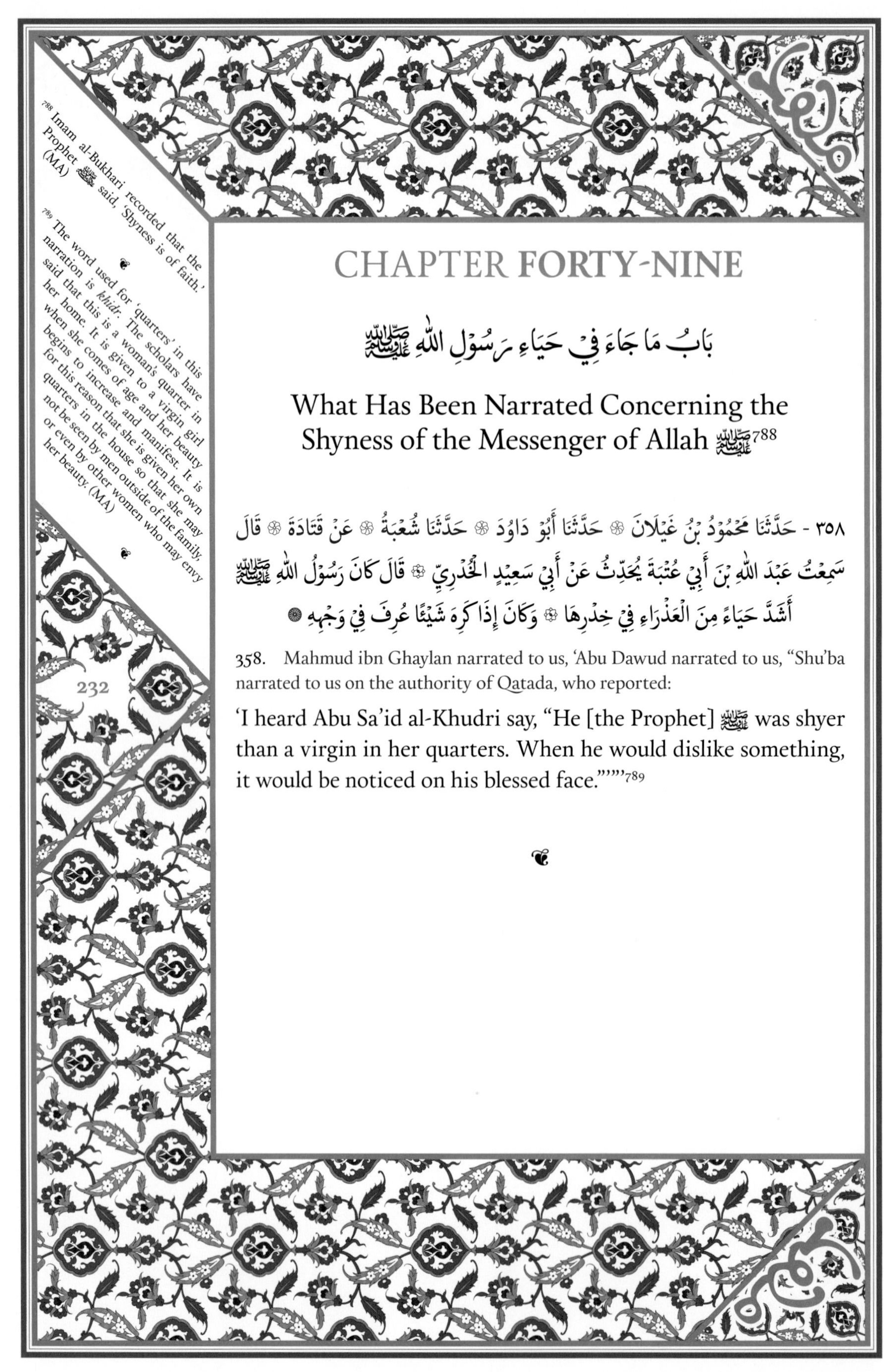

CHAPTER FORTY-NINE

بَابُ مَا جَاءَ فِي حَيَاءِ رَسُولِ اللهِ ﷺ

What Has Been Narrated Concerning the Shyness of the Messenger of Allah ﷺ[788]

٣٥٨ - حَدَّثَنَا مَحْمُودُ بْنُ غَيْلَانَ ۞ حَدَّثَنَا أَبُو دَاوُدَ ۞ حَدَّثَنَا شُعْبَةُ ۞ عَنْ قَتَادَةَ ۞ قَالَ سَمِعْتُ عَبْدَ اللهِ بْنَ أَبِي عُتْبَةَ يُحَدِّثُ عَنْ أَبِي سَعِيدٍ الْخُدْرِيِّ ۞ قَالَ كَانَ رَسُولُ اللهِ ﷺ أَشَدَّ حَيَاءً مِنَ الْعَذْرَاءِ فِي خِدْرِهَا ۞ وَكَانَ إِذَا كَرِهَ شَيْئًا عُرِفَ فِي وَجْهِهِ ۞

358. Mahmud ibn Ghaylan narrated to us, 'Abu Dawud narrated to us, "Shu'ba narrated to us on the authority of Qatada, who reported:

'I heard Abu Sa'id al-Khudri say, "He [the Prophet] ﷺ was shyer than a virgin in her quarters. When he would dislike something, it would be noticed on his blessed face."'"'[789]

---

[788] Imam al-Bukhari recorded that the Prophet ﷺ said, 'Shyness is of faith.' (MA)

[789] The word used for 'quarters' in this narration is *khidr*. The scholars have said that this is a woman's quarter in her home. It is given to a virgin girl when she comes of age and her beauty begins to increase and manifest. It is for this reason that she is given her own quarters in the house so that she may not be seen by men outside of the family, or even by other women who may envy her beauty. (MA)

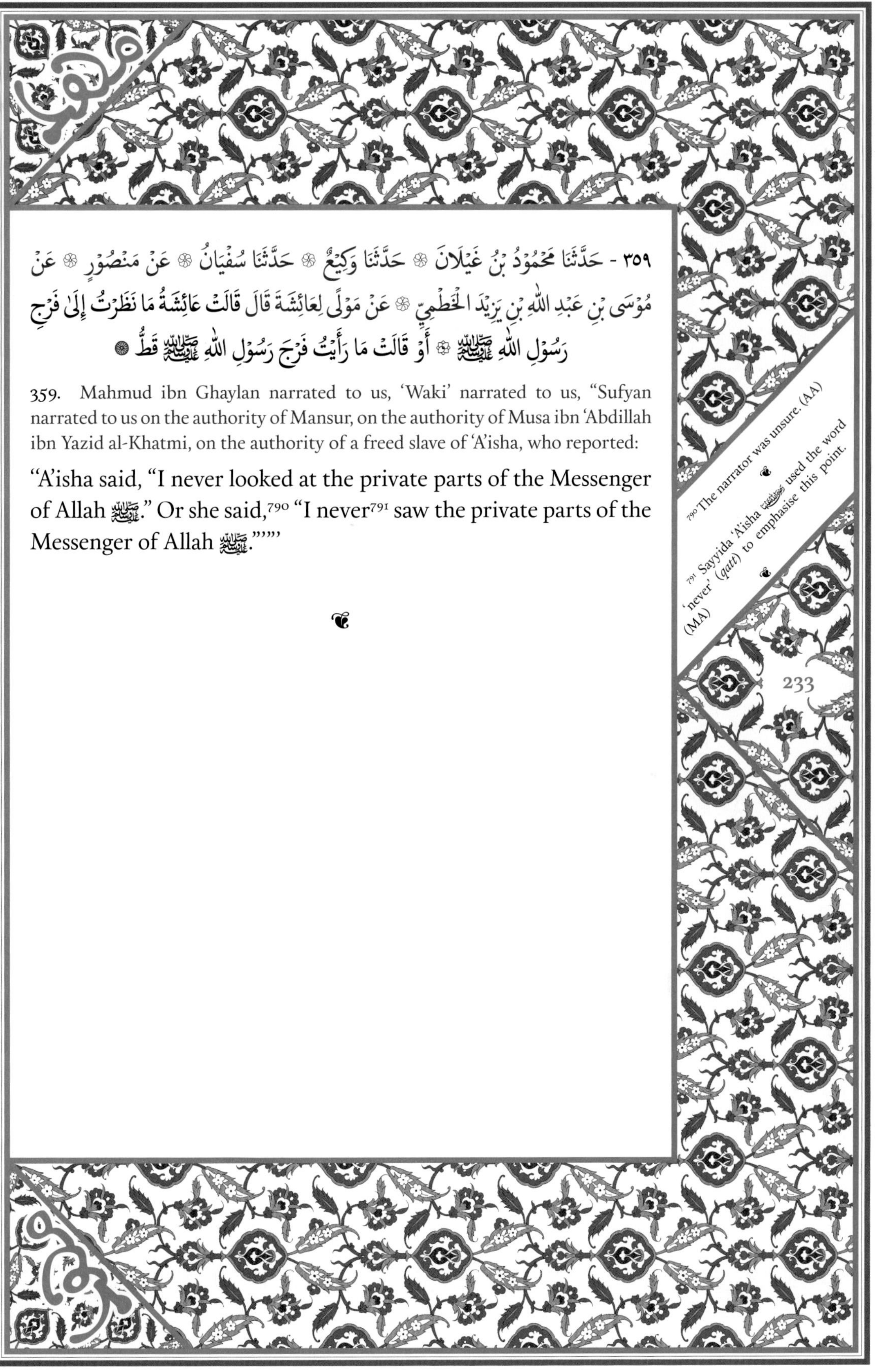

٣٥٩ - حَدَّثَنَا مَحْمُودُ بْنُ غَيْلَانَ ۞ حَدَّثَنَا وَكِيعٌ ۞ حَدَّثَنَا سُفْيَانُ ۞ عَنْ مَنْصُورٍ ۞ عَنْ مُوسَى بْنِ عَبْدِ اللهِ بْنِ يَزِيدَ الْخَطْمِيِّ ۞ عَنْ مَوْلًى لِعَائِشَةَ قَالَ قَالَتْ عَائِشَةُ مَا نَظَرْتُ إِلَى فَرْجِ رَسُولِ اللهِ ﷺ ۞ أَوْ قَالَتْ مَا رَأَيْتُ فَرْجَ رَسُولِ اللهِ ﷺ قَطُّ ۞

359. Mahmud ibn Ghaylan narrated to us, 'Waki' narrated to us, "Sufyan narrated to us on the authority of Mansur, on the authority of Musa ibn 'Abdillah ibn Yazid al-Khatmi, on the authority of a freed slave of 'A'isha, who reported:

"A'isha said, "I never looked at the private parts of the Messenger of Allah ﷺ." Or she said,[790] "I never[791] saw the private parts of the Messenger of Allah ﷺ.""""

[790] The narrator was unsure. (AA)

[791] Sayyida 'A'isha used the word 'never' (*qatt*) to emphasise this point. (MA)

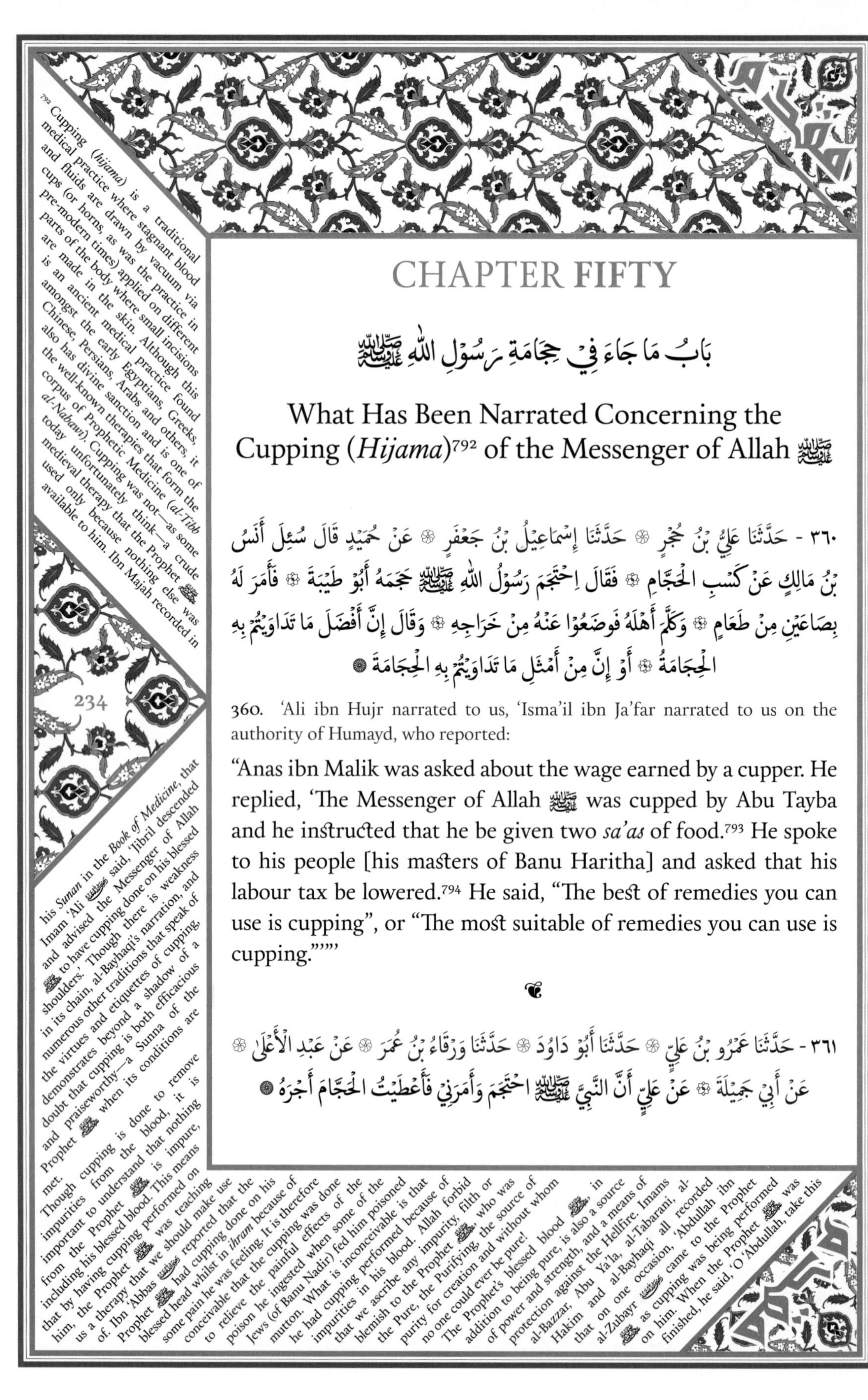

CHAPTER FIFTY

بَابُ مَا جَاءَ فِي حِجَامَةِ رَسُولِ اللهِ ﷺ

What Has Been Narrated Concerning the Cupping (*Hijama*)[792] of the Messenger of Allah ﷺ

٣٦٠ - حَدَّثَنَا عَلِيُّ بْنُ حُجْرٍ ۞ حَدَّثَنَا إِسْمَاعِيلُ بْنُ جَعْفَرٍ ۞ عَنْ حُمَيْدٍ قَالَ سُئِلَ أَنَسُ بْنُ مَالِكٍ عَنْ كَسْبِ الْحَجَّامِ ۞ فَقَالَ احْتَجَمَ رَسُولُ اللهِ ﷺ حَجَمَهُ أَبُو طَيْبَةَ ۞ فَأَمَرَ لَهُ بِصَاعَيْنِ مِنْ طَعَامٍ ۞ وَكَلَّمَ أَهْلَهُ فَوَضَعُوا عَنْهُ مِنْ خَرَاجِهِ ۞ وَقَالَ إِنَّ أَفْضَلَ مَا تَدَاوَيْتُمْ بِهِ الْحِجَامَةُ ۞ أَوْ إِنَّ مِنْ أَمْثَلِ مَا تَدَاوَيْتُمْ بِهِ الْحِجَامَةَ ۝

360. ʿAli ibn Hujr narrated to us, ʿIsmaʾil ibn Jaʿfar narrated to us on the authority of Humayd, who reported:

"Anas ibn Malik was asked about the wage earned by a cupper. He replied, 'The Messenger of Allah ﷺ was cupped by Abu Tayba and he instructed that he be given two *saʿas* of food.[793] He spoke to his people [his masters of Banu Haritha] and asked that his labour tax be lowered.[794] He said, "The best of remedies you can use is cupping", or "The most suitable of remedies you can use is cupping."'"

❦

٣٦١ - حَدَّثَنَا عَمْرُو بْنُ عَلِيٍّ ۞ حَدَّثَنَا أَبُو دَاوُدَ ۞ حَدَّثَنَا وَرْقَاءُ بْنُ عُمَرَ ۞ عَنْ عَبْدِ الْأَعْلَى ۞ عَنْ أَبِي جَمِيلَةَ ۞ عَنْ عَلِيٍّ أَنَّ النَّبِيَّ ﷺ احْتَجَمَ وَأَمَرَنِي فَأَعْطَيْتُ الْحَجَّامَ أَجْرَهُ ۝

[792] Cupping (*hijama*) is a traditional medical practice where stagnant blood and fluids are drawn by vacuum via cups (or horns, as was the practice in pre-modern times) applied on different parts of the body where small incisions are made in the skin. Although this is an ancient medical practice found amongst the early Egyptians, Greeks, Chinese, Persians, Arabs and others, it also has divine sanction and is one of the well-known therapies that form the corpus of Prophetic Medicine (*al-Tibb al-Nabawi*). Cupping was not—as some today unfortunately think—a crude medieval therapy that the Prophet ﷺ used only because nothing else was available to him. Ibn Majah recorded in his *Sunan* in the *Book of Medicine*, that Imam ʿAli ؓ said, 'Jibril descended and advised the Messenger of Allah ﷺ to have cupping done on his blessed shoulders.' Though there is weakness in its chain, al-Bayhaqi's narration, and numerous other traditions that speak of the virtues and etiquettes of cupping, demonstrates beyond a shadow of a doubt that cupping is both efficacious and praiseworthy—a Sunna of the Prophet ﷺ when its conditions are met.

Though cupping is done to remove impurities from the blood, it is important to understand that nothing from the Prophet ﷺ is impure, including his blessed blood. This means that by having cupping performed on him, the Prophet ﷺ was teaching us a therapy that we should make use of. Ibn ʿAbbas ؓ reported that the Prophet ﷺ had cupping done on his blessed head whilst in *ihram* because of some pain he was feeling. It is therefore conceivable that the cupping was done to relieve the painful effects of the poison he ingested when some of the Jews (of Banu Nadir) fed him poisoned mutton. What is inconceivable is that he had cupping performed because of impurities in his blood. Allah forbid that we ascribe any impurity, filth or blemish to the Prophet ﷺ, who was the Pure, the Purifying, the source of purity for creation and without whom no one could ever be pure!

The Prophet's blessed blood ﷺ, in addition to being pure, is also a source of power and strength, and a means of protection against the Hellfire. Imams al-Bazzar, Abu Yaʿla, al-Tabarani, al-Hakim and al-Bayhaqi all recorded that on one occasion, ʿAbdullah ibn al-Zubayr ؓ came to the Prophet ﷺ as cupping was being performed on him. When the Prophet ﷺ was finished, he said, 'O ʿAbdullah, take this

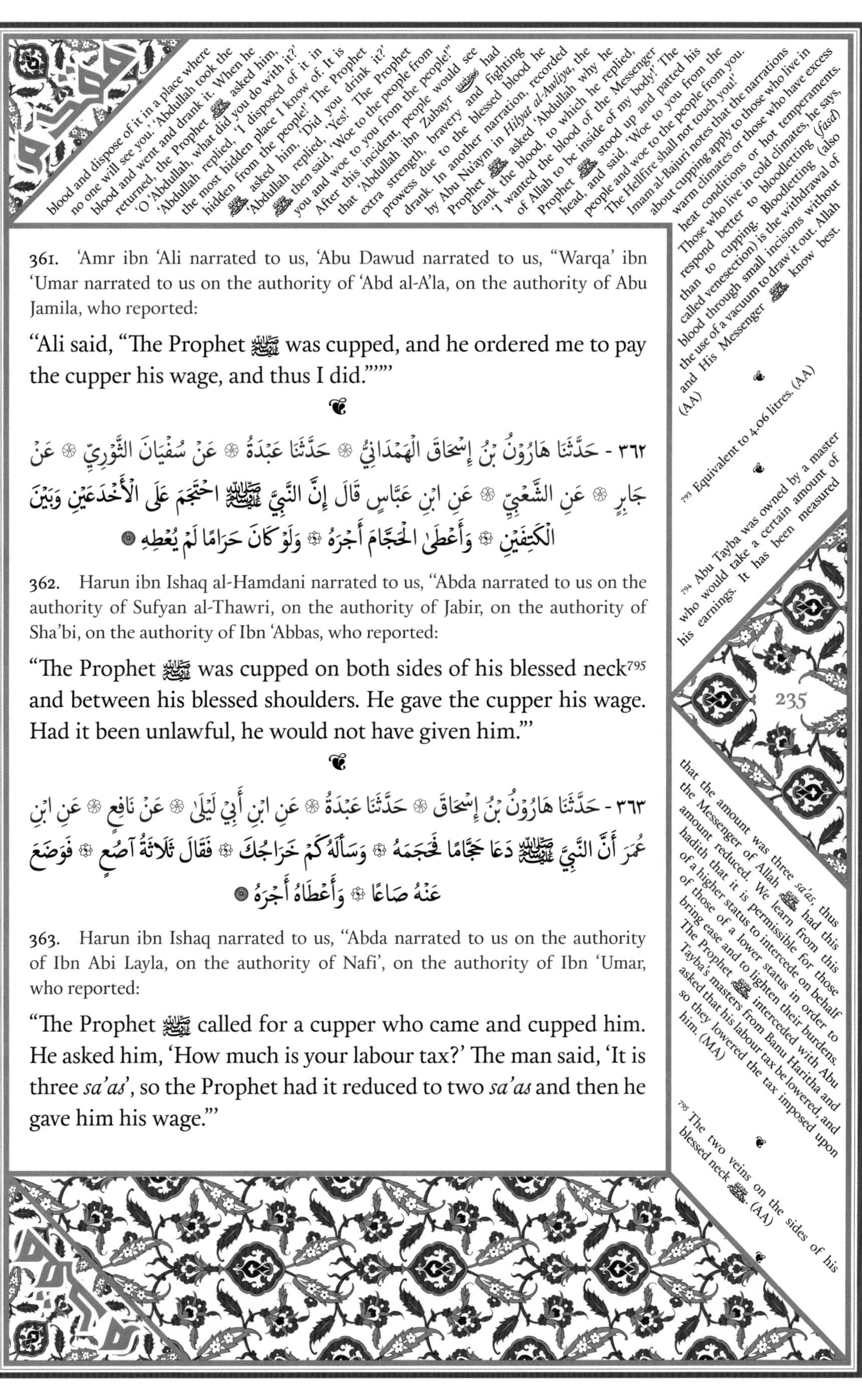

blood and dispose of it in a place where no one will see you.' 'Abdullah took the blood and went and drank it. When he returned, the Prophet ﷺ asked him, 'O 'Abdullah, what did you do with it?' 'Abdullah replied, 'I disposed of it in the most hidden place I know of. It is hidden from the people!' The Prophet ﷺ asked him, 'Did you drink it?' 'Abdullah replied, 'Yes!' The Prophet ﷺ then said, 'Woe to the people from you and woe to you from the people!" After this incident, people would see that 'Abdullah ibn Zubayr رضي الله عنهما had extra strength, bravery and fighting prowess due to the blessed blood he drank. In another narration, recorded by Abu Nu'aym in *Hilyat al-Awliya*, the Prophet ﷺ asked 'Abdullah why he drank the blood, to which he replied, 'I wanted the blood of the Messenger of Allah to be inside of my body!' The Prophet ﷺ stood up and patted his head, and said, 'Woe to you from the people and woe to the people from you. The Hellfire shall not touch you!' Imam al-Bajuri notes that the narrations about cupping apply to those who live in warm climates or those who have excess heat conditions or hot temperaments. Those who live in cold climates, he says, respond better to bloodletting (*fasd*) than to cupping. Bloodletting (also called venesection) is the withdrawal of blood through small incisions without the use of a vacuum to draw it out. Allah and His Messenger ﷺ know best. (AA)

361. 'Amr ibn 'Ali narrated to us, 'Abu Dawud narrated to us, "Warqa' ibn 'Umar narrated to us on the authority of 'Abd al-A'la, on the authority of Abu Jamila, who reported:

"Ali said, "The Prophet ﷺ was cupped, and he ordered me to pay the cupper his wage, and thus I did.""""

٣٦٢ - حَدَّثَنَا هَارُوْنُ بْنُ إِسْحَاقَ الْهَمْدَانِيُّ ۞ حَدَّثَنَا عَبْدَةُ ۞ عَنْ سُفْيَانَ الثَّوْرِيِّ ۞ عَنْ جَابِرٍ ۞ عَنِ الشَّعْبِيِّ ۞ عَنِ ابْنِ عَبَّاسٍ قَالَ إِنَّ النَّبِيَّ ﷺ احْتَجَمَ عَلَى الْأَخْدَعَيْنِ وَبَيْنَ الْكَتِفَيْنِ ۞ وَأَعْطَى الْحَجَّامَ أَجْرَهُ ۞ وَلَوْ كَانَ حَرَامًا لَمْ يُعْطِهِ ۞

362. Harun ibn Ishaq al-Hamdani narrated to us, "Abda narrated to us on the authority of Sufyan al-Thawri, on the authority of Jabir, on the authority of Sha'bi, on the authority of Ibn 'Abbas, who reported:

"The Prophet ﷺ was cupped on both sides of his blessed neck[795] and between his blessed shoulders. He gave the cupper his wage. Had it been unlawful, he would not have given him."'

٣٦٣ - حَدَّثَنَا هَارُوْنُ بْنُ إِسْحَاقَ ۞ حَدَّثَنَا عَبْدَةُ ۞ عَنِ ابْنِ أَبِي لَيْلَى ۞ عَنْ نَافِعٍ ۞ عَنِ ابْنِ عُمَرَ أَنَّ النَّبِيَّ ﷺ دَعَا حَجَّامًا فَحَجَمَهُ ۞ وَسَأَلَهُ كَمْ خَرَاجُكَ ۞ فَقَالَ ثَلَاثَةُ آصُعٍ ۞ فَوَضَعَ عَنْهُ صَاعًا ۞ وَأَعْطَاهُ أَجْرَهُ ۞

363. Harun ibn Ishaq narrated to us, "Abda narrated to us on the authority of Ibn Abi Layla, on the authority of Nafi', on the authority of Ibn 'Umar, who reported:

"The Prophet ﷺ called for a cupper who came and cupped him. He asked him, 'How much is your labour tax?' The man said, 'It is three *sa'as*', so the Prophet had it reduced to two *sa'as* and then he gave him his wage."'

[793] Equivalent to 4.06 litres. (AA)

[794] Abu Tayba was owned by a master who would take a certain amount of his earnings. It has been measured that the amount was three *sa'as*, thus the Messenger of Allah ﷺ had this amount reduced. We learn from this hadith that it is permissible for those of a higher status to intercede on behalf of those of a lower status in order to bring ease and to lighten their burdens. The Prophet ﷺ interceded with Abu Tayba's masters from Banu Haritha and asked that his labour tax be lowered, and so they lowered the tax imposed upon him. (MA)

[795] The two veins on the sides of his blessed neck ﷺ. (AA)

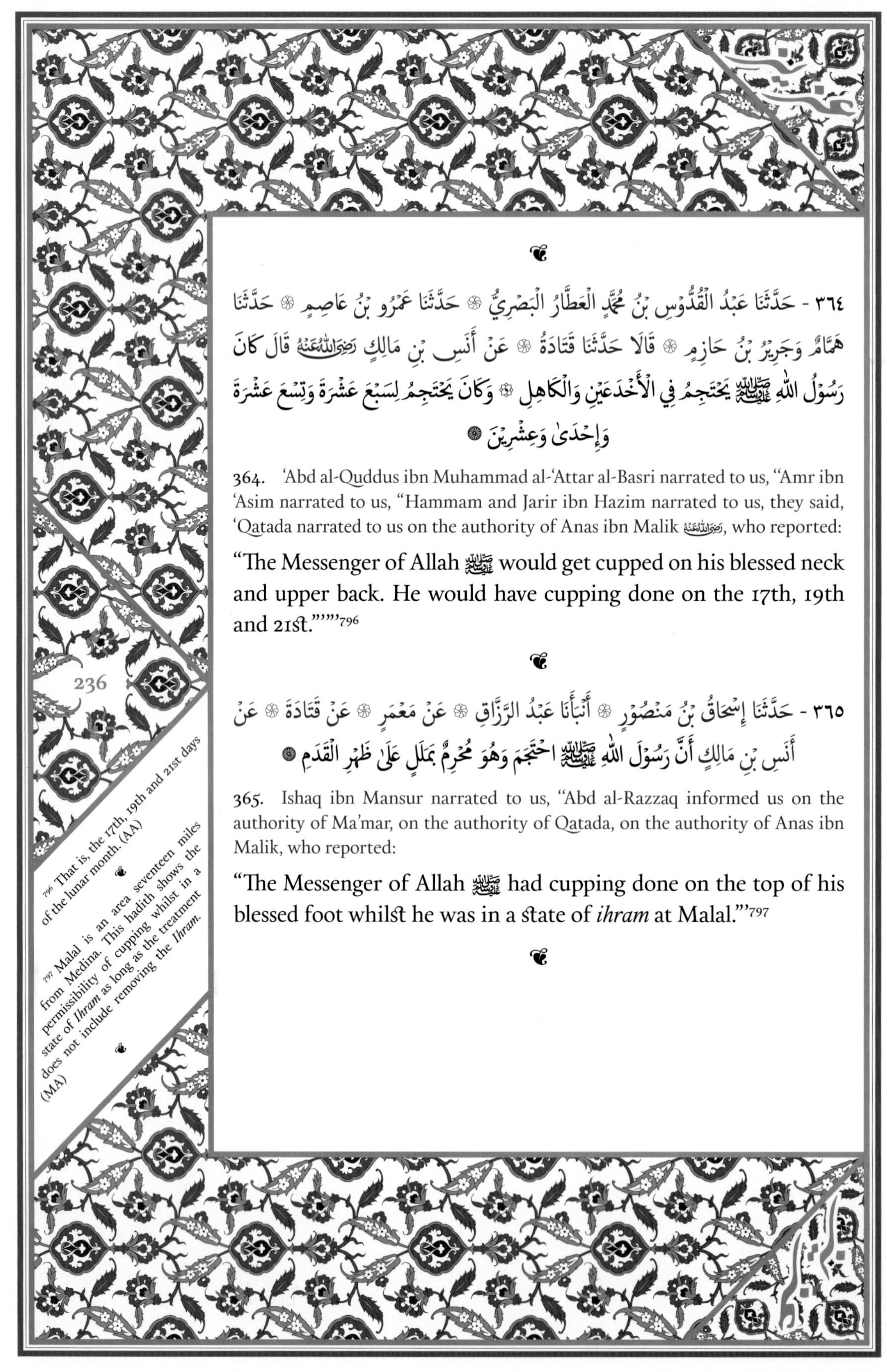

٣٦٤ - حَدَّثَنَا عَبْدُ الْقُدُّوسِ بْنُ مُحَمَّدٍ الْعَطَّارُ الْبَصْرِيُّ ❁ حَدَّثَنَا عَمْرُو بْنُ عَاصِمٍ ❁ حَدَّثَنَا هَمَّامٌ وَجَرِيرُ بْنُ حَازِمٍ ❁ قَالَا حَدَّثَنَا قَتَادَةُ ❁ عَنْ أَنَسِ بْنِ مَالِكٍ رَضِيَ اللَّهُ عَنْهُ قَالَ كَانَ رَسُولُ اللَّهِ ﷺ يَحْتَجِمُ فِي الْأَخْدَعَيْنِ وَالْكَاهِلِ ❁ وَكَانَ يَحْتَجِمُ لِسَبْعَ عَشْرَةَ وَتِسْعَ عَشْرَةَ وَإِحْدَى وَعِشْرِينَ ❁

364. ʿAbd al-Quddus ibn Muhammad al-ʿAttar al-Basri narrated to us, "Amr ibn ʿAsim narrated to us, "Hammam and Jarir ibn Hazim narrated to us, they said, ʿQatada narrated to us on the authority of Anas ibn Malik رضي الله عنه, who reported:

"The Messenger of Allah ﷺ would get cupped on his blessed neck and upper back. He would have cupping done on the 17th, 19th and 21st."'"'[796]

٣٦٥ - حَدَّثَنَا إِسْحَاقُ بْنُ مَنْصُورٍ ❁ أَنْبَأَنَا عَبْدُ الرَّزَّاقِ ❁ عَنْ مَعْمَرٍ ❁ عَنْ قَتَادَةَ ❁ عَنْ أَنَسِ بْنِ مَالِكٍ أَنَّ رَسُولَ اللَّهِ ﷺ احْتَجَمَ وَهُوَ مُحْرِمٌ بِمَلَلٍ عَلَى ظَهْرِ الْقَدَمِ ❁

365. Ishaq ibn Mansur narrated to us, "Abd al-Razzaq informed us on the authority of Ma'mar, on the authority of Qatada, on the authority of Anas ibn Malik, who reported:

"The Messenger of Allah ﷺ had cupping done on the top of his blessed foot whilst he was in a state of *ihram* at Malal."'[797]

[796] That is, the 17th, 19th and 21st days of the lunar month. (AA)

[797] Malal is an area seventeen miles from Medina. This hadith shows the permissibility of cupping whilst in a state of *Ihram* as long as the treatment does not include removing the *Ihram*. (MA)

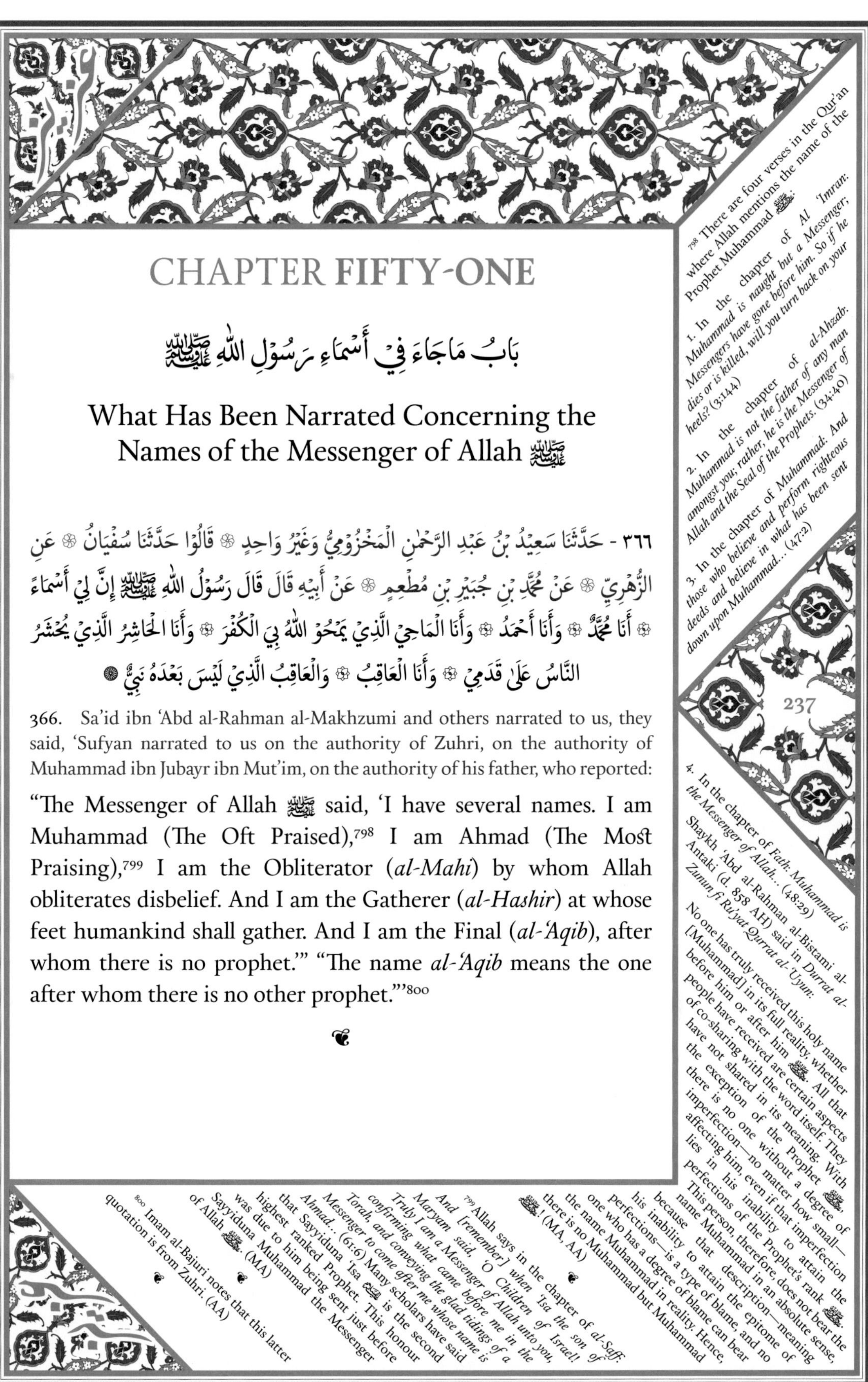

CHAPTER FIFTY-ONE

بَابُ مَا جَاءَ فِي أَسْمَاءِ رَسُولِ اللهِ ﷺ

What Has Been Narrated Concerning the Names of the Messenger of Allah ﷺ

٣٦٦ - حَدَّثَنَا سَعِيدُ بْنُ عَبْدِ الرَّحْمٰنِ الْمَخْزُومِيُّ وَغَيْرُ وَاحِدٍ ۞ قَالُوْا حَدَّثَنَا سُفْيَانُ ۞ عَنِ الزُّهْرِيِّ ۞ عَنْ مُحَمَّدِ بْنِ جُبَيْرِ بْنِ مُطْعِمٍ ۞ عَنْ أَبِيهِ قَالَ قَالَ رَسُولُ اللهِ ﷺ إِنَّ لِي أَسْمَاءً ۞ أَنَا مُحَمَّدٌ ۞ وَأَنَا أَحْمَدُ ۞ وَأَنَا الْمَاحِي الَّذِي يَمْحُو اللهُ بِيَ الْكُفْرَ ۞ وَأَنَا الْحَاشِرُ الَّذِي يُحْشَرُ النَّاسُ عَلَىٰ قَدَمِي ۞ وَأَنَا الْعَاقِبُ ۞ وَالْعَاقِبُ الَّذِي لَيْسَ بَعْدَهُ نَبِيٌّ ۞

366. Sa'id ibn 'Abd al-Rahman al-Makhzumi and others narrated to us, they said, 'Sufyan narrated to us on the authority of Zuhri, on the authority of Muhammad ibn Jubayr ibn Mut'im, on the authority of his father, who reported:

"The Messenger of Allah ﷺ said, 'I have several names. I am Muhammad (The Oft Praised),[798] I am Ahmad (The Most Praising),[799] I am the Obliterator (*al-Mahi*) by whom Allah obliterates disbelief. And I am the Gatherer (*al-Hashir*) at whose feet humankind shall gather. And I am the Final (*al-'Aqib*), after whom there is no prophet.'" "The name *al-'Aqib* means the one after whom there is no other prophet."'[800]

[798] There are four verses in the Qur'an where Allah mentions the name of the Prophet Muhammad ﷺ:

1. In the chapter of Al 'Imran: *Muhammad is naught but a Messenger; Messengers have gone before him. So if he dies or is killed, will you turn back on your heels?* (3:144)
2. In the chapter of al-Ahzab: *Muhammad is not the father of any man amongst you; rather, he is the Messenger of Allah and the Seal of the Prophets.* (34:40)
3. In the chapter of Muhammad: *And those who believe and perform righteous deeds and believe in what has been sent down upon Muhammad...* (47:2)
4. In the chapter of Fath: *Muhammad is the Messenger of Allah...* (48:29)

Shaykh 'Abd al-Rahman al-Bistami al-Antaki (d. 858 AH) said in *Durrat al-Zunun fi Ru'yat Qurrat al-'Uyun*:

No one has truly received this holy name [Muhammad] in its full reality, whether before him or after him ﷺ. All that people have received are certain aspects of co-sharing with the word itself. They have not shared in its meaning. With the exception of the Prophet ﷺ, there is no one without a degree of imperfection—no matter how small—affecting him, even if that imperfection lies in his inability to attain the perfections of the Prophet's rank ﷺ. This person, therefore, does not bear the name Muhammad in an absolute sense, because that description—meaning his inability to attain the epitome of perfections—is a type of blame, and no one who has a degree of blame can bear the name Muhammad in reality. Hence, there is no Muhammad but Muhammad ﷺ! (MA, AA)

[799] Allah says in the chapter of *al-Saff*: *And [remember] when 'Isa the son of Maryam said, 'O Children of Israel! Truly I am a Messenger of Allah unto you, confirming what came before me in the Torah, and conveying the glad tidings of a Messenger to come after me whose name is Ahmad...'* (61:6) Many scholars have said that Sayyiduna 'Isa ﷺ is the second highest ranked Prophet. This honour was due to him being sent just before Sayyiduna Muhammad the Messenger of Allah ﷺ. (MA)

[800] Imam al-Bajuri notes that this latter quotation is from Zuhri. (AA)

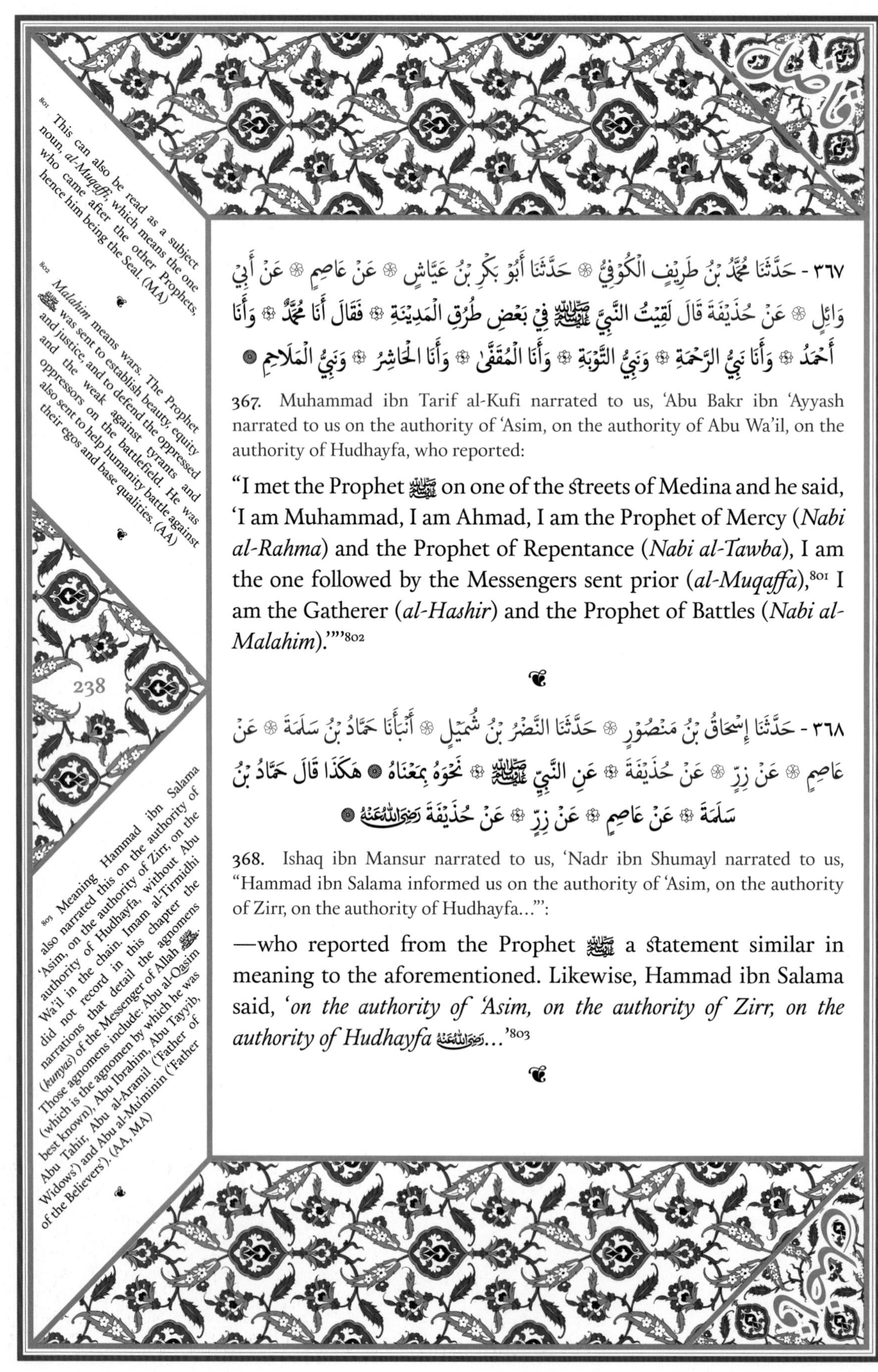

٣٦٧ - حَدَّثَنَا مُحَمَّدُ بْنُ طَرِيفٍ الْكُوفِيُّ ۞ حَدَّثَنَا أَبُو بَكْرِ بْنُ عَيَّاشٍ ۞ عَنْ عَاصِمٍ ۞ عَنْ أَبِي وَائِلٍ ۞ عَنْ حُذَيْفَةَ قَالَ لَقِيتُ النَّبِيَّ ﷺ فِي بَعْضِ طُرُقِ الْمَدِينَةِ ۞ فَقَالَ أَنَا مُحَمَّدٌ ۞ وَأَنَا أَحْمَدُ ۞ وَأَنَا نَبِيُّ الرَّحْمَةِ ۞ وَنَبِيُّ التَّوْبَةِ ۞ وَأَنَا الْمُقَفَّى ۞ وَأَنَا الْحَاشِرُ ۞ وَنَبِيُّ الْمَلَاحِمِ ۞

367. Muhammad ibn Tarif al-Kufi narrated to us, 'Abu Bakr ibn 'Ayyash narrated to us on the authority of 'Asim, on the authority of Abu Wa'il, on the authority of Hudhayfa, who reported:

"I met the Prophet ﷺ on one of the streets of Medina and he said, 'I am Muhammad, I am Ahmad, I am the Prophet of Mercy (*Nabi al-Rahma*) and the Prophet of Repentance (*Nabi al-Tawba*), I am the one followed by the Messengers sent prior (*al-Muqaffa*),[801] I am the Gatherer (*al-Hashir*) and the Prophet of Battles (*Nabi al-Malahim*).'"'[802]

٣٦٨ - حَدَّثَنَا إِسْحَاقُ بْنُ مَنْصُورٍ ۞ حَدَّثَنَا النَّضْرُ بْنُ شُمَيْلٍ ۞ أَنْبَأَنَا حَمَّادُ بْنُ سَلَمَةَ ۞ عَنْ عَاصِمٍ ۞ عَنْ زِرٍّ ۞ عَنْ حُذَيْفَةَ ۞ عَنِ النَّبِيِّ ﷺ ۞ نَحْوَهُ بِمَعْنَاهُ ۞ هَكَذَا قَالَ حَمَّادُ بْنُ سَلَمَةَ ۞ عَنْ عَاصِمٍ ۞ عَنْ زِرٍّ ۞ عَنْ حُذَيْفَةَ رَضِيَ اللَّهُ عَنْهُ ۞

368. Ishaq ibn Mansur narrated to us, 'Nadr ibn Shumayl narrated to us, "Hammad ibn Salama informed us on the authority of 'Asim, on the authority of Zirr, on the authority of Hudhayfa..."':

—who reported from the Prophet ﷺ a statement similar in meaning to the aforementioned. Likewise, Hammad ibn Salama said, '*on the authority of 'Asim, on the authority of Zirr, on the authority of Hudhayfa* رضي الله عنه*...*'[803]

801 This can also be read as a subject noun, *al-Muqaffi*, which means the one who came after the other Prophets, hence him being the Seal. (MA)

802 *Malahim* means wars. The Prophet ﷺ was sent to establish beauty, equity and justice, and to defend the oppressed and the weak against tyrants and oppressors on the battlefield. He was also sent to help humanity battle against their egos and base qualities. (AA)

803 Meaning Hammad ibn Salama also narrated this on the authority of 'Asim, on the authority of Zirr, on the authority of Hudhayfa, without Abu Wa'il in the chain. Imam al-Tirmidhi did not record in this chapter the narrations that detail the agnomens (*kunyas*) of the Messenger of Allah ﷺ. Those agnomens include: Abu al-Qasim (which is the agnomen by which he was best known), Abu Ibrahim, Abu Tayyib, Abu Tahir, Abu al-Aramil ('Father of Widows') and Abu al-Mu'minin ('Father of the Believers'). (AA, MA)

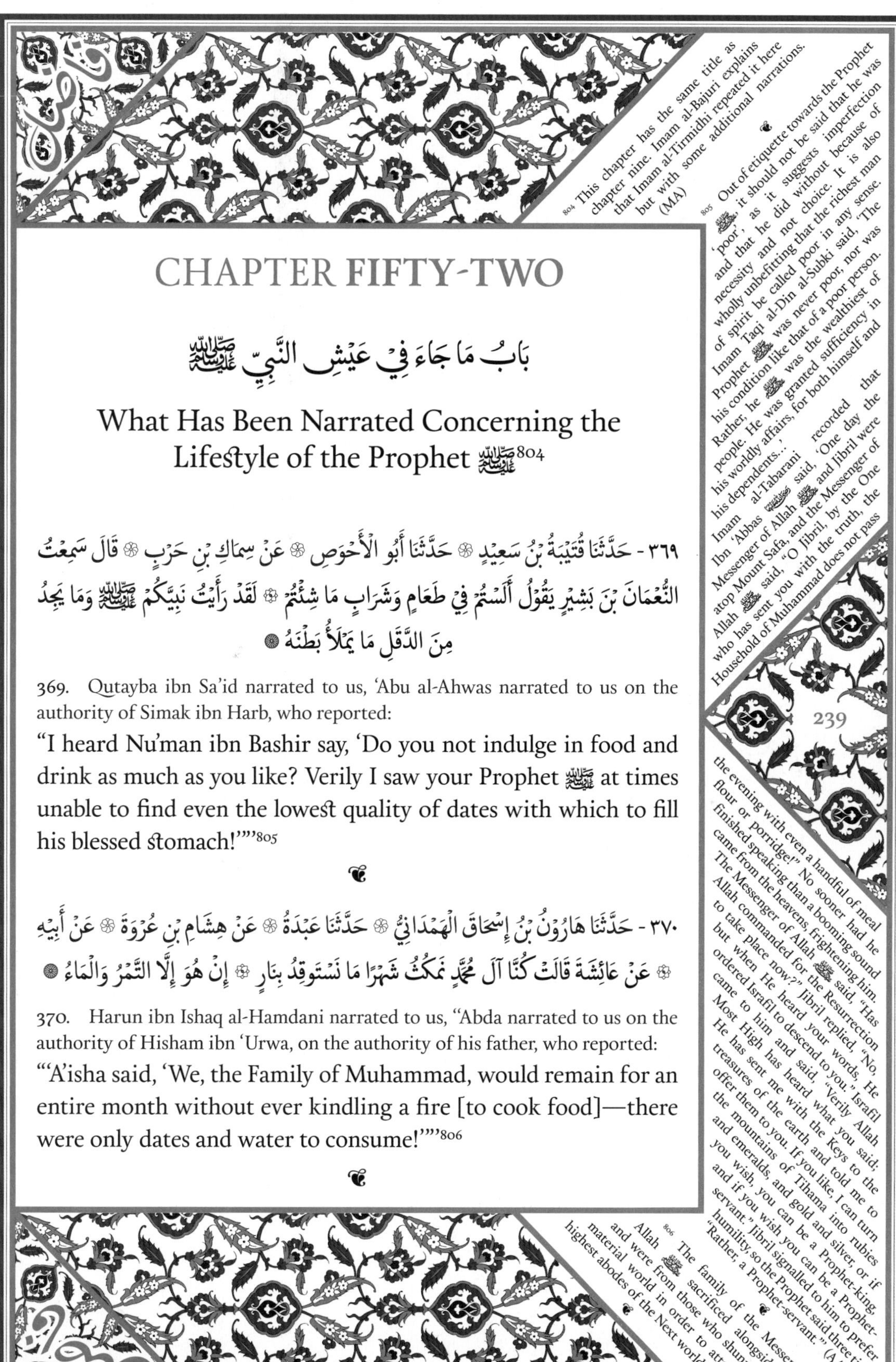

CHAPTER **FIFTY-TWO**

بَابُ مَا جَاءَ فِي عَيْشِ النَّبِيِّ ﷺ

What Has Been Narrated Concerning the Lifestyle of the Prophet ﷺ[804]

٣٦٩ - حَدَّثَنَا قُتَيْبَةُ بْنُ سَعِيدٍ ❀ حَدَّثَنَا أَبُو الْأَحْوَصِ ❀ عَنْ سِمَاكِ بْنِ حَرْبٍ ❀ قَالَ سَمِعْتُ النُّعْمَانَ بْنَ بَشِيرٍ يَقُولُ أَلَسْتُمْ فِي طَعَامٍ وَشَرَابٍ مَا شِئْتُمْ ❀ لَقَدْ رَأَيْتُ نَبِيَّكُمْ ﷺ وَمَا يَجِدُ مِنَ الدَّقَلِ مَا يَمْلَأُ بَطْنَهُ ❁

369. Qutayba ibn Sa'id narrated to us, 'Abu al-Ahwas narrated to us on the authority of Simak ibn Harb, who reported:

"I heard Nu'man ibn Bashir say, 'Do you not indulge in food and drink as much as you like? Verily I saw your Prophet ﷺ at times unable to find even the lowest quality of dates with which to fill his blessed stomach!'"[805]

❦

٣٧٠ - حَدَّثَنَا هَارُونُ بْنُ إِسْحَاقَ الْهَمْدَانِيُّ ❀ حَدَّثَنَا عَبْدَةُ ❀ عَنْ هِشَامِ بْنِ عُرْوَةَ ❀ عَنْ أَبِيهِ ❀ عَنْ عَائِشَةَ قَالَتْ كُنَّا آلَ مُحَمَّدٍ نَمْكُثُ شَهْرًا مَا نَسْتَوْقِدُ بِنَارٍ ❀ إِنْ هُوَ إِلَّا التَّمْرُ وَالْمَاءُ ❁

370. Harun ibn Ishaq al-Hamdani narrated to us, "Abda narrated to us on the authority of Hisham ibn 'Urwa, on the authority of his father, who reported:

"'A'isha said, 'We, the Family of Muhammad, would remain for an entire month without ever kindling a fire [to cook food]—there were only dates and water to consume!'"[806]

❦

[804] This chapter has the same title as chapter nine. Imam al-Bajuri explains that Imam al-Tirmidhi repeated it here but with some additional narrations. (MA)

❦

[805] Out of etiquette towards the Prophet ﷺ, it should not be said that he was 'poor', as it suggests imperfection and that he did without because of necessity and not choice. It is also wholly unbefitting that the richest man of spirit be called poor in any sense. Imam Taqi al-Din al-Subki said, 'The Prophet ﷺ was never poor, nor was his condition like that of a poor person. Rather, he ﷺ was the wealthiest of people. He was granted sufficiency in his worldly affairs, for both himself and his dependents...' Imam al-Tabarani recorded that Ibn 'Abbas said, 'One day the Messenger of Allah ﷺ and Jibril were atop Mount Safa, and the Messenger of Allah ﷺ said, "O Jibril, by the One who has sent you with the truth, the Household of Muhammad does not pass the evening with even a handful of meal flour or porridge!" No sooner had he finished speaking than a booming sound came from the heavens, frightening him. The Messenger of Allah ﷺ said, "Has Allah commanded for the Resurrection to take place now?" Jibril replied, "No, but when He heard your words, He ordered Israfil to descend to you." Israfil came to him and said, "Verily Allah Most High has heard what you said; He has sent me with the Keys to the treasures of the earth and told me to offer them to you. If you like, I can turn the mountains of Tihama into rubies and emeralds, and gold and silver, or if you wish, you can be a Prophet-king, and if you wish you can be a Prophet-servant." Jibril signalled to him to prefer humility, so the Prophet said three times, "Rather, a Prophet-servant."' (AA, MA)

❦

[806] The family of the Messenger of Allah ﷺ sacrificed alongside him and were from those who shunned the material world in order to attain the highest abodes of the Next world. (MA)

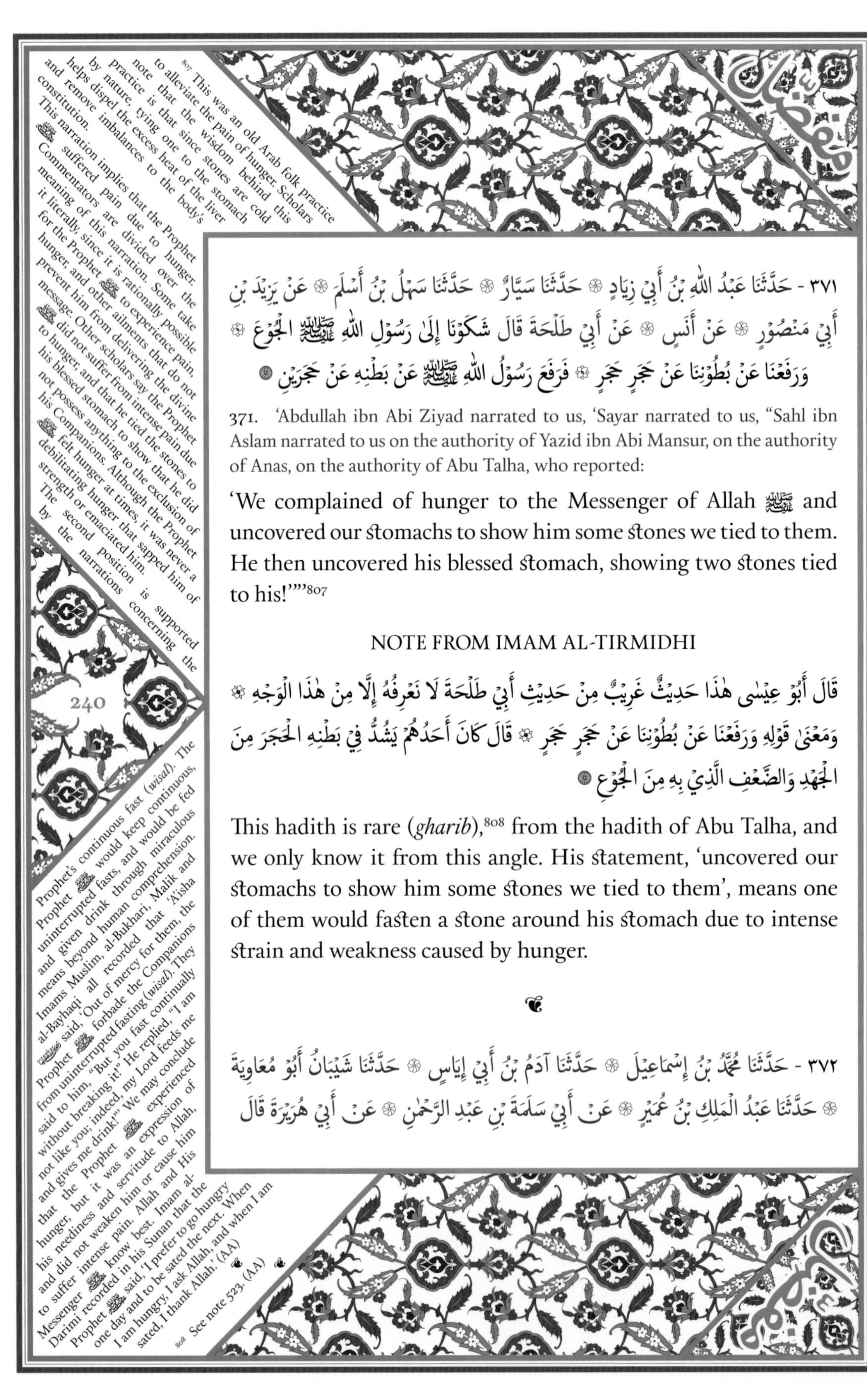

٣٧١ - حَدَّثَنَا عَبْدُ اللهِ بْنُ أَبِي زِيَادٍ ۞ حَدَّثَنَا سَيَّارٌ ۞ حَدَّثَنَا سَهْلُ بْنُ أَسْلَمَ ۞ عَنْ يَزِيدَ بْنِ أَبِي مَنْصُورٍ ۞ عَنْ أَنَسٍ ۞ عَنْ أَبِي طَلْحَةَ قَالَ شَكَوْنَا إِلَىٰ رَسُولِ اللهِ ﷺ الْجُوعَ ۞ وَرَفَعْنَا عَنْ بُطُونِنَا عَنْ حَجَرٍ حَجَرٍ ۞ فَرَفَعَ رَسُولُ اللهِ ﷺ عَنْ بَطْنِهِ عَنْ حَجَرَيْنِ ۞

371. 'Abdullah ibn Abi Ziyad narrated to us, 'Sayar narrated to us, "Sahl ibn Aslam narrated to us on the authority of Yazid ibn Abi Mansur, on the authority of Anas, on the authority of Abu Talha, who reported:

'We complained of hunger to the Messenger of Allah ﷺ and uncovered our stomachs to show him some stones we tied to them. He then uncovered his blessed stomach, showing two stones tied to his!'"'[807]

NOTE FROM IMAM AL-TIRMIDHI

قَالَ أَبُو عِيسَىٰ هٰذَا حَدِيثٌ غَرِيبٌ مِنْ حَدِيثِ أَبِي طَلْحَةَ لَا نَعْرِفُهُ إِلَّا مِنْ هٰذَا الْوَجْهِ ۞ وَمَعْنَىٰ قَوْلِهِ وَرَفَعْنَا عَنْ بُطُونِنَا عَنْ حَجَرٍ حَجَرٍ ۞ قَالَ كَانَ أَحَدُهُمْ يَشُدُّ فِي بَطْنِهِ الْحَجَرَ مِنَ الْجَهْدِ وَالضَّعْفِ الَّذِي بِهِ مِنَ الْجُوعِ ۞

This hadith is rare (*gharib*),[808] from the hadith of Abu Talha, and we only know it from this angle. His statement, 'uncovered our stomachs to show him some stones we tied to them', means one of them would fasten a stone around his stomach due to intense strain and weakness caused by hunger.

٣٧٢ - حَدَّثَنَا مُحَمَّدُ بْنُ إِسْمَاعِيلَ ۞ حَدَّثَنَا آدَمُ بْنُ أَبِي إِيَاسٍ ۞ حَدَّثَنَا شَيْبَانُ أَبُو مُعَاوِيَةَ ۞ حَدَّثَنَا عَبْدُ الْمَلِكِ بْنُ عُمَيْرٍ ۞ عَنْ أَبِي سَلَمَةَ بْنِ عَبْدِ الرَّحْمٰنِ ۞ عَنْ أَبِي هُرَيْرَةَ قَالَ

[807] This was an old Arab folk practice to alleviate the pain of hunger. Scholars note that the wisdom behind this practice is that since stones are cold by nature, tying one to the stomach helps dispel the excess heat of the liver and remove imbalances to the body's constitution. This narration implies that the Prophet ﷺ suffered pain due to hunger. Commentators are divided over the meaning of this narration. Some take it literally, since it is rationally possible for the Prophet ﷺ to experience pain, hunger, and other ailments that do not prevent him from delivering the divine message. Other scholars say the Prophet ﷺ did not suffer from intense pain due to hunger, and that he tied the stones to his blessed stomach to show that he did not possess anything to the exclusion of his Companions. Although the Prophet ﷺ felt hunger at times, it was never a debilitating hunger that sapped him of strength or emaciated him. The second position is supported by the narrations concerning the Prophet's continuous fast (*wisal*). The Prophet ﷺ would keep continuous, uninterrupted fasts, and would be fed and given drink through miraculous means beyond human comprehension. Imams Muslim, al-Bukhari, Malik and al-Bayhaqi all recorded that 'A'isha ﷺ said, 'Out of mercy for them, the Prophet ﷺ forbade the Companions from uninterrupted fasting (*wisal*). They said to him, "But you fast continually without breaking it!" He replied, "I am not like you; indeed, my Lord feeds me and gives me drink!"' We may conclude that the Prophet ﷺ experienced hunger, but it was an expression of his neediness and servitude to Allah, and did not weaken him or cause him to suffer intense pain. Allah and His Messenger ﷺ know best. Imam al-Darimi recorded in his Sunan that the Prophet ﷺ said, 'I prefer to go hungry one day and to be sated the next. When I am hungry, I ask Allah, and when I am sated, I thank Allah.' (AA)

[808] See note 523. (AA)

خَرَجَ رَسُوْلُ اللهِ ﷺ فِي سَاعَةٍ لَا يَخْرُجُ فِيهَا وَلَا يَلْقَاهُ فِيهَا أَحَدٌ ۞ فَأَتَاهُ أَبُو بَكْرٍ ۞ فَقَالَ مَا جَاءَ بِكَ يَا أَبَا بَكْرٍ ۞ قَالَ خَرَجْتُ أَلْقَى رَسُوْلَ اللهِ ﷺ وَأَنْظُرُ فِي وَجْهِهِ وَالتَّسْلِيمَ عَلَيْهِ ۞ فَلَمْ يَلْبَثْ أَنْ جَاءَ عُمَرُ ۞ فَقَالَ مَا جَاءَ بِكَ يَا عُمَرُ ۞ قَالَ الْجُوْعُ يَا رَسُوْلَ اللهِ ۞ قَالَ ﷺ وَأَنَا قَدْ وَجَدْتُ بَعْضَ ذٰلِكَ ۞ فَانْطَلَقُوْا إِلَىٰ مَنْزِلِ أَبِي الْهَيْثَمِ بْنِ التَّيِّهَانِ الْأَنْصَارِيِّ ۞ وَكَانَ رَجُلًا كَثِيْرَ النَّخْلِ وَالشَّاءِ ۞ وَلَمْ يَكُنْ لَهُ خَدَمٌ ۞ فَلَمْ يَجِدُوْهُ ۞ فَقَالُوْا لِامْرَأَتِهِ أَيْنَ صَاحِبُكِ ۞ فَقَالَتْ اِنْطَلَقَ يَسْتَعْذِبُ لَنَا الْمَاءَ ۞ فَلَمْ يَلْبَثُوْا أَنْ جَاءَ أَبُو الْهَيْثَمِ بِقِرْبَةٍ يَزْعَبُهَا فَوَضَعَهَا ۞ ثُمَّ جَاءَ يَلْتَزِمُ النَّبِيَّ ﷺ وَيُفَدِّيهِ بِأَبِيهِ وَأُمِّهِ ۞ ثُمَّ انْطَلَقَ بِهِمْ إِلَىٰ حَدِيقَتِهِ فَبَسَطَ لَهُمْ بِسَاطًا ۞ ثُمَّ انْطَلَقَ إِلَىٰ نَخْلَةٍ فَجَاءَ بِقِنْوٍ فَوَضَعَهُ ۞ فَقَالَ النَّبِيُّ ﷺ أَفَلَا تَنَقَّيْتَ لَنَا مِنْ رُطَبِهِ ۞ فَقَالَ يَا رَسُوْلَ اللهِ إِنِّي أَرَدْتُ أَنْ تَخْتَارُوْا أَوْ تَخَيَّرُوْا مِنْ رُطَبِهِ وَبُسْرِهِ ۞ فَأَكَلُوْا وَشَرِبُوْا مِنْ ذٰلِكَ الْمَاءِ ۞ فَقَالَ النَّبِيُّ ﷺ هٰذَا وَالَّذِي نَفْسِي بِيَدِهِ مِنَ النَّعِيمِ الَّذِي تُسْأَلُوْنَ عَنْهُ يَوْمَ الْقِيَامَةِ ۞ ظِلٌّ بَارِدٌ وَرُطَبٌ طَيِّبٌ وَمَاءٌ بَارِدٌ ۞ فَانْطَلَقَ أَبُو الْهَيْثَمِ لِيَصْنَعَ لَهُمْ طَعَامًا ۞ فَقَالَ النَّبِيُّ ﷺ لَا تَذْبَحَنَّ لَنَا ذَاتَ دَرٍّ ۞ فَذَبَحَ لَهُمْ عَنَاقًا أَوْ جَدْيًا فَأَتَاهُمْ بِهَا فَأَكَلُوْا ۞ فَقَالَ ﷺ هَلْ لَكَ خَادِمٌ ۞ قَالَ لَا ۞ قَالَ فَإِذَا أَتَانَا سَبْيٌ فَأْتِنَا ۞ فَأُتِيَ النَّبِيُّ ﷺ بِرَأْسَيْنِ لَيْسَ مَعَهُمَا ثَالِثٌ ۞ فَأَتَاهُ أَبُو الْهَيْثَمِ ۞ فَقَالَ النَّبِيُّ ﷺ اِخْتَرْ مِنْهُمَا ۞ قَالَ يَا رَسُوْلَ اللهِ اِخْتَرْ لِي ۞ فَقَالَ النَّبِيُّ ﷺ إِنَّ الْمُسْتَشَارَ مُؤْتَمَنٌ ۞ خُذْ هٰذَا فَإِنِّي رَأَيْتُهُ يُصَلِّي ۞ وَاسْتَوْصِ بِهِ مَعْرُوْفًا ۞ فَانْطَلَقَ أَبُو الْهَيْثَمِ إِلَى امْرَأَتِهِ فَأَخْبَرَهَا بِقَوْلِ رَسُوْلِ اللهِ ﷺ ۞ فَقَالَتِ امْرَأَتُهُ مَا أَنْتَ بِبَالِغٍ حَقَّ مَا قَالَ فِيهِ النَّبِيُّ ﷺ إِلَّا بِأَنْ تَعْتِقَهُ ۞ قَالَ فَهُوَ عَتِيقٌ ۞ فَقَالَ ﷺ إِنَّ اللهَ لَمْ يَبْعَثْ نَبِيًّا وَلَا خَلِيفَةً إِلَّا وَلَهُ بِطَانَتَانِ ۞ بِطَانَةٌ تَأْمُرُهُ بِالْمَعْرُوْفِ وَتَنْهَاهُ عَنِ الْمُنْكَرِ ۞ وَبِطَانَةٌ لَا تَأْلُوْهُ خَبَالًا ۞ وَمَنْ يُوقَ بِطَانَةَ السُّوْءِ فَقَدْ وُقِيَ ۞

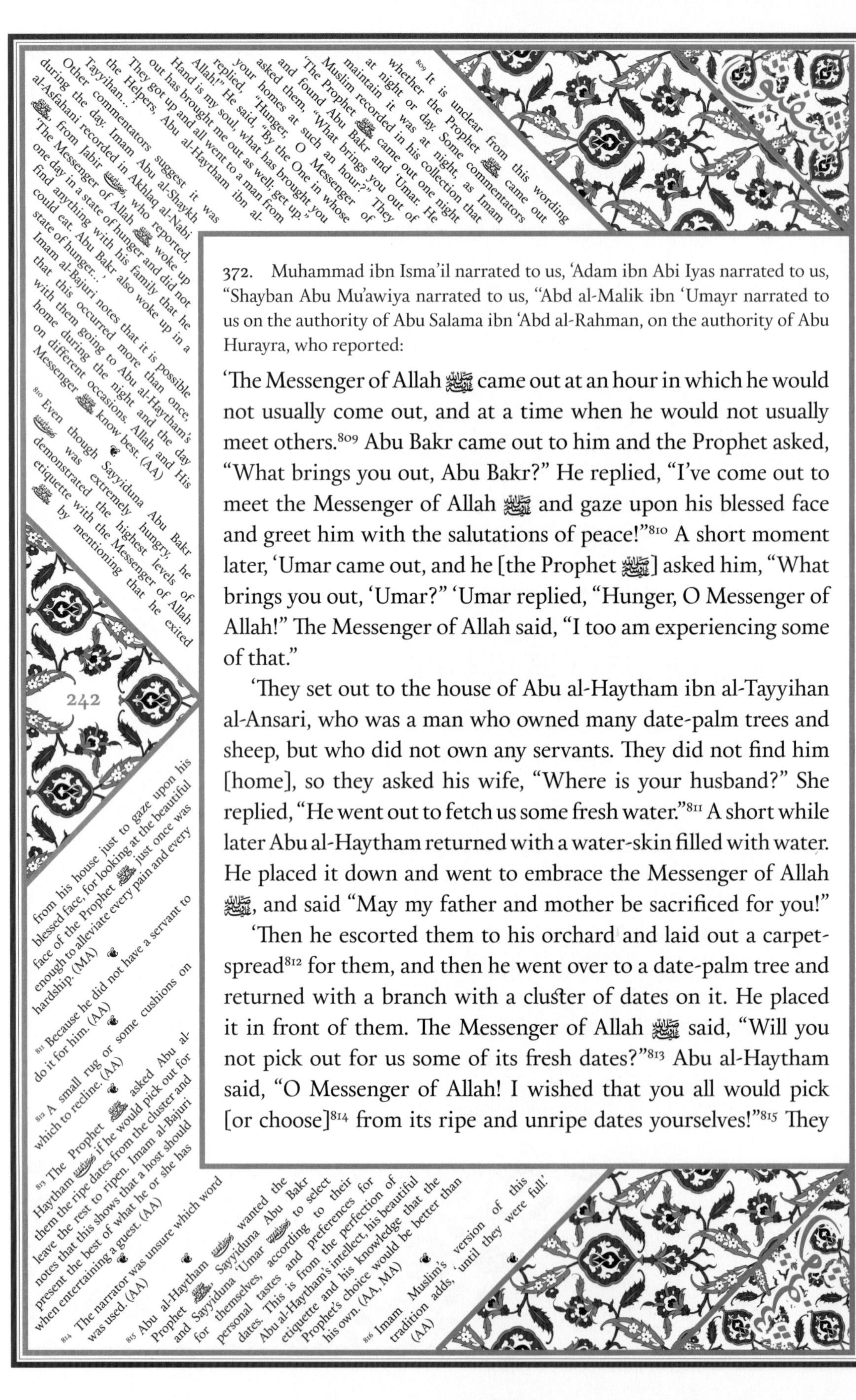

372. Muhammad ibn Isma'il narrated to us, 'Adam ibn Abi Iyas narrated to us, "Shayban Abu Mu'awiya narrated to us, "Abd al-Malik ibn 'Umayr narrated to us on the authority of Abu Salama ibn 'Abd al-Rahman, on the authority of Abu Hurayra, who reported:

'The Messenger of Allah ﷺ came out at an hour in which he would not usually come out, and at a time when he would not usually meet others.[809] Abu Bakr came out to him and the Prophet asked, "What brings you out, Abu Bakr?" He replied, "I've come out to meet the Messenger of Allah ﷺ and gaze upon his blessed face and greet him with the salutations of peace!"[810] A short moment later, 'Umar came out, and he [the Prophet ﷺ] asked him, "What brings you out, 'Umar?" 'Umar replied, "Hunger, O Messenger of Allah!" The Messenger of Allah said, "I too am experiencing some of that."

'They set out to the house of Abu al-Haytham ibn al-Tayyihan al-Ansari, who was a man who owned many date-palm trees and sheep, but who did not own any servants. They did not find him [home], so they asked his wife, "Where is your husband?" She replied, "He went out to fetch us some fresh water."[811] A short while later Abu al-Haytham returned with a water-skin filled with water. He placed it down and went to embrace the Messenger of Allah ﷺ, and said "May my father and mother be sacrificed for you!"

'Then he escorted them to his orchard and laid out a carpet-spread[812] for them, and then he went over to a date-palm tree and returned with a branch with a cluster of dates on it. He placed it in front of them. The Messenger of Allah ﷺ said, "Will you not pick out for us some of its fresh dates?"[813] Abu al-Haytham said, "O Messenger of Allah! I wished that you all would pick [or choose][814] from its ripe and unripe dates yourselves!"[815] They

809 It is unclear from this wording whether the Prophet ﷺ came out at night or day. Some commentators maintain it was at night, as Imam Muslim recorded in his collection that 'The Prophet ﷺ came out one night and found Abu Bakr and 'Umar. He asked them, "What brings you out of your homes at such an hour?" They replied, "Hunger, O Messenger of Allah!" He said, "By the One in whose Hand is my soul, what has brought you out has brought me out as well; get up." They got up and all went to a man from the Helpers, Abu al-Haytham ibn al-Tayyihan..' Other commentators suggest it was during the day. Imam Abu al-Shaykh al-Asfahani recorded in Akhlaq al-Nabi ﷺ, from Jabir, who reported, 'The Messenger of Allah ﷺ woke up one day in a state of hunger and did not find anything with his family that he could eat. Abu Bakr also woke up in a state of hunger..' Imam al-Bajuri notes that it is possible that this occurred more than once, with them going to Abu al-Haytham's home during the night and the day on different occasions. Allah and His Messenger ﷺ know best. (AA)

810 Even though Sayyiduna Abu Bakr was extremely hungry, he demonstrated the highest levels of etiquette with the Messenger of Allah ﷺ by mentioning that he exited from his house just to gaze upon his blessed face, for looking at the beautiful face of the Prophet ﷺ just once was enough to alleviate every pain and every hardship. (MA)

811 Because he did not have a servant to do it for him. (AA)

812 A small rug or some cushions on which to recline. (AA)

813 The Prophet ﷺ asked Abu al-Haytham if he would pick out for them the ripe dates from the cluster and leave the rest to ripen. Imam al-Bajuri notes that this shows that a host should present the best of what he or she has when entertaining a guest. (AA)

814 The narrator was unsure which word was used. (AA)

815 Abu al-Haytham wanted the Prophet ﷺ, Sayyiduna Abu Bakr and Sayyiduna 'Umar to select for themselves, according to their personal tastes and preferences for dates. This is from the perfection of Abu al-Haytham's intellect, his beautiful etiquette and his knowledge that the Prophet's choice would be better than his own. (AA, MA)

816 Imam Muslim's version of this tradition adds, 'until they were full.' (AA)

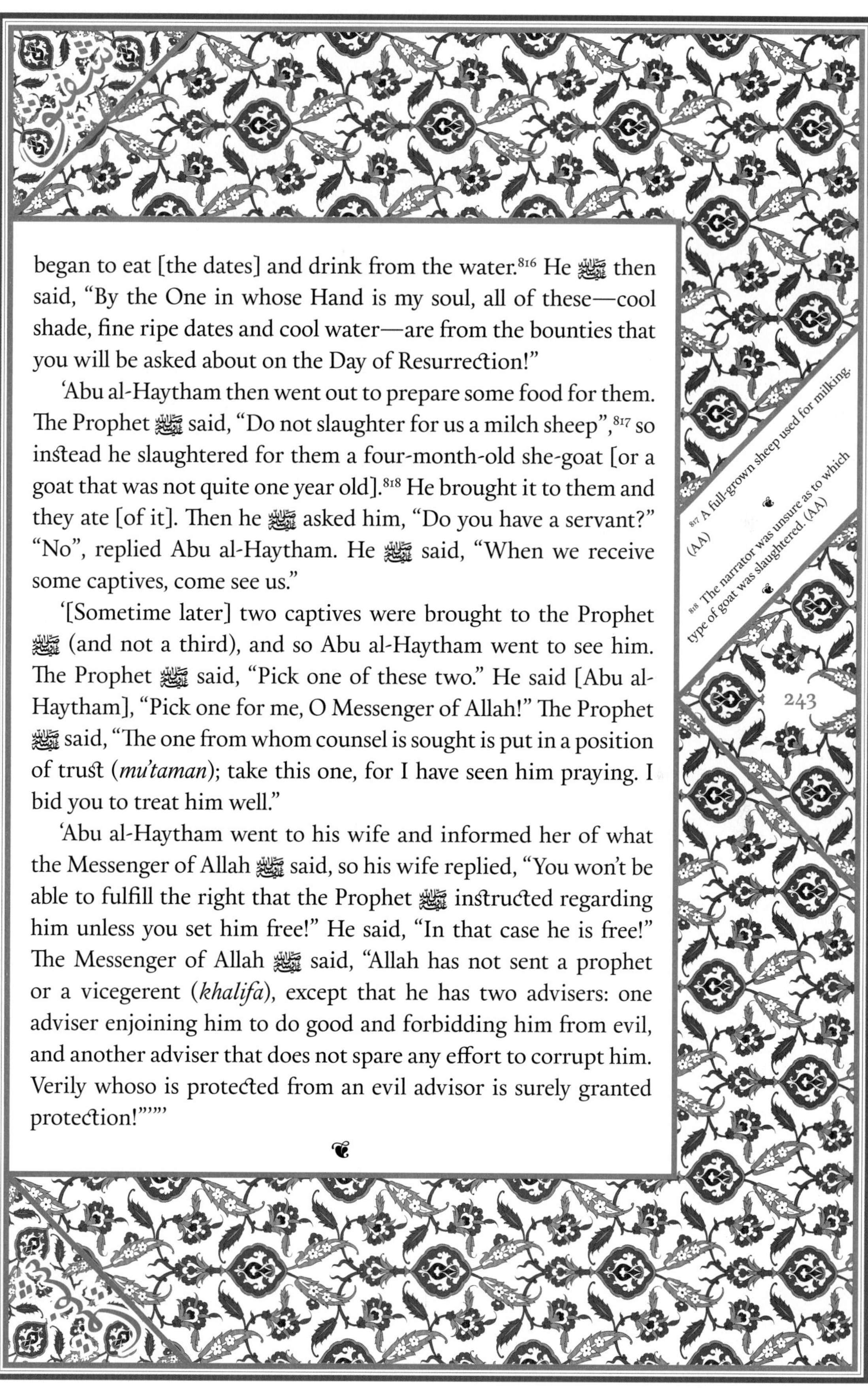

began to eat [the dates] and drink from the water.[816] He ﷺ then said, "By the One in whose Hand is my soul, all of these—cool shade, fine ripe dates and cool water—are from the bounties that you will be asked about on the Day of Resurrection!"

'Abu al-Haytham then went out to prepare some food for them. The Prophet ﷺ said, "Do not slaughter for us a milch sheep",[817] so instead he slaughtered for them a four-month-old she-goat [or a goat that was not quite one year old].[818] He brought it to them and they ate [of it]. Then he ﷺ asked him, "Do you have a servant?" "No", replied Abu al-Haytham. He ﷺ said, "When we receive some captives, come see us."

'[Sometime later] two captives were brought to the Prophet ﷺ (and not a third), and so Abu al-Haytham went to see him. The Prophet ﷺ said, "Pick one of these two." He said [Abu al-Haytham], "Pick one for me, O Messenger of Allah!" The Prophet ﷺ said, "The one from whom counsel is sought is put in a position of trust (*mu'taman*); take this one, for I have seen him praying. I bid you to treat him well."

'Abu al-Haytham went to his wife and informed her of what the Messenger of Allah ﷺ said, so his wife replied, "You won't be able to fulfill the right that the Prophet ﷺ instructed regarding him unless you set him free!" He said, "In that case he is free!" The Messenger of Allah ﷺ said, "Allah has not sent a prophet or a vicegerent (*khalifa*), except that he has two advisers: one adviser enjoining him to do good and forbidding him from evil, and another adviser that does not spare any effort to corrupt him. Verily whoso is protected from an evil advisor is surely granted protection!""""

[817] A full-grown sheep used for milking. (AA)

[818] The narrator was unsure as to which type of goat was slaughtered. (AA)

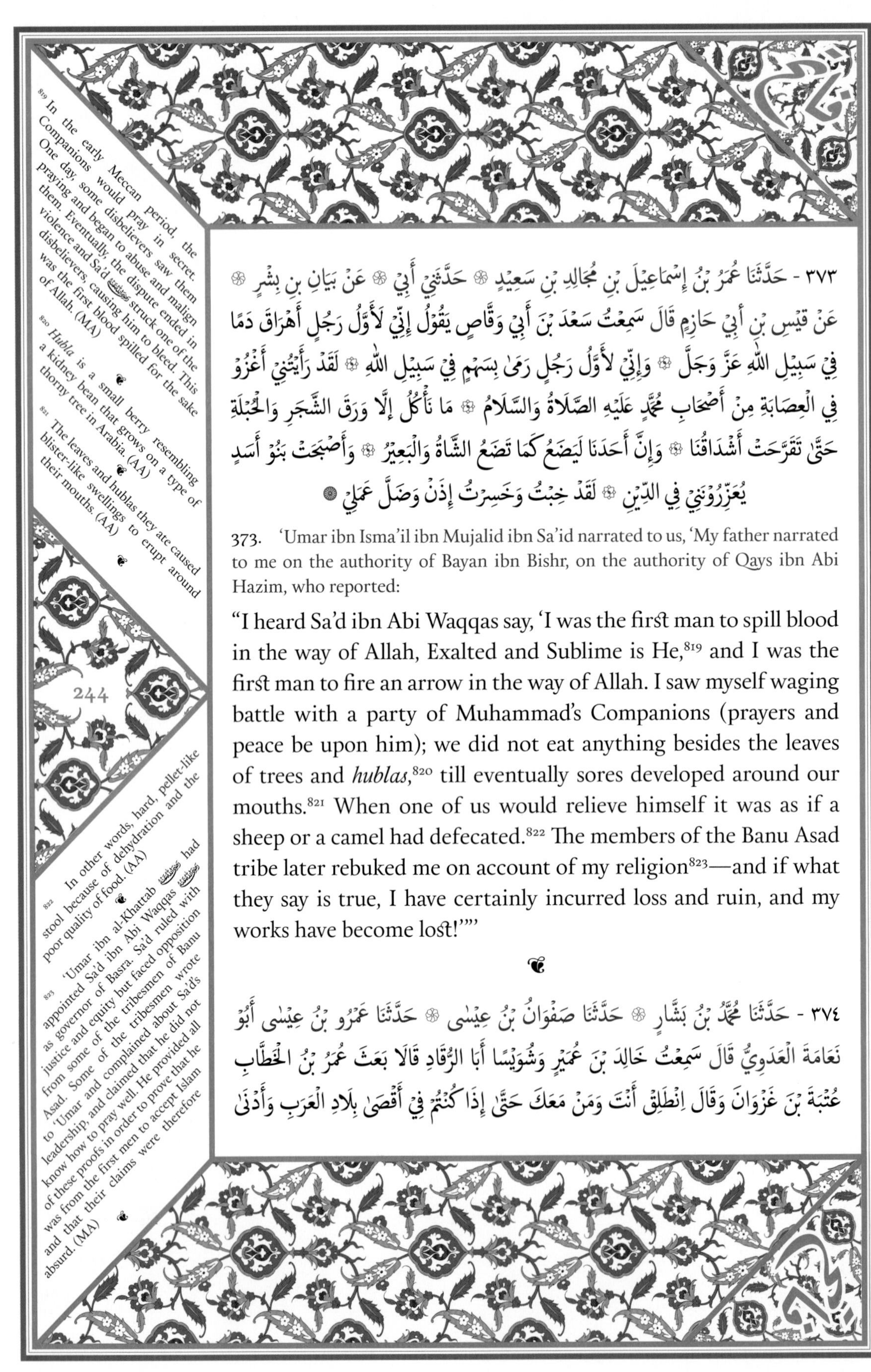

٣٧٣ - حَدَّثَنَا عُمَرُ بْنُ إِسْمَاعِيلَ بْنِ مُجَالِدِ بْنِ سَعِيدٍ ۞ حَدَّثَنِي أَبِي ۞ عَنْ بَيَانِ بنِ بِشْرٍ ۞ عَنْ قَيْسِ بْنِ أَبِي حَازِمٍ قَالَ سَمِعْتُ سَعْدَ بْنَ أَبِي وَقَّاصٍ يَقُولُ إِنِّي لَأَوَّلُ رَجُلٍ أَهْرَاقَ دَمًا فِي سَبِيلِ اللهِ عَزَّ وَجَلَّ ۞ وَإِنِّي لَأَوَّلُ رَجُلٍ رَمَىٰ بِسَهْمٍ فِي سَبِيلِ اللهِ ۞ لَقَدْ رَأَيْتُنِي أَغْزُو فِي الْعِصَابَةِ مِنْ أَصْحَابِ مُحَمَّدٍ عَلَيْهِ الصَّلَاةُ وَالسَّلَامُ ۞ مَا نَأْكُلُ إِلَّا وَرَقَ الشَّجَرِ وَالْحُبْلَةِ حَتَّىٰ تَقَرَّحَتْ أَشْدَاقُنَا ۞ وَإِنَّ أَحَدَنَا لَيَضَعُ كَمَا تَضَعُ الشَّاةُ وَالْبَعِيرُ ۞ وَأَصْبَحَتْ بَنُو أَسَدٍ يُعَزِّرُونَنِي فِي الدِّينِ ۞ لَقَدْ خِبْتُ وَخَسِرْتُ إِذَنْ وَضَلَّ عَمَلِي ۞

373. 'Umar ibn Isma'il ibn Mujalid ibn Sa'id narrated to us, 'My father narrated to me on the authority of Bayan ibn Bishr, on the authority of Qays ibn Abi Hazim, who reported:

"I heard Sa'd ibn Abi Waqqas say, 'I was the first man to spill blood in the way of Allah, Exalted and Sublime is He,[819] and I was the first man to fire an arrow in the way of Allah. I saw myself waging battle with a party of Muhammad's Companions (prayers and peace be upon him); we did not eat anything besides the leaves of trees and *hublas*,[820] till eventually sores developed around our mouths.[821] When one of us would relieve himself it was as if a sheep or a camel had defecated.[822] The members of the Banu Asad tribe later rebuked me on account of my religion[823]—and if what they say is true, I have certainly incurred loss and ruin, and my works have become lost!'"'

٣٧٤ - حَدَّثَنَا مُحَمَّدُ بْنُ بَشَّارٍ ۞ حَدَّثَنَا صَفْوَانُ بْنُ عِيسَىٰ ۞ حَدَّثَنَا عَمْرُو بْنُ عِيسَىٰ أَبُو نَعَامَةَ الْعَدَوِيُّ قَالَ سَمِعْتُ خَالِدَ بْنَ عُمَيْرٍ وَشُوَيْسًا أَبَا الرُّقَادِ قَالَا بَعَثَ عُمَرُ بْنُ الْخَطَّابِ عُتْبَةَ بْنَ غَزْوَانَ وَقَالَ انْطَلِقْ أَنْتَ وَمَنْ مَعَكَ حَتَّىٰ إِذَا كُنْتُمْ فِي أَقْصَىٰ بِلَادِ الْعَرَبِ وَأَدْنَىٰ

[819] In the early Meccan period, the Companions would pray in secret. One day, some disbelievers saw them praying and began to abuse and malign them. Eventually, the dispute ended in violence and Sa'd struck one of the disbelievers, causing him to bleed. This was the first blood spilled for the sake of Allah. (MA)

[820] *Hubla* is a small berry resembling a kidney bean that grows on a type of thorny tree in Arabia. (AA)

[821] The leaves and hublas they ate caused blister-like swellings to erupt around their mouths. (AA)

[822] In other words, hard, pellet-like stool because of dehydration and the poor quality of food. (AA)

[823] 'Umar ibn al-Khattab had appointed Sa'd ibn Abi Waqqas as governor of Basra. Sa'd ruled with justice and equity but faced opposition from some of the tribesmen of Banu Asad. Some of the tribesmen wrote to 'Umar and complained about Sa'd's leadership, and claimed that he did not know how to pray well. He provided all of these proofs in order to prove that he was from the first men to accept Islam and that their claims were therefore absurd. (MA)

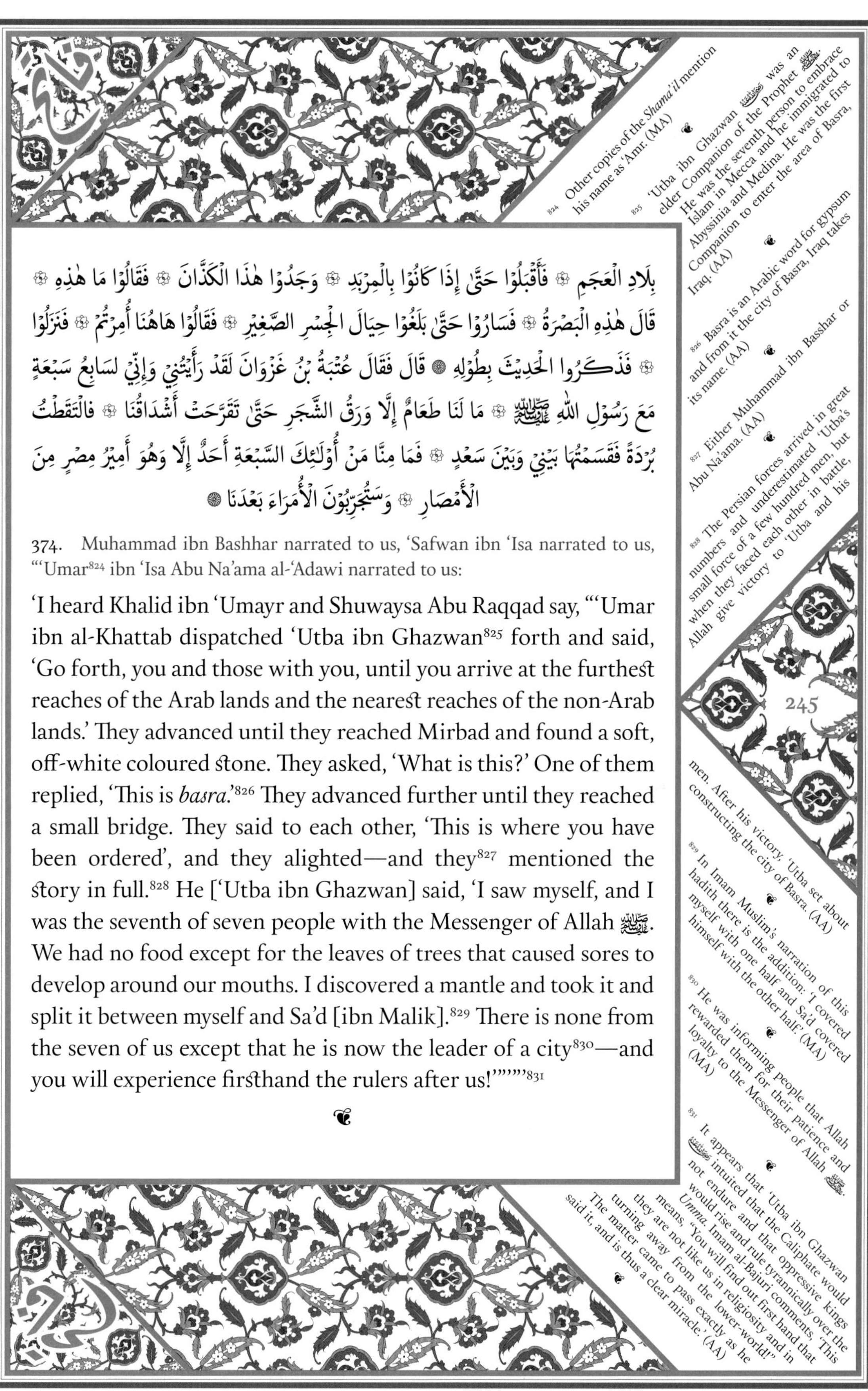

بِلَادِ الْعَجَمِ ۞ فَأَقْبَلُوا حَتَّىٰ إِذَا كَانُوا بِالْمِرْبَدِ ۞ وَجَدُوا هَٰذَا الْكَذَّانَ ۞ فَقَالُوا مَا هَٰذِهِ ۞
قَالَ هَٰذِهِ الْبَصْرَةُ ۞ فَسَارُوا حَتَّىٰ بَلَغُوا حِيَالَ الْجِسْرِ الصَّغِيرِ ۞ فَقَالُوا هَاهُنَا أُمِرْتُمْ ۞ فَنَزَلُوا
۞ فَذَكَرُوا الْحَدِيثَ بِطُولِهِ ۞ قَالَ فَقَالَ عُتْبَةُ بْنُ غَزْوَانَ لَقَدْ رَأَيْتُنِي وَإِنِّي لَسَابِعُ سَبْعَةٍ
مَعَ رَسُولِ اللهِ ﷺ ۞ مَا لَنَا طَعَامٌ إِلَّا وَرَقُ الشَّجَرِ حَتَّىٰ تَقَرَّحَتْ أَشْدَاقُنَا ۞ فَالْتَقَطْتُ
بُرْدَةً فَقَسَمْتُهَا بَيْنِي وَبَيْنَ سَعْدٍ ۞ فَمَا مِنَّا مِنْ أُولَئِكَ السَّبْعَةِ أَحَدٌ إِلَّا وَهُوَ أَمِيرُ مِصْرٍ مِنَ
الْأَمْصَارِ ۞ وَسَتُجَرِّبُونَ الْأُمَرَاءَ بَعْدَنَا ۞

374. Muhammad ibn Bashhar narrated to us, 'Safwan ibn 'Isa narrated to us, "'Umar[824] ibn 'Isa Abu Na'ama al-'Adawi narrated to us:

'I heard Khalid ibn 'Umayr and Shuwaysa Abu Raqqad say, "'Umar ibn al-Khattab dispatched 'Utba ibn Ghazwan[825] forth and said, 'Go forth, you and those with you, until you arrive at the furthest reaches of the Arab lands and the nearest reaches of the non-Arab lands.' They advanced until they reached Mirbad and found a soft, off-white coloured stone. They asked, 'What is this?' One of them replied, 'This is *basra*.'[826] They advanced further until they reached a small bridge. They said to each other, 'This is where you have been ordered', and they alighted—and they[827] mentioned the story in full.[828] He ['Utba ibn Ghazwan] said, 'I saw myself, and I was the seventh of seven people with the Messenger of Allah ﷺ. We had no food except for the leaves of trees that caused sores to develop around our mouths. I discovered a mantle and took it and split it between myself and Sa'd [ibn Malik].[829] There is none from the seven of us except that he is now the leader of a city[830]—and you will experience firsthand the rulers after us!'"'"[831]

[824] Other copies of the *Shama'il* mention his name as 'Amr. (MA)

[825] 'Utba ibn Ghazwan (ra) was an elder Companion of the Prophet ﷺ. He was the seventh person to embrace Islam in Mecca and he immigrated to Abyssinia and Medina. He was the first Companion to enter the area of Basra, Iraq. (AA)

[826] Basra is an Arabic word for gypsum and from it the city of Basra, Iraq takes its name. (AA)

[827] Either Muhammad ibn Basshar or Abu Na'ama. (AA)

[828] The Persian forces arrived in great numbers and underestimated 'Utba's small force of a few hundred men, but when they faced each other in battle, Allah give victory to 'Utba and his men. After his victory, 'Utba set about constructing the city of Basra. (AA)

[829] In Imam Muslim's narration of this hadith there is the addition: 'I covered myself with one half and Sa'd covered himself with the other half.' (MA)

[830] He was informing people that Allah rewarded them for their patience and loyalty to the Messenger of Allah ﷺ. (MA)

[831] It appears that 'Utba ibn Ghazwan (ra) intuited that the Caliphate would not endure and that oppressive kings would rise and rule tyrannically over the *Umma*. Imam al-Bajuri comments, 'This means, "You will find out first hand that they are not like us in religiosity and in turning away from the lower-world!" The matter came to pass exactly as he said it, and is thus a clear miracle.' (AA)

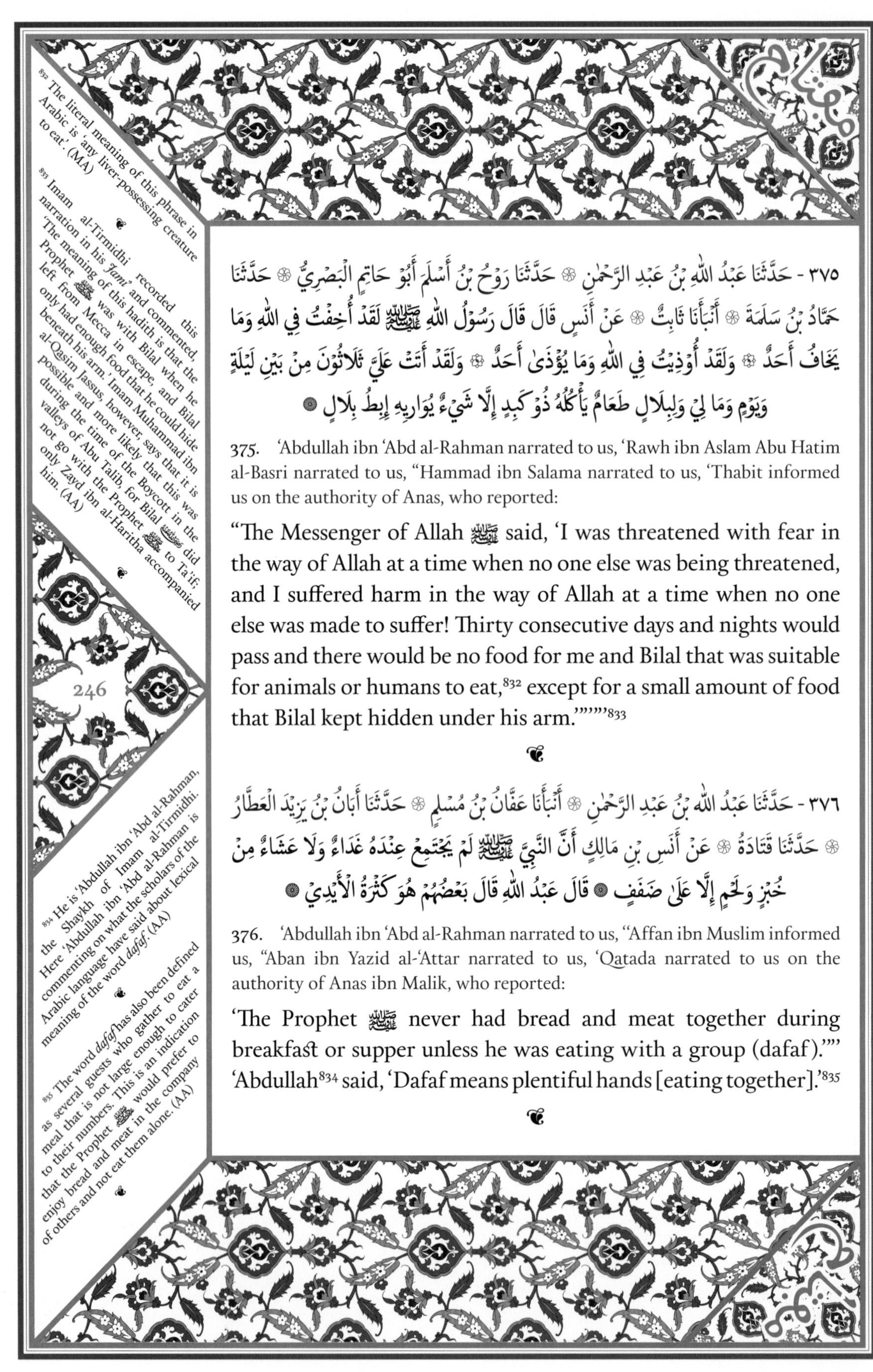

٣٧٥ - حَدَّثَنَا عَبْدُ اللهِ بْنُ عَبْدِ الرَّحْمٰنِ ۞ حَدَّثَنَا رَوْحُ بْنُ أَسْلَمَ أَبُو حَاتِمٍ الْبَصْرِيُّ ۞ حَدَّثَنَا حَمَّادُ بْنُ سَلَمَةَ ۞ أَنْبَأَنَا ثَابِتٌ ۞ عَنْ أَنَسٍ قَالَ قَالَ رَسُولُ اللهِ ﷺ لَقَدْ أُخِفْتُ فِي اللهِ وَمَا يَخَافُ أَحَدٌ ۞ وَلَقَدْ أُوذِيتُ فِي اللهِ وَمَا يُؤْذَىٰ أَحَدٌ ۞ وَلَقَدْ أَتَتْ عَلَيَّ ثَلَاثُونَ مِنْ بَيْنِ لَيْلَةٍ وَيَوْمٍ وَمَا لِي وَلِبِلَالٍ طَعَامٌ يَأْكُلُهُ ذُو كَبِدٍ إِلَّا شَيْءٌ يُوَارِيهِ إِبِطُ بِلَالٍ ۞

375. 'Abdullah ibn 'Abd al-Rahman narrated to us, 'Rawh ibn Aslam Abu Hatim al-Basri narrated to us, "Hammad ibn Salama narrated to us, 'Thabit informed us on the authority of Anas, who reported:

"The Messenger of Allah ﷺ said, 'I was threatened with fear in the way of Allah at a time when no one else was being threatened, and I suffered harm in the way of Allah at a time when no one else was made to suffer! Thirty consecutive days and nights would pass and there would be no food for me and Bilal that was suitable for animals or humans to eat,[832] except for a small amount of food that Bilal kept hidden under his arm.'"'"[833]

❦

٣٧٦ - حَدَّثَنَا عَبْدُ اللهِ بْنُ عَبْدِ الرَّحْمٰنِ ۞ أَنْبَأَنَا عَفَّانُ بْنُ مُسْلِمٍ ۞ حَدَّثَنَا أَبَانُ بْنُ يَزِيدَ الْعَطَّارُ ۞ حَدَّثَنَا قَتَادَةُ ۞ عَنْ أَنَسِ بْنِ مَالِكٍ أَنَّ النَّبِيَّ ﷺ لَمْ يَجْتَمِعْ عِنْدَهُ غَدَاءٌ وَلَا عَشَاءٌ مِنْ خُبْزٍ وَلَحْمٍ إِلَّا عَلَىٰ ضَفَفٍ ۞ قَالَ عَبْدُ اللهِ قَالَ بَعْضُهُمْ هُوَ كَثْرَةُ الْأَيْدِي ۞

376. 'Abdullah ibn 'Abd al-Rahman narrated to us, "Affan ibn Muslim informed us, "Aban ibn Yazid al-'Attar narrated to us, 'Qatada narrated to us on the authority of Anas ibn Malik, who reported:

'The Prophet ﷺ never had bread and meat together during breakfast or supper unless he was eating with a group (dafaf).'"' 'Abdullah[834] said, 'Dafaf means plentiful hands [eating together].'[835]

❦

[832] The literal meaning of this phrase in Arabic is 'any liver-possessing creature to eat.' (MA)

[833] Imam al-Tirmidhi recorded this narration in his *Jami'* and commented, 'The meaning of this hadith is that the Prophet ﷺ was with Bilal when he left from Mecca in escape, and Bilal only had enough food that he could hide beneath his arm.' Imam Muhammad ibn al-Qasim Jassus, however, says that it is possible and more likely that this was during the time of the Boycott in the valleys of Abu Talib, for Bilal did not go with the Prophet ﷺ to Ta'if; only Zayd ibn al-Haritha accompanied him. (AA)

[834] He is 'Abdullah ibn 'Abd al-Rahman, the Shaykh of Imam al-Tirmidhi. Here 'Abdullah ibn 'Abd al-Rahman is commenting on what the scholars of the Arabic language have said about lexical meaning of the word *dafaf*. (AA)

[835] The word *dafaf* has also been defined as several guests who gather to eat a meal that is not large enough to cater to their numbers. This is an indication that the Prophet ﷺ would prefer to enjoy bread and meat in the company of others and not eat them alone. (AA)

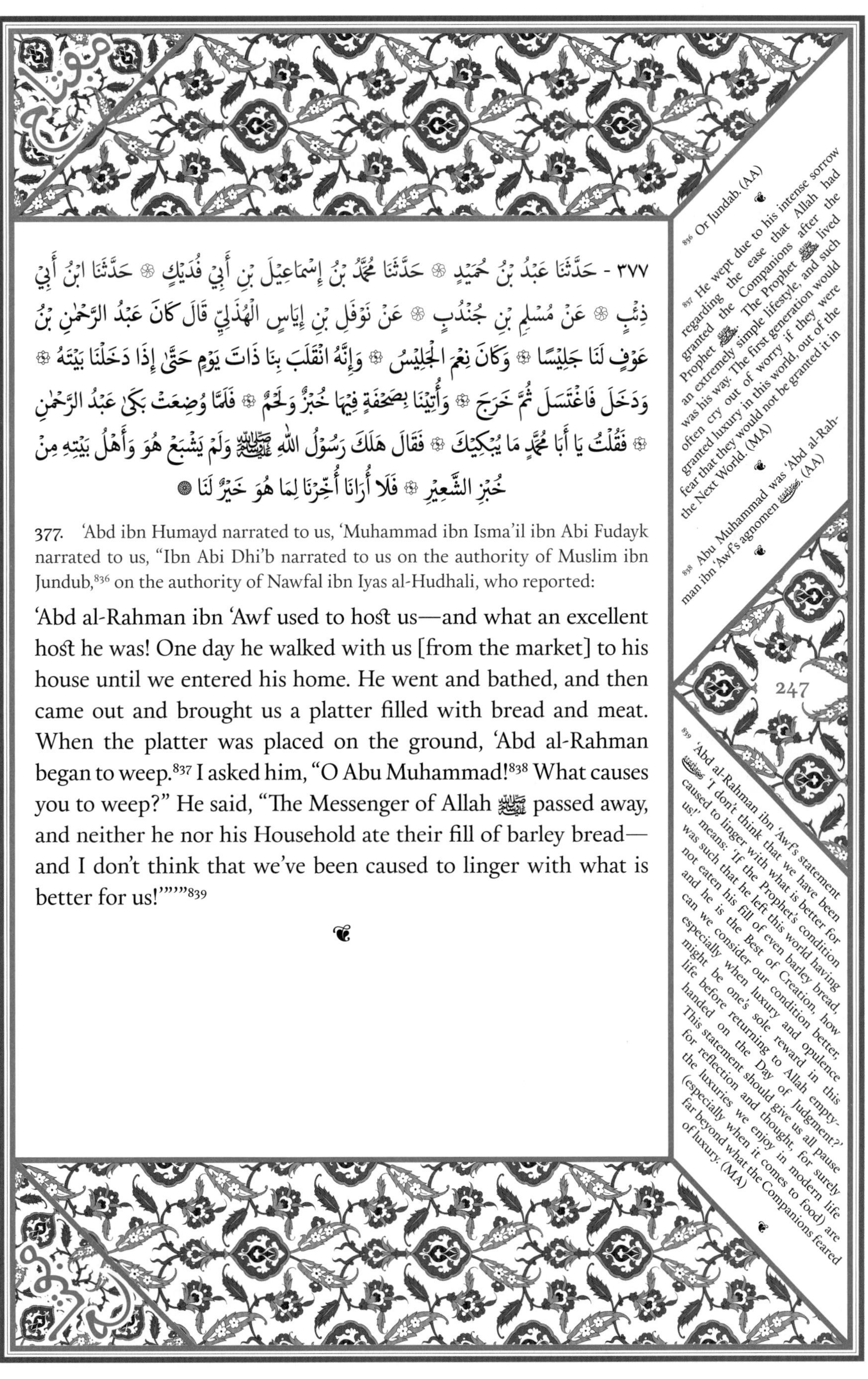

٣٧٧ - حَدَّثَنَا عَبْدُ بْنُ حُمَيْدٍ ۞ حَدَّثَنَا مُحَمَّدُ بْنُ إِسْمَاعِيلَ بْنِ أَبِي فُدَيْكٍ ۞ حَدَّثَنَا ابْنُ أَبِي ذِئْبٍ ۞ عَنْ مُسْلِمِ بْنِ جُنْدُبٍ ۞ عَنْ نَوْفَلِ بْنِ إِيَاسٍ الْهُذَلِيِّ قَالَ كَانَ عَبْدُ الرَّحْمٰنِ بْنُ عَوْفٍ لَنَا جَلِيسًا ۞ وَكَانَ نِعْمَ الْجَلِيسُ ۞ وَإِنَّهُ انْقَلَبَ بِنَا ذَاتَ يَوْمٍ حَتَّىٰ إِذَا دَخَلْنَا بَيْتَهُ ۞ وَدَخَلَ فَاغْتَسَلَ ثُمَّ خَرَجَ ۞ وَأُتِينَا بِصَحْفَةٍ فِيهَا خُبْزٌ وَلَحْمٌ ۞ فَلَمَّا وُضِعَتْ بَكَىٰ عَبْدُ الرَّحْمٰنِ ۞ فَقُلْتُ يَا أَبَا مُحَمَّدٍ مَا يُبْكِيكَ ۞ فَقَالَ هَلَكَ رَسُولُ اللهِ ﷺ وَلَمْ يَشْبَعْ هُوَ وَأَهْلُ بَيْتِهِ مِنْ خُبْزِ الشَّعِيرِ ۞ فَلَا أُرَانَا أُخِّرْنَا لِمَا هُوَ خَيْرٌ لَنَا ۞

377. 'Abd ibn Humayd narrated to us, 'Muhammad ibn Isma'il ibn Abi Fudayk narrated to us, "Ibn Abi Dhi'b narrated to us on the authority of Muslim ibn Jundub,[836] on the authority of Nawfal ibn Iyas al-Hudhali, who reported:

'Abd al-Rahman ibn 'Awf used to host us—and what an excellent host he was! One day he walked with us [from the market] to his house until we entered his home. He went and bathed, and then came out and brought us a platter filled with bread and meat. When the platter was placed on the ground, 'Abd al-Rahman began to weep.[837] I asked him, "O Abu Muhammad![838] What causes you to weep?" He said, "The Messenger of Allah ﷺ passed away, and neither he nor his Household ate their fill of barley bread—and I don't think that we've been caused to linger with what is better for us!'""''[839]

836 Or Jundab. (AA)

837 He wept due to his intense sorrow regarding the ease that Allah had granted the Companions after the Prophet ﷺ. The Prophet ﷺ lived an extremely simple lifestyle, and such was his way. The first generation would often cry out of worry if they were granted luxury in this world, out of the fear that they would not be granted it in the Next World. (MA)

838 Abu Muhammad was 'Abd al-Rahman ibn 'Awf's agnomen ﷺ. (AA)

839 'Abd al-Rahman ibn 'Awf's statement ﷺ 'I don't think that we have been caused to linger with what is better for us!' means: 'If the Prophet's condition was such that he left this world having not eaten his fill of even barley bread, and he is the Best of Creation, how can we consider our condition better, especially when luxury and opulence might be one's sole reward in this life before returning to Allah empty-handed on the Day of Judgment?' This statement should give us all pause for reflection and thought, for surely the luxuries we enjoy in modern life (especially when it comes to food) are far beyond what the Companions feared of luxury. (MA)

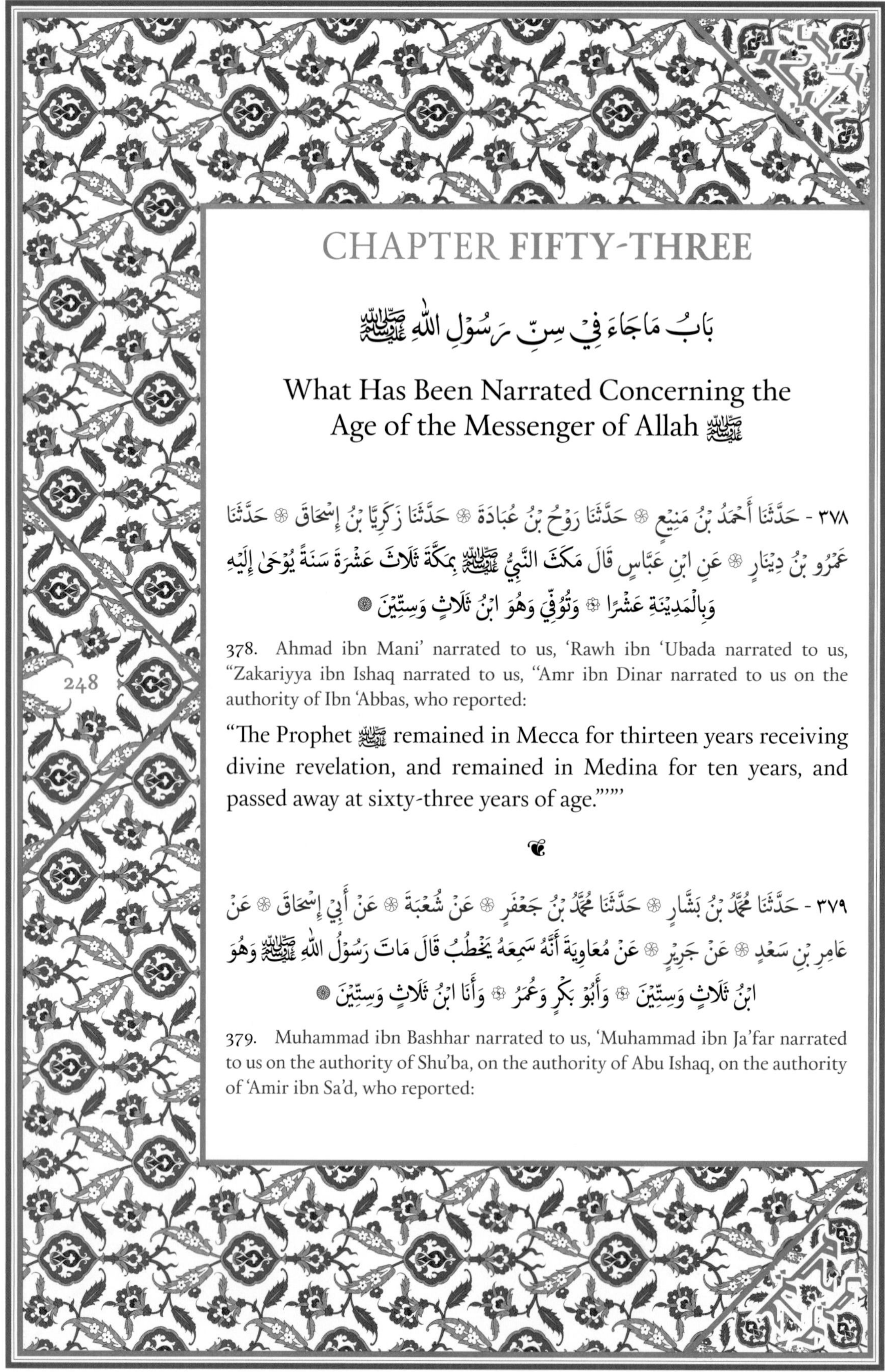

CHAPTER **FIFTY-THREE**

بَابُ مَا جَاءَ فِي سِنِّ رَسُولِ اللهِ ﷺ

What Has Been Narrated Concerning the Age of the Messenger of Allah ﷺ

٣٧٨ - حَدَّثَنَا أَحْمَدُ بْنُ مَنِيعٍ ❀ حَدَّثَنَا رَوْحُ بْنُ عُبَادَةَ ❀ حَدَّثَنَا زَكَرِيَّا بْنُ إِسْحَاقَ ❀ حَدَّثَنَا عَمْرُو بْنُ دِينَارٍ ❀ عَنِ ابْنِ عَبَّاسٍ قَالَ مَكَثَ النَّبِيُّ ﷺ بِمَكَّةَ ثَلَاثَ عَشْرَةَ سَنَةً يُوحَى إِلَيْهِ وَبِالْمَدِينَةِ عَشْرًا ❀ وَتُوُفِّيَ وَهُوَ ابْنُ ثَلَاثٍ وَسِتِّينَ ❀

378. Ahmad ibn Mani' narrated to us, 'Rawh ibn 'Ubada narrated to us, "Zakariyya ibn Ishaq narrated to us, "Amr ibn Dinar narrated to us on the authority of Ibn 'Abbas, who reported:

"The Prophet ﷺ remained in Mecca for thirteen years receiving divine revelation, and remained in Medina for ten years, and passed away at sixty-three years of age."""'

٣٧٩ - حَدَّثَنَا مُحَمَّدُ بْنُ بَشَّارٍ ❀ حَدَّثَنَا مُحَمَّدُ بْنُ جَعْفَرٍ ❀ عَنْ شُعْبَةَ ❀ عَنْ أَبِي إِسْحَاقَ ❀ عَنْ عَامِرِ بْنِ سَعْدٍ ❀ عَنْ جَرِيرٍ ❀ عَنْ مُعَاوِيَةَ أَنَّهُ سَمِعَهُ يَخْطُبُ قَالَ مَاتَ رَسُولُ اللهِ ﷺ وَهُوَ ابْنُ ثَلَاثٍ وَسِتِّينَ ❀ وَأَبُو بَكْرٍ وَعُمَرُ ❀ وَأَنَا ابْنُ ثَلَاثٍ وَسِتِّينَ ❀

379. Muhammad ibn Bashhar narrated to us, 'Muhammad ibn Ja'far narrated to us on the authority of Shu'ba, on the authority of Abu Ishaq, on the authority of 'Amir ibn Sa'd, who reported:

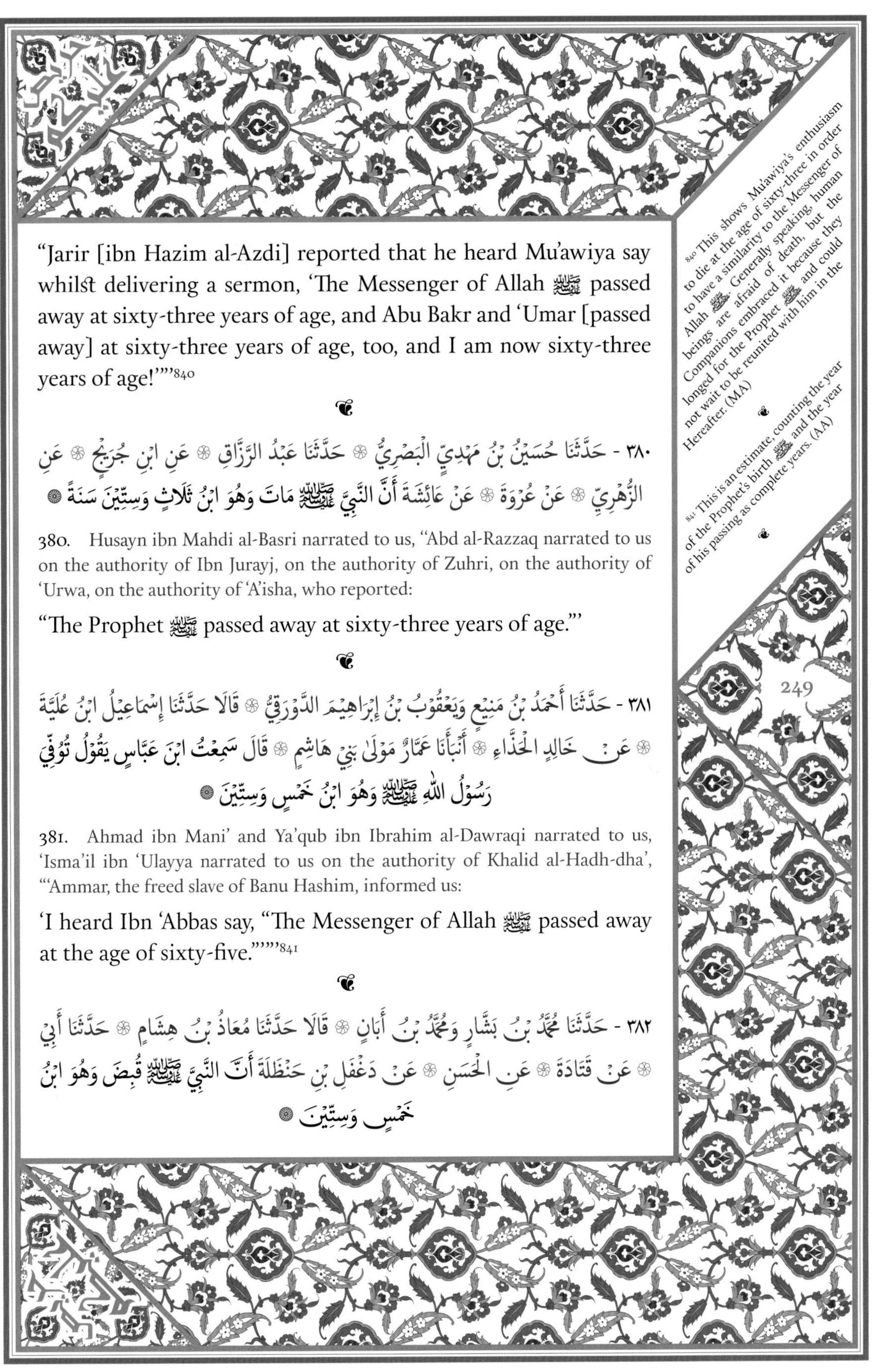

“Jarir [ibn Hazim al-Azdi] reported that he heard Mu’awiya say whilst delivering a sermon, ‘The Messenger of Allah ﷺ passed away at sixty-three years of age, and Abu Bakr and ‘Umar [passed away] at sixty-three years of age, too, and I am now sixty-three years of age!’”’[840]

❦

٣٨٠ - حَدَّثَنَا حُسَيْنُ بْنُ مَهْدِيٍّ الْبَصْرِيُّ ❁ حَدَّثَنَا عَبْدُ الرَّزَّاقِ ❁ عَنِ ابْنِ جُرَيْجٍ ❁ عَنِ الزُّهْرِيِّ ❁ عَنْ عُرْوَةَ ❁ عَنْ عَائِشَةَ أَنَّ النَّبِيَّ ﷺ مَاتَ وَهُوَ ابْنُ ثَلَاثٍ وَسِتِّينَ سَنَةً ❁

380. Husayn ibn Mahdi al-Basri narrated to us, “Abd al-Razzaq narrated to us on the authority of Ibn Jurayj, on the authority of Zuhri, on the authority of ‘Urwa, on the authority of ‘A’isha, who reported:

“The Prophet ﷺ passed away at sixty-three years of age.”’

❦

٣٨١ - حَدَّثَنَا أَحْمَدُ بْنُ مَنِيعٍ وَيَعْقُوبُ بْنُ إِبْرَاهِيمَ الدَّوْرَقِيُّ ❁ قَالَا حَدَّثَنَا إِسْمَاعِيلُ ابْنُ عُلَيَّةَ ❁ عَنْ خَالِدٍ الْحَذَّاءِ ❁ أَنْبَأَنَا عَمَّارٌ مَوْلَى بَنِي هَاشِمٍ ❁ قَالَ سَمِعْتُ ابْنَ عَبَّاسٍ يَقُولُ تُوُفِّيَ رَسُولُ اللَّهِ ﷺ وَهُوَ ابْنُ خَمْسٍ وَسِتِّينَ ❁

381. Ahmad ibn Mani’ and Ya’qub ibn Ibrahim al-Dawraqi narrated to us, ‘Isma’il ibn ‘Ulayya narrated to us on the authority of Khalid al-Hadh-dha’, “‘Ammar, the freed slave of Banu Hashim, informed us:

‘I heard Ibn ‘Abbas say, “The Messenger of Allah ﷺ passed away at the age of sixty-five.”’”’[841]

❦

٣٨٢ - حَدَّثَنَا مُحَمَّدُ بْنُ بَشَّارٍ وَمُحَمَّدُ بْنُ أَبَانٍ ❁ قَالَا حَدَّثَنَا مُعَاذُ بْنُ هِشَامٍ ❁ حَدَّثَنَا أَبِي ❁ عَنْ قَتَادَةَ ❁ عَنِ الْحَسَنِ ❁ عَنْ دَغْفَلِ بْنِ حَنْظَلَةَ أَنَّ النَّبِيَّ ﷺ قُبِضَ وَهُوَ ابْنُ خَمْسٍ وَسِتِّينَ ❁

[840] This shows Mu’awiya’s enthusiasm to die at the age of sixty-three in order to have a similarity to the Messenger of Allah ﷺ. Generally speaking, human beings are afraid of death, but the Companions embraced it because they longed for the Prophet ﷺ and could not wait to be reunited with him in the Hereafter. (MA)

❦

[841] This is an estimate, counting the year of the Prophet’s birth ﷺ and the year of his passing as complete years. (AA)

❦

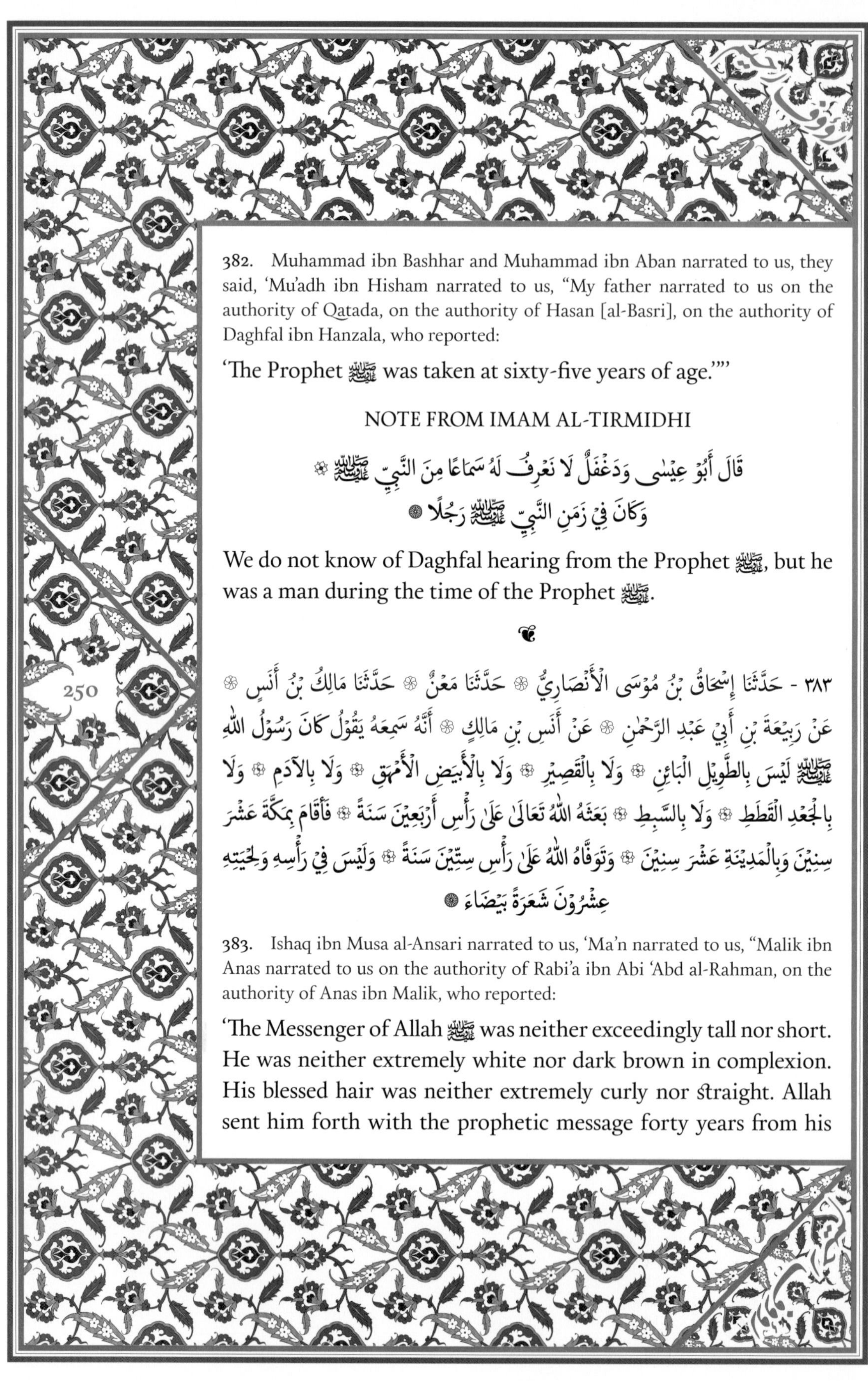

382. Muhammad ibn Bashhar and Muhammad ibn Aban narrated to us, they said, 'Mu'adh ibn Hisham narrated to us, "My father narrated to us on the authority of Qatada, on the authority of Hasan [al-Basri], on the authority of Daghfal ibn Hanzala, who reported:

'The Prophet ﷺ was taken at sixty-five years of age.'"'

NOTE FROM IMAM AL-TIRMIDHI

قَالَ أَبُو عِيسَى وَدَغْفَلٌ لَا نَعْرِفُ لَهُ سَمَاعًا مِنَ النَّبِيِّ ﷺ ۞
وَكَانَ فِي زَمَنِ النَّبِيِّ ﷺ رَجُلًا ۞

We do not know of Daghfal hearing from the Prophet ﷺ, but he was a man during the time of the Prophet ﷺ.

٣٨٣ - حَدَّثَنَا إِسْحَاقُ بْنُ مُوسَى الْأَنْصَارِيُّ ۞ حَدَّثَنَا مَعْنٌ ۞ حَدَّثَنَا مَالِكُ بْنُ أَنَسٍ ۞ عَنْ رَبِيعَةَ بْنِ أَبِي عَبْدِ الرَّحْمٰنِ ۞ عَنْ أَنَسِ بْنِ مَالِكٍ ۞ أَنَّهُ سَمِعَهُ يَقُولُ كَانَ رَسُولُ اللهِ ﷺ لَيْسَ بِالطَّوِيلِ الْبَائِنِ ۞ وَلَا بِالْقَصِيرِ ۞ وَلَا بِالْأَبْيَضِ الْأَمْهَقِ ۞ وَلَا بِالْآدَمِ ۞ وَلَا بِالْجَعْدِ الْقَطَطِ ۞ وَلَا بِالسَّبِطِ ۞ بَعَثَهُ اللهُ تَعَالَى عَلَى رَأْسِ أَرْبَعِينَ سَنَةً ۞ فَأَقَامَ بِمَكَّةَ عَشْرَ سِنِينَ وَبِالْمَدِينَةِ عَشْرَ سِنِينَ ۞ وَتَوَفَّاهُ اللهُ عَلَى رَأْسِ سِتِّينَ سَنَةً ۞ وَلَيْسَ فِي رَأْسِهِ وَلِحْيَتِهِ عِشْرُونَ شَعَرَةً بَيْضَاءَ ۞

383. Ishaq ibn Musa al-Ansari narrated to us, 'Ma'n narrated to us, "Malik ibn Anas narrated to us on the authority of Rabi'a ibn Abi 'Abd al-Rahman, on the authority of Anas ibn Malik, who reported:

'The Messenger of Allah ﷺ was neither exceedingly tall nor short. He was neither extremely white nor dark brown in complexion. His blessed hair was neither extremely curly nor straight. Allah sent him forth with the prophetic message forty years from his

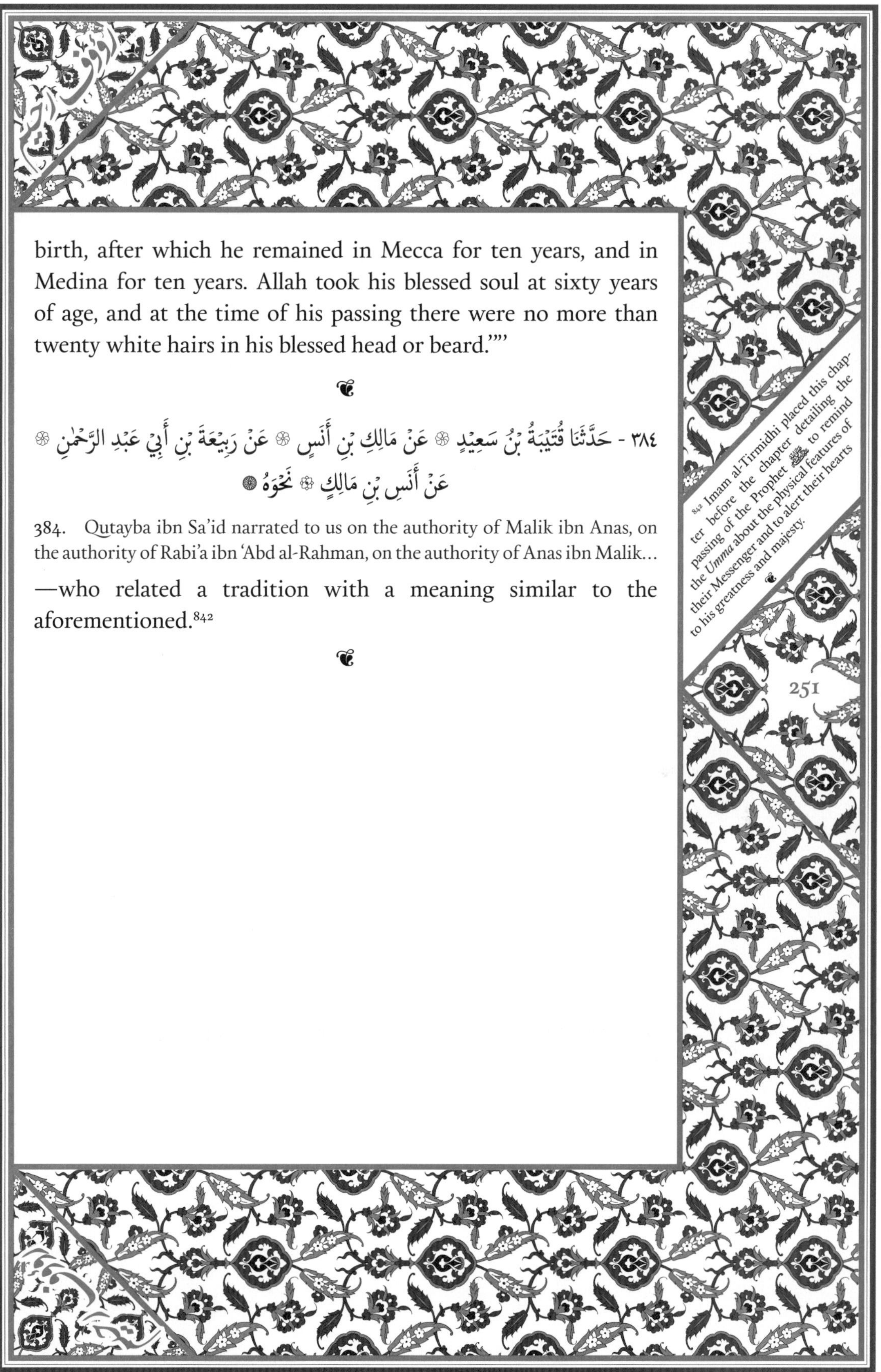

birth, after which he remained in Mecca for ten years, and in Medina for ten years. Allah took his blessed soul at sixty years of age, and at the time of his passing there were no more than twenty white hairs in his blessed head or beard.'"'

٣٨٤ - حَدَّثَنَا قُتَيْبَةُ بْنُ سَعِيدٍ ❁ عَنْ مَالِكِ بْنِ أَنَسٍ ❁ عَنْ رَبِيعَةَ بْنِ أَبِي عَبْدِ الرَّحْمَٰنِ ❁ عَنْ أَنَسِ بْنِ مَالِكٍ ❁ نَحْوَهُ

384. Qutayba ibn Sa'id narrated to us on the authority of Malik ibn Anas, on the authority of Rabi'a ibn 'Abd al-Rahman, on the authority of Anas ibn Malik...

—who related a tradition with a meaning similar to the aforementioned.[842]

842 Imam al-Tirmidhi placed this chapter before the chapter detailing the passing of the Prophet ﷺ to remind the *Umma* about the physical features of their Messenger and to alert their hearts to his greatness and majesty.

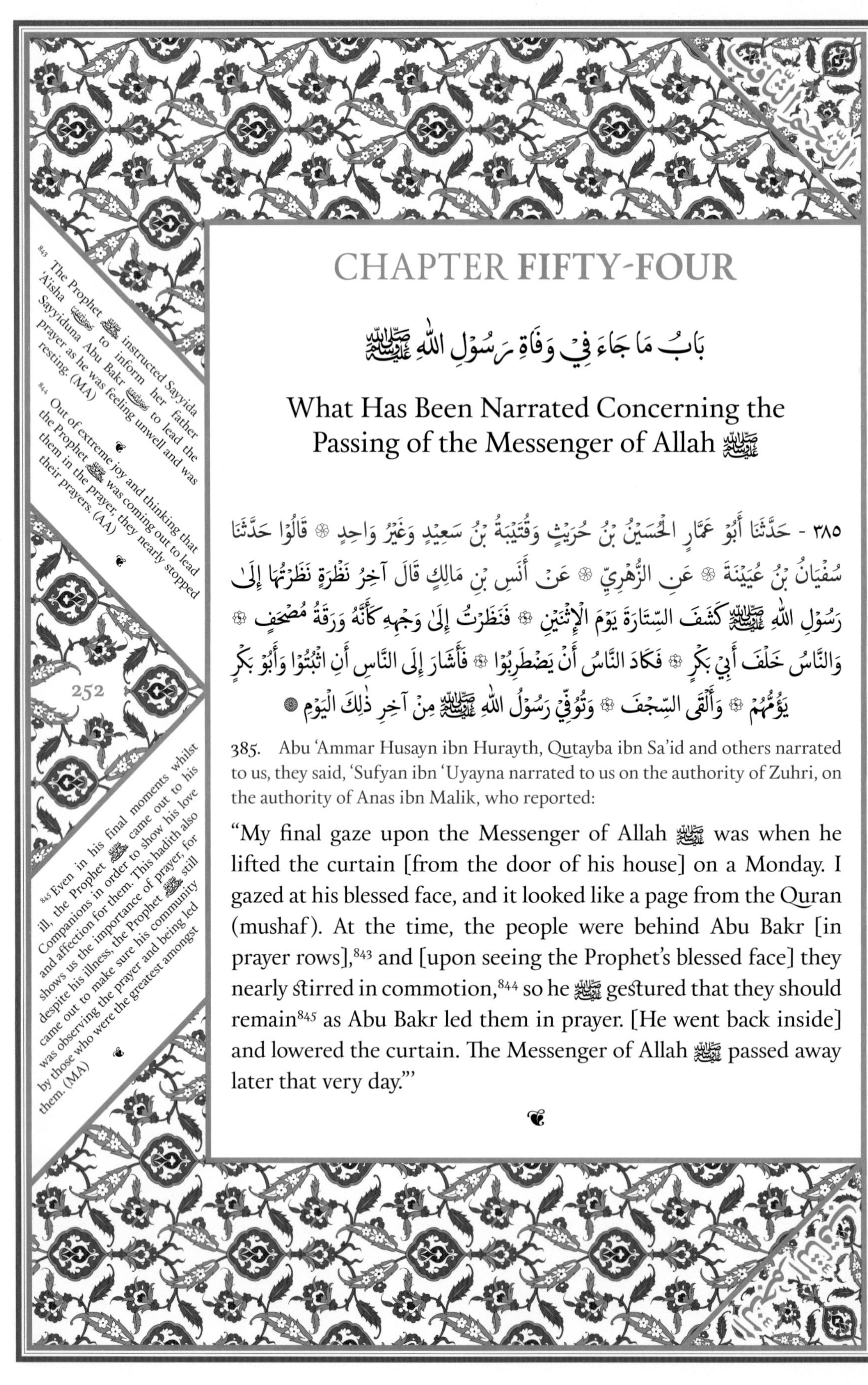

CHAPTER FIFTY-FOUR

بَابُ مَا جَاءَ فِي وَفَاةِ رَسُولِ اللهِ ﷺ

What Has Been Narrated Concerning the Passing of the Messenger of Allah ﷺ

٣٨٥ - حَدَّثَنَا أَبُو عَمَّارٍ الْحُسَيْنُ بْنُ حُرَيْثٍ وَقُتَيْبَةُ بْنُ سَعِيدٍ وَغَيْرُ وَاحِدٍ ۞ قَالُوا حَدَّثَنَا سُفْيَانُ بْنُ عُيَيْنَةَ ۞ عَنِ الزُّهْرِيِّ ۞ عَنْ أَنَسِ بْنِ مَالِكٍ قَالَ آخِرُ نَظْرَةٍ نَظَرْتُهَا إِلَى رَسُولِ اللهِ ﷺ كَشَفَ السِّتَارَةَ يَوْمَ الْإِثْنَيْنِ ۞ فَنَظَرْتُ إِلَى وَجْهِهِ كَأَنَّهُ وَرَقَةُ مُصْحَفٍ ۞ وَالنَّاسُ خَلْفَ أَبِي بَكْرٍ ۞ فَكَادَ النَّاسُ أَنْ يَضْطَرِبُوا ۞ فَأَشَارَ إِلَى النَّاسِ أَنِ اثْبُتُوا وَأَبُو بَكْرٍ يَؤُمُّهُمْ ۞ وَأَلْقَى السِّجْفَ ۞ وَتُوُفِّيَ رَسُولُ اللهِ ﷺ مِنْ آخِرِ ذٰلِكَ الْيَوْمِ ۞

385. Abu 'Ammar Husayn ibn Hurayth, Qutayba ibn Sa'id and others narrated to us, they said, 'Sufyan ibn 'Uyayna narrated to us on the authority of Zuhri, on the authority of Anas ibn Malik, who reported:

"My final gaze upon the Messenger of Allah ﷺ was when he lifted the curtain [from the door of his house] on a Monday. I gazed at his blessed face, and it looked like a page from the Quran (mushaf). At the time, the people were behind Abu Bakr [in prayer rows],[843] and [upon seeing the Prophet's blessed face] they nearly stirred in commotion,[844] so he ﷺ gestured that they should remain[845] as Abu Bakr led them in prayer. [He went back inside] and lowered the curtain. The Messenger of Allah ﷺ passed away later that very day."'

[843] The Prophet ﷺ instructed Sayyida 'A'isha رضي الله عنها to inform her father Sayyiduna Abu Bakr رضي الله عنه to lead the prayer as he was feeling unwell and was resting. (MA)

[844] Out of extreme joy and thinking that the Prophet ﷺ was coming out to lead them in the prayer, they nearly stopped their prayers. (AA)

[845] Even in his final moments whilst ill, the Prophet ﷺ came out to his Companions in order to show his love and affection for them. This hadith also shows us the importance of prayer, for despite his illness, the Prophet ﷺ still came out to make sure his community was observing the prayer and being led by those who were the greatest amongst them. (MA)

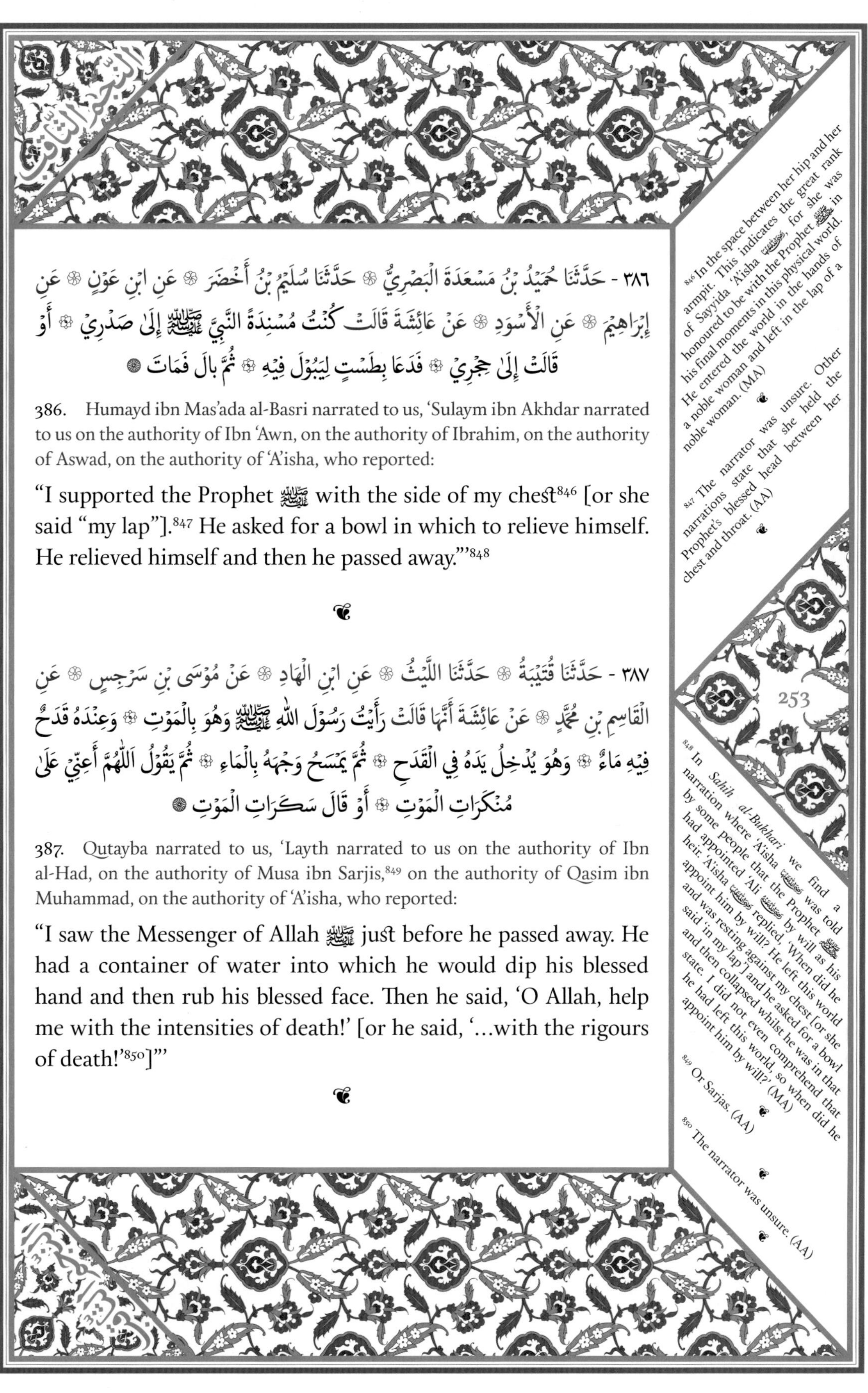

٣٨٦ - حَدَّثَنَا حُمَيْدُ بْنُ مَسْعَدَةَ الْبَصْرِيُّ ۞ حَدَّثَنَا سُلَيْمُ بْنُ أَخْضَرَ ۞ عَنِ ابْنِ عَوْنٍ ۞ عَنْ إِبْرَاهِيمَ ۞ عَنِ الْأَسْوَدِ ۞ عَنْ عَائِشَةَ قَالَتْ كُنْتُ مُسْنِدَةَ النَّبِيِّ ﷺ إِلَى صَدْرِي ۞ أَوْ قَالَتْ إِلَى حِجْرِي ۞ فَدَعَا بِطَسْتٍ لِيَبُوْلَ فِيهِ ۞ ثُمَّ بَالَ فَمَاتَ ۞

386. Humayd ibn Mas'ada al-Basri narrated to us, 'Sulaym ibn Akhdar narrated to us on the authority of Ibn 'Awn, on the authority of Ibrahim, on the authority of Aswad, on the authority of 'A'isha, who reported:

"I supported the Prophet ﷺ with the side of my chest[846] [or she said "my lap"].[847] He asked for a bowl in which to relieve himself. He relieved himself and then he passed away."'[848]

٣٨٧ - حَدَّثَنَا قُتَيْبَةُ ۞ حَدَّثَنَا اللَّيْثُ ۞ عَنِ ابْنِ الْهَادِ ۞ عَنْ مُوْسَى بْنِ سَرْجِسٍ ۞ عَنِ الْقَاسِمِ بْنِ مُحَمَّدٍ ۞ عَنْ عَائِشَةَ أَنَّهَا قَالَتْ رَأَيْتُ رَسُوْلَ اللهِ ﷺ وَهُوَ بِالْمَوْتِ ۞ وَعِنْدَهُ قَدَحٌ فِيهِ مَاءٌ ۞ وَهُوَ يُدْخِلُ يَدَهُ فِي الْقَدَحِ ۞ ثُمَّ يَمْسَحُ وَجْهَهُ بِالْمَاءِ ۞ ثُمَّ يَقُوْلُ اللَّهُمَّ أَعِنِّي عَلَى مُنْكَرَاتِ الْمَوْتِ ۞ أَوْ قَالَ سَكَرَاتِ الْمَوْتِ ۞

387. Qutayba narrated to us, 'Layth narrated to us on the authority of Ibn al-Had, on the authority of Musa ibn Sarjis,[849] on the authority of Qasim ibn Muhammad, on the authority of 'A'isha, who reported:

"I saw the Messenger of Allah ﷺ just before he passed away. He had a container of water into which he would dip his blessed hand and then rub his blessed face. Then he said, 'O Allah, help me with the intensities of death!' [or he said, '...with the rigours of death!'[850]]"'

[846] In the space between her hip and her armpit. This indicates the great rank of Sayyida 'A'isha ﷺ, for she was honoured to be with the Prophet ﷺ in his final moments in this physical world. He entered the world in the hands of a noble woman and left in the lap of a noble woman. (MA)

[847] The narrator was unsure. Other narrations state that she held the Prophet's blessed head between her chest and throat. (AA)

[848] In *Sahih al-Bukhari* we find a narration where 'A'isha ﷺ was told by some people that the Prophet ﷺ had appointed 'Ali ﷺ by will as his heir. 'A'isha ﷺ replied, 'When did he appoint him by will? He left this world and was resting against my chest [or she said 'in my lap'] and he asked for a bowl and then collapsed whilst he was in that state. I did not even comprehend that he had left this world, so when did he appoint him by will?' (MA)

[849] Or Sarjis. (AA)

[850] The narrator was unsure. (AA)

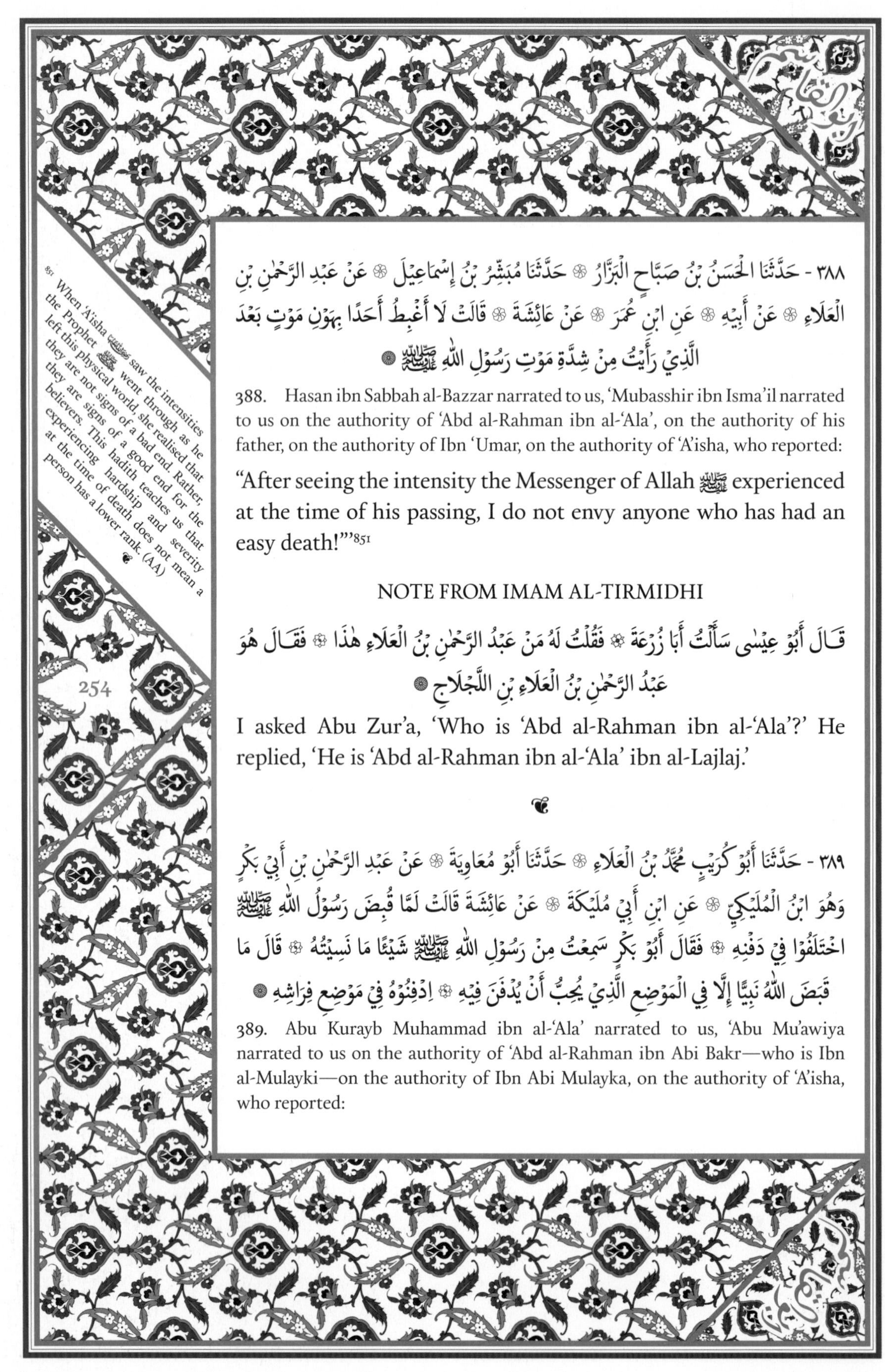

٣٨٨ - حَدَّثَنَا الْحَسَنُ بْنُ صَبَّاحٍ الْبَزَّارُ ۞ حَدَّثَنَا مُبَشِّرُ بْنُ إِسْمَاعِيلَ ۞ عَنْ عَبْدِ الرَّحْمٰنِ بْنِ الْعَلَاءِ ۞ عَنْ أَبِيهِ ۞ عَنِ ابْنِ عُمَرَ ۞ عَنْ عَائِشَةَ ۞ قَالَتْ لَا أَغْبِطُ أَحَدًا بِهَوْنِ مَوْتٍ بَعْدَ الَّذِي رَأَيْتُ مِنْ شِدَّةِ مَوْتِ رَسُولِ اللّٰهِ ﷺ ۞

388. Hasan ibn Sabbah al-Bazzar narrated to us, 'Mubasshir ibn Isma'il narrated to us on the authority of 'Abd al-Rahman ibn al-'Ala', on the authority of his father, on the authority of Ibn 'Umar, on the authority of 'A'isha, who reported:

"After seeing the intensity the Messenger of Allah ﷺ experienced at the time of his passing, I do not envy anyone who has had an easy death!"'[851]

NOTE FROM IMAM AL-TIRMIDHI

قَالَ أَبُو عِيسٰى سَأَلْتُ أَبَا زُرْعَةَ ۞ فَقُلْتُ لَهُ مَنْ عَبْدُ الرَّحْمٰنِ بْنُ الْعَلَاءِ هٰذَا ۞ فَقَالَ هُوَ عَبْدُ الرَّحْمٰنِ بْنُ الْعَلَاءِ بْنِ اللَّجْلَاجِ ۞

I asked Abu Zur'a, 'Who is 'Abd al-Rahman ibn al-'Ala'?' He replied, 'He is 'Abd al-Rahman ibn al-'Ala' ibn al-Lajlaj.'

❦

٣٨٩ - حَدَّثَنَا أَبُو كُرَيْبٍ مُحَمَّدُ بْنُ الْعَلَاءِ ۞ حَدَّثَنَا أَبُو مُعَاوِيَةَ ۞ عَنْ عَبْدِ الرَّحْمٰنِ بْنِ أَبِي بَكْرٍ وَهُوَ ابْنُ الْمُلَيْكِيِّ ۞ عَنِ ابْنِ أَبِي مُلَيْكَةَ ۞ عَنْ عَائِشَةَ قَالَتْ لَمَّا قُبِضَ رَسُولُ اللّٰهِ ﷺ اخْتَلَفُوا فِي دَفْنِهِ ۞ فَقَالَ أَبُو بَكْرٍ سَمِعْتُ مِنْ رَسُولِ اللّٰهِ ﷺ شَيْئًا مَا نَسِيتُهُ ۞ قَالَ مَا قَبَضَ اللّٰهُ نَبِيًّا إِلَّا فِي الْمَوْضِعِ الَّذِي يُحِبُّ أَنْ يُدْفَنَ فِيهِ ۞ ادْفِنُوهُ فِي مَوْضِعِ فِرَاشِهِ ۞

389. Abu Kurayb Muhammad ibn al-'Ala' narrated to us, 'Abu Mu'awiya narrated to us on the authority of 'Abd al-Rahman ibn Abi Bakr—who is Ibn al-Mulayki—on the authority of Ibn Abi Mulayka, on the authority of 'A'isha, who reported:

[851] When 'A'isha ﷺ saw the intensities the Prophet ﷺ went through as he left this physical world, she realised that they are not signs of a bad end. Rather, they are signs of a good end for the believers. This hadith teaches us that experiencing hardship and severity at the time of death does not mean a person has a lower rank. (AA)

❦

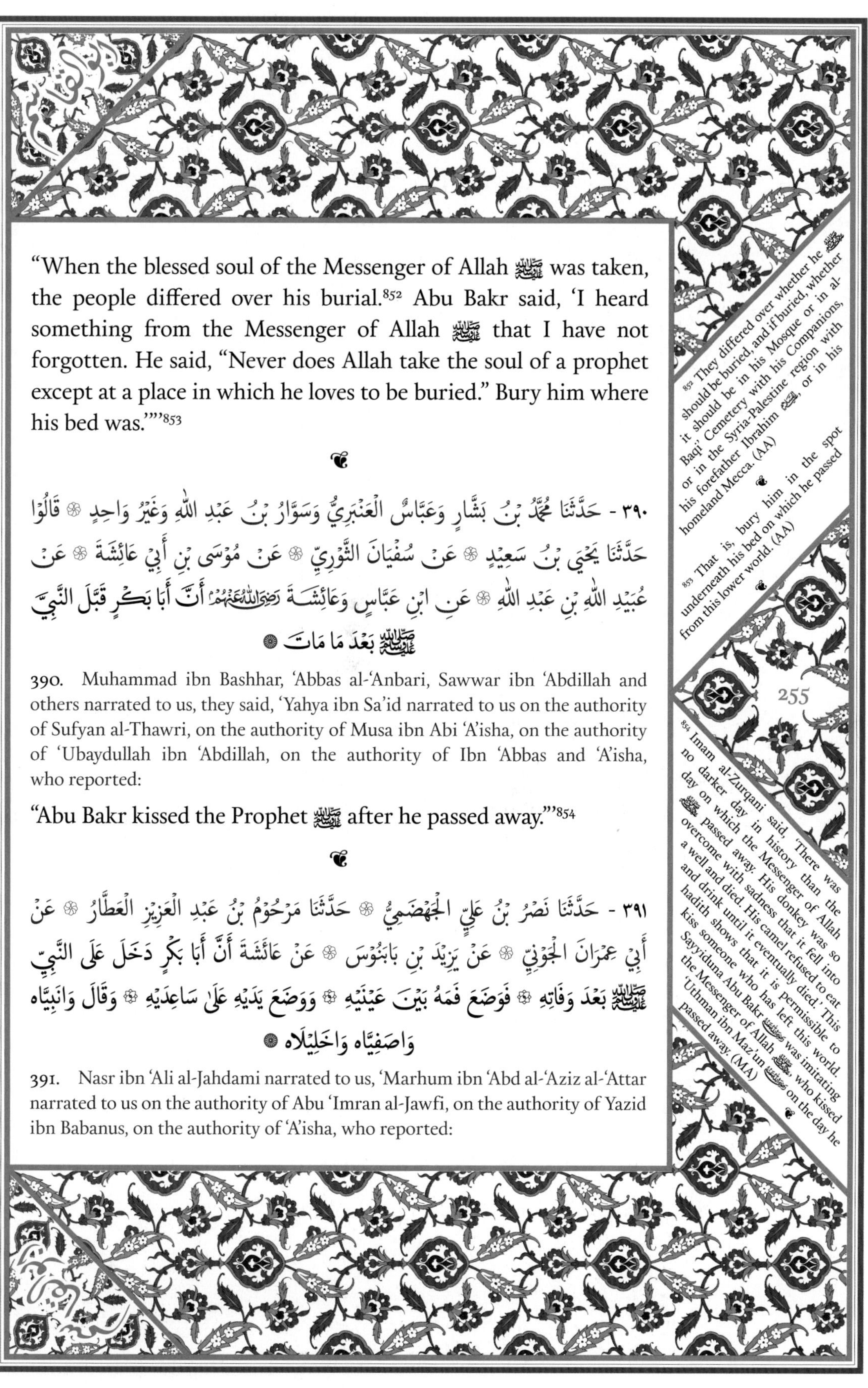

"When the blessed soul of the Messenger of Allah ﷺ was taken, the people differed over his burial.[852] Abu Bakr said, 'I heard something from the Messenger of Allah ﷺ that I have not forgotten. He said, "Never does Allah take the soul of a prophet except at a place in which he loves to be buried." Bury him where his bed was.'"[853]

٣٩٠ - حَدَّثَنَا مُحَمَّدُ بْنُ بَشَّارٍ وَعَبَّاسٌ الْعَنْبَرِيُّ وَسَوَّارُ بْنُ عَبْدِ اللهِ وَغَيْرُ وَاحِدٍ ۞ قَالُوا حَدَّثَنَا يَحْيَى بْنُ سَعِيدٍ ۞ عَنْ سُفْيَانَ الثَّوْرِيِّ ۞ عَنْ مُوسَى بْنِ أَبِي عَائِشَةَ ۞ عَنْ عُبَيْدِ اللهِ بْنِ عَبْدِ اللهِ ۞ عَنِ ابْنِ عَبَّاسٍ وَعَائِشَةَ رَضِيَ اللهُ عَنْهُمْ أَنَّ أَبَا بَكْرٍ قَبَّلَ النَّبِيَّ ﷺ بَعْدَ مَا مَاتَ ۞

390. Muhammad ibn Bashhar, 'Abbas al-'Anbari, Sawwar ibn 'Abdillah and others narrated to us, they said, 'Yahya ibn Sa'id narrated to us on the authority of Sufyan al-Thawri, on the authority of Musa ibn Abi 'A'isha, on the authority of 'Ubaydullah ibn 'Abdillah, on the authority of Ibn 'Abbas and 'A'isha, who reported:

"Abu Bakr kissed the Prophet ﷺ after he passed away."'[854]

٣٩١ - حَدَّثَنَا نَصْرُ بْنُ عَلِيٍّ الْجَهْضَمِيُّ ۞ حَدَّثَنَا مَرْحُومُ بْنُ عَبْدِ الْعَزِيزِ الْعَطَّارُ ۞ عَنْ أَبِي عِمْرَانَ الْجَوْنِيِّ ۞ عَنْ يَزِيدَ بْنِ بَابَنُوسَ ۞ عَنْ عَائِشَةَ أَنَّ أَبَا بَكْرٍ دَخَلَ عَلَى النَّبِيِّ ﷺ بَعْدَ وَفَاتِهِ ۞ فَوَضَعَ فَمَهُ بَيْنَ عَيْنَيْهِ ۞ وَوَضَعَ يَدَيْهِ عَلَى سَاعِدَيْهِ ۞ وَقَالَ وَانَبِيَّاه وَاصَفِيَّاه وَاخَلِيلَاه ۞

391. Nasr ibn 'Ali al-Jahdami narrated to us, 'Marhum ibn 'Abd al-'Aziz al-'Attar narrated to us on the authority of Abu 'Imran al-Jawfi, on the authority of Yazid ibn Babanus, on the authority of 'A'isha, who reported:

[852] They differed over whether he ﷺ should be buried, and if buried, whether it should be in his Mosque or in al-Baqi' Cemetery with his Companions, or in the Syria-Palestine region with his forefather Ibrahim (peace be upon him), or in his homeland Mecca. (AA)

[853] That is, bury him in the spot underneath his bed on which he passed from this lower world. (AA)

[854] Imam al-Zurqani said, 'There was no darker day in history than the day on which the Messenger of Allah ﷺ passed away. His donkey was so overcome with sadness that it fell into a well and died. His camel refused to eat and drink until it eventually died.' This hadith shows that it is permissible to kiss someone who has left this world. Sayyiduna Abu Bakr (may Allah be pleased with him) was imitating the Messenger of Allah ﷺ who kissed 'Uthman ibn Maz'un (may Allah be pleased with him) on the day he passed away. (MA)

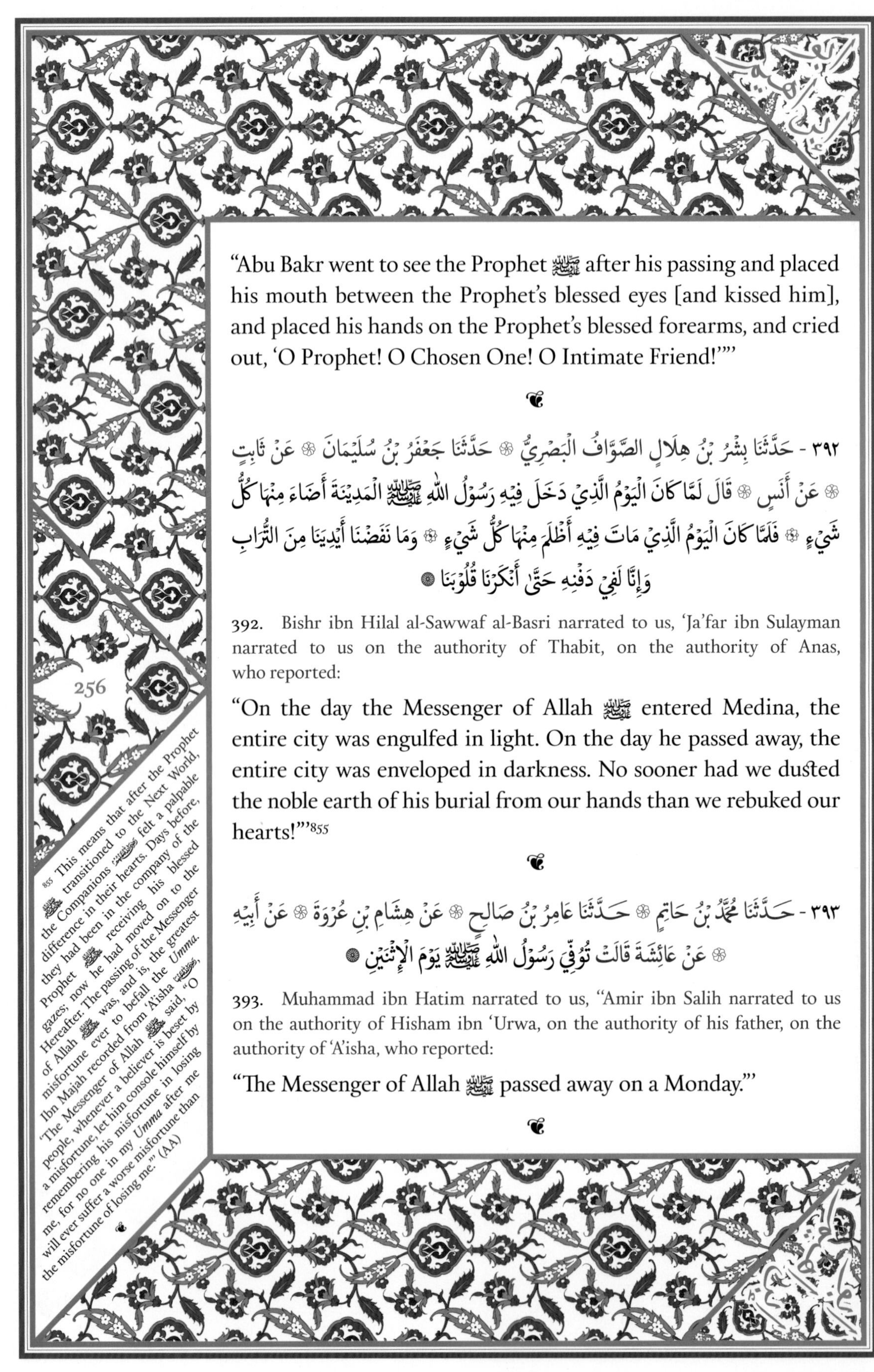

“Abu Bakr went to see the Prophet ﷺ after his passing and placed his mouth between the Prophet’s blessed eyes [and kissed him], and placed his hands on the Prophet’s blessed forearms, and cried out, ‘O Prophet! O Chosen One! O Intimate Friend!’”

❦

٣٩٢ - حَدَّثَنَا بِشْرُ بْنُ هِلَالٍ الصَّوَّافُ الْبَصْرِيُّ ❁ حَدَّثَنَا جَعْفَرُ بْنُ سُلَيْمَانَ ❁ عَنْ ثَابِتٍ ❁ عَنْ أَنَسٍ ❁ قَالَ لَمَّا كَانَ الْيَوْمُ الَّذِي دَخَلَ فِيهِ رَسُولُ اللهِ ﷺ الْمَدِينَةَ أَضَاءَ مِنْهَا كُلُّ شَيْءٍ ❁ فَلَمَّا كَانَ الْيَوْمُ الَّذِي مَاتَ فِيهِ أَظْلَمَ مِنْهَا كُلُّ شَيْءٍ ❁ وَمَا نَفَضْنَا أَيْدِيَنَا مِنَ التُّرَابِ وَإِنَّا لَفِي دَفْنِهِ حَتَّى أَنْكَرْنَا قُلُوبَنَا ❁

392. Bishr ibn Hilal al-Sawwaf al-Basri narrated to us, ‘Ja’far ibn Sulayman narrated to us on the authority of Thabit, on the authority of Anas, who reported:

“On the day the Messenger of Allah ﷺ entered Medina, the entire city was engulfed in light. On the day he passed away, the entire city was enveloped in darkness. No sooner had we dusted the noble earth of his burial from our hands than we rebuked our hearts!’”[855]

❦

٣٩٣ - حَدَّثَنَا مُحَمَّدُ بْنُ حَاتِمٍ ❁ حَدَّثَنَا عَامِرُ بْنُ صَالِحٍ ❁ عَنْ هِشَامِ بْنِ عُرْوَةَ ❁ عَنْ أَبِيهِ ❁ عَنْ عَائِشَةَ قَالَتْ تُوُفِّيَ رَسُولُ اللهِ ﷺ يَوْمَ الْإِثْنَيْنِ ❁

393. Muhammad ibn Hatim narrated to us, “Amir ibn Salih narrated to us on the authority of Hisham ibn ‘Urwa, on the authority of his father, on the authority of ‘A’isha, who reported:

“The Messenger of Allah ﷺ passed away on a Monday.’”

❦

[855] This means that after the Prophet ﷺ transitioned to the Next World, the Companions felt a palpable difference in their hearts. Days before, they had been in the company of the Prophet ﷺ receiving his blessed gazes; now he had moved on to the Hereafter. The passing of the Messenger of Allah ﷺ was, and is, the greatest misfortune ever to befall the *Umma*. Ibn Majah recorded from ‘A’isha, ‘The Messenger of Allah ﷺ said, “O people, whenever a believer is beset by a misfortune, let him console himself by remembering his misfortune in losing me, for no one in my *Umma* after me will ever suffer a worse misfortune than the misfortune of losing me.”’ (AA)

❦

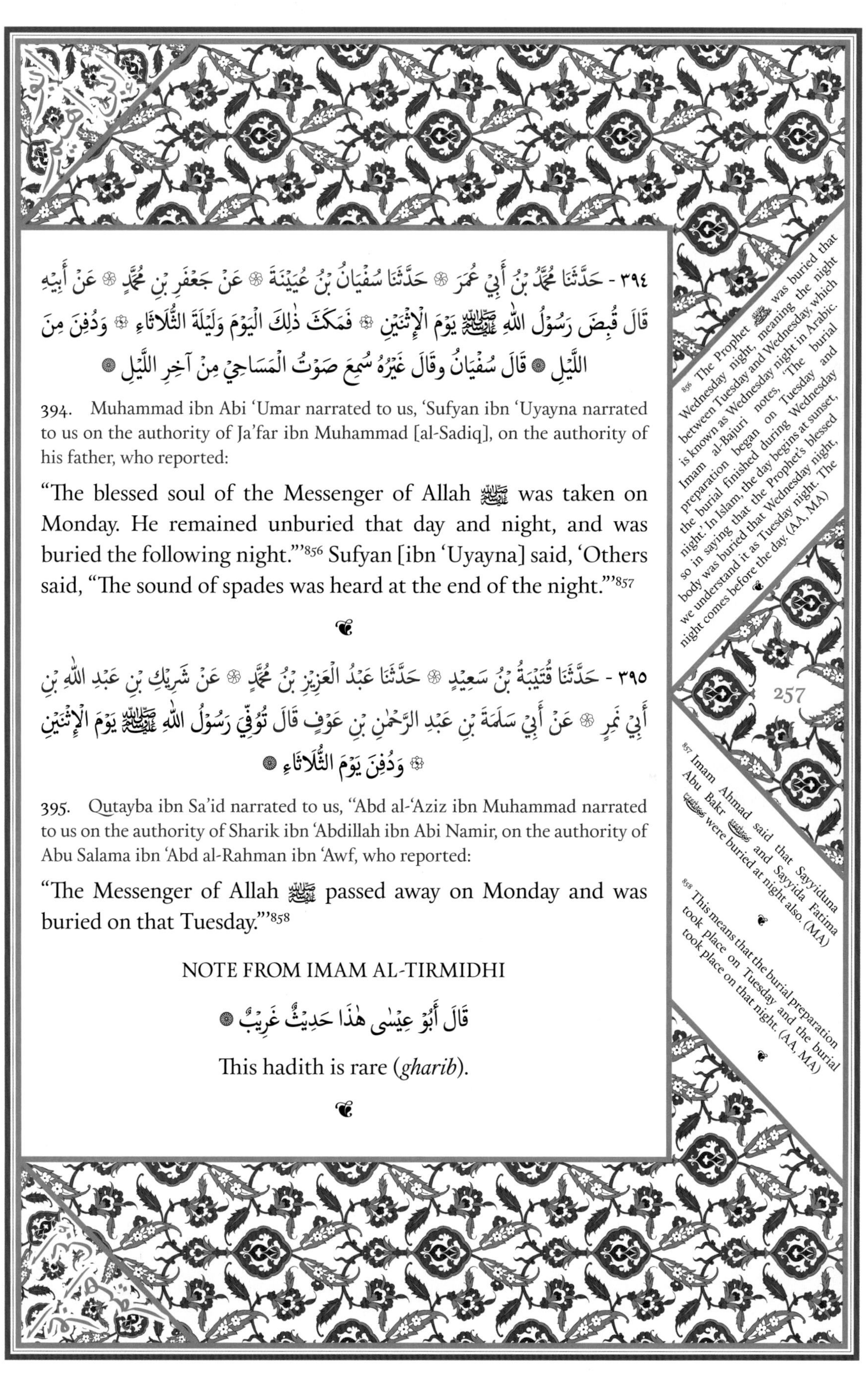

٣٩٤ - حَدَّثَنَا مُحَمَّدُ بْنُ أَبِي عُمَرَ ۞ حَدَّثَنَا سُفْيَانُ بْنُ عُيَيْنَةَ ۞ عَنْ جَعْفَرِ بْنِ مُحَمَّدٍ ۞ عَنْ أَبِيهِ قَالَ قُبِضَ رَسُولُ اللهِ ﷺ يَوْمَ الإِثْنَيْنِ ۞ فَمَكَثَ ذٰلِكَ الْيَوْمَ وَلَيْلَةَ الثُّلَاثَاءِ ۞ وَدُفِنَ مِنَ اللَّيْلِ ۞ قَالَ سُفْيَانُ وقَالَ غَيْرُهُ سُمِعَ صَوْتُ الْمَسَاحِيْ مِنْ آخِرِ اللَّيْلِ ۞

394. Muhammad ibn Abi 'Umar narrated to us, 'Sufyan ibn 'Uyayna narrated to us on the authority of Ja'far ibn Muhammad [al-Sadiq], on the authority of his father, who reported:

"The blessed soul of the Messenger of Allah ﷺ was taken on Monday. He remained unburied that day and night, and was buried the following night."'[856] Sufyan [ibn 'Uyayna] said, 'Others said, "The sound of spades was heard at the end of the night."'[857]

❦

٣٩٥ - حَدَّثَنَا قُتَيْبَةُ بْنُ سَعِيدٍ ۞ حَدَّثَنَا عَبْدُ الْعَزِيزِ بْنُ مُحَمَّدٍ ۞ عَنْ شَرِيكِ بْنِ عَبْدِ اللهِ بْنِ أَبِي نَمِرٍ ۞ عَنْ أَبِي سَلَمَةَ بْنِ عَبْدِ الرَّحْمٰنِ بْنِ عَوْفٍ قَالَ تُوُفِّيَ رَسُولُ اللهِ ﷺ يَوْمَ الإِثْنَيْنِ ۞ وَدُفِنَ يَوْمَ الثُّلَاثَاءِ ۞

395. Qutayba ibn Sa'id narrated to us, "Abd al-'Aziz ibn Muhammad narrated to us on the authority of Sharik ibn 'Abdillah ibn Abi Namir, on the authority of Abu Salama ibn 'Abd al-Rahman ibn 'Awf, who reported:

"The Messenger of Allah ﷺ passed away on Monday and was buried on that Tuesday."'[858]

NOTE FROM IMAM AL-TIRMIDHI

قَالَ أَبُو عِيْسٰى هٰذَا حَدِيثٌ غَرِيبٌ ۞

This hadith is rare (*gharib*).

❦

[856] The Prophet ﷺ was buried that Wednesday night, meaning the night between Tuesday and Wednesday, which is known as Wednesday night in Arabic. Imam al-Bajuri notes, 'The burial preparation began on Tuesday and the burial finished during Wednesday night.' In Islam, the day begins at sunset, so in saying that the Prophet's blessed body was buried that Wednesday night, we understand it as Tuesday night. The night comes before the day. (AA, MA)

❦

[857] Imam Ahmad said that Sayyiduna Abu Bakr ﷺ and Sayyida Fatima ﷺ were buried at night also. (MA)

❦

[858] This means that the burial preparation took place on Tuesday and the burial took place on that night. (AA, MA)

❦

٣٩٦ - حَدَّثَنَا نَصرُ بنُ عَلِيٍّ الجَهضَمِيُّ ۞ حَدَّثَنَا عَبدُ اللهِ بنُ دَاوُدَ ۞ حَدَّثَنَا سَلَمَةُ بنُ نُبَيطٍ ۞ أُخبِرنَا عَن نُعَيمِ بنِ أَبِي هِندٍ ۞ عَن نُبَيطِ بنِ شَرِيطٍ ۞ عَن سَالِمِ بنِ عُبَيدٍ وَكَانَت لَهُ صُحبَةٌ قَالَ أُغمِيَ عَلَىٰ رَسُولِ اللهِ ﷺ فِي مَرَضِهِ فَأَفَاقَ ۞ فَقَالَ حَضَرَتِ الصَّلَاةُ ۞ فَقَالُوا نَعَم ۞ فَقَالَ مُرُوا بِلَالًا فَليُؤَذِّن ۞ وَمُرُوا أَبَا بَكرٍ أَن يُصَلِّيَ لِلنَّاسِ ۞ أَو قَالَ بِالنَّاسِ ۞ قَالَ ثُمَّ أُغمِيَ عَلَيهِ فَأَفَاقَ ۞ فَقَالَ حَضَرَتِ الصَّلَاةُ ۞ فَقَالُوا نَعَم ۞ فَقَالَ مُرُوا بِلَالًا فَليُؤَذِّن ۞ وَمُرُوا أَبَا بَكرٍ فَليُصَلِّ بِالنَّاسِ ۞ فَقَالَت عَائِشَةُ إِنَّ أَبِي رَجُلٌ أَسِيفٌ ۞ إِذَا قَامَ ذٰلِكَ المَقَامَ بَكَىٰ فَلَا يَستَطِيعُ ۞ فَلَو أَمَرتَ غَيرَهُ ۞ قَالَ ثُمَّ أُغمِيَ عَلَيهِ فَأَفَاقَ ۞ فَقَالَ مُرُوا بِلَالًا فَليُؤَذِّن ۞ وَمُرُوا أَبَا بَكرٍ فَليُصَلِّ بِالنَّاسِ ۞ فَإِنَّكُنَّ صَوَاحِبُ أَو صَوَاحِبَاتُ يُوسُفَ ۞ قَالَ فَأُمِرَ بِلَالٌ فَأَذَّنَ ۞ وَأُمِرَ أَبُو بَكرٍ فَصَلَّىٰ بِالنَّاسِ ۞ ثُمَّ إِنَّ رَسُولَ اللهِ ﷺ وَجَدَ خِفَّةً ۞ فَقَالَ انظُرُوا لِي مَن أَتَّكِئُ عَلَيهِ ۞ فَجَاءَت بَرِيرَةُ وَرَجُلٌ آخَرُ ۞ فَاتَّكَأَ عَلَيهِمَا ۞ فَلَمَّا رَآهُ أَبُو بَكرٍ ذَهَبَ لِيَنكُصَ ۞ فَأَومَأَ إِلَيهِ أَن يَثبُتَ مَكَانَهُ حَتَّىٰ قَضَىٰ أَبُو بَكرٍ صَلَاتَهُ ۞ ثُمَّ إِنَّ رَسُولَ اللهِ ﷺ قُبِضَ ۞ فَقَالَ عُمَرُ وَاللهِ لَا أَسمَعُ أَحَدًا يَذكُرُ أَنَّ رَسُولَ اللهِ ﷺ قُبِضَ إِلَّا ضَرَبتُهُ بِسَيفِي هٰذَا ۞ قَالَ وَكَانَ النَّاسُ أُمِّيِّينَ لَم يَكُن فِيهِم نَبِيٌّ قَبلَهُ ۞ فَأَمسَكَ النَّاسُ ۞ فَقَالُوا يَا سَالِمُ انطَلِق إِلَىٰ صَاحِبِ رَسُولِ اللهِ ﷺ فَادعُهُ ۞ فَأَتَيتُ أَبَا بَكرٍ وَهُوَ فِي المَسجِدِ ۞ فَأَتَيتُهُ أَبكِي دَهِشًا ۞ فَلَمَّا رَآنِي قَالَ لِي أَقُبِضَ رَسُولُ اللهِ ﷺ ۞ قُلتُ إِنَّ عُمَرَ يَقُولُ لَا أَسمَعُ أَحَدًا يَذكُرُ أَنَّ رَسُولَ اللهِ ﷺ قُبِضَ إِلَّا ضَرَبتُهُ بِسَيفِي هٰذَا ۞ فَقَالَ لِي انطَلِق ۞ فَانطَلَقتُ مَعَهُ ۞ فَجَاءَ وَالنَّاسُ قَد دَخَلُوا عَلَىٰ رَسُولِ اللهِ ﷺ ۞ فَقَالَ يَا أَيُّهَا النَّاسُ أَفرِجُوا لِي ۞ فَأَفرَجُوا لَهُ ۞ فَجَاءَ حَتَّىٰ أَكَبَّ عَلَيهِ وَمَسَّهُ ۞ فَقَالَ ﴿إِنَّكَ مَيِّتٌ وَإِنَّهُم مَّيِّتُونَ﴾ ۞ ثُمَّ قَالُوا يَا صَاحِبَ رَسُولِ اللهِ ﷺ أَقُبِضَ رَسُولُ اللهِ ﷺ ۞ قَالَ نَعَم ۞ فَعَلِمُوا أَن قَد صَدَقَ ۞ قَالُوا يَا صَاحِبَ رَسُولِ اللهِ ﷺ أَيُصَلَّىٰ

عَلَىٰ رَسُولِ اللهِ ﷺ ۞ قَالَ نَعَمْ ۞ فَقَالُوا وَكَيْفَ ۞ قَالَ يَدْخُلُ قَوْمٌ فَيُكَبِّرُونَ وَيُصَلُّونَ
وَيَدْعُونَ ثُمَّ يَخْرُجُونَ ۞ ثُمَّ يَدْخُلُ قَوْمٌ فَيُكَبِّرُونَ وَيُصَلُّونَ وَيَدْعُونَ ثُمَّ يَخْرُجُونَ حَتَّىٰ يَدْخُلَ
النَّاسُ ۞ قَالُوا يَا صَاحِبَ رَسُولِ اللهِ أَيُدْفَنُ رَسُولُ اللهِ ﷺ ۞ قَالَ نَعَمْ ۞ قَالُوا أَيْنَ ۞
قَالَ فِي الْمَكَانِ الَّذِي قَبَضَ اللهُ فِيهِ رُوحَهُ ۞ فَإِنَّ اللهَ لَمْ يَقْبِضْ رُوحَهُ إِلَّا فِي مَكَانٍ طَيِّبٍ
۞ فَعَلِمُوا أَنْ قَدْ صَدَقَ ۞ ثُمَّ أَمَرَهُمْ أَنْ يُغَسِّلَهُ بَنُو أَبِيهِ ۞ وَاجْتَمَعَ الْمُهَاجِرُونَ يَتَشَاوَرُونَ
۞ فَقَالُوا انْطَلِقْ بِنَا إِلَىٰ إِخْوَانِنَا مِنَ الْأَنْصَارِ نُدْخِلْهُمْ مَعَنَا فِي هٰذَا الْأَمْرِ ۞ فَقَالَتِ الْأَنْصَارُ
مِنَّا أَمِيرٌ وَمِنْكُمْ أَمِيرٌ ۞ فَقَالَ عُمَرُ بْنُ الْخَطَّابِ مَنْ لَهُ مِثْلُ هٰذِهِ الثَّلَاثَةِ ﴿ثَانِيَ اثْنَيْنِ إِذْ هُمَا
فِي الْغَارِ إِذْ يَقُولُ لِصَاحِبِهِ لَا تَحْزَنْ إِنَّ اللهَ مَعَنَا﴾ مَنْ هُمَا ۞ قَالَ ثُمَّ بَسَطَ يَدَهُ فَبَايَعَهُ ۞
وَبَايَعَهُ النَّاسُ بَيْعَةً حَسَنَةً جَمِيلَةً ۝

396. Nasr ibn 'Ali al-Jahdami narrated to us, "Abdullah ibn Dawud narrated to us, he said, "Salama ibn Nubayt narrated to us, 'It was related to us on the authority of Nu'aym ibn Abi Hind, on the authority of Nubayt ibn Sharit, on the authority of Salim ibn 'Ubayd, who was a Companion, who reported:

"During his illness, the Messenger of Allah ﷺ was overcome.[859] When he came to, he said, 'The time for the prayer has arrived!'[860] They[861] said, 'Yes!' He said, 'Enjoin Bilal to give the call for prayer, and enjoin Abu Bakr to lead the people in prayer.' Then he was overcome again. When he came to [the second time], he said, 'The time for the prayer has arrived!' They said, 'Yes!' He said, 'Enjoin Bilal to give the call for prayer, and enjoin Abu Bakr to lead the people in prayer.' 'A'isha said [to the Prophet ﷺ], 'My father is a sensitive man; if he stands in that position[862] he will be overcome with tears. He will be unable; if only you would order someone else [that would be good]!' He said, 'Then the Prophet was overcome again. When he came to [the third time], he said, 'Enjoin Bilal to

859 This phrase in Arabic, *ughmiya*, literally means 'fainted' or 'fell unconscious'. The Companions used ambiguous words to describe some of the states the Prophet ﷺ experienced. The root meaning of 'fainting' is to lose sense perception (*faqd al-hiss*). The Prophet's 'fainting', however, was not like the fainting of ordinary human beings. For ordinary humans, fainting is usually the result of a decrease of blood flow to the brain, resulting in unconsciousness. Some scholars have said that this 'fainting' was a spiritual state (*hal*) the Prophet ﷺ had experienced because his sublime essence was completely immersed (*istighraq*) in the divine disclosures of the final moments before his transition from the worldly realm (*dunya*) to the intermediate realm (*barzakh*). Based on this interpretation, I have translated the phrase *ughmiya* as 'overcome' instead of the cruder 'fainted' or 'passed out'. Scholars have clarified that 'fainting' is possible for prophets, since it is similar to other forms of illness which they may experience and which do not prevent them from conveying the divine message. Imams Taqi al-Din al-Subki and Siraj al-Din al-Bulqini argued that the 'fainting' of the prophets was not like the fainting of others, and that it in no way made their hearts unaware. In the hadith about his perpetual fasting (*wisal*), the Prophet ﷺ said, 'I am not like you.' Neither is he like us in his 'fainting'. If the eyes of the Prophet Muhammad ﷺ slept but his blessed heart did not, how could he have entered a period of deep unconsciousness or a coma-like state and been oblivious to his surroundings? The root meaning of this word in Arabic is *ighma*, which indicates an enveloping. The *ighma* that the Prophet ﷺ experienced was an increase of light flooding his consciousness, an increase in disclosures from the Divine. When the intensities of these disclosures subsided, the Prophet 'came to'. During this entire episode, the Prophet ﷺ was aware. We see this clearly in his statement after he came to, 'The time for the prayer has arrived!' We see beautiful parallels between this incident and the Miraculous Ascent (*Mi'raj*), when Allah took the Prophet ﷺ on the journey past the seven heavens and to the Lote-tree of the Furthest Boundary (*Sidrat al-Muntaha*). When the beloved of Allah ﷺ was taken on the Ascension, he received the command to establish the daily prayers and he conveyed it to his *Umma* upon his return; and when he 'came to' after being 'overcome', he instructed those around him to establish the prayer! Allah and His Messenger ﷺ know best. (AA)

860 This part of the hadith is key to understanding something of the nature of his being 'overcome'. In this wording, the Prophet ﷺ is making an emphatic statement, telling his Companions that the time for the prayer has arrived. Many commentators have said that this was an implied question, since other narrations record that he asked, 'Has the time for prayer arrived?' There is no contradiction here, for in asking them if the time of the prayer had arrived, the Prophet ﷺ was gently reminding them to be mindful of it despite the distress they were suffering. Allah and His Messenger ﷺ know best. The essential lesson of this incident is to uphold the five daily prayers even in the most difficult of circumstances. (AA)

861 The Companions in his presence. (AA)

862 Leading the people in prayer, standing in the place where the Prophet ﷺ would stand. (AA)

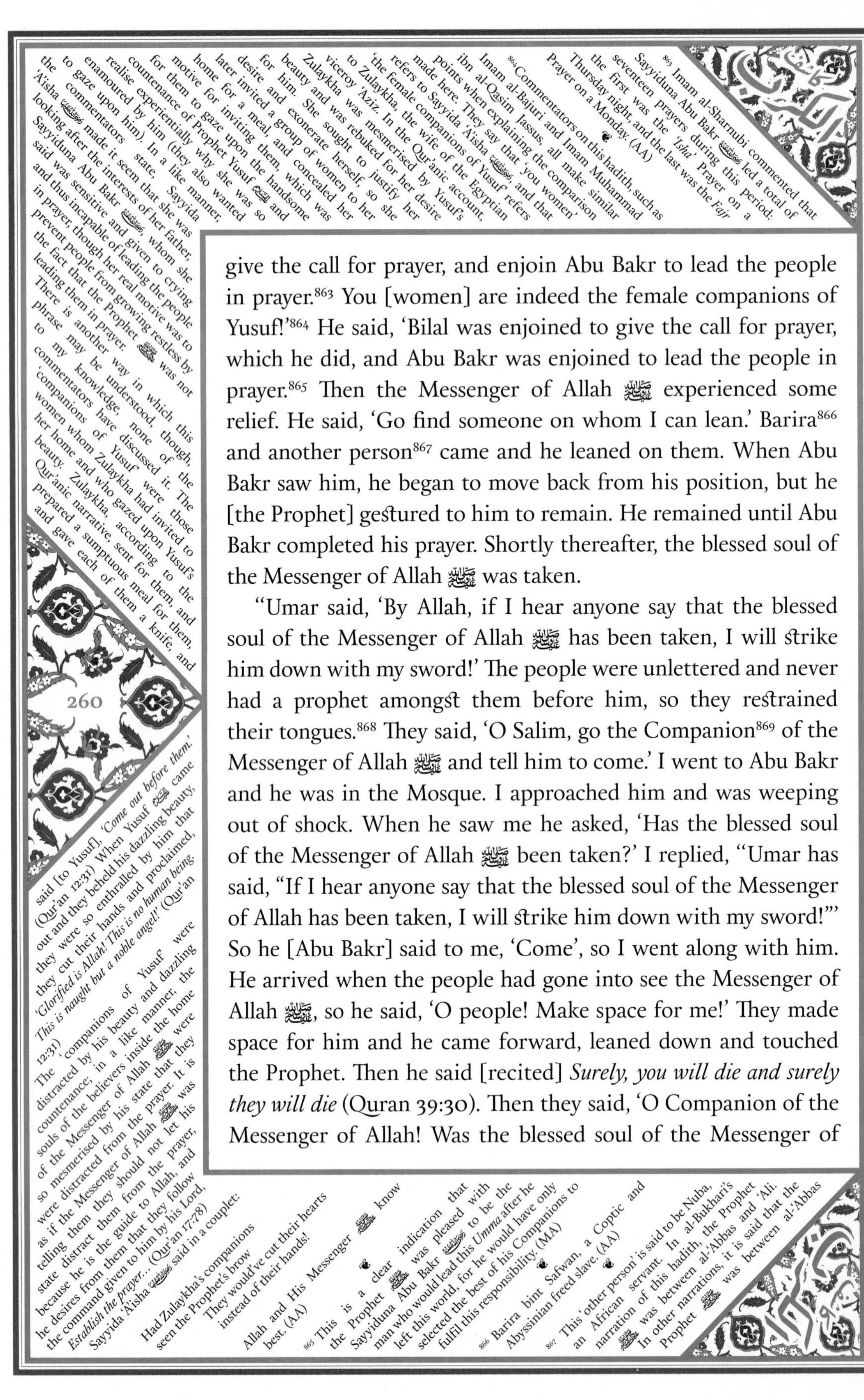

give the call for prayer, and enjoin Abu Bakr to lead the people in prayer.[863] You [women] are indeed the female companions of Yusuf!'[864] He said, 'Bilal was enjoined to give the call for prayer, which he did, and Abu Bakr was enjoined to lead the people in prayer.[865] Then the Messenger of Allah ﷺ experienced some relief. He said, 'Go find someone on whom I can lean.' Barira[866] and another person[867] came and he leaned on them. When Abu Bakr saw him, he began to move back from his position, but he [the Prophet] gestured to him to remain. He remained until Abu Bakr completed his prayer. Shortly thereafter, the blessed soul of the Messenger of Allah ﷺ was taken.

"Umar said, 'By Allah, if I hear anyone say that the blessed soul of the Messenger of Allah ﷺ has been taken, I will strike him down with my sword!' The people were unlettered and never had a prophet amongst them before him, so they restrained their tongues.[868] They said, 'O Salim, go the Companion[869] of the Messenger of Allah ﷺ and tell him to come.' I went to Abu Bakr and he was in the Mosque. I approached him and was weeping out of shock. When he saw me he asked, 'Has the blessed soul of the Messenger of Allah ﷺ been taken?' I replied, "Umar has said, "If I hear anyone say that the blessed soul of the Messenger of Allah has been taken, I will strike him down with my sword!"' So he [Abu Bakr] said to me, 'Come', so I went along with him. He arrived when the people had gone into see the Messenger of Allah ﷺ, so he said, 'O people! Make space for me!' They made space for him and he came forward, leaned down and touched the Prophet. Then he said [recited] *Surely, you will die and surely they will die* (Quran 39:30). Then they said, 'O Companion of the Messenger of Allah! Was the blessed soul of the Messenger of

863 Imam al-Sharnubi commented that Sayyiduna Abu Bakr led a total of seventeen prayers during this period: the first was the *'Isha'* Prayer on a Thursday night, and the last was the *Fajr* Prayer on a Monday. (AA)

864 Commentators on this hadith, such as Imam al-Bajuri and Imam Muhammad ibn al-Qasim Jassus, all make similar points when explaining the comparison made here. They say that 'you women' refers to Sayyida 'A'isha, and that 'the female companions of Yusuf' refers to Zulaykha, the wife of the Egyptian viceroy 'Aziz. In the Qur'anic account, Zulaykha was mesmerised by Yusuf's beauty and was rebuked for her desire for him. She sought to justify her desire and exonerate herself, so she later invited a group of women to her home for a meal, and concealed her motive for inviting them, which was for them to gaze upon the handsome countenance of Prophet Yusuf and realise experientially why she was so enamoured by him (they also wanted to gaze upon him). In a like manner, the commentators state, Sayyida 'A'isha made it seem that she was looking after the interests of her father, Sayyiduna Abu Bakr, whom she said was sensitive and given to crying and thus incapable of leading the people in prayer, though her real motive was to prevent people from growing restless by the fact that the Prophet ﷺ was not leading them in prayer. There is another way in which this phrase may be understood, though, to my knowledge, none of the commentators have discussed it. The 'companions of Yusuf' were those women whom Zulaykha had invited to her home and who gazed upon Yusuf's beauty. Zulaykha, according to the Qur'anic narrative, sent for them, and prepared a sumptuous meal for them, and gave each of them a knife, and said [to Yusuf], *'Come out before them.'* (Qur'an 12:31) When Yusuf came out and they beheld his dazzling beauty, they were so enthralled by him that they cut their hands and proclaimed, *'Glorified is Allah! This is no human being. This is naught but a noble angel!'* (Qur'an 12:31) The 'companions of Yusuf' were distracted by his beauty and dazzling countenance; in a like manner, the souls of the believers inside the home of the Messenger of Allah ﷺ were so mesmerised by his state that they were distracted from the prayer. It is as if the Messenger of Allah ﷺ was telling them they should not let his state distract them from the prayer, because he is the guide to Allah, and he desires from them that they follow the command given to him by his Lord, *Establish the prayer...* (Qur'an 17:78) Sayyida 'A'isha said in a couplet:

Had Zulaykha's companions seen the Prophet's brow
They would've cut their hearts instead of their hands!

Allah and His Messenger ﷺ know best. (AA)

865 This is a clear indication that the Prophet ﷺ was pleased with Sayyiduna Abu Bakr to be the man who would lead this *Umma* after he left this world, for he would have only selected the best of his Companions to fulfil this responsibility. (MA)

866 Barira bint Safwan, a Coptic and Abyssinian freed slave. (AA)

867 This 'other person' is said to be Nuba, an African servant. In al-Bukhari's narration of this hadith, the Prophet ﷺ was between al-'Abbas and 'Ali. In other narrations, it is said that the Prophet ﷺ was between al-'Abbas

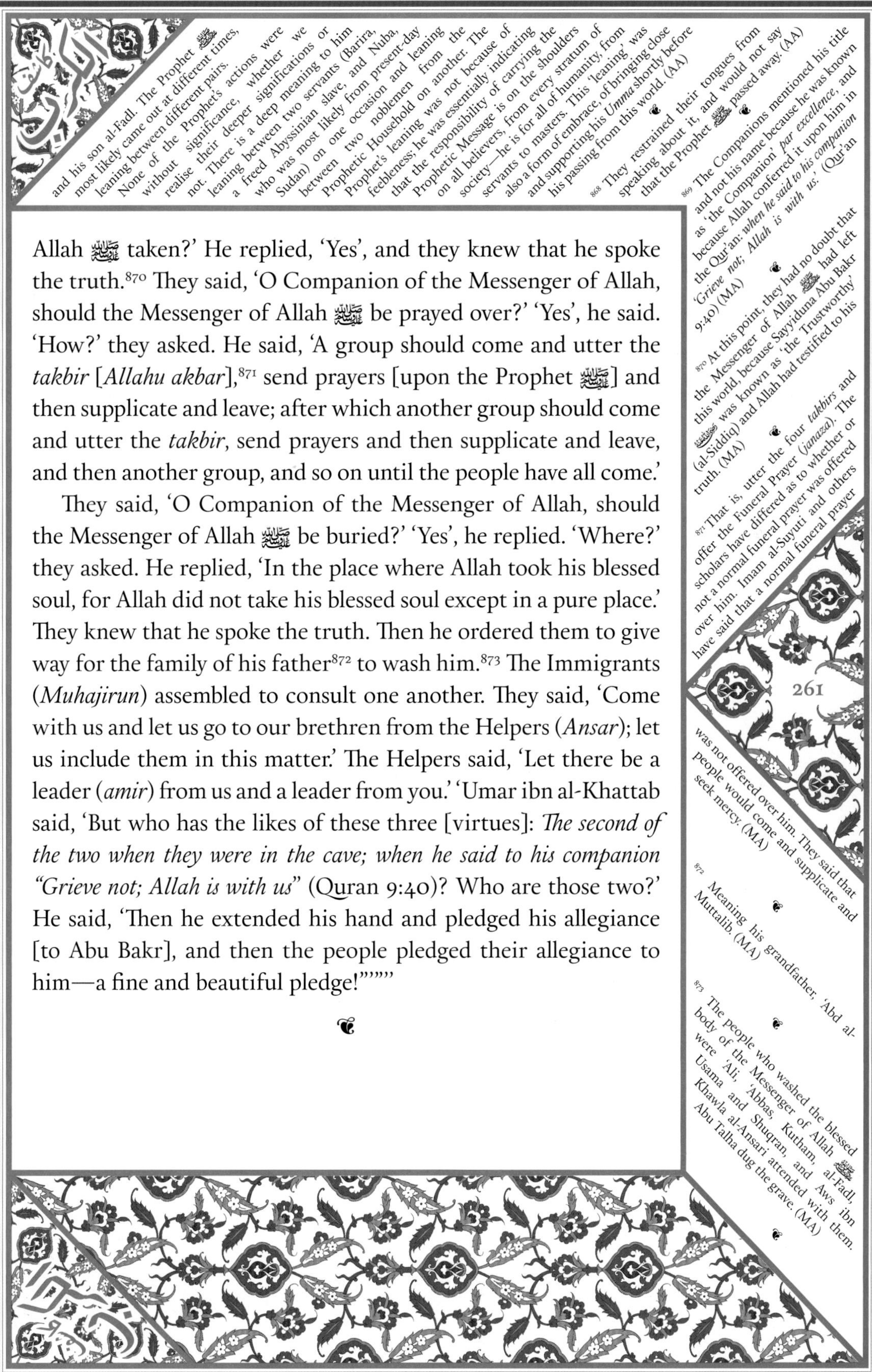

and his son al-Fadl. The Prophet ﷺ most likely came out at different times, leaning between different pairs. None of the Prophet's actions were without significance, whether we realise their deeper significations or not. There is a deep meaning to him leaning between two servants (Barira, a freed Abyssinian slave, and Nuba, who was most likely from present-day Sudan) on one occasion and leaning between two noblemen from the Prophetic Household on another. The Prophet's leaning was not because of feebleness; he was essentially indicating that the responsibility of carrying the Prophetic Message is on the shoulders on all believers, from every stratum of society—he is for all of humanity, from servants to masters. This 'leaning' was also a form of embrace, of bringing close and supporting his *Umma* shortly before his passing from this world. (AA)

Allah ﷺ taken?' He replied, 'Yes', and they knew that he spoke the truth.[870] They said, 'O Companion of the Messenger of Allah, should the Messenger of Allah ﷺ be prayed over?' 'Yes', he said. 'How?' they asked. He said, 'A group should come and utter the *takbir* [*Allahu akbar*],[871] send prayers [upon the Prophet ﷺ] and then supplicate and leave; after which another group should come and utter the *takbir*, send prayers and then supplicate and leave, and then another group, and so on until the people have all come.'

They said, 'O Companion of the Messenger of Allah, should the Messenger of Allah ﷺ be buried?' 'Yes', he replied. 'Where?' they asked. He replied, 'In the place where Allah took his blessed soul, for Allah did not take his blessed soul except in a pure place.' They knew that he spoke the truth. Then he ordered them to give way for the family of his father[872] to wash him.[873] The Immigrants (*Muhajirun*) assembled to consult one another. They said, 'Come with us and let us go to our brethren from the Helpers (*Ansar*); let us include them in this matter.' The Helpers said, 'Let there be a leader (*amir*) from us and a leader from you.' 'Umar ibn al-Khattab said, 'But who has the likes of these three [virtues]: *The second of the two when they were in the cave; when he said to his companion "Grieve not; Allah is with us"* (Quran 9:40)? Who are those two?' He said, 'Then he extended his hand and pledged his allegiance [to Abu Bakr], and then the people pledged their allegiance to him—a fine and beautiful pledge!"""'

[868] They restrained their tongues from speaking about it, and would not say that the Prophet ﷺ passed away. (AA)

[869] The Companions mentioned his title and not his name because he was known as 'the Companion' *par excellence*, and because Allah conferred it upon him in the Qur'an: *when he said to his companion 'Grieve not; Allah is with us.'* (Qur'an 9:40) (MA)

[870] At this point, they had no doubt that the Messenger of Allah ﷺ had left this world, because Sayyiduna Abu Bakr was known as 'the Trustworthy' (al-Siddiq) and Allah had testified to his truth. (MA)

[871] That is, utter the four *takbirs* and offer the Funeral Prayer (*janaza*). The scholars have differed as to whether or not a normal funeral prayer was offered over him. Imam al-Suyuti and others have said that a normal funeral prayer was not offered over him. They said that people would come and supplicate and seek mercy. (MA)

[872] Meaning his grandfather, 'Abd al-Muttalib. (MA)

[873] The people who washed the blessed body of the Messenger of Allah ﷺ were 'Ali, 'Abbas, Kutham, al-Fadl, Usama and Shuqran, and Aws ibn Khawla al-Ansari attended with them. Abu Talha dug the grave. (MA)

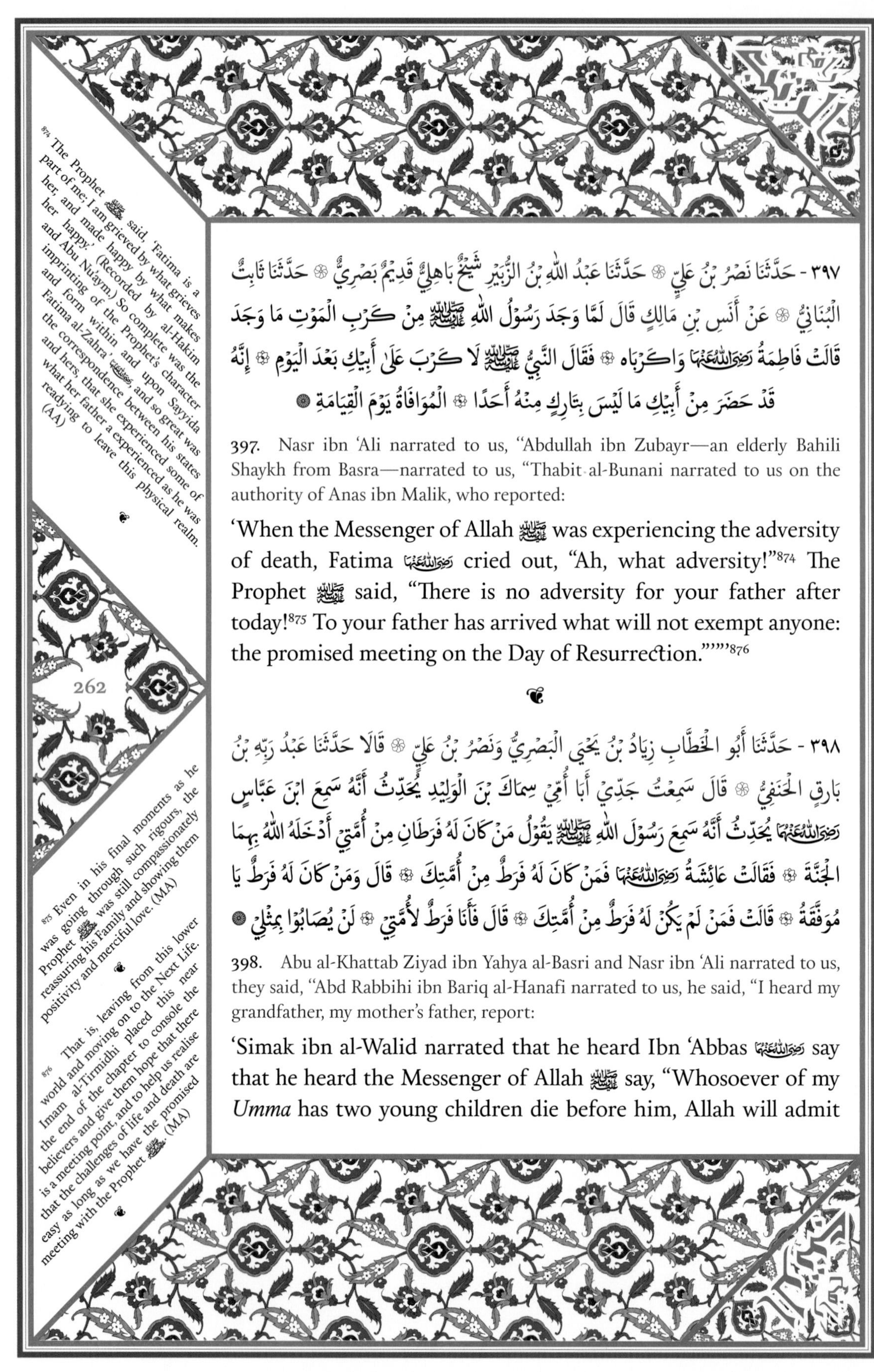

٣٩٧ - حَدَّثَنَا نَصرُ بْنُ عَلِيٍّ ۞ حَدَّثَنَا عَبدُ اللهِ بْنُ الزُّبَيرِ شَيخٌ بَاهِلِيٌّ قَدِيمٌ بَصرِيٌّ ۞ حَدَّثَنَا ثَابِتٌ الْبُنَانِيُّ ۞ عَنْ أَنَسِ بْنِ مَالِكٍ قَالَ لَمَّا وَجَدَ رَسُولُ اللهِ ﷺ مِنْ كَرْبِ الْمَوتِ مَا وَجَدَ قَالَتْ فَاطِمَةُ رضي الله عنها وَاكَرْبَاه ۞ فَقَالَ النَّبِيُّ ﷺ لَا كَرْبَ عَلَى أَبِيكِ بَعْدَ الْيَوْمِ ۞ إِنَّهُ قَدْ حَضَرَ مِنْ أَبِيكِ مَا لَيْسَ بِتَارِكٍ مِنْهُ أَحَدًا ۞ الْمُوَافَاةُ يَوْمَ الْقِيَامَةِ ۞

397. Nasr ibn 'Ali narrated to us, "Abdullah ibn Zubayr—an elderly Bahili Shaykh from Basra—narrated to us, "Thabit al-Bunani narrated to us on the authority of Anas ibn Malik, who reported:

'When the Messenger of Allah ﷺ was experiencing the adversity of death, Fatima رضي الله عنها cried out, "Ah, what adversity!"[874] The Prophet ﷺ said, "There is no adversity for your father after today![875] To your father has arrived what will not exempt anyone: the promised meeting on the Day of Resurrection."'""[876]

❦

٣٩٨ - حَدَّثَنَا أَبُو الْخَطَّابِ زِيَادُ بْنُ يَحْيَى الْبَصرِيُّ وَنَصرُ بْنُ عَلِيٍّ ۞ قَالَا حَدَّثَنَا عَبْدُ رَبِّهِ بْنُ بَارِقٍ الْحَنَفِيُّ ۞ قَالَ سَمِعْتُ جَدِّي أَبَا أُمِّي سِمَاكَ بْنَ الْوَلِيدِ يُحَدِّثُ أَنَّهُ سَمِعَ ابْنَ عَبَّاسٍ رضي الله عنهما يُحَدِّثُ أَنَّهُ سَمِعَ رَسُولَ اللهِ ﷺ يَقُولُ مَنْ كَانَ لَهُ فَرَطَانِ مِنْ أُمَّتِي أَدْخَلَهُ اللهُ بِهِمَا الْجَنَّةَ ۞ فَقَالَتْ عَائِشَةُ رضي الله عنها فَمَنْ كَانَ لَهُ فَرَطٌ مِنْ أُمَّتِكَ ۞ قَالَ وَمَنْ كَانَ لَهُ فَرَطٌ يَا مُوَفَّقَةُ ۞ قَالَتْ فَمَنْ لَمْ يَكُنْ لَهُ فَرَطٌ مِنْ أُمَّتِكَ ۞ قَالَ فَأَنَا فَرَطٌ لِأُمَّتِي ۞ لَنْ يُصَابُوا بِمِثْلِي ۞

398. Abu al-Khattab Ziyad ibn Yahya al-Basri and Nasr ibn 'Ali narrated to us, they said, "Abd Rabbihi ibn Bariq al-Hanafi narrated to us, he said, "I heard my grandfather, my mother's father, report:

'Simak ibn al-Walid narrated that he heard Ibn 'Abbas رضي الله عنهما say that he heard the Messenger of Allah ﷺ say, "Whosoever of my *Umma* has two young children die before him, Allah will admit

[874] The Prophet ﷺ said, 'Fatima is a part of me; I am grieved by what grieves her, and made happy by what makes her happy.' (Recorded by al-Hakim and Abu Nu'aym.) So complete was the imprinting of the Prophet's character and form within and upon Sayyida Fatima al-Zahra' رضي الله عنها, and so great was the correspondence between his states and hers, that she experienced some of what her father a experienced as he was readying to leave this physical realm. (AA)

❦

[875] Even in his final moments as he was going through such rigours, the Prophet ﷺ was still compassionately reassuring his Family and showing them positivity and merciful love. (MA)

[876] That is, leaving from this lower world and moving on to the Next Life. Imam al-Tirmidhi placed this near the end of the chapter to console the believers and give them hope that there is a meeting point, and to help us realise that the challenges of life and death are easy as long as we have the promised meeting with the Prophet ﷺ. (MA)

❦

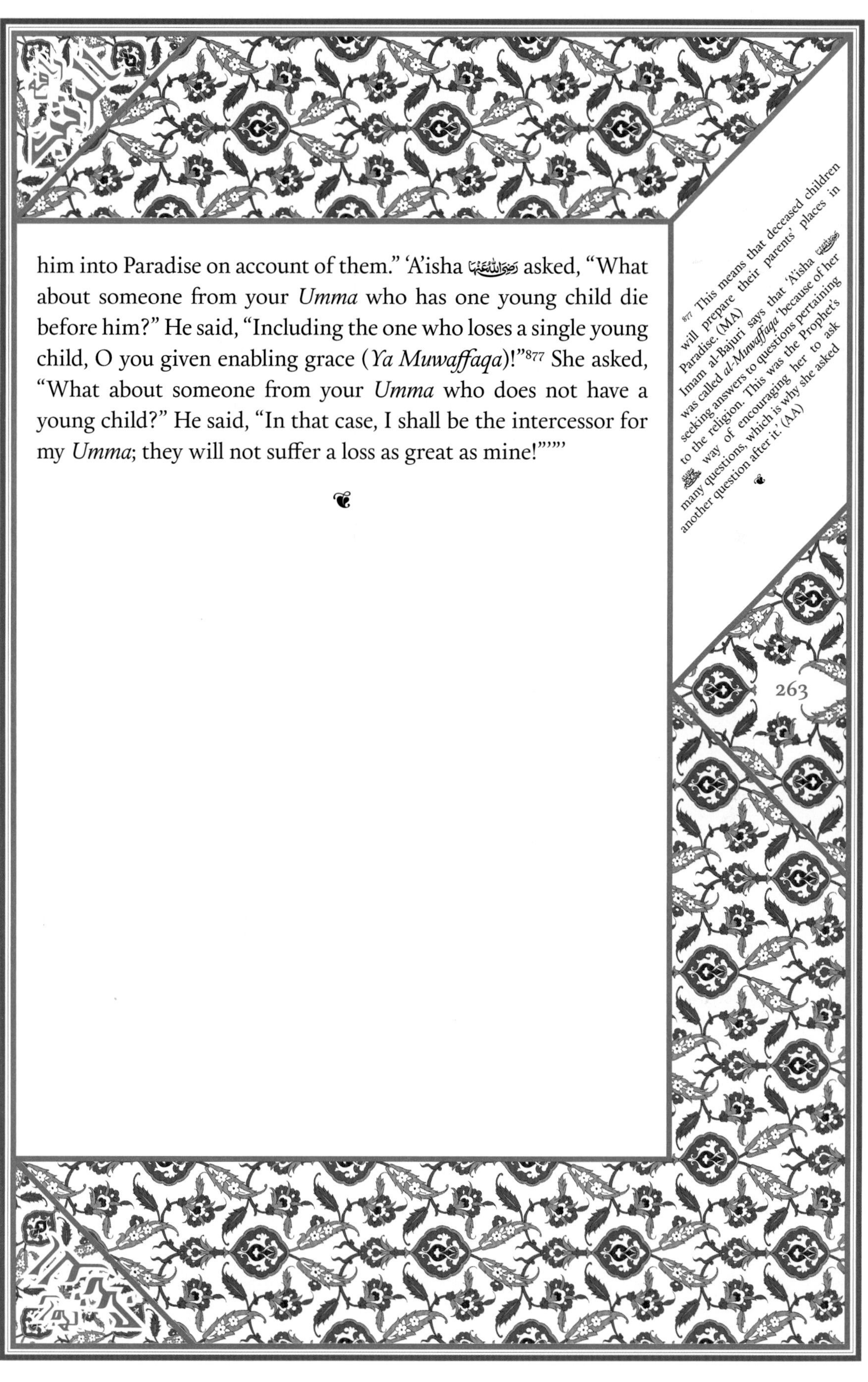

him into Paradise on account of them." 'A'isha رضي الله عنها asked, "What about someone from your *Umma* who has one young child die before him?" He said, "Including the one who loses a single young child, O you given enabling grace (*Ya Muwaffaqa*)!"[877] She asked, "What about someone from your *Umma* who does not have a young child?" He said, "In that case, I shall be the intercessor for my *Umma*; they will not suffer a loss as great as mine!""""

❦

[877] This means that deceased children will prepare their parents' places in Paradise. (MA) Imam al-Bajuri says that 'A'isha رضي الله عنها was called *al-Muwaffaqa* 'because of her seeking answers to questions pertaining to the religion. This was the Prophet's ﷺ way of encouraging her to ask many questions, which is why she asked another question after it.' (AA)

❦

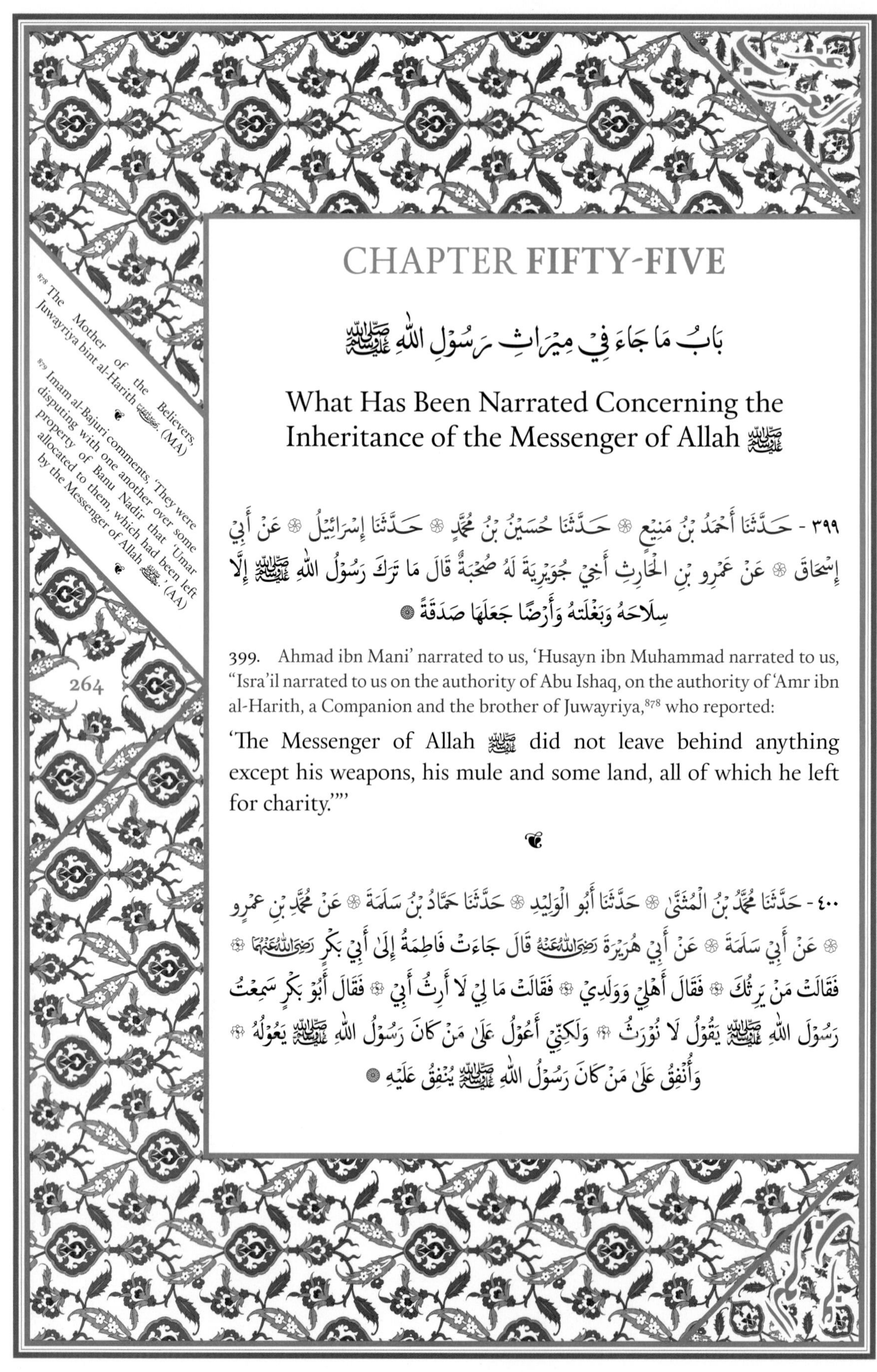

CHAPTER FIFTY-FIVE

بَابُ مَا جَاءَ فِي مِيرَاثِ رَسُولِ اللهِ ﷺ

What Has Been Narrated Concerning the Inheritance of the Messenger of Allah ﷺ

٣٩٩ - حَدَّثَنَا أَحْمَدُ بْنُ مَنِيعٍ ۞ حَدَّثَنَا حُسَيْنُ بْنُ مُحَمَّدٍ ۞ حَدَّثَنَا إِسْرَائِيلُ ۞ عَنْ أَبِي إِسْحَاقَ ۞ عَنْ عَمْرِو بْنِ الْحَارِثِ أَخِي جُوَيْرِيَةَ لَهُ صُحْبَةٌ قَالَ مَا تَرَكَ رَسُولُ اللهِ ﷺ إِلَّا سِلَاحَهُ وَبَغْلَتَهُ وَأَرْضًا جَعَلَهَا صَدَقَةً ۞

399. Ahmad ibn Mani' narrated to us, 'Husayn ibn Muhammad narrated to us, "Isra'il narrated to us on the authority of Abu Ishaq, on the authority of 'Amr ibn al-Harith, a Companion and the brother of Juwayriya,[878] who reported:

'The Messenger of Allah ﷺ did not leave behind anything except his weapons, his mule and some land, all of which he left for charity.'"'

٤٠٠ - حَدَّثَنَا مُحَمَّدُ بْنُ الْمُثَنَّى ۞ حَدَّثَنَا أَبُو الْوَلِيدِ ۞ حَدَّثَنَا حَمَّادُ بْنُ سَلَمَةَ ۞ عَنْ مُحَمَّدِ بْنِ عَمْرٍو ۞ عَنْ أَبِي سَلَمَةَ ۞ عَنْ أَبِي هُرَيْرَةَ رَضِيَ اللهُ عَنْهُ قَالَ جَاءَتْ فَاطِمَةُ إِلَى أَبِي بَكْرٍ رَضِيَ اللهُ عَنْهُمَا ۞ فَقَالَتْ مَنْ يَرِثُكَ ۞ فَقَالَ أَهْلِي وَوَلَدِي ۞ فَقَالَتْ مَا لِي لَا أَرِثُ أَبِي ۞ فَقَالَ أَبُو بَكْرٍ سَمِعْتُ رَسُولَ اللهِ ﷺ يَقُولُ لَا نُورَثُ ۞ وَلَكِنِّي أَعُولُ عَلَى مَنْ كَانَ رَسُولُ اللهِ ﷺ يَعُولُهُ ۞ وَأُنْفِقُ عَلَى مَنْ كَانَ رَسُولُ اللهِ ﷺ يُنْفِقُ عَلَيْهِ ۞

[878] The Mother of the Believers, Juwayriya bint al-Harith رضي الله عنها. (MA)

[879] Imam al-Bajuri comments, 'They were disputing with one another over some property of Banu Nadir that 'Umar allocated to them, which had been left by the Messenger of Allah ﷺ.' (AA)

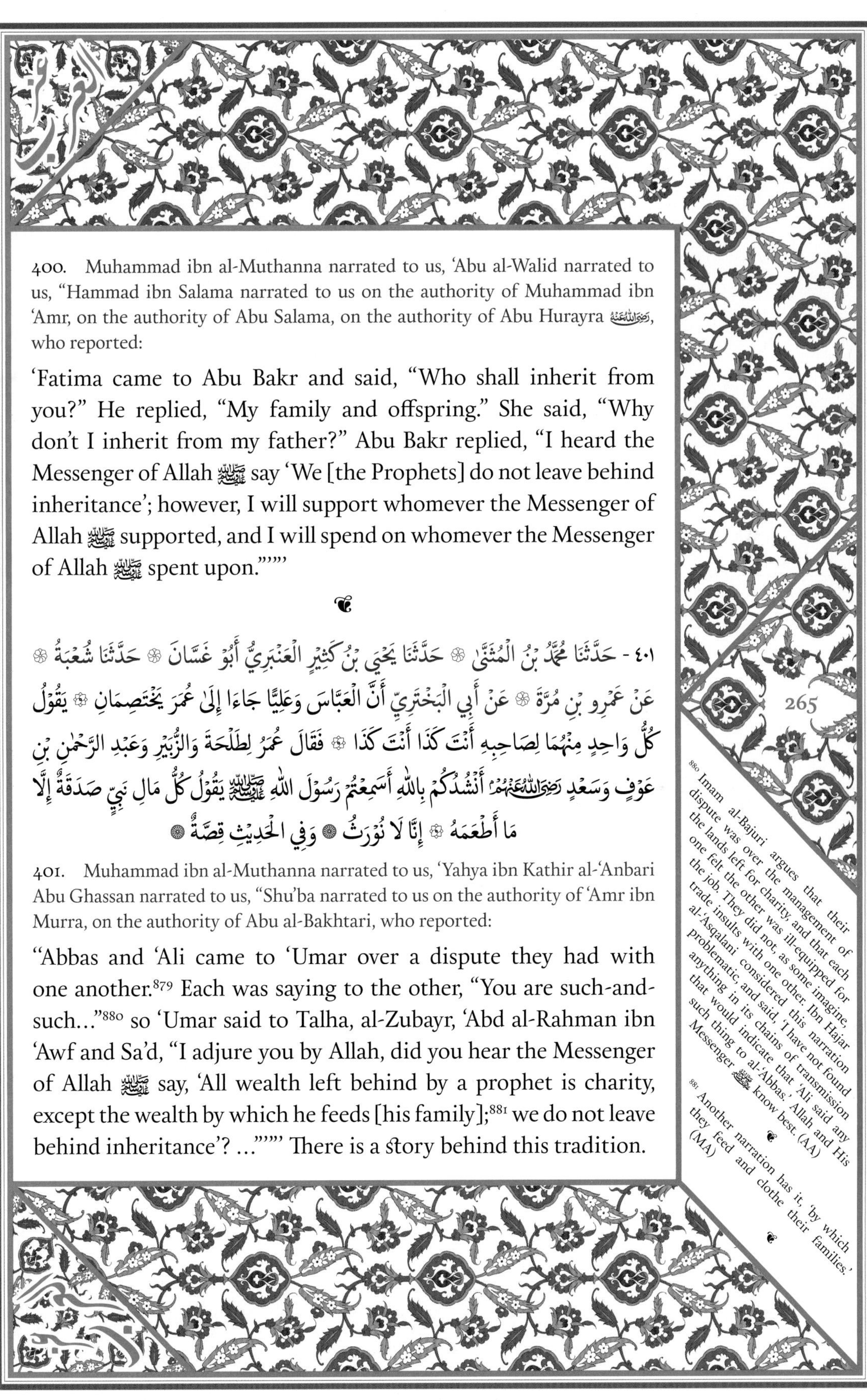

400. Muhammad ibn al-Muthanna narrated to us, 'Abu al-Walid narrated to us, "Hammad ibn Salama narrated to us on the authority of Muhammad ibn 'Amr, on the authority of Abu Salama, on the authority of Abu Hurayra رضي الله عنه, who reported:

'Fatima came to Abu Bakr and said, "Who shall inherit from you?" He replied, "My family and offspring." She said, "Why don't I inherit from my father?" Abu Bakr replied, "I heard the Messenger of Allah ﷺ say 'We [the Prophets] do not leave behind inheritance'; however, I will support whomever the Messenger of Allah ﷺ supported, and I will spend on whomever the Messenger of Allah ﷺ spent upon."'"'

٤٠١ - حَدَّثَنَا مُحَمَّدُ بْنُ الْمُثَنَّى ۞ حَدَّثَنَا يَحْيَى بْنُ كَثِيرٍ الْعَنْبَرِيُّ أَبُو غَسَّانَ ۞ حَدَّثَنَا شُعْبَةُ ۞ عَنْ عَمْرِو بْنِ مُرَّةَ ۞ عَنْ أَبِي الْبَخْتَرِيِّ أَنَّ الْعَبَّاسَ وَعَلِيًّا جَاءَا إِلَى عُمَرَ يَخْتَصِمَانِ ۞ يَقُولُ كُلُّ وَاحِدٍ مِنْهُمَا لِصَاحِبِهِ أَنْتَ كَذَا أَنْتَ كَذَا ۞ فَقَالَ عُمَرُ لِطَلْحَةَ وَالزُّبَيْرِ وَعَبْدِ الرَّحْمَٰنِ بْنِ عَوْفٍ وَسَعْدٍ رَضِيَ اللَّهُ عَنْهُمْ أَنْشُدُكُمْ بِاللَّهِ أَسَمِعْتُمْ رَسُولَ اللَّهِ ﷺ يَقُولُ كُلُّ مَالِ نَبِيٍّ صَدَقَةٌ إِلَّا مَا أَطْعَمَهُ ۞ إِنَّا لَا نُورَثُ ۞ وَفِي الْحَدِيثِ قِصَّةٌ ۞

401. Muhammad ibn al-Muthanna narrated to us, 'Yahya ibn Kathir al-'Anbari Abu Ghassan narrated to us, "Shu'ba narrated to us on the authority of 'Amr ibn Murra, on the authority of Abu al-Bakhtari, who reported:

"Abbas and 'Ali came to 'Umar over a dispute they had with one another.[879] Each was saying to the other, "You are such-and-such..."[880] so 'Umar said to Talha, al-Zubayr, 'Abd al-Rahman ibn 'Awf and Sa'd, "I adjure you by Allah, did you hear the Messenger of Allah ﷺ say, 'All wealth left behind by a prophet is charity, except the wealth by which he feeds [his family];[881] we do not leave behind inheritance'? ..."'"' There is a story behind this tradition.

880 Imam al-Bajuri argues that their dispute was over the management of the lands left for charity, and that each one felt the other was ill-equipped for the job. They did not, as some imagine, trade insults with one other. Ibn Hajar al-'Asqalani considered this narration problematic, and said, 'I have not found anything in its chains of transmission that would indicate that 'Ali said any such thing to al-'Abbas.' Allah and His Messenger ﷺ know best. (AA)

881 Another narration has it, 'by which they feed and clothe their families.' (MA)

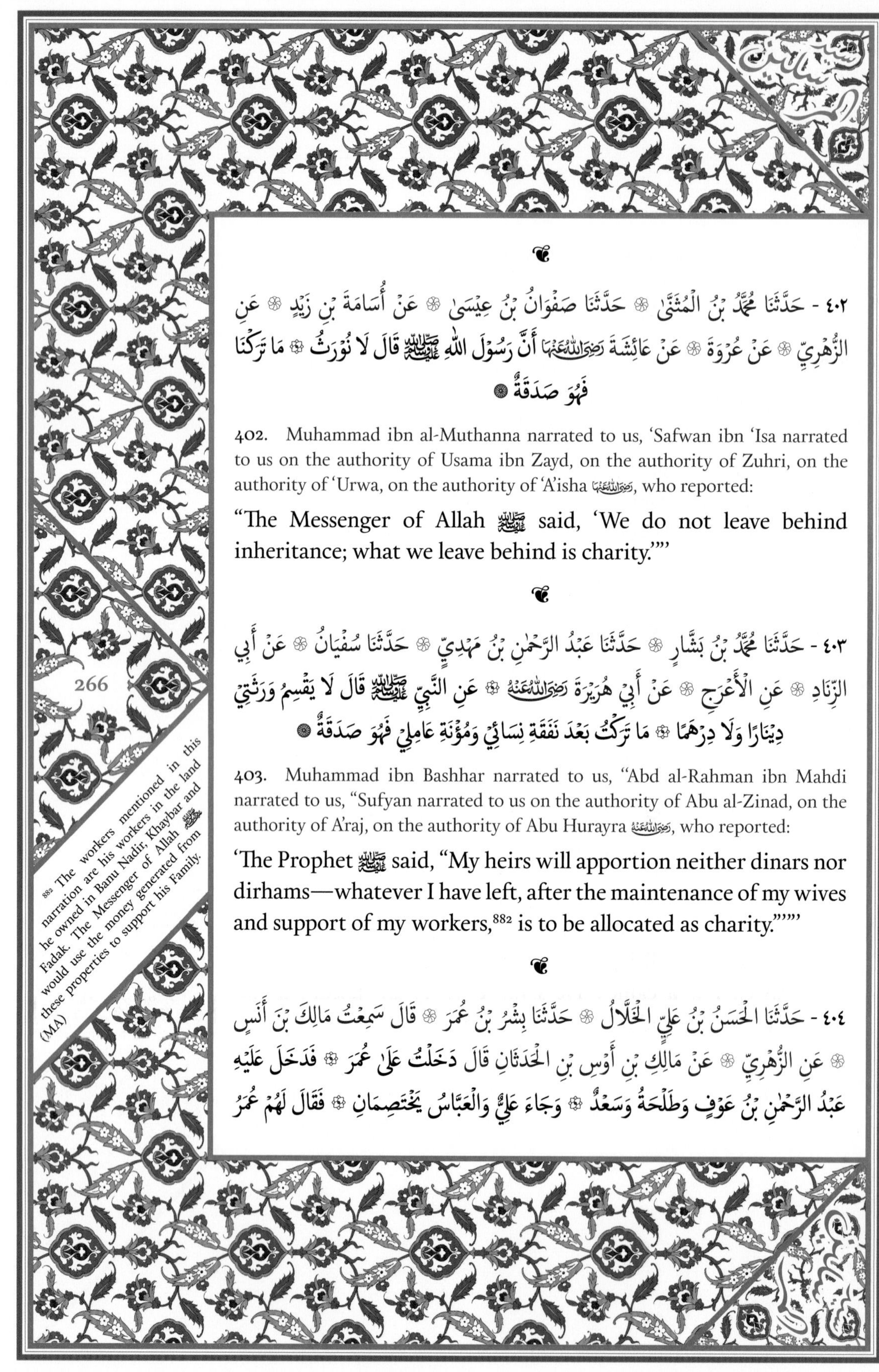

٤٠٢ - حَدَّثَنَا مُحَمَّدُ بْنُ الْمُثَنَّىٰ ❁ حَدَّثَنَا صَفْوَانُ بْنُ عِيسَىٰ ❁ عَنْ أُسَامَةَ بْنِ زَيْدٍ ❁ عَنِ الزُّهْرِيِّ ❁ عَنْ عُرْوَةَ ❁ عَنْ عَائِشَةَ رَضِيَ اللَّهُ عَنْهَا أَنَّ رَسُولَ اللهِ ﷺ قَالَ لَا نُورَثُ ❁ مَا تَرَكْنَا فَهُوَ صَدَقَةٌ ❁

402. Muhammad ibn al-Muthanna narrated to us, ‘Safwan ibn ‘Isa narrated to us on the authority of Usama ibn Zayd, on the authority of Zuhri, on the authority of ‘Urwa, on the authority of ‘A’isha رضي الله عنها, who reported:

“The Messenger of Allah ﷺ said, ‘We do not leave behind inheritance; what we leave behind is charity.’”’

٤٠٣ - حَدَّثَنَا مُحَمَّدُ بْنُ بَشَّارٍ ❁ حَدَّثَنَا عَبْدُ الرَّحْمَٰنِ بْنُ مَهْدِيٍّ ❁ حَدَّثَنَا سُفْيَانُ ❁ عَنْ أَبِي الزِّنَادِ ❁ عَنِ الْأَعْرَجِ ❁ عَنْ أَبِي هُرَيْرَةَ رَضِيَ اللَّهُ عَنْهُ ❁ عَنِ النَّبِيِّ ﷺ قَالَ لَا يَقْسِمُ وَرَثَتِي دِينَارًا وَلَا دِرْهَمًا ❁ مَا تَرَكْتُ بَعْدَ نَفَقَةِ نِسَائِي وَمُؤْنَةِ عَامِلِي فَهُوَ صَدَقَةٌ ❁

403. Muhammad ibn Bashhar narrated to us, “Abd al-Rahman ibn Mahdi narrated to us, “Sufyan narrated to us on the authority of Abu al-Zinad, on the authority of A’raj, on the authority of Abu Hurayra رضي الله عنه, who reported:

‘The Prophet ﷺ said, “My heirs will apportion neither dinars nor dirhams—whatever I have left, after the maintenance of my wives and support of my workers,[882] is to be allocated as charity.”’””

٤٠٤ - حَدَّثَنَا الْحَسَنُ بْنُ عَلِيٍّ الْخَلَّالُ ❁ حَدَّثَنَا بِشْرُ بْنُ عُمَرَ ❁ قَالَ سَمِعْتُ مَالِكَ بْنَ أَنَسٍ ❁ عَنِ الزُّهْرِيِّ ❁ عَنْ مَالِكِ بْنِ أَوْسِ بْنِ الْحَدَثَانِ قَالَ دَخَلْتُ عَلَى عُمَرَ ❁ فَدَخَلَ عَلَيْهِ عَبْدُ الرَّحْمَٰنِ بْنُ عَوْفٍ وَطَلْحَةُ وَسَعْدٌ ❁ وَجَاءَ عَلِيٌّ وَالْعَبَّاسُ يَخْتَصِمَانِ ❁ فَقَالَ لَهُمْ عُمَرُ

882 The workers mentioned in this narration are his workers in the land he owned in Banu Nadir, Khaybar and Fadak. The Messenger of Allah ﷺ would use the money generated from these properties to support his Family. (MA)

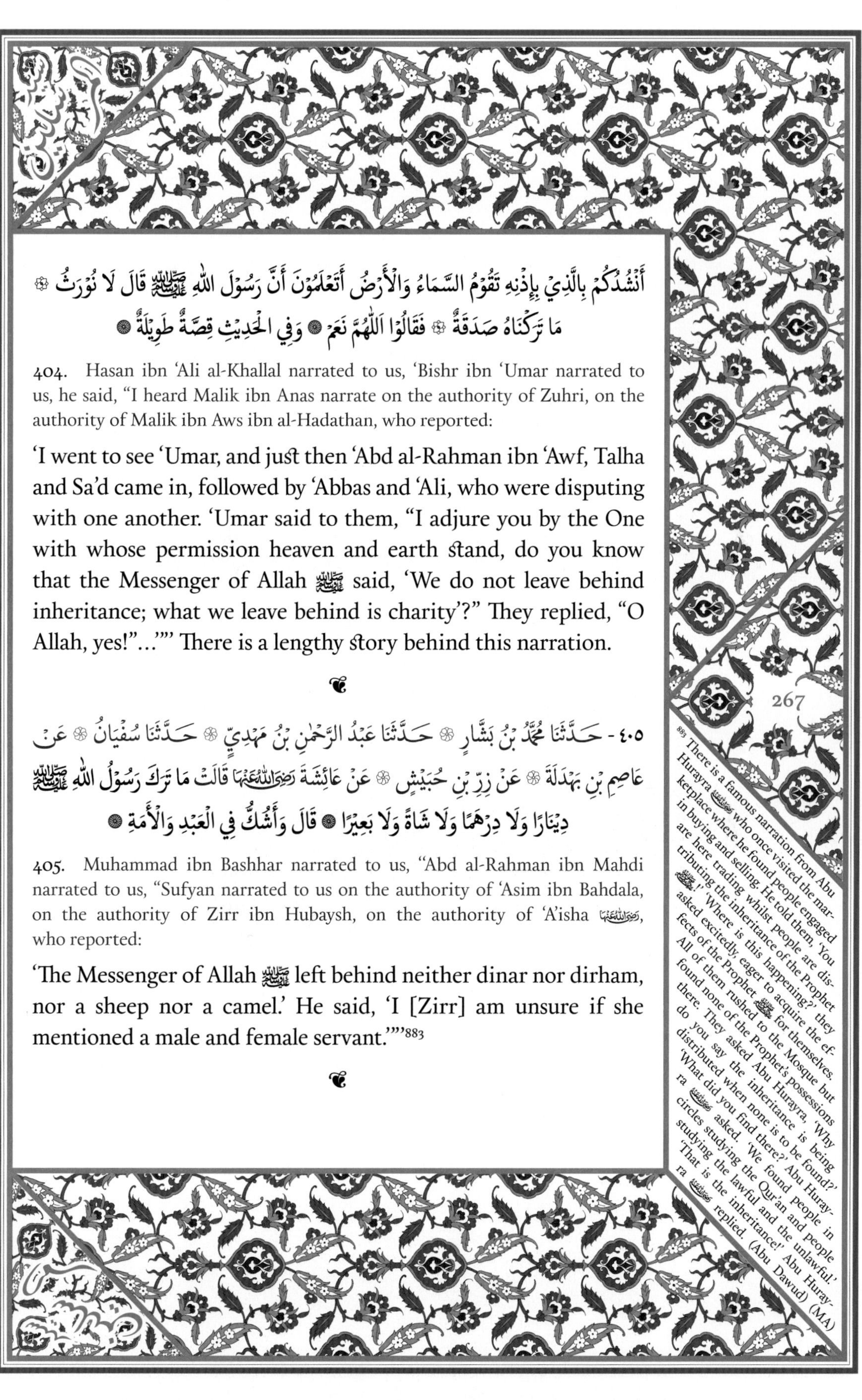

أَنْشُدُكُمْ بِالَّذِي بِإِذْنِهِ تَقُومُ السَّمَاءُ وَالْأَرْضُ أَتَعْلَمُونَ أَنَّ رَسُولَ اللهِ ﷺ قَالَ لَا نُورَثُ ۞ مَا تَرَكْنَاهُ صَدَقَةٌ ۞ فَقَالُوا اللّٰهُمَّ نَعَمْ ۞ وَفِي الْحَدِيثِ قِصَّةٌ طَوِيلَةٌ ۞

404. Hasan ibn 'Ali al-Khallal narrated to us, 'Bishr ibn 'Umar narrated to us, he said, "I heard Malik ibn Anas narrate on the authority of Zuhri, on the authority of Malik ibn Aws ibn al-Hadathan, who reported:

'I went to see 'Umar, and just then 'Abd al-Rahman ibn 'Awf, Talha and Sa'd came in, followed by 'Abbas and 'Ali, who were disputing with one another. 'Umar said to them, "I adjure you by the One with whose permission heaven and earth stand, do you know that the Messenger of Allah ﷺ said, 'We do not leave behind inheritance; what we leave behind is charity'?" They replied, "O Allah, yes!"...''' There is a lengthy story behind this narration.

٤٠٥ - حَدَّثَنَا مُحَمَّدُ بْنُ بَشَّارٍ ۞ حَدَّثَنَا عَبْدُ الرَّحْمٰنِ بْنُ مَهْدِيٍّ ۞ حَدَّثَنَا سُفْيَانُ ۞ عَنْ عَاصِمِ بْنِ بَهْدَلَةَ ۞ عَنْ زِرِّ بْنِ حُبَيْشٍ ۞ عَنْ عَائِشَةَ رَضِيَ اللهُ عَنْهَا قَالَتْ مَا تَرَكَ رَسُولُ اللهِ ﷺ دِينَارًا وَلَا دِرْهَمًا وَلَا شَاةً وَلَا بَعِيرًا ۞ قَالَ وَأَشُكُّ فِي الْعَبْدِ وَالْأَمَةِ ۞

405. Muhammad ibn Bashhar narrated to us, "Abd al-Rahman ibn Mahdi narrated to us, "Sufyan narrated to us on the authority of 'Asim ibn Bahdala, on the authority of Zirr ibn Hubaysh, on the authority of 'A'isha رضي الله عنها, who reported:

'The Messenger of Allah ﷺ left behind neither dinar nor dirham, nor a sheep nor a camel.' He said, 'I [Zirr] am unsure if she mentioned a male and female servant.''''[883]

[883] There is a famous narration from Abu Hurayra رضي الله عنه who once visited the marketplace where he found people engaged in buying and selling. He told them, 'You are here trading whilst people are distributing the inheritance of the Prophet ﷺ!' 'Where is this happening?' they asked excitedly, eager to acquire the effects of the Prophet ﷺ for themselves. All of them rushed to the Mosque but found none of the Prophet's possessions there. They asked Abu Hurayra, 'Why do you say the inheritance is being distributed when none is to be found?' 'What did you find there?' Abu Hurayra رضي الله عنه asked. 'We found people in circles studying the Qur'an and people studying the lawful and the unlawful.' 'That is the inheritance!' Abu Hurayra رضي الله عنه replied. (Abu Dawud) (MA)

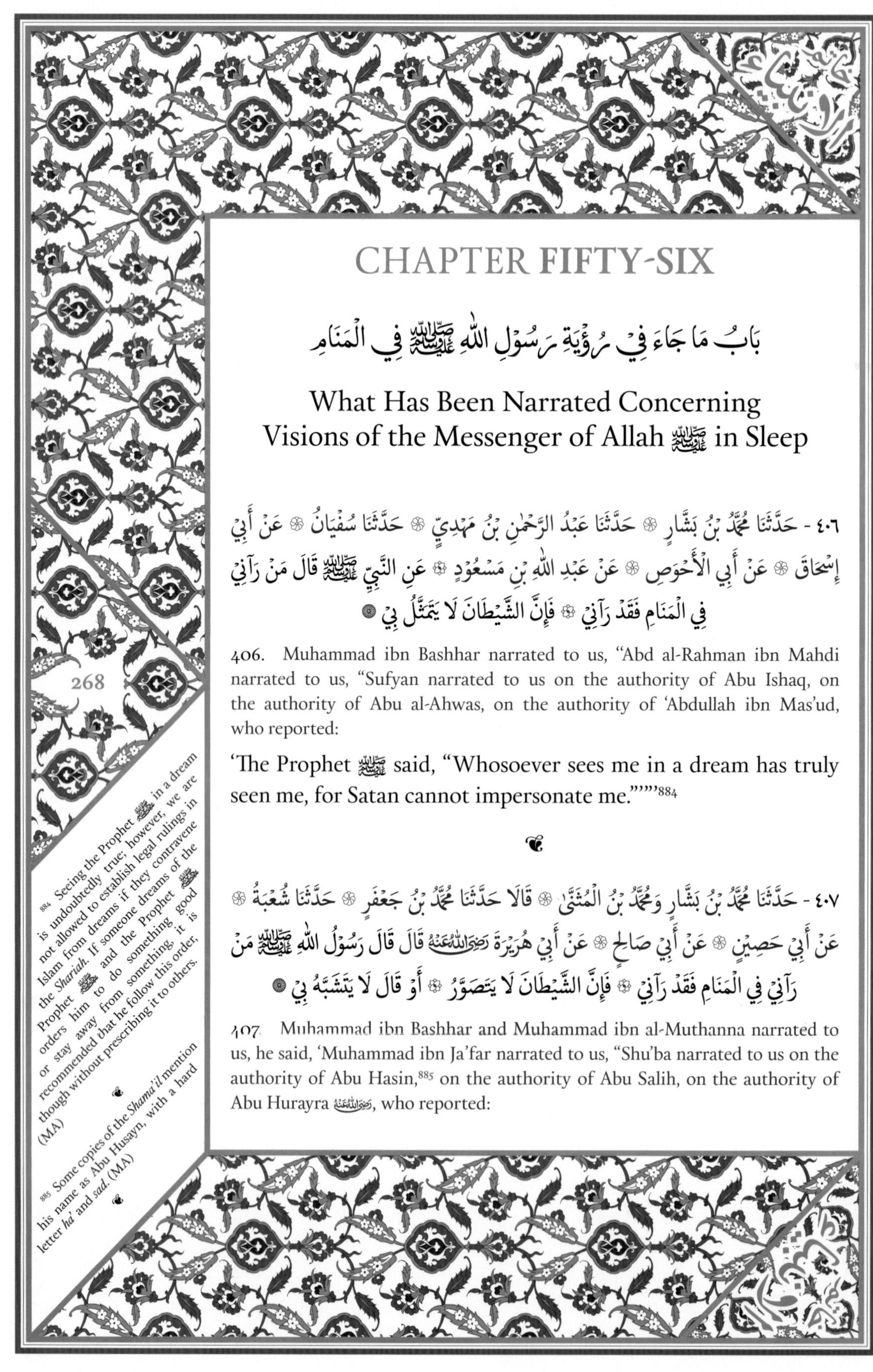

CHAPTER FIFTY-SIX

بَابُ مَا جَاءَ فِي رُؤْيَةِ رَسُولِ اللهِ ﷺ فِي الْمَنَامِ

What Has Been Narrated Concerning Visions of the Messenger of Allah ﷺ in Sleep

٤٠٦ - حَدَّثَنَا مُحَمَّدُ بْنُ بَشَّارٍ ❁ حَدَّثَنَا عَبْدُ الرَّحْمٰنِ بْنُ مَهْدِيٍّ ❁ حَدَّثَنَا سُفْيَانُ ❁ عَنْ أَبِي إِسْحَاقَ ❁ عَنْ أَبِي الْأَحْوَصِ ❁ عَنْ عَبْدِ اللهِ بْنِ مَسْعُودٍ ❁ عَنِ النَّبِيِّ ﷺ قَالَ مَنْ رَآنِي فِي الْمَنَامِ فَقَدْ رَآنِي ❁ فَإِنَّ الشَّيْطَانَ لَا يَتَمَثَّلُ بِي ❁

406. Muhammad ibn Bashhar narrated to us, "Abd al-Rahman ibn Mahdi narrated to us, "Sufyan narrated to us on the authority of Abu Ishaq, on the authority of Abu al-Ahwas, on the authority of 'Abdullah ibn Mas'ud, who reported:

'The Prophet ﷺ said, "Whosoever sees me in a dream has truly seen me, for Satan cannot impersonate me."'"'[884]

❦

٤٠٧ - حَدَّثَنَا مُحَمَّدُ بْنُ بَشَّارٍ وَمُحَمَّدُ بْنُ الْمُثَنَّى ❁ قَالَا حَدَّثَنَا مُحَمَّدُ بْنُ جَعْفَرٍ ❁ حَدَّثَنَا شُعْبَةُ ❁ عَنْ أَبِي حَصِينٍ ❁ عَنْ أَبِي صَالِحٍ ❁ عَنْ أَبِي هُرَيْرَةَ رَضِيَ اللهُ عَنْهُ قَالَ قَالَ رَسُولُ اللهِ ﷺ مَنْ رَآنِي فِي الْمَنَامِ فَقَدْ رَآنِي ❁ فَإِنَّ الشَّيْطَانَ لَا يَتَصَوَّرُ ❁ أَوْ قَالَ لَا يَتَشَبَّهُ بِي ❁

407. Muhammad ibn Bashhar and Muhammad ibn al-Muthanna narrated to us, he said, 'Muhammad ibn Ja'far narrated to us, "Shu'ba narrated to us on the authority of Abu Hasin,[885] on the authority of Abu Salih, on the authority of Abu Hurayra رضي الله عنه, who reported:

[884] Seeing the Prophet ﷺ in a dream is undoubtedly true; however, we are not allowed to establish legal rulings in Islam from dreams if they contravene the *Shariah*. If someone dreams of the Prophet ﷺ and the Prophet ﷺ orders him to do something good or stay away from something, it is recommended that he follow this order, though without prescribing it to others. (MA)

[885] Some copies of the *Shama'il* mention his name as Abu Husayn, with a hard letter *ha'* and *sad*. (MA)

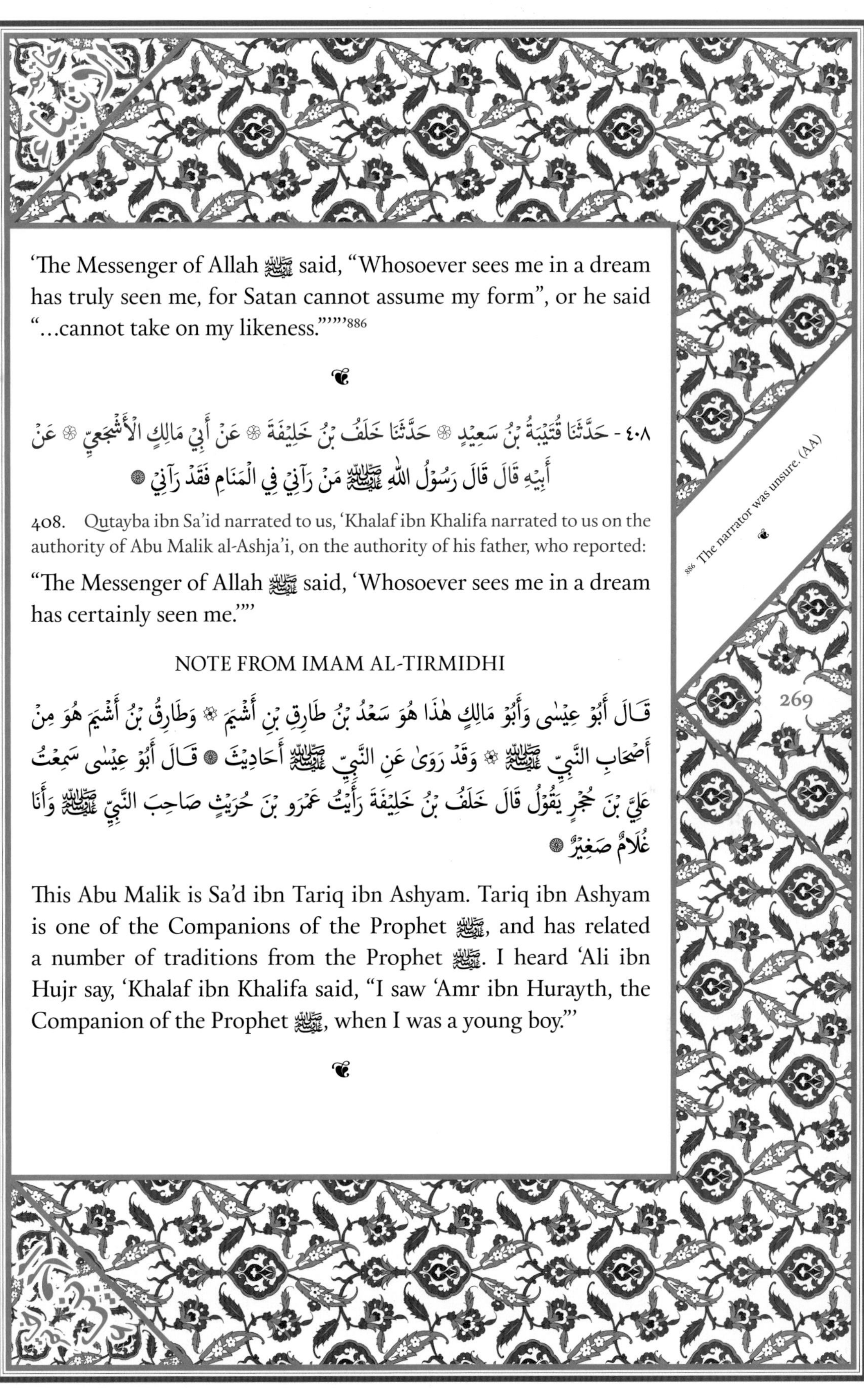

'The Messenger of Allah ﷺ said, "Whosoever sees me in a dream has truly seen me, for Satan cannot assume my form", or he said "...cannot take on my likeness."""'[886]

❦

٤٠٨ - حَدَّثَنَا قُتَيْبَةُ بْنُ سَعِيدٍ ۞ حَدَّثَنَا خَلَفُ بْنُ خَلِيفَةَ ۞ عَنْ أَبِي مَالِكٍ الْأَشْجَعِيِّ ۞ عَنْ أَبِيهِ قَالَ قَالَ رَسُولُ اللهِ ﷺ مَنْ رَآنِي فِي الْمَنَامِ فَقَدْ رَآنِي ۝

408. Qutayba ibn Sa'id narrated to us, 'Khalaf ibn Khalifa narrated to us on the authority of Abu Malik al-Ashja'i, on the authority of his father, who reported:

"The Messenger of Allah ﷺ said, 'Whosoever sees me in a dream has certainly seen me.'"'

NOTE FROM IMAM AL-TIRMIDHI

قَالَ أَبُو عِيسَى وَأَبُو مَالِكٍ هٰذَا هُوَ سَعْدُ بْنُ طَارِقِ بْنِ أَشْيَمَ ۞ وَطَارِقُ بْنُ أَشْيَمَ هُوَ مِنْ أَصْحَابِ النَّبِيِّ ﷺ ۞ وَقَدْ رَوَى عَنِ النَّبِيِّ ﷺ أَحَادِيثَ ۝ قَالَ أَبُو عِيسَى سَمِعْتُ عَلِيَّ بْنَ حُجْرٍ يَقُولُ قَالَ خَلَفُ بْنُ خَلِيفَةَ رَأَيْتُ عَمْرَو بْنَ حُرَيْثٍ صَاحِبَ النَّبِيِّ ﷺ وَأَنَا غُلَامٌ صَغِيرٌ ۝

This Abu Malik is Sa'd ibn Tariq ibn Ashyam. Tariq ibn Ashyam is one of the Companions of the Prophet ﷺ, and has related a number of traditions from the Prophet ﷺ. I heard 'Ali ibn Hujr say, 'Khalaf ibn Khalifa said, "I saw 'Amr ibn Hurayth, the Companion of the Prophet ﷺ, when I was a young boy."'

❦

886 The narrator was unsure. (AA)

❦

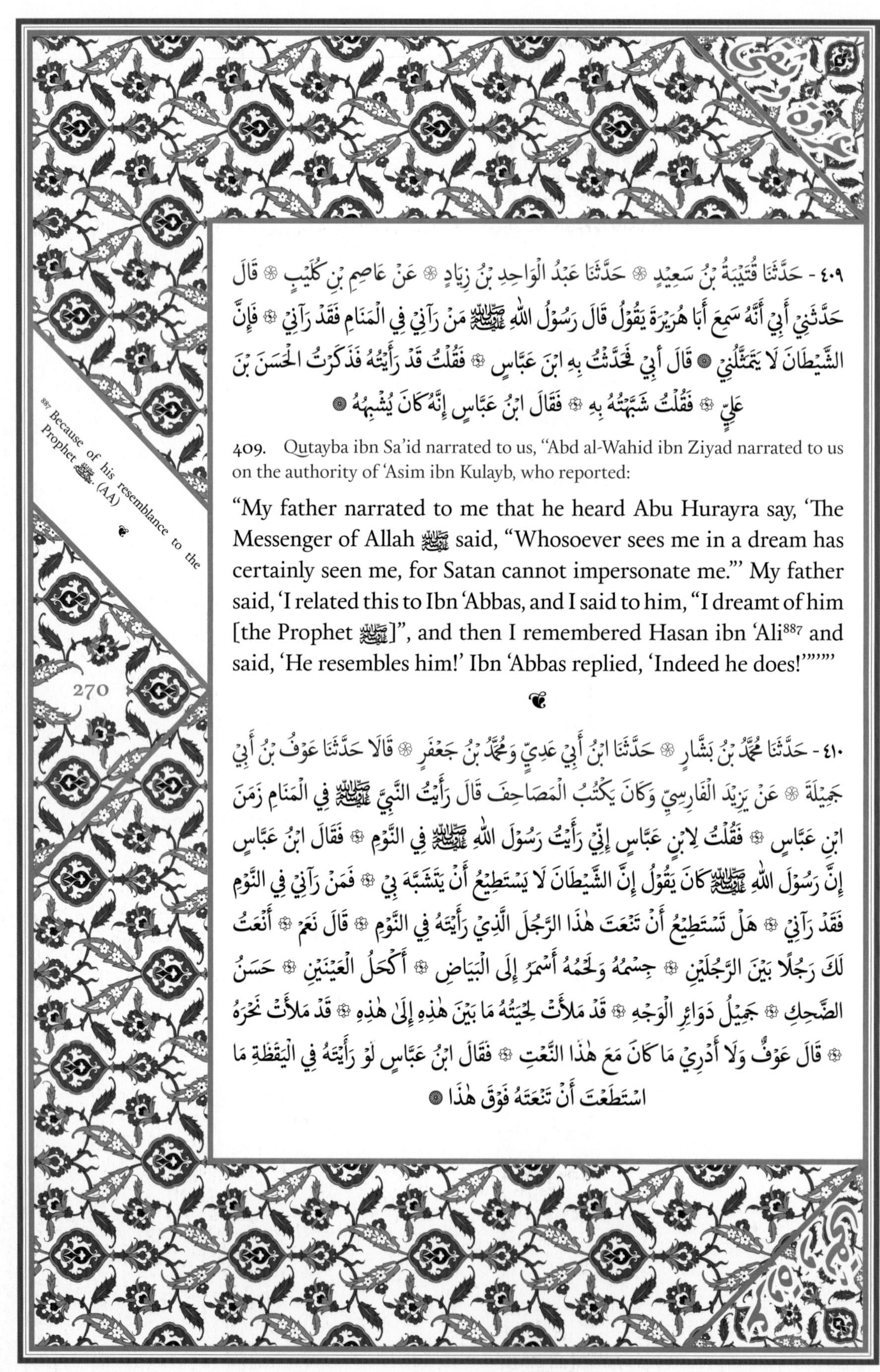

٤٠٩ - حَدَّثَنَا قُتَيْبَةُ بْنُ سَعِيدٍ ۞ حَدَّثَنَا عَبْدُ الْوَاحِدِ بْنُ زِيَادٍ ۞ عَنْ عَاصِمِ بْنِ كُلَيْبٍ ۞ قَالَ حَدَّثَنِي أَبِي أَنَّهُ سَمِعَ أَبَا هُرَيْرَةَ يَقُولُ قَالَ رَسُولُ اللهِ ﷺ مَنْ رَآنِي فِي الْمَنَامِ فَقَدْ رَآنِي ۞ فَإِنَّ الشَّيْطَانَ لَا يَتَمَثَّلُنِي ۞ قَالَ أَبِي فَحَدَّثْتُ بِهِ ابْنَ عَبَّاسٍ ۞ فَقُلْتُ قَدْ رَأَيْتُهُ فَذَكَرْتُ الْحَسَنَ بْنَ عَلِيٍّ ۞ فَقُلْتُ شَبَّهْتُهُ بِهِ ۞ فَقَالَ ابْنُ عَبَّاسٍ إِنَّهُ كَانَ يُشْبِهُهُ ۞

409. Qutayba ibn Sa'id narrated to us, "Abd al-Wahid ibn Ziyad narrated to us on the authority of 'Asim ibn Kulayb, who reported:

"My father narrated to me that he heard Abu Hurayra say, 'The Messenger of Allah ﷺ said, "Whosoever sees me in a dream has certainly seen me, for Satan cannot impersonate me."' My father said, 'I related this to Ibn 'Abbas, and I said to him, "I dreamt of him [the Prophet ﷺ]", and then I remembered Hasan ibn 'Ali[887] and said, 'He resembles him!' Ibn 'Abbas replied, 'Indeed he does!'""""

٤١٠ - حَدَّثَنَا مُحَمَّدُ بْنُ بَشَّارٍ ۞ حَدَّثَنَا ابْنُ أَبِي عَدِيٍّ وَمُحَمَّدُ بْنُ جَعْفَرٍ ۞ قَالَا حَدَّثَنَا عَوْفُ بْنُ أَبِي جَمِيلَةَ ۞ عَنْ يَزِيدَ الْفَارِسِيِّ وَكَانَ يَكْتُبُ الْمَصَاحِفَ قَالَ رَأَيْتُ النَّبِيَّ ﷺ فِي الْمَنَامِ زَمَنَ ابْنِ عَبَّاسٍ ۞ فَقُلْتُ لِابْنِ عَبَّاسٍ إِنِّي رَأَيْتُ رَسُولَ اللهِ ﷺ فِي النَّوْمِ ۞ فَقَالَ ابْنُ عَبَّاسٍ إِنَّ رَسُولَ اللهِ ﷺ كَانَ يَقُولُ إِنَّ الشَّيْطَانَ لَا يَسْتَطِيعُ أَنْ يَتَشَبَّهَ بِي ۞ فَمَنْ رَآنِي فِي النَّوْمِ فَقَدْ رَآنِي ۞ هَلْ تَسْتَطِيعُ أَنْ تَنْعَتَ هَذَا الرَّجُلَ الَّذِي رَأَيْتَهُ فِي النَّوْمِ ۞ قَالَ نَعَمْ ۞ أَنْعَتُ لَكَ رَجُلًا بَيْنَ الرَّجُلَيْنِ ۞ جِسْمُهُ وَلَحْمُهُ أَسْمَرُ إِلَى الْبَيَاضِ ۞ أَكْحَلُ الْعَيْنَيْنِ ۞ حَسَنُ الضَّحِكِ ۞ جَمِيلُ دَوَائِرِ الْوَجْهِ ۞ قَدْ مَلَأَتْ لِحْيَتُهُ مَا بَيْنَ هَذِهِ إِلَى هَذِهِ ۞ قَدْ مَلَأَتْ نَحْرَهُ ۞ قَالَ عَوْفٌ وَلَا أَدْرِي مَا كَانَ مَعَ هَذَا النَّعْتِ ۞ فَقَالَ ابْنُ عَبَّاسٍ لَوْ رَأَيْتَهُ فِي الْيَقَظَةِ مَا اسْتَطَعْتَ أَنْ تَنْعَتَهُ فَوْقَ هَذَا ۞

887 Because of his resemblance to the Prophet ﷺ. (AA)

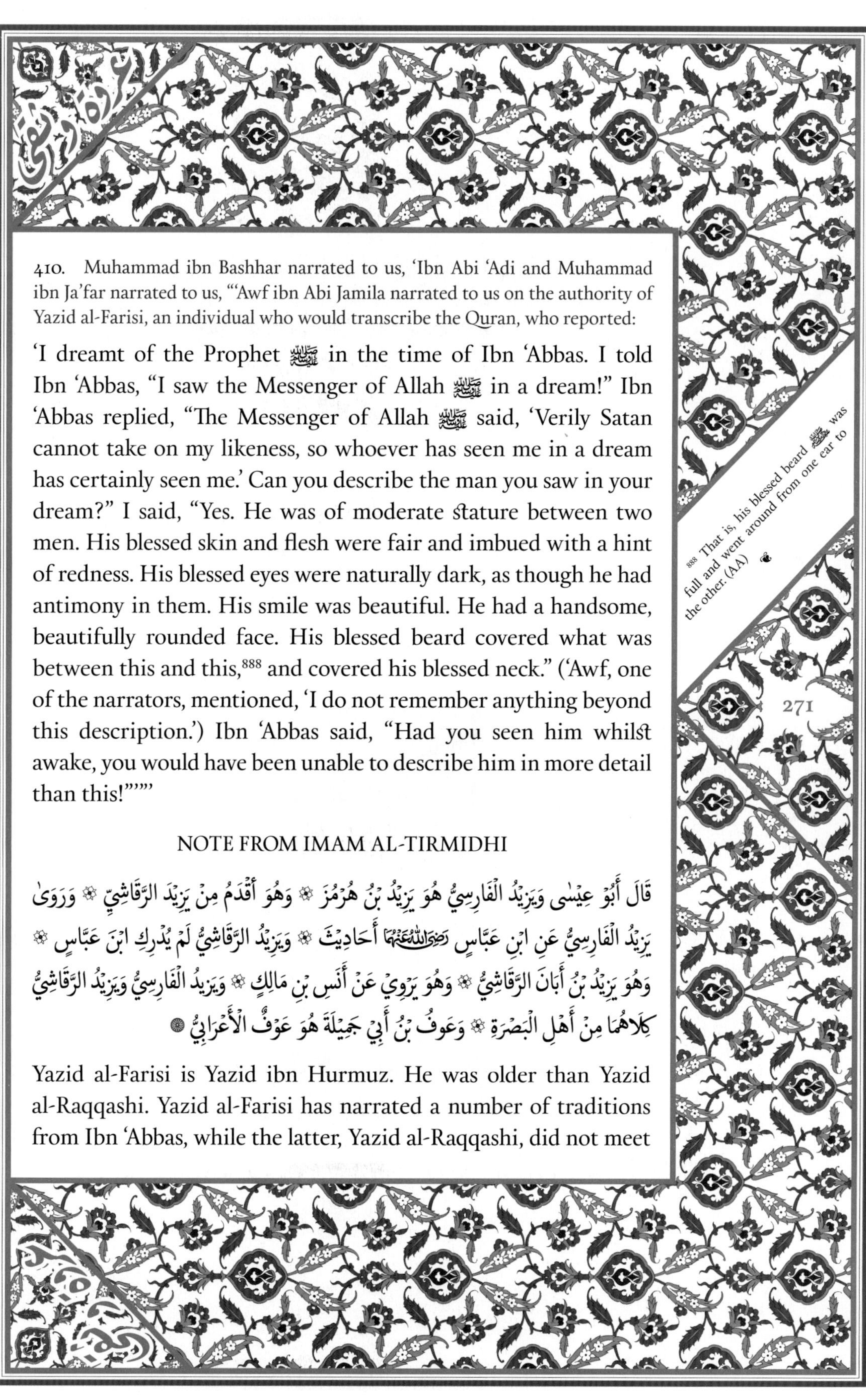

410. Muhammad ibn Bashhar narrated to us, 'Ibn Abi 'Adi and Muhammad ibn Ja'far narrated to us, "'Awf ibn Abi Jamila narrated to us on the authority of Yazid al-Farisi, an individual who would transcribe the Quran, who reported:

'I dreamt of the Prophet ﷺ in the time of Ibn 'Abbas. I told Ibn 'Abbas, "I saw the Messenger of Allah ﷺ in a dream!" Ibn 'Abbas replied, "The Messenger of Allah ﷺ said, 'Verily Satan cannot take on my likeness, so whoever has seen me in a dream has certainly seen me.' Can you describe the man you saw in your dream?" I said, "Yes. He was of moderate stature between two men. His blessed skin and flesh were fair and imbued with a hint of redness. His blessed eyes were naturally dark, as though he had antimony in them. His smile was beautiful. He had a handsome, beautifully rounded face. His blessed beard covered what was between this and this,[888] and covered his blessed neck." ('Awf, one of the narrators, mentioned, 'I do not remember anything beyond this description.') Ibn 'Abbas said, "Had you seen him whilst awake, you would have been unable to describe him in more detail than this!"""'

NOTE FROM IMAM AL-TIRMIDHI

قَالَ أَبُو عِيسَى وَيَزِيدُ الْفَارِسِيُّ هُوَ يَزِيدُ بْنُ هُرْمُزَ ❁ وَهُوَ أَقْدَمُ مِنْ يَزِيدَ الرَّقَاشِيِّ ❁ وَرَوَى يَزِيدُ الْفَارِسِيُّ عَنِ ابْنِ عَبَّاسٍ رَضِيَ اللهُ عَنْهُمَا أَحَادِيثَ ❁ وَيَزِيدُ الرَّقَاشِيُّ لَمْ يُدْرِكِ ابْنَ عَبَّاسٍ ❁ وَهُوَ يَزِيدُ بْنُ أَبَانَ الرَّقَاشِيُّ ❁ وَهُوَ يَرْوِي عَنْ أَنَسِ بْنِ مَالِكٍ ❁ وَيَزِيدُ الْفَارِسِيُّ وَيَزِيدُ الرَّقَاشِيُّ كِلَاهُمَا مِنْ أَهْلِ الْبَصْرَةِ ❁ وَعَوفُ بْنُ أَبِي جَمِيلَةَ هُوَ عَوْفٌ الْأَعْرَابِيُّ ۞

Yazid al-Farisi is Yazid ibn Hurmuz. He was older than Yazid al-Raqqashi. Yazid al-Farisi has narrated a number of traditions from Ibn 'Abbas, while the latter, Yazid al-Raqqashi, did not meet

888 That is, his blessed beard ﷺ was full and went around from one ear to the other. (AA)

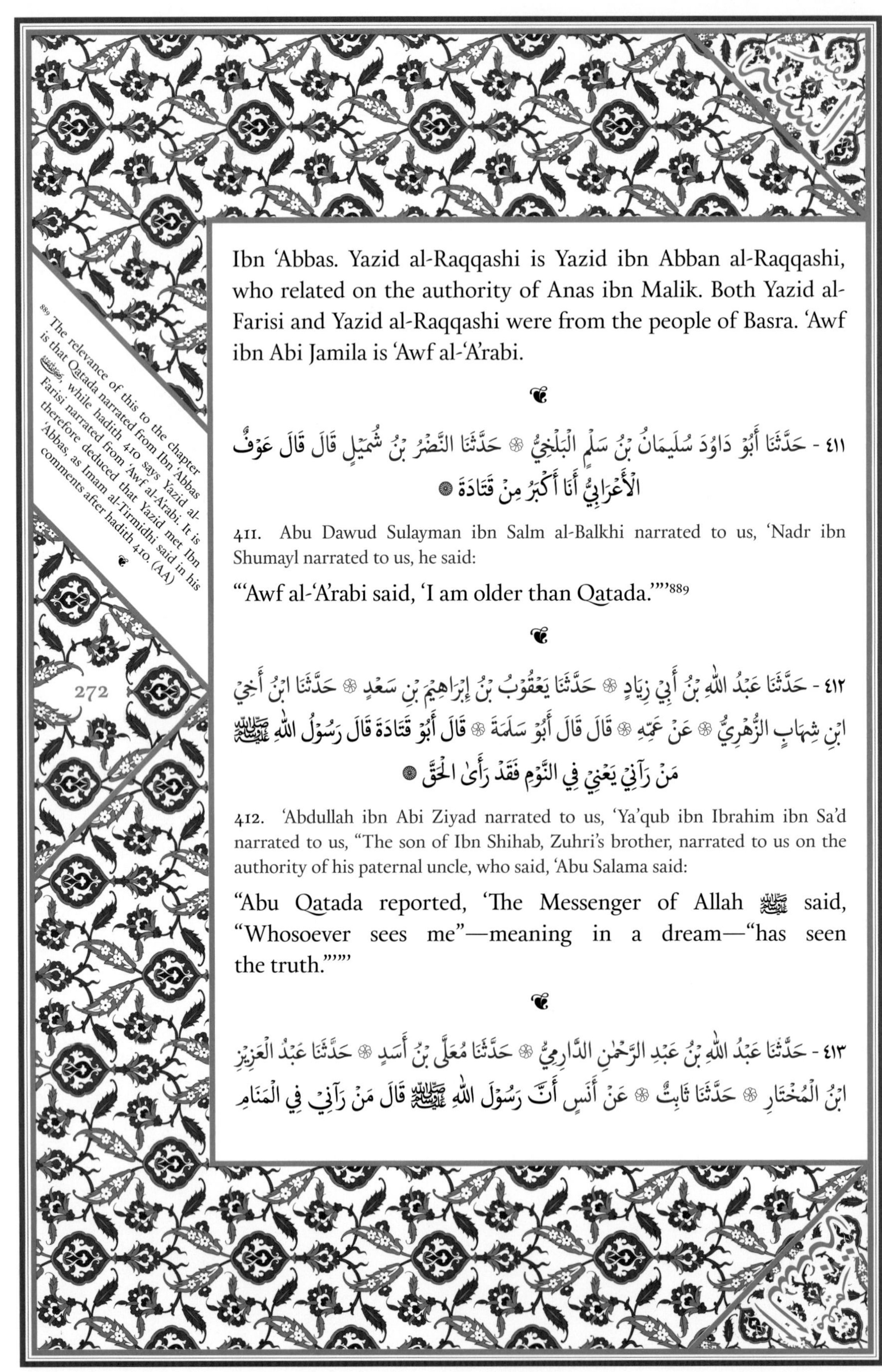

Ibn 'Abbas. Yazid al-Raqqashi is Yazid ibn Abban al-Raqqashi, who related on the authority of Anas ibn Malik. Both Yazid al-Farisi and Yazid al-Raqqashi were from the people of Basra. 'Awf ibn Abi Jamila is 'Awf al-'A'rabi.

❦

٤١١ - حَدَّثَنَا أَبُو دَاوُدَ سُلَيمَانُ بْنُ سَلْمٍ الْبَلْخِيُّ ۞ حَدَّثَنَا النَّضْرُ بْنُ شُمَيْلٍ قَالَ قَالَ عَوْفٌ الْأَعْرَابِيُّ أَنَا أَكْبَرُ مِنْ قَتَادَةَ ۞

411. Abu Dawud Sulayman ibn Salm al-Balkhi narrated to us, 'Nadr ibn Shumayl narrated to us, he said:

"'Awf al-'A'rabi said, 'I am older than Qatada.''"[889]

❦

٤١٢ - حَدَّثَنَا عَبْدُ اللهِ بْنُ أَبِي زِيَادٍ ۞ حَدَّثَنَا يَعْقُوبُ بْنُ إِبْرَاهِيمَ بْنِ سَعْدٍ ۞ حَدَّثَنَا ابْنُ أَخِي ابْنِ شِهَابٍ الزُّهْرِيِّ ۞ عَنْ عَمِّهِ ۞ قَالَ قَالَ أَبُو سَلَمَةَ ۞ قَالَ أَبُو قَتَادَةَ قَالَ رَسُولُ اللهِ ﷺ مَنْ رَآنِي يَعْنِي فِي النَّوْمِ فَقَدْ رَأَى الْحَقَّ ۞

412. 'Abdullah ibn Abi Ziyad narrated to us, 'Ya'qub ibn Ibrahim ibn Sa'd narrated to us, "The son of Ibn Shihab, Zuhri's brother, narrated to us on the authority of his paternal uncle, who said, 'Abu Salama said:

"Abu Qatada reported, 'The Messenger of Allah ﷺ said, "Whosoever sees me"—meaning in a dream—"has seen the truth.""'"

❦

٤١٣ - حَدَّثَنَا عَبْدُ اللهِ بْنُ عَبْدِ الرَّحْمَنِ الدَّارِمِيُّ ۞ حَدَّثَنَا مُعَلَّى بْنُ أَسَدٍ ۞ حَدَّثَنَا عَبْدُ الْعَزِيزِ ابْنُ الْمُخْتَارِ ۞ حَدَّثَنَا ثَابِتٌ ۞ عَنْ أَنَسٍ أَنَّ رَسُولَ اللهِ ﷺ قَالَ مَنْ رَآنِي فِي الْمَنَامِ

[889] The relevance of this to the chapter is that Qatada narrated from Ibn 'Abbas, while hadith 410 says Yazid al-Farisi narrated from 'Awf al-A'rabi. It is therefore deduced that Yazid met Ibn 'Abbas, as Imam al-Tirmidhi said in his comments after hadith 410. (AA)

❦

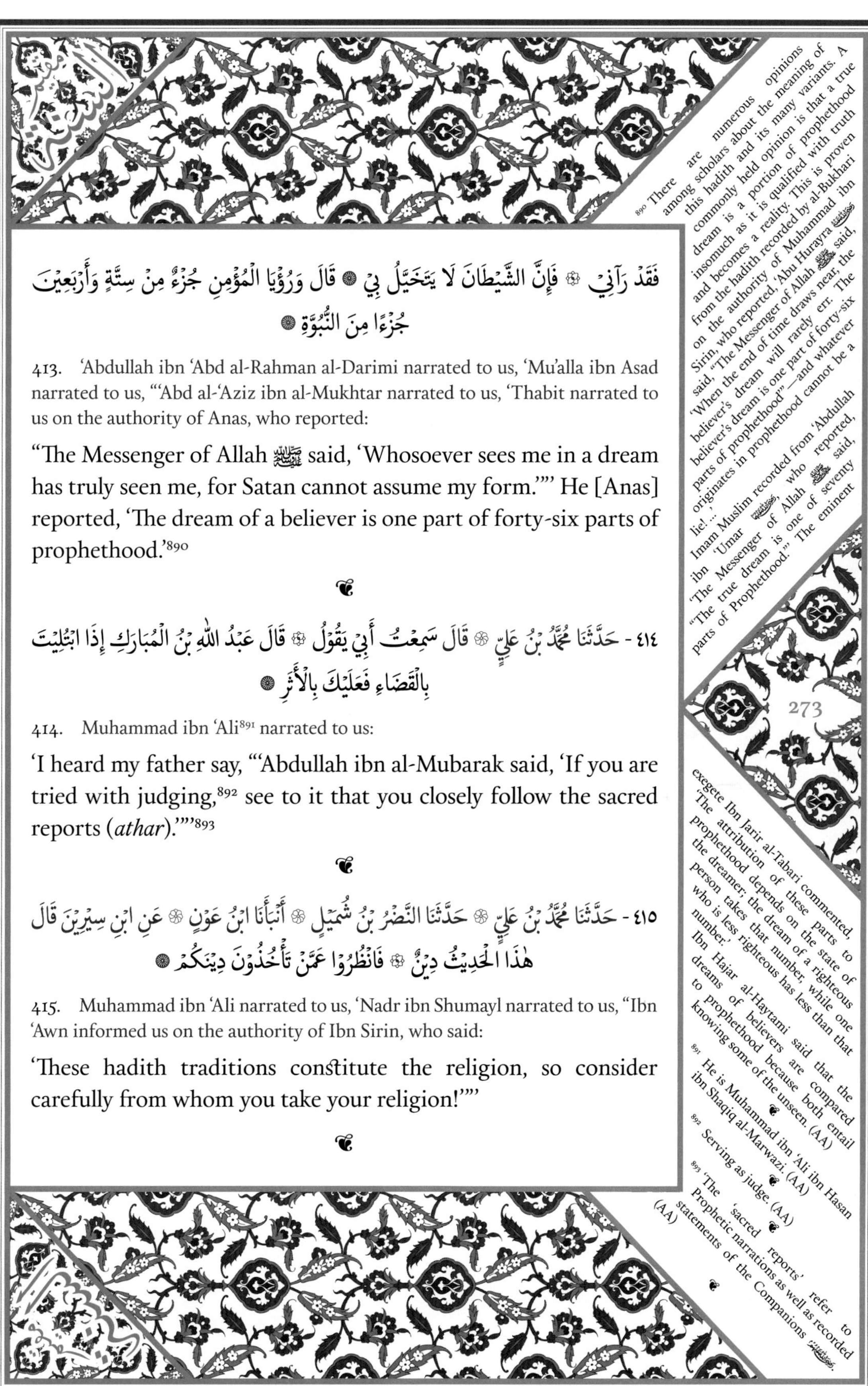

فَقَدْ رَآنِي ۞ فَإِنَّ الشَّيْطَانَ لَا يَتَخَيَّلُ بِي ۞ قَالَ وَرُؤْيَا الْمُؤْمِنِ جُزْءٌ مِنْ سِتَّةٍ وَأَرْبَعِينَ جُزْءًا مِنَ النُّبُوَّةِ ۞

413. 'Abdullah ibn 'Abd al-Rahman al-Darimi narrated to us, 'Mu'alla ibn Asad narrated to us, "'Abd al-'Aziz ibn al-Mukhtar narrated to us, 'Thabit narrated to us on the authority of Anas, who reported:

"The Messenger of Allah ﷺ said, 'Whosoever sees me in a dream has truly seen me, for Satan cannot assume my form.'"' He [Anas] reported, 'The dream of a believer is one part of forty-six parts of prophethood.'[890]

❦

٤١٤ - حَدَّثَنَا مُحَمَّدُ بْنُ عَلِيٍّ ۞ قَالَ سَمِعْتُ أَبِي يَقُولُ ۞ قَالَ عَبْدُ اللهِ بْنُ الْمُبَارَكِ إِذَا ابْتُلِيتَ بِالْقَضَاءِ فَعَلَيْكَ بِالْأَثَرِ ۞

414. Muhammad ibn 'Ali[891] narrated to us:

'I heard my father say, "'Abdullah ibn al-Mubarak said, 'If you are tried with judging,[892] see to it that you closely follow the sacred reports (*athar*).'"'[893]

❦

٤١٥ - حَدَّثَنَا مُحَمَّدُ بْنُ عَلِيٍّ ۞ حَدَّثَنَا النَّضْرُ بْنُ شُمَيْلٍ ۞ أَنْبَأَنَا ابْنُ عَوْنٍ ۞ عَنِ ابْنِ سِيرِينَ قَالَ هٰذَا الْحَدِيثُ دِينٌ ۞ فَانْظُرُوا عَمَّنْ تَأْخُذُونَ دِينَكُمْ ۞

415. Muhammad ibn 'Ali narrated to us, 'Nadr ibn Shumayl narrated to us, "Ibn 'Awn informed us on the authority of Ibn Sirin, who said:

'These hadith traditions constitute the religion, so consider carefully from whom you take your religion!'"'

❦

[890] There are numerous opinions among scholars about the meaning of this hadith and its many variants. A commonly held opinion is that a true dream is a portion of prophethood insomuch as it is qualified with truth and becomes a reality. This is proven from the hadith recorded by al-Bukhari on the authority of Muhammad ibn Sirin, who reported, 'Abu Hurayra said, "The Messenger of Allah ﷺ said, 'When the end of time draws near, the believer's dream will rarely err. The believer's dream is one part of forty-six parts of prophethood'"—and whatever originates in prophethood cannot be a lie!...' Imam Muslim recorded from 'Abdullah ibn 'Umar, who reported, 'The Messenger of Allah ﷺ said, "The true dream is one of seventy parts of Prophethood." The eminent exegete Ibn Jarir al-Tabari commented, 'The attribution of these parts to prophethood depends on the state of the dreamer; the dream of a righteous person takes that number, while one who is less righteous has less than that number.' Ibn Hajar al-Haytami said that the dreams of believers are compared to prophethood because both entail knowing some of the unseen. (AA)

❦

[891] He is Muhammad ibn 'Ali ibn Hasan ibn Shaqiq al-Marwazi. (AA)

[892] Serving as judge. (AA)

[893] 'The 'sacred reports' refer to Prophetic narrations as well as recorded statements of the Companions. (AA)

❦

صممت هٰذه النّسخة المباركة من كتاب الشّمائل المحمّدية والخصائل المصطفويّة،
من تأليف الإمام أبي عيسى محمد بن عيسى بن سورة السّلمي التّرمذي المتوفّى
٢٧٩ هجريّة رحمه الله تعالى رحمة واسعة وطيّب آثاره ونوّر ضريحه وضرائح المدفونين
حوله، العبد الضّعيف الفقير إلى رحمة الرّبّ العليّ القدير
محمّد إدريس جلاليّ بن كمال باشا بن حسن محمّد
غفر الله له ولوالديه ولمشايخه ولأحبابه ولجميع
المسلمين، في شهر ربيع الأوّل ١٤٤١ هجريّة ببلدة
الحبيب نوح بن محمّد الحبشي قدّس الله سرّه
الشّريفة سنغافورة، و
الحمد لله ربّ
العالمين
آمين
م

The design & typesetting of this edition of the blessed work *al-Shama'il al-Muhammadiyya wa al-Khasa'il al-Mustafawiyya* by AL-IMAM ABU 'ISA MUHAMMAD B. 'ISA B. SAWRA AL-SULAMI AL-TIRMIDHI (D. 279 AH)—Allah Most High have mercy on him with deep affection; perfume his words & works; illuminate his resting abode & those around him—was completed in the noble month of *Rabi' al-Awwal* 1441 AH in SINGAPORE—the honoured land of AL-HABIB NUH B. MUHAMMAD AL-HABSHI (Allah sanctify his secret)—by the weak & needy slave who is in need of the kindness of the Exalted & Omnipotent Lord: MOHAMED IDRIS JALALI B. KAMAL BATCHA B. ASAN MOHAMED—Allah forgive him, his parents, *Shuyukh*, loved ones & all Muslims. All-Praise to Allah, Lord of the entire cosmos. *Amin!*

لَا يُؤْمِنُ أَحَدُكُمْ حَتَّىٰ أَكُونَ أَحَبَّ إِلَيْهِ
مِنْ وَلَدِهِ وَوَالِدِهِ وَالنَّاسِ أَجْمَعِينَ

"None of you have truly believed until I am more beloved to him than his children, parents and all of humanity."

SAHIH AL-BUKHARI 15, SAHIH MUSLIM 44

GENERAL INDEX

A

B

C

D

Q

R

S

T

QUR'ANIC VERSE INDEX

الشَّمائِلُ المُحَمَّدِيَّة

والخصائل المصطفويّة

لِلإِمَامِ أَبِي عِيسَى مُحَمَّدِ بْن عِيسَى بْن سَوْرَة السُّلميّ التِّرمِذِيّ

المتوفى سنة ٢٧٩ هجريّة

النَّص العَرَبي مُقَابِل ترجمته بالإنجليزيَّة مَع التَّعليقات

ترجمه وعلّق عليه

عبد العزيز سراقة و محمد أسلم

عفا الله عنهما

ناشران

أكاديميّة
مدينة العلم
برمنغهام، بريطانيا

معهد
الامام الغزّاليّ
نيويورك، أمريكا

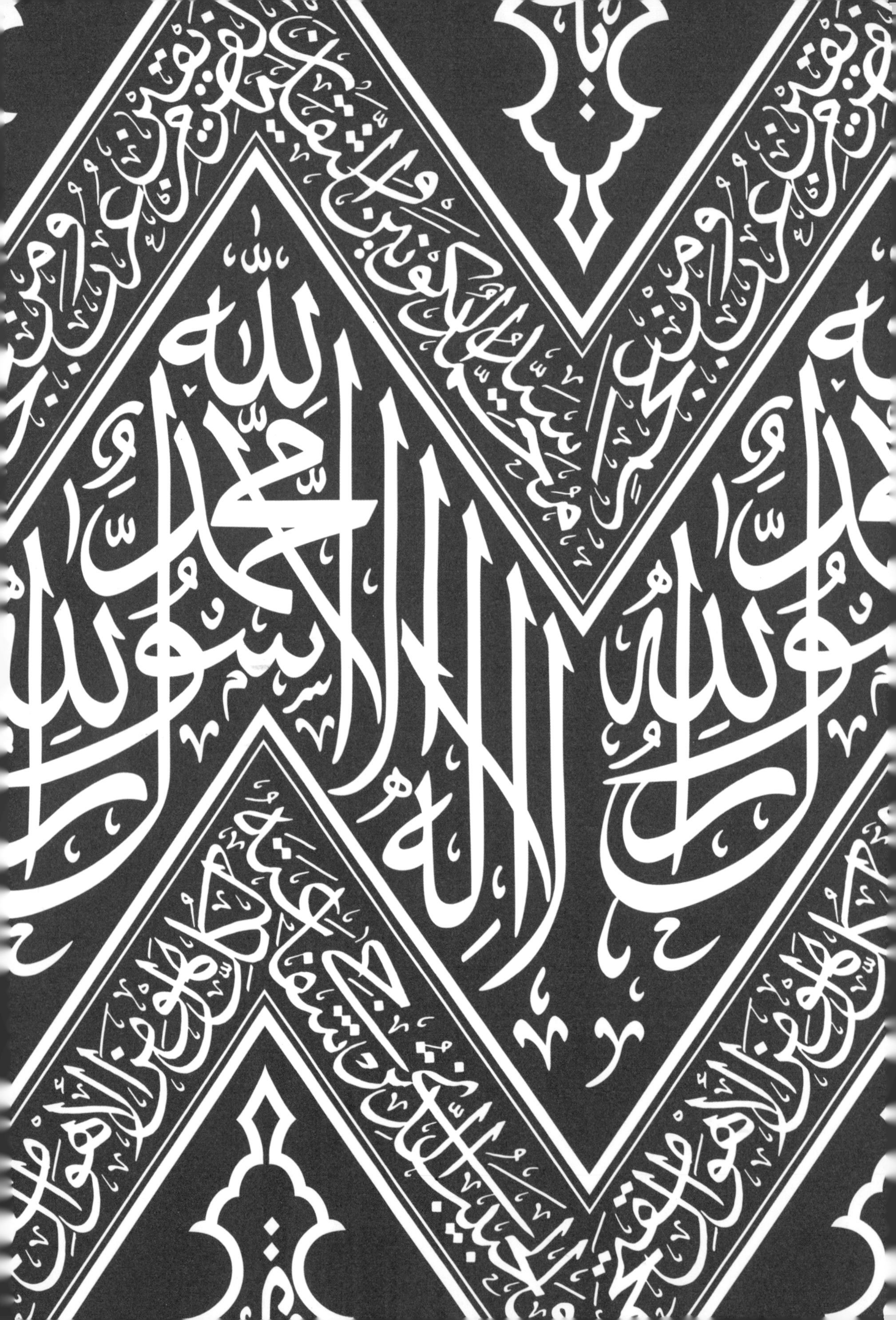
لا إله إلا الله محمد رسول الله